Textbook on

Immigration and Asylum Law

Fifth edition

Gina Clayton
BA (Hons), LLM
Visiting Lecturer, Middlesex University

Chapter 3 revised & updated by

Caroline Sawyer
BA (Hons), MA, PhD
Senior Lecturer, Victoria University of Wellington

Chapters 5 & 6 revised & updated by

Helen Toner
BA (Hons), LLM, DPhil
Dean of students, University of Warwick

Chapters 9, 10 & 11 revised & updated by

Helena Wray
BA (Hons), PhD
Senior Lecturer, Middlesex University

OXFORD
UNIVERSITY PRESS

OXFORD
UNIVERSITY PRESS

Great Clarendon Street, Oxford, OX2 6DP,
United Kingdom

Oxford University Press is a department of the University of Oxford.
It furthers the University's objective of excellence in research, scholarship,
and education by publishing worldwide. Oxford is a registered trade mark of
Oxford University Press in the UK and in certain other countries

Second Edition published 2006
Third Edition published 2008
Fourth Edition published 2010
Impression: 1

British Library Cataloguing in Publication Data
Data available

Library of Congress Cataloging in Publication Data
Library of Congress Control Number: 2012938463

ISBN 978-0-19-969943-8

Printed in Great Britain by
Ashford Colour Press Ltd, Gosport, Hampshire

Textbook on Immigration and Asylum Law

OUTLINE CONTENTS

SECTION 6 **Enforcement** 527

DETAILED CONTENTS

16 Deportation 568

17 Removal 588

18 Expulsions and Article 8 610

PREFACE

This fifth edition of *Textbook on Immigration and Asylum Law* is the first in which we have not had to incorporate a new immigration law statute. The pace of change at the level of primary legislation has slowed down. However, for those who are studying or applying immigration and asylum law, the subject remains fast-moving. For instance, the period January 2010 to January 2012 has seen 17 Statements of Changes in the immigration rules, many of them governing the points-based system of entry for work and study, and as ever there have been important policy changes.

The successful study and application of immigration law requires a range of skills and qualities. Among these are an understanding of the principles of public law, human empathy, and an appreciation of political forces. Also essential is a willingness to question. Some of the most outstanding decisions of the Supreme Court could only be arrived at because a lawyer did not simply accept that the rules as applied had the last word.

One of the characteristics of immigration law which makes challenges difficult is its reliance on policy. For instance, the UK Border Agency's Case Resolution Directorate, established to clear the backlog of old asylum cases, was closed in July 2011, the target date, despite the fact that many thousands of old cases still remained unresolved. Although the rump body, the Case Assurance and Audit Unit, purports to apply the same criteria as the CRD, their policy is to grant three years discretionary leave rather than indefinite leave as was given before. The result is that people who have waited perhaps the longest for resolution of their status will be deprived of the opportunity to have their families join them, as a result of administrative categorization. Such is the nature of immigration law: where provisions are established in policy rather than a binding legal source, the only obstacle to change is political. Challenges to such a change in policy are difficult to mount, but the impact on the lives of individuals is enormous.

Immigration law is sometimes concerned with controlling the use of power. Again an understanding of public law and a willingness to challenge are important. For instance, the points-based system (PBS) of entry for work and study, introduced in 2008, has generated voluminous administrative guidance and new rules in an ongoing attempt to routinize and codify the grant or refusal of leave to enter the UK for work or study. Guidance notes for applicants have been treated as binding by the Home Office, even in relation to bureaucratic detail. Challenges to this practice culminated in the Court of Appeal judgment in *SSHD v Pankina and others* [2010] EWCA Civ 719, in which the Court ruled that guidance, which has not been laid before Parliament, is not binding. The government had been subject to a similar challenge in relation to its cap on numbers permitted to enter for work, and with a similar result (*R (on the application of JCWI) v SSHD* [2010] EWHC 3524 (Admin)).

In both cases, having been required to lay provisions before Parliament, the government obliged, and achieved the result it had at first desired. One might then ask, what was the point of the litigation? The point is transparency, accountability, and upholding the rule of law in its broad sense.

Once the rule is made, what if the rule itself gives an unfair result or makes unfair demands? Although there are only limited appeal rights left in immigration law, the tribunal is called upon to find a way to achieve substantive fairness, to use some creativity with public law concepts in order to produce justice. Increasing codification makes for increasing inflexibility and this, paradoxically, generates more unfairness. For instance in *Naved (Student – fairness – notice of points) Pakistan* [2012] UKUT 00014(IAC), the appellant had been refused because of 'failure to produce a document that he was never asked to produce'. The tribunal found this unfair and thus not in accordance with the law, even though it was permitted by statute and the terms of the scheme. In cases like this the concept of fairness can be used to moderate the imposition of trivial and arbitrary restrictions. As people's private lives may be interfered with by disruption of their work or study, Article 8 ECHR also comes into play as a moderating influence on the inflexibility of the points-based system.

Underlying all this, although there is no enforceable right to freedom of movement, people will move. It has always been the case even before there were borders to move across, and today's ease of transport routes and global information network mean that the demands to experience a different country and to live, work and study elsewhere will only increase. Naturally, individuals are unwilling to allow their life plans to be blighted by minor bureaucratic requirements, and so the inflexibility of the PBS will continue to attract challenge, and immigration law, as a branch of public law, will need to continue to find ways to give expression to the need for substantive as well as procedural challenge.

Immigration lawyers need to have an understanding of European law. This book includes two chapters which provide a brief introduction to free movement law and some of the areas where EU law impacts on UK immigration and asylum law. Free movement law interacts with immigration provisions for instance where they apply to non-EU citizen members of the families of EU nationals (see e.g. the case of *Zambrano* discussed in chapter 5). The Court of Justice of the European Union's new jurisdiction in immigration and asylum law is binding on the UK and brings the possibility of embedding new principles, including human rights.

The potential of the law to have a liberalizing effect on the rules which govern the lives of individuals is demonstrated in recent decisions of the UK Supreme Court, for instance *ZH Tanzania*, *Quila*, and *HJ (Iran) and HT (Cameroon)*, all of which are discussed in this volume. Immigration and asylum are fascinating areas of law to study, and I hope that students will continue to find that this book supports and stimulates their interest.

I am extremely grateful to Helena Wray, Helen Toner, and Caroline Sawyer for once again updating and in some cases substantially rewriting six chapters of this book. Their contribution, as before, enhances scholarship of the book, and makes its continuation possible. The diversity of styles between us all is also an enhancement for the reader, and I greatly appreciate their continued commitment.

My increased involvement in grassroots asylum organizations in the last two years has also made a contribution to the asylum chapters. The many refugees I have met who have shared their story with me have deepened my education and understanding, and I offer my thanks to those individuals, too numerous to mention.

Thank you to the team at OUP, to Emily Uecker and Caroline Quinnell. Though the production of the book has become more straightforward with time, on this occasion we have had to deal with technical matters generated by the change to digital formats. Both have been very patient in explaining and dealing with the effects on the manuscript.

Finally, thanks as ever to my husband Mike Fitter, whose generosity and patience make all the rest possible.

Gina Clayton
1 April 2012

GUIDE TO USING THE BOOK

Incorporated in this textbook are a number of features that are designed to help you in your studies.

SUMMARY

This chapter examines the definition of a 'refugee' four
Relating to the Status of Refugees 1951 and the Refuge
Although at the time of drafting the Convention this pa
preoccupation of contracting states, every phrase of it l
courts and tribunals worldwide.

Chapter summaries provide an overview of what will be addressed in each chapter, so you are aware of the key learning outcomes for each topic.

Key Case

EM (Lebanon) v SSHD [2008] UKHL 64

The appellant's asylum claim failed and she faced ren
Lebanon. The accepted evidence was that if returned t
tody of the child to her husband who had previously
Saudi Arabia and had subjected her to extreme violenc
automatically give custody to the father if he did not ap

Key case boxes highlight important cases in each subject area and provide a valuable summary of the significant points to note.

QUESTIONS

1 Was the ECJ right to refuse entitlement to b
with the Commission's view that Article 18
the Union should not be impeded by being
After all, Mr Collins would only have qualif
was genuinely seeking work.
2 Do you agree with the Court in *Akrich* that r
rights arising from *Surinder Singh*?
3 *Akrich* and *Metock* take very different views a
States and Community law in relation to co
of EU citizens. Which do you find more con
4 In *Forster*, the Advocate General takes a diffe
differences, which you prefer, and why.

For guidance on answering questions, visit ww

At the end of each chapter is a selection of **questions**. These allow you to check your understanding of the topics covered, and help you engage fully with the material in preparation for further study, writing essays, and answering exam questions.

Guidance on answering these questions is available on the Online Resource Centre: **www.oxfordtextbooks.co.uk/orc/clayton5e/**

FURTHER READING

Buck, Trevor (2006) 'Precedent in Tribunals and the Deve
Quarterly no. 25, October, pp. 458–484.
Buxton, Richard 'Application of Section 13(6) of the Tribu
to Immigration Appeals from the Proposed Upper Trib
pp. 225–227.
Carnwath, Robert 'Tribunal Justice – A New Start' [2009]
Chowdhury, Zahir 'The Concept of "Error of Law" in Pub
Immigration Cases' *Immigration Law Digest* vol. 15, no.

Each chapter concludes with a list of recommended **further reading**.

These suggestions include books and journal articles, and will help to supplement your knowledge and develop your understanding of the subjects covered.

ONLINE RESOURCE CENTRE

www.oxfordtextbooks.co.uk/orc/clayton5e/

This book is accompanied by an Online Resource Centre – a website providing free and easy-to-use resources designed to support the book.

> 'Clayton is able to keep the reader up to date with the textbook's on-line companion website, which is easily accessible and very useful in this particular area'
> *Legal Information Management*

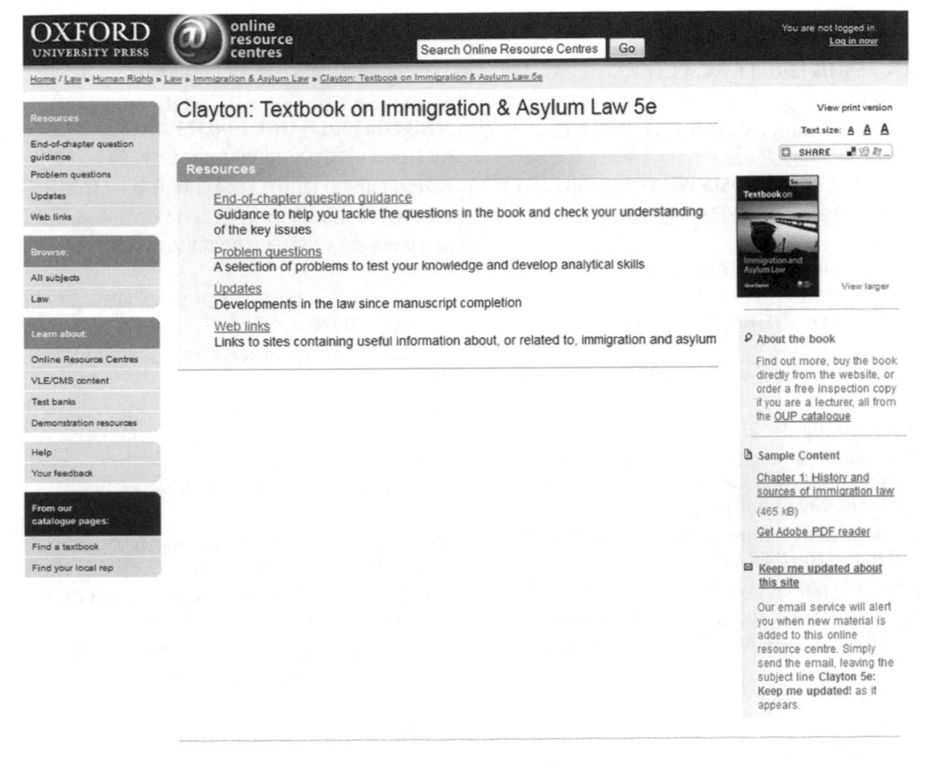

- Yearly updates provide easy access to changes and developments in the law, helping you to stay up-to-date in this fast-moving area
- Problem questions develop your analytical skills and put your knowledge to the test
- Guidance on answering end-of-chapter questions allows you to check your understanding of the key issues
- A selection of web links allow you to research topics of particular interest

TABLE OF CASES

*Cases and page references in **bold** indicate a 'Key Case'*

TABLE OF STATUTES

TABLE OF STATUTORY INSTRUMENTS

TABLE OF EUROPEAN LEGISLATION

TABLE OF TREATIES AND CONVENTIONS

TABLE OF IMMIGRATION RULES

LIST OF ABBREVIATIONS

AIT	Asylum and Immigration Tribunal
AITOCA	Asylum and Immigration (Treatment of Claimants, etc.) Act 2004
APG	Asylum Policy Guidance
API	Advanced Passenger Information
API	Asylum Policy Instructions
APU	Asylum Policy Update
ARC	Application registration card
BAPIO	British Association of Physicians of Indian Origin
BCIA	Borders, Citizenship and Immigration Act 2009
BDTC	British dependent territories citizenship
BIA	Border and Immigration Agency
BID	Biometric immigration document
BIOT	British Indian Ocean Territory
BN(O)	British national (overseas)
BNA	British Nationality Act
BOC	British overseas citizen
BOTA	British Overseas Territories Act
BOTC	British overseas territories citizen
BPP	British protected person
BRP	Biometric residence permit
CAS	Confirmation of Acceptance for Studies
CAT	Convention Against Torture
CEAS	Common European Asylum System
CEDAW	Convention on the Elimination of All Forms of Discrimination Against Women
CEEC	Central and Eastern European Agreements
CEFR	Common European Framework of Reference for Languages
CERD	Convention on Ending Racial Discrimination
CJEU	Court of Justice of the European Union
CO	Crown Office
CRC	Convention on the Rights of the Child
CRD	Case Resolution Directorate
CRE	Commission for Racial Equality
CTA	Common Travel Area
CUKC	Citizen of the UK and Colonies
DFT	Detained fast track
DL	Discretionary leave
DoH	Department of Health
ECHR	European Convention on Human Rights
ECO	Entry clearance officer
ECtHR	European Court of Human Rights
EEA	European Economic Area

EIG	Enforcement Instructions and Guidance
ELR	Exceptional leave to remain
ESOL	English for speakers of other languages
EURODAC	European Dactyloscopy
EWCA	England and Wales Court of Appeal
FCC	Five Countries Conference
FCO	Foreign and Commonwealth Office
FGM	Female genital mutilation
GCI	Government-controlled Iraq
HASC	Home Affairs Select Committee
HLR	Housing Law Reports
HP	Humanitarian protection
HRLR	Human Rights Law Reports
HSMP	Highly skilled migrants programme
IAA	Immigration and Asylum Act 1999
IANA	Immigration, Asylum and Nationality Act 2006
IANL	Journal of Immigration, Asylum and Nationality Law
IAT	Immigration Appeal Tribunal
ICCPR	International Covenant on Civil and Political Rights
IDI	Immigration Directorate Instructions
ILPA	Immigration Law Practitioners' Association
ILR	Indefinite leave to remain
ILU	Immigration Law Update
IND	Immigration and Nationality Directorate
INLP	Immigration and Nationality Law and Practice
INLR	Immigration and Nationality Law Reports
JCHR	(Parliamentary) Joint Committee on Human Rights
JCWI	Joint Council for the Welfare of Immigrants
MAC	Migration Advisory Committee
MOU	Memorandum of Understanding
NAM	New Asylum Model
NGO	Non-Governmental Organization
NI	Nationality Instructions
NIAA	Nationality Immigration and Asylum Act 2002
NSA	Non-suspensive appeal
OISC	Office of the Immigration Services Commissioner
PBS	Points-based system
PMI	Prime Minister's Initiative
QMV	Qualified majority voting

RABITs	Rapid Border Intervention Team
RALON	The Risk and Liaison Overseas Network
SEF	Statement of Evidence
SEF	Statement of Evidence Form
SIAC	Special Immigration Appeals Commission
SIS	Schengen Information Systems
SOCA	Serious Organised Crime Agency
SSHD	Secretary of State for the Home Department
TCEA	Tribunals Courts and Enforcement Act 2007
TCNs	Third country nationals
TFEU	Treaty on the Functioning of the European Union
UDHR	Universal Declaration of Human Rights
UKBA	United Kingdom Border Agency
UNHCR	United Nations High Commissioner for Refugees
UNHRC	United Nations Human Rights Committee
UTIAC	Upper Tribunal Immigration and Asylum Chamber

Introduction

The notion of a textbook might be taken to imply that there is a standard body of legal knowledge which can be imparted with neutrality and understood in isolation from its context. Nowhere is this less true than in immigration law. To use the words of Legomsky, 'Ensconced as it is in sensitive and controversial policy considerations, immigration law is an area in which the need to place legal doctrine within its larger social and political context is especially acute' (*Immigration and the Judiciary* 1987:5).

As a legal textbook, although this book does not examine in detail the historical and political circumstances, it does introduce the historical and political context in which the law is formed. It gives the historical context of many of the topics covered, and includes references to political debates and some of the current research into the social dimensions of migration. This is not comprehensive, but is an encouragement to the reader to pursue some of these matters further using the wealth of literature in this area, and reference should be made to reading lists at the end of each chapter.

The key themes emerge across different sections and chapters of the book. For instance, the current focus on security and prevention of terrorism lies behind the e-borders scheme described in chapter 7, the detention provisions in chapter 15, and deprivation of nationality in chapter 3. Suspicion of asylum seekers and their motives – connected with the security issue also – is apparent in the material in chapter 12 on the asylum process and in chapter 14 on criminalization and exclusion. The integration agenda, also appearing as a form of control on private life, is apparent in chapter 9 on family life as well as chapter 3 on nationality. Control of entry for work (chapter 10) has taken a new form which integrates it with the new style of border control discussed in chapter 7. The imperative for enforcement in tension with the human reality of individual lives and with international dynamics, infuses the account of appeals and challenges (chapter 8), deportation and removals (chapters 16 and 17) and detention and the asylum process (chapters 15 and 12).

Section 1 sets the foundation for the rest of the book. Chapter 1 gives an outline of the historical development of immigration law in the UK, and an introduction to the sources of immigration law, including discussion of the immigration rules and their special status. Chapter 2 introduces some of the policy issues which provide themes that run throughout the book. The institutional basis of immigration control is described. Security and economic migration are touched on, and there are sections on the treatment of asylum seekers while in the UK and the role of the media. Chapter 3 explains who is subject to immigration control by looking at who has the right of abode in the UK and at key aspects of British nationality law, setting this in the context of nationality law generally. Chapter 4 deals with the application of the Human Rights Act to immigration and asylum law by looking at the content of the rights and their scope of application. The approach of this book is to look at the law through the prism of that Act, and the human rights dimension is addressed in each chapter as it arises.

Section 2 covers the European dimension. Chapter 5 describes the rights of entry of European nationals and others through European free movement provisions for workers. Chapter 6 sets out some of the framework issues arising from European membership, explaining how non-EU nationals are treated in the legal structures.

Section 3 deals with the system of immigration control. Chapter 7 follows the process of entering the UK by examining the legal hurdles encountered before and on arrival, discusses the powers of decision-making held by immigration and entry clearance officers, and concludes with an explanation of the kinds of leave that can be obtained. It integrates an examination of the new e-borders scheme, and the way in which the UK is extending its borders into other countries as part of the changing nature of immigration control, which is becoming more akin to policing. Chapter 8 outlines the structure of the appeals system and examines the grounds of appeal and the ways in which judicial review is used to challenge some of the exercises of executive power in the immigration system.

Section 4 examines the main legal bases for obtaining entry to the UK in immigration law. There is a chapter devoted to joining family members for those who are settled and temporarily resident. A chapter examines the rapidly changing area of entry for work, business, and study, examining in detail the workings of the new points system. A short chapter deals with entry as a visitor.

Section 5 is concerned with asylum claims. Chapter 12 considers the process of making an asylum claim and the special procedures such as fast tracking and certification of claims which enable claims to be decided in a minimum time and with minimum opportunity for challenge. It also examines the issues which are special to asylum appeals. Chapter 13 is devoted to an examination of the criteria which must be fulfilled in order to attain refugee status. Chapter 14 considers criminalization particularly of asylum seekers, and the laws which exclude them from protection when they are considered to have acted in ways that undermine human security.

Section 6 is about enforcement. Chapter 15 concerns the grounds for immigration detention and the means of challenging it. The book ends with three short chapters on deportation, removal, and the application of Article 8 ECHR to these enforced departures. Removal ends the book as it is the end of the process. In a sense, however, it brings us back to the beginning, as the capacity to remove those with no claim in law to stay is seen as a key to the credibility and capacity of government. The countering of this power by claims to the right to respect for private and family life balances the needs of the individual against this political imperative.

SECTION 1

Laying the foundations

1

History and sources of immigration law

SUMMARY

This chapter divides into two parts. The first gives a brief history of immigration law in the UK, focusing on key legislative developments and noting the themes which arise in that history. The second part introduces the reader to the sources of immigration law, including the immigration rules and concessions.

1.1 Introduction

One of the reasons for having at least a passing acquaintance with the history of immigration law in the UK is that themes repeat themselves over time, and it is possible to gain a greater perspective and understanding when we know that the current trend is not new. Particular kinds of legal provisions are created, abolished, and then recreated. For instance, sanctions on airlines for carrying passengers who do not carry full documents were introduced in the latter part of the twentieth century by the Immigration (Carriers Liability) Act 1987, but in 1905 the Aliens Act had provided for fines to be levied on carriers of unauthorized passengers.

Bevan identified nine themes in UK immigration policy: lack of planning, the Commonwealth, the importance of the European Community, international law, bipartisan policy, concern for civil liberties, race relations, the question of assimilation or diversity, and the use of language (1986:22–28). These themes are still important in the twenty-first century, though the balance has changed since 1986. We would now need to add the preoccupation with deterring false asylum claims and terrorism. Each of these will emerge to varying degrees in the course of this book. In enabling us to see that the issues of today are not new, a historical perspective creates the possibility of learning from history.

1.1.1 Attitudes to immigration

Every history of immigration shows that in Britain each new group of arrivals has been regarded with suspicion and hostility. Allegations against Jews at the turn of the twentieth century, West Indians in the 1950s, people from the Asian subcontinent in the 1960s, and in the 1990s, and at the turn of the twenty-first century, against asylum seekers, are all remarkably similar: 'every mass immigrant group was liable to be pronounced unconventional, unclean, unprincipled and generally unwelcome' (Jones in

Juss 1993:71). To this we can add that they are accused of being inveterate liars and scrounging from, or alternatively taking the jobs of, native British people, sometimes even the last two at the same time.

A linked phenomenon is the assertion that the issue is not one of race but of numbers. This is strongly correlated with a political objective of assimilation rather than diversity. If an immigrant group gains sufficient strength in numbers, it is thought that it will have more capacity to retain an identity distinct from that of the host population. Interestingly, while denying that the control of entry is to do with race, it is generally said that it is to do with race relations. Politicians often justify a curb on immigration by saying that it is good for race relations. The basis for this is the numbers idea again, and the goal of assimilation. Immigrant groups are thought to be assimilable in small numbers (see for instance the report of Political and Economic Planning discussed in Dummett and Nicol 1990:174). In larger numbers they are said to generate resentment in the host population. Established immigrant groups have sometimes also supported this line of argument, though others have opposed any form of immigration controls. Examples of the latter are the action of Jewish trade unions in the nineteenth century and the Indian, West Indian and Pakistani Workers' Association in the twentieth century (see Cohen, Humphries, and Mynott 2002).

The link between immigration and race relations was enshrined in government in the former Home Affairs Select Committee on Race Relations and Immigration. Just by way of example, this Committee's report of 1990 asserted that 'the effectiveness and fairness of immigration controls affect both the maintenance of good race relations at home and Britain's standing in the world'. The European Court of Human Rights did not accept this argument for the maintenance of immigration rules that discriminated against women (*Abdulaziz, Cabales and Balkandali v UK* (1985) 7 EHRR 471). The Commission did not accept that the restriction on the entry of husbands was justifiable on the grounds advanced by the government, which included the protection of employment opportunities for the indigenous population and the maintenance of 'public tranquillity'. The numbers involved were so small that the effect on the employment situation was insignificant, and no link had been demonstrated between excluding such men and 'good race relations'. The effect could equally be the reverse, in that although the rules addressed the fears of some members of the population, they could create resentment in others, particularly the immigrant population which would regard the rules as unfair (para 77). The Court endorsed the Commission's view (para 81).

Protection of race relations is often advanced as a reason for government policy. However, Lester and Bindman say that this thinking is an expression of 'the ambivalence of public policies. One face confronts the stranger at the gate; the other is turned towards the stranger within' (1972:13–14). Roy Hattersley, who at one time considered that strict immigration control was necessary to maintain good race relations, ultimately came to the conclusion that:

> Good community relations are not encouraged by the promotion of the idea that the entry of one more black immigrant into this country will be so damaging to the national interest that husbands must be separated from their wives, children denied the chance to look after their aged parents and sisters prevented from attending their brothers' weddings. It is measures like the Asylum and Immigration Bill – and the attendant speeches – which create the impression that we cannot 'afford to let them in'. And if we cannot afford to let them in, then those of them who are already here must be... doing harm. (*The Guardian* 26 February 1996)

1.2 History of immigration law

In studying immigration, we are focusing on movement into a country, in this case the UK. However, this is only one small part of a worldwide movement of peoples which has gone on since time immemorial. Until at least around 1994 (Home Affairs Committee, Fifth Report 2005–06, para 8), Britain was a country of net emigration; in other words, more people left the UK than entered it. Many of the people who have come to the UK have been from areas with a long history of migration, and in paying attention to their arrival in the UK we are only selecting a tiny portion of history.

A complex body of statute, rules, and case law governing entry into the UK is a twentieth-century phenomenon. Before this there was not a developed body of law, but there were numerous provisions controlling the movement of 'aliens'. Aliens were people who did not owe allegiance to the Crown, defined as those who were not British subjects, (British Nationality and Status of Aliens Act 1914 s 27). See chapter 3. Sometimes, sweeping measures have been employed; for example, in 1290, Edward I, following an increasing campaign of hatred against Jews, expelled all Jews from England. Some of those expelled would have been aliens, and some British subjects. The latter, according to Magna Carta, had a right to remain in the kingdom and travel freely in and out; the royal decree was illegal as well as immoral, but there was no remedy.

Measures controlling the movement of aliens were often connected with hostilities with other countries. In the sixteenth century, when England was at war with Spain, Ireland gave assistance to the Spaniards, and Ireland and England were in continual conflict. There were by this time a significant number of Irish people resident in England. As Dummett and Nicol comment, regardless of the individual views or affiliations of these people, Queen Elizabeth I issued a proclamation that 'no manner of person born in the realm of Ireland... shall remain in the realm' (1990:45). The Irish were either expelled from England or imprisoned. Again, in 1793, a statute was passed to control the entry of aliens, this time directed towards travellers from France; following the French Revolution, it was feared they might stir up similar fervour in England. While some echoes of these earlier practices may be detected in modern law, by and large the immigration law of the last 100 years is a very different creature from the Royal Proclamations of Edward and Elizabeth.

The beginning of modern-day immigration control can be traced to the persecution of Jews in Eastern Europe at the end of the nineteenth century. From being an envied and romanticized minority as they had been in the nineteenth century, Jews once again became a target of violence and hostility. Many took refuge in Western Europe, including England. However, such movements of hatred are not generally confined within national boundaries, and the new arrivals also found themselves the subject of a campaign in Britain. They were concentrated in areas of poor housing and working conditions, and Parliament debated as it does now whether the immigrants exacerbated these conditions, or whether their industry and creativity were an asset. A Jewish family living in overcrowded rooms, and taking in lodgers to cover the rent, was said to be 'lowering the social standard very greatly' (HL Debs 5 July 1898 vol 60 col 1098). The counter-argument was made that overcrowding should be dealt with by domestic law, not immigration control (HL Debs 20 June 1898 vol 59 col 729). 'Foreigners' were few in number: 'but they settle down in one or two limited areas, and this handful of foreigners becomes a very large quantity in these limited areas' (col 738).

Both in former times and later in the twentieth century, immigrants are associated with overcrowded housing, disease, crime, and either taking jobs and keeping down wages, or refusing to work and taking up welfare provision. The contrary nature of maintaining both these propositions was also noted a century ago (HL Debs 20 June 1898 vol 59 col 729).

A campaign against alien workers followed, and the government responded by setting up a Royal Commission to investigate the effect of immigrant workers upon housing and employment conditions and upon public health and morals, the allegations being that they were unclean and spread disease and crime. The conclusion of the Royal Commission was that there was no threat to the jobs and working conditions of British workers, and immigrants did not create poverty, disease, and crime. There was a slightly higher rate of crime among some alien groups, though Dummett and Nicol suggest that 'the figures were crude and took no account of social class' (1990:101), and immigrants were living in overcrowded housing. The balance of the report was not obviously in favour of immigration control; nevertheless, the Royal Commission recommended control. The result was the Aliens Act 1905, the first major piece of modern immigration legislation.

This Act marked the inception of the immigration service and the appeals system. It set up an inspectorate which operated at ports of entry to the UK. It was called the Aliens Inspectorate and its officers (the first immigration officers) had the power to refuse entry to aliens who were considered 'undesirable'. Undesirability was defined as lacking in the means to support oneself and dependants, and lacking in the capacity to acquire such means; mentally ill; likely through ill health to become dependent on the public welfare system or to endanger the health of others; or as having been previously expelled or convicted abroad of an extraditable nonpolitical crime. As a result of successful argument in Parliament, those opposed to controls on aliens had managed to limit the inspectorate's powers to those who travelled on the cheapest tickets (steerage class) on immigrant ships, which were defined as those carrying more than 20 aliens. These categories bear a striking similarity to the requirements for entry in modern-day immigration rules. Under present rules, all categories of entrant are required to show that they will not be reliant on public funds, long-term entrants are required to undergo a medical examination (HC 395 para 36) and the commission of criminal offences may give grounds for deportation (Immigration Act 1971 s 3(5)(a)). Note also that the standards in the Act do not clearly correspond to the findings of the Royal Commission; instead, they compromise between averting real problems which had been identified and pandering to fears which had been shown to be unfounded. The overall effect is somewhat mitigated by the arguments in Parliament of those concerned with civil liberties. Here we see Bevan's themes of lack of planning and bipartisan policy enacted, the latter meaning that political parties would tend to take opposing positions on immigration (though it would also be true to say that it is an issue which does not always split on party lines).

The Act also marked the beginning of an appeals system, by providing for Immigration Appeals Boards. They were set up in every major port of entry and immigrants refused leave to enter had a right of appeal to them.

As we have seen in relation to earlier conflicts with France and Spain, war has been used to impose severe restrictions upon foreigners. During the First World War, the Aliens Restriction Act 1914 s 1 gave the Secretary of State a great deal of power to regulate the entry, stay, and deportation of aliens, and even to pass regulations 'on any other matters which appear necessary or expedient with a view to the safety of the realm'. The Aliens Restrictions (Amendment) Act 1919 extended these wartime powers to apply at any time, subject to a yearly review. This was the pattern also with Prevention of

Terrorism Acts, introduced in 1974 as an emergency measure subject to annual review, but culminating in a permanent Terrorism Act in 2000. The effects of the 1919 Act were far-reaching. Not only did the wide powers given to the Secretary of State for wartime now also apply in peacetime, but the Act also set the pattern, as Bevan describes, for the legal structure of immigration control. The legislation, like many modern statutes, was skeletal in form, having few substantive provisions but giving wide powers to the Secretary of State to make rules.

The 1919 Act was followed by the Aliens Order of 1920, which laid out the more detailed control of aliens and initiated today's system of work permits. Both passports and work permits grew out of wartime controls, as before 1914 it was possible to travel between a number of countries without a passport.

The Second World War had a very significant effect upon patterns of immigration to the UK. War was declared at a time when the Commonwealth was a strong bond which held together a number of nations in allegiance to the monarch of the UK. The UK was regarded by many as the 'mother country'. The fact that British and Commonwealth soldiers were fighting alongside one another contributed to the development of the idea of family, a sense of partnership, and belonging. Additionally, some Commonwealth service people had contributed to the war effort by doing essential work in the UK and so developed real familiarity with Britain. The media talked in terms of loyalty and gratitude to other Commonwealth citizens. This sense of belonging was not a thought-out policy based on a concept of rights enforceable by individuals, but more of a pleasing sentiment which was not expected to have any legal effect.

The reality of post-war entry to the UK was somewhat different. Spencer (1997) describes the deliberations of an interdepartmental working party set up in 1948, and also the later work of a committee of the Ministry of Labour, to consider where there were labour shortages and whether citizens from Commonwealth countries could or should be recruited to make up any shortfall. Writers differ as to the extent of any labour shortage and of recruitment policies aimed at remedying such shortage. The main focus was on the West Indies, and the question of whether workers should be recruited from there. Spencer reports negative conclusions as far as the recruitment of West Indians was concerned; they were not considered suitable workers or acceptable to the unions in the UK. Spencer also reports a refusal by the unions to cooperate with a recruitment scheme, and a preference by the government committees for workers from the continent of Europe. The reasons for this preference were that European workers would integrate more easily and it would be easier for the government to return them when no longer needed. The latter is in part because European workers would not have any claim as British subjects whereas Caribbean workers would. That Europeans would be regarded as easier to integrate could be surprising in view of the fact that English would be a native language for Caribbean workers though not for any European. However, Spencer's analysis of the Cabinet papers of the time, released under the 30-year rule, strongly suggests that colour was at the root of the government's objection to West Indian workers. An analysis of Cabinet papers of the following few years relating to attempts to restrain immigration in the early 1950s reveals the same concerns (Carter, Harris, and Joshi 1987).

All the authors previously mentioned, whose work is based on Cabinet papers, recount obstructive practices that were instituted in the Caribbean, West Africa, India, and Pakistan, making it more difficult for citizens of those countries to travel to Britain despite their being Commonwealth citizens. Examples of tactics employed were the delay in issuing passports and the omission of the reference to British subject status on travel documents, even though the holder was entitled to such a reference.

The passage of the British Nationality Act in 1948 did not affect right of entry into the UK; it dealt with nationality rather than immigration. However, it did so in a rather theoretical sense, being more a matter of labelling than of delivering enforceable rights. Indeed, it was not within the contemplation of those who produced this legislation that the millions of Commonwealth citizens and citizens of the UK and Colonies would attempt to use their theoretical right to enter the UK. It expressed the rather theoretical and symbolic idea that legislators had of the meaning of British subject status, and began the division between citizens of independent Commonwealth countries and other British subjects, which laid the foundation for the later development of immigration control (see chapter 3).

Despite the disincentives mentioned earlier, immigration into Britain continued. There were opportunities for work, and these were attractive. By far the largest number of entrants was from Ireland and the countries known as the Old Commonwealth, i.e., Australia, Canada, and New Zealand. Immigration from the Caribbean was also rising, though not keeping pace with Ireland and the old Commonwealth. Until the release of the Cabinet papers relating to the 1950s, it was widely believed that there was a disproportionate rise in that period of immigration from the Caribbean and of social problems associated with this immigration. The popular account also entailed that the government was dedicated to retaining the rights of British subjects from the Caribbean to enter the UK, but then as social problems escalated, they were reluctantly forced to legislate in the form of the Commonwealth Immigrants Act 1962 to restrict the right of some Commonwealth citizens. Political speeches of the time focused on the familiar theme of numbers. Only a certain number of immigrants, it was asserted, could be assimilated – in other words absorbed – into the majority culture in Britain without noticeable impact or making demands. The studies mentioned earlier suggest a contrary view, namely that in working parties established specifically to consider the role of 'coloured' workers, the link of immigrants with social problems was not proven, and immigrants from the West Indies were far outnumbered by those from Ireland and the old Commonwealth. The initiative to control black immigration seemed to come, not from the identification of a social problem, but from an independent agenda within the Home Office and Cabinet Office. The government moved to impose a quota system on immigrants from the West Indies. However, official descriptions of them became more favourable after arrivals increased from India and Pakistan. Those who were formerly lazy were now industrious and English-speaking, and it was the South Asians who were 'unassimilable'. The British government succeeded in obtaining cooperation from West Indian, Indian, and Pakistani governments to restrain migration, and Paul comments:

> The range of administrative methods used by territories of origin and the United Kingdom to prevent colonial migration was so extensive that one might suggest that those migrants who did succeed in obtaining a passport, completing an English language interview, bearing up to scrutiny and accepting the propaganda at its true value were indeed hardy souls. (1997:153)

After years of political debate and manoeuvring, the Commonwealth Immigrants Act was finally passed in 1962. The significance of the Act was immense. For the first time, there was a restriction on the rights of certain Commonwealth citizens to come to the UK.

The Act distinguished between Commonwealth citizens based on parentage. Those who were born in the UK or Ireland or who held a passport issued by the government of those countries would not be subject to immigration control; others would. The immigration control consisted of conditions that a Commonwealth citizen would have to satisfy to gain entry. Whether these conditions were satisfied was to be determined by an immigration officer who was given a wide measure of discretion.

One of the peculiar features of British immigration law, to which we shall return time and again, is the heavy reliance on formerly unpublished instructions, guidelines, and concessions. These less formal sources in practice often determine the outcome of applications. In the course of the implementation of the Commonwealth Immigrants Act 1962, it was made clear by internal guidance that the discretion given to immigration officers to refuse entry on the basis that requirements were not met, would not be applied in practice to immigrants from Canada, Australia, or New Zealand. The system of control that was established therefore discriminated at two levels against black would-be entrants. Initially, the terms of the Act itself, while neutral on their face as regards race or colour, were based on a requirement of birth in the UK or possession of a passport issued by the UK government, both of which would be satisfied more often in practice by white people. At the second level of internal instructions, the discrimination was closer to being explicit. As with the Jews in the thirteenth century, though less publicly, the distinction was made on the basis of ethnicity, not nationality.

For the Commonwealth citizens subject to immigration control, a three-tier system of work vouchers was instituted. Dummett and Nicol comment that this founded a bureaucratic system for processing immigration rather than a method of controlling it. The actual effect of the Commonwealth Immigrants Act was very different from the government's intention. There was a substantial rise in immigration from the Indian subcontinent in particular around the time of the 1962 Act. The Act has often been presented as the response to this increased immigration, but as Spencer (1997) and Bevan (1986) recount, it is more likely to have caused it. Spencer suggests four ways in which the Commonwealth Immigrants Act actually encouraged immigration, as follows.

First, the build-up to the legislation had taken years. The proposal to restrict immigration was therefore known long in advance and during the years 1960–62 this created a rush to 'beat the ban'.

Second, prior to the 1962 Act, those who had come from the Indian subcontinent to Britain were mainly men who had come for a temporary period to work and to send money back to their families. Often this was in a tradition in their original locality, and they came to Britain because at that time there was a good chance of employment, particularly in the textile industry in the north. These men's travels were therefore not immigration as it is sometimes understood 40 years later, i.e., they had not come to settle. The 1962 Act made it less likely that men retiring from this role could be replaced by younger relatives as the work voucher system would not have favoured their entry. The Act therefore tended to encourage those men to apply for leave to remain in the UK.

Following on from the last point, the Act permitted unification of families, and so for the men who had come as sojourners, the provisions of the Act combined to make remaining in the UK and being joined by their families the more viable option. It might be said (though Spencer does not make this point) that the Act encouraged and established the growth of an immigrant population modelled on British assumptions of working and family life, rather than an understanding of what migration meant to those who were doing it.

Spencer's final point is also made by Dummett and Nicol (1990): that the Act established a regime that regulated and therefore to a degree allowed people to enter the UK, namely the system of entry control and work vouchers.

The 1962 Act was formative in that it laid the foundation of the distinction between entry as a right and entry subject to the fulfilment of conditions, and did so by using the criterion of connection with the UK. The particular history of this Act reminds us not to take at face value assertions of cause and effect in relation to legislation; it also introduces the role of internal guidance in the operation of immigration law.

The history of the Commonwealth Immigrants Act 1968 is discussed by many writers including Shah, P. (2000), Bevan (1986), and Dummett and Nicol (1990). It provides a stark illustration of the difference between immigration policy based on loyalty to those whom the Empire and then the Commonwealth gave the status of British subject, and immigration policy based on fear of admission of numbers of non-white people. The key events were the independence of, first, Kenya and, later, Uganda and Tanzania. Each of these countries at independence had an established minority population which had come from the Indian subcontinent, some of whom had been introduced into East Africa by Britain which, as colonial power, had employed them on construction projects. Many had left India before its independence and before the creation of Pakistan, and their only citizenship was that of the UK and Colonies. The East African countries, on attaining independence, pursued a policy of Africanization that required residents to demonstrate their allegiance to the new state. Many Asians either did not fulfil the conditions for acquiring the new citizenship or did not register within the time limit, preferring to wait and see how their fortunes were likely to go in the new regime before committing themselves. Some may have been reluctant to lose their British connection. For many of those who did not acquire the new citizenship, serious consequences ensued. They lost their employment or their livelihood, and sought to use whatever protection their citizenship of the UK and Colonies could offer them. Their passports had been issued by the British High Commission and, therefore, under the 1962 Act they were not subject to immigration control. They had, as British subjects, right of entry into the UK. Inflated figures of likely entrants were quoted in the media, and the Commonwealth Immigrants Act 1968 was rushed through Parliament. The new Act provided that British subjects would be free from immigration control only if they, or at least one of their parents or grandparents, had been born, adopted, registered, or naturalized in the UK. The issue of a passport by a British High Commission thus ceased to be a qualification for entry free of control. For those subject to control, another voucher system was introduced. This one was based on tight quotas, reflecting the government's contention that numbers were the problem.

The story of the East African Asians illustrates how a British government was prepared to mix together issues of nationality and immigration. This is one of the themes identified by Bevan. While the East African Asians retained their CUKC (citizen of the UK and Colonies) status, it was in effect worthless as it no longer conferred a right of entry to their country of nationality.

The issue of colour (which was the terminology then used, and which was quite accurate) continued to dominate public debate about immigration. When the Immigration Act 1971 was passed, the racial definition of those with rights of entry and those without was complete. While later statutes have made substantial changes to the immigration process and the rights of immigrants, the 1971 Act remains the source of Home Office and immigration officers' powers to make decisions on entry, stay, and deportation. Its significance in terms of the history we are now tracing is its division of the world into patrials and non-patrials. Previously, UK law had divided the world into British subjects and aliens. This was the fundamental category which determined whether a person had right of entry into the UK. Legislation then, as we have seen, restricted the rights of some British subjects to the extent that these rights became practically worthless. The Immigration Act 1971 gave right of abode in the UK to those it defined as 'patrials'. These were:

(i) citizens of the UK and Colonies who had that citizenship by birth, adoption, naturalization, or registration in the UK;

(ii) citizens of the UK and Colonies whose parent or grandparent had that citizenship by those same means at the time of the birth of the person in question;

(iii) citizens of the UK and Colonies with five years' ordinary residence in the UK;

(iv) Commonwealth citizens whose parent was born or adopted in the UK before their birth;

(v) Commonwealth citizens married to a patrial man.

Commonwealth citizens who had been settled in the UK for five years when the Act came into force (1 January 1973) also had the right to register and thus possibly the right of abode. Others would be subject to immigration controls. Apart from the five-year residence qualification, the right to live in the UK and to enter free from immigration control was determined by birth or parentage, not by nationality. The British Nationality Act 1981 carried this classification into British nationality law, and it is still the case that there are some, though a dwindling number, of British nationals who do not have a right of entry to the UK. More detail is given of all these provisions in chapter 3.

On the same day that the Immigration Act 1971 came into force, the UK entered the European Community (EC). One of the cornerstones upon which the EC is built is freedom of movement, not only of goods but also of workers and their families. Despite this timing, the Immigration Act made no reference to European membership or the principle of freedom of movement. It continues to be the case up to the present that UK immigration law has developed quite separately from European law on freedom of movement (*R v IAT and Surinder Singh ex p SSHD* [1992] Imm AR 565) and that, at the same time that immigration restrictions were confirmed for Commonwealth citizens with a traditional allegiance to Britain, a new category of privilege was created for European nationals. The free movement rights of EU nationals are now implemented in UK law by the Immigration (European Economic Area) Regulations 2006, SI 2006/1003.

Primary immigration, that is of people coming to establish a life on their own rather than to join family members, virtually ceased with the Acts of 1968 and 1971; nevertheless, in the 1980s, the general trend in immigration provisions remained towards increasing restriction. Attention switched from primary immigration to family settlement, and more demanding rules for the entry of spouses were introduced. These raised such a political storm that, most unusually, there was a debate in Parliament concerning new immigration rules (see the discussion in chapter 9).

On the whole, however, toward the end of the twentieth century, immigration policy (as distinct from asylum) did not play such a prominent part in the political life of the UK as it did previously. The Labour government's abolition of the infamous primary purpose rule in 1997 was a reversal of one of the most punitive provisions on family settlement (again see chapter 9) and the reduced tension around immigration and increased awareness of rights made this possible. The increasingly restrictive nature of immigration law did not arise from concerns about immigration as such, but from concerns about increased asylum claims. The rapid growth of a visa regime, now affecting travellers from potentially any country in the world, is an example of this (see chapter 7). The Immigration and Asylum Act 1999 made significant inroads into the rights of appeal of those alleged to be in breach of immigration law, but this was to address the backlog of cases at the Home Office and to expedite the removal of unsuccessful asylum seekers. The backlog, rather than issues of entry and entitlement, became the immigration scandal of the late 1990s in its own right.

The other major development in immigration law particularly in the last 20 years has been the introduction of internal controls. This entails the requirement for housing officers, benefits officers, employers, registrars of births, marriages, and deaths, and airline officials to interpret immigration status, upon which entitlement to civil benefits such as housing or employment increasingly depends. Juss dates the introduction of these provisions from the first report of the Select Committee on Race Relations and Immigration in 1978. The effect has been to exclude from social benefits those people who have, or who may have, or who may be thought to have, a questionable immigration status. The introduction of biometric identity documents for foreign nationals in 2007 heralded the entrenchment of immigration status into everyday life.

Both the development of internal controls and the reduction of appeal rights ride on the back of the issue which has attracted public attention since the 1990s – that of asylum. The bulk of the case law reported in the Immigration Appeal Reports for some years concerned asylum rather than immigration issues. There was an escalation of legislation principally aimed at controlling asylum seekers: the Asylum and Immigration Appeals Act 1993, Asylum and Immigration Act 1996, Immigration and Asylum Act 1999, Nationality, Immigration and Asylum Act 2002, the bizarrely named Asylum and Immigration (Treatment of Claimants, etc.) Act 2004, and the Immigration, Asylum and Nationality Act 2006. However, although the target group is different, the themes are recognizable.

The 1993 Act introduced an appeal right for asylum seekers, but also the concept of a claim 'without foundation' (Sch 2 para 5). Again, this is based on the idea of a potential entrant as dishonest. Claims so certified would attract only limited appeal rights, the government's avowed intention being to speed through the system claims which could be identified at an early stage as unmeritorious. This provision is based not only on the idea of the deceptive applicant but also on addressing the backlog. Juss gives a stinging account of the origins of the 1993 Act in which he suggests that the problem of the backlog was self-inflicted, resulting from a recruitment freeze in the Immigration and Nationality Department (IND). Opportunities for applicants to manipulate the system arose as a result of increasing delays, and these manipulations in turn extended the delays. His account may be borne out by the fact that the backlogs were tackled in the year 2000 by recruiting extra personnel in the IND.

Delay and cheating the system, and the relationship between the two, became the political issues of the 1990s. The alleged cheating was both at the point of entry (the concept of the 'bogus' asylum seeker) and after entry (the concept of the 'scrounger'). These ideas underlie further provisions in the Asylum and Immigration Act 1996 such as, for instance, the creation of a new offence of obtaining leave to remain by deception (s 4). The kinds of claims that would be subjected to restricted appeal rights (known then as the short procedure) were extended to include those from a designated country of origin. Designation, according to the promoting minister in Parliament, would be on the basis that there had been a high number of applications and a high number of refusals from that particular country and that there was, in general, no serious risk of persecution in that country (HC Debs 11 December 1995 col 703). This provision has a similar basis to the 'without foundation' provision, that of expediting applications on the basis that they may be identified without full examination as being unmeritorious. Similar provisions followed in the 1999 Act ('manifestly unfounded') and in the 2002 Act ('clearly unfounded'). The list of designated countries became known as the 'White List'. It was abandoned after a successful challenge, in *R v SSHD ex p Javed and Ali* [2001] Imm AR 529, to the inclusion of Pakistan because of known widespread discrimination against women and against Ahmadis, which had been accepted in the higher courts in the UK (*Shah and Islam v IAT and SSHD* [1999] Imm AR 283 and *Ahmed (Iftikhar) v Secretary of State for the Home Department* [2000] INLR 1). Where sectors of society could be said to be at risk, it could not be reasonable to say there was, in general, no serious risk of persecution. A new 'white list' was produced in the 2002 Act and has been extended by ministerial orders and the 2004 Act (see chapter 12).

Section 2 of the 1996 Act also introduced a power for the Secretary of State to certify that asylum seekers could be returned, before their claim was considered, to a 'safe third country'. This was the beginning of the UK's effort to stop asylum seekers being 'bounced around' Europe, i.e., shuttled from one country to another, each one declining to hear their asylum application but finding a reason to return them to another Member State. The UK was a signatory to the Dublin Convention, the treaty by which EC countries sought to find a way of determining which state should hear an asylum application. However, as international law, this treaty was not directly binding in the UK. As the Common European Asylum System has been coming into effect, the treaty has been superseded by a regulation, binding in the UK, discussed in chapter 12.

Other provisions of the 1996 Act continued the dual themes of deception and internal controls. More criminal offences were devised, targeting the racketeering of those who arrange entry to the UK for gain (s 5), and more internal controls were set up, including recruiting employers into the system of detection of residents with potentially irregular immigration status (ss 8 and 9).

The history of immigration law is full of examples of legislation swiftly introduced to reverse higher court decisions. Section 11 of the 1996 Act was one such example. The Social Security (Persons from Abroad) Miscellaneous Amendment Regulations 1996, SI 1996/30, had removed benefits from almost everyone who was subject to immigration control. The regulations were declared ultra vires by Simon Brown LJ because they were beyond the tolerance level of a 'civilised nation'. 'Something so uncompromisingly draconian can only be achieved by primary legislation' (*R v Secretary of State for Social Security ex p JCWI* [1997] 1 WLR 275). As Macdonald puts it: 'The government duly obliged, enacting the condemned regulation as section 11 of the 1996 Act' (2001:9).

The Immigration and Asylum Act 1999 continued the trend by, according to Statewatch, 'hugely increasing surveillance, monitoring and compulsion'. Registrars of births, marriages, and deaths were brought into the internal control system (s 24). Penalties for carrying passengers without full documentation increased once again, being extended to include trains, buses, and coaches to cover entry via the Channel Tunnel (Part II of the Act). There were also provisions for penalizing private car and lorry drivers who carried clandestine entrants. Asylum seekers were excluded from the mainstream benefits system, and a dispersal system was instituted which would distribute them around the country (Part VI). Appeal rights were further curtailed, both for asylum seekers and other deportees (Part IV). Limited appeal rights for family visitors were reinstated. The 1990s had seen a massive increase of asylum seekers detained in detention centres and prisons. One of the anomalous features of immigration detention generally, including that of asylum seekers, is that it is not subject to any compulsory supervision by the courts, and there is no presumption of a right to bail, as there is when someone is charged with a criminal offence. In the 1999 Act, the government took the opportunity to address this issue by introducing a routine bail hearing (Part III). However, these provisions were never implemented, and were repealed by the Nationality, Immigration and Asylum Act 2002. The 1999 Act contained the first statutory presumptions of the safety of a third country to which an asylum seeker could be returned. This appeared to be a government reaction to having the Secretary of State's certificates of safety issued under the 1996 Act regularly struck down by the courts.

In the Immigration and Asylum Act 1999 s 11, the certificates in relation to European countries were made immune to judicial review by a statutory presumption that such countries were deemed safe. This proved unassailable (*R (Thangasara) v SSHD* [2002] UKHL 36).

The 1999 Act was proclaimed as a radical overhaul of the immigration and asylum system. It expressed the political agenda of its day – suspicion that there is a large volume of unmeritorious asylum claims; the cost of welfare benefits obtained by people who made such claims; the progressive extension of internal controls; the problem of backlog and delay in the system both before dealing with claims and before removal from the country of those who did not succeed; and the shifting of blame to the morally more acceptable targets of 'racketeers' rather than the obviously vulnerable asylum seekers. There was another influence at the time of debates on the 1999 Act, namely, the Human Rights Act 1998 (HRA), which had received Royal Assent but was not yet in force. The 1999 Act removed some rights to have an appeal heard in the UK. The counterbalance was to provide an in-country appeal on human rights grounds. The 1999 Act provided the first statutory right of appeal against immigration decisions on human rights grounds (s 65, now in the Nationality, Immigration and Asylum Act 2002 s 84). Further discussion of the implications of the introduction of the HRA is reserved for chapter 4.

1.2.1 Twenty-first century

Five immigration statutes have been passed already in this century. There have also been four anti-terrorism statutes, three of which derived from and interact with policies to restrict the activities of foreign nationals. A further provision restricting immigration status was inserted into a criminal justice statute (Criminal Justice and Immigration Act 2008). In parallel throughout this same period the higher courts have been occupied with working out the application of the Human Rights Act to immigration and immigration-related decisions. At first the tension was severe between the government which had drafted, promoted, and secured the passage of the Human Rights Act through Parliament and the judiciary who were applying it to immigration and asylum cases. Amidst a 'gathering storm in relations' between the executive and judiciary (Rawlings 2005:380), the government attempted to stop all immigration and asylum issues from being heard by the courts, whether on appeal or review, by means of an ouster clause in the Asylum and Immigration (Treatment of Claimants, etc.) Bill 2003. More recently, the government proposes new legal structures to curtail the powers of judges to apply human rights, both in the 2011 consultation on family migration (*Family Migration: A Consultation*), by which they proposed to statutorily fix the interpretation of Article 8 ECHR, and through the UK's term as chair of the Council of Europe, running from November 2011, during which they propose reforms to limit the jurisdiction of the Court when the interference complained of results from primary legislation or a decision of the Supreme Court.

During the same period there has been an intensified focus on security. This predated 11 September 2001, but was accelerated by the events of that day. Also during this period the completion of the first phase of the Common European Asylum System and latterly the acquisition by the Court of Justice of the EU of competence in immigration and asylum matters have meant that first EU legislation on asylum, and then EU case law, have had a direct effect in the UK.

At the time of the passing of the 1999 Act, it was widely predicted there would be another immigration statute within three years, and so it turned out (see for this point and generally, McKee 2002). The Nationality, Immigration and Asylum Act 2002 was preceded by a White Paper: *Secure Borders, Safe Haven; Integration with Diversity in Modern Britain* (Cm 5387), announced by Home Secretary David Blunkett in the following terms:

> The White Paper takes forward our agenda by offering an holistic and comprehensive approach to nationality, managed immigration, and asylum that recognises the interrelationship of each element in the system. No longer will we treat asylum seekers in isolation or fail to recognise that there must be alternative routes to entry into this country. (HC Debs 7 February 2002 col 1028)

The Act deals with changes to nationality law, the provision of accommodation centres for asylum seekers, restrictions on the asylum support system, the provision of removal centres and expansion of powers of detention and removal, extension and amendment of the carriers' liability scheme, and the introduction of further criminal offences. At least as much as the 1999 Act, this Act was dominated by objectives concerning the asylum system.

McKee refers to 'divergent and contradictory goals', specifically:

- to keep asylum seekers out, but to provide a welcome for genuine refugees;
- to integrate refugees and ethnic minorities into mainstream British culture, but to celebrate cultural diversity;
- to include a raft of authoritarian and repressive measures under the same anodyne umbrella of 'modernisation' as liberal measures to allow economic migration and facilitate easier travel. (2002:181)

Within the broad purposes identified by McKee, the Act and the White Paper have a number of underlying policy themes which may be characterized as:

1. developing an all-pervasive control system for asylum seekers;
2. a controlled development of the possibility of entry for work;
3. the creation of a class of people without rights or status;
4. development of extra-territorial immigration control;
5. combating terrorism; and
6. the strengthening of executive power.

Taking each of these in turn: the all-pervasive control system is an attempt to repair the damaged credibility of the asylum system, which had been criticized for unfairness, inefficiency, and delay. Accommodation and removal centres were elements in this development. Restrictions on welfare support which made it conditional on reporting or residence also tightened the level of continuous control that the government is able to exercise over asylum seekers. Increased powers of detention and removal served the same purpose.

The second policy underlying the 2002 White Paper was a cautious encouragement of economic migration. This was the first evidence for decades that immigration policy might be directed towards encouragement of entry, and received a general welcome. Shah, R. (2002:315), for instance, saw this as evidence of 'a new dynamism' in the Home Office. However, this apparent shift in policy was not reflected in the 2002 Act. Extensions of various schemes permitting entry of workers were implemented by concessions and developments in administrative practice which, in some cases, resulted in changes to the immigration rules. The retention of government control over entry into the UK is presaged in the White Paper, para 12: 'We have taken steps to ensure that people with the skills and talents *we need* are able to come to the UK on a sensible and managed basis' (emphasis added). The retention of control and the words emphasized lend support to the argument of Cohen that such proposals represent nothing new; rather, they replicate a historical tendency to manipulate overseas labour, 'labour which can be turned on and off like a tap' (2002). Bevan made the same comment in relation to earlier provisions (1986:278). Scepticism it seems was warranted. A further White Paper in 2005 announced a tiered system of managed migration that aimed to bring entry for work and study into a more routinized, bureaucratized system, dominated by immigration control. But this is to anticipate.

The growth of a class of people without rights or status is evident in a number of disparate developments, and three provisions of the 2002 Act in particular are part of that development. Section 4 substantially extended the power of the Secretary of State to deprive a person of their British nationality. In the case of people who acquired their British nationality by naturalization or registration, there is no requirement to have regard to whether doing so will leave them stateless. In the case of others, although they may not strictly speaking be left stateless, as the Joint Parliamentary Committee on Human Rights pointed out:

> deprivation of British citizenship would entail loss of British diplomatic protection; loss of status; loss of the ability to participate in the democratic process in the United Kingdom; and serious damage to reputation and dignity. The Home Office argument assumes that the real threat to human rights would derive from any subsequent decisions taken as part of the immigration control process. In that process, there would usually be adequate opportunity to ensure that effect is given to Convention rights, and that other rights are given appropriate weight. However, we are concerned about the wider implications of loss of British citizenship. (Parliamentary Joint Committee on Human Rights Session 2001–02 Seventeenth Report para 26)

While recognizing that there is no right to British nationality, the Committee was concerned about the consequences of statelessness, and that if the other country refused a passport, the alternative nationality would be 'an empty shell' (para 26). The Committee's report reveals that the civic limbo in which persons would find themselves was not recognized by the Home Office. The difficulties of being left in a condition of no status or rights are easily underestimated, and in *Ahmed v Austria* 24 EHRR 62 had resulted in Mr Ahmed taking his own life.

Section 76 of the 2002 Act enables the Secretary of State to revoke a person's indefinite leave to remain if the person 'is liable to deportation but cannot be deported for legal reasons'. The legal reasons which would prevent deportation are likely to be that the person would face a serious violation of their human rights in their country of origin and no other country is willing to accept them. Without indefinite leave to remain, a person may neither work nor claim benefits. They are without status and without means.

The 2002 Bill was amended in the House of Lords so that citizenship by birth (though not by application) could only be removed in reliance on acts committed after s 4 came into force (1 April 2003). However, indefinite leave to remain may be revoked in reliance on anything done before s 76 came into force (10 February 2003) and leave granted before that date may be revoked, giving the section retrospective effect.

Finally, s 67(2) in combination with its interpretation in *R v SSHD ex p Khadir (Appellant)* [2005] UKHL 39 means that a person who is granted temporary admission – a status without rights – may remain in that position for years, even though there is no possibility of being removed (see chapter 15). The status of temporary admission, on which many asylum seekers remain for years, is a bar to rights of many kinds. The government has maintained that people on temporary admission are not 'lawfully present' for the purpose of social security rules and housing rules. Arguments on this and other issues have even led to the legal fiction that people temporarily admitted are not present at all, let alone lawfully. This was scotched in *Szoma v Secretary of State for the Department of Work and Pensions* [2005] UKHL 64, in which their Lordships held that the appellant was lawfully present.

The concern with undocumented migrants both throughout Europe and further afield is marked by this paradox; ever-increasing control measures are developed alongside measures to exclude some people from the system altogether. The Criminal Justice and Immigration Act 2008 contains a further power of this kind, discussed later.

The development of extra-territorial immigration control is strongly signalled in the 2002 White Paper but barely appears in the Act. It was indeed a very significant development, but was introduced by a single enabling section. Ann Dummett submitted to the Parliamentary Joint Committee on Human Rights (JCHR) that the chief threat which the 2002 Bill represented to human rights arose from

> the character it shares with all the immigration legislation of the twentieth century: it is an enabling Bill...Many of its provisions are vague and general, allowing for subsequent, more precise provisions contained in statutory instruments and rules. The nature of these precise provisions is to be to a very large extent discretionary. (Memorandum 5 to JCHR 17th Report Session 2001–02)

The detail of the export of immigration control is contained in secondary legislation and administrative arrangements. The notable exceptions are Sch 8, which extends and amends the liability of carriers (lorry drivers, rail companies, and so on) for clandestine entrants hidden in their vehicles. Section 141 permits a law of the UK to have effect abroad. This is the enabling section which laid the foundation for UK immigration control to operate at French ports. In fact, the legislative foundation for exporting the border in other ways had already been laid in the 1999 Act. Nevertheless, posting immigration officers alongside their counterparts at European ports, with the aim of deterring asylum claims constituted a significant change. These measures are discussed fully in chapter 7.

Combating terrorism is a thread which runs throughout legislation and government policy much more strongly since 11 September 2001. The Anti-terrorism, Crime and Security Act 2001 contains significant provisions affecting refugee claims, discussed in chapter 14, but the connection with prevention of terrorism is not explicit in the Immigration Acts. There are not, for instance, sections headed 'terrorism'. Nevertheless, in the 2002 Act, the strengthened and extended border controls, the new offences created, and the intensive monitoring of asylum seekers all have security as a background theme and objective (see McKee 2002 and Shah, R. 2002).

The asylum support provisions of the 2002 Act were among its most contentious. Despite research suggesting that welfare policies are not an effective deterrent (Home Office Research Study 243, 2003), the government was dedicated to a path of reducing welfare provision. As welfare support is not covered as a subject in its own right in this book, the main issues will be outlined here. The crucial provision in the 2002 Act was s 55 which provided that the Secretary of State has no obligation to provide welfare support (money or accommodation) where a claim for asylum has not been made 'as soon as reasonably practicable' unless this is necessary to avoid a breach of the claimant's human rights. Challenges to denial of benefit multiplied in the High Court. In the first year of the Act, judges made over 800 emergency orders for the payment of interim benefit (Sedley LJ annual Legal Action Group lecture November 2003). After people were refused support even when they claimed asylum on the day of their arrival in the UK, the case of *R (on the application of Q) v SSHD* [2003] EWCA Civ 364 considered the meaning of s 55. The Court of Appeal accepted that the asylum seeker's circumstances should be taken into account in determining what was 'as soon as reasonably practicable' and this could include advice given by someone arranging their passage. In January 2004, the government was obliged to introduce fairer procedures and a three-day period to allow people to find their way to relevant government offices (Macdonald and Webber 2005:868).

The government still pursued to the House of Lords the question of whether actual or imminent destitution would amount to a breach of Article 3 – the right to be free of inhuman or degrading treatment. The House of Lords found that it did (*R v SSHD ex p Adam, Limbuela and Tesema* [2005] UKHL 66; see further in chapter 4). Despite the inroads which court decisions at all levels have made into the operation of s 55, the Parliamentary Joint Committee on Human Rights reiterated their concern that:

> the levels of homelessness and destitution which reliable evidence indicates have in practice resulted from section 55 are very likely to breach both the obligation of progressive realisation of rights under Articles 9 and 11 International Covenant on Economic Social and Cultural Rights (since they represent a regression in the protection of these rights for asylum seekers), and the obligation to ensure minimal levels of the Covenant rights to the individuals affected by section 55. (JCHR Session 2005–06 Eighth Report HL paper 104 HC 850 para 121)

Welfare support continued to be a major preoccupation in the 2004 Act. The proposal in the consultation letter which preceded the Act which provoked the most opposition was that welfare support and accommodation should be withdrawn from failed asylum seekers with families. The 1999 Act had already withdrawn support from asylum seekers whose claim had failed, but it was not thought appropriate then to inflict destitution on children. In 2003, the government had a different solution – take the children into care. Section 9 enables support to be withdrawn once a claim has failed and appeals are exhausted in a case where the Secretary of State certifies that the claimant 'has failed without reasonable excuse to take reasonable steps to leave the UK voluntarily' (s 9 of the 2004 Act, inserting para 7A into Sch 3 of the 2002 Act). Section 10 drew almost as much criticism as it enables the Secretary of State to make regulations making continuation of accommodation for a failed asylum seeker dependent upon performing community service.

The Parliamentary Joint Committee on Human Rights noted that an asylum seeker 'who has exhausted their rights of appeal, cannot return to their country for reasons beyond their control and who has no other means of support is in an analogous position to a UK citizen or any other person in the UK who is entitled to emergency state assistance to prevent destitution' (Fourteenth Report 2003–04 HL 130/HC 828 para 18). An obligation to perform community service as a condition of receiving emergency social assistance was not, as claimed by the government 'a normal civic obligation'. On the contrary, it was 'without precedent or even analogy' (para 15). There was a significant risk of breach of Article 4(2) ECHR through forced or compulsory labour (para 16). Singling out asylum seekers would breach Article 14 as it was unjustifiably discriminatory (para 21), and a withdrawal of support if someone did not perform the labour could breach Article 3 by subjecting them to inhuman and degrading treatment (para 24). In the event, s 10 proved impossible to implement as no community organizations could be found who were willing to provide the community service in question.

The operation of s 9 was piloted in late 2005 in East London, Manchester, and West Yorkshire. Organizations representing social workers lobbied against it as their members baulked at taking asylum seekers' children into care when this would not be in the children's best interests. The Joint Committee on Human Rights considered that it would be difficult to implement s 9 without breaches of Articles 3 and 8 (Session 2003–04 Fifth Report HL Paper 35 HC 304 para 45). Reports of children's charities and refugee organizations concluded that the pilot of s 9 had caused enormous distress and destitution. Families were considered to be at low risk of absconding, but some did disappear when faced with the prospect of parents being separated from children (Refugee Action and Refugee Council 2006). The Immigration Asylum and Nationality Act 2006 contains a provision (s 44) allowing s 9 to be repealed by ministerial order, but this has not been implemented.

The 2002 Act demonstrated the strength of executive power not only in its content but also in the nature of its passage through Parliament. One of the most hotly debated provisions in the Bill, according to Judith Farbey, was the proposal that the Secretary of State should be able to certify asylum claims 'clearly unfounded' and that this certificate should prevent any appeal from taking place in the UK. This late amendment prevented proper parliamentary scrutiny of the removal of appeal rights for people who, if they have been wrongly refused, may face the most serious human rights violations. This was announced after the end of the Commons Standing Committee, leaving any effective debate only to the House of Lords. A further amendment to this clause was one of many announced even after Committee stage in the House of Lords. This led to the unusual step of the Bill being sent back to the Lords Committee for further consideration.

This practice of introducing late amendments on significant matters was a characteristic of the passage of both the 2002 and 2004 Act. The Parliamentary Joint Committee on Human Rights also commented adversely on the Home Office practice in relation to the 2002 Act of not replying to the Committee's questions until crucial parliamentary stages had been passed (JCHR Session 2001–02 Seventeenth Report para 4). In relation to the 2004 Act 'we find ourselves once again in the very same position so soon after having made clear that such a practice undermines parliamentary scrutiny of legislation for compatibility with human rights' (JCHR Session 2003–04 Fourteenth Report HL 130 HC 828 para 3). Lord Lester commented that an unfortunate effect of this lack of scrutiny is that 'the matter will end up in court' (HL Debs 6 July 2004 col 722) as, in fact, happened on the very matter upon which that comment was made (regulations on marriage, discussed in chapter 9).

Haste and lack of consultation characterized the 2003 AITOC Bill. It was introduced in November 2003, with minimal consultation and during the currency of a Home Affairs Committee inquiry into Asylum Applications. The Committee had to break off its work to provide a response to the Bill, and said:

> we have not had the benefit of a draft Bill, nor – in common with other interested parties – were we given more than a few weeks' notice of the proposals even in outline. In view of the fact that since March 2003 we have been conducting a major inquiry into asylum applications, we find this regrettable. (Home Affairs Committee Session 2003–04 Second Report HC 218 para 3)

The Bill contained a clause which would have prevented all higher courts from hearing any immigration or asylum case whether by way of appeal or review. The government's stated reason was to streamline the appeals process and end unmeritorious appeals, but the measure contained no means of separating the meritorious from the unmeritorious, and that decision is precisely the one the courts can make. In addition to the plain injustice to foreign nationals, the development of international refugee law would be denied the contribution of the British House of Lords.

There was unanimous opposition from the legal establishment. The Law Society, Bar Council, Joint Parliamentary Committee on Human Rights, and senior judiciary, including two former Lord Chancellors, agreed the ouster clause violated the rule of law. Matrix Chambers published an opinion quoting Lord Denning: 'If tribunals were at liberty to exceed their jurisdiction without any check by courts the rule of law would be at an end' (*ex p Gilmore* [1957] 1 QB 574 at 586). The Constitutional Affairs Committee said:

> The new proposals do little to address the failings at the initial decision making level and the low level of Home Office representation at initial appeals, which must add to the delays in the system. We think it unlikely that the abolition of a tier of appeal can by itself increase 'end to end' speed and achieve improvements in the quality of judicial decisions. We doubt whether many of the proposals contained in the new Bill are necessary to deal with the current issues in relation to asylum and immigration appeals. (Constitutional Affairs Committee Session 2003–04 Second Report HC 211 summary)

The government was forced to concede, and on introducing the Bill for its second reading in the House of Lords the Lord Chancellor Lord Falconer accepted that the ouster clause could not stand (HL Debs 15 March 2004 col 51).

The Bill contained other reforms of the appeals system which, after reformulation, gained acceptance in Parliament. The principal one was collapsing the former two-tier system of immigration appeals into one.

The 2004 Act added a number of enforcement powers. It is a fairly short miscellany of mainly punitive or enforcement measures, the Bill being referred to by Lord Lester as 'mean spirited and reactionary' (2004:263). It received Royal Assent on 22 July 2004.

In February 2005, the White Paper entitled *Controlling our Borders: Making Migration Work for Britain* (Cm 6472) was announced as a 'five-year strategy for asylum and immigration'. The Immigration, Asylum and Nationality Act 2006 was said to provide the legislative base for implementing the proposals, but includes fresh initiatives not raised in the White Paper; it is apparent that the White Paper is not a five-year plan in any comprehensive sense. Much of its content referred to changes that had already been agreed or made. New proposals included:

- the introduction of a points system for all migration for work or study, privileging the most skilled and ending settlement rights for the low skilled;
- detaining more failed asylum seekers;
- giving recognized refugees only temporary leave (five years);
- abolishing appeals against work and study immigration decisions;
- increasing use of new technology and intelligence coordination at borders, and reintroducing exit monitoring.

Most of these did not require legislation, and the majority of the 2006 Act provisions concern tightening enforcement powers, whether through immigration officers' powers or sanctions on employers.

The most radical and far-reaching proposals of *Controlling our Borders* were those to end appeal rights and to institute a comprehensive points system for work and study. The points-based system was modelled on that of other countries, for instance Australia, in which a certain number of points are required to gain entry, and these are gained for qualifications and other characteristics such as age, available money, and so on. Once published, the points-based system consisted of five tiers to encompass all routes to entry for work and study. The vision promoted by the government was of a routinized system, with applications beginning with an online self-assessment form for the applicant to check whether they would qualify for entry, and applications for entry made at overseas posts instead of through the specialized system at Work Permits (UK). The first stage of implementation, for highly skilled people, started in March 2008, and by March 2009 all five tiers were in force. The points-based system is discussed in chapter 10.

As each tier of the points-based system came into effect, appeal rights for that tier were removed using s 4. It removes the right of appeal against refusal of entry clearance in all but specified family visitor and dependant cases. Those who retain the right of appeal are not defined in the statute but by regulations. The new system encompasses students and all those who apply to work in the UK. The change is radical. A swell of opposition to the removal of appeal rights from students and the enlistment of universities in immigration control, including from University Vice-Chancellors and Principals (letter from Universities UK to *Financial Times*, Tuesday, 5 July 2005), was to no avail.

The government regards appeal rights as less important in the points-based system because of the claimed objectivity. However, Parliament was all but required to take this on trust. The points system that would replace the existing system had not been published in any detail at the time of parliamentary debate on the Bill. This made it difficult for Parliamentarians to debate the Bill effectively and test the government's assertion that the new system would guarantee fair and objective decisions, warranting removal of the right of appeal. Eventually, at report stage in the House of Lords, the government agreed that the tiered migration system would be published before their Lordships went on to the third reading, so that they could assess the safeguards for themselves. This was done by publishing an outline in the document, 'A Points Based System: Making Migration Work for Britain', and the Bill was passed.

Lest we be tempted to think that haste and lack of consultation are purely modern practices, the requirement for entry certificates, which laid the foundation for the whole system of entry clearance, was a last-minute amendment to the Immigration (Appeals) Act 1969. The draconian Commonwealth Immigrants Act 1968 was rushed through Parliament in only five days. One difference now is that statutes are prefaced with a declaration that they are compatible with the Human Rights Act (under HRA s 19), but often there has not been enough consideration of whether this is the case.

The points-based system extends the policy of end-to-end monitoring to all who enter for work and study. A key feature of the system is 'compliance checking': this involves sponsors reporting that migrants are here and are doing what their terms of entry permitted them to do, and whether people have left the UK at the end of their permitted period of stay. Educational institutions are sponsors of overseas students, and employers of their employees.

In the meantime, entry for work became less welcome after all. Romanian and Bulgarian workers were given more limited rights to work than A8 nationals, and the terms of entry for medical graduates and highly skilled workers were dramatically restricted during 2006 (see chapters 8 and 10). Families once again came under the government spotlight, as a certificate of approval scheme was introduced for marriages of foreign nationals (see chapter 9), and proposals issued to raise the age for marriage once again (implemented in 2008) and introduce language testing for spouses. The first two of these initiatives have since been found to be unlawful by the Supreme Court (see chapter 9) and the third is the subject of litigation.

The 2006 Act, in addition to removing rights of appeal as mentioned previously, develops the provisions for information exchange between carriers and immigration control personnel, including a power for the Secretary of State or an immigration officer to compel disclosure to them of passenger lists. This is an element in 'exporting the border', as introduced in the 2002 White Paper. The Act's other miscellaneous provisions are enforcement oriented, including a provision which makes it far easier to exclude people charged with terrorist-related offences from the protection of the Refugee Convention (s 54, see chapter 14). As discussed earlier, the 2002 Act made it possible for the first time for people to lose British nationality acquired by birth or parentage. The 2006 Act made this substantially easier, equating the grounds with the grounds for deportation – simply that the deprivation of nationality was 'conducive to the public good' (s 56).

Continuing the control theme, *Controlling our Borders* introduced a 'new asylum model' (NAM), an administrative system designed to streamline applications and make greater use of detention. The accommodation centres proposed in the 2002 Act did not prove viable, and induction centres were introduced as another attempt to process as many asylum claims as possible while keeping the claimant in some form of detention or controlled accommodation. The NAM is in place for all new asylum decisions from March 2007 onwards. Its workings are discussed further in chapter 12. In tandem with the NAM, in July 2006, the Home Office announced that there was a 'legacy' of 450,000 cases that were outstanding and would not come within the NAM, and they undertook to clear this backlog within five years. The 'Case Resolution' directorate was set up within the Home Office to be proactive in achieving this. By the deadline of July 2011, some 18,000 cases remained officially to be completed, and were transferred to a new unit: Case Assurance and Audit. Another 98,000 asylum cases were placed in a 'controlled archive'. As these were reviewed, it began to appear that the majority might be duplicate files for cases that had already been concluded. This would be consistent with the outcome of the CRD's work, as 56 per cent of the outcomes in July 2011 were 'other' – i.e., duplicates, errors (for instance the person was an EU national), or placed in the controlled archive. In parallel with the passage of the 2006 Act through Parliament, the Home Affairs Committee was conducting an inquiry into immigration control. A number of recent reforms may be traced to their report. Perhaps their main message was that the immigration system was stuck in the era of seeing itself, and being seen, as concerned with preventing entry. The focus now needed to be different. Two aspects were important: facilitation of legitimate travel; and control of immigration after arrival in the country. When people's leave to remain expired, the government should be aware of that and able to act on it.

Also in 2006, the Home Office instituted a root and branch review of the immigration system, following the disclosure that foreign prisoners had been released without being considered for deportation. The review went beyond this issue, resulting in a programme of far-reaching organizational reforms. An independent inspectorate replaced the former monitoring roles.

Developing the policy of internal controls, the UK Borders Act 2007 introduced a scheme of biometric identity documents for foreign nationals. Sections 5 to 15 provide that any non-European Economic Area (EEA) national in the UK, whether lawfully resident or not, may be required to apply for a 'biometric immigration document'. This means any kind of document recording external physical characteristics including in particular fingerprints, features of the iris, and digital photographs which may be scanned by facial recognition technology. Exactly who is required to apply for these documents is specified by the Secretary of State in regulations. Section 19 removes the right to introduce new documentary evidence at appeals against a refusal to vary leave under the points-based system, thus underscoring the policy of the PBS that the first decision should be the final decision.

The 2007 Act introduces automatic deportation for those who have committed certain criminal offences (ss 32–39). Although the Home Affairs Committee endorsed this idea for 'serious criminals', it may be doubted whether all those caught by this provision could really be described as such (see chapter 16 for discussion). A further provision in the Criminal Justice and Immigration Act 2008 removes all status from people who cannot be deported for legal reasons. This is to prevent the government from being obliged to give a protective status to people who have been convicted of a criminal offence, but cannot be returned to their home country because of feared human rights abuses. They will not be removed, but may be kept in the UK without any right to claim any social benefits or to work. The Act also provides for powers to restrict their residence and work, and for electronic tagging. This is some steps short of the house arrest introduced under the Prevention of Terrorism Act's control orders, but more oppressive than mere temporary admission. It is another example of the government legislating to overturn a decision of the courts, this time the decision in the Afghan hijackers' case, discussed in chapters 2 and 8.

The 2006 Act gave increased powers of arrest to immigration officers. The 2007 Act gave them increased powers of detention. The 2006 Act created a duty for immigration, revenue, and customs officers to share information. These steps contributed to the creation of the unified border force, announced by the Prime Minister in July 2007. This heralded a major new development in immigration control. The defining document was *Security in a Global Hub*, emanating in 2007 from the Cabinet Office. The document proclaimed the new agency as an integration of the Immigration Department of the Home Office, by this time known (transitionally) as the Borders and Immigration Agency, UKVisas (the entry clearance operation overseas), and the border operations of HM Revenue and Customs. The UK Border Agency came into being in April 2008. UKBA, though located in the Home Office, reports jointly to the Chancellor of the Exchequer and the Home Secretary. Although UKBA's 2009–12 Business Plan says that it 'supports the delivery objectives' of the Foreign and Commonwealth Office, this department looks like the junior partner. The intelligence- and technology-led system of e-borders established under the auspices of UKBA is described in chapter 7.

Alongside these institutional changes, the government attempted to achieve a goal often referred to by earlier administrations, that of consolidating all immigration statutes into one. The aim of consolidation was itself consolidated with another aim, to 'simplify' immigration law. In July 2008, a 'Draft Partial Simplification Bill' was published. The Bill was not a great success, the House of Commons Home Affairs research paper describing it as 'not what one might call "simple": it is still full of complex clauses, sub-clauses, exceptions, qualifications and cross-references, and in some cases reproduces sections of previous Acts wholesale'. On 11 November 2008, the Home Affairs Committee suspended its scrutiny of the Bill, taking the view that it was unable to continue until the whole Bill had been published, and the Bill was withdrawn.

The elements of the Bill which dealt with the new idea of an earned progression towards citizenship were skeletally enacted in the Borders, Citizenship and Immigration Act 2009, in particular by providing for the status of 'probationary citizenship'. This was intended to place a hurdle between temporary and indefinite leave, and to allow government to change the criteria and qualification periods from time to time depending upon policy. The then government envisaged a points-based system for settlement, which could incorporate various tests of integration, again depending on 'current interests' ('Earning the Right to Stay: A New Points Test for Citizenship'). These plans were abandoned by the coalition government in November 2010.

The main body of the 2009 Act is concerned with provisions for officials of UKBA to carry out the functions of HMRC and other related powers which progress the creation of the single border agency. The Act contains a short miscellany of other items, including a new duty on the Secretary of State to make arrangements to ensure that immigration, asylum, and nationality functions are discharged 'having regard to the need to safeguard and promote the welfare of children' who are in the UK (s 55). This recognized the UK's withdrawal of its reservation to the UN Convention on the Rights of the Child. The Parliamentary Joint Committee on Human Rights said that this represented 'a most welcome change in policy' (Legislative Scrutiny: Borders, Citizenship and Immigration Bill, Ninth Report of Session 2008–09 HL 62, HC 375) which would provide an opportunity to begin to address the serious human rights concerns the Committee had previously expressed, including the inappropriate detention of children, the effect on them of 'heavy handed enforcement methods such as dawn raids and forced removals', and inappropriate methods for testing their age (para 1.14). Joint guidance on the performance of the new duty has been issued by the Home Office and the Department for Children, Schools and Families, and its importance was emphasized by the Supreme Court in *ZH (Tanzania)* [2011] UKSC 4.

The coalition government which came to power in May 2010 has not yet produced primary legislation on immigration or asylum law. Its most public act on immigration has been a commitment to reduce net immigration. Detailed consultations in 2011 on family migration and on settlement were promulgated in the context of reducing net migration. Proposals in *Family Migration: A Consultation* include introducing specified detailed questions to ascertain whether the marriage is 'genuine', setting a minimum income threshold to sponsor a partner or relative, extending the probationary period for partners from two years to five years, abolishing immediate settlement for partners with a four-year relationship, giving immigration control functions to marriage registrars, and introducing a probationary period for elderly relatives. The family migration consultation also contains a very ambitious section in which UKBA proposes statutory constraints on the application and interpretation of Article 8. The consultation on *Employment-Related Settlement* proposed to abolish settlement for Tier 2 skilled workers and abolish the domestic worker category, together with the protections for domestic workers that accompanied that route, limiting stay in Tier 5 to 12 months and abolishing the right for the family of Tier 5 workers to accompany them.

1.3 Sources of immigration law

There is no doubt that immigration control is an exercise of executive power; that is, it is exercised by the executive arm of government, in this case principally by the Home Secretary, Home Office civil servants, immigration officers, and entry clearance officers. Less clear are the source and limits of that power. Immigration law is, in a sense, all about the exercise of executive power and the limits upon it. A characteristic that will be encountered over and over again in the study of immigration law is the retention of discretion, which is of course less amenable to control than the application of specific rules. The discretionary nature of immigration law is at the root of much of the criticism that has been directed at it. While challenges to decisions and initiatives towards accountability and openness seek to put limits on the power of the executive, in other ways the scope to use discretion is continually reasserted. In order to ascertain the extent to which decisions can be challenged, it is necessary to consider the source of the power which is exercised. A purely statutory power is subject to public law constraints and perhaps the exercise of appeal rights; something with a more nebulous origin may be harder to control. So we will begin with that question – where does it come from?

1.3.1 **Prerogative origins?**

The right of nation states to control the entry and expulsion of foreign nationals is often said to be an essential aspect of sovereignty, and arguably exercised under the prerogative. The prerogative was originally the power of the Crown. The Bill of Rights 1689 decreed that the prerogative could not be extended any further and that statute could supersede the prerogative. From this time on, the prerogative had a residual character (see, for instance, Loveland, *Constitutional Law; Administrative Law and Human Rights: A Critical Introduction* 2003). In the present day, relevant prerogatives, if any, are at the disposal of the government, which now holds the authority of the Crown for most purposes. There are personal prerogatives of the monarch such as dispensing certain honours, but we are not concerned with these.

The extent of the prerogative has been a matter of argument even in quite recent times. In *R v Secretary of State ex p Northumbria Police Authority* [1989] QB 26, the Court of Appeal found that there was a prerogative to keep the peace even though it had not been written down anywhere. However, Vincenzi argues that there are specific recognized areas of prerogative power, not an amorphous pool which could be used for purposes convenient to the government (1992:300). Following *CCSU v Minister for the Civil Service* [1985] AC 374 (the GCHQ case) in which the House of Lords decided that the exercise of the prerogative was reviewable, a number of prerogative powers have been considered, and the reviewability of each decided as a separate question (see, e.g., *R v Secretary of State for Foreign and Commonwealth Affairs ex p Everett* [1989] QB 811 CA, *R v SSHD ex p Bentley* [1993] 4 All ER 442). This seems to support Vincenzi's argument. Indeed, this approach seems to flow from Lord Diplock's list in the GCHQ case of potentially non-reviewable prerogative powers, and the question was not resolved in *ex p Northumbria Police Authority*.

Those prerogative powers which have been identified include matters such as the conduct of foreign affairs, the power to conduct the internal affairs of the civil service, and the issue of passports (Vincenzi 1998). It would be a brave person now who suggested that there was a major prerogative power left undiscovered, and in the area of immigration control it is reasonable to assume that whatever prerogative power exists is known about. Chapter 4 of Vincenzi's book explores the relationship between the prerogative and immigration control, and reference should be made to that for a full account. All the authorities agree that there is a prerogative power to deal with aliens, but there is disagreement over its extent.

Immigration control in the UK is now largely governed by statute and immigration rules made pursuant to the statutory duty to do so (Immigration Act 1971 s 3(2)). The Immigration Act 1971, however, expressly reserves a prerogative power in mysterious terms: 'This Act shall not be taken to supersede or impair any power exercisable by Her Majesty in relation to aliens by virtue of her prerogative' (s 33(5)). In its reference only to aliens, the subsection conforms with the established view that the prerogative does not apply to those who owe allegiance to the Crown, that is, British and Commonwealth citizens (cp. *DPP v Bhagwan* [1972] AC 60 and *R v IAT ex p Secretary of State for the Home*

Department [1990] 3 All ER 652). However, what power over 'aliens' does the section reserve, and over which 'aliens'? The whole Act and all subsequent immigration statutes, deal with those who are subject to immigration control. If there was a prerogative of immigration control, this would, as a normal rule, be in abeyance to the extent of the statutory power (*AG v de Keyser's Royal Hotel Ltd* [1920] AC 508). It would be both superseded and impaired. Section 33(5) is not thought to displace this rule. Immigration control is exercised pursuant to the statute and rules as indeed the rule of law requires. It is not empowered by a mysterious source which somehow lurks behind the rules. Vincenzi suggests that the only non-contentious prerogative in relation to aliens is to imprison enemy aliens, that is, nationals of those countries with whom the UK is at war. Macdonald in his 5th edition (2001:708) suggested there was a power to deport, and as we have seen, Edward and Elizabeth I behaved as though they thought so. However, this was in relation to aliens regarded as enemies, not those regarded as friends. In the 6th edition, Macdonald revised his views (2005:3) and, following the work of Shah and Vincenzi, adopts the view that there was no distinction in common law between the rights of subjects and friendly aliens. The first appearance of a reservation of a prerogative power was in the Aliens Restriction Act 1914, passed at the outbreak of the First World War. A clause to ensure that the Crown did not, by the Act, diminish its power to deal with the enemy would be consistent with its context and purpose. Thus this reservation seems highly likely to have been referring to enemy aliens.

There is undoubtedly a power to make immigration decisions outside the immigration rules, but this can simply derive from the wide powers in the statute to give or refuse leave to enter or remain (the Immigration Act 1971 ss 3A, 3B, and 4), and there is no need to employ the prerogative as an explanation (Macdonald 1995:41). Glidewell LJ in *R v Secretary of State for the Home Department ex p Rajinder Kaur* [1987] Imm AR 278 took the view that this power to make decisions outside the rules is derived from the prerogative. However, that case concerned a Commonwealth citizen, and Glidewell LJ cannot have been right in this. Vincenzi argues that immigration control cannot be a prerogative power because the concept of immigration control is a modern one, originating in the Aliens Act 1905. The innovation that the Act represented is clear from parliamentary debates. For instance, Sir Charles Dilkes, the MP for Gloucestershire, Forest of Dean, said that the measure 'for the first time' would prevent 'free men' from coming to a 'free country' (HC Debs 29 March 1904 vol 132 col 991). The basis of the Bill was that statutory power was needed to interfere with the entry of aliens. If immigration control is seen as a 'prerogative power clothed in statute', its amenability to regulation is that much less. If it is seen as a purely statutory power, it must be exercised in accordance with the power granted by that statute and in accordance with principles of statutory interpretation, and not otherwise. Evans notes:

> The reluctance of the courts to challenge the Executive's exercise of statutory powers on matters touching national security may also have been influenced by the Crown's claim that the exclusion and expulsion of aliens were within its prerogative, the scope of which was never definitely established, but which still maintains a shadowy existence alongside immigration control. (1983:422–423)

Although the conclusion here is that it is unlikely that the prerogative is the source of immigration control, the idea that it is continues to appear. In *Odelola* [2009] UKHL 25, the House of Lords expressed the view, obiter, that the source of the power to make the immigration rules was the prerogative. This subject is revisited later in connection with the immigration rules.

1.3.1.1 *A modern equivalent?*

The danger of relying on the prerogative is that it allows reliance upon a supposed reserve of undefined power to supplement explicit provisions. However, even without reliance on the prerogative, two other principles, sovereignty and the judgement of the executive, may be observed in more recent case law to be playing a similar role. The first is explanatory and the second is justificatory.

Sovereignty in dealing with foreign nationals is curtailed by treaties to which the state is a party such as, in the UK's case, the European Convention on Human Rights, and the 1951 UN Convention Relating to Refugees. In the age of internationalism, the development of international human rights norms, and an international criminal court, the nation state can no longer be properly regarded as the ultimate legal authority. It is well recognized that national legal authority must now be tempered by regard for international law, and that international regulation is a fact of life.

Ironically, it is through the Human Rights Act 1998, bringing the rights of the European Convention into UK law, that the idea of sovereignty seems to make something of a comeback. In immigration cases, the European Court of Human Rights routinely begins its reasoning with the statement that states have the right, as a recognized principle of international law, and subject to their treaty obligations, to control the entry of non-nationals (see *Abdulaziz Cabales and Balkandali* (1985) 7 EHRR 471 para 67). This statement has an understandable place in the judgment of an international court, but has been transposed into the UK courts' and tribunals' reasoning in human rights cases. It is not inaccurate, but is unnecessary in the national context, where the task of the decision-maker is to apply and interpret law which is already made by the sovereign law-maker (Parliament) or is of a lesser status (immigration rules) or is case law which arises or can be argued to have a place in the jurisdiction. Sovereignty, if it arises at all, is being exercised, not challenged, and the reiteration of it in national courts has an effect similar to that noted by Evans in relation to the prerogative. This was demonstrated in *R v SSHD ex p Saadi, Maged, Osman and Mohammed* [2002] 1 WLR 3131, HL, in which the principle of sovereignty was itself used to interpret, and thus restrict, human rights (see chapter 15). The outcome was endorsed by the European Court of Human Rights (ECtHR). As Dauvergne comments, 'Migration law is transformed into the new last bastion of sovereignty' (2004:588), and correspondingly, sovereignty is invoked to buttress the state's right to control migration. A number of writers now argue that the territorial notion of sovereignty is also breaking down (e.g., Thomas and Kostakopoulou, Dauvergne), and that sovereignty is now exercised over people and information more than over territory. The shift in the UK's border control strategy could be argued to demonstrate just that.

In the early days of the Human Rights Act, the idea that immigration control is a matter for the executive influenced the courts and tribunals as they began to explore the application of qualified rights, which require them to judge the proportionality of the harm done to the individual against the public interest. The doctrine of deference to the executive was developed from judicial review, but in *Huang and Kashmiri v SSHD* [2007] UKHL 11, the House of Lords held that deference is not really a proper constitutional principle at all. The judiciary are competent to decide whether in a particular case they should give special weight to the Secretary of State's judgement or not. To argue for deference is not the same thing as to argue for a prerogative power, but the effect may be similar in that, in both instances, it is posited that there is an area of exercise of judgement which is somehow the special preserve of the government. For instance, in the case of indefinite detentions of foreign nationals, the Court of Appeal deferred to the judgement of the executive that discrimination on grounds of nationality was necessary for security reasons (*A v SSHD* [2002] EWCA Civ 1502). In the House of Lords, Lord Bingham in particular set out the UK's obligations under international treaties as an important part of the reasons why this deference was not warranted (*A v SSHD* [2004] UKHL 56).

1.3.2 Statutory origins

For the avoidance of doubt, the present-day legal source of the power of immigration control is statutory. The main statutes are the Immigration Act 1971, the Immigration and Asylum Act 1999, the Nationality, Immigration and Asylum Act 2002, the Asylum and Immigration (Treatment of Claimants, etc.) Act 2004, and the Immigration, Asylum and Nationality Act 2006, supplemented by the UK Borders Act 2007 and the Borders Citizenship and Immigration Act 2009. All of these have been discussed earlier.

The fundamental legal authority for the power to control immigration is found in the Immigration Act 1971 s 4(1), which says:

> The power under this Act to give or refuse leave to enter the United Kingdom shall be exercised by immigration officers, and the power to give leave to remain in the United Kingdom, or to vary any leave under section 3(3)(a) (whether as regards duration or conditions), shall be exercised by the Secretary of State.

Perhaps surprisingly, the statutes contain none of the specific provisions which govern whether a person may gain entry to the UK or leave to remain, although they do contain the basic grounds upon which they may be required to leave. The requirements to be met to gain entry or leave to remain are mainly contained in the immigration rules.

1.3.3 Immigration rules

Immigration Act 1971 s 1(4) contains the only requirement as to the content of the rules. They must

> include provision for admitting (in such cases and subject to such restrictions as may be provided by the rules...) persons coming for the purpose of taking employment, or for the purposes of study, or as visitors, or as dependants of persons lawfully in or entering the UK.

Section 3(2) provides that this

> shall not be taken to require uniform provision to be made by the rules as regards admission of persons for a purpose or in a capacity specified in section 1(4) (and in particular, for this as well as other purposes of this Act, account may be taken of citizenship or nationality).

The rules are now voluminous and run into several hundreds. (Numbering stops at 395 but this is not indicative as many are divided into sub-rules: A to Z and so on.) The last set of new rules was in 1994, so that all changes since then are amendments to those rules (coincidentally called HC 395). They are frequently amended in major or minor respects. The rules govern almost all immigration cases and also have an impact on asylum cases. They contain the practical substance of immigration law.

On reading the rules, it is apparent that they are the language of the administrator rather than the lawyer. They are practical and descriptive, stating what action should be taken in given sets of circumstances. This being the case, they should not be treated as a legal text in the English tradition, namely as language which has been created with great precision and therefore must be interpreted strictly. The accepted approach (*Alexander v IAT* [1982] 2 All ER 766) to interpretation is:

> These Rules are not to be construed with all the strictness applicable to the construction of a statute or a statutory instrument. They must be construed sensibly according to the natural meaning of the language which is employed. (para 11)

This was confirmed again by the House of Lords in *Odelola* and in *Mahad and others v ECO* [2009] UKSC 16. The rules have become more specific over the years. They have also become more and more comprehensive, as matters formerly dealt with by concessions and policies are absorbed into the rules. The Home Affairs Committee has called for their redrafting and consolidation 'to provide a clear, comprehensive and realistic framework for decisions', though this did not exclude properly exercised judgement (Fifth Report 2005–06). The immigration rules may be divided into points-based rules and the rest. In the non-points-based rules, there is scope for judgement as to whether specified criteria are met, for instance whether a couple intend to live together as husband and wife. This is not a discretion in a pure sense, but it is a matter on which an entry clearance officer and an applicant could disagree. By comparison in the points-based rules, the idea of adequacy of maintenance is replaced by specified sums, and subjective states such as 'intention to leave' do not appear. For details of the points-based scheme see chapter 10.

The status of the immigration rules has been a subject of much legal argument. The Immigration Act 1971 s 3(2) says that the Secretary of State 'shall from time to time lay before Parliament statements of the rules... to be followed in the administration of this Act'. They are thus in form not delegated legislation. The House of Lords, in *Odelola*, thought that this section did not impose a statutory duty to make the rules, but rather that the duty was procedural – to lay them before Parliament, subject to the negative resolution procedure. *Pearson v IAT* [1978] Imm AR 212 has been followed, and confirmed in *Odelola*, that the Rules are not delegated legislation or rules of law, but rules of practice for the guidance of those who administer the Act. Despite this, the rules have a status well beyond that of normal administrative guidelines. Previous statutes provided that an adjudicator 'must allow an appeal if he considers that the decision or action against which the appeal is brought was not in accordance with the law or any immigration rules applicable to the case' (Immigration Act 1971 s 19 and Immigration and Asylum Act 1999 Sch 4 para 21). The current equivalent provision is that the appeal must be allowed if the decision 'is not in accordance with the law (including immigration rules)' (Nationality, Immigration and Asylum Act 2002 s 86(3)(a)). This seems to represent a shift towards recognizing the rules as a form of law. This was explicitly stated for the first time by Sedley LJ in *SSHD v Pankina and others* [2010] EWCA Civ 719:

> In my judgement the time has come to recognize that, by a combination of legislative recognition and executive practice, the rules made by Home Secretaries for regulating immigration have ceased to be policy and have acquired a status akin to that of law. (para 17)

Sedley LJ confirmed that the rules are not subordinate legislation. The arrangements for their creation are 'not merely unusual but unique' (para 13), and he draws his conclusion that they have a status akin to law in part from the requirement that they be laid before Parliament:

> The rules were being... made the source of justiciable rights – something which, in the domestic sphere... the Crown as executive has no power to do. It can make law only with the authority of Parliament. It follows that only that which enjoys or secures Parliament's authority... is entitled to the quasi-legal status of immigration rules. (para 21)

The rules are subject only to very limited parliamentary scrutiny, and if Parliament wants to reject them it must reject the rules as a whole: there is no provision for amendment (though in February 2008, a debate in Parliament secured promises from the government to deal with some objections to new grounds for refusing leave to enter the UK. See chapter 7). Rules have been rejected on very few occasions, the most notable perhaps being in December 1982 (HC Debs 15 December 1982 col 355) when the Labour Party opposition succeeded in defeating the Conservative government's proposed new marriage rules. These would have introduced a burden on the applicant to show that the marriage was genuine (later introduced anyway) and a two-year probationary period (defeated on that occasion but introduced on 1 April 2003 without parliamentary debate). In *Huang and Kashmiri v SSHD* [2007] UKHL 11, the House of Lords rejected an argument that the negative resolution procedure meant that the immigration rules were the product of democratic debate. The immigration rules are 'not the product of active debate in Parliament, where non-nationals seeking leave to enter or remain are not in any event represented' (para 17).

Key Case

***SSHD v Pankina and others* [2010] EWCA Civ 718**

Applicants for leave to remain under the points-based system met the requirement of the rules to have £800 in their bank accounts, but did not meet the requirements in the guidance for this sum to be in their accounts for a continuous period of three months prior to their application. The Secretary of State purported to incorporate this guidance into the rules, although it had not been laid before Parliament. The Court of Appeal held that although there was no obstacle in principle to incorporating a policy into a legally enforceable measure, a policy was simply guidance as to the usual case, and was to be interpreted. So if an applicant's bank balance fell below £800 for one day, there would be consideration of whether the spirit and intention of the policy was nevertheless met. In this case the Secretary of State did not rely on the guidance as policy, but as an extension of the rule and thus mandatory. This was impermissible as it had not been laid before Parliament, affected individuals' status and entitlement, and could be changed at any time by the Secretary of State. If the provision was to have the force of law (as an immigration rule did) it must be certain (para 33).

Even though the rules are subject only to a limited parliamentary scrutiny they are subject to challenge by way of judicial review on the usual grounds of illegality, irrationality, and procedural impropriety (following Lord Diplock's classification in *CCSU v Minister for the Civil Service* [1985] AC 374). Unsuccessful attempts have been made to challenge the rules on the basis that they fetter discretion, this being an aspect of illegality (*R v Secretary of State for the Home Department ex p Rajinder Kaur* [1987] Imm AR 278). For the purpose of a challenge for irrationality, the rules are treated like by-laws, and so may only be struck down if they are 'impartial or unequal in their operation as between classes; manifestly unjust; made in bad faith; or involving such oppressive or gratuitous interference with the rights of those subject to them as could find no justification in the minds of reasonable persons' (*Kruse v Johnson* [1898] 2 QB 91). This has succeeded on one occasion, when the rule on admission of family dependants was challenged for its requirement that the elderly dependent relative, in order to gain entry, must be living at a standard substantially below that in their country. This discriminated against applicants in poor countries, for whom even a small amount of financial help would lift their standard of living above a low level for their country (*R v IAT ex p Manshoora Begum* [1986] Imm AR 385).

The rules are subject to directly applicable EC law, and in *R (on the application of Ezgi Payir) v SSHD* [2005] EWHC 1426 (Admin), the High Court made a declaration that rr 92–94 were unlawful insofar as they purported to exclude the right to an extension of stay for a Turkish au pair, contrary to Article 6 of Decision 1/80 of the Council of the Association between the EU and Turkey. This outcome was upheld on a preliminary reference to the ECJ (Case C–294/06).

The decision in *Odelola*, that the rules were not subordinate legislation, meant that the Interpretation Act 1978 did not apply to them, and so the appellant did not obtain that Act's protection against retrospective effect. In similar wording, the Human Rights Act defines subordinate legislation in s 21(1) as including 'rules... made under primary legislation'. *Pankina* proceeded on the basis, though not fully argued, that the immigration rules are not included in s 21 HRA. The effect of this is that the interpretive duty in HRA s 3 does not apply to the rules. This was the view of the Court of Appeal in *AM (Ethiopia), and others v Entry Clearance Officer* [2008] EWCA Civ 1082, though in a passing comment.

Even without s 3, those who implement the rules are public authorities under s 6 and their actions must be in accordance with the Convention. In effect, immigration rules must be applied in a way that upholds Convention rights, as Sedley LJ said in *Pankina*:

> In exercising her powers, whether within or outside the rules of practice for the time being in force, the Home Secretary must have regard and give effect to applicants' Convention rights. (para 45)

The Court of Appeal in *R (on the application of Syed) v SSHD* [2011] EWCA Civ 1059 confirmed this interpretation.

The judgment in *Huang* referred to earlier confirmed that the immigration rules do not already embody human rights standards. The consideration of a human rights claim begins once an applicant has failed under the rules. Human rights standards are additional to the rules, which, as previously discussed, are simply guidance in the administration of the powers to grant and refuse leave to enter or remain.

One of the critical issues concerning the effect of the rules is the question of which set of rules applies if the rules are changed between the date of the application and the date of the decision, as happened in *Odelola* (see chapter 10). The House of Lords' answer was that the applicable rules are those in force at the date of the decision. Different considerations apply in the integrated scheme for highly skilled migrants – see chapter 8.

1.3.4 Policies and concessions

Internal government instructions are highly influential in the implementation of immigration law as they guide immigration officers and Home Office officials in their response to individual cases. These may be of a formal or informal kind. Mention has already been made of the exclusion of black passport-holders from the UK by means of internal government instructions which accompanied the Commonwealth Immigrants Act 1962. These, of course, were not the kind of instructions to which the public would have access. The secrecy which was a hallmark of immigration law has changed in recent years, and the body of internal instructions is now disclosed on the Home Office website. Internal instructions as they now exist may be divided into three kinds.

First, there are policy documents which give guidance on the exercise of a discretion. The criteria for immigration detention are found entirely in guidance documents of this kind, disclosed on the IND website in the Enforcement Instructions and Guidance.

Second, there is guidance on the application of the immigration rules. Lord Justice Sedley in *ZH (Bangladesh) v SSHD* [2009] EWCA Civ 8 described this guidance as being directions about the implementation of the rules (para 26) and said that Home Office officials should not depart from the Immigration Directorate Instructions (IDIs) without good reason. This reflected the legal obligation of the government not to act inconsistently with its own policy unless there was a good reason for doing so (*British Oxygen v Board of Trade* [1971] AC 610, *ZH* para 33). On the other hand, the IDIs did not have the force of law. They were not an aid to construction of the immigration rules, but sat 'within the four corners of the rule' to which they related (para 32).

These kinds of guidance are mainly disclosed on the UKBA website, but the location of particular subjects is often unpredictable and the usability is marred by poor indexing and lack of dating (so that it is difficult to tell whether the particular guidance was in force at the date of a decision, as in *R (on the application of I and O) v SSHD* [2005] EWHC 1025 (Admin)). Third, there are various kinds of concessions. One of the features of immigration law is the extent of provision which has been contained in discretionary practices outside the rules. Sometimes, these have been standard practices, established for many years. Although the rules have become more and more comprehensive, they still do not cover every eventuality. An example of this was the grant of indefinite leave to remain to a person who attains refugee status. This had the appearance of an established rule, as it was invariable practice for some years, but when practice was changed in August 2005, this could be done simply by an announcement. Such announcements may be given, for instance, by notice on the IND website, in Parliament, by letter to interested organizations.

There are also temporary concessions often in periods of upheaval or emergency. An example was a policy not to return people to active war zones, a policy which has now been revoked.

What all these forms of guidance have in common is that if an individual comes within their terms they can expect to be treated in accordance with the policy. This may be enforced, depending on circumstances, either by appeal or judicial review, and these forms of redress are discussed in chapter 8. *R v SSHD ex p Amankwah* [1994] Imm AR 240 was the first case which held that even if the policy was undisclosed, if its existence was known, a decision which did not take the policy properly into account was unreasonable and unfair. The existence of a policy on marriage and deportation had become known by accident, having been referred to in a Home Office letter in a previous case.

Since then, policies have been gradually disclosed. At first, selected documents were sent to practitioner organizations. Now the majority of internal instructions of substance are available on the Home Office website.

Case law has developed to say that the Home Office should apply the policy in a relevant case even if the individual is unaware of it (*R (on the application of Rashid) v SSHD* [2005] EWCA Civ 744 – see chapter 8).

Individual exceptions may be made, and as Macdonald describes (1995:44–45), may become established concessions as the compassionate circumstances which led to their first being recognized are replicated in other cases. It is possible to argue that the particular circumstances of the case warrant more lenient treatment than the rules seem to provide. The source of the power for Home Office and immigration officers to do this has been discussed earlier, and is the Immigration Act 1971, not the prerogative.

Guidance in the points-based system is a different phenomenon again. It is referred to in the immigration rules as binding and is phrased in mandatory terms. It is addressed not to UKBA officials, as are the policies discussed earlier, but to applicants on what is required of them, and is mainly procedural (what kind of documents are accepted, when to submit them, and so on). This guidance was described by the Tribunal in *NA & Others (Tier 1 Post-Study Work-funds)* [2009] UKAIT 00025 as a 'hybrid of a new kind' (para 46). As held by the Court of Appeal in *Pankina,* guidance cannot be given the same force as a rule.

1.3.5 Tribunal decisions

A specialist source of law in the immigration and asylum field is the body of case law emanating from the Tribunal. The structure of the Tribunal and grounds of appeal to it are discussed more fully in chapter 8. Here we simply consider Tribunal decisions as a source of law.

Studies by Buck (2006) and Thomas (2005) examine the unique phenomenon of the Tribunal and its case law. The early idea of tribunals, as fact-finding bodies which were somehow closer to the people and the facts than the courts could be, is a misleading picture of the Tribunal which hears immigration and asylum appeals. Its characteristics are described by Thomas as: high volume; fact-based; compulsory (in that claimants have little alternative); no compromise is possible; serving public interest; not bound by usual rules of evidence; and an exceptionally high rate of challenge.

Buck notes that the intention of Tribunal case law was that it would not be binding in the way that the decisions of higher courts are. Wade and Forsyth say that the Tribunal's duty is to reach the 'right decision in the circumstances of the moment' (p. 931). The authority of the new Upper Tribunal is intended to be enhanced by its constitution as court of record, explicitly equal in the court hierarchy with the High Court. The transfer to the new Tribunal structure has highlighted issues about the nature and authority of Tribunal case law. In *AH (Sudan),* Baroness Hale said that rarely should the decision of a specialist Tribunal be interfered with, unless it was plainly wrong in law. However, the specialist quality of the Tribunal has been doubted, on the grounds that its jurisdiction is too diverse to permit of real specialization, and that many decisions are taken by an immigration judge sitting alone, unlike other Tribunal jurisdictions in which lay people with relevant expertise act as wing members (Chowdhury 2009). In the transfer of judicial review jurisdiction to the Upper Tribunal, there is potentially a trade-off between Tribunal specialism and the capacity of High Court judges to maintain coherence with the wider body of law, in particular public law principles (see Thomas 2009). Tribunal decisions are not all reported, and a practice direction prevents unreported cases from being cited in tribunals except in defined circumstances. The decision as to which decisions are reported is made by a Reporting Committee, following guidance published by the President of the Upper Tribunal Immigration and Asylum Chamber (Guidance note 2011 no. 2). The procedure of the Reporting Committee has been questioned as contravening the principles of fairness and due administration of justice (Toal 2012). There is a system of factual precedents called country guidance cases, discussed in chapter 12.

Tribunal decisions may be accessed by searching on www.bailii.org or www.justice.gov.uk/guidance/courts-and-tribunals/tribunals/immigration-and-asylum/upper/index.htm.

1.4 Conclusion

Whether the focus of attention is the Jews in the nineteenth century, West Indians in the 1960s, East African Asians in the 1970s, or more recently asylum seekers, immigration legislation is passed with a target group in mind. The political agenda of the day moulds the law in a very direct way. The current targets include the illegally resident population, and terrorists. The first is a diverse group of people not abroad, but present in the UK, and mainly unaccounted for. As far as UK law is concerned, the same could perhaps be said of the second group. The result is a concentration on security and the dissemination of points of immigration control through many aspects of life. Another current target, to regularize entry for work, has become enmeshed in similar processes.

QUESTIONS

1 How have the themes identified by Bevan in 1986 developed in the present day?
2 The minister introducing a Draft Immigration Bill in 2009 said that it would 'ensure that Parliament and not case law determines immigration policy'. To what extent is this a realistic or desirable objective, given the nature and sources of immigration law?
3 Given the use and origin of the immigration rules, it appears that the Secretary of State both makes and implements much of immigration law. Is this a problem?

For guidance on answering questions, visit www.oxfordtextbooks.co.uk/orc/clayton5e/.

FURTHER READING

Bevan, Vaughan (1986) *The Development of British Immigration Law* (Beckenham: Croom Helm).

Bingham, Lord 'The Rule of Law' *Cambridge Law Journal* (2007) 66, pp. 67–85.

Carter, Bob, Harris, Clive, and Joshi, Shirley [1987] *The 1951–55 Conservative Government and the Racialisation of Black Immigration* Policy Papers in Ethnic Relations no. 11 CREC.

Chowdhury, Zahir (2009) 'The Doctrine of Deference to Tribunal Expertise and the Parameters of Judicial Restraint' *Immigration Law Digest* vol. 15, no. 3, Autumn, pp. 15–21.

Cohen, Steve, Humphries, Beth, and Mynott, Ed (eds) (2000) 'Never Mind the Racism... Feel the Quality' *Immigration and Nationality Law and Practice* vol. 14, no. 4, pp. 223–226.

—— (2002) *From Immigration Controls to Welfare Controls* (London: Routledge).

Dauvergne, Catherine (2004) 'Sovereignty, Migration and the Rule of Law in Global Times' *Modern Law Review* vol. 67, no. 4, pp. 588–615.

Dummett, Ann and Nicol, Andrew (1990) *Subjects, Citizens, Aliens and Others* (London: Weidenfeld and Nicolson).

Fryer, Paul (1984) *Staying Power: The History of Black People in Britain* (London: Pluto).

Gillespie, Jim (1996) 'Asylum and Immigration Act 1996: An Outline of the New Law' *Immigration and Nationality Law and Practice* vol. 10, no. 3, pp. 86–90.

Gilroy, Paul (2002) *There Ain't no Black in the Union Jack* (London: Routledge).

Harvey, Colin (2005) 'Judging Asylum' in Shah, P. (ed.) *The Challenge of Asylum to Legal Systems* (London: Cavendish).

HJT Training Professionals and ILPA (2009) *A Compilation of Immigration and Asylum Policies of the Home Office. Volume 1: Regular Migration Under the Immigration Rules. Volume 2: Asylum and Other Forms of Protection; Enforcement Action* (London: HJT/ILPA).

Joint Council for the Welfare of Immigrants (JCWI) (2005) *Recognise Rights, Realize Benefits, JCWI analysis of the five-year plan* (London: JCWI).

Juss, Satvinder (1993) *Immigration, Nationality and Citizenship* (London: Mansell).

Layton-Henry, Zigg (1992) *The Politics of Immigration* (Oxford: Blackwell).

Macdonald, Ian and Toal, Ronan (2008) *Macdonald's Immigration Law and Practice*, 7th edn (London: Butterworths), chapter 1.

McKee, Richard (2006) 'The Immigration, Asylum and Nationality Act 2006 and other developments' *Journal of Immigration, Asylum & Nationality Law* vol. 20, no. 2, pp. 86–93.

Moore, Robert and Wallace, Tina (1975) *Slamming the Door* (London: Martin Robertson and Co.).

Paul, Kathleen (1997) *Whitewashing Britain: Race and Citizenship in the Postwar Era* (New York: Cornell).

Poole, Tom (2005) 'Harnessing the Power of the Past? Lord Hoffmann and the Belmarsh Detainees Case' *Journal of Law and Society* vol. 32, no. 4, pp. 534–561.

Rawlings, Richard (2005) 'Review, Revenge and Retreat' *Modern Law Review* vol. 68, no. 3, pp. 378–410.

Shah, Prakash (2000) *Refugees, Race and the Legal Concept of Asylum in Britain* (London: Cavendish).

Shah, Ramnik (2002) 'Secure Borders, Safe Haven' *New Law Journal* vol. 152, no. 7021, pp. 315–317.

Singh, Rabinder (2004) 'Equality: The Neglected Virtue' *European Human Rights Law Review* 2, pp. 141–157.

Spencer, Ian (1997) *British Immigration Policy since 1945: The Making of Multi-Racial Britain* (London: Routledge).

Stevens, Dallal (1998) 'The Asylum and Immigration Act 1996: The Erosion of the Right to Seek Asylum' *Modern Law Review* vol. 61, no. 2, pp. 201–222.

—— (2001) 'The Immigration and Asylum Act 1999: A Missed Opportunity?' *Modern Law Review* vol. 64, no. 3, pp. 413–438.

—— (2004) 'The Nationality, Immigration and Asylum Act 2002: Secure Borders, Safe Haven?' *Modern Law Review* vol. 67, no. 4, pp. 616–631.

—— (2004) *UK Asylum Law and Policy* (London: Sweet & Maxwell), chapters 1 and 2.

Thomas, Robert (2003) 'Asylum Appeals Overhauled Again' *Public Law* Summer, pp. 260–271.

—— (2009) 'Tribunalising Immigration and Asylum Judicial Reviews' *Immigration Law Digest* vol. 15, no. 4, Winter, pp. 2–4. (2003)

Toal, Ronan (2012) 'The Reporting Committee of the Upper Tribunal, Immigration and Asylum Chamber: Country Guidance Decisions' *Journal of Immigration Asylum and Nationality Law* vol. 26 no.1 pp. 64–67.

Vincenzi, Christopher (1992) 'Extra-statutory Ministerial Discretion in Immigration Law' *Public Law* Summer, pp. 310–321.

—— (1998) *Crown Powers, Subjects and Citizens* (London: Cassell).

Virdee, Satnam (1999) 'England: Racism, Anti-racism and the Changing Position of Racialised Groups in Economic Relations' in Dale, G., and Cole, M. (eds) *The European Union and Migrant Labour* (Oxford: Berg).

2

Policy, politics, and the media

SUMMARY

This chapter is an introduction to some of the policy issues which shape immigration law. These issues are raised so that as they appear, embedded within the law throughout this book, they may be more easily recognized. The role of the media is discussed, because it is a powerful actor in moulding immigration and asylum policy, though in discussing the law, usually an invisible one. Some of the provisions which govern the treatment in the UK of asylum seekers are also covered here. These, too, have no other place in this book, not being an aspect of the law of entry, but they affect and are affected by the climate of policy on entry, and give rise to human rights issues. The institution and operation of the UK Border Agency is introduced as both a tool and an expression of policy.

2.1 Introduction – migration policy in a global context

In 2006, shortly after taking up his post as Home Secretary, John Reid pronounced that the immigration system was 'not fit for purpose'. His comment, dramatic, publicly given, and headline-catching, obscures the assumption behind it – that there is a recognized or agreed purpose for the immigration system. The Home Affairs Committee, in a measured introduction to the report of their inquiry into immigration control, posed the question, 'what is the purpose of the immigration system in the twenty-first century?' (Fifth Report of Session 2005–06 HC 775 para 5).

Before considering how this question is answered in policy and practice in the UK, we will take a step back to look through a wider lens. The study of migration is a vast field, engaging many disciplines including economics, politics, history, philosophy, international relations, as well as law. The main subject of this book is a tiny corner of that field: the national law which regulates entry to the UK. Though the policies implemented are national, the context for them is international. Evidence to the Home Affairs Committee was that:

> the great contradiction in migration today is that it is a global issue that people try to manage at a national level

and

> the root causes of migration are so powerful – it is about underdevelopment, disparities in demographic processes, in development, and in democracy – that to an extent … immigration control is treating the symptom rather than the cause. (para 7)

One of the key questions in the study of migration is 'What causes people to migrate?' Views that are held about this may in turn influence policy if policy makers seek to influence behaviour. Yash Ghai (1997) suggests that the market was historically, and remains, the key determinant of international movement. From the establishment of plantations and their demand for labour, the aspirations of employers fuelling illicit migration, and the balancing demand of the market for stability, labour mobility, and competition, these economic forces, he argues, predominate. Demetrios Papademetriou (2003) suggests that two drivers are particularly important in the present era: political, social, and cultural intolerance, which at the extreme turns into gross, group-based violations of human rights; and the systematic failure of governments to address multiple disadvantages faced by their populations. Papademetriou acknowledges that these phenomena are always present, and suggests additional triggers precipitate a pattern of migration:

- a long-term political, social, and economic relationship between the country of origin and destination country;
- economic benefits of migration sufficient to motivate the destination country to organize structures to receive migrants;
- a mature and influential 'anchor' ethnic community in the destination state, who may welcome and facilitate new arrivals; and
- interest groups in the destination state who oppose the circumstances from which migrants are escaping, thus carving out a social space into which they can be welcomed, and political support for permissive migration policies.

It may be noted that of the two drivers which Papademetriou identifies as being particularly relevant at the present time, flight from human rights violations is one which would generate a need for international protection, perhaps a claim for refugee status. The failure of governments to address disadvantage might have that result, but might also generate what is often called economic migration. The trigger factors do not sit neatly in either category. While the law, particularly in Western countries (see discussion of EU policy in chapter 6), distinguishes sharply between economic migration and asylum-seeking, the actual causes of international movement are not necessarily so sharply distinguished. Savitri Taylor (2005:6) regards the attempt to make this distinction as problematic. She says that 'the explanation for most international migration is to be found in a combination of economic and non-economic factors'. She considers that Western governments' attempts to *control* 'irregular' migration by controlling borders are an attempt to do the impossible. She proposes cooperation with countries of origin to *manage* migration for the benefit of all concerned at the same time as the long-term work of tackling root causes – poverty, armed conflict, and human rights abuse.

This kind of approach, seeing the management of migration as requiring international cooperation, is reflected in the work of the Global Commission on Migration, convened to move 'beyond the political deadlock which had effectively paralysed international discussion on migration for more than a decade' (Grant 2006:13). The Commission proposed that migration should become 'an integral part of national, regional and global strategies for economic growth' (2005:2). Moving beyond the deadlock involved recognizing migration as a potential benefit for the host country, the country of origin, and the migrant themselves, and developing policies that enable all those benefits to flow freely. Their recommendations included measures to prevent the benefit to states of origin from being lost. For instance, a 'brain drain' should be replaced by a 'brain circulation', and taxation or appropriation of remittances – the money that migrants send home – should be prevented. The money sent in remittances is 'second only to foreign direct investment in countries. In some countries remittances can be higher than official development assistance' (DFID 2007:13).

The Global Commission set an ambitious objective:

> Women, men and children should be able to realise their potential, meet their needs, exercise their human rights and fulfil their aspirations in their country of origin, and hence migrate out of choice rather than necessity. Those women and men who migrate and enter the global labour market should be able to do so in a safe and authorised manner, and because they and their skills are valued and needed by the states and societies that receive them. (2005:11)

These ideas echo a view put forward by the economist John Maynard Keynes, that migration is 'the oldest action against poverty', and recognized in the UK by the Department for International Development (DFID):

> migration and development are linked ... The objectives of both fields are more likely to be achieved if migration and development policies begin to acknowledge the benefits and risks of migration for poor people and developing countries. (DFID 2007:33)

Interestingly, the UK government's consultation paper, *Earning the Right to Stay: A New Points Test for Citizenship*, contained a section headed 'Migration and International Development'. This section set out some ideas for encouraging circular migration in order to reduce the impact of a brain drain on developing countries. It suggested, for instance, developing codes of practice for different sectors, such as the one in force with the NHS whereby the UK reduces active recruitment from countries with vulnerable healthcare systems, or giving credits in the earned citizenship scheme for development work in a migrant's home country. This consultation was abandoned.

Immigration law attempts to influence the behaviour of migrants. Some would say this is an exercise which should not be undertaken. Jonathon Moses, for instance, argues that the globalization of labour is the necessary next step after the globalization of capital and trade. Some research suggests that the economic impact of an open border would be minimal, but that the difficulties which would be faced are the cultural ones of our capacity to live together.

Whatever is the case, the operation of laws is influential on migration in ways that are not fully understood. Economics, human rights, and regulatory laws are part of a complex web which interacts with the subjective reasons that people have for moving.

By way of example, there may be a trade-off between rights and the availability of opportunities for migrants to work. Martin Ruhs (2009) cites as extremes the Gulf States and Sweden. In 2005, migrants accounted for a relatively high percentage of the population in the Gulf States, ranging between 24.4 per cent in Oman and 78.3 per cent in Qatar. He describes labour migration in the Gulf States as an 'employer-led, large-scale guest worker programme', entailing minimal rights without opportunities for settlement. In Sweden, by contrast, labour migration is minimal; perhaps 400 people per year (OECD 2008), but rights are comprehensive. He argues that this trade-off should be acknowledged, recognizing that the opportunity for migration has value and is conducive to human development, but also that a core minimum of rights should be identified.

The examples of the Gulf States and Sweden clearly show how governments attempt to influence behaviour through law, and the simple figures presented show that these attempts can have an impact, though from this brief information we cannot deduce the whole effect. Papademetriou warns that: 'The attempt to manage ... complex transnational processes through unilateral and single purpose policies will be of ever diminishing value.' He cites three escalating drivers of migration in the twenty-first century:

exclusion of ethnic or religious groups, the deterioration of ecosystems, and flight from natural and human-made disasters. These are events for which border-oriented long-term policy responses are unlikely to be adequate. Papademetriou finds present policy constructs for dealing with migration dated and 'disturbingly binary'. Categories of 'sending and receiving' countries, 'permanent and temporary migrants' and 'economic migration and seeking refuge' are not, he suggests, an adequate foundation for policy.

As we look at the UK's law and policy, we can expect to see this tension between what we might call the old binary view and the awareness of a transnational reality. Yash Ghai observes that the law is contradictory as its underlying principles are confused. Although 'governments welcome economic flows – especially of finance and trade' they are more ambivalent on flows of people (Castles 2007:12).

There is unlikely to be a simple answer to the question which the Home Affairs Committee posed: the purpose of the immigration system. How the answer is currently seen in the UK may be partly indicated by where responsibility is located in government.

2.2 Institutional basis of immigration control – an overview

A number of parts of government have a significant role to play in migration policy: the Department of Education and Skills in relation to overseas students and registers of colleges; local authority social service departments in relation to children at risk; the Department for Business, Enterprise and Regulatory Reform in relation to illegal working; and so on. As a result of the Home Affairs Committee's recommendation, a Cabinet sub-committee was created to remedy 'the absence of any place within government with overall responsibility . . . for determining . . . migration strategy'. In so recommending, the Home Affairs Committee was drawing attention, not to an absence of immigration control, which is a more limited activity, but to an absence of an overall migration strategy. Migration policy in the UK has tended to be strongly identified with immigration control – a more familiar phrase, and the title of this section. Publicly available documentation does not suggest that this sub-committee survived the 2010 General Election.

The present authority to control immigration is given by Immigration Act 1971 s 4(1) to 'the Secretary of State'. Though the Act does not specify which Secretary of State this is, in long-standing policy and practice this has been the Home Secretary. In *Pearson v IAT* [1978] Imm AR 212, the Court of Appeal held that the Secretary of State, referred to throughout the immigration statute, must 'by reason of the subject matter' be the Home Secretary. We might note in passing that the Department of Health guidance which prohibited doctors who had qualified in another country from getting work in English hospitals – although it was the subject of a successful challenge in the courts – was so in part precisely because another government department than the Home Office had unlawfully attempted to lay down an immigration measure (*R (on the application of BAPIO Action Ltd) v SSHD and Department of Health* [2008] UKHL 27; see chapter 10).

The immigration service, although answerable to the Home Secretary, was originally a distinct service. Immigration officers' powers concerned entry, and the Secretary of State's powers, exercised through Home Office civil servants (*Carltona Ltd v Commissioner of Works* [1943] 2 All ER 560) were to deal with those already in the country by making decisions on further leave to remain or deportation (Immigration Act 1971 s 4).

The distinction between the Secretary of State's powers and immigration officers' powers has diminished (Immigration and Asylum Act 1999 s 1 and is now of limited significance.

The 1971 Act did not deal with work permits, which remained the responsibility of the Secretary of State for Employment. Entry clearance officers remained answerable to the Foreign and Commonwealth Office. At the turn of this century, there were substantial changes. Chapter 1 has related how the Immigration and Asylum Act 1999 enlisted more of society in immigration control and laid the foundations to export the UK's border, the detail of which is discussed in chapter 7. This policy of more seamless and pervasive control was mirrored in institutional changes. In 2000, the Home Office and Foreign Office set up a joint unit to manage entry clearance. Following this, the Entry Clearance operation was rebranded 'UKVisas', and is now the International Group of the UK Border Agency. In June 2001, responsibility for work permit applications transferred from the Department of Education and Employment to the Home Office. It retained a separate identity as 'Work Permits UK' until 2008, with the creation of UKBA and the introduction of the points-based system. Now it is subsumed within UKBA. As immigration control was both extended beyond the UK's border and introduced into civil affairs, so the Home Office became the department with overall control.

2.2.1 The 2006 reviews

From December 2005 to June 2006, the Home Affairs Select Committee of the House of Commons conducted a major inquiry into immigration control. During the period of that inquiry, there was a public outcry over the release of foreign national prisoners who had not been considered for deportation. An observer would be forgiven for thinking that this was due to 'weak laws' or possibly even the Human Rights Act. Neither of these was the case, and the problem was poor communication within the Home Office. Factors contributing to this included overload on those working in the system and an over-concentration on asylum issues at the expense of other Home Office work. The affair as treated in the media is discussed later in the chapter. It was in reaction to this that John Reid's review took place, looking at strategic objectives, core processes, culture, and organization of the Immigration and Nationality Directorate (as it then was) (as stated to the Committee, HC 775 para 537).

The first published fruit of the review, issued shortly before the Home Affairs Committee reported, included an intention to 'make IND a more powerful agency, more clearly accountable to Parliament and the public'. The objectives of the reforms associated with the review were to:

- strengthen borders; use tougher checks abroad so that only those with permission can travel to the UK; monitor who leaves 'so that we can take action against those who break the rules';
- fast-track asylum decisions, removing those who fail, and integrating those who need protection;
- enforce compliance with immigration laws, 'removing the most harmful people first and denying the privileges of Britain to those here illegally'; and
- 'Boost Britain's economy by bringing the right skills here from around the world, and ensuring that this country is easy to visit legally' (*Fair, Effective, Transparent and Trusted*, July 2006).

These largely repeated the objectives of the five-year strategy launched in 2005. The agency was divided into regions in the interest of accountability and visibility. The message was that the immigration system was to be run in a way that ordinary people understood. Strategic direction was divided into management areas: asylum; borders; enforcement; human resources and organizational development; managed migration; and resource management; and the Director of UKVisas was given a seat on the board. An immigration casework review was undertaken to simplify and standardize activities and put in place an electronic caseworking system and improved information and knowledge management systems.

A critical area of need for reform was that of asylum decision-making (see chapter 12 for the ongoing history and importance of this). This system was also radically changed and regionalized. The Case Resolution Directorate was established to deal with the backlog of cases. The New Asylum Model, discussed in chapter 12, was introduced for all asylum claims made after April 2007. It applies the principles associated with the reforms, of speed, simplicity, and accountability by allocating an asylum case, after a screening interview, to a 'case owner' who then in theory sees it through to a conclusion. See chapter 12 for further discussion.

In the organizational culture, speed of decision-making became a highly prized quality in response to problems and injustice caused by delay. Already by this time, the prevailing governmental approach to a need to show achievement was to work to targets, mainly described in terms of numbers and time (e.g., 30,000 removals per year). The Home Affairs Committee identified the following problems with targets:

- Major political targets meant that other work may have been sidelined or even deliberately manipulated (para 572).
- For instance, prioritizing asylum claims and asylum removals had created backlog in other areas, and contributed to the foreign prisoner issue not being acted on more quickly.
- Targets were set for one part of a system without considering the effects elsewhere.
- This includes a problem with numerical targets per se in that, if a target of dealing with 90 per cent of claims in a certain time is met, 'what happens to the remaining 10% is irrelevant from the point of view of meeting targets' (para 583); so a target culture can also contribute to a black hole into which more difficult cases disappear because nobody can afford to spend the time on them.
- Targets on speed had a negative impact on quality.
- Targets might be met, but still have no impact on the underlying objective because they were the wrong targets. They might be set because they could be met rather than because they were designed to address a problem.

Despite these criticisms by the Committee, and perhaps fuelled by new efforts at accountability, the culture of speed and targets intensified after the 2006 reviews, most strikingly exemplified by the regular publication of 'milestones'. The effects of speedier initial decision-making in asylum cases, when treated in isolation from a larger-scale perspective, are discussed in the section on the treatment of asylum seekers.

2.2.2 UKBA

Before the 2006 reviews, as we have seen, some areas of work that had traditionally been outside Home Office control had come within it. From the outside at least, this looked like a one-way process associated with the exported border and the development of internal immigration controls. The Home Affairs Committee report took a different angle on the case for integrating government functions. As noted earlier, they successfully argued for a Cabinet Committee to take overall responsibility for immigration, as it affects the work of so many departments and they had noted a lack of liaison and overall judgement about the balance between competing interests (para 561).

In early 2007, the Home Secretary announced that the Home Office would be split into two. The focus of the new Home Office was to be terrorism, policing, security, and immigration. This allocation gave a clear signal about the way that immigration was perceived, and the direction that further institutional change would take. One of the effects is that the international protection nature of the work of dealing with asylum claims is even more invisible. In a 2004 proposal for division of the Home Office, a department for justice would deal with all crime-related matters, and 'department for rights' with human rights, immigration and asylum, family law and civil disputes, freedom of information, constitutional reform, electoral law and devolution (HL Constitution Committee Session 2006–07 Sixth Report para 19). This would have given a very different message.

As late as November 2006, the Minister for Immigration, Nationality and Citizenship said that the idea of a single border force was 'damaging, distracting and disruptive. That idea is outdated and is rooted in a concept of a frontier that is long past.' It should be consigned to 'the bin where it belongs' (HC Debs 2 November 2006 col 182WH). However, in a transitional phase from April 2007 the IND became the Border and Immigration Agency, reflecting the shifting emphasis, and on 25 July 2007 the government announced the creation of a new unified border force, called the UK Border Agency. It incorporates the BIA, UKVisas, and the border work of HM Revenue and Customs, and involves closer cooperation with the police Special Branch and with transport organizations, and regulators.

Interestingly, the full public launch of the new border concept did not come from the Home Secretary but from the Prime Minister. The Cabinet Office report *Security in a Global Hub* (2007) proposes 'dual and symmetrical' lines of accountability to the Chancellor and the Home Secretary. Migration in this vision is more a matter of border security than of foreign relations. The border as envisaged is not a 'purely geographical entity' (para 6). Much of the improved security that the document promises is delivered by 'exporting the border'. This is described in chapter 7, where we follow the various processes of border crossing. It relies on biometric data and cross-database checking at entry clearance posts, advance passenger information and juxtaposed controls in France and Belgium. *Security in a Global Hub* is an extensive document, describing a strategy of deterrence, intelligence sharing, and an integrated operation of policing and immigration control. Passengers are checked electronically against databases and watch lists, in advance through a visa application and again at the border.

On 1 March 2008, the first regulations took effect which created a duty to share information between immigration authorities, police, revenue and customs in relation to a range of matters including 'passenger information' and 'notification of non-EEA arrivals on a ship or aircraft'. These were made under powers that already existed (Immigration, Asylum and Nationality Act 2006 (Duty to Share Information and Disclosure of Information for Security Purposes) Order 2008, SI 2008/539). The legislative foundation for closer cooperation between the three bodies was developed in the UK Borders Act 2007.

By April 2009, UKBA was fully established. The public face of UKBA is markedly more security and enforcement oriented than its immediate predecessor, the Border and Immigration Agency, inevitably if not only because immigration functions are now institutionally combined with the work of crime prevention and raising revenue. UKBA's Business Plan April 2009–March 2012 states its purpose as follows: 'To secure our border and control migration for the benefit of our country' (UKBA Business Plan April 2009–March 2012:10). The strategic objectives arising from this are three, and are stated as articles of intent:

> We will protect our border and our national interests.
> We will tackle border and tax fraud, smuggling and immigration crime.
> We will implement fair and fast decisions.

It would be easy to lose sight of the purposes of immigration control as anything other than these. However, they are not the whole story. In its response to a report from the House of Lords Committee on Economic Affairs: 'The Economic Impact of Immigration' (session 2007–08 HL 82) the government said that the objectives of Britain's immigration system were threefold:

- To offer humanitarian protection to people requiring sanctuary and fleeing persecution;
- To welcome the loved ones of UK citizens and those with permission to be in the UK who want to be re-united with their families;
- To attract those with the skills who can make a positive contribution to the UK, through work and study.

These objectives attract little attention in UKBA's business plan, but this should come as no surprise. These differences reflect the tensions indicated by Papademetrios and others, and they are no doubt also influenced by the media, which we discuss later. Nevertheless, UKBA marks a consciously different approach from BIA, who stated their purpose as being to 'manage immigration in the interests of Britain's security, economic growth and social stability', in keeping with the tenor of the 2002 White Paper, *Secure Borders, Safe Haven: Integration with Diversity in Modern Britain* Cm 5387. Management instead of control implies dealing with a resource, something that is inherently beneficial, and while setting rules and processes for how to handle the resource, getting the best out of it. The reversion to the language of control marks a more hard-nosed attitude to economic migration, and a more absolute approach to enforcement and border control. As UKBA says, 'We will deliver increasingly visible action in our efforts on migration, with a stronger emphasis on controlling rather than managing migration' (Business Plan:35). The emphasis on achieving speedier decision-making remains, in the most recent internal review of working practices, see *Asylum Improvement Project, Report on Progress*, May 2011.

The HASC has remained, since its 2006 inquiry, intensely interested in the workings of UKBA, and has instituted a practice of requiring four-monthly reports.

We will now examine four policy areas which continue to be important.

2.3 Security

Security has been high on the government and public agenda since the attacks on the World Trade Centre on 11 September 2001. The presence of terrorist networks in the UK, many of whose members were born abroad, brought allegations that the government did not know who was in the UK. Increasingly, immigration control became wrapped up with the anti-terrorism programme. The indefinite detention provisions in the Anti-terrorism, Crime and Security Act 2001, the government's legislative response to the September 11 attacks, have been extensively commented upon, but the relevant point here is that the connection made in those provisions between protection against terrorism and immigration was held by the House of Lords in *A v SSHD* [2004] UKHL 56 to be unjustifiable. The provisions, later declared unlawful also by the ECtHR in *A v UK* (2009) 49 EHRR 29, enabled foreign nationals to be detained without trial if the Secretary of State certified that they were suspected of international terrorist connections and if they could not be deported because there was a real risk that they would be tortured abroad (see chapter 15). As a security measure, it had the drawback that British suspects could not be detained, and the targeting of those who were not British could not be rationally justified before the courts. Refugee law has been changed by the drive against terrorism, and the climate created by connecting the two has contributed towards the ease with which detention and criminalization have been visited upon asylum seekers. Chapters 14 and 15 of this book include a more detailed exploration of these matters.

Criticism of the immigration system was compounded on 26 July 2005 when, immediately after failed attempts at bombings in London, one of the suspects departed on Eurostar. This brought to public attention that there was no longer any monitoring of people leaving the country, as controls on departure had been abolished in the 1990s. The Prime Minister's statement on security on 5 August 2005 set out a number of anti-terror measures that would be taken. While not all have materialized in the form that the Prime Minister suggested, the speech does provide a guide to the security purpose of a number of immigration-related measures that have been taken and that are still ongoing. These are remarkably wide. They reveal four main areas of action on law and legal policy which are relevant for our purposes:

- Extending grounds for deportation to include 'unacceptable behaviour' such as 'glorifying terrorism'. Following this, a policy was adopted of relying on such behaviour as evidence that deportation or exclusion met the statutory requirement that it was 'conducive to the public good' (see for instance *Naik v SSHD* chapter 7). At the same time, the new offence of encouraging terrorism was introduced in the Terrorism Act 2006. The UK Borders Act 2007 and the Criminal Justice and Immigration Act 2008 strengthened the connection between deportation, loss of immigration status, and criminal offences. See chapter 16.
- Action on nationality law. This included reviewing the oath of allegiance and language testing, and expanding the grounds for depriving British citizens of their nationality (Immigration, Asylum and Nationality Act 2006 s 56). These matters are discussed in chapter 3.
- Implementation of the e-borders scheme. This is discussed in chapter 7.
- Measures to make it easier to prevent anyone with terrorist connections from obtaining refugee status (e.g., ss 54 and 55 of the Immigration, Asylum and Nationality Act 2006, discussed in chapter 14). Likelihood of causing harm was also a reason for prioritizing an asylum decision within the backlog dealt with by the Case Resolution Directorate.

The creation of the UK Border Agency did not feature in the Prime Minister's speech. As mentioned earlier, at that time, a unified force was not government policy.

The law barely deals with the question of what really is security. It is not confined to combating terrorism, however, as the deportation of serious criminals is also said to be in aid of public security. Security is usually concerned with a threat to the public or a section of the public. In *SSHD v Rehman* [2001] 3 WLR 877, the House of Lords said that they had jurisdiction to decide what national security was, while the Secretary of State was the only proper judge of what was *in the interests* of national security (see chapter 16). Controversially, their Lordships decided that an action which threatened the security of another country was a matter of national security in the UK.

There is a great volume of writing on the effect of increased security measures on immigration and on asylum-seeking in the UK, in Europe, and worldwide. Much of it charts increased monitoring and controls, and examines the risks of asylum claims being wrongly prevented or denied. While the rhetoric of governments often counterposes civil liberties and security, writers make the point that these can be on the same side. Related to this, some writers question the notion of 'security' as used in these debates. For instance, Nana Poku, Neil Renwick, and John Glenn argue that the idea of security which underlies the panoply of legal provisions is an outdated one tied to a national society, seen as military security and political and territorial integrity. They argue for replacing this with an idea of 'human security' (as opposed to 'state security') which values basic welfare of the population. This would entail taking into account that the pressures which cause migration often have their source outside the borders of a state, and that these may be events which fundamentally affect the security of a population, such as environmental degradation, economic deprivation, and conflict. They give examples of where such causes of insecurity have come from outside a state's borders: the 'speculative activities that resulted in the economic meltdown in South East Asia which led to the mass expulsion of "guest" workers from those states', and 'the sale of armaments to oppressive regimes'. They conclude that acknowledging this causal interdependence 'lies at the heart of sustainable common security'. This is an interesting counterpart to the House of Lords' identification of the security of one nation with the security of another – or of all.

UKBA's Business Plan, despite the involvement of the FCO on its board, is written from a very different perspective, and has a predominant concern with achieving a state border that is impenetrable except in accordance with stringent monitoring processes. Any idea of the body responsible for immigration having a facilitative internationally oriented role is absent from the document. Instead, the UKBA claims to be 'one of the largest law enforcement agencies in the UK'. A key task is 'to prevent harmful people and goods ever coming to the UK'.

2.4 Economic growth and economic migration

While there has been pressure on the UK government to close the border to entry for work, encapsulated in the slogan 'British jobs for British workers', the actual economic impact of migration is complex, and very different in different sectors of the economy. The Migration Advisory Committee is an expert group which takes evidence from an extensive range of sources and has the job of advising the government on the need for, and to an extent the impact of, migrant workers, in particular on where there are shortages of skilled workers which could appropriately be filled by migration. Government decisions on controlling the opportunities to enter for work are based on advice from this body. For discussion of its work see chapter 10. Problems for government in relation to entry for work include attracting the people with the skills for which there is an unmet demand and tackling illegal working.

The Global Commission commends the practice of granting settlement to those who enter for work. Granting the right to stay often contributes to economic growth in the destination country and plays a role in meeting the needs of migrants. However, they also point out two disadvantages. One is that the public mood is not always welcoming, and may be less willing to accept long-term migrants. The other is that countries of origin stand to gain more if migrants return. Although it is difficult to devise programmes of temporary entry for work that protect migrant workers' rights, the Commission advises that this should be attempted as well as settlement routes. In such cases, workers' rights, including access to proper working conditions, information and to transfer employers, should be respected (2005:17–18).

These standards support the capacity of migration to alleviate poverty. If routes to work within the law are too restricted so that enterprising migrants are pushed into using illegal means, there is an overall loss (though note the arguments of Ruhs earlier, which suggest that there may be an optimum balance). The individual migrant may suffer poor or dangerous living and working conditions, never be able to earn enough to pay off debts owed to smugglers or traffickers, let alone send home, and yet not be able to bring any of their troubles to the attention of the authorities because of their own illegal status. In the meantime, their country of origin may receive little or no benefit from their migration. The host country loses taxation, working conditions for other workers may be driven down, the immigration system is brought into disrepute, and migrants suffer from being associated with illegality. Where the rights of migrant workers are respected, their autonomy increases and they are able to leave abusive employers, send money home, return home when they are ready, or if they want to settle in the new country, are free to do so lawfully rather than 'disappearing' into the illegal economy (see Ryan MRN 2006).

In the UK, entry for work has been subject to intense scrutiny following the government's commitment to cut net immigration to tens of thousands. Students account for by far the largest group of immigrants (64 per cent of non-EEA visas in 2009), although the HASC argues that they should not be included in immigration figures unless and until they apply to stay after their studies, which the vast majority do not. Family settlement also accounts for a far greater number than workers. However, as human rights and domestic race relations are critically involved in family settlement, this is difficult to control. Similarly, EEA nationals account for significant numbers of immigrants, but have a right to enter. The government introduced a 'cap' on numbers of non-EEA workers who can enter for skilled work (20,700 in Tier 2 (General) between April 2011 and April 2012 – see chapter 10), and in December 2010 closed the general category for entry for highly skilled workers to all except 'those who have won international recognition in scientific and cultural fields, or who show exceptional promise', limited to 1,000 grants of entry clearance.

The Migration Advisory Committee was asked to report on the level at which the cap should be set in order to achieve the government's target of reducing net migration to 'tens of thousands'. The entry of non-EEA nationals for work – arguably the only group which could be so tightly numerically controlled – accounts for about one quarter of the net immigration figure or one tenth of the gross immigration figure (i.e., without off-setting emigration). The HASC observed that 'the proposed cap—unless it is set close to 100%—will have little significant impact on overall immigration levels' (para 31). The Migration Advisory Committee was unequivocal that the target could only be achieved by 'cutting net migration on study and family routes'. These limitations on entry for skilled work were controversial among employers' organizations. The focus on limiting entry for work gave rise to advice from the HASC to the government 'not to treat the routes it can control too stringently in order to compensate for the routes it cannot control' (*Immigration Cap* First Report of Session 2010–11 HC 361 para 28). Employers' organizations opposed capping the numbers of intra-company transfers, which accounted for about 60 per cent of entries for skilled work. The HASC also advised against including intra-company transfers, while pointing out that without doing so there would be minimal impact on numbers.

The decision to cap migration for work is discussed again in chapter 10, in the context of the legal provisions governing entry for work.

2.5 Undocumented migrants and removal

The director of immigration enforcement and removals, when asked by the Home Affairs Committee how many illegal migrants there were in the UK, famously replied: 'I have not the faintest idea' (HC 775 para 74). The media seized upon this as evidence of government incompetence in numerous ways. The political credibility of the immigration and asylum system rests in part on the timely and humane departure of those who have no right to be here. However, there is much confusion and misinformation about who such people are, how many there are, and what harm their continued presence does, if any. The undocumented or 'irregular' population (thought to be around half a million) consists mainly of people who have overstayed their original leave, people who have entered clandestinely or on false documents without being detected, and people whose removal has been directed, but who have not left, such as asylum seekers whose claim has failed (see, e.g., JCWI 2006). There are also many migrants who are legitimately in the UK but who are in breach of their conditions of stay, for instance by working. Irregular migrants include those who have been trafficked. So when figures, known or guessed at, are used in debating these matters, it is generally unknown who is included. Describing such people as 'illegal' carries connotations of criminality that are often quite inappropriate. 'Illegal immigrant' – the term beloved of the media – has no precise meaning. To describe someone as an illegal immigrant who has worked in breach of their conditions of stay is equivalent to describing someone who has committed a speeding offence as an 'illegal driver'.

The circumstances of people with irregular status are more various than imagination can encompass. For instance, the history that led to the Court of Appeal case of *Bibi and others v SSHD* [2007] EWCA Civ 740 was that a man had entered the UK in the 1960s using documents that were not his, and obtained a British passport in that identity. He had worked in the UK ever since, and made regular trips home to Bangladesh. It was only after his death when the rights of his family were affected that his deception came to light. He had probably lived and worked and paid taxes with nothing apparently to distinguish his situation from that of another naturalized British citizen. This man's situation was very different from that of the cockle-pickers who died in Morecambe Bay, and others who live in hiding because their illegal status and their, in effect, debt bondage to their traffickers means that they have no option but to hide from the authorities.

Evidence given to the Home Affairs Committee suggested that by far the largest number among undocumented migrants are people who have at some point been lawfully resident, and may still be so. A number of NGOs take the same view:

> Anecdotal evidence suggests that pressures exist with the experiences of migration which buffet against plans and intentions to remain lawfully and which convert a minority of migrants into

rule breakers and overstayers. Many of these pressures are financial, involving the discovery that recovery of the cost of the original investment in migration (visa fees, student fees, travel costs, legal advice and other facilitation, etc) is not as easily recoverable from the meagre wages available to migrants as had been thought. In other instances migrants will come under pressure from family abroad to remain to take full advantage of earnings opportunities which can be remitted abroad. In these cases migrants may be tempted to work more hours than permitted or overstay their leave in order to claim to the benefits of migration. (MRN 2007)

The weight of evidence and opinion is that action needs to be taken on many different fronts to tackle this problem, but that some regularization of existing irregular migrants and the protection of migrant workers' rights are important elements. Enforcement by removal is not the only strategy. Ruhs and Anderson (2007) point out some non-compliance is partial and tolerated by all concerned. For instance, how does the law evaluate a request by a student's employer that she works a couple of extra hours so that she exceeds the permitted hours that week? These compromises, they suggest, need to be understood.

2.5.1 Carrying out forced removals

Even when a removal decision has been made and directions issued to carry it out, carrying this into effect is not a simple matter. The obstacles to removal are real, and not always understood by critics. As JCWI relates:

Removal of failed asylum seekers may be impeded for a variety of practical reasons, such as a lack of travel documents, a lack of co-operation from the authorities of the country of origin in issuing such documents, or because there are no safe routes of return, or simply because that country is unsafe to return to. (2006:17)

In addition to these reasons, Phuong discusses a host of other practical factors. Airlines may be reluctant to take people who are being removed against their will:

Each person to be removed from the UK is subject to a risk assessment in order to determine his suitability for escorted or unescorted removal via commercial air services...In any case, the International Air Transport Association...has decided that the number of persons to be removed should be limited to one escorted and three unescorted on each flight. (2005:124)

Additionally, many passengers do not like to see people forced onto a plane and 'may take their business to another airline' (2005:125). In Germany, under pressure from the public, Lufthansa decided it would not carry passengers who were resisting deportation (2005:125). Because of the limited flights to removal destinations and the growing reluctance of commercial airlines, governments including the UK have begun to use charter planes for returns. Clearly this is an expensive method, as planes with a capacity of hundreds of passengers may only carry a few dozen returnees at any one time (2005:125), although flights to, e.g., Afghanistan have been known to carry as many as 90 passengers.

The Home Affairs Committee noted that, despite the tone of much public debate, public opinion is another factor which explains the low number of removals relative to government targets and the numbers of those who are liable in law to removal (para 418). (See also the section on media.) Phuong notes that, although public opinion may be in favour of removals in the abstract, when it comes to people being removed by force, and sometimes even injured or killed in the attempt, especially if they know them personally or they 'seem likeable (especially if they are well educated and have small children) they can become quite opposed to a particular forced removal' (2005:126).

In almost any government statement of immigration policy objectives in recent years, 'increase removals' has appeared as a key item. The practical reality is that it is a hard and unpleasant business for all involved and often unfeasible. Phuong concludes that one should also ask 'why are there so many people to be removed in the first place?' She, too, speculates that limited routes to legal migration may be part of the reason, and that opening up economic migration could assist. The Global Commission on International Migration recommends: 'States should address the conditions that promote irregular migration by providing additional opportunities for regular migration and by taking action against employers who engage migrants with irregular status.' The Commission also recommends 'dialogue and cooperation among states' (2005:36). Other commentators, too, consider that action on illegal working would alleviate the problems of undocumented migrants. Ryan (2006) explains that giving migrants the same basic workers' rights as other employees could solve some of the problems of exploitation not only directly but also indirectly, and help resolve immigration irregularity at the same time. The Home Affairs Committee recommends that action is taken more swiftly when, for instance, leave is refused or an appeal lost, while people are still in contact with the system. They criticize the practice of removing families as a 'soft target'.

The conduct of removals is also a cause for concern. The Joint Committee on Human Rights heard evidence of small children taken out of their beds early in the morning by officials, bundled into cold vans and then into detention. There were also many instances of violence, for instance people on the way to removal being beaten in the back of vans. The Committee recommended that people should be properly prepared for removal and that the removals should be carried out with dignity (HL 81 HC 60 para 337). Since then, the report *Outsourcing Abuse* in 2008 documented nearly 300 assaults against asylum detainees, and in 2011 HM Chief Inspector of Prisons inspected and reported on removals to Jamaica and Nigeria, voicing concerns about excessive mild restraints used on individuals who offered no resistance, and racist and offensive language used at what is a very distressing time for most people who are removed. In October 2010, Jimmy Mubenga died in the course of restraint by G4S escorts while being placed on a plane for deportation to Angola. He is the second person to have died in the course of deportation from the UK.

2.6 Treatment of asylum seekers

This section concerns the conditions of support for asylum seekers during their time in the UK. For reasons that appear later in this chapter and elsewhere in this book, there is in the UK a population of people who have sought refuge here unsuccessfully. Many, no-one knows how many, would say that their first asylum decision was badly made and the appeal system was unable to put that right (see chapter 12 for some reasons as to why that might be).

The Tenth Report of the Parliamentary Joint Committee on Human Rights in Session 2006–07, *The Treatment of Asylum Seekers*, is an important document in the immigration and asylum debate. The Committee explains the importance of their report in this way:

> 12. The treatment of asylum seekers is important for the men, women and children seeking asylum in the UK. But it is also important for those of us who are not asylum seekers. This is because the UK's approach to migration – and its treatment of asylum seekers in particular – says something about the society we live in and the kind of country we want to be. The human rights principles

and values of democratic societies must guide the country's behaviour towards asylum seekers and its relationships with other countries from which asylum seekers originate.

Asylum seekers who have no other means of material support are entitled to a basic level of assistance (currently approximating to 54 per cent of the income support rate) and accommodation while their claim is being considered (Immigration and Asylum Act 1999 s 95). This can be refused if they do not claim asylum as soon as reasonably practicable after their arrival (Nationality, Immigration and Asylum Act 2002 s 55). As discussed in chapter 1, the application and interpretation of this section left hundreds (at least) of asylum seekers destitute. Following the *Limbuela* judgment, discussed in chapter 1, asylum seekers should no longer be denied support where they are destitute. In the JCHR enquiry, witnesses including from the Home Office confirmed that s 55 of the 2002 Act was still being used to deny support to people who had somewhere to sleep but no food. Also, anyone who took more than three days after arrival to claim might well not receive support. However, the difficulties of finding one's way to an unknown location in an unknown country, perhaps not speaking the language, and without the information that this journey was necessary and how to do it, were minimized or overlooked (para 78). The Committee concluded that the continued application of s 55 did not comply with the *Limbuela* judgment, that there were clear breaches of Article 3 ECHR, and that s 55 ought to be repealed.

Where an asylum claim has failed, as most do, entitlement to support under s 95 ends. An asylum seeker may then be able to claim support under s 4 of the 1999 Act if they are taking all reasonable steps to go home, or the Secretary of State accepts that they are physically not able to leave, either because of illness or there is no viable route of return, or failure to support would entail a breach of their human rights, or they have children who would otherwise require local authority support. Section 4 support consists of accommodation and a card (Azure card) credited with £35 per week. Asylum seekers are not permitted to work, though see *ZO Somalia* discussed later in this chapter.

The Committee found that a disturbingly high number of people had not even obtained the support to which they were entitled because of inefficiency and incompetence. Examples of how the system worked included that people could only claim asylum at either Liverpool or Croydon between 9 a.m. and 1 p.m., Monday to Friday. This placed an impossible burden on people who did not know the country and had nowhere to stay overnight and no means to pay for a bed. Now claims may only be made in Croydon. For some people, the system had proved so daunting that they did not manage to get into it at all. Refugee Action gave evidence to the JCHR that these difficulties increased the likelihood of potential asylum seekers 'disappearing without engaging in the asylum process, as they simply may not make it to an asylum screening unit' (para 80).

As the JCHR found, 'the government's approach to asylum has, in large part, been based on the assumption that many of those who arrive in the UK and claim asylum are not genuinely in need of protection but rather are economic migrants seeking a better life for themselves and their families' (para 3). The Committee criticized the frequent moves of asylum seekers, interrupting children's schooling and causing other hardship, the use of vouchers to buy food and toiletries – once abandoned by the government as too degrading and inefficient but now revived – and the poor housing provided as the only option for asylum seekers, sometimes overcrowded with collapsing ceilings. With the prohibition on doing paid work, there was no escape from the degrading conditions. The Committee concluded:

The treatment of asylum seekers in a number of cases reaches the Article 3 threshold of inhuman and degrading treatment. This applies at all stages of the asylum process.

Then, most damningly:

> We have been persuaded by the evidence that the government has indeed been practising a deliberate policy of destitution of this highly vulnerable group. We believe that the deliberate use of inhumane treatment is unacceptable.

Research by the Joseph Rowntree Trust revealed that, among the 21 countries of origin represented by the destitute asylum seekers surveyed, those most strongly represented were known for conflict and human rights abuses. The largest groups were from Eritrea (25 per cent), Sudan (14 per cent), and Iran (12 per cent). This may in part be an indicator of the very real obstacles to return even when an individual asylum claim has failed. For such a person, fast progress through the asylum system may mean that they are plunged more rapidly into destitution or, one of the few options for survival, illegal working. Other options are charities, begging, sleeping rough or staying with friends. For a fuller account of survival strategies see Crawley, Hemmings, and Price, 2011. For the government, meeting targets of fast processing may mean an increase in the number of people who have no regular status but cannot be removed, a phenomenon which causes them much political embarrassment, an increase in illegal working which they are pledged to reduce, or an increase in destitution for which they are also criticized.

The Joseph Rowntree research showed that some of the destitute asylum seekers in Leeds had been through the New Asylum Model. The same research showed that people may remain in the UK, destitute, for long periods. Fast initial decision-making may increase illegal working and poverty in another way. Asylum seekers cannot apply for permission to work unless the initial decision on their asylum claim is outstanding for more than 12 months. However, this does not apply to a delay in appeals. So an initial decision may be very fast, but then the appeal process drags on for years, and the opportunity to apply for permission to work is no longer available (JCHR para 77). EC Reception Directive 2003/9 Article 11(2) requires that if a decision has not been taken within one year through no fault of the applicant, the Member State must 'decide the conditions for granting access to the labour market for the applicant'.

Key Case

***ZO (Somalia) and MM (Burma) v SSHD* [2010] UKSC 36**

The Supreme Court held that Article 11(2) of the Directive also applied to fresh claims for asylum, so that if a person whose first claim had failed later found further evidence and was able to make a fresh claim, that would trigger the start of a further 12-month period after which permission to work could be sought. Many asylum seekers do make fresh claims. The government's common practice was to decide that further representations did not amount to a fresh claim and then refuse that claim on the same day. The representations might be waiting for years for a decision as to whether they met the requirements (see chapter 12) to be treated as a fresh claim, but during that time the Home Office would not treat time as running for the purposes of permission to work. The Court said that to interpret the rules in that way deprived the right to apply for permission to work of all utility.

The judgment of the Court of Appeal was to the same effect as that of the Supreme Court, but was never implemented. Once the Supreme Court judgment was given, UKBA introduced a policy that the only work for which asylum seekers could be considered was that in the list of shortage occupations.

Funding for English classes for asylum seekers has also been intermittently stopped and started. The Refugee Council commented:

> The removal of automatic ESOL and FE funding for asylum seekers is a major blow toward their ability to function and communicate effectively during the time when their claim is being considered... English language brings greater self-sufficiency which, amongst other benefits, means less reliance on support services. It also allows people to make connections with the local community that they would not have otherwise. We are particularly concerned that these changes further disempower people who have already undergone significant loss. (ESOL and Further Education Funding Changes 2007/08 announced by the Learning and Skills Council. Briefing November 2007)

In addition to the government responses to John Reid's view that the immigration system was 'not fit for purpose', an independent group of people was convened to investigate the asylum system in depth. This became the Independent Asylum Commission, which reported in 2008 on whether the asylum system was 'fit for purpose yet'. The foreword to their final report said:

> We lose control over the movements of the asylum seeker at exactly the point – after refusal – that the incentive for the asylum seeker to maintain contact disappears. And we lose moral authority by using destitution to 'encourage' refused asylum seekers to return home 'voluntarily'.

Their recommendations included that 'robust independent research should be undertaken into the reasons why different categories of refused asylum seeker do not return home voluntarily, and the results should inform a pilot project to increase take-up of voluntary return'. The Commission made many detailed and practical recommendations, and though it is not possible to summarize them all, it may be fair to say that their reports indicate, as in the recommendation referred to earlier in the chapter, a need for far more information about the real human situation of those who are caught in the asylum system, and a political will to feed that information into policy-making in order to create a system that is both more effective and more humane.

2.7 Immigration control within the borders

The introduction in the UK Borders Act of biometric immigration documents (BIDs) for all foreign nationals may initially have been a trial run for identity cards for all UK residents; however, identity cards for all have now been abandoned. BIDs, also called biometric residence permits (BRPs), are being introduced for different groups of foreign nationals at a time, and are intended to integrate with e-borders.

The requirement to apply for a BRP at the same time as making an immigration application first came into effect on 25 November 2008 for extensions of leave for students, spouses, civil and unmarried partners. In March 2009, it was extended to more groups, including medical and academic visitors and workers who are outside the points-based system. From January 2010, skilled workers applying to remain under Tier 2 of the points-based were required to have a BRP. They are now issued to all foreign nationals who obtain leave to remain in the UK for more than six months. From February 2012 they will be issued to all who are granted indefinite leave to remain or refugee status.

There is no obligation to carry the BRP, but it may be used to gain access to public services, education, or employment. This generates potential for discrimination if cards *become* a requirement where access to the benefit in question does not in fact depend on immigration status, or where the BRP is not well understood. Beynon reported a speech of the former Home Secretary at the launch of *Enforcing the Rules*, the March 2007 instalment of the reform programme, to the effect that BRPs were to be used to 'refine and upscale a project already in hand – the enforced destitution of irregular migrants such as failed asylum applicants and visa overstayers so as to encourage them to return to their sending countries' (2007:328)

The use of BRPs to access health care is in keeping with the government's current programme of attempting to end access to the National Health Service for various groups of foreign nationals, in particular refused asylum seekers. The JCHR has already commented on the infringements of basic rights that are occurring as vulnerable pregnant women are refused ante-natal care, and how this sometimes results in an emergency which could have been prevented when a woman is rushed to hospital.

Following up on these concerns, UKBA conducted an online survey in 2011 of BRP users, inquiring into their experiences of the ease or otherwise of use, and any problems of discrimination or obstruction in its use. About half of the respondents had not used the card to access education or employment. Of those that had, while some problems with the use of the card were indicated – e.g., that replacement cards did not contain a full immigration history, thus giving an impression perhaps of an irregular status, and that the cards were not well understood by officials – on the whole results were evenly balanced between those who found the card convenient and those who found it inconvenient. Among the respondents, there was no significant impact on protected groups (i.e., based on immigration status, race or gender). Sixty-four per cent of the respondents were male, and 81 per cent were between 21 and 44 years old (*Securing our Border: Controlling Migration – Biometric Residence Permit Surveys 2011 Summary Analysis* December 2011).

The integration policy revealed in current legal changes and proposals is marked by a tendency to harmonize to a conception of British life that is based on the majority culture. Changes include the introduction of tests on English language and 'life in the UK', initially as a condition of obtaining British citizenship, and indefinite leave to remain, and now proposed also for leave to enter or remain for marriage, discussed in chapter 9.

2.8 Media

The final subject in this chapter is the media. They have been present, though without mention, in much of what has gone before. Policy is presented and framed in the way it is because the government expects that the media will publicize what they have said. Without the news media, many of the policy statements we have been discussing might not be made at all. Lord Woolf described the relationship between the media and the judiciary as one of a common interest, and a need to be independent of one another while also recognizing that each has some power to uphold the other's independence. The media and judiciary each act as a check on the power of government, particularly when that government has a large majority and can become 'impatient of interference and criticism' (2003). When there is tension in the relationship between the judiciary and executive, the media is an interested party.

Constitutional Reform Act 2005 s 3 affirms convention by requiring ministers to uphold the independence of the judiciary. The House of Lords Constitution Committee explained that this does not mean that ministers may not comment on individual cases. They may, but they should say that they disagree with the decision and that they will appeal if that is the case, and not imply that there is something wrong with the judge for making that decision (2006–07 Sixth Report para 40).

This convention has been infringed in immigration and asylum cases in recent years. In a number of cases, the judge has come under personal attack. Even more than this, ministers have implied that there is something unconstitutional and anti-democratic in the judges upholding the rights of asylum seekers. Remarkably, in relation to *R (on the application of Q and M) v SSHD* [2003] 2 All ER 905, the then Home Secretary David Blunkett said that he would not put up with judges interfering with the democratic process in this way. The case was one of statutory interpretation, using the Human Rights Act to interpret the Nationality, Immigration and Asylum Act 2002. Commenting on Mr Blunkett's response, Geoffrey Bindman in *The Independent* newspaper in February 2003 pointed out that it is the constitutional task of the judiciary to interpret legislation, and in a democracy, judicial review is the essential constitutional check by the judiciary of the executive.

A personal attack on the judge was combined with misinformation in the case of *S v SSHD*, in which the government apparently used the media to publish a distorted account of a court case, with damaging results for the courts, the Human Rights Act and the appellants. This case was serious enough that, in combination with two other incidents, it prompted an enquiry by the JCHR.

The legal aspects of the case of S are dealt with in chapter 8. Briefly, this was the case of the nine people who had hijacked a plane as a desperate measure to leave Afghanistan. They were members of a group opposed to the government, and were in fear for various reasons, including that one member of their group had been tortured, killed, and then delivered to their door. After an eight-day hearing by a specially convened Tribunal, their claims for asylum were turned down because of the crime they had committed by hijacking the plane, but it was held that they should have temporary protection because of their fears of human rights abuses. This would entail a grant of discretionary leave. They were convicted of the hijacking and served prison sentences, though later cleared by the Court of Appeal because the jury had been misdirected on the question of duress.

The government accepted before the Tribunal that the appellants did not present any security risk to the UK, but refused to accept the ruling of the Tribunal. They did not challenge it, but just kept the appellants on temporary admission, even though there was no basis in law for this. Discretionary leave, although temporary, would entitle them to work or claim benefits, neither of which they could do on temporary admission.

As the hijack itself was such a high-profile event, the media would be interested in the fate of the appellants, so anticipation of press coverage must have been in the government's mind in the conduct of this case. The question was whether the government was willing to take the lead in explaining to the public that the hijackers had paid the penalty in law for their criminal actions, what they had suffered, why they needed protection, and to take credit for Britain upholding its proud tradition of giving sanctuary, albeit temporary. Unfortunately, they did nothing, leaving the appellants in limbo for 18 months.

When the case eventually came to the High Court, and Sullivan J ordered that the Secretary of State act lawfully and grant discretionary leave, the government appealed to the Court of Appeal. The High Court judgment was castigated in the press and by the Prime Minister as 'an abuse of common sense'. The response of the Prime Minister and Home Secretary implied that the High Court had only just decided that the claimants could not return for human rights reasons and that they were amazed and outraged by this, rather than acknowledging that the human rights decision had been made 18 months earlier and was no surprise. Their response also implied that these people had hijacked a plane and got off scot-free. Crucially, the Home Secretary commented in the press:

> When decisions are taken which appear inexplicable or bizarre to the general public, it only reinforces the perception that the system is not working to protect or in favour of the vast majority of ordinary decent hard-working citizens in this country.

The media did not apparently notice that the 'ordinary decent hard-working citizens of this country' were not in any way adversely affected by the decision, but were being invoked in support of the indignation of the Home Secretary and Prime Minister. Over the next few days, they picked up the case as a call to repeal the Human Rights Act. The Daily Telegraph contrasted the 'hijack at gunpoint' with the right to stay. There was no mention of the basis for the appellants' fear, nor the abuse of power by the Home Secretary. The press coverage painted the claimants as the villains of the piece, and the Home Secretary as amazed and outraged. Eventually the Court of Appeal applauded Sullivan J's judgment as 'impeccable'.

At the special inquiry by the Parliamentary Joint Human Rights Committee, the Lord Chancellor was asked whether he regarded Sullivan J's judgment as 'impeccable' or 'inexplicable and bizarre'. His response sets out a fairly standard piece of legal reasoning which implicitly endorses that it was 'impeccable'.

Comment has not all been in one direction. As discussed in chapter 1, in recent years, there has sometimes been a high level of tension between the executive and judicial branches of government. One indication of this was that senior judiciary broke their time-honoured tradition of not commenting on government policy. The battle over the proposed ouster clause in the AITOC Bill brought out the senior and retired judiciary in powerful opposition, not only in Parliament but also outside it. Lord Woolf's trenchant criticism in his Squire Centenary lecture marked a new point in executive/judicial relations. Lord Steyn was prepared to count himself out of hearing the challenge to the British government's role in detention in Guantanamo Bay, which he described as a 'legal black hole' (2004:256), in order to be free to warn publicly against an 'unprincipled and exorbitant executive response' (*The Independent* 26 November 2003).

The use of the media in relation to S was a low watermark. However, the release of foreign prisoners reported in 2006 was, if anything, a lower point. In this case, neither the judiciary nor the Human Rights Act had any part to play. Journalism revealed a failing in government, and the government then blamed the judiciary and the Human Rights Act. The story is best told in the words of the JCHR report:

> 22. When it came to light that a substantial number of foreign prisoners had been released at the end of their sentences without being considered for deportation, some of whom had re-offended, the then Home Secretary, Rt Hon Charles Clarke MP announced plans, in a statement to the House of Commons on 3 May 2006, to change the system governing deportation of foreign prisoners.
>
> 23. The new Home Secretary, Dr Reid, said in a newspaper article on 7 May: 'the vast majority of decent, law-abiding people...believe that it is wrong if court judgments put the human rights of foreign prisoners ahead of the safety of UK citizens. They believe that the Government and their wishes are often thwarted by the courts. They want the deportation for foreign nationals [sic] to be considered early in their sentence, and are aware that this was overruled by the courts' (*News of the World*).

The cause of the prisoners not being considered for deportation was actually a failure of communication between different parts of the Home Office, and nothing at all to do with the Human Rights Act. This was admitted by the government in evidence given to the JCHR enquiry. This admission of course gained almost no press coverage by comparison with the outcry over the release of the prisoners, which was full of misinformation of all kinds. After the assertion by the Home Secretary that the Human Rights Act was to blame, the Prime Minister followed up in Parliament with a speech referring to the government's plans to change the law on deportation, and said that the vast majority of people 'would be deported, irrespective of any claim that they have that the country they are returning to may not be safe' (HC Debs 17 May 2006 col 990). The implication was not only that the Human Rights Act was to blame but also that the government had the power to legislate to override fundamental rights. The press coverage also implied that the prisoners *would* have been deported if they had been considered, but deportation is a discretion to be exercised on the merits of the individual case. There were said to be 1,000 prisoners freed without consideration of their cases, but the fact that this total was accumulated over seven years was lost from public view.

A serious result of the media outcry was that the government was under pressure to find and deport as many of the freed prisoners as they could. This meant that recently released foreign nationals, even if they would not normally be deported on the facts of their case, were at higher risk. One such case was that of Sakchai Makao, a popular young Thai man who had lived in Shetland most of his life. After one crime that was out of character, he served an eight-month prison sentence, but was welcomed back to Shetland. He was re-arrested for deportation in the aftermath of the foreign prisoners issue, but the islanders said he had been picked up as a 'soft target', and they campaigned for him to stay. The Tribunal agreed he should.

Not only foreign nationals were at risk in this operation. Some of the alleged foreign national prisoners turned out to be British. It seemed that prisoners' nationality was not routinely checked (see Shah, R. 2007).

None of this was to do with the Human Rights Act or, in fact, the state of the law at all, but it was nevertheless a platform upon which the government could launch its idea of 'automatic' deportation for serious offences. In chapter 16, we discuss how automatic this actually is. Although the UK Borders Act 2007 has created a strong presumption in a wide range of criminal cases, even the strongest presumption cannot displace human rights, as the JCHR noted. Government representatives before the Committee were forced to agree.

The foreign national prisoners issue also provoked a published letter from the Prime Minister to the Home Secretary, in which he alleged that British courts overruled the government in a way that was inconsistent with other EU countries' interpretation of the ECHR. A parliamentary question and inquiries by the JCHR were unable to unearth any such case, but if they had, the implication that this would be somehow illegal, unethical or unconstitutional is simply wrong. The suggestion was withdrawn before the JCHR, but again without media attention.

Sometimes, of course, the press itself misrepresents the law, and has also done this in a way that inaccurately disparages the Human Rights Act. An instance of this was press coverage of the case of Learco Chindamo, the young man who killed Philip Lawrence. A teenager killing a respected head teacher generated particularly strong feeling, and once again the Human Rights Act was wrongly credited with the fact that the Asylum and Immigration Tribunal held that he could not be deported. Chindamo, as an EU national, could only be deported 'on imperative grounds of public policy', which would not apply in this case where he was agreed not to present a future risk. Undeterred by facts, the *Daily Mail* and other newspapers reported that the Human Rights Act was the reason for the ruling which it described as 'profoundly stupid and amoral' (21 August 2007). The Shadow Home Secretary was apparently also taken in, saying that the case demonstrated 'a stark demonstration of the clumsy incompetence of this Government's human rights legislation'. In fact, it was an EC Directive which bound the Tribunal.

The concern in cases of this kind, and one reason that *S* and the foreign prisoners issue warranted investigation by the JCHR, was that such inaccurate reporting, and particularly when led by government, undermines attempts to build a human rights culture. It feeds racism, though this was not discussed by the JCHR, as the implication of the Home Secretary's remark, not voiced openly by him but quickly picked up on by newspapers such as the Daily Mail, is that human rights are delivered to failed asylum seekers in preference to long-term residents. There was no foundation for this in the cases in question.

The role and power of the press in creating a climate around asylum has been researched in a number of studies. This, too, is not new. Greenslade for the Institute of Public Policy Research shows that press reports have encouraged ill-feeling against migrants since the early part of the twentieth century, including anti-Jewish material in the newspapers of the late 1940s and press coverage of street fighting in Notting Hill in the 1950s, inaccurately reported as 'race riots'. The study shows how 'newspapers, either by exaggerating race disputes or covering them in such a way as to suggest that migrants were the cause of trouble, helped to set the political agenda which led to immigration legislation' (2005:17). A similar story may be told about disturbances in Brixton in 1981, also inaccurately dubbed 'race riots'. Greenslade gives up-to-date examples of misinformation in newspapers which directly resulted in violence. For instance, the misleading claim that 'luxury pads' were being prepared for asylum seekers resulted in homes being broken into and damaged before refugees had moved in.

In October 2003, the Press Complaints Commission issued a brief guidance note to editors about terminology. It explained, for instance, that an asylum seeker is 'someone currently seeking refugee status or humanitarian protection'. Consequently 'there can be no such thing in law as an "illegal asylum seeker"'. This guidance on terminology, while welcome, only scratched the surface. The JCHR recommended the PCC go further and provide practical guidance on professional practice of journalists in reporting matters of legitimate public interest, while not encroaching on free speech (para 366).

A study for the Information Centre about Asylum and Refugees in the UK (ICAR) assessed the impact of media and political images of refugees and asylum seekers on community relations in London (Media Image, Community Impact 2004). This report uses a range of methods and is a theoretically grounded study. It was inconclusive about the link between unbalanced press reporting and violence against asylum seekers. It did find under-reporting of violence against asylum seekers and refugees, and the frequent use of emotive language and inaccurate information. The writers noted that 'local papers were more likely than national ones to interpret their role as providing a balanced picture on issues that affect local people' (2004:98). This finding was repeated in a later study by ICAR of the effect of the Press Complaints Commission Guidelines (ICAR 2007).

The ICAR research found that during the period of the study (in 2005) only 1 per cent of newspaper articles contained inaccurate terminology such as 'illegal asylum seeker'. Of 2,000 articles assessed, 37 were singled out for further investigation and 'analysed for possible mixing of fact, comment and conjecture. Examples were found of misuse of statistics, stories whose main claims were misleading and misrepresentations of quotes or facts' (2007:12). The most inaccurate reporting was in the daily newspapers with the top six circulation figures. The most common theme in these papers was the system being 'out of control'. The study found 'most political reporting to be "tired, repetitive and unquestioning". Stories reflected the obsession with chaos, and failed to offer alternative perspectives.' Another finding was that regional papers ran more individual stories, which ICAR considered 'an important means of increasing understanding of how policies and attitudes affect real people' (2007:13). 'In particular, it is interesting that local concern about asylum seekers facing deportation featured highly' (2007:11). ICAR contrasted the sympathetic response in individual situations with the national political focus on the desirability of deportation.

This finding is important, given the enormous power attributed in the immigration and asylum field to an invisible factor called 'public opinion'. There is now a range of initiatives by NGOs and by individuals and community groups to tackle 'public opinion' directly by the provision of direct information about and contact with refugees and asylum seekers and their human experience. See, for instance, the Refugee Awareness Project originating in Refugee Action, in which local people and refugees talk and work together, and the City of Sanctuary movement, an initiative to build a climate of welcome and hospitality. These and other initiatives working directly on this form of 'climate change' illustrate that public opinion and the question of accurate and inaccurate information is a major driver in the field of asylum policy.

As government solutions to an ill-defined problem proliferate, so do the solutions of civil society, migrants themselves, activists, and people at various levels of organization. The London-based Strangers into Citizens campaign commissioned a telephone poll of 1,004 British adults in April 2007. Of these, 66 per cent believed that undocumented migrants who have been in the UK for more than four years and pay taxes should be allowed to stay and not called 'illegal'; and 67 per cent believed that asylum seekers should be allowed to work (Strangers into Citizens press release 24 April 2007). Following this, a coalition of 40 organizations formed a campaign called 'Still Human Still Here' which aims to end the destitution of refused asylum seekers.

An important role played by the media in immigration and asylum issues is in investigative journalism. Journalists have revealed many human stories and uncovered malpractice in government, for instance when a chief immigration officer was alleged to have pressurized an 18-year-old asylum seeker for sex in return for asylum status (Observer 21 May 2006). Sometimes also press reports from their country of origin may be an important source of evidence for asylum seekers. It is difficult to establish their claim outside their country, but they may be able to obtain newspaper reports through contacts or online, or occasionally witness statements from investigative journalists (for instance in *BK (DRC)* [2007] UKAIT 00098).

Some of the major human rights violations occurring in connection with migration have been uncovered by investigative journalists, for instance, the Joseph Rowntree Foundation note in their report on contemporary slavery a 'formidable body of work by investigative journalists' (2007:24) which has uncovered stories of trafficking adults and children for sex and other forms of forced labour, and abuse. John Pilger's film, *Stealing a Nation*, brought the little-known story of the Chagos Islanders (see chapter 3) to the attention of the general public when it was shown on ITV.

2.9 Conclusion

This chapter just touches on some of the issues surrounding the making of legal policy. This is the edge of a very large field. Some other policy issues are addressed throughout this book as they arise.

QUESTIONS

1 Under what conditions is it possible to make immigration policy in a way that is truly democratically accountable? Is this desirable?

2 What elements would you like to see in a code of practice for the media on reporting on immigration and asylum issues?

For guidance on answering questions, visit www.oxfordtextbooks.co.uk/orc/clayton5e/.

FURTHER READING

Andreouli, Eleni and Stockdale, Janet E. (2009) 'Earned Citizenship: Assumptions and Implications' *Journal of Immigration, Asylum and Nationality Law* vol. 23, no. 2, pp. 165–180.

Beynon, Rhian (2007) 'The Compulsory Biometric Registration of Foreign Nationals in the UK: Policy Justifications and Potential Breaches of Human Rights' *Journal of Immigration, Asylum and Nationality Law* vol. 21, no. 4, pp. 324–333.

Billings, Peter and McDonald, Ian (2007) 'The Treatment of Asylum Seekers in the UK' *Journal of Social Welfare and Family Law* vol. 29, no.1, March 2007, pp. 49–65.

Birnberg Peirce & Partners, Medical Justice and NCADC (2008) 'Outsourcing Abuse' (London: Medical Justice).

Crawley, Heaven, Hemmings, Joanne, and Price, Neil, (2011) 'Coping with Destitution: Survival and Livelihood Strategies of Refused Asylum Seekers Living in the UK' Centre for Migration Policy Research (CMPR), Swansea University (Swansea: Oxfam and Swansea University).

Department of International Development (DFID) (2007) 'Moving out of Poverty – Making Migration Work better for Poor People' (London: DFID).

Fancott, Nancy and York, Sheona, (2008) 'Enforced Destitution: Impediments to Return and Access to Section 4 "Hard Cases" Support' *Journal of Immigration, Asylum and Nationality Law* vol. 22, no. 1, pp. 5–26.

Flynn, Don and Williams, Zoe (eds) (2007) 'Towards a Progressive Immigration Policy' (London: Migrant Rights Network).

Ghai, Yash, (1997) 'Migrant Workers, Markets and the Law' in Wang Gungwu (ed.), *Global History and Migration* (Boulder, CO: Westview Press), pp. 145–182.

Global Commission on International Migration (GCIM) (2005) 'Migration in an Interconnected World: New Directions for Action' (GCIM).

Grant, Stephanie (2006) 'GCIM Report: Defining an "Ethical Compass" for International Migration Policy' *International Migration* vol. 44, no. 1, pp. 13–19.

Greenslade, Roy (2005) 'Seeking Scapegoats' IPPR Asylum and Migration Working Paper (London: Institute for Public Policy Research).

Home Office, *Borders, Immigration and Identity Action Plan* (Policy document, December 2006) (London: Home Office).

——*Fair, Effective, Transparent and Trusted: Rebuilding Confidence in our Immigration System* (Policy document, July 2006) (London: Home Office).

House of Commons Home Affairs Committee (2011) *The Work of the UK Border Agency* April–July 2011 HC 1497, and earlier reports in the series.

——(2012) *Rules Governing Enforced Removals from the UK* 18th report of session 2012–12 HC 563.

Independent Asylum Commission (IAC) (2008) *Deserving Dignity* (London: IAC).

Independent Chief Inspector of Prisons (2011) *Detainees under Escort: Inspection of escort and removals to Jamaica* 24–25 March 2011 (London: ICIP).

——*Detainees under Escort: Inspection of escort and removals to Nigeria* 20–21 April 2011 (London: ICIP).

Information Centre about Asylum and Refugees (ICAR) (2004) *Media Image, Community Impact* (London: ICAR).

—— (2006) *Reporting Asylum: the UK Press and the Effectiveness of PCC Guidelines* (London: ICAR).

Joint Council for the Welfare of Immigrants (JCWI) (2006) 'Recognising Rights, Recognising Political Realities: The Case for Regularising Irregular Migrants' (London: JCWI).

Joint Parliamentary Committee on Human Rights *The Treatment of Asylum Seekers*, Tenth Report of 2006–07 HL Paper 81 HC 60.

Migrants Rights Network (2007) 'Enforcement Policy: The Heart of Managed Migration?' (London: Migrants Rights Network).

Moses, Jonathon (2006) *International Migration: Globalization's Last Frontier* (London: Zed Books).

Phuong, Catherine (2005) 'The Removal of Failed Asylum Seekers', *Legal Studies* vol. 25, no. 1, 117–141.

Poku, Nana, Renwick, Neil, and Glenn, John (2000) 'Human Security in a Globalising World' in David T. Graham and Nana K. Poku (eds) *Migration, Globalisation and Human Security* (London: Routledge), pp. 9–12.

Ruhs, Martin (2009) 'Migrant Rights, Immigration Policy and Human Development' Human Development Research Paper 2009/23, United Nations Development Programme (UNDP).

Ruhs, Martin and Anderson, Bridget (2006) 'Semi-Compliance in the Migrant Labour Market' Compas Working Paper 30 (Oxford: Compas).

Ryan, Bernard (2008) 'Integration Requirements: A New Model in Migration Law' *Journal of Immigration, Asylum and Nationality Law* vol. 22, no. 4, pp. 303–316.

Shah, Ramnik (2007) 'The FNP Saga' *Journal of Immigration, Asylum and Nationality Law* vol. 21, no. 1, pp. 27–31.

Somerville, Will (2007) *Immigration under New Labour* (Bristol: Policy Press).

Taylor, Savitri (2005) 'From Border Control to Migration Management: The Case for a Paradigm Change in the Western Response to Transborder Population Movement' *Social Policy and Administration* vol. 39, no. 6, December pp. 563–586 (24).

Woolf, Lord (2003) 'Should the Media and the Judiciary be on Speaking Terms?' www.judiciary.gov.uk/media/speeches/2003/should-media-judiciary-be-on-speaking-terms.

3

Nationality, citizenship, and right of abode

SUMMARY

Nationality law lies behind issues of immigration and asylum. The question of who belongs to a nation may be answered in various ways, and the way a country defines its own nationals may change over time. This chapter considers the bases of nationality and citizenship and traces the development of British nationality law, focusing on changes from 1948 to the present day. It looks at the effects on particular groups of people of those changes, characterized to a significant extent by progressive exclusion, based on views of who 'belongs' to Britain. The fundamental incident of citizenship, the right to live in one's own country, is considered, both as to the interaction of nationality and immigration law and as to the overall effect of full inclusion as a citizen. The bases for obtaining British nationality by registration and naturalization are discussed, as are the developing powers of deprivation of citizenship.

3.1 Introduction

Nationality law has consequences for immigration law. The greatest incident of nationality or citizenship is the right to live in one's own country. Those who wish to live in a country of which they are not nationals may or may not be permitted to immigrate. As Juss says (1993:48), 'those individuals who are nationals of a state are deemed...to be its citizens...and the state uses its immigration law to prevent the entry and residence of non-nationals'. Not all British nationals have the right to enter the UK; some non-nationals, however, such as European citizens, do.

Some countries have nationality systems within which all their people are regarded as 'citizens' of the political entity, reserving the word 'nationality' for an identity within that overarching category. Thus, for example, in the old Soviet Union, a person would be a citizen of the Soviet Union but have a subsidiary and essentially ethnic identity, such as Ukrainian, which would also appear on their passport. Moreover, even for citizens, a permit was required to live in a popular area such as Moscow; this 'propiska' system persists, albeit officially under another name. The UK has used the terms 'nationality' and 'citizenship' in its laws since 1948, but the former has tended to refer to a more historical, inclusive, and imperial version of Britishness and the latter to a more modern political adherence to the state. Some non-citizens may have the right of abode (the right to live) in the UK because of their status in countries that used to be part of the British Empire. This structure is the opposite of having an overall citizenship referable to the territorial boundaries of the state but with ethnic subdivisions and internal residence permit requirements. It has no official acknowledgement of ethnic diversity but broadens the right of residence to those whose citizenship lies outside the UK's boundaries. UK nationality law has recently gone through considerable change, which is not yet concluded. Much of it involves shedding the remnants of post-imperial rules, long after the Empire itself has been officially disposed of.

British nationality law was historically riddled with inequalities of sex and birth status where British people sought to pass citizenship to their children born abroad or outside marriage. The discriminatory aspects of citizenship by descent have largely been dealt with, but the UK's attitude to race discrimination in nationality law remains hard to pinpoint. The UK refused to accept an opinion of the European Commission of Human Rights in 1973 that elements of its laws were racist (*East African Asians v UK* (1973) [1981] 3 EHRR 76), and the Race Relations (Amendment) Act 2000 made a partial exclusion for nationality functions as it did for immigration functions. This was, however, removed by s 6 of the Nationality, Immigration and Asylum Act 2002, so nationality functions are now included within the general duty on public authorities to avoid race discrimination. An ethnic group, as defined in law for the purposes of the Race Relations Act 1976, involves a shared history and some of the practices regarded as culture, such as language or sometimes religious practice (*Mandla v Dowell Lee* [1983] 2 AC 548 HL). Thus, Sikhs are an ethnic group, as are the English, and Roma (also called Gypsies). Nationality functions are not, however, the same as nationality laws, so that the latter may still indirectly discriminate by tending in effect to exclude some ethnic groups more than others.

3.1.1 Nature of nationality and its structure

Nationality and citizenship law is inherently controversial, because the question of how a state defines who belongs is itself disputed. A country may be defined by its geographical boundaries. It may be defined by its members, when it is often described as a 'nation'. If a country is identified by its existence as a political entity, it will often be referred to as a 'state'. The definitions may conflict: a group of people within a state may define itself as a nation that is politically subjugated by another nation. Some groups who feel they constitute nations, or states, may not be recognized as such by more established countries. Andrew Grossman (2001) has described how nationality may function for people who feel that they ought to have a country but have not achieved self-determination, pointing out how some of the trappings of individual citizenship may work, such as being able to use travel documents. It is also commonplace that even long-established states and populations may have continuing political disputes over who belongs. The law is often unclear too, and the nationality laws of other countries are increasingly relevant across jurisdictions: if a person is to be expelled from Britain, another country must take them in, and this may give rise to legal and practical difficulties (see for example the discussion in *MS (Palestinian Territories)* [2010] UKSC 25). An entitlement to citizenship elsewhere may deprive a person of the benefit of British refugee law (*ST (Ethnic Eritrean – nationality – return) Ethiopia CG* [2011] UKUT 00252 (IAC)), or may mean they can be deprived of British nationality as the deprivation would not leave them stateless (*Al-Jedda v SSHD* [2010] EWCA Civ 212).

Different countries have different rules of national belonging, but there are four basic ideas that may lie behind it: geography, allegiance, descent, or choice. The Universal Declaration of Human Rights Article 15 and the International Covenant on Civil and Political Rights Article 24(3) assert a right to a nationality, but the sovereign right of countries to define their own nationals is fundamental to international law. The coexistence of a variety of systems means that some people are eligible for more than one citizenship – though some countries do not allow their citizens to be citizens of other countries at the same time – and some people are stateless and have no citizenship at all.

The simplest way of recognizing someone as a national is perhaps by geography, ascribing membership to anyone born on the territory. This is the *jus soli* (law of the soil) principle. Allegiance is perhaps a still more ancient system of defining membership. It belongs to a world in which power was obtained by claiming territories through conquering their peoples. The system of allegiance is also inclusive, and children born within the monarch's territory in this type of system are generally born nationals, owing allegiance, whoever their parents are.

Membership by descent is the idea sometimes referred to as 'bloodlines' or the *jus sanguinis* (law of blood), so that the children of nationals are themselves born nationals, regardless of where they are born, and this may carry through many generations of a family living abroad. The children of non-nationals, however, are by definition also non-nationals even if they are born on the territory to lawful residents. In a pure form of this system, one cannot become a national if born outside it. A system of this type was operated in Germany until 2000, leading to large populations of German-born and educated people who were regarded as foreigners because their parents were from, say, Turkey. Although there were limited provisions for naturalization (becoming a national), this was, in effect, racially discriminatory and had to be changed.

Most countries do have some system for granting citizenship to the children of nationals who are born abroad, usually with a limit of one or two generations. This is also known as a 'law of return'. In the UK, nationality has long been transmissible at least one generation, and there are advantageous provisions for the second generation born abroad to register.

In addition, a country may admit a person who requests membership, perhaps after the satisfaction of requirements such as a period of residence on the territory or commitment to certain national values. The basis on which naturalization is allowed varies amongst countries; in the UK, the most striking element is probably its fundamentally discretionary nature.

3.1.2 International and regional law on nationality and statelessness

Although Article 15 of the Universal Declaration of Human Rights of 1948 says that 'everyone has the right to a nationality', not only is international law rarely enforceable in any way, but also no system of working out which nationality any individual ought to have is prescribed. The provision may be a sign of the national conflicts that gave rise to the UDHR itself. In Europe in the 1930s and 1940s, many people found themselves stateless as they did not fall within the nationality definition of any existing country. There are also UN Conventions that relate to statelessness, but these have attracted relatively few signatories. Nevertheless, many countries, including the UK, have provisions in their domestic laws which grant citizenship to people born in the territory if they did not get a nationality at birth and so were born stateless.

There also exists a European Convention on Nationality, made by the Council of Europe in 1997. Though very few states have signed this, so it is not a useful legal tool, its contents are interesting as an example of some contemporary consensus. Until the later twentieth century, Europe showed a wide range of systems of nationality law, but by the earliest years of the twenty-first century, they had converged, on a broadly similar basis to the 1997 Convention. That asks states to recognize those born on the territory to parents who are lawfully resident, and to make provision for granting citizenship to lawful foreign residents of ten years' standing, or certain residents who are stateless. It does not invite states to operate the *jus soli*, by which a country recognizes as nationals all those born on the territory. It does require an element of the *jus sanguinis*, in that it asked states to recognize the children of citizens even if those children are born abroad. Its provisions in relation to deprivation of citizenship require that it should not be arbitrary, and that, with some exceptions, it should not be used so as to leave a person stateless. Avoidance of statelessness is one of the objectives of the Convention, according to its preamble, and its Article 4 provides that the rules of each state party should be based on the principles that everyone has a right to a nationality and that statelessness should be avoided. Although the UK has not signed the European Convention on Nationality, British law now broadly accords with its provisions in relation to the attribution of citizenship, though perhaps not in relation to deprivation of nationality and the risk of statelessness.

It should be noted that the European Convention on Human Rights (ECHR) contains no right to citizenship, nor a positive right to live in one's own country. The right not to be expelled from one's own country might seem a basic incident of citizenship, and perhaps one particularly apposite to the circumstances of civil collapse that gave rise to the ECHR itself. However, that right is contained only in Optional Protocol No. 4, which the UK has so far not signed, although it has been acknowledged that it contains important rights. In the White Paper, *Bringing Rights Home*, which presaged the Human Rights Act of 1998, the incoming Labour government of Tony Blair said that the Protocol should be ratified 'if potential conflicts with our domestic law can be resolved' (para 4.11), these 'conflicts' being the position of British nationals from outside the UK, who were often not permitted to enter the UK. The ECHR, unlike most other international instruments, is enforceable at the instance of the individual victim. The omission of nationality rights from the core of the ECHR, and the failure of the UK to sign up to Protocol No, 4, is therefore of very practical significance.

A further practical point in relation to the structure of British nationality law in the European context is that citizenship of the European Union, a very valuable status giving rise to rights all over the continent, is defined by the membership rules of each individual Member State. UK-British citizens are European citizens, but this does not include overseas British nationals. In December 1992, on the point of joining the European Community, Britain issued a Declaration stating that overseas British nationals – those who were subject to immigration control in the UK – would not be British for the purpose of European Community law. This was later confirmed in the European Court of Justice at Luxembourg in Case C–192/99 *R v Secretary of State for the Home Department ex p Manjit Kaur* Case C–192/99 *Kaur* [2001] ECR I–1237.

3.1.3 Belonging in the UK: settlement, citizenship, and residence

The first clear legal affirmation of the principle that anyone born in the monarch's realm was therefore a subject of the monarch was *Calvin's Case* [1608] 7 Co. Rep 1a; 11 Digest 496, 2. This case dealt with the question of whether someone born in Scotland after the union of England and Scotland was then a subject of the monarch, and it was held that they were. This clearly established the *jus soli* in the UK, later formally codified in the British Nationality and Status of Aliens Act 1914. Section 1 of the 1914 Act said that a person 'born within His Majesty's dominions and allegiance' was a British subject. By then, the British Empire covered about 20 per cent of the world and everyone in it was equally British by birth – or this was at least the theoretical position: Shah has discussed the way in which in reality non-white British people were subjected to institutionalized racial prejudice (Shah 2000:70). Nevertheless, the *jus soli* remained formally in place up to and beyond the dismantling of the Empire, and by the end of the Second World War there were about 600 million British people eligible to enter and live in the UK and exercise full civic rights while they lived here.

Since the end of the Second World War, British nationality law has become gradually more restrictive, first of all providing for formal subdivision of the citizenship of British subjects amongst their countries of residence in the British Nationality Act 1948 (see 3.1.4), and then closing the doors of the UK to overseas British nationals from the 1960s onwards. In 1983, the principle of the *jus soli* was removed from British law, marking a great break of principle, even though the new legal provisions meant that almost everyone born in the UK was still a full British citizen. At the level of everyday life then access to social benefits such as health care or education depended on need or place of residence, not nationality or immigration status. As Hale LJ said in *O v London Borough of Wandsworth; Bhika v Leicester City Council* [2000] EWCA Civ 201 the National Assistance Act was 'about needs, not morality', and she also pointed out that status was difficult to determine. From the 1990s onwards, those without status were gradually excluded from such benefits, in a process which is still continuing. An identity card system has been instituted to try to deal with the problems of ascertaining status, as discussed in chapters 2 and 7. Originally intended to cover the whole resident population, it now applies only to foreign nationals.

This marks a complete change from the traditional system of belonging in the UK, which reflected the mediaeval system of settlement within a parish. 'Settlement' remains a term used within the UK system, and the concept is often still more important than that of citizenship (see chapter 7). One might say that indefinite leave to remain reflects the formal mediaeval concept of 'denizenship', bringing most of the benefits of Britishness without naturalization. The lack of focus on citizenship and formerly on immigration status as the fount of social entitlement has meant that these areas are not a major part of a general legal education, and this remains the case. The political climate has moved on, though, so that the government's appointee, Peter Goldsmith, who wrote a report on *Citizenship: Our Common Bond* in 2007, could be bemused at the lack of a bright line between citizens and others, speaking of 'a muddle that probably exists for honourable reasons' (Goldsmith 2007:77). It is, however, simply the traditional structure.

Many foreign nationals have lived in the UK for very protracted periods on ILR, being effectively British for everyday purposes but with travel documents in another nationality. If they have refugee status, they will have UK-issued travel documents. Living in the UK on ILR was often useful for those whose countries of origin do not allow dual nationality, but who are unwilling to renounce their original nationality for some reason. For Mr Al-Rawi, whose family left Iraq and settled in New Malden, the reason was that he was the family member 'chosen' to maintain Iraqi nationality and so retain claims on land in Iraq. Unfortunately, when Mr Al-Rawi was then detained in Guantanamo Bay, and the British government obtained the release of British citizens, because he was not a British citizen he was not released. In *Al-Rawi v SSHD* [2006] EWCA Civ 1279, the Court held that despite his not being a citizen as such, the UK had the right to intervene with the US about how he was treated. However, following *R (on the application of Abbassi) v Secretary of State for Foreign and Commonwealth Affairs* [2003] UKHRR 76, the Court did not have the power to compel the government to do that in a particular way.

The fact that these cases on the difference between citizens and non-citizen residents are tested so late in the development of nationality laws is a symptom of the longstanding fuzziness of the dividing lines between the two. It is also interesting to see that it is opposite in thrust to the previous notable case law where a defendant accused of treason tried to establish that he was not British enough to be convicted. William Joyce, who was also known as 'Lord Haw-Haw' because of his haughty manner of speaking, had made broadcasts from Nazi Germany during the Second World War. He was a citizen of the United States of America, but had travelled to Germany on a British passport obtained because his father had been Irish when Ireland was under British rule. On that basis, it was held that he had obtained the protection of Britain and so owed allegiance. Joyce was hanged for treason in 1946 (*Joyce v DPP* [1946] AC 347).

Many long-term British residents have neither British citizenship nor indefinite leave to remain. There is a variety of other statuses, and both the meaning of the statuses and the entitlements of those who hold them are often unclear. Many people live and work in the UK who are not strictly entitled to do so. Others may be entitled to live in the UK but not to claim welfare benefits. The position may be further confused by qualifications such as 'habitual residence' or 'ordinary residence' which also apply to British people (Larkin 2007). This has considerable effects for the everyday life of those people, and also those who come into contact with them and so for British society in general.

3.1.4 British nationality in transition: restructuring the Empire

British nationality was originally based on birth in the land controlled by the monarch, wherever it was. It was after the Second World War that the distinction between UK-based and non-UK-based British people began to be drawn. Former colonies became independent, their populations largely transferring their allegiance into the new countries. These newly independent countries often did not allow dual nationality and required people, in order to belong as a citizen of the new country, to cease to be British. Canada passed its own citizenship laws in 1946; India followed shortly afterwards. Britain responded with the British Nationality Act 1948, acknowledging the control of the newly independent states over their own affairs and at the same time retaining some idea of universal Empire. This was embodied in the concept of the Commonwealth, which has moral but not political power. Most current members are former British territories, though Mozambique is a longstanding member and applications to join have also been made by, for example, the Palestinian National Authority. Rwanda was the most recent country to join, in November 2009. Not all former British territories are members: Ireland left on independence and other countries such as South Africa, Zimbabwe, or Fiji have variously been suspended as a measure of disapproval.

The British Nationality Act 1948 retained the overall status of 'subject' for all British people in the Empire, but superimposed on it the new (to British law) idea of 'citizenship'. The idea was that people would be either citizens of the UK and Colonies (CUKCs) in the UK or where their countries of residence remained colonies, or, where their countries gained independence, they would be citizens of those countries and British subjects as well. CUKCs were people born, adopted, registered, or naturalized in the UK or the Colonies, or whose father was such a person. The 1948 Act itself had no immediate impact on the status of members of either group. There was also movement between the two groups. Citizens of independent Commonwealth countries, or of Ireland, had the right to register as CUKCs if they had been resident in the UK or a colony for 12 months, though later the Commonwealth Immigrants Acts would affect these registration rights. CUKCs would, if they met any necessary criteria, become citizens of independent Commonwealth countries when their home country gained independence.

Some people, however, fell outside both categories of citizenship (ss 13 and 16 BNA 1948), if their country of residence became independent but for some reason they did not gain citizenship of it. These people became British subjects without citizenship. Others were not British subjects because they were born, not in a British colony, but in a British protectorate such as Iraq. The difference between colonies and protectorates was established during the Empire, when colonies were countries governed by Britain where the common law applied, whereas at least in theory in protectorates government was by local rulers, and the common law did not apply. Those who were connected with protectorates were not CUKCs but British Protected Persons, and because this status could not be transmitted to children, there are now few of them left.

3.1.5 The end of Empire: the Commonwealth Immigrants Acts and the East African Asians

After the war, Britain began to close its borders to British nationals from outside the UK. The structure and infrastructure of Britain needed rebuilding, inviting substantial labour immigration, especially from the British Caribbean in the 1950s. There was also substantial non-white, visible immigration to the UK from Africa, for reasons connected with Empire and decolonization. The reaction of the newly independent former colonies in East Africa to past white domination was policies of Africanization. Kenya, Tanganyika (Tanzania), and Uganda had substantial populations of Asian descent, often families who had for generations served in the British civil service. Many decided against renouncing their status as CUKCs, or even BPPs, in favour of the new African citizenship, so that if life became too difficult they could go to the UK.

The reaction in the UK was to close the border to non-white immigration from East Africa, in a domestic climate of growing racial tension. In 1962, the Commonwealth Immigrants Act made British subjects subject to immigration control unless they had a UK passport issued by the UK government rather than the government of a colony, or by a High Commission even in a colony. The 1968 Commonwealth Immigrants Act then divided CUKCs into those who could enter the UK without restriction, and those who could not. The atmosphere of racial tension in which this legislation was passed was not universally discouraged by government figures: the speech made by Enoch Powell, MP for Wolverhampton South West, in April 1968 is still famous as the 'Rivers of Blood speech'. In it, he talked of rioting by white people against the non-white population unless immigration was stopped. In this climate, the Commonwealth Immigrants Act 1968 passed through Parliament with great rapidity. Though Powell was sacked from the Shadow Cabinet for his speech, the effects of the Acts remained in place and were consolidated in the Immigration Act 1971, which is still in force.

The effect of these Acts was to divide British people into those who had the 'right of abode' in the UK and those who were subject to immigration control, with the former being described in the original terms of s 2 of the 1971 Act as 'patrials'. CUKCs who were born, adopted, naturalized, or registered in the UK (s 2(1)(a)), or whose parents or grandparents were (s 2(1)(b)), were 'patrials'. So were CUKCs who had been ordinarily resident in the UK for five years (s 2(1)(c)). The right of abode was more restricted for Commonwealth citizens, who had it if they had a parent born or adopted in the UK (s 2(1)(d)) or were married to patrial men (s 2(2)). The ancestral connection for Commonwealth citizens thus needed to be closer than for CUKCs in order to obtain the right of abode. The value of a British passport for those without the requisite parental connections suddenly diminished. The Act took away the right of abode for the majority of East African Asians, who were thus left with no country in which they had any right to live. Their chance of entry to the UK depended on a voucher scheme which operated on a quota system.

Section 1 of the 1968 Act was the subject of the challenge before the European Commission of Human Rights in *East African Asians v UK* (1973) [1981] 3 EHRR 76. The successful basis of the claim was that the Act was racially discriminatory and that such treatment was degrading and thus in breach of Article 3 of the Convention. This decision was of historic importance in finding as fact that the statute was passed with a racial motive. This was strenuously denied by the government on the basis that requiring a familial connection had nothing to do with colour but only with defining who 'belongs' to the UK. However, the evidence for this emerges clearly from the Cabinet papers and other official records of the time, which refer to 'coloured' immigration (see Lester 2002) and the Commission was satisfied about the effects of the legislation:

> persons who belong to the category of 'patrials' have the 'right of abode' in the United Kingdom... such persons would normally be white Commonwealth citizens.... The Asian citizens of the United Kingdom and Colonies in East Africa, on the other hand, would not normally be 'patrials' and thus have no 'right of abode' in the United Kingdom, the State of which they are citizens. (*East African Asians v UK* para 202)

The second significant aspect of the Commission's decision was the finding that racial discrimination can amount to a breach of Article 3 in itself. If it is sufficiently severe it amounts to degrading treatment, doing away with the need to identify another Convention right in respect of which discrimination may be alleged under Article 14 (see chapter 4 for further discussion of these Articles). If the UK had ratified Protocol 4 of the Convention the applicants would have had a very strong case under Protocol 4, being nationals denied entry, and also under Article 14 read with Protocol 4. However, the decision could be said to have greater significance because of the use of Article 3, though the Strasbourg Court has tended to be less radical since then in its defence of rights of nationality and citizenship.

3.2 British citizenship under the British Nationality Act 1981

There are six categories in British nationality law: British citizens (the most privileged category, and the only one that always carries a right of abode in the UK); British Overseas Territories citizens; British Overseas citizens (BOTC); British subjects; British nationals (Overseas); and British protected persons. The broad trajectory of the development of British nationality law is to focus on British citizens and to lose the other categories (see Table 3.1).

3.2.1 Acquisition of British citizenship by birth

Section 1 of the British Nationality Act 1981 (BNA 1981) deals with the acquisition of British citizenship by people born after the commencement of the 1981 Act on 1 January 1983. It provides that a person born in the UK after commencement is a British citizen if, at the time of their birth, their mother or father is a British citizen or settled in the UK. This ended the longstanding tradition of the *jus soli*, establishing instead a form of the *jus sanguinis*, tempered by broad provisions for registration and naturalization of those born outside the UK. For the first time, the UK-born children of, say, migrant

Table 3.1 Right of abode

Legislative era	Right of abode	Subject to immigration control
Pre-1948	All British subjects	Aliens
British Nationality Act 1948	All British subjects	Aliens
Commonwealth Immigrants Act 1962	Those born in the UK	Aliens
	Irish citizens	Commonwealth citizens with passports issued by colonial or Commonwealth government
	Commonwealth citizens (i.e., British subjects) with passports issued by UK government	
Commonwealth Immigrants Act 1968	Those born in the UK	Aliens
	Irish citizens	Commonwealth citizens with passports issued by colonial or Commonwealth government
	Commonwealth citizens (i.e., British subjects) with passports issued by UK government and whose parent or grandparent was born, naturalized or adopted in the UK	Commonwealth citizens with passports issued by UK government, but without parental connection
Immigration Act 1971	CUKCs born, naturalized or adopted in UK or with parent or grandparent born, adopted, or naturalized in UK	Aliens
	CUKC resident in UK for five years	CUKCs without parental connection or residence
		Other Commonwealth citizens without parent born in UK
	Other Commonwealth citizens whose parent was born (only) in UK	Irish citizens (in theory subject to control but mainly exempt because of Common Travel Area)
	Commonwealth citizens married before 1 January 1973 to a man with right of abode	
British Nationality Act 1981	British citizens	Aliens
	Commonwealth citizens who had right of abode at commencement (1 January 1983)	Citizens of Commonwealth countries
		British Dependent Territories citizens
		British Overseas citizens
		British Dependent Territories citizens

workers or refugees could be born stateless in the UK if they did not gain a nationality through their parents.

The British Overseas Territories Act 2002 (BOTA) Sch 1 amended British Nationality Act s 1 so that since 21 May 2002, birth in an overseas territory also results in British citizenship if the child's parents are British or settled in the territory. Their parents are likely now to be British following BOTA s 3 (see 3.3.1). British Overseas territories are currently: Anguilla, Bermuda, the British Antarctic Territory (so-called, although this is also claimed by Chile and Argentina and has no inhabitants), British Indian Ocean Territory, Cayman Islands, Falkland Islands, Gibraltar, Montserrat, Pitcairn, Henderson, Ducie and Oeno Islands, St Helena and Dependencies, Turks and Caicos Islands, and the Virgin Islands. The Sovereign base areas on Cyprus are British Overseas Territories, but birth there does not give rise to British citizenship. The BOTA is discussed more fully at 3.3.1.

Under BNA 1981 s 1, British citizenship is acquired by birth in the UK if the child's parents are either British or settled. To be settled means to be ordinarily resident in the UK without any immigration restrictions (Immigration Act 1971 s 33). Settlement is discussed more fully in chapter 7. European nationals exercising free movement rights in the UK used to be regarded as settled for nationality purposes, i.e., their child born in the UK could have British nationality. However, the Immigration (European Economic Area) Regulations (SI 2000/2326) limited the definition of European nationals who would be regarded as settled for nationality purposes, and this limitation is continued in the 2006 Regulations (SI 2006/1003) to apply to those who have acquired permanent residence under those regulations. Therefore, children born to EEA nationals who are exercising EC rights in the UK will be British if born before 2 October 2000, but not if born after that date unless their parents have permanent residence in the UK. Section 42 of the Borders, Citizenship and Immigration Act 2009 provides that British citizenship is transmissible to children by serving members of the British armed forces even if they are not themselves British or settled.

3.2.2 Acquisition under the Act by those born before commencement

Section 11 of the British Nationality Act gave British citizenship to anyone born before commencement of the Act who was a CUKC with right of abode before the Act. In other words, it gave British citizenship to patrial CUKCs as defined in the old s 2 of the 1971 Act, discussed earlier. These were the people with a parental or grandparental connection with the UK who were citizens of the UK itself, or a colony, but not Commonwealth countries.

On 21 May 2002, British citizenship was also acquired by existing citizens of the British Overseas Territories listed earlier (British Overseas Territories Act 2002 s 3), whatever their date of birth.

3.2.3 British citizenship by descent

Citizenship by birth in the UK was historically a matter of the common law; citizenship by descent, which is of the essence of the *jus sanguinis*, has always been statutory. At the time of implementation of the 1971 Immigration Act, nationality passed through men to the children of their marriage, and through women only to non-marital children. A person born to married parents outside the UK and Colonies could only acquire CUKC status if their father was British. The CUKC citizenship so acquired was citizenship by descent, which in UK law cannot be passed to a child also born outside the UK. Transmission of nationality outside the UK and Colonies could therefore only occur for one generation, and this is still the position under the 1981 Act, although rights of registration help the next generation (see at 3.4.1).

Where a person is born to a British parent (or, under s 42 BCI Act 2009, a serving member of the British armed forces) outside the UK, they are a British citizen by descent (BNA s 2). Therefore if a British couple, A and B, go abroad, say to work, and have a child C while they are abroad, but later return, C's children, if born in the UK, will be British, and the line of British citizenship continues unbroken. If, however, C stays abroad, or goes to work abroad herself and has children there, they will not be British unless their other parent is British otherwise than by descent. C's children have an entitlement to register as British if they meet certain conditions (set out at 3.4.1), but this ends with them, and is not available to their children. The provision maintains a distinction between those who are British and those who are settled. The children of a settled couple, neither of whom is British, are British if born in the UK, but otherwise are not. The exception, since 21 May 2002, is that birth in an overseas territory to British parents will now give rise to British citizenship otherwise than by descent (i.e., full British citizenship), regardless of whether the parents are settled in the UK or in the overseas territory where the birth takes place. British citizenship by descent in the overseas territories continues only for those who had that status before 2002.

Prior to the 1981 Act, citizenship could pass only through a married father. The 1981 Act provided for citizenship to pass through the mother also, and this applied to the citizenship of British Dependent Territories as well as British citizenship. Section 13 of the Nationality, Immigration and Asylum Act 2002 subsequently allowed those born between 7 February 1961 and 1 January 1983 to register as British if they would have been British by descent if, at the time of their birth, nationality could pass through a woman (see *SSHD v Hicks* [2006] EWCA Civ 400). Under the Borders, Citizenship and Immigration Act 2009, that right is extended to include those born earlier, so that these provisions are no longer gender discriminatory.

Even following the 1981 Act, children could not obtain British citizenship from their father, however, if their parents were unmarried (s 50 BNA 1981). This was challenged in *R on the application of Montana v SSHD* [2001] 1 WLR 552 CA, where a British citizen man had a son born in Norway to a Norwegian mother to whom the father was not married. After the relationship ended, the father applied to have his child registered as a British citizen under the discretionary power in s 3, but the Secretary of State declined. On the application for judicial review of the decision, it was said that the basis for the refusal was that the child had insufficient connection with the UK. The appellant argued that the child would have British citizenship if his parents had been married, so the exercise of the Secretary of State's discretion was in breach of human rights, namely, Article 8, the right to respect for private and family and Article 14, freedom from discrimination in relation to Convention rights. The Court of Appeal held that common nationality was not a requirement of family life, so Article 8 was not engaged. It considered that there was no true comparison between those who obtained citizenship under s 2, by descent, and those who did so by registration under s 3, and therefore there was no discrimination. Under s 9 Nationality, Immigration and Asylum Act 2002, British citizenship is, however, now available to children born to unmarried British fathers, including those treated as the father of a child under the Human Fertilisation and Embryology Act 1990 and any other person 'who satisfies prescribed requirements as to proof of paternity'. This means either naming the father on the child's birth certificate within one year of their birth, or proving the matter to the Secretary of State's satisfaction by 'any evidence which [the Secretary of State] considers to be relevant, including, but not limited to' DNA test reports and court orders (British Nationality (Proof of Paternity) Regulations 2006 (SI 2006/1496)). Section 9 NIAA 2002 came into force in July 2006 and refers to children born from that date.

3.2.4 British nationality in European law

For the purposes of EC law Britain has defined 'British nationals' as British citizens, British overseas territories citizens deriving their citizenship from Gibraltar (though since the British Overseas Territories Act 2002 s 3 came into force these people have been British citizens), and British subjects with the right of abode. This excludes British overseas citizens (see *Manjit Kaur*), British protected persons, and Commonwealth citizens with right of abode.

3.3 Other categories of British nationality

The less privileged classes of British nationality were created to answer immigration concerns at particular moments in history (see Table 3.2), and can best be understood in the context of the UK's relationship with the groups who were the targets of the legislation.

3.3.1 British Overseas Territories Citizens

In older documentation and in the British Nationality Act 1981, this nationality status is referred to as British Dependent Territories Citizenship. But, in recognition that many territories are not dependent but thriving communities (see White Paper, *Partnership for Progress and Prosperity* (Cm 4264)), they were renamed in s 1 British Overseas Territories Act 2002 as 'overseas' rather than 'dependent'. Since the British Overseas Territories Act 2002 came fully into force on 21 May 2002, the majority of people in this citizenship category have become British citizens.

Given that, there seems to be little reason for retaining BOTC status at all. One remaining function is that the 2002 Act does not amend the British Nationality Act in relation to naturalization. Therefore, residence in an overseas territory can only lead to naturalization as a BOTC, not a British citizen (under the British Nationality (British Overseas Territories) Regulations 2007, SI 2007/3139). This prevents British citizenship from being attained by going to live in a British Overseas Territory. The parliamentary debates also reveal another reason. Birth in the Sovereign base areas in Cyprus (Akrotiri and Dhekelia) gives only BOTC status, not British citizenship. Ben Bradshaw, then Foreign Office Minister, said this was because those areas were 'for use as military bases only, and not for the establishment of a wider community' (HC Debs 22 November 2001 col 543). A more detailed answer is to be found in his words to the Standing Committee:

> Hon. Members should also bear in mind that Cyprus is at an important crossroads between the middle east and Europe.... if we extended the treaty's provisions to cover the bases, there would not just be a handful of people who might be eligible for British citizenship. The fear is that more people would be attracted to go to Cyprus and make applications for asylum. (6 December 2001 Standing Committee D)

Here we see the development of trends as described in chapter 1. Whereas in the mid-twentieth century, a desire to curb non-white immigration drove immigration law and policy and that of nationality, in the late twentieth and early twenty-first centuries, a desire to curb asylum claims is the driver. This policy shapes not only immigration law, but also, as we see here, an otherwise incomprehensible and even obscure provision of nationality law.

Table 3.2 Effect of legislation determining immigration and nationality status

Legislation	Legal principle	Effect
Pre-1948	In theory, all British subjects had the right to enter UK	In reality, there was less travel than now, and informal means were used to control non-white entry
British Nationality Act 1948	Divided British subjects into CUKCs and Citizens of Independent Commonwealth Countries. British subjects also called Commonwealth citizens	Laid foundation for distinctions to be made between CUKCs and other British subjects/Commonwealth citizens
Commonwealth Immigrants Act 1962	Introduced first immigration control on Commonwealth citizens	Linking freedom from control to passports issued by UK government or birth in UK meant expatriate white British more likely to be exempt than non-white colonial or Commonwealth residents
Commonwealth Immigrants Act 1968	Parental connection with UK more fully established as basis for freedom from immigration control	Developing blood tie as basis of UK citizenship, many UK passport holders, especially East African Asians, excluded
Immigration Act 1971	Parental or birth connection with UK becomes main means of establishing freedom from control. More generous provisions for CUKCs than for Commonwealth citizens	Consolidating blood tie and effects of 1968 Act. In simultaneous legislation European Nationals granted rights of free movement
British Nationality Act 1981	Birth in UK no longer enough for exemption from immigration control. Crucial emphasis on parentage Citizens of Dependent Territories excluded	British Citizenship finally established, and on basis of earlier immigration law. Immigration law considerations have informed who is deemed fully British
British Overseas Territories Act 2002	BDTCs renamed BOTCs, made BCs and given right of abode	Hong Kong's independence is now established. There are very few overseas territories left and British government grants right of abode to their citizens

3.3.1.1 *The status as it was created*

The category originally called British Dependent Territories Citizenship was created by the BNA 1981 for those people who were CUKCs by virtue of a close connection with what would have formerly been called a colony, then called a dependent territory, and now an overseas territory. The close connection was birth in the territory when at the time of the birth their father or mother was either a BDTC, or settled there or in another overseas territory (BNA 1981 s 15). Under s 23 BNA 1981, a person became a BDTC on commencement if they were a CUKC before commencement by their birth, naturalization, or registration in a dependent territory, or if their parent or grandparent had CUKC citizenship by one of these means. There are also provisions for naturalization and registration as BOTCs, and for obtaining BOT citizenship by descent if born outside the territories to a BOTC parent. As well as being capable of being passed through generations, BOTC status can also be acquired by descent by birth outside the territory, in the same way as British citizenship and with the same consequences.

At the time of the passing of the British Nationality Act 1981, the promoting minister made it clear that all BDTCs were to have the same citizenship status, although this did not give them entry to other dependent territories. More significantly, it did not give them entry to Britain as BDTC status did not carry a right of abode. It may appear that the 1981 Act removed the right of abode from this group of CUKCs. However, as discussed earlier, the Commonwealth Immigrants Act 1968 and the Immigration Act 1971 had already restricted the right of abode so that in practice most CUKCs living in overseas territories would not have had a right of abode. In relation to this group, the 1981 Act therefore did little more than crystallize into nationality law existing rules which, though previously found apparently in immigration law, dealt with the greatest incident of citizenship, namely the right to live in one's own country.

3.3.1.2 *Hong Kong*

In the 2002 Act, BOTCs from all overseas territories apart from the Cyprus bases (see previous discussion) have become British citizens, with full rights of abode, with a limited exception in the case of the British Indian Ocean Territory, discussed further later in the chapter. The reader might feel moved to ask why these rights could not have been accorded in 1983, instead of these British nationals going through 20 years of nationality wilderness. It is not possible to give a full answer to this question. There have been changes of government in the meantime, and the political climate has changed since 1981. The government has stated its wish to advance towards ratification of Protocol 4. Another relevant factor is certainly Hong Kong.

Hong Kong had been held by Britain since the Victorian era on a long lease from China, and returned to Chinese hands in 1997. When, during the parliamentary debate on the 1981 Act, the question was raised of whether each dependent territory should have its own citizenship status, the government opposed the idea. Opposition members argued the case for Gibraltar and the Falklands, but it was noticeable that opposition parties conceded that Hong Kong was a special case, and no one was prepared to argue for concessions for Hong Kong. This was surely because of fears that many Hong Kong CUKCs would want to enter the UK rather than live under Chinese control. Dummett and Nicol's analysis is that: 'No British politician was ready to consider a redefinition of British nationality which would give right of abode in the UK to 2.6 million British Chinese in Hong Kong' (1990:242). Before 1997, Macdonald had said that:

> The population of Hong Kong consists of some 3.2 million British Dependent Territories Citizens who will become Chinese nationals after 1997, 10, 000 who will not, 2 million Chinese nationals, 17,000 British citizens with the right of abode, 150,000 foreign nationals (ie not British or Chinese) and about 11, 000 stateless persons (mainly refugees from Vietnam). (1995:147)

The figures are slightly at variance but the point is clear: the right of abode in the UK would not be given to the people of Hong Kong in general.

About 50,000 'key' people were however given British citizenship under the British Nationality (Hong Kong) Act 1990. They were selected for their importance to the economy of Hong Kong, which was a major centre of international trade and finance. These people, being well off, were particularly well placed to leave, but it was particularly important to the UK that they stay and continue running Hong Kong, as it appeared that the Chinese government would be willing to allow its economic role to continue even after the handover of sovereignty. The idea was that, knowing they could leave easily for the UK if necessary, they would feel able to stay and see what happened. Indeed, this appeared to work.

Some possibility of entry to the UK was given to a limited number of Hong Kong BDTCs when Article 4 of the Hong Kong (British Nationality) Order 1986 created a new category of citizenship: British National (Overseas). This applied only to BDTCs who had that citizenship by virtue of birth, parentage, naturalization, or registration in Hong Kong. This status was awarded only on application before a cut-off date and does not carry any right of entry to the UK. The holder may register as a British citizen after five years' lawful residence in the UK, providing the last year is free of immigration restrictions, and Hong Kong BDTCs in any event have those rights under s 4(1) BNA. It seems that most of those entitled to register as BN(O)s did so, although the vast majority were ethnically Chinese and therefore obtained Chinese nationality as well. The Nationality, Immigration and Asylum Act 2002 s 14 later provided that no one may be registered as a BOTC by virtue of a connection with Hong Kong.

Some Hong Kong residents were, however, left adrift by the system, especially those who were not ethnically Chinese (especially the numbers of people of Indian origin) and so did not get Chinese nationality, and who held a form of British nationality that did not carry the right of abode or were British Protected Persons. After much pressure on their behalf, the British Nationality (Hong Kong) Act 1997 was passed; such people who were ordinarily resident in Hong Kong immediately before the handover and would otherwise have been left stateless were entitled to register as British citizens. A discretionary right to register was also given to Hong Kong war widows.

3.3.1.3 *Gibraltar and the Falkland Islands*

For reasons of political strategy, Britain was unwilling to let some of its overseas territories go, and maintaining the link with the population was the way to retain the territorial claim. The residents of Gibraltar and the Falkland Islands particularly benefited from the position of their home countries on the international political scene.

Gibraltar is a British territory physically in southern Spain and to which Spain lays claim. In order not to weaken the British claim, Gibraltarians were included in the UK's declaration of British nationality for EU purposes. Strengthening that position, Gibraltarian BDTCs were given the right to register as British citizens by s 5 BNA 1981.

In 1983, Argentina attempted military seizure of the Falklands Islands, a British territory off the coast of South America. The population of the islands is largely a farming community of British origin. Britain wanted to retain sovereignty, not least because the islands could be important in asserting title to land or mineral resources. The British Nationality (Falkland Islands) Act 1983 granted British citizenship to the islanders and provided that anyone born in the Falklands after the date of commencement to a parent born or settled in the Falklands would be a British citizen.

Had these provisions not been made, Gibraltarians and Falkland Islanders would have benefited from the British Overseas Territories Act 2002 by becoming British citizens in any event. British citizenship of course brings with it EU citizenship, but Britain is not the only EU country to have territories and populations physically well outside Europe. France, for example, has its overseas lands, 'régions d'outre-mer,' such as Guadeloupe and Martinique.

3.3.1.4 *The Chagos Islands*

The nationality story of the Chagos Islanders (also, and perhaps more properly, known as the Ilois) is overshadowed by the political tale. The Chagos Islands form part of the British Indian Ocean Territory, which until 1965 was part of the British colony of Mauritius but then became a separate dependent territory. Mauritius itself was to become independent in 1968, but well before then the US had identified the largest island, Diego Garcia, as somewhere it would like to build a military base. The UK agreed to lease it to them and went on to expel the islanders, by a mixture of trickery and legislation, largely to Mauritius and the Seychelles. In 2000, the Divisional Court, examining the implementation of the legislative provisions the UK government had called in aid, found in *R v Secretary of State for the Foreign and Commonwealth Office ex p Bancoult* [2001] 2 WLR 1219 that 'a power to make laws for the "peace, order and good government" of a territory...required its people to be governed, not removed', and Mr Bancoult won the right for the Chagossians to return.

In the Standing Committee debate on the British Overseas Territories Bill, the Foreign Office minister stated that 'such treatment would be impossible today' (HC Standing Committee D 6 December 2001). Nevertheless, it took some lobbying, the case of *Bancoult*, and an amendment to the Bill before those Chagossians who had lost the opportunity of BDTC status were included in the provisions of the 2002 Act. As nationality prior to the 1981 Act passed only through married fathers, those born to Chagossian (CUKC) mothers but whose father was not Chagossian (but was, for instance, Mauritian) after the enforced exile but before the 1981 Act did not obtain CUKC status. If they had been born in the Chagos Islands they would have been CUKCs by birth. Section 6 of the British Overseas Territories Act 2002 provided that a person born in these circumstances between 26 April 1969 and 1 January 1983 would obtain British citizenship by descent. This put them in the same position as they would have been if their citizenship had been transmitted through their mother, but not the same position as if the exile had never happened, as they would then have become British citizens under the 2002 Act like other BOTCs. The government's justification for this at the time was that they were now free to return to the Chagos Islands, and if they did so their children would be British citizens. If they did not, there would be no reason for them to have any more enduring form of British citizenship than any other British citizen who chooses to stay abroad.

The victory of the right to return, however, proved hollow, as no practical arrangements could be made and, despite promises, the British government did not assist, but produced a feasibility study suggested the low-lying islands would not be habitable. A claim for compensation by the Islanders was dismissed in the QBD by Ouseley LJ in 2003 (*Chagos Islanders v AG HMs BIOT Commissioner* [2003] EWHC 2222). On 10 June 2004, hidden behind the publicity given to European and local election day, two Orders in Council were signed by the Queen. The British Indian Ocean Territory (Constitution) Order appointed a Commissioner to rule over the territory and stated as a constitutional principle that no person has any right of abode in the territory or has unrestricted access to any part of it. The British Indian Ocean Territory (Immigration) Order provided for a system of permits to visit the islands, decisions being appealable only to the Commissioner. These orders were made under the Royal Prerogative and, in the words of Baroness Symons 'restore the legal position to what it had been understood to be before the High Court decision' in *ex p Bancoult* (HL Debs 15 June 2004 col WS27). The executive had overturned the judicial decision and stopped the repopulation of the islands. This undermined the justification offered by the government for limiting the nationality entitlement of Ilois people born between 1969 and 1981, as they have no right of return to enable them to pass British citizenship to their children.

The announcement of the prerogative orders provoked outrage in a number of quarters, including in Mauritius, where the government threatened to withdraw from the Commonwealth to enable it to sue the UK in the International Court of Justice. On 7 July, an early day motion secured a debate in the House of Commons at which the Parliamentary Under-Secretary of State for Foreign and Commonwealth Affairs had an opportunity to defend the government's reasons. He also took this opportunity to disclose that two days earlier, the government had amended its declaration accepting the jurisdiction of the International Court of Justice to exclude not only current Commonwealth countries (an existing exception retained by a number of Commonwealth members) but also former Commonwealth countries (Hansard 7 July 2004 col 294WH). In other words, Mauritius would not be able to sue in any event.

The orders were challenged by judicial review and once again found unlawful (*R (on the application of Bancoult) v SSFCA* [2006] EWHC 1038 (Admin)). The government appealed but lost again in the Court of Appeal (*SSFCA v R (on the application of Bancoult)* [2007] EWCA Civ 498). The Secretary of State argued that an Order in Council was not subject to judicial review. The prerogative orders were made nominally by the Queen in a process even less open to scrutiny than secondary legislation; there was no debate in the Privy Council on the matter, and by constitutional convention the Queen signed the orders on the advice of a single minister. The Court of Appeal held that it was a fiction to regard these orders as acts of the monarch. They were in reality acts of the executive and as such subject to judicial review. It held that, like the ordinance that was successfully challenged in 2000, the prerogative power exercised by the Orders in Council was not in reality an act of governance at all, let alone one for peace and good order. For the population of the Chagos Islands, the case concerned 'not its governance, but its elimination as a population' (para 66). There was no relevant change of circumstance since the ministerial assurance after the 2000 Divisional Court decision that the Chagossians would be allowed to return home. The prerogative orders that once again removed their right were a defeat of a substantive legitimate expectation and were 'so profoundly unfair... as to amount to an abuse of power' (para 73).

The government appealed to the House of Lords, who granted them leave to appeal on condition that they paid all the costs, regardless of the outcome. In (*R (on the application of Bancoult) v SSFCA* [2008] UKHL 61), the House of Lords considered the issue of whether a constitutional right of abode exists in British law and, if so, how that applies in an overseas territory, or colony. The House held that, although the Colonial Laws Validity Act 1865 meant that colonial laws could not be found void by local courts because they were 'repugnant to the laws of England', it had not ousted the jurisdiction of the English courts to review the exercise of the prerogative. The right of abode was described as 'fundamental and, in the informal sense in which that is necessarily used in a United Kingdom context, constitutional' (per Lord Mance, para 151). Nevertheless, the House found there was 'no basis for saying that the right of abode is in its nature so fundamental that the legislative power of the Crown simply cannot touch it' (per Lord Hoffman, para 45). By a 3:2 majority, the House found for the government, holding that the right of abode was in the gift of Parliament, and that what Parliament had given, Parliament could also take away. A commentator suggested that 'their Lordships' deference fails to reflect a judicial commitment to substantive legality' (Cohn, 2009). The Chagos Islanders had complained to Strasbourg in 2004, under Articles 3, 8, 6, and 14 of the ECHR, and their claim began to proceed in February 2009 (Application no. 35622/04).

The case has other continuing ramifications. The journalist John Pilger made a documentary about the expulsion of the Chagos Islanders in 2004 (see www.archive.org/details/John_Pilger). Some Islanders came to the UK as British citizens and found establishing a life here difficult because of the rules excluding people without a period of residence from welfare provisions, which in this context may appear ironic ([2007] UKSSCSC CJSA_1223_2206). The use of Diego Garcia, the biggest island, by the US remains politically controversial. Following confirmation that it was used as a refuelling stop for US 'extraordinary rendition' flights, carrying terrorism suspects to places where they could be tortured, in November 2009 the All-Party Parliamentary Group on Extraordinary Rendition proposed that the practice be outlawed. In 2010, it was announced that a marine reserve was to be established in the Islands, and a US cable made public on Wikileaks suggested that one motivation was to engage environmental arguments to defeat any subsequent return by the islanders. Mauritius has approached the International Tribunal for the Law of the Sea in order to contest the plans. The US lease on Diego Garcia expires in 2016.

Another British territory with exceptional nationality arrangements is Ascension Island, which is administratively part of the territory of St Helena, and like Diego Garcia is devoted largely to military use. Here, no one has a right of abode. A Foreign Office promise to grant this was revoked in early 2006, and government policy is that 'All those working and living on Ascension Island are required by Ascension law to leave once their contracts expire' (Geoff Hoon, SSFCA, Hansard Written Answers 23 May 2007 col 1311W).

3.3.2 British Overseas Citizens

This kind of nationality was created by s 26 BNA 1981 to cover those CUKCs who did not at commencement obtain British citizenship or British Dependent Territories citizenship. It carries no right of abode in the UK (see *AL and others (Malaysia BOCs) Malaysia* [2009] UKAIT 00026), and the number of people holding this status is diminishing as it cannot be transmitted to children.

Those most affected by the creation of BOC status were people of Asian origin living in East African countries. The situation of people and families from India and Pakistan who had moved to Kenya and Uganda has been briefly described in chapter 1. The legislative history is one of the longest-running human rights issues in UK nationality and immigration law.

East African Asians did not have the necessary connection with the UK to obtain British Citizenship on 1 January 1983 (see 3.1.5), nor with an overseas territory to become a BDTC. Accordingly, under the BNA 1981 they obtained the residual status of BOC with no right of abode and no transmission to children. There was a significant lobby to include them in what became the 2002 British Overseas Territories Act, but this failed. A Private Member's Bill was proposed to fill this deficit, but did not receive government support. East African Asians thus remained BOCs without right of abode while citizens of overseas territories attained full British citizenship. The government gave as a reason for not including BOCs in the 2002 Act that many had access to or had acquired dual nationality, or had access to the UK through the voucher scheme. While this was generally correct for most people with BOC status, namely those of Malaysian nationality living in Singapore, it was not true of East African Asians. They could only use the discretionary voucher system, which was ended on 4 March 2002 by announcement in Parliament without any prior warning. The reason given was that it was not much used (Angela Eagle, Minister of State for Home Office HC Debs 5 March 2002 col 162W), though evidence given in *ECO Mumbai v NH (India)* [2007] EWCA Civ 1330 para 6 was that there were 500 applications per year at that stage.

The matter was finally addressed by a late amendment to the Nationality, Immigration and Asylum Bill 2002 to provide that BOCs have a right to register as British citizens if they have no other nationality or have not deprived themselves of such nationality after 4 July 2002 when the provision (s 4B inserted in BNA 1981) was announced.

The present position for BOCs may be summarized as follows:

(a) BOCs who have no other nationality may register as British citizens.

(b) If they do so, unlike other British citizens, they do not have the option of dual nationality.

(c) They may not relinquish another nationality in order to gain British nationality.

(d) Those who entered under the voucher system or can otherwise obtain leave to enter, have a right to register after five years' residence.

(e) This applies also for a dual national (see s 4 at 3.4.1).

(f) Dependants of former BOCs now BCs may apply to enter the UK under the usual family rules for settlement, which are more stringent than the rules for families under the voucher scheme.

(g) Any qualifying person may become a British citizen, whereas only heads of families could obtain vouchers under that scheme.

The abolition of the special voucher scheme and creation of a right to register was accompanied by an assertion that no one would be worse because of the scheme's abolition and that the provisions were intended to right a historic wrong. However, there were no transitional provisions to ensure that individuals did not suffer, and the changes have thrown up numerous problems. In *ECO Mumbai v NH* [2007] EWCA Civ 1330, the Court of Appeal found for a woman who wished to sponsor the entry of her adult son from India. Although the immigration rules did not allow for his entry, to refuse it to 'families like this... prevented for over thirty years from settling in the country of which some or all of their members once were, and are now again, citizens' (para 21) was a disproportionate interference with the right to family life under Article 8 ECHR. The legislation that had prevented the family from settling was racially discriminatory, and the refusal to accept the sponsor as a head of household because she was a married woman discriminated against her on the grounds of sex. What was necessary in a democratic society was 'consideration of all the circumstances including the previous history of any previous wrongful act' (para 18, quoting the Tribunal).

In later cases in the Tribunal, *NH* has been distinguished. For instance, in *JB and others (children of former BOC – limits of NH) India* [2008] UKAIT 00059, the Tribunal said that in applications by over-age children of former BOCs, Article 8 had to be applied to the actual situation to ascertain whether it would be breached by refusing entry. The 'historic wrong' referred to in *NH* would not create an Article 8 right of itself. This was further applied in *PV & ors* [2009] UKAIT 00033, where the Tribunal found that the BOC sponsor's financial position only allowed maintenance of his wife, and was insufficient to maintain his four children in their teens and twenties. After examining the family history, the Tribunal ruled that a refusal was not so 'conspicuously unfair', that Article 8 should override the maintenance requirements of the Rules.

The UK's declaration on nationality for purposes of EU membership still excludes BOCs. Therefore, BOCs do not, by virtue of that status, obtain citizenship of the European Union (*Manjit Kaur*), though following the new s 4B, the discrimination inherent in this situation is much reduced.

3.3.3 British subjects under the Act

This name is given by the 1981 Act to the people known under earlier nationality statutes as British subjects without citizenship. If such people acquire any other citizenship, they lose their British subject status. In addition to those mentioned in the historical section, this group includes some Irish citizens who exercised a right to retain their British subject status. They have effective right of abode in the UK by virtue of the Common Travel Area (see chapter 7) though most others do not. The new right to register for citizenship under BNA 1981 s 4B applies also to this group.

3.3.4 British Protected Persons

Before the majority of countries that had been under British rule during the Empire obtained independence, millions of people were British Protected Persons. Now there are very few. They, too, have the new right to register under BNA 1981 s 4B. This is a part of a process which may be summarized as one of gradual exclusion from the most favoured class of British nationality, which carries the right of abode, until the group remaining became so small that steps towards inclusion were finally taken.

3.4 Becoming British: registration and naturalization

If a person is not a national or citizen of a country, they might want to become one. British law historically had two very separate ways of doing this, but the processes of registration and naturalization are now much closer to each other than they used to be. Traditionally, registration is for those not born British but, nevertheless, entitled to apply to become so because of specified connections with the UK, such as UK-born British ancestors or certain types of established residence in the UK, and naturalization was for anyone else. The two processes are converging particularly as requirements of good character are creeping into the registration process, making it more akin to an exercise of discretion.

3.4.1 Registration

Registration broadly provides a method for those who fall just outside the provisions for British citizenship, to apply for it nevertheless. The process has been available for a very long time, as the case of *Bibi and others v SSHD* [2007] EWCA Civ 740 shows. Mr Jabbar entered the UK using someone else's identity and after five years of residence registered as a CUKC in 1967. After he died, his widow and children claimed that they had right of abode through his citizenship. The Court of Appeal held that his registration as a CUKC was void. The person identified on the documents had not been in the UK for five years, so no registration had taken place. Thus, the family had no basis upon which to claim right of abode.

Some people are entitled to register as British citizens, namely:

(a) Children of a British citizen by descent, if either the child and both parents have lived in the UK for three years prior to the date of the application (BNA 1981 s 3(5)) or application is made for registration while the child is a minor (s 3(2) as amended by s 43 BCI Act 2009), and providing at least one of the grandparents was a British citizen otherwise than by descent (s 3(2) and (3)). This is the provision referred to earlier which limits the transmission of citizenship by descent to one generation by birth and a second generation by registration (s 4C). This section is amended by s 45 BCI Act 2009 to remove the gender discrimination so that those born before 1961 are now able to trace entitlement through the female line. In the case of the entitlement to register as the child of a British citizen by descent, the British parent by descent must also have lived in the UK for at least three years prior to the birth (s 3(3)). In the case of registration under s 3(5), i.e., where the child and parents have returned to live in the UK for three years, both parents must consent to the registration. If the parents are divorced or legally separated or one has died, the three-year residence requirement only applies to one parent. These rules thus provide a mixture of *jus soli* and *jus sanguinis*. Where a British citizen by descent returns to the UK and lives here with their child, this demonstrates an intention to make the UK their home, which gives the child a kind of restored *jus soli*. They have not actually been born in the UK, but their presence here and that of their family suggests that they should be treated as though they were. Where the child is not resident, a stronger blood tie with the UK is required (s 3(3)).

(b) British Overseas Territories Citizens, British Nationals (Overseas), British Overseas Citizens, British subjects under the 1981 Act, and British Protected Persons, so long as they have been resident in the UK for five years, are entitled to register as British citizens under BNA 1981 s 4. As mentioned earlier, since the British Overseas Territories Act 2002, the only BOTCs who remain to use the right to register are those who have naturalized in the overseas territories or who are BOTCs solely by virtue of birth in a Cyprus base (unlikely to be the case as the parent's nationality will generally have superseded this). The rest will be British citizens automatically. BOCs, BPPs, and British subjects under the Act who have no other nationality can now register under s 4B without the five-year residence condition. Whilst British Nationals (Overseas) were originally excluded from this provision, s 44 BCI Act 2009 includes them. Now residents of Hong Kong have won the rights previously attained by the East Africans Asians and the Chagossians.

(c) Children born in the UK whose parent becomes British or settled, providing the application is made while they are still minors (BNA s 1(3)).

(d) Children born in the UK who live here until they are 10 years old (BNA s 1(4)).

(e) Persons born stateless in the UK, providing they have lived in the UK for five years at the date of the application and apply before they reach the age of 22 (BNA Sch 2 para 3, as amended by the Nationality, Immigration and Asylum Act 2002).

(f) A new s 4D is added by s 46 the BCI Act 2009 to give a right of registration to the children of non-British serving members of the armed forces who are born abroad.

Other people may be registered at the discretion of the Secretary of State. Under BNA s 3(1), s/he has discretion to register any minor. Children registered under s 3(1) are British citizens by descent if one of their parents was British at the time of their birth (s 14(1)(c)). This discretion may be used to fill gaps in the entitlements listed previously, for instance where a child has been adopted abroad by British parents, though it paradoxically means that the children of British parents are disadvantaged by comparison to the children of foreign nationals, since citizenship by descent is a less privileged status (see *Azad Ullah*, later in the chapter). Nationality Instructions chapter 9 gives guidance on the exercise of the discretion. Section 9.15.2 says 'the most important criterion is that the child's future should clearly be seen to lie in the UK'. If the child and family seem to have an established way of life in the UK, then the Home Office 'should accept at face value that the child intends to live here'. The parents' immigration status is relevant to this. Where the mother had indefinite leave to remain and had applied for British Citizenship, the Home Office was wrong to place emphasis on the fact that the father's leave was still limited (*R (on the application of Ali) v SSHD* [2007] EWHC 1983 (Admin)). He had also applied for indefinite leave to remain. The reason it had not yet been granted was delay in the Home Office, and his application showed where the children's future lay.

Section 47 of the BCI Act 2009 has controversially inserted a 'good character' requirement for most types of registration where the applicant is an adult or a child aged over ten years.

3.4.2 Naturalization

Naturalization is another process for obtaining British nationality by application. After many years focused in the areas of asylum and immigration, legislative reform has now moved onto naturalization, with considerable new provisions appearing in Part 2 of the Borders, Citizenship and Immigration Act 2009. There are conditions to be fulfilled, and especially fees to be paid, but even then there is no entitlement to naturalization. It is an exercise of discretion by the Secretary of State. As an exercise of discretion subject to statutory requirements and published criteria, it is open to judicial review on usual administrative law grounds (see 3.6). There are no limits on who may apply to naturalize. The way naturalization works does vary, however, according to the status of the applicant.

As seen earlier, British Overseas Citizens who become British have a more restricted status than outright foreigners who naturalize. British citizens by descent cannot naturalize in order to 'switch' to being British citizens otherwise than by descent, in order to rid themselves of the disadvantage of the secondary British citizenship status. In *SSHD v Azad Ullah* [2001] EWCA Civ 659, Mr Ullah was a British citizen by descent who had lived in the UK for some time with his Indian wife. Their children born in the UK were British citizens otherwise than by descent because Mr Ullah was British, but the Ullahs planned to spend a protracted period in India and wanted any children who might be born to them there to be British. Mr Ullah therefore applied to naturalize as a British citizen otherwise than by descent. The Court of Appeal held that this was not permissible.

In the programme of reform, the procedures of naturalization were changed first, with a 'Knowledge of Life in the UK' test and citizenship ceremonies, introduced under the Nationality, Immigration and Asylum Act 2002. These were modelled on procedures in other countries, replacing a low-key, private process with a more public one. The content of the process, however, did not change a great deal. Considerable media attention was also devoted to the introduction of the new pledge and oath of allegiance, and to the obligation on those naturalizing to be able to speak English (or, in fact, Welsh or Scots Gaelic), but these were both longstanding provisions. The oath of allegiance was made part of the new citizenship ceremony, rather than being the somewhat desultory declaration it had been previously, made privately before a solicitor, with the process of naturalization being completed by post. The method of testing for language skills is more formalized, though for fluent English-speakers a pass is inferred from passing the 'Life in the UK' test (see 3.4.2.6).

The requirements for naturalization are now in the process of change, following some years of the promotion of 'citizenship' in its meaning of 'being a good citizen', especially as taught in schools. Closer government interest and consultation on nationality issues followed, which were then tied to the roles and especially voluntary work that might be expected of those who wished to become British. First of all, the Prime Minister, Gordon Brown, asked Peter Goldsmith, the former Attorney-General, to report on the 'legal rights and responsibilities associated with British citizenship... as a basis for defining what it means to be a Citizen in Britain's open democratic society'; on the difference between the categories of British nationality; on the relationship amongst residence, citizenship, and British national status and on the incentives for long-term residents to become citizens; and on the civic roles of citizens and residents, including voting, jury service, and other forms of participation. Goldsmith's subsequent report *Citizenship: Our Common Bond*, leant very heavily on the idea of civic participation, especially the willingness to undertake unpaid work, as something the British government would wish to see in would-be citizens. The government's Green Paper, *The Path to Citizenship*, followed in 2008, and then a 'Simplification Bill', which aimed to replace the accumulation of immigration and nationality laws with one clear and workable piece of legislation. Unfortunately, that Bill was felt to fulfil neither demand and it was withdrawn, but followed by the Borders, Citizenship and Immigration Act in 2009. Most noticeable amongst its provisions are those extending the period for which many people will have to live in the UK, before being eligible for naturalization unless they are 'active citizens' who undertake some form of unpaid work (s 41(1)).

The requirements which must be fulfilled in order to qualify to apply for naturalization are found in BNA 1981 s 6 and Sch 1. Applications may only be made by persons of 'full age and capacity'.

3.4.2.1 *Capacity*

Full capacity is defined in BNA 1981 s 50(11) as 'not of unsound mind'. The Nationality Instructions chapter 18 annex A says that the question is whether the applicant is sufficiently mentally competent to know that they want to become British citizens. Where applicants have lodged their own applications, it should be assumed that they meet the requirement 'unless there is information on the Home Office papers to cast doubt on this'. By Immigration, Asylum and Nationality Act 2006 s 49, the Secretary of State may waive the capacity requirement 'if he thinks it in the applicant's best interests'. This is a very minimal standard compared with the demanding approach of the new tests of knowledge of English language and life in the UK, but this, too, may be waived in suitable cases (see later).

3.4.2.2 *Period of residence and 'earned citizenship'*

Naturalization requires a period of residence in the UK. The present qualifying period is three years for a person married to or in a civil partnership with a British citizen (s 6(2)), otherwise, it is five years (s 6(1)). Schedule 1 allows certain periods of absence from the UK without jeopardizing the application (270 days for spouses or 450 days for others, provided that not more than 90 of these days are in the last 12 months), and there is a discretion to disregard the residence requirement, at least to an extent (see NI chapter 18 annex B paras 4 and 5). The exceptions to the rule that there is no discretion to waive the requirement for presence at the beginning of the qualifying period are very limited.

The Borders, Citizenship and Immigration Act 2009 provides that an extra three years of residence will be required from applicants for citizenship who have not 'earned' that citizenship by carrying out unpaid work. The government is consulting on how to implement these requirements which would seem, for example, to exclude particularly those with child care responsibilities. Whilst exclusion of the economically less viable might be desirable in terms of the general economic wellbeing, if – as is likely – the people, nevertheless, live in the UK, the impact of making the position of children in particular precarious could be alienating and socially destabilizing to their communities in the longer term.

3.4.2.3 *Type of residence*

Residence during the majority of the qualifying period is only required to be physical presence, not a particular immigration status. However, at the date of application a spouse or civil partner, and for the last year of residence a s 6(1) applicant, must be free of immigration restrictions on their stay (Sch 1 para 1(2)(b)). Residence must also not have been in breach of immigration laws (1(2)(d)), though once again there is a discretion to regard periods so spent as lawful (para 2(d)). NI chapter 18 annex B para 8.10 gives examples of when the Home Office would normally exercise discretion to disregard a breach, which it would not normally do 'when the breach was substantial and deliberate' or could affect the good character requirement (see 3.4.2.4). Because of the historical complexity and laxity of the immigration system, many people, especially asylum seekers, could be in breach of immigration laws, and it is not always easy to say how far someone's status may be lawful.

There is a special provision concerning periods spent in detention or on temporary admission (as to which, see chapter 15). BNA 1981 Sch 1 gives a discretion to regard periods of 'technical absence' as residence for naturalization purposes. This is generally used for members of the forces and diplomatic staff. People in detention without leave are physically present in the UK but in immigration law they are not legally present. Those on temporary admission used not to be considered legally present, but since the House of Lords' decision in *Szoma v DWP* [2005] UKHL 64 have been so. The acceptance of this is, however, grudging: see immigration rules para 276A(b)(ii), where it is admitted only where there is a subsequent full grant of leave, and NI 9.7 says that if at the end of detention or temporary admission the person was given leave to enter, their time in detention or on temporary admission should count as residence, but not if they are removed or depart voluntarily.

3.4.2.4 *Good character requirement*

Schedule 1 para 1(1)(b) requires 'that he is of good character'. The Act gives no further explanation as to how this requirement should be interpreted. Home Office guidance is to be found in NI chapter 18 annex D. Criminal activity is clearly an indication that the person may be regarded as not of good character: however, not all criminal activity will debar an applicant. The Home Office applies the Rehabilitation of Offenders Act 1974 for this purpose, and in Northern Ireland the Rehabilitation of Offenders (Northern Ireland) Order 1978. On 5 December 2007, the Home Secretary made an announcement that, henceforth, unspent convictions would generally debar an application. Some offences can never be spent under the statutory provisions. The Home Office used to look in these cases for a period clear of offending, but have not suggested what their approach will be now. The whole issue is discretionary. The question used to be whether it seems that the person intends to abide by the law (para 2.1), but the Home Secretary's announcement suggests that the goal posts have moved. The Home Office confirmed to Bindman's (solicitors), in a letter dated 4 September 2001, that homelessness of itself did not put a person's good character in doubt. Other matters which should not be held against the applicant include 'Eccentricity, including beliefs, appearance and lifestyle' (para 5.2). Notoriety may be a reason to refuse an application, taking account of 'anticipated public reaction' (para 5.4).

3.4.2.5 *Language requirement*

This requirement came into the public spotlight with the publication, in February 2002, of the White Paper, *Secure Borders, Safe Haven* (Cm 5387). The White Paper proposed that applicants for British citizenship should be required to demonstrate a level of language proficiency in English, Welsh, or Scottish Gaelic, these being regarded as the British languages. The BNA 1981, in fact, already required that the applicant 'had sufficient knowledge of the English, Welsh or Scottish Gaelic language' (Sch 1 para 1(1)(c)). As the White Paper observed, this was assumed to be the case unless there was evidence to the contrary. The new proposal was for actual testing of language ability as in other countries cited in the White Paper, for instance Australia, Canada, France, Germany, and the US. The proposal came into being in the Nationality, Immigration and Asylum Act 2002 as an addition to the rule-making powers in BNA s 41, enabling rules to be made 'for determining whether a person has sufficient knowledge of a language for the purpose of an application for naturalization' (s 1(3)). Accordingly, the British Nationality (General) (Amendment) Regulations 2005, SI 2005/2785 provide that the level of language qualification is ESOL (English for Speakers of Other Languages) level 3. Someone who is already fluent in the English language may meet the language requirement by taking and passing the test on Life in the UK (see next section). Someone not yet fluent to ESOL level 3 is required to learn and pass a separate language test.

Schedule 1 BNA 1981 contains provision for waiving the language requirement if 'because of the applicant's age or physical or mental condition it would be unreasonable to expect him to fulfil it' (para 2(e)). The 2002 Act does not repeal this provision and so exemption may be given to ill or elderly people or those with learning difficulties. The measure has been controversial, not because there is doubt about the value of fluency in British languages, but because of concern about the alienating effects of compulsion.

3.4.2.6 *Knowledge of British society*

This was a highly contentious provision in the 2002 Act in s 1(1), adding a requirement 'that he has sufficient knowledge about life in the United Kingdom', backed up with an addition to the rule-making power to enable this to be assessed as for language. The proposal was a manifestation of the government's policy, mentioned at the beginning of this chapter, to make citizenship a meaningful concept, and to link it with nationality. The phrase 'life in the United Kingdom' suggests something about habits and practices, usual ways of behaving, and so on. This suggests culture and raises connotations of ethnicity rather than nationality. In a state made up of many ethnicities, this raises the question of whose life the candidate for naturalization should know about. In the words of Jim Marshall MP in the second reading debate in the House of Commons, is the measure concerned 'to improve civic participation and awareness' or to 'promote cultural uniformity' (HC Debs 24 April 2002 col 366). Answers may be found in *Life in the United Kingdom: A Journey to Citizenship*, the handbook produced by the 'Life in the United Kingdom' Advisory Group, set up to advise the Home Secretary on implementation of these proposals. A critique of the handbook from a South Asian perspective noted the relative absence of information in the book that would be useful to immigrants, and the invisibility of minority ethnic groups, the writing seeming to come from a perspective of being 'born and bred' in the UK with little attention paid to crucial issues of racism and religion other than Christianity (Noor 2007). A second and expanded edition in 2007 recognized that 'immigration and diversity' and history are important (Kiwan 2007). Contributions to the Citizenship Review revealed that the thinking behind the new naturalization process is at least in part a vision of education and integration, but its impact is unresearched (Kiwan 2007).

There is a programme of studies which can accompany the handbook for all applicants for naturalization. Knowledge of life in the UK is a requirement for applications for naturalization made after 1 November 2005, when s 1(1) and (2) came into force. Since April 2007, this is also part of the requirements for indefinite leave to remain (see chapter 7).

3.4.2.7 *Pledge*

Along with the requirement for knowledge of British society was the institution of a pledge to be taken as well as the oath of allegiance, which is the formal moment at which new citizenship is acquired. Contrary to what an observer might glean from much of the media discussion at the time of the 2002 Bill, the oath of allegiance to the monarchy had always been part of obtaining citizenship. However, it was administered by a Commissioner for Oaths (usually a solicitor) or magistrate, in private and without ceremony.

The additional pledge, in Sch 1 to the 2002 Act, is as follows:

> I will give my loyalty to the United Kingdom and respect its rights and freedoms. I will uphold its democratic values. I will observe its laws faithfully and fulfil my duties and obligations as a British Citizen.

This is administered in formal ceremonies for nationality applications made after 1 January 2004.

Part of the legacy of the focus on immigration considerations as a basis for nationality law is that the 'duties and obligations' of a British citizen have never been identified and most people who are British by birth or descent would have no idea what these are. It is therefore debatable whether those who acquire their nationality by a formal process should be asked to promise to fulfil them. The formal ceremonies, after an initial blaze of publicity, have largely become a matter of routine once more (Rimmer 2007).

3.4.2.8 *Intention to live in UK*

The final requirement for naturalization is that the applicant intends to make their future home in the UK (Sch 1 para 1(1)(d)). Where the applicant has an established home in the UK, or there is no reason to doubt this intention, then it will be regarded as met (NI chapter 18 annex F para 2). An intention to travel should not debar the applicant unless it appears that they do not intend to return.

3.4.2.9 *Becoming British by adoption*

A child can become British by adoption if at least one of the adoptive parents is a British citizen on the date of adoption, and the adoption order is made by a court in a British territory, or after May 2003 under the 1993 Hague Convention on Intercountry Adoption and the adopters are habitually resident in the UK at the relevant date. If, for example, the parents are resident overseas and this does not apply, it may be possible register the child as British. An application for registration should be made before the child is 18, and would be likely to succeed if the child would have been British had s/he been the adopters' biological child. The child's British status will survive any annulment of an adoption order. More interestingly, if a British person is adopted abroad, they do not cease to be British for that reason.

3.5 Renunciation and deprivation of nationality

3.5.1 Renunciation

It is possible to renounce British citizenship. The right and process are in s 12 BNA 1981. Renunciation takes effect only when accepted by the Secretary of State, who will not accept any renunciation of British citizenship that would leave the individual in question stateless. A common reason for renouncing British citizenship is that the person concerned wishes to take up the nationality of a country that does not allow dual citizenship. In such cases, British citizenship may subsequently be resumed as of right (subject to any good character requirement), but only once. All other resumptions of British citizenship after renunciation are discretionary, like ordinary naturalization.

3.5.2 Deprivation of nationality, citizenship, and the right of abode

Section 40 of the British Nationality Act 1981 deals with deprivation of citizenship. The provision that citizenship obtained by fraud, false representation, or concealment of a material fact may be removed is of long standing. Where a person registers as a British citizen on a factual basis that later turns out to be untrue, the fact that this was simply due to mistake will not cure the withdrawal of the passport or the invalidity of the claim to British citizenship, even if this results in statelessness: see *Burnett's Application* [2010] NICA 2. The Secretary of State also had the power to deprive a person of their citizenship if he was satisfied that the person had been guilty of 'disloyalty or disaffection to Her Majesty', helping an enemy in time of war, or a criminal offence within five years of obtaining citizenship. The provisions as to deprivation have, however, been extended considerably in recent years, by the Nationality, Immigration and Asylum Act 2002 and then by the Immigration, Asylum and Nationality Act 2006.

The 2002 Act was passed in a climate of suspicion about 'foreign terrorists' and a media scandal about the inability to deport Abu Hamza al-Masri, an Egyptian Muslim cleric who had naturalized following marriage to a British woman, before exciting press and other attention by preaching violence and religious hatred. Section 4 of the 2002 Act allowed deprivation of citizenship if the person had done something seriously prejudicial to the vital interests of the UK or a British overseas territory. This also applied to those born British in the UK: this was new and caused considerable public disquiet at the time. It also did not work in respect of Mr al-Masri, because he would have been left stateless, which was prohibited.

Given the public concern over the 2002 Act, reforms passed in 2006 excited little attention, although the powers of deprivation under the IANA 2006 are so strong as to allow in practice for something close to arbitrary deprivation. They appear to be the result of the Home Secretary's losing the case of *SSHD v Hicks* [2006] EWCA Civ 400, though they form part of a longer trajectory. David Hicks was an Australian citizen, who, after the 2002 legislative reforms, acquired a right under BNA 1981 s 4C to register as a British citizen by descent because his mother was British. He applied to register as a citizen in 2005 because he was detained by the US government in Guantanamo Bay for terrorism-related activities, and British citizens obtained more assistance from the UK government than Australians did from Canberra. The Secretary of State declined to register him and alternatively proposed, should he have the right to register, to deprive him of that citizenship simultaneously with granting it. The Court of Appeal held in *SSHD v Hicks* [2006] EWCA Civ 400 that he was entitled to register. It was agreed that the original 1981 version of the section applied, so in 2000 and 2001 when he was in Afghanistan Mr Hicks owed no duty to the British Crown and there were no grounds for the deprivation. It also held that he could not be deprived of the resulting British nationality on the basis of 'disaffection', because at the time of his terrorist training in Pakistan and Afghanistan he was not a British citizen; as he owed no duty of allegiance, he could not breach it. The response of the government was to give the Secretary of State the power to deprive a person of their citizenship if s/he 'is satisfied that it is conducive to the public good' (s 56 IANA 2006). This provision was passed, and used in relation to Mr Hicks, almost immediately. A corresponding provision was passed in relation to deprivation of the right of abode (s 57 IANA 2006). Section 58 of the Immigration, Asylum and Nationality Act 2006 also introduced a requirement of good character that would have made it possible for the Home Office to refuse to register him as he was accused of involvement in terrorism (which he later admitted).

Section 40 of the BNA 1981 thus now allows the Secretary of State to deprive a person of British citizenship if it is considered conducive to the public good, provided the person is not thereby left stateless. There is no requirement for the decision to be based on reasonable grounds, and although administrative law imports a requirement of reasonableness, any appeal would have the limited scope of judicial review. This applies even to those born British in the UK, though it is, as Majid (2008) has pointed out, the criterion previously applied in relation to deportation of foreign nationals. The government indicated at the time that the kind of behaviour which could found deprivation of citizenship under this subsection would include that in the 'list of unacceptable behaviours' made public by the Home Secretary on 24 August 2005 (Standing Committee E 27 October 2005 col 254) as part of the government's public strategy to counter terrorism after the London bombings of 7 July 2005 (see chapter 16).

The prohibition on leaving people stateless in relation to this form of deprivation means in effect that only British people who are dual nationals are likely to be affected by this provision. One question that may have to be answered is whether for these purposes a person is considered stateless if they could, on application, obtain the nationality of another country even if they do not currently hold it. Those who have naturalized may now, however, be deprived of their British citizenship if they have obtained it by fraud, misrepresentation, or concealment of a material fact even if that would leave them stateless.

These are wide and draconian powers and demonstrate a new attitude to nationality. It has become more conditional upon conduct. In the case of people who have obtained their nationality by registration or naturalization, the possibility that they could be left stateless if they have obtained it by fraud conveys a powerful message.

The Nationality Instructions chapter 55 give an account of the difference between fraud which means that nationality will be taken away, and fraud which means that the original grant of nationality was a nullity – i.e., had no effect. In *Bibi and others v SSHD* [2007] EWCA Civ 740 discussed previously, the grant was a nullity because Mr Jabbar took on the identity of another person, so a grant of nationality to him did not happen. If he had falsified certain details, such as the time he had spent in the UK, the grant of nationality would have taken effect. He could have been deprived of it once the fraud came to light, but he would have actually been a British Citizen in the interim. In some cases (though problematic on the facts of that case as he had died), this difference could affect the rights of relatives.

As mentioned in chapter 1, the Parliamentary Joint Committee on Human Rights raised concerns with the Home Office about the use of deprivation of nationality, particularly 'loss of British diplomatic protection; loss of status; loss of the ability to participate in the democratic process in the United Kingdom; and serious damage to reputation and dignity' (Joint Committee on Human Rights Session 2001–02 Seventeenth Report para 26). The Home Office, somewhat disingenuously, replied that the person would have another nationality and so the harm to them would be limited, but did not mention that this may not be the case where nationality is removed because of fraud.

3.6 Challenging nationality decisions

Under the old s 40, a proposal to make an order depriving a person of their citizenship could be referred to a committee of inquiry. The 2002 Act introduced a full right of appeal to the Tribunal, but not if the Secretary of State certifies that the decision was taken wholly or partly in reliance on information which in his opinion should not be made public in the interests of national security or the relationship between the UK and another country, or 'otherwise in the public interest'. This is a very wide provision, and given the grounds for deprivation in s 40(2) there is potential for it to apply in almost any case. In these cases, an appeal will lie to the Special Immigration Appeals Commission. As discussed in chapter 8, the proceedings of this Commission may be closed to the public and evidence may be withheld from the appellant. Section 4 of the Asylum and Immigration (Treatment of Claimants, etc.) Act 2004 made appeals against deprivation orders non-suspensive.

Under the BNA 1981, there is no appeal against a refusal of naturalization or registration, and this remains unchanged. The 2002 Act has, however, provided some increased rights for aggrieved applicants. It repeals s 44(2) and (3), which provided that no reasons should be given for discretionary nationality decisions. In practice, this had already become a discredited provision, as in Mohammed al Fayed's well-known challenge to the Home Secretary's refusal of his naturalization application, the Court of Appeal held that in some cases the Secretary was under a duty to give the applicant notice of the reasons for refusal (*Fayed v SSHD* [1997] 1 All ER 228). The Secretary of State followed this with an announcement in Parliament that reasons would generally be given and this is in accordance with the 1997 Convention. The method of legal challenge to a refusal of naturalization is judicial review on usual administrative law grounds on the basis of reasons given. In practice, if an application fails through not meeting the factual criteria, the remedy would be to re-apply when the criteria were met, or point out the Home Office error if there had been one.

In *Harrison v SSHD* [2003] INLR 284, the appellant had wanted to be recognized as British through a disputed ancestral claim, but been refused. He cited his right under Article 6 ECHR to a fair trial in relation to matters of his civil rights, but the Court of Appeal held that being recognized as a citizen was not a civil right within the meaning of Article 6 ECHR. It did, however, say that Mr Harrison could apply to the Court for a declaration of his citizenship and that this hearing would follow normal requirements of fairness. As with Mr Fayed, this amounts to much the same thing. As will be seen elsewhere in this book, the courts are reluctant to imply any private rights for affected parties to challenge the state's power to control its membership or borders. The application of Article 6 is considered more fully in chapter 4.

One of the most important incidents of citizenship is surely the right to live in one's own country. A current legal issue is the counterbalancing of the rights of British children to live in Britain if their carer parents are foreign nationals without separate status. See *ZH (Tanzania)* [2011] UKSC 4, discussed in chapter 9.

3.7 Conclusion

This chapter has sought to show that in the second half of the twentieth century, the UK's nationality law was shaped largely by its relationships with its former colonies and by the desire to restrict immigration from the majority of these. From the early part of the twentieth century when millions of people could claim the status of British subject and the theoretical right of abode that went with this, we have now come to a time when only the status of British citizen carries the right of abode. Obtaining this by birth is restricted to those with a close connection with the UK or its few remaining overseas territories. The process of changing the basis of entitlement seems to be coming to an end, but some people, particularly British Overseas Citizens, have had to fight long and hard not to be entirely left out of the concluding arrangements of the Empire.

A new phase was heralded by the Nationality, Immigration and Asylum Act 2002. The Act demonstrates the exclusive power of the state, as noted at the beginning of this chapter, to determine who are its nationals. In earlier legislation, the government was preoccupied with the question of who 'belonged' to the UK, largely seen in terms of birth and parentage. Exclusion on the basis of heritage has increased, though some overseas-based groups have become entitled to British citizenship; discrimination based on gender or parental marriage status has decreased. In the 2002 and 2006 legislation, the state's power of determination is turned in a further new direction, testing allegiance not only by bloodline but by conduct and participation as a citizen. As one era ends, a new one is dawning.

QUESTIONS

1 Are the UK's nationality laws closer to a principle of *jus soli* or *jus sanguinis*? Whichever you think, what elements can you find in UK nationality law of the other principle?

2 How do registration and naturalization fit in with the way the UK embodies the *jus soli* or *jus sanguinis* principles?

3 Is it possible to give content to the idea of 'belonging' to a country? How does British nationality law do it? How would you do it?

4 How would you structure a law of deprivation of nationality or citizenship? What safeguards would you put in place?

For guidance on answering questions, visit www.oxfordtextbooks.co.uk/orc/clayton5e/.

FURTHER READING

Anderson, Benedict (2006) *Imagined Communities* (new edn) (London: Verso).

Blake, Charles (1982) 'Citizenship, Law and the State: The British Nationality Act 1981' *Modern Law Review* vol. 45, pp. 179–197.

Clayton, Gina (2008) 'Right of Abode and National Insecurity', *Immigration Law Digest* vol. 14, no. 4, Winter, pp. 2–9.

Cohn, Margit (2009) 'Judicial Review of Non-Statutory Executive Powers after Bancoult: A Unified Anxious Model' *Public Law* pp. 260–286.

Dummett, Ann (2006) 'The United Kingdom', in Rainer Baubock, Eva Ersboll, Kees Groenendjik, and Harald Waldrauch (eds) *The Acquisition and Loss of Nationality: Policies and Trends in 15 European Countries* (IMISCOE Research) (Amsterdam: University of Amsterdam Press).

Dummett, Ann and Nicol, Andrew (1990) *Subjects, Citizens, Aliens and Others* (London: Weidenfeld and Nicolson), chapter 7.

Elliott, Mark and Perreau-Saussine, Amanda (2009) 'Pyrrhic public law: Bancoult and the sources, status and content of common law limitations on prerogative power' *Public Law* pp. 697–722.

Fransman, Laurie (2011) *British Nationality Law* (3rd edn) (London: Bloomsbury), this is the major authoritative work, for reference on all issues.

Gellner, Ernest (1983) *Nations and Nationalism* (Ithaca, NY: Cornell University Press).

Goldsmith, Peter (2007) *Citizenship: Our Common Bond* accessed at: www.justice.gov.uk/reviews/docs/citizenship-report-full.pdf.

Grossman, Andrew (2001) 'Nationality and the Unrecognised State' *International and Comparative Law Quarterly* vol. 50, pp. 849–876.

Hansen, Randall S. (2001) 'From Subjects to Citizens: Immigration and Nationality Law in the UK' in Randall S. Hansen and Patrick Weil (eds), *Towards a European Nationality: Citizenship, Immigration and Nationality Law in the EU* (New York/ Houndsmills: Palgrave), pp. 69–94.

Hogenstijn Maarten and van Middelkoop, Daniel (2005) 'Saint Helena: Citizenship and Spatial Identities on a Remote Island' *Tijdschrift voor Economische en Sociale Geografie* vol. 96, no. 1, pp. 96–104.

Immigration Law Practitioners' Association (2000) 'The Overseas Territories White Paper and Protocol 4 of the ECHR – the ILPA response' *Journal of Immigration, Asylum and Nationality* vol. 14, no. 3, pp. 142–150.

Joint Council for the Welfare of Immigrants (JCWI) (2006) *Immigration, Nationality and Refugee Law Handbook* (6th edn) (London: JCWI).

Kiwan, Dinah (2007) 'Becoming a British Citizen: A Learning Journey', Goldsmith Citizenship Review, Ministry of Justice.

Larkin Philip (2007) 'Migrants, Social Security, and the "Right to Reside": A Licence to Discriminate?' *Journal of Social Security Law* pp. 61–85.

Lester, Anthony (2002) 'Thirty Years On: The *East African Asians Case* Revisited' *Public Law* Spring, pp. 52–72.

—— (2008) 'Citizenship and the Constitution' *Political Quarterly* vol. 79, no. 3, pp. 388–403.

Levy, Andrea (2004) *Small Island* (London: Headline).

Majid, Hina (2008) 'Protecting the Right to Have Rights: The Case of Sect. 56 of the Immigration, Asylum and Nationality Act 2006' *Immigration, Asylum and Nationality Law* vol. 22, no. 1, pp. 27–44.

Mole, Nuala (1995) 'Constructive Deportation and the European Convention' *European Human Rights Law Review* launch issue, pp. 63–71.

Noor, Osman (2007) 'Review of Life in the UK' 21 *Journal of Immigration, Asylum and Nationality Law* vol. 12, no. 2, pp. 166–168.

Paul, Kathleen (1997) *Whitewashing Britain: Race and Citizenship in the Postwar Era* (New York: Cornell University Press), chapter 1.

Pilger, John (2004) 'Stealing a Nation' documentary film about the Chagos Islanders.

Rimmer, Mark (2007) 'The Future of Citizenship Ceremonies', Goldsmith Citizenship Review (London: Ministry of Justice).

Sawyer, Caroline (2004) 'A Losing Ticket in the Lottery of Life: Expelling British Children' *Public Law* Winter, pp. 750–758.

—— (2006) 'Not Every Child Matters: The UK's Expulsion of British Children' *International Journal of Children's Rights* vol. 14, no. 2, pp. 157–185.

—— (2009) *EUDO Citizenship Observatory Country Report: United Kingdom*, accessed at: eudo-citizenship.eu/docs/CountryReports/United%20Kingdom.pdf

Shah, Prakash (2000) *Refugees, Race and the Legal Concept of Asylum* (London: Cavendish), chapter 5.

Shah, Ramnik (2003) 'Special Voucher Scheme Abolished' *Journal of Immigration, Asylum and Nationality Law* vol. 16, pp. 108–110.

—— (2003) 'A Wrong Righted: Full Status for Britain's 'Other Citizens' *Journal of Immigration, Asylum and Nationality Law* vol. 17, pp. 19–24.

Smith, Anthony D. (1996) *Nations and Nationalism in a Global Era* (Cambridge: Polity Press).

The Home Office in the UK Advisory Group (2007) *Life in the United Kingdom: A Journey to Citizenship* 2nd edn (London: The Stationery Office).

Tomkins, Adam (2001) 'Magna Carta, Crown and Colonies' *Public Law* pp. 571–585.

White, Robin M. (2002) 'Immigration, Nationality, Citizenship and the Meaning of Naturalisation: Brubaker, the United Kingdom EU Citizens, Third Country Nationals and the European Union' *Northern Ireland Law Quarterly* vol. 53, no. 3, pp. 288–319.

Winder, Robert (2004) *Bloody Foreigners* (London: Little Brown).

Woollacott, Simon (2005) 'Persons Granted British Citizenship, 2004', *Home Office Statistical Bulletin* 08/05.

4

Immigration law and human rights

SUMMARY

This chapter discusses the relationship between human rights law and immigration law in the UK, including the effect on unsuccessful asylum claimants. It introduces relevant aspects of the operation of the Human Rights Act. There is a detailed discussion of the application of Article 3 and Article 8 to immigration situations, and there is briefer treatment of the remaining Articles.

4.1 Introduction

4.1.1 The relationship between immigration law and human rights

There is an obvious connection between migration and human rights. In moving between countries fundamental rights are often being exercised, for instance to be reunited with one's family or to be free from torture or discrimination. Some accounts of human rights would include the right to freedom of movement itself, or the right to work. Immigration law enforcement may involve *prima facie* violations of other rights; for instance, people who are not even suspected of crime can be detained under immigration powers. However, there is no human right to move to a particular country. States have the right to a system of law which, within the constraints of international law, regulates who may enter. Whatever the origins of that power, which we briefly considered in chapter 1, immigration law is primarily concerned with defining and giving enforceable substance to it. It has been concerned with regulating the numbers, origin, and material and other circumstances of those to whom entry will be granted, not primarily with the protection of their rights.

In the context of migration and human rights, seeking asylum is a special case as an application for asylum is an application for a specialized form of international human rights protection. This chapter is not concerned with making an asylum claim, which is dealt with in section 5 of this book, but is concerned with the application of human rights law in the UK in immigration decision-making, including to a person whose asylum claim has failed. In fact, many human rights claims heard by the immigration appellate bodies are made by people whose asylum claims have been unsuccessful.

This chapter will focus on the use of the European Convention on Human Rights in the UK, both directly and through the Human Rights Act 1998. But many other international conventions may be relevant to immigration cases, for instance, the International Covenant on Civil and Political Rights (ICCPR), the Convention on Ending Racial Discrimination (CERD), the Convention on the Elimination of All Forms of Discrimination Against Women (CEDAW), the Convention Against Torture (CAT), and the Convention on the Rights of the Child (CRC). Human rights principles may also be drawn from the deliberations of bodies whose work is to develop human rights, for instance the United Nations Commission on Human Rights. Case law from other jurisdictions where there are constitutionally enshrined rights is relevant, including in particular from Commonwealth jurisdictions and judgments of the Privy Council.

4.1.2 Development of immigration law and human rights

The rights of foreign nationals have been controversial throughout the life of the European Convention on Human Rights and, in the UK, of the Human Rights Act. Adverse political reactions to the prospect and the actuality of rights granted to foreign nationals have had a significant impact on the development of human rights law. When the UK first ratified the ECHR, it did not immediately grant the individual right of petition. This meant that, although the UK was a party to the Convention in international law, no one in the UK's jurisdiction who suffered an infringement of their rights could actually go to the Court of Human Rights and complain. The delay may be attributed to the government's fear of applications from overseas territories, of which Britain had 42 in 1953 when the Convention was ratified. Macdonald cites a minister in Parliament: 'among emerging communities political agitators thrive and one may well imagine the use which political agitators would make of the right of individual petition' (Blake and Fransman (1999:vii). By the end of 1966, when the UK granted the individual right of petition, the number of overseas territories had dropped to 24.

As discussed in the previous chapter, the UK has not ratified Protocol 4 because of its inability to comply, principally on account of the position of British overseas citizens.

Since the right of individual petition was granted, the UK government has tested other arguments that would exclude the rights of foreign nationals from the reach of the Convention, or limit their access to it. The UK has not been alone in this endeavour, as case law discussed in this chapter will show. In *Abdulaziz, Cabales and Balkandali v UK* (1985) 7 EHRR 471, the UK government argued that Protocol 4, Article 4, which simply says: 'Collective expulsion of aliens is prohibited', was the only reference in the Convention to immigration control, and that accordingly no other immigration decision came within the reach of the Convention. The European Court of Human Rights (ECtHR) rejected this argument.

The Court's judgment established the principle that Convention rights, and in this case the right to respect for family life (Article 8), do apply to a state's immigration decisions. They made the following important statement:

> the right of a foreigner to enter or remain in a country was not as such guaranteed by the Convention, but immigration controls had to be exercised consistently with Convention obligations, and the exclusion of a person from a State where members of his family were living might raise an issue under Article 8. (para 59)

This principle remains a crucial foundation of the relationship between immigration decisions and human rights, and Article 8 in particular. Immigration decisions are acts of the state with the potential to affect the rights of individuals. Where rights are affected, interference with them may be challenged in the ECtHR, or in the UK's national courts in reliance on the Convention rights secured by the Human Rights Act 1998.

Since *Abdulaziz* the application of Convention rights to immigration decisions has been litigated in a wide range of situations. As the scope of human rights law has expanded, its principles have become more sophisticated and its limits tested. The body of this chapter will explore in more detail the gradual expansion of the application of

Convention rights, and the contrary developments by which their application has been restricted.

Pursuant to the Lisbon Treaty (the Treaty on the Functioning of the European Union OJ C 83/49), the CJEU acquired jurisdiction in immigration and asylum matters, and the fundamental rights contained in the EU Charter of Fundamental Rights became justiciable in EU law. This has introduced the first binding supranational authority in relation to human rights applied to immigration and asylum issues. The first judgment on these points was in C–411/10 *NS v SSHD* and C–493/10 *ME and others v Refugee Applications Commissioner and Minister for Justice, Equality and Law Reform*.

Key Case

C–411/10 *NS v SSHD* and C–493/10 *ME and others v Refugee Applications Commissioner and Minister for Justice, Equality and Law Reform*

The applicants were asylum seekers who had travelled through Greece and claimed asylum in the UK and Ireland respectively. The legal challenges were to the UK and Ireland's practice and legislation, which allowed no opportunity for the asylum seekers to argue that their return to Greece, pursuant to the EC regulation known as Dublin II, would breach their human rights. In the UK, return to Greece was deemed safe by the Asylum and Immigration (Treatment of Claimants, etc) Act 2004, and as such could not be challenged.

The judgment of the CJEU Grand Chamber was delivered after that of the ECtHR in *MSS v Belgium and Greece*. In *MSS* the ECtHR had accepted evidence from 'regular and unanimous reports of international non-governmental organizations' to reach a conclusion that the fundamental rights of asylum seekers under Article 3 ECHR were infringed in Greece. The CJEU concluded that 'there existed in Greece at the time of the transfer of the applicant MSS, a systemic deficiency in the asylum procedure and the reception conditions of asylum seekers' (para 89).

The CJEU held that, contrary to the submissions of governments, the discretion that Member States have to decide an asylum application themselves, instead of sending the applicant to another Member State under the Dublin Regulation, is a discretion which implements EU law. Accordingly it must be exercised consistently with the principles of EU law including respect for fundamental rights. The Court held that where the Member State could 'not be unaware' that systemic deficiencies existed in the asylum procedure in the receiving country such that there were substantial grounds for believing that there was a real risk of violations of Article 4 of the Charter (equivalent to Article 3 ECHR) then the Charter prohibited an asylum seeker from being transferred to that country. EU law prohibited a conclusive presumption that the destination state complied in its asylum procedures with the Charter of Fundamental Rights.

The workings of the Dublin regulation and the case of *MSS* are discussed more fully in chapter 12. The point here is the radical effect of the CJEU's judgment on human rights law in the EU. While the Court said that minor infringements would not nullify Dublin transfers, as the need for a common system in the EU required assumptions to be made, in the face of evidence of real risk of inhuman or degrading treatment or punishment, or torture, regulations made for the operation of the Common European Asylum System would give way to human rights.

The two sources of legal authority which had been applied in the UK, the Dublin regulation and AITOCA, are both binding sources of law. The CJEU judgment therefore has far-reaching implications as it means that, through the Charter of Fundamental Rights in the Lisbon Treaty, national primary legislation and EU secondary legislation must be operated compatibly with human rights in areas where EU law applies.

4.2 Applying the Human Rights Act

Since October 2000, human rights are statutorily embedded in immigration and asylum decision-making. Immigration decisions are acts of public authorities under s 6 of the Human Rights Act and as such are required by s 6 to be compatible with the Convention rights derived from the ECHR.

This obligation is reinforced by s 84 of the Nationality Immigration and Asylum Act 2002 which makes a breach of Convention rights a ground of appeal against an immigration decision. Human rights appeals are discussed further in chapter 8.

4.2.1 Duty of interpretation

Section 3 creates a principle of interpretation which has far-reaching consequences. By s 3(1), so far as it is possible to do so, primary and subordinate legislation must be read and given effect in a way which is compatible with Convention rights. The phrase 'and given effect' makes it clear that the purpose is to uphold rights and echoes the principle of ECHR case law that human rights law should be practical and effective. The duty is to read statute and secondary legislation so as to protect rights whenever possible. While immigration decisions may depend on interpretation of primary legislation, the questions of interpretation often concern procedural matters such as the availability of appeal rights, the standard to be applied in judging a claim (both at issue in *BA Nigeria and PE Cameroon* [2009] UKSC 7), or the procedure adopted by the Secretary of State (e.g., *Sapkota*). In reality, it is often these kinds of procedural points that determine the outcome of an immigration appeal, and any human rights involved in it. In this broad sense, the interpretation of statute is concerned with delivery of rights, but Convention rights protected by the Human Rights Act are not directly in issue. The reader might object that access to a court is a right protected by Article 6. However, Article 6 rights are, according to established case law, not applicable in immigration and asylum cases (see *Maaouia* later in this chapter). So, although the strong interpretive duty in s 3 applies in interpretation of immigration statutes, in practice it is rarely possible to invoke it.

The second question concerning the section 3 duty of interpretation is whether it can be applied to the interpretation of the immigration rules. The immigration rules are now accepted not to be subordinate legislation (*Odelola* and *Pankina*). Current authority is that the section 3 duty of interpretation therefore does not apply, but this makes little difference in practice, as each decision which applies the rules is an act of a public authority governed by s 6 HRA and therefore must uphold Convention rights (*AM v ECO Ethiopia* [2008] EWCA Civ 1082 and *Pankina*).

4.2.2 Relationship between the ECtHR and UK courts

The case law of the ECtHR is an important source for UK courts of explication of human rights law. The extent and authority of the actual influence of Strasbourg case law on UK law is however contentious, and has become a focus of intense debate.

The HRA s 2 obliges courts and tribunals to 'take into account' the judgments and opinions of the European Court of Human Rights and the other Strasbourg decision-making bodies which operate the Convention. It was the policy of the government which introduced the HRA in 1998, endorsed by Parliament, not to require that UK courts should be bound by Strasbourg decisions. However, 'taking into account' has been interpreted in different ways. Klug and Wildbore describe three approaches: the 'mirror' approach, by which the UK courts regard themselves as effectively bound by Strasbourg; the 'dynamic' approach, in which Strasbourg decisions are treated as a floor but not necessarily a ceiling; and the 'municipal' approach, in which the courts consider the Strasbourg case law, but seek to develop a domestic interpretation of Convention rights in specific circumstances. For example, Singh J suggested in *Amirthanathan* that UK courts should be moving towards 'an autonomous human rights jurisdiction by reference to principles to be found animating the Convention rather than an over-rigid approach' (para 59).

The courts regularly say, consistently with the mirror and dynamic approaches, that they should follow ECtHR case law where there is, in the words of Lord Slynn, 'a clear and constant jurisprudence' on a particular matter (*R (Alconbury Developments Ltd) v Secretary of State for the Environment* [2001] 2 WLR 1389 at para 26). Indeed, in the same passage, Lord Slynn suggested that 'in the absence of some special circumstances' that would be the proper course of action. A less liberal approach by the UK courts would invite an application to Strasbourg, and should be carefully justified (suggesting the dynamic approach). This is not to say that ECtHR decisions are always radically rights-oriented, as they are not.

In the early days of the Human Rights Act, while some judges took the approach of Singh J in *Amirthanathan,* on the whole in immigration law at least there was deference to the Strasbourg court. The application of Article 8, the right to respect for family and private life, to decisions to remove someone from the UK or refuse them leave to enter, presented particular challenges to the judiciary in calibrating their relationship both with the government and with Strasbourg. With these decisions they entered the arena, in effect, of evaluating the weight to be given to the government's implementation of immigration control, when that had the effect of breaking up or uprooting a family, or preventing them from living together.

Since 2 October 2000, UK courts have been called upon to interpret Convention rights directly for the purpose of the case before them. In doing so they become a source of authority on the interpretation of the ECHR as on any other question of law. A House of Lords or Court of Appeal decision on the meaning or application of the Convention therefore binds lower courts, whereas a decision made by the ECtHR must be taken into account.

The relationship between Strasbourg and UK case law, as used in the UK courts and tribunals, has however become far more fluid and nuanced as this new jurisdiction has developed (see evidence given by Supreme Court judges to the Joint Committee on Human Rights on 15 November 2011 HC 873-ii). In *Quila,* the Supreme Court broke new ground by expressly declining to follow *Abdulaziz v UK* (1985) 7 EHRR 471. This was not a radical departure in Article 8 case law, because the Supreme Court cited a number of cases since *Abdulaziz* which showed that the direction of ECtHR case law had changed (see chapter 9). However, the explicit departure from *Abdulaziz* demonstrated the independent growth of UK human rights jurisprudence. Lord Wilson said:

> Having duly taken account of the decision in *Abdulaziz* pursuant to section 2 of the Human Rights Act 1998, we should in my view decline to follow it. It is an old decision. There was dissent from

it even at the time. More recent decisions of the ECtHR, in particular *Boultif* and *Tuquabo-Tekle* [2006] 1 FLR 798, are inconsistent with it. There is no 'clear and consistent jurisprudence' of the ECtHR which our courts ought to follow: see *R (Alconbury Developments Ltd) v Secretary of State for the Environment, Transport and the Regions* [2001] UKHL 23, [2003] 2 AC 295 at para 26, per Lord Slynn. (para 43)

2011 saw the culmination of a dialogue between the Strasbourg court and the UK Supreme Court. The ECtHR Chamber had found that the UK's standards for determining the admissibility of hearsay evidence departed from those of Article 6 (*Al-Khawaja and Tahery v UK* (2009) 49 EHRR 1). The Supreme Court declined to follow that judgment:

The requirement to 'take into account' the Strasbourg jurisprudence will normally result in this court applying principles that are clearly established by the Strasbourg Court. There will, however, be rare occasions where this court has concerns as to whether a decision of the Strasbourg Court sufficiently appreciates or accommodates particular aspects of our domestic process. In such circumstances it is open to this court to decline to follow the Strasbourg decision, giving reasons for adopting this course. This is likely to give the Strasbourg Court the opportunity to reconsider the particular aspect of the decision that is in issue, so that there takes place what may prove to be a valuable dialogue between this court and the Strasbourg Court. This is such a case. (*Horncastle v R* [2009] UKSC 14 para 11)

The ECtHR's Grand Chamber reconsidered the domestic law (*Al-Khawaja and Tahery v UK* [2011] ECHR 2127) resulting in a judgment which found that the UK's rule on hearsay evidence had violated the Article 6 rights of the claimant where a witness did not attend due to fear, but not where the witness had died.

This dialogue between Strasbourg and national courts is endorsed by Sir Nicholas Bratza, UK judge in the ECtHR and president of the Court from November 2011. He challenges a populist view that the Strasbourg court oversteps its role, noting that in 2010 1,200 cases were lodged with the Court from the UK. 1,177 were declared inadmissible. Only 23 resulted in a judgment of the Court, and in several of these there was a finding of no violation (2011:507). He suggests, endorsing Baroness Hale, that the national courts should 'sometimes consciously leap ahead of Strasbourg'. Two cases where they have notably done that were asylum and immigration cases discussed later: *Limbuela* and *EM (Lebanon)*. He also says that 'it is right and healthy that national courts should continue to feel free to criticize Strasbourg judgments where... they have misunderstood national law or practice' (2011:512). Bratza supports the national courts' freedom to depart from Strasbourg in either direction when appropriate.

The UK government is using its present period as chair of the Council of Europe to promote reforms to the jurisdiction of the Court which would restrict the individual right of petition in the interests of efficiency and the principle of 'subsidiarity' i.e., that the national governments are the primary guarantors or rights. To date this principle has been protected by the doctrine of the margin of appreciation, most classically defined in *Handyside v UK* (1979–80) 1 EHRR 737.

Key Case

***Handyside v UK* (1979–80) 1 EHRR 737**

By reason of their direct and continuous contact with the vital forces of their countries, state authorities are in principle in a better position than the international judge to give an

> opinion on the exact content of these requirements [for the protection of morals] as well as on the 'necessity' of a 'restriction' or 'penalty' intended to meet them '...it is for the national authorities to make the initial assessment of the reality of the pressing social need implied by the notion of "necessity" in this context. Consequently, Article 10.2 leaves to the Contracting States a margin of appreciation. This margin is given to both the domestic legislator ("prescribed by law") and to the bodies, judicial amongst others, that are called upon to apply and interpret the laws in force'. (para 48)

Where the Court employs a wide margin of appreciation this means it is less willing to interfere with the acts of governments.

Conversely, as seen for instance in *Al-Skeini v UK,* 55721/07 [2011] ECHR 1093, and *A and Others v the United Kingdom,* 3455/05, [2009] ECHR 301, the Grand Chamber declined to hear an argument put forward by the government that had not been tested in the House of Lords. To do so would be inconsistent with its role as 'subsidiary to the national systems safeguarding human rights' (*Al-Skeini* para 99).

Commonly, legal reasoning uses both ECtHR and UK cases when interpreting the Convention, and this is the practice followed in this book. In the course of discussing one topic, we may move from ECtHR case law to UK case law and back again. The ECtHR is not a precedent-setting court. Nevertheless, the court does attempt to create a consistent jurisprudence, so ECtHR case law will give an indication of how the ECtHR might approach an issue. If a decision is old, and the subject matter is one in which there have been significant developments, then the decision may provide less reliable guidance as to how the court may approach a similar matter now.

4.2.3 Declarations of incompatibility

There is a unique power in the Human Rights Act to declare primary or secondary legislation incompatible with human rights. Although this does not affect the continuing force of primary legislation, it creates pressure on the government to consider amending it and report to Parliament on its reasoning. This power has been used in relation to the certificate of approval scheme which required the Secretary of State's consent to the marriage of foreign nationals. The High Court's declaration that the exemption from the scheme for Church of England marriages was incompatible with Articles 12 and 14 declaration was upheld by the Court of Appeal (*SSHD v Baiai and Trzcinska, Bigoku and Agolli and Tilki* [2007] EWCA Civ 478, discussed in more detail in chapter 9). The Home Office did not appeal this point to the House of Lords. The regime of indefinite detention imposed on foreign suspected terrorists by the Anti-terrorism, Crime and Security Act 2001, improperly presented as immigration law, was declared incompatible with Article 14 (*A v SSHD* [2004] UKHL 56).

4.3 Scope of human rights claims

Immigration, by its nature, raises questions of the scope of the human rights jurisdiction. It does so in terms of those who can make a human rights claim, and where, geographically, liability for breaches of human rights begins and ends.

4.3.1 Who may make a human rights claim?

Anyone present in the jurisdiction may make a human rights claim. There is no requirement of lawful presence. Article 1 ECHR provides that the rights and freedoms of the Convention must be secured to everyone within the state's jurisdiction. This Article was not included in the HRA, but the statute contains no exclusions of people on grounds of their status, and anyone may apply who claims that their Convention rights have been violated, 'if he would be a victim for the purposes of Article 34 of the Convention if proceedings were brought in the ECtHR' (HRA s 7). This requires that the applicant be directly affected by the act or omission in question. The effect may be actual, as, for instance, in *Berrehab v Netherlands* (1988) 11 EHRR 322, where the applicant's right to have contact with his child was interfered with by the order to remove him from the Netherlands. Alternatively, the effect may be prospective, as, for instance, in *Campbell and Cosans v UK* (1982) 4 EHRR 293 where two children attended a school which permitted corporal punishment. They themselves had not been punished in this way, but by being at the school they were at risk of being so.

Appeals against immigration decisions on the basis that the decision infringes a human right are made on the ground that the decision, or a removal consequent upon it, 'is unlawful under s 6 of the Human Rights Act 1998... as being incompatible with the appellant's Convention rights' (Nationality, Immigration and Asylum Act 2002 s 84(1)). Section 84(1) does not permit an appeal to be brought by someone else whose human rights are interfered with by an immigration decision. However, in Article 8 cases, the Article 8 rights of others cannot in practice be separated from those of the appellant. The question of whether the rights of others could be taken into account in an appeal based on family life was moot until the House of Lords judgment in *Beoku-Betts v SSHD* [2008] UKHL 39.

Key Case

***Beoku-Betts v SSHD* [2008] UKHL 39**

The appellant was a citizen of Sierra Leone who came to the UK as a student in 1997 after a coup, during which, as members of a politically active family, he and his elder brother had been subject to mock executions. His asylum claim failed, and his case continued to the House of Lords on the basis of his Article 8 claim. He had a close relationship with his family, most of whom were in the UK, and their needs and interests and the close-knit quality of the family had been treated as important by the adjudicator who had allowed the appeal. The Secretary of State objected to this approach.

The House of Lords said:

> To insist that an appeal to the Asylum and Immigration Tribunal consider only the effect upon other family members as it affects the appellant, and that a judicial review brought by other family members considers only the effect upon the appellant as it affects them, is not only artificial and impracticable. It also risks missing the central point about family life, which is that the whole is greater than the sum of its individual parts. The right to respect for the family life of one necessarily encompasses the right to respect for the family life of others, normally a spouse or minor children, with whom that family life is enjoyed. (para 4 *per* Baroness Hale)

The House held that the life of the family could be considered on an appeal based on Article 8, and the parties agreed that this principle applied to decisions of the Secretary of State, so that initial Home Office decisions must also be made with regard to the rights of other family members. These points are now settled, and earlier Tribunal decisions to the contrary effect (e.g., SS Malaysia [2004] Imm AR 153 and Kehinde* 01/TH/02688) are overruled. The application of *Beoku-Betts* is discussed in chapter 9.

Where a human rights challenge touches on a question of policy, or affects a wider group of people than just the claimant, a public interest organization may be involved in the case. Where an organization is directly affected by the action it may be joined as an interested party. Alternatively, the organization may provide expert evidence on the impact of the issue on their client group, or apply to appear as intervenors in order to argue wider points that may not be made by the parties. In appeals and judicial review, you will sometimes notice that a human rights or refugee organization appears in the title to the case. For instance in *R (on the application of Q) v SSHD* [2003] EWCA Civ 364, a challenge to withholding benefits from asylum seekers, both Liberty and the Joint Council for the Welfare of Immigrants were represented. In *Quila* the AIRE Centre, the Asian Community Action Group, Southall Black Sisters, and the Henna Foundation all intervened. The United Nations High Commissioner for Refugees sometimes intervenes in asylum cases of particular significance.

4.3.2 **Which decisions are subject to a human rights appeal?**

An appeal to the tribunal on human rights grounds can only be made against an immigration decision listed in Nationality, Immigration and Asylum Act 2002 s 82. The most significant decisions not listed are removal directions, discussed in chapter 17 and a decision to detain. In the case of an action or decision not covered by s 82, the decision-maker as a public authority is still bound by the Human Rights Act itself, but the interference with the right can only be challenged in the forum which is already available to challenge that decision (HRA s 7). In the case of a decision to detain, this is a bail hearing or judicial review. Removal directions may only be challenged by judicial review. By HRA s 8 each court in which a human rights matter is heard may only deliver the remedies that are normally within its jurisdiction. Therefore, applications under the 2002 Act are limited to the remedies which the Tribunal can normally award. It can, for instance, allow an appeal against refusal of leave to enter, but not grant damages.

Immigration officers, entry clearance officers, and Home Office officials are public authorities within the meaning of the Human Rights Act. However, some detention-related activities are now contracted to commercial bodies. For instance, private security firms run detention centres, provide escorts accompanying people being removed, and airline employees may prevent a passenger from travelling if they do not have the correct documents.

Independent contractors running detention centres take on full responsibility for detainees both in common law (*Quaquah v Group 4 Securities Ltd (No 2), The Times*, June 27 2001) and under the Human Rights Act (*R (on the application of D and K) v SSHD* [2006] EWHC 980 (Admin)). In preliminary issues determined in litigation arising from the fire at Yarl's Wood Immigration Removal Centre, the private companies running the centre were held to be carrying out public functions and to be public authorities in the context of liability for damage caused by riot (*Yarl's Wood Immigration Limited; GSL UK Limited; Creechurch Dedicated Limited v Bedfordshire Police Authority* [2009] EWCA Civ 1110). This appears consistent with the conclusion of the Parliamentary Joint Committee on Human Rights that a body functions as a public authority where there is an exercise of a 'function that has its origin in governmental responsibilities in such a way as to compel individuals to rely on that body for realisation of their Convention human rights' (JCHR report Seventh of 2003–04, The Meaning of Public Authority under the Human Rights Act HL Paper 39 HC 382 para 157).

Sometimes however a commercial company acts as a buffer between the public authority (the immigration officer) and a person affected. In *Farah v British Airways, The Independent*, 18 January 2000 the appellants were prevented from boarding an aircraft by an airline relying on an immigration officer who advised that the documents were not valid. The decision not to carry the passengers was treated as a decision taken under the terms of the contract.

Section 6(3) excludes Parliament from the definition of 'public authority', so Parliament's actions in legislating or failing to legislate are not challengeable. The inclusion of courts and tribunals as public authorities means that their decisions must uphold Convention rights.

4.3.3 Geographical scope – expulsions

Many human rights cases in the immigration and asylum context are concerned with the effect of removing a person from the country, and this includes both the damage to their life here and what may happen to them abroad. As the consequence may be experienced outside the UK, expulsions engage the question of geographical scope.

The case of *Soering v UK* (1989) 11 EHRR 439 was the first to establish that, where a state expelled a person to face treatment in breach of a Convention article, the expelling state could be held to be in breach. This is not vicarious liability for the actions of the other state, but because the expulsion itself amounts to a breach. In *Soering* a German national challenged extradition to the US state of Virginia to face the death penalty on a charge of murdering his girlfriend's parents. The threat to his life could not be challenged because Article 2, the right to life, permits the death penalty and at that time the UK had not ratified Protocol 6 which outlaws it. However, the ECtHR decided that expulsion to face the phenomenon of being on death row was a breach of Article 3 because of the inordinate delays and suspense, during which the condemned person might wait for years to know whether they would be killed or not. *Cruz Varas v Sweden* [1991] 14 EHRR 1 confirmed that expulsion itself may amount to a violation in the case of deportation as well as extradition. The principle is expressed in *Soering* as follows:

> A decision by a contracting State to expel a fugitive may give rise to an issue under Article 3, and hence engage the responsibility of that State under the Convention, where substantial grounds have been shown for believing that the person concerned, if extradited, faces a real risk of being subjected to torture or inhuman or degrading treatment or punishment in the requesting country. The establishment of such responsibility inevitably involves an assessment of conditions in the requesting country against the standards of Article 3 of the Convention. Nonetheless, there is no question of adjudicating on or establishing the responsibility of the receiving country, whether under general international law, under the Convention, or otherwise. Insofar as any liability under the Convention is or maybe incurred, it is liability incurred by the extraditing Contracting State by reason of its having taken action which has as a direct consequence the exposure of an individual to proscribed treatment. (para 91)

This phenomenon is referred to loosely as 'extra-territorial' application of the Convention right. This is a convenient shorthand as the expulsion is a breach because of what is likely to happen elsewhere.

Soering and *Cruz Varas* put the application of Article 3 to expulsions beyond doubt. By extension, it would be difficult rationally to exclude Article 2, and despite some case law to the contrary, this is now established (see account of Article 2 later in this chapter).

Soering itself seems to suggest there may be scope for extraterritorial application of Article 6, and this was applied in *Othman (Abu Qatada) v UK* application no. 8139/09 in which the ECtHR held for the first time that unfairness of a trial abroad would mean that expulsion breached Article 6 (see later in this section).

Engagement of the responsibility of the sending state has been more contentious where the feared breach abroad is of a qualified right. In *Bensaid v UK* (2001) 33 EHRR 205, the applicant failed in his challenge to removal on the ground of a feared breach of Articles 3 and 8, but the ECtHR found no obstacle to his arguing a feared breach of Article 8.

In the early days of the Human Rights Act, a number of cases, without deciding the point, assumed the possibility of extra-territorial application of qualified rights, that is, those which allow the state to interfere with the right when necessary for the protection of listed public interests. See, for instance, *Nhundu and Chiwera* 01TH00613 and *SSHD v Z, A v SSHD, M v SSHD* [2002] Imm AR 560, *Kacaj* [2002] Imm AR 213.

The question of responsibility where breaches of qualified rights are feared abroad was settled by the House of Lords in *R v Special Adjudicator ex p Ullah and Do v SSHD* [2004] UKHL 26.

Key Case

***R v Special Adjudicator ex p Ullah and Do v SSHD* [2004] UKHL 26**

Both Mr Ullah and Ms Do feared infringement of their rights to freedom of religion (Article 9), and Mr Ullah additionally freedom of expression (Article 10) and freedom of association (Article 11) on return to their countries of origin. They had each claimed asylum as they feared persecution for their religious beliefs, but their asylum claims had failed. Mr Ullah was a citizen of Pakistan and a member of the Ahmadhiya, a minority faith. Ms Do was a Roman Catholic teacher from Vietnam.

The House of Lords held that:

- theoretically, a real risk of breach of any Convention right on return may make the expulsion a breach of the UK's obligations (overturning the CA that only Article 3 could be engaged in an extra-territorial case);
- such a feared breach would need to be flagrant, or in the case of a qualified right, amount to a fundamental denial of that right in order to engage the responsibility of the UK (departing from CA in which a breach of any other right would only be so regarded if it amounted to a breach of Article 3);
- it is not the case that the Convention rights were not intended to interfere with the state's sovereign rights in relation to foreign nationals (refuting the CA's obiter comments in this respect);
- the expelling state cannot relieve itself of responsibility by saying the breach happens elsewhere. The action of expulsion takes place within the jurisdiction;
- *Soering* and *Cruz-Varas* clearly stated the law and may be followed. They are not exceptions.

On the facts, the appellants failed in their claims, but the points of principle are important. The third point refutes the argument made for the UK government in *Abdulaziz* and which did not find favour with the ECtHR in that case. Indeed, 20 years of ECtHR case law since *Abdulaziz* had proceeded on the basis that immigration decisions are subject to human rights considerations. As mentioned in the introduction to this chapter, this exclusion of foreign nationals is an argument that resurfaces in different forms. The reader may be able to see the link with arguments about deference to the executive (chapter 8), and see discussion of *Saadi v UK* in chapter 15. These are doctrines which tend to make rights connected with immigration non-justiciable.

In *R v SSHD ex p Bagdanavicius (FC) & another* [2005] UKHL 38 the House of Lords explained that the assessment of risk on return does not mean that the court is making a decision in law about that receiving country, which after all is not represented in the court. It only means there has to be an assessment of risk to the appellant (para 22).

Although the House of Lords held in *Ullah and Do* that expulsions may engage qualified rights as a result of anticipated treatment in the destination state, this is not a straightforward matter to assess. The appeals in *SSHD ex p Razgar* [2004] UKHL 27 concerned claims based on Articles 3 and 8, that the claimants would suffer deterioration in their mental health if returned to France or Germany. The House of Lords held that the right to respect for private life can be engaged by the foreseeable consequences for health or welfare of removal from the UK when removal does not violate Article 3, if the facts relied on by the appellant are sufficiently strong. The threshold is said to be a high one. Such a claim could not be successfully made simply by showing relative disadvantage in care between the sending and receiving state (para 9). Where the consequences of removal for family or private life are felt in the UK, the House of Lords called this a 'domestic' case. It is settled law that removal can engage Article 8 because of the consequences for family or private life in the UK, and this is dealt with extensively later. Where the consequences are feared abroad, they called it a 'foreign' case. The difference between these two is expressed by Baroness Hale:

> 42.... In a domestic case the state must always act in a way which is compatible with the Convention rights. There is no threshold test related to the seriousness of the violation or the importance of the right involved. Foreign cases, on the other hand, represent an exception to the general rule that a state is only responsible for what goes on within its own territory or control... the Strasbourg court has not yet explored the test for imposing this obligation in any detail. But there clearly is some additional threshold test indicating the enormity of the violation to which the person is likely to be exposed if returned.
>
> 43.... Lord Bingham also refers to a third, or hybrid category. Here 'the removal of a person from country A to country B may both violate his right to respect for private and family life in country A and also violate the same right by depriving him of family life or impeding his enjoyment of private life in country B'... On analysis, however, such cases remain domestic cases. There is no threshold test of enormity or humanitarian affront. But the right... protected by Article 8 is a qualified right, which may be interfered with if this is necessary to pursue a legitimate aim. What may happen in a foreign country is therefore relevant to the proportionality of the proposed expulsion.

Since *Razgar*, there have been comments in the Court of Appeal that all expulsion cases are foreign cases (*SV v SSHD* [2005] EWCA Civ 1683 para 13) and even, in the Tribunal, that a case was a foreign case because the appellant was not settled in the UK (*BK Serbia and Montenegro* [2005] UKIAT 00001). This view may safely be regarded as incorrect. Guidance to Home Office caseworkers refers to 'domestic' and 'foreign' cases in the terms used in *Razgar*, and the distinction and its effects as delineated by Baroness Hale must be taken to represent the current state of the law.

The latest authority on the breach of qualified rights abroad is that of *EM (Lebanon) v SSHD* [2008] UKHL 64.

Key Case

EM (Lebanon) v SSHD [2008] UKHL 64

The appellant's asylum claim failed and she faced removal with her 10-year-old child to Lebanon. The accepted evidence was that if returned to that country she would lose custody of the child to her husband who had previously attempted to remove the child to Saudi Arabia and had subjected her to extreme violence. This was because the law would automatically give custody to the father if he did not approve the mother as custodian. She claimed that removal would breach her right to respect for family life under Article 8.

The House of Lords held that where the appellant claimed a breach of qualified rights abroad, the question was whether the treatment she feared would constitute a flagrant breach so as to amount to a nullification or destruction of the very essence of the right. This was a single question, and there was no distinction between a flagrant breach and a complete denial of the right (as the Court of Appeal had suggested).

Their Lordships said that, in the absence of exceptional circumstances, an appellant could not claim entitlement to remain in the UK to escape the discriminatory effects of family law in their country of origin. However, exceptional circumstances were present here. The appellant's son had never had a personal relationship with his father. All he knew of him was as someone who had inflicted serious violence on his mother before he was born. There would be no opportunity in Lebanon for the appellant to oppose the transfer of custody. There was a close relationship between mother and son and a real risk that the mother would not be permitted any contact with her son at all. Consequently, the removal of mother and son to Lebanon would breach their Article 8 rights. The breach was flagrant because the mother would not have any opportunity to oppose the award of custody to the father.

The decision inevitably entails a reflection on Sharia law as applied in Lebanon, though Baroness Hale and Lord Bingham were careful to say that their decision was not a judgment on Sharia law. Their Lordships referred to the discriminatory nature of the system, but made no explicit finding on Article 14.

The House of Lords in *B (Algeria) v SSHD; OO (Jordan) v SSHD* [2009] UKHL 10 confirmed that the flagrant breach standard applies to the risk of violation of Articles 5 and 6 abroad. They held that Mr Othman (Abu Qatada) was unlikely to be detained without trial for the legal maximum of 50 days in Jordan, but even if he was, this was not a flagrant or fundamental breach of Article 5. The ECtHR agreed with this. However, the House of Lords held that the risk that evidence used against him in trial had been obtained by torture did not amount to a flagrant or fundamental breach of Article 6. Here the ECtHR disagreed. The Court considered that the use at trial of evidence obtained by torture would amount to a flagrant denial of justice (*Othman v UK* para 263). The Court did not consider it necessary to determine whether a flagrant denial of justice only arose when the trial would have serious consequences for the applicant (para 262). The central issue was the use of evidence obtained by torture.

4.3.4 Geographical scope – entry decisions

The other main question concerning geographical scope is the application of human rights when the applicant is outside the UK. This is a trickier question in legal theory than in expulsion cases, though in practice it is often treated as much simpler.

The description of immigration control in chapter 7 shows that whether someone is outside the UK or not when they apply for leave to enter is in part a matter of factual accident. When an application for leave to enter is made in the UK, there is no doubt that the Human Rights Act applies. When the applicant is abroad, does their location make a difference? As chapter 7 shows, decisions on leave to enter may now be made anywhere in the world. The Court of Appeal in *Naik v SSHD* [2011] EWCA Civ 1546 remarked that:

> It is difficult to see any logic in treating an applicant less favourably because he takes the sensible course of applying for entry clearance from abroad, rather than simply arriving at border control at Heathrow. (para 31)

The argument against human rights applying to entry clearance cases is that these decisions are taken outside the jurisdiction. For ECHR purposes the jurisdiction is primarily territorial, but there are exceptions including the acts of a consular official (e.g., *Bankovic v Belgium* (2001) 11 BHRC 435). The question is whether entry clearance officers and their decisions come within this consular exception. The closest authority in terms of facts is *R (on the application of B) v Secretary of State for Foreign and Commonwealth Affairs* [2004] EWCA Civ 1344, where the Court of Appeal considered a wealth of ECtHR authorities, none conclusive, on the question of whether the Convention applied to the actions of consular officials who gave temporary protection to asylum seekers in Australia. Being unable to reach a concluded view, the court was content to assume that the applicants were sufficiently within the jurisdiction of the UK.

Much of the growing case law on the jurisdictional reach of the ECHR outside the respondent state derives from conflict situations and does not translate directly to entry clearance. The leading case now on this question is *Al-Skeini v UK*. There was no factual dispute in that it was accepted that the relatives of the six claimants had died at the hands of the British forces. The government had already accepted, following a House of Lords ruling to this effect, that the UK could be liable under the HRA for the death in UK military custody of Baha Mousa. The question brought before the Court was whether the actions of the troops in the streets of Basra fell within the UK's jurisdiction so as to be actionable under the HRA or ECHR, and if so, whether the UK had breached Article 2 by not conducting an independent investigation into the other deaths. The Court held that 'the exercise of physical power and control over the person in question' was decisive in establishing extra-territorial jurisdiction (para 136). Applying this, they held that the UK had assumed in Iraq the exercise of some public powers normally exercised by a sovereign government:

> In particular, the United Kingdom assumed authority and responsibility for the maintenance of security in South East Iraq. In these exceptional circumstances, the Court considers that the United Kingdom, through its soldiers engaged in security operations in Basrah during the period in question, exercised authority and control over individuals killed in the course of such security operations, so as to establish a jurisdictional link between the deceased and the United Kingdom for the purposes of Article 1 of the Convention. (para 149)

In practice, Article 8 is treated as applying in entry cases. For instance, the House of Lords in *Chikwamba v SSHD* [2008] UKHL 40 (discussed later in the chapter) based their decision on the expectation that if the appellant were required to leave the UK and apply for entry clearance to join her spouse, she would have a right of appeal under Article 8 against a refusal. They pointed to the duty of entry clearance officers in the immigration rules to act in accordance with human rights.

The Court of Appeal in *Farrakhan* (see later in relation to Article 10) held that Article 10 was engaged in an immigration decision made abroad because the Secretary of State had refused entry partly in order to prevent Mr Farrakhan from exercising freedom of expression. However, the Court had accepted the Secretary of State's concession that the fact that the appellant was outside the UK did not affect his right to a human rights appeal. The Court of Appeal in *Naik v SSHD* [2011] EWCA Civ 1546 also found that this question did not arise for decision as the Court accepted the judge's finding that those who would have wanted to hear Dr Naik speak had the right under Article 10 to hear his words, though the interference with that right was justified. Thus Article 10 was engaged, applying Article 10 collectively, much as *Beoku-Betts* applies Article 8. The result seems to be that whether a Convention right is engaged by a decision on entry is a question of fact in each case.

The direction of the case law both in Strasbourg and the UK is to minimize any difference between the application of Article 8 to entry and removal decisions. In *Tuquabo-Tekle v Netherlands* the Netherlands government attempted to raise a late objection to the admissibility of the application on the basis that the applicant for a residence permit was outside the territory, and the 'day-to-day responsibility for the regulation and control of the entry of aliens' was not an exception to the primarily territorial jurisdiction of the ECtHR. The Court did not allow the point to be argued, as the case had already been accepted as admissible. In the UK, in *T (s.55 BCIA 2009 – entry clearance) Jamaica* [2011] UKUT 00483(IAC) the tribunal cited without remark *Tuquabo-Tekle* and other cases in the context of applying Article 8 to an entry decision, simply to show that the Strasbourg court also applied Article 3 of the UN Convention on the Rights of the Child to all administrative decision-making. The application of Article 8 was uncontroversial.

Refusal of entry clearance may be appealed on human rights grounds according to Nationality, Immigration and Asylum Act 2002 ss 82 and 84, and the suggestion of the Tribunal that this was a mistake by Parliament (*Rev Sun Myung Moon v ECO Seoul* [2005] UKIAT 00112 para 56) must now be regarded as mistaken. However, the attempt of the Netherlands government in *Tuquabo-Tekle* to argue that immigration decisions taken abroad do not engage Convention rights might suggest that there will still be a case in the ECtHR which will consider the application of *Al-Skeini* to entry clearance posts.

4.4 Convention rights – Article 3

Not all the Convention rights will be examined in detail here. This section will concentrate on those rights which are most commonly encountered in the immigration and asylum contexts.

4.4.1 Treatment contrary to Article 3

Article 3 provides that:

No-one shall be subjected to torture or inhuman or degrading treatment or punishment.

In relation to persecution, Goodwin-Gill and Macadam say that it is 'a concept only too readily filled by the latest examples of one person's inhumanity to another, and little purpose is served by attempting to list all its known measures' (2007:93–4). The same could be said of treatment that contravenes Article 3. Cross-reference may be made here to discussion of 'severe harm' in the refugee definition discussed in chapter 13, and no catalogue of violations is attempted in either chapter. Other common questions are the degree of risk, whether the treatment can be justified (is the protection absolute?), and the parameters around contentious areas such as denial of welfare support or medical treatment. Treatment that falls short of torture may still be inhuman or degrading treatment but it must pass a certain threshold of severity in order to come within Article 3. The Convention moves with the times, and in *Selmouni v France* (1999) 29 EHRR 403 the ECtHR held that the interrogation techniques (hooding, exposure to noise, deprivation of food and drink, deprivation of sleep, and enforced standing against a wall) found to be degrading and inhuman in *Ireland v UK* (1978) 2 EHRR 25 would now be found to be torture. This is the case, even if some local public opinion lags behind. In the case of *Tyrer v UK* birching a schoolboy on the Isle of Man was held to be a violation of Article 3, as this form of punishment, once considered acceptable, was now generally regarded as degrading. The court's conclusion was not affected by evidence of belief by the public on the Isle of Man in the deterrent effect of such treatment. This is a necessary consequence of the absolute nature of the Article. The police force cannot, for instance, say that such treatment is necessary to extract a confession.

Whether treatment is degrading will depend on the circumstances of the individual. Adverse treatment on grounds of race may amount to degrading treatment if it is institutionalized, as in the *East African Asians cases* (1981) 3 EHRR 76. Here, the European Commission on Human Rights found that the refusal of entry to the UK to the British passport holders resident in Uganda, Tanzania, and Kenya (discussed in chapter 3) amounted to institutionalized racism. Such consistent adverse treatment of people on account of their race was degrading, and passed the threshold of severity to amount to a violation of Article 3.

A breach of Article 3 normally requires actual or threatened physical or psychological ill-treatment which is deliberately applied. In *Q and M* [2003] EWCA Civ 364, there was argument as to what might constitute treatment. The Court of Appeal found:

> The imposition by the legislature of a regime which prohibits asylum seekers from working and further prohibits the grant to them, when they are destitute, of support amounts to positive action directed against asylum seekers and not to mere inaction. (para 57)

The denial of benefits was therefore 'treatment' for the purposes of Article 3, and this was endorsed by the House of Lords in *R v SSHD ex p Adam, Limbuela and Tesema* [2005] UKHL 66. If the asylum seeker has, by some other means, for instance friends or a charity, obtained shelter, sanitary facilities, and some money for food, the denial of benefit does not reach the threshold to be regarded as degrading (*R (on the application of S, D, T) v SSHD* [2003] EWHC 1951 (Admin)). The House of Lords' judgment in *Adam, Limbuela and Tesema* explores individual circumstances to assess whether the threshold for a breach of Article 3 has been reached: 'section 55 asylum-seekers...are not only forced to sleep rough but are not allowed to work to earn money and have no access to financial support by the state. The rough sleeping which they are forced to endure cannot be detached from the degradation and humiliation that results from the circumstances that give rise to it' (Lord Hope, para 60). This application of Article 3 to the imposition of absolute destitution on asylum seekers is confirmed by the ECtHR's judgment in *MSS v Belgium and Greece*. The Court held that in the light of the particular vulnerability of destitute asylum seekers, and their absolute dependency on the host state for their material needs, the conditions in which MSS lived were in breach of Article 3. He had no accommodation, and no regular source of food or shelter. He slept in a park.

Reference may be made to human rights literature to pursue further the question of whether Article 3 contains both positive and negative obligations. The positive duty to investigate alleged breaches may occasionally be relevant in immigration and asylum matters. It was held to extend to alleged breaches of Article 3 in the administration of a detention centre in the UK (*R (on the application of AM) v SSHD and Kalyx, BID intervening* [2009] EWCA Civ 219).

One of the difficult issues where individuals rely on Article 3 to oppose their removal is the question of whether removal can be opposed on the basis of conditions that are general, not particular to the applicant. For instance, in *N (Burundi)* [2003] UKIAT 00065, the Tribunal rejected the argument of the claimant that the ravages of civil war in her country were such that it would be inhuman to return her. In this respect the judgment of the ECtHR in *Sufi and Elmi v UK* represents a new development.

Key Case

***Sufi and Elmi v UK* 8319/07 [2011] ECHR 1045**

The Court found, in applications made by refused asylum seekers against their removal to Somalia, that 'the violence in Mogadishu is of such a level of intensity that anyone in the city, except possibly those who are exceptionally well-connected to "powerful actors", would be at real risk of treatment prohibited by Article 3' (para 250). In relation to risks in other parts of the country the Court made detailed findings, including for instance that an applicant might not be at risk in parts of central and southern Somalia if they had close family who could protect them. In regions controlled by Al-Shabaab, or in the camps for internally displaced people, a returnee would be at risk of treatment contrary to Article 3.

The court's detailed engagement with the risks in different parts of a war-torn country demonstrates the demands that are now being made of human rights law. The majority of asylum claimants in the UK come from countries where there is ongoing conflict. Returning unsuccessful claimants to such countries may raise issues under Article 15(C) of the Refugee Qualification Directive (see chapter 13), and under Article 3 ECHR.

4.4.2 Inadequate medical treatment and Article 3

Where there is torture or other severe physical or psychological ill-treatment, there is little doubt that the treatment will cross the high threshold necessary to amount to a breach of Article 3. Other kinds of ill treatment are more controversial. The case of *D v UK* (1997) 24 EHRR 423 broke new ground in this respect, although it has generally been distinguished in subsequent cases where applicants have sought to rely on it. The Secretary of State sought to deport D after he had served a long prison sentence for supplying prohibited drugs. He was by this time in an advanced stage of AIDS. He was receiving terminal care in a hospice. The treatment he had been receiving had slowed down the progress of the disease and relieved his symptoms, and he was receiving support as he faced death. His life expectancy was short in any event, but if he was deported to St. Kitts the treatment upon which he depended would not be available at all, and he had no family or social network to support him. The end of his life would be marked by much greater suffering. The ECtHR held that to return him in these circumstances would breach Article 3.

In *Bensaid v UK* (2001) 33 EHRR 205, the applicant was suffering from schizophrenia, and argued both that the upheaval would aggravate his condition, and that suitable treatment would not be available in Algeria. He failed on the second point. In rare cases there is scope for arguments under Article 8 in relation to loss of medical care, as indicated in *Razgar* and discussed further later in the chapter.

The leading case in relation to medical care is that of *N v SSHD [2005] UKHL 31.*

Key Case

***N v SSHD* [2005] UKHL 31**

N was an AIDS sufferer facing deportation to Uganda. In the UK, where she had been living for five years, her condition had stabilized on medication. This medication would not be available to her in Uganda. Her brothers and sisters had died of AIDS and her life expectancy would be reduced to a year or two. The House of Lords unanimously and carefully distinguished *D v UK.* It held that in *D*, the removal was a breach of Article 3 because it would mean that his death, which was imminent, would take place in far more distressing circumstances. Here, death was not imminent, although their Lordships acknowledged there could be no real difference in humanitarian terms between removing someone to face imminent death and removing someone to face death within a year or two. The difference came in that the Convention could not be taken to have imposed upon the parties an obligation to provide medical treatment. Lord Brown identified *D* as concerning a negative obligation – not to deport D to 'an imminent, lonely and distressing end' (*N v SSHD* [2005] UKHL 31 para 93). *N*, he thought, concerned a positive obligation – to provide N with medical treatment. Not to allow N to remain but not give her medical care would not answer her needs.

All their Lordships expressed strong sympathy with N, and distaste for having to make this decision. Lord Brown came very close to suggesting that the Secretary of State should exercise discretion to let N stay (para 99). In the end, social policy considerations had to be overt in order to make sense of this case. Lord Nicholls and others acknowledged 'If the appellant were a special case I have no doubt that, in one way or another, the pressing humanitarian considerations of her case would prevail'. However, given the prevalence of AIDS in Africa in particular and the shortage of treatment, her case was 'far from unique' (para 9). Their Lordships saw the issue as being outside their capacity to resolve. The problem arose from 'Uganda's lack of medical resources compared with those available in the UK' (para 8) and the better answer than migration and human rights claims was, in the words of Lord Hope, 'for states to continue to concentrate their efforts on the steps which are currently being taken, with the assistance of the drugs companies, to make the necessary medical care universally and freely available' (para 53).

The ECtHR by a majority of 14 to 3 confirmed the House of Lords decision (*N v UK* (2008) 47 EHRR 885). They considered that Article 3 usually only applied to intentional acts or omissions of a state or non-state body. In medical cases, Article 3 applied only in very exceptional circumstances. The Convention was essentially directed to the protection of civil and political rights, and a fair balance between the interests of the community and the rights of the individual was inherent in the Convention. Article 3 could not be relied upon to address the disparity in medical care between contracting states and an applicant's state of origin.

The court in *N v UK* applied Article 3 in a very different way from that used when the risk on return is a risk of torture, arguably treating Article 3 more like a qualified right. In reported cases at least, it remains, following *N*, extremely difficult for anyone to resist removal on health grounds using Article 3. In *GS (Article 3 –exceptionality) India* [2011] UKUT 35 (IAC) the appellant had only one kidney, and was dependent on dialysis every two or three days for his survival. The Secretary of State decided to remove him. In India the nearest hospital to his home which could provide dialysis was 300 kilometres away, and GS had no means to pay for that treatment or support himself near the hospital. Without dialysis he would die within a week or two. The Upper Tribunal upheld his removal, relying on *N*. In *CA v SSHD* [2004] EWCA Civ 1165 the appellant was HIV positive, and the adjudicator found that she would not necessarily lack the requisite treatment on return to Ghana. However, her baby, who at the time of the hearing had not yet been born, would have little chance of staying well as he or she could not be breastfed, and dried formula milk would be mixed with unsafe water. There was a reasonable likelihood that the baby would die, therefore it was a breach of Article 3 to return the mother. Laws LJ, giving the leading judgment, said 'It seems to me obvious simply as a matter of common humanity that for a mother to witness the collapse of her new-born child's health and perhaps its death may be a kind of suffering far greater than might arise by the mother's confronting the self-same fate herself'. *DM (Zambia) v SSHD* [2009] EWCA Civ 474 shows that, following *Razgar*, Article 8 may also be argued on facts of this kind, although it was unsuccessful in that case as evidence suggested that the appellant would have access to support, resources, and medication beyond that often available to a person in Zambia.

A risk of suicide is also dealt with in the context of Articles 3 and 8. In *J v SSHD* [2005] EWCA Civ 629, the Court of Appeal said that, in a case where there is a real risk that the appellant will take their life if they are returned to their home country, relevant questions for the court include whether there is a causal link between the removal and the risk of suicide, and whether the applicant's fear of ill-treatment is objectively well founded. An Article 3 claim could in principle succeed in a suicide case, but the threshold would be high because it is a 'foreign' case (i.e., the feared risk would materialize abroad) and higher still because the harm feared would not be directly caused by the authorities but as a result of an illness (following *D v UK* and *Bensaid v UK*). Finally, the decision-maker must assess 'whether the removing and/or the receiving state has effective mechanisms to reduce the risk of suicide' (para 31).

Key Case

***Y and Z (Sri Lanka) v SSHD* [2009] EWCA Civ 362**

The appellants, who were brother and sister, were Sri Lankan Tamils. They had been tortured by the Sri Lankan security forces as suspected LTTE members or sympathizers, both had been raped in captivity, and suffered from post-traumatic stress disorder and depression. The second appellant's husband and daughter were killed by the security forces. Two cousins had been executed by the security forces, and their mother (the appellants' aunt) had starved herself to death in a public protest.

Their asylum claim in the UK failed because it was found that, although they had suffered such serious violations, there was no real risk of repetition. After their arrival in the UK, 50 members of their extended family were killed in the 2004 tsunami. The appellants claimed to be at risk of suicide if they were returned.

Sedley LJ in the Court of Appeal said that, in applying *J*, in relation to suicide, what mattered was whether there was a real and overwhelming fear, not whether it was well-founded. Where there was considered to be no objective risk to the asylum seeker on return, but the individual was said to be at risk of suicide if returned, it was right to scrutinize the claim with care. But there came a point at which an undisturbed finding that an appellant had been tortured and raped in captivity had to be conscientiously related to credible and uncontradicted expert evidence that the likely effect of the psychological trauma, if return was enforced, would be suicide. In such a case, return was a breach of Article 3.

In *J*, the court had at first characterized the risk of suicide as the result of a naturally occurring illness, thereby bringing the case into a similar category to *N v UK*. However, in *Y & Z* the Court of Appeal said that the anticipated self-harm would be the consequence of the acts of the Sri Lankan security forces, not of a naturally occurring illness. It would be the product of fear and humiliation brought about by the brutality to which both appellants had been subjected before they fled.

Rory Dunlop questions this analysis on the basis of inconsistency with *N v UK*. He says that N claimed that her HIV infection resulted from rape by security forces, but that this was not pursued by the courts. Dunlop concludes that the reason for this is that the cause of illness is irrelevant.

4.4.3 Absolute right under challenge

Article 3 confers an absolute right, the breach of which cannot be justified by any interest of the state. Despite the arguments used in the medical cases discussed earlier, this is a settled principle of law, and the ECtHR confirmed in *Chahal v UK* (1996) 23 EHRR 413 that this means that even a person who may be a danger to national security cannot be expelled to face torture. This simple assertion, confirmed in *N v Finland* (2005) 43 EHRR 12, has become the focal point of an international debate, in which states bent on defeating terrorism seek ways to circumvent the absolute nature of this prohibition.

In the UK, both the government and the Opposition have talked of withdrawing from the whole European Convention, and then re-ratifying without Article 3 (e.g., British Prime Minister on television's 'Frost Programme' on 26 January 2003). Legal opinion, unsurprisingly, was that 'it is strongly arguable that the ECHR does not permit a contracting state to use the power of denunciation... as a device to secure a reservation which could not otherwise validly be made, and therefore the proposal floated by the Prime Minister would be invalid and unlawful' (29 January 2003, Blackstone Chambers, D. Pannick and S. Fatima, for Liberty). This call became, for the Coalition government which took power in 2010, a proposal for a 'British bill of rights'. A Commission was set up to consider this proposal and consult. Consultation responses have largely been to the effect that the Human Rights Act already fulfils the need, and any amendment should be in the direction of adding for instance economic and social rights.

The government attempts to avoid the absolute protection of Article 3 also by intervening in challenges in the ECtHR, for instance, *Saadi v Italy* [2008] ECHR 179.

Key Case

Saadi v Italy **[2008] ECHR 179**

Italy wanted to deport the applicant to Tunisia where he would face a risk of torture. The Italian government gave evidence that he was a risk to national security. The UK intervened to support the Italian government's argument that an expelling state should be able to balance the risk to its society against the risk to the deportee. The ECtHR disagreed. The Court held unanimously that the protection of Article 3 against torture was absolute and fundamental in a democratic society. The fact that the feared ill-treatment would take place abroad did not prevent the responsibility of the contracting state from being engaged nor did it affect the standard of proof. In attempting to deal with the threat of terrorism, states were not permitted to weigh any threat to the security of the host state against the risk of torture in the destination state. These two risks were of different kinds.

The absolute nature of the prohibition on returning someone to a risk of torture was energetically reasserted by the ECtHR in *Saadi v Italy*, and subsequent decisions in the ECtHR have followed that judgment.

Where removal is blocked by human rights law, the UK government has sought other measures to keep people out of circulation and obviate the risk they are thought to pose to national security where there is insufficient evidence to bring criminal charges:

- indefinite detention without trial – found unlawful by the House of Lords in *A v UK* [2004] UKHL 56;
- control orders – many in force and accepted as lawful, but the most extreme conditions approximating to house arrest in solitary confinement found unlawful by the House of Lords in *SSHD v MB* [2007] UKHL 46; and
- deprivation of any immigration status and associated civil rights (Criminal Justice and Immigration Act 2008).

Meanwhile, there is a possibility (sometimes a probability, e.g., C. Murray, speech at Chatham House, 8 November 2004) that evidence of the risk they are thought to pose to national security may have been obtained by torture, ruled unacceptable by the ECtHR in the case of *Othman (Abu Qatada) v UK*. As evidence obtained by torture may be unreliable, some of the people upon whom these measures are imposed may be no risk at all. As national security cases are heard by the Special Immigration Appeals Commission those accused may also not be able to test the evidence against them (see chapters 8 and 16).

4.4.3.1 *Memoranda of understanding (MOU)*

In addition to restrictive measures within the UK, the government has sought other ways to effect returns. One is to obtain assurances from receiving governments that returnees will not be subject to torture. Memoranda of understanding (MOU) that returnees will not be tortured have been signed with countries including Ethiopia, Jordan, Libya, and Lebanon. The reliability of assurances has been seriously doubted (see Human Rights Watch 2005 and Amnesty International 2007 and 2010). The courts have maintained the position that it is for them to determine 'the factual question of whether an individual faces a substantial risk of torture on his return, and in reaching that decision the courts will properly take into account the assurances given as part of all the relevant evidence, including evidence about the likelihood of those assurances being delivered in practice' (Counter-Terrorism Policy and Human Rights Joint Committee on Human Rights Third Report of sessions 2005–06 HL 75–I, HC 561–I para 145).

Thus, the means and standard of evaluation of the reliability of assurances is said not to be a question of law, but rather one of assessing evidence to draw a conclusion of fact (see, e.g., *BB v SSHD* [2006] UKSIAC 39/2005 para 4, confirmed in *RB, U and OO v SSHD* [2009] UKHL). The Special Immigration Appeals Commission said that the following conditions should be fulfilled for assurances to be adequate:

(i) the terms of the assurances must be such that, if they are fulfilled, the person returned will not be subjected to treatment contrary to Article 3;

(ii) the assurances must be given in good faith;

(iii) there must be a sound objective basis for believing that the assurances will be fulfilled;

(iv) fulfilment of the assurances must be capable of being verified.

BB concerned return to Algeria. The same case, joined with that of another Algerian and that of Mr Othman who was to be returned to Jordan, reached the House of Lords. One of the issues in the Lords was that the appellants wanted to challenge SIAC's assessment of the reliability of the memoranda of understanding, or assurances. However, the House of Lords held that this could only be challenged before them if SIAC had made its decision unreasonably, i.e., if its decision would be susceptible to challenge in judicial review. Their Lordships held that there was nothing in SIAC's assessment of the reliability of the memoranda of understanding which suggested an error of that kind (see chapter 8 for further discussion). Lord Phillips said that the ECtHR cases did not establish that assurances must eliminate all risk of inhuman treatment before they could be relied upon.

In *AS & DD (Libya) v SSHD*, Liberty intervening [2008] EWCA Civ 289, SIAC had found that Libya signed the MOU in good faith, but assurances would be honoured when Colonel Qadhafi or his regime considered it was in their interests to do so. Colonel Qadhafi's assessment of his interests was unpredictable, and, based on past conduct, he might at times act in ways that the outside world thought damaged his long-term interests, but which he would assess according to a different priority. The Court of Appeal approved this approach by SIAC, and the assurances were held not to give sufficient protection. Accordingly, deportation to Libya risked breaching Article 3.

Metcalfe is highly critical of SIAC's assessment in the cases that became *RB, U and OO* in the House of Lords. As he points out, MOU only become an issue in a country in which torture has already taken place in breach of international agreements, so an assurance of adherence to international agreements is not *prima facie* a new protective step. He also considers that SIAC showed little awareness of the difficulties involved in detecting torture and ill-treatment, and minimized the need for scrutiny and redress.

The ECtHR has taken a similar approach in that it has decided each case of MOU on its merits. *Saadi v Italy* was itself a case of assurances, in which the ECtHR said that even if the Tunisian government had provided more detailed assurances,

> that would not have absolved the Court from the obligation to examine whether such assurances provided, in their practical application, a sufficient guarantee that the applicant would be protected against the risk of treatment prohibited by the Convention. The weight to be given to assurances from the receiving State depends, in each case, on the circumstances obtaining at the material time. (para 148)

This fairly robust approach to assurances was maintained in another case against Italy and three against Russia in the following two years; in each case the ECtHR found diplomatic assurances insufficient. The foundational case in affirming the absolute nature of Article 3, *Chahal v UK*, was also a case of assurances which the Court found unconvincing. Against the trend, in *Mamatkulov v Turkey* [2005] 41 EHHR 25, the Court decided that assurances by Uzbekistan were sufficient to prevent Turkey from being in breach by returning the applicant, and the assurances of Jordan, which were given at a very high level and specifically in relation to Mr Othman (Abu Qatada), were held to be sufficient protection for him against torture (*Othman (Abu Qatada) v UK*).

The UK's practice of sending people back to countries with proven records of torture on the basis of diplomatic assurances was strongly criticized by Thomas Hammarberg, the Commissioner for Human Rights of the Council of Europe, in a report following his visit to the UK in 2008 (CommDH(2008)23 Strasbourg, 18 September 2008). In the Amnesty International report *Dangerous Deals*, the UK is described as 'the most influential and aggressive promoter in Europe of the use of diplomatic assurances to forcibly return people it considers threats to national security to countries where they would face a real risk of serious human rights violations' (2010:27). The report says that the UK has relied on post-return monitoring arrangements to strengthen the assurances. However, the reality of post-return monitoring is described by the report as inadequate (and in an Ethiopian case was found to be so – see *XX v SSHD* [2010] UKSIAC 61/2007). Detainees are not visited in conditions where they may remain anonymous. The fear of reprisals is therefore a major constraint. The monitoring bodies have no powers of enforcement.

The House of Lords in *RB* held that effective verification was essential for assurances to be protective. Verification could be achieved by means, formal and informal, of which monitoring was only one. Other means could include contact by the British Embassy and investigation by Amnesty International and other non-governmental agencies.

4.4.3.2 *Evidence obtained by torture*

The absolute nature of Article 3 is undermined when evidence is accepted which has been obtained by torture. In no case would evidence obtained by torture within the UK be admissible (*A v SSHD* [2005] UKHL 71), but the question of admitting evidence which may have been obtained by torture abroad may arise in national security cases, in which the evidence that a person poses a risk to national security may have been obtained through intelligence and may then found their deportation or exclusion. It may also arise in exclusion from refugee status on account of acts said to have been committed abroad (*Al-Sirri v SSHD* [2009] EWCA Civ 222).

In *A and others v SSHD* [2005] UKHL 71, a committee of seven Law Lords unanimously rejected the Secretary of State's argument that evidence which might have been obtained by torture could, as a matter of law, be admitted before the Special Immigration Appeals Commission. The judgment is a complex one, and the distinctions between the majority and minority views are not easy to follow – as Lord Brown expresses (para 173). The majority (Lords Brown, Rodger and Hope) considered that SIAC should refuse to admit the evidence if it concluded, on a balance of probabilities, that the evidence *was* obtained by torture. Lords Bingham and Hoffmann thought that evidence should be excluded if there was a *real risk* that it had been obtained by torture, probably meaning that it should be excluded if SIAC was not satisfied that evidence had not been obtained by torture. In *RB, U & OO*, the House of Lords held that no higher standard than that which applied in SIAC could be applied to the risk of Mr Othman being convicted abroad in a trial in which evidence might have been obtained by torture. This was the issue on which the ECtHR disagreed with the national Court. The Strasbourg Court found that:

- admitting evidence obtained by torture would only serve to legitimate indirectly the sort of morally reprehensible conduct which the authors of Article 3 of the Convention sought to proscribe;
- torture evidence is excluded because it is 'unreliable, unfair, offensive to ordinary standards of humanity and decency and incompatible with the principles which should animate a tribunal seeking to administer justice' (quoting Lord Bingham in *A and others*);
- fundamentally, no legal system based upon the rule of law can countenance the admission of evidence – however reliable – which has been obtained by such a barbaric practice as torture. The trial process is a cornerstone of the rule of law. Torture evidence damages irreparably that process; it substitutes force for the rule of law and taints the reputation of any court that admits it. Torture evidence is

excluded to protect the integrity of the trial process and, ultimately, the rule of law itself (para 264).

The Court affirmed the 'Court of Appeal's view that there is a crucial difference between a breach of Article 6 because of the admission of torture evidence and breaches of Article 6 that are based simply on defects in the trial process or in the composition of the trial court' (para 265).

In *Al-Sirri v SSHD* [2009] EWCA Civ 222, the Court of Appeal held that it was wrong to admit evidence which had probably been obtained by torture. This was in the context of a decision to exclude the appellant from refugee status on the grounds of convictions obtained abroad.

In an interim report to the UN General Assembly on 1 September 2004, the UN Special Rapporteur on Torture criticized attempts by governments to circumvent the absolute nature of the prohibition on torture and other inhuman treatment on the ground of combating terrorism. The UN General Assembly in November 2011 repeated its stand against torture, passing a resolution which included condemnation of

> any action or attempt by States or public officials to legalize, authorize or acquiesce in torture and other cruel, inhuman or degrading treatment or punishment under any circumstances, including on grounds of national security or through judicial decisions.

The resolution urged states not to expel a person to another state 'where there are substantial grounds for believing that the person would be in danger of being subjected to torture, and recognized that 'diplomatic assurances, where used, do not release States from their obligations under international human rights, humanitarian and refugee law, in particular the principle of non-refoulement' (doc. A/C.3/66/L.28/Rev.1). The ECtHR's judgment in *Othman (Abu Qatada)* now strongly reinforces that resolution.

In the course of increased international cooperation against terrorism, there were allegations that the UK had been complicit in torture abroad of people in whom it has an interest, even including its own citizens. The Detainee Inquiry has been launched to investigate these allegations, though there have been criticisms of its powers and remit (see, e.g., BBC News UK 'Torture Inquiry: UN's Juan Mendez calls for openness' 13 November 2011). The Parliamentary Joint Committee on Human Rights has remained very concerned about this issue, and has questioned the government on it in its now regular reports on national security, counter-terrorism, and human rights. See for instance JCHR 17th report of session 2009–2010 HL 86 HC 111.

4.4.3.3 *Extraordinary rendition*

The practice of 'extraordinary rendition' is that of transporting people to extra-territorial locations for interrogation 'in circumstances that make it more likely than not that the individual will be subjected to torture or cruel, inhuman or degrading treatment' (All Party Parliamentary Group on Extraordinary Rendition, December 2005). These locations include US bases and countries known for their record of torture (Amnesty International 2005:4). The All Party Parliamentary Group on Extraordinary Rendition has engaged in litigation and Freedom of Information requests, and has succeeded in obtaining disclosure of the MOU between the UK and US concerning the 'transfer of captured persons in Iraq'. The group has challenged the secrecy surrounding these practices and the denial by the UK government that it has had any role in the US' extraordinary rendition programme. The Council of Europe's Committee for the Prevention of Torture in its 17th report in September 2007 concluded: 'in the light of information now in the public domain, there can be little doubt that the interrogation techniques applied in the CIA-run facilities concerned have led to violations of the prohibition of torture and inhuman or degrading treatment'.

There was a breakthrough in December 2011 when the Court of Appeal granted an application for a writ of habeas corpus in relation to a Pakistani national who had been captured by UK forces in Iraq, handed over to US forces, and detained for seven years in Bagram in Afghanistan (*Rahmatullah v Secretary of State for the Foreign and Commonwealth Affairs and the Ministry of Defence* [2011] EWCA Civ 1540). The Court accepted that, under the MOU and the Geneva Conventions, the UK had sufficient control of Mr Rahmatullah that the UK government was able to make a request of the US government to release Mr Rahmatullah. Initially the UK government had denied that Mr Rahmatullah was detained. A US tribunal had found in 2010 that he was not an enduring security threat, but he remained in detention.

This decision, the Court of Appeal said, was not inconsistent with *Abbassi* [2002] EWCA Civ 1598 and *Al-Rawi* [2008] QB 289, in which the Court had refused, in judicial review, to make an order that the Foreign and Commonwealth office use its diplomatic powers in relation to detainees in Guantanamo Bay. The basis of the successful habeas corpus application was that Mr Rahmatullah was within the control of the UK. To require the government to require his release was not trespassing on the forbidden area of foreign relations.

Finally, the Danish government in 2007 launched an initiative to establish a new basis of international cooperation in the handling of detainees in military operations. This so-called Copenhagen process, involving 28 governments, aims to address the new legal and practical difficulties experienced by troops in international military situations, in particular in Afghanistan and Iraq. The Copenhagen process has been criticized by groups including Amnesty International, who are concerned that agreements reached will undercut existing protections for detainees and will rely heavily on the device with which we began this discussion: diplomatic assurances.

A risk of extraordinary rendition can be viewed as a kind of *refoulement*. For instance, an applicant in *Ahmad, Aswat, Ahsan and Mustafa v UK* Application nos 24027/07, 11949/08 and 36742/08 attempted to resist extradition to the US on the basis that he feared extraordinary rendition – i.e., that he would be taken out of the jurisdiction in order to be treated in a way that he could not lawfully be treated within it.

4.4.4 Relationship with asylum claims

There is a substantial overlap between the treatment which might form the substance of an asylum claim and treatment which would breach Article 3. The majority of Article 3 claims are thus from people whose asylum claim has failed or are made concurrently with an asylum claim. The case of *Kacaj* established that the standard of proof is the same for a refugee claim and for a human rights claim. The standard to be applied is to enquire whether there is a real risk of the feared treatment occurring. This was further explained by Sedley LJ in *Batayav v SSHD* [2003] EWCA Civ 1489: 'If a type of car has a defect which causes one vehicle in ten to crash, most people would say that it presents a real risk to anyone who drives it, albeit crashes are not generally or consistently happening' (para 38).

Kacaj also established that the approach in the asylum case of *Horvath v SSHD* [2000] 3 WLR 370 to the question of state protection applies in Article 3 cases. In that case, the Roma applicant had been subjected to attacks by skinheads, and the case in the House of Lords turned on whether the system of criminal law in Slovakia gave him adequate protection. It was held that where there is a system of criminal law which makes violent attacks punishable, and a reasonable willingness by the enforcement agencies to enforce that law, then the state is held to protect its citizens sufficiently. Therefore, when treatment contrary to Article 3 is feared from people who are not part of the state machinery themselves, if there is such a system in place there will be no sustainable claim under Article 3.

The ECtHR has now said in a line of cases that:

> the existence of the obligation not to expel is not dependent on whether the source of the risk of the treatment stems from factors which involve the responsibility, direct or indirect, of the authorities of the receiving country. Having regard to the absolute character of the right guaranteed, Article 3 may extend to situations where the danger emanates from persons or groups of persons who are not public officials. What is relevant in this context is whether the applicant is able to obtain protection against and seek redress for the acts perpetrated against him or her. (*Auad v Bulgaria* [2011] ECHR 1602)

The House of Lords in *Bagdanavicius* reaches a similar conclusion but with a different emphasis, saying that serious harm without a failure of state protection did not amount to inhuman or degrading treatment or punishment. Only the state was capable in law of inflicting these, and the prospect of a brutal attack by non-state agents where there was a reasonable system of protection did not constitute the treatment proscribed by Article 3 (para 24).

An Article 3 claim may succeed where an asylum seeker is unable to prove that the ill-treatment they fear is for a reason laid down by the Refugee Convention (see chapter 13). The Jamaican case of *A v SSHD* [2003] EWCA Civ 175, discussed later in the chapter, was one such, where violent reprisals were feared from a criminal gang. *AS (Appeals raising Articles 3 and 8) Iran* [2006] UKAIT 00037 also provided an example where the immigration judge found that there was a real risk of punishment by lashes but not for a reason recognized by the Refugee Convention. This treatment would contravene Article 3.

4.5 Convention rights – Article 2

Article 2(1) provides that:

> Everyone's right to life shall be protected by law. No-one shall be deprived of his life intentionally save in the execution of a sentence of a court following conviction of a crime for which this penalty is provided by law.

Article 2 does not outlaw the death sentence. This is done by Protocol 13, which the UK ratified on 10 October 2003. Protocol 13, unlike Protocol 6, outlaws the death penalty in all circumstances. The inclusion of Protocol 13 in the rights in Sch 1 to the Human Rights Act means that there are substantial constitutional problems in the way of any future government which might wish to re-introduce the death penalty, including in time of war.

Article 2(1) entails both that the state must take some positive steps to prevent life being taken and that the state must not itself take life.

4.5.1 Positive obligation

The positive duty to protect life is of a limited kind. In *Osman v UK* (2000) 29 EHRR 245, the police were aware that a schoolteacher who had developed an obsession with his pupil was harassing him. The European Court of Human Rights held that there was no breach of Article 2 in their failure to apprehend him and to prevent the killing which he committed, because there was no decisive stage at which the police knew or ought to have known that the lives of the applicant family were at real and immediate risk. The corollary of this is that if, in another case, there were such a decisive stage at which the risk was real and immediate then there could be a breach of Article 2. Case law on this protective aspect of Article 2 more often concerns the death of someone who was already in the care of the state, for instance in custody. More generally, in *Osman,* the Court interpreted the duty of protection in Article 2 to mean that the state has a general duty to establish and maintain an effective system of criminal law to deter, detect, and punish offenders. Such a duty would be fulfilled by the maintenance of a police and criminal justice system such as that in the UK.

4.5.2 Negative obligation

The negative obligation not to take life is qualified by Article 2(2), which sets out possible defences the state may be able to maintain where death results accidentally from the use of force which is no more than absolutely necessary:

(a) in defence of any person from unlawful violence;

(b) in order to effect a lawful arrest or to prevent the escape of a person lawfully detained; and

(c) in action lawfully taken for the purpose of quelling a riot or insurrection.

The terms of this paragraph are strictly construed by the Court, and in determining whether the use of force was no more than absolutely necessary attention may be paid to whether adequate guidelines for the situation were in place and followed. This was demonstrated in the case of *McCann v UK* (1996) 21 EHRR 97 (the 'deaths on the Rock' case) where the lack of training in shooting to wound rather than to kill was one of the reasons that the UK government was found in breach of Article 2 for the killing of IRA suspects in Gibraltar.

The negative aspect of the duty is less likely to be relevant as a defence to removal but is relevant to the conduct of immigration functions in the UK. There have been two deaths at the hands of officials during deportations in the UK. In 1993, a woman called Joy Gardner suffocated to death when she was bound and gagged by the police Alien Deportation Group. Prosecution and complaints failed. In October 2010 an Angolan man, Jimmy Mubenga, died while being restrained by escorts employed by a private security firm as he was being put onto a plane for deportation. What Article 2 may add to legal routes is a further element of state responsibility. If the individuals were exonerated because sufficient justification was found for their actions at the time, given their training, responses, and state of knowledge, this does not exonerate the state from providing a level of training that would prevent such incidents from occurring. In the case of McCann, the SAS officers were not trained to shoot to wound rather than kill. They were not held individually to blame but the state was in breach of Article 2. In the case of Joy Gardner, it seems that the officers were insufficiently aware of the effect of binding someone's head with 13 feet of surgical tape. The positive obligation also requires diligent and prompt investigation of a death at the hands of the state (*Kaya v Turkey* (1999) 28 EHRR 1). The Supreme Court in *In the matter of an application by Brigid McCaughey and another for Judicial Review (Northern Ireland)* [2011] UKSC 20 held that an inquiry into a death must comply with the procedural requirements of Article 2, even if the death occurred before the commencement of the Human Rights Act. This meant that the inquests could, as the Coroner proposed, consider the purpose and planning of the operation in which the deceased met their deaths. The inquest would thus be capable of considering whether they were, as their surviving relatives alleged, the victims of a 'shoot to kill' policy. The Supreme Court was following a new development in the ECtHR in *Silih v Slovenia* (2009) 49 EHRR 37 where the Court held that the duty to investigate deaths had evolved into a separate and autonomous duty.

4.5.3 Article 2 and expulsions

Article 2 is relevant in the case of threatened expulsion of someone from the UK to a risk of death. This would usually refer to deliberate killing against which there is insufficient protection in the destination country, and not to the circumstances in *N*. Earlier case law suggested that the risk of death must be 'near certain' in order to engage the responsibility of the expelling state, following a Commission decision, *Dehwari v Netherlands* (2001) 29 EHRR CD 74. However, in *A v SSHD* [2003], the Court of Appeal applied the same standard to a risk of violation of Article 2 as to Article 3, namely that there was a 'real risk'. The risk to the appellant in that case came from gang members seeking revenge for her giving a name to the police of the person she thought killed her son. There was substantial other evidence of reprisals her family had already suffered and of the risk to her life should she return to Jamaica. Note an example here of the effect of the Human Rights Act on the doctrine of precedent. Prior to a decision of the Court of Appeal there was no binding authority on the level of risk to be proved where Article 2 was applied to an expulsion because of risk of death in the receiving state (so-called 'extra-territorial application'). Since the UK Court of Appeal has decided the matter this is now binding on subsequent tribunals, and *Dehwari* ceases to have effect.

The case of *A* illustrates that it is immaterial whether the danger comes from the state or, as here, criminal gangs, if there is a real risk that the applicant will not be protected. This confirms the approach in *Kacaj*, referred to previously, in relation to state responsibility.

4.5.4 Death penalty

If the danger to life comes from the state, this may be by way of extra-judicial killing or by the death penalty. The imposition of the death penalty raises different legal questions, which are changed and possibly simplified by the inclusion of Protocol 13 in the Human Rights Act. A minister in a parliamentary written answer (WA 40 28 November 2001) confirmed that there would not be expulsions to face the death penalty. Extradition requests to the UK now contain an assurance that the death penalty will not be imposed.

The way in which the death penalty is carried out may involve an expelling state in a breach of Article 3. This is a small extension of the outcome of *Soering*, and is demonstrated in cases such as *Jabari v Turkey* [2001] INLR 136. Here, the applicant was granted refugee status by the UNHCR in Turkey, but because she had not made her application within five days, under Turkish law she was still vulnerable to expulsion from Turkey. There was a real risk that if returned to Iran she would face death by stoning for adultery. Returning her to face this was held to be a breach of Article 3.

4.6 Convention rights – Article 4

Article 4 is potentially relevant to protect victims of trafficking, and where domestic workers are kept in forced conditions. An important development in the ECtHR is *Rantsev v Cyprus and Russia* Application no. 25965/04,[2010] ECHR 22. Here the police had handed a young woman back to her employer who had taken her to the police, asking for her to deported, without investigating whether she might have been trafficked. The ECtHR found Cyprus to have violated Article 4. The case is discussed further in chapter 14.

4.7 Convention rights – Article 6

4.7.1 Content of the right

Article 6, the right to a fair hearing, is one of the most litigated Articles in the Convention. It sets out minimum requirements of a fair hearing which apply to the determination of 'civil rights and obligations' and criminal trials and provides further minimum rights for a person charged with a criminal offence, for instance to have information of the charge, facilities and time for preparing a defence, and so on.

In addition to the express rights set out, Article 6 also imports a general requirement of fairness into trials, which is open to interpretation by the Court. It has been held to require access to a court (*Golder v UK* (1979–80) 1 EHRR 524), the right to put one's case on equal terms with one's opponent, which may, depending on the circumstances entail the right to legal representation, and the right to participate effectively in proceedings (e.g., *Goddi v Italy* (1984) 6 EHRR 457).

4.7.2 Defining a 'civil right'

Where an immigration offence such as illegal entry is charged, then Article 6 applies as to any other criminal matter. However, the majority of immigration issues only come within the ambit of Article 6(1) if they are regarded as civil rights. In the case law of the ECtHR civil rights are personal to the individual, and are distinguished from public or administrative matters. The ECtHR does not necessarily take the same view as a domestic authority of what constitutes a private and what a public matter. For example, in *Salesi v Italy* (1993) 26 EHRR 187, the Court found that payment of a social security benefit falls within Article 6. In *Adams & Benn v UK* (1996) 23 EHRR 160 CD, the Commission referred to personal, economic, or individual aspects as characteristic of a private law and thus a civil right. It could be argued that immigration matters have these characteristics. In *Uppal v UK* (1979) 3 EHRR 391, the Commission found that decisions to deport were of an administrative nature and so not covered by Article 6(1). Challenging extradition (*Farmakopoulous v Greece* (1990) 64 DR 52), nationality (*S v Switzerland* (1988) 59 DR 256), and entry for employment (*X v UK* (1977) 9 DR 224) have all been found not to qualify as civil rights for Article 6.

The issue came before the Grand Chamber of the ECtHR in the case of *Maaouia v France* (2001) 33 EHRR 42.

Maaouia v France (2001) 33 EHRR 42

Mr Maaouia was unaware of a deportation order made against him as it was not served on him. The following year, he went to the Nice Centre for Administrative Formalities to regularize his immigration status and was served with the deportation order. He refused to leave the country in compliance with the order, and was sentenced to one year in prison and ten years' exclusion from French territory. He appealed through the French system against his exclusion, but his appeals were finally dismissed in 1994 on the ground that he had not challenged the deportation order in the lower courts, though it was eventually quashed because it had not been served. Mr Maaouia then applied for rescission of the exclusion order, which clearly could not stand as the deportation order on which it was based no longer existed. Rescission is a remedy available on mainly humanitarian grounds. He continued to take steps to regularize his immigration status. Eventually, in 1998, the exclusion order was rescinded and he obtained a residence permit.

Mr Maaouia claimed in the ECtHR that the four-year delay in rescinding the exclusion order was unreasonable and thus a breach of Article 6 as he had not had a fair hearing within a reasonable time in determination of his civil rights (6:1).

The Court, by a majority of 15 to 2, decided that Article 6:1 did not apply. Rescission of the exclusion order was not a criminal matter because the original merits of the criminal charges were not examined. The majority also thought that the exclusion order was not a penalty but an administrative measure particular to immigration control. It was also not 'civil' within the meaning of Article 6, for two principal reasons. The first was the view which the majority took of the existence and rationale of Protocol 7 Article 1, which provides procedural safeguards relating to the expulsion of aliens. They considered that the purpose of this Protocol was to give protection to aliens which had not previously existed. If there had been no previous protection then it must be the case that Article 6 did not apply to aliens faced with expulsion.

The Court's second main reason was that the Commission had previously expressed a consistent view, in cases such as those referred to earlier, that the rights of aliens faced with expulsion were not within Article 6. Given that the matter was referred to a full court because of its importance and the lack of previous decisions of the Court, for the Court to follow the less authoritative earlier decisions rather than look at the matter afresh is disappointing.

Personal and economic effects of rescission were not considered sufficient to bring the matter within Article 6. The Court said 'the fact that the exclusion order incidentally had major repercussions on the applicant's private and family life and on his prospects of employment cannot suffice to bring those proceedings within the scope of civil rights'.

Powerful dissenting judgments from Judges Loucaides and Traja argued that insufficient attention had been paid to the history of Article 6 and to Article 31 of the Vienna Convention on the Law of Treaties. This Article requires that if a term is capable of more than one interpretation, the meaning which enhances individual rights should be preferred. Their view of the history of Article 6 was that the phrase 'civil rights and obligations' was meant to catch all non-criminal matters, rather than to develop a new and specialized meaning. The result of limiting its application to private law matters is that the individual has less protection against the power of the state than against other individuals, which they said was 'absurd' and flouted the purpose of the Convention. Their view of Protocol 7 was that it was designed to furnish 'additional special protection' for people liable to be expelled. It refers to administrative safeguards rather than judicial safeguards, and it was the latter which were the realm of Article 6.

As the sole judgment on this matter of a full court, Maaouia is an important statement of the interpretation of Article 6. Later applications to the ECtHR that deportation or asylum proceedings (*Eskelinen v Finland* (2007) 45EHRR 43) were unfair under Article 6 have been rejected without discussion. In the UK, *Maaouia* has been consistently followed and the non-applicability of Article 6 to immigration matters is treated as settled law. The House of Lords in *RB, U & OO* held that the fact that other rights were also at stake did not change this, and Article 6 did not apply to a challenge before SIAC to a decision to deport. The Court of Appeal in *W (Algeria) v SSHD* [2010] EWCA Civ 898 confirmed that, in a case where the appellant was the subject of both a control order under the Terrorism Act and a deportation order, Article 6 applied to the control order, so that he must be 'provided with the essence of the allegations against him' (following *A v UK* [2009] ECHR 301) but not to the deportation order, following *Maaouia*.

In *R (on the application of MK(Iran)) v SSHD* [2010] EWCA Civ 115 the appellant argued that the EC Qualification Directive required the inapplicability of Article 6 to asylum claims to be re-examined. 'With reluctance' the Court of Appeal, while accepting that this argument had force, held that such a re-examination was outside its remit. Article 47 of the EU Charter, also giving the right to a fair hearing, was unsuccessfully argued to give the appellant the right to a prompt determination of his asylum claim (see also chapter 8). It may be that this issue will come before the CJEU in time.

The majority of procedural issues which would affect a fair hearing in the immigration appeal tribunals are covered in the Tribunal's procedure rules. In the previous chapter, we noted the case of *Harrison v SSHD* [2003] INLR 284 in which the Court of Appeal held that the right to be recognized as a British citizen was not a civil right for Article 6 purposes. In a similar vein, the High Court in *MH and others v SSHD* [2008] EWHC 2525 (Admin) held that decisions of the Secretary of State relating to naturalization were exercises of public law discretion, and disputes about refusal of nationality did not relate to the determination of civil rights or obligations. In that case, the Court of Appeal held that 'the same principles of fairness should apply in every case, whether the ECHR applies or not' (*SSHD v AHK, GA, AS, MH, FT and NT* [2009] EWCA Civ 287).

In *AM (Upgrade appeals: Article 6) Afghanistan* [2004] Imm AR 530, the Tribunal held that an appeal by which a person with exceptional leave to remain could upgrade his status to that of refugee was not a 'civil right' and thus did not engage Article 6.

In *SSHD v MB and AF* [2007] UKHL 46 the House of Lords was unanimous that proceedings challenging a control order under the Prevention of Terrorism Act 2005 were civil proceedings for the purposes of Article 6, and that a control order was not a criminal charge. Though replacing the former unlawful controls on foreign nationals, these are not immigration provisions.

Finally the Special Immigration Appeals Commission rejected the application of Article 6 to a bail application to them by a person detained pending deportation (*R on the application of BB v SIAC and SSHD* [2011] EWHC 2129 (Admin)).

4.8 Convention rights – Article 8

Article 8 is discussed at length here because of its central relevance to immigration and asylum cases. Applications to enter to join family members and challenges to a removal or deportation which would break up a family are the substance of many cases in the courts and tribunals. Challenges based on Article 8 may also follow unsuccessful asylum claims where a person has built up a life in the UK while waiting for their case to be determined. The House of Lords in *Huang* and *Kashmiri* stated the 'core value' which Article 8 exists to protect:

> Human beings are social animals. They depend on others. Their family, or extended family, is the group on which many people most heavily depend, socially, emotionally and often financially. There comes a point at which, for some, prolonged and unavoidable separation from this group seriously inhibits their ability to live full and fulfilling lives. (para 18)

This expresses the importance of the Article 8 right, which in immigration control may come into direct conflict with the exercise of state power. Thus, legal doctrine surrounding it has become highly developed, and its application raises all the difficult questions about proportionality and jurisdiction.

The text of the Article is:

> 8.1 Everyone shall have the right to respect for his private and family life, his home and correspondence.
>
> 8.2 There shall be no interference with the exercise of this right except such as is in accordance with the law and is necessary in a democratic society in the interests of national security, public safety or the economic well-being of the country, for the prevention of disorder or crime, for the protection of health or morals, or for the protection of the rights and freedoms of others.

A structured approach is used in the ECtHR to applying the Article, and in one of the first UK cases using Article 8, *Nhundu and Chiwera* (01/TH/000613), the Tribunal expressed this as follows:

> Article 8 is to be analysed according to a step-by-step approach, asking first whether there is an existent private or family life, second whether there is an interference with that private or family life, third whether that interference pursues a legitimate aim, fourth whether it is in accordance with the law and finally whether it is proportionate.

This was elaborated by Lord Bingham in the House of Lords in *Razgar* (para 19) in the following way:

> (1) Will the proposed removal be an interference by a public authority with the exercise of the applicant's right to respect for his private or (as the case may be) family life?
>
> (2) If so, will such interference have consequences of such gravity as potentially to engage the operation of article 8?
>
> (3) If so, is such interference in accordance with the law?
>
> (4) If so, is such interference necessary in a democratic society in the interests of national security, public safety or the economic well-being of the country, for the prevention of disorder or crime, for the protection of health or morals, or for the protection of the rights and freedoms of others?
>
> (5) If so, is such interference proportionate to the legitimate public end sought to be achieved?

These are referred to as 'Lord Bingham's five steps' and are often used as a foundation for Article 8 reasoning. *Razgar* was a case about the application of Article 8 to the health consequences of removal, abroad as well as in the UK. As discussed previously in relation to extra-territorial scope, where the feared breach of qualified rights is abroad (*EM (Lebanon)*), the threshold is much higher. Court of Appeal cases have confirmed that it is a mistake to elevate Lord Bingham's point 2 to create a high threshold for the engagement of Article 8 where, as is usually the case, the claim is for protection of family or private life in the UK. See on this point *AG (Eritrea)* [2007] EWCA Civ 801 para 28, *VW (Uganda) v SSHD and AB (Somalia) v SSHD* [2009] EWCA Civ 5, and Baroness Hale's refutation in *Razgar* of a threshold in domestic cases, set out at 4.3.3. With this caveat, the five steps are a widely accepted formulation, and we now examine each in turn.

4.8.1 Does private or family life exist?

In an immigration context, the issue is rarely of interference with home or correspondence. Interference with private or family life is usually the question. These are ECHR concepts which are given their meaning by the ECtHR. In accordance with HRA s 2, the UK courts are obliged to take account of these meanings.

4.8.1.1 *Private life*

The concept of private life in Article 8 is a wide one. The ECtHR in *Niemietz v Germany* (1992) 16 EHRR 97 has said that it is not possible or desirable to define all the situations to which the concept of private life can apply. In *Marckx v Belgium* (1979) 2 EHRR 330, the Court identified the central purpose of Article 8 as to protect the individual from arbitrary interference by public authorities, and this principle may be used to help determine new situations which may come within the protection of Article 8. The range of circumstances which the Court has accepted as coming within Article 8 includes the right to have one's own body free from invasion or harm (as in, e.g., *Costello-Roberts v UK* 19 EHRR 112 in which the issue, also raised under Article 3, was corporal punishment), and self-determination (see *Pretty v UK* (2002) 35 EHRR 1 where, although the Court did not find in the applicant's favour, Article 8 was held to be engaged in the question of the applicant's desire to end her life in the way she chose). In *Niemietz*, private life was held to 'comprise to a certain degree the right to establish and develop relationships with other human beings'. This includes the most intimate relationships as in *Dudgeon v UK* (1981) 4 EHRR 149 and may include professional relationships, especially where these are not easily separated from the rest of life. The case of *Botta v Italy* (1998) 26 EHRR 241 is one of a number of cases endorsing the principle that private life includes physical and psychological integrity.

More recently, in the case of *Maslov v Austria* [2008] ECHR 546, the ECtHR held that 'the totality of social ties between settled migrants and the community in which they are living constitutes part of the concept of "private life" within the meaning of Article 8'. This is a very important judgment for the application of Article 8 to immigration cases. Private life can also be established when the individual knows that their stay in the country is temporary, as in *MM (Tier 1 PSW; Art 8; 'private life') Zimbabwe* [2009] UKAIT 00037. MM had been a student in the UK and then obtained limited leave for post-study work. In the UK she had developed social and professional ties and relationships, and her daughter was at school. The temporary nature of the immigration leave held by someone like MM does not displace the fact that she has a private life in the UK, but is relevant when the proportionality of not extending leave is considered. In the Court of Appeal, in *DM (Zambia)* [2009] EWCA Civ 474, Sedley LJ gave some further guidance about the nature of private life. He said that to remove an AIDS sufferer 'from free care and treatment in one of the best health services in the world, which had rescued her from what would otherwise have been a terminal condition', was a 'clear interference with her physical and psychological integrity and thus an invasion of her private life requiring justification', although justification was found in that case. This follows *Razgar* where the House of Lords held that the right to respect for private life can be engaged by the foreseeable consequences for health or welfare of removal from the UK, and endorses a holistic concept of private life which extends 'to those features which are integral to a person's identity or ability to function socially as a person' (para 9).

To complete the application of Article 8 to health care cases, it is worth noting that in *ES (Tanzania) v SSHD* [2009] EWCA Civ 1353, the Court found that it was insufficient to follow *N v UK*, which did not deal with the application of Article 8 where, as here, the appellant had been given leave to remain in the UK specifically for medical treatment for AIDS, then had the continuation of that leave refused. The case was remitted to the Tribunal for a structured decision, taking into account the de facto commitment which the UK had made to ES.

The courts have made distinctions between family and private life, depending on the gender and legal relationship of the partners. However, this distinction is breaking down in favour of an approach which focuses on the reality of relationships. In *JN (Uganda)* [2007] EWCA Civ 802, the appellant had lived a 'decent and industrious' life in the UK for 12 years. She was doing paid work, voluntary work, was deeply involved with her church, and had a relationship with a man whom she had not married in case she was returned to Uganda. This was accepted as private life. The Court held that the reasoning of the House of Lords in *Huang* concerning respect for family life applied equally to private life (para 16). This is reflected also in the ECtHR's judgment in *AA v UK* discussed later in the chapter.

4.8.1.2 *Family life*

Family life includes the society of close relatives. The ECtHR regards a 'lawful and genuine' marriage as amounting to family life, even if the couple have not yet been able to establish a home together (*Abdulaziz, Cabales and Balkandali v UK* and *Berrehab v Netherlands*). This principle has been confirmed and applied in the UK (e.g., in *A (Afghanistan) v SSHD* [2009] EWCA Civ 825). *J (Pakistan)* [2003] UKIAT 00167 illustrated that there must either be a valid marriage with a plan to cohabit, or a marriage which the parties believed, even if mistakenly, to be valid, with actual cohabitation. In this case, the marriage had taken place by telephone and was not valid in the UK. The wife had gone to live with her mother-in-law, symbolizing the union, but the husband and wife had not yet lived together. The Tribunal held that there was no family life as required by Article 8.

Minor children are also regarded as having a relationship of family life with biological or adoptive parents, even if they do not live together, and the ECtHR has repeatedly held that in the absence of exceptional circumstances the parent–child relationship automatically gives rise to family life (but see *Khan v UK* discussed later). In *Berrehab*, the parents were not married and no longer lived together. Nevertheless, the father had contact with the child four times a week for several hours at a time. The Court found that family life between father and child had not been broken by the ending of the partnership between the parents. The Court of Appeal in *Singh v ECO New Delhi* [2004] EWCA Civ 1075 had to consider an application for entry clearance following an intra-family adoption which did not and never could meet the requirements of the immigration rules. The case had had a very protracted history, including a decision by the ECtHR that an application was admissible because the refusal to recognize adoptions carried out in India was *prima facie* discriminatory. The Court of Appeal followed the ECtHR's approach in *Lebbink v Netherlands* (Application no. 45582/99) para 36: 'The existence or non-existence of "family life" for the purposes of Article 8 is essentially a question of fact depending upon the real existence in practice of close personal ties.' It had no doubt that the substantial relationship between the child and adoptive parents amounted to family life. The fact that it did not meet the UK's stringent requirements in the immigration rules should not be allowed to impede the reality of genuine family life and entry clearance should be granted. The concept of family life must be understood in the context of the UK's multicultural society.

In *R (on the application of G.K. Ahmed) v SSHD* [2009] EWHC 2403 (Admin) the High Court held that the birth of a child and four months of cohabitation following that birth until the claimant was arrested made a substantial difference to the way that the relationship would be regarded. It was a new family, but nonetheless a family.

A recent case in the ECtHR took into account the quality of the relationship even in the case of minor children. In *Khan v UK* [2011] ECHR 2533 the children had not seen their father for ten years prior to his deportation. The eldest had been four years old when he last saw his father. Given this and the evidence that he had not been a positive influence in the children's lives, the Court held that his family life was not strong.

The approach to family relationships in the context of Article 8 has been rethought following the House of Lords' judgment in *Beoku-Betts*, which, as discussed earlier, introduces the concept that the whole family is the proper subject for consideration under Article 8. The anti-discrimination provisions of Article 14 mean that the marital status of the parents should not make any difference to the degree of respect accorded to the family under Article 8. The case of *Marckx v Belgium* expounded on this point: 'Article 8 makes no distinction between the legitimate and illegitimate family. Such distinction would not be consonant with the word "everyone" in Article 1 and this is confirmed by Article 14 with its prohibition... of discrimination grounded on birth.'

Somewhat in contradiction of these principles, Commission cases have not treated couples of the same sex in the same way as married couples (e.g., *Kerkhoven v Netherlands* Application no 15666/89). In the UK, following the Civil Partnership Act 2004 and the inclusion of registered partners in the immigration rules, it appears there is no justification for continuing to distinguish between couples on the basis of whether they are of the same or different sexes. In *Krasniqi v SSHD* [2006] EWCA Civ 391, there was no issue raised against respect for the same-sex relationship being for family life, though Sedley LJ said the characterization of same-sex relationships remained 'problematical'. In so saying he referred to *Secretary of State for Work and Pensions v M* [2006] UKHL 11, but the ambivalence which characterizes that case arises in part from the very different context of child support calculations.

It can be assumed that family life exists between brothers and sisters who are living together as children. In the case of adult siblings or adults and their parents, the approach of the ECtHR, and following that, domestic courts, has been to treat the quality of emotional ties as relevant in determining whether there is family life. Often the Court looks for 'more than normal emotional ties'. In *Anam v UK* [2011] ECHR 940 the ECtHR held that there was family life between the claimant and his parents because of a 'higher degree of reliance on his mother and adult siblings than other adults as a result of his diagnosed mental health problems'. But this is not always required. In *Moustaquim v Belgium* (1991) 13 EHRR 802, family life was held to exist between the applicant and his brothers and sisters and his parents. He was an adult no longer living with the family, but he maintained contact with them. Similarly, in *Boughanemi v France* (1996) 22 EHRR 228, family life was engaged in a deportation which separated the applicant from his ten siblings who all lived in France. The Court of Appeal in *Senthuran v SSHD* [2004] EWCA Civ 950 confirmed that family life may exist between adult siblings where the requisite level of connection and dependency is present. The ECtHR is moving away from placing reliance on the distinction between private and family life. See *Omojudi v UK* [2009] ECHR 1942 and this passage in *AA v UK* [2011] ECHR 1345:

> An examination of the Court's case-law would tend to suggest that the applicant, a young adult of 24 years old, who resides with his mother and has not yet founded a family of his own, can be

> regarded as having 'family life'. However, it is not necessary to decide the question given that, as Article 8 also protects the right to establish and develop relationships with other human beings and the outside world and can sometimes embrace aspects of an individual's social identity, it must be accepted that the totality of social ties between settled migrants and the community in which they are living constitutes part of the concept of 'private life' within the meaning of Article 8. Thus, regardless of the existence or otherwise of a 'family life', the expulsion of a settled migrant constitutes an interference with his right to respect for private life. While the Court has previously referred to the need to decide in the circumstances of the particular case before it whether it is appropriate to focus on 'family life' rather than ' private life', it observes that in practice the factors to be examined in order to assess the proportionality of the deportation measure are the same regardless of whether family or private life is engaged. (para 49)

This approach was followed in *RG (Automatic deportation Section 33(2)(a) exception) Nepal* [2010] UKUT 273(IAC) in which the Tribunal found, in the case of a young man of 20, that the essence of the case was one of a family that 'have strong mutual links and that have always lived together and who expected to continue to live together in the UK' . They concluded that 'substantial respect was due to those links by way of family life or private life different in kind from the mere number of years of residence here'. (para 28)

The evaluation of the level of contact between family members raises particular difficulties where adult children and parents are living in different countries. There must be 'an irreducible minimum' of actual and effective relationship (*Kugathas v SSHD* [2003] INLR 170 CA). In *Kugathas*, the appellant was a man of 38 who had lived away from Sri Lanka for 17 years and had no family there. However, he had a mother, brother, and sister in Germany and had lived with them before coming to the UK three years earlier. His sister had visited him and he had maintained contact by telephone. The Court of Appeal held there had been no family life with them since he left Germany. In *ZB (Pakistan)*, the Court commented that decisions should 'demonstrate a proper appreciation that a person's family was the group on which many people most heavily depended socially, emotionally and often financially' following the House of Lords' statement in *Huang* to this effect.

4.8.2 What does 'respect for private or family life' entail?

What a positive obligation of respect requires depends upon the situation. The implications of this are considered more fully in chapter 9, in the context of family settlement.

As discussed there, the trend in the courts is increasingly to make no real distinction of principle between what respect requires when a removal threatens to break up a family and what respect requires when a person applies to join their family in the UK. In *Tuquabo-Tekle v The Netherlands* [2006] 1 FLR 798 the Court asserted that boundaries between the state's positive and negative obligations under Article 8 did 'not lend themselves to precise definition', and that the applicable principles were similar.

The leading case of *Huang and Kashmiri v SSHD* [2007] UKHL 11 concerned applications for leave to remain in the UK, though as both applicants were in the UK, in practice they also concerned the prospect of removal. In following *Huang and Kashmiri*, the courts and tribunals often make no distinction between leave to remain, entry, and removal. In *QJ (Algeria) v SSHD* [2010] EWCA Civ1478 the appellant argued that SIAC had erred in law by saying that *Huang* applied only to entry and not to deportation cases. The Court held that SIAC had made no error of law because they had applied the test of proportionality, and this was what *Huang* was affirming.

4.8.3 Has there been an interference with the right?

The next question in applying Article 8 is whether there has been an interference with the right to respect for private or family life. There is normally little doubt about the act of interference in the immigration context. The most obvious and damaging interference with family life by a removal is the break-up of the family. It can also easily be argued that the upheaval and disruption of support networks, wider family relationships, and so on is an interference with family and private life. If other family members are removed, the upheaval to the whole family must be considered as the potential breach (*Beoku-Betts*). The Tribunal in *Nhundu* said that where a family is established, removal will constitute an interference with family life. In some later cases, this has been doubted, but this has generally been based on an erroneous interpretation of Lord Bingham's second step to create a high threshold for engagement of Article 8. In *DM (Zambia) v SSHD* [2009] EWCA Civ 474, the Court said:

> Once the existence of private or family life in the UK is established, its character and intensity affect the proportionality of the proposed interference with it, not its existence or the engagement of Article 8. (para 17)

In other words, the real issue in Article 8 cases is whether the upheaval caused by removal or refusal of entry is proportionate to the public interest served. This is now affirmed by the Supreme Court in *Quila* which held that 'forcing a married couple to choose either to live separately for some years or to suspend their plans to live in one place and go to live where neither of them wishes to live' was 'a colossal interference' with their right to respect for family life. (para 32 and 72) 'The only sensible enquiry can be into whether the refusals were justified.' (para 43).

The ECtHR does not hesitate to find an interference in removal cases, but has also gone beyond this to find that prolonged uncertainty and insecurity of status generated by immigration decisions can also amount to an interference. For instance in *Shevanova v Latvia* a deportation order amounted to an interference with private life even though it was never enforced, because of the uncertainty and insecurity it created, and in *Sisojeva v Latvia* (Application no. 60654/00) prolonged refusal to recognize a stateless Russian family's right to permanent residence in Latvia constituted an interference with their right to respect for their family life.

4.8.4 Can the interference be justified?

This is the main question in the majority of Article 8 cases. It is governed by Article 8.2 which, like the other qualified rights, has the following substantive requirements. The interference with the right, to be permitted, must be:

- in accordance with the law;
- in pursuit of a legitimate aim;
- necessary in a democratic society in the interests of that aim; and
- proportionate to the aim pursued.

Finally, the reasons given by the state must be relevant and sufficient (*Handyside v UK*). These are established principles of Convention case law, referred to in almost every

ECtHR case decided using the qualified rights. According to the ECtHR in *Smith and Grady v UK* (1999) 29 EHRR 493, these principles 'lie at the heart of the Court's analysis of complaints under Article 8 of the Convention' (para 138). We shall consider each in turn.

4.8.4.1 *In accordance with the law*

This has the same meaning as 'prescribed by law', which is the wording used in the other qualified Articles. It requires that the provision which interferes with the right not only complies with domestic law, but also that the law itself is accessible (*Silver v UK* (1983) 5 EHRR 347) and precise enough to enable an individual to regulate their conduct accordingly (*Sunday Times v UK* (1979) 2 EHRR 245). In immigration and asylum cases, this requirement is very rarely an issue. The interference normally arises from the application of statute or rules, which easily meet these criteria. A rare case of an immigration provision not being 'in accordance with the law' was *KK (Jamaica)* [2004] UKIAT 00268, which concerned the concession that children under 12 only needed to show adequate accommodation with their parent in order to obtain settlement. The terms of the concession were held to be insufficiently precise as it was not clear whether it only applied to entry clearance cases, nor whether the applicant had to be informed that the concession applied to them.

In *Estrikh v Latvia* [2007] ECHR 57 the ECtHR, held that a deportation was not in accordance with the law because it had taken place on the day that the applicant lodged an appeal against the deportation, in contravention of the Criminal Procedure Code, which, as in the UK, deemed that the order was not final until appeals had been exhausted.

In the UK, the inaccessibility of policies governing immigration-related decisions has been an important basis of challenge. These challenges are more usually brought on public law principles rather than Convention rights, and more often concern detention, and so potentially Article 5 ECHR, rather than Article 8. See *Lumba and Mighty* in chapter 15.

4.8.4.2 *In pursuit of a legitimate aim*

This requirement is rarely the subject of case law, but in immigration cases the importance of identifying the aim correctly has been recognized. See for instance *AA v UK* where the Court takes pains to identify which legitimate aim the government contends is served, before going on to consider whether deportation is proportionate. The legitimate aims are listed in para 2 of the qualified Articles (see Article 8 earlier in the chapter). They differ slightly as between the different qualified rights.

Importantly, this list of aims is exhaustive. The Court in *Golder v UK* said that the words 'There shall be no interference...except such as...' left 'no room for the concept of implied limitations' (para 44). Article 18 provides that restrictions on Convention rights cannot be used for any purposes other than those prescribed. Indeed, for this to be otherwise would subvert the purpose of the Convention, which is to control the situations in which governments can legitimately interfere with the rights of individuals. The aims listed are quite wide in their coverage, and it is not usually problematic for a government to bring their action within them. In the case of deportations, 'prevention of disorder or crime' or 'protection of health or morals' are usually cited as public interests served by the deportation. In removals, the legitimate aim may be less easy to identify. Removal is directed towards immigration enforcement, but this is not listed in para 2 as a legitimate aim. Blake and Husain (Immigration, Asylum and Human Rights 2003:190) summarize the position as follows:

Immigration control has consistently been held by the European Court to relate to the preservation of the economic well-being of the country, the prevention of disorder or crime, the protection of health and morals, and the protection of the rights and freedoms of others. Exclusions and expulsions of illegal entrants are therefore likely to fall easily within a permissible competing interest under Article 8(2). It is important to note that immigration control is not of itself a valid end capable of justifying an interfering measure; it is rather the medium through which other legitimate aims are promoted.

The evaluation of the legitimate aim in cases which are about enforcing immigration rules has been affected in the UK by the case of *Chikwamba*. See chapters 9 and 18. The identification of the legitimate aim is a fundamental requirement for considering proportionality. Without identifying the legitimate aim, there is nothing to which the interference must be proportionate. Richards LJ in *JO (Uganda) and JT (Ivory Coast) v SSHD* [2010] EWCA Civ 10 stressed that in deportation cases (based on criminal behaviour) and in removal cases (based on immigration enforcement)

> The difference in aim is potentially important because the factors in favour of expulsion are in my view capable of carrying greater weight in a deportation case than in a case of ordinary removal. (see chapter 18)

There must be a rational connection between the aim and the means by which it is pursued (*de Freitas v Permanent Secretary of Ministry of Agriculture, Fisheries, Lands and Housing* [1999] 1 AC 69). This means not just that the aim generally is a legitimate one, but that it can be served by interfering with individual rights in this particular case.

Following *Huang and Kashmiri*, it is the Court's task to investigate the connection between the aim and the measures employed, and to weigh up the competing considerations on each side and according appropriate weight to the judgment of a person with responsibility for a given subject matter and access to special sources of knowledge and advice (para 16). This is the question of whether the interference is necessary in a democratic society and proportionate to the aim pursued. In a similar vein to Richards LJ quoted earlier, the Supreme Court in *ZH (Tanzania)* remarked, in the context of considering whether the removal of a parent of British children was in the interests of the economic well-being of the country, that:

> Each of the legitimate aims... may involve individual as well as community interests ... In reality, however, an argument that the continued presence of a particular individual in the country poses a specific risk to others may more easily outweigh the best interests of that or any other child than an argument that his or her continued presence poses a more general threat to the economic well-being of the country. (para 28)

4.8.4.3 *Necessity in a democratic society*

The question of whether the interference is necessary in a democratic society was said by the ECtHR in *Smith and Grady* to be the core of rights protection. Necessity has been equated with serving a 'pressing social need' (*Sunday Times v UK*). There is a question as to the relationship of this requirement with that of proportionality. Is it the same thing in different words? The approach often used in the judgments of the ECtHR is to ask these questions: first, is it necessary to interfere with this person's rights in order to achieve a legitimate aim? If it is, is the actual interference proportionate to this aim? Finally, are the reasons advanced by the state relevant and sufficient to support that interference? For further discussion of this issue, see Fasti (2002). Sometimes, the questions of proportionality and necessity seem to flow into each other. In *Miao v SSHD* [2006] EWCA Civ 75, Sedley LJ said that to treat the two issues separately is to overcomplicate the issue. For instance in *AA v UK* the ECtHR treated necessity in a democratic society as the question to be answered, but approached the case in the same way as if they had called it proportionality.

The question of necessity is considered in the context of a democratic society. The characteristics of a democratic society according to the ECtHR are tolerance, pluralism, broad-mindedness, and willingness to tolerate ideas that shock or offend (*Handyside v UK*). These qualities are derived from the context of freedom of expression cases, and have limited relevance to immigration, although the idea of tolerance is apparent in the ECtHR's reasoning in *AA*. It is relevant that a democratic society is evidently not one in which all people think or behave in the same way. Necessity should be distinguished from reasonableness. The priority is given to the right, the interference permitted by paragraph 2 is the exception rather than the rule. This was explicitly stated in *Sunday Times v UK*, but in principle applies to all the qualified rights.

Necessity in a democratic society is rarely explicitly mentioned in UK immigration cases, perhaps for the reasons given by Sedley LJ, but it had a particular relevance in the case of *ECO Mumbai v NH (India)* [2007] EWCA Civ 1330. Here, the Court of Appeal endorsed the Tribunal's examination of the history of discriminatory legislation preventing British East African Asians from obtaining residence in the UK in deciding whether it was proportionate to refuse entry to an 18-year-old son of the sponsor. The Tribunal said:

> We regard this history and context as of the utmost relevance. We agree with the Appellants' representatives that the assessment of what is necessary in a democratic society in Article 8 terms should involve a consideration of all the circumstances including the previous history of any previous wrongful act and an understanding of how the convention rights have to be enforced. We accept the submission that 'in Strasbourg cases the Courts have looked at the history of development of legislation in assessing what is the right thing to do in the modern context when acknowledgements of past wrongful treatment are made'. (quoted in CA para 18)

4.8.4.4 *What is proportionality?*

Proportionality is a relatively new concept in UK law, though it is established in some other countries and in the ECHR and in European law. A classic formulation may be found in *de Freitas*, which was a Privy Council case from Antigua and Barbuda. Here, Lord Clyde observed, at p. 80, that in determining whether a limitation on a right was arbitrary or excessive the Court should ask itself:

> whether: (i) the legislative objective is sufficiently important to justify limiting a fundamental right; (ii) the measures designed to meet the legislative objective are rationally connected to it; and (iii) the means used to impair the right or freedom are no more than is necessary to accomplish the objective.

In the context of Convention rights, point (i) here overlaps with identifying the legitimate aim and the question of necessity in a democratic society. The second and third points are a useful guide in considering the question of whether an infringement of a right is proportionate to the aim pursued. Proportionality requires a rational connection between the interference and the aim pursued, and that the interference is no more than is necessary.

The *de Freitas* formulation was added to by the House of Lords in *Huang and Kashmiri*. They said that in addition to these points 'the need to balance the interests of society with those of individuals and groups' was something 'which should never be overlooked or discounted' (para 19). This gives a slight weighting to the interests of society as compared with the *de Freitas* formulation. In *de Freitas*, the interests of society do not feature unless they are weighty enough to justify limiting a fundamental right. In *Huang*, the interests of society do not need any further justification beyond being identified as the interests of society. Who identifies these and what kind of society they represent are questions left unasked. This statement of the need for balance between society and the individual is not new with *Huang*, and was said by the House of Lords in *Razgar* to be 'inherent in the whole of the Convention' (para 20).

Proportionality is very fact-specific. It is only possible to form a judgement about the infringement of an individual's rights in the light of all the circumstances of a particular case. Often, in judgments, one sees the phrase 'in all the circumstances'. In the context of proportionality, these are not empty words but may actually be the nub of the issue. It may be justifiable policy in general to remove people who have entered the UK illegally, and still disproportionate in a particular case, given that person's situation. Where human rights are concerned, even within the context of a policy, the state must justify an infringement on the merits of the individual case. The question of proportionality involves a close examination of facts but it is not a factual question, it is a judgment based upon an investigation into facts. In *A v SSHD* [2004] UKHL 56, Lord Bingham said: 'The European Court does not approach questions of proportionality as questions of pure fact...Nor should domestic courts do so' (para 44).

The nature of the proportionality exercise has been a vital and contentious question since the inception of the Human Rights Act. Many of the questions that have been debated have now been settled by the House of Lords in *Huang*, *Chikwamba*, and *EB (Kosovo)*, and although there remains uneven application of these judgments in the lower courts and tribunals, and difference of opinion on individual cases, it is now possible to give an authoritative account in general terms of the proper approach to proportionality. The House of Lords judgment in *Huang* set it out as follows:

> The question for the appellate immigration authority is whether the refusal of leave to enter or remain, in circumstances where the life of the family cannot reasonably be expected to be enjoyed elsewhere, taking full account of all considerations weighing in favour of the refusal, prejudices the family life of the applicant in a manner sufficiently serious to amount to a breach of the fundamental right protected by article 8. If the answer to this question is affirmative, the refusal is unlawful and the authority must so decide. (*Huang* para 20)

The House of Lords rejected many of the doctrines which have complicated the issue. Determining proportionality, they say, 'is not, in principle, a hard task to define, however difficult the task is, in practice, to perform' (para 14).

It has proved in many immigration cases to be the nub of the responsibility given to the judges by Parliament in the Human Rights Act. It is also, of course, a requirement of primary decision-makers in the Home Office. The proportionality exercise is not a special one for the judges.

Chikwamba v SSHD [2008] UKHL 40, unlike *Huang*, did not deal with the structure or principles of proportionality but with its application. The House of Lords held unanimously and in vigorous terms that it was disproportionate to expect the wife of a Zimbabwean refugee, herself a Zimbabwean, to return to Zimbabwe with her small child to make an application for entry clearance. All that prevented her Article 8 application to remain to live with her husband from being decided in the UK was a rule that as she did not have entry clearance for this purpose she should leave to obtain it. To require this was to elevate a policy beyond reason. This case is discussed further in chapters 9 and 18.

EB (Kosovo) v SSHD [2008] UKHL 41 is also discussed in more detail in chapter 18, where we consider the effect of delay by the Home Office on enforcement of decisions by removal. Again, the House of Lords took a humane view of the situation, both in respect of inevitable imperfections in a 'complex and overloaded system' and in respect of delay in decision-making on the individual who is the subject of that decision. In addition to the decision on the relevance of delay, Lord Bingham also considered that the decision of the adjudicator had not 'accurately or adequately addressed the human problems' raised by the appellant's appeal, in that he had not considered the proportionality of separating the appellant from his girlfriend, informally adopted child, and expected child, or alternatively, of requiring his girlfriend 'to move to a country which was entirely unfamiliar and whose language she could not speak' (para 18).

These human points are the substance of proportionality decisions.

4.9 Other qualified rights

Article 10, which protects freedom of expression, is regarded as one of the most central Articles of the Convention. It protects freedom of expression in written or spoken words, action, and through any medium such as theatre, film, photography, or painting. There have been occasional applications to immigration law where speaking tours have been prevented by the Secretary of State exercising her powers to exclude a speaker. In *Farrakhan* [2002] 3 WLR 481 it was held that refusal of entry to the Nation of Islam leader Louis Farrakhan engaged his right to freedom of expression but did not breach it. Mr Farrakhan had been refused entry to the UK to conduct a speaking tour on the grounds that his exclusion was conducive to the public good. The Court of Appeal, relying on the ECtHR cases of *Piermont v France* [1995] 20 EHRR 301, *Swami Omkarananda and Divine Light Zentrum v Switzerland* (1997) 25 DR 105, and *Adams and Benn v UK* (1997) 88A DR 137, held that where, as here, an immigration decision was made with the purpose of preventing the exercise of Article 10 rights, then the Article is engaged. However, the Secretary of State's reason for excluding Farrakhan was a justifiable one relating to public order and a legitimate restriction on the right within Article 10.2. The Court of Appeal upheld the exclusion of Dr Naik (see 4.3.4 and chapter 7) on similar grounds.

4.10 Other derogable rights

Article 12 provides that:

> Men and women of marriageable age have the right to marry and to found a family according to the national laws governing the exercise of this right.

What the law requires by way of respect for this right in the context of immigration policy has been considerably strengthened by case law. In the UK the decision of the Supreme Court in *Quila* has given more substance to the right to marry. The Court departed from *Abdulaziz, Cabales and Balkandali v UK* to the extent that it held that an application for entry as a spouse engaged Article 8, otherwise the notion of the right to found a family becomes rather meaningless.

Article 12 cannot be used to establish a right of entry for a spouse married according to traditions regarded as unlawful in the UK, for instance, the marriage of a person under the age of 16. The Article expressly provides only the right to marry 'according to the national laws governing the exercise of this right'. This means according to the national laws of the country where Article 12 is or would be invoked, not the laws of the country where the marriage took place. In *R (on the application of Baiai and others) v SSHD* [2008] UKHL 53, discussed in chapter 9, the House of Lords held that the right to marry was fundamental, and not subject to the same qualifications as the right to respect for family life. Article 12 allowed for the right to be subject to national laws governing its exercise, but these should govern regulatory matters. Any rules of substance must only be for a generally recognized public interest and must never impair the substance of the right. They thought that the fixed fee of £295 impaired the essence of the right to marry. The condition that a person must have a certain number of months' leave remaining was not related to the genuineness of the marriage and was an unreasonable restriction on the right. The ECtHR also came to the conclusion that the scheme of certificates of approval for marriage was a breach of Article 12 (*O'Donoghue and Others v the UK* (Application no. 34848/07). The Court's objections were that the scheme did not differentiate between genuine and sham marriages (the supposed purpose of the scheme) but imposed a blanket requirement on marriages based purely on immigration status. The fee was prohibitive for some couples.

Article 13 of the Convention provides a right to an effective remedy and is not included in the scope of the HRA. The government justified its omission by arguing that the Act itself was the guarantee of a remedy, but its omission may exclude the greater opportunity for judicial creativity which would have been generated by the right to a remedy.

Article 14 is potentially of wide application. The full text of Article 14 is:

> The enjoyment of the rights and freedoms set forth in this Convention shall be secured without discrimination on any ground such as sex, race, colour, language, religion, political or other opinion, nationality or social origin, association with a national minority, birth or other status.

Article 14 was successfully used by the applicants in *Abdulaziz, Cabales and Balkandali v UK*. In that case, the applicants succeeded in pleading sex discrimination in the application of Article 8 rights, even though no breach of Article 8 was found.

Key Case

Abdulaziz, Cabales and Balkandali v UK **(1985) 7 EHRR 471**

Three women who were settled in the UK challenged the immigration rules then in force (HC 394) on the basis that they discriminated against women. The rules allowed virtually automatic admission of wives of British men, but there were more hurdles to be overcome for the husbands of British women.

The ECtHR found that the rules were discriminatory. The British government's response to this was to alter the rules to make the more restrictive process applicable to wives as well as husbands. The inequality between the sexes was thus rectified, but British citizens of different ethnic origins were more sharply differentiated as more people who have family connections abroad are likely to want to marry someone from abroad. The Court considered this question in relation to Mrs Balkandali who was a British citizen born outside the UK, but concluded that the government was not obliged to provide equal rights between citizens of different ethnic origins. They said: 'there are in general persuasive social reasons for giving special treatment to those whose link with a country stems from birth within it' (para 88).

Article 14 guarantees non-discrimination in the delivery of the other Convention rights, but is not a free-standing right. In order to lodge a claim under Article 14, it is necessary that discrimination is alleged in some area that is within the ambit of one of the other Convention rights. For instance, in *Abdulaziz*, the applicants alleged that the immigration rules interfered with their Article 8 rights to family life and discriminated against them as women because it would have been easier for men to bring their spouses into the country. The Court found in their favour on the discrimination issue but not on the family life issue as it was not impossible for them to set up family life in another country. It was necessary to claim under Article 14 that the Article 8 issue of the interference with family life was involved, but there did not need to have been a violation of Article 8 in order for the applicants to succeed under Article 14.

Discrimination for Article 14 entails a difference in treatment which is not based upon 'an objective and reasonable justification' and is not proportionate to the social objective of that difference in treatment. These principles were established in the *Belgian Linguistics case (No 2)* (1968) 1 EHRR 252. Although the wording of Article 14 makes no reference to any defences or justification, this potential defence is held to be inherent in the concept of discrimination, i.e., it is differential treatment which cannot be justified. The principles of discrimination and its justification are not fully developed in the law of the ECHR, but by analogy with cases in the Court of Justice of the EU the defence must be strictly construed, and the justification must exist independently of any discriminatory reasoning (Case 170/84 *Bilka Kaufhaus GmbH v Weber von Hartz* [1986] ECR 1607).

In UK law, a distinction is made between direct discrimination, which entails that one group is treated less favourably than another (e.g., men are paid more than women for the same work) and indirect discrimination, which entails that a requirement or condition is applied equally to all groups but has a disproportionate impact on one group (e.g., part-time workers have fewer rights, but more part-time workers are women, so women are indirectly discriminated against). Neither European law nor the law of the ECtHR expressly distinguishes between direct and indirect discrimination. In Article 14 arguments, therefore, there is no need to make this distinction.

One of the most significant decisions on Article 14 in recent times concerned not immigration, but why it was discriminatory to categorize an issue as one of immigration. The challenge by those detained under the powers of indefinite detention in the Anti-terrorism, Crime and Security Act 2001 was mounted partly on the basis that the statutory power was discriminatory as it allowed the detention of only foreign nationals (*A v SSHD* [2004] UKHL 56). The government's case was that the power was not discriminatory because these detainees could not be deported because they faced a real risk of treatment contrary to Article 3, and the relevant comparison was with non-UK nationals who *could* be deported. The House of Lords accepted the appellants' argument that the appropriate comparator for the purpose of assessing discrimination was a British suspected international terrorist. The difference in treatment between British and non-British suspects (i.e., the detention) had no bearing on the objective of defeating terrorism but was purely immigration or nationality related, an impermissible basis under Article 14. The Home Office's proposed comparator group were not the appropriate ones because they did not share the most relevant characteristics of the appellants, namely non-removability. British nationals did share that characteristic, and to say that they were not comparable because they had a right of abode whereas the appellants could not be removed, as did the Court of Appeal, was to accept the Secretary of State's treatment of the matter as an immigration issue, which it patently was not. The decision is discussed again in chapter 15.

The marriage provisions challenged in *R (on the application of Baiai and others) v SSHD* were also found to be in breach of Article 14 as they made an unwarranted exception for Church of England marriages.

Article 5 protects the right to liberty and security of person and is discussed in chapter 15. Immigration detention raises many human rights issues. At the same time, the use of detention is growing, in particular to control asylum seekers and those who are or may be subject to deportation. Article 5 is the Article from which the UK has derogated on a number of occasions. The first derogations were all in relation to overseas territories during their struggles for independence. Later, there was a derogation from Article 5 in relation to detention in Northern Ireland, which was withdrawn as part of the peace process. In 2001, there was the derogation discussed earlier in relation to 'international terrorists', also discussed further in chapter 15.

The UK government has no plans to sign Protocol 12 ECHR, which provides for a free-standing right not to be discriminated against in any action by a public authority and in delivery of 'rights set forth by law' (see their response to the Parliamentary Joint Committee on Human Rights report on the International Covenant on Economic Social and Cultural Rights, Session 2005–06 Eighth Report HC 850 HL paper 104).

4.11 Conclusion

In simple terms, human rights are a counterbalance to the exercise of executive power. While the 'new human rights era' shifted the balance, it has also thrown existing tensions into sharper relief. House of Lords' decisions, particularly in *Huang and Kashmiri*, *Chikwamba*, *EB (Kosovo)*, and *Beoku-Betts* have laid out humane principles as a foundation for a distinctive UK jurisprudence in Article 8 cases. The scope of Article 3 protection is limited by political and economic considerations in medical cases, though remains absolute where there are real risks of torture or inhuman or degrading treatment. The impact of the higher courts is increasingly to create a UK human rights jurisprudence that has real protective power. As other chapters of this book show, however, these advances are in a context in which legislation and policy is moving in the opposite direction.

QUESTIONS

1 How would you have decided the case of *N*?

2 Does it or should it make any difference to rights under Article 8 whether family life has been formed while waiting for an asylum claim to be processed or while spending time in the UK as, say, a student?

3 Is proportionality really a question of law?

online resource centre

For guidance on answering questions, visit www.oxfordtextbooks.co.uk/orc/clayton5e/.

FURTHER READING

All Party Parliamentary Group on Extraordinary Rendition (December 2005) *Briefing: Torture by Proxy: International Law Applicable to 'Extraordinary Renditions'*.

Amnesty International (2007) *United Kingdom: Deportations to Algeria at all Costs*, AI Index: EUR 45/001/2007.

Bratza, Nicholas (2011) 'The Relationship between the UK Courts and Strasbourg' *European Human Rights Law Review* vol. 5, pp. 505–512.

Clayton, Gina (2008) 'Article 3 Jurisprudence – *N v UK*: Not a Truly Exceptional Case?' *Immigration Law Digest* vol.14, no. 3, Autumn, pp. 6–14.

Clayton, Richard (2004) 'Judicial Deference and Democratic Dialogue: The Legitimacy of Judicial Intervention under the Human Rights Act' *Public Law* 33–47.

Dunlop, Rory (2009) 'Case Analysis: *Y & Z (Sri Lanka) v SSHD*' *European Human Rights Law Review* vol. 6, pp. 805–810.

Gough, Roger, McCracken, Stuart, and Tyrie, Andrew (2011) *Account Rendered: Extraordinary Rendition and Britain's Role* (London: Biteback Publishing).

Hickman, Tom (2008) 'The Court and Politics after the Human Rights Act: A Comment' *Public Law* Spring, pp. 84–100.

Klug, Francesca and Wildbore, Helen (2010) 'Follow or Lead? The Human Rights Act and the European Court of Human Rights' *European Human Rights Law Review* vol. 6, pp. 621–630.

MacDonald, Ian (2008) 'ECHR Article 8: Bringing UK Courts back in Step with Strasbourg' *Journal of Immigration, Asylum and Nationality Law* vol. 22, no. 4, pp. 293–302.

McKee, Richard (2008) 'Deference Deferred: Article 8 Appeals: Recent House of Lords Decisions' *Immigration Law Digest* vol. 14, no. 4, Summer, pp. 8–15.

Metcalfe, Eric (2009) 'The False Promise of Assurances against Torture' *JUSTICE Journal* vol. 6, no. 1, pp. 63–92.

Mole, Nuala (2007) 'Asylum and the European Convention on Human Rights' AIRE Centre, Council of Europe.

Schaefer, Max (2011) '*Al-Skeini* and the Elusive Parameters of Extraterritorial Jurisdiction' *European Human Rights Law Review* vol. 5, pp. 566–581.

Shah, Prakash (2000) 'The Human Rights Act 1998 and Immigration Law' INLP vol. 14, no. 3, pp. 151–158.

Shah, Sangeeta and Poole, Thomas (2009) 'The Impact of the Human Rights Act on the House of Lords' *Public Law* April, pp. 347–371.

Steyn, Lord (2005) 'Deference – A Tangled Story' *Public Law* pp. 346–359.

Weiss, Wolfgang (2011) 'Human Rights in the EU: Rethinking the role of the ECHR after Lisbon' *European Constitutional Law Review* vol. 7, no. 1, pp. 64–95.

SECTION 2

European law and migration

5

Freedom of movement for EU nationals

SUMMARY

This chapter introduces freedom of movement within the European Union (EU). The focus is on rights of entry and residence, particularly for employed workers and their families. A brief account is given of the increasing impact of EU citizenship, and there is discussion of the public policy reasons for excluding rights.

5.1 Introduction

Chapter 4 mainly concerned the application of rights found in the European Convention on Human Rights, the most well-known treaty of the Council of Europe. This chapter concerns a different European system, that of the European Union. Both the Council of Europe and the European Community had their origins in the desire of states after the Second World War to avoid such a conflict ever occurring again. The European Community (EC) began as the European Economic Community (EEC), one of three associations of states which aimed to build close trading links in Europe, and was established by the EEC Treaty, also known as the Treaty of Rome. Economic interdependence was seen as a means to promote peaceful cooperation. The EEC was renamed the EC in 1992. The EC Treaty contains the four freedoms upon which the Community is built, the free movement of goods, persons, services, and capital, all of which serve the central purpose, stated in Article 14 EC (ex 7a), of establishing an area of freedom of movement 'without internal frontiers'. It also established supranational institutions with certain law-making, enforcement, and judicial powers, and the entire legal order has come to be characterized as a 'new legal order of international law' with distinct legal effects such as direct effect within Member States' legal systems and supremacy over national law.

The European Union (EU) was the political union of the Member States of the EC, encompassing a number of intergovernmental areas of cooperation as well as the institutions of the EC. It was established by the Treaty on European Union 1992 (Treaty of Maastricht). The EU is developing a political vision which far exceeds in scope the economic idea of a free market and EU law is expanding to serve that goal. The creation by the Treaty on European Union of EU citizenship seems to prefigure a political union within which free movement derives from citizenship status rather than economic function.

The Treaty of Amsterdam 1997 extended the EC's competence in areas of social policy, the environment, public health, consumer protection, cooperation in policing and civil and criminal justice, and immigration and asylum. It had become apparent that market issues could not be seen in a vacuum. The employment of workers raises questions of their rights and health and safety; the establishment of businesses has an impact on the environment; the presence of transient nationals of other states has implications for policing; and so on.

The next stage of European integration was to be furthered by the Treaty establishing a Constitution for Europe. However, the Constitution was rejected in referenda in France and the Netherlands in 2005. Many of the ideas of the Constitutional Treaty are now incorporated in a new Treaty, called the Lisbon Treaty. We shall examine this later in the chapter as it applies to immigration and asylum. This now renames the EC Treaty the 'Treaty on the Functioning of the European Union' (TFEU) and 'collapses' the previous pillar structure that distinguished between the EC and the EU. Henceforth, it is simply the EU, and we will follow this terminology in this chapter and the next unless the historical context specifically requires otherwise. The new numbering of Treaty Articles after amendments by the Treaty of Lisbon is used, with the old number in brackets, e.g., 'Article 45 TFEU (ex 39 EC)' so that the connection can be made with older cases and materials.

This chapter concerns the law which governs the free movement of people within the European Union (EU). As such, it is principally about the movement of EU nationals, but the movement of non-EU nationals, known in European law as third country nationals, may come within the ambit of EU law as a result of their connection with EU nationals, for instance as a spouse or employee. The chapter concentrates on the rights of EU nationals as workers to move within the EU. The rights of establishment and to provision of services are not covered in detail, and for these, as for a fuller account of free movement generally, reference should be made to textbooks on EU law.

5.2 Sources of law

Free movement law is primarily contained in Treaty Articles and secondary legislation, and is given effect in UK law by statute and rules. In the event of a European provision not being given effect by these mechanisms, the main relevant provisions are directly effective, and take precedence over any inconsistent national provision (Case 6/64 *Costa v ENEL* [1964] ECR 585). Thus, EU law takes effect where UK law fails to deliver an enforceable EU right, but does not prevent UK law from giving greater rights than are contained in EU law.

Appeals against decisions made under the European provisions are made to the same appellate bodies as other UK immigration appeals (Immigration (European Economic Area) Regulations 2006, SI 2006/1003 part 6). This means that there are decisions of the Tribunal and higher courts on European free movement issues. Domestic courts may rule on matters of EC law, but where it is necessary, under Article 267 TFEU (ex 234 EC) any court or tribunal may refer a question to the European Court of Justice for a preliminary ruling, which will then return to the domestic court for application. Only courts against whose decision there is no legal remedy are obliged to refer, and even this obligation is subject to the exception that a reference need not be made if the point is abundantly clear – Case 283/81 *CILFIT*.

On 30 April 2006, Directive 2004/38/EC on the right of citizens of the Union and their families to move and reside freely within the territory of Member States became binding on Member States. This Directive replaced many of the earlier directives and regulations concerning entry and residence. Commonly known as the Citizens' Directive, it is now a major source of law which consolidates and enhances free movement rights. The Commission has released its first report on the implementation of the Directive (COM(2008)840) and issued guidance for better transposition (COM(2009)313), although this is not legally binding. The detailed implementation in UK law is by the Immigration (European Economic Area) Regulations 2006, SI 2006/1003, (as subsequently amended in 2009 and 2011, and supplemented on an operational level by European Casework Instructions), intended to give effect to the Citizens' Directive, though whether they do so fully is a matter we shall consider.

Section 7 of the Immigration Act 1988 implements in UK law the basic principle of free movement by providing that those who have an 'enforceable Community right' shall not require leave to enter under the Immigration Act 1971. This means that although they are technically subject to immigration control, within that system of control they have a right to enter to exercise their freedom of movement. This may be seen at any port of entry to the UK where there is a channel for EU citizens who are normally waved through on presentation of proof of right to travel. Those with an enforceable Community right are nationals of the European Economic Area (EEA), that is, EU countries, Iceland, Norway, and Liechtenstein, and the UK Regulations include Swiss nationals also (Immigration (European Economic Area) Regulations 2006, SI 2006/1003, reg 2(1)). Nationals of Bulgaria and Romania are still subject to transitional provisions limiting their rights to work and permitting Member States to retain national measures restricting access to the labour market.

5.2.1 Determination of EU citizenship

Nationality of a Member State – and thus EU citizenship – is determined by each Member State, having regard to EU law. This leaves matters primarily in the hands of Member States but it is not out of the question that certain determinations or revocations of nationality may be questionable under EU law.

In Case 21/74 *Airola v Commission* [1975] ECR 221, this entailed that staff regulations should be applied so as to disregard a nationality imposed on a female employee by operation of a discriminatory domestic law over which she had no control. Normally, however, the Court, as in Case C–369/ 90 *Micheletti* [1992] ECR I–4329 (a case of dual Italian/Argentinian nationality) and *Chen* (an unusual case of Irish nationality acquired by birth in the North of Ireland, even though this was UK territory), will expect one EU Member State to recognize the nationality conferred on an individual by another. However, mere possession of another Member State nationality by someone who had never been economically active in their state of residence nor exercised any Treaty rights abroad in another Member State was held to involve a purely internal situation in Case C–434/09 *McCarthy*. Deprivation of nationality (and thus of EU citizenship and its benefits) where the individual does not also have a second EU Member State nationality is also to some extent a matter of EU law, see the recent case, Case C–135/08 *Rottmann*.

5.2.2 UK nationals for EU purposes

A number of Member States, including the UK, have made declarations, appended to the Maastricht Treaty, as to whom they regard as their nationals for EC purposes. The UK's Declaration ([1983] OJ C23/1) defines as nationals for EU purposes British citizens, British subjects with the right of abode in the UK, and British 'dependent' (now overseas) territories citizens who acquire that citizenship from connection with Gibraltar. This appears to exclude Commonwealth citizens with right of abode in the UK, unless the Immigration Act 1971 definition of 'British citizens' can be implied into the declaration. Such people are treated by the Immigration Act 1971 as British citizens, indeed their right of abode in the UK is the same as that of a British citizen. However, it appears they do not obtain freedom of movement rights in the EU, even though they may well have lived in the UK all their lives, have the right to vote, and are in every other respect the equivalent in law of a British citizen (see comment by Dell'Olio 2002). The exclusion of British overseas territories citizens who are not from Gibraltar no longer has any significance: they became British citizens by virtue of the British Overseas Territories Act 2002. It may be noted that the Act did not give other European nationals the right to enter the British Overseas Territories. Other categories of British national remain excluded, namely British overseas citizens, British nationals (overseas), and British subjects under the Act or British protected persons.

A challenge to the exclusion of British overseas citizens arose before the ECJ in Case C–192/99 *Manjit Kaur*, an attempt to reverse the underprivileged immigration status of British overseas citizens, as discussed in chapter 3. The applicant was born in Kenya in 1949 of a family of Asian origin. As a citizen of the United Kingdom and Colonies, she had a right of abode in the UK. She lost this through the operation of the immigration statutes of the 1960s, and by the British Nationality Act 1981 she became a British overseas citizen with no right of abode. In 1990, she claimed a right to enter and remain in the UK as an EU national, but her claim was denied on the basis of the UK's declaration defining UK nationals for EU purposes as excluding British overseas citizens.

Article 6(2) of the Treaty on European Union, as amended by the Treaty of Amsterdam, recognized fundamental rights as a principle of Community law. Ms Kaur argued that her right of abode in the UK was a fundamental right, recognized by Article 3, Protocol 4 of the European Convention on Human Rights which says that nationals shall not be deprived of the right to enter their country of nationality. The UK's failure to ratify this Protocol, at least in part because of a wish to avoid obligations to British overseas citizens, had no bearing on the case, as under Article 6(2), the Convention is used as a source of principle for EU law rather than being directly applied. The ECJ, however, reaffirmed the pre-Maastricht principle that it was for Member States, with due regard to EU law, to determine who would be their nationals and thus nationals of the Union. The Court would therefore not interfere with Ms Kaur's status as determined by Britain. The High Court in *ex parte Zaunab Upadhey* 31 January 2000 (unreported) ILU vol. 3 no. 13 confirmed that a British protected person was also not a British national for EU purposes.

The British government's position on categories of British nationals is revealed in a 2006 amendment (Regulation 1932/2006) to the European Common Visa List regulation. The amendment adds to the list of those who require visas to enter the EU: BOTCs who do not have right of abode in the UK; BOCs; British Subjects who do not have rights of abode in the UK; and BPPs. It adds British Nationals (Overseas) to the list of those who do not require visas.

5.3 Free movement of Union citizens

EU law is founded on the principle of the 'four freedoms' of movement of goods, persons, services/establishment of businesses, and capital. Here we focus on the free movement of persons. This freedom has primarily developed in connection with economic activities but the Treaty on European Union created EU citizenship, and in what is now Article 20 TFEU (ex 18 EC), a general right to move and reside freely within the territory of the Member States.

The objective of the Citizens' Directive is to develop Union citizenship as the 'fundamental status of nationals of the member states when they exercise their rights of free movement and residence' (preamble para 2). Here, the Directive quotes the ECJ in Case C–184/99 *Grzelczyk* [2002] 1 CMLR 19, where the Court's finding that a student lawfully residing in another Member State could claim a benefit available to other residents (other EU migrants and Belgian students) in that state made a significant advance in developing the rights of EU citizens. We therefore begin with the rights of entry and residence of Union citizens, the term used in the Citizens' Directive for nationals of a Member State.

The ECJ suggested, in both *Grzelczyk* and *Baumbast*, that EU citizenship and Article 20 meant that free movement is increasingly to be detached from the exercise of economic activity. As we shall see, this is indeed increasingly the case, but economic status remains highly relevant in some situations.

5.3.1 Union citizens' rights of entry and residence

The Citizens' Directive 2004/38 Article 5.1 provides that Member States must allow Union citizens entry simply on production of an identity card or passport, and no entry visa requirement or similar may be imposed. Where a Union citizen or family member does not have the necessary travel documents, they must be given every opportunity to obtain them or have them brought before they are turned back at a border between Member States (Article 5.4). On production of an identity document or passport and confirmation of employment an EU state national must be issued with a registration certificate (Article 8.3). This is proof of the existing entitlement to free movement rights, and so possession of such a document cannot be required as a condition of exercising the rights (*Martinez Sala*). These provisions are implemented in the UK by reg 11 of the 2006 Regulations. There are also special provisions for temporary permits for seasonal workers, those on short-term temporary contracts, and frontier workers. Third country national family members who qualify under the directive are to be issued with residence cards, not registration certificates (Article 9).

Member States must, 'acting in accordance with their laws', issue identity documents or passports to their own nationals (Article 4.3). A failure to issue a passport in the UK could be challenged as a breach of this Directive, which may only be permitted on the restricted grounds allowed by Article 27.

Having entered, any Union citizen and their family members have an initial right to reside for three months without any qualifying conditions (Article 6). After the first three months there is a further indefinite right of residence so long as qualifying conditions exist (Article 7). The conditions are that the person is a worker, self-employed, economically self-sufficient, a student with adequate means and sickness insurance, or the family member of any of these. How these conditions are met is discussed more fully below. In principle, it appears that removal of persons not exercising Treaty rights because they satisfy none of these conditions is not excluded by the Directive, although recourse to public funds must not 'automatically' result in revocation of a right of residence and subsequent removal. Questions and concerns have been raised about attempts to remove homeless EEA nationals in the UK (see further at 5.8.2.5).

5.3.1.1 *Permanent residence*

Article 17(1)(b) of the Directive gives a right to remain to those who have ceased work through permanent incapacity, either through pensionable industrial disease or injury, having lived in the Member State continuously for two years or more. This is implemented in the same terms in the UK Regulations, reg 5(3). Article 17(1)(a) gives the right to remain to workers who retire in a Member State, having lived there for three years and worked there for one year, prior to retirement. Regulation 5(2) implements this in the UK. There is also a right of permanent residence for those who, after three years' continuous employment and residence in the host Member State, obtain employment in another Member State, but who return at least weekly to the first Member State. Again this is implemented in the UK Regulations.

In addition to these particular situations, Article 16 gives a right of permanent residence to all Union citizens and their families after five years of continuous lawful residence. Provisions are made about breaks in continuity. This right includes the right to have accompanying family members enter and join the migrant, without complying with the 'sufficient resources' condition (Case E-4/11 *Clauder*), according to the EFTA Court. Another important question concerning the interpretation of this right has recently been clarified. There was a view, based on recital 17 in the preamble to the Directive, that Article 16 refers to five years' residence in accordance with the Directive, in other words, exercising a right given by the Treaty or Directive for those five years. Case C–162/09 *Lassal* confirms that this is not the case in so far as five years of residence before the Directive came into force does confer the right to permanent residence, but Case C–235/09 *Dias* also makes clear that a formal residence card which had not been revoked is not in itself proof of ongoing compliance with conditions of stay under EU law if the individual had not in fact complied with conditions that would have made the residence lawful throughout the five years. It also indicated that, once this five-year period is completed, periods of absence or periods of residence that do not fully comply with the Directive's conditions before the 2006 date do not necessarily interrupt the continuity of residence to result in loss (or rather, non-acquisition) of the permanent residence status. Case 424/10 *Ziolkowski* raises the question of lawful residence under national law of an A8 national prior to accession and acquisition of the status of EU citizen. The case indicates that such prior residence may be counted, but the applicant must have complied with the conditions set out in the Directive.

5.4 Freedom of movement for workers

Free movement of persons is one of the four fundamental freedoms of the EU. Consonant with the original purpose of the Treaty, the free movement of persons was linked to economic activity. However, even without consideration of Article 20 TFEU (ex 18 EC), this is not limited to actually carrying out work, as the Community institutions, including the ECJ in interpreting EU law, take a liberal and purposive approach to the EU's legal provisions in order to make the free market effective. Case law and secondary legislation flesh out the content of the free movement right, but it begins with Article 45 TFEU (ex 39 EC), which reads as follows:

1. Freedom of movement of workers shall be secured within the Community.
2. Such freedom of movement shall entail the abolition of any discrimination based on nationality between workers of the Member States as regards employment, remuneration, and other conditions of work and employment.

3. It shall entail the right, subject to limitations justified on grounds of public policy, public security, or public health:
   (a) to accept offers of employment actually made;
   (b) to move freely within the territory of Member States for this purpose;
   (c) to stay in a Member State for the purpose of employment in accordance with the provisions governing the employment of nationals of that State laid down by law, regulation, or administrative action;
   (d) to remain in the territory of a Member State after having been employed in that State, subject to the conditions which shall be embodied in implementing regulations to be drawn up by the Commission.
4. The provisions of this Article shall not apply to employment in the public service.

Paragraph 1, setting out the objective of the Article, may be regarded as an agenda for the Court in its decisions and for the other EU bodies in making secondary legislation. Unlike UK legislation which usually prohibits a certain sort of activity, or sets out a power that may be exercised in defined circumstances, Treaty articles, which are the EU's primary legislation, are often phrased in terms of a purpose. The Court's interpretive task is to promote that purpose within the framework of EU law.

In terms of achieving the purpose set out in para 1 of Article 45, the listed rights a, b, c, and d within para 3 may be regarded as the minimum content of the freedom. Paragraph 2 expresses one of the key policies of the EU, the abolition of discrimination based on nationality. Paragraph 4 on the other hand represents a concession to the sovereignty of states, permitting them, for national security or related purposes, to retain some posts specifically for their nationals. In a series of cases, Article 45 has been held to be sufficiently clear, precise, and unconditional to be directly effective, e.g. Case 167/73 *Commission v French Republic* [1974] ECR 359. It may therefore be relied upon directly by a worker to protect their freedom of movement, which means it may be used as a basis for argument in national courts.

5.4.1 Personal scope – to whom Article 45 applies

The definition of who is a worker has been consistently held by the Court to be a matter of EU law, not domestic law, so Member States cannot narrow the effect of Article 45 TFEU by using their own definition. In the Immigration (European Economic Area) Regulations 2006, SI 2006/003, reg 4(1), 'worker' means a worker within the meaning of Article 45.

5.4.1.1 *People in work*

The term 'worker' refers to someone who is or has been employed. The rights of self-employed people are dealt with separately by the provisions on the rights of establishment and provision of services. Case C–66/85 *Lawrie-Blum* [1986] ECR 2121 held that a worker in EU law was someone who, for a period of time, performs services under the direction of another in return for remuneration. Case C–53/81 *Levin* [1982] ECR 1035 concerned a part-time worker refused a residence permit by the Dutch authorities on the grounds that she was not in gainful employment because she earned less than Dutch law regarded as a subsistence level of income, i.e., the minimum on which someone could live. The ECJ took account of the contribution low part-time wages can make to a family. The need to engage in such work was a real economic need. Concerning part-time work which paid less than subsistence wages, the ECJ said that it 'constitutes for a large number of persons an effective means of improving their living conditions'.

Freedom of movement should not be restricted to full-time workers who were earning more than the minimum wage. However, there would have to be some lower limit on the amount of work which would qualify. The ECJ held that the Article guaranteed freedom of movement only for those 'who pursue or are desirous of pursuing an economic activity' and that that activity had to be 'genuine and effective'. It would exclude activities 'on such a small scale as to be marginal and ancillary'.

Case 139/85 *Kempf* [1986] ECR 1741 established that low-paid work may be supplemented not only by the earnings of other family members, but also from other sources including public funds. In *Kempf* the applicant was a music teacher who taught 12 lessons per week and supplemented his income by a claim on public funds. The Court held that:

> It is irrelevant whether those supplementary means of subsistence are derived from property or from the employment of a member of his family, as was the case in Levin, or whether, as in this instance, they are obtained from financial assistance drawn from the public funds of the Member State in which he resides, provided that the effective and genuine nature of his work is established.

Remuneration is crucial to worker status, but need not be in the form of a wage. The economic nature of the work is the key, and provision for basic needs such as accommodation, food, pocket money, etc., in return for participation in the activities and work of a religious community can satisfy this – Case 196/87 *Steymann*. However, in Case 344/87 *Bettray* [1989] ECR 1621, the applicant did not convince the ECJ that he was a worker as the work that he did was rehabilitative in purpose, and not economic. This was so even though he was paid a wage for his work. The work was selected because of its suitability for him rather than he for the work. In Case C–456/02 *Trojani*, the ECJ held that a resident in a homeless hostel working for about 30 hours a week under its direction, as part of a personal re-integration programme in return for benefits in kind and 'pocket money' cash, could claim residence as a worker if the paid activity was real and genuine (*Steymann*) rather than rehabilitative (*Bettray*). It would be for the national court to examine the facts to discover if this was the case.

The wage does not have to be the full rate for the job. In *Lawrie-Blum* the applicant was regarded as a worker while working as trainee teacher. The wage was less than the full rate for a qualified teacher but the Court noted that a trainee was giving lessons to pupils and thus providing a service of economic value to the school.

In Case 413/01 *Ninni-Orasche* the ECJ held that the fact that the employment contract was for a fixed short term and that she knew that in advance did not affect Ms Ninni-Orasche's claim to receive the benefits of a worker. The question is an objective one as to whether the employment is effective and genuine.

5.4.1.2 *People seeking work*

Article 45 itself does not mention people seeking work, but for the freedom of movement for workers to be fully meaningful it is necessary for that freedom to be extended to those who have not yet secured a job offer in another European country but wish to work there. The expectation that job-seekers will also benefit from freedom of movement provisions is implicit in Council Regulation 1612/68 Article 5, which says:

> A national of a Member State who seeks employment in the territory of another Member State shall receive the same assistance there as that afforded by the employment offices in that State to their own nationals seeking employment.

In Case 316/85 *Lebon* [1987] ECR 2811, the ECJ held that those who were seeking work should be entitled to equality of treatment in access to employment under Article 45 and under Articles 2 and 5 of Regulation 1612/68.

Case C–292/89 *Antonissen* [1991] ECR I 745 considered more fully the position of unemployed job-seekers. Mr Antonissen, a Belgian national, had entered the UK, but did not find work. The UK government proposed to deport him following his conviction for drugs offences. Part of his challenge was to the immigration rule then in force, para 143 of HC 169, which limited to six months the stay of an EC national seeking work. The Court held that a job-seeker should be allowed a reasonable period within which to become acquainted with the job opportunities available in the country to which they had moved, and that, in the context of that case, six months was a reasonable period. However, at the end of that time the person could still not be deported if they could show that they were genuinely seeking, and had a chance of obtaining, work. The UK 2006 Regulations expressly include a job-seeker as a 'qualified person', i.e., a beneficiary of EC rights (reg 6).

In *Lebon and Antonissen*, a job-seeker was not treated as a worker for all purposes. The right to remain to seek work was simply a necessary corollary of Article 45, required to give effect to the freedom of movement for workers, but not in itself giving entitlement to all the rights which attach to a worker. In Case C–85/96 *Martinez Sala* [1998] ECR I 2691, the Court said that there was no single definition of 'worker' in EU law: 'it varies according to the area in which the definition is to be applied'. In the context of Article 45, 'a person who is genuinely seeking work must...be classified as a worker'.

5.4.1.3 *Unemployment after having been in work*

In the case of unemployment, as appears from *Antonissen* and *Martinez Sala* just discussed, there is a distinction between retaining the status of worker in the context of social rights, and the status of worker giving a right to reside in a Member State. The Citizens' Directive 2004/38 provides that the status of worker will be retained where s/he is temporarily unable to work because of illness or accident; s/he has been in employment for more than one year and is now involuntarily unemployed, registered and seeking work; s/he has been in employment for less than a year and is now involuntarily unemployed, though in this case the status may only be retained for a further six months, or s/he embarks on vocational training. If the unemployment was voluntary, then the vocational training must be related to the previous employment (Directive 2004/38 Article 7(3)). This enacts the decision in Case C–39/86 *Lair* [1988] ECR 3161, and reg 6(2) of the UK Regulations implements these provisions precisely. The Citizens' Directive provides that where the worker becomes involuntarily unemployed during the first 12 months the status of worker is retained for a minimum of 6 months after that (Article 7(3)(c)). The UK Regulations implement this by requiring that after 6 months the worker retains the status if they can provide evidence of seeking employment in the UK and of a 'genuine chance of being engaged' (reg 6(2)(b)(ii)). The Citizens' Directive protects a worker on the expiry of a short fixed-term contract, enacting an aspect of *Ninni-Orasche* (see 5.4.1.1). The UK Regulations make no such reference, but as the meaning of 'worker' in Article 45 is incorporated into the Regulations by reg 4(1), the decision in *Ninni-Orasche* is also incorporated, and so a worker whose short fixed-term contract ends should still be regarded as a worker under reg 6(2)(b).

In *RP (EEA Regs – worker – cessation)* [2006] UKAIT 00025, the appellant entered the UK in 1999, worked for four months, and was then unemployed for five years, except for one week in 2001. The Tribunal held that he was a worker in 1999, and for some time thereafter. They were not convinced that he had been genuinely seeking work since then, and the week of employment in 2001 was 'marginal and ancillary'. Thus, at some time before his application for an EEA residence document in 2004, he had lost the status of worker. He was thus no longer a qualified person under the EEA regulations.

More drastically, the worker registration scheme for A8 Nationals (see later in the chapter) excluded workers from the protection of the normal 6-month retention of worker status on losing their job until they had completed one full uninterrupted and correctly registered year of work. This was upheld by the House of Lords in *Zalewska* [2008] UKHL 67, despite some criticism and unease about the compatibility of this exclusion with EU law and even a subsequent reasoned opinion by the Commission in 2010 requesting the UK authorities to end this discrimination against A8 nationals in the WRS. Since the A8 WRS has now been abolished this infringement process has been suspended.

5.4.2 Material scope – the content of free movement rights for workers

The underlying premise of European free movement law is that equality in conditions after arriving in another Member State, such as rights to social benefits or access to employment, all support the freedom to move, though this book's focus on migration and constraints of space mean that the main emphasis is on rights of entry and residence.

To give a fuller picture we briefly touch here on some of the social rights. They derive from the Treaty's statement of principle and are expanded and interpreted in accordance with situations brought before the Court, and new Directives.

Many employment contracts are, of course, with private employers. Case C–281/98 *Angonese* [2000] ECR I–4139 established beyond doubt that equality of treatment in Article 45 applies to collective agreements and contracts between individuals ('horizontal effect'). In that case, the requirement to obtain a certificate of bilingualism issued only by the local authority in order to obtain employment at a bank was a discriminatory restriction contrary to the Article. The certificate would serve its purpose just as well if it was provided by a competent authority elsewhere.

5.4.2.1 *Entry and residence*

Article 45(3) provides the right to enter the territory of another Member State and to reside there in order to take up an offer of employment. Directive 2004/38 ensures that there are not administrative obstacles to the exercise of this right, and the right of entry for workers is as described in 5.3.1 for all Union citizens.

5.4.2.2 *Working conditions*

One of the fundamental principles of the Treaty is the abolition of discrimination between nationals of Member States. Article 45(2) requires the abolition of discrimination between workers of Member States as regards 'employment, remuneration and other conditions of work and employment'. The provision has been held to apply to obvious working conditions such as the length and security of employment contracts, e.g., in Case C–272/92 *Maria Chiara Spotti* [1993] ECR I–5185. It also applies to matters not within the direct province of the employer such as the refund of tax deductions, Case C–175/88 *Biehl* [1990] ECR I–2779.

Regulation 1612/68 Article 7 which governs equality in relation to social and tax advantages may be interpreted to give effect to the right of non-discrimination in relation to working conditions. See, for instance, Case C–195/98 *Österreichischer Gewerkschaftbund, Gewerkschaft Öffentlicher Dienst v Austria* [2000] ECR I–10497.

5.4.2.3 *Access to employment*

The most fundamental right relating to work is of course the opportunity to obtain a job in the first place. Article 45 provides that the worker has the right to 'accept offers of employment actually made'. In addition to this, domestic legal systems must not put in place provisions which discriminate against other Member State nationals in being able to obtain such an offer of employment (Article 45(2)). Regulation 1612/68 gives further effect to these Articles:

> Any national of a Member State shall . . . have the right to take up an activity as an employed person, and to pursue such activity, within the territory of another Member State in accordance with the provisions laid down by law, regulation or administrative action governing the employment of nationals of that State. He shall, in particular, have the right to take up available employment in the territory of another Member State with the same priority as nationals of that State. (Article 1)

This prohibits indirectly discriminatory provisions, i.e., those which apply both to foreign and home state nationals but which would deter other Member State nationals, in addition to directly discriminatory provisions, i.e., those which discriminate between home and foreign workers. This is made explicit in Article 3 of the regulation which makes 'provisions laid down by law, regulation or administrative practices of a member state' of no effect if they

> limit application for and offers of employment, or the right of foreign nationals to take up and pursue employment or subject these to conditions not applicable in respect of their own nationals; or though applicable irrespective of nationality, their exclusive or principal aim or effect is to keep nationals of other Member States away from the employment offered.

One of the best-known cases dealing with this principle, though in the application of Article 45 rather than the regulation, is the *Bosman* case from the world of football.

Key Case

Case 415/93 *Union Royale Belge des Sociétés de Football Association v Bosman* [1995] ECR I–4921

Bosman was a goalkeeper with the Belgian team, RC Liege, who challenged the nationality rules which limited the number of foreign players a club could field in official matches (he also challenged the post-contract transfer fee rules, but this raised different issues involving restrictive rules that did not discriminate on the grounds of nationality). The ECJ ruled in his favour. The Court said that a limit on the matches in which a foreign player could appear obviously discouraged a club from employing them.

One of the arguments used by the Belgian Football Association was that the rules promoted cultural identity and thus were supported by Article 162 TFEU (ex 151(1) EC) which was one of the measures introduced by the TEU 'to contribute to the flowering of the cultures of the member states'. The TEU marked a move away from the strictly economic base of EC law and began the process of increasing the (then) EC's competence in educational and cultural areas. The Court rejected this argument as applied to *Bosman*. It said that sport and culture should not be confused, and that the case concerned the freedom of professional sportspeople to move between Member States. *Bosman* was controversial, partly because it put players more in charge and partly because it meant that there was nothing to stop a football club from fielding a team which included no 'home' players from the home nation. UEFA has subsequently entered into an agreement to try to protect the number of locally trained players, but this agreement has also proved controversial. Intergovernmental discussions have not yet exempted sport from freedom of movement provisions, though the sporting bodies have promoted that view (see McAuley 2003). The Court has restated that sportspeople are protected by Article 45 in Case C–176/96 *Lehtonen* [2001] 1 All ER (EC) 97, though accepting rules to ensure the regularity of sporting competitions, subject to a test of necessity. Most recently, in Case C–325/08 *Olympique Lyonnais*, the Court appears to have refined its position confirming that trainee players may be subject to a proportionate regime to ensure some compensation to their training club if they chose not to continue playing there if offered a contract, but to move elsewhere. A further and more general discussion of sport is found in the Commission's Communication COM(2011)12.

Some job requirements may have a genuine cultural purpose which would be protected by the Treaty, even though they are discriminatory in their effect. One of the most obvious is language, and explicit provision is made for this in Article 3 of Regulation 1612/68. This article and its effect were considered in Case 379/87 *Groener*. Groener was a Dutch national who had been working in Ireland as a part-time art teacher. After two years she applied for a full-time post and was recommended for the job. However, she was not appointed as she failed a mandatory Irish language test, even though the lessons would be given in English. Groener argued that as Irish would not be required for the lessons it could not be required, as provided in Article 3(1) of Reg 1612/68, 'by reason of the nature of the post to be filled'. However, the Court supported the lawfulness of the Irish government's policy which was that the use of Irish was being promoted in schools a means of expressing national culture and identity. The requirement was not disproportionate to this objective, and could be upheld within Article 3(1).

Even where a condition of employment explicitly or implicitly constitutes an obstacle to the free movement of workers, by for instance requiring prior experience in the host state, it may be lawful if it pursues a legitimate aim compatible with the Treaty, is justified by pressing reasons of public interest, and if application of the measure ensures achievement of that aim and does not go beyond what is necessary for that purpose. This has been illustrated in numerous cases in the ECJ, of which the following are but recent examples.

Case C–40/05 *Kaj Lyyski* concerned a Swedish government scheme to recruit and train teachers to remedy a shortage. Candidates had to be employed in a Swedish school. This would discriminate against non-Swedish candidates. The ECJ accepted that the scheme's aim was legitimate, and that it was more difficult to monitor practical training if it was taking place outside Sweden. However, as some colleges were exempting trainees from the practical part of the training, and as candidates could be allowed to carry out their training at a different school from the one where they were employed, it could not be said that current employment in a Swedish school was necessary to achieve the Swedish government's aim.

In *Kaj Lyyski*, the requirement indirectly affected applicants from other Member States. In Case C–371/04 *Commission v Italy*, the Member State directly refused to take into account experience gained in other Member States when recruiting for the civil service, on the grounds that the recruitment process in other Member States would be different from that in Italy. The ECJ held that this justification was insufficient. The aim of getting qualified people for the job was appropriate, but if someone was doing equivalent work in a different Member State their experience was what counted and Italy could not discount that experience on the basis of how the person was employed.

5.4.2.4 *Social and tax advantages*

Article 7 of Reg 1612/68 is central in creating a legal basis for equality of social condition and opportunity. The social advantages covered by the Article are not confined to those arising from employment, as a result of Case 207/78 *Ministère Public v Even* [1979] ECR 2019. Even was a French national working in Belgium. He took early retirement, and his pension was reduced on the basis of the number of years early he had received the pension. This was the usual practice, but it did not apply to Belgian nationals who received a war service pension. Even received a French war service pension and so argued that his pension should not be subject to the early retirement reduction. Like nationality, war service is regarded as a quasi personal relationship between the individual and the state, and the Belgian provision was to give the country's own nationals 'an advantage by reason of the hardships suffered for that country'. Therefore, Mr Even lost his claim. However, the statement of principle made by the Court in the case has wider impact:

> The advantages which this regulation extends to workers who are nationals of other Member States are all those which, whether or not linked to a contract of employment, are generally granted to national workers primarily because of their objective status as workers or by virtue of the mere fact of their residence on the national territory.

This principle has been built upon in succeeding cases. For example, Case 65/81 *Reina* [1982] ECR 33 demonstrates that this objective approach may prevent a national social policy from creating disadvantage for other Member State nationals. In Reina, an Italian couple living in Germany applied for a discretionary childbirth loan. The loan could only be granted where one member of the couple was German. It was means tested, and based on a policy of promoting population growth in Germany. The Landeskreditbank refused the Reinas' application, and defended their claim in the ECJ on the basis that the political objective meant that the loan was not an Article 7(2) social advantage. The ECJ looked at the question from the point of view of the impact upon workers. The actual effect of denying the loan to non-German families was that families from other Member States would be living with less material support than German families. This flew in the face of the purpose and the wording of Regulation 1612/68. Article 7(2) could include benefits granted on a discretionary basis, and the ECJ was not debarred from making decisions on social advantages which might have a political effect.

Case 137/84 *Mutsch* [1985] ECR 2681 invoked Even to endorse the right of a Luxembourg national to use the German language in certain court proceedings, as Belgians were allowed to do. This social advantage had no connection with employment, and was unlikely to influence nationals of other Member States in their desire or otherwise to travel to Belgium for work. However, the Court recognized that the ability to conduct court proceedings in their own language 'plays an important role in the integration of a migrant worker and his family into the host country, and thus in achieving the objective of free movement for workers'. The objective of the law is not only to ensure equality in working conditions, but also to remove obstacles to the social integration of workers in pursuit of a vision of a European Community in which people are genuinely free to live wherever their occupation takes them.

The judgment in Case 249/83 *Hoeckx* [1985] ECR 973 showed that Article 7(2) of Directive 1612/68 may be used to fill a gap left by another provision, in this case Regulation 1408/71 on social security benefits. The minimum income allowance, the 'minimex', was granted to people who could show five years' residence in Belgium, which the applicant could not as her residence in Belgium had been interspersed with periods in France. The Court found that the benefit was not one of those covered by Regulation 1408/71, but that it did constitute a social advantage in accordance with Article 7(2). Moreover, the residence condition discriminated against nationals of other Member States in access to this social advantage. It did not apply to Belgian nationals, but even if did it would still be indirectly discriminatory as non-nationals would be less likely to be able to fulfil it.

5.4.2.5 *Social assistance*

However, Reg 1612/68 does not give entirely open access for Union citizens to the welfare benefits systems of Member States. Not all benefits of a host state are open to Union citizens who migrate there for work, and conversely migrants may, in moving, lose benefits that would have been payable in their home state. For full coverage of this subject, including discussion of the coordination of social security systems and payments under what was Reg 1408/71, now Reg 883/04, reference should be made to EU law sources such as those listed at the end of this chapter. The following cases illustrate some of the main principles.

In *Lebon*, the Court held that a work seeker did not qualify for equal social and tax advantages under Article 7 of Regulation 1612/68. The outcome was similar in Case C–138/02 *Collins* [2005] QB 145, although here the ECJ significantly, affirmed the possibility of a work seeker claiming social benefits intended to facilitate access to the labour market. Mr Collins was in a similar position to Mr Antonissen, having come to the UK to seek work but not yet found it. Although he would have a right under Articles 1 to 6 of Reg 1612/68 to equal treatment in job opportunities, unlike Ms Martinez Sala, he had not made any economic contribution in the EU for 17 years. The Court held that his status as worker did not, for all purposes, remain intact for that period. It was relevant that his current search for work was unrelated to his casual employment 17 years earlier. He could not return to the UK and claim means-tested benefits immediately. Even though the job-seeker's allowance might not be outside the scope of equal treatment in principle, it was therefore permissible and compatible with Article 45 TFEU (ex 39 EC) for the UK to maintain and enforce a reasonable and proportionate residence requirement to demonstrate some link with the UK job market before granting the benefit.

This is consistent in principle with Case C–184/99 *Grzelczyk* [2002] 1 CMLR 19, in which the denial of a student's claim for the 'minimex' benefit in his fourth year of university was held to be discriminatory. The situation would have been different if he had arrived in Belgium and claimed straight away, but he was in his fourth year of study, had worked and supported himself so far, and thus had a claim that to accord him the benefits that a Belgian student (or indeed a migrant EU citizen worker) would be able to obtain in this situation was not an 'unreasonable' burden on the host state. This outcome resulted from weight placed on Article 20 TFEU (ex 18 EC), and the Union citizen's right to reside in another state.

In Case C–22/08 *Vatsouras*, benefit claims by work-seekers that were argued to be excluded by Article 24(2) of the Citizen's Directive were considered. Article 24(2) allows derogation from the provision of social assistance during the first three months of residence and longer for job-seekers. Although the Court considers – and implicitly upholds the validity of – Article 24(2), it again distinguishes between different kinds of benefits, stating that 'benefits of a financial nature which, independently of their status under national law, are intended to facilitate access to the labour market cannot be regarded as constituting social assistance within the meaning of Article 24(2) of Directive 2004/38'. This means that such benefits will apparently not be covered by the legislative exclusion from equal treatment laid down in Article 24(2).

A number of cases on social security benefits concern frontier workers, that is people who work in one Member State and are resident in another. In Case C–213/05 *Geven*, Ms Geven worked between 3 and 14 hours per week in Germany, but lived in the Netherlands with her husband (who also worked in Germany) and her son. The ECJ upheld the refusal of the German child-raising allowance to Ms Geven, as it required a minimum of 15 hours per week. They accepted the German government's rationale for introducing the allowance: that it was to encourage the birth rate in Germany. Although Ms Geven's work was more than marginal and ancillary, so she was a worker for the purposes of Article 45, and although the child-raising allowance was a social advantage within Reg 1612/68, the conditions for entitlement to it were rightly within the power of the Member State, which had exercised them rationally in accordance with a legitimate policy. By way of contrast, on the same day (18 July 2007), the ECJ also decided Case C–212/05 *Hartmann*. Here again, a couple lived in Austria and one worked in Germany while the other cared for the child in Austria. Her claim for the child-raising allowance was endorsed by the Court on the basis that the allowance was a social advantage acquired by her partner, and extended to her as a spouse. Perhaps Ms Geven's claim might have had a greater chance of success if she had claimed as her partner's dependant?

In a different factual situation, the ECJ held that the worker could claim a care allowance from the authorities in Austria, where he worked and paid taxes and national insurance. The care allowance was to support his disabled daughter who lived at home with him in Germany (Case C–286/03 *Hosse*). Entitlement may be lost to certain special non-contributory benefits relating to disability if the holder migrates to another Member State. See, for instance, Case C–154/05 *Kersbergen-Lap & Dams-Schipper.*

5.4.2.6 *The 'Right to Reside' test and* Patmalniece

In 2004, in an attempt to enforce the limits of entitlement to benefits by migrant EU citizens, particularly those newly arrived, a new test was introduced (and subsequently amended in 2006) for access to a range of income-related benefits. This involved both factual habitual residence and a legal right to reside in the UK (we leave aside the special position of the Common Travel Area and Irish citizens). Naturally this 'right to reside' was satisfied by UK nationals but only by some EU citizens – and in particular it excluded those not entitled to reside under EU law, i.e., as working or self-sufficient, or now under the new Directive and Regulations, those who might have obtained a legally secure right of permanent residence. In *Patmalniece* [2011] UKSC 11, this was held by the House of Lords to be indirectly discriminatory, drawing on the ECJ's reasoning in *Bressol* (see 5.4.2.7) in which Belgium had incorporated a fairly similar (but 'permanent') right to reside test in its student admissions policy in certain university sectors. However, the Court considered the test justified in the particular case, pension credit, which was covered by the specific Social Security Regulation (at the time Regulation 1408/71). Interestingly, the Commission has started infringement proceedings against the UK in respect of the right to reside test being applied to a range of benefits covered by the social security co-ordination Regulation, 883/04. Media reports suggest that the government intends to defend its position on this, so formal court proceedings may well follow.

5.4.2.7 *Education*

Education is the subject of specific provisions in secondary legislation. Article 7(3) of Reg 1612/68 gives workers access to vocational schools and retraining on the same basis as national workers. As we have already seen, in the Citizens' Directive the status of worker is retained where training following work was either linked to the former occupation or was necessary re-training after the worker had become involuntarily unemployed.

Articles 165 and 166 TFEU (ex 126 and 127 EC) provide for the development of education and vocational training within the EU. Students have a specific right of residence for vocational education by virtue of Directive 2004/38 Article 7(1)(c) provided they can satisfy the relevant national authority: (a) that they have sufficient resources to avoid becoming a burden on the social assistance system of the host Member State; (b) they are enrolled in a recognized educational establishment for the principal purpose of following a course of study; and (c) they are covered by sickness insurance in respect of all risks in the host state. In common with many other 'self sufficient' residents, students here for more than six months are entitled to NHS treatment, but the status of this entitlement as fulfilling or defeating the condition of having comprehensive medical insurance remains somewhat problematic. Case C–209/03 *Bidar* established that student maintenance support was no longer entirely outside the scope of the Treaty. Although requiring evidence of integration into the host society by a period of residence before granting such assistance is permissible, it also suggested that Member States must not act disproportionately in setting the conditions of eligibility, including any period of residence required. In the case, UK Regulations had effectively precluded Bidar from attaining 'settled' status even though his length of prior residence was sufficient, and this was seen as disproportionate. However, the subsequently finalized Directive 2004/38 restricts any obligation of payment of maintenance grants by the host state until permanent residence is obtained, usually five years (Article 24) and this raises an interesting tension between the proportionality approach suggested by *Bidar* and the clear rule inserted into the Directive. Case C–158/07 *Forster* suggests that Member States will not be prevented from relying on the Directive to maintain a clear 'bright-line' rule of five-year residence before allowing access to student maintenance support. *Grzelczyk*, (at 5.4.2.5), however, established that general social assistance payments may be available for migrant students where they are to host state national students and that recourse to such benefits should not be an automatic reason for ending a student's lawful residence status, particularly where the individual has been resident for some time. Case C–73/08 *Bressol* affirmed the theoretical possibility of placing numerical restrictions on non-resident students entering specific higher education courses. The Court accepted that this was indirectly discriminatory (the Belgian residency test included satisfying not just a test of residence but other criteria including having a permanent right to reside in Belgium), but insisted that such must be justified. Whilst suitable and proportionate measures to guard against real risks of future shortages of health professionals could be a possible public health justification for imposing indirectly discriminatory conditions on access to university training courses, vague assertions of securing future workers to provide health services in the host state in question were scrutinized somewhat sceptically as a measure justifying the kind of residency tests and quotas applied, although the final decision will rest with the national court.

By Article 12 of Reg 1612/68, children dependent on a worker have the same right of access to the education system of the host country as do nationals of that state.

5.5 Family members

The right to be accompanied by family members is one of the most significant and litigated rights accorded to workers. Directive 2004/38 replaces Articles 10 and 11 of Reg 1612/68 in respect of family members' right of entry, residence, and employment. Family members are 'qualifying persons' in the UK Regulations.

Rights are granted to members of Union citizens' families without reference to the nationality of those family members, and this is one of the ways in which a third country national may come directly within the ambit of EU law. As rights derive from the relationship with the Union citizen, the family member may be left vulnerable if that relationship is disrupted by for instance death, divorce, or migration. The Citizens' Directive goes some way to enhance the rights of family members, though TCNs still have fewer rights than EEA nationals, and as we shall see, the UK Regulations may not fully implement the Directive.

5.5.1 Who is a family member?

Full rights under the 2004 Directive apply to the Union citizen's spouse, their registered partner if the host Member State treats such partnerships as equivalent to marriage, children or grandchildren under 21, dependent children or grandchildren if over 21, parents or grandparents if they are dependent, in each case, on either partner. A registered partnership must be contracted in a Member State. *Netherlands v Reed* [1986] ECR 1283 established that rights applied to cohabitees to the extent that the host state treated such partnerships as equivalent to marriage, as a 'social advantage' under Art 7(2) of Reg 1612/68. According to Article 3, Member States must also facilitate the admission of other dependants of the Union citizen, including where health grounds strictly require personal care by them, and a partner with whom the Union citizen has 'a durable relationship, duly attested'. This wider group of family members is called in the Directive 'beneficiaries'. In the UK Regulations, they are similarly defined, but called 'extended family members'. The precise meaning of 'facilitation' and other questions relating to the nature and duration of dependency and significance of prior residence in the same country as the primary EU citizen migrant have been referred to the Court of Justice in Case C–83/11 *Rahman*.

In relation to all except partners and children under 21, rights only accrue where the family member is 'dependent' on the Union citizen. In Case 316/85 *Lebon* [1987] ECR 2811, dependants were treated as those who were in actual fact dependent upon the worker. There was no need for an assessment of the reasons for the need for support, but simply of whether the worker is actually providing support for that person. In Case C–1/05 *Jia v Migrationsverket,* the ECJ effectively endorsed more inquiry into the matter by holding that a family member was only dependent on an EU state national if they needed the material support provided to meet their essential needs in their state of origin. This test of necessity is closer to the UK's domestic immigration rules applying to dependent relatives, and is the current authority for interpretation of the Citizens' Directive.

Children may include not only biological children of the worker but, for instance, in *Baumbast* the worker's stepchild benefited from Reg 1612/68. This is in keeping with the purpose of European secondary legislation and family life as defined by Article 8 of the European Convention on Human Rights, which takes account not only of biological relationships but also of the actuality of relationships.

In Case C–370/90 *Surinder Singh* [1992] ECR I–4265, a British national entered the UK with her Indian husband after they had both been living and working in Germany. If she had never left the UK, she would have had to use UK law to bring her husband in. However, as she had exercised her rights of free movement by going to work in another EU country, it was held that her husband had the right of entry with her under EU law when she returned to her home state, the UK. In Case C–109/01 *Akrich,* the appellants sought to use this principle to rely on EU rights for the husband on returning to the UK after the couple had spent what might be termed a 'working holiday' of six months or so in Dublin. The Court held that the reasons for the couple's attempting to exercise

Treaty rights in this way were irrelevant, providing the marriage was genuine. This aspect of the Court's reasoning in *Akrich* still seems sound even though other aspects have been over-ruled (see 5.5.2, *Metock*).

On the other hand, in the UK Tribunal, a UK national's exercise of her free movement rights without her spouse could not confer a right of residence on him. He had never left the UK since his illegal entry some 10 years earlier. The fact that his wife worked in Ireland for six months could not legitimize his stay. This was not the purpose of the right to be accompanied by one's spouse (*GC (China)* [2007] UKAIT 00056, [2008] EWCA Civ 623).

5.5.2 Family rights of entry and residence

Under Directive 2004/38, family members acquire rights in parallel with their Union citizen family member: to entry, to three months' residence without conditions (Article 6), to a longer period of residence while the Union citizen is a 'qualified person', i.e., a worker, self-employed, self-sufficient, or a student (Article 7), or a permanent resident pursuant to Article 16, and to an independent right of permanent residence after five years' residence. Additionally, the family member acquires rights to residence in the particular circumstances detailed at 5.5.4 where their relationship with the Union citizen is severed. Exceptionally, family members may acquire rights to residence outside the provisions of the Directive to make the right of the Union citizen effective (see discussion on *Chen* at 5.5.5).

Family members should be admitted on proof of their entitlement, i.e., of their identity and relationship. For third country nationals, this includes a passport, though for EU nationals identity may be proved by a national identity card. The right of entry of a non-EU family member may be subject to a visa requirement, but it is disproportionate and therefore prohibited to send them back at the border for lack of a visa provided they are able to prove their identity and relationship and there is no evidence to suggest they present a risk to public policy, etc (Case C–459/99 *Mouvement Contre le Racisme, l'Antisemitisme et la Xenophobie Asbl (MRAX) v Belgium* [2002] 3 CMLR 25).

The UK Regulations on the issue of a family permit departed from the requirements of the Directive. Regulation 12 required that the family member be either lawfully resident in another Member State, or meet the requirements of the UK immigration rules. This applied to all family members, whether a spouse, child, parent or other relative. This regulation relied on *Akrich*, in which the ECJ ruled that a family member must have been lawfully resident in one Member State in order to benefit from free movement rights in another state. It stated:

> Regulation No 1612/68 covers only freedom of movement within the Community. It is silent as to the rights of a national of a non-Member State, who is the spouse of a citizen of the Union, in regard to access to the territory of the Community. In order to benefit in a situation such as that at issue in the main proceedings from the rights provided for in Article 10 of Regulation No 1612/68, the national of a non-Member State, who is the spouse of a citizen of the Union, must be lawfully resident in a Member State when he moves to another Member State to which the citizen of the Union is migrating or has migrated. (paras 49, 50)

The Citizens' Directive is similarly silent. The interpretation adopted by the UK and Ireland, although supported by some other governments, was controversial and departed from the traditional understanding of the scope of EU law rights. Further clarification was required and a challenge was inevitable. Ireland had introduced rules similar to those in the UK immigration rules and these were challenged in Case

C–127/08 *Metock*, which made it clear that on this point, *Akrich* was no longer to be relied upon.

Case C–127/08 *Metock & Others v Minister for Justice, Equality and Law Reform*

A number of failed asylum seekers who had married EU citizens from other Member States sought to rely on EU Law rights to remain in Ireland. None of them had been previously lawfully resident in any EU Member State, nor would they have satisfied the domestic immigration regulations in force in Ireland for immediate entry and settlement as a spouse. Relying on *Akrich* and domestic regulations similar to the UK's Regulation 12, the Irish authorities refused their applications and the case was referred to the ECJ. The Court of Justice held in their favour, stating,

> It is true that the Court held in paragraphs 50 and 51 of *Akrich* that, in order to benefit from the rights provided for in Article 10 of Regulation No 1612/68, the national of a non-member country who is the spouse of a Union citizen must be lawfully resident in a Member State when he moves to another Member State to which the citizen of the Union is migrating or has migrated. However, that conclusion must be reconsidered. The benefit of such rights cannot depend on the prior lawful residence of such a spouse in another Member State (see, to that effect, MRAX, paragraph 59, and Case C–157/03 *Commission v Spain*, paragraph 28). The same interpretation must be adopted a fortiori with respect to Directive 2004/38 (paragraphs 58 and 59).

It also clarified that a third country national spouse of Member State national 'benefits from the provisions of that directive, irrespective of when and where their marriage took place and of how the national of a non-member country entered the host Member State' (paragraph 99).

The judgment was unwelcome in some Member States and, unusually, was even discussed in the Justice and Home Affairs Council. The UK, in particular, was slow to comply, with initial indications from the Border Agency and the Tribunal which seemed to deny or underestimate the need for change in the light of the judgment. Although guidance was altered to bring practice into compliance, Reg 12 was only formally amended in 2011.

5.5.3 Extended family members

As mentioned earlier, the Directive provides that Member States must facilitate the entry of extended family members in accordance with national law. These are defined to include:

- A partner in a duly attested durable relationship.
- Another family member who is either dependent on the Union citizen, or lived as a member of their household, or 'on serious health grounds, strictly requires the personal care of the EEA national or their registered partner'.

The UK Regulations (reg 8) repeat this definition and add the category of a relative who would come within the UK's immigration rules for dependent family members. The UK Regulations implement the Directive by providing that extended family members may be issued with a family permit to join or accompany an EEA national if 'in all the circumstances, it appears to the ECO appropriate to issue' it. By comparison, the ECO must issue a family permit for immediate family members.

The effect is that a married or registered civil partner may enter as of right, but an unregistered partner apparently only does so technically as a matter of discretion, subject also to application of *Netherlands v Reed*, see 5.5.1. Family members who would not come within the UK's immigration rules for dependent relatives (HC 395 para 317, see chapter 9), e.g., a cousin, would only be admitted on the ECO's discretion and if they had been dependent on the Union citizen or a member of their household. Extended family members who would come within the UK's immigration rules (an adult sister, brother, uncle, or aunt living alone in the most exceptional compassionate circumstances) are also subject to the discretion of the immigration officer. This also raises a question of priority between the parts of the Regulation. For instance, if an adult sister had been living with a couple who migrated to the UK using European free movement rights, would her claim to enter depend simply upon her having been a member of the Union citizen's household (reg 8(2)(a)) or upon meeting the immigration rules (reg 8(4))? In the latter case she would have to show she was (now) living alone in the most exceptional compassionate circumstances and was mainly financially dependent on the Union citizen.

The Tribunal in *AK (Sri Lanka)* [2007] UKAIT 00074 relied on the requirement in Article 3.2 of the Citizens' Directive that the admission of extended family members be facilitated in accordance with national law. They held (upholding *AP and FP (Citizens' Directive Article 3(2); discretion; dependence) India* [2007] UKAIT 00048) that this referred to the substantive national law, and the facilitation was procedural, meaning that difficult hurdles should not be put in the way of such relatives. However, they rejected the argument for the appellant that, as a relative who did not come within the terms of the Regulations (a cousin who had not been dependent on the Union citizen nor a member of her household), he gained a right of residence directly from the Directive. Article 3.2 did not, they thought, create rights of residence; it only defined who would benefit from the requirement to have their entry facilitated. Thus, the Secretary of State was permitted to apply the immigration rules, and a cousin's entry would be a matter of discretion. Although *Metock* concerned close family members, the Court of Appeal in *Bigia v ECO* [2009] EWCA Civ 79 has clarified that a general requirement of prior residence in another EU Member State is not applicable to 'extended'/'other' family members either for the same reasons. *KG (Sri Lanka) v Secretary of State for the Home Department* [2008] EWCA Civ 13 held that, in relation to such extended family members, the relationship of dependency or membership of the household should exist in the country from which the Union Citizen has most recently come, and *Bigia* confirms that this conclusion is not affected by *Metock*. As noted at 5.5.1, a number of questions concerning 'extended family members' await clarification from the Court of Justice in Case C–83/11 *Rahman*, including the nature and circumstances of the dependency and prior residence of the claimant family member, and the nature of the obligation to 'facilitate'.

5.5.4 Residence without the Union citizen

Family members may acquire or retain rights of residence in certain circumstances even if their relationship with the Union citizen comes to an end. In these cases there is an explicit difference in the Directive between family members who are not nationals of a Member State and those who are. For family members who are nationals of a Member State, their right of residence is not affected by the death or departure from the country of the Union citizen, nor by divorce, annulment of marriage, or termination of registered partnership. This means that such right as they already have is not affected. In order to obtain permanent residence they must themselves become a worker, self-employed, student or self-sufficient, or once again become a family member joining or accompanying a Union citizen who satisfies these conditions (Articles 12.1 and 13.1).

Third country national family members are subject to additional requirements. In the case of death of the Union citizen the family member's rights are not affected if they lived as family for one year prior to the death. There is no provision for protecting a third country national where the Union citizen leaves the country. In the case of divorce, annulment and partnership termination, there are four circumstances in which the right of residence is retained: the marriage or registered partnership lasted three years, at least one of which was in the host state; the third country national has custody of the Union citizen's children; residence is warranted because of particularly difficult circumstances such as domestic violence; or the third country national partner has access rights to a minor child and the Court has ruled that access must happen in the host state.

Third country national family members may only acquire permanent residence in these circumstances if they become workers, self-employed, self-sufficient or if they are members of a family 'already constituted in the host state' of a person who fulfils these conditions. This presumably means that a child of a marriage between a third country national and a Union citizen, who has not acquired an EU nationality, would acquire permanent residence after their parents' divorce if their TCN parent acquired it, say, by being a worker. However, if their TCN parent could not establish their own right to permanent residence, but remarried another EU national then the rights of both child and parent would depend on those of the new EU partner (Articles 12.2 and 13.2).

In the UK's 2006 Regulations, children at school of a qualified person (EU worker, self-employed, self-sufficient, or student) who has died or left the UK retain rights of residence (reg 10(3)) as do parents with custody of such a child (reg 10(4)). Third country nationals retain residence under any of the conditions listed in the Directive for the ending of the relationship but only if they themselves are workers, self-employed or self-sufficient, or they are still a family member of an EEA national in one of these categories (reg 10(5)). This creates a substantial disadvantage for TCN family members in the Regulations as compared with the Directive. Additionally, if their EU partner dies they obtain a permanent right of residence if they lived with the qualified person immediately before their death and for the two years preceding, or the death was due to industrial accident or injury (reg 15(e)). So, if a TCN spouse lived with their EU citizen spouse for two years and then that person dies, they acquire permanent residence. If a TCN spouse retains their right of residence due to having custody of a child and being self-employed, at the end of five years' residence (subject to points below) they acquire permanent residence.

A family member who retains the right to reside obtains permanent residence after five years' residence, as they would if their relationship had continued without disruption (reg 15(1)(f)). The condition above concerning death of a partner under reg 15(e) of the UK Regulations applies also to EU citizens. Strangely, no provision is made in the UK Regulations for EU national partners on the end of a relationship, except as the parents of children at school. They would of course have a right to work, and to acquire rights of residence as workers, and permanent residence after five years as a custodial parent or worker etc.

The failure in the UK Regulations to provide for the departure of the Union citizen is in line with court and tribunal decisions based on the earlier Regulations. In *DA (EEA – revocation of residence document)* [2006] UKAIT 00027, the Tribunal held that where the EU spouse had left the UK the Secretary of State was entitled to revoke a residence document on the basis that the appellant was no longer the spouse of a qualifying person.

This was because the qualifying person had ceased to qualify, having left the country. See also *Kungwegwe v SSHD* [2005] EWHC 1427 (Admin). The 2006 Regulations make it clear that a residence document can be revoked where the holder has 'ceased to have a right to reside' under the Regulations.

Case C–267/83 *Diatta v Land Berlin* [1985] ECR 567 held that, while a couple are still married, the non-EU spouse retains their rights of residence whether or not they continue to live under the same roof. In the light of the UK Regulations it seems that this right is retained for an EU spouse, but only for a non-EU spouse if the Union citizen can be proved to be still exercising Treaty rights in the UK or if the relationship is legally ended and one of the conditions set out in reg 10(5) applies.

5.5.5 *Chen* – the self-sufficient child

Case law has also developed a right to reside for TCN parents where their presence is necessary to give effect to the right of an EU citizen national child, but this right is hedged about with many qualifications and conditions. In Case C–413/99 *Baumbast v SSHD* [2002] 3 CMLR 23, the Court considered the situation of a German man who had been running a business in the UK, but when that failed, left his Colombian wife and children in the UK, which he considered his family home, while he worked outside the EU. The ECJ held that the child of an EU national former worker had a right to remain in education in the host state, and the fact that the EU national parent was now mainly working elsewhere would not affect that right. To hold otherwise would interfere with the mobility of workers within the EU. To make the child's right effective, Mrs Baumbast, too, must have a right to reside with the child. Children and their accompanying TCN parent (still married but separated), need not be self-sufficient if the children remain for education in a *Baumbast*-type situation after one parent has exercised rights as a worker, see Cases C–310/08 *Ibrahim* and C–480/08 *Teixeira*.

Zhu and Chen v SSHD [2004] Imm AR 333 broke new ground in establishing the right to be accompanied by a parent.

Key Case

Case C–200/02 *Zhu and Chen v SSHD* [2004] Imm AR 333

The claimants were a mother and her child. The mother and her husband were Chinese nationals who worked for a large chemical production company which exported to various parts of the world. In the course of the husband's work he frequently travelled to the EU including the UK. The couple wished to have a second child, against China's one child policy, and decided to have the child in Northern Ireland. The effect of Irish law at the time was that a child born on the island of Ireland acquired Irish nationality. The baby was an EU citizen and so had free movement rights within the EU. As she had adequate sickness insurance and sufficient resources, she had a right of residence for an indeterminate period of time under then Directive 90/36, now the Citizens' Directive (*Chen* para 78).

The mother and daughter sought to remain in the UK to exercise this right. The mother was not the daughter's dependant, but she had a right to reside with the child in order to give effect to the child's right. The child was too young to live alone and her right of residence was otherwise meaningless. The conscious use by the couple of EU law was not an abuse because it did not distort the purpose and objectives of EU law, but rather 'took advantage of them by legitimate means to attain the objective which the EU provision sought to uphold; the child's right of residence' (para 122).

Following *Chen*, a range of cases came to the Tribunal and the Court of Appeal in which parents sought to establish a right to reside. In particular, the question of whether the child's economic support may come from the parent's employment in the host Member State arose. The Chens had sufficient income, so the question did not arise for them. The UK immigration rules prevented the family income from coming from employment in the UK. This has also been the approach in the Tribunal, confirmed in the Court of Appeal in *W (China) and X (China) v SSHD* [2006] EWCA Civ 1494, *ER and others (Ireland)* [2006] UKAIT 00096, *GM & AM* [2006] UKAIT 00059, and in *Ali v SSHD* [2006] EWCA Civ 484. However, Case C–34/09 *Zambrano* suggests that Member States may be required to permit a parent to work. In that case it was made clear that the (Colombian) parents should be given the right to work in Belgium to provide for the child. Interestingly, it was also an 'internal situation' case as the situation involved a Belgian-born and national child of Colombian parents seeking to remain in Belgium, so a distinction might be made on that point and further clarification may be required.

5.5.6 Article 20

Although the ECJ has accepted in *Baumbast* that the right of residence now in Article 20(2)a TFEU (ex 18 EC) is directly effective, arguments that this right is entirely unconstrained by the requirements of self-sufficiency in secondary legislation have been unsuccessful. The text of Article 20 TFEU is qualified: 'in accordance with the conditions and limits defined by the Treaties and by the measures adopted thereunder'. Although this qualification is expressed slightly differently from the previous text, there is nothing to indicate that the effect will be any different. In *Chen* itself, the ECJ held that a child had a right to reside under Article 20 which she could exercise because she was economically self-sufficient, as required by secondary legislation. If she had not been able to fulfil these requirements, Article 20 would not have provided an independent right. *Baumbast* and *Grzelczyk* do suggest that, in suitable cases, proportionality may be invoked to place some restraint on the application of the strict letter of the law in the implementation of secondary legislation, but *Trojani* clearly indicates that there are limits to this (as does *Forster* in the case of equal treatment).

5.5.7 Article 8 ECHR

In the cases discussed in the preceding sections, the whereabouts and activities of the parent(s) were crucial in practice to the European child's exercise of their rights.

In Case C–60/00 *Carpenter*, however, it is the Union citizen's wife whose residence is in question. Mr Carpenter was a UK national living in the UK from where he ran a business which had clients in and involved some travel to other Member States. Mrs Carpenter was a Philippine national who had overstayed her visitor's visa and married Mr Carpenter. She was refused leave to remain in the UK because of her irregular immigration status at the time of her marriage. She challenged the decision that she should return to the Philippines to apply for entry clearance and a residence permit on the basis that she had EU law rights. The fundamental question in the case is whether these law rights were engaged at all. The ECJ concluded that they were. Mr Carpenter was exercising his rights under Article 56 TFEU (ex 49 EC) to provide services in another Member State. His capacity to do this was hindered by the disruption to his family life – amongst other things, his wife had to return to the Philippines and so could not look after the children during his absences, and could not travel freely with him because she would not gain re-entry to the UK, but it is not clear how heavily these practical issues weighed with the Court compared with the basic issue of the separation of a married couple.

The ECJ placed emphasis on the infringement of Article 8 ECHR which was entailed by separating Mr and Mrs Carpenter. Deportation was disproportionate as, although she had infringed immigration law, there was no other complaint against her. Therefore, Mr Carpenter's Article 56 rights were infringed by requiring his wife to leave the country.

Both here and in the context of deportations (see 5.8), ECHR rights are in principle highly relevant but in practice the well-established secondary free movement law (Directive 2004/38) often gives as much or indeed better protection. Indeed this was why Mrs Carpenter and Mr Akrich sought to rely on EU law.

5.5.8 Social and tax advantages

Citizens' Directive Article 24 provides that family members who obtain a right to remain are entitled to equality of treatment. In Case 32/75 *Fiorini*, an Italian woman and her children were resident in France. She was the widow of an Italian man who had worked in France and died in an industrial accident. During his life, he had been entitled to a fare reduction card for large families, but when she claimed this after his death it was refused on the grounds that she was not French. She claimed nationality discrimination in breach of Article 18 TFEU (ex 12 EC) and of Article 7(2) Reg 1612/68. This case predated *Even*, but the ECJ still took the view that the social advantages referred to in Article 7(2) did not have to arise from a contract of employment. The Article was intended to refer to all social and tax advantages. As the family had a right to remain in France after Mr Fiorini's death, pursuant to Reg 1251/70, they also had a right to equal treatment in relation to these social advantages. Combining the effects of Article 7 of Reg 1251/70 and Article 7(2) of Reg 1612/68 they were entitled to the fare reduction card as would be any French family in a comparable situation.

An important right for families established in Reg 1612/68 Article 11 and continued in Directive 2004/38 Article 23 is to 'take up any activity as an employed person throughout the territory of that same state'. Case C–10/05 *Mattern and Cikotic* [2006] ECR I–03145 emphasized that the spouse's right to work is to work in the host state, not another Member State.

As mentioned earlier, the worker's children's right to education is the same as that of host state nationals, and continues after their parent has ceased work. Entitlement to educational grants is now dealt with in the Citizens' Directive Article 24(2), and benefits families of workers, the self-employed, and those with permanent residence.

5.5.9 Marriages of convenience

A spouse is held not to qualify as a spouse for the purpose of the Treaty or secondary legislation if the marriage is one of convenience (see *Akrich* at 5.5.1). By a non-binding resolution of 4 December 1997, the European Council defines this as a marriage entered into 'with the sole aim of circumventing the rules on entry and residence'. This is a more stringent test than the old primary purpose rule in UK law. Evasion must be the sole aim of the marriage, rather than one motive among many. The resolution sets out a list of factors which may provide grounds for believing that the marriage is one of convenience. They include for instance that the parties do not live together after the marriage, that they do not speak a language understood by both, and they are inconsistent about details such as each other's nationality and job. These provisions are directed at obvious subversion of the rules, are more objective, and have not given rise to the invasions of privacy and voluminous case law that have accompanied national marriage rules. On the other hand, Member State authorities claim that this leads to greater opportunities for cases of abuse to go undetected and are concerned to maintain as much surveillance to prevent such abuse as their resources, and EU law, will allow. The Citizens' Directive permits measures to combat fraud or abuse of rights, including marriages of convenience (Article 35), but these must be proportionate and subject to the procedural safeguards in Articles 30 and 31 of the Directive.

5.6 Internal effect

In a number of cases, applicants have sought to use rights granted by European law in situations which have not involved the crossing of national borders. The ECJ has held that these situations must be regarded as internal to Member States and thus not involving freedom of movement. In Case C-175/78 *R v Saunders* [1979] ECR 1129, a British national from Northern Ireland who was convicted of an offence in England was required to return to Northern Ireland and keep out of England and Wales for three years. The ECJ declined to interfere with this. They took the position that the state was entitled to impose restrictions within the Member State upon its own nationals where this was done in the course of criminal law.

Cases 35 and 36/81 *Morson & Jhanjhan* took a similar approach in relation to family rights and Cases C-64 and 65/96 Uecker & Jaquet confirmed that EU citizenship does not in the Court's view alter this fundamentally. A number of commentators have suggested that if borders within the EU are to be removed, the requirement of movement across borders in order to trigger family reunion rights is artificial. The artificiality was recognized by the Commission in early drafts of the Family Reunion Directive in proposing to abolish this discrimination in respect of family reunion but this did not survive to the final version of the directive. In *Carpenter v SSHD*, *Surinder Singh*, and *Chen* (all discussed earlier), the ECJ rejected the argument that the situation was purely internal and found sufficient link to the exercise of community law rights – the time spent working in Germany, the services provided regularly in other Member States, and the residence as an Irish national in the UK. Three recent cases emphasize that the reach of EU law into apparently 'internal situations' is by no means fully settled yet.

Key Case

C-34/09 *Ruiz Zambrano v Office national de l'emploi*

In Case C-34/09 *Zambrano*, the question of the internal effect of Articles 18 and 20 TFEU (ex 12, 17, and 18 EC) was raised to question whether an EU citizen in their state of birth and sole EU Member State nationality could assert a right of residence under EU law and rely on the *Chen* principle to acquire residence for a TCN parent/carer. As alluded to earlier, the Court established the capacity of EU law and the status of EU citizenship to protect the residence right of the whole family in this situation, on the basis that the family otherwise faced exile from the whole of the EU and this would be a denial of the genuine enjoyment of the substance of citizenship rights of the infant EU citizen. The Court comments that 'Article 20 TFEU precludes national measures which have the effect of depriving citizens of the Union of the genuine enjoyment of the substance of the rights conferred by virtue of their status as citizens of the Union (see, to that effect, *Rottmann*, paragraph 42)... A refusal to grant a right of residence to a third country national with dependent minor children in the Member State where those children are nationals and reside, and also a refusal to grant such a person a work permit, has such an effect... It must be assumed that such a refusal would lead to a situation where those children, citizens of the Union, would have to leave the territory of the Union in order to accompany their parents. Similarly, if a work permit were not granted to such a person, he would risk not having sufficient resources to provide for himself and his family, which would also result in the children, citizens of the Union, having to leave the territory of the Union. In those circumstances, those citizens of the Union would, in fact, be unable to exercise the substance of the rights conferred on them by virtue of their status as citizens of the Union' (paragraphs 42–44)

Key Case

C–434/09 *Shirley McCarthy v SSHD*

On a different note, Case C–434/09 *McCarthy* is perhaps an indication that *Zambrano* does not herald the end of the 'internal situation' for good. The ECJ perhaps rather surprisingly refused to recognize the effect of the dual (Irish/British) nationality of a British resident wife who wished to assert her Irish nationality as defeating the 'internal situation' argument so that her Jamaican husband could rely on EU rights rather than the domestic UK immigration regulations. She had apparently never worked in the UK or Ireland and was dependent on benefits. The Court comments that 'no element of the situation of Mrs McCarthy, as described by the national court, indicates that the national measure at issue in the main proceedings has the effect of depriving her of the genuine enjoyment of the substance of the rights associated with her status as a Union citizen, or of impeding the exercise of her right to move and reside freely within the territory of the Member States, in accordance with Article 21 TFEU. Indeed, the failure by the authorities of the United Kingdom to take into account the Irish nationality of Mrs McCarthy for the purposes of granting her a right of residence in the United Kingdom in no way affects her in her right to move and reside freely within the territory of the Member States, or any other right conferred on her by virtue of her status as a Union citizen.' '... by contrast with the case of *Ruiz Zambrano*, the national measure at issue in the main proceedings in the present case does not have the effect of obliging Mrs McCarthy to leave the territory of the European Union. Indeed, as is clear from paragraph 29 of the present judgment, Mrs McCarthy enjoys, under a principle of international law, an unconditional right of residence in the United Kingdom since she is a national of the United Kingdom' (paragraph 50).

Like *Zambrano*, the conclusion in this case was somewhat unexpected and has provoked much comment. *Zambrano* and *McCarthy* sit uneasily together and it is clear that the reach of EU law in situations where the 'internal situation' argument is raised still remains in a state of uncertainty. The follow-up to this does not eliminate the tension between these two cases but provides some answers.

Key Case

C–256/11 Murat Dereci v Bundesministerium für Inneres

In Case C–256/11 *Dereci*, the Court still maintains that the Zambrano family faced the choice of staying in Belgium or exile from the entire EU, without explaining why any right to work would not also apply in France not Belgium as parents of a migrant infant EU citizen and thus allow them to settle there (as in *Chen*, in a state other than that of the child's nationality). It emphasizes however that in the normal situation of a married couple or adult children, who wish to reunite the family in the EU citizen's home Member State, the frustration of that wish by the home Member State's immigration regulations will not necessarily lead to the loss of the core of the EU citizenship right by being obliged to leave the entire EU territory. The Court comments that 'the criterion relating to the denial of the genuine enjoyment of the substance of the rights conferred by virtue of European Union citizen status refers to situations in which the Union citizen has, in fact, to leave not only the territory of the Member State of which he is a national but also the territory of the Union as a whole... the mere fact that it might appear desirable to a national of a Member State, for economic reasons or in order to keep his family together in the territory of the Union, for the members of his family who do not have the nationality of a Member State to be able to reside with him in the territory of the Union, is not sufficient in itself to support the view that the Union citizen will be forced to leave Union territory if such a right is not granted' (paragraphs 66 and 68).

A very different situation raising acutely the 'internal situation' question has arisen in respect of the differences in tuition fees in different parts of the UK – resulting for example in English domiciled students being charged much higher fees than Scottish or other EU domiciled students to attend Scottish universities. A legal challenge arguing breach of human rights is underway, including on grounds of discrimination under national law, although it is not clear whether EU law will be a major part of this challenge. The orthodox view would be that it would not apply to an English student studying elsewhere in the UK but requires other EU students to be charged equally with Scottish students – but an argument to the contrary might yet be advanced at some stage of the proceedings.

5.7 Public service exceptions

The EU Treaty recognizes that some kinds of work may require a particular affiliation to the state, and where this is the case it may be legitimate for the state to restrict work to its own nationals. Accordingly, Article 45 TFEU (ex 39 EC) includes an exception for employment in the public service, giving the state the right to discriminate on the basis of nationality in opportunities to be admitted to such jobs.

What this exception covers is one of those issues, like the definition of a worker, which the ECJ regards as a matter of Community law. The definitions of Member States will not be conclusive as this would give them power to define the terms of their own exemption, which would not be appropriate. Two approaches to the question have been identified: the 'institutional approach' and the 'functional approach'. The institutional approach says that because a person is employed by a particular body, say, a national railway, this employment is defined as employment in the public service. The functional approach looks at what is entailed in the work and determines whether this should qualify as public service. The ECJ prefers the latter approach, while Member States have tended to argue (unsuccessfully) in favour of the former.

In Case 149/79 *Commission v Belgium*, the Court set out some characteristics which could bring employment within the definition of public service. First, the post presumes on the part of the employee and employer a 'special relationship of allegiance to the State'. Second, there is a reciprocity of rights and duties which form the foundation of the bond of nationality. Third, the post must involve the exercise of powers conferred by public law and duties designed to safeguard the general interests of the state.

Commission (non-binding) guidance suggests when the exception might apply, including certain functions within the armed services, police, judiciary, tax authorities, and certain public bodies engaged in preparing or mounting legal actions. It would generally not include nursing, teaching, and non-military research (1988 OJ C 72/2).

If and when a non-national is actually employed in public service, Article 45(4) cannot be used to treat them less favourably than national workers. In Case 195/98 *Österreicher Gewerkschaftbund, Gewerkschaft Öffentlicher Dienst v Austria* [2000] ECR I–10497, a union challenged the practice of discounting periods of service spent in other Member States when reckoning periods of service for the purposes of pay and promotion. The government argued that teachers were employed in the public service and therefore exempt under Article 45(4). This argument was doomed as it was already settled law that teachers were not covered by the public service exception, but the Court also held that non-recognition of earlier periods of service was not a matter connected with access to employment but to conditions of employment once in post, and thus not covered by Article 45(4).

For the self-employed, the exception in Article 51 (and 62) TFEU (ex 55 and 66) takes effect in relation to 'activities which in that state are connected, even occasionally, with the exercise of official authority'. In Case 2/74 *Reyners v Belgium* [1974] ECR 631, a Dutch lawyer had obtained his legal education in Belgium, but was refused admission to the Belgian bar on the grounds that he was not of Belgian nationality. The Court said that the extension of the exception to the whole profession was not permissible where activities connected with the exercise of official authority were separable from professional activity as a whole. The exercise of official authority in the legal profession was the exercise of judicial authority by judges, and not contact with the courts by advocates.

5.8 Public policy exceptions

The public policy, security, and health exception is the only basis for deportation of an EEA national, and should be compared with grounds for other foreign nationals, discussed in chapter 16. Substantial differences will be seen as the deportation of an EU citizen is in almost every case an interference with their Treaty right to freedom of movement. Any ECHR rights are additional to this. Directive 2004/38 replaces Directive 64/221 in implementing this exception, and enhances protection for the individual.

5.8.1 Public health

This may be dealt with briefly. Article 29 of the Directive says:

> 1. The only diseases justifying measures restricting freedom of movement shall be [those] with epidemic potential as defined by...the World Health Organisation and other infectious or contagious parasitic diseases if they are the subject of protective provisions applying to nationals of the host Member State.
> 2. Diseases occurring after three months from the date of arrival shall not constitute grounds for expulsion from the territory.

Article 29(1) represents a tighter policy than its predecessor, as Directive 64/221 listed specific diseases in addition to those listed by the World Health Organization. Article 29(2) allows for some possibility of expulsion as opposed to refusal of entry; Directive 64/221 did not.

Medical examinations may only be required 'where there are serious indications that it is necessary' within the first three months after arrival. By way of comparison, UK immigration law may require a medical examination of any applicant for settlement.

5.8.2 Public policy

This is the more contentious and frequently used ground which also encompasses public security. There is no definition of public policy in the Directive or by the ECJ, but the Court interprets the Directive restrictively in order not to interfere with the purposes of the Treaty.

Article 27(2) of the Directive provides:

> Measures taken on grounds of public policy or public security shall comply with the principle of proportionality and shall be based exclusively on the personal conduct of the individual concerned. Previous criminal convictions shall not in themselves constitute grounds for the taking of such measures.
>
> The personal conduct of the individual concerned must represent a genuine, present and sufficiently serious threat affecting one of the fundamental interests of society. Justifications that are isolated from the particulars of the case or that rely on considerations of general prevention shall not be accepted.

To appreciate the radical nature of this paragraph comparison needs to be made with grounds for UK deportations discussed in chapter 16, where it will be seen that a general policy of deterrence has often been accepted by the courts as justifying an individual deportation. This new element in Article 27(2) reinforces the social objectives of free movement law, showing that the power of the state in relation to the individual is curbed by EU law.

Accordingly, one of the earliest and foundational decisions on the application of the public policy exception would almost certainly not be decided the same way today. Case 41/74 *Van Duyn* [1974] ECR 1337, concerned whether association with an organization could amount to personal conduct. Ms Van Duyn was a member of the Church of Scientology and was refused leave to enter the UK to work for the Church because the UK government considered its activities to be socially harmful. The ECJ concluded that this was within the permissible range of discretion for a Member State, and this was the case even if (as was the case here) the organization had not been made unlawful, and its nationals could participate in it without legal sanction. It would be an undesirable distortion of social policy to require a government to outlaw an activity so that it could prevent people from entering the country to take part in it. The Court would however expect to see some administrative measure taken against the activity. In the *Van Duyn* case a statement in Parliament sufficed for that.

Case 115/81 *Adoui and Cornouaille* takes a different approach, and one more likely to be used if *Van Duyn* were heard again today. The ECJ would be concerned to see that effective measures were taken against nationals who engaged in the activity in question before regarding it as a suitable basis for excluding a non-national. Prostitution was not illegal in Belgium and there was not a strong enough policy reason to exclude non-nationals for engaging in an activity that was not prohibited, or at least subject to effective repressive and deterrent measures, for nationals.

EU nationals should not be deported as a sanction for administrative lapses or irregularities. In Case C–215/03 *Oulane*, it was disproportionate to detain and deport a French national who did not produce proof of identity on two occasions when requested.

5.8.2.1 *Criminal convictions*

The most common basis for derogation on grounds of public policy is criminal conduct. The ECJ has reinforced on a number of occasions that previous convictions do not in themselves constitute grounds for exclusion or expulsion, although such convictions may be taken into account in determining whether someone should be deported on the grounds of public policy. The leading case is Case 30/77 *R v Bouchereau* [1977] ECR 1999. The defendant, a French national working in the UK, was convicted for a second time of unlawful possession of drugs. The sentencing court wished to recommend that he be deported and referred two questions to the ECJ. The Court ruled, first, that a recommendation for deportation was a 'measure' within Article 3; and, second, that 'the existence of previous criminal convictions can only be taken into account in so far as the circumstances which gave rise to that conviction are evidence of personal conduct constituting a present threat to the requirements of public policy'. Elaborating, the Court went on, 'recourse…to the concept of public policy presupposes…a genuine and sufficiently serious threat to the requirements of public policy affecting one of the fundamental interests of society'. However, the Court also issued a caveat that in sufficiently serious cases, conduct alone might warrant deportation. Directive 2004/38 adopts these words from *Bouchereau*.

By contrast, the personal conduct of the applicant in Case 67/74 *Bonsignore* [1975] ECR 297 could not be said to pose any threat to public policy affecting one of the fundamental interests of society. He was an Italian worker resident in Germany who, while handling a gun (which he had purchased illegally) accidentally but negligently killed his younger brother. The incident was a tragic accident, and there was no reason to deprive Mr Bonsignore of his German residence on the grounds of public policy.

There is thus no scope for *automatic* expulsion connected to the commission of criminal offences (Case C–50/06 *Commission v Netherlands*, also Case C–348/96 *Donatella Calfa* [1999] ECR I–0011). This must mean, as Macdonald suggests, that para 320(18) of the immigration rules HC 395 cannot be applied to EEA nationals as it provides that entry clearance or leave to enter the UK should normally be refused where the applicant has committed an offence punishable in the UK with imprisonment of 12 months or more. The UK Borders Act 2007 ss 32–39, which introduce compulsory deportation for certain criminal convictions (see chapter 16), sensibly contain an exception for those protected by EU law so that deportation will not be automatic, although now the threshold for *consideration* for removal of even EU/EEA nationals in cases of drugs, violent, or sexual offences has recently been reduced from sentences of two years to 12 months.

5.8.2.2 *Weighing up the conduct*

We can usefully compare the EC public policy proviso with the UK law concept of a deportation being 'conducive to the public good'. Theoretically, the emphasis in both is not on what the individual has done in the past but on the effect on society of their continued presence but the European law standard makes more demands on the state than the UK law standard, as the state's argument must be sufficient to outweigh the right of freedom of movement, within a system in which this freedom is the primary purpose, and the Court has repeatedly stated that this power of derogation must be interpreted restrictively.

In UK courts and tribunals, the caveat in *Bouchereau*, permitting deportation when past conduct is sufficiently serious, has been applied in offences involving Class A drugs, for instance the case of *Marchon* [1993] Imm AR 384 in which a Portuguese doctor had been convicted of importing 4.5 kilos of heroin. This view has been regarded as 'unsound as a matter of Community law' by the Tribunal in *MG and VC (EEA Regulations 2006; 'conducive' deportation; Ireland)* [2006] UKAIT 00053.

In cases where the proposed deportee has a family or private life in the UK, the disruption to this must be proportionate to the public interest pursued in accordance with Article 8 ECHR, and various factors relevant to such a balancing assessment are enumerated in Article 28 of Directive 2004/38. These are equivalent to the widest possible interpretation of Article 8 ECHR, including 'social and cultural integration into the host member state'.

5.8.2.3 *Protection for long-term residents*

Directive 2004/38 introduces new protections against expulsion where the individual has long residence in the host state. This means that there are now three tiers of protection against expulsion decisions, as follows:

1. A decision against any Union citizen or their family member, only on grounds of public policy, public health, or public security. Considerations as just discussed, Article 27(1).
2. An expulsion decision against a Union citizen or their family member who has the right of permanent residence may only be taken on 'serious grounds of public policy or public security', Article 28(2).

3a. An expulsion decision against a Union citizen who has resided for 10 years may only be taken on 'imperative grounds of public security', Article 28(3)a.

3b. An expulsion decision against a minor, unless expulsion is necessary for the best interests of the child, also may only be taken on 'imperative grounds of public security', Article 28(3)b.

It is clear that expelling an EU national is intended to be a rarity.

'Imperative grounds of public security' were interpreted in *MG and VC* [2006] UKAIT 00053 to mean something more than 'the ordinary risk to society arising from the commission of further offences by a convicted criminal' (para 34). The Home Office representative suggested that what was intended was the commission or suspicion of terrorist offences, but the Court of Appeal in *LG (Italy) v SSHD* [2008] EWCA Civ 190 said that 'imperative grounds of public security' did not necessarily connote a terrorist threat.

Key Case

Case C–145/07 *Land Baden-Württemberg v Panagiotis Tsakouridis*

Tsakouridis was a Greek national who was born and had lived in Germany all his life and had an unlimited residence permit there since 2001. He then returned briefly to Greece a couple of times in 2004/5 but was returned under an arrest warrant and eventually convicted of various narcotics offences and in 2007 was sentenced to six and a half years in prison. This was not his first conviction however as he had a criminal record going back to 1998. He was informed that his permanent residence was revoked and he was liable to expulsion to Greece, relying (apparently decisively and exclusively) on the five-year sentence threshold in relevant German regulations. This expulsion was overturned on appeal to the Stuttgart Administrative Court on the grounds that there were no 'imperative' grounds of public security and that crossing the five-year sentence threshold making expulsion *possible* did not *automatically* lead to this conclusion. On reference to the Court of Justice during the course of a further appeal against the quashing of the expulsion, the ECJ made it clear that narcotics offences were not necessarily excluded from being viewed either as 'serious grounds of public policy or security' or as 'imperative reasons of security' if they were serious enough. However it also made clear that any national regulation purporting to use the length of sentence alone as an indication of such 'serious' or 'imperative' reasons being established without taking into account all the factors involved could not be sustained. On this point the initial decision seems to have been unsustainable and its quashing by the Stuttgart Administrative Court justified, although the case would not automatically be precluded for *consideration* as one of 'imperative reasons of public security' purely because it involved a drugs offence, if it were serious enough.

5.8.2.4 *Procedural rights*

Directive 2004/38 provides for a right to judicial procedures for all expulsion decisions. Furthermore, it provides that where an application is made for an interim order to suspend enforcement, with limited exceptions for repeat cases and where expulsion is based on 'imperative grounds of national security', no enforcement action may be taken until that application has been heard.

An important decision in terms of European law's impact in the UK was C–357/98 *R v SSHD ex p Yiadom* [2000] ECR I–9265. A decision refusing leave to enter after the applicant had been in the UK for seven months on temporary admission was in reality a decision to remove her, not a decision on entry. This would therefore attract a right under Article 9 Directive 64/221 to have an appeal before removal, which was not available to a non European. As mentioned in chapter 1, one of the sub-themes of immigration and asylum law in the UK at present is the creation of a kind of non-status; a condition of being present in body but not in law. Here, the European Court of Justice takes a very realistic approach. It is not appropriate to give someone a temporary status in the country, then make a decision which means they must leave, but to label it a decision on entry rather than removal and so deprive them of appeal rights (compare *Khadir*, discussed in chapter 15).

5.8.2.5 *Expulsion of those not exercising Treaty rights: the case of homeless EEA nationals*

The UK authorities have indicated their intention to enforce more strictly the limits of EU residence rights against those not in fact entitled to be here because they are not, or are no longer, 'qualified persons' exercising Treaty rights (see Weiss, IANL 2010). As noted at 5.3.1, this appears to be permitted by EU law, after individual consideration and not automatically, on the basis of being or becoming an 'unreasonable burden' on the social assistance system. Some however have questioned the use of removal powers against those who are by and large because of the 'right to reside' test (see 5.4.2.6) not entitled to claim income-related welfare benefits. If such individuals are not entitled under national legislation to such assistance, how can they be an 'unreasonable burden' on the system from which they are excluded by law? argues Weiss – although after the Court of Appeal judgment in *Lekpo-Bouza* [2010] EWCA Civ 909, his suggestion that reliance on access to NHS care would normally fulfil rather than negate the 'health insurance' condition may be more questionable. Despite concerns being raised at national level and with the Commission, a pilot programme has been operating and some such removals have been carried out. The legality of removals on the basis of lack of exercise of Treaty rights on both points (means and health insurance) remains to be fully clarified.

5.9 European enlargement and freedom of movement

The fundamental status of Union citizen applies to nationals of states recently acceded to the EU. There is no status such as 'new union citizen'. Nevertheless, the right reserved to old Member States to phase in their recognition of the rights of nationals of the states that acceded in 2004 and 2007 delayed the full implementation of rights for nationals of the A8 (2004) states and nationals of the A2 (2007) states do not yet have full rights of free movement in the UK.

Prior to their accession, the new Member States had various levels of agreement giving some access to self-employment in the EU. However, despite the fact that some as a consequence may be quite established in old Member States, as we have seen in 5.3.1.1, the requirement for residence to be 'according to the Directive' may defer their right to permanent residence.

Their right to work in an employed capacity was also in many cases deferred. Under the 2004 Act of Accession, the old Member States had an option to derogate from free movement provisions and to continue to apply their national law for two years after accession. There then followed a three-year period during which old Member States could continue restrictions on notice to the Commission. During this time the UK opened access to the labour market (more generously than some other Member States) but enforced a 'worker registration scheme' and put in place restrictions on many 'out of work' benefits until a full year of employment had been completed. This had serious consequences for numbers of A8 nationals who found themselves vulnerable to refusal of benefits and destitution if they became unemployed before completing a year of registered employment, sometimes purely due to lack of completion of registration formalities. As we have seen this was the subject of an unsuccessful challenge in the House of Lords in the *Zalewska* case [2008] UKHL 67 and an uncompleted infringement procedure by the Commission. The transition period was intended then to be complete after five years (i.e., in May 2009), but an old Member State which had not achieved full access to the labour markets for new Member State workers might, in the case of threatened or actual 'serious disturbance to its labour market', have a further two years in which to achieve full access. Amidst growing unemployment and a severe recession, the UK government retained the derogation in respect of A8 nationals on the basis of the 'serious disturbance in the labour market' criterion until 2011. The justification for this appears questionable and this provoked serious criticism, but now the final two-year period has expired, the A8-WRS has been abolished.

As regards Bulgaria and Romania (the A2 states), similar transitional arrangements applied in the 2007 Treaty of Accession. The UK announced that it would not be opening its labour market fully to Bulgarian and Romanian nationals. In fact, some access is given, again subject to a registration scheme, but only to employment in listed categories (see chapter 10). These restrictions still remain in force in 2011.

5.10 Conclusion

Directive 2004/38 represents a significant advance in developing rights of free movement. However, in the UK, the interpretation of the Directive by the Court of Appeal and in Regulations maintains a consistently restrictive approach. While, in theory, Article 20 TFEU provides a right of residence, in practice the extent of rights of residence are still largely dictated by and subject to the limitations and conditions laid down in secondary legislation.

QUESTIONS

1. Was the ECJ right to refuse entitlement to benefit to Mr Collins? Do you have any sympathy with the Commission's view that Article 18 (now 20) requires that the mobility of citizens of the Union should not be impeded by being unable to claim benefits while they look for work? After all, Mr Collins would only have qualified for income-based job-seeker's allowance if he was genuinely seeking work.
2. Do you agree with the Court in *Akrich* that motivation is irrelevant when a couple relies on the rights arising from *Surinder Singh*?
3. *Akrich* and *Metock* take very different views about the division of competence between Member States and Community law in relation to control of first entry into the EU by family members of EU citizens. Which do you find more convincing?
4. In *Forster*, the Advocate General takes a different view from the Court of Justice. Explain the differences, which you prefer, and why.
5. How do you reconcile the judgments in *Zambrano*, *McCarthy*, and *Dereci*?

For guidance on answering questions, visit www.oxfordtextbooks.co.uk/orc/clayton5e/.

FURTHER READING

Barnard, Catherine (2010) *The Substantive Law of the EU: The Four Freedoms* (3rd edn) (Oxford: Oxford University Press).

Carlier, Jean-Yves (2005) 'Case Note on *Chen*', (2005) *Common Market Law Review* vol. 42, pp. 1121–31.

Costello, Cathryn (2009) 'Free Movement and "Normal Family Life" in the Union' *Common Market Law Review* vol. 46, p. 587.

Craig, Paul and de Búrca, Gráinne (2007) *EU Law: Text, Cases and Materials* (4th edn) (Oxford: Oxford University Press).

Currie, Samantha (2006) '"Free" Movers? The Post-accession Experience of Migrant Workers in the UK' *European Law Review*, April, pp. 207–299.

—— (2009) 'Accelerated Justice or a Step too far? Residence Rights of Non-EU Family Members and the Court's ruling in Metock' *European Law Review* vol. 34, no. 2, p. 310.

Dautricourt, Camille and Thomas, Sebastian (2009) 'Reverse Discrimination and Free Movement of Persons under Community Law: All for Ulysees, nothing for Penelope?' *European Law Review* vol. 34, no. 3, p. 433.

Guild, Elspeth (ed.) (1999) *The Legal Framework and Social Consequences of Free Movement of Persons in the European Union* (London: Kluwer Law International).

Handoll, John (1988) 'Article 48(4) EEC and Non-National Access to Public Employment' *European Law Review* vol. 13, no. 4, pp. 223–241.

Jacqueson, Catherine (2002) 'Union Citizenship and the Court of Justice: Something New under the Sun? Towards Social Citizenship' *European Law Review* vol. 27, no. 3, pp. 260–281.

Journal of Immigration, Asylum and Nationality Law vol. 21, no. 3 is a special issue devoted to EC law, focusing on the implementation of the Citizens' Directive in the UK. All seven articles are relevant.

Kubal, Agnieszka (2009) 'Why Semi-legal? Polish Post-2004 EU Enlargement Migrants in the United Kingdom' *Journal of Immigration, Asylum and Nationality Law* vol. 23, no. 2, p. 148.

McAuley, Darren (2003) 'Windows, Caps, Footballs, and the European Commission. Confused? You Will Be' *Competition Law Review* vol. 24, no. 8, pp. 394–399.

McKee, Richard (2007) 'Regulating the Directive? The AIT's Interpretation of the Family Members Provisions in the EEA Regulations' *Journal of Immigration, Asylum and Nationality Law* vol. 21, no. 4, pp. 334–340.

Oosterom-Staples, Helen (2005) 'Case Note on *Collins*', *Common Market Law Review* vol. 42, pp. 205–233.

Peers, Steve (2001) 'Dazed and Confused: Family Members' Residence Rights and the Court of Justice' *European Law Review* vol. 26, no. 1, pp. 76–83.

Spaventa, Eleanor (2005) 'Case Note on *Akrich*', *Common Market Law Review* vol. 42, pp. 225–239.

—— (2008) 'Seeing the woods for the trees? On the scope of Union Citizenship and its effects' *Common Market Law Review* vol. 45, p. 13.

Toner, Helen (2004) '*Chen* – Judgment of the ECJ' *Journal of Immigration, Asylum and Nationality Law* vol. 18, no. 4, pp. 265–266.

—— (2006) 'New Regulations Implementing Directive 2004/38' *Journal of Immigration, Asylum and Nationality Law* vol. 20, no. 3, pp. 158–178.

Van Eicken, and H. de Vries, S. (2011) "A New Route Into the Promised Land? Being a European Citizen After Ruiz Zambrano" *European Law Review* vol. 36, p. 704.

Van Eulsweg, P. and Kochenov, D. (2011) 'On the Limits of Judicial Intervention" EU Citizenship and Family Reunification Rights' *European Journal of Migration and Law* vol. 13, no. 1, p. 443.

Wiesbrock, A. (2011) 'Disentangling the "Union Citizenship Puzzle" the *McCarthy* case' *European Law Review* vol. 37, p. 861.

6

Immigration and asylum for third country nationals under EU law

SUMMARY

This chapter introduces the law and policy of the European Union concerning immigration and asylum. It is concerned with third country nationals who are not beneficiaries of the Union's free movement provisions (see chapter 5): the distinction between the EU's Free Movement law and Immigration and Asylum law is a longstanding and very significant one. The focus of EU policy on asylum deterrence is introduced as part of the context for UK law on asylum. 'Fortress Europe' is described in terms of stratification of rights according to nationality, and there is discussion of the rights of Turkish nationals and the UK's definition of British national for EU purposes. The chapter briefly charts the progress towards implementing the new immigration and asylum provisions deriving from the Treaty of Amsterdam, and the developments introduced by the Treaty of Lisbon. The UK's opt-in position is noted, as are its choices to date. Finally, there is an introduction to the EU dimension of human rights.

6.1 Introduction

The UK's immigration and asylum law is formed in the context of its membership of the EU, whose influence is both political and legal. At the present stage of development, the UK has not opted into many of the implementing provisions concerning immigration, and while it is not impossible that at some point in the future much of immigration law will be at least partly subject to European law, currently we are a long way from that position. The UK for the most part opted into the first stage of the Common European Asylum System (CEAS), and the UK's asylum system is increasingly not just politically influenced by European developments but subject to them in law, although the position is complicated further by the UK's more recent reluctance to opt into the recasting and amending of the various Directives and Regulations involved in the *second* stage of the CEAS. First, we will outline how rights in EU law are layered and stratified according to different categories of nationality, before examining the current Treaty structure and outlining the main features of the secondary legislation relating to the EU's Immigration and Asylum law.

6.2 European system of stratification of rights

Until recently, very broadly speaking, the EU's stratification was into three groups: EU nationals, nationals of countries with which the EC has association agreements, and other third country nationals. Now there are changes in these groupings. First, there is differentiation within the category of 'favoured EC nationals' (a phrase occasionally used in case law). By the European Economic Area Agreement, and the Swiss Agreement, the specific free movement rights (but not all the benefits of EU citizenship) are extended to nationals of Iceland, Liechtenstein, Norway, and Switzerland, in addition to the Member States of the EU. With the accession of ten new Member States in 2004 and two in 2007, not all rights were automatically acquired on accession, but Malta and Cyprus were exempt from the derogations which old Member States could apply to new Member States in relation to freedom of movement. Therefore, within the category of EU nationals, there are some with more rights than others. This currently only applies to Bulgaria and Romania, but there is the possibility of similar arrangements being made on any future accessions of new Member States. The rights which accompany EU citizenship have been addressed in chapter 5. Secondly the Directive on long-term resident third country nationals creates some rights at a European level on the basis of residence rather than nationality, though it did not go as far as opening European citizenship to long-term resident third country nationals. Finally, the common list of visa countries makes further differentiation between different groups of TCNs.

6.2.1 The favoured group: EU nationals

As we have seen, the most extensive rights in freedom of movement attach to EU nationals, and on the face of it those who qualify for this status, are simply 'nationals of EU Member States'. The Member States, upon entering into the Treaty on European Union, declared that in cases of disputed nationality status, the question should be settled solely by reference to the national law of the Member State concerned. The jurisprudence of the Court has tended to follow this approach with the proviso that in making its determination, the Member State must have due regard to EU law, which may give some jurisdiction to the ECJ on a question affecting entitlement under EC law.

6.2.1.1 *Europeans in UK immigration law: shifting allegiances, freedom, and restriction*

The EU's stratification of rights coexists with Member States' own system of immigration control, but as European law takes precedence where it applies, EU membership has changed previous legal relationships. A brief excursus into the position under UK law is helpful here.

European countries (leaving aside the particular historical connection with Ireland) are not and were not part of the British Empire or the Commonwealth, and European nationals were 'aliens' in immigration statutes prior to 1971. However, twentieth-century development of British immigration policy and law targeted the New Commonwealth. In 1973, as full immigration control was consolidated for Commonwealth citizens and foreign nationals generally, EC Member State (as it then was) nationals became exempt from the requirement to have leave to enter.

Since the Second World War, European countries have been for the UK not only neighbours but also allies. In EU law, EU citizens have freedom to come and go, and Commonwealth citizens, who before 1962 had the right of abode in the UK, are 'third country nationals'. This term also encompasses nationals of the main refugee-producing countries. However, while the aim of UK immigration law is immigration control, the aim of the EU Treaties and their implementing legislation is to promote freedom of movement within Europe.

The second target group of policy, particularly in the last 25 years, has been asylum seekers, and the imposition of visa regimes has been used to deter travellers from countries which are considered to produce a high number of refugee claims. Some of the new members of the European Union are countries from which there have in the past been significant numbers of asylum claims, for instance the Czech Republic and the Slovak Republic. Asylum applications between EU Member States are so rare as to be almost unknown. They would normally be unnecessary as a potential claimant may exercise rights of free movement if economically active or self-sufficient (see chapter 5), and the Qualification Directive does not provide for them.

6.2.2 Association Agreements

Returning to the issue of stratification of rights in EU law, we turn to Association Agreements. These agreements with non-EU countries give rights to nationals of those countries to engage in economic activity in the EU, although fewer than the rights available to EU nationals. Each agreement provides for the establishment of a Council which has the responsibility for the development and implementation of the agreement. Many of the countries which entered into these agreements have now become EU Member States, and their agreements with the EU operate as a minimum standard below which new rights on accession could not fall, even during transitional phases, but are now of largely historic interest with Transitional Arrangements drawing to a close or already completed. The key exception is Turkey, which was the first country with which the EU entered into an agreement of this kind. The position of Turkish nationals is complex and increasingly litigated, so it is worth outlining a few key points here. Interested readers should consult more detailed works at the end of the chapter for further information.

6.2.2.1 *EC–Turkey Agreement*

Many provisions of the EC–Turkey Agreement have direct effect, and Articles 12–14 provide that the contracting parties are to be guided by the relevant articles of the EC Treaty in progressively securing freedom of movement for workers, freedom of establishment, and provision of services. As in all the Association Agreements, there is no right of entry – the national law of the host country applies. However, once they have entered, there is a principle of non-discrimination as between Turkish and EU nationals. Council Decision 1/80 Article 6 sets out the specific rights for a worker:

(i) after one year's legal employment, to renewal of the work permit to work for the same employer;

(ii) after three years' legal employment, to respond to an offer of employment from another employer; and

(iii) after four years' legal employment, to any paid employment of the worker's choice.

The meaning of 'a worker' under Decision 1/80 was considered by the ECJ in Case C–294/06 *Payir, Aykuz and Ozturk v SSHD*. Ms Payir came to the UK as an au pair, and applied for leave to remain to stay with the same employer. Her application was refused by the Secretary of State on the basis that the Turkey Agreement did not apply because she was not a worker. The High Court, Court of Appeal, and ECJ disagreed. She fulfilled the objective conditions to come within the definition of worker in Decision 1/80, and the fact that her work was taken up with the motive of 'acquisition of cultural experience and deepening of linguistic knowledge' (Advocate General's opinion) could not affect that classification. Her work was a genuine and effective economic activity, she was 'duly registered' as belonging to the UK labour force (Article 6). There was no encroachment upon the competence of Member States in regulating the entry of Turkish nationals.

This right only applied to a Turkish national who had been admitted pursuant to domestic law. The Court in addition held that these principles also applied to Mr Aykuz and Mr Ozturk, students who were working the full 20 hours per week permitted.

Article 7 of Decision 1/80 provides that members of a Turkish worker's family who have been authorized by national law to join them may take up offers of work although they must first have three years of lawful residence. Children may enter education once one of their parents has been working for a period, and if they have been in vocational training in the host state are then free to enter employment, providing their parent has been legally employed for three years.

The Turkey Agreement has a protective effect which ensures that the movement is towards the integration of Turkish workers, not against it. This purposive approach also benefits family members, as demonstrated in Case C–325/05 *Derin*. The ECJ held that a family member of a Turkish worker who had acquired the right to free access to employment would only lose the right of residence if his deportation was justified under the stringent test required for EU nationals (see chapter 5), or if he left the territory for a significant length of time without legitimate reason. This was so, even though he was over 21 years of age and no longer dependent on his parents.

Many, though not all, of the key ECJ cases concerning the EC–Turkey Agreement are on reference from courts in Germany. This is an example of how one may see patterns of migration behind the case law. Just as the UK invited workers from the Caribbean in the 1960s, so the German government in 1961 issued an invitation to Turkish workers to fill the labour shortages that arose after the Second World War. This established Germany as a key destination for Turkish migrant workers of succeeding decades: around a quarter of Germany's non-German registered population is Turkish.

The standstill clause

In Case C–37/98 *Savas* [2000] All ER (EC) 627, the ECJ held that the standstill provision in Article 41 of the Additional Protocol to the Agreement meant that the UK could not apply provisions on establishment to Turkish workers that were more restrictive than those which obtained at the time of the commencement of the Turkey Agreement (1 January 1973 when the UK joined the EC). Consequently, the old – and more favourable – rules on self-employment must be applied to Turkish workers.

The scope of the standstill clause was considered by the ECJ in Case C–16/05 *Tum and Dari v SSHD*. The Court held that unsuccessful Turkish asylum seekers were not debarred from benefiting from *Savas* and the standstill clause, which was a procedural limitation applying to decisions on entry just as much as any other decision.

Key Case

Case C–16/05 *The Queen (Tum and Dari) v SSHD*

Mr Tum and Mr Dari were Turkish nationals who entered the UK and made asylum applications. Pending the outcome of their asylum applications, they were granted temporary admission, which is a provisional permission to be in the UK, and not the same as being granted entry. The asylum claims were unsuccessful, and decisions were made to remove them to European countries through which they had travelled, pursuant to the Dublin Convention. However, they were not actually removed, and made applications to enter the UK to set up in business. Although they were physically present, the applications had to be for leave to enter because they did not yet have this. By this time, Mr Dari was running a successful pizza business.

The Secretary of State refused their applications on the grounds that the standstill clause did not apply to provisions on entry. Mr Tum and Mr Dari would not be able to comply with the more stringent requirements for setting up in business which applied at the date of their application, and it was fraudulent and thus an abuse of EC law for asylum seekers whose claim had failed to rely on the EC–Turkey Agreement and the standstill clause. Before the ECJ the Secretary of State also argued that it would undermine the competence of national authorities if the standstill clause applied to provisions on entry.

The ECJ preferred the interpretation put forward by Mr Tum and Mr Dari. The standstill clause did not grant a substantive right of entry and thus did not interfere with the state's right to control immigration. It was only a procedural limitation, preventing states from imposing any new obstacles after the entry into force of the EC–Turkey Agreement. It applied to provisions governing admission or entry. Community law could not be used for fraudulent purposes, but the national courts 'which gave rulings on the substance of these cases... expressly stated that Mr Tum and Mr Dari could not be accused of any fraud'. Additionally, the protection of public interests such as order or security was not in issue. The fact that they had made unsuccessful asylum applications was irrelevant to their claim relying on the EC–Turkey Agreement.

Fraud exception to Tum and Dari

It was accepted by the ECJ and by the Court of Appeal that 'Community law cannot be relied upon for fraudulent or abusive ends' (ECJ para 64). In *Tum and Dari* itself, the ECJ and UK courts held that merely making an asylum application which was unsuccessful did not amount to fraud or deception, and no fraud or deception was alleged in Mr Tum or Mr Dari's conduct. In *R (on the application of Aksu) v SSHD* [2006] EWHC 1382 (Admin), the claimant made an unsuccessful asylum claim in Germany, but when he arrived in the UK denied that he had made any prior claim and claimed asylum again. In *R (on the application of Semsek) v SSHD* [2006] EWHC 1486, the adjudicator found that the claimant's asylum claim was based on untrue facts. In *Yilmaz v SSHD* [2005] EWHC 1068, the claimant attempted but failed to gain entry using false endorsements in his passport. In all these cases it was accepted that fraud precluded reliance on Association Agreement rights. In *Sonmez* [2009] EWCA Civ 582, however, the situation was more alleged abuse of rights rather than outright fraudulent conduct. The applicants were relying on businesses started by them in breach of the conditions under which they had earlier been admitted to the UK for temporary purposes (either as students or visitors). The Court of Appeal held this was a case covered by the 'fraud or abuse' exception to *Tum and Dari*. Further clarification has been provided in Case C–186/10 *Oguz*, which suggests otherwise. The ECJ made it clear that establishing a business in breach of the conditions of initial leave to remain did not in fact preclude reliance on rights contained in the Protocol for an application for further leave to remain. Being unconditional and an essentially 'procedural' mechanism not granting substantive rights but preventing more stringent conditions being imposed by national law, the Court considered that an 'abuse of rights' exception was out of place to preclude reliance on the standstill clause. The alleged abuse however (consisting of breaching conditions of entry by setting up a business and retrospectively, even a very short time later, relying on this) could be relied upon in examining the application for leave to remain under the relevant national provisions dating from the UK's accession in 1972 which did provide for the applicant's conduct to be taken into consideration.

Limitation on Tum and Dari

The Tribunal in the UK in *OY v ECO Nicosia* [2006] UKAIT 00028 distinguished *Tum and Dari* on the basis that the case referred to the standstill clause relating to freedom of establishment, whereas *OY* concerned the standstill clause in Decision 1/80 referring to 'access to employment'. Arguably at variance with principles of EC free movement law discussed in the previous chapter, the Tribunal held that being accompanied by one's family was not related to access to employment. Furthermore, the standstill clause could not govern conditions of entry. This last point will need to be reconsidered in the light of the subsequent ECJ judgment in *Tum and Dari*.

Extension of Tum and Dari

The ECJ ruled in Case C–226/08 *Soysal* that the imposition of visa requirements will be a breach of the standstill clause in a Member State where such requirements were not in place at the time the standstill clause came into effect (in the case of Germany, 1973). It also appears from Case C–256/11 *Dereci* that the standstill clause will apply to prevent more generous measures put in place in national law being reversed, even if this reversal is only partial and does not fall below the original position.

6.2.2.2 *Other Association Agreements*

There were Association Agreements (the CEEC – Central and Eastern European Agreements) with Bulgaria, the Czech Republic, Estonia, Hungary, Lithuania, Poland, Romania, Slovakia, and Slovenia. These countries are now all members of the EU. The CEEC agreements are relevant still for the new Member States as a minimum standard for their rights to work in the old Member States during the transition period (see Chapter 5). The CEEC agreements are less far-reaching than the agreement with Turkey. They set out some anti-discrimination provisions for employed workers, and rights of establishment (that is, to set up business) and provide services.

There are less advantageous cooperation agreements with Algeria, Morocco, and Tunisia, the so-called 'Maghreb agreements'. These provide for equality of treatment for employed workers only.

6.2.3 New Member States

Under the Acts of Accession in 2004 and 2007, old Member States had an option for the first two years after accession of new Member States to continue to apply their national law, that meant until 1 May 2006 for A8 countries, and 1 January 2009 for Bulgaria and Romania. There followed a three-year period during which old Member States agreed to introduce greater freedom of access to labour markets. The transition period should then end (i.e., after five years), but a Member State which has not achieved full access to the labour markets for new Member State workers may, in case of threatened or actual 'serious disturbances to its labour market', have a further two years in which to achieve full access. While full rights do not apply, the Association Agreements will continue to have effect and so the option to restrict access only applies to employment. Full integration must be achieved after seven years, so only Romania and Bulgaria are now subject to transitional arrangements. The UK's scheme permitting Accession nationals to enter employment under certain conditions is discussed in chapters 5 and 10.

6.2.4 Third country nationals

Technically, third country nationals (TCNs) are nationals of non-EU countries. In practice we may regard them as nationals of non-EEA countries, as defined by the

UK Immigration (European Economic Area) Regulations 2006, because nationals of Iceland, Liechtenstein, Norway, and Switzerland have rights almost equivalent to EU citizens. The entry and status of what we might call the residual category of TCNs – covered by none of the agreements either personally or materially in relation to the particular issue at hand (such as entry, family reunification, or right to work) – has traditionally been and remains primarily governed by the national law of Member States. However EU law provisions increasingly set out limitations upon what national law may specify. Note that the UK has not opted into any of these provisions (leaving aside asylum, dealt with in more detail later in the chapter) hence the brevity with which they are treated here.

First, there is a Common Visa List (Council Regulation EC 539/2001 as amended, most recently in 2010 and 2011). The Regulation lists those countries whose nationals require a visa to enter Europe and those whose nationals do not require a visa. Those who do not require a visa, e.g., nationals of the US, Japan, and Singapore, may enter for up to three months without a visa. Nationals of countries on the visa list require visas for any purpose. Recent changes move towards harmonization of the EU and UK visa lists, but the UK has still not opted into this provision as the European list includes a number of Commonwealth countries which the UK has not yet included on its own visa list, for instance Trinidad and Tobago and Botswana. The EU visa list is longer than the UK's, and note the changes in relation to British nationals mentioned in chapter 5. There is also now a visa code and a long stay visa code outlining conditions for granting visas and a Visa Information System containing a database of information (including biometric) on applicants.

Some secondary EU legislation governing entry and stay of TCNs for specific purposes, and the Directives on resident TCNs and family reunion provide some rights for TCNs who are already resident. These are discussed further later.

Finally (although often the most attractive option that TCNs may attempt to establish), nationals of third countries may be able to enter a European country by virtue of an EU Freedom of Movement provision based on their connection with a European exercising free movement rights – if employed by a European business exercising its right of establishment in another Member State, or if a family member of a European citizen who was moving between Member States. These have already been outlined in chapter 5.

6.3 The Treaty of Amsterdam

We now turn to examine the Treaty provisions and secondary legislation generally applicable to all non-EEA nationals.

The hardening of European immigration policies towards nationals of other countries has earned the EU the nickname 'Fortress Europe'. Until 1997, immigration and asylum were matters of intergovernmental cooperation. Now, the Treaty sets legal objectives to be attained by all the Member States. These are developed in secondary legislation on immigration and asylum enacted by EU institutions, and the European Court of Justice (ECJ) has competence to rule on these matters.

The Treaty of Amsterdam came into force on 1 May 1999, and inserted into the EC Treaty a new Title IV governing immigration, asylum, and visas. The Title makes the dual purpose of EC law on migration very plain. Old Article 61(1)(a) EC says that the Council must adopt:

measures aimed at ensuring the free movement of persons in accordance with Article 14, in conjunction with directly related flanking measures with respect to external border controls.

In other words, Member States must open their borders to each other and control their borders to those from outside. As the internal market developed, so, as Guild says, 'one member state's third country nationals become those of the whole unified territory' (in Guild and Harlow (eds) 2001:90). Member States would want to be assured that others were admitting third country nationals on similar terms to themselves. The stronger external border could be seen in part as a consequence of the more relaxed internal borders.

The required controls on external borders include 'standards and procedures' for external border checks and rules on visas, including a 'list of third countries whose nationals must be in possession of visas when crossing the external borders' (Old Article 62 EC). The required asylum measures include minimum standards on a range of matters and, a particular concern of European states: 'criteria and mechanisms for determining which member state is responsible for considering an application for asylum submitted by a national of a third country in one of the member states' (Old Article 63(1) EC). Measures on immigration policy must include 'conditions of entry and residence' including for family reunion, and measures on 'illegal immigration and illegal residence' (Old Article 63(3)EC).

None of these provisions suggest what the standards or objectives of these measures should be. For instance, is the list of visa countries to be short, and thus permissive, or long, and thus restrictive? European law is interpreted in accordance with its purpose, and the purpose of Title IV is: 'In order to establish progressively an area of freedom, security and justice.'

The meaning of this phrase has been extensively debated (see, for instance, P. Boeles in Guild and Harlow (eds) 2001). In general terms, the freedom referred to is the freedom to move within the Union, and security is safety from threats largely seen as external. This leaves the question of 'and justice for whom?' – an important one in the understanding of the Union's objectives in establishing the AFSJ. On the whole, justice is understood as criminal justice – but there is also the alternative perspective of access to justice for those affected by these legal measures. The purpose of Title IV, therefore, largely seems to be to replicate the strong external and relaxed internal controls which have already characterized the EU. There is only one requirement to promote the rights of third country nationals in Title IV, and that is that there must be provision for family reunion. The extent of this provision depends on secondary legislation.

Title IV allowed a period of five years after the entry into force of the Treaty of Amsterdam for the new measures to be adopted, which gave a deadline of 1 May 2004. There were exceptions to this deadline for provisions on the rights of legally resident third country nationals, conditions of entry and residence, and the promotion of balanced effort between Member States in receiving refugees ('burden sharing').

6.4 Implementing the Amsterdam Treaty – the Tampere Programme

For the most part, the UK's law on immigration of third country nationals, aside from those seeking asylum, is not directly affected by the developing immigration law of the EU. The entry of TCN family members of EEA nationals is governed by the EC free movement provisions discussed in chapter 5. The development of EU immigration law is, however, part of the political and legal context in which UK immigration law is formed, and a brief account is given here of developments pursuant to the Treaty of Amsterdam. The provisions on asylum are outlined here and discussed in more detail where they affect the UK's substantive law covered in later chapters.

Shortly after the Treaty of Amsterdam came into force, there was a meeting of the European Council at Tampere, devoted to the development of the 'area of freedom, security and justice'. It was a key opportunity to formulate some objectives for policy on migration. Four main principles emerged:

- partnership with countries of origin;
- moving towards a common European asylum system, which should in time lead towards a common asylum procedure and a uniform status for those granted asylum;
- fair treatment of third country nationals; and
- more efficient management of migration flows.

6.4.1 Tampere conclusions – partnership with countries of origin

The Tampere conclusions set wide-ranging objectives in terms of partnership with countries of origin. The tone of the conclusions was liberal, although there was also scepticism as to whether this was form or substance (see, for instance, Statewatch vol. 9, no. 5). The Council recognized the need for a 'comprehensive approach to migration addressing political, human rights and development issues in countries and regions of origin and transit'. This would require 'combating poverty, improving living conditions and job opportunities, preventing conflicts and consolidating democratic states and ensuring respect for human rights, in particular rights of minorities, women and children' (Commission of the EC 2001 Conclusions para 11).

A High Level Working Group set up in 1998 was to continue its work to look at the causes of migration, including forced migration. The group's work was concentrated on six countries which were all perceived to produce large numbers of refugees, and action plans were adopted.

The main legislative result of the focus on partnerships with countries of origin has been to use the EU's political and economic power to conclude readmission agreements, the aim of which is to ensure that illegal entrants to the EU from these countries can be repatriated. Incentives for third countries to conclude such agreements with the EU include favourable trade terms and facilitating the grant of visas to their nationals. Readmission agreements have been entered into with a number of countries including Hong Kong, Sri Lanka, Macao, and Albania. Negotiations were completed during 2007 with several candidate and prospective candidate countries for admission to the EU – Macedonia, Montenegro, Bosnia, and Serbia. Other concluded agreements are with countries on the EU's new borders: Russia, Moldova, and Ukraine. Most recently, agreements with Pakistan and Georgia have entered into force. There are also negotiations ongoing with Morocco, Algeria, China, and Belarus, and re-negotiations of existing agreements with Russia, Ukraine, and Moldova. There are concerns in the creation of readmission agreements about 'guarantees of human rights in the accelerated readmission procedure and about respect for the status in international law of asylum seekers and stateless persons' (European Parliament debate 14 February 2007). The agreements generally require that the non-EU country agrees to accept people returned from the

EU, even when they are not nationals of that country, or are stateless, if they have entered the EU irregularly through that country. Negotiations with Pakistan almost broke down on this issue, but, as with other negotiating partners, Pakistan's trade interests were too much at risk for it to pull out. The European Council of Refugees and Exiles explains how important that risk is: 'The EU is Pakistan's largest trading partner, accounting for 28 per cent (EUR 3 billion) of its exports and 17 per cent (EUR 2 billion) of its imports in 2004' (ECRAN weekly update 19/3/2007) and EU–Pakistan trade grew 8 per cent annually from 2003–07. As the size and wealth of the EU grows, so does its negotiating power.

Pressure on third countries to control the irregular migration of their nationals into the EU has direct effects in those countries on the prospective immigrants. For instance, a crackdown by the Moroccan authorities included rounding up would-be migrants and leaving them in the desert without food or water (Spijkerboer 2007:130, quoting Human Rights Watch and the *Financial Times*). Cooperation with Libya, and especially Italy's involvement, has been particularly controversial and provoked a storm of protest in recent years, both in 2005 and more recently when in May 2009, Italian ships intercepted boats on the high seas and returned them to Libyan territorial waters (see Human Rights Watch 2009 and further on cooperation with Libya see Hamood 2008). Often, increased controls in target countries may mean that would-be migrants make longer and more hazardous journeys to avoid such controls.

In September 2005, the Commission issued a further communication on integrating migration issues into relations with third countries (COM (2005) 390). A key focus is the economic role of money paid by migrant workers to families back home ('remittances', see chapter 2). Partnerships with countries of origin and patterns of 'circular migration' have gained a high profile in recent years – see the Commission's Communication on Circular Migration and Mobility Partnerships between the European Union and Third Countries COM(2007)248, and the follow-up document SEC(2009)1240.

6.4.2 Tampere conclusions – fair treatment of third country nationals

The treatment of long-term resident third country nationals was one of the most liberal of the Tampere conclusions. Following Tampere, the Commission proposed two Directives: one to enhance and consolidate the rights of long-term resident third country nationals, and the second to give rights of entry and residence to their family members. In a number of respects, the first draft Directives could have heralded an equalization of rights within the EU based, not on nationality but on residence, but the provisions of the Directives were much reduced during subsequent negotiations. Lawful residence, not just nationality, still becomes a basis for the acquisition of rights, but of a lesser kind. The watered-down Family Reunion Directive 2003/86 EC was finally adopted on 22 September 2003, and implemented by October 2005. The reduced nature of the rights given by the Directive drew criticism, not only from non-governmental groups, but also from the European Parliament which launched a legal action against the European Council on the grounds that the limitations imposed on family reunification for children were incompatible with the right to respect for family life and the principle of equality of treatment, as was the waiting period of up to three years for the issue of a residence permit. The ECJ rejected this challenge (Case C–540/03 *European Parliament v Council of the EU* [2006] ECR I–05769), although in Case C–758/08 *Chakroun* the challenge under the Directive to the minimum income requirements imposed in the Netherlands did succeed, indicating some willingness on the part of the ECJ to take seriously the task of policing compliance with the limits of Member States' discretion in implementing the Directive.

Directive 2003/109/EC on the status of long-term resident TCNs was finally agreed in 2003, after refugees were removed from its ambit, and discretion restored to Member States in a number of respects. Broadly speaking, the Directive gives to third country nationals who have been lawfully resident in Europe for five years security of status and a qualified right to move to other Member States. It was implemented in January 2006. The question of long-term residence rights for refugees has been revisited, and resulted in Directive 2011/55 amending the initial 2003 Long Term Residence Directive. The Commission proposal concerning the entry of third country nationals for study or voluntary work has borne fruit in Directive 2004/114, and Directive 2005/71 concerns the admission of researchers. Discussions on what, if any, role the EU should have in regulating entry and conditions of stay for the purposes of employment has been long and controversial. A 2001 Commission Proposal was dropped but a Directive on the admission of highly skilled workers (the EU 'Blue Card' scheme), based on a less ambitious 2007 Proposal, was eventually adopted in 2009 – Directive 2009/50 EC. This provides enhanced rights to highly skilled workers once admitted to one Member State and a 'fast-track' route to onward mobility to another EU Member State after 18 months. Control over first admission, however, remains in the hands of each individual Member State, and some have questioned how attractive these conditions really are for highly skilled workers. This Directive was closely followed by one (Directive 2009/52) providing for sanctions against employers of illegally staying third country nationals (on both of these Directives, see Peers 2009a). A draft Directive intended to streamline admissions procedures and bring together procedures for granting residence and work permits COM(2007)638 remains under discussion, although a deal was reached in 2011 and formal adoption of the agreed text is likely soon. Proposals on intra-corporate transferees and seasonal workers were presented in 2010 (COM(2010)378, 379) and remain under discussion.

6.4.3 The Hague and Stockholm Programmes

In November 2004, the Member States approved a second five-year plan to further the creation of an area of 'freedom, security and justice'. The objectives of the Hague Programme include:

> improvement of the common capability of the Union and its Member States to guarantee fundamental rights, minimum procedural safeguards and the access to justice, to provide protection in accordance with the Geneva Convention and other international treaties to persons in need, to regulate migration flows and to control the external borders of the Union, to fight organised cross-border crime and repress the threat of terrorism... development of a Common Asylum System... the approximation of law and the development of common policies.

The European Council's introduction to the programme reveals an emphasis on security 'in the light of terrorist attacks in the United States on 11 September 2001 and in Madrid on 11 March 2004', and exhorts Member States to 'take full account of the security of the Union as a whole'.

Returning irregular migrants is prioritized in the Hague Programme, and a Directive on common policy on returns of those who have stayed irregularly has finally been agreed – Directive 2008/115. It includes a radical new provision for a re-entry ban that would be valid throughout the EU, reinforcing a European-wide approach to removals.

The French Council presidency in 2008 presided over the development of a 'Pact on Immigration and Asylum', a political declaration which some have seen as driven by nationalism and intergovernmentalism (Carrera and Guild 2008). Five major commitments are:

> (1) to organize legal immigration to take account of priorities needs and reception capacities determined by each member state, and to encourage integration, (2) control illegal immigration by ensuring that illegal immigrants return to their countries of origin or to country of transit (3) to make border controls more effective (4) to construct a Europe of Asylum and (5) to create partnerships with countries of origin and transit to encourage the synergy between migration and development.

The new programme inaugurated in 2009 is called the 'Stockholm Programme' as Sweden held the presidency of the EU in the second half of 2009. Immigration and asylum continue to occupy a significant place in the new multi-annual programme. The draft agenda includes: consolidating and developing the 'Global approach to migration'; maximizing the positive and minimizing the negative effects of migration; developing policies that will respond to labour market requirements while 'having due regard to Member States competences and the principle of community preference'; a pro-active policy 'based on a European Status for migrants'; effective policies to combat illegal immigration, including monitoring the newly adopted employer sanctions and returns directives; addressing the position of unaccompanied minors; creating a 'Common Area of protection and Solidarity', including the second phase of the Common European Asylum System; and further action on management of external borders and visa policy. The pace of discussion and developments in this area seems unlikely to slow.

6.5 Immigration, asylum and the Lisbon Treaty

The Lisbon Treaty will have some significant effects in the area of immigration and asylum. As noted, the EC Treaty becomes the TFEU – but there are also some changes of substance. First, legislation in almost all the remaining areas not yet covered by the 'ordinary legislative procedure' is now decided by qualified majority voting among the Member States (QMV) rather than unanimity, and co-decision with the European Parliament not just non-binding consultation. Most significantly, this now includes legal migration, as much of the rest already operated under these procedures by the time the Lisbon Treaty had been agreed. Jurisdiction of the Court of Justice is normalized. A new set of competences will come into force, with some differences in detail (see Peers 2008b). Borders and visas are dealt with in Article 77 TFEU (formerly 62 EC), asylum in Article 78 TFEU (formerly 63(1) and (2) EC), and immigration (including irregular immigration) in Article 79 TFEU (formerly 63(2) and 63(3) EC). These move from minimum harmonization towards developing 'common' policies on immigration and on asylum (discussed further in the relevant chapters). One striking new express limitation of competence is that reserving to Member States the determination of numbers of third country nationals entering from third countries in order to seek work (Article 79(5) TFEU), a reminder of the continuing political sensitivity of economic migration.

6.6 UK's position

In accordance with protocols appended to the Treaty of Amsterdam, the UK, Ireland, and Denmark have anomalous positions. The UK is able to remain outside the new immigration and asylum provisions unless it opts in. The UK has not yet opted into any substantial provisions on legal migration or protection of third country nationals but has opted into many of the provisions concerning irregular migration, including: Directive 2001/40 on mutual recognition of expulsion decisions; Directive 2001/51 on carrier sanctions; a Framework decision on trafficking in persons (OJ 2002 L 203/1); a Directive and Framework Decision on facilitation of illegal entry and residence (OJ 2002 L 328); and Directive 2004/82 creating an obligation for carriers to communicate passenger data to immigration services. The UK has not opted into the majority of provisions on borders and visas, but has opted into the European common visa format (Reg 334/2002), and the format for residence permits (Reg 1030/2002).

Where the UK has not opted in there is not a consistent pattern as to whether the UK or EU provisions are the more generous, and the main reason given by the UK government for not opting in is to retain control and flexibility.

In terms of asylum policies, the UK has been more enthusiastic about European cooperation, and has opted into most of the legal measures involved in the first stage of the Common European Asylum System.

The UK keeps its opt-out under the Treaty of Lisbon, but there are some slightly complex issues concerning what happens to the UK's opted-in status and the original (unamended) legislation in the UK when legislation is amended or 're-cast' for other Member States (see Peers 2008). The first re-cast directive to be agreed (recast to the Qualification Directive) awaits formal adoption. The UK and Ireland opted out, as they were entitled to do. Despite different views being expressed, the position as currently understood appears to be that they will remain bound by the *previous* first-stage Qualification Directive 2004/83.

6.7 Security – the Schengen Agreement

The Schengen Agreement 1985, and its 1990 implementing convention, was entered into outside the framework of what was then EC law by all the then member countries of the EU with the exception of the UK and Ireland, with the objective of achieving the gradual abolition of checks at common borders. The Schengen Agreement also declared an intention to reinforce cooperation between the customs and police authorities of the contracting states 'notably in combating crime, particularly illicit trafficking in narcotic drugs and arms, the unauthorized entry and residence of persons, customs and tax fraud and smuggling' (Article 9). To this end, the Schengen Information System (SIS) was established, facilitating exchange of intelligence between the contracting states. The Treaty of Amsterdam brought the Schengen acquis into either the first or third pillars of the EU, depending on the subject matter. The Schengen provisions are aimed at maintenance of external borders as well as dissolution of borders within the Community. The provisions of the Schengen acquis (i.e., the collection of authoritative documents) apply to third country nationals wherever the context so allows. Most recently, the communitarized Schengen provisions on visas have been replaced by a new Regulation establishing a Community Code on Visas (Melloni 2009).

Under the Treaty of Amsterdam, the UK needs the consent of other Schengen states to opt into elements of the Schengen acquis. Council Decision 2000/365/EC determines in which Schengen provisions the UK participates, following its request to do so. Accordingly, there are limited provisions relating to border control which have effect in the UK. These concern security issues such as protection of personal data and the entry of individuals carrying narcotic drugs (Articles 75–76 and 126–127 of the Convention applying the Schengen Agreement). In Case C–77/05 *UK v Council*, the UK argued that it has the power unilaterally to opt into those provisions which build upon the Schengen acquis without the consent of the other Member States. The ECJ held that this was a misinterpretation; the UK could not opt into 'Schengen-building' measures without the consent of the other Schengen states.

The accession of 12 new Member States to the EU necessitated a new information system (SIS II), but the opportunity is being taken to extend its use and capacities, and in particular to accommodate biometric data. The new system is now under construction. The SIS works on the basis of records (alerts) being created for five categories of people and for lost and stolen objects. Records suggest that Italy and Germany have been using the category of 'people to be refused entry to the Schengen area' to register all failed asylum seekers (Statewatch News Online April 2005: statewatch.org/news/). New categories of alert are being created for SIS II, widening the scope for creating records, and enabling greater data sharing, and this is not only for passport control. The Justice and Home Affairs ministers of the EU, at a meeting in June 2003, agreed the addition of new categories of data and the possibility of access to that information being granted for other purposes, principally law enforcement. Development of SIS II is proceeding in accordance with the UK's proposal that law enforcement officers should have access to information that someone has been refused entry because they are believed to constitute a threat to public order, national security or safety, or there are grounds to believe they will commit a serious offence. Previously, this information was only made available to immigration officers for the purposes of border control. The UK will participate in SIS II to the extent of criminal law and policing information, but not in relation to immigration information. The new SIS is accompanied by a new Visa Information System (see Peers 2009b), but the UK has not yet opted into this. For a full discussion of the UK's role and of the progress, purposes, and politics of SIS II, see the House of Lords European Union Committee Session 2006–07 Ninth Report HL paper 49.

6.8 Frontex

A major new development in Europe's control of its borders is the institution of Frontex, the European agency for the management of operational cooperation at the external borders of the European Union. This was established by Reg 2007/2004 in October 2004, but the UK was excluded from discussions on the Frontex Regulation, and it was this Regulation and the creation of Frontex that the UK challenged in Case C–77/05 *UK v Council* (discussed at 6.7). Frontex came into being at a time of rising concern about illegal entry on the southern borders of the EU, and in particular about deaths at sea. The role of Frontex in these situations is to ensure the integration of border forces between Member States, and their cooperation with third countries, rather than to provide border guards. Having said this, two more developments followed hard on the heels of the creation of Frontex: a new emergency force came into being in 2007, the

Rapid Border Intervention Team, known as RABITS; and Decision 574/2007/EC establishing a European Border Fund, to provide financial assistance 'to support the member states who bear, for the benefit of the Community, a lasting and heavy financial burden' (recital 4 to the Decision). Questions arise about the role and accountability of the RABITS: when they act in conjunction with Member State border guards, to whom are they accountable? RABITS came into being not long after the political spotlight turned onto new groups of illegal entrants arriving in the Canary Islands. Irregular migration on Europe's southern border generates two particular policy concerns: preventing unauthorized entry; and preventing deaths at sea. The irregular migrants who come by sea, while they may still be paying amounts beyond their means for the crossing, are also those who cannot afford forged papers for land or air border crossings. Spijkerboer argues that 'intensifying the EU's external borders has not decreased the number of irregular migrants, but, rather, has led irregular migrants to use alternative and increasingly dangerous routes' (2007:127), including, for instance, taking much longer journeys, such as travelling south first to Senegal or Mauritania, or travelling in bad weather, and the dangerous practice of unloading potential migrants at sea without life jackets.

Although the UK was prevented from joining in Frontex by its non-participation in the Schengen Agreement, the UK government appears to be creating its own 'border guards', an occupation not formerly recognized in the UK. The UK Border Agency, whose work and creation is discussed in chapters 2 and 7, will inevitably enter into a working relationship with Frontex.

Frontex is now well and truly operational – the first Frontex Joint Operations (Hermes and Poseidon) and the first deployment of RABITs along the Greek-Turkish border in 2010/2011 have already taken place – further details, press releases, and information on these can be accessed on the Frontex website.

6.9 Europe and asylum

In absolute numbers, the highest refugee populations by far in recent years have been in Pakistan and Iran. Germany has come a close third. If the ratio of refugees to other inhabitants or to gross domestic product is measured, no country in the EU featured in the top ten refugee-receiving countries in 2000 nor probably since (UNHCR). Nevertheless, globally, including in Europe, the number of refugees grew during the 1980s and 1990s. There was a dip from 2000 to 2003, then a gradual rise, and a sharp rise in global figures in 2006, accompanied by a decrease in Europe. The rise was attributable to 1.2 million people seeking refuge from Iraq in Syria and Jordan and a change in the method of counting in the US. The drop in Europe was attributable to the naturalization of refugees in Serbia and a consolidation of Germany's statistics. Whatever the numbers, there is a widespread perception within Europe that asylum is a problem. The refugee determination process in Europe is centred on individuals proving their case in a legalistic framework according to the criteria in the 1951 UN Convention Relating to the Status of refugees. This has in part led to a popular perception that a successful applicant is a 'genuine' refugee and an unsuccessful one is a 'bogus' refugee. Some popular thinking also equates the unsuccessful asylum claimant with an 'economic migrant'. As the EU has not had a migration policy which enables economic entry, this motivation has not been regarded as legitimate.

Europe's more recent recognition of its need for labour has only very marginally penetrated asylum policy for fear that the asylum route will be used by economic migrants. There is a volume of research on causes and patterns of migration. Key findings are that:

- Repression and/or discrimination against minorities and/or ethnic conflict exists in all the main refugee-producing countries.
- Conflict seems to be a major cause of refugee movements.
- Poverty or underdevelopment may precipitate conflict but is not of itself apparently a cause of refugee movement.
- Where a country is undergoing rapid change or crisis, the motivations of individuals for leaving may be mixed – it is therefore difficult to distinguish between someone in need of protection (a Convention refugee) and someone seeking economic stability (an economic migrant).
- A reputation for democratic institutions, the rule of law, and developed social systems make Europe an attractive destination for people who decide to leave a situation of conflict and crisis.
- Existing personal, familial or other known links, knowledge of the language, and past colonial links are a strong influence on an individual's choice of a particular European country. (Castles, Crawley, and Loughna 2003)

These findings suggest that addressing the causes of forced migration requires addressing the causes of conflict, and that distinguishing between a Convention refugee and an economic migrant may not be simple. EU policy, however, has concentrated on prevention of illegal migration and the deterrence of asylum seekers. It may be argued that such measures 'make it more difficult for those who are genuinely in need of protection to seek asylum and at the same time have created a "migration industry" of smugglers, facilitators and traffickers' (Castles et al 2003:v). Asylum policy then must deal with controlling the smugglers and traffickers, and a further range of penal provisions has been introduced to this end.

6.9.1 The First Stage of the Common European Asylum System

The asylum provisions adopted under Title IV have completed the first stage of creating a Common European Asylum System and include the following provisions in force:

- Decisions to establish a European Refugee Fund, which concerns exceptional support for the costs of asylum. The second of such funds has been agreed.
- Regulation 2725/2000 on Eurodac, a Europe-wide fingerprint database for asylum seekers, and Regulation 407/2002 implementing it.
- Directive 2001/55 on temporary protection, limiting the obligations of states in the case of a mass exodus.
- Directive 2003/9, setting minimum reception conditions.
- 'Dublin II' Regulation 343/2003, making provision for the criteria for establishing which Member State is responsible for an application. Regulation 1563/2003 gives the detailed rules.
- Directive 2004/83, giving the definition of a refugee or one who may obtain subsidiary protection, and the content of that protection ('the Qualification Directive').
- Directive 2005/85 on minimum standards on procedures for granting and withdrawing refugee status ('the Procedures Directive').

Minimum standards for dealing with asylum claims have taken longer to complete than the more explicitly deterrent and burden-sharing aspects of the Common European Asylum System. Negotiations on a common list of safe countries of origin were shelved in order to complete the Procedures Directive as the list could not be agreed (see chapter 12 for further discussion). The European Parliament mounted a successful legal challenge to the constitutionality of the provisions whereby a common list of safe countries of origin (being countries from which Member States would be obliged to consider an application as unfounded) was to be compiled by qualified majority voting (Case C–133/06 *European Parliament v European Council*). As noted the UK (and Ireland) have generally opted into these and insofar as their implementation is relevant to the development of UK asylum law the provisions are discussed in more detail elsewhere in this book.

6.9.2 CEAS Stage Two

The second stage of the CEAS is now underway under the Stockholm Programme, with a Policy Plan on Asylum COM(2008)360 in 2008. Various proposals have already been presented, including for amendment of the Reception Conditions Directive, EURODAC and Dublin Regulations in 2008, and of the Qualification and Procedures Directives in 2009. The recast Qualification Directive was formally adopted at the end of 2011, but new amended Proposals in relation to the EURODAC Regulation, Reception Conditions, and Procedure Directives, presented by the Commission in 2010 and 2011, will take longer to complete. The UK and Ireland have not opted into all of these amending measures, for instance they have not opted into the recast Qualification Directive. The Parliament and Council consider that they will remain bound by the 2004 Qualification Directive.

One significant aspect of the second stage of the CEAS is the establishment of the European Asylum Support Office in November 2010. It role is to (1) provide support for practical cooperation between Member States, (2) to provide support for Member States under particular pressure, and (3) contribute to the implementation of the CEAS, including by collecting and exchange of information and drafting documents such as guidance on the implementation of EU legal instruments. The EASO is based in Malta.

6.10 UK implementation

The UK has opted into all existing provisions on asylum and must give effect to them. Where directives are in force, the UK must adopt (or adapt) its own legal provisions to bring its law into compliance with the Directive by the date set for this purpose.

The Directive on reception conditions (2003/9/EC) was given legal force in the UK on 5 February 2005 by the Asylum Support (Amendment) Regulations 2005, SI 2005/11, the Asylum Seekers (Reception Conditions) Regulations 2005, SI 2005/7, and a new Part 11B of the immigration rules HC 395. SI 2005/7 provides for minimum standards, for instance, in accommodating families to have regard to family unity and 'so far as...reasonably practicable' to accommodate families together (reg 3), and to take into account the needs of a vulnerable person, though not to assess for such needs (reg 4). SI 2005/11 deals mainly with discontinuation or suspension of asylum support. The new immigration rules deal mainly with obligations to give written information to asylum seekers. They also give the right to apply to the Secretary of State for permission to take up paid work if the asylum decision is still outstanding after one year (see Baldaccini 2005 for discussion).

The Directive on minimum standards for procedures in assessing an asylum claim (2005/85/EC) is discussed in the context of the asylum claim process in chapter 12, and the Directive concerned with the conditions for qualifying as a refugee (2004/83/EC) is discussed in chapter 13.

The Dublin II (Regulation (EC) 343/2003), governing criteria and mechanisms for determining the Member State responsible for examining an asylum application, is considered more fully in chapter 12 in the context of the development of so-called 'safe third country provisions'.

The UK did not need to bring in further measures to ensure compliance with the Eurodac Regulation as the power to collect fingerprints from asylum seekers had already been granted in the Immigration and Asylum Act 1999 s 141 (see chapter 7).

6.11 Human rights in the EU

Human rights and fundamental freedoms occupy an important place in the EU legal order. They were initially developed by the ECJ, then recognized in Article 6 of the TEU at Maastricht and Amsterdam as 'general principles of law' upon which the EU is founded and which it respects. The source of these rights may be the legal traditions of the Member States, the ECtHR, or other international treaties to which Member States have contributed or to which they are parties (see, e.g., Case 4/73 *Nold v Commission* [1974] ECR 491).

6.11.1 The developing relationship of human rights and Community law

The EU has not acquired a general human rights competence. In other words, it is not yet the case that the EU promotes human rights separately from EU issues, but rather that it upholds human rights when these are potentially violated within the existing bounds of EU law. As the European Parliament's challenge to the Family Reunion Directive shows, this may include a direct challenge to secondary legislation even before it is applied.

The ECJ has on many occasions stated that fundamental human rights are a foundation of EU law, and is not a stranger to independent application of fundamental rights to the cases that come before it. For instance, in Case C–63/83 *R v Kirk* [1984] ECR 2689, the question was of the validity of the Sea Fish Order 1982 which prohibited fishing in UK waters by Danish fishing vessels. This, of course, is discriminatory. Council Regulation 170/83 Article 6(1) purported to allow Member States to derogate from the non-discrimination principle in relation to sea fishing, and to do so retroactively. The ECJ held that this would amount to retroactive imposition of a penalty which was equivalent to a criminal penalty. The Court said at para 3:

> The principle that penal provisions may not have retroactive effect is one which is common to all the legal orders of the member states and is enshrined in article 7 of the European Convention for the Protection of Human Rights and Fundamental Freedoms as a fundamental right; it takes its place among the general principles of law whose observance is ensured by the Court of Justice.

Before the TEU Article F (now 6(2)) expressly recognized fundamental rights as a principle of EU law, the Court can be seen here employing a principle of fundamental rights by reference both to 'all the legal orders of the member states' and to the ECHR. Also before the TEU, in Case C–5/88 *Wachauf* [1989] ECR 2609, the ECJ referred to general principles of fundamental rights as enshrined in numerous international instruments to which the Member States were parties. Without naming any particular treaty or any particular right, the Court found that rules which, on the expiry of an agricultural lease, had the effect of depriving the tenant of the fruits of his labour, would breach such fundamental rights. The Court, at para 18, enunciated the following principle:

> The fundamental rights recognized by the Court are not absolute, but must be considered in relation to their social function. Consequently, restrictions may be imposed on the exercise of those rights, in particular in the context of a common organization of a market, provided that those restrictions in fact correspond to objectives of general interest pursued by the Community and do not constitute, with regard to the aim pursued, a disproportionate and intolerable interference, impairing the very substance of those rights.

The Court's first assertion here must be qualified as the ECHR, and in many cases, criminal law makes some rights absolute which in theory might be interfered with in the name of free movement of workers. The right to be free from slavery is an example of such a right. The principle of free movement of workers could not be advanced to promote for instance abusive domestic labour or sex-trafficking.

Having said this, the principle of balancing economic and fundamental rights appears so far to prevail in EC law. Case C–112/00 *Schmidberger* [2003] 2 CMLR 34 broke new ground in this respect, for the first time weighing an interference with an EU right against the exercise of a fundamental right protected by the ECHR. A transport firm challenged the decision of the Austrian government to permit a demonstration by environmental protesters which blocked the Brenner highway, a major international route, for 30 hours. There had been forewarning and advertising of alternative routes. The Austrian government took its decision bearing in mind the protesters' right under Article 11 ECHR to demonstrate peacefully. The ECJ held that, although the EU law 'right to free movement of goods' was engaged, the state's decision to uphold the Article 11 right, given all the measures that were taken, was not disproportionate and did not infringe EC law.

The ECJ also found it was necessary to balance rights of freedom of establishment and rights of workers to organize and take industrial action in *Viking Line* (Case C–438/05). This was an instance of the phenomenon known rather unattractively in EU discourse as 'social dumping'. This refers to the practice of producing goods for export in a country with low standards of pay and protection for workers, thus making the exporter's costs artificially lower than those of its competitors in countries with higher standards, and giving an advantage in international trade at the expense of lower-paid or less-protected workers. The Court held that industrial action by the union was a restriction on the freedom of establishment, but

> that restriction may, in principle, be justified by an overriding reason of public interest, such as the protection of workers, provided that it is established that the restriction is suitable for ensuring the attainment of the legitimate objective pursued and does not go beyond what is necessary to achieve that objective.

The ECJ has sometimes of its own motion introduced an argument based on fundamental rights. In *Carpenter*, *Gloszczuk*, and *Kondova*, the first ECJ cases to refer to the right to respect for the family life of third country nationals, the Court said that any removal of the applicants would have to be carried out in accordance with Article 8, i.e., with due respect for their right to family life and only if necessary in a democratic society in the interests of a legitimate aim. The Court's approach in Carpenter suggests that mere regulation of immigration would not be sufficient to justify removal – perhaps a more generous interpretation and application than would be seen from Strasbourg. The ECJ may draw upon 'the constitutional traditions common to the member states' as a source of principle or fundamental rights, and not only on the specific rights protected by the ECHR. In Case 36/02 *Omega Spielhallen* [2004] ECR I 9609, the German public authority had prohibited the parts of Laserdrome activity which were 'playing at killing' or simulated homicide, in the interests of public order and the protection of human dignity. In upholding the prohibition, the ECJ reiterated that fundamental rights play an integral part in EU law, and then said that EU law also 'strives to ensure respect for human dignity as a general principle of law'. This case is an unusual and interesting one in protecting human dignity as a fundamental principle.

Note the comparison with *Manjit Kaur*, where on a strong challenge to national sovereignty, the ECJ did not uphold an argument based on fundamental rights. A less direct challenge to a state's authority on nationality issues succeeded in *Airola*, where the fundamental human right in question, not to be subject to sex discrimination, derived from the original economic purposes of the Community.

6.11.2 Challenging EC primary legislation

Case C–540/03 *European Parliament v European Council* was a challenge to secondary legislation. What happens if the EU's own primary legislation appears to conflict with fundamental rights? In the normal course of things, the ECJ does not have power to examine the validity of primary EU legislation, and human rights do not function in the EC as a constitutional standard which would give the ECJ any special jurisdiction in this respect. This limitation on the jurisdiction of the ECJ was revealed in *Matthews v UK* (1999) 28 EHRR 361. The case could not be heard in the ECJ but was considered by the European Court of Human Rights. The Court held the UK and the other Member States to be in breach of the ECHR by entering into a decision and primary legislation which excluded the people of Gibraltar from voting in European Parliamentary elections. This breached their rights under Article 3 of Protocol 1 to the ECHR which guarantees free and fair elections. Primary legislation could not be challenged within the EU's own legal order. The ECtHR but not the ECJ could judge the matter.

6.11.3 Charter of Fundamental Rights, ECHR, and the Lisbon Treaty

In an initiative separate from the main Treaties, the European Charter of Fundamental Rights (OJ 2000 C 3641) was formally adopted by a solemn declaration at the European Council in Nice in December 2000. It recognizes a wide range of fundamental rights, but initially had a declaratory, non-binding status. It has already been used by the ECJ as a source of reference for the nature of rights which should be respected in the Union. Its status is further enhanced by being given legal force in the Treaty of Lisbon, although there are 'opt-out' declarations by Poland and the UK also annexed to the Treaty. The relationship between the Charter and the ECHR is not fully resolved. The two documents are intended to be compatible, though the scope of the Charter is wider. Concerning the relationship between the two documents, the Charter's Article 52(3) says:

In so far as this Charter contains rights which correspond to rights guaranteed by the Convention for the Protection of Human Rights and Fundamental Freedoms, the meaning and scope of those rights shall be the same as those laid down by the said Convention. This provision shall not prevent Union law providing more extensive protection.

There is a contradiction here, but a plausible interpretation is that the Charter may be interpreted so as to be more protective of rights than the ECHR, but not less, and the principle of consistent interpretation cannot be used to defeat rights granted in Union law. An interesting relevant example of where the Charter could extend protection is in Article 47(2), which broadens the scope of the right to a fair hearing to 'rights and freedoms guaranteed by the law of the Union'. This would include any rights arising from the immigration and asylum provisions under Title IV, which as we have seen in chapter 4, are excluded from the right to a fair hearing under the present case law of the ECHR. There has been much discussion over the years of the possibility of accession of the EU to the ECHR, and the Lisbon Treaty now provides for this in Article 218 TFEU; negotiations are now well underway to settle the terms of accession and necessary practical arrangements. It also reaffirms the place of fundamental rights from the ECHR and constitutional traditions of the Member States as general principles of the Union's law (Art 6(3) TEU).

6.11.4 Fundamental rights and EU migration law directives and regulations

It is clear that protection of fundamental rights is a significant part of any system of immigration and asylum law. The Stockholm Programme makes significant references to this, as do the preambles to all legislation asserting compliance with the fundamental rights that form part of EU law, including the Charter and ECHR. Nonetheless, NGOs and migrant organizations have challenged a number of specific provisions and also have persistent concerns about the reality of compliance when it comes to implementation on the ground. The relationship between fundamental rights protection and the interpretation and implementation of the secondary legislation is one of the key questions for the next few years. Perhaps one of the most recent and high profile examples of ongoing concerns has been the number of requests by asylum seekers to suspend removals to other Member States on the basis of fear of violation of fundamental rights and unfair processes, particularly but not exclusively in Greece. This resulted in a successful challenge under the ECHR in the Strasbourg Court in *MSS v Greece and Belgium* Application no. 30696/09, in which both Belgium and Greece were held by the ECHR to be in violation of obligations – Belgium in its refusal to suspend the transfer of an asylum seeker to Greece under the Dublin Regulation and deal with the case itself in the face of real and significant evidence of non-compliance by Greece. Similar conclusions have been reached by the CJEU concerning the same point of principle under EU law in Case C–411/10 *NS v UK* (see chapter 12). Although suggesting a clear principle that not every breach of the Directives in a proposed destination state would engage this obligation, if there is real credible evidence of a serious risk of breaches constituting violations of fundamental rights, including the EU Charter, the sending state itself would be in breach of EU law in not operating its discretion in favour of the applicant to process the asylum application itself. A presumption of compliance by other Member States is permissible, but such a presumption must be rebuttable, and there must be a realistic practical opportunity to do so.

This undermines the more or less 'automatic' nature of the transfer system in the Dublin Regulation and emphasizes that Member States must take seriously concerns about violations of fundamental rights in treatment of asylum seekers by other Member States, at the risk of being implicated and condemned for violation of fundamental rights themselves in knowingly sending applicants to face such treatment elsewhere in the EU when the evidence is strong enough that this may happen. This must be taken into account when Member States exercise their discretion not to transfer under the Dublin system. This point, and what Member States should do when one of them appears to be so overwhelmed by the practical and financial demands on its asylum system that standards are being compromised in this way, is being considered further in the re-casting of the Dublin Regulation.

6.12 Conclusion

This chapter has raised some of the policy issues which dominate immigration and asylum law in Europe, and the UK's negotiated opt-in arrangement to the provisions arising under Title IV of the Amsterdam Treaty. To date, the UK has taken a leading part in discussions on asylum and has opted into all provisions on that subject, although not all the recent proposed amending measures. It has also opted into some of the increased security measures in the Schengen acquis, which now forms part of EU law. The EU as a whole has been slower to implement a full range of provisions creating rights for third country nationals, and the UK shows far less inclination to opt into these. The European legal system provides a base for migration law that is purposive in its reasoning, and this provides part of the context for the development of UK migration law, not only politically and in terms of binding legal provisions, but also in terms of a different kind of thinking about law.

QUESTIONS

1. Why do you think the UK negotiated an opt-in arrangement to the Treaty of Amsterdam? Why do you think the EC agreed to this?
2. What are the benefits to the UK of opting into the EU measures on asylum?
3. What are the interests at stake in the case of *Tum and Dari*, and how did the ECJ deal with these?

For guidance on answering questions, visit www.oxfordtextbooks.co.uk/orc/clayton5e/.

FURTHER READING

Baldaccini, Anneliese (2005) 'Asylum Support and EU Obligations: Implementation of the EU Reception Directive in the UK' *Journal of Immigration, Asylum and Nationality Law* vol. 19, no. 3, pp. 152–160.

—— (2009) 'The Return and Removal of Irregular Migrants under EU Law: An Analysis of the Returns Directive' *European Journal of Migration and Law* vol. 11, no. 1, pp. 1–17.

Biondi, Andrea (2004) 'Free Trade, a Mountain Road and the Right to Protest: European Economic Freedoms and Fundamental Individual Rights' *European Human Rights Law Review* no. 1, pp. 51–61.

Boelaert-Suominen, Sonja (2005) 'Non-EU Nationals and Council Directive 2003/109 EC on Status of TCNs who are Long-term Resident: 5 Paces forward and Possibly 3 Paces back' *Common Market Law Review* vol. 42, no. 4, pp. 1011–1052.

Boeles, Pieter (2001) 'Introduction: Freedom, Security and Justice for All' in Elspeth Guild and Carol Harlow (eds), *Implementing Amsterdam: Immigration and Asylum Rights in EC Law* (Oxford: Hart), pp. 1–12.

Boeles, Pieter, den Heijer, Maarten, Lodder, Gerrie, and Wouters, Kees (2009) *European Migration Law* (Antwerp: Intersentia).

Carrera, Sergio and Guild, Elspeth (2008) 'The French Presidency's European Pact on Immigration and Asylum: Intergovernmentalism vs Europeanisation?' Centre for European Policy Studies Policy Brief No. 170.

Castles, Stephen, Crawley, Heaven, and Loughna, Sean (2003) *States of Conflict: Causes and Patterns of Forced Migration to the EU and Policy Responses* (London: Institute of Public Policy Research).

Dale, Gareth and Cole, Mike (1999) *The European Union and Migrant Labour* (Oxford: Berg).

Dell'Olio, Fiorella (2002) 'The Redefinition of the Concept of Nationality in the UK: Between Historical Responsibility and Normative Challenge', *Politics*, vol. 22, no. 1, pp. 9–16.

European Commission (2004) *Area of Freedom, Security and Justice: Assessment of the Tampere Programme and Future Orientations*, COM (2004) 4002, final, 2 June.

European Council on Refugees and Exiles (2004*), Broken Promises – Forgotten Principles: An ECRE Evaluation of the Development of EU minimum standards for Refugee Protection* Tampere 1999 Brussels 2004.

Facenna, Gerry (2004) '*Eugen Schmidberger, Internationale Transporte und Planzüge v Austria*: Freedom of Expression and Assembly vs Free Movement of Goods' [2004] *European Human Rights Law Review* vol. 1, pp. 73–80.

Guild, Elspeth (2001) 'Primary Immigration: The Great Myths' in Elspeth Guild and Carol Harlow (eds), *Implementing Amsterdam: Immigration and Asylum Rights in EC Law* (Oxford: Hart), pp. 65–94.

—— (1999) 'Free Movement of Persons in Europe: The Amsterdam Treaty and its Implications for the UK' *Immigration and Nationality Law and Practice* vol. 13, no. 4, pp. 128–132.

Guild, Elspeth, and Harlow, Carol (eds) (2001) *Implementing Amsterdam: Immigration and Asylum Rights in EC Law* (Oxford: Hart).

Gumus, Yasin Karem (2010) 'The EU Blue Card Scheme: a Step in the Right Direction?' *European Journal of Migration and Law* vol. 12, p. 435.

Hailbronner, Kay (1998) 'European Immigration and Asylum Law under the Amsterdam Treaty' *Common Market Law Review* vol. 35, no. 5, pp. 1047–1067.

Hall, Stephen (1996) 'Loss of Union Citizenship in Breach of Fundamental Rights' *European Law Review* vol. 21, pp. 129–143.

Hamood, Sara (2008) 'EU–Libya Co-operation on Migration: A Raw Deal for Refugees and Migrants?' *Journal of Refugees Studies* vol. 21, no. 1, pp. 19–42.

Higgins, Imelda and Hailbronner, Kay, (2004) *Migration and Asylum Law and Policy in the EU FIDE 2004, National reports* (Cambridge: Cambridge University Press).

House of Lords EU Committee 'Frontex: the EU External Borders Agency' (Ninth Report of Session 2007/08).

Human Rights Watch (2009) *Pushed Back, Pushed Around* (Human Rights Watch, online).

Lyasky, O. 'Complementing and Completing the CEAS: A Legal Analysis of the Emerging Extraterritorial Elements of EU Refugee Protection Policy' (2006) *European Law Review* vol. 31, pp. 230–235.

Meloni, Annalisa (2009) 'The Community Code on Visas: Harmonisation at Last?' *Common Market Law Review* vol. 34, no. 5, p. 671.

Mitselegas, Valsamis (2006) 'The Directive on the Reception of Asylum Seekers and its Implementation in the UK', *Journal of Immigration, Asylum and Nationality Law* vol. 20, no. 1, pp. 42–45.

Peers, Steve (1998) 'Building Fortress Europe: The Development of EU Migration Law' *Common Market Law Review* vol. 35, no. 6, pp. 1235–1272.

—— (2003) 'Key Legislative Developments on Migration in the European Union' *European Journal of Migration and Law* vol. 5, no. 1, pp. 107–141.

—— (2008a), Legislative update: EU immigration and asylum competence and decision-making in the Treaty of Lisbon *European Journal of Migration and Law* vol. 10, no. 2, p. 219.

—— (2008b) 'In a World of their own? Justice and Home Affairs Opt-outs and the Treaty of Lisbon' *Cambridge Yearbook of European Legal Studies* vol. 10 (2007/08), p. 383.

—— (2009a) 'Legislative Update: EC Immigration and Asylum Law Attracting and Deterring Labour Migration – the Blue Card and Employer Sanctions Directives' *European Journal of Migration and Law* vol. 11, no. 4, pp. 387–426.

—— (2009b) 'Legislative Update: EC Immigration and Asylum Law, 2008: Visa Information System' *European Journal of Migration and Law* vol. 11, no. 1, pp. 69–94.

—— (2009c) 'Turkish Visitors and Turkish Students: New Rights from the European Court of Justice' *Journal of Immigration, Asylum and Nationality Law* vol. 23, no. 2, pp. 197–203.

Rogers, Nicola (2006) 'Turkish Association Agreement Applications – A Myriad of Problems and some Solutions' *Journal of Immigration, Asylum and Nationality Law* vol. 20, no. 4, pp. 283–288.

Shah, Prakash (2002) 'Why some British Nationals are not European Union Citizens' *Journal of Immigration, Asylum and Nationality Law* vol. 16, no. 2, pp. 82–96.

Stevens, Dallal (2004) *UK Asylum Law and Policy* (London: Sweet & Maxwell), chapter 9.

—— (2005) 'Asylum Seekers in the New Europe: Time for a rethink?' in P. Shah (ed.), *The Challenge of Asylum to Legal Systems* (London: Cavendish).

SECTION 3

The system of immigration control

7

Crossing the border and leave to remain

SUMMARY

This chapter is concerned with the legal processes of crossing the border to enter the UK and the stages at which that crossing is encountered before and on arrival. The extra-territorial powers of immigration officers and the increasing role of new technologies are discussed as characteristics of an increasingly diffuse, intelligence-based, and security-oriented system. The chapter describes the role and powers of entry clearance officers and immigration officers, and considers the general grounds for refusal of leave or entry clearance. The Common Travel Area (CTA) is introduced. Finally, there is discussion of the grant of leave, and of how the most secure immigration status of settlement may be achieved.

7.1 Introduction

The legal processes described in this chapter apply to all those who are subject to immigration control (Immigration Act 1971 s 3(1)). The law relating to the various categories of entry such as spouse, dependent child, worker, is dealt with in the fourth part of this book and asylum claims in the fifth part. The provisions discussed in this chapter apply to those whose applications are discussed in section 4 of this book, and, where relevant, to asylum seekers. The power to give or refuse leave to enter is the foundation of immigration control, and the study of these powers and of their interpretation by civil servants and judicial bodies tells us about the nature of immigration control and the way that it is changing.

7.1.1 Changing nature of immigration control

The development of immigration control from the Aliens Act 1905 up to the end of the twentieth century was increasingly complex in detail but quite simple in concept. At the borders, whether sea or air, immigration officers determined whether a passenger needed leave to enter, and if so whether and on what terms to grant it. The exception to this was the Common Travel Area which expressed a recognition that the land border between Britain and Ireland required a more flexible approach, and, from 1969, entry clearance, which formalized a pre-entry stage of immigration control in British embassies and High Commissions abroad.

At the end of the twentieth century, this traditional model was dissolving, in part as a result of membership of the European Union, as discussed in chapter 6. Although the UK has not yet opted into many immigration provisions made under the Treaty of Amsterdam, it is a full partner in the Common European Asylum System, and participates in security measures such as the Schengen information system and the Eurodac fingerprinting system. The UK's movement towards harmonization with the rest of Europe brings a dual preoccupation with freedom of movement on the one hand, and security on the other. Increasingly sophisticated international intelligence networks and communication media make this possible. Immigration control is becoming a matter of interception, policing, and international information exchange, not granting leave by a stamp in a passport at a port of entry.

Now in the twenty-first century, the system still bears some of the features of geographical border control, but also of the newer and more dispersed system, which has statutory foundations in the Immigration and Asylum Act 1999. In the traditional model, immigration control is exercised principally at two points. One is the port of entry, administered by the immigration service, the other is an entry clearance post at an embassy, high commission, or diplomatic post overseas. In the emerging model, an integrated system considers visa applications and grants the effective leave abroad, having checked security details with immigration, police, taxation, and security services in the UK. Passengers are vetted before embarking on a journey. The physical border, the point of arrival, becomes a place of checking and policing, of potential arrest and detention. The UK Border Agency, created in 2007, carries out all these functions. Monitoring for immigration infringement becomes a function distributed through a range of practices and legal provisions to educational bodies, local authorities, other public bodies, commercial bodies, and even private individuals.

7.2 Scope of immigration control

7.2.1 Common Travel Area

7.2.1.1 *Common Travel Area – introduction*

Entry from another part of the Common Travel Area is an exception to the requirement for leave to enter. Agreements on absence of immigration controls between the UK and Ireland have existed in various forms since the founding of the Irish Free State in 1922. Although there were restrictions on travel during and for a short while after the Second World War, these were relaxed after an exchange of letters between the two governments in 1952 proposed a similar and mutually enforced immigration policy. This laid the foundation for the present day Common Travel Area (see Ryan 2001). The UK implemented this by repealing the requirement for aliens to obtain leave to land from Ireland (Aliens (No 2)) Order 1952, SI 1952/636. The arrangement for an absence of immigration control between the two countries and mutual assistance with enforcement included passing information between governments about the movement of aliens. In particular, there was, and still is, a sharing of intelligence about those who appeared on the other country's list of undesirable aliens.

The present-day Common Travel Area (CTA) consists of the United Kingdom of Great Britain and Northern Ireland, the Channel Islands, the Isle of Man, and the Republic of Ireland. It was established by Immigration Act 1971 s 1(3) which provides that journeys which are purely between any of these places (i.e., they do not start or end outside the CTA) are free of immigration control. This does not mean, however, that the whole of the immigration law of the CTA is entirely harmonized or that it is subject to the same laws (see Immigration Act 1971 s 9). The UK, Islands, and Ireland remain different jurisdictions. Neither does it mean that no individual travelling is subject to any restriction, as there are exceptions to this freedom of movement. The effect of the CTA is to create an area somewhat similar to the Schengen system, in which there is mutual enforcement of each other's immigration laws but which does not facilitate entry to the area from outside. Critically, however, leave to enter the UK does not also constitute leave to enter the Republic of Ireland, and vice versa. See discussion of the case of *Emmanson* in the next section.

7.2.1.2 *Common Travel Area – operation*

While their inhabitants have British nationality, the Isle of Man and Channel Islands, have their own immigration laws. In practice, the Island authorities adopt British provisions selectively; for instance they do not permit the collection of biometric information for entry clearance, thus putting the Islands outside a major part of the UK government's e-borders programme, discussed later in this chapter. Islanders are not subject to British immigration control, and vice versa. Immigration Act 1971 Sch 4 gives effect in the UK to the immigration laws of the Islands. The result is that limited leave granted in the UK or Islands has effect with the same limitations throughout the UK and Islands. Similarly, deportation orders made in the UK or Islands are given effect in each other's jurisdiction and illegal entry into one is illegal entry into the others.

Citizens of the Republic of Ireland on the other hand, are subject to British immigration control (and vice versa). The CTA means that British and Irish citizens may enter Ireland and Britain respectively without leave and without having to present a passport to establish their status, but like other EEA nationals they may be deported. There is an additional provision for the exclusion of Irish citizens if the Secretary of State personally directs that their exclusion is conducive to the public good (Immigration (Control of Entry through Republic of Ireland) Order 1972, SI 1972/1610 article 3(1)(b)(iv) and (2)).

The CTA effects mutual enforcement of immigration controls. An illegal entrant to Ireland for instance is not permitted by the CTA to enter Britain, and requires leave to do so. The UK and Ireland enforce each other's deportation orders, though not without question. The IDI 9.2.3.4, June 2004, advises that an Irish deportation order is a relevant consideration, but an application for entry should still be considered on its merits. Visa nationals who do not, on entering another part of the CTA, have a valid visa for the UK, do not have this omission wiped out on entering the UK. They still need a visa. The Immigration (Control of Entry through Republic of Ireland) Order 1972, SI 1972/1610 article 3(1)(b) makes this plain in relation to entry through Ireland. The applicant in *R (on application of Alinta)* [2006] NIQB 61 lived in Northern Ireland but had overstayed his UK visa. On attempting to cross the border to the Republic of Ireland on a shopping trip, he was detained and in due course served with notice of removal signed by a UK immigration officer. He was escorted by security personnel back to Northern Ireland. He contended that he was not an overstayer as he was not in the UK at the time of the service of the notice, and he was not liable to removal as he had been brought back to the UK under the control of the law so his presence could not be unlawful. These ingenious arguments failed. According to Article 3 of the Order, as a person who had overstayed in the UK he needed fresh leave to re-enter. Without this, he was an illegal entrant. The mutuality provisions have the same effect in relation to the Islands.

SI 1972/1610 article 4 allows a limited stay in the UK for certain people entering through the Republic of Ireland. If someone's leave to remain in the UK has expired while they were in Ireland, the Order itself grants seven days' leave on return to the UK, unless they were a visitor on a short visa in which case it grants one month. If they have entered Ireland from outside the CTA they may only remain in the UK for three months and may not take paid work. The Court of Appeal in *Kaya v SSHD* [1991] Imm AR 572 confirmed that someone who exceeds this period is correctly treated as an overstayer.

The CTA has been criticized as a weak point in the UK's border controls, and the Labour government in 2009 included a clause in the Borders, Citizenship and Immigration Bill which would in effect have reintroduced immigration controls within the CTA. The clause was defeated in the House of Lords. The Coalition government has dropped proposals for legislative reform of the CTA but instead has strengthened internal controls by changes of practice. Operation Gull was a programme introduced in November 2010, in which UKBA ended the secondment of police officers at Scottish sea ports, and increased its enforcement staff at Northern Irish sea ports. A report on the operation cited a 65 per cent increase in immigration offenders detected at Scottish and Northern Irish sea ports (*Common Travel Area: Review of Arrangements at Northern Ireland Sea Ports*). As the report explains, ferry routes between Northern Ireland and Scotland are domestic UK services 'and are, legally and in immigration control terms, no different to [sic] ferry services between... Hampshire and the Isle of Wight. The Northern Irish Court of Appeal in *Emmanson (Fyneface), Re Judicial Review* [2010] NICA 35 was asked to rule that checking the status of passengers on these routes was unlawful. The Secretary of State relied on Immigration Act 1971 Sch 2 para 2A, giving a power to 'examine a person who has arrived' in order to establish whether their leave should be cancelled (see 7.6.5), and the case of *Baljinder Singh v Hammond* [1987] 1 All ER 829 where the High Court held that an immigration officer might examine a person outside the port of entry and at a date subsequent to entry, provided they had information to found an enquiry as to the person's immigration status. The Court of Appeal declined to rule on the lawfulness of Operation Gull, on the basis that Mr Emmanson had consented to the examination and so no authority had been exercised.

The case raises questions about the operation of the CTA. Mr Emmanson had obtained entry clearance to the UK as a visitor. Before he left Nigeria he had obtained both sterling and euros, and bought presents for a woman living in Dublin. He was detained on arrival in Belfast from Stranraer. Mr Emmanson said that he was not aware that as a visitor to the UK he was not allowed to visit Ireland. Indeed, the CTA operates on the usual presumption that a visitor's visa to one part of the CTA is valid for all. However, as Mr Emmanson had not declared his intention to visit Dublin, the immigration officer considered that his entry clearance had been obtained by deception and that he was an illegal entrant. The NICA endorsed this view. The effect of this decision is that an applicant for entry clearance to any part of the CTA must declare their intention to travel to other parts, otherwise they may be treated as an illegal entrant. The Chief Inspector of UKBA pointed out the vulnerability of the operation of the CTA to challenge on the basis of misuse of the power to examine. His report emphasizes that the law following *Singh v Hammond* is that examination on in-country journeys is only authorized where the immigration officer *has information* which would found an inquiry into whether the person examined had breached immigration law.

The impact on the common law right of freedom of movement within the territory was raised by Mr Emmanson's counsel, but was left without comment also because of his consent to examination.

The CTA does not fit easily with the e-borders programme, and the Isle of Man's government, the Tynwald, has made it clear that the Isle of Man will not introduce collection of data for e-border purposes.

7.2.2 Who is subject to immigration control?

British citizens and Commonwealth citizens with right of abode, as defined and discussed in chapter 3, are not subject to immigration control (Immigration Act 1971 s 3(1)). The following groups are, strictly speaking, subject to immigration control but do not need leave to enter: nationals of the European Economic Area (Immigration Act 1988 s 7); air and sea crews making a lawful stop within s 8(1) of the 1971 Act; service people, diplomats, and their households; people arriving from another part of the Common Travel Area (1971 Act s 8); and prisoners brought to the UK to give evidence in drug-trafficking cases (Criminal Justice (International Co-operation) Act 1990 s 6). Certain representatives of governments and those benefiting from immunities conferred by Orders in Council referring to international tribunals and other international bodies are exempt from immigration control under the Immigration (Exemption from Control) Order 1972, SI 1972/1613, as amended. All other passengers need leave to enter. Visa nationals, and all non-EEA nationals who intend to stay for more than six months, need entry clearance which must be obtained at an entry clearance post overseas. The list of visa national countries is appended to the immigration rules and is frequently updated (usually lengthened).

Although asylum claimants need leave to enter, this cannot be granted until their asylum claim has been processed. This cannot be done at the port as the investigation is too complex, and by the nature of the claim cannot be done before arrival. Asylum claimants are therefore normally given a status called temporary admission pending determination of their claim (Immigration Act 1971 Sch 2 para 21); alternatively, they may be detained. Detention and temporary admission are discussed in chapter 15.

Recognized refugees are issued with a travel document pursuant to the obligation in the 1951 UN Convention Relating to the Status of Refugees, and these are recognized for travel by signatory states. From 11 February 2004, the UK suspended its participation in the 1959 Council of Europe Agreement on the Abolition of Visas for Refugees 'on public order and security grounds', with the effect that refugee travel documents must now be endorsed with a visa to obtain entry to the United Kingdom.

7.3 Before entry – entry clearance

An entry clearance application is the earliest point in time at which an intending immigrant might encounter UK immigration control. Entry clearance applications are granted or refused by entry clearance officers (ECOs) based in British posts abroad, that is, in embassies, high commissions, and consulates. Entry clearance officers perform a vital function in the implementation of immigration control. Given this, it is surprising both that entry clearance officers are not mentioned in any of the legislation, and that until June 2000 they were answerable to the Foreign and Commonwealth Office (FCO) rather than to the Home Office. The defining reference to entry clearance officers in the immigration rules is in para 26, which says that where appropriate the term 'entry clearance officer' should be substituted for 'immigration officer'. The UKBA website gives ready access to the Entry Clearance Guidance (ECG) used by ECOs.

Where entry clearance is required, it must be obtained before setting out for the UK (HC 395 para 28). It is mandatory for all non-EEA passengers coming to the UK for more than six months, and for nationals of visa national countries also for shorter stays. Those people for whom entry clearance is not mandatory may apply for entry clearance as a precaution (HC 395 para 24) to establish their eligibility for entry and so avoid the risk of being turned away at the port. This may be advisable since those without entry clearance have no right of appeal (Nationality Immigration and Asylum Act 2002 s 89 as amended).

7.3.1 Development of entry clearance and the need for reform

Visas were instituted during the First World War for all those who were not nationals of Commonwealth countries. After the war, visas remained available as an ad hoc mechanism and were used for temporary controls for particular groups, including, even then, to deter refugees. For instance, in 1938, anticipating Jewish refugees, the UK reinstated a visa requirement for Austria and Germany (see Dummett and Nicol:157).

Another form of prior entry clearance, the entry certificate, was introduced by the Immigration Appeals Act 1969 for Commonwealth citizens applying to join family members in the UK. This control was aimed at limiting entry from the New Commonwealth. It began with a written parliamentary answer in 1969, announcing a system of entry certificates for Commonwealth men seeking entry to join wives and fiancées. This was rapidly followed by the requirement in the Immigration Appeals Act 1969 for all dependent relatives to obtain an entry certificate. The government introduced this as a late amendment to the Bill, incurring criticism of the 'last minute inclusion of yet another control – perhaps the most restrictive of all – the mandatory entry certificate' (National Council for Civil Liberties, quoted by Juss 1994:44). People required to apply for an entry certificate as opposed to a visa had in theory a right to enter. However, the application system created notorious delays, which in themselves operated as an illegitimate form of immigration control (*R v SSHD ex p Phansopkar* [1975] 3 WLR 322 CA).

Perhaps strangely, the brief period during which the 1969 Act was in force was the only time when entry clearance has been required by statute. The Immigration Act 1971 contains no requirement for entry clearance, nor any indication of who may be required to hold entry clearance, though it is defined in the Act as 'a visa, entry certificate or other document which, in accordance with the immigration rules, is to be taken as evidence [or the requisite evidence] of a person's eligibility, though not [a British citizen] for entry into the UK' (s 33). Where entry clearance is mandatory, this is achieved by the immigration rules.

The number of visa national countries, that is, those whose nationals require entry clearance for any purpose, is now around 113. To put that number in perspective, the United Nations currently recognizes 191 countries. Countries are added to the list when circumstances suggest that asylum claims from there will increase. For instance, during the three months of July to September 2002, a total of 2,105 Zimbabweans sought asylum in the United Kingdom, almost as many as in the whole of 2001. In November 2002, the Secretary of State announced that Zimbabwe would become a visa national country.

In the early days of entry clearance applications, information was gathered largely from interviews. Entry clearance posts were not well distributed, so an applicant might have a long and arduous journey to get to the interview. A research report by the UK Immigration Advisory Service described a common journey as follows:

> The train journey from Sylhet to Dacca alone takes 13 hours, added to that, of course, the cumbersome boat, bus journey, including miles of walking to reach Sylhet town from the village. [Most wives were also] carrying an infant and other children of very young age through the long journey. (p. 11, as quoted by Juss:73)

On arrival, an applicant, who would not have the resources to rest in a hotel before attending the interview, would be exhausted and not really fit for an important interview. Despite this, researchers reported that applicants would never answer in the negative the standard question asked by the ECO as to whether they were fatigued, nervous, or unwell. The reason was the fear that if they were unfit for interview on arrival, the interview would be postponed for a long period (CRE:36).

The conduct of the interview could be oriented to catching people out rather than examining their application in the light of the immigration rules. ECOs used the 'discrepancy system', the practice of interviewing separately members of the same family, then turning down claims to be related from people who differed in minor detail in their accounts of events or circumstances. The events in question could be years in the past, thereby increasing the likelihood of difference in memories in *bona fide* applicants.

Major studies in the early 1980s, later work by Juss (1997), research conducted into family visitor appeals, and the working holidaymaker scheme, all revealed concerns with the quality of entry clearance decisions. These were repeated in government-sponsored reviews by the Entry Clearance Monitor, the National Audit Office, and the FCO.

Problems identified mainly concerned:

- delays in processing the application;
- cursory or poor quality consideration of the application;
- oppressive conduct and conditions of interview; and
- use of discrepancy system by ECOs.

The Home Affairs Committee (Fifth Report of Session 2005–06 HC 775) commented that the immigration rules were vague, allowing too much scope for inconsistency in decision-making. An additional pressure on ECOs is sheer numbers. The numbers of people requiring entry clearance are swelled by the increase in global travel generally. The need to address these problems combined with an increased concern with security to create a momentum for change.

7.3.2 The new system: entry clearance as part of e-borders

The new system of entry clearance, which has been coming into effect from 2003, is part of the government's plan to create a security ring around the UK which is not a physical barrier but is a system of 'e-borders' – i.e., an electronic border. The new system has the following characteristics:

- collection of information by biometrics and other electronic processes;
- a consequent enhanced role for database information in decision-making;
- increasing points of access to the system through online applications, 'hub and spoke' working and delegation of the public interface to commercial bodies;
- for decisions on entry for work and study, routinized decision-making by the use of purportedly measurable, objective, and transparent criteria, replacing much of the former discretion (though see chapter 10 for actual operation);
- limited appeal rights; and
- greater reliance on management rather than judicial processes for quality control.

Each of these points will be addressed in turn.

7.3.2.1 *Biometrics*

The introduction of compulsory biometric data for all entry clearance applicants was enabled by the Nationality, Immigration and Asylum Act 2002 s 126 which granted the power to require biometric information. Digital photographs and fingerprinting are now a compulsory requirement in any visa application (Immigration (Provision of Physical Data) Regulations 2006, SI 2006/1743). This method makes it easier to transfer to other parts of the border control operation unique information about applicants. The scanned fingerprints are checked against police and immigration records to identify if a prospective traveller has already been fingerprinted in the UK by the immigration authorities, has been arrested, charged, cautioned or convicted, is on a security watch-list, or has made an asylum application in the UK. Failure to provide biometric data is a discretionary reason for refusing entry clearance (HC 395 para 320(20)).

The only way that an individual can challenge the accuracy of a match of their fingerprints with those in a database is in the course of appealing against a consequent refusal of entry clearance; but in the case of a decision on entry for work or study or a non-family visit, there is no such appeal, except on human rights or race discrimination grounds. This makes it less surprising that there is no case law yet on the refusal of entry clearance on the basis of biometric information. Concerning challenges to fingerprint matches in the Eurodac system (the European database which records fingerprints of asylum claimants), in *YI (Previous claims – fingerprint match – EURODAC) Eritrea* [2007] UKAIT 00054, the Tribunal held that it was right to require further evidence in addition to a bare assertion that the prints matched in order to be satisfied that the fingerprint records proved that the claimant had made a previous claim for asylum in Italy. An example of such further evidence would be a photograph of the person who supplied the prints said to be matched by the claimant's. This was in the context of an allegation of fraud, and the High Court in *R (on the application of YZ, MT and YM v SSHD* [2011] EWHC 205 (Admin) held that this did not give a right to challenge the Eurodac system. In *RZ (Eurodac – fingerprint match – admissible) Eritrea [2008] UKAIT 00007*, the Tribunal held that the standard of proof was the balance of probabilities, though the burden of proof was on the Secretary of State to show the accuracy of the match. A successful challenge would be difficult to mount as the evidence was that the system was highly reliable.

7.3.2.2 *Use of electronic information*

Fingerprints and photographs are evidence of identity supporting an application. Entry clearance may be refused when a match of this information with police, immigration, or security records indicates that the applicant has a criminal record, is a security risk, or has a previous immigration history which might found a reason for refusal. This can arise through the fingerprint match revealing that the applicant is now using, or has in the past used, a false document (such as a forged passport) to gain entry, or through information coming to light which the applicant had not disclosed. The applicant need not have committed a wrong before, or be telling any lies or using any false documents concerning the content of their present application. A simple non-disclosure of a previous refusal of entry clearance is a mandatory reason to refuse entry clearance on this occasion (HC 395 para 320(7A)).

Although fingerprint records introduce a technological measure of genuineness, this does not dispense with the exercise of judgement by a human being. For instance, to determine whether there has been disclosure of a previous refusal requires judgement, as revealed in the April 2009 report of the Independent Monitor for Entry Clearance, where a previous refusal notice had been enclosed with the application although the correct box on the application form had erroneously not been ticked.

7.3.2.3 *Increased points of access*

There are two developments which have had an impact on the accessibility of the visa application system. One is that many applications may now be made online. The other is that UKBA has contracted with commercial organizations to provide Visa Application Centres (VACs). The processes used vary from country to country. A typical example is that of Manila, where applicants complete an online visa application form, then attend a commercially run Visa Application Centre where they pay their fee, provide biometric data, and submit a paper copy of their application form. The VAC sends the documents to the British Embassy where ECOs make the decision.

UKBA has also adopted a method of 'hub and spoke' working, whereby many diplomatic posts no longer make entry clearance decisions, but pass them to 'hub' posts where the decision is made. For instance, the Madrid office decides applications made in Portugal as well as those made in Spain; Canberra handles applications from New Zealand. Warsaw has become the hub for applications from non-EU nationals from eight countries. Very few applicants now personally meet the ECO who makes the decision on their case, as compared with the days of the long journeys and interviews described at 7.3.1. The Independent Monitor estimated in evidence to the Home Affairs Committee that 8 per cent are now interviewed.

7.3.2.4 *Measurable, objective, and transparent criteria*

In the points-based system for entry for work and study, criteria such as 'adequate' maintenance have been replaced by fixed, specified amounts which the applicant must possess to meet the requirements of the rules. Criteria such as 'intention to leave at the end of studies', which used to form part of the student rules, have been dropped altogether. Similarly, the assessment of whether a person is able to follow the course of study for which they have applied no longer forms part of an immigration decision. The new rules and the effect of their application are discussed in detail in chapter 10.

7.3.2.5 *Reduced appeal rights*

Refusals of entry clearance for non-family visitors, workers, and students are subject to a right of appeal only on human rights and race discrimination grounds. Any other challenge may be made only by an internal administrative review conducted by an Entry Clearance Manager who was not involved in the original decision. In an administrative review, the applicant may only claim that 'a mistake has been made' relating to the specified criteria. Unlike in an appeal, they may not request sight of the evidence or cross-examine. They cannot submit documents that were missing from the original application and request administrative review on that basis. The decision-maker may not request missing documents in order to make a fully informed decision on the first occasion. An application may be made for judicial review of the decision, but this is a daunting and expensive task for an applicant abroad, and relies on permission being granted by the Court. In practice, disappointed applicants apply again and pay another fee.

7.3.2.6 *London Olympics and Paralympics 2012*

There is a contemporary short-term exception to the requirement for entry clearance and to provide biometric data. Athletes, coaches, support staff, umpires, technical staff, media personnel, and other individuals associated with the Olympic or Paralympic Games are required to obtain accreditation for the Games and to undergo security checks, but not to apply for a visa or supply biometric information. They receive an Olympic or Paralympic identity and accreditation card which they can use in lieu of a visa from 30 March 2012 to 8 November 2012. This concession was a contractual commitment for the Olympic host city. Secondary legislation was adopted to enable UKBA to collect biometric information when a Games participant applies for leave to remain during the Games (Immigration (Provision of Physical Data) (Amendment) Regulations 2011, SI 2011/1779).

7.3.3 Monitoring entry clearance applications

With each step as appeal rights were removed, the government appointed an independent monitor to oversee the quality of the decisions in question. By 2007 this had resulted in a number of monitors, each with a different remit. Following consultation, the government abolished the monitors, and appointed instead a Chief Inspector of UKBA, whose remit covers all the work of the Agency. The inspector's remit concerning entry clearance is broader than that of the monitor, in that it includes grants of entry clearance as well as refusals. Like the monitor, the inspector is unable to make recommendations in individual cases, and systemic recommendations are not enforceable. The House of Commons Home Affairs Committee questioned the outgoing monitor and the incoming inspector on the implications of the transition (Monitoring UKBA, First Report of Session 2008–09 HC 77), and expressed concern that it was too burdensome for the Chief Inspector to take on the work of monitoring the visa operation ('The Work of the UK Border Agency' (Second Report of Session 2009–10 HC 105)). In practice, the reports of the Chief Inspector have been thorough and robust. Entry clearance was one of the first areas of UKBA work to which the Inspectorate's attention turned, and there are now reports of the entry clearance operation in Abuja, Rome, Guangzhou, Chennai, Kuala Lumpur, Amman, Istanbul, and New York. The Chief Inspector has paid particular attention to decision-making at entry clearance posts in Pakistan, after a comparative inspection of entry clearance practices in Abu Dhabi and in Islamabad suggested that adverse discrimination occurred in Islamabad.

Against this background, we now consider the legal effect of entry clearance once granted. The grounds upon which entry clearance may be refused are almost identical to reasons for refusal of leave to enter, and are discussed later in that context.

7.3.4 Effect of entry clearance

Before the changes introduced by the Immigration and Asylum Act 1999, entry clearance and leave to enter were two distinct stages of the entry control process. Although possession of entry clearance made it highly likely that leave to enter would be granted on arrival, it was not in itself a grant of leave. From 28 April 2000, the Immigration (Leave to Enter and Remain) Order 2000, SI 2000/1161 enabled entry clearance to have effect as leave to enter, provided it specifies the purpose for which the holder wishes to enter the UK, and is endorsed with any conditions to which it is subject or a statement that it is to have effect as indefinite leave (Article 3). In most cases now, therefore, entry clearance will function as leave to enter. The exception is for refugee travel documents. Entry clearance endorsed on these after 27 February 2004 does not have effect as leave to enter (Immigration (Leave to Enter and Remain) (Amendment) Order 2004, SI 2004/475).

As a consequence of this extended effect of entry clearance, the role of immigration officers at the port of entry has changed to more of a policing function, checking the traveller's identity and the validity of existing documents. Immigration Act 1971 Sch 2 para 2A says that, in the case of a passenger who arrives with leave, the powers of the immigration officer are to examine that person to ascertain whether any grounds exist to cancel that leave, and, as discussed at 7.6.5, in limited circumstances the immigration officer has the authority to refuse entry to someone holding an entry clearance (para 321 of the Rules). An implication of the changed nature of the examination at the border became apparent in *Khaliq v Immigration Officer, Gawtick* [2011] UKUT 00350(IAC). The appellant had entry clearance as a student. On arrival in the UK, it was apparent that he did not meet the college's minimum requirement for English language, and he accepted that he had bought the certificate purporting to verify his level of English. However, the points-based system no longer requires examination of qualifications by an entry clearance or immigration officer; the offer letter issued by the college is conclusive. There was no evidence before the Tribunal as to whether the language certificate had been sent to the college. There was therefore no evidence that the appellant had made any false representation in relation to his application for leave. Para 321A permits an immigration officer to cancel leave granted by entry clearance if false representations (see 7.6.5) were made to obtain that leave. As the appellant is not making an application at the port of entry, a certificate produced at that time is not a representation for the purposes of obtaining leave and so cannot result in cancellation. Before 2000, where a holder of entry clearance applied for leave to enter at the border, a false representation of this kind would have resulted in refusal. The grant of entry clearance which has effect as leave to enter bears two dates, one when the entry clearance becomes effective, 'valid from...' and one which marks its expiry, 'valid until...'. The passenger may travel once the entry clearance/leave to enter is effective. Entry clearance officers are advised to ask the passenger when they are planning to travel, and are permitted to make the entry clearance/leave to enter valid from a date up to three months after the date when they granted it. ECO Guidance ECB9.4 advises:

> For applicants in long-term categories who are subject to either a qualifying period before applying for settlement, or to a limit on their total length of stay in that category, leave to enter should begin on the date they arrive in the UK. This will ensure that they are able to meet the qualifying period within the validity of their entry clearance and avoid unnecessary applications for extensions of stay.

If a person arrives before the 'valid from . . .' date, the immigration officer on arrival has a discretion to cancel the entry clearance (HC 395 para 30C) and grant a new period of leave (para 31A). This discretion must, of course, be exercised reasonably.

7.4 Development of the exported border

A flow of new measures to export border control has been built upon the power in the Immigration (Leave to Enter and Remain) Order 2000, SI 2000/1161, to grant leave to enter outside the UK. The power to grant or refuse leave to enter from abroad was not only granted for convenience of some travellers, but also for deterrence of others, namely asylum seekers. Simon Brown LJ in *European Roma Rights Centre and Others v Immigration Officer, Prague Airport and SSHD* [2003] 4 All ER 247 explains:

> There are difficulties, however, of a political nature in imposing a visa regime on certain friendly states and so Parliament in 1999 authorized the Home Secretary to introduce in addition a scheme enabling the immigration rules to be operated extra-territorially rather than simply at UK ports of entry. Intending asylum seekers would in this way be refused leave to enter the UK by immigration officers operating abroad and so be unable to travel to the UK to claim asylum here. (para 2)

First, we consider the Order itself, then the uses that have been made of it so far.

7.4.1 Immigration (Leave to Enter and Remain) Order 2000, SI 2000/1161

The Immigration (Leave to Enter and Remain) Order 2000 was made pursuant to a widely phrased power in Immigration and Asylum Act 1999 s 1 (which inserted a new section 3A into the Immigration Act 1971):

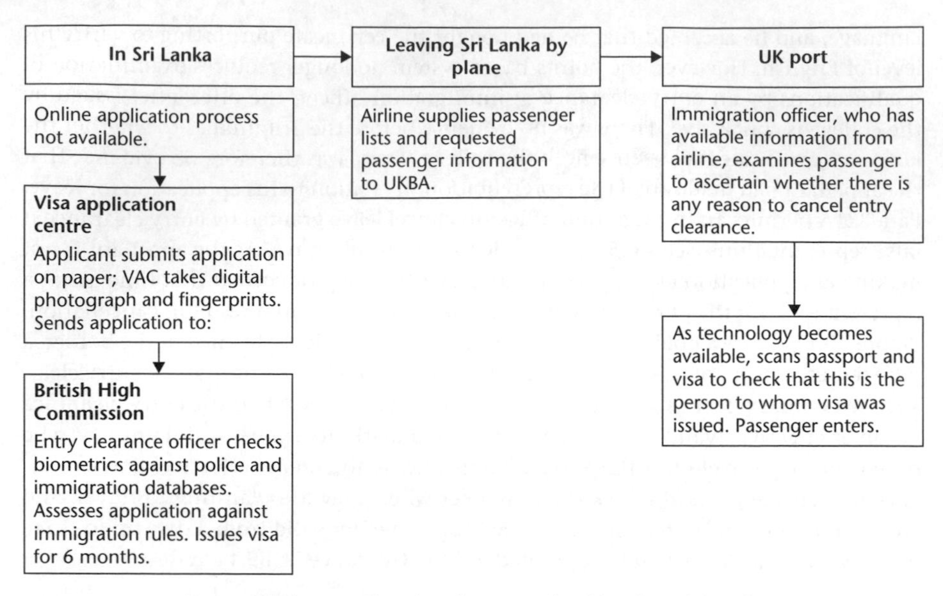

Figure 7.1 Stages of immigration control – visitor from Sri Lanka

1. The Secretary of State may by order make further provision with respect to the giving, refusing or varying of leave to enter the United Kingdom.
2. An order under subsection (1) may, in particular, provide for leave to be given or refused before the person concerned arrives in the United Kingdom;
   (a) the form or manner in which leave may be given, refused or varied;
   (b) the imposition of conditions;
   (c) a person's leave not to lapse on his leaving the common travel area.

This was the first time since the 1971 Act that there had been a substantive change in the power to grant or refuse leave to enter. It should be noted that the power in s 3A is simply to 'make further provision with respect to the giving, refusing, or varying of leave to enter'. The specific powers which follow in subsection 2 are not necessarily an exhaustive account of how this power will be exercised.

The power was first exercised by making the Immigration (Leave to Enter and Remain) Order 2000, SI 2000/1161. By Article 7 of that order, 'an immigration officer *whether or not in the United Kingdom*, may give or refuse a person leave to enter the United Kingdom *at any time before his departure for, or in the course of his journey to*, the United Kingdom' (emphases added). This means that neither the immigration officer nor the grant of leave are fixed to the port of entry. Leave may be given before or during travel, and the immigration officer need not be based at the port. Article 8 provides that notice giving or refusing leave to enter, instead of being given in writing as required by s 4(1) of the 1971 Act, may be given by fax or e-mail, or, in the case of visitors, orally including by telephone. Article 8A, inserted by Immigration (Leave to Enter and Remain) (Amendment) Order, SI 2010/957, implements e-borders by providing for leave to be given as a visitor by entry through an automated gate under specified conditions. Leave to enter may also be given to responsible third parties, not just to the passenger directly (Article 9). This flexibility in the means of communicating a grant of leave to enter may have drawbacks if, for instance, a question of proof arises at a later date (see Luqmani,

Randall, and Scannell 2000:12). However, it was intended to be for the convenience of those regarded as 'low risk' passengers, for instance those on school trips or other organized tours. In these cases, a passenger list may be presented and endorsed with leave to enter, even before setting out on the trip, and this is intended to minimize delay at the port of entry. An example of the process is given in Figure 7.1.

In addition to grant by entry clearance, and advance clearance for groups of 'low risk' passengers, the power to grant or refuse leave to enter before travel is designed for schemes established abroad to deter unauthorized passengers.

7.4.2 Juxtaposed control

The first of these initiatives considered here is known as 'juxtaposed control'. This involves a reciprocal arrangement whereby British immigration officers work at ports abroad, and border guards of those countries work in the ports in the UK, each country carrying out its immigration controls *before* the passenger embarks on the journey to cross the border. Presently, these reciprocal arrangements are in place between the UK and France and Belgium.

The first juxtaposed controls were a development of the Channel Tunnel project, as the opening of the Channel Tunnel was seen to create new opportunities for clandestine migrants to enter the UK by hiding in containers and lorries. The Sangatte Protocol to the Treaty of Canterbury was agreed between France and the UK, establishing the principles of and authorizations for juxtaposed controls. This is given effect within the UK's legal system, by the Channel Tunnel (International Arrangements) Order 1993, SI 1993/1813 (the 1993 Order), made using powers in the Channel Tunnel Act 1987.

The Sangatte Protocol and the 1993 Order provide for officials of each country to carry out their functions in a 'control zone' in the other. Control zones are: 'the part of the territory of the host State determined by mutual agreement between the two Governments within which the officers of the adjoining state are empowered to effect controls'. The actions of these officials were to be governed by 'frontier control enactments' of each state which were permitted by the Sangatte Protocol to have effect in the control zone in the other.

These first controls operated on the shuttle trains which carried road vehicles, and also enabled immigration officers of each state to operate on board Eurostar passenger trains. However, an increase in undocumented arrivals and asylum claims at Waterloo led to an Additional Protocol being agreed between France and the UK authorizing juxtaposed controls in railway stations. Following amendments because of changes to the Eurostar route, and an agreement with Belgium, juxtaposed controls for Eurostar passengers are now operating in London St Pancras, Ebbsfleet International and Ashford on British territory, Paris Gare du Nord, Calais Fréthun, and Lille-Europe on French territory, and the Gare du Midi in Brussels.

While the first Channel Tunnel juxtaposed controls were wide-ranging, dealing with animal health, consumer goods, and traffic issues as well as immigration, the Eurostar controls were purely aimed at immigration, and in particular at the deterrence of asylum claims. The Additional Protocol Article 3 provided that controls exercised by the state of departure were to check whether the person was free in law to leave its territory, and controls by the state of arrival were to check whether the passenger was in possession of the necessary travel documents and fulfilled any other conditions for entry to its territory. Additionally, to meet the UK government's interest in preventing asylum seekers from reaching the UK through the Tunnel, the Additional Protocol with France provided that claims for refugee status must be made and processed in the state of departure if made at any time before the train doors closed at the last scheduled stop in that state (Article 4). The responsibility for receiving asylum claims was thus imposed, by agreement, on France. The same applies to a claim for protection made on the basis of human rights rather than as a refugee.

A main source of impetus for the extension of juxtaposed controls to sea ports was the furore surrounding the Red Cross refugee camp at Sangatte in northern France. There were daily illegal entries to the UK by asylum seekers waiting in the camp; and this, combined with the associated breaches of security, danger, and injury to individuals, and delays to freight and other traffic, created a three-year dispute over causes and responsibilities between the two governments. Accordingly, in 2002, British immigration officers began working alongside French border police in Calais, in an informal arrangement to cooperate, and for this a new legal foundation was needed.

In 2003, France and the UK entered into a Frontier Control Treaty at le Touquet 'concerning the implementation of frontier controls at the sea ports of both countries on the Channel and North Sea' (Cm 5832, in force on 1 February 2004). The Treaty is given effect in UK law by the Nationality, Immigration and Asylum Act 2002 (Juxtaposed Controls) Order 2003, SI 2003/2818, made under the power in the Nationality, Immigration and Asylum Act 2002 s 141. This power broke new ground in allowing an order to provide for 'a law' of England and Wales to have effect in a specified area outside the UK.

The Treaty says that the powers which may be exercised in sea port control zones are 'all the laws and regulations of the Contracting Parties concerning immigration controls and the investigation of offences relating to immigration' (Article 2). However, the 2003 Order specifically lists those statutes which apply.

As new enforcement powers are effected in the UK, many have been added to the sea port juxtaposed control regime. For instance, the Nationality, Immigration and Asylum Act 2002 (Juxtaposed Controls) (Amendment) Order 2006, SI 2006/2908, extends to a control zone the power to take fingerprints of someone who fails to provide a valid passport or equivalent on arrival. The offences of absconding from detention and obstructing a search (Immigration, Asylum and Nationality Act 2006 ss 40 and 41) are also extended to the control zone. By means of these incremental changes the control zones are increasingly treated as part of UK jurisdiction, and the network of border control is established outside the actual territory, including by the use of new detection technology to find people hiding in vehicles. However, it is not at all clear that the appeal provisions of the Nationality Immigration and Asylum Act 2002 apply in control zones. The Act is not referred to, though the Order is made under that Act, and it does seem that appeals under the 2002 Act are probably not available in sea ports.

In its reply to concerns raised in the consultation process on juxtaposed controls, the Home Office said that passengers would be able to contact their embassy at any time, though it is unlikely that an asylum seeker would feel safe to do so, and 'those passengers refused entry who have a right of appeal from abroad will be served with a notice of refusal which will include information about the Refugee Legal Centre and Immigration Advisory Service' (Juxtaposed Control Implementation, Dover–Calais, Consultation Process Report, Response 1). However, both these organizations have gone into administration, and there are few immigration decisions taken in a control zone for which the legal foundation can be found for an appeal. Even those that may exist in theory are not supported by any practical arrangements for their exercise. The Home Office's Control of Immigration Statistics show that, typically, between 23 per cent and 27 per cent of 'non-asylum' refusals of entry at ports of entry are at juxtaposed controls. Of course as an asylum claim cannot be made to the destination country in a control zone, these figures do not reveal how many of those refused might have had asylum as their ultimate aim, or what happened to them.

The Nationality, Immigration and Asylum Act 2002 (Juxtaposed Controls) (Amendment) Order 2011, SI 2011/1786 allows for biometric details to be taken in control zones where holders of Olympic accreditation cards apply for leave to enter, thus enabling the UK to carry out security checks on a proportion of Games participants.

7.4.3 Airline liaison officers

Another role taken abroad by immigration officers is as airline liaison officers (ALOs), to advise airlines on the validity of documents presented to them for travel to the UK. These immigration officers do not grant or refuse leave to enter, but advise airlines which may then refuse to allow the passenger to board. In answer to a question in Parliament, the immigration minister said that in the five years up to January 2009, Airline Liaison Officers had assisted in preventing nearly 210,000 people from boarding planes, 'equivalent to about two jumbo jets a week' (HC Debs 27 January 2009 288W). The liability of the officers for wrong advice is a matter of concern, given that there is no appeal against what is in formal terms advice to the airline rather than an immigration decision (see discussion of *Farah v British Airways & Home Office* TLR 26 January 2000, at 7.5.3.5). Asylum seekers may travel on false documents as this may be the only way to leave their country. For obvious reasons, the effect on asylum seekers turned away from flights after such advice is unknown.

ALOs play a part in the development of intelligence-led immigration control. In October 2008 the ALO Network amalgamated with the overseas Risk Assessment Unit Network, which provided intelligence support to entry clearance officers. The resulting body, RALON – The Risk and Liaison Overseas Network, provides an intelligence link between posts overseas and the UK, enabling individuals to be targeted more easily if they are identified as a threat. When a requirement for visas is implemented in relation to nationals of a country, RALON provides country-specific risk assessments. RALON also connects with SOCA (the Serious Organised Crime Agency) to track stolen British passports and detect or prevent their re-use.

7.4.4 Passenger information

As part of developing the Schengen area, the UK opted into EC Directive 2004/82, binding from 5 September 2006. This entails that Member States have systems requiring carriers to transmit passenger data to immigration authorities. The Immigration and Asylum Act 1999 first required carriers to provide immigration officers 'such information relating to the passengers carried, or expected to be carried... as may be specified' (Immigration Act 1971 Sch 2 para 27(2) as amended). An additional power was inserted by the Asylum and Immigration (Treatment of Claimants, etc.) Act 2004 to require provision of 'a copy of all or part of a document that relates to the passenger'. The 2006 Act has added powers for the police to require passenger and freight information (ss 32 and 33) and a duty for the border agencies (UKBA, police, and HMRC) to share information among themselves (s 36). Passenger information may be provided electronically and so may be checked against 'multi-agency watchlists' prior to boarding. By these means, passenger information provided by carriers becomes part of the 'e-borders' scheme as announced in the five-year strategy ('Controlling our Borders' Cm 6472).

The Immigration and Police (Passenger, Crew and Service Information) Order 2008, SI 2008/5 provides that an immigration officer or the police may require a responsible person in respect of a ship or aircraft to provide a passenger list showing the names and nationality of passengers on board, whether arriving in or leaving the UK. They may also be required to provide, if they have it, dozens of items of data specified in the Order, including, for instance, in relation to passengers the number of pieces and description of any baggage carried, their ticket number, its date and place of ticket issue, the identity of any person who made the reservation, and more. Information must be provided electronically.

The House of Commons Home Affairs Committee has requested regular reports on the e-borders scheme since it appeared that targets for implementation would not be met and that advance passenger information requirements were ill-suited to ferry and rail travel. It also appeared that the scheme might breach EU law because it imposed a requirement other than the simple production of ID or a passport as a condition of entry.

The EU Commission gave its view that the programme would be compatible with EU law provided that the following guarantees given by UKBA were met 'in their entirety and in a legally binding manner' and 'in the everyday operation of the e-Borders scheme':

- Passengers who are EU citizens or their family members will not be refused entry/exit or incur sanctions on the basis that their passenger data is unavailable to the UK authorities for whatever reason;
- Carriers will not incur sanctions if they are unable to transmit data through no fault on their part;
- Carriers will be instructed by the UK authorities not to deny boarding to travellers, regardless of their nationality, who do not communicate Advanced Passenger Information (API) data to the operator, and that the provision of API data to operators is neither compulsory nor is made a condition of purchase and sale of the ticket;
- UK authorities will make available to persons travelling to/from the UK the information required by Article 10 of Directive 95/46/EC [on the protection of personal data] and will assist carriers to communicate this information to travellers;
- A single contact point will be established by UK authorities to allow data subjects to exercise their data protection rights;
- Appropriate safeguards will be applied to transfers of data to third countries, in line with requirements of the UK data protection authority.

These conditions effectively undermine the advance passenger information scheme as envisaged by the UK government.

7.4.5 Pre-clearance

Successive Home Secretaries have asserted that it would be desirable to pre-sift asylum claims abroad, and the third initiative discussed here is an example of an attempt to do this. The pre-clearance scheme at Prague in the Czech Republic was an experiment in overseas activity of the British immigration service aimed at deterring unauthorized passengers from travelling, and targeting Roma asylum seekers. In this case, leave to enter was granted or refused before embarkation on a flight for the UK. In *European Roma Rights Centre (ERRC) v Immigration Officer at Prague Airport and SSHD* [2002] EWHC 1989 (Admin), the evidence of the Secretary of State confirmed that 'the Prague operation is not a pre-screening which is a prelude to a subsequent consideration of eligibility at a United Kingdom airport. Rather it takes the place of that consideration of that eligibility' (para 25). The judgments in the Court of Appeal [2003] 4 All ER 247 and House of Lords [2004] UKHL 55 confirmed what critics and the UK government had agreed upon, namely that the effect of such a scheme was to prevent asylum claims being made. The difference between the parties was whether this was lawful or not. This case was a dramatic illustration of the potential of the Immigration (Leave to Enter and Remain) Order 2000. Where an asylum claim is made at a UK port of entry there is an obligation implied by the 1951 UN Convention Relating to the Status of Refugees to consider it. However, the Courts in the ERRC case found there was no obligation to allow the claimant to reach the UK in order to make that claim. As discussed in chapter 8, the House of Lords found this scheme to be discriminatory on racial grounds and therefore unlawful.

The Prague scheme ran from 18 July 2001 to 26 February 2003. Following the Czech Republic's accession to the European Union in 2004, the scheme would have no basis.

7.5 Trans-border controls – carriers' liability

A feature of current government policy is to extend the responsibility for immigration control to people in many walks of life. Liability placed on those who transport people and goods is not a new phenomenon, but until the 1980s it was relatively unimportant. Its use has expanded enormously in the UK since 1987 and it now represents a major plank in the government's policy to control asylum claims.

7.5.1 International context

Germany, Belgium, the USA, Canada, and Australia have all introduced measures imposing liability on carriers for the transport of passengers who either hide themselves and gain entry without being detected ('clandestine entrants') or who do not have the appropriate documents for travel, for instance their passport is forged or stolen or does not show the requisite entry clearance ('inadequately documented' passengers). Articles 26 and 27 of the Schengen Convention, which became part of EC law following the Treaty of Amsterdam, require the imposition of carrier sanctions by means of legislation, and the UK has been active in these measures.

7.5.2 Summary of legislative history

Under the Aliens Act 1905, a shipping company committed an offence punishable by a fine if a person subject to immigration control disembarked without leave to enter. If an immigrant who needed leave was admitted to the UK but expelled within six months, the Home Office could recover the cost of the return journey from the shipping company which had brought that passenger. Similar provisions persist to the present day. Immigration Act 1971 Sch 2 paras 26 and 27 set out various supplementary duties of shipping companies and airlines, which show how closely these commercial bodies are required to cooperate with the immigration service. For instance, if they carry passengers who require leave to enter, ships or aircraft may only call at designated ports of entry, and must ensure that passengers disembarking pass through designated control areas. Liability could be imposed without any fault on the part of the carriers.

Although the risk of penalties gave an incentive to carriers to check the documentation of passengers and refuse passage where they had doubts as to someone's status, there was no statutory obligation to do so until the Immigration (Carriers' Liability) Act 1987. The Act imposed fines on airlines and shipowners or their agents of £1,000 for each person carried by them who entered without a valid passport, and, where required, visa. This was increased to £2,000 in 1991. This amount was per passenger, not per journey. Therefore, if 50 inadequately documented passengers were found on one ship, the fine imposed on the owner or agent would be £50,000, or, after 1991, £100,000. In 1993, the Asylum and Immigration Appeals Act 1993 s 12 added liability for carrying people who did not have the required transit visas. In 1998, legislation was introduced to include trains following the opening of the Channel Tunnel (Channel Tunnel (Carriers' Liability) Order 1998, SI 1998/1015).

In 1999, the Immigration and Asylum Act introduced liability for clandestine entrants as opposed to just passengers with improper documentation, and increased the scope of legislation to cover road transport. Later amending regulations have included rail freight (Carriers Liability (Clandestine Entrants) (Application to Rail Freight) Regulations 2001, SI 2001/280). These provisions represented an enormous extension of liability. Whereas a professional passenger carrier such as an airline would have in place procedure for checking documentation, the extension to clandestine entrants and road transport meant that other commercial organizations and individuals, who had no professional expertise in transporting passengers, could be held liable to a penalty for people who had hidden in their car or lorry. The Immigration (Carriers' Liability) Act 1987 was repealed. Current law is governed by the 1999 Act, as amended by Nationality, Immigration and Asylum Act 2002 Sch 8 and the Carriers' Liability Regulations 2002, SI 2002/2817, amending regulations and codes of practice.

7.5.3 The statutory scheme of carriers' liability

7.5.3.1 *Liability for clandestine entrants*

Section 32(5) of the 1999 Act imposed liability for clandestine entrants arriving in the UK on the owner or captain of the ship or aircraft, the owner, hirer, or driver of another vehicle, including, if the vehicle is a detached trailer, its operator. Since amendment by the 2002 Act, a penalty is imposed for each clandestine entrant, the maximum being £2,000 (Carriers' Liability Regulations 2002, SI 2002/2817, reg 3). In respect of each clandestine entrant, a penalty may be collected from more than one responsible person. In this case, there is a maximum aggregate penalty of £4,000 per entrant (reg 3). If the driver is an employee of the vehicle's owner or hirer, the employer is jointly and severally liable for the penalty. The maximum applies to the passenger, not the carrier. So, up to £4,000 may be paid by a number of different carriers for the one clandestine entrant, but if a carrier carries several clandestine entrants, the maximum penalty is £2,000 per passenger.

The definition of 'clandestine entrant' in s 32(1) as amended is striking. There are two aspects to it, first of all the concealment. A person is a clandestine entrant if they arrive concealed in a vehicle, ship, rail freight wagon, or aircraft or pass or attempt to pass through immigration control concealed in a vehicle. Arrival includes in a control zone as prescribed for the purposes of juxtaposed control (Carriers' Liability (Amendment) Regulations 2004, SI 2004/244). The definition catches both a person who stowed away on a ship, but disembarks on foot, and someone who continues or attempts to continue through immigration control hidden in a vehicle. The second part of the definition is that the person evades, or attempts to evade, immigration control, or, which is more surprising, they claim, or indicate that they intend to claim, asylum in the UK. There can be no doubt that this provision catches a genuine asylum claimant. The penalty is on those who transport them rather than the clandestine entrants themselves, but of course the effect of this is to make carriers more wary of carrying clandestine entrants. There is a non-statutory scheme of refunding penalties paid for carrying inadequately documented travellers where the passenger ultimately succeeds in an asylum claim, but this does not apply when the passenger is granted humanitarian protection or discretionary leave (see *Charging Procedures – a Guide for Carriers*, Appendix B). A successful asylum claim might of course be years down the line and so of small comfort to the carrier.

There is a defence in s 34 to liability for the penalty if the carrier can show that they were acting under duress, or that they had an effective system for preventing the carriage of clandestine entrants, which was operated properly, and they did not know, and had no reasonable grounds for suspecting, that someone might be concealed.

In determining whether a system is effective, account will be taken of the code of practice for vehicles issued by the Secretary of State under s 32A. The code contains detailed provision for road haulage and other commercial vehicles concerning the sealing of containers and repeated inspections. It also contains provisions for buses and coaches concerning the locking of doors and inspections and even for private vehicles such as cars and caravans, making equivalent provision.

Following the extension of liability to rail freight operators by the Carriers' Liability (Clandestine Entrants) (Application to Rail Freight) Regulations 2001, SI 2001/280, a Code of Practice for securing rail freight has also been adopted, and a further code for rail freight shuttle wagons.

The carrier may serve a notice of objection to the penalty (Carriers' Liability Regulations 2002, SI 2002/2817) which the Secretary of State must consider. If the notice is upheld, the Secretary of State may sue to recover the amount of the penalty. Importantly, following the *Roth* case discussed shortly, the 2002 Act introduced a right of appeal to a court against the imposition of the penalty (1999 Act s 35A; *International Transport Roth GmbH and Other v SSHD* [2002] 3 WLR 344).

The penalty is backed up by the power in s 36(1) for a senior officer to detain vehicles pending payment of the charge, if 'there is a significant risk that the penalty will not be paid' and no satisfactory alternative security. This power was extended by the 2002 Act to detaining a vehicle while the matter is being considered (1999 Act s 36(2A) and (2B)). The Court may order the release of a transporter if it considers that there is satisfactory security, or there is no significant risk that the penalty will not be paid or it considers that the penalty was not payable (s 37(3A) and (3B)). If the Court does not order the release of the transporter and the penalty is not paid within 84 days, the transporter may be sold (s 37(4)).

7.5.3.2 *Improperly documented passengers*

Since the 2002 Act, liability for improperly documented passengers does not apply to bus, coach, and train operators but only to owners of ships or aircraft. The penalty is payable on demand to the Secretary of State like an 'on the spot' fine. Section 40(4) provides a defence if the carrier can show that the passenger embarked with the proper documentation. The *Charging Procedures— Guide for Carriers* sets out situations in which the penalty will be waived, including that the carrier acted on the advice of an airline liaison officer.

7.5.3.3 *Effect of scheme*

The new carrier provisions in the 1999 Act came into effect between 6 December 1999 and 18 September 2000. Simon Brown LJ, in the case of *International Transport Roth GmbH & Others* at para 10, described the effect as follows:

> By June 2001, 988 penalty notices had been served in respect of 5,433 clandestine entrants. 249 vehicles had been detained, of which 190 were subsequently released on payment of the penalty or a substantial security. In some 25 per cent of cases where clandestine entrants were discovered, either no penalty notice was served or, following the carrier's notice of objection, the Secretary of State decided, under section 35(8), that the penalty was not payable. The average penalty payable is some £12,000 (in respect, therefore, of six clandestine entrants). The bulk of the penalties are paid by companies, but some 10 per cent are paid by individuals including occasional car drivers. By October 2001 the value of the penalties paid or agreed to be paid was £2,432 million. In some cases instalment payments have been agreed, in the most extreme case at the rate of £40 per month for 12.5 years (£6,000).

In the *Roth* case, three of the appellants only discovered clandestine entrants when they were travelling up the motorway to London. They 'would never have been penalized had they not themselves alerted the police'.

The effect on small businesses of these penalties may be imagined, and the scheme generated an outcry. It was subject to a number of challenges.

7.5.3.4 *Redress for carriers*

When the system under the 1999 Act came into effect, there was no appeal against the imposition of a penalty. In *R (on the application of Balbo B &C Auto Transport Internazional) v SSHD* [2001] 1 WLR 1556, the Secretary of State had decided to uphold the penalty and in the absence of a right of appeal the claimants applied for judicial review of that decision. The Administrative Court held that judicial review was not appropriate, but when the Secretary of State began enforcement proceedings then liability could be challenged.

The claimants in *Roth* challenged the harshness of the scheme, demonstrated by the fixed penalty, by the carriers bearing the burden of establishing that they were not blameworthy, and the lack of compensation for loss of business while a vehicle was detained, even if the carrier was determined not to be liable in the end. They suggested this was a disproportionate response to the problem of clandestine entrants. They challenged the lack of discretion and flexibility and the lack of provision for a fair hearing or a right of appeal, alleging under the Human Rights Act 1998 a breach of Article 6 and of Protocol 1, Article 1.

The specific procedural requirements of a fair trial in Article 6 apply only to a criminal matter, though the general principle of fairness applies also to the determination of civil rights and obligations. The requirements of fairness would therefore be greater if the proceedings were regarded as criminal. In the Act the charge levied is referred to as a 'civil penalty', there is no criminal charge and the penalty is recoverable as a civil debt. However, what a proceeding is called by the domestic authorities is not conclusive of whether it will be regarded as criminal or civil for the purposes of Article 6 ECHR. The Court of Appeal agreed (by a majority) with the carriers that the penalty scheme should be regarded as criminal, mainly because the carriers were in fact being punished, and the punishment meted out was severe.

It was a small step from this conclusion to decide that the scheme violated Article 6, though not necessarily for the reasons advanced by the carriers. Simon Brown LJ held: 'The hallowed principle that the punishment must fit the crime is irreconcilable with the notion of a substantial fixed penalty' (para 47). He accepted the claimants' characterization of the scheme as 'harsh', and this was his main reason for finding a breach of Article 6. In a similar vein, he concluded that the heavy burden on the carriers violated the principle of proportionality inherent in Protocol 1, Article 1, and that even if there was no violation of Article 6, then there was of this Article.

Jonathan Parker LJ found the scheme incompatible with Article 6 for a different reason, namely that the Secretary of State had an exclusive role in determining liability, and the role of the courts was subsidiary. 'Accordingly, for the simple yet fundamental reason that the scheme makes the Secretary of State judge in his own cause, the scheme in my judgment is plainly incompatible with Article 6' (para 157).

Following the Court of Appeal's decision, a right of appeal was introduced and a flexible penalty.

7.5.3.5 *Redress for travellers*

While the carriers' liability scheme, particularly in relation to clandestine entrants, has clearly caused great problems for carriers, the scheme also carries particular hazards for potential passengers. The greatest hazard of the scheme is to an asylum seeker, who, by reason of their situation, may lack proper documents, and who is turned away from a flight, or discovered and removed from a lorry, perhaps directly into the hands of the authorities whose persecution they seek to escape. There has been considerable criticism of carrier penalties for the risks they may create for undocumented asylum seekers. There is also a potential problem for any traveller whose documents are not correctly understood.

This problem arose in *Farah v British Airways & Home Office, The Times* 26 January 2000. In this case, the Somali appellants had been prevented from embarking on a flight from Cairo to London. One had a passport. The other four appellants, all members of the same family, had declarations of identity documents issued by the British Embassy in Addis Ababa. The immigration liaison officer advised the airline that the passengers were incorrectly documented and should not be allowed to travel. As a consequence, they were detained in Cairo airport for five days, then deported to Ethiopia. The *Times* report is of the Court of Appeal's judgment that the judge should not have struck out the part of the particulars of claim which claimed negligence. This was held to be an arguable matter which would turn on the particular facts and should be heard.

The liability of airlines and of ALOs in this situation is as yet undetermined, though the *European Roma Rights Centre* case found that the Race Relations (Amendment) Act 2000 applied to decisions of immigration officers abroad (see 7.4.5).

The Council of Europe's Parliamentary Assembly considered the issue of sanctions against airlines in 1991 and commented:

> Airline sanctions... undermine the basic principles of refugee protection and the rights of refugees to claim asylum, while placing a considerable legal, administrative and financial burden upon carriers and moving the responsibility away from the immigration officers.

Research on people illegally resident in the UK shows that different routes of entry are more likely to be taken by people of different nationalities. It would suggest that airline controls impact more on travellers from West and Sub-Saharan Africa, and carrier sanctions would bite more on travellers from Albania, Ukraine, and Sri Lanka (Home Office 20/05 chapter 4).

Although energetic use has been made of carrier sanctions, this does not seem to have been sustained. The first annual report of the UKBA inspector commented, in relation to an inspection of juxtaposed controls, that penalties on carriers were not being fully used (*Independent Chief Inspector of UKBA report July 2008–September 2009*:39).

7.6 Immigration officers' powers on arrival

On arrival at a UK port, a passenger with or without entry clearance will encounter an immigration officer. By s 4(1) of the 1971 Act, immigration officers have specific statutory responsibility for giving or refusing leave to enter. Although this responsibility is no longer exclusive to them, as discussed at 7.7, in non-asylum cases, leave to enter is still granted by immigration officers where it has not already been granted by way of entry clearance.

Until April 2000, leave to enter was only granted at the port of entry by means of a date stamp in the passport. For travellers receiving leave to enter at the port it may still be granted by this method, unless and until e-borders make that redundant. Leave to enter may be refused on any of the grounds discussed at 7.6.4.

The extensive powers of immigration officers contained in Sch 2 of the 1971 Act are largely geared towards giving them the necessary scope of action in determining applications for leave to enter. Powers of examination, search, detention, and so on have all been granted and developed to lead ultimately to being able to make the decisive judgement – whether or not a person should have leave to enter the UK. Even the power to issue removal directions began as an administrative power to enforce a refusal of leave to enter. The integration of customs and immigration functions within UKBA, the statutory basis for which is provided in the Borders Citizenship and Immigration Act 2009, entails that immigration officers may also be designated as customs officials (s 3), thus extending further their powers on arrival.

The most widely applicable of the immigration officer's powers is to examine any person arriving (Sch 2 para 2). This includes where entry clearance has been granted (para 2A) and even where leave to enter is not required, as Immigration Act 1971 s 1(1) provides that freedom to come and go, enjoyed for instance by British citizens, may be hindered 'to enable their right to be established'. Any person arriving may be examined to ascertain whether they need leave to enter, and may be required to produce 'either a valid passport with photograph or some other document satisfactorily establishing his identity and nationality or citizenship' (Immigration Act 1971 Sch 2(1) and (4)). Therefore, a British passport-holder must show their passport to gain entry, even though they do not need leave to enter, and without such proof they may be refused entry (see also Immigration Act 1971 s 3(9) and HC 395 para 12). A 'valid' passport means a current one. The case of *Akewushola v Immigration Officer Heathrow* [2000] 2 All ER 148 CA established that an expired passport plus other proof of identity was not sufficient. Case C 378/97 *Wijsenbeek* [1999] I–6207 established that an EEA national passenger could be required to prove their entitlement despite their right to free movement, although a valid identity card is all that is necessary to establish the right to travel. In the case of other nationals, passports or refugee travel documents will be required (Table 7.1).

The legal process called 'examination' is at minimum a cursory inspection of a passport, and may go on from there (*R (on the application of Ogilvy) v SSHD* [2007] EWHC 2301 (Admin)) to involve an interview or a series of interviews. These may be on different dates so that the whole examination may be spread over a considerable period

Table 7.1 Entry and arrival

Method of arrival and entry decision	Consequence for entry
At a port. No leave granted but allowed physically to remain pending further inquiries (probably on temporary admission – see chapter 15)	Has arrived but not entered
At a port. Leave granted or already held and not cancelled	Arrives on disembarking from ship or boat and enters lawfully when passes through immigration control
Not at a port. Crosses land border (Republic of Ireland to N. Ireland). Leave granted or already held and not cancelled	Arrives and enters lawfully on crossing border (see *R v Javaherifard and Miller* [2005] EWCA Crim 323)
Not at a port. Arrives by sea or air (e.g., on a remote beach). No leave	Arrives on disembarking. Enters at time of arrival, but not lawfully
Not at a port. Arrives by sea or air (e.g., private landing strip). Has leave	Arrives on disembarking. Enters at time of arrival, lawfully

of time. The examination also includes other investigations carried out by the immigration officer which may not involve the passenger directly (*Thirukumar* [1989] Imm AR 270). In between interviews, the applicant may be in detention or released in the UK on a status known as temporary admission (Sch 2 para 21). Paragraph 4 imposes a duty on people who are undergoing examination to provide all information required for the examination including documentation. There is in law no 'duty of utmost good faith' to disclose everything which might conceivably be relevant (*Khawaja* [1984] AC 74 HL). However, *Khawaja* is also authority that silence as to a material fact is capable of amounting to deception or fraud depending on the circumstances, and this was relied on by the Court of Appeal in the case. The collection and rapid electronic transmission of passenger data now means that when a traveller arrives at a UK port, advance information about them may already be available to the immigration officer.

Documents may be retained by the immigration officer until the examination is over (para 4(2A) and (4)). This power was extended by Immigration, Asylum and Nationality Act 2006 s 27 to allow retention of documents, including a passport, from arrival until the person 'is about to depart or be removed'. In other words, the passport can be retained throughout a person's stay in the UK. The immigration officer also has power to search the passenger and their luggage (para 3). Powers are further extended by the UK Borders Act 2007 which provides that trained immigration officers may be 'designated', and these designated officers may detain a person suspected of a listed immigration offence (ss 1 and 2). This merges immigration and criminal policing functions.

Where a person arrives in the UK at a port, they are deemed not to have entered until they have passed through the designated area for immigration control (Immigration Act 1971 s 11). The repercussions of this are as shown in Table 7.1.

7.6.1 E-borders

There are a number of dimensions to the government's plan to establish 'e-borders'. In broad terms, this is the idea that personal details will be recorded and checked electronically and that this will become the paramount form of immigration control. The UK's e-borders system, if made fully effective in the way that the government envisaged, would be one of the most intensive in the world according to Statewatch. The current target date is 2015, though the Home Affairs Committee doubted the feasibility of this (*The Work of the UK Border Agency (November 2010–March 2011)* Ninth report of Session 2010–12 HC 929). UKBA aims to create a comprehensive record of passenger movements which it considers will strengthen security by:

- identifying in advance passengers who are a potential risk;
- telling us who plans to cross our border;
- checking travellers against lists of people known to pose a threat; and
- enabling us to link a person's journeys in order to form a detailed travel history, so that we can provide background checks to other agencies and compile a profile of suspect passengers and their travel patterns and networks.

The integration of immigration control with security issues was expressed in the Prime Minister's 'Statement on Security' in Parliament on 25 July 2007:

> Our first line of defence against terrorism is overseas at other countries' ports and airports where people embark on journeys to our country, and from where embassies issue visas.

As we have seen, the introduction of biometric information into the visa application process is the first step in the creation of e-borders. The Prime Minister goes on:

> The way forward is electronic screening of all passengers... at ports and airports... The Home Secretary will enhance the existing E-borders programme to incorporate all passenger information.
>
> The second line of defence is at our borders where biometrics... are already in use.

Since 30 November 2009, those people who arrive with biometric entry clearance have their fingerprints scanned on arrival to ensure that they match the prints of the person to whom entry clearance was issued.

British citizens also need to be able to travel in and out of the UK through electronic borders. The UK is moving towards embedding biometric details in the passports of British citizens, at the same time trying to ensure technological compatibility with new minimum security standards for European passports, including biometric fingerprint and facial data (Reg 2252/2004), although the Regulation is part of the Schengen *acquis* which does not apply to the UK.

Personal interviews are now used for first-time British passport applications, at which identity is confirmed through biographical details, facial features are scanned, and fingerprints taken. The information is recorded in a microchip which is read by an electronic reader at immigration control. The Identity Cards Act 2006 s 38 allows orders to be made compelling disclosure of information from other government departments for the purposes of issuing a passport.

For non-EEA nationals, the introduction of biometric residence permits (see chapter 2) performs a role in the e-borders project. The Immigration (Biometric Registration) Regulations 2008, SI 2008/3048 (as amended) require all applicants for specified categories of leave in the UK, and their dependants, to apply for a BRP. SI 2009/819 extends the requirement to those who are updating their passport or travel document. Thus, at the point of application, foreign nationals are brought into the electronic system. Details of leave granted are held on a chip in the BRP, and are therefore machine-readable and capable of being directly compared electronically with databases.

Data sharing with other countries is also at the heart of the e-borders scheme. Electronic collection and transmission of data has enabled the UK to enter into an agreement with the Five Countries Conference (FCC) nations: the USA, Canada, Australia, and New Zealand. Under a Protocol, the five countries are each able to check an agreed number (initially 3,000) per year of fingerprint sets in immigration cases against databases of the other FCC countries. The UK states it will use the Protocol primarily to check asylum cases where, e.g., the person cannot be identified or there is reason to believe the person may be known to another FCC country, and to check foreign nationals who have been convicted of criminal offences but are difficult to remove due to questions about identity and documentation.

A voluntary iris recognition system for frequent travellers is in place at nine airport terminals, including Heathrow, Gatwick, and Birmingham. In return for the provision of biometric data, those registered with the scheme gain a privileged status in the e-borders system, with unhindered entry and exit. Exit is now relevant as checks on departure from the country, which were abolished for journeys to Europe in 1994, and for other departures in 1998, are being reintroduced.

7.6.2 Extended powers in relation to terrorism

Immigration officers have powers under Sch 7 to the Terrorism Act 2000 as amended to stop, detain, search, and question any person at an air or sea port for the purpose of determining whether that person appears to be concerned or to have been concerned in the 'commission, preparation or instigation of acts of terrorism' (s 40(1)(b)). A person at a port may have arrived in the UK from anywhere. There is a wider power in relation to journeys into Northern Ireland from the Republic of Ireland when a person may be stopped not only at the port, but also within the border area. This is defined as any place up to a mile from the border with the Republic, or, if the journey is by train, the first train stop in Northern Ireland (Sch 7 para 4). This places a limit on the freedom of movement given by the Common Travel Area, and consistently with current trends these constraints on movement are not immigration restrictions but are security restrictions entailing policing activity. The Nationality, Immigration and Asylum Act 2002 (Juxtaposed Controls) Order 2003, SI 2003/2818 applies these powers to sea port control zones.

However, the 2000 Act contains no equivalent of the exclusion powers which were part of earlier anti-terrorism legislation. Under the Prevention of Terrorism (Temporary Provisions) Act 1989 and its predecessors, it was possible for individuals to be restricted to living in either Great Britain or Northern Ireland. These exclusion orders affecting British citizens did not appear in the 2000 Act, the omission being an aspect of the peace process in Northern Ireland.

Powers under the schedule do not require a basis of reasonable suspicion. They may be exercised 'for the purpose of determining whether' the person may have terrorist involvement, in other words, simply in order to find out. These powers are also given a wide scope by the broad definition of terrorism used in s 1 (discussed more fully in chapter 14). The exercise of these powers is subject to the usual administrative law restraints and theoretically to the Equality Act 2010, as discussed in chapter 8. However, this places the burden on the complainant to show that the powers were unlawfully exercised, rather than on the immigration officer to show that there was a reasonable basis for their actions.

In similar vein, an immigration officer may search a ship, aircraft, or anything on or which he reasonably believes to have been or be about to be on a ship or aircraft (e.g., a container) 'for the purpose of satisfying himself whether there are any persons he may wish to question under paragraph 2' (para 7).

The maximum period of detention for these powers to be exercised is nine hours (Sch 7 para 6), although the person may be detained for longer by the police if there are grounds for suspicion.

7.6.3 The decision on leave to enter

If satisfied that the passenger meets the requirements of the specific rules applying to the kind of leave they want (e.g., spouse, visitor, etc), and does not fall foul of the general grounds for refusal (see 7.6.4) the immigration officer (or in practice often the entry clearance officer) may grant them leave to enter. This decision is subject to all the constraints of public law and to appeal, where available, on grounds listed in Nationality, Immigration and Asylum Act 2002 s 84. Since the amendment of s 89 by the 2006 Act, there has been no appeal on arrival for a passenger who does not have entry clearance except on grounds of race discrimination, human rights or asylum. An immigration officer must act in accordance with the immigration rules and instructions given by the Secretary of State (Immigration Act 1971 Sch 2 para 1(3)). There is fuller discussion of these legal constraints in the next chapter on appeals.

7.6.4 Refusal of leave to enter

The immigration rules contain general grounds for refusal, which apply to leave to enter or entry clearance. The grounds for refusal in para 320 are divided into those upon which leave to enter or entry clearance 'is to be refused' and those upon which leave to enter 'should normally be refused'. With effect from 31 August 2011 new guidance has been issued on the application of these rules. The new guidance is available on the UKBA website, but by comparison with the former guidance the published parts are skeletal. Much of the substance is marked as non-disclosable, and the text that remains is mainly procedural and repeats the rules. A collection of general guidance dating from 2004 survives in the IDI. Before considering some of the grounds individually we shall consider their standing in administrative law.

The wording of the rules indicates that when a reason in the first group applies, refusal of leave is mandatory and when a reason in the second set applies, refusal is discretionary. However, although 'is to be refused' clearly implies an intention for refusals to be mandatory, the administrative law principle against fettering discretion does not permit prescription of a set of circumstances in which there must always be a refusal. The power to grant or refuse leave is given by statute (s 4(1) Immigration Act 1971), and the immigration rules may not lawfully restrict the statutory power, though they guide it. The principle against fettering discretion, or, it may be said, against having a rigid policy, entails that an authority acts lawfully in having a policy as long as it is prepared to listen to someone who has something new to say which might justify dealing with them in a different way (*R v Port of London Authority ex p Kynoch Ltd* [1919] 1 KB 176 and *British Oxygen Co Ltd v Minister of Technology* [1971] AC 610). This principle was applied to the immigration rules by the Court of Appeal in *Pearson v Immigration Appeal Tribunal*. Paragraph 5 of the immigration rules then in force, HC 80, provided that if the Department of Employment did not approve an extension of leave for work, then the application 'should be refused'. The Court of Appeal said, at 225, that in making such a rule:

> The Home Secretary did, in our opinion, make a rule as to how he would in future, as a matter of general policy, exercise his discretion, but not how he would exercise it in every case without

considering the circumstances of a particular case and whether to make an exception to that policy.

Following *Pearson,* the existence of so-called mandatory reasons for refusal is not an unlawful fetter on discretion according to administrative law, because there exists a power to act outside the rules. This discretion is acknowledged in the remnant of the old Immigration Directorate Instructions (IDI) Chapter 9 section 1, but there is no guidance remaining on how to exercise it.

In *R(on the application of P and Q) v SSHD* [2001] EWCA Civ 1151, the Court of Appeal held that the prison service was entitled to have a policy that when mothers were in prison, children should be separated from them at 18 months old. Article 8 ECHR would not prevent such a policy from existing, but it would require that the application of the rule to the individual case should be examined. Article 8 therefore goes further than the existing administrative law rule in that it requires a decision-maker to show that infringement of the right to respect for family life caused by adherence to the policy was proportionate to the aim sought to be achieved. The result of this for the application of mandatory grounds for refusal is that they may be regarded as a legitimate statement of policy and therefore of what will normally happen, but that the immigration officer or entry clearance officer must be prepared to act outside the policy if individual circumstances warrant doing so. When a qualified Convention right is infringed by the refusal, then the infringement must be proportionate to the public interest which the officer seeks to protect.

In the case of refusal of leave to enter or entry clearance, the courts will not readily find that a Convention right other than Article 8 is at stake. See the discussion of *R (on the application of Farrakhan) v SSHD* [2002] Imm AR 447 CA in chapter 4.

7.6.4.1 *Immigration officer is satisfied*

A number of the reasons for refusal in para 320 entail the immigration officer being satisfied that something is the case. This formula requires that the officer approaches the enquiry in a reasonable manner. *Secretary of State for Education v Tameside MBC* [1977] AC 1014 established that even though the statute said that the minister could exercise his powers if he was 'satisfied that' the local authority was acting unreasonably, this was not just a matter of his subjective judgement but of assembling all the relevant information and making a rational decision based on that evidence. He was required to act reasonably, and this requirement is implicit in any immigration rule using a similar phrase. *JC (China) v ECO Guangzhou* [2007] UKAIT 00027 confirmed that the burden of proof is on the Secretary of State on the balance of probabilities to prove any fact upon which a refusal under para 320 relies.

7.6.4.2 *Reasons for refusal*

The first reason given in para 320 is that 'entry is sought for a purpose not covered by the rules'. The obligation is on the applicant to show that the reason for entry is within the categories provided for by the rules (*Abid Hussain v ECO Islamabad* [1989] Imm AR 46). However, the applicant is not a lawyer (usually) and the obligation on them is modified 'where there is an obvious link or connection' with another rule. For instance, in *SZ (Applicable immigration rules) Bangladesh* [2007] UKAIT 00037, a child who could not gain entry as an adopted child could possibly have done so under another rule applying to children, and the decision-maker could have considered that without the applicant having to advance it.

Paragraph 320(1) gives the clearest example of when, although the rule might appear to mandate refusal, discretion could be exercised outside the rules. The application might be within the general scope of a category, for instance dependent relatives in exceptional compassionate circumstances (HC 395 para 317), but the particular applicant, for instance, a nephew, does not actually qualify because the family relationship to the sponsor is not one of those for which the rule provides. Refusal is possible under para 320(1), but so also is a grant of entry exceptionally outside the rules if the circumstances are sufficiently compelling to make this an appropriate exercise of discretion.

7.6.4.3 *Evidential, documentary or status requirements*

A number of the general reasons for refusal relating to evidential or documentary requirements or other matters concerning the status of the applicant are in the following sub-paragraphs of rule 320:

(3) failure to produce a valid national passport or other document satisfactorily establishing identity and nationality;

(4) failure to satisfy the Immigration Officer, in the case of a person who intends to enter another part of the common travel area, that he is acceptable to the immigration authorities there;

(5) failure, in the case of a visa national, to produce a valid and current entry clearance issued for the purpose for which entry is sought;

(6) failure to furnish the Immigration Officer with information required for deciding whether leave to enter is required and on what terms leave should be given;

(8A) where the person seeking leave is outside the UK, failure to supply any information, documents, copy documents or medical report requested by an Immigration Officer;

(13) failure, except by a person eligible for admission for settlement as a spouse or civil partner under paragraph 282, to satisfy the Immigration Officer that he will be admitted to another country after a stay in the United Kingdom;

(20) failure to provide physical data as required by regulations made under section 126 of the Nationality, Immigration and Asylum Act 2002.

These grounds are largely self-explanatory. The last one has been mentioned in relation to the role of biometrics in entry clearance. It is clear from the report of the Independent Monitor (April 2009) that sub-rule 8A should apply only to specific requests made to an individual. It was wrong to apply it, as the ECO did, 'in the light of the information disseminated by the Embassy through a variety of media – all of which you could reasonably be expected to have access to' (para 134).

7.6.4.4 *Grounds relating to public good*

Paragraph 320(6) provides that leave must be refused where the Secretary of State has personally directed that the exclusion of a person from the United Kingdom is conducive to the public good. The discretionary ground in para 320(19) is similarly worded, except that it is not based on a personal direction of the Secretary of State but on the discretion of the immigration officer. Paragraph 320(18) allows for refusal on the basis of conviction of an offence imprisonable for 12 months or more.

Personal directions such as that permitted by para 320(6) are used when there is a perceived risk to national security when the individual has some degree of notoriety or political prominence, or there is intelligence information suggesting risk. For instance, in *Murungaru v SSHD, ECO Nairobi, British High Commissioner Nairobi* [2008] EWCA Civ 1015, the Secretary of State received information that the Kenyan MP and minister was engaging in activities concerned with corruption in Kenya during his medical visits to the UK. It was partly to show support for the Kenyan government that the Secretary of State acted quickly under para 320(6) to prevent his next visit.

In *Farrakhan*, the Secretary of State had information that, because Mr Farrakhan had expressed anti-Semitic views, and because two members of the Nation of Islam had been arrested for public order offences outside the Stephen Lawrence Inquiry, his presence in the UK might give rise to disorder. As a personal decision of the Secretary of State, a decision under para 320(6) may only be appealed through the restricted procedure of the Special Immigration Appeals Commission (Nationality, Immigration and Asylum Act 2002 s 98). The Court of Appeal in *Farrakhan* considered that this indicated that Parliament had taken the view that in this area of decision-making, the courts should accord the Secretary of State's opinion a significant degree of deference.

The direction made by the Secretary of State that the person's exclusion is for the public good is not itself made under the immigration rules, and the source of the power is not discussed in the case law. It was used in relation to Dr Zakir Naik, a Muslim teacher who planned to visit the UK in July 2010 (his 15th visit) on a public lecture tour. Dr Naik's teachings were highly controversial. The Secretary of State regarded some of his public statements as unacceptable, and contrary to the Home Office's published policy on so-called 'unacceptable behaviours' (see chapters 2 and 16). She regarded his comments as supporting the 9/11 attacks and as anti-Jewish and decided to exclude him from the UK. Dr Naik's challenge failed (*Naik v SSHD and ECO Mumbai* [2011] EWCA Civ 1546).

In *EV v SSHD* [2009] UKSIAC 67/2008, the Special Immigration Appeals Commission held that in challenges to a personal direction of the Secretary of State they should use an approach similar to that which they adopted in appeals against deportation. Namely, SIAC should, to the extent possible, make findings of fact. As to past events, findings would be on balance of probabilities. Then, giving 'due deference' to the view of the Secretary of State, SIAC would review her decision in the light of the facts as found (para 6).

Exclusion under sub-para 19 is on the basis that where, from information available to the Immigration Officer, 'it seems right' to refuse leave to enter on the ground that exclusion is conducive to the public good; 'for example, in the light of the character, conduct or associations of the person'. The old IDI elaborated, saying 'the immigration officer must specify what past or future action of the person makes his exclusion conducive to the public good. Vague generalisations...will not suffice' (IDI 9.2.21 June 2004). However, the present version is linked to criminal conduct and no guidance on the exercise of the discretion is published. The case of *Ramanathan v Secretary of State for the Foreign and Commonwealth Office* [1999] Imm AR 97 gives an example of the kind of activities which formerly did and probably still would found refusal under this paragraph. Here, the appellant was suspected of facilitating unlawful immigration. The appellant remained outside the UK and no criminal charges were brought, but suspicions expressed in communications between British High Commissions in Sri Lanka (his country of origin) and Singapore (his country of residence) were sufficient to support a refusal on this ground.

The information founding the decision might be prior information, perhaps revealed through a fingerprint match, which would then found a refusal of entry clearance. Alternatively, it might be information gathered at the port of entry, for instance if the passenger is found to be in possession of illegal drugs or quantities of pornography sufficient to suggest that they are intending to sell it rather than use it personally. Paragraph 320(18) provides for the refusal of leave to enter or entry clearance on the basis of a criminal conviction 'save where the immigration officer is satisfied that admission would be justified for strong compassionate reasons'. In both cases discretion must be exercised fairly (*R v SSHD ex p Moon* [1996] COD 54, *Secretary of State for Education v Tameside MBC*), and in a case where the right to respect for private or family life is interfered with by a refusal of leave, discretion must be exercised proportionately in accordance with Article 8. As 'strong compassionate reasons' often relate to private or family life, the arguments in pre-October 2000 case law about what would amount to 'strong compassionate reasons' are now largely superseded by human rights arguments and the requirement for proportionality.

The admission of the boxer Mike Tyson to the UK gave the occasion for the Divisional Court to consider the nature of the discretion given to the immigration officer in this sub-paragraph (*R v SSHD ex p Bindel* [2001] Imm AR 1). As Mike Tyson had been convicted of rape and had been sentenced to six years' imprisonment, he would have been liable for exclusion under this sub-paragraph. Exercising his power to issue instructions to immigration officers, the Secretary of State directed that Mike Tyson should be admitted. A group called Justice for Women argued in judicial review proceedings that the Secretary of State was not entitled to give such an instruction, however, as we have seen (chapter 1), the Secretary of State is not bound by the rules and may direct immigration officers to act more generously towards an applicant. Sullivan J went further than this. He held that the discretion to admit Tyson was exercisable within the rule, and the instruction by the Secretary of State was thus not inconsistent with the rule. There were reasons of public interest for admitting Tyson, such as the economic benefit that the boxing match would bring, the fact that tickets for the fight had already been sold, and business interests were depending on it. As Justice for Women argued, these are clearly not 'strong compassionate reasons', they are economic reasons. However, Sullivan J held that the reference to 'strong compassionate reasons' in the sub-paragraph was not an exhaustive description of the basis for exercising discretion. Macdonald refers to it as 'distressingly vague' (5th edn 2001:84).

The Rehabilitation of Offenders Act 1974 applies to entry to the UK, so that a person should not be refused entry on the basis of a conviction which is 'spent' under the Act. Returning residents are not exempted from this sub-paragraph, so a settled person could be refused re-entry on the basis of a conviction (see *Ogilvy* at 7.8.1), though Article 8 rights are almost certain to be engaged in such a case. Arguments about the rights of long-term residents to remain despite criminal convictions are considered more fully in the section on enforcement.

7.6.4.5 *Travel bans*

Increasingly, there are international interests involved in restricting certain people from travelling between countries. These centre around the prevention of crime, particularly terrorist and drugs offences, and restriction of the movements of war criminals and national leaders upon whom groups of nations wish to bring pressure to bear. This was effected in UK law by s 8 of the Immigration and Asylum Act 1999, inserting a s 8B into the Immigration Act 1971. The section provides for a new category of 'excluded persons'. These are people named or referred to in a resolution of the United Nations Security Council or Council of the European Union which is designated for this purpose by an Order made by the Secretary of State. Since s 8B came into force, the Secretary of State has made a number of Immigration (Designation of Travel Bans) Orders designating European resolutions concerning for instance former President Milosevic of Yugoslavia, and President Mugabe of Zimbabwe, and members of the Syrian regime. The effect of these designations is, according to s 8B, that the excluded person 'must be refused' leave to enter or leave to remain in the UK. These resolutions and orders are targeted upon particular figures and will not often be encountered. Their significance lies not in the scope of their application, but in that they demonstrate the increase in concerted international action on issues which are seen as relating to violations of human rights on a large scale, or to the spread of criminal activity. However, EU orders banning travel to the EU do not apply in the Vatican. This became publicly apparent when Robert Mugabe travelled to the Vatican for Pope John Paul II's funeral in 2005 and beatification in 2011.

7.6.4.6 *Medical reasons*

The immigration rules require that a person who intends to remain in the UK for more than six months is referred to the medical inspector for a medical examination (HC 395 para 36). This applies to anyone who is coming to the UK to settle with family members. Referral to the medical inspector may also be made if the person seeking entry 'mentions health or medical treatment as a reason for his visit or appears not to be in good health' (para 36). An immigration officer may also refer a person for further medical examination after entry 'in the interests of public health' (Immigration Act 1971 Sch 2 para 7). A scheme implemented in 2007 requires applicants for more than six months' stay from designated high risk countries to have a medical test for tuberculosis *before* making their entry clearance application. Testing centres for those countries are established in Bangladesh, Cambodia, Ghana, Kenya, Pakistan, Sudan, and Thailand. Medical procedures related to applications for entry clearance are now clearly described in the entry clearance guidance on the UKBA website..

Refusal to undergo a medical examination is a discretionary reason for refusal of leave to enter or entry clearance (para 320(17)) and so is failure to supply a medical report when an application is proceeding outside the UK (para 320(8A) and Immigration (Leave to Enter and Remain) Order 2000, SI 2000/1161, Article 7(4)). The effect of this is that, when an immigration officer or ECO (HC 395 para 39) refers a person for a medical examination, that person is compelled to attend the medical examination if they want leave to enter.

Earlier ambiguities in the rules about the relative standing of the medical inspector's report and the immigration officer's decision, and about the basis of a medical certificate, have been cleared up in the new IDI on 'cross-cutting factors in entry decisions', which says:

> Medical inspectors will only issue certificates when satisfied the person's condition is a significant risk to public health. If they do issue a medical certificate or following a medical examination they recommend the person must not enter because of medical reasons you must refuse entry or leave to remain in the UK. (p. 27)

This IDI suggests that the substantive decision is in effect delegated to the medical inspector, whose opinion is conclusive. However, it must be read with the IDI on entry decisions, which retains the immigration officer's discretion, in accordance with the rule:

> When a port medical officer has issued a certificate which recommends that it is undesirable for medical reasons to admit a passenger, you should refuse leave to enter under paragraph 320(7). However, you may use your discretion not to do so if you think there are strong compassionate reasons. In such cases, you must judge the case on its merits and refer your decision to a chief UK Border Agency officer. The hardship of being refused should not in itself warrant your use of discretion.

A serious illness such as AIDS or HIV is not enough reason alone to refuse leave to enter for public health reasons. In such cases:

- The port medical inspector will provide an estimate of the cost of treatment required.
- You must consider the information against the Immigration Rules.

The medical inspector is a doctor employed by the Home Office to make reports on potential immigrants and asylum seekers (Immigration Act 1971 s 4(2) and Sch 2 para 1(2)) and medical officers attached to British posts abroad carry out examinations there. The IDI stresses that medical inspectors should not be asked to examine passengers to discover whether they have borne children or had sexual relations nor to X-ray them to determine their age. The prohibition is worded strictly, and this is because precisely these practices were carried out in the 1970s. The former refers to the virginity tests carried out on the claimed basis that a good Muslim or Hindu woman would not engage in sexual relations before marriage, nor would a respectable man of those faiths marry someone who had. Therefore genuine fiancées could be detected by their virginity. The ensuing scandal prompted the Commission for Racial Equality's investigation into immigration control, but the scale of the practice was only revealed in May 2011 after confidential Home Office files were disclosed (*The Guardian* 8 May 2011 'Virginity tests for immigrants reflected "dark age prejudices" of 1970s Britain').

The immigration officer may override the medical inspector's opinion if there are 'strong compassionate circumstances'. The inspector's opinion may not be challenged on its own merits (*Al-Tuwaidji v Chief Immigration Officer Heathrow* [1974] Imm AR 34 followed in *Mohazeb v Immigration Officer Harwich* [1990] Imm AR 555, and note the exclusive grounds for appeal in Nationality, Immigration and Asylum Act 2002 s 84), but the immigration officer's exercise of discretion may be appealed (s 84(1)(f)). This ground for refusal does not apply to people with settled status who, having travelled abroad, may not be refused re-entry on medical grounds.

7.6.4.7 *Immigration breaches*

Previous breaches of immigration law used to be a discretionary reason for refusing entry clearance or leave to enter, but became mandatory on 1 April 2008 (HC 321). Paragraph 320 7(A) added grounds that false representations or information has been submitted or there has been a material non-disclosure in relation to the application, and these are also a reason for refusal of leave to remain for people who have leave in the UK but are applying to extend it (para 322(1A)). The meaning of these terms is considered at 7.6.5.1 in relation to the case of *AA*.

Introduced at the same time, para 320 7(B) was a radical new departure. It effects a re-entry ban. It sets a mandatory ground for refusal of entry clearance or leave to enter where the applicant has breached immigration laws by: *(a)* overstaying; *(b)* breaching a condition attached to their leave; *(c)* being an illegal entrant; and *(d)* using deception in an application for entry clearance, leave to enter or remain (whether successful or not). In these cases, entry clearance or leave to enter may only be granted if certain periods of time have elapsed, as follows:

- 28 days for an overstayer who left voluntarily without expense to the Secretary of State;
- 12 months for anyone else who left the UK voluntarily not at the expense of the Secretary of State;
- 5 years for anyone who left the UK voluntarily at the expense of the Secretary of State;
- 10 years for anyone who used deception in an application for entry clearance or was removed or deported.

Previously, it was only a deportation order which resulted in a period of exclusion from the UK. Through this new rule, the impact of immigration enforcement has been greatly intensified The effect of enforcement is a matter which now enters into judicial decisions (see *Chikwamba* para 45). The Court of Appeal in *AS (Pakistan) v SSHD* [2008] EWCA Civ 1118 held that the duration of exclusion was a relevant factor to be taken into account when assessing the proportionality of the deportation. The Tribunal in *NA & others (Cambridge College of Learning)* [2009] UKAIT 00031 took account of the effect of a finding against the appellants that they had used false representations to obtain leave to remain in confirming that the standard of proof for such a finding was a high one. In *MA (Nigeria) v SSHD* [2009] EWCA Civ 1229, the Court of Appeal held that a failure to take account of the effect of the re-entry ban amounted to an error of law, and in *AA v SSHD* [2010] EWCA Civ 773 (see 7.6.5.1) the Court of Appeal was influenced by the re-entry ban in reaching its conclusion. In the same spirit, the Upper Tribunal in *Ozhogina and Tarasova v SSHD* [2011] UKUT 00197 (IAC) held that where the Secretary of State refused an application for entry clearance on the basis that the appellant had breached the UK's immigration laws by using deception in an application for entry clearance (para 320(7B) (d)), the Secretary of State must show that a false statement was deliberately made for the purpose of securing an immigration advantage. Paragraph 320(7B) does not apply to the applications of adult partners and family members (para 320(7C)).

A further ground for discretionary refusal, added on 30 June 2008, is that the applicant 'has previously contrived in a significant way to frustrate the intentions of these Rules' (para 320(11)). The application of this paragraph is fraught with difficulty, but cases in the Upper Tribunal have begun to clarify how it should be applied. In *SD v ECO Chennai* [2010] UKUT 276 (IAC) the Tribunal held that:

- The substance of paragraph 320(11) refers to an applicant's previous history.
- If an application for entry clearance is refused on the ground of forged documents in a previous application, the Entry Clearance Officer has the burden of proof that the documents were forged.
- If there was no judicial determination of that issue, and the appellant did not admit it, there would need to be evidence to establish a forgery.

In *PS v ECO New Delhi* [2010] UKUT 440 (IAC) the Tribunal observed that the combination of para 320(7B), (7C), and (11) produce a 'somewhat complicated and uncertain system'. In this case the appellant's asylum application had failed. He had married lawfully in the UK, and could comply with the immigration rules. He left the UK voluntarily and went to India, where he applied for entry clearance. The Tribunal overturned the refusal of the ECO and the First Tier Tribunal, observing that the automatic prohibition of entry clearance was disapplied because of his family reasons for entry (para 320(7C)). Paragraph 320(7B) did not apply because he had left the UK voluntarily more than 12 months before he applied for entry clearance. The Tribunal thought that a proper purpose of the rules was that the provisions of paragraph 320(7B) and (7C) encouraged a person in the position of Mr S voluntarily to leave the United Kingdom, to remain outside the UK for a significant period, and then to seek to regularize his immigration status by applying properly for leave to enter to join his wife. Refusing his entry by application of para 11 would defeat that proper purpose of the rules.

7.6.4.8 *General and specific grounds*

The points-based rules (see chapter 10) have made a new linkage between general and specific requirements as the rules for applications in the PBS include the requirement that: 'the applicant must not fall for refusal under the general grounds for refusal' (see, e.g., rule 245C for Tier 1 and rule 245ZD for Tier 2).

In *NA & others (Cambridge College of Learning)* [2009] UKAIT 00031, the Tribunal endorsed the general grounds for refusal of leave (to remain rather than to enter, thus under para 322(1A) of the immigration rules) as the applicants for Post-Study Work made false representations by relying on diplomas for courses that had never run. The Tribunal went on to say that even if the high standard of proof which was required to show false representations had not been met, reasonable doubts about what was proved by documents were relevant to assessing whether the appellant met the substantive requirements of the rules.

7.6.5 Cancellation or refusal of leave to enter

Where entry clearance has effect as leave to enter, that leave to enter may be cancelled on arrival. In the less common situation where entry clearance does not have effect as leave to enter, leave may be refused on arrival (HC 395 paras 321 and 321A). On the same grounds, entry clearance may be revoked before travel (para 30A). This is rare, but was done in the case of Mr Naik – see 7.6.4.4. The effect of cancellation is that at the port, the passenger, though without leave to enter, may be admitted temporarily to pursue an appeal; people who have entry clearance issued for the same purpose as that for which they now seek to enter (s 89(1) Nationality Immigration and Asylum Act 2002 as amended) are among the dwindling few who still have a right of appeal that can be exercised in the UK. Cancellation does not have retrospective effect (*NM (Zimbabwe)* [2007] UKAIT 00002) so that, when the appellant in that case applied for a variation of leave before the cancellation decision, he had current leave which meant his leave was extended until his appeal was heard.

In addition to medical grounds and the public good (Immigration Act 1971 Sch 2A (2)(c) and (3) and HC 395 para 321A), leave to enter may be cancelled or refused on the following grounds: *(a)* the leave or entry clearance was obtained by false representations; *(b)* the leave or entry clearance was obtained as a result of material facts not being disclosed; or *(c)* there has been a material change of circumstances since the leave or entry clearance was obtained (see *Khaliq* at 7.3.4). Where the person is outside the UK, failure to provide requested documents may also generate a cancellation of leave to enter (para 321A(6)). In *Murungaru v SSHD* [2008] EWCA Civ 1015, the claimant had a multiple entry visa for the UK which was revoked without notice about three months after it had been granted. He wanted to travel to the UK to continue his private medical treatment and challenged the revocation of the visa by judicial review. One of his arguments was that the revocation interfered with his rights under Article 1 of Protocol 1 of the ECHR, the right to peaceful enjoyment of his possessions, that is, to his contract with his doctors. The Court of Appeal held that Dr Murungaru's contractual rights had none of the qualities of possessions. They were intangible, not assignable, not transmissible, not realizable and had no present economic value. They could not be described as an asset. They did not count as a possession for the purposes of A1P1.

7.6.5.1 *False representations and non-disclosure of material facts*

The Court of Appeal in *A v SSHD* [2010] EWCA Civ 773 considered the meaning of 'false representations' in the context of an application for leave to remain. Previous authority (*Akhtar* [1991] Imm AR 326 CA) was that in order to be considered false, representations did not have to be fraudulent, simply inaccurate.

Key Case

***AA v SSHD* [2010] EWCA Civ 773**

Mr A was a student who had, at the date of his application for further leave to remain, been in the UK for nine years. He had studied and worked continuously through that time, had not breached the immigration rules, had obtained a first class undergraduate degree, and a masters degree, and now applied for leave to remain as a Tier 1 (post-study work) migrant.

In his application he failed to disclose that he had three convictions for driving without a licence or insurance. The application form clearly asked for disclosure of criminal offences including driving offences, but Mr A did not think that these convictions were criminal, and so did not disclose them. He was refused leave on the basis that 'material facts were not disclosed' and that he had used deception. In view of the finding that he had used deception, the re-entry ban in para 320(7B) applied, the period dating from his date of leaving the UK.

Mr A's appeal to the Tribunal was refused on the basis that his statement was false, that this was a mandatory ground for refusal, and thus there was no discretion and his intention was irrelevant.

The Court of Appeal noted that deception is defined in para 6 of the immigration rules as:

> making false representations or submitting false documents (whether or not material to the application), or failing to disclose material facts.

The Court of Appeal drew on the immigration rules, guidance in the IDIs, Lord Bassam's assurance in the House of Lords that mistakes of fact would not be treated as deception, and a letter from Mr Liam Byrne MP, Minister of State at the Home Office. On the basis of these, the Court came to the conclusion that 'false' was not to be used in its meaning of 'untrue' or 'incorrect', but in its meaning of 'lying' or 'deceitful'. Consequently, 'dishonesty or deception is needed, albeit not necessarily that of the applicant himself, to render a "false representation" a ground for mandatory refusal' (para 76).

The Court noted that in *Akhtar* the representation was a dishonest one (by the husband that he had no other wife) although transmitted through someone who was not aware of that (his second wife, the applicant). Also, at the time of *Akhtar*, the finding that there had been a false statement did not result in liability to a re-entry ban of several years. For these reasons, *Akhtar* was not authority for the proposition that in the present context falsity did not require deception.

In *AA* the Court did not deal with the interpretation of the ground of material non-disclosure. However, a failure to disclose traffic-related offences has been the reason for several of the reported appeals in the Upper Tribunal based on this rule. *F. Ahmed v SSHD* [2011] UKUT 00351 (IAC) was a case before the Upper Tribunal in which the appellant, the holder of an Oyster card, had assumed that it was valid for travel to Gravesend. It was not, and he was fined £80, to which were added compensation of £4.50, a victim surcharge of £15, and costs of £35. Like Mr A, he did not think this was a criminal conviction, and so did not disclose it in his application for further leave to remain as a student. The Upper Tribunal held that in the light of *AA*, the material on the basis of which Rix LJ concluded that dishonesty was required for 'false representations' applied equally to the interpretation of non-disclosure within the context of paragraph 322(1A). UT Judge Mckee said: 'In many, if not most, cases false representations and material non-disclosure will be opposite sides of the same coin'.

In the case of cancellation of leave to enter, the rule requires that the applicant themselves must have made the false statement (para 321A(2)). Leave may not be cancelled on the basis of a statement by a third party. Older case law on refusal of leave to enter or revocation of entry clearance may now need to be revisited in the light of *AA*. One reason that the Court of Appeal did not discuss the issue of material non-disclosure was that there has been, as the Court said, some 'uneasy jurisprudence' on the question of materiality. The implication is that older cases (see, e.g., *Sukhjinder Kaur* [1998] Imm AR 1 CA), may need to be revisited. So far as the power to cancel is concerned, this is contained in Immigration Act 1971 Sch 2 para 2A (2) and (8) as well as in the immigration rules. Thus, while the conditions for *refusal* of leave to enter are still governed only by the immigration rules, those for *cancelling* existing leave which was granted outside the UK are governed by statute. Para 2A (2) refers to leave obtained 'as a result of' false information or failure to disclose material facts. The implication of this is that false representations or non-disclosure must be at least material and possibly decisive in order to warrant cancellation of leave. An applicant cannot oppose the cancellation or refusal of leave to enter on the basis that if the true facts had been known they would have gained entry anyway (*Bugdaycay* [1987] AC 514 HL).

The proof of a false representation must be made to a high standard, though not the criminal standard. This was confirmed by the Tribunal in *NA & others (Cambridge College of Learning)* [2009] UKAIT 00031, making the distinction between refusal of leave to remain and a criminal charge in that the former did not carry penal consequences. Refusal under the immigration rules did not inherently deprive an applicant of any right or privilege in the same way as a criminal conviction did. Nevertheless, the Tribunal agreed that the consequences of refusal under Part 9 (general reasons) could be serious, particularly as the appellants might be faced with a re-entry ban of 5 to 10 years under para 320(7B).

7.6.5.2 *Change of circumstances*

A change of circumstances, in order to warrant refusal of leave to enter or revocation of entry clearance, must be so fundamental that it undermines the basis upon which the original application was made. In the case of a visitor who changes their itinerary or their sponsor, the change would not normally be regarded as fundamental. It is in each case a question of fact and degree (*Immigration Officer Heathrow v Salmak* [1991] Imm AR 191). Changes in visitors' plans are discussed further in chapter 11.

Again, cancellation of leave granted by entry clearance is governed by statute (Immigration Act 1971 Sch 2 para 2A) which permits cancellation where 'the person's purpose in arriving in the UK is different from the purpose specified in the entry clearance'. A former but similarly worded rule had harsh consequences in *Angur Begum* [1989] Imm AR 302, in which the Divisional Court held that there was a change of circumstances removing the basis for admission when the sponsoring father and husband of the applicants had died since the application was made.

7.7 Leave to enter granted in the UK

As mentioned at 7.6, entry to the UK is a legal event which may or may not coincide with physical arrival. So a person may be living in the UK for a period of months or even years on temporary admission, but still not be treated as having entered.

Referring back to s 4(1), it is apparent that in 1971 the statute contemplated a clear division of function between immigration officers and other Home Office civil servants. Immigration officers were to have the power to give or refuse leave to enter, and the Secretary of State, in practice the Immigration department, had power to give leave to remain or to vary leave. Decisions on leave to remain or varying leave are the 'in country' decisions, taken once a person is in the UK. These may be contrasted with the border control decisions allocated by s 4 to the immigration service. Decisions on asylum claims are made by the Home Office. The effect of this used to be that at the end of a claim for asylum, the papers related to the claim went back to the immigration service to grant or refuse leave to enter. This added to the administrative complexity of dealing with asylum cases and was nonsensical in the case of someone who had been living in the UK on temporary admission for perhaps years.

Accordingly, the Immigration (Leave to Enter) Order 2001, SI 2001/2590, made under Immigration Act 1971 s 3A, provides that the Secretary of State may give or refuse leave to enter to an asylum or human rights applicant, and may exercise all the powers of an immigration officer (examination, requiring medical examinations, etc.) for that purpose. The trend towards eroding the distinction between immigration officers and Secretary of State powers is a concomitant of the creation of an integrated border agency.

7.8 The leave obtained

In this section, there is discussion of the possible kinds of leave that a person may acquire, and of the effects of such leave.

7.8.1 Non-lapsing or continuing leave

A further change made by the Immigration (Leave to Enter and Remain) Order 2000, SI 2000/1161 was the introduction of so-called 'non-lapsing' or 'continuing' leave. Before 30 July 2000, the position was governed entirely by Immigration Act 1971 s 3(4), which provides: 'A person's leave to enter or remain in the United Kingdom shall lapse on his going to a country or territory outside the Common Travel Area...' There were a few exceptions to this rule, but in general what it meant was that people on limited leave, such as students, could go away from the UK for a weekend break, and be refused entry on their return.

From 30 July 2000, s 3(4) remains in force, but its effects are considerably modified. Article 13(2) of the 2000 Order provides that leave will not lapse on the holder's leaving the Common Travel Area if 'it was conferred by means of an entry clearance...or for a period exceeding six months'. The effect of this is that most people with limited leave are able to come and go during the currency of that leave without fear of being refused entry on return. Article 13(5) of the Immigration (Leave to Enter and Remain) Order 2000 applies the cancellation powers in Immigration Act 1971 Sch 2 para 2A to non-lapsing leave. The immigration officer is therefore entitled to examine people returning to discover whether any such reason applies (Immigration Act 1971 Sch 2 para 2A). In *R (on the application of Ogilvy) v SSHD* [2007] EWHC 2301 (Admin), the High Court held that this applied to someone who had indefinite leave to remain. There was suspicion that the claimant was involved in criminal offences, and the Court held that the Home

Office acted lawfully in using this immigration power to hold his passport, suspend his leave, and grant temporary admission while further criminal inquiries were conducted. The power was not limited to investigation of his current immigration status. Criminal offences might after all be a reason to cancel leave. This meant that a long-term resident of the UK could be deprived of leave to remain, and, thus, unlike a British citizen, be unable to work or claim benefits pending trial. This is the case whether or not they are ultimately convicted and even if they would not be liable to deportation. Where leave is varied so that a person has no leave, or it is revoked, s 3D of the Immigration Act 1971 provides that leave is continued pending appeal, but this does not expressly cover the suspension of leave applied in *Ogilvy*. This is a temporary measure pending investigation (Sch 2 para 2A(7)) and seems to deprive the applicant of all status.

The non-lapsing provisions do not apply to leave to enter as a visitor, but Article 4 of the 2000 Order has a similar effect, providing that a visit visa 'during its period of validity, shall have effect as leave to enter the United Kingdom on an unlimited number of occasions'. Visit visas, though usually valid for six months, may be granted for periods of up to five years, on the basis that any stay as a visitor is limited to six months, but permitting multiple entries during the five-year period. These visas are particularly used by business people. The leave to enter lapses on the visitor leaving the Common Travel Area (2000 Order Article 13(2)) but on their return within the period of validity of the visa it operates as leave to enter again (Article 13(2)). The Immigration (Leave to Enter and Remain) (Amendment) Order 2005, SI 2005/1159, makes an exception to this provision for visitors under an Approved Destination Status Agreement with China. These visas are normally for one entry unless endorsed for two.

The visitor who does not benefit from the 2000 Order is the non-visa national visitor who obtains leave to enter at the port which lapses on their departure (Article 13(2)), but who does not possess a visa which can operate as leave to enter on their return. Therefore, they must re-apply for leave to enter on arrival at the port on each occasion.

7.8.2 24-hour rule

The 24-hour rule has effectively been nullified by the Immigration (Leave to Enter and Remain) Order 2000, SI 2000/1161 Article 12, but it remains on the statute book and is briefly discussed here so that Article 12 may be understood. It applied to lawful entrants applying at the port for leave to enter for a limited period. This is now restricted to non-visa nationals wishing to enter as a visitor. Immigration Act 1971 Sch 2 para 6(1) provides that if the immigration officer fails to give notice of their decision to the passenger within 24 hours of the conclusion of the examination, the passenger is automatically granted six months deemed leave with a prohibition on working. This is equivalent to the leave that a visitor would be routinely granted. Article 12 provides that notice given *on any date* after the end of the examination is to be regarded as having been given within the period of 24 hours specified in paragraph 6(1) of Sch 2 (emphasis added). The 24-hour rule is thus deemed to be satisfied in any case in which a decision is made.

7.8.3 Limited leave to enter or remain

Leave to enter may be for an indefinite or a limited period of time. Limited leave may be subject to conditions:

- restricting or prohibiting employment,
- requiring the holder to maintain themselves and any dependants without recourse to public funds,
- requiring the holder to register with the police,
- reporting to an immigration officer or the Secretary of State, and
- about residence (Immigration Act 1971 s 3(1)(c)).

The last two conditions were added by UK Borders Act 2007 s 16 as part of the government's intention to keep track of people, particularly asylum seekers and unaccompanied children seeking asylum. There were objections (e.g., from Liberty, see Public Bill Committee 1 March 2007 col 121) about the width of the condition about residence. There is no limit on the face of the condition as to *what* can be specified about residence, so it could in theory be used like house arrest. A proposal to insert a test of necessity and explicit human rights protection in the clause was defeated. No other conditions are possible. If and when the time limit is lifted on the holder's stay in the UK, any conditions will also be lifted, as indefinite leave may not be subject to conditions (s 3(3)).

If the holder of limited leave does not intend to leave the country on the expiry of the leave, an application to extend or vary the terms of leave must be made before it expires, otherwise the person becomes an overstayer and is liable to removal (Immigration Act 1999 s 10). Such an application to vary or extend leave is an application for leave to remain. Leave to remain for a person already in the UK is granted by the Secretary of State under the power in Immigration Act 1971 s 4(1). The power includes giving further limited leave to remain, either by way of extending the existing leave or by varying it to a different immigration category, or giving indefinite leave to remain. Where limited leave is extended or varied, the Secretary of State may also vary or continue any conditions attaching to the earlier leave (Immigration Act 1971 s 3(3) and HC 395 para 31). The Immigration (Leave to Enter and Remain) Order 2000, SI 2000/1161 Article 13(6) extends the scope of the power to vary leave by providing that it may be exercised while the holder of leave is outside the UK (immigration rules para 33A).

Section 3C of the Immigration Act 1971 provides a statutory extension of leave where an application for variation is made within the currency of existing leave. It is quite likely that, for reasons outside the control of the applicant, such as Home Office delays, existing leave may expire before the application for variation is decided. This would result in an injustice if a person were then treated as an overstayer simply because their application had not been heard. Section 3C extends the existing leave, on the existing conditions if any, until the decision has been taken and any appeal finally determined.

7.8.4 No-switching rules

The 'no-switching' rules restrict the categories between which changes may be made. These restrictions are mainly apparent from the immigration rules. However, there are certain changes which, although not provided for or even prohibited by the rules, are permitted either exceptionally or as a matter of policy ascertainable through the IDIs. Permissible switching is now generally very limited. Until 2003, all categories could change to spouse, though not fiancé(e). Rule changes following the 2002 White Paper *Secure Borders, Safe Haven*, Cm 5387, now prevent visitors from staying in the UK for marriage (see HC 395 para 284(i)). Some provisions for students and visitors are covered in chapters 10 and 11. For full details of current permitted and prohibited switches, reference should be made to the immigration rules and updates to the JCWI Immigration, *Nationality and Refugee Law Handbook*. Where the change of category is permitted, there must be an application for a variation of leave.

7.8.5 Indefinite leave

When leave is indefinite there may be no further contact with the Home Office and there is no further stage to pass through in terms of immigration status. For most entrants, indefinite leave to remain may only be granted after a period of limited leave. The government is proposing to abolish indefinite leave to enter in most of the remaining cases where this is possible (*Family Migration: A Consultation* July 2011).

Many immigration categories cannot lead to indefinite leave, and the individual must leave at the end of their permitted time, unless they can make a successful application to vary their leave under the immigration rules, or removal would breach their human rights. For instance, leave to enter or remain as a student or Tier 5 worker cannot be converted directly to indefinite leave. By contrast, people who have leave to enter or remain as a spouse or a Tier 1 worker may apply for indefinite leave once they have fulfilled the qualifying number of years' residence without breach of conditions. With effect from 6 April 2011, applicants for indefinite leave to remain must show that they have no unspent convictions (as defined by the Rehabilitation of Offenders Act 1974). This requirement has been added to each rule which provides for indefinite leave to remain.

A person with indefinite leave to remain has full access to the National Health Service and may freely change employment as no conditions may be attached to indefinite leave (Immigration Act 1971 s 3(3)(a)). They may have recourse to public funds, unless their sponsor has signed an undertaking to support them for a fixed period after entry. During this period, no claim for welfare benefits may be made by them or on their behalf.

Since 2 April 2007, all applicants for indefinite leave to remain must pass a test on Life in the UK or complete a course for speakers of other languages which includes citizenship materials and obtain a specified qualification. Where people's English language is at ESOL level 3 or above, they take the Life in the UK test. Where it is not, they must attend the course. EEA nationals are exempt from this requirement, but must comply with it if they apply for British nationality. There are also exemptions for certain medical conditions and those under 18 or over 66. The tests must be taken by any non-exempt person who is applying for indefinite leave, on any basis. If the applicant has not passed the test by the time their existing leave expires, they can be granted an extension for this purpose.

Residence without immigration restriction is one of the qualifications to apply for naturalization as a British citizen (British Nationality Act 1981 Sch 1 paras 1 and 3). Once a person gains indefinite leave they may begin to count time towards qualifying to naturalize as British if they so wish.

UK practice was to grant indefinite leave to people on acquisition of refugee status, but since 31 August 2005, a grant of five years has been normal practice. The first reviews of these grants of leave fell due in August 2010, and are generally being treated, under what is called the Protection Route, as applications for indefinite leave.

There are other concessions entailing a grant of indefinite leave. One which attracted public attention during 2009 was that Commonwealth citizens who have served in the armed forces may obtain indefinite leave to remain in the UK if they were discharged from service in the UK. This had never applied to Gurkhas, Nepalese soldiers of the Gurkha Brigade, as, due to the agreement made between India, the UK, and Nepal at the time of the formation of the Brigade, Gurkhas were to return to Nepal at the end of their service. In 2004, the immigration rules were changed to incorporate the former 'Armed Forces Concession', giving a right to indefinite leave to those with four years of service. However, this did not include Gurkhas discharged before 1 July 1997 because before that date, when Hong Kong was returned to Chinese rule, the Gurkhas had a base in Hong Kong, and were thus not discharged in the UK as the rule required. There was still a discretion to grant ILR to Gurkhas who fell outside that rule.

In *R (on the application of D.P. Limbu, C.P. Limbu, Shrestha, Rai, Gurung and Mukhiya) v SSHD, ECO Kathmandu and ECO Hong Kong* [2008] EWHC 2261 (Admin), a number of ex-members of the Gurkha Brigade challenged the refusal to them of indefinite leave under the discretionary policy. Part of the reason for the discretionary policy was to honour the exceptional service record of Gurkhas. These claimants had given long and distinguished military service and served in the UK's military campaigns, including the Falklands. The judge concluded that it was irrational to refuse them leave, and quashed the refusal.

On 24 April 2009, the government published guidance for applications for settlement from Gurkhas who were discharged before 1 July 1997. One of the criteria was that anyone with 20 or more years of service could settle in the UK. The standard length of army service by Gurkhas was 15 years. After a public campaign (famously spearheaded by the actress, Joanna Lumley) a Liberal Democrat motion in the House of Commons voted to overturn the government policy and give all Gurkhas equal rights of residence, and on 21 May 2009 the Home Secretary announced that any former Gurkha with more than four years' service who had been discharged from the Brigade of Gurkhas before 1 July 1997 would be eligible for settlement in the UK (HC Debs 16 July 2009 col 251W).

7.8.5.1 *Long residence*

It is appropriate that people who have been living for a long time in a country should have some security of residence, when they have not otherwise obtained a secure immigration status. This principle was given effect in the UK by a concession, which in April 2003 became part of the immigration rules. The residence requirement in both the rule and the concession is ten years' or more continuous lawful residence or 14 years' or more continuous residence of any legality. The concession gave effect to Article 3(3) European Convention on Establishment, which the UK ratified on 14 October 1969, and which provides that nationals of any contracting party who have been lawfully residing for more than ten years in the territory of another party may only be expelled for reasons of national security or for particularly serious reasons relating to public order, public health, or morality. The concession extended this provision in three respects:

- it included all foreign nationals, not just those of contracting states;
- granting indefinite leave rather than simply refraining from removing such a person; and
- allowing those who have been in the UK illegally to benefit.

The UK's long residence provisions do not give immunity from expulsion, nor limit the grounds for it in the way that the Convention suggests. The concession provided a presumption for the grant of indefinite leave, but the presumption is weakened in the rule which replaced it. The rule, instead of requiring strong countervailing factors to refuse leave after long residence, says that indefinite leave may be granted if 'having regard to the public interest there are no reasons why it would be undesirable'. The words 'should normally' have been removed. The rule requires that reasons not to grant leave should be ascertained in the light of the individual circumstances such as age, domestic circumstances, personal history, including character, conduct, associations, and employment record, and this also weakens the presumption (para 276B(ii)). It emerged in *FH (Bangladesh) v SSHD* [2009] EWCA Civ 385 that the concession remained in force alongside the rule until 1 or 2 March 2006. However, applications made now are made under the rules.

Short absences of up to six months will not break continuity if the person has leave when they are abroad (para 276A(a)). There are exceptions, and the person's intention is also relevant. Sometimes, longer ones will also be accepted as part of the period of residence, depending on the intention shown. In *LL (China) v SSHD* [2009] EWCA Civ 617, the appellant failed in her application for leave based on ten years' residence. She had undergone all her schooling in the UK from the age of 13, and then completed an undergraduate degree, and began a full-time course in accountancy. Her residence had been lawful at all times, but she had gone home to China in all her school and university holidays. As a consequence, her cumulative absences totalled more than 18 months – a limit set in the rules para 276A (a)(v). She was not accepted to have the requisite period of continuous residence.

In the case of a claim based on ten years of lawful residence, the former concession allowed for a short break in legality, where, for instance, an application was filed late, providing it was then granted. However, the Court of Appeal in *MD (Jamaica) and GE Canada v SSHD* [2010] EWCA Civ 213 held that such an allowance could not be implied into the rule. The IDI allows for a single break of up to 10 days if an application for further leave to remain has been made out of time (see *Syed and Patel v SSHD* [2011] EWCA Civ 1059).

The 14-year rule enables overstayers, people in breach of condition, and illegal entrants to declare themselves to the Home Office and obtain a status which enables lawful working, an application to be joined by relatives, entitlement to welfare benefits, and so on. The Court of Appeal in *ZH (Bangladesh) v SSHD* [2009] EWCA Civ 8 commented that the long residence rules were in the nature of an amnesty, which gives a guide to their application. The rule does not require a person with 14 years' residence to have any lawful residence. Typically, such a person might have been working illegally, as in *ZH (Bangladesh)* itself. The Court said that the point of the rule was to enable such a person to regularize their stay. To hold the illegality against them and refuse leave was to destroy the point of the rule. The extended stay (14 years) and its unlawfuless were neutral gateway factors for inclusion in the rule. *ZH (Bangladesh)* affirms the earlier case of *Aissaoui v SSHD* [2008] EWCA Civ 37, which was to a similar effect, and disapproves the Tribunal case *MO (Long residence rule – public interest proviso) Ghana* [2007] UKAIT 14.

However, an applicant under the 14-year rule cannot count time after enforcement proceedings have been commenced against them (HC 395 para 276B(i)(b)). The way this works was illustrated in the case of *R v SSHD ex p Ofori* [1994] Imm AR 581. Here, the applicant had six years' leave, then overstayed for five. He then applied for indefinite leave to remain but was refused. At the date of decision, he had been in the UK for 12 years. A decision was made to deport him and he appealed. At the (unsuccessful) end of the appeal process he had been in the UK for 14 years. He applied again for indefinite leave to remain, relying on the long residence concession. The High Court supported the Secretary of State's decision that he could not rely on time spent during the appeal process towards his 14 years.

There was a practice, now abandoned, of serving notice of intention to deport 'on the file', i.e., where a person could not be traced, the notice was issued but left to lie on the file. There are still people in relation to whom this was done at some point in the past. *Popatia* [2001] Imm AR 46 establishes that this does not count as service for the purpose of the long residence provisions and service on the file does not commence enforcement proceedings.

7.8.5.2 *Returning residents*

A person with indefinite leave has no immigration restrictions on their stay in the UK, but they are still subject to immigration control in that if they leave the country they may be examined by an immigration officer on their return and refused entry on limited grounds. Prior to the Immigration (Leave to Enter and Remain) Order 2000, SI 2000/1161, the position of such people was governed by the so-called returning resident rules, found in HC 395 paras 18–20. These rules were based on the fact that indefinite leave lapsed when the holder left the UK, but enabled the holder to be readmitted provided they had not been absent for more than two years, that when they last entered they had indefinite leave, that they now returned for settlement and that they did not leave the UK with the assistance of public funds (i.e., using a government repatriation scheme). These rules are still in existence, but must now be read together with SI 2000/1161. The effect of the 2000 Order is that leave does not lapse during an absence of less than two years. So, a person with indefinite leave who returns within two years no longer has to re-apply for leave. The effect of the change removes the basis for confusion and distressing refusals of leave to enter provided the person returns within two years. They may only be examined at the port to see if the leave should be cancelled, for the reasons discussed in the earlier section on this subject.

After two years, even so-called non-lapsing leave actually lapses (Immigration (Leave to Enter and Remain) Order 2000, SI 2000/1161 Article 13(4)). Outside the two-year period, re-entry is a matter of discretion, but if the only factor preventing return is that the person has been away too long, they should be admitted if, for example, they have lived in the UK for most of their life (HC 395 para 19). This is a wide discretion, and the example of when it should be exercised is no more than an indication of a basis for exercising it. Reference may be made to the IDIs for more examples. Visa nationals returning after more than two years will need a new entry clearance.

Returning residents may be refused readmission on grounds under para 320, in the limited situations where these are relevant, but not on medical grounds. Refusal is possible on grounds of exclusion being conducive to the public good, and para 320(9) gives the basis for refusal of leave where the requirements of para 18 are not met.

7.8.5.3 *Revoking indefinite leave*

The security of indefinite leave to remain is somewhat undermined by the power in Nationality, Immigration and Asylum Act 2002 s 76. Under this section the Secretary of State may revoke a person's indefinite leave to enter or remain if the person is liable to deportation but 'cannot be deported for legal reasons'. In a similar vein, under s 76(2) indefinite leave can be revoked if it was obtained by deception but the person cannot be removed for legal or practical reasons. A person whose leave is revoked will not be able to work or claim benefits and therefore will have no basis for economic support unless they are detained or work illegally. Their children will not be British, and depending on the laws of their country of nationality may be born stateless. They will have no right to be joined by other members of their family. This raises the prospect of a new group of people forced into destitution. There is no exemption in the section for children. Section 76 does not require that national security is in issue and the application of this section may raise issues under Human Rights Act Articles 3, 8, and 14. Those with indefinite leave but not with British nationality do not have a right to the protection of the state nor a formal obligation of allegiance (see *Al-Rawi* and chapter 3).

Section 76 may be cross-referenced with the designation power in the Criminal Justice and Immigration Act 2008, see chapters 1 and 14.

7.9 Settlement

The terms 'settlement' and 'settled' are used widely in immigration law, and it is important to grasp their meaning. Settled status must be distinguished from right of abode, indefinite leave to remain, and ordinary residence.

The Immigration Act 1971 s 33(2)A defines a person who is 'settled' as subject to no immigration restrictions on length of stay and ordinarily resident in the UK. These two components of the definition are both important. Someone who has no immigration restrictions on their length of stay may be in that position either because they have indefinite leave to remain or because they have right of abode. Right of abode, it may be recalled from the chapter on nationality, is the right to come and go 'without let or hindrance' (Immigration Act 1971 s 1) and is held only by British citizens and the relatively few Commonwealth citizens with right of abode. Settlement includes indefinite leave to remain but carries the additional requirement of ordinary residence.

The meaning of the term 'ordinary residence' was considered by the House of Lords in *Shah v Barnet London Borough Council* [1983] 2 AC 309, not an immigration but an education case, concerning a student's entitlement to a grant, which also, under statute, depended upon 'ordinary residence'. The House of Lords held that it was possible to have more than one ordinary residence. The country of ordinary residence was the person's home, chosen as part of a settled way of life for the time being. It could be of long or short duration and did not imply permanence. The reason for being present was irrelevant providing it was voluntary, and immigration status had no bearing on the matter, providing the person was not in breach of immigration law. This meant that someone with limited leave could be ordinarily resident. In the context of defining 'settled status' it means that there is no need to prove that the person intends to be in the UK for the rest of their life. The case of *Chugtai* [1995] IAR 559 developed *Shah* in holding that a person could be ordinarily resident in two countries at the same time. In *AB Bangladesh* [2004] UKIAT 00314 the Tribunal held that this could include where the appellant intended to spend six months of each year in each country. He could therefore be said to be coming to the UK 'for settlement'.

Colloquially, it is often said that when a person obtains indefinite leave to remain they 'get settlement', as for instance when a worker has lived for five years in the UK and obtains indefinite leave to remain, or a spouse whose restrictions are lifted after their probationary period. The words 'settlement' and 'indefinite leave to remain' are often used interchangeably and for practical purposes this is quite valid. However the two are not exactly the same. Settled status is not awarded by the Secretary of State explicitly. It is a description of a state of affairs rather than an immigration status awarded. It is necessary to be able to identify when a person is settled as important rights accrue to someone with settled status. Children born in the UK to a settled person will be British (British Nationality Act 1981 s 1), and in the immigration rules a settled person is qualified to sponsor a partner or relative to come to the UK (HC 395, e.g., paras 281, 317).

In practical terms, settlement and indefinite leave to remain are virtually coterminous. As we have seen, a person with indefinite leave to remain who stays away from the UK for more than two years may lose that leave. Therefore, an ordinary residence requirement is implied in retaining indefinite leave to remain. Although it is technically accurate to refer to a British citizen ordinarily resident in the UK as 'settled', these entitlements are of greater real significance to people who are not British. In general, therefore, the word 'settled' is used to refer to people who have indefinite leave to remain and are ordinarily resident in the UK.

Settled status in this usual sense does not carry full rights of citizenship. A settled person can be deported on the ground that deportation is conducive to the public good (Immigration Act s 3(5)(a)) and does not have the right to vote or stand for Parliament. In these respects, as well as the possible loss of status after two years' absence, settled status is less secure than right of abode.

7.10 Conclusion

This chapter has considered some of the legal provisions relating to crossing the UK's borders and obtaining an immigration status here. The border itself is described as an increasingly distributed, intelligence-led, and security-focused system, rather than a geographical boundary. The widening scope of control is accompanied by its transformation into a technologically driven policing and deterrence system. The dominance of executive discretion in immigration law has been problematic, and difficult for the individual to challenge, but so is a machine reading. Issues of technological reliability and data protection will enter into immigration law. It is debatable which is more transparent as befits a democracy.

QUESTIONS

1 How do you think the Immigration (Leave to Enter and Remain) Order 2000 changes the substance and nature of immigration control?
2 What would you consider to be appropriate medical grounds for refusal of leave to enter and who do you think should make that decision? How does your idea compare with the present law?
3 What do you think are the reasons for limiting the categories of leave to and from which a person can switch?

online resource centre

For guidance on answering questions, visit www.oxfordtextbooks.co.uk/orc/clayton5e/.

FURTHER READING

Cabinet Office (2007) *Security in a Global Hub* (London: Cabinet Office).

Commission for Racial Equality (1985) *Immigration Control Procedures: Report of a Formal Investigation* (London: Commission for Racial Equality), chapter 3.

Guild, Elspeth (2000) 'Entry into the UK: The Changing Nature of National Borders' INLP vol. 14, no. 4, pp. 227–238.

House Of Commons Home Affairs Committee (2011) *UK Border Controls* 17th report of session 2010–12 HC 1647 .

Juss, Satvinder (1997) *Discretion and Deviation in the Administration of Immigration Control* (London: Sweet & Maxwell).

Ryan, Bernard (2001) 'The Common Travel Area between Britain and Ireland' *Modern Law Review* vol. 64, November 2001, pp. 855–874.

Shah, Ramnik (2007) 'Language Test for Permanent Residents' *Journal of Immigration, Asylum and Nationality Law* vol. 21, no. 1, pp. 26–27.

Statewatch Bulletin 'UK: E-Borders Plan to Tackle "Threats"' vol. 15, no. 3/4.

Toal, Ronan (2008) 'The New "General Grounds for Refusal"' *Journal of Immigration, Asylum and Nationality Law* vol. 22, no. 2, pp. 135–146.

United Kingdom Borders Agency (UKBA) (2011) 'Common Travel Area: Review of new arrangements at Northern Ireland Sea Ports' (London: UKBA).

Wray, Helena (2006) 'Guiding the Gatekeepers: Entry Clearance for Settlement on the Indian Sub-Continent' *Journal of Immigration, Asylum and Nationality Law* vol. 20, no. 2, pp. 112–129.

8

Challenging decisions: appeals and judicial review

SUMMARY

This chapter describes the structure of the appeals bodies, both the Tribunal and the Special Immigration Appeals Commission, the grounds of appeal, and some of the significant uses of judicial review, in particular as a means of challenging unfairness in asylum decision-making. UKBA's duty as a public body not to discriminate on racial grounds is also considered, and the authorized exceptions to that. The chapter ends with a section on those who represent immigrants and asylum seekers and the regulation of their services.

8.1 Introduction

The only possible grounds for appeal in immigration law are set out in statute. The grounds themselves are quite comprehensive, but access to appeal rights is restricted by complex legislation. The more technical aspects of law relating to appeals are outside the scope of this book, and for this reference should be made to practitioner works such as Macdonald's *Immigration Law and Practice*, or JCWI's *Immigration, Nationality and Refugee Law Handbook*.

The first part of this chapter describes the structure of the appeals system and then we discuss the principles of law which are the grounds for appealing immigration decisions.

8.2 The Appeal Tribunal

A two-tier system of immigration appeals was instituted in 1969 for Commonwealth citizens and in 1973 for all immigrants. There was an initial appeal to an adjudicator, with a second appeal to an Immigration Appeal Tribunal (IAT). The Asylum and Immigration (Treatment of Claimants, etc.) Act 2004 abolished that two-tier system, replacing it with a single-tier, Asylum and Immigration Tribunal (AIT), with effect from 4 April 2005. Members of the AIT were called Immigration Judges, and adjudicators and legally qualified members of the IAT transferred immediately to this role and title (2004 Act Sch 2 paras 27 and 28). Non-legally qualified members of the IAT became non-legally qualified members of the AIT (para 28).

The system of challenging a decision of the AIT was complex. In brief, challenge was by way of an application for 'reconsideration', not appeal, to a panel of the Tribunal, the underlying idea being that the Tribunal on reconsideration was constitutionally the same judicial body, looking again at their decision, even though different personnel of different seniority would be involved (see *DK (Serbia)* [2006] EWCA Civ 1747). This resulted in complex and sometimes inconsistent rules, found partly in the procedure rules but developed in case law, to deal with issues such as whether findings of fact of the first Tribunal were binding at the reconsideration hearing, and whether issues of law on the reconsideration hearing should be restricted to those which had been identified by the judge who decided to order reconsideration (see *HS (Afghanistan) v SSHD* [2009] EWCA Civ 771).

The AIT has now in turn been abolished. The Tribunals, Courts and Enforcement Act (TCEA) 2007 created a new unified Tribunal structure, to encompass tribunals in all areas of law. On 15 February 2010, the Asylum and Immigration Tribunal was abolished and its functions incorporated into the new Tribunal structure (Transfer of Functions of the Asylum and Immigration Tribunal Order 2010, S1 2010/21). The new Tribunal once again has two tiers: the First Tier and the Upper Tribunal, each of which has an Immigration and Asylum Chamber. Article 3 of the Transfer of Functions Order provides for immigration judges of the AIT to be transferred in as First Tier Tribunal judges. The 2004 Act created a new tier of 'designated immigration judges' in an initiative to create a supervisory structure within the Tribunal. They are transferred in as First Tier Tribunal judges and deputy judges of the Upper Tribunal. Senior immigration judges and non-legal members become judges and members of the Upper Tribunal. The Upper Tribunal was newly created as a court of record.

Appeals may be made from the First Tier to the Upper Tribunal on the grounds of error of law. As discussed later in relation to appeals to the Court of Appeal, an error of law must be more than a disagreement on the facts. By way of not uncommon example, in *AP (Trinidad and Tobago) v SSHD* [2011] EWCA Civ 551 the Court of Appeal allowed the appeal on the basis that the First Tier Tribunal had not made an error of law in deciding that the public interest in deporting the appellant because of his offending did not outweigh his right to respect for family life. In such a case, if all the relevant facts are carefully considered, with reasons given, it is difficult to substantiate a claim of error of law.

Permission for such an appeal is sought from the First Tier Tribunal in the first instance, and if refused, then directly from the Upper Tribunal. On hearing an appeal, the Upper Tribunal can decide the matter for itself, or remit the case back to the First Tier if it considers that the matter needs to be reheard (TCEA s 12). If the Upper Tribunal refuses permission to appeal, this decision is not appealable (TCEA s 13(8)(c)). TCEA s 13(6) empowered the Lord Chancellor to make permission to appeal to the Court of Appeal conditional on that court considering that the proposed appeal raises an important point of principle or practice, or that there is some other compelling reason to hear the appeal. The Joint Committee on Human Rights argued that this extra test should not apply to immigration and asylum appeals (see Buxton 2009), but their proposal was resisted. The Lord Chancellor made the order, and its application to immigration and asylum cases is discussed later (*PR (Sri Lanka) v SSHD* [2011] EWCA Civ 988).

In addition to concern about the threshold for permission to appeal from the Upper Tribunal to the Court of Appeal, the statutory conditions for the new Tribunal presented questions for asylum and immigration judicial review cases:

- Would final decisions of the Upper Tribunal be open to judicial review, and if so, what would be the threshold for granting an application for permission?
- Some judicial review functions of the High Court were to be transferred to the Upper Tribunal. Would this include any immigration and asylum matters?

Non-appealable decisions of the AIT had been open to judicial review but as the Upper Tribunal was a court of record, there was an argument that its decisions would not be open to judicial review. In immigration and asylum law an important non-appealable decision of the Upper Tribunal is its refusal of permission to appeal from a decision of the First Tier Tribunal. This was the substance of MR's challenge in the case of *Cart* before the Supreme Court.

In *R (on the application of Cart, U and XC) v Upper Tribunal and SIAC* [2009] EWHC 3052 (Admin), government parties – the Secretary of State for Justice, the Secretary of State for the Home Department, and the Child Maintenance and Enforcement Commission – initially argued that the designation of a judicial body as a superior court of record prevented its decisions from being susceptible to judicial review. This argument was rejected by the High Court, which held that as a court of limited jurisdiction the Upper Tribunal could not in principle be unreviewable. The case reached the Supreme Court on the issue of what test the Court should apply in considering whether to grant permission for judicial review of a decision of the Upper Tribunal.

Key Case

***R (on the application of Cart) v Upper Tribunal and R (on the application of MR (Pakistan)) v Upper Tribunal and SSHD* [2011] UKSC 28**

The Supreme Court held that it would be inconsistent with the new structure introduced by the 2007 Act to distinguish between the scope of judicial review in the various jurisdictions which had been gathered together in the new structure (para 37). There was no question of ousting the judicial supervision that judicial review provided; the question was, the threshold at which this should be permitted. The Court was faced with three alternative propositions:

1. Judicial review of the tribunal was limited to 'pre-*Anisminic* excess of jurisdiction and the denial of fundamental justice'.
2. Nothing had changed – judicial review of the new tribunal could be granted on the same basis as before.
3. Judicial review of Upper Tribunal decisions should be limited to the grounds upon which permission to make a second-tier appeal to the Court of Appeal would be granted.

The Court chose the third option as a 'rational and proportionate' solution. As the Lord Chancellor had made the order under s 13(6) TCEA, the grounds upon which permission to make a second-tier appeal to the Court of Appeal may be granted are that '(a) the proposed appeal would raise some important point of principle or practice; or (b) there is some other compelling reason for the relevant appellate court to hear the appeal' (Appeals from the Upper Tribunal to the Court of Appeal Order 2008, SI 2008/2834, art 2). 'Second tier appeals' are those where the decision of the Upper Tribunal is itself a decision on appeal. Lord Dyson said:

> Care should be exercised in giving examples of what might be 'some other compelling reason', because it will depend on the particular circumstances of the case. But they might include (i) a case where it is strongly arguable that the individual has suffered what Laws LJ referred to at para 99 as 'a wholly exceptional collapse of fair procedure' or (ii) a case where it is strongly arguable that there has been an error of law which has caused truly drastic consequences. (para 131)

The threshold for judicial review having been settled, in *PR (Sri Lanka v SSHD* [2011] EWCA Civ 988, the Court of Appeal considered whether the threshold in the Lord Chancellor's order should be applied to immigration and asylum appeals, and how it should be interpreted. In particular, what could be encompassed in the phrase 'some other compelling reason'? The Court held that the test should be applied the same way in immigration and asylum cases as in other matters. The Supreme Court's judgment in *Cart* rejected any special test. Lady Hale quoted Sullivan LJ in the Court of Appeal:

> The immigration and asylum jurisdiction was not the only one in which claimants might be unrepresented, or particularly vulnerable, or where fundamental human rights were involved, or where the law was complex. (para 36)

Part of the rationale of the new unified tribunal system was that access to appeals did not depend on the subject matter under appeal. (para 28) The Court said, '"compelling" means *legally* compelling, rather than compelling, perhaps, from a political or emotional point of view, although such considerations may exceptionally add weight to the legal arguments' (para 36).

The TCEA s 19 mandated the transfer of judicial reviews to the Upper Tribunal when specified conditions are met. Asylum and immigration judicial reviews were originally excluded from such transfers. The Joint Human Rights Committee thought that cases which raised complex issues of fact and law, or in which human rights such as life, liberty or freedom from torture were at stake should continue to be heard by High Court judges. The result was a compromise. Section 53 of the Borders Citizenship and Immigration Act 2009 requires the High Court to transfer to the Upper Tribunal judicial reviews which challenge the refusal of the Secretary of State to treat an asylum claimant's representations as a fresh claim (see chapter 12), and this was brought into effect on 17 October 2011 (SI 2011/2342).

The existing Asylum and Immigration Tribunal (Procedure) Rules 2005, SI 2005/230 form the foundation for the practice of the First Tier Tribunal, though the rules of the new Tribunal are governed by an independent Procedure Rules Committee. On 19 December 2011 the payment of fees was introduced for immigration and asylum appeals. Appeals against most enforcement processes are exempt from fees, and appellants on asylum support are exempt. There is also a procedure for applying for individual exemption (HM Courts and Tribunals Service: Immigration and Appeals Tribunal fees guidance). See chapter 1 for comment on the work of the Tribunal.

8.2.1 The procedure of the Tribunal

The overriding objective of procedure rules provides a principle by which they can be interpreted and which may guide discretionary decisions. In the 2003 Procedure Rules, the overriding objective was to 'secure the just, timely and effective disposal of appeals and applications'. This was changed in the 2005 Rules to handling proceedings 'as fairly, quickly and efficiently as possible' (r 4), suggesting that expediency may take precedence over fairness. The UNHCR had recommended that the rule be 'amended to reflect more clearly the emphasis that should be given to the fundamental concern of correctly identifying those who are in need of international protection' (UNHCR December 2004 para 2). While speed and efficiency are generally desirable for all concerned, the main purpose of a refugee determination and appeal procedure is to make accurate decisions about those in need of protection and not to put claimants at risk.

The rules allow short time limits for appealing (ten days, or five for someone who is in detention: r 7, and even less in the fast track). This can create severe problems in a situation where legal advice is hard to come by, public funding for cases equally scarce (see later section on representation), and the appellant's first language may well not be English. Even the calculation of these time periods is complex and critical (see *R (on the application of Semere) v AIT* [2009] EWHC 335 (Admin)). In *FP (Iran) and MB (Libya) v SSHD* [2007] EWCA Civ 13, r 19(1) read with r 56(2) of the Asylum and Immigration Procedure Rules 2005, allowed an appeal to go ahead in the absence of the appellant when his former solicitors had closed down and failed to inform the tribunal of their clients' new address. This went to 'the very essence' of the right to be heard and was unlawful. The rule was amended and now allows for a hearing not to go ahead in a party's absence if the Tribunal is aware that there could be good reasons not to do so.

In asylum cases, the Tribunal's determination is served on the Home Office who must then serve it on the appellant (r 23(4) and (5)), though in non-asylum cases it is served by the Tribunal on both parties within ten days (r 22). Conversely, notice of appeal must be filed by the appellant on the Tribunal, who must then serve it on the Home Office 'as soon as reasonably practicable' (r 12). This is intended to prevent the delays which used to ensue after the appellant had lodged their appeal with the Home Office and then had to wait for lengthy periods before the Home Office informed the Tribunal (see McKee 2005:99). However, it also opens up the possibility that the Home Office, having no notice of the appeal, may arrest, detain, and even remove the appellant before the appeal is heard, though it could be unlawful to do so.

Initial appeals to the First Tier Tribunal are rehearings of the whole case, and the Tribunal may 'consider evidence about any matter which it thinks relevant to the substance of the decision' (Nationality, Immigration and Asylum Act 2002 s 85(4)). In entry clearance and certificate of entitlement cases, i.e., those where the applicant is outside the UK, evidence is limited to evidence of matters arising before the date of the decision, and in appeals against points-based decisions *no* new evidence is allowed except to prove the validity of a document (s 85A). The Tribunal may adopt an inquisitorial style, asking questions of the Home Office representative and the applicant, but the proceedings are in most respects adversarial in nature.

The burden of proof is on the appellant, and the standard of proof in immigration cases is the balance of probabilities (confirmed in *ECO Dhaka v Shamim Box* [2002] UKIAT 02212). There is sometimes debate as to whether this standard is properly applied, though it is to be hoped that examples of contrary practice as extreme as this one identified by Juss (1997) would not be encountered now. In *Walayat Begum v Visa Officer Islamabad* TH/13561/75, the Tribunal had before it the passport of the appellant's first wife, whom he claimed had died. The passport was endorsed: 'The holder of this passport has died. Passport has been cancelled and returned.' There was other evidence also. The Tribunal held 'There is no really direct or solid evidence that Manzoor Begum has died' (1997:129).

The Nationality, Immigration and Asylum Act 2002 has simplified the statutory grounds for immigration appeals, although the procedures for ascertaining a right to exercise such an appeal and for actually exercising it have become ever more complex. There are broadly four questions to consider:

- Is this the kind of decision against which an appeal may be brought?
- Are there grounds for the appeal (i.e., reasons in law why it is said to be wrong)?
- Is the appeal available in this case?
- If so, is it available in the UK or only from abroad?

Section 82 of the Nationality Immigration and Asylum Act 2002 sets out the decisions against which appeals may be brought. They are all the major decisions made in relation to a person's stay in the UK, including refusal of leave to enter, refusal of entry clearance, refusal to vary leave, a decision to remove, and a decision to deport. Appealable decisions do not include the issue of removal directions, i.e., the actual implementation of the decision to remove (see chapter 17). The second question is answered by s 84, which sets out the grounds upon which appeals may be made. These are discussed in the body of this chapter.

The third and fourth questions are answered by reference to a voluminous body of highly technical rules, most of which are scattered unpredictably across a range of statutes both in the body of legislation and the schedules. These may be found in practitioner works, and are largely outside the remit of this book, though occasional reference is made to broad and important rules. Two to be aware of are that the refusal of applications for entry clearance for work, study, and non-family visits carry no right of appeal except on human rights and race discrimination grounds (Immigration and Asylum Act 1999 ss 59 and 60 and Immigration, Asylum and Nationality Act 2006 s 4), and there is no right of appeal against refusal of leave to enter for someone who does not hold entry clearance on arrival, issued for the purpose for which they now seek entry (s 89 Nationality Immigration and Asylum Act 2002 as amended by 2006 Act s 6).

A determination of the Upper Tribunal may be appealed to the Court of Appeal, with permission, on a point of law. What an individual must show to obtain permission was discussed earlier in relation to *PR (Sri Lanka)* and *Cart*. It is not always easy to distinguish between an error of fact and an error of law. In *E v SSHD and R v SSHD* [2004] EWCA Civ 49, there was a delay of some months between the hearing and the Tribunal decisions being promulgated. During that period, human rights reports were produced on the country to which the appellants would be sent. These reports significantly affected the factual basis on which the decisions had been made. The Court of Appeal held that the Tribunal could have reviewed its decision. They made the further important statement that:

> It was time to accept that a mistake of fact giving rise to unfairness was a separate head of challenge in an appeal on a point of law, at least in those statutory contexts where the parties shared an interest in cooperating to achieve the correct result. Asylum law was such an area. For a finding of unfairness there must have been a mistake as to an existing fact, including a mistake as to the availability of evidence on a particular matter. The fact or evidence must have been 'established' in the sense that it was uncontentious and objectively verifiable. The appellant must not have been responsible for the mistake and the mistake must have played a material part in the tribunal's reasoning.

In immigration and asylum cases, a wide and flexible approach is taken to the concept of error of law. The Court in *R (Iran) v SSHD* [2005] EWCA Civ 982 gave guidance on the kinds of errors of law which might arise in immigration proceedings, including, for example, failing to give any or adequate reasons for findings on material matters or to take into account or resolve conflicts of fact. The Supreme Court has urged the Court of Appeal not to be quick to 'characterise as an error of law what is no more than a disagreement with the AIT's assessment of the facts' (*MA (Somalia) v SSHD* [2010] UKSC 49). This was borne out in *AP (Trinidad and Tobago)* mentioned at 8.2, where the Upper Tribunal made an error of law by considering that the First Tier Tribunal had done so.

8.3 Special Immigration Appeals Commission

There is a separate system for appeals involving national security. This used to be a secret procedure before a panel of advisers, known as the 'Three Wise Men', but the conduct of these proceedings was very restricted. The panel was required to make the case against the person known to them as far as they considered national security would allow, but there was no obligation to disclose evidence or identify witnesses. The individual had no right to legal representation, and perhaps most strangely of all, no right to see the decision in their case.

Article 5(4) ECHR requires that someone who is detained should have the right to challenge their detention in a court. The applicant in the case of *Chahal v UK* (1997) 23 EHRR 413 was detained for a total of six years following a decision to deport him on national security grounds. The ECtHR held that there was a violation of Article 5(4) of the Convention in that there was no provision for him to challenge his detention before a court as the 'Three Wise Men' procedure could not be called a court. The ECtHR recognized that there may be a necessity for matters to be heard in a private forum where disclosure of some issues to the public could cause harm to national security. Nevertheless, some countries, Canada for example, had devised procedures which gave more protection to the rights of the individual while still taking account of the state's need for security. The procedure was also found to breach Article 13 of the Convention, as the panel of special advisers did not provide an effective safeguard for Mr Chahal against removal from the UK to a place where he could suffer torture or inhuman or degrading treatment or punishment in breach of Article 3.

In response to the judgment of the ECtHR, the UK replaced the 'Three Wise Men' with the Special Immigration Appeals Commission (SIAC), set up by the Special Immigration Appeals Commission Act 1997 (SIACA). The Commission must consist of one member who has held (or holds) high judicial office, one member who either is or has been a legally qualified member of the Tribunal and a third member who would normally be someone with experience of national security matters (SIACA 1997 Sch 1). The Commission has power to exclude anybody from a hearing, including the appellant and their representative if the Commission accepts a submission from the Secretary of State that it is necessary to rely on 'closed' material – that is, material which it would be against the public interest to disclose, even to the appellant. If the Commission decides to hold a closed hearing, the interests of the appellant are represented by a Special Advocate, appointed by the Attorney-General (or in Scotland, by the Lord Advocate) for that purpose. The Special Advocate is not at liberty to discuss those proceedings with the appellant. This procedure is intended to comply with Article 5 ECHR, while still providing some protection for government concerns about national security.

8.3.1 Jurisdiction

The jurisdiction of the SIAC is to hear appeals against immigration decisions, usually exclusion, refusal of entry as an asylum seeker, deportation, or deprivation of nationality, if the Secretary of State certifies that he or she took the decision personally, wholly or partly in the interests of national security or the relationship between the UK and another country (Nationality, Immigration and Asylum Act 2002 s 97). Section 99 allows the Secretary of State to issue a certificate under s 97 while an appeal is pending before the Tribunal, thereby compelling its transfer to SIAC. The use of special advocates and closed evidence has spread to other jurisdictions outside SIAC, including challenge to control orders and judicial reviews concerned with national security issues. There are now at least 21 different contexts in which special advocates are used in the UK (JCHR 2010 para 58).

The Commission can hear appeals on the same grounds as those which may be raised in the Tribunal (1997 Act s 2(2)(e), as substituted by 2002 Act Sch 7 para 20). The Commission has similar powers to those of the Tribunal on appeals, in that it must allow the appeal if it considers that the decision appealed is not in accordance with the law or the immigration rules, or that a discretion should have been exercised differently (SIACA 1997 s 2(3)(b), as substituted by 2002 Act Sch 7 para 20). In *SSHD v Rehman* [2001] 3 WLR 877, the first case to come before SIAC, the House of Lords agreed with the Court of Appeal and SIAC that the Commission's role was to review the merits of the case in full, which could include reviewing the Secretary of State's findings of fact. The deportation appeals heard by SIAC are discussed fully in chapter 16.

Appeals from SIAC are to the Court of Appeal on a point of law. In *B (Algeria) v SSHD; OO (Jordan) v SSHD* [2009] UKHL 10, there was a challenge to SIAC's assessment of the reliability of assurances given by the governments of Jordan and Algeria that the appellants would not be tortured if they were returned there. The House of Lords held that the Court of Appeal had been wrong to overturn SIAC's assessment. This should only be done if their assessment was clearly not sustainable on the evidence such that their judgment on this factual issue amounted to an error of law.

8.3.2 Evidence and procedures in SIAC

The standard of proof in SIAC proceedings is the balance of probabilities as regards allegations of past actions (*Rehman v SSHD and ZZ v SSHD* [2008] UKSIAC 63/2007), even though in content and implications for an unsuccessful appellant the proceedings have much in common with criminal cases. The assessment of risk to national security is, however, a speculative matter which is considered to be chiefly within the remit of the executive (see *ZZ v SSHD* [2011] EWCA Civ 440 and discussion of Rehman in chapter 16). The House of Lords in *A and others v SSHD* [2005] UKHL 71 held that SIAC could not admit evidence if there was evidence that it could have been obtained by torture (see chapter 4 for full discussion).

Two aspects of SIAC's procedure have attracted particular attention. One is the use of closed evidence. The other is the role of the Special Advocate. After an inquiry by the Constitutional Affairs Committee, the procedure rules were amended to improve the fairness of the process (Special Immigration Appeals Commission (Procedure) (Amendment) Rules 2007, SI 2007/1285). The House of Lords and the ECtHR have both laid down requirements for the fair use of closed material.

The ECtHR heard a challenge from people who had been subjected to indefinite detention under the 2001 Act (see chapter 15), including a challenge under Article 5(4) to the fairness of the procedure before SIAC, which determined whether the Secretary of State was reasonable in believing each applicant to be a risk to national security and in suspecting them of involvement in international terrorism (*A v UK* (2009) 49 EHRR 29). The ECtHR said that 'in view of the dramatic impact of the lengthy – and what appeared at that time to be indefinite – deprivation of liberty on the applicants' fundamental rights, Article 5 para 4 must import substantially the same fair trial guarantees as Article 6 para 1 in its criminal aspect' (para 217). The Court accepted the reasons for keeping some evidence secret, but held that where full disclosure was not possible, Article 5(4) required that the detainee must be provided with sufficient information about the allegations to enable him to give effective instructions to the special advocate and to challenge the allegations against him. Even if the detail and sources of evidence remained undisclosed, if the allegations contained in the open material were sufficiently specific, it should be possible for the applicant to provide information to refute them. An example was the allegation that several of the applicants had attended a terrorist training camp at a stated location between stated dates; an applicant could have provided an alibi or an alternative explanation for his presence there. Where, however, the open material consisted purely of general assertions and SIAC's decision was based to a decisive degree on closed material, the procedural requirements of Article 5(4) would not be satisfied (para 220).

This standard of disclosure has been endorsed by the House of Lords in relation to challenges in the High Court to control orders under the Prevention of Terrorism Act 2005 (*SSHD v AF* [2009] UKHL 28), which are the present equivalent of the detentions challenged in *A v UK*, but has been held not to apply in SIAC proceedings concerning deportation or exclusion (*W (Algeria) v SSHD* [2011] EWCA Civ 898). In *RB (Algeria) v SSHD; OO (Jordan) v SSHD* [2009] UKHL 10 the House of Lords drew a distinction between the control order jurisdiction and that under the 1997 Act. Lord Brown said that Article 6 did not apply to SIAC proceedings because, unlike in control order cases, the appellants were not facing a charge against them, but rather were opposing their deportation. Article 6 applied to control order cases because these were domestic and not immigration proceedings in which the UK government was restricting liberty. Principles could not be drawn across from one to another. Under the amended procedure rules, the Special Advocate may now call evidence and cross-examine witnesses. The Secretary of State must search for and serve on the appellant any evidence which might tend to show that the allegations against the appellant are untrue ('exculpatory evidence'). The rules also give the Commission a power to order the Secretary of State to serve a summary of the closed evidence on the appellant. There are still restrictions on the Special Advocate's role however. They may not take instructions upon the closed evidence. Even if evidence in closed material shows that the case in the open material is flawed, they may not deal with this in an open hearing or take further instructions on inconsistencies.

We now move from the appeals system to the content of appeals.

8.4 Grounds of appeal to the Tribunal

The grounds of appeal are set out in Nationality, Immigration and Asylum Act 2002 s 84, and are as follows:

(a) that the decision is not in accordance with the immigration rules;
(b) that the decision is unlawful by virtue of Race Relations Act 1976 s 19B;
(c) that the decision is unlawful under Human Rights Act s 6...as being incompatible with the appellant's Convention rights;
(d) that the appellant is an EEA national or a member of the family of an EEA national and the decision breaches the appellant's rights under the Community Treaties;
(e) that the decision is otherwise not in accordance with the law;
(f) that the person taking the decision should have exercised differently a discretion conferred by immigration rules;
(g) that removal of the appellant in consequence of the immigration decision would breach the UK's obligations under the Refugee Convention or...Human Rights Act s 6.

Section 86 provides that the Tribunal must allow the appeal 'in so far as it thinks that' one of these is the case. This largely repeats an earlier provision found both in the Immigration and Asylum Act 1999 (Sch 4 para 21) and in the Immigration Act 1971 (s 19).

Breach of the Refugee Convention forms the subject of the chapters on asylum law. European Community rights are explored in chapter 5. The substance of rights under the Human Rights Act is discussed in chapters 4 and 18, but the jurisdiction to hear that ground is discussed here, as are the other grounds.

8.4.1 Not in accordance with the immigration rules

The effect of s 86 and its predecessors is to give binding force to the immigration rules. Immigration officers, Home Office officials, and entry clearance officers are bound to act in accordance with the rules in the sense that if they do not their decisions are appealable. This means that at the appeal stage, if the Tribunal considers that requirements for, e.g., entry are met, the appeal must be allowed and entry granted. Although the applicant, as we saw in chapter 1, cannot at the beginning insist on obtaining entry if they consider they meet the requirements, at the stage of appeal, the rules have the force of law.

The status of the immigration rules, which, as discussed in chapter 1 is unique, has implications for appeals. *Odelola v SSHD* [2009] UKHL 25 was one of many cases arising out of the changes to the rules for postgraduate doctors to complete their training in the UK.

Key Case

***Odelola v SSHD* [2009] UKHL 25**

Ms Odelola came to the UK in 2005 as a postgraduate doctor and completed two clinical attachments in order to progress with her training. In January 2006, she received confirmation that her basic surgical training was regarded as 'acceptable' by the UK's Postgraduate Medical Education and Training Board. She applied for leave to remain as a postgraduate doctor. On 3 April 2006, there was a radical restructuring of the immigration rules relating to medical graduates, including that only a UK medical degree would now suffice as a basis for leave. Ms Odelola's application was refused on 26 April. She appealed on the basis that the rules applied to her should be those in force at the time of her application, in accordance with which she would have obtained leave to remain. The House of Lords confirmed the decisions of the Tribunal and Court of Appeal, and held that the immigration rules, even though they had the force of law for appeals, represented policy. They were not subordinate legislation within the terms of the Interpretation Act 1978 and so not subject to s 16(1)(c) of that Act which prevented subordinate legislation from affecting existing rights. Ms Odelola had no vested right under the immigration rules. The Secretary of State was free to change them and to implement start dates as a matter of policy and without transitional provisions. The applicable rules were those at the time of the decision.

Odelola establishes that in the majority of cases, the immigration rules according to which decisions will be taken, are those in force at the time of the decision. The finding against retrospectivity in the *HSMP Forum* case (see 8.5.3) was on the different basis that the HSMP rules promised a scheme that operated as a whole, and implied that its terms would be kept stable.

Following the Court of Appeal judgment in *Pankina* (see chapters 1 and 10), there have been numerous tribunal appeals against decisions in the points-based system which are based on guidance that has been treated as binding, but which does not meet the requirements of *Pankina*. For example in *Owolabi (Tier 2 – skilled occupations) Nigeria* [2011] UKUT 313 (IAC) the Tribunal held that the decision was not in accordance with the immigration rules where the applicant had been refused on the basis of requirements in a list of skilled occupations that had been published *after* the rules which referred to it were laid in Parliament. The means of publishing was simply by putting the list on UKBA's website which meant that it could be changed by the Secretary of State at any time. The case of *Alvi* (see 10.3.2) had found that a list of occupations was a substantive matter, i.e., the kind of provision which must, if it was to be treated as binding, be laid before Parliament (*Pankina).*

8.4.2 Race discrimination as a ground of appeal

The changes to the immigration rules on international medical graduates, which affected Ms Odelola, had a major impact on doctors of Indian origin, but race discrimination as a ground of appeal under the Nationality, Immigration and Asylum Act 2002 s 84(1)(b) is not a challenge to the *making* of a such a rule, but rather to the discriminatory application of rules. Strangely, the race discrimination provision on which the s 84(1)(b) appeal is based was repealed by the Equality Act 2010. The resulting abolition of this ground in immigration appeals may have been accidental. This section assumes that the ground will be restored (see online resource centre).

In *SK India* [2006] UKAIT 00067, the Tribunal gave general guidance on making race discrimination claims in the Tribunal. They said that the usual principles of discrimination law apply, so that it is necessary to identify a comparator who would be better treated than the appellant, and where indirect discrimination is alleged then statistics may be used to show differential impact of a rule or policy. Where this is done, the populations chosen must be comparable. In that case, the appellant presented information that some entry clearance posts, including New Delhi, had a much lower rate of granting working holidaymaker applications than others, for instance in Canada and Australia. This could not establish discrimination without information on other characteristics of the applicants.

An appeal on race discrimination grounds is unlike other appeals because the grounds refer to how the decision was taken, and success on that point may not in itself be enough to decide the claim in the appellant's favour (see Quayum and Chatwin 2004:97). For instance, in *CS (Race discrimination; proper approach) Jamaica* [2006] UKAIT 00004, the entry clearance officer made sweeping generalizations about Jamaican men, which the adjudicator accepted must have influenced the refusal of entry clearance. Unlike in *SK India* direct discrimination of this kind does not require statistical evidence. However, for separate reasons she found that without this discrimination the requirements for entry clearance would still not have been fulfilled, and the Tribunal agreed that the finding of race discrimination did not necessarily vitiate the refusal if there were other objective grounds.

Where an appeal on the merits is allowed, it is still necessary for the Tribunal to make a finding on the race discrimination issue (Nationality, Immigration and Asylum Act 2002 s 86(2)(a)), although a pending application in the ECtHR suggests that this does not always happen (*Mbuisa v UK* Application no. 22897/09). This may then generate a claim in the County Court for damages for injury to feelings arising out of the same facts (Quayum and Chatwin p. 98). Generally, if entry clearance is granted while an appeal is pending, the appeal is treated as abandoned (2002 Act s 104). This could mean that race discrimination would then be without a remedy – 'a particularly unfortunate consequence of the abandonment provisions' (*VE Nigeria* [2005] UKIAT 00057 para 21). The Immigration, Asylum and Nationality Act 2006 now prevents the appeal from being treated as abandoned where it was brought on race discrimination grounds so that the appellant may still claim damages in the County Court.

Race discrimination may also found a human rights appeal under Article 14 where the discrimination occurs in the ambit of another Convention right. Therefore, where, for instance, it is claimed that an alleged breach of an Article 8 right affected one racial group more severely or even exclusively, a complaint of discrimination may be made under Article 14. Race discrimination was found in itself to be capable of amounting to a breach of Article 3 in the *East African Asians Case* (1973) 3 EHRR 76, it being a 'special affront to human dignity' to single out a group of people for differential treatment on racial grounds. This does not mean that in all circumstances race discrimination can be regarded as a free-standing breach of Article 3. The level of severity to cross the threshold for Article 3 would have to be met in each case.

8.4.3 Human rights appeals

Entry clearance officers (though see discussion on scope in chapter 4), immigration officers, and officials in the Home Office are all public authorities for the purposes of Human Rights Act 1998 s 6, and therefore bound not to act in breach of a person's Convention rights. This obligation is confirmed in HC 395 para 2, and a breach of it is the basis for an appeal against an immigration decision under s 84.

Determining a human rights appeal is not an exercise of discretion (*AG and others (Policies; executive discretions; Tribunal's power) Kosovo* [2007] UKAIT 00082), it is a judgment on whether a decision is lawful. Therefore, if the decision is overturned on appeal the Tribunal's judgment must be implemented if there is no further appeal. It is not something which needs to return to the Secretary of State for further consideration, as an exercise of discretion might sometimes do.

There is some ambiguity about the form of leave that follows a successful appeal based on Article 8. Where it is a breach of human rights to apply an immigration rule strictly, or, to put in another way, where a lawful decision is to apply the rule so as to uphold human rights, the proper grant of leave would seem to be according to the rule. So if it is a breach of Article 8 to disregard family income from the daughter of a man who applies to join his wife in the UK, one consequence is that leave is granted as a spouse in the same way as the rule allows. However, some favourable decisions under Article 8 are followed by a grant of discretionary leave. This use of policy is currently under review, and may give rise to further litigation. In *Abdelghani* (see 9.4.5) the judge left the point open, after deciding that it was not discriminatory to grant discretionary leave instead of indefinite leave in the particular case.

The human rights appeal introduced into the appeals jurisdiction the concepts and principles of human rights law and the European Court of Human Rights. In the case of the qualified rights this also entails taking into account countervailing public interests. So, for instance, the right to respect for family life may be outweighed by the need for the prevention of disorder or crime. In the context of deportation and removal, the courts have declined to evaluate the necessity for the social policy upon which these decisions are based. Principles of the following kind are often advanced as reasons for restraint by the judiciary:

- executive decision-makers are accountable to a democratic body
- the primary decision-maker will have evaluated the facts
- the allocation of a kind of decision to a particular decision-maker is the will of Parliament (e.g., the Home Secretary is entrusted by Parliament with immigration control) (Attrill 2003).

Others are sceptical of this view of the executive: 'routine decision-making by civil servants' should not be elevated to a constitutionally protected act just because a minister somewhere up the chain of command was put in post by an elected government (Richard Clayton 2004:40).

It is also commonly said that an executive decision-maker has more expertise in the relevant matter, although through the Human Rights Act, Parliament has made the judiciary the guardian of rights, a matter in which it, as the traditional arbiter of justice, has expertise (see *Huang v SSHD* [2005] EWCA Civ 105 para 55).

However, there is no doubt that in making the judgments involved in human rights cases, judges enter the field of social policy, although they carefully limit the way in which they do so. For instance in *Quila* the Supreme Court, having considered the evidence for raising the age at which settled people can sponsor partners as a means of preventing forced marriage, decided that the interference with the rights of young couples was disproportionate to the disputed impact on forced marriages.

Lord Bingham in *A v SSHD* [2004] UKHL 56 adopted the idea of 'relative institutional competence', rather than suggesting that one branch of government gives way to the other (para 29). Furthermore, the independence of the judiciary is in itself a constitutional safeguard and a 'cardinal feature of the modern democratic state, a cornerstone of the rule of law itself' (*A v SSHD* [2004] UKHL 56 para 42).

Human rights law does not displace the executive's responsibility for immigration control and give it to judges, but brings in a counterweight. This was perhaps most fully illustrated in *Chikwamba v SSHD* [2008] UKHL 40 where the House of Lords held that it was disproportionate and a breach of Article 8 to expect the appellant, who was the wife of a Zimbabwean refugee, and her small child, to return to Zimbabwe, with all the difficulties that that would involve, just for the technical purpose of applying for an entry clearance which she could expect to be granted. This is a clear example of how human rights law introduces an evaluation of the administrative requirements of immigration control, rather than accepting that government policy should prevail over individual circumstances in all cases. This is not to say that *Chikwamba* can be followed in every case where leaving to obtain a visa causes problems for the family (see chapters 9 and 18).

The effort to strike a new balance resulted, in the early years of the Human Rights Act, in various formulations of the idea of 'deference' to the executive (see earlier editions of this book, and the reading list at the end of the chapter). Finally, the House of Lords in *Huang and Kashmiri v SSHD* [2007] UKHL 11 established that such an idea has no place in human rights appeals. Their Lordships said that the Court would weigh in the balance factors such as the Home Secretary's judgement that a particular person presented a threat, or that there was a need to deter others from breaking the law, but that:

> The giving of weight to factors such as these is not, in our opinion, aptly described as deference: it is performance of the ordinary judicial task of weighing up the competing considerations on each side and according appropriate weight to the judgment of a person with responsibility for a given subject matter and access to special sources of knowledge and advice. (para 16)

Refining elements of this judgment process with concepts such as 'due deference, discretionary areas of judgment...and so on' they regarded as 'a tendency...to complicate and mystify what is not, in principle, a hard task to define, however difficult the task is, in practice, to perform' (para 14).

8.4.3.1 *The jurisdiction of appeal bodies in human rights cases*

One of the important issues for tribunals in deciding human rights appeals is whether they have jurisdiction to substitute their judgment for that of the Secretary of State, and re-assess the merits of the issue. The judicial review case of *R (on the application of Mahmood) v SSHD* [2001] 1 WLR 840 was at an early stage adopted by tribunals as an authority in Article 8 appeals, thus importing a pre-Human Rights Act judicial review standard into first-tier human rights appeals. This approach reached its high water mark in *Edore v SSHD* [2003] 3 All ER 1265, the first Court of Appeal case actually on the issue, where the Court said that the Tribunal could not overturn the decision of the primary decision-maker unless it was irrational.

A contrary authority, which had not been followed, was that of one of the first reported Tribunal decisions after the commencement of the Human Rights Act, *Nhundu and Chiwera* 01TH00613, which held that the courts and tribunals were not only able but bound to consider the merits of the case for themselves, in accordance with their duty under Human Rights Act s 6. This view was finally adopted by the House of Lords in *Huang and Kashmiri* [2007] UKHL 11.

Key Case

***Huang and Kashmiri* [2007] UKHL 11**

Mrs Huang was 58 years old. She had been staying with her daughter, son-in-law and their child in the UK. She was estranged from her husband. She applied to stay in the UK so that she could live with her daughter and son-in-law, but she did not come within the requirements of the immigration rules. She appealed on the basis that to compel her return to China would breach her right to respect for family life under Article 8.

Mr Kashmiri came to the UK at the age of 20. His father already had leave to remain as a refugee, together with his wife and younger sons. Mr Kashmiri's own asylum claim failed, and at the age of 20 he was held not to qualify as his father's dependant, so leave was refused. He also appealed on Article 8 grounds.

Both appellants' cases fell outside the immigration rules but both had family reasons for wanting to be in the UK.

The House of Lords, in relation to the question of jurisdiction, held:

> the task of the appellate immigration authority, on an appeal on a Convention ground against a decision of the primary official decision-maker refusing leave to enter or remain in this country, is to decide whether the challenged decision is unlawful as incompatible with a Convention right or compatible and so lawful. It is not a secondary, reviewing, function dependent on establishing that the primary decision-maker misdirected himself or acted irrationally or was guilty of procedural impropriety. The appellate immigration authority must decide for itself whether the impugned decision is lawful and, if not, but only if not, reverse it. (para 11)

Earlier authorities to the contrary are now displaced. The question now is not whether tribunals have jurisdiction to judge the merits of a human rights appeal, but whether and how in practice they exercise it.

8.4.3.2 *Human rights, the immigration rules, and the mistaken doctrine of exceptionality*

The House of Lords in *Huang* also settled two other questions following from interlinked doctrines whose propagation the Court of Appeal, in *AG (Eritrea) v SSHD* [2007] EWCA Civ 801, described as something 'going wrong'.

The first was the proposition referred to earlier that 'the Rules have themselves struck the balance between the public interest and the private right' (para 57). The Court of Appeal in *Huang* suggested that the immigration rules had the democratic authority of having been subject to parliamentary scrutiny, and as such the Tribunal should defer to the provisions in the rules. The House of Lords rejected this view, saying that the immigration rules are 'not the product of active debate in Parliament, where non-nationals seeking leave to enter or remain are not in any event represented'. Furthermore, the statutory right of appeal on human rights grounds which was enacted by Parliament was based on the supposition that 'an applicant may fail to qualify under the Rules and yet may have a valid claim by virtue of Article 8' (para 17). This equation of the immigration rules with human rights standards falls with the House of Lords judgment.

The second point, however, did not lie down so easily. Equating a proper balance of interests with the immigration rules, the Court of Appeal went on to say that cases which can be shown to succeed on the basis of human rights would therefore be exceptional. The Court also based this proposition on dicta of Lord Bingham in *Razgar v SSHD* [2004] UKHL 27:

> Decisions taken pursuant to the lawful operation of immigration control will be proportionate in all save a small minority of exceptional cases, identifiable only on a case by case basis. (para 20)

This Court of Appeal decision in *Huang* created a flood of cases in which litigants and the Tribunal searched for or denied the existence of 'exceptional' features in order to establish or refute a human rights claim. Rapidly there arose 'the test of exceptionality', downgrading human rights protection into a search for the unusual, and this was what was 'going wrong' according to the Court of Appeal in *AG (Eritrea)*, where the Tribunal had overturned a well-reasoned first instance appeal decision by looking for the individual's whole circumstances to be exceptional.

The House of Lords in *Huang and Kashmiri* resolved the question of what Lord Bingham meant in *Razgar*:

> He was there expressing an expectation, shared with the Immigration Appeal Tribunal, that the number of claimants not covered by the Rules and supplementary directions but entitled to succeed under Article 8 would be a very small minority. That is still his expectation. But he was not purporting to lay down a legal test. (para 20)

Exceptionality is a prediction, not a precondition. The House of Lords' judgment in Huang does away with a test of exceptionality, but it is not so clear what meaning can be given to the expectation that not many cases will succeed. The Court of Appeal judgment in *AG (Eritrea)* was given in order to clarify *Huang* in this respect. They said:

> While its practical effect is likely to be that removal is only exceptionally found to be disproportionate, it sets no formal test of exceptionality and raises no hurdles beyond those contained in the article itself. (para 25)

This has been repeated in the Court of Appeal, and in *EB (Kosovo) v SSHD* [2008] UKHL 41 where the House of Lords reiterated their main points in *Huang*, with particular reference to Article 8 which may be summarized as follows:

- the jurisdiction to decide on an Article 8 claim is that of the immigration judge, it is not a reviewing function entailing deference to the Secretary of State
- an Article 8 claim is not required to be exceptional in order to succeed
- family life is a crucial human experience and value
- the imperatives of immigration control should be treated as an important matter to weigh against the right to respect for family life
- the decision as to how to weigh up these matters cannot be reduced to a formula; it is a difficult judgment which must be exercised.

Interpretation of Lord Bingham's comments in *Razgar* generally leaves out of account the origin of his prediction, which was the case of *Kacaj*. *Kacaj*, like *Razgar*, concerned a 'foreign' case in the terms of *Ullah and Do* (see chapter 4), i.e., a case in which the effects of the infringement of the right would be experienced outside the UK. These cases, according to *Razgar* and *Ullah and Do*, involve a higher threshold of risk and of breach in order to succeed. Therefore, it follows that very few will. It was in this context that Lord Bingham expressed his expectation. Subsequent decisions have lost sight of this context, and it must be admitted that Lord Bingham himself did not refer to it in *Huang*. Nevertheless, it remains the case that it is mistaken to seek for exceptionality in a human rights appeal.

Another point about the scope of *Huang* arose in *RG (Automatic deport Section 33(2)(a) exception) Nepal* [2010] UKUT 273 (IAC) where the Tribunal said that the observations in *Huang* were directed to 'cases where despite failure to comply with the immigration rules admission may be required by Article 8'. In a deportation case of a lawful resident it was obvious that the question was not whether the case was 'exceptional'. Whether this distinction will be pursued, in a climate in which the ECtHR is reducing the gap between removal and entry cases, remains to be seen.

Finally, where the right of appeal can only be exercised on a point of law – which is the case for appeals to the higher courts – the exercise of determining proportionality when adjudicating on a qualified right is not in itself a question of law. The appeal cannot succeed only on the basis that the higher court might have decided the case differently. Sedley LJ remarked on an apparent resulting anomaly:

> The reason why the Court of Human Rights, in cases such as *Uner* and *Maslov* 1638/03 [2007] ECHR 224 (22 March 2007), makes its own appraisal of proportionality is that it possesses the unique status of a court both of first instance and of last resort. It may be anomalous that, despite the underlying legislative policy of patriating the Convention rights, the superior courts of the United Kingdom lack the same power of reappraising merits as the Strasbourg court, but without doubt they do lack it. (*PE (Peru) v SSHD* [2011] EWCA Civ 274 para 28)

8.4.4 Not in accordance with the law

The ground that the decision is not in accordance with the law has played an important part in the development of immigration appeals. Where the decision is said not to comply with statute or common law, this ground may be used. It may also be a ground for appeal where a decision is not in accordance with a policy or concession. It may be recalled (from chapter 1) that a basis for entry may be contained in policies and concessions outside the immigration rules, and that failure to apply a published policy can result in the decision being quashed in judicial review proceedings (*R v SSHD ex p Amankwah* [1994] Imm AR 240). However, judicial review as a remedy is limited in that it only compels the decision-maker to take the decision again properly. It is expensive, and subject to strict time limits and the hurdle of the permission stage. In the case of *Abdi v SSHD* [1996] Imm AR 148, the Court of Appeal decided that a failure to take into account a published policy was contrary to established principles of administrative law, and therefore not 'in accordance with the law' as required by Immigration Act 1971 s 19, the relevant section then in force. The decision would therefore be subject to appeal. This was a major breakthrough for immigration appeals as it made failure to implement a policy appealable. This ground of appeal is retained in the 2002 Act, but its effect is limited by the exclusive prescription of appealable decisions in s 82. Where a concession (policy) directly affects an appealable decision, such as leave to enter, then it is appealable under s 84(1)(e). For example, in *SSHD v HH (Iraq)* [2009] EWCA Civ 727, a decision had been taken to deport an Iraqi national in breach of a policy which said: 'Enforcement action should not be taken against nationals who originate from countries which are currently active war zones.' The Court of Appeal held that this decision was not in accordance with the law.

Where the concession does not directly affect an appealable decision, for instance, a procedural waiver concerning the application process as applied to Kosovan families in 2000, then there is no appeal, only judicial review. Macdonald puts it that there is still room for argument that a decision is not in accordance with the law where 'the purpose of the stay is recognized by the rules, although waiver of part of the rule's requirement, or an extension of its application, is sought in accordance with Home Office policy' (2008:1196). This is apparent in the cases discussed later challenging the operation of UKBA's asylum decision-making process.

It is still not always clear what is not in accordance with a policy. The wording of many of the IDIs is loose, and certainly cannot be construed like a statute. Failure to apply a policy is the basis of challenge, and this does not always mean that the appellant will gain the benefit of it as the policy itself may suggest otherwise. The Court itself may construe a policy, as it did in *R (on the application of K) v SSHD* [2010] EWHC 3102 (Admin). The policy governed cases in which a person missed a grant of ILR for which they would have been eligible if their case had been promptly dealt with. The judge held that it was not restricted to people who were still in the UK. He arrived at this conclusion from the part of the wording of the policy which had not been publicly disclosed but was nevertheless purportedly relied on. It is unusual for a policy to have reach outside the UK, but the purpose of this policy was protective, and the protective purpose would be lost if people could be removed in breach of it and then have no remedy. (See *R (on the application of S) v SSHD* [2007] EWCA Civ 546 at 8.5.4.)

Where a policy conflicts with a rule of general law, it is not binding. The Court of Appeal in *Ishtiaq v SSHD* [2007] EWCA Civ 86 held that they could not be bound by the IDI to refuse to accept evidence of domestic violence that was not in a list of kinds of evidence which purported to be exclusive. Where policy in the published instructions conflicts with the immigration rules the situation is complicated. Immigration Act 1971 Sch 2 para 1(3) provides that immigration officers must act in accordance with the law and the rules, and instructions given to them by the Secretary of State, provided these are not inconsistent with the rules. However, the purpose of instructions is often to supplement or supersede the rules. This purpose could not be achieved if officers refused to obey instructions where they were inconsistent with the rules. The rules on the other hand have a superior authority in law to policy. In *ZH (Bangladesh) v SSHD* [2009] EWCA Civ 8, the Court of Appeal said that the IDIs did not have the force of law. The instructions sat within the four corners of the rule. They were not an aid to the construction of the immigration rules.

More recent litigation has been concerned with the relationship between the immigration rules and published guidance which form the points-based system of entry for work and study. Here, much of the voluminous 'policy guidance' takes the form of instructions to applicants on a wide range of matters from the kind of occupation that might qualify them for entry to the form that must be filled in. Determining the true substance of these provisions and accordingly the effect they should have has generated a number of challenges following *Pankina*. The case law is discussed in chapter 10.

As the statutory power to give leave to enter is not made subject to the immigration rules, there is a residual power based on s 4 to make decisions which are more favourable towards the applicant than the rules permit. As Vincenzi (1992) discusses, this does not do away with the problem of Sch 2 para 1(3). It results in a complete contradiction.

Where the proper result on applying the policy is ascertainable from the facts before the Court, an appeal court itself may apply the Secretary of State's policy and decide the issue (*AB (Jamaica) v SSHD* [2007] EWCA Civ 1302). Where this is not possible, the court or tribunal may send the case back to the Secretary of State to take the decision in accordance with the policy (see, further, Glossop 2007).

An immigration decision can be challenged as not in accordance with the law if the decision is taken in breach of public law principles, e.g., by failing to take into account a relevant consideration, or, as in *AA and others v SSHD* [2008] UKAIT 00003, that there was a breach of a legitimate expectation.

The Court of Appeal addressed a complex issue of this kind in *Sapkota v SSHD* [2011] EWCA Civ 132. A series of cases had addressed the situation in which an individual is refused leave to remain, but then not served with removal directions. In *TE (Eritrea) v SSHD* [2009] EWCA Civ 174 the Court of Appeal held that this could be unfair, and was so in that case. The problem for the individual is that if they lose an appeal against the refusal of leave to remain, they no longer have leave to be in the UK, cannot work or claim benefits, but also they do not have a forum in which they can argue why they should not be removed from the UK under the immigration rules relating to removal (para 395C – see chapter 17). They are thus without means to continue their usual life but also without a forum to argue their case in full, although in *JM (Liberia)* [2006] EWCA Civ 1402 Laws LJ held that the tribunal judge should have heard Article 8 arguments to be heard when leave was refused.

In *Sapkota,* the Court of Appeal held that a refusal of leave to remain, which was not followed or accompanied by a decision to remove, was not in accordance with the law because it was not in accordance with the policy of all grounds being raised and heard together and of avoiding the same appellant bringing numerous appeals. This policy is enshrined in statute by the 'one-stop' notice procedure in s 120 Nationality Immigration and Asylum Act 2002 and in the provision of s 47 Immigration and Asylum Act 2006, allowing removal directions to be served while an appeal is pending. Though the judgment is dense and complex, it is interesting for its reliance on this policy as demonstrated in statute as a basis for finding the decisions to refuse leave to remain to be not in accordance with the law. The basis of the decision is not statutory construction, but public law principle.

The government's response to *Sapkota* has embraced that public law point with a vengeance. It has deleted para 395 of the immigration rules, thus deleting the requirement for the personal and compassionate factors listed there to be taken into account in making a removal decision (HC 1733 effective from 13 February 2012). Accordingly, all appeals can be heard together.

8.4.5 Exercise of discretion

The power to allow an appeal if the Tribunal considers that a discretion should have been exercised differently appears to be a wide power, but its scope is diminishing as the number of discretions in the rules diminishes. Where there has been an exercise of discretion, the Tribunal can decide that it should have been exercised differently and substitute its own decision. The power to deport has been a key example of this but, as discussed in chapter 16, the discretion in that power is vanishing.

The appeal body's power is also limited by Nationality, Immigration and Asylum Act 2002 s 86(6), which replicates earlier similar provisions. The subsection says that a refusal to depart from the rules is not to be regarded as an exercise of discretion. This means that where, for instance, leave has been refused in accordance with the rules, an applicant cannot appeal on the grounds that they asked for discretion to be exercised outside the rules but were refused. The only appeal in this situation would be that the decision was not in accordance with the law if a relevant policy had not been applied.

8.5 Judicial review

Because appeal rights in immigration and asylum matters have been so frequently curtailed, and their scope limited, judicial review has been and continues to be a very important recourse. Immigration decisions are subject to judicial review in accordance with usual public law principles, including since 2 October 2000 on the basis that they infringe Convention rights. In accordance with the normal rules of judicial review, any relevant appeal rights must first be exhausted (e.g., *Cinnamond v British Airports Authority* [1980] 2 All ER 368).

A number of general principles of administrative law have been established in immigration cases. Examples include: the Court's power to examine the factual basis of a decision-maker's exercise of power where this is necessary to see that the decision-maker has jurisdiction (*Khawaja v Secretary of State for the Home Department* [1983] AC 74 concerning illegal entry); the publication of an express promise or undertaking will lead to a legitimate expectation of its being honoured (*Attorney General for Hong Kong v Ng Yuen Shiu* [1983] 2 AC 629); the right to reasons for a decision (*R v Secretary of State for the Home Department ex p Fayed* [1998] 1 All ER 228, CA, a challenge to refusal of British nationality); and the obligation to hear both sides of a case which affects fundamental rights, even where strict rules of natural justice do not apply (*R v Secretary of State for the Home Department ex p Moon* (1996) 8 Admin LR 477, concerning the issue of entry clearance).

Often, judicial review is the only way to restrain an impending removal if all appeal rights have been exhausted, or would be of no avail once the person is removed. Ascertaining the correct proceedings is not a straightforward matter, and for fuller discussion reference should be made to practitioner works on this issue. Where there is a right of appeal against removal, except where human rights are in issue, the right of appeal must be exercised in preference to judicial review, even if this can only be exercised from abroad. In *SSHD v R (on the application of Lim and another)* [2007] EWCA Civ 773, Mr Lim, a work-permit holder, was detained with removal directions set for the following day for the minor immigration infraction of being thought to be working at a different restaurant from the one for which he had permission, though in the same town and owned by the same employer. The Court of Appeal, while judging detention and removal a 'colossal overreaction', found that the appeal mechanism was the correct one, except in cases where the facts showed there was no jurisdiction to remove. Precedent facts involved in a decision to remove could be the subject of judicial review. Such facts would include the identity of the person being removed and whether they were a British citizen. In relation to other factual issues on which the decision to remove was based, the Court should 'calibrate the use of judicial review...to the nature of the issue or issues'. Where the remedy of an appeal existed, it should be used, unless the circumstances were exceptional.

An important aspect of the changes brought by the Tribunals Courts and Enforcement Act is the judicial review jurisdiction conferred on the Upper Tribunal. Initially this excluded any decisions made under the Immigration or Nationality Acts. Disputes about age assessment (see chapter 15) do not as such involve immigration decisions, and in *R(FZ) v LB Croydon* [2011] EWCA Civ 59, the Court pointed out the suitability for transfer of age disputes:

> Some of them may be orthodox judicial review grounds. But the core challenge is likely in most cases to be a challenge to the age which the local authority assessed the claimant to be. Thus most of these cases are now likely to require the court to receive evidence to make its factual determination. (para 6)...Transfer to the Upper Tribunal is appropriate because the judges there have experience of assessing the ages of children from abroad in the context of disputed asylum claims. (para 31)

As mentioned at 8.2, s 53 of the Borders, Citizenship and Immigration Act 2009 has lifted the restriction on transferring immigration cases to the Upper Tribunal where these are challenges to the refusal to treat further representations as fresh claims. Some of these transfers will take place where a pending removal is challenged by the submission of further representations.

Most judicial reviews concern the application of law or policy. Occasionally, its actual making is subject to challenge. Amit Kapadia, the executive director of HSMP Forum, explained the advantages of judicial review as a way to challenge changes to the HSMP programme itself: 'if individuals had to wait for their refusals, only then to appeal in tribunals, it would be a lengthy process and the hardships involved would break the individuals' (p. 191). In *R (on the application of BAPIO Action Ltd) v SSHD and Department of Health* [2008] UKHL 27, the facts of which are given in chapter 10, BAPIO challenged guidance issued by the Department of Health to NHS employers that international medical graduates with limited leave should only be offered a vacant training post if the resident labour market criterion was satisfied. This was in effect an immigration restriction, but discussions between the DoH and the Home Office to achieve the restriction had broken down, as the Home Office considered that a fundamental change in the immigration rules would be required (para 60). So the Department of Health went ahead anyway. The guidance was found unlawful for reasons given at 8.5.3.

In principle, all the usual grounds of judicial review apply, but there are some which have particular relevance.

8.5.1 Natural justice or fairness

Administrative law recognizes a distinction between a judicial function and an administrative function. A judicial function is one which decides between competing arguments on the basis of evidence, and determines an outcome which will be decisive of rights or entitlements (e.g., *Ridge v Baldwin* [1964] AC 40), for example, imposing a criminal sentence or granting compensation. An administrative function is to process an application or otherwise follow a procedure according to the rules and principles governing that action. This may include the use of discretion where the rules permit. So, for instance, issuing a driving licence is an administrative matter. While administrative decisions must be made fairly and in accordance with relevant procedures, a judicial decision must be made in accordance with the principles of natural justice, giving both sides a fair hearing and acting without bias. Sometimes fairness and natural justice are equated, for instance in *Lloyd v McMahon* [1987] AC 625.

There is not always a clear distinction between administrative and judicial decisions, and immigration decisions may have qualities of each. In *Re HK* [1967] QB 617, Lord Parker CJ held that in making inquiries to ascertain the age of a child seeking to enter the UK the immigration officer should act fairly, 'only to that limited extent do the so-called rules of natural justice apply, which in a case such as this is merely a duty to act fairly'. The role of immigration officers in deciding applications was considered in *R v SSHD ex p Mughal* [1973] 3 All ER 796 not to be a judicial but an administrative one. The same goes for entry clearance officers and Home Office officials. Strictly, this means they are not bound by the rules of natural justice, but they are bound to act fairly. In *R v SSHD ex p Moon, The Times*, 8 December 1995, the Divisional Court held that in dealing with an application for entry clearance the entry clearance officer should give the applicant an opportunity to deal with objections to their application. As immigration decision-making becomes more tightly circumscribed by rules and guidance, legal challenges to the adequacy of these processes to meet the standards of fairness become more complex and difficult to make, particularly in the points-based system.

In asylum and human rights cases, the matters at stake are of such importance that only the highest levels of fairness are sufficient. The Court of Appeal in *R v SSHD ex p Thirukumar* [1989] Imm AR 270 held that this includes providing a copy to the applicant of their answers at previous interviews. The Court of Appeal in *R (on the application of Dirshe) v SSHD* [2005] EWCA Civ 421 held that, where the applicant had no public funding either for a representative or for their own interpreter, the overall fairness of the process required that the applicant be able to tape record the asylum interview, although there is not necessarily a principle of equality of arms, as there would be between private litigants.

According to *Maaouia v France*, Article 6 ECHR, the right to a fair hearing, does not apply in immigration matters (see chapter 4). Where the right to respect for private or family life is at stake, Article 8 imposes procedural obligations (*IR (Sri Lanka) & others v SSHD* [2011] EWCA Civ 704), but only to the extent that the person affected must have access to adversarial proceedings.

However, as Lord Steyn said in *R v SSHD ex p Anufrijeva*, 'the Convention is not an exhaustive statement of fundamental rights under our system of law' (para 27) and fundamental principles may still be found and applied. In *Anufrijeva*, the appellant's asylum claim had been turned down but she was not informed. Shortly after that, the welfare benefits she had received as an asylum seeker (90 per cent of the usual income support rate) were stopped as her asylum claim was no longer current, but she was not given a reason. She argued that the asylum decision could not be treated as effective because she had not been notified. Her case was not isolated as this practice was part of Home Office policy at the time. Lord Steyn said:

> The arguments for the Home Secretary ignore fundamental principles of our law. Notice of a decision is required before it can have the character of a determination with legal effect because the individual concerned must be in a position to challenge the decision in the courts if he or she wishes to do so. This is not a technical rule. It is simply an application of the right of access to justice. That is a fundamental and constitutional principle of our legal system. (para 26)

He referred to the view that an uncommunicated administrative decision could bind an individual as 'an astonishingly unjust proposition' (para 30). Where the individual is excluded not from an administrative but a judicial process, as we saw in *FP (Iran)*, there may be a breach of natural justice.

The Court of Appeal applied principles of natural justice in reaching the conclusion in *AK (Iran) v SSHD* [2008] EWCA Civ 941 that when an appellant's representative withdrew the day before the hearing, the immigration judge should have adjourned the hearing to give him a fair chance to secure representation. He was an Iranian national, and a transsexual, and was afraid that he would be perceived as homosexual in Iran and persecuted as such. The appellant had been found credible, but two previous immigration judges had made opposite assessments of the objective evidence. The importance of legal representation was clear. Sedley LJ made the point that a review based on natural justice was not confined to questions of rationality, but must consider what was 'right', in the light of what fairness required.

In R (on application of *AM (Cameroon)) v AIT and SSHD (interested party)* [2008] EWCA Civ 100, allegations concerning the behaviour of the immigration judge in connection with the hearing of the asylum claimant's appeal included that he had refused to allow oral evidence to be admitted by telephonic link from a barrister whom the claimant said had represented her in getting her out of detention. The fact of her detention was doubted by the Home Office and in issue in the asylum claim. The judge also refused an adjournment to allow the claimant's medical condition to stabilize and described as 'mere supposition' a medical report stating that AM's blood pressure was critically high. After AM collapsed, the judge granted an adjournment to a date when her representative was not available, refusing a longer adjournment as requested by her doctor. On the renewed date, the hearing proceeded without the participation of either the appellant or her representative, although the claimant's credibility was a live issue in the case.

The Court of Appeal held that the appellant's allegations raised the question of whether the immigration judge should have continued to hear the case, and there needed to be a process that could wipe that hearing and decision from the slate. A challenge based on natural justice was able to do this, where an appeal was not. This was a rare situation where a challenge to an interlocutory decision was appropriately brought by way of judicial review because these issues of natural justice could only be decided in that forum. Such an application and outcome would still be possible in relation to the new Upper Tribunal following the Supreme Court's dicta in *Cart*.

In conclusion, even though full rules of natural justice entailing equality of arms may not be applicable in immigration and asylum cases, a high degree of fairness and openness is required, consistent with the importance of the matters at stake and fundamental principles of access to justice and the rule of law.

8.5.2 Unfairness amounting to an abuse of power

This head of judicial review has developed as a response to serious flaws in the decision process for asylum claims.

Key Case

***R (on the application of Rashid) v SSHD* [2005] EWCA Civ 744**

Mr Rashid was an Iraqi Kurd who sought asylum in the UK in December 2001. At that time there was a Home Office policy that people who had a well-founded fear in other parts of Iraq would not be forcibly returned on the basis they could find safety in the Kurdish Autonomous Zone (KAZ). The policy was based on the stance of the Kurdish authorities who, because of a lack of infrastructure and resources after the 1991 Gulf War, were not able to admit people who had been living in other parts of Iraq. The policy was not applied to Mr Rashid and his asylum claim was refused within a week on the basis he could relocate in the KAZ.

Six months later, in correspondence, the Home Office reiterated the refusal. A year later, on appeal to the adjudicator, relocation to the KAZ was fully argued by the Home Office Presenting Officer. The policy was still in force. The Home Office resisted an application for leave to appeal, then unsuccessfully opposed an application for permission for judicial review on the same point. Until late February 2003, the argument was maintained. There were two other applicants in a situation legally identical to Mr Rashid, M and A. By letter of 6 March 2003, A's legal representatives were told that the Secretary of State was not, 'as a matter of policy...relying on the availability of internal relocation' to the KAZ and that A would be granted refugee status. On 12 March 2003, Mr Rashid's solicitors wrote to the Treasury solicitors asking that he too be granted refugee status, as the Home Office had already accepted that his case was on the same point. On 21 March 2003, it was announced that, because of the military action in Iraq, decision-making on Iraqi nationals had been suspended. The suspension lasted until June 2003. The Home Office agreed in March to reconsider Mr Rashid's case, but did not do so until January 2004, by which time, they said, he could return, and he was refused refugee status.

The judicial review on Mr Rashid's behalf successfully claimed that he had a legitimate expectation that the policy would be applied to him, and that the repeated failure to do so was 'conspicuous unfairness amounting to an abuse of power'. In earlier cases, this has been described as something 'illogical' or 'immoral' (*R v Inland Revenue Commissioners, ex parte Unilever plc* [1996] STC 681), or, as counsel for Mr Rashid said, something which 'leaps off the page'. Other factors which induced the Court to find in his favour were the lack of consistency with M and A, 'the persistence of the conduct, and lack of explanation for it' (para 36), particularly in a country which at the time was in the focus of the Secretary of State's attention, Iraq being a source of the one of the highest numbers of refugees.

A number of attempts to follow Rashid have failed in cases where delay in making a decision has meant that a different policy has been applied to the applicant than would have been if the decision had been made more promptly. In Rashid, there was no initial delay in making a decision, but rather a number of points over a 16-month period in which decisions and representations were made about his case, but always on the wrong basis. There was then a delay in applying the policy to him once it was acknowledged that it should be (March 2003 to January 2004), but this was only another in a catalogue not of periods of inaction, as is often the case, but of actual errors.

Rashid was followed successfully, if success is an appropriate word, where once again, three Iraqi Kurds had been refused asylum on the basis they could relocate in the KAZ, in ignorance of the same policy (*A, H and AH v SSHD* [2006] EWHC 526 (Admin)). As in *Rashid*, only a finding of extreme unfairness could warrant going against the *Ravichandran* principle, which entails that asylum decisions are to be made on the basis of the situation as it stands at the time of the hearing. Application of that principle would mean that if it is safe at the time of the hearing the claimants would be expected to return.

In 2006, the Home Office issued a policy bulletin to provide guidance to decision-makers on the implications of the judgments in *Rashid* and *R (A) (H) and (AH)*. It said that:

> we should not seek to enforce the removal of failed asylum seekers whose cases have the potential to fall within the scope of the *Rashid* judgment and/or the cases of *R (A): (H) and (AH)*, pending consideration of their cases.

An Annex to the Iraq policy bulletin set out factual requirements for inclusion within it, namely that the application was decided between April 1991 and 20 February 2003, that the applicant was accepted as being from Government-controlled Iraq (GCI), that s/he was found to have no well-founded fear of persecution for a Convention reason, and had not been granted four years' ELR. In *R (on the application of AM & SS) v SSHD* [2009] EWCA Civ 833, the claimants fell within the factual situation described in the Annex, except that their origin in GCI had originally been disputed, and only found as fact on appeal. The Court held that the purpose of the policy bulletin was to make indefinite leave to remain (ILR) available for those who fell potentially within the scope of *Rashid* or *AH*, in relation to whom there had been the same type of conspicuous unfairness and maladministration. In the case of *AM and SS*, there had not been a wrongful failure to apply the policy, because the Home Secretary had not accepted that the claimants came from GCI. The later finding that they had did not require the policy to be applied.

Rashid is not a remedy for delay, or even for gross administrative errors. In *R (on the application of S, H & Q) v SSHD* [2009] EWCA Civ 142, the Home Office had delayed in dealing with three asylum claims and had made significant administrative errors. For example, S's Statement of Evidence (SEF) was not linked to his file. His claim was refused on the basis that he had not sent the SEF but he was not notified of that. In 2002, his solicitors were informed both that his claim had been refused because of a failure to return the SEF, and that the claim was being considered. In 2005, S applied for indefinite leave on the basis that he should have been granted exceptional leave based on a policy in existence at the time of the original non-compliance refusal, in which case he would now have qualified for ILR. The Court did not accept these arguments. They held that the facts in *Rashid* were extreme. It would be rare that even a catalogue of errors such as these would found an expectation of a grant of indefinite leave. The Home Office's failure to implement its policies correctly did not mean that an application now for ILR should be granted.

Individuals affected by delays and mistakes in the Home Office continue to seek ways to obtain redress, and there has been an increase in actions claiming damages for the effects of such failings. In *R (on the application of MK) (Iran) v SSHD* [2010] EWCA Civ 115 the claimant had arrived in the UK as a minor, via Greece. There was an attempt to remove him to Greece pursuant to the Dublin Regulations (see chapter 12) which was abandoned when it was accepted that he was a minor, in April 2005. No asylum interview was conducted until April 2008. He failed in his action for damages. The Court accepted that the delay was unreasonable in domestic law, but this, as a public law determination, did not give rise to an action for damages. The Court held that neither EU nor ECHR law remedied that deficit (see chapter 4). The Court had sympathy with the argument that the Qualification Directive has the capacity to change the established principle that asylum claims do not engage the right to a fair hearing under Article 6 ECHR, but considered that this was too great a step for the domestic courts to take.

The case of *R (on the application of S and others) v SSHD* [2006] EWCA Civ 1157 disclosed another form of abuse of power. It was discussed in chapter 2 as an example of the misrepresentation in the media which sometimes distorts public debate on immigration and asylum cases.

Key Case

***R (on the application of S and others) v SSHD* [2006] EWCA Civ 1157**

The case was the application for judicial review by a group of people from Afghanistan who in February 2000 hijacked an aeroplane in order to enter the UK. They were convicted of criminal offences. Then their convictions were set aside by the Court of Appeal because the jury had not been directed properly on the issue of duress, but by this time they had served their prison sentences.

They opposed the Taleban government, and belonged to a group, four of whom had been detained. Not long after this, the dead body of one had been returned bearing marks of torture. They had devised the plan to hijack an aircraft as a means of escape. Their asylum claim was turned down. In an unusual step, a panel of adjudicators was convened to hear their appeal. The panel generally believed their accounts, but held that they were debarred from refugee status because of their action in hijacking the aircraft. There were mitigating circumstances certainly, but there would also have been alternatives. However, they did face a real risk of treatment contrary to Article 3 if they returned, so they succeeded on human rights grounds. Under the policy then in force they should have been granted six months' discretionary leave, which would be reviewed and was renewable. Instead, they were kept on temporary admission with the consequence that they could not work or claim benefits. This situation went on for a year, after which the Secretary of State inserted into the policy a caveat that leave would not be granted when 'Ministers decide, in view of all the circumstances of the case, that it is inappropriate to grant any leave and instead place or keep the person on temporary admission.'

After a further period of time and sustained pressure by the claimants' solicitors the Secretary of State wrote to say that he had decided not to grant the claimants' discretionary leave but to keep them on temporary admission.

This inserted clause may readily be recognized as a claim of arbitrary power. There is a policy, but the Minister decides when it will and will not apply. In the High Court, Sullivan J said:

> the policy does not give any, or any effective, protection against arbitrary interference by Ministers... It is a paradigm of an unfettered administrative discretion to depart from a published policy whenever the Minister thinks it appropriate to do so. It therefore leaves them 'vulnerable to interference by [ministers] acting on any personal whim, caprice, malice, predilection, or purpose other than that for which the power was conferred.' (para 113, referring to Lord Bingham in *R (Gillan) v Commissioner of Police for the Metropolis* [2006] 2 WLR 537)

Sullivan J found the failure to grant discretionary leave and the insertion into the policy unlawful and the Court of Appeal agreed. It was not open to the Secretary of State to extend those who could be subject to temporary admission without the sanction of Parliament. Temporary admission is allowed by statute only where a person would otherwise be detained. This was not the case here.

Once the appeal body had decided that the human rights claim succeeded, there should have been no significant delay in the grant of discretionary leave. There was a clear policy which applied without question in the situation. The Secretary of State is of course entitled to change his policy. The mistake here was:

- to change it as a substitute for implementing it;
- to claim untrammelled power by the change; and
- to claim a new power to grant a status awarded by statute without consulting Parliament.

The Secretary of State dealt with defeat by legislation. In the Criminal Justice and Immigration Act 2008 ss 130–137 there is a power to take away the right to any kind of leave for someone in the position of these appellants, and keep them on temporary admission with residence conditions and electronic tagging.

8.5.3 Legitimate expectation

Policy is designed to provide a degree of predictability and transparency in the exercise of executive power, and consistent treatment between comparable individuals. The public law doctrine of legitimate expectation may be invoked where an applicant is deprived of the benefit of a policy which should have been applied to them. This is a dynamic and evolving area of law, but it is settled that, in cases where the policy applies specifically to the individual and they have relied upon it to their detriment, there can be substantive as well as procedural expectation (*R v North and East Devon HA ex p Coughlan* [2001] QB 213, *Nadarajah and Abdi v SSHD* [2005] EWCA Civ 1363). If an individual comes within the terms of a policy, they can expect to be treated in accordance with it (e.g., *R v SSHD ex p Khan* [1985] 1 All ER 40), though as we have seen, when no proper decision is made through maladministration, this will not necessarily found a legitimate expectation (*S, H & Q*). In another case of delay, *Obienna v SSHD* [2008] EWHC (Admin) 1476, concerning an application for indefinite leave on the basis of long residence, the statement of an 'aim' to deal with applications within three weeks and more complex cases 'normally' within 13 weeks did not amount to a representation which would found a legitimate expectation.

Nevertheless, if there is *no* policy, and thus no way of ensuring fairness and consistency, this may be unlawful. In *Obienna* the Court did comment that at an earlier stage, when there had been no system to deal with the backlog of cases, this was unlawful. From May 2007 until December 2007, the system was conspicuously unfair because all resources were devoted to new intake and expedited cases. Since December 2007, there had been a system for dealing with the backlog in chronological order. Provided that was sufficiently resourced so as to avoid excessive delays, this was likely to be lawful. The failure to acknowledge letters which asked relevant questions about matters of importance to the writer was a serious failure in public administration, giving cause to question whether the policy was being applied fairly and consistently.

As discussed at 8.5.2, delay in dealing with an application so that the claimant misses the benefit of a policy (*S, H & Q*) does not amount to conspicuous unfairness nor even breach of legitimate expectation. A complementary argument would be that the policy should not be changed to the applicant's detriment.

This was dealt with directly in *R (on the application of Rechachi, Kalobo, Fodil, Yusuf)* [2006] EWHC 3513 (Admin). In 2005, the Home Office changed its practice of giving recognized refugees indefinite leave to remain, and replaced it with a routine grant of five years' leave. Mr Rechachi claimed asylum in 2002, submitted medical evidence in 2003, and his claim was finally refused in April 2005. His appeal was heard in May 2005, decided in June, and the decision promulgated in July. The policy change took effect on 30 August 2005. On 20 December 2005, after much chasing by his solicitors, he received five years' leave to remain.

The High Court held that:

- There can be no challenge to the Secretary of State's right in principle to change his policy.
- Refugee status is recognized, not granted.
- Five years' leave is an adequate discharge of the obligation under the Refugee Convention.
- The Secretary of State in changing his policy specifically decided that the five-year period would apply to leave granted as a consequence of an appeal which

succeeded before 30 August 2005. This was to avoid inconsistency and for administrative convenience (*Rechachi* para 44). The Secretary of State was entitled to make policy of this kind and on this basis. The application of the policy to these claimants was intentional and not an oversight.

These conclusions only left open the question of whether the delay in each case was unreasonable. The Court held it was not, though only just in the case of Mr Rechachi. Similar issues arose under the Highly Skilled Migrants' Programme, but with a different result, because of the terms of the scheme.

In *R (on the application of HSMP Forum Ltd) v SSHD* [2008] EWHC 664 (Admin), the Court found that the HSMP was a single integrated programme, and migrants on the HSMP had a legitimate expectation that once they had gained leave to enter, which was initially for a year, the terms of the scheme would remain as they had been when they gained leave. It was, accordingly, an unlawful breach of that expectation to change the terms for granting the next stage of leave.

In the *BAPIO* case, Lords Mance and Rogers thought that the guidance issued by the Department of Health breached a legitimate expectation held by migrants on the HSMP scheme that they would not be prohibited by domestic rules from taking work – a substantive legitimate expectation. Lords Bingham and Carswell found the guidance unlawful on the different ground that the Department of Health had no power to, in effect, alter the immigration rules.

Rechachi deals with a deliberate change of policy which still discharged the obligation to which it was addressed. *Rashid* and cases following dealt with decisions which ignored policy. A further basis for a legitimate expectation, perhaps more similar to S, was demonstrated in *R (on the application of Tozlukaya) v SSHD* [2006] EWCA Civ 379. The family came within the scope of the policy that where children had spent seven years in the UK there was a presumption that the family would not normally be removed (DP5/96/99). The Secretary of State denied the family the benefit of the policy on the basis that each decision must be taken on its own merits, a basis for decision-making which denied any substance to the policy at all. Evidence for the Home Office was that caseworkers did not have access to the statement in Parliament, or an approved summary of the policy. The Court of Appeal held that 'all this is contrary to the basic principles of good administration' (para 89). There was a legitimate expectation that the policy would be applied.

Knowledge of relevant policies was an issue in *Rashid* not only for caseworkers but also for Mr Rashid. It was argued that he could not have a legitimate expectation that the policy applied if he did not know about it. However, his legitimate expectation is that decisions will be taken in accordance with relevant polices, i.e., according to law. The Court of Appeal built on earlier principles (e.g., in *R v SSHD ex p Ahmed and Patel* [1998] INLR 570) by holding that the legitimate expectation applied even though he was not aware of the policy:

> Whether the claimant knows of the policy is not in the present context relevant. It would be grossly unfair if the court's ability to intervene depended at all upon whether the particular claimant had or had not heard of a policy, especially one unknown to relevant Home Office officials. (para 25)

However, in *SSHD v Rahman* [2011] EWCA Civ 814 the Court of Appeal held that the appellant could not rely on this principle to found an expectation that the policy DP5/96/99 concerning families with children (see earlier) should not be withdrawn. The appellants applied for leave to remain after the policy had been withdrawn, although they had completed the period of seven years' residence before the policy was withdrawn. The Court of Appeal rejected the arguments that there was a duty to consult on the withdrawal of the policy, that the change should have been laid before Parliament, and that the appellants had a legitimate expectation of its being applied to them. The Court held that the appellants could not have a legitimate expectation if they did not know of the policy. Furthermore, it was a policy to deal with people whose stay was unlawful, and as such they could have no legitimate expectation; the Secretary of State was entitled to change her policy 'whenever she considered it in the public interest to do so' (para 43). It may be that the family's lack of knowledge of the policy would not have been treated as so significant, in accordance with previous authority, if the case had concerned a failure to apply an extant policy to them, rather than a challenge to its withdrawal.

8.5.4 Fettering discretion

There is a complex relationship in public law between policy and discretion. Policy is not binding like statute; it is a guide to the exercise of discretion. To protect against arbitrariness, the person who comes within it may expect the benefit of it, but if a decision has been properly considered and the policy applied, the individual may still be excluded from benefiting by the terms of the policy itself. Another relevant principle is that discretion is to be exercised, and when a decision-maker fails to do this, there may be an unlawful fetter.

The claimant in *SSHD v R (on the application of S)* [2007] EWCA Civ 546 alleged a conspicuous unfairness, amounting to abuse of power, following *Rashid*, but the Court saw it differently.

Key Case

***SSHD v R (on the application of S)* [2007] EWCA Civ 546**

The claimant had entered the UK as an asylum seeker from Afghanistan in 1999 at the same time as his cousin. The cousin's application was dealt with, but R's was not. If R's application had been dealt with during the first couple of years of his stay he would have received the benefit of a policy which would have entailed his being granted ILR. The first substantive response from the Home Office to R came in 2002 and informed him that applications made prior to 2001 had been put on hold. The reason for this, not given to him at the time, was the government's desire to meet targets for dealing with later applications, as set out in a Public Service Agreement.

The Court of Appeal said: 'All other considerations, including fairness and consistency in the treatment of individual applicants, were ignored in order to meet the target' (para 19). The claimant and those in this position were 'sacrificed so that it could be said that the government was meeting a target' (para 18, the CA adopting the 'suspicion' of the Court below).

Unlike Rashid, this was not a decision made in ignorance of a policy that should have been applied. It was rather a failure or even refusal to make decisions, which Carnwath LJ identified as a 'textbook case' of fettering discretion, contrary to an established principle of public law (para 50). The exercise of discretion requires that individual cases are treated individually, and in accordance with any relevant policy. Mr S, who was granted indefinite leave to remain after this successful claim, attempted to sue for damages. He sued in the tort of misfeasance in public office, which required 'evidence from which it can properly be inferred that those responsible for the policy knew that they had no power to introduce it, and were acting in bad faith in as much as they did not have an honest belief that they were acting lawfully' (*FS v SSHD* [2011] EWHC 1858 (QB) para 41). The Court found that there was no such evidence and S's claim for damages failed.

The need to deal with the backlog of asylum cases that resulted in part from the policy to clear more recent cases in accordance with the PSA targets was an element, in the 2006 review (see chapter 2), in establishing the Case Resolution Directorate for so-called 'legacy' cases. Once a system of priority had been established within that system, delays in making individual decisions are not unlawful providing the policy is properly applied. So in *HG, AK, AM, MN, IR, HW v SSHD* [2008] EWHC 2685 (Admin), the claimants, who had been in the same position as S, could not claim any further priority in the legacy system to move their cases further up the queue. Their claims had been outstanding since 2000, but were in the legacy system and would be dealt with in accordance with the priority accorded them by that policy.

8.6 Race discrimination

We have already briefly discussed race discrimination as a ground of appeal against an immigration decision. This section considers further provisions applying to UKBA as a public body. Paragraph 2 of the HC 395 requires immigration officers, entry clearance officers, and Home Office staff to carry out their duties 'without regard to the race, colour or religion of persons seeking to enter or remain in the UK'. After the McPherson Inquiry into the death of Stephen Lawrence, and the public disquiet that followed, public authorities were brought within the ambit of the Race Relations Act 1976 by the Race Relations (Amendment) Act 2000. This meant that public authorities had a duty to promote equality, and were prohibited from discriminating on racial grounds in performance of their functions.

This application of the Race Relations Act to immigration matters also brought with it a duty to carry out a racial equality impact assessment of policy changes. A failure to do this was challenged by the British Association for Physicians of Indian Origin (BAPIO) when entry conditions were changed for overseas doctors (*R (on the application of BAPIO Action Ltd and Yousaf) v SSHD and Secretary of State for Health* [2007] EWHC 199 (Admin).

Under the Race Relations Act as amended, immigration and asylum matters were subject to exceptions under the Race Relations Act. These allowed decisions to be taken on grounds of nationality or ethnic or national origin, but not on grounds of race or colour, and only in accordance with authorization by a minister. Authorizations were made regularly from 27 March 2001 onwards. They permitted discrimination in immigration decision-making, on the basis of a person's nationality where the minister was satisfied that:

(a) specific intelligence suggests that a significant number of person of that nationality have breached or will attempt to breach the immigration laws, or
(b) there is statistical evidence showing that in the preceding month the total number of adverse decisions or breaches of the immigration laws by persons of that nationality exceeded 50 in total and 5 for every 1,000 admitted persons of that nationality, or that there is an emerging trend of breaches.

Following ministerial authorization, on the basis of nationality, a person could be subjected to more rigorous examination, refused leave to enter, required to submit to language analysis, or documents or information could be requested from them or priority may be given to setting removal directions.

The power was exercised in relation to nationals of numerous countries, including Zimbabwe, Somalia, Turkey, Iran, Iraq, and Sudan, Afghanistan, Albania, China, and those of Kurdish and Tamil ethnicity. The fast-track schemes discussed in chapter 12 were initially authorized by this power.

The lawfulness of the first authorization was tested in *R (on the application of Tamil Information Centre) v SSHD* [2002] EWHC 2155 (Admin). As the actions permitted by the authorizations are acts of discrimination which would otherwise be unlawful, on principle they should be construed narrowly. Section 19D which gave the power to make the authorization said explicitly that the permitted discrimination could be carried out only by a Minister of the Crown acting personally, or in accordance with 'a requirement imposed or express authorization given with respect to a particular case or class of case by a Minister of the Crown acting personally' (s 19D(3)(a)).

Forbes J found for the claimant in holding that the terms 'delegated the essential task of actually identifying and defining any such case or class of case entirely to the decision-making of immigration officials, and what is more, by reference to their standards and/or thresholds rather than his own' (at para 19). Finally, a Race Monitor was appointed, in accordance with Race Relations Act 1976 s 29E, to monitor the likely effect of the authorizations and their operation. A constant theme of her annual reports was that basing selection on previous adverse decisions meant that passengers of the identified nationalities were less likely to be given the benefit of the doubt, and so more likely to receive a refusal, and thus the authorization could be self-fulfilling (Annual Report 2004–05 paras 2.31–2.35).

The authorizations permit discrimination in procedure, not outcome. In July 2008, the role of the Race Monitor was subsumed within the new UKBA Inspectorate.

8.6.1 Authorizations under the Equality Act 2010

The Race Relations Act has been repealed by the Equality Act 2010 which provides a new scheme for ministerial authorizations to discriminate. The evidential basis is as before, but there is no obligation to disclose the authorizations. No public information is given about which nationalities are targeted.

The breadth of the exceptions under the 2010 Act is extraordinary. The central protective provision in the Act is in section 29, which requires public authorities not to do anything that constitutes discrimination, harassment, or victimization. This obligation is made subject to wide exceptions in relation to immigration by Schedule 3 part 4. The protection of section 29 on grounds of disability is excluded for decisions on leave to enter or remain. It is excluded for discrimination based on religion or belief for decisions on entry or leave to remain or exclusion from the UK where these are taken on the basis that they are conducive to the public good. It is excluded for the exercise of functions in relation to the Immigration Acts and Special Immigration Appeals Commission Act in relation to discrimination based on nationality or 'ethnic or national origins' (para 17(1)). The functions in relation to which discrimination is permitted are those exercised by a Minister of the Crown personally, or by a person acting in accordance with an authorization given, with respect to a particular case or class of case, by a Minister of the Crown acting personally; or with respect to a particular class of case, by relevant legislation or an instrument made under it (para 17(4)). The only functions under Immigration Acts which may not be subject to discrimination under this provision are powers of arrest and search.

The key difference between the new authorizations to discriminate on grounds of race, and the former system, is that the new authorizations are not published and the nationalities on the list are not disclosed. It follows that authorizations may be made on grounds of ethnicity as well as nationality without that being disclosed. Reinforcing the secrecy, entry clearance officers are prohibited by internal instructions from referring to the list when making decisions (FOI request 17943). The purpose of evidence-based statutorily authorized discrimination is in part to make the basis of decisions more accountable and transparent. The reverse seems to be the impact of these changes.

The first authorization under the Equality Act followed a report from the Independent Chief Inspector of UKBA which found that

> customers from Gulf Cooperation Council countries, who provided limited evidence to support their applications, were granted entry clearance, whereas customers from Pakistan were also being refused for not providing enough information, even when such evidence was not stipulated as a requirement in the guidance provided by UK Border Agency. (para 6.17)

If a ministerial authorization were in place to mandate discrimination of this kind, the only way for an affected individual to find out would be to compel disclosure in legal proceedings.

8.6.2 Where a whole immigration scheme is racially discriminatory

The *Roma Rights* case was a challenge to a pre-clearance scheme (see chapter 7).

Key Case

***European Roma Rights Centre and other v Immigration Officer, Prague Airport and SSHD* [2004] UKHL 55**

The scheme entailed immigration officers stationed at Prague Airport refusing leave to enter to passengers before they could board the plane. It was located in Prague because there was a high number of asylum claims refused from the Czech Republic and the scheme was to deter claims that were considered to be not well founded. The great majority of claims were made by people of Roma ethnicity, and they generally failed because the applicant was considered to be experiencing discrimination rather than persecution, or the treatment they feared was not at the hands of the state (*Horvath v SSHD* [2000] 3 All ER 577 HL). Perhaps surprisingly, the Secretary of State did not use an authorization under s 19D to operate the scheme, but rather said that it was not discriminatory at all. When it was challenged, the Court of Appeal found that although Roma were selected for more intensive questioning and were more likely to be refused passage, they were not refused as Roma, but as potential asylum claimants. This fine distinction was explained by Simon Brown LJ saying that the higher refusal rate for Roma was not because they were being stereotyped, but because 'they are less well placed to persuade the immigration officer that they are not lying in order to seek asylum' (para 86).

The House of Lords looked at the matter quite differently. Baroness Hale gave the leading judgment on the issue of discrimination:

> The Roma were being treated more sceptically than the non-Roma. There was a good reason for this. How did the immigration officers know to treat them more sceptically? Because they were Roma. That is acting on racial grounds. If a person acts on racial grounds, the reason why he does so is irrelevant. (para 82)

As Baroness Hale pointed out, direct discrimination cannot, in law, be justified, and this was direct discrimination.

There was in existence an authorization under s 19D which permitted more intensive examination of Roma. Although the Secretary of State decided it had no application in this case and did not rely on it, Baroness Hale found that it was not irrelevant:

> The combination of the objective of the whole Prague operation and a very recent ministerial authorization of discrimination against Roma was, it is suggested, to create such a high risk that the Prague officers would consciously or unconsciously treat Roma less favourably than others that very specific instructions were needed to counteract this. (para 89)

This is very similar to the point made by the Independent Race Monitor. Authorizations, while intended to limit discrimination to particular cases, may in themselves contribute to an atmosphere of discrimination which needs to be positively countered. 'It is worth remembering that good equal opportunities practice may not come naturally' (Baroness Hale, para 90).

The Prague scheme was found to be discriminatory in its operation, contrary to Race Relations Act 1976 s 1, and a declaration made to that effect.

Some of the difficulties in litigating on race discrimination grounds in immigration matters are illustrated by the *BAPIO* case. There could be no doubt that Indian doctors would be adversely affected by the changes to the rules for international medical graduates. BAPIO's standing to bring the action, and to challenge the failure to consult them, depended on precisely this. A timely Racial Equality Impact Assessment would have forced the government to consider these questions openly. Why was the challenge not made on the grounds that the rule changes were discriminatory? The probable reason is that there would be no chance of winning an argument that in effect challenges the basis of immigration control. The change to the rules limited training posts to graduates of UK medical schools. The government can lawfully favour its own nationals in the matter of access to employment and training, and some would say they are obliged to do so.

8.7 Representation

In such a complex and powerful system, effective, knowledgeable, and affordable representation is essential. Procedural points are often essential to the outcome of an immigration case, and many issues can only be tested on judicial review, which is a virtually impossible task for an unrepresented applicant. The importance of the matter to the individual also will often mean that representation is highly desirable.

Organizations of experienced representatives also have an important role in commenting on the almost continuous flow of legislation and policy-making and in responding to consultations. In fact they are in a better position than most to assist government to see the implications of their proposals. This has political significance also as immigration and, to a greater extent, asylum are fields in which political battles are fought with legal tools. However, immigration and asylum law practice is underfunded and now, highly regulated.

Prior to 2000 it was possible for unqualified people to represent clients both in dealings with the Home Office and at tribunals. The combination of lack of public funding and the freedom given to unqualified and unregulated advisers gave scope for unscrupulous individuals to set themselves up as immigration practitioners and charge high fees for work of dubious quality and sometimes of no value at all. It would be wrong to suggest that poor practice was the preserve of the unqualified. It was also the case that, due perhaps partly to the absence of immigration law from most legal professional training, bad work for high prices was done by legal professionals. Added to this was the vulnerability of immigration and asylum clients due to the profound importance to them of the matter, the scarcity of sound knowledge of the subject, and the possibility that they may not be fluent in English.

8.7.1 **Regulatory system**

Part V of the Immigration and Asylum Act 1999 provided the first statutory controls of the provision of immigration advice and representation by prohibiting such work from being done by an unqualified person (s 84(1)). A qualified person is, broadly speaking, an authorized member of a legal professional body (the Law Society, Institute of Legal Executives, or General Council of the Bar), or someone registered with the Immigration Services Commissioner. Voluntary organizations such as citizens' advice bureaux, and other publicly funded organizations providing immigration advice must comply with the requirements of the scheme. To provide immigration advice outside these provisions is an imprisonable offence under s 91.

The Immigration Services Commissioner's role is (s 83) to promote good practice in immigration advice and representation and to maintain a register of qualified advisers (s 85). Their powers and duties include preparing a code setting standards of conduct which applies to registered individuals and exempt bodies, i.e., all except legal professionals and government employees (Sch 5). The Commissioner's Rules and Codes of Standards allow for registration at a number of different levels, depending on the scope and level of competence of the organization or registered individual. This does not include representation in immigration offences as these are a branch of criminal law. The 2004 Act amended and increased the OISC's powers, introducing a power of entry and search of premises and seizure of documents including a power to seize materials that are subject to legal privilege (s 38). The 1999 Act also makes provision, in s 87, for an Immigration Services Tribunal which hears complaints from those aggrieved by a decision of the Commissioner, or disciplinary matters referred by the Commissioner. Non-practising barristers must apply for regulation with the Office of the Immigration Services Commissioner (OISC news April 2002).

Both the Law Society and the Bar Council set up voluntary panel and accreditation schemes, but the greater impact on legal professionals is from compulsory accreditation for publicly funded work. This was instituted by the Law Society and Legal Services Commission together. Since 1 April 2005, all advisers must be accredited. In early 2004, the allowable amount of public funding for each asylum case was radically reduced, as was legal aid firms' capacity to authorize their own expenditure (see for instance 'Asylum Advisers Face Axe' *The Guardian* 11 October 2004, 'Open and Shut case' *Law Gazette* 10 February 2005). Further waves of legal aid reductions have followed.

Though the causes are disputed, following further cuts in the legal aid allocation for immigration and asylum cases, the two main NGO providers of advice and representation went into administration: Refugee and Migrant Justice in 2010 and Immigration Advisory Service in 2011. The High Court has given permission for the administrators of IAS to destroy client files not retrieved after a retrieval period ending in May 2012. The Office of the Immigration Service Commissioner Codes and Standards requires client files to be kept for six years, the same period as solicitors. Despite regulation, obtaining reliable legal representation and the assurance of proper standards in relation to immigration and asylum legal work remains a huge challenge.

The Legal Aid Sentencing and Prevention of Offences Bill, proceeding through Parliament in 2011/12, proposes to remove legal aid from the majority of immigration cases, including those based on Article 8. Asylum claims will remain within the scope of legal aid, but legal aid will be removed from ancillary matters such as refugee family reunion.

8.8 Conclusion

The final subject treated here, the restricted availability of legal representatives, in practice has an enormous impact on the actual accessibility of courts and tribunals to people affected by immigration and asylum decisions. Obtaining good legal advice is a significant hurdle for would-be appellants to cross, before the highly technical rules concerning the scope and availability of appeals can be navigated effectively.

QUESTIONS

1 Consider the case for and against transferring judicial review cases to the Upper Tribunal.
2 Is it appropriate to use discrimination on the grounds of nationality in making immigration or asylum decisions? What about ethnic group? How does this differ from making decisions on the basis of colour?
3 Who should decide whether legal advisers are abusing the system?

online resource centre

For guidance on answering questions, visit www.oxfordtextbooks.co.uk/orc/clayton5e/.

FURTHER READING

Buck, Trevor (2006) ‘Precedent in Tribunals and the Development of Principles’ *Civil Justice Quarterly* no. 25, October, pp. 458–484.

Buxton, Richard (2009) ‘Application of Section 13(6) of the Tribunals Courts and Enforcement Act 2009 to Immigration Appeals from the Proposed Upper Tribunal’ *Judicial Review* vol.14, no. 3 pp. 225–227.

Carnwath, Robert (2009) ‘Tribunal Justice – A New Start’ *Public Law* January, pp. 48–69.

Chowdhury, Zahir (2009) ‘The Concept of “Error of Law” in Public Law and its Application in Immigration Cases’ *Immigration Law Digest* vol. 15, no. 2, Summer, pp. 8–20.

Clayton, Gina (2007) ‘Prediction or Precondition? The House of Lords Judgment in *Huang and Kashmiri*’ *Journal of Immigration, Asylum and Nationality Law* vol. 21, no. 4, pp. 311–323.

Coussey, Mary (2004, 2005, and 2006) *Annual Reports of the Independent Race Monitor* (London: UKBA).

Joint Parliamentary Committee on Human Rights *Counter-Terrorism Policy and Human Rights (Seventeenth Report): Bringing Human Rights Back in.* Sixteenth Report of Session 2009–10 HL Paper 86 HC 111.

Kapadia, Amit, (2008) ‘Experiencing Judicial Review’ *Judicial Review* vol. 13, no. 3, pp. 191–192.

Knight, C. J. S. (2009) 'Expectations in Transition: Recent Developments in Legitimate Expectation' *Public Law* January, pp. 15–24.

Mitchell, Harry (2005) 'The Roma Case in the House of Lords and the Question of the 2001 Authorisation' *Journal of Immigration, Asylum and Nationality* Law vol. 19, no. 1, pp. 34–38.

Office of the Immigration Services Commissioner – codes and standards, press releases, annual reports, accessed at: http://oisc.homeoffice.gov.uk/.

Thomas, Robert (2005) 'Evaluating Tribunal Adjudication: Administrative Justice and Asylum Appeals' *Legal Studies* vol. 25, no. 3, pp. 462–498.

—— (2008) 'The Immigration Appeals Consultation Paper' *Immigration Law Digest* vol. 14, no. 3, Autumn, pp. 2–5.

Vaughan, Anthony 'The Tribunal's New Role in Article 8 Statutory Appeals' *Journal of Immigration, Asylum and Nationality Law* vol. 21, no. 2, pp. 129–136.

SECTION 4

Entry to the UK

9

Family life

SUMMARY

This chapter mainly concerns non-EEA nationals who wish to live permanently with family members who are settled in or are nationals of the UK although the family members of those coming to work or study and of refugees are also briefly considered. It starts by considering some preliminary issues before examining marriage-related applications, that is, applications to join a spouse, fiancé(e), civil or long-term partner. The rules relating to adult family members and to children are then considered. At the end of the chapter, there is brief consideration of those with limited leave, and finally of refugees and asylum seekers.

9.1 Introduction

Family migration most commonly occurs through marriage or parenthood as rules for admission of other relatives are very restrictive. In 2009 (the last year for which figures are available), around 55,000 non-EEA family members were admitted to the UK, More than 39,000 of the total were spouses, fiancé(e)s, and civil partners, while nearly 11,000 were children. Around 5,000 other family members also entered and were given indefinite leave immediately (Home Office *Control of Immigration Statistics: United Kingdom 2009*: Supplementary Table 1c).

Since family migration first became an issue in the mid-1960s, the main focus has been on the admission of family members from the Indian subcontinent. This has always been the largest single region of origin, although it has become less important as migration from other regions has increased. Home Office statistics show that, in 1999, 38.5 per cent and, in 2009, 32.31 per cent of spouses entering the UK were from the subcontinent (*Control of Immigration Statistics 2009* p. 62, and *Control of Immigration: Statistics 2003* Table 1.6). The next largest groups were the rest of Asia and Middle East (14.07 per cent in 1999 and 24.78 per cent in 2009) and Africa (13.79 per cent in 1999 and 17.85 per cent in 2009). As Charsley (2012a) points out, the range of nationalities involved in family migration should not be overlooked. She has identified more than 70 nationalities involved in spousal migration, with significant numbers settling in the UK from countries such as the Philippines, South Africa, China, and the US. She has also shown (2012b) that refusal rates of spousal migrants have risen in the past few years and vary widely between countries of origin.

Family migration presents a particular challenge for the government. A decision to admit a migrant for work or business can be made purely on the basis of the UK's economic or other interests. However, the admission of family members involves the personal interests of British residents and restrictive policies may be unpopular. On the other hand, family migration may permit the entry of those who would not qualify under other channels and whom the government would prefer not to admit. This tension has been evident since family migration first became a controversial issue in the mid-1960s. There are thus two perspectives: that of the government seeking to manage migration on behalf of the country and that of the UK resident or national who wishes to re-unite with their family member. Very often, it has been the former which is foregrounded and the issue is seen primarily as one of immigration control.

9.2 The politics of family life

Much contention surrounds family settlement applications as a result of differences and perceived differences between the practices of immigrant and host communities, raising questions about marriage and child-rearing practices, concepts of the family, individual freedom, and family duties. The law has often been dominated by an overriding concern with preventing abuse and the entry of undesirable migrants. Marriage, in particular, has 'offered an opportunity to vent a gamut of powerful and well-rehearsed emotions' (Bevan 1986:253) while Jackson observes that it has 'attracted the most controversial immigration rules' (Jackson, Immigration Law and Practice 1996:395). These emotions have intensified in recent years due to concerns about forced marriage and the integration of foreign spouses, resulting in new measures, some of which have been legally problematic. These were in addition to those rules already aiming to ensure the economic independence of the migrant and the 'genuineness' of the marriage.

Over the years, many of the measures regulating entry through marriage have particularly affected arranged marriages, as practised in UK-based communities of South Asian origin. This is not accidental. Many members of these communities have continued to marry spouses from their region of origin, leading to concerns about chain migration, the continued entry of unskilled non-English-speaking migrants, and the perpetuation of forms of family life that some consider archaic and oppressive.

Husbands have often been suspected of being disguised economic migrants. The first major attempt to control marriage migration to the UK after the Commonwealth Immigrants Act 1962 involved a ban between 1969 and 1974 on the entry of Commonwealth husbands unless 'special features' were present. In the 1970s and 1980s, the primary purpose rule, discussed later in this chapter, was a more focused means of minimizing the entry of spouses, particularly husbands from the Indian subcontinent, while wives and children were affected by controversial administrative methods adopted by the entry clearance system. The entry of very young spouses and of more than one spouse in a polygamous marriage were ended between 1986 and 1990.

The primary purpose rule was removed in 1997 but marriage migration has remained controversial. There have been two major themes in recent regulation: firstly, encouraging the integration of spouses and protecting the victims of forced marriage, and, secondly, preventing bogus or sham marriages.

The 2002 White Paper, *Secure Borders, Safe Haven* (Cm 5387), whose subtitle was *Integration with Diversity in Modern Britain*, suggested that young people from British Asian families should consider marrying someone who lived in the UK (p. 18). Incoming spouses must now pass the knowledge of language and life in the UK tests before settlement. The government introduced a pre-entry language requirement for spouses in 2010, using arguments more commonly associated with labour migration even though partners are not required to work. A rejected challenge to this requirement is subject to appeal (*R (on the application of Chapti) v SSHD* [2011] EWHC 3370 (Admin)). The minimum age for sponsorship and entry was raised to 18 in 2003 and 2004, respectively, in response to concerns about forced marriage and to 21 in 2008 although, as you will see, this was found by the Supreme Court to breach Article 8 ECHR and was withdrawn in late 2011. The government also adopted an inflexible approach to the maintenance of migrant family members by their extended family, a position that was undermined by the Supreme Court (see *Mahad (Ethiopia) and others v ECO* [2009] UKSC 16, discussed later in the chapter).

Despite some sympathetic decisions such as *Mahad* and other cases discussed in this chapter, cultural differences in attitudes towards marriage and family are also sometimes visible in the case law, particularly in marriage. For example, disapproval of polygamous marriage arrangements may be detected in the interpretation of the requirement to show intention to live together in *AB Bangladesh* [2004] UKIAT 00314 (see 9.6.4.3).

Meanwhile, rules governing other forms of family life have been liberalized, reflecting changing values amongst the majority population. Unmarried and civil partners are now recognized within the rules. Although aspects of these provisions are problematic such as the protection for victims of domestic violence, their presence suggests that 'modern' values and relationships have achieved a degree of official acknowledgement that often still eludes 'traditional' forms of family life.

Many claims for leave to remain as a spouse are made by those who have married a UK or EEA national after entering the UK. This has given rise to suspicions of sham marriages, particularly when the spouse entered on short-term leave (for example, as a visitor) or was without leave (including many asylum seekers). In 2002, the government prohibited these migrants from 'switching' into marriage, requiring them to return to their country of origin to make an entry clearance application, a policy substantially undermined by the House of Lords (*Chikwamba v SSHD* [2008] UKHL 40). The Certificates of Approval scheme established by Asylum and Immigration (Treatment of Claimants, etc.) Act 2004 required non-EEA nationals to obtain permission of the Secretary of State to marry, which was almost always refused when migrants did not have long-term leave. Aspects of the scheme were found by the House of Lords to be incompatible with Convention Rights (*R (on the application of Baiai and others v SSHD* [2008] UKHL 53). These cases and others, discussed in this chapter, reflect an increasing level of engagement by the higher courts in questions involving respect for the family life of migrants under Article 8 ECHR or, in the case of *Baiai*, Article 12, the right to marry. Several government policies have been successfully challenged in the courts using human rights.

The Coalition government, which came to power in 2010, is committed to a vast reduction in 'net migration', a problematic objective discussed in chapter 2, and family migration is included in this target for reduction. In July 2011, the government launched a consultation on family migration which contained many radical proposals, most of which will, if implemented, reduce the numbers and change the characteristics of family migrants. Specific proposals in the consultation (referred to here as the Family Migration Consultation) are discussed at various points in this chapter but the Foreword by the Home Secretary, Theresa May, sets the tone:

> This government is determined to bring immigration back to sustainable levels and to bring a sense of fairness back to our immigration system...Of course, those with a legitimate right to come here must still be able to do so. But we need to crack down on abuse of the family route and to tighten up the system.

Many recent or proposed changes to the control of family migration resemble those implemented elsewhere in Europe, for example, raising the age of entry and sponsorship of spouses, minimum income requirements, pre-entry language testing, more demanding integration criteria, and so on. In the Family Migration Consultation, the government considers implementation of a 'combined attachment' requirement, a criterion adopted in Denmark which requires some couples to show that their combined attachment to Denmark is greater than to any other country. Increasingly, policy developments are taking place and must be analysed in a European context (see, for example, the work of Van Oers, Ersbøll and Kostakopoulou (2010) or Groenendijk (2011)),

9.3 Legal context

There is no enshrined right for a British resident to be joined in the UK by their family members. Section 1(4) Immigration Act 1971, which obliges the Secretary of State to make rules to govern certain types of entry, does not require these to cover the admission of family members, an omission that cannot be challenged under the Human Rights Act 1998 as this is an omission of the legislature which is immune from action (s 6(3)). Entry is governed by the immigration rules and the applicant is not the UK resident but the foreign national family member who wishes to enter and who must meet the requirements of the rules.

As discussed in chapter 1, the legal status of the immigration rules is ambiguous. Recent case law, such as *Odelola* and *Mahad*, has confirmed that they represent statements of policy rather than legal rights but they are nonetheless binding on the government, as *Pankina* demonstrated. As we have already seen, the immigration rules are made by a minister after, usually, cursory scrutiny by Parliament and the requirements change frequently. While consultation exercises take place in immigration as elsewhere, there is no duty to consult nor to abide by the outcome of a consultation. The lack of statutory grounding for the entry of family migrants makes it easier to restrict rights in line with popular or government concerns.

As this chapter will show, some restrictive government policies have been successfully challenged in the courts, often using human rights, particularly Article 8 ECHR. The government is unhappy at such constraints on its power and, in the Family Migration Consultation, Theresa May referred to a government-established commission to investigate the creation of a UK Bill of Rights and expressed her 'sincere hope that the commission will bring some common sense back to this, admittedly difficult, area'.

Whether a family member gets leave to enter depends upon the judgement of an entry clearance officer as to whether they fulfil the requirements of the rules. While an unsuccessful applicant can appeal, the appellant remains abroad and it is the sponsor in the UK who attends the appeal and whose presence is, in practice, often decisive. However, under the rules, they have no official standing, reflecting the absence of any positive right attaching to UK residents to be joined by their family members.

Immigration law and practice in the UK are affected by both European Union law and human rights norms. As explained in chapter 5, free movement rights in EU law have often permitted British nationals to avoid restrictive UK rules on family migration. These rights are an increasingly important backdrop to the law and policy discussed in this chapter. As already noted, human rights, particularly under Article 8 ECHR (right to respect for private and family life), have been influential in the development of the law in the past period. The Human Rights Act 1998 and Convention rights in general have been discussed in chapter 4. The application of Article 8 in particular family situations is discussed as it arises in this chapter. However, there are some important preliminary issues which are discussed here before the main content of the chapter.

9.4 Right to respect for family life

The right to respect for private and family life is not confined to the ECHR but is a universally recognized fundamental human right. It is included in the Universal Declaration of Human Rights 1948 and the International Covenant on Civil and Political Rights 1966, both of which forbid arbitrary and unlawful interference with family life. The International Covenant on Economic, Social and Cultural Rights 1966 says, in Article 12, that 'the widest possible protection and assistance should be accorded to the family, which is the natural and fundamental group unit of society'. The European Charter of Fundamental Rights says, at Article 7, that '[e]veryone has the right to respect for his or her private and family life, home and communications'.

In domestic law, remedies for breach of the right are available through the Human Rights Act 1998, particularly under Article 8 ECHR, the right to respect for private and family life. Breach of Article 8 gives grounds for appealing against an immigration decision including a refusal of entry clearance or leave to remain (Nationality, Immigration and Asylum Act 2002 s 84(1)(c)). The scope and application of Article 8 is discussed fully in chapter 4. In this chapter, we do not consider private life but we will consider how the obligation to respect family life is manifested or otherwise in the law concerning the settlement of family members.

The Article provides:

1. Everyone has the right to respect for his private and family life, his home and his correspondence.
2. There shall be no interference by a public authority with the exercise of this right except such as is in accordance with the law and is necessary in a democratic society in the interests of national security, public safety, or the economic well-being of the country, for the prevention of disorder or crime, for the protection of health or morals, or for the protection of the rights and freedoms of others.

It will be recalled that the application of Article 8 requires a structured approach which considers the determinative issues in an ordered way. The relevant issues are:

- Does family life exist?
- What does 'respect for family life' require?
- Has there been an interference with the exercise of this right?
- Is the interference in accordance with the law?
- Is it necessary in a democratic society to protect one of the interests set out in Article 8(2)?
- If so, is the interference proportionate to the legitimate aim pursued?

Most disputed cases centre on the Article 8(2) question of proportionality. However, it is not always clear from the courts' reasoning whether it is proportionality or the existence of, or interference with, family life that is being decided. Nor is it always clear which Article 8(2) interest is protected by immigration control. Immigration control is usually presumed to serve one or more of these interests and the question does not receive detailed consideration. However, identifying the interest served by interference affects the weight of the case for interference. In *JO (Uganda) v SSHD* [2010] EWCA Civ 10, Lord Justice Richards, at para 29, pointed out that deportation cases, where the migrant has been involved in wrong-doing, serve the interests of preventing disorder or crime, issues not at stake in ordinary removal cases. Thus, where an appellant's drink-driving convictions had been insufficient to merit a deportation order, they were also insufficient to refuse indefinite leave to remain as a spouse where economic aims were in issue (*LD (Article 8 – best interests of a child) Zimbabwe* [2010] UKUT 278 (IAC).

Critically, as discussed in chapter 8, *Huang* made it clear that it is for the Court or Tribunal to reach its own decision on proportionality, a point made again by the Supreme Court in *Quila* which proceeded to carry out its own detailed examination of proportionality, discussed later in this chapter. The immigration rules do not necessarily represent the correct balance between the interests of the individual and the interests of the state, and it is for the state to justify the proportionality of the Article 8(2) interference. Cases must be decided on their particular facts and, in the words of Lord Bingham in *EB (Kosovo) v SSHD* [2008] UKHL 41 at para 12:

> there is in general no alternative to making a careful and informed evaluation of the facts of the particular case. The search for a hard-edged or bright-line rule to be applied to the generality of cases is incompatible with the difficult evaluative exercise which article 8 requires.

It is also worth recalling the words, already quoted in chapter 4, of their Lordships in *Huang and Kashmiri* (para 18), when they referred to the 'core value' of Article 8:

> Human beings are social animals. They depend on others. Their family, or extended family, is the group on which many people most heavily depend, socially, emotionally and often financially. There comes a point at which, for some, prolonged and unavoidable separation from this group seriously inhibits their ability to live full and fulfilling lives.

The tension between humans' emotional needs and the complex individual evaluation demanded by Article 8, on the one hand, and the demands of a generally applicable and often restrictive immigration policy on the other has driven much recent case law as discussed in this chapter.

9.4.1 Does family life exist?

The application of a family member to enter the UK engages the positive obligation in Article 8 to 'respect' private and family life. While the other qualified Articles use the formula 'everyone has the right to freedom' whether of religion, expression or assembly, Article 8 does not provide a right to family life, but to 'respect for' private or family life. This has two implications. First, Article 8 does not provide a right to establish a family life. To the extent that this is covered in the Convention, it is dealt with in Article 12, the right to marry and found a family. The prior existence of family life must therefore be established under Article 8(1). The question of what constitutes family life has been discussed in chapter 4, including the situations in which adult relationships may or not may be treated by the courts as requiring respect under Article 8.

The need for an established family life can have hard results where compassionate factors are present but pre-existing family life cannot be shown. The Tribunal in *ECO Lagos v Imoh* [2002] UKIAT 01967 held that Article 8 did not apply where a four-year-old girl wanted to move to the UK to live with her aunt whom she had only visited once. The minimal prior contact meant that this would be to establish family life, not to respect family life that was already extant. It may also mean that the type of family life that is protected under Article 8(1) may be reduced due to circumstances beyond the parties' control. The Court of Appeal in *MB (Somalia) v ECO* [2008] EWCA Civ 102 found that a ten-year involuntary separation of an elderly mother and adult son after he came to the UK as a refugee adversely affected the quality of established family life for the purposes of Article 8.

9.4.2 What requires respect and what respect requires

The courts have emphasized that family life may take many forms and it is the family life in the particular case that must be respected. In *EM (Lebanon) v SSHD* [2008] UKHL 64, Lord Bingham said (at para 37):

> Families differ widely, in their composition and in the mutual relations which exist between the members, and marked changes are likely to occur over time within the same family. Thus there is no pre-determined model of family or family life to which article 8 must be applied.

Here, the family consisted of a mother and her 12-year-old son. If the family were returned to Lebanon, the son's father, who had been violent to the mother and who had not seen his son since birth, would be entitled to custody and the mother, at best, to visits. Lord Bingham found that the family life in this case involved, not only practical matters of physical care, but a bond of 'deep love and mutual dependence' (para 40) and returning them to Lebanon would 'flagrantly violate, or completely deny and nullify' their right to respect for that family life (para 42).

Family life that takes other forms must also be respected. In *MS (Ivory Coast)* [2007] EWCA Civ 133, the appellant could not live with her children due to her previous violence but she was applying for a contact order. The Court of Appeal held that she was entitled to consideration of her Article 8 rights. In *R (on the application of Fawad and Zia Ahmadi)* [2005] EWCA Civ 1721, Zia, a refugee, suffered from schizophrenia. His brother, Fawad, was refused refugee status but provided effective support to Zia. Fawad claimed that respect for his family life required the opportunity to do that. Although the Secretary of State had certified that the claim was 'clearly unfounded' (see chapter 12), the Court disagreed and held that it should be considered.

The wording of Article 8(1) implies a positive obligation on the part of the state to respect existing private and family life (*Marckx v Belgium*) not just a negative duty to avoid expulsion. However, for many years, it was assumed that any positive obligation would rarely extend to admission. This belief was established by the majority view in *Abdulaziz v United Kingdom*, at para 68, that: 'The duty imposed by article 8 cannot be considered as extending to a general obligation on the part of a contracting state to respect the choice by married couples of the country of their matrimonial residence and to accept the non-national.'

In cases since *Abdulaziz*, the European Court of Human Rights has questioned the clear-cut nature of the demarcation. In *Sen v Netherlands* (2003) 36 EHRR 7, refusal to admit a minor child was found to breach article 8 ECHR. In *Tuquabo-Tekle v the Netherlands* [2006] 1 FLR 798, the daughter's admission was sought in order to allow reunification with her family. The Court observed at paras 41 and 42, that 'the boundaries between the state's positive and negative obligations under this provision do not lend themselves to precise definition' and that 'the applicable principles are, nonetheless, similar'. In *Rodrigues da Silva, Hoogkamer v Netherlands* (2006) 44 EHRR 729, the mother was entitled to remain in the Netherlands to continue contact with her daughter, a finding that the Court acknowledged entailed a positive act.

In the Supreme Court case of *R (on the application of Quila and another) v SSHD* [2011] UKSC 45 (discussed further later in the chapter), Lord Wilson declined to follow *Abdulaziz* because later cases, including those just cited, were inconsistent with it. As Lady Hale observed in the same case, what the later cases taken together show is that each case demands its own examination and where family life exists, a similar approach to interference should now be taken in all types of cases.

This seems a correct approach and not only because it recognizes the development of the European jurisprudence since *Abdulaziz*. A rigid demarcation between the negative duty to refrain from expulsion and the positive duty to admit is artificial. A married couple is regarded as having family life so an application to join one's spouse engages the right to respect for family life even if they have never lived together. There is also a strong presumption of family life between minor children and their parents. Thus, while Article 8 only protects family life that already exists, its existence does not necessarily depend upon there already being cohabitation (even if that is what its respect ultimately requires). The distinction is even more tenuous when migrants are physically present but lack status as allowing them to stay involves both the positive act of granting leave and the negative act of refraining from expulsion. It is not clear why, in terms of establishing interference, these cases are materially different from those cases where the migrant has limited leave (although compliance with immigration law may be a factor in determining proportionality).

While all forms of family life must be respected and the engagement of the state's positive and negative obligations arise in similar ways, it does not follow that respect will require cohabitation in the same country in all instances. For some relationships, contact through letters, phone calls, and visits is sufficient to maintain family life. This is particularly so as regards adult family members who are not in a relationship of dependency and who do not normally expect to live together, although each situation needs to be considered on its own facts and cohabitation may be required in some cases.

9.4.3 Whose family life?

Section 84(1) of the Nationality, Immigration and Asylum Act 2002 provides that an appeal against an 'immigration decision' (as defined in s 82 of that Act) may be brought on the grounds that 'the decision is unlawful under section 6 of the Human Rights Act 1998... as being incompatible with the appellant's Convention rights', suggesting that only the appellant's own human rights may be the subject of the appeal. This interpretation caused numerous practical difficulties. Other members of the family (children or elderly relatives, for example) might be equally or even more affected by the immigration decision but were not part of the appeal and their interests were not considered. They had to bring separate proceedings under s 7 of the Human Rights Act 1998. Yet, if a human rights case proceeds to the ECtHR, all the parties' interests are taken into account.

Case law on the question had been conflicting until, in 2008, the House of Lords found in *Beoku-Betts v SSHD* [2008] UKHL 39 that, notwithstanding the narrow wording of the Act, it should be construed widely and the family unit considered as a whole for Article 8 purposes. In the words of Baroness Hale (at para 4), a narrow approach is not only artificial and impracticable but 'risks missing the central point about family life, which is that the whole is greater than the sum of its individual parts'.

The difference that the judgment in *Beoku-Betts* might make was highlighted in obiter dicta of Baroness Hale in a subsequent House of Lords decision *AS (Somalia) v*

SSHD [2009] UKHL 32. The case concerned two war orphans from Somalia whose care was undertaken by the sponsor's mother and, after she died, the sponsor and then, following forcible separation, the sponsor's mother-in-law. When the sponsor was granted refugee status in the UK, the two children and the sponsor's natural daughter applied for entry. The natural daughter was admitted but the other two children had no right of entry under the immigration rules and their Article 8 claims, heard before *Huang* and *Beoku-Betts*, failed. Baroness Hale commented, at para 26, that, had the totality of family life enjoyed by the sponsor and all three of the children been looked at in the round, the initial decision might have been different.

Just how family life is more than the sum of its parts is illustrated by the Court of Appeal decision in *ZB v SSHD* [2009] EWCA Civ 834. Here, the applicant's husband, eight adult children, and 19 grandchildren lived and were settled in the UK. The AIT considered that she could not show sufficient family life with any single member of the family (she had voluntarily lived apart from her husband for substantial periods of the marriage). The Court of Appeal found that this failed to consider family life as a whole rather than as a series of disconnected segments.

If there is a failure to respect family life, the question moves on to whether the interference is necessary in a democratic society for a reason permitted in Article 8(2). These tests have been discussed fully in chapter 4 but some issues that are particularly relevant to family life are discussed here.

9.4.4 Living together abroad

An important issue is whether the family can continue its family life by living together abroad. The issue often arises in removal cases where one party has established a family life in the UK without having the appropriate leave or any leave at all and this is discussed more fully in chapter 18. It may also arise when parties make an entry clearance application but, for whatever reason, are unable to meet the requirements of the immigration rules. If it is found that the family can satisfactorily be reunited abroad, there is no breach of Article 8. Thus, the ECtHR found in *Abdulaziz* that there were no obstacles to establishing family life elsewhere or 'special reasons why that could not be expected of them' (*Abdulaziz* para 68). More recent ECtHR cases on refusal of admission weigh the factors which indicate whether the family could live together elsewhere and regard this as an important question but not necessarily critical (see, for instance, *Gul v Switzerland* (1996) 22 EHRR 93, *Ahmut v Netherlands* (1996) 24 EHRR 62, and *Sen v Netherlands* (2003) 36 EHRR 7). The issue has been confused by the use in certain ECtHR cases of the term 'insurmountable obstacles' to living abroad. The phrase was used by Lord Phillips in *R (on the application of Mahmood) v Home Secretary* [2001] 1 WLR 840 and was subsequently deployed to establish an unnecessarily high hurdle in Article 8 cases without a full appreciation of the term's meaning in the context in which it had been used.

After some years in which many Article 8 cases failed because there were not found to be 'insurmountable obstacles' to the family living abroad, the question received much needed clarification. The proper approach was identified in *Huang and Kashmiri v SSHD* [2007] UKHL 11 as a question of whether 'the life of the family cannot reasonably be expected to be enjoyed elsewhere' (para 20). In *EB (Kosovo) v SSHD* [2008] UKHL 41, Lord Bingham (at para 12) found that it would rarely be proportionate to remove a spouse, where there is a close and genuine bond and the other spouse 'cannot reasonably be expected' to go abroad or the effect would be to sever the relationship between parent and child. In *Muse and others v ECO* [2012] EWCA Civ 10, the Court of Appeal pointed out that deciding if it is reasonable for the UK-based family member to move abroad is not straightforward and 'the harshness of such an expectation is a matter of degree which forms part of an overall evaluation whether or not a decision refusing entry would be disproportionate' (para 34).

9.4.5 Removal to make an entry clearance application

For a long period, government policy was to regard the removal of adult relatives as proportionate because there is the opportunity to apply for entry from abroad and the entry clearance officer must take Article 8 considerations into account. In this way, those who were not entitled to be in the UK or to switch status were said not to gain an unfair advantage over those who apply from abroad and wait their turn. The numbers affected by this approach increased after 2002, when those present without leave or on short-term leave were banned from switching into marriage.

This policy was problematic, however, as even temporary removal often risks destabilizing family life and financial self-sufficiency (which might jeopardize the outcome of the entry clearance application). In *LH (Truly exceptional – Ekinci applied) Jamaica* [2006] UKIAT 00019 for example, the applicant's child was disabled and the mother was unable to cope alone. The applicant would lose his job as a result of removal, putting the family onto benefits. Nonetheless, he had to return to Jamaica to make an entry clearance application.

These problems were exacerbated where removal was to a country which was unstable and which might not even have entry clearance facilities. For instance, in *HC (Availability of Entry Clearance Facilities) Iraq* [2004] UKIAT 00154, it was considered reasonable for the applicant to return to Iraq (shortly after the Second Gulf War), obtain travel documents, negotiate Jordanian border controls, and endure the cost and danger of travelling from Iraq to Jordan to make a visa application.

After much litigation on the question, the House of Lords considered the question in *Chikwamba v SSHD* [2008] UKHL 40 (discussed also in chapters 4 and 18). The case involved a failed asylum seeker from Zimbabwe. Removals to Zimbabwe had been suspended and she was not returned. She married a Zimbabwean refugee and had a child. Once removals were reinstated, the Secretary of State sought her removal, arguing that she could apply for entry clearance from Zimbabwe. The House of Lords upheld an appeal against that decision and judgments were given in unusually frank terms. Lord Scott (at paras 3–4) expressed astonishment that the case had come this far and said that:

> policies that involve people cannot be, and should not be allowed to become rigid inflexible rules. The bureaucracy of which Kafka wrote cannot be allowed to take root in this country and the courts must see that it does not.

Lord Brown (at paras 39–42) was sceptical about the government's argument that the policy was necessary to prevent applicants 'jumping' the entry clearance queue, suggesting (at para 41) that the 'real rationale' of the policy was 'the rather different one of deterring people from coming to this country in the first place without having obtained entry clearance and to do so by subjecting those who do come to the very substantial disruption of their lives involved in returning them abroad?' He found (at para 44) that:

> only comparatively rarely, certainly in family cases involving children, should an article 8 appeal be dismissed on the basis that it would be proportionate for the appellant to apply for leave from abroad.

Requiring applicants to leave and reapply for entry clearance is not always disproportionate but all the relevant circumstances of the case must be taken into account (see para 42). Not of relevance, however, is the likelihood that an entry clearance application will succeed or fail (para 36).

Chikwamba was an important case and alleviated the difficulties of many applicants with families. It is consistent with the approach taken in *Beoku-Betts* promulgated on the same day and discussed earlier. However, their Lordships distinguished the situation of the appellant in *Chikwamba* from those in previous authorities, notably *R (on the application of Ekinci) v SSHD* [2003] EWCA Civ 765. While the appellant in *Ekinci* had a child, he was also described as having 'an appalling immigration history' (para 30) and he would only be required to travel to Germany and wait a month for a visa. *Chikwamba* does not assist every migrant who wishes to have their spouse claim decided in-country, although the Court of Appeal, in *MA (Pakistan) v SSHD* [2009] EWCA Civ 953, observed that the principle in the case is not confined to cases where children are involved and the Upper Tribunal in *Hayat (nature of Chikwamba principle) Pakistan* [2011] UKUT 00444 (IAC) found that it need not involve a relationship with a UK-settled party. Whether a case falls outside the scope of *Chikwamba* is a question that must be determined on a case by case basis. Home Office policy after *Chikwamba* states that '[r]eturning an applicant to his/her home country in order to make an entry clearance application may still be proportionate in a small number of cases. All cases must therefore be considered on their own merits.'

In his lead judgment in *Chikwamba*, Lord Brown (at para 43) indicated factors to consider when deciding if return is proportionate. These included the immigration history, the length of time needed to process the application, the disruption to the family, delay by the government in dealing with the applicant's case while in the UK, and whether the ECO abroad is better placed than the UK authorities to investigate the claim. *R (on the application of Kotecha and Das) v SSHD* [2011] EWHC 2070 (Admin) illustrates where the line may be drawn. Mr Kotecha was an overstayer from Tanzania working in the UK, having originally been granted leave as a student. He married a British woman who studied and worked but there were no children. An entry clearance application would take only one month to decide and it was found that the parties could either go together to Tanzania or accept a short separation. The claim failed, the judge being uncertain whether even Article 8(1) was engaged in these circumstances.

By contrast, Mrs Das' claim succeeded. She was a Bangladeshi national who entered with her husband and infant son. Her husband died and she remained in the UK, assisted by her husband's brother, who had indefinite leave and with whom she first had a child and then married some two years after her first husband's death by which point, she had overstayed. Her new husband's job and connections were in the UK and her eldest child was at school. Making an entry clearance application would take between one and four months. Given her childcare responsibilities and her husband's employment, it was not realistic for the family to travel to Bangladesh nor for her to go alone and requiring her return would be disproportionate.

A drawback of succeeding in a *Chikwamba*-type case is that an applicant, even one who meets all the requirements for entry clearance save that of valid leave, may receive discretionary leave, under which an entitlement to indefinite leave arises only after six years compared to two years under a spouse visa. A claim for judicial review on this point failed (*R (on the application of Abdelghani) v SSHD* [2010] EWHC 1227 (Admin)). Although the Court had sympathy for the applicant, the claim had been made on the basis of the immigration rules whereas the defect lay in the application of the provisions for discretionary leave.

9.5 Maintenance and accommodation

The immigration rules require that all family member applicants must show that they will be adequately maintained and accommodated without recourse to public funds and this question is considered here as a preliminary matter, although it appears separately in the rules in relation to each type of applicant. The requirement aims to protect the public purse and prevent migrants and their families falling into extreme poverty. Its interpretation, however, has caused considerable controversy.

9.5.1 Maintenance

The wording of the maintenance requirements is slightly different for each type of family member. For spouses and allied categories, the requirement in para 281 is that 'the parties will be able to maintain themselves and any dependants adequately without recourse to public funds'. Under para 297(v), children 'can, and will, be maintained adequately by the parent, parents or relative the child is seeking to join without recourse to public funds'. For adult dependant relatives, the criterion is that the applicant 'can, and will, be maintained adequately, together with any dependants, without recourse to public funds' (para 317(iva)). The possible differences of meaning of these various formulations, together with the different contexts in which each appears, have caused considerable difficulty, recently clarified by the Supreme Court in *Mahad and others v ECO* [2009] UKSC 16 and discussed at 9.5.1.3.

The essence of the rule is that the family's financial position must be sufficiently strong to avoid the need to claim the state benefits found in para 6 of the immigration rules (although recent migrants are anyway ineligible for most of them). In *Konstatinov v Netherlands* Application no. 16351/03, the ECtHR said that there was no objection in principle to rules that require a minimum level of income sufficient to meet the basic costs of subsistence of family members (para 50). The list of public funds in para 6 includes virtually all means-tested and disability benefits, apart from emergency provision, including child benefit and housing support. National Health Service treatment and state education are not classified as public funds. However, health care for migrants is a controversial issue and the Family Migration Consultation suggests requiring future family migrants to obtain medical insurance before entry, which would, at best, impose a heavy additional financial burden and, at worst, exclude the elderly and infirm who may be uninsurable.

'Recourse to public funds' means recourse to additional public funds over and above those to which the sponsor is already entitled (para 6A). The fact that a new claim might be made in future is not an issue. The test is whether maintenance would be adaquate without a claim.

9.5.1.1 *Adequacy*

The rules require that the parties can maintain themselves 'adequately'. This means that their standard of living must not fall below the minimum considered acceptable in the UK. Adequacy is an objective standard even if some families can live more frugally *(KA (Pakistan)* [2006] UKAIT 00065 para 6). In determining adequacy, the yardstick is income support together with passport benefits (such as housing benefit, council tax benefit, and free school meals and prescriptions; *KA (Pakistan)* [2006] UKAIT 00065, approved by the Court of Appeal in *AM (Somalia) and others v ECO* [2008] EWCA Civ

1082 at para 79). It is not necessary to show there is sufficient money for an indefinite period. In the case of *Ishtiaq Ali* (11568), the Tribunal commented:

> to require some certainty that the parties to the marriage will at all times in the future be able to support and accommodate themselves would make it virtually impossible for a young couple with modest means to meet the requirements of the rule.

In *Shakila Kauser* (17428) INLP vol. 13(2), p. 78, the Tribunal considered there was no need to look further ahead than six months after the appellant's arrival to ascertain whether the couple could maintain themselves adequately. This approach is commonly taken also in indefinite leave applications at the end of the probationary period for married couples and has been confirmed in case law (see, for instance, *Adesegun v ECO Lahore* [2002] UKIAT 02132).

Savings may be taken into account in deciding whether maintenance is adequate. Clearly, where savings will make up a shortfall in income, they will eventually run out. However, as a marriage applicant usually receives leave for only a two-year period initially and must meet the maintenance criterion again when applying for settlement, sufficient savings to cover the two-year period will be acceptable (*Jahangra Begum and others (maintenance – savings) Bangladesh* [2011] UKUT 00246 (IAC). How long savings must last where applicants are entitled to indefinite leave immediately has not been determined but, in addition to the principles discussed in the previous paragraph, it should be recalled that proof is on the balance of probabilities and absolute certainty about the future is not required. A balanced approach based on all the evidence should be taken.

The Family Migration Consultation of July 2011 argued that too many family migrants are reliant on the low wages of their sponsor and risk needing welfare support. It proposed imposing a specific minimum threshold and asked the Migration Advisory Committee to report on the level needed to avoid such risk. The Committee found that an income of between £18,600 and £25,700 would be required for a couple (more where there are children), figures that are in excess of the income earned by between 45 per cent (on the lower figure) and 64 per cent (on the higher figure) of current sponsors. The Family Migration Consultation also envisaged removing recognition of the potential contribution of the incoming partner in spouse cases and 'review' of the provision of third-party support. If all these proposals are implemented, a huge proportion of family members will be unable to meet the conditions of entry. A further possible tightening lies in the suggestion that those who have claimed specified welfare benefits in the period before the application or who are undischarged bankrupts should be excluded from sponsorship.

9.5.1.2 *Disabled sponsor*

Some disabled sponsors receive additional benefits because of their greater needs and it has often been argued that these can be used to support a spouse (who might also perform caring duties that would otherwise be performed, for pay, by others). Tribunal cases had been inconsistent but the Court of Appeal, in *MK Somalia* [2007] EWCA Civ 1521, found by a majority that the sponsor could use the benefit in question (disability living allowance) howsoever she chose, including to maintain a spouse. Pill LJ, dissenting, feared that disabled sponsors might, as a result, be placed under pressure to use their funds in this way (at para 15), perhaps reflecting concerns that have been expressed elsewhere about the exploitation of disabled sponsors in international marriages. Although it was not in issue in *Mahad*, Lord Brown noted the finding and seemed to suggest, as would be logical, that it was not confined to spouse applications.

The decision in *MK Somalia* assists those disabled sponsors who can save out of their additional benefits. However, the Tribunal suggested in *NM (Disability Discrimination)*

Iraq [2008] UKAIT 00026 that this will arise only occasionally. Disabled individuals will often find it difficult to meet the maintenance requirement due to their weak financial position, which may obtain for all their lives so that they are indefinitely precluded from sponsorship. However, the Tribunal in *NM* did not consider that this disadvantage amounted to unlawful discrimination either under the Disability Discrimination Act 1995 or Article 14 ECHR. The Court of Appeal came to the same conclusion, after detailed consideration, on Article 14 (the DDA point not being argued) in *AM (Somalia) v ECO* [2009] EWCA Civ 634.

9.5.1.3 *Third-party maintenance*

One of the major questions concerning maintenance is whether the applicant must be supported from his or her own resources and those of the sponsor or whether they may rely on support from the wider family or from friends to meet the requirements of the rule.

In *Arman Ali* [2000] INLR 89, Collins J, in the High Court, found that an absolute bar on third-party funding breached Article 8 and the rules should be construed purposively to avoid placing more hurdles than are necessary to the enjoyment of family life in the UK. As a consequence of *Arman Ali*, the rule governing the maintenance of children was changed in 2000 to a more restrictive wording and, it was argued by the Home Office, this required children to be entirely maintained by the parents or relatives whom they were joining in the UK.

This interpretation was challenged in *MW (Liberia)* [2007] EWCA Civ 1397. MW was a child whose mother fled civil war, leaving her and her brother in the care of a family friend in Ivory Coast. The mother came to the UK, where she was granted exceptional leave to remain. She enrolled as a student and was in receipt of benefits. Friends in the church gave regular money every week which she sent to look after MW, her brother having gone missing. Her friends were willing to maintain this level of support if MW came to the UK. In the Court of Appeal, it was argued that permitting third-party support would reflect 'changing ideas of family life in a pluralist society where wider communities or extended families support each other in various ways' (para 11). This argument did not persuade the Court who believed that the rules were clear and prohibited third-party support.

That seemed to close the issue so far as children were concerned but the rules for spouses and other relatives were more ambiguously expressed. The government's position at the time was that third-party support for couples would be 'accepted exceptionally' and for a limited period. Third-party maintenance for other relatives was not envisaged. This ignored the decision in *Arman Ali*, an omission described as 'regrettable' in *Mahad*.

The Court of Appeal decision, *AM (Ethiopia) and others v ECO* [2008] EWCA Civ 1082, involved several parties who had been refused admission on maintenance grounds despite, in some instances, offers of third-party support. They included an elderly infirm Somali husband wanting to join his wife and five children. His daughter, who had a well-paid job, and a cousin were willing to maintain him. Another was a Sri Lankan national wanting to join his disabled son. A family friend was willing to provide financial support. The Court found that these, and the other offers of third-party support in this case, could not be relied upon to meet the maintenance requirement. Joint sponsorship was suggested as a possible solution in appropriate cases, although the Court did not rule on whether that was permissible under the current rules.

AM failed to establish a principled basis for distinguishing between the various resources that may be available to a sponsor, for example, from a relative, friend, church or employer. One of the objections to third-party support was that it is difficult to ensure its future continuation. Yet, that is an evidential question to be established in each case and other more acceptable forms of support, such as from employment, may be equally or more precarious. Unsurprisingly, the issue came before the Supreme Court.

Key Case

***Mahad and others v ECO* [2009] UKSC 16**

This case was an appeal by some of the appellants in *AM (Ethiopia)* and the appellant in *AM (Somalia)*, discussed previously, whose disability discrimination claim had been rejected by that Court and who also wished to rely on third party support. The Supreme Court found that, in the words of Lord Kerr, the overall purpose of the maintenance provisions 'is to ensure that there is no resort to public funds by family members entering the United Kingdom... If it can be shown that funds are reliably available from a third party, that eventuality is avoided and the purpose of the rules is fulfilled' (para 51).

In his lead judgment, Lord Brown found that all three categories of family member should be treated according to the same principles, despite the differences in wording. The particular wording used in relation to children was stated to be purely a protection measure designed to ensure that children lived with the relatives named in the application. He observed that third-party maintenance was not materially different from nor less reliable or harder to ascertain than other types of support already accepted, such as employment or help with accommodation, and that, unlike passages elsewhere in the rules, a prohibition on such support was not apparent from the wording of the rules. As the rules, as construed by him, already permitted third-party support, it was not necessary to decide whether a construction in accordance with Article 8 was required or whether Article 8 rights should remain the subject of a separate application outside the rules. He also found that it was open to ECOs to ask a third party to become a joint sponsor and give an undertaking.

The decision recognizes the plurality of family norms and of the mutual support that members of migrant communities and extended families often provide for each other. The decision is strictly obiter so far as the maintenance of children is concerned as none of the applications was made under para 297, but the views of their Lordships were unambiguous and effectively settle the question for all applicants.

The Immigration Directorate Instructions (chapter 8, annex F, para 5.1) now recognize that third-party support for all relatives is permitted provided that satisfactory evidence is provided, and that joint sponsorship is possible. As already mentioned, the Family Migration Consultation proposed a review of third-party support. If the rules are amended to exclude its application, challenges under Article 8 ECHR are likely to follow.

9.5.2 Accommodation

In addition to financial maintenance, the rules require that new entrants must be accommodated adequately. *Mushtaq* (9342) established a base-line requirement that accommodation is 'adequate' if occupation would not be an offence. This means that it is not statutorily overcrowded according to the standard laid down by the Housing Act 1985 s 326. Reports from independent Environmental Health Officers are often prepared to establish that standards are met. Although this is not obligatory at present if satisfactory evidence can be provided in other ways, it may become compulsory according to the Family Migration Consultation. On the other hand, compliance with the overcrowding standard does not in all cases automatically mean that the accommodation is adequate. In *S (Pakistan)* [2004] UKIAT 00006, the Tribunal held that a small terraced house, although it would not be statutorily overcrowded, was not adequate for two adult couples and four small children. There were three bedrooms and a through living-room from which the stairs went up.

HC 395 para 6A applies equally in the case of accommodation. Consequently, the provision of accommodation without recourse to public funds means without additional recourse. In *Rahman* (14257) INLP (1997) vol. 11(4), p. 135, a husband applied to join his wife who lived at her parents' house and was not working. Housing costs were met by housing benefit. The Tribunal held that the question it had to consider was whether there would be any additional claim as a consequence of his arrival. As there would not, his appeal was allowed on the accommodation issue.

The accommodation must be owned or occupied exclusively by the parties. Ownership may be of any form of legal interest in land, freehold or leasehold. Occupation must be by virtue of some legal right to occupy, but this can be as a licensee or a lodger. The requirement to own or occupy exclusively was introduced into the immigration rules in 1994. There was concern that it would discriminate against people living as an extended family. A letter from Nicholas Baker MP, Minister of State for the Home Office, to Giles Shaw MP in October 1994 said that:

> Arrangements whereby the applicant joins his or her married partner in an established household with other residents are...acceptable providing...the applicant and their married partner have at least a small unit of accommodation e.g. a bedroom for their exclusive use.

The Immigration Directorate Instructions reflect the correct position but the presence of the word 'exclusively' may still cause difficulty, as shown in *KJ ('Own or occupy exclusively') Jamaica* [2008] UKAIT 00006. Here, the applicant lived with his girlfriend and her son in a two-bedroom flat of which she was the tenant. There was no overcrowding even if his own son, with whom he did not live, stayed overnight. However, the application was refused by the Home Office because it could not be said that the applicant had 'exclusive' occupation of any part of the property. The Tribunal disagreed and declined to give the word a technical legal meaning, finding it to mean that:

> there is somewhere that the person or people in question can properly, albeit without any legal accuracy, describe as their own home.

As long as this condition is met and satisfactory evidence is provided, it is not necessary that the parties pay a market rent; third-party assistance with accommodation is permitted *(AB (Third party provision of accommodation)* [2008] UKAIT 00018), a position approved by the Supreme Court in *Mahad*.

9.6 Immigration rules for married partners

When the Civil Partnership Act 2004 was implemented in December 2005, the immigration rules on married partners were amended to include civil partners, and the rules are now the same for the two groups. The terms 'married partner' or 'spouse' are used here to include both groups.

Anyone who is subject to immigration control (i.e., is not an EEA national and does not have right of abode) who wants to enter the UK as the married partner of someone settled here, must obtain prior entry clearance even if they do not come from a visa national country. The requirements are set out in para 281 of the current immigration rules. Entry clearance obtained as a married partner will also operate as leave to enter providing its duration and any conditions are endorsed on it (Immigration (Leave to Enter and Remain) Order 2000, SI 2000/1161).

Most of the requirements to obtain leave as a married partner are the same, whether the applicant is applying for entry clearance from abroad or is already in the UK in another capacity. Therefore, case law on a leave to remain case may sometimes be used to illustrate the same point on leave to enter.

9.6.1 Present and settled sponsor

The first requirement is that 'the applicant is married to a person present and settled in the UK or who is on the same occasion being admitted for settlement'. This person is referred to as the 'sponsor'. Paragraph 6 of the rules provides that 'sponsor' means:

> the person in relation to whom an applicant is seeking leave to enter or remain as their spouse, fiance, civil partner, proposed civil partner, unmarried partner, same-sex partner or dependent relative.

Paragraph 281(i)(a) says that the sponsor must be 'present and settled or on the same occasion being admitted for settlement'. As discussed in chapter 7, a 'settled' person includes both a person who has acquired indefinite leave to remain under immigration law and one who has a right of abode. Settled immigrants, Commonwealth citizens with right of abode, and British citizens therefore all qualify as sponsors, providing they are settled, i.e., are ordinarily resident in the UK (Immigration Act 1971 s 33(2)(A)) or are entering on the same occasion for settlement. The Entry Clearance Guidance (SET 3.4) notes that, strictly speaking, someone with the right of abode is not 'being admitted for settlement' but, where there is the intention to return to the UK to reside, they should be regarded as present and settled. In *Rourke v ECO Pretoria* [2002] UKIAT 05666, the sponsor was regarded as present and settled although he had been living and working abroad since 1992. In *Zarda Begum* [1983] Imm AR 175, the Tribunal took the view that the rule permits an applicant to join a partner ordinarily resident in the UK but not to be installed there while their partner lives elsewhere. This does not prevent a settled person, including a British citizen, from having a home in the UK where their partner lives, and another outside the UK, providing they can be said to be ordinarily resident in their UK home (*AB Bangladesh* [2004] UKIAT 00314).

The applicant will normally be awarded leave for 27 months initially and can apply for settlement after two years. Where the sponsor and applicant have lived abroad together for at least four years, indefinite leave will be granted immediately under para 281(i)(b) provided the applicant passes the test of knowledge of language and life in the UK. If the test is not passed, leave is granted for 27 months. Such an applicant may apply for indefinite leave as soon as they have passed the test (SET 3.23). The four-year rule applies both to those with the right of abode (mostly nationals) and those who have indefinite leave to remain although the latter group may find it more difficult to meet the condition of four years' cohabitation abroad as they risk losing their indefinite leave status if they are absent for more than two years (paras 18 and 19: see chapter 7).

In the Family Migration Consultation, the government proposed removal of the four-year rule so that all new spouses would have to undergo the probationary period (due to be raised to five years) no matter how long the couple had lived together outside the UK.

9.6.2 That the applicant has passed a test in English speaking and listening from an approved English language test provider

This requirement entered the rules in November 2010. It requires applicants (subject to narrowly drawn exemptions for age, infirmity and 'exceptional compassionate circumstances') to take and pass an English language speaking and listening test to A1 standard (the lowest level of the Common European Framework of Reference for Languages). Nationals of countries deemed to be 'majority English speaking' (which includes Canada but not, for example, Nigeria or Ghana) or where a single test centre is not available, and those with certain higher education qualifications in English are also exempt.

This apparently simple and undemanding new criterion has proven to be highly problematic in practice. Access to suitable tuition can be a major hurdle for those living in rural areas and some individuals find learning a new language particularly difficult although they do not qualify for exemptions. However, the largest problem has been the small number of approved test providers and the unavailability of tests that only involve speaking and listening. Most tests require literacy in English either to pass the test (as only a combined grade for reading, writing, speaking, and listening is given) or to take it (as literacy skills are needed to take the speaking and listening test, for example, to read a passage aloud or to select multiple choice answers). In addition, the benefits for post-entry integration of requiring proven competence in English at such a low level have not been established. In other European countries where such a test has been implemented, the outcome has been a reduction in the number of spousal migrants (see Groenendijk 2011).

As already mentioned, the compatibility of the test with Articles 8, 12, and 14 ECHR was unsuccessfully challenged in *Chapti*, the decision in which was, at the time of writing, under appeal to the Court of Appeal.

9.6.3 That the parties have met

The next requirement, that the parties have met, is usually straightforward for married couples. Proxy marriages are valid in some countries (see, for example, *CB (Validity of marriage: proxy marriage) Brazil* [2008] UKAIT 00080). Muslim marriages may also sometimes take place by proxy, provided there is an offer and acceptance before witnesses (e.g., as in the case of *Akhtar* 2166) but this is relatively rare. The requirement to have met may also affect fiancé(e)s who meet online or enter very traditional arranged marriages.

The requirement to have met was introduced into the rules in 1979 by a newly elected Conservative government, alongside other proposals including the prohibition on the entry of more than one wife to a polygamous marriage, a question discussed further at 9.6.7.2. The proposed changes were so far-reaching that the rules (HC 394) were debated in the House of Commons. The opposition accused the government of equating arranged marriages with marriages of convenience. Alex Lyon MP went on: 'it is intended to hit the genuine arranged marriages of Asian girls, whether or not they were born in this country' (HC Debs 14 November 1979 col 1336). The Home Secretary in his response did not deny that this was the case, but revealed another objective for the rule:

> I remember the Hon. Member for Ealing, Southall telling me that in the future it will increasingly be the practice that Asian girls in this country will wish to marry Asian boys in this country. I should have thought that was a position that we should encourage.

HC 394 was challenged in *Abdulaziz, Cabales and Balkandali*, but the European Court of Human Rights found that the requirement for the parties to have met was not racially discriminatory under Article 14 of the Convention.

Where there has not been a recent meeting, the test in *Meharban v ECO Islamabad* [1989] Imm AR 57 may be applied. In that case, the sponsor and her fiancé had played together as children, but she could not recall his appearance or other characteristics. His application for entry clearance was refused. The Tribunal found that, while there was no need for the parties to have met each other in the context of marriage or marriage arrangements, they should have an appreciation of each other's appearance or personality. In *Hashmi* (4975), the families found a way to satisfy both the immigration rules and their religious tradition. The fiancé and his parents stayed for a few days at the same house as the sponsor and her mother. This was arranged in order to comply with the rule, but, because of religious tradition, they did not speak to each other. The Tribunal accepted that there had been a 'meeting' within the rule.

The Entry Clearance Guidance (SET 3.10) does not refer to *Hashmi* but cites the earlier case of *Jaffer* (4284). Here, the parties had stayed in the same house when the sponsor was 14 and had seen each other from one room to another but had not spoken. They were found not to have met. There is a tension between this case and *Hashmi* and the entry clearance service prefers the more restrictive interpretation.

9.6.4 Intention to live permanently with each other

The parties must show that 'each of the parties intends to live permanently with the other as his or her spouse or civil partner' (para 281(iii)). The rule provides an opportunity to test the genuine nature of the marriage. Anxiety about marriages of convenience, or 'sham' or 'bogus' marriages as they have more recently been described, has been a recurrent theme in immigration control, although Wray (2006a) has argued that measures to combat them have often gone much wider, targeting unwanted migrants in genuine marriages. Before considering application of the test of intention to live together therefore, it is worth considering briefly both problems with the concept of a sham marriage and the historical context from which the rule has emerged.

9.6.4.1 *What is a sham marriage?*

There have been several attempts to define a sham marriage in legislation. Perhaps the clearest has been that used in EU law: a marriage concluded 'with the sole aim of circumventing the rules on entry and residence' (Council Resolution 97/C 382/01 of 4 December 1997). If a marriage has no purpose except to gain admission to another country and the parties do not intend to have a married life, measures to prevent that happening are unobjectionable. However, measures under UK law have often targeted marriages where intentions are more mixed. As Wray (2006a) points out, motives for choosing a spouse may include the social and economic benefits, including immigration, which will flow from the marriage even though the parties fully intend to live together and may be deeply attached.

As a result, there is a substantial grey area where immigration plays a role in decision-making but the relationship is entirely genuine. It includes not only marriages where immigration status is an added inducement but marriages that take place sooner than they otherwise might to secure immigration status and parties to arranged marriages where the families have negotiated the marriage bearing in mind the immigration consequences. Such marriages are far removed from a sham marriage, which may be entered into for money and where the parties have no relationship and no intention to live together yet may easily be caught by measures purporting to prevent only sham marriages as may marriages where there is no immigration motive at all. An example of such broad measures is the 'primary purpose rule', removed from the immigration rules in 1997 and discussed in the next section, and the Certificates of Approval scheme discussed later in this chapter and also now abolished.

9.6.4.2 *The historical context*

Entry through marriage first became a prominent issue in the mid-1960s. After Commonwealth immigration controls were imposed by the Commonwealth Immigrants Act 1962, migrants had to decide whether to return definitively to their country of origin or remain in the UK and bring over their families, as male migrants were entitled to do under the Act. The issue particularly affected South Asian workers who had often left their families behind, envisaging only a temporary sojourn. The result was a large increase in the number of wives and children arriving. Growing hostility to their arrival led to claims of abuse and long queues at airports while their credentials were checked. The problem was eventually exported through the imposition of a compulsory entry clearance system under the Immigration Appeals Act 1969, leading to long delays and a suspicious approach to decision-making on the subcontinent and elsewhere that led to lasting resentment. These applicants often lacked official documentation, such as birth or marriage certificates, to prove their status and there was heavy reliance on the so-called 'discrepancy system', under which different family members were interviewed separately and asked about their lives and homes, sometimes in great detail. If their answers differed, this would be used to cast doubt upon their relationship and applicants were rejected as being 'not related as claimed'. Some years later, DNA testing revealed that most of those who had been refused were telling the truth.

As they reached marriageable age, some young women of migrant origin in the UK entered marriages with men from their country of origin and sought to bring them to the UK. As it was more usual for a wife to move to her husband's place of residence, these marriages were regarded with great suspicion, even though such customs are liable to evolve as circumstances change and this new pattern represented a pragmatic response to a new situation in which the wife's place of residence offered more opportunities. However, the entry of non-white men of working age was seen as unacceptable and, in 1969, the entry of all Commonwealth husbands was banned unless there were 'special features'. The ban proved unpopular as its effects were felt well beyond migrant communities and, following extensive campaigning, it was removed in 1974 and, over the succeeding years, a new tool evolved: the 'primary purpose rule'. This rule required the applicant to prove that 'the marriage was not entered into primarily to gain admission to the UK' (HC 395 para 281 before amendment). Applicants were faced with the difficult task of proving a negative, that any immigration motivation was not the primary purpose of the marriage. For those who had entered arranged marriages, this was particularly difficult as the reasons for marriage that are familiar in the West, such as romantic attachment, were often absent at this early stage and marriages were entered for reasons of family obligation that could easily be presented as driven by emigration. Many thousands of husbands, particularly from South Asia, were refused during the currency of the rule, although, as time went on, some concessions were made for long-lasting marriages.

The primary purpose rule was rarely applied outside South Asia and the Caribbean. Macdonald and Blake said in 1991 that they had 'still to hear of an American, Australian or New Zealander who [had] failed the primary purpose test' (1991:260–261). It is unsurprising that Macdonald later referred to the 'primary purpose' rule as one which 'generated more anger and anguish than perhaps any of the other Immigration Rules' (1995:343).

In accordance with its manifesto commitment, the incoming Labour government removed 'primary purpose' from the immigration rules in June 1997. The test of 'intention to live together', which had been present in the rules since 1977 but little used in the era of primary purpose, became the main way of determining whether the marriage is genuine.

9.6.4.3 *Applying 'intention to live together'*

While the 'primary purpose' rule was criticized for going beyond the detection of sham marriages, the test of 'intention to live together' relies on a major characteristic of most genuine marriages. Most spouses intend to live with each other, although a few couples prefer to maintain separate homes or to spend substantial periods apart. Nonetheless, 'intention to live together' is a test that is designed to fulfil its stated purpose of distinguishing between genuine and sham marriages. Most couples are able to satisfy the test by providing evidence of their relationship or that their marriage conforms to the norms of their culture. There seem to be relatively few refusals on 'intention' alone. Compared to the era of primary purpose, acceptance rates have improved and the issue has lost much of its heat.

Nonetheless, some problems have been associated with its application, particularly in the Indian subcontinent (see Wray 2006b). Some entry clearance officers have had difficulty understanding the difference between 'primary purpose' and 'intention'. The former is concerned with the motives for the marriage and the latter with the parties' intentions for the future, regardless of the reasons for the marriage. Even if emigration was one or even the major reason for the marriage, if the parties intend to cohabit, the 'intention' test is satisfied, a point made explicitly in the case of *Canas* (20557) INLP vol. 13(3) (1999) p. 109. In *Alaezihe v ECO Dublin* [2002] UKIAT 01168, the Tribunal overturned the adjudicator's decision because he had placed too much reliance on the appellant's adverse immigration history, from which he had gleaned an intention to come to the UK. This, however, was not the question. The appropriate question was, given that the parties were married, whether they had the intention to live together permanently.

The discrepancy approach has also sometimes been inappropriately applied to the requirement to show intention to live together. In *Anju Malik v ECO New Delhi* [2002] UKIAT 00738, the point was made that discrepancies do not have the same significance in an arranged marriage as in a love match, a point also made in the cases of *Sabar Gul v ECO Islamabad* TH/5118/99 and *Choudhury v ECO Dhaka* [2002] UKIAT 00239. In both these cases, the adjudicator had looked for evidence of personal knowledge of each other's circumstances, which should not be expected where the marriage had been arranged and the parties had little prior direct knowledge of each other.

Intention to live together does not require a willingness to cohabit anywhere. It is present even if the parties are willing to cohabit only in the UK (*R (on the application of Olofunisi) v IAT* [2002] EWHC 2106), although the Entry Clearance Guidance (SET 3.6) suggests that the entry clearance service regards this as relevant. A couple may intend to live permanently together even though present circumstances, such as work or family commitments, prevent them from cohabiting all the time, as in *Kumar* (17779) INLP vol. 13(3) p. 109 (1999), *Niksarli* (21663) (INLP vol. 14, no. 2, p. 110), and *Satnam Singh*

(19068) INLP vol. 13(2) (1999) p. 78. On the other hand, where a sponsor had, at the time of the marriage, committed an offence leading to a nine-year prison sentence, the Tribunal held that no intention to live together could be formed. An intention is more than a wish (*Shabbana Bibi v ECO Islamabad* [2002] UKIAT 06623).

Past periods of separation are irrelevant if future intention is established. In *Janat Bi* (16929), the couple had lived together for 11 years followed by separation during most of the next 40 years because of the wife's family commitments. Their intention to live together was accepted. In *Barlas* TH/ 03975/2000, there were four years of separation before the appellant applied to come to the UK. The Tribunal did not see this as counting against intention to live together, particularly in the context of an arranged marriage. However, there are limits to the types of separation that will be countenanced. In *AB Bangladesh* [2004] UKIAT 00314, the Tribunal held that the appellant's intention to live six months of each year with his British wife and the other six months with his wife in Bangladesh could not amount to an intention to live permanently together.

Cohabitation does not require sexual relations but the precise content of 'living together' sometimes seems elusive. In *ZB and HB (Validity and recognition of marriage) Pakistan* [2009] UKAIT 00040, the applicant wished to join her severely disabled spouse. Although the central issue was that of capacity, the Tribunal was not persuaded that intention to live together was present, saying that the requirements of the rule 'are not met simply by a wish to share a house, nor by a wish to look after the sponsor, or a wish to alleviate the care responsibilities imposed upon the sponsor's mother by her relatives' (para 16). Given that the parties had a sex life and a child, it is difficult to pinpoint exactly what the Tribunal required although it seems that the lack of mutual interaction and previous visits was a decisive factor, a finding that is reminiscent of primary purpose with its emphasis on the motivation for the marriage.

Generally, a balanced approach should be taken, looking at the marriage as a whole, not one episode or aspect of it. In *Bryan* (14694) INLP vol. 11(3) (1997), immigration officers apparently caught the sponsor on a bad day. When they called, he expressed his doubts about the appellant, thought she might be having a relationship with another man, that the marriage was just being used to enable her to stay in the UK, and so on. She was not interviewed. The Tribunal allowed her appeal, saying that the question of intention to live together did not turn upon the credibility of what was said or done on a particular day, but on the position in the light of all the evidence. As *Noisaen* and a number of other cases such as *Chowdhury* (16080), *Hanif* (17561) both INLP vol. 12, (4), p. 146 (1998), and *Iqbal* (17293) in June 1999 demonstrate, enquiries into intention should be confined to whether the surrounding circumstances and context of the marriage suggest that intention exists. The fact, for example, that the parties have a house that they intend to live in together is more important than the particular conversations that they have had about the house (*Chowdhury*).

9.6.5 The marriage is subsisting

Paragraph 281(iii) also requires that the marriage be subsisting. In *GA ('subsisting' marriage) Ghana* [2006] UKAIT 00046, the Tribunal treated this as a separate requirement to legal validity and to intention to live together. A subsisting marriage, they said, is one which has some real substance in terms of relationship. This couple had lived apart for 20 years and there was a legal tie, but the marriage was not subsisting. This was a starred decision and the ruling was therefore binding on subsequent tribunals, overturning the earlier view in *BK* [2005] UKAIT 00174 that 'subsisting' only meant the marriage was current in law.

In the Family Migration Consultation, the government expressed a wish 'to find objective means of identifying whether a relationship, marriage or partnership is genuine and continuing or not'. It proposed defining 'more clearly what constitutes a genuine and continuing relationship, marriage or partnership (one that is "subsisting" for the purposes of the Immigration Rules)'. Possible indicators include a common account of the 'core facts' of the relationship, a common language, the parties' relative ages, the nature of the wedding celebrations, and the parties' immigration histories. The problem with any such checklist is that many genuine marriages may fail under one or more of those headings. There is a danger that such indicators will be used to reinforce pre-existing stereotypes about which migrants engage in bogus marriages.

9.6.6 Time when requirements must be met

What happens if an application is refused, but circumstances change so that by the time of the appeal, the rules have been met, for example, through employment or an offer of accommodation? After the Court of Appeal judgment in *R v IAT ex p Kotecha* [1982] Imm AR 88, account could be taken of arrangements which were positively and reasonably foreseeable at the time of the decision. Section 85(5) Nationality, Immigration and Asylum Act 2002 provides that, in entry clearance cases, the Tribunal 'may consider only the circumstances appertaining at the time of the decision to refuse', i.e. in existence at the time of the decision to refuse. Therefore, in an entry clearance application, evidence which arises after the date of the decision will not be admissible except to the extent that it sheds light on the situation at the date of the decision. The rule is exemplified by a starred decision, *DR Morocco* [2005] UKIAT 00038, where intense correspondence between a couple after refusal of entry clearance was admissible evidence that, at the date of the refusal, they did, in fact, have an intention to live permanently together. What is not admissible, however, is evidence of a fact necessary for entry when that fact arises only after the decision has been made. In *SF (Afghanistan) v ECO* [2011] EWCA Civ 758, the Court of Appeal found that the applicant could not rely on a job offer made after the decision because there was no evidence put forward at the time of the decision to show that such an offer was at all probable. As the Court said in *DR Morocco* (at para 28), 'the fact that something happened does not logically demonstrate its likelihood anyway, because unlikely events do happen'.

The exclusion of post-decision evidence, except when light is shed on the state of affairs at the time of the decision, does not apply to a refusal of an application of leave to remain as a spouse made in-country. In *AS (Somalia) v SSHD* [2009] UKHL 32 at para 9, Lord Phillips considered that the distinction was justified because, in applications made outside the jurisdiction, the entry clearance officer is best placed to make factual judgements. The exception for entry clearance applications was not, in itself, incompatible with Article 8, although there might be particular cases where its effects, in terms of delay and expense, would be disproportionate.

9.6.7 Legal issues concerning marriage and divorce

Applicants must establish a valid marriage, required under the rules by inclusion of the simple phrase in para 281 'is married'. The validity of the marriage is adjudged at the date of the marriage and is established by showing that both parties had the legal capacity to marry and that the celebration took place in accordance with appropriate formalities. The second of these requirements is the more straightforward to apply in law, although there may be practical difficulties in obtaining evidence. If the marriage is properly conducted according to the law of the country in which it is celebrated, its formal validity is accepted in English law (the principle of *lex loci celebrationis*). This means that in a country where same-sex marriage is recognized, a properly conducted same-sex marriage will be recognized for immigration purposes.

The country in which the marriage is celebrated is usually where both parties are physically present. The only exceptions are where the marriage is conducted by telephone or by proxy. The Entry Clearance Guidance says at SET 3.17 that in countries where marriage consists of an offer by a man accepted by a woman, a telephonic marriage is celebrated in the country where the woman is. Therefore, where the wife is resident in the UK and the offer made from overseas, the marriage is considered as having been celebrated in the UK and so not valid in UK law. If the husband is in the UK and the wife in a country where telephone marriages are valid and the formalities are observed, the marriage should be valid. However, the Entry Clearance Guidance and the Immigration Directorate Instructions state that a telephone marriage celebrated whilst one of the parties is in the UK is not valid. In *J (Pakistan)* [2003] UKIAT 00167, it was conceded that a telephonic marriage where the man was present and domiciled in the UK was not valid as the law of the UK governed his personal capacity to marry and does not recognize telephonic marriages.

However, this approach is arguably incorrect. The rules on domicile, which govern these matters, are concerned with capacity to enter the marriage (matters such as age, consanguinity, and so on) and not the form of the marriage. If the marriage is entered in a country where telephone marriages are valid, the location and domicile of the other party should be irrelevant. In *KC and NNC v City of Westminster* [2008] EWCA Civ 198, the Court of Appeal accepted a telephone marriage between a man in the UK and a woman in Bangladesh as valid in Bangladesh (although the point was not fully argued). Its non-recognition by the Court was because of the husband's mental incapacity.

Proxy marriage is lawful in some countries and such marriages, provided they are celebrated according to local rules, are valid regardless of the domicile of the parties (*CB (Validity of marriage: proxy marriage) Brazil* [2008] UKAIT 00080). The Tribunal in *CB*, relying on *Apt v Apt* [1947] P 127, found that there was no public policy reason to invalidate proxy marriages. This is acknowledged in the IDI chapter 8, annex B, para 3.1.

Aside from such rare situations, a marriage certificate is normally enough to prove formal validity. In *Babul* (16466), it was held that where a marriage certificate is produced which provides prima facie proof of a valid marriage, the party asserting that the marriage is not valid has the burden of proof to a high standard. If a finding is made that the marriage is not valid, this only has a direct effect for immigration purposes. There would need to be a separate declaration under the Family Law Act 1986 to affect the marriage for any purpose other than immigration. The issues which have a greater effect on the recognition of marriages in the UK are the questions of the legal capacity to enter into the marriage in question and the recognition of previous divorces.

9.6.7.1 *Capacity*

The capacity to marry is determined for each individual separately, and is governed by the law of the country which is their domicile. Halsbury's Laws (vol. 8(1) para 680) explains:

> A person is domiciled in that country in which he [sic] either has or is deemed by law to have his permanent home. Every individual is regarded as belonging, at every stage in his life, to some community consisting of all persons domiciled in a particular country... Although a person may have no permanent home, the law requires him to have a domicile.

Domicile differs from ordinary residence, in that a person may have more than one ordinary residence but not more than one domicile. Domicile may also differ from nationality and the personal civil law which applies to an individual is the law of their domicile. Domicile of origin is acquired at birth and is the domicile of the father for a child born inside marriage and of the mother for a child born outside marriage. *Cramer v Cramer* [1986] Fam Law 333 CA confirms an old rule that there is a strong presumption in favour of retaining one's domicile of origin. A domicile of choice is acquired by residence in a country where one intends to stay permanently. This intention must be proved by objective criteria. Statements of intention will not suffice. The House of Lords in *Mark v Mark* [2005] UKHL 42 held that, if a person's presence is illegal in immigration law, this does not affect their domicile. The House of Lords made the distinction between a status which would give some benefit against the state, when illegality ought not to benefit an individual, and domicile, which is a private law matter and a question of fact. Domicile simply determines which legal system will govern private law matters such as divorce proceedings. The burden of proving that the domicile of origin has been lost rests on the person making the assertion. If they do not succeed in discharging the burden of proof, the domicile remains the domicile of origin.

To say that the law of a person's domicile governs their capacity to marry means that conditions for entering into a marriage, such as age and mental capacity, are according to that country's law. The law of the UK requires that a person must be 16 years old and not married to anyone else in order to enter a valid marriage. Although the age at which someone may sponsor their married partner is now 18 (after rising to 21), this does not prevent the marriage taking place at whatever age is allowed by the law of the parties' domicile. It only means that a married partner cannot enter the UK until both parties are 18.

Domicile is also relevant where one party lacks the capacity to marry under English law but may do so under the law where the marriage is celebrated. The issue has become prominent in the recent past because of a number of marriages between mentally disabled adults resident in the UK and applicants living abroad. From a UK perspective, these marriages may be regarded, in the words of Wall LJ in *KC* as, 'exploitative and indeed abusive' (para 45). Motives may, however, on examination, prove less malign than first appear, being concerned with procuring long-term care for the relative rather than their abuse, although these marriages are controversial, particularly where they also involve sexual relations.

Key Case

***KC and NNC v City of Westminster Social and Community Services Department* [2008] EWCA Civ 198**

This case has already been discussed in relation to telephone marriages. The marriage involved a young man with serious mental disabilities and a woman living in Bangladesh. The man was domiciled in England and Wales and lacked capacity to consent to marriage under UK law, although it seemed (although was not fully argued) that the marriage was valid in Bangladesh. Social services intervened and sought various orders, including one as to the validity of the marriage in the UK. As the man lacked capacity to marry, his marriage was voidable under s 12 Matrimonial Causes Act 1973. A voidable marriage remains in existence until the Court has issued a decree of nullity. The Court of Appeal found that the question was therefore one of recognition rather than validity. The marriage would not be recognized by the English courts as, while it was not void, it was 'offensive to the conscience of the English court' (para 101). This was a decision of policy rather than law, the Court finding such a marriage repugnant to its values.

9.6.7.2 *Polygamy*

Where a polygamous marriage has been validly entered into in another country, English law does not recognize it as valid where one party to the marriage is domiciled in the UK (Matrimonial Causes Act 1973 s 11(d)). *Hussain v Hussain* [1982] 3 All ER 369 CA found that this applied to the marriages of British women to men domiciled in countries that permitted polygamy and celebrated in that country, as they were potentially polygamous. The Private International Law (Miscellaneous Provisions) Act 1995 s 5 provided that s 11(d) only applies to actually polygamous marriages. The effect is that where the practical reality of the marriage is that it is monogamous it will be treated as such by UK law, wherever it is celebrated.

Where a marriage is in fact polygamous, if one of the parties is domiciled in the UK, the marriage is void under s 11(d). If neither party is domiciled in the UK, the validity of the polygamous marriage is recognized if it was recognized in the country where the parties are domiciled. However, para 278 of the immigration rules prevents entry clearance being granted to a wife where another wife of the same man has, since her marriage to him, visited the UK or been granted entry clearance or a certificate of entitlement.

9.6.7.3 *Recognition of divorce*

Because the UK does not recognize polygamy for people domiciled in the UK and does not permit entry of further married partners, entry clearance will be refused where an earlier divorce is not recognized as the person will be regarded as still married to the previous spouse. Religious divorces, such as the Islamic talaq divorce or the Jewish Get, if obtained in the UK, will not be regarded as valid as, within the jurisdiction, divorce may only be granted by a civil court (see, for instance, *ECO Islamabad v Tanzeela Imran* [2002] UKIAT 07383). A divorce obtained partially in the UK and partially abroad is not recognized in the UK even if it follows the formalities of the other country. This is the outcome of the House of Lords decision in *R v SSHD ex p Ghulam Fatima* [1986] AC 527. In that case, a talaq was pronounced in the UK and notice sent to the Union Council in Pakistan. The House of Lords found that it should not be recognized in the UK, a decision that was criticized for prolonging 'limping marriages' where the divorce is recognized in one jurisdiction and not in another.

The law in relation to recognition of divorces obtained entirely in other countries is set out in Family Law Act 1986 ss 44–54. A divorce obtained in a foreign jurisdiction will be recognized if it complies with the legal requirements of the country where it was obtained, if it was obtained by proceedings and if either party was habitually resident, domiciled in, or a national of that country (Family Law Act 1986 s 46(1)).

The majority of divorces obtained abroad, including many talaq divorces, are obtained through proceedings and are capable of recognition under s 46(1). For example, in Bangladesh and most of Pakistan, the Muslim Family Law Ordinance of 1961 requires registration of the talaq with the Union Council. The divorce then becomes effective in civil law after a period allowed for reconciliation. A talaq so registered will be recognized in UK law if the other conditions for recognition are met. This should be distinguished from the situation in *Naseem Akhtar* (15412) INLP vol. 12(1) (1998), p. 30, where there had been ancillary proceedings carried out after a bare talaq. This was not sufficient to convert a bare talaq into a talaq by proceedings.

The Tribunal in *Baig v ECO Islamabad* [2002] UKIAT 04229 laid down guidance as to the proper approach to ascertaining whether a divorce was obtained by proceedings. The Tribunal made an important distinction between tradition and proceedings. The talaq in question in this case was not a bare talaq, but a talaq al-hasan, which entailed formal declarations of divorce at monthly intervals. The appellant argued that this was by way of proceedings as it entailed more ritual and process than a bare talaq. The Tribunal said, however, that talaq al-hasan:

> lacks any formality other than the ritual performance. It lacks the invocation or assistance of any organ of the state. It does not even require an organ of the state to act as a registrar or recorder of what has happened. (para 39)

Accordingly, it was regarded as a purely personal act and not a divorce obtained by proceedings. Section 46(2) of the Family Law Act 1986 provides that a divorce obtained otherwise than by means of proceedings may still be recognized if it is effective in the country in which it was obtained, both parties are domiciled in a country which recognizes the divorce, and neither party was habitually resident in the UK for a period of one year prior to the divorce. This assists parties who are relying on a divorce obtained before commencing residence in the UK. For example, in *NC (bare talaq – Indian Muslims recognition) Pakistan* [2009] UKAIT 00016, both parties had previously been divorced using the bare talaq procedure but as both had been domiciled and resident in countries that permitted bare talaq (the Kashmir region of Pakistan and India), the earlier divorces were recognized.

Recognition of marriage and divorce is made even more complex by the prevalence in some countries of customary unofficial ceremonies for which there is little or no paperwork. In the past, the absence of formal documentation was used regularly as a means to divide families who were clearly related. Registration in countries such as India has become more commonplace and the issue has become less prominent. Nonetheless, there are still frequent reports of instances when applicants have had difficulty establishing their entitlement with consequences in terms of delay, expense, and refusal (see Menski 2007; Shah 2011a, 2011b).

Where written evidence of a customary marriage or divorce is not available, evidence may be provided by a statutory declaration or affidavit from family members or others able to confirm that the ceremony took place. There is no obligation to register a ceremony if to do so is optional under local law (*NA (Customary marriage and divorce – evidence) Ghana* [2009] UKAIT 00009). The Entry Clearance Guidance provides that evidence of a marriage may also be obtained through separate interview of the parties (SET 3.15).

If a person is not free to marry another, their application to enter as a married partner cannot be treated as an application to enter as a fiancé(e) and granted on that basis *(ECO Islamabad v Mohammad Rafiq Khan* 01/TH 2798 and *ECO Islamabad v Shakeel* [2002] UKIAT 00605).

9.6.8 Leave to enter and the probationary period

If all these conditions are met, together with those relating to maintenance and accommodation, a married partner is given leave to enter the UK for up to 27 months (HC 395 para 282). This allows the applicant time to arrange entry after issue of the visa and still to fulfil the two-year probationary period. Since 8 November 1996, spouse visas have been routinely subject to the condition not to have recourse to public funds. The Social Security (Persons from Abroad) Miscellaneous Amendment Regulations 1996 also removed entitlement to non-contributory benefits from people with limited leave, such as married partners in their first two years, so most benefits cannot be accessed anyway. However, recourse to contributory benefits may still arise and breach of the condition is a criminal offence and potentially a basis for removal. However, the IDIs (chapter 8, Annex F) says that this may be overlooked if a person has become dependent on public funds for a short time through no fault of their own.

The Family Migration Consultation proposes extending the spouse probationary period from two years to five years with a prohibition on receiving means-tested benefits for the whole of that period. The effect would be that couples must maintain not only their relationship but their economic independence, accommodation etc. for a much longer period than at present. Where a marriage breaks down or jobs or homes are lost before the five years have expired, the migrant spouse would become liable to removal. A likely outcome, particularly where there are children, would be an increase in claims under Article 8 ECHR.

9.6.8.1 *Indefinite leave to remain*

Shortly before the end of the two-year period, the married partner may apply for indefinite leave to remain if they continue to meet the requirements of the rules as to maintenance and accommodation, valid and subsisting marriage, intention to live together, has passed the knowledge of life and language in the UK test and does not have any unspent convictions (para 287).

Paragraph 287 requires the applicant to have received leave as the spouse of the party upon whom the indefinite leave application is based and to have lived in the UK for two years. It does not require the applicant to have current leave and, in an unreported Tribunal case, it was successfully argued that where the leave had expired and the applicant had overstayed, the applicant still qualified for indefinite leave if he met the other conditions, including those in para 322 regarding circumstances in which leave to remain should be refused (Appeal no. IA/20825/2010).

Once indefinite leave is granted, the married partner from abroad is free of immigration restrictions on their stay, may claim benefits, and may come and go freely, subject to the requirements of para 18 of the rules (see chapter 7). After three years' residence as a married partner, they may apply to become a British citizen (British Nationality Act 1981 s 6 and Sch 1, amended by Civil Partnership Act 2004 Sch 27 para 72), but until they acquire that citizenship, the married partner with indefinite leave remains liable to deportation and may lose their status if they leave the UK for a period of two years (see chapters 3 and 7 on naturalization and settlement).

9.6.8.2 *Leave to remain as a married partner*

As mentioned earlier, a person with limited leave under some other categories of the immigration rules may apply in the UK to stay as a married partner (para 284). Rules as to accommodation and maintenance, the marriage, and so on, apply as for an application for entry clearance and the applicant must not have remained in breach of immigration laws. The 2002 White Paper, *Secure Borders, Safe Haven* (Cm 5387), argued that many marriages entered into by people who had been in the UK for less than six months were not genuine (para 7.11). Consequent rule changes ended the possibility of extending leave to stay as a married partner for those granted six months' leave or less. Where a person who is not eligible to switch into marriage wishes to remain on that basis, their application may be considered in accordance with Article 8 ECHR.

An applicant for an extension of stay as a married partner will be granted for two years in the first instance, placing them on a similar footing to a married partner who comes directly from abroad (para 285) and they will be subject to conditions as to public funds.

9.6.9 Domestic violence and bereavement

On the basis of the rules discussed so far, a married partner has no claim to remain if the marriage breaks down or their partner dies during the first two years. This caused particular anguish to those bereaved and serious problems for those who suffer violence from their spouse during the probationary period. The latter group could not remain safely in their marriage but might feel unable to leave, particularly if return to their country of origin was financially or socially impossible.

Under para 287(b), the bereaved may obtain indefinite leave if the relationship was still in existence at the time of death. Paragraph 289A of the immigration rules provides for indefinite leave for victims of domestic violence under certain conditions. It applies to those who have entered or been given leave as a spouse, civil partner, or as an unmarried or same sex partner but not, the Tribunal has found, to partners granted discretionary leave outside the immigration rules (*Guzman Barrios (domestic violence – DLR – Article 14 ECHR) Columbia* [2011] UKUT 00352 (IAC)). The relationship must have broken down permanently as a result of domestic violence before the expiry of limited leave. Violence is not confined to physical violence but includes '[a]ny incident of threatening behaviour, violence or abuse (psychological, physical, sexual, financial or emotional)" (Modernised Guidance 'Victims of Domestic Violence' p. 7) although a certain minimum threshold of seriousness must be crossed (*AN (Pakistan) v SSHD* [2010] EWCA Civ 757). While the Guidance sets out the kinds of evidence required to prove domestic violence, that cannot be taken to limit the discretion implicit in the rule to admit whatever evidence the decision-maker thinks fit (*AI (Pakistan) v SSHD* [2007] EWCA Civ 386).

The violence must cause the relationship to break down before the probationary period expires and the rule cannot not be used to remedy overstaying (*IN (domestic violence IDI policy)* [2007] UKAIT 00024). However, a domestic violence sufferer may lose track of time or may be prevented from applying for indefinite leave as part of the abuse. Cultural factors also inhibit some victims from coming forward when the violence first occurs. The Modernised Guidance does envisage that out-of-time applications may be made (pp.13–14) but the violence must have caused the breakdown before the end of the probationary period, and that can be difficult to establish retrospectively. In *IN*, the wife told her GP that she did not report the violence before 'because of the Asian culture'. While there was evidence of earlier abuse, her attempts at reconciliation meant that she could not show that the marriage had ended during the probationary period.

The violence does not have to be the immediate or the only cause of the breakdown (*R (on the application of B) v SSHD* [2002] EWCA Civ 1797; *AG (India) v SSHD* [2007] EWCA Civ 1534). The Tribunal in *LA (Pakistan) v SSHD* [2009] UKAIT 00019 sensibly pointed out that, while a relationship usually ends at the moment one or both parties declare an intention to leave, the cause of the breakdown, here the 'boorish conduct' of the husband over an extended period, can only be assessed by looking at the relationship as a whole.

A major practical issue facing those fleeing violent relationships is the 'no recourse to public funds' requirement of their leave. Refuges cannot offer places to those who are unable to claim benefits, while social housing is also not available to victims. In 2011, the government amended the rules to exclude those with unspent criminal convictions from obtaining indefinite leave including on domestic violence grounds (see para 289a(v) HC 395). On 12 October 2011, in response to a parliamentary question, the Minister for Equalities, Lynne Featherstone, said that: '[n]o one with a minor conviction has been or will ever be denied their stay in this country'. The Minister for Immigration, Damian Green, in a letter to ILPA dated 4 April 2011, stated that instances of minor unspent criminality would be considered on a case-by-case basis outside the rules although settlement would not always follow.

9.7 Restricting the right to marry

Section 24 of the Immigration and Asylum Act 1999 imposed a duty on marriage registrars to report to the Secretary of State any marriage which they have reasonable grounds for suspecting is a 'sham marriage'. A 'sham marriage' is defined in s 24(5) as one entered into by a person 'who is neither a British Citizen nor a national of an EEA state other than the UK... for the purpose of avoiding the effect of one or more provisions of the UK immigration law or rules'.

The number of reports by registrars under the 1999 Act rose from 756 in 2001 to 2,712 in 2003, and 2,251 in just the first half of 2004 (Hansard 15 June 2004 col 681). This rise, which may have been due to increased incidence or increased reporting, was cited in support of the 'Certificates of Approval' scheme introduced under ss 19–25 Asylum and Immigration (Treatment of Claimants, etc.) Act 2004 (AITOCA).

AITOCA s 20 requires those subject to immigration control and who wish to marry outside the Church of England to give notice of their marriage in specified form to designated registrars. Section 25 formerly provided that the registrar could enter the marriage in the marriage notice book (necessary for the marriage to proceed) only if the party or parties subject to immigration control had entry clearance for the purpose of marriage (i.e., a fiancé(e) or marriage visitor visa), written permission of the Secretary of State to marry, or belonged to a class exempted from the Act by the Secretary of State.

Implementation of s 25 was highly controversial. All those subject to immigration control but without indefinite leave or a fiancé(e) or marriage visit visa had to apply for a certificate of approval to marry, costing £135 later raised to £295. Those on short-term leave, without leave, or whose leave would shortly expire were refused unless compassionate circumstances (narrowly defined) were present. Given the blanket ban and the discrimination in favour of Church of England marriages, legal challenge was inevitable. The government was defeated in the High Court, the Court of Appeal, and, finally, the House of Lords.

Key Case

***R (on the application of Baiai and others) v SSHD* [2008] UKHL 53**

The applicants in this case all wished to marry but at least one of the parties in each relationship needed a certificate of approval to do so. These had initially been refused because of their immigration status. The genuine nature of the relationships had not been challenged. The House of Lords found that the right to marry under Article 12 was a strong right, which could be regulated by national law but could not be subject to conditions that impaired the essence of the right. While governments could impose conditions on the marriages of foreign nationals in order to ascertain whether there was a marriage of convenience, the scheme as implemented breached Article 12 ECHR (the right to marry) because of its broad and over-inclusive nature. The fee of £295 for each party needing a certificate could also be expected to 'impair the essence' of the right to marry. These were matters determined by regulations and guidance and did not affect the compatibility of the statute with Convention rights. The statutory scheme itself was discriminatory only because of the exemption for marriages in the Church of England. The government having accepted this conclusion, the declaration of incompatibility was set aside.

The effect of the judgment was that the government could still require foreign nationals to obtain permission from the government before getting married but those marrying in the Church of England must not be treated differently, the cost of the application must be reasonable, and permission must not be refused on the basis of immigration status alone.

In addition to the *Baiai* judgments, the scheme was found to breach Articles 12 and 14 ECHR by the European Court of Human Rights in *O'Donoghue and others v UK* (Application no. 34848/07 [2010] ECHR 2022). The Court was particularly critical of the blanket nature of the scheme based purely on immigration status, the fee, and of the exemption for Church of England marriages.

Despite these multiple unfavourable findings, the government's response was slow and unsatisfactory. The fee was finally removed in April 2009 but refunds of fees already paid were available only to those who could show that payment caused them 'real financial hardship'. Section 25, requiring a certificate of approval, remained on the statute books until May 2011. The requirement to give particular notice for non-Church of England marriages in s 20 remains unrepealed.

After the *Baiai* judgment but before being abolished, the certificates of approval scheme still permitted the authorities to investigate marriages involving those subject to immigration control even if permission would not be refused to those in genuine marriages. The utility of the scheme, from the government's perspective, was clear. Parties without leave who applied were making their whereabouts known to the authorities and could be targeted for removal. Whether or not this actually occurred, it was a disincentive to marry and thereby to establish a family life that is better protected against removal under Article 8 ECHR.

Nonetheless, the inability to recover costs through fees made it an expensive regulatory tool and the scheme was eventually abandoned. The Family Migration Consultation has made new suggestions for tackling sham marriages, including combining some of the functions of registration officers and immigration officers at weddings, greater documentary requirements, making 'sham' a lawful impediment to marriage, and preventing those who entered as a spouse or who have previously sponsored a spouse from acting as sponsors in further marriages.

9.8 Forced marriages

Forced marriages have become a prominent issue in the recent past, with many government initiatives aimed at protecting victims. The issue of forced marriage goes far beyond immigration but the discussion here is confined to how forced marriages are treated in immigration law.

The Forced Marriage Unit was created by the Home Office and Foreign and Commonwealth Office in 2005 and operates out of the Foreign and Commonwealth Office. It also has units at some entry clearance posts and particularly assists those forced into marriage abroad. Where the victim of a forced marriage is willing to state publicly that they have been coerced, a marriage visa may be refused on the grounds that there is no intention to live together or the marriage is not subsisting. However, in many cases, victims are too frightened of reprisals to acknowledge their situation openly. Given the need to give reasons for a refusal and the existence of appeal rights, it is difficult to refuse a spousal visa application if the victim is not willing to speak out.

In response to concerns about forced marriage, the minimum ages for sponsorship and entry were raised to 18 in 2003 and 2004. In December 2007, the government published a Consultation Document (Home Office/Border and Immigration Agency, *Marriage to Partners From Overseas*). This proposed several measures to prevent forced marriages including raising the minimum age for entry and sponsorship to 21 and this happened in 2008 (HC 1113). New guidance for entry clearance staff on forced marriage was inserted into the IDI (chapter 8, Annex A2).

Providing assistance to victims of forced marriages is vital but there was uneasiness about the increase in the age of entry and sponsorship. In part, this is based on history. The 'reluctant sponsor' was often invoked by those hostile to the continuation of arranged marriages, and forced and arranged marriages were often conflated. For example, in 1985, following newspaper reports about Asian girls 'sold' by their parents, the Home Secretary, David Waddington, commented that '[t]he so-called "primary purpose" rule has been much attacked but these stories show that it can protect women against exploitation' ('Scandal of the Brides for Sale' Daily Mail 5 August 1985). There was also concern that raising the minimum age for sponsorship and entry is not the most effective means of preventing forced marriages which do not only involve that age group. It was argued that raising the age limit would mean only that victims were held abroad until of age to sponsor. The campaigning group, Southall Black Sisters, gave evidence to the Home Affairs Committee that this happened after the age was raised from 16 to 18 (HC 263-II Ev 334). Research commissioned by the Home Office but not published by them questioned the effectiveness of the proposal and the Home Affairs Select Committee, while sympathetic to arguments for raising the age, recommended more research before implementation (HC263–I p. 139).

The measure affected all who wish to enter early marriages, not just those who are forced into it and, in 2011, the Supreme Court found that the policy breached Article 8 ECHR:

Key Case

***Quila and others v SSHD* [2011] UKSC 45**

Appeals were brought by parties to two unforced marriages involving partners under 21. The Supreme Court (Lord Brown dissenting) accepted that, as married couples, family life existed even if it was relatively undeveloped and that refusal to allow the overseas spouse admission amounted to an interference, described by Lord Wilson as 'colossal' (para 32), so as to engage Article 8 ECHR. As discussed earlier in this chapter, the Court declined to follow the majority finding in the ECtHR case of *Abdulaziz v UK* (1985) 7 EHRR 471 that Article 8 was more difficult to engage in entry cases, on the grounds that it was an old decision and inconsistent with later jurisprudence. In carrying out its own review of the proportionality of the rule, in accordance with the principle established in *Huang*, the Court found that, while the rule was rationally connected to the aim of preventing forced marriage, the government had failed to establish that it was no more than necessary to accomplish its objective nor that it struck a fair balance between the rights of parties to unforced marriages and the interests of the community in preventing forced marriage: 'On any view it is a sledge-hammer but she [the Secretary of State] has not attempted to identify the size of the nut' (Lord Wilson, para 58). While the findings were confined to the particular couples in the case, in the words of Lady Hale (at para 80), 'it is difficult to see how she [the Home Secretary] could avoid infringing article 8 whenever she applied the rule to an unforced marriage'.

In November 2011, the government amended the immigration rules so that the minimum age of entry and sponsorship reverted to 18. However, the issue is likely to remain a live one. At present, while a forced marriage may involve many criminal acts such as abduction or rape, for which the perpetrators may be convicted, forcing someone into marriage is not currently a specific criminal offence although this has been discussed on many occasions. In the Family Migration Consultation, the government proposed the creation of such a criminal offence as well as sponsorship bans for those convicted of domestic violence or forced marriage offences and the involvement of social services in international marriages involving vulnerable sponsors.

9.9 Unmarried couples

The right of unmarried couples to be reunited in the UK did not obtain a stable place in the immigration rules until 2 October 2000. In April 2003, the requirement for a legal obstacle to marriage was abolished and the minimum prior period of cohabitation reduced to two years. The current rule (para 295A) provides that, to enter the UK, an unmarried couple, whether of the same or different genders, must show that any previous marriage or comparable relationship has broken down, they have lived together for two years before applying for entry, and that they are not so closely related that the law would prevent their marriage. Where they have lived together for four years, the applicant partner is still, at the time of writing, able to gain immediate settlement as married partners do, subject to passing to passing the knowledge of language and life in the UK, although the Family Migration Consultation proposes abolition.

Paragraph 295D provides that those who already have leave to enter or remain in the UK may switch into leave as an unmarried partner subject to similar conditions that govern switching as a married partner. In calculating the two-year period, IDI Ch 8 Annex Z, para 2 concedes 'short breaks apart for up to six months are acceptable for good reason, such as work commitments or looking after a relative', provided it is clear that the relationship continued throughout the period. Visiting often will not amount to cohabitation, but the cohabitation does not have to have been in one country, and there does not need to be an established joint home if they have, for instance, been living alternately at each other's separate homes using the 'visitor' category.

Other requirements for unmarried partners such as the present and settled sponsor, accommodation and maintenance, are as for married couples and are interpreted in the same way. The relationship is protected by Article 8 ECHR. In *Marckx v Belgium* (1979) 2 EHRR 330, the ECtHR held that there should be no discrimination between the married and unmarried in relation to the status of their children.

9.10 Fiancé(e)s

Finally, it is possible for an individual engaged to be married to a settled person to apply for entry clearance as a fiancé(e). The requirements are set out in para 290 of the rules and are similar to the requirements for a married partner except that some conditions will apply only after marriage and the fiancé(e) must show they are seeking leave to enter for marriage or civil partnership with a settled person.

If the application succeeds, leave is granted for a period of six months, during which time the ceremony must take place, there is a prohibition on working and leave is conditional on not having recourse to public funds. If the marriage does not take place during the six-month period, a further extension 'for an appropriate period' (para 294) may be granted to enable the marriage to take place, provided the Home Office is satisfied that there is good cause for the delay, there is satisfactory evidence that the marriage will take place at an early date, and all the other conditions for leave to enter continue to be met (para 293).

9.11 Other adult relatives

9.11.1 Admissible relatives

Other adult relatives may be admitted for settlement if they qualify under para 317 of the rules. Their admissibility is determined by their relationship to the sponsor. Applicants must be:

(i) parent or grandparent who is divorced, widowed, single, or separated, aged 65 years or over;

(ii) parents or grandparents travelling together at least one of whom is 65 or over;

(iii) a parent or grandparent aged 65 or over who has remarried or entered into a second civil partnership but cannot look to the married partner or children of the second relationship for financial support; and

(iv) a parent or grandparent under the age of 65, or son, daughter, sister, brother, uncle, or aunt over the age of 18 if living alone in the most exceptional compassionate circumstances.

Other relatives may be considered outside the rules, but only where there is a close emotional bond and very strong compassionate circumstances. Thus, only a very narrow range of relatives can enter and, in future, the range may be narrower still. Amongst other measures aimed at this relatively small group of migrants, the Family Migration Consultation suggests raising the age threshold of 65 in line with rises in the UK state pension age. It also proposes that dependent relatives under 65 should meet an English language requirement, a demanding provision given that these are amongst the most vulnerable of new migrants.

Until November 2011, single, separated, or divorced parents over 65 were not provided for in the Rules and policy was to treat them in the same way as parents under 65 This caused some hard results. In *MB (Somalia) v ECO* [2008] EWCA Civ 102, the 73-year-old applicant had been separated from her husband in 2001 due to the war in Somalia and did not know his whereabouts. She wanted to join her son who was a refugee in the UK. Her application was refused because she was not a widow over 65 and she was not living alone in the most exceptional compassionate circumstances as her situation was no worse than many thousands of other refugees. The Court found that it was not irrational or discriminatory to distinguish between widowed parents and the less easily defined class of separated parents while, as mentioned earlier in this chapter, the Article 8 claim was weakened by the 10-year separation of mother and son which had affected the quality of the family life entitled to protection. Fortunately for those in the position of this applicant, the rules were amended in November 2011 by HC 1151.

9.11.2 Financial dependency

All applicants in this category must be 'financially wholly or mainly dependent on the sponsor'. Until November 2011, the rules specified that relatives under 65 had to be 'mainly dependent on relatives living in the UK' whereas now only the support of the sponsor can be brought into account. After *Mahad*, third-party support post-entry is permissible and it is arguable that this should also be the case before entry (although relatives may be advised to channel their support through the likely sponsor).

Dependency must be of necessity as 'the question of dependency has to be construed in the context of immigration control. The question of genuineness runs through all the immigration regulations... dependants have to show their genuine need' (*Chavda v ECO Bombay* [1978] Imm AR 40). This not only interprets the term narrowly, but also involves a judgement as to what is necessary, a concept which may vary between cultures.

This was illustrated in the case which established the test of 'necessary dependence', *Zaman v ECO Lahore* [1973] Imm AR 71. An elderly farmer and his wife applied to join their son in the UK. They were financially dependent upon him because, in accordance with custom, Mr Zaman gave the modest income from the farms to his sons who were still resident in Pakistan. The Tribunal held that their dependence was not necessary. This case contrasts with *ECO New Delhi v Malhan* [1978] Imm AR 209. Here, the appellant's eldest son had voluntarily taken over his mother's support out of a desire to fulfil his moral obligations. The Tribunal held that she was entitled to look to him for support and not to 'more distant' relatives (her brother and father).

What steps to maximize income should an applicant take? In *Chavda*, it was accepted that a widow could not compel her three sons, who lived with her, to work and the dependency on her eldest son in the UK was necessary and not contrived. Where sons can clearly get work this might be different, as in *Hasan v ECO Bombay* [1976] Imm AR 28. In *Piara Singh* (19579) INLP vol. 13(3) (1999), p. 107, elderly parents had a spare room which they kept for visits by family members. It was held that they should not be expected to let this out to reduce their financial dependency on the sponsor.

In *Bibi v ECO Dhaka* [2000] Imm AR 385, the Court of Appeal confirmed that financial dependency may be in the form of money or money's worth. If someone has their needs for accommodation, clothing, food, and other necessities provided in kind, they are financially dependent on the provider. Here, the appellant lived with her son, daughter-in-law, and their children, and was applying to join another son in the UK who regularly sent money to the family. This was used mainly for the children's education. The Court of Appeal found that the true situation was that the family had some dependency on the sponsor, but the appellant was dependent on the family she lived with, not the sponsor in the UK. The principle, therefore, is that there must be direct financial dependency. This was confirmed in *VS (para 317(iii) no 3rd party support)* [2007] UKAIT 00069. Here the sponsor, who was severely disabled, sent a regular £100 per month to the appellant, but it was provided by a distant relative who gave evidence that he was willing and able to continue this support into the future. The Tribunal held that the sponsor was just a conduit for the relative's money, and that the appellant was not financially dependent on him. It is questionable whether this case would still stand after *Mahad*.

If a relative comes to the UK for a visit and then applies under para 317, they must prove that they were dependent on the sponsor before they entered the UK (*MB (para 317: in-country application) Bangladesh* [2007] Imm AR 389). This decision makes plain the underlying spirit and purpose of para 317. It is not a means by which people settled in the UK may make arrangements for the care of their elderly relatives, and in this respect a settled UK family of immigrant descent does not have the choices available to families whose extended family live in the UK. The rule depends on material and physical need and is more of a safety net than a positive support to family life.

The Family Migration Consultation suggests that, in future, the remittance of funds to dependent relatives may be seen not as evidence of a claim to enter but as an alternative means of meeting their needs. If so, the result would be a Catch 22. Without showing dependency, the claim for entry will fail. If dependency is shown, it will be argued that this can continue. The desire of many families to spend time with and care for their elderly relatives would thus become even more irrelevant and, as already discussed in this chapter, Article 8 will offer little assistance as it protects only the existing life of family members not the life they wish to have.

9.11.3 No close relatives to turn to

The applicant must be without close relatives in their own country to whom they can turn for financial support. The rule did not previously include the words 'for financial support' and the leading judgment on its meaning concerned its previous formulation. Dillon LJ in the Court of Appeal case of *R v IAT ex p Swaran Singh* [1987] 1 WLR 1394 read the phrase 'as importing "to turn to in case of need" – any sort of need which may afflict elderly parents'. He gave examples of illness or accident and said that the rule was one of 'broad humanity'. Family relationships should be borne in mind, and where relatives are hostile or unwilling to help, they are clearly not relatives to turn to. In a more recent case, the Tribunal has found that the issue of dependency and no close relative to turn to are 'two sides of the same coin'. Where a person was found to be dependent as of necessity on the sponsor, this would normally mean that there was no other close relative to whom they could turn (*Parekh* (14016) INLP vol. 11 (2) (1997), p. 73).

ECO Islamabad v Rehmat Bi (16074 March 1998 Legal Action) provides useful guidance on financial dependency and another close relative to turn to. It suggests that both requirements should be assessed starting with the needs of the applicant. Here, her needs were for house repairs, frequent contact with her son, medical treatment, and assistance with mobility. Her son funded the repairs, the cost of telephone calls between them, and his own air fares and arranged the medical treatment. When he was there, he gave her the practical assistance which she needed to get around. He had also paid for his father's funeral. She was emotionally dependent on him and, in an earlier case, *R v IAT ex p Bastiampillai* [1983] 2 All ER 844, it was held that, where there was emotional dependency, this could tip the balance to show that dependency existed.

9.11.4 Living alone in the most exceptional compassionate circumstances

Adult relatives who are under 65 must show, in addition to the other conditions, that they are 'living alone in the most exceptional compassionate circumstances'. Being financially dependent on a relative in the UK and having no other close relatives to turn to do not, on their own, amount to exceptional compassionate circumstances (*Nessa* (16391) INLP vol. 13(2) (1999), p. 75) and families may be kept apart because there is nothing exceptional about their situation. However, the Court of Appeal has held that it is not a breach of Article 8 for the government 'to confine the circumstances in which dependent relatives of persons living in the United Kingdom are permitted indefinite leave to enter in the way that they have done in paragraph 317' (*Husna Begum* para 12).

Living alone does not always require that there is literally no other person in the home, but that there is no one able to meet the needs of the applicant. Severe mental or physical disabilities without the necessary care being available will normally be regarded as the most exceptional compassionate circumstances (e.g., *Visa Officer Islamabad v Sindhu* [1978] Imm AR 147). In *EK v ECO Colombo* [2006] EWCA Civ 926, the appellant was not found to be living alone merely because her mother, with whom she had always lived, was now in the UK. She was 23 and lived with her father's two sisters who 'were not treating her unkindly or harshly' (para 22). The compassionate circumstances may have arisen since the applicant's arrival in the UK, if they have been here for instance on a visit. In *Alyha Begum* (17162) INLP vol. 13(3) (1999), p. 107, the applicant's brothers-in-law had been taking away her possessions in her absence, and she would be isolated if she returned.

In *Akhtar Bi v ECO Islamabad* 01/BH/0002, the appellant was a widow under 65 living alone as her sons and daughter had moved to the UK. The Tribunal Chair found her situation to be similar to that of any widowed mother whose children have left home and, while her sadness was understandable, her situation was not exceptional. The other two members of the Tribunal considered her situation to be exceptional because she had always previously had at least one child living with her and now faced living alone for the first time at the age of 57.

There are broadly two approaches taken to this rule. One, following *Swaran Singh* referred to earlier, construes the rule as one of 'broad humanity' and which therefore should not be interpreted in a strict and literal way. The other, which has become more dominant, denies that the rules embody any such policy. In particular, Dyson LJ in *MB (Somalia)* observed that the rule represents a policy decision as to where the balance should be struck between humanity and immigration control so that stating that the rule is one of broad humanity does not assist in assessing the legality of the policy.

There are difficulties about how the financial support of the sponsor affects the applicant's situation. The Court of Appeal in *Zohra Begum* held that the rule should not be interpreted as if the sponsor's contribution was not there. On the other hand, the Tribunal in *Nessa Bibi v ECO Dhaka* (21162A) arguably went too far in regarding the support provided by the sponsor as a reason to find that she was not living in exceptionally compassionate circumstances. In *Azza Mohamed v SSHD* [2012] EWCA Civ 31, the Court of Appeal held that the correct test is whether exceptional circumstances exist, taking into account support by relatives settled in the UK.

In *Husna Begum,* the Court of Appeal found in favour of a woman of 22, all of whose immediate family were now living or about to live in the UK. Evidence suggested that, as a young single woman in rural Bangladesh, she would be isolated and at risk. This cannot be generalized to all women in this position, as each case must be decided on its facts. In *Sayania v IAT* [2001] EWHC Admin 390, the High Court refused a young woman left alone in India leave to appeal to the Tribunal. Burnton J did not think that Article 8 assisted or that her lonely position could bring her within the rule. The Immigration Directorate Instruction (chapter 8, section 6) reflects that view, saying that the situation of such a woman may be taken into account, but does not of itself bring her within the rule.

9.11.5 Terms of stay for a successful relative

Entry clearance for dependent relatives will function as leave to enter and remain indefinitely providing the entry clearance is endorsed to that effect (Immigration (Leave to Enter and Remain) Order 2000, SI 2000/1161). There is, at present, no probationary period. However, the Family Migration Consultation proposes introducing a five-year probationary period for adult dependants. Given that, by definition, these will all be elderly or very vulnerable, this would add a harsh degree of added insecurity. It is possible that concern is primarily about the potential burden that these migrants may place on public services. However, as will be seen in the next paragraph, sponsor undertakings may be taken in respect of benefit claims. Medical treatment has never been the subject of restrictions or undertakings but the Consultation notes the high cost of providing such medical care and suggests the possibility of requiring medical insurance for dependent relatives. Such insurance is likely to be exorbitant in cost (and is unlikely to cover existing medical conditions) and may be unobtainable for some. It would certainly exclude all but the very wealthy from sponsoring an elderly relative.

Maintenance and accommodation requirements are similar to those for married partners, and must be met for the application to succeed. Paragraph 35 of the rules gives power to immigration authorities to require the sponsor to sign an undertaking that they will be responsible for their relative's maintenance. The effect of this is to disbar the sponsored relative from any claim to key means-tested benefits for five years from the date of admission to the UK. If the relative does make a claim, the paying authorities may seek to recover from the person who gave the undertaking. Refusal by the sponsor to give an undertaking is a discretionary ground for refusal of entry clearance under para 320.

An undertaking is a formal document. In *Ahmed v Secretary of State for Work and Pensions* [2005] EWCA Civ 535, the Court of Appeal held that a statement by the sponsor that he was 'able and willing' to maintain and accommodate his uncle was designed to show to the entry clearance officer that the requirements for granting entry clearance were met and did not amount to an undertaking, which was a solemn promise for the future. The sponsor's uncle therefore was not debarred from a claim for backdated benefit on the grounds of being a person who had leave to enter the UK 'as a result of a maintenance undertaking' (Immigration and Asylum Act 1999 s 115).

9.12 Children

9.12.1 Introduction

The migration of children involves domestic and private international law provisions concerning abduction, custody, and adoption as well as complex nationality rules. The UK's immigration law on children is only a small part of the picture which cannot effectively be considered in isolation. This is an area of increasing complexity now warranting specialist texts (see, for instance, Coker, Finch, and Stanley 2002). This section is therefore limited in its aim and scope. It aims to explain some of the particular immigration rules relating to the admission of children for settlement.

In November 2008, the UK withdrew its reservation to the UN Convention on the Rights of the Child, which had exempted the UK from the Convention in relation to immigration matters and had been widely criticized. The obligations in the Convention extend to children within the jurisdiction of the contracting state, which, in this context, means within the territory of the UK and there is no obligation to ensure that the rules governing the entry of children are compliant. Moreover, the Convention does not give rise to directly enforceable rights. However, the government will have to report on its compliance to the UN Committee on the Rights of the Child.

Article 3(1) of the Convention provides that the best interests of the child shall be a 'primary consideration'. Following withdrawal of the reservation, s 55 Borders,

Citizenship and Immigration Act 2009 imposed a duty on the Secretary of State to ensure that immigration- and asylum-related duties are carried out having due regard to the need to safeguard and promote the welfare of children who are in the United Kingdom. Lady Hale, at para 23 of *ZH (Tanzania)*, regarded this as representing 'the spirit, if not the precise language' of the obligation and also found, at para 24, that the ECHR requires national states to make children's interests 'a primary consideration' so that a decision made without such consideration would not be 'in accordance with the law' for the purposes of Article 8(2). The acknowledgement of such a principle moves immigration decision-making about children who are in the UK much further towards welfare principles, an advance that may be contrasted with the situation that still obtains in entry cases, where immigration considerations still predominate.

The s 55 obligation may also affect decisions that are made about those who are caring for a child as *ZH (Tanzania)* demonstrated.

Key Case

***ZH (Tanzania) v SSHD* [2011] UKSC 4**

The case involved a Tanzanian woman national whose immigration history was described as 'appalling'. There was little doubt that, were only her own interests at stake, she would have been unable to resist removal. However, she had two children born in the UK to a British father and who were British citizens. Their father had serious health problems and it was doubtful that he could care for them if the mother were removed. Her removal would therefore almost inevitably entail their departure with her to Tanzania.

As Lady Hale noted, the duty to make a child's interests 'a primary consideration' is not the same as to make them 'the primary consideration' or 'the paramount consideration', as required by s 1(1) Children Act 1989 in respect of decisions regarding a child's upbringing. Immigration decisions generally do not affect a child's upbringing directly and the s 55 obligation is to make a child's interests the first consideration although the strength of other factors may still outweigh them. However, Lord Kerr said, at para 46:

> This [best interests] is not, it is agreed, a factor of limitless importance in the sense that it will prevail over all other considerations. It is a factor, however, that must rank higher than any other. It is not merely one consideration that weighs in the balance alongside other competing factors. Where the best interests of the child clearly favour a certain course, that course should be followed unless countervailing reasons of considerable force displace them.

As the government conceded, the principle applies not only to the care of children pending immigration decisions but to the decisions themselves. Lady Hale enumerated the matters that might be relevant in such an assessment including nationality and its connection with lifestyle, the social and linguistic disruption of children's childhood and the loss of homeland, the loss of educational opportunities, and loss of contact with wider family members.

The children's nationality, while not a 'trump card', was of particular importance in assessing their best interests. They had an unqualified right of abode and had lived in the UK for their entire lives, were being educated and had other social links there, and a good relationship with their father. They also had citizenship rights which they would be unable to exercise if they could not remain. While there were strong countervailing factors, they did not outweigh, in this case, the interests of the children. Even if the children had been conceived in the hope of strengthening the mother's claim to remain, they themselves were innocent of her shortcomings.

The decision in *ZH* is congruent with the decision of the CJEU, reached on different legal grounds, in *Zambrano v Onde* (C–34/09) delivered a month later in March 2011 and discussed in chapter 5. Although the main application of *ZH* is in relation to removal or deportation, dealt with in chapters 17 and 18, it will also be relevant when children or parents make further claims to remain in the UK under the immigration rules. It was cited, for example, in *R (on the application of Mansoor) v SSHD* [2011] EWHC 832 (Admin) which concerned a citizen father and seven children who had indefinite leave. The mother was admitted for a two-year probationary period. Shortly before it expired, the husband lost his job, was obliged to claim benefits, and her claim for indefinite leave was refused. The refusal was over-turned, amongst other reasons, for its failure to consider the interests of the children as a primary consideration.

While *ZH* focused on the weight to be awarded to nationality, the findings as to the importance of the child's interests apply to all children present in the UK, irrespective of their nationality. Subsequent cases have explored further the nature of the obligation. Where children have another nationality, particularly one that is shared with their parents, the arguments against return will have less force, particularly for young children whose interests are still primarily wrapped up in their immediate family life which will continue overseas. Even so, other factors concerning their interests—education, social links, and so on—will apply and the issue is to be decided as part of the overall Article 8 assessment with, however, the children's interests addressed first as a distinct enquiry. Decision-makers must be proactive in establishing what those interests are as well as the child's own wishes and views (accorded due weight according to the child's age and maturity) and must give proper and informed consideration to them (*AJ (India) and others v SSHD* [2011] EWCA Civ 1191; *R (on the application of Tinizaray) v SSHD* [2011] EWHC 1850 (Admin); *E-A (Article 8 – best interests of child) Nigeria* [2011] UKUT 00315 (IAC); *MK (best interests of child) India* [2011] UKUT 00475 (IAC)).

Section 55 is stated to apply only to children in the UK so that it does not apply in entry cases where immigration concerns carry much greater weight. However, Lady Hale's observation in *ZH (Tanzania)* that the interests of children are a primary consideration under Article 8(2) should apply equally when ECHR issues arise in entry cases. The s 55 guidance, to which regard must be had under s 55(3) of the 2009 Act, states at para 2.34, that 'UK Border Agency staff working overseas must adhere to the spirit of the duty and make enquiries when they have reason to suspect that a child may be in need of protection or safeguarding, or presents welfare needs that require attention'. Thus, there does seem to be an obligation on UKBA to consider the welfare of children. The Upper Tribunal in *T (s.55 BCIA 2009 – entry clearance) Jamaica* [2011] UKUT 00483 (IAC) found that s 55 indeed does not apply to children outside the UK but that the application of the immigration rules, Article 8, and the guidance should all be taken into account and investigations made if necessary. As Lady Hale suggested in *ZH,* it is difficult to envisage a situation in which s 55 applied and the outcome would be different from that required by Article 8.

The rules for the admission of children for settlement are found in paras 297–303 HC 395. The child must be under 18 at the time of the application. If he or she reaches 18 before a decision is made, they will not be refused for that reason (para 27). The IDI (chapter 8, Annex M, para 2.1) says that a child who reaches 18 after issue of the visa but before entry should not be refused entry for that reason alone. However, the Family Migration Consultation suggests that children, in future, should be no more than 17 years and 6 months at the time of the application so that they enter before they are 18. Children who are close to 18 would no longer be given indefinite leave but finite leave to expire on their eighteenth birthday, when they 'will be able to apply for leave to remain in the UK in their own right', even though the options for such young adults are very limited. It is also proposed that children aged 16 or above should demonstrate a basic level of English before admission.

According to para 6 of the rules, a parent includes a step-parent, an adoptive parent, and an unmarried father, if paternity is accepted or proved. If, after DNA testing, the child turns out, as happened in *ECO Accra v Attafuah* [2002] UKIAT 05922, not to be the father's natural child, it seems there is no provision parallel to that in nationality law to treat the child as the child of that person. However, the Entry Clearance Guidance (SET 7.11.8) emphasizes the need for discretion and says that where an illegitimate child has been brought up as a child of the family, it would normally be appropriate to admit the child under para 297(i)(f), that there are serious and compelling family or other considerations why exclusion is undesirable.

When children come to join both parents, or where one parent is dead, the position is relatively straightforward. Principles of accommodation and maintenance are already familiar, and the only additional requirement is that the child is 'not leading an independent life, is unmarried and has not formed an independent family unit' (para 297(iii)).

Adequate accommodation was given an unusually extended meaning by the Court of Appeal in *M & A v ECO* [2003] EWCA Civ 263. Other children of the same parents had been taken into care, and one had died as a result of abuse. The Court had, at that time, no remit to consider welfare in an entry case but the gap in the protective capacity of the rules was filled by the Tribunal's creative decision that the accommodation was not adequate because the children would not be safe.

There are special rules which apply when the child is only joining one parent or relative. Either the sponsoring parent must have sole responsibility for the child or there must be serious and compelling family or other considerations which make exclusion of the child undesirable.

9.12.2 Sole responsibility

When the other parent of the child is still living, it must be shown that the sponsoring parent has 'sole responsibility' for them (HC 396 para 297(i)(c)). Given that the sponsor will usually have been living in the UK without the child, sole responsibility does not mean sole care or most applications would fail as relatives, not only the other parent, may also share care. If there is a residence order in favour of the UK parent, this is a strong indicator of sole responsibility for immigration purposes. Some custody orders obtained overseas are similarly regarded (IDI chapter 8, Annex M, para 4.4). Otherwise, both the Instructions (IDI Annex M, para 4.3) and the Entry Clearance Guidance (SET 7.8) set out some relevant factors. These include the legal relationship between all the parties, financial support, and arrangements for care. It is expected that the child will have been cared for by the sponsor's own relatives and not those of the other parent.

The sole responsibility rule does not give separated parents and children the power to choose where the child should live. An example given in the IDI makes this apparent:

> Two foreign nationals living abroad have a child, then separate. One parent comes to the United Kingdom and obtains settlement. The child remains with the parent abroad for several years, then at the age of 13+ wishes to join the parent in the United Kingdom to take advantage of the educational system. There is no reason why the child should not remain with the parent who lives abroad. In this case the parent who lives in the United Kingdom would not be considered to have sole responsibility. (chapter 8, Annex M, para 4.1)

The example cited here implies manipulation of the immigration system; however, the outcome would be the same if the child and custodial parent had started to argue and the family thought it was time for a change in the interests of the child.

The Court of Appeal in the case of *Nmaju v IAT* [2001] INLR 26 held that there were two points of principle in determining sole responsibility. One is the quality of control, the other is for what period of time that control must be exercised. The quality of control which will give rise to a finding of sole responsibility requires retention of ultimate responsibility for the child even if someone else is doing the day-to-day care provided this is 'under the direction' of the responsible parent. The parent would be expected to show a continuous interest in the child's welfare and upbringing.

Where there are two parents actually involved, the Tribunal in the case of *Zahir* 00/TH/02262 held that sole responsibility is still capable of arising, for instance, if one parent's role was clearly subsidiary, though it was not so on the facts in that case. *TD Yemen* [2006] UKAIT 00049 sets out the approach to sole responsibility cases:

(i) The question of sole responsibility is a factual one.
(ii) 'Responsibility' may be undertaken by individuals other than a child's parents and may be shared. The issue of sole responsibility is not just a matter between the parents.
(iii) If both parents are involved in the upbringing of the child, it will be exceptional that one will have sole responsibility.
(iv) If it is said that one is not involved, one of the indicators will be that they have abandoned or abdicated their responsibility.
(v) If day-to-day responsibility (or decision-making) is shared with others (such as relatives or friends) that does not prevent the parent having sole responsibility within the meaning of the Rules.
(vi) The test is whether the parent has continuing control and direction of the child's upbringing including making all the important decisions in the child's life. If not, responsibility is shared and not 'sole'.

In *TD*, the child had lived with his mother in Yemen and been brought up by her. His father phoned him every week and was entirely responsible for his financial support. He took part in major decisions, though there had been few of these. The Tribunal concluded that responsibility was shared, not sole. They referred to the underlying purpose of para 297 as being 'to effect family unity'. This, they thought, would be undermined if the provision was interpreted so as to allow a child to join a parent who was not, in fact, solely responsible for them (para 48).

The other issue in *Nmaju* is the period of time for which sole responsibility must be assumed. In that case, three children were left in the care of their father who, in September 1996, said that he was too old to look after them any longer and left them in the care of a maid. In November of that year, their application to join their mother was refused on the basis that, if she had sole responsibility, it was only for two months and that was too short a period of time. The reality of the situation at the time of the entry clearance decision was that the mother had sole responsibility and this was sufficient to meet the requirements of the rule. *TD Yemen* confirms this result.

9.12.3 Exclusion undesirable

The welfare of the child takes greater priority under the next sub-paragraph of the rule, 'that there are serious and compelling family or other considerations which make exclusion of the child undesirable'. This is not a question of whether it would on balance be better for the child to move to the UK. For instance, in *Dawson v ECO Accra* 01/TH/1358, the Tribunal, in refusing the appeal on this ground, noted that there was no evidence of mistreatment of the appellant or of his mother or stepfather according him a lack of respect.

The rule may be used to join a relative other than a parent, although it was suggested in *OU (Nigeria) and others v SSHD* [2008] EWCA Civ 128 that this must be a blood relative. The IDI (chapter 8, Annex M, para 1) emphasize that this basis for entry is only to be used when parents or relatives in the child's own country are unable to care for him or her and the circumstances surrounding the child are exceptional in relation to those of other children living in that country.

Where a child is seeking to join a parent, the circumstances of the UK parent, both of an emotional and of a physical nature, for example, illness or infirmity, may be taken into account. Where the application is to join another relative, the relative's circumstances should not form part of the consideration. This appears to be an attempt to avoid children being brought in as carers for other relatives in need.

Previous case law suggested that only if the living conditions in the child's country of origin were intolerable would entry to the UK be considered on this ground. However, it was later found that an overall view must be taken, including such factors as the willingness and availability of the overseas adult to look after the child; the living conditions available for them; the greater vulnerability of small children, and the need for family unity (*Hardward* 00/TH/01522). In *Hardward* itself, there is still an emphasis on conditions abroad as a starting point, although, in that case, the appellant was already in the UK. The appellant lost because, although there were compelling family reasons why she should remain, it was not shown that her father in Jamaica was unable to care for her.

The case of *Hardward* predated the implementation of the Human Rights Act by a few months. The application under the 'exclusion undesirable' rule was turned down, but the Tribunal considered whether, given the imminence of the Human Rights Act, it should make a recommendation using Article 8. The Tribunal suggested that para 298(i) of the rules was incompatible with the Human Rights Act:

> the onus of justifying that interference under Art 8(2) shifts to the immigration authorities. That is in clear contrast with the wording of the rule set out at paragraph 298(i) which places the burden throughout on the appellant to justify why her exclusion would be undesirable. (para 19)

This argument seems to have much force.

9.12.4 Adoption

Inter-country adoption is a growing and complex subject, combining immigration and family law. This brief coverage just raises some issues associated with it. It is necessary to distinguish between adoption of a non-British child in the UK, and adoption overseas with the intention or consequence that the child moves to the UK.

9.12.4.1 *Adoption in the UK*

The adoption of a non-British child in the UK by a British citizen confers British nationality immediately upon the making of the adoption order (British Nationality Act 1981 s 1(5)). In the case of *In re B (a minor (AP)* [1999] 2 AC 136, the House of Lords established new principles for immigration considerations in the adoption of children in the UK.

Key Case

In re B (a minor (AP) [1999] 2 AC 136

B had visited the UK with her mother. She attended school in Leeds while they stayed with her grandparents, and appeared to be thriving, so her mother left her there and returned to Jamaica. B and her grandparents applied for exceptional leave for B to stay in the UK as it appeared to be in her best interests, all the more as her father in Jamaica had now died, and her mother and sister were living in reduced circumstances. Her application was refused. The parties were advised that B could only stay in the UK if she was adopted by her grandparents. Her mother consented, but the Home Secretary intervened to oppose the adoption. He also made it clear that if just a residence order were made in favour of the grandparents, he would still seek to deport B. As Lord Hoffmann says in his judgment at 140:

> Ms B had only two years of minority left. And although the benefits to her from being able to spend those two important years living with her grandparents and going to school in Leeds were plain and obvious, it would not ordinarily be necessary for her to be adopted. Were it not for her precarious immigration status, she could simply have stayed with her grandparents or, if the situation needed to be formally regulated, the Court could have made a residence order under the Children Act 1989. But the Home Office made it clear that if the Court merely made a residence order, it would nevertheless order her deportation. Thus the acquisition of British citizenship by adoption was an essential element in securing her the advantages of living with her grandparents and continuing at her school.

The Court of Appeal had accepted the Home Office's proposition that 'the court should ignore benefits which would result solely from [a] change in immigration status when determining whether the child's welfare calls for adoption' (at 141). As the acquisition of the right of abode was the main benefit, it discharged the adoption order. The House of Lords considered that this interpretation flouted the terms of the Adoption Act, which required the judge to 'have regard to "all the circumstances" and to treat the welfare of the child "throughout his childhood" as the first consideration'. It was impossible to ignore the immigration benefits of the adoption. Lord Hoffmann continues with a passage (at 141) which has great significance for adoptions:

> No doubt the views of the Home Office on immigration policy were also a circumstance which the court was entitled to take into account, although it is not easy to see what weight they could be given. Parliament has not provided, as I suppose it might have done, that the adoption of a non-British child should require the consent of the Home Secretary. On the contrary, it has provided that the making of an adoption order automatically takes the child out of the reach of the Home Secretary's powers of immigration control. The decision whether to make such an order is entirely one for the judge in accordance with the provisions of section 6. In cases in which it appears to the judge that adoption would confer real benefits upon the child during its childhood, it is very unlikely that general considerations of 'maintaining an effective and consistent immigration policy' could justify the refusal of an order. The two kinds of consideration are hardly commensurable so as to be capable of being weighed in the balance against each other.

The criteria for deciding whether an adoption order should be made were amended after *Re B* was heard. In *B v S* [2009] EWHC 2491 (Fam), the High Court considered that these changes did not affect the underlying position which was that, where an adoption is merely to facilitate immigration and there is no genuine transfer of parental control, it is unlikely to be in the child's interests and would fail under the criteria.

Where there is a true intention to adopt, the child's welfare is paramount and would not be outweighed by breaches of the immigration rules although courts should be on their guard against misuse of adoption proceedings.

9.12.4.2 *Adoption outside the UK*

A child adopted outside the UK in accordance with the 1993 Hague Convention on the Protection of Children and Co-operation in Respect of Inter-Country Adoptions will be a British citizen if one of the parents is a British citizen and both parents are habitually resident in the UK (s 1(5) British Nationality Act 1981). In that case, the immigration authorities do not need to be involved. However, where parents are settled in the UK but not citizens, the child will not be a British citizen and is subject to immigration control. In such cases, a child may enter the UK for settlement if the requirements of HC 395 para 310 are met. As will be demonstrated in this section, the rules are not entirely satisfactory, particularly where intra-family adoptions are involved. If the child cannot be admitted under the adoption rules, it may be possible to apply using the rule that exclusion is undesirable (*SK ('Adoption' not recognised in UK) India* [2006] UKAIT 00068). However, a further UK adoption procedure may be necessary after entry.

Two types of adoption are recognized under para 310: those made by the competent authorities in countries of origin or residence whose adoption orders are recognized by the UK under the Adoption (Designation of Overseas Adoption) Order 1973, SI 1973/19, and 'de facto' adoptions. Alternatively, a child may be admitted, under para 316A, to join parents with a view to adoption under UK law after entry.

The 1973 Order, based on the 1993 Hague Convention, appears now to be outdated. In particular, it does not include India, although India has now ratified the Convention. The rules have been found not to discriminate on grounds of race in this respect (*MN (Non-recognised adoptions: unlawful discrimination?) India* [2007] UKAIT 00015). De facto adoptions must comply with the conditions set out in para 309A. The adoptive parent or parents, if both are involved, must have been living abroad (together if a couple) and have assumed the role of the child's parents for at least 18 months prior to the application and the child must have lived with the adoptive parent or parents for the 12 months immediately preceding the application. These provisions aim to provide for situations where a child has been treated as part of the family prior to the family's entry. The lengthy period of residence abroad means that it is rarely appropriate for UK-based parents who want to adopt from abroad. It is also often unsuitable for refugees who have cared for orphaned or abandoned children in areas of conflict. By the time that refugee status has been granted and an application for their entry made, the relationship no longer qualifies as a de facto adoption (although Article 8 may sometimes assist); *MK (Somalia v ECO* [2008] EWCA Civ 1453; *Mohamoud (paras 352D and 309A – de facto adoption) Ethiopia* [2011] UKUT 00378 (IAC).

The rules for adoption therefore create particular difficulties for parents who have adopted children in countries whose adoptions do not comply with the Hague Convention (such as Pakistan or Bangladesh) or where the parents are not citizens and the adoption is not recognized by the 1973 Order (such as India). This was the case for the couple in *MN (India) v ECO (New Delhi)* [2008] EWCA Civ 38, the appeal from the Tribunal case of the same name referred to earlier, and which demonstrates how the technicalities of adoption law can interact with immigration law against the interests of the child.

MN (India) v ECO (New Delhi) **[2008] EWCA Civ 38**

The parents of the adoptive child in this case were settled in the UK and one parent was a British citizen. They were of Indian origin. The child's birth mother had worked as a servant for the adoptive father's family in India and was in poor health. Her birth father had died. The adoptive father assumed responsibility for her education and health care and subsequently went through an adoption ceremony which was registered in the local court and conformed with Indian law as it then stood. Shortly afterwards, India ratified the Hague Convention. There was no suggestion that this was anything other than a genuine adoption in the interests of the child.

The parents wished to bring their adopted daughter to live with them in the UK but the application was refused, a refusal upheld by the Court of Appeal. The Court identified four possible routes of entry:

- Adoption in a country whose adoption orders are recognized by the UK under the 1973 Order. As already indicated, this does not include India.
- *De facto* adoption: this did not apply here. Although the adoptive father and his wife had spent time in India with the girl, they did not meet the particular requirements for a *de facto* adoption.
- Entry for the purposes of being adopted in the UK under para 316A. This would require a lengthy assessment procedure which would have caused uncertainty and delay. Given that the child was already 14 at the time of the appeal and had been lawfully adopted in India, the parents were unwilling to consider this option.
- Adoption in India under the Hague Convention which was ratified in 2003 by both India and the UK. If adopted in conformity with the Convention, the daughter would have been a British citizen through her father. However, it was doubtful whether such an order could be obtained in India, given that she was regarded as already adopted under Indian law.

The Court considered that the parents should have given more consideration to obtaining an adoption order in the UK, enabling them to use the third route of entry. The Article 8 claim was dismissed on the basis that there was no impediment to the continuation of family life as it had previously been enjoyed.

Recognition of the country's adoption process (or of a de facto adoption) is not enough to bring the child within the requirements of the immigration rules as there are additional criteria to be met. Paragraph 310 requires that, at the time of the adoption, both of the adoptive parents were resident together abroad or that either or both were settled in the UK. In addition, it lays down requirements for the adoption, namely that the adopted child has the same rights and obligations as any other child of the marriage; that the child was adopted due to the inability of others to care for them; that there is a genuine transfer of parental responsibility to the adoptive parents; that the child has lost or broken ties with their family of origin; and that the adoption is not one of convenience to facilitate admission to the UK. These requirements are more stringent than those for an adoption order in the UK which would not necessarily require that the child was adopted 'due to the inability of others to care for them' nor that the child has lost or broken ties with their family of origin. Indeed, it is no longer thought good practice in family law to insist upon a child severing contact with their family of origin. In *Boadi v ECO Ghana* [2002] UKIAT 01323, the Tribunal took account of this in its interpretation of the rule, holding that severing ties with a family of origin did not mean severing emotional ties, but just that the adoption was not an arrangement which could be seen as reversible. A different view of the rules had been taken in the case of *Kamande v ECO Nairobi* [2002] UKIAT 06129 a few months earlier, in which the Tribunal refused to recognize the adoption for the purposes of the rules because, although responsibility had been transferred, the appellant still retained a strong emotional relationship with his grandparents who had brought him up.

When an adoption is arranged within the family, for instance the adoption of a niece or nephew, it may not be possible to show that the parents are unable to care for the child or that all ties have been severed with the birth family. Case law on this has been mixed. In *H (A Minor) (Adoption: Non-Patrial), Re* [1997] 1 WLR 791, the Court of Appeal declined to overturn an adoption when the motivation arose from the adoptive parents' infertility. In *J (A Minor) (Adoption: Non-Patrial), Re* [1998] 1 FLR 225, the Court of Appeal, in a comparable case, again refused to overturn the adoption order. The Court distinguished between deception used to gain entry to achieve a genuine adoption and deception as to the nature of the adoption itself. The Court expressed a view that, while the adoption rules were so restrictive, it was difficult to argue that they should not be circumvented by genuine applicants (see Macdonald 2001:455).

In *Radhika Sharma v ECO New Delhi* [2005] EWCA Civ 89, the Court of Appeal adopted a strict interpretation of the requirement to show that the birth family cannot care for the child. They held that inability to care did not include unwillingness, as in the present case. This seems a harsh finding which ignores the psychological factors that may cause rejection of a child and that it may be in the child's interests to live with willing adoptive parents rather than reluctant birth parents. The decision here was perhaps connected to doubts about the veracity of the sponsor's story.

By contrast, in *Singh v ECO New Delhi* [2004] EWCA Civ 1075, the Court had to consider an application for entry clearance following an intra-family adoption which could not meet the requirements of the immigration rules because the child had not severed ties with his family of origin. Indeed, he was being cared for well by his birth parents while he waited to join his adoptive parents, his aunt and uncle, with whom he had a strong relationship. The case had a very protracted background, including a decision by the ECtHR that an application was admissible because the refusal to recognize adoptions carried out in India was prima facie discriminatory. The Court of Appeal heard and decided an application purely upon Article 8 grounds. It had no doubt that the substantial relationship between the child and adoptive parents amounted to family life. That it did not meet the UK's stringent immigration requirements should not impede genuine family life and entry clearance should be granted. However, as the earlier discussion on *MN* demonstrates, it is relatively unusual that an adoption case will demonstrate sufficient pre-existing family life for an Article 8 claim to succeed.

Singh did not decide anything about the validity of the restrictions on adoption in the immigration rules. The Court simply rejected a 'rigid and formulaic approach' (para 33) which would require adherence to legal form at the expense of particular facts. The Tribunal decision in *SK India* [2006] UKAIT 00068 held that the non-recognition of Indian adoptions was not a matter that the Tribunal could or should overrule, as adoptions had a wider significance than immigration and there were other effects to be reckoned with. The UK was entitled to require certain formalities of an adoption. This approach was, as indicated, endorsed in *MN India* [2007] UKAIT 00015, where the Tribunal rejected an argument that the rules were discriminatory (see Chowhury 2007 for discussion of the issues and a critique of these decisions).

There are other regulations also governing adoption of children abroad. The Adoptions with a Foreign Element Regulations 2005, SI 2005/392, as amended, lay down an extensive system of regulation and approval for adoptive parents. However, they only apply to adoptions under the Hague Convention, adoptions of a foreign child in the UK, or adoptions abroad effected less than six months before the child enters the UK, and so not all those that are permitted in the immigration rules. The Children and Adoption Act 2006 also provides for special restrictions on adopting children from abroad where there is a suspicion of harm to children.

9.12.5 Parents of children in the UK

So far, this chapter has focused on children who wish to enter the UK to join their parents. The immigration rules make provision for separated or divorced parents who need to enter for contact with children under 18. Under para 246 HC 395, where a child is resident in the United Kingdom with the other parent and the applicant can show either a contact or residence order from a UK court or a certificate from a district judge confirming the parent's intention to maintain contact, then entry for up to 12 months will be granted, subject to conditions of maintenance and accommodation and to the applicant showing their intention to take an active role in the child's upbringing. The Immigration Directorate Instructions observe that it is, in fact, impossible to obtain a certificate from a district judge as required by the rules and a sworn affidavit from the other parent is acceptable instead (Chapter 7, section 1, para 2.1).

Leave to remain may also be granted under para 284A to those who have leave to remain as spouses or partners of the parent of the child in question subject to similar conditions although a statement from the other parent may replace the court order and there must already be ongoing contact. Indefinite leave is available to either category after 12 months.

These provisions do not cover all the circumstances in which parents may wish to enter or remain for contact. In particular, they do not apply to parents who are present without leave or who wish to enter but do not have a court order and cannot count on the cooperation of the other parent. *MS (Ivory Coast)* [2007] EWCA Civ 133 found that a decision to remove an applicant in the process of seeking a contact order may violate Article 8. If such a parent were successful, discretionary leave would still be required, in most cases, as the parent would not meet the criteria of para 284A. Under s 55, the interests of the child would now be a primary consideration in any such decision.

9.13 Family life for those with limited leave

The preceding material in this chapter has dealt with applications to join people settled in the UK. People entering for a limited time, for instance for work or study, may have the right to bring their immediate family with them. Those entering under Tiers 1, 2, and 4 (but, in most cases, only graduate students coming for at least 12 months), and Tier 5 (Temporary Worker) (collectively described in the rules as 'Relevant Points Based Migrants') may bring family members with them subject to the conditions set out in paras 319A–K of the rules. Rules similar to those for spouses and relating to valid and subsisting marriage, the length and nature of any unmarried partnership, and intention to live together apply to the spouses, civil partners, unmarried or same sex partners of relevant PBS migrants. Those entering for 12 months or more may work and all must not intend to stay in the UK beyond the expiry of their partner's leave. Children of the same categories of PBS migrants are permitted to enter, subject to the conditions of para

296. The specific maintenance requirements for the family members of each Tier are set out in Appendix E.

Migrants regarded as purely temporary do not have the right to be accompanied by family members. These include visitors, seasonal workers, those on the sectors-based scheme, Tier 5 (Youth Mobility), and the currently unimplemented Tier 3. The children of people with limited leave who are born in the UK will not be British, as their parents are not settled.

9.14 Refugees and asylum seekers

Once a person has obtained refugee status or, after 30 August 2005, a grant of humanitarian protection, they may be joined by a partner and minor children whom they left behind in their country of origin. However, the right only accrues once status has been granted and applies only to relationships that existed and to children who were part of the household prior to departure from the country of origin. Children who have been adopted informally, a common occurrence in strife-torn countries where birth parents may die or disappear, are not covered by the right and must rely on Article 8 (*MK (Somalia) and others v ECO* [2008] EWCA 1453).

The spouse of such a person must also show that the parties intend to live together and the marriage is subsisting, and the applicant would not, themselves, be excluded by Article 1F of the Refugee Convention (see chapter 14 (para 352A–(iii)). Minor children may also apply to join a refugee provided they are under 18, not married or leading an independent life, were part of the family unit before the refugee sponsor left the country of origin, and would also not be excluded under Article 1F (para 352D). Similar rules apply to the family members of those granted humanitarian protection (paras 352FA and FD and 352FG).

Around 12 per cent of refugee claims are made by minors but there is no provision in the rules nor in current policy for such children to be joined by their parents, a policy that appears to be at odds with the government's obligations under s 55 Borders, Citizenship and Immigration Act 2009.

The refugee family reunion rules are more generous than those for citizens and residents as maintenance and accommodation requirements do not apply. In *ZN (Afghanistan) v ECO* [2011] UKSC 21, the Supreme Court held that the immigration rules, as then worded, permitted a naturalized refugee to rely on the refugee family reunion rules. The government responded by amending the rules so that, now, only those who are 'currently' refugees or have humanitarian protection can sponsor relatives under these more expansive provisions. The Court of Appeal has found that those granted indefinite leave as the spouse of a refugee cannot, themselves, rely on the refugee family reunion rules to sponsor other family members (*MS (Somalia) v SSHD* [2010] EWCA Civ 1236).

Since 30 August 2005, refugees have been given five years' leave, which is renewed in the light of conditions in the country of origin (previously, they received indefinite leave at once). Their family members are given limited leave, to run for the same period as the refugee. This policy contributes to instability and uncertainty for refugee families who must decide whether to remain separated or undergo the upheaval of relocation for a possibly finite period.

The rules left an extraordinary lacuna that operated against a refugee who formed a family after departure from the country of origin and whose partner did not themselves have settled status in the UK. As the refugee had five years' leave rather than indefinite leave they did not qualify as a sponsor under the marriage rules for settled people. As their new relationship post-dated their departure, they could not qualify as a sponsor under the refugee rules. However, it is unrealistic to expect refugees, who may well have been single when they left, not to form relationships over such a prolonged period.

In *A (Afghanistan) v SSHD* [2009] EWCA Civ 825, the Court of Appeal considered this restriction. In the previous hearing, the Tribunal had been unable to identify any relevant public interest and the Home Office could not do so in time for this hearing. The Court held that there was therefore nothing which could be weighed against the interference with Article 8, the breach of which was disproportionate. Policy arguments were put forward by the government in the subsequent Upper Tribunal case of *FH (Post-flight spouses) Iran* [2010] UKUT 275 (IAC), presided over by Lord Justice Sedley, but were found unpersuasive. The Tribunal concluded that, where an applicant met all the requirements for entry as a spouse of a settled resident (including maintenance and accommodation), exclusion was unlikely to be proportionate. They also recommended giving urgent attention to amending the rules. In 2011, the rules were amended to allow those with limited leave as refugees or through humanitarian protection to sponsor spouses, civil partners, unmarried partners, and minor children on a similar basis to settled residents and nationals (paras 319L and 319V). Fiancé(e)s are not included in these rules nor under the rules applicable to pre-flight family members. In *Aswatte (fiancé(e)s of refugees) Sri Lanka* [2011] UKUT 0476 (IAC), the Tribunal found that where, as here, there was a long-standing relationship, the principle in *FH* applied and refusal to allow entry under the fiancé rules for settled residents was disproportionate.

9.15 Conclusion

The rules on family settlement still carry the burden of policy on integration and diversity. The continuing proposals for change and the reasons given for these changes indicate that they continue to be instruments of social policy.

In comparison with the 1960s and 1970s, the law relating to family settlement is now relatively transparent. The IDI and entry clearance guidance are published and concessions are increasingly integrated into the rules. This greater transparency, combined with the albeit limited effect of Article 8, is no more than is necessary and appropriate, given that decisions about family members have a fundamental effect on the welfare and happiness of those settled in the UK. In substance, however, the rules continue to restrict the possibilities for family life of such residents. Family migration continues to be an area of frequent and continuing intervention. The contrast with the position of EEA nationals exercising Treaty rights in the UK, and discussed in chapter 6, is marked and will become more marked if the proposals contained in the Family Settlement Consultation are implemented.

QUESTIONS

1 What is the purpose of the probationary period for partners? Is the government right to propose a probationary period for other adult relatives?
2 What role is there for immigration control in the prevention of forced marriages?

3 Why are governments resistant to allowing third-party support to meet the maintenance requirement?
4 Draft your own immigration rule for the admission of children, taking into account the policy priorities you would consider most important. How does this compare with the existing rules?

online resource centre

For guidance on answering questions, visit www.oxfordtextbooks.co.uk/orc/clayton5e/.

FURTHER READING

Charsley, Katharine (2012a) 'Marriage-related migration to the UK' *International Migration Review* vol. 46, forthcoming.

Charsley, Katharine and Benson, Michaela (2012b) 'Marriages of Convenience and Inconvenient Marriages: Regulating Spousal Migration to Britain' *Journal of Immigration Asylum and Nationality Law* vol. 26, no. 1, pp. 10–26.

Chowdhury, Zahir (2007) 'Recognition of Foreign Adoption: The Immigration Rules and English Conflict of Laws' *Immigration Law Digest* vol. 13, no. 2, Summer, pp. 10–16.

Clayton, Gina (2008) 'Section 3 of the Human Rights Act and the Immigration Rules' *Immigration Law Digest* vol. 14, no. 1, Spring, pp. 7–13.

Coker, Jane, Finch, Nadine, and Stanley, Alison (2002) *Putting Children First: A Guide for Immigration Practitioners* (London: Action Group).

Drew, Sandhya and Nastic, Dragan (2009) 'The Immigration Reservation to the Convention on the Rights of the Child: An Insuperable Difficulty no More' *Journal of Immigration, Asylum and Nationality Law* vol. 23, no. 2, pp. 119–134.

Finch, Nadine (2007) 'Family and Immigration Cases: Implications for Practice' *Family Law* vol. 37, August, pp. 716–720.

Groenendijk, Kees (2011) 'Pre-departure Integration Strategies in the European Union: Integration or Immigration Policy?' *European Journal of Migration and Law* vol. 13, pp. 1–30.

James, Charles (2006) '50 Years of Family Immigration: Changes in British Legislation for Partner and Family Immigration: 1955–2005' *Journal of Immigration, Asylum and Nationality Law* vol. 20, no. 1, pp. 21–36.

Jones, Adele (2002) 'A Family Life and the Pursuit of Immigration Controls', in S. Cohen, B. Humphries, and E. Mynott (eds), *From Immigration Controls to Welfare Controls* (London: Routledge).

McKee, Richard (1999) 'Primary Purpose by the Back Door? A Critical Look at "Intention to Live Together"' *Immigration and Nationality Law and Practice* vol. 13, no. 1, pp. 3–5.

Menski, Werner (2007) 'Dodgy Asians or Dodgy Laws? The Story of H' *Journal of Immigration, Asylum and Nationality Law* vol. 21, no. 4, pp. 284–294.

Mole, Nuala (1987) *Immigration: Family Entry and Settlement* (Bristol: Jordan & Sons).

Pearl, David (1986) *Family Law and the Immigrant Communities* (Bristol: Jordan & Sons).

Pearl, David and Menski, Werner (1998) *Muslim Family Law* (3rd edn) (London: Sweet & Maxwell).

Pilgram, Lisa (2009) 'Tackling "Sham Marriages": The Rationale, Impact and Limitations of the Home Office's "certificate of approval" scheme' *Journal of Immigration, Asylum and Nationality Law* vol. 23, no. 1, pp. 24–40.

Rogers, Nicola (2003) 'Immigration and the ECHR: Are New Principles Emerging?' *European Human Rights Law Review* 1, pp. 53–64.

Sachdeva, Sanjiv (1993) *The Primary Purpose Rule in British Immigration Law* (Stoke on Trent: Trentham).

Shah, Prakash (2002) 'Children of Polygamous Marriage: An Inappropriate Response' *Immigration and Nationality Law and Practice* vol. 16, no. 2, pp. 110–112.

—— (2011a), 'When South Asians Marry Trans-jurisdictionally: Some reflections on immigration cases by an "expert"' in Holden, L. ed. *Cultural Expertise and Litigation: Patterns, Conflicts, Narratives* (London: Routledge).

—— (2011b) *Transnational Family Relations in Migration Contexts: British Variations on European Themes* available at: www.religareproject.eu/content/transnational-family-relations-migration-contexts-british-variations-european-themes.

Sondhi, Ranjiv (1987) *Divided Families: British Immigration Control in the Indian Subcontinent* (London: Runnymede Trust).

Stanley, Alison (2006) 'Children First, Migrants Second' *Legal Action* March, pp. 7–8.

Van Oers, Ricky, Ersbøll, Eva. and Kostakopoulou, Dora (2010) *A Re-Definition of Belonging? Language and Integration Tests in Europe* (Leiden: Martinus Nijhoff).

Wray, Helena (2006a) 'An Ideal Husband? Marriages of Convenience, Moral Gate-Keeping and Immigration to the UK' *European Journal of Migration and Law* vol. 8, pp. 303–320.

—— (2006b) 'Hidden Purpose: Ethnic Minority International Marriages and "Intention to Live Together"' in P. Shah and W. Menski (eds) *Migration, Diasporas and Legal Systems in Europe* (London and New York: Routledge-Cavendish), pp. 163–184.

—— (2009) 'Moulding the Migrant Family' *Legal Studies* vol. 29, no. 4, pp. 592–618.

—— (2011) *Regulating Marriage Migration into the UK: A Stranger in the Home* (Farnham: Ashgate).

Yeo, Colin (2009) 'Raising the Spouse Visa Age' *Journal of Immigration, Asylum and Nationality Law* vol. 23, no. 4, pp. 365–370.

10

Entry for work, business, and study: the points-based system

SUMMARY

This chapter deals with the law relating to entry for work, self-employment, and study, the areas covered by the points-based system (PBS). Some of those who are currently in the UK entered under the former rules, and these still govern their stay, although, when they renew their leave, most will have to meet the requirements of the PBS. This chapter is organized around the five tiers of the PBS but makes reference to some of the old rules as well as providing some historical perspective. It also considers those few schemes remaining outside the PBS and, briefly, illegal working.

10.1 Introduction

Until implementation of the points-based system (PBS), entry for work, business, or study was governed by many disparate schemes within the immigration rules. Most of these were incorporated into the PBS or eliminated. Leave to enter for work or study is always for a limited period. Although some routes lead to settlement, the current policy trend is to reserve this only for the wealthy or the most skilled workers.

The provisions of this chapter do not apply to those who do not need the permission of the immigration authorities to work in the UK. These are:

(a) British citizens and those with a right of abode in the UK (see chapter 3);

(b) Irish citizens, who are exempted from immigration control in the Common Travel Area (Immigration Act 1971 s 1(3) and see chapter 7);

(c) EEA nationals, who have freedom of movement under the EC Treaties, though the ability to work is limited for A2 nationals (see 10.9.1 and chapter 5);

(d) Those with indefinite leave to remain in the UK (see chapter 7);

(e) Those with entry clearance in the form of a certificate of entitlement (see chapter 7);

(f) Those on their 'probationary period' as a married, civil, or unmarried partner (HC 395 paras 282 and 295B, see chapter 9); and

(g) Refugees.

This section is followed by a short history of the law prior to the PBS. There is then a general introduction to the PBS before consideration of each Tier and, finally, routes outside the PBS.

10.2 A brief history of entry to the UK to work and the development of the work permit scheme

Work permits began in 1916 as a form of permission to undertake certain types of skilled work and were issued only to aliens, i.e., non-Commonwealth citizens including Europeans, although Dummett and Nicol (1990:111) comment that the purpose of the scheme was 'not very clear'. Relatively few foreign nationals came to work in the UK at that time and the scheme was, in part, a carryover from the wartime practice of monitoring the presence of 'aliens'. Commonwealth citizens were British subjects and had, in theory, an unfettered right to enter the UK, though few actually did so.

After the Second World War, there was active recruitment to fill Britain's labour needs. Thousands of work permits were issued for specific groups and purposes, e.g., to Italian men for coalmining. In 1945, the government instituted the European Voluntary Workers' Scheme (EVWS), which, for six years, recruited Europeans in refugee camps for three-year contracts in jobs assigned by the Ministry of Labour. These were single people without dependants and, initially, settlement rights. Paul's (1997:84) work reveals that, despite its short-term origins, the government soon began to think of 'the benefits that come from the assimilation of virile, active and industrious people into our stock' and permitted the long-term settlement and integration of this much-needed labour, although not of those who '"through ineptitude or general low mental capacity" or "undesirable character" proved useless' or who were disabled refugees or married women with children (Paul 1997:79). The welcome was conditional, and strongly controlling, but national resources were devoted to making it work.

The EVWS met local opposition from, for example, the National Union of Mineworkers (Dummett and Nicol 1990:176). In the meantime, Commonwealth citizens, who did not need work permits, were filling vacancies. As described in chapter 1, Commonwealth nationals who had served Britain during the Second World War, returned to make a living and a future in the UK. Others were recruited locally during the 1950s by major employers, for example, London Transport, and the British Hotels and Restaurants Association, with inducements such as the payment of fares. Much of this work was low paid. As with the EVWS, public opinion was ambivalent. Paul argues that the government was hostile towards the 492 British subjects who arrived from the West Indies on the Empire Windrush in 1948: 'The colonials were met and housed to avoid "disorder" and with the determination that this was to be a once-only affair' (1997:118). British subjects from the Commonwealth could not be controlled in terms of their conditions and length of stay, unlike alien workers. The latter were also seen as more easily assimilated, being white and European. The links between labour market issues and race are covered in chapter 1, and the reader is referred to that chapter for fuller discussion.

During this period, then, there were two systems of entry for work operating in parallel. For foreign nationals, the work permit system continued. Public attention, however, focused on Commonwealth citizens, who entered by virtue of their right as British subjects. Under the Commonwealth Immigrants Act 1962, they became subject to a voucher system, allocated primarily according to skills and need for labour. Vouchers, unlike the work permits issued to aliens, carried a right to immediate settlement but, as Commonwealth citizens already had the right to settle, the scheme represented a curtailment of rights. The voucher system was an attempt to subject Commonwealth citizens to the UK's market needs and their settlement was a necessary concession (see, for instance, Bhabha, Klug, and Shutter (eds)), and Holmes (1988)).

The 1965 White Paper restricted entry under the voucher system further. The Immigration Act 1971 completed the process by bringing foreign nationals and Commonwealth citizens into the same work permit scheme, and work vouchers were abolished. The remaining work-related advantages of being a Commonwealth citizen were lost, with the exception of the right of entry for Commonwealth citizens with a UK-born grandparent, discussed briefly later in this chapter. On the same day that the 1971 Act came into force, the UK became a member of the European Communities, giving European nationals the right to travel to the UK for work.

In 1979, a time of high unemployment, the work permit scheme was reviewed and work permits made more difficult to obtain, becoming available only for workers with high levels of skill, qualifications, or experience. In 1989, economic circumstances were different, and a further review had a different outcome. Devine and Barrett-Brown (2001) note that 'there was sustained economic growth with an increasing demand for highly skilled labour, an increase in internationalization in the way business was operating and substantial inward investment by foreign companies'. The Department of Employment, then responsible for the work permit scheme, modified its traditional policy of protecting the resident labour force to support the development of an enterprise economy. Applications that were clearly furthering business growth and investment would be processed more quickly with fewer demands on employers. The result was a two-tier system within the work permit scheme.

Early twenty-first century labour market conditions were different again as were the terms of debate. A research report for the Home Office, *International Migration and the UK: Recent Patterns and Trends*, summarized the issues as being 'the contribution labour migration can make to alleviating the possible impacts of demographic change; a need to compete in a global skills market to remain economically competitive; and a need to recruit overseas workers to meet specific labour shortages' (Dobson, Koser, Mclaughlan, and Salt 2001). Projections of the numbers of migrant workers needed to sustain European economies briefly became headline news, although the Labour Migration Survey cast doubt on these projections. The Minister for Immigration, Barbara Roche, announced a change of policy, including a new route of primary immigration for the highly skilled (*The Independent* 21 July 2000). The 2002 White Paper *Secure Borders, Safe Haven* (Cm 5387) indicated, for the first time since the 1960s, that there might be a positive role for new primary 'managed migration'. Globalization meant that transnational companies needed to move their own skilled workers about the globe, and economic development increased the supply of skilled labour and demand for study. After a review, the work permit scheme was significantly opened up in 2001. The qualifications needed were reduced, applications to fill shortage occupations were expedited, and switching employers within the UK became easier. In June 2001, Work Permits (UK) was transferred from the Department of Education and Employment to the Home Office and their powers extended to the issue of work permit extensions and in-country grants of leave, without a separate application to the immigration department. The new lawful routes for economic migration proposed in the 2002 White Paper were implemented, not through primary legislation, but in schemes and rules, for instance the Highly Skilled Migrants Programme (HSMP), aimed at the most skilled and which led to settlement. Anticipating the PBS, both the HSMP and a new Innovators' scheme were based on a points system, common in other Commonwealth countries but not previously used in the UK. There was expansion of the Working Holidaymakers Scheme and of the Seasonal Agricultural Workers Scheme (SAWS), both considered later in this chapter, and, in May 2003, a new Sectors Based Scheme (SBS), also discussed later, was introduced extending the work permit scheme from its traditional professional base through short-term permits in food-processing and the hotel and catering industry.

On 1 May 2004, ten countries acceded to the European Union. The UK, unlike most of its European partners, granted nationals of the new Member States an immediate right to work, subject to registration under the Workers' Registration Scheme. Accession Monitoring Reports showed Accession State nationals engaged in a wide range of occupations, including bus, lorry, and coach drivers, care workers, teachers, researchers, classroom assistants, and health-related posts, but the immediate impact was primarily in agriculture and fishing, where employment grew sharply (Portes and French 2005).

The positive tone towards economic migration which emerged in the 2002 White Paper was not sustained. In 2004, quotas were introduced and then reduced in SAWS and quotas were reduced also in the SBS. Criteria for the Working Holidaymaker Scheme tightened again soon after having been relaxed. In April 2004, the government announced a '"top to bottom review" of managed migration routes to assess the extent to which they were subject to abuse or otherwise open to improvement' (*Selective Admission* para 4.8). The results were a number of measures tightening immigration control. In February 2005, the publication of the White Paper, *Controlling our Borders: Making Migration Work for Britain* (Cm 6472), announced plans for a tiered points system encompassing all immigration for work or study and favouring the most skilled both for entry and settlement. In July, a consultation document was published, entitled *Selective Admission*, in which the criteria were uncompromisingly economic. Details of the new managed migration scheme were published in March 2006 as Cm 6741, *A Points-Based System: Making Migration Work for Britain*. Implementation started in 2008 and now covers almost all migrants coming for work or study.

The implementation of the PBS coincided with a sharp recession, rising unemployment, and new concerns about immigration and security. The trend has been towards more restriction and this is evident in many aspects of the PBS discussed later in the chapter. While 2008 saw a record number of foreigners living in the UK (*ONS Population Trends No. 138*), government rhetoric began to suggest that the principal effect of the PBS would not be to manage migration, as originally conceived, but to reduce it. This theme has continued in even more marked terms since the Coalition government came to power in 2010. Its commitment to reducing net migration to the 'tens of thousands' means that very few (1,000 per year) highly skilled migrants without a job offer may now enter the UK while the number of skilled work migrants filling vacancies has been capped and new restrictions placed on students.

10.3 The points-based system (PBS): Introduction

The structure of the PBS is similar to the outline in the consultation paper. Most non-family migration routes were consolidated into one of five Tiers, although some were deleted and a very few, discussed later, still operate outside the PBS. To qualify in each Tier, applicants must have sufficient points according to the criteria of the scheme. The government vigorously promoted the transparency, objectivity, and flexibility of the PBS. However, in significant respects, the PBS lacks these characteristics, at least so far as applicants are concerned.

The Select Committee on Home Affairs reported on the PBS in July 2009 (*Managing Migration: The Points Based System*, Thirteenth Report of Session 2008–09 HC 217–I).

Some of its specific findings are discussed later in the chapter. Its overall conclusion was that, while the scheme as a whole, received a 'cautious welcome', several key structures required further consideration.

10.3.1 Flexibility

The defining characteristic of a points system is that applicants who do not fully meet one criterion can compensate by scoring well elsewhere. That type of flexibility was initially present in Tiers 1 and 2 to a limited extent but has now entirely disappeared. Elsewhere within the PBS, applicants have always been required to attain full points by meeting a specific requirement. A Tier 4 student, for example, needs 30 points for attributes. These can be obtained only by obtaining a 'Confirmation of Acceptance for Studies'. Ten points are needed for maintenance. These can be awarded only by possession in the manner specified of the sum specified in Appendix C. In other words, points are simply another way of saying that the applicant must meet all the requirements of the immigration rules. The Select Committee noted that the PBS had a degree of 'rigidity and inflexibility', even though a sensitive and flexible allocation of points is important given the absence of discretion by decision-makers.

10.3.2 Complexity and accountability

The PBS is difficult to navigate successfully. Criteria for entry are set out in the immigration rules. The rules themselves must be cross-referenced with the appendices. There is additional lengthy guidance for each Tier and in relation to each application form. The Tier 2 Guidance, for instance, is 58 pages long and contains detailed instructions as to all the evidence needed for a successful application. Guidance is subject to frequent change, raising questions of certainty and clarity (the Tribunal in *NA and others v SSHD* [2009] UKAIT 00025 noted five versions for the Tier 1 Post-Study Work route between June 2008 and March 2009).

Guidance outside the immigration rules has long existed in the form of the Immigration Directorate Instructions and Entry Clearance Guidance. However, the PBS guidance is of a different order of complexity and specificity and is expressed as instructions to applicants or sponsors not as guidance to officials. Paragraph 245A HC395 provides that where the Rules state that specified documents must be provided, that means the documents specified in the Points-Based System Policy Guidance for that route. If they are not provided, the application will fail. The role of guidance, which is not subject to even the limited legislative scrutiny of the immigration rules, in determining the acceptability of an application is thus of critical practical importance to applicants.

Early Tribunal decisions on the PBS (for example, *NA and others v SSHD*) found that guidance was binding on applicants. In *NA*, three individuals had been refused leave under the Tier 1 (Post-Study Work) scheme because they failed to meet the guidance requirements as to the period of time for which funds must be shown as available. The Tribunal found that they could not rely on other evidence to show financial solvency. One applicant had been ill during the relevant period but had recovered and her ability to maintain herself was not questioned. However, because she could not show the requisite funds for the three-month period required by the guidance, she had to leave the UK, losing her job and the life she had created for herself. Given the difficulties faced by such applicants, it was unsurprising that the issue came before the higher courts.

SSHD v Pankina and others **[2010] EWCA Civ 719**

This case has already been discussed in chapter 1 because of what it says about the constitutional position of the immigration rules. The particular issue in the case arose out of the maintenance requirement for applicants for a Tier 1 Post-Study Work visa. Appendix C of the immigration rules required applicants 'to have the level of funds shown in the table below' and to provide 'specified documents', said in the policy guidance to be 'personal bank or building society statements covering the three month period immediately before the application' and showing always a balance of at least £800.

Sedley LJ found that the immigration rules, while they remain statements of policy, have acquired, through the negative resolution procedure required by the Immigration Act 1971, a status akin to law, which is not shared by the guidance. While it is permissible to incorporate extraneous material into legal instruments by reference to it, this cannot be used as a way to create new legally effective rules that are liable to further change without parliamentary scrutiny. He found in favour of the applicants who had met the requirements of the rules but failed to meet those contained in the guidance.

The principle in *Pankina* was applied in several subsequent cases. *R (on the application of English UK) v SSHD* [2010] EWHC 1726 (Admin), concerned an attempt to increase the standard of English required of incoming language students via amendment to guidance. Foskett J found the *ratio* of *Pankina* to be that a material or substantive change to the administration of immigration control must be subject to parliamentary scrutiny as required by s 3(2) Immigration Act 1971. This rendered the change via guidance unlawful.

The distinction between substantive or material and minor criteria was discussed by the Divisional Court in *R (on the application of JCWI) v SSHD* [2010] EWHC 3524 (Admin). Sullivan LJ accepted that 'there is a spectrum and that, in enacting section 3(2) Parliament did not intend that every alteration to the Secretary of State's practice, however minor should be subject to the scrutiny of Parliament' (para 43). The point at which scrutiny was not required did not need to be identified here as the use of guidance to impose a cap on numbers permitted entry under Tiers 1 and 2 was clearly on the wrong side of it. This approach was endorsed by the Court of Appeal in *R (on the application of Alvi v SSHD* [2011] EWCA Civ 681 which found that a list of approved occupations which referred to a minimum skill equivalent to NVQ level 3 could not be relied on to refuse a Tier 2 application when this minimum requirement was not in the immigration rules. Similarly, in *Owolabi (Tier 2 – skilled occupations) Nigeria* [2011] UKUT 00313 (IAC), the Upper Tribunal found that the Secretary of State could not rely on a list of skilled occupations that was created after the immigration rule which refers to it.

Given the distinction between material and minor criteria, not every requirement in the guidance can be challenged but where to draw the line is difficult to determine. The applicant in *R (on the application of Ahmed) v SSHD* [2011] EWHC 2855 (Admin) applied in April 2010 for leave as a Tier 4 student, relying on a 'visa letter' from his institution. The rules at that time provided that the applicant must provide a Confirmation of Acceptance for Studies (CAS) whose form was not specified under the rules. From February 2010, UKBA had accepted only CAS in electronic form, although a visa letter had previously been acceptable, and guidance to this effect was published before he made the application. Singh J formulated the distinction as being between substantive requirements and those relating to the means of proving eligibility. The requirement to submit the CAS in a particular form did not offend the principle in *Pankina*. This reflects Lord Justice Sedley's dicta at para 6 of *Pankina*, that the requirements challenged in that case went 'well beyond simply specifying the means of proving eligibility and introduce a substantive further criterion'. However, the weight of both his judgment and subsequent ones was on the distinction between 'substantive or material', i.e., significant changes and minor ones, rather than evidential issues. Thus, in *FA and AA (PBS: effect of Pankina) Nigeria* [2010] UKUT 00304, the immigration rules required the applicant to show that the necessary funds were available to her. The guidance specified that funds must be held by the applicant or her parents. The funds were in her husband's name and her application was rejected. The Upper Tribunal, which included the President and Vice-President, held that *Pankina* applied and the requirement in the guidance was not enforceable.

Although *Pankina* ensures applicants can usually rely on the rules, the PBS remains complex to navigate. When first established, the aim was to provide an objective and transparent set of criteria (see, for example, *Controlling Our Borders* pp. 15–16) but this does not appear to be the case. A survey published in 2009 found that, while the new system worked well for many students, for a significant number, 'difficulties with the forms and procedures, or errors and obstruction from ECOs and commercial partners resulted in students being confused, tripped up, put off by, or even refused' (*Tier 4: Students' Experiences (Applying from outside the UK) Summary*, p. 5). Nor is it clear that the PBS has reduced the level of fraud or non-compliance. Some applicants may, for example, borrow the funds needed for the maintenance requirements and repay them once the application has been granted. Numbers of students entering the UK from the Indian subcontinent increased dramatically following introduction of the PBS and it was claimed that this was due to widespread fraud, particularly as regards the maintenance requirements ('Immigration Rules Result in Flood of Bogus Applications', *Sunday Telegraph*, 6 December 2009).

There is no appeal against refusal of a PBS application made through entry clearance, except on human rights grounds. The government justified loss of entry clearance appeal rights by the 'objective and verifiable' criteria of the PBS (*Controlling Our Borders* 2005 p. 2), yet there is no evidence that human error has been eliminated. Independent appeal rights were replaced by a system of administrative review and by scrutiny by the Chief Inspector of the UK Border Agency. Administrative review mirrors a long-standing system whereby an entry clearance manager reconsiders a refusal. These were previously criticized as ineffective (see National Audit Office (2004) *Visa Entry to the United Kingdom: The Entry Clearance Operation* HC 367 at p. 27). The review may not be used to introduce new evidence (except as relates to previous use of deception), even though according to *Odelola v SSHD* [2009] UKHL 25, the rules to be applied to the application are those in force at the date of the decision, and not of the application. If rules change against the applicant after the application, the applicant has no opportunity to demonstrate compliance with new requirements.

The PBS is also subject to independent monitoring by the Chief Inspector of the UK Border Agency, a post created by the UK Borders Act 2007 and which took over the functions previously carried out by the Independent Monitor for Entry Clearance and others (see chapter7). Monitoring is not a substitute for appeal rights. Only a small sample of decisions is examined and there is no power to overturn poor decisions. The Select Committee on Home Affairs (*Fifth Report of Session 2007–8* HC 425, Conclusions and Recommendations) recommended that the Chief Inspector should be given the power to investigate individual cases and provide appropriate remedies.

Appeal rights remain in place for in-country applications. but have been attenuated further since implementation of s 19 UK Borders Act 2007, which prohibits the introduction of new evidence at a PBS appeal (unless the appeal is on human rights or EU free movement grounds) even if it relates to the state of affairs at the time of the application. Examples would include bank statements that show that the applicant did, in fact, possess the requisite funds when the application was made. The outcome is that only evidence included in the application may be taken into account, even though, in accordance with *Odelola*, the applicable rules may have changed after the application was made.

Judicial review is also available but, as *Rhandawa v SSHD* [2008] EWHC 3042 (Admin) demonstrates, that is not the same as an appeal. Here, an application under the Highly Skilled Migrant Programme had been refused because of evidence of false claims about employment which were challenged by the applicant. Mr Justice Sullivan said that, had this been an appeal on the merits, he might have been cautious about accepting the unfavourable evidence but that, in a judicial review, he was confined to deciding whether the defendants had been unreasonable to rely on it.

The combined effect of all these measures is that an applicant under the PBS only has one shot at getting the application right despite the complexity of the process and the possibility of last minute or even post-application changes to the criteria. The early evidence of the PBS does not suggest that the quality of decision-making is better than under the previous rules and there have been some well-publicized reports of doubtful decisions (see Wray 2009:239). The report by the UK Council for International Student Affairs, referred to earlier, found that 10 per cent of student applicants had to apply more than once to get a visa and believed that their first application had been unreasonably refused. This was likely to have a lasting effect on their own and their families' and friends' perception of the UK as a destination (Summary p. 6). The Chief Inspector of the UKBA undertook a thematic inspection of Tier 2 applications in 2010 and, while he found much to commend in staff practice and attitudes, he also found that the complexity of the system and inconsistencies in practice between posts created difficulties for applicants and made good and consistent decision-making harder to achieve (Chief Inspector UK Border Agency (2010) *A Thematic Inspection of the Points-Based System: Tier 2 (Skilled Workers) July – August 2010*).

The position was made more difficult by para 34C inserted into the immigration rules in 2008. This renders an application invalid if it does not comply with all the formal requirements and the result for an in-country applicant may be inadvertent overstaying with drastic consequences. Such an applicant may be able to rely on a concession announced by Lord Bassam, during parliamentary debate on the PBS, that applications made within 28 days of leave expiring (which means the end of the appeal process) will be treated as having been made in time (HL Hansard 17 March 2008 cols 97–98). However, a combination of complexity, administrative rigidity, and delay means that minor errors can still have serious effects as the lengthy tale of Mr Kobir demonstrates (*R (on behalf of Mahsud Kobir) v SSHD* [2011] EWHC 2515 (Admin)). Mr Kobir had studied in the UK for several years in compliance with the immigration rules. In May 2009, he applied for further leave to study for a postgraduate qualification, the first time he had done so under the PBS. He did so using a 55-page application form, 50 pages of Tier 4 guidance, and 21 pages of guidance as to the form. By error, he failed to include the application fee for his two children. The application was returned as invalid on 26 June 2009, after expiry of his leave. He resubmitted it on 3 July 2009 but it was not decided until July 2010, one year later. In the meantime, he had no leave and could not enroll on the course for which he had applied and paid. Unknown to him, the delay was due to investigation and suspension of his intended institution but the suspension was eventually lifted and his application considered. It was refused because, as at the date of his re-application, his bank statements were out of date. They had to be dated no more than one month before the application, a requirement fulfilled in the first application but not by the time of the second. Because he had no valid leave at the time of the second application, he had no right of appeal and was warned that if he did not leave the UK voluntarily, he was liable to prosecution (even though, at that time, the Home Office had possession of the family's passports).

Undeterred, Mr Kobir enrolled at a further college and submitted a third application with up-to-date bank statements. This application was refused because, although he now met all the criteria for an in-country application, he was not eligible to apply in-country because he did not have leave. Eventually, the application was reconsidered but again refused because his maintenance did not meet the more onerous out-of-country criteria. These decisions were eventually quashed on judicial review for their lack of proportionality and it is to be hoped that Mr Kobir's application finally received proper attention.

Leaving aside the immigration consequences of making invalid applications, it is unsatisfactory that applicants must make and pay for a new application if they make a minor error. Opportunities for a particular job or course may be permanently foregone. The Select Committee recommended that an applicant should be able to submit additional paperwork, where this is requested, without having to make a fresh application or pay another fee. In his report on Tier 2, the Chief Inspector made a similar recommendation and noted variable practice in that regard.

Sedley LJ in *Pankina,* found that, in applying the immigration rules, the government must have regard to applicants' Convention rights. An in-country applicant may have established an Article 8 private or family life that will suffer interference if an application for further leave fails and refusal for minor errors that do not affect the applicant's substantive eligibility may be disproportionate. In *CDS (PBS: 'available': Article 8) Brazil* [2010] UKUT 00305 (IAC), the Upper Tribunal observed out that there is no hard and fast rule about which aspects of the Rules may be overlooked to render a decision compliant: '... even central requirements are not determinative if the countervailing claim is of sufficient weight'. This however does not mean that Article 8 is 'a means whereby the immigration rules can be ignored or re-written, because a judicial fact-finder regards a person as having only narrowly failed to comply with the relevant rules' (*MM and SA (Pankina: near miss) Pakistan* [2010] UKUT 481 (IAC)). Nor may serious breaches be ignored. In *SAB and others (students – serious breach of conditions – Article 8) Ghana* [2010] UKUT 441, the applicant had worked in excess of the hours permitted under his Tier 4 visa, a flagrant breach that could not be overlooked.

When all else fails, MPs may make representations to the UK Border Agency on behalf of their constituents. The Home Affairs Select Committee in 2009 foresaw that these would increase as a result of the removal of appeal rights and was highly critical of the existing quality and speed of responses.

10.3.3 Role of the sponsor

All PBS applicants, except those for Tier 1, need a sponsor. This will be the employer for Tier 2, the educational establishment for Tier 4, or may be a religious body, charity, sporting, or cultural body or even a government under Tier 5. Tier 2 and Tier 5 sponsors are rated 'A' or 'B'. The 'B' rating is regarded as transitional and the sponsor must either improve their performance under a 'sponsorship action plan' or lose their licence. A new category of 'Highly Trusted Sponsor' is available for Tier 4 sponsors. Since September 2011, new sponsors must get at least an 'A' rating and are expected to move to Highly Trusted Sponsor status within 12 months. Sponsors who were previously accepted as 'B' rated must move to an 'A' rating or face revocation.

Sponsors are drawn deeper into the control of migrants under the PBS. They now have many positive obligations. For instance, employer and student sponsors must report the following:

- failure to turn up for the first day of work or enrolment at college (or other educational establishment);
- unauthorized absences from work of more than ten working days or from ten 'expected contacts' at college;
- termination of the contract of employment or termination of studies;
- changes in circumstances or information that indicate that the employee or student is breaching their conditions of entry.

Sponsors make a considerable investment to obtain and maintain a licence and the success of a sponsor's business may depend upon its continuation. Because of the penalties that attach to non-compliance, there is a temptation to over-report possible violations and more than 35,000 reports were made by educational institutions in just two years ('UK Universities "over-report" on foreign students' *University World News* 2 October 2011).

As you will see later, migrants' ability to enter or remain is also often, in practice, determined by the conduct of their sponsor. However, the system of licensing is not based on statute and is still regulated through guidance. An unsuccessful claim under *Pankina* principles was made in respect of sponsors' guidance in *R (on the application of New London College Ltd) v SSHD* [2011] EWHC 856 (Admin). Here, the claimant was a college whose licence had been withdrawn. However, it was found that the guidance to sponsors did not have to be incorporated into the immigration rules as it did not constitute a material or substantive change to the rules which merely authorize the licensing of sponsors and require applicants to have a sponsor.

This is logical given that the rules are statements 'as to the practice to be followed... for regulating the entry into and stay in the United Kingdom' of those who need leave to enter or remain (s 3(2) Immigration Act 1971) and sponsors are not such individuals. However, it means that the regulation of sponsors remains discretionary with consequences both for sponsors themselves and for applicants. As the High Court explained in *R (on the application of The London Reading College Ltd) v SSHD* [2010] EWHC 2561 (Admin), at para 9:

> ...establishing a college and achieving both accreditation and licensing is a substantial business undertaking for an establishment. Having achieved this status and opened for business teaching students, the college will inevitably have made substantial financial commitments. The loss of a licence would have the most serious professional and financial consequences for the college and its proprietors. It would also have a serious impact upon both its students and its prospective students.

Yet, these serious impacts are regulated outside statute and may be challenged only by judicial review (see, for instance, the unsuccessful claims in *R (on the application of San Michael College) v SSHD* [2011] EWHC 642 (Admin) or *R (on the application of Westech College) v SSHD* [2011] EWHC 1484 (Admin)). In the words of Ian Macdonald QC, 'there is not a whiff of statutory authority to inaugurate or run this new innovation... By what authority all this is being carried out is not at all clear' (Speech to ILPA AGM 27 November 2010).

10.3.4 Stratification and settlement

The PBS is highly stratified. The rights attaching to migrant status are dependent upon the Tier in which entry is granted which, in turn, is largely determined by the migrant's skills and education. In particular, only Tier 1, Tier 2, and a very few Tier 5 migrants may settle. The numbers of Tier 1 migrants has been dramatically reduced and settlement for Tier 2 and Tier 5 migrants may become more difficult in future (Home Office/ UK Border Agency (2011) *Employment-Related Settlement, Tier 5 and Migrant Domestic Workers: A Consultation*). The conditions for further leave and settlement are set out in the rules and require migrants to continue to meet the original terms of entry. Research commissioned by the Equalities and Human Rights Commission was concerned that women and other less favoured groups may be adversely affected by requirements such as the need to maintain employment at minimum income levels for a prolonged period (Kofman et al 2009).

The UKBA website advises that '[i]f you are considering applying for settlement in the future, please note that the Immigration Rules are subject to change. You must meet all the requirements of the Immigration Rules at the time when you make your application.' This warning is a wise precaution after the government tried and failed to change the terms upon which those who had already entered the UK under the HSMP (now replaced by Tier 1) could obtain further leave to remain. The HSMP was amended without notice in November 2006, applying new criteria to extension of leave applications by those who had already migrated to the UK. The reason given by the government was that many were not in highly paid employment as the scheme envisaged, but were working as, inter alia, taxi drivers (Letter of Minister of State to JCHR 18 May 2007).

The High Court found, in *R (on the application of HSMP Forum Ltd) v SSHD* [2008] EWHC 664 (Admin), that the HSMP scheme from entry to settlement composed one whole and could not be retrospectively amended for those who had already embarked upon it. The position was different for new entrants. Similarly, the extension of the minimum period of leave before settlement from four to five years also could not be retrospectively applied (*R (on the application of HSMP Forum (UK) Ltd v SSHD* [2009] EWHC 711 (Admin)).

The HSMP scheme had particular characteristics, which enabled these claims to succeed. It was aimed at those planning to migrate permanently and applicants had to intend to make the UK their main home. The Court observed that the government could have prevented its difficulties by expressly stating that there was no guarantee that the criteria for further stay would not change. In fact, it chose to imply the opposite as the HSMP guidance advised applicants that 'once you have entered under the programme you are in a category that has an avenue to settlement'. By contrast, the High Court found (although before the HSMP cases) that those who entered with work permits could not establish any such entitlement (*R (on the application of Ooi and others) v SSHD* [2007] EWHC 3221 (Admin)).

The underlying issue in the HSMP litigation, i.e., the extent to which the government can change the terms of continuing leave after entry, has also arisen in other work-related contexts. The terms on which overseas medical graduates may complete their medical training or work in the UK have changed frequently in the past 20 years. In 2006, the options for foreign medical graduates to complete their training and obtain work in the UK were dramatically reduced by the removal of provision for permit-free medical training in the UK. The government also tried to prevent doctors who could no longer qualify under the permit-free provisions from qualifying under the HSMP, not, as might be expected, by changing the HSMP rules but by sending guidance to NHS employers advising them that overseas medical graduates should only be employed if certain conditions were met.

Key Case

***R (on the application of BAPIO Action Limited) v SSHD* [2008] UKHL 27**

The situation of the second claimant to the original High Court challenge, Dr Imran Yousaf, was representative of the difficulties faced by those affected by the changes although Dr Yousaf tragically took his own life shortly before the High Court decision. He had obtained his primary medical qualification in Pakistan, working there as a junior doctor for two years. He came to the UK in 2004 to continue his training, taking and passing the necessary conversion tests. The test and visa fees and the costs of travel represented a significant commitment and he had incurred considerable debts. However, he did not obtain a post before the abolition of permit-free training and transitional arrangements did not apply to him.

In the House of Lords, the outstanding issue was the legality of the guidance issued to NHS employers, which aimed to prevent those in Dr Yousaf's position from remaining in the UK under the HSMP. It was found that the guidance was unlawful because, in effect, it changed the terms of leave without complying with the requirements in the Immigration Act 1971 for amendment of the immigration rules. Two of their Lordships also found that those doctors who had already been admitted under the HSMP (so, not Dr Yousaf) had a legitimate expectation that they could proceed to settlement under that scheme.

These cases, although decided under pre-PBS rules, highlight a major tension within the government's thinking about skilled migration. Skilled migrants are unlikely to come to the UK if they do not have the option of long-term residence for themselves and their families. Yet, the government wishes to retain the power to adjust rights as it deems necessary. As will be seen, the PBS requires migrants to prove their worth on entry, when they apply for further leave and again on settlement. As the position is clear from the outset, migrants cannot claim that they have been misled. However, the greater degree of uncertainty that migrants now face may be a disincentive to those whose skills allow them to choose between destinations.

10.3.5 The Migration Advisory Committee

The Migration Advisory Committee (MAC) has played an extensive role in the development of the PBS. It is an advisory, non-statutory committee established by the government in 2007. According to its terms of reference, it:

> will provide independent and evidence-based advice to Government on specific sectors and occupations in the labour market where shortages exist which can sensibly be filled by migration...The government may, from time to time, ask the MAC to advise on other matters relating to migration.

The MAC is based in UK Border Agency offices but is independent of government. It has a number of functions but the most significant are to identify which jobs come within the description of graduate (formerly 'skilled') employment for the purposes of Tier 2 and to review the list of shortage occupations. It has also, at the request of government, carried out other tasks including reviews of the position of A2 and A8 nationals, an analysis of

Tiers 1 and 2 and their dependants, and a list of graduate level occupations. The MAC is central to government claims that the PBS is determined by objectively assessed criteria.

10.4 Tier 1 migrants

Tier 1 now provides the only route to entry as a highly skilled worker, entrepreneur, or investor and is the only Tier for which a sponsor is not required. Entry clearance is always required before entry and switching in-country is possible only in limited circumstances. Tier 1 replaced a range of schemes such as the Highly Skilled Migrant Programme, Writers, Composers and Artists, Innovators and Investors. Not all of them have their equivalents under Tier 1. The Coalition government has also substantially reduced the ability of migrants to enter under this Tier through the closure of Tier 1 (General) and its replacement by the much more restrictive Tier 1 (Exceptional Talent). Similarly, the closure of the Tier 1 (Post-Study Work) route also excludes many former overseas students previously able to stay and work in the UK after graduation.

There are three active sub-categories in the Tier: Exceptional Talent, Entrepreneurs, and Investors, and two which are no longer open to new entrants, General and Post-Study Work.

10.4.1 Tier 1 (Exceptional Talent) and Tier 1 (General)

Tier 1 (Exceptional Talent) was introduced in August 2011 to replace the Tier 1 (General) which closed to new entrants at the same time. Tier 1 (General) had been a popular scheme, with almost 14,000 main visas and more than 10,000 dependant visas issued in 2009. It was a primary target in the Coalition government's drive to reduce net migration through a cap on numbers. In June 2010, the government asked the MAC to advise on the level at which the Tier 1 and 2 caps should be set in 2011/12. The Committee concluded that, on balance, Tier 1 and 2 migrants make a small but cumulatively significant positive net fiscal contribution, i.e., the benefits of their presence outweigh the costs but that, if the objective was to reduce migration, those who entered should be the most productive. It therefore proposed a small reduction in the number of Tier 1 visas, more regular recalibration of the points awarded and a requirement of graduate level employment at the renewal stage. These cautious proposals were not in line with the government's radical plans and, in July 2010 and before the publication of the MAC report, the government announced an interim cap of 600 Tier 1 (General) acceptances per month.

Despite the MAC's views, the government argued that many Tier 1 migrants were not doing highly skilled work. In October 2011, the government published research which showed that 25 per cent of Tier 1 visa holders were working in skilled occupations and earning over £25,000 pa and 29 per cent were working in unskilled employment and/or were earning under £25,000 pa. The position of the remaining 46 per cent was unclear and other factors may have affected the findings; for example, the data was drawn only from Tier 1 migrants with dependants (Home Office/UK Border Agency *Points Based System Tier 1: An Operational Assessment*). Nonetheless, in March 2011, Damian Green, Minister for Immigration, said that this tier 'supposedly the route for the best and the brightest – has not attracted highly-skilled workers. At least 30% of Tier One migrants work in low-skilled occupations such as stacking shelves, driving taxis or working as security guards and some don't have a job at all.' The closure of the Tier 1 (General) route was announced in November 2010 and implemented from December 2010 for overseas applications and from August 2011 for in-country applicants, when Tier 1 (Exceptional Talent) also opened.

The Exceptional Talent scheme is much more restrictive than Tier 1 (General). Its purpose, according to para 245B of the rules is to provide a route for exceptionally talented individuals in the fields of science, humanities, engineering, and the arts who 'are already internationally recognized at the highest level as world leaders... or who have already demonstrated exceptional promise and are likely to become world leaders'. Applicants must apply from outside the UK and switching is not permitted. They need a minimum of 75 points under Appendix A (para 245BB), which can be obtained only through endorsement by a Designated Competent Body, which is defined in para 4(b) of Appendix A as The Arts Council (allocated 300 endorsements for arts and culture), The Royal Society (300 endorsements for natural and medical sciences), The Royal Academy of Engineering (200 endorsements), and the British Council (300 endorsements for humanities and social sciences). Thus, in the year 2011–12, only 1,000 migrants can enter under this heading. There are no language or maintenance requirements.

Entry clearance is for three years and four months and is subject to conditions as to public funds, registration with the police, and some limits on employment. Further leave is obtainable provided the applicant is economically active in his expert field through employment or self-employment or both, the Designated Competent Body has not withdrawn its endorsement and the applicant has a level of English equivalent to B1 Common European Framework of Reference for Language Learning (CEFR). Indefinite leave is obtainable after five years subject to meeting the same requirement as before regarding economic activity and the other criteria for settlement.

Tier 1 (Exceptional Talent) is not an equivalent to Tier 1 (General) being capped, far more restrictive and lacking the flexibility of a points system. Tier 1 (General) was not only uncapped but had a more flexible system for awarding points. Those who scored less well under one heading might make them up under another. Points could be earned under four headings: Qualifications, Previous Earnings, UK Experience, and Age although it was impossible to score sufficient points without scoring highly in either Qualifications or Previous Earnings. When first implemented, points for earnings were capped at £40,000 pa. In December 2009, the MAC argued that earnings were a good proxy for skills and, rather than introducing an explicit and difficult skills criterion, points for earnings should be expanded above the £40,000 ceiling (Migration Advisory Committee (MAC), *Analysis of the Points Based System – Tier 1, December 2009*, p. 145). From April 2010, those earning £150,000 per annum or above could gain all the points needed for entry while, as also recommended by the MAC, points for earnings below £25,000 were removed. Points were available for academic qualifications but not for professional qualifications unless these could be independently verified. Points were not awarded for a medical degree, which lasts for a minimum of five years. A qualified doctor might well have insufficient points for Tier 1 and had to apply under Tier 2, resulting in reports of local shortages ('Rule change over doctor jobs' *BBC News* 30 July 2009). In its December 2009 report, the MAC recommended that appropriate professional qualifications should be treated as equivalent to a Master's degree.

The rules for Tier 1 (General) are now of direct relevance only to those who entered under the scheme (or its predecessor schemes) before the category was closed and are now seeking further leave or settlement. Applicants for settlement must have completed five years in the UK in a skilled work category, must still qualify for the points under which they originally qualified for entry, and meet the usual conditions of settlement. Their other point of interest is as a historical comparison with its replacement, the Exceptional Talent scheme. Unlike the new scheme, Tier 1 (General) was one of the very few instances of a true points-based approach within the PBS. It was also open to anyone who qualified, unlike the new regime which is capped.

10.4.2 Tier 1 (Entrepreneur)

Paragraph 245D of the immigration rules explains that this route is for migrants who wish to establish, join, or take over one or more businesses in the UK. A business means an enterprise as a sole trader, a partnership, or a UK-registered company. The applicant must have 75 points under the relevant paragraphs of Appendix A, 10 under Appendix B (English language), and 10 under Appendix C (maintenance).

A new applicant can gain the 75 points for attributes under Appendix A only by meeting all three of the following criteria:

- the applicant has access to at least £200,000 or to at least £50,000 from various approved sources;
- held in one or more regulated financial institutions;
- disposable in the UK.

Each of these characteristics is awarded 25 points each and must be met in full, an example of where the PBS does not really operate on a points basis but merely as a means of ensuring that certain criteria are met. The rules explain the meaning of 'regulated financial institution' and 'disposable in the UK'. The applicant must also have a minimum of ten points for English language under Appendix B, acquired through reaching level C1 of the CEFR, graduation from a university course certified as taught in English, or nationality of an English speaking country. The applicant also needs 10 points for maintenance under Appendices C and E, which stipulate that the applicant must show that he has £2,800 for himself and £1,600 for each dependant available to him as at the date of the application.

Initial leave is for three years and four months and is subject to conditions as to public funds, police registration, and no employment except in the businesses upon which the application was based. Under para 245DE(c), leave may be curtailed if, within six months of entry or the grant of leave to remain, the applicant has failed to register with HM Revenue and Customs as self-employed, register a new business of which they are a director, or register as a director of an existing business. When an application for further leave is made, the applicant must show, as well as meeting language and maintenance criteria, that they fulfilled and continue to fulfil the requirements of para 245DE(c), that they invested the funds upon which they founded the application directly into one or more businesses in the UK and that, as a consequence, the equivalent of two new full-time UK jobs have been created.

A Tier 1 (Entrepreneur) migrant may obtain indefinite leave after five years in that category or former related categories or three years if the applicant has created at least 10 new jobs, established a business with an income of at least £5 million during a three-year period, or joined or invested in a business and, as a consequence, there was a net increase in income of £5 million over a three-year period.

10.4.3 Tier 1 (Investor)

According to para 245E of the rules, the purpose of this category is to provide a route 'for high net worth individuals making a substantial financial investment to [sic] the UK'.

This category is aimed at the independently wealthy as, to obtain the 75 points needed under Appendix A, a first-time applicant must have at least £1 million of his own under his control and at his disposal in the UK or must own assets with a net value of £2 million and have £1 million available to him in the UK, and loaned to him by a UK regulated financial institution. There are no language or maintenance requirements. Leave is granted for three years and four months. Under paragraph 245EE(c) leave may be curtailed if the applicant has not invested at least £750,000 in UK government bonds or share or loan capital in active and trading UK companies and used the remainder used to purchase UK assets or placed on deposit in a UK regulated financial institution. This must have happened within three months of entry or leave to remain.

The period of time before settlement is obtainable depends upon the wealth of the applicant. The super-rich who have £10 million under their control in the UK may settle after two years provided they have invested 75 per cent of that £10 million in UK government bonds or companies and the remainder is on deposit in a UK regulated financial institution. Those with £5 million so available and so invested can settle after three years while the merely wealthy who have £1 million under their control and invested in the UK must wait five years. The other usual conditions for settlement must also be met.

10.4.4 Tier 1 (Post-Study Work)

This scheme is due to close in April 2012. Its purpose was described in para 245F as being 'to encourage international graduates who have studied in the UK to stay on and do skilled or highly skilled work'. However, the government believed that, given high levels of graduate unemployment in the UK, overseas graduates should no longer have open access to the labour market, even for a limited period. The closure of the route, however, was also a possible disincentive to overseas students who could no longer count on being able to work after graduation and thereby to recoup the cost of their overseas studies and the Select Committee on Home Affairs recommended reform rather than abolition (Select Committee on Home Affairs *Student Visas* Seventh Report of Session 2010–11 para. 58). The government's attitude towards overseas students is further discussed in 10.7.

Post-study work was not a direct route to settlement but provided a bridge between graduation and other skilled categories. Applicants needed 75 points under Appendix A, which required that the applicant must have a suitable higher qualification from a recognized UK institution, gained while lawfully present and the application was made within 12 months of graduation.

Applicants also needed points for maintenance and English language although this was met through UK study. Leave was granted for two years, after which the applicant had to switch into another Tier 1 or Tier 2 category if they wished to remain. Time spent as a Tier 1 (Post-study work) migrant did not count towards settlement in these other categories.

10.4.5 Tier 1 discussion

Tier 1 has recently seen dramatic changes as a result of the Coalition government's policy of reducing net migration. It was perhaps inevitable that a government seeking to reduce immigration would limit open-ended schemes such as Tier 1 (General) although reductions could have been obtained by tightening the criteria rather than its destruction. However, the creation of the Exceptional Talent route was a politically useful way of emphasizing the government's willingness to consider entry for a small elite perceived to have most to offer. There was also a marked emphasis on attracting the wealthy and entrepreneurial with accelerated settlement available for those shown to have made a particularly large contribution in terms of investment or job creation. This contrasts with the closure of other routes in this tier and reflects government policy. Damian Green said in March 2011 that '[e]ntrepreneurs and investors can play a major part in our economic recovery, and I want to do everything I can to ensure that Britain remains an attractive destination for them. Last year we issued far too few visas to those who wish to set up a business or invest in the UK – I intend to change that.'

10.5 Tier 2 migrants

10.5.1 The work permit scheme

Tier 2, which was implemented in November 2008, replaced the long-established work permit scheme (which still, however, applies to A2 nationals; see 10.9.1). The work permit scheme had been seen as an efficient and responsive system (see, for example, Home Affairs Committee *Managing Migration: Points-Based System Oral Evidence* HC217–iv, Qs.227, 228). Entry was a two-stage process. The prospective employer applied for a work permit and, if that was issued, the applicant applied for entry clearance and/or leave to enter or remain. The immigration decision was usually secondary to the work permit decision (although see the discussion of the Sectors Based Scheme later in this chapter for an instance when immigration considerations predominated).

The legal basis for the work permit scheme was uncertain (for more discussion, see earlier editions of this book). Their issue was an area of executive power largely beyond democratic or judicial scrutiny, although it was subject to judicial review. The conditions of eligibility were in guidance notes, which, over time, became publicly available on government websites. However, their discretionary and non-statutory basis meant that, as with the PBS guidance, they could be amended without debate or scrutiny. The only appeal was against the immigration decision, which was unlikely to succeed as lack of a work permit was a valid reason for refusal of leave. Parties argued unsuccessfully that the Secretary of State had therefore unlawfully confined his discretion under the immigration rules, as the immigration decision was dependent on the work permit decision (*Pearson v IAT* [1978] Imm AR 212).

10.5.2 Structure of Tier 2

According to para 245H of the rules, the purpose of Tier 2 (other than the Intra-Company Transfer route which is dealt with under separate rules) is to 'enable UK employers to recruit workers from outside the EEA to fill a particular vacancy that cannot be filled by a British or EEA worker'. All applicants coming from outside the UK need entry clearance. There are four sub-categories within Tier 2: General; Minister of Religion; Sportsperson; and Intra-Company Transfer.

Those applying under the General, Minister of Religion and Sportsperson routes are all dealt with under para 245H. All must have sufficient points for attributes, language and maintenance under Appendices A, B, and C, be at least 18 (or have parental consent if between 16 and 18), and have a sponsor which is not a company in which they own more than 10 per cent of the shares. Initial leave is for the period of engagement plus one month or for three years, whichever is the shorter. Periods of further leave are granted, subject to the applicant still qualifying for sufficient points. Conditions of leave include a prohibition on working except for the sponsor (although voluntary work and supplementary work of up to 20 hours per week in the same profession and at the same level as the main employment are permitted). This means that a new application must be made if the employee changes jobs or their conditions of employment change so that they no longer work under the same job classification or within the shortage occupation list or their pay is reduced below the level indicated on the Certificate of Sponsorship. Switching is permitted from other work-related categories. Settlement is possible after five years have been spent in a work-related category with the last part as a Tier 2 migrant, provided the employer confirms that the applicant's services are still required and that the salary is at the appropriate rate for the job as set out in the Tier 2 Codes of Practice (para 245HF(d). This latter requirement may cause difficulty for those who entered under old rules when lower salaries were permitted. In an unreported Tribunal case, reliance on the Code of Practice was found to be unlawful under *Pankina* principles and senior care workers recruited under old rules had a legitimate expectation of settlement without being subject to a minimum salary. Article 8 was also engaged (JCWI *Senior carers win stage in fight for right to settle* 14 December 2011).

10.5.3 Tier 2 (General)

These migrants need 50 points for Attributes from Appendix A, 10 points for language from Appendix B, and 10 points for maintenance from Appendix C. Attributes are found in paras 76–84A of Appendix A. Thirty points are awarded if the job offer:

- relates to a 'shortage occupation'; or
- the Resident Labour Market Test has been passed; or
- the post carries a salary of at least £150,000; or
- the applicant has already worked for the employer for 6 months on a Post-Study Work visa and will continue to do the same work.

The remaining 20 points are gained through having an 'appropriate salary' which, for a new entrant, must be at least £20,000 pa and not less than the appropriate rate stated in UKBA codes of practice.

All applicants need a Certificate of Sponsorship. The Certificate must relate to a job that appears on the UK Border Agency's list of graduate level occupations and the salary must be at or above the appropriate rate for the job. Under para 80 of Appendix A, inserted in March 2011, the Secretary of State may limit the number of Certificates of Sponsorship available in any specific period and, in addition to meeting the criteria for entry, new applicants will be awarded a visa only if that limit has not been reached or they are to be paid a salary of at least £150,000. The limit for the period 6 April 2011 to 5 April 2012 is 20,700. One thousand five hundred of these are available monthly and they are rolled over if there are insufficient qualifying applications.

The minimum requirement for a Certificate of Sponsorship is a job that passes the Resident Labour Market test and carries a salary of of £20,000. However, if there are more applications than Certificates available, then under a complex formula set out in para 83B of Appendix A, preference will be given to applications in shortage occupations or which are very highly skilled and well-paid. In fact, after the cap was introduced, numbers of applications were much lower than expected and, by October 2011, there was a reported accumulation of more than 9,300 Certificates of Sponsorship (*Breytanbach's Immigration News* 18 October 2011). The reasons are unclear but may be due to a combination of economic retrenchment by employers and uncertainty about the process ('Confusion leaves visas going spare' *Financial Times* 5 May 2011).

10.5.3.1 *The shortage occupation list*

The shortage occupation list identifies those occupations where it is recognized that the skill level of the job and domestic labour shortages make it sensible to recruit outside the EEA. Being on this list is one way to gain 30 points for attributes. It is drawn up by the government following recommendations by the MAC and is updated every six months, although the Home Affairs Committee, in its 2009 report *Managing Migration: The Points Based System*, suggested that this should happen more frequently. Occupations may be added or removed from the list in line with market conditions and the tendency in the recent past has been for the list to contract. By December 2011, around 190,000 posts were covered by the list compared to around 1 million in 2007 (although, of course, not all these posts had been filled by migrants).

There are some problematic areas in the list. In 2009, the MAC found that many chefs did not meet its definition of skilled work but, recognizing shortages in that area, recommended their inclusion subject to a minimum pay and experience threshold. The issue is that skills learnt within one tradition may not transfer to other cultures. Many Indian, Chinese, and other non-British restaurants, for example, have relied on migrant chefs and it has been pointed out that these cannot easily be replaced by domestic labour. The need to speak the language of the restaurant and to appreciate its overall culture (as well as the willingness to work long unsocial hours) were cited by the MAC as reasons why shortages persisted even in a recession (*Second review of the shortage occupation lists for the UK and Scotland: Autumn 2009*).

Others, however, have argued that EEA nationals of ethnic minority origin could be trained in these skills, reducing the need for imported labour ('Caterers Call for School of Curry in UK' *The Observer* 15 March 2009). The Home Affairs Committee called for more efforts to link skills shortages to training. However, while this may satisfy some demand, there is still a perceived need for highly skilled chefs at top end restaurants and chefs remain on the shortage occupation list but only where there is a sufficient level of skill and the salary is above a minimum figure. The result has been reports of up to one in four vacancies in less prestigious restaurants remaining unfilled, which plans to set up 'curry colleges' will not resolve in the short term (See 'The Curry Crisis' *The Guardian* 8 January 2012).

Certificates of Sponsorship for posts on the shortage occupation list automatically attract 30 points for attributes. When applying for further leave, the applicant must again be awarded points under Appendix A but, if an occupation has moved out of the shortage occupation list, the points are still awarded.

10.5.3.2 *Graduate level occupations*

Paragraph 77E of Appendix A requires that a new applicant for a Tier 2 (General) post not on the shortage occupation list must be entering for a job that is included in the UKBA's list of graduate level occupations (equivalent to Level 4 of the National Qualifications Framework). Those applying to renew leave must be working to Level 3, the standard that previously applied. The requirement to be working at graduate level was introduced in April 2011 and reflects the Coalition government's concern to limit immigration only to the highly skilled. As a consequence, 71 formerly eligible occupations were excluded.

Some skilled work may exist independently of formal qualifications. Care work, for example, involves interpersonal skills that are not easily measurable and many experienced care workers have few academic qualifications. Care workers were excluded from the first list of skilled occupations published by the MAC in September 2008. In its April 2009 review, the MAC recommended inclusion of senior skilled care workers if criteria were met including qualifications at NVQ level 2, minimum experience and pay, and supervisory responsibility in the post to which they are recruited. They thus returned to the list but were again removed when occupations below graduate level became ineligible. As senior care workers are not on the current shortage occupation list, such an occupation cannot currently form the basis of a new application. However, those permitted to enter under the old rules may apply for further leave and settlement.

10.5.3.3 *Resident Labour Market Test*

If a graduate level post does not appear on the shortage occupation list, the employer must carry out the Resident Labour Market Test (RLMT). The test is designed to ensure that EEA labour is not available to fill the post. To pass the test, the vacancy must be advertised to settled workers for 28 calendar days at the necessary skill level and at the market rate. Subject to a few exceptions, the post must be advertised through Jobcentre Plus and by one other method as permitted under a Code of Practice. The employer cannot refuse to employ an EEA national only because of the absence of skills or qualifications not specifically requested in the advertisement. If no suitable resident worker applies, a Certificate of Sponsorship may be issued within six months of the advertisement appearing.

The RLMT has been criticized as too undemanding and the Home Affairs Committee (2009) recommended that its operation be reviewed to ensure its rigorous enforcement. There have also been repeated calls, during the recession, for the test to be withdrawn so that only occupations on the shortage list may be filled by migrants. This question was, at the government's request, investigated by the MAC who did not find that there was an economic case for the RLMT route to be closed although it made some recommendations for change, including a longer period of advertisement, later implemented, and more enforcement measures.

10.5.3.4 *English language and maintenance*

Tier 2 General Migrants applying for entry clearance must gain 10 points under Appendix B for English language competence at level B1 CEFR whether or not this skill is necessary to do the job (for example, if the migrant will be employed in the arts or in an ethnic minority business such as a restaurant). However, the Home Affairs Committee (2009) regarded it as necessary for living in and integrating into British society.

Applicants also must have £800 in funds for themselves to gain the 10 points needed under Appendix C for maintenance and £533 for each family member under Appendix E. The maintenance requirements are waived for periods of further leave or if an A-rated sponsor undertakes to provide maintenance and accommodation for the family for the first month of employment.

10.5.4 **Tier 2 (Minister of Religion)**

Before the PBS, the immigration rules enabled minority faiths to recruit fully trained ministers from abroad and to undertake exchanges although these were subject to complex rules and instructions. The White Paper of 2002, *Secure Borders, Safe Haven*, argued that religious leaders needed to be able to communicate effectively with leaders of other faiths (para 3.31), and in 2004, an English language requirement was introduced. This anticipated the introduction of language requirements in the naturalization, then settlement, and finally entry requirements for other migrants.

Ministers of religion coming to the UK for an extended period now fall within Tier 2, while temporary religious workers come under Tier 5 and are discussed at 10.8.1.3. A minister of religion entering under Tier 2 must score 50 points under paras 85–92 of Appendix A, which are awarded for possession of a Certificate of Sponsorship. The sponsor must confirm that the Resident Labour Market Test has been performed, the applicant is qualified to do the job, intends to base himself in the UK, will comply with the conditions of his leave, and will be accommodated and maintained by the sponsor. Under Appendix B, ministers of religion must demonstrate a higher level (B2 CEFR) of English language competence than other Tier 2 migrants. The Appendix C and E maintenance requirements apply to new applicants unless an 'A'-rated sponsor undertakes to maintain the applicant and his family for the first month.

10.5.5 Tier 2 (Sportsperson)

Applicants in this category also need 50 points under paras 93–100 of Appendix A which are awarded for possession of a Certificate of Sponsorship. The sponsor must confirm that the applicant is qualified to do the job, has been endorsed by the sport's governing body as being internationally established at the highest level, will make a significant contribution to the sport's development, the post could not be filled domestically, and the migrant intends to base him or herself in the UK and will comply with the conditions of his leave. Maintenance and a basic English language requirement apply.

10.5.6 Intra-company transfer

The Intra-Company Transfer (ICT) route 'enables multinational employers to transfer their existing employees from outside the EEA to their UK branch for training purposes or to fill a specific vacancy that cannot be filled by a British or EEA worker' (para 245G HC 395). Numbers entering as ICTs increased from 33,645 in 2004 to 49,710 in 2008. In 2009, they accounted for 60 per cent of all Tier 2 visas and 40 per cent of Tier 1 and 2 combined (Select Committee on Home Affairs (2010) *Immigration Cap* First Report of Session 2010–11). The Chair of the MAC criticized the ITC route as prone to abuse and used to bypass the more rigorous demands of the Tier 2 (General) route, particularly in IT ('Migration Adviser Says Companies Should Train UK Staff' *The Guardian* 20 March 2009). The MAC recommended, alongside improved enforcement, that ICTs should no longer be a route to settlement and that the minimum period of prior employment should be extended to 12 months. Graduate trainees should enter on a separate scheme, involving a three-month minimum period of prior employment and a 12-month maximum stay.

However, restricting ICTs is not straightforward. The UK is subject to various international agreements and international businesses expect to transfer staff globally with relative ease. They were thus not included in the numerical cap imposed on other Tier 2 migrants. However, they were made the subject of further regulation introduced in April 2011 and the ICT route is now divided into four sub-categories:

- Short-term staff coming for 12 months or less;
- Long-term staff coming for more than 12 months;

- Graduate trainees;
- Skills transfer.

All ITC applicants need 50 points under Appendix A. Thirty points are available for the Certificate of Sponsorship and 20 points are available for the appropriate salary. Understanding the criteria, in practice, requires close reading of the rules (paras 245GA–GF) and Appendix A, not an easy task given the complex exceptions and convoluted paragraphs. In essence, the position is that:

- The ICT applicant must be coming to do a job that is on the list of graduate level occupations (with exceptions only in respect of further leave for those who entered under the old rules);
- Short-term and long-term staff must have been employed by the sponsor for a continuous period of 12 months immediately prior to the date of application (with allowances for parental and long-term sick leave);
- Graduate trainees must be taking part in a structured graduate training programme, and have been working for the sponsor outside the UK for at least 3 months. No more than five such trainees may be sponsored by a single employer in the year April 2011 to April 2012;
- Skills transfer applicants must be entering for the sole purpose of transferring skills to or from the sponsor's UK work environment and the appointment is additional to staffing requirements;
- Long-term staff must be paid a salary of at least £40,000 per year and the other sub-categories at least £24,000 per year and not less than the appropriate rate published in Tier 2 Codes of Practice;
- Applicants must meet the maintenance requirements for Tier 2 migrants;
- Short-Term, Graduate Trainee and Skills Transfer applicants for entry must not have been present on an ICT visa in the 12 months preceding the application;
- Short-Term and Graduate Trainee ICTs may enter for one year maximum, Skills Transfer ICTs for 6 months and Long Term ICTs for 3 years and one month;
- Entry clearance prohibits recourse to public funds and working except for the sponsor as permitted, supplementary employment and voluntary work;
- Further leave in the Long-Term sub-category is possible provided the employer remains the same, up to a maximum of five years in total. Short-Term and Graduate Trainee staff can apply for further leave in the same sub-category with the same employer up to a maximum of twelve months in total. Skills Transfer ICT staff can apply for further leave up to six months in total. In all cases, the points requirement must be met;
- There is no language requirement on entry but an applicant seeking grant of leave beyond three years (who will be a Long-Term ICT or one who entered under previous rules) must have basic language skills so as to score ten points under Appendix B;
- Those who complete five years as an ICT (in practice, now only Long-Term staff) may apply for indefinite leave. However, in its settlement consultation (Home Office/ UK Border Agency (2011) *Employment Related Settlement, Tier 5 and Overseas Domestic Workers: A Consultation*) the government proposed removing the entitlement of ICTs to settle in the UK.

10.6 Tier 3 migrants

Tier 3 was designed for low-skilled migrants. The 2006 White Paper, *A Points Based System: Making Migration Work for Britain*, anticipated that any PBS scheme would be open only to nationals of countries with a satisfactory returns policy, while other control options such as compulsory remittances and pre-purchased return tickets were also under consideration. Low-skilled migrants would receive only temporary visas with no dependants and no route to settlement. There was never a strong commitment to the scheme and it has never opened. The five-year strategy for immigration, published in 2005, had anticipated that new sources of EEA labour would fill low-skilled vacancies. The Select Committee (2009) heard evidence of a shortage of labour in the catering industry but regarded this as primarily due to poor wages and conditions.

Prior to the PBS, low-skilled migration was governed by the Sectors Based Scheme (SBS) and the Seasonal Agricultural Workers Scheme (SAWS, discussed further in 10.9.1.2). SBS visas were short-term with no dependants, no switching, and no route to settlement. They were introduced in 2003 on a quota basis to meet shortages in the hotel and catering and food processing businesses (mainly meat and fish), occupations which would not meet the usual skill requirements of the work permit scheme. In Bangladesh, in particular, there was a rush to apply for permits. However, 89 per cent of the prospective workers were refused entry clearance, usually on the grounds of absence of intention to leave the UK. From January 2008, the SBS was available only to workers from Romania and Bulgaria aged between 18 and 30. Although deleted from the rules in 2009, it remains in place for these A2 nationals with a quota in 2012 and 2013 of 3,500 workers in food processing. Tier 3, meanwhile, remains indefinitely suspended. With the exception of SAWS and of domestic workers, there are currently no opportunities for non-EEA nationals to enter the UK to perform low-skilled work, even on a temporary basis.

10.7 Tier 4 (Students)

10.7.1 Introduction

There is a long tradition of travel to other countries, including the UK, in pursuit of learning and education and study is a common reason for entry. In its student visa consultation (Home Office/UK Border Agency (2010) *The Student Immigration System: A Consultation*) the government claimed that 468,000 people entered on student-related visas in 2009, compared to 272,000 entrants in 1999, but the higher figure includes nearly 40,000 student visitors, a short-term category that was introduced only in 2007 and may also have included an element of double counting. 71 per cent of entrants came from Asia (including 29 per cent from the Indian subcontinent), 14 per cent from the Americas, and 9 per cent from Africa (Home Office (2010) *Control of Immigration Statistics 2009* Statistical Bulletin 15/10 p. 20).

Despite historical Commonwealth ties, the UK now competes for international students with other English-speaking destinations (US, Australia, or Canada, for example) in a global marketplace, while students come to the UK from many countries outside the Commonwealth. Global education is an important tool in maintaining and creating international influence, as well as benefiting developing countries and providing an income stream for educational institutions. It follows that immigration questions should not be the only concern. However, although most students only remain for a limited period, the entry of students is regarded principally as an immigration issue by the Coalition government and a reduction in their numbers forms part of its strategy for reducing immigration.

From the Commonwealth Immigrants Act 1962 to the end of the twentieth century, the rules relating to students changed from brief and welcoming to complex and restrictive. In June 1999, the government launched the Prime Minister's Initiative (PMI) to welcome international students, addressed particularly to those who intended to train for shortage occupations. Despite this stated policy change and some liberalization, the rules and their interpretation by tribunals subsequently became again more restrictive. Phase 2 of the PMI was launched in April 2006 as a marketing campaign, targeting international students particularly in identified priority countries but did not result in changes to the rules governing entry.

Until the implementation of Tier 4 in March 2009, the rules governing the entry of students required decision-makers to determine matters such as the applicant's ability or intention to follow the course. These questions, which formed the basis of many refusals and appeals under the old rules (see previous editions of this book for more information), are now mostly determined by the sponsor. In some respects, this is sensible as educational establishments are best placed to decide academic questions such as ability to follow the course. However, they are also accountable for these decisions, which must be evidenced in ways satisfactory to the immigration service. It is part of the deeper enmeshment of sponsors in the immigration system, which includes the complex systems, already alluded to, for monitoring student compliance. Further, as discussed in this chapter, the Coalition government has now reintroduced elements of monitoring by the immigration authorities.

Implementation of Tier 4 was controversial. Numbers of applications increased dramatically, and it was argued that this was due to fraudulent applications which officials lacked the power to refuse ('Immigration Rules Result in Flood of Bogus Students' *Sunday Telegraph* 6 December 2009). Some applications in some regions were temporarily suspended, for example applications to study English and NVQ level 3 courses at some Chinese posts. In November 2009, the then Prime Minister announced a review of the criteria for admission as a student ('Brown to Get Tough on Student Visas and Foreign Skilled Workers' *The Independent* 13 November 2009). In March and April 2010, restrictions were introduced on the amount of work that could be done by students studying below degree level and on the institutions that could sponsor such students. The Coalition government regards students primarily as a source of immigration. In a speech to the Royal Commonwealth Society made on 7 September 2010 outlining the government's immigration policy, Damian Green, the Minister for Immigration, said that:

> [t]he largest group of cases in our study granted visas in 2004 were to students, around 186,000. We think of students as people coming here for a short period, normally up to three years, to do a course. But more than a fifth of those 186,000 were still here after five years...To those who say that these are precisely the brightest and the best who Britain needs, I would say let's look at the facts. We estimate that around half, I repeat, around half of the students coming here from abroad only, are coming to study a degree level (or above) course.

In November 2010, the Coalition government launched a consultation on student visas. This proposed limiting courses below degree level, raising the language criterion, requiring academic progression if further leave is to be granted, reducing entitlements to work and to bring in dependants, and stricter accreditation procedures. As you will see, several of these proposals have now been implemented. It has been reported that numbers have decreased substantially as a consequence (*Bogus Colleges: What about their Genuine Students* JCWI 22 November 2011). Nonetheless, while students are regarded as a source of immigration, the government has not capped their numbers as it has done with Tier 1 and Tier 2 migrants. This presumably reflects the economic contribution of overseas students, described by the Home Affairs Committee as the UK's seventh largest export industry and the second biggest contributor to the UK's net balance of payments (House of Commons Home Affairs Committee (2011) *Student Visas* Seventh Report of Session 2010–11, para 15).

10.7.2 The sponsorship system

Educational institutions wishing to recruit overseas students must obtain a sponsorship licence from UKBA. As already discussed, sponsors are now expected either to be highly trusted or to achieve this status within a short period of time. Sponsors who are not highly trusted are limited as to the number of students they may sponsor and the type of course and even highly trusted sponsors operating in the private sphere may sponsor only limited numbers of students (see para 115 Appendix A). Once registered, sponsors will issue a Confirmation of Acceptance for Studies (CAS) to students whom they wish to sponsor and this forms the basis of the student's visa application. Students with a CAS cannot now be refused even if the immigration authorities suspect that they may not be able or intending to study and it appears that institutions are sometimes put under unofficial pressure to withdraw CAS (ILPA members mailing December 2011; see also *R (on the application of Hazret Kose) v SSHD* [2011] EWHC 2594 (Admin)).

Registered sponsors have a range of obligations including record keeping responsibilities and the reporting obligations discussed earlier in the chapter. While, following *Pankina,* applicants may rely on the immigration rules rather than guidance, the position of sponsors remains largely determined by policy and guidance (see the previous discussion). Operation of the sponsorship system however may have serious consequences for applicants, particularly where a college loses its sponsorship licence.

There have long been allegations of bogus educational providers. After 1 January 2005, students had to enrol with educational providers on an approved list. In March 2009, this was replaced by the UK Border Agency's register of sponsors. As at May 2009, only around 1,500 educational institutions had registered as sponsors, compared to 15,000 on the old list and one quarter of applications had been refused. By December 2011, this had increased but only to 2,125. In a report published in July 2009 (*Bogus Colleges* – Eleventh Report of 2008–9 HC595), the Home Affairs Committee found that previous quality assurance procedures had been insufficient, leading to increases in the numbers of bogus colleges. It considered the PBS accreditation regime to be more effective but recommended more robust inspections The introduction of the Highly Trusted Sponsor status in September 2011 created an enhanced regulatory regime whereby only institutions who meet a series of demanding criteria are permitted to continue to sponsor.

From the student's perspective, a registered sponsor is a prerequisite for obtaining leave. However, that may not be the end of the matter if the sponsor is subsequently suspended or removed from the list of registered sponsors. The increasingly rigorous regulatory regime means institutions may have their status revoked after the CAS has been issued or during the period of study. According to JCWI writing in November 2011 (*Bogus Colleges: What about their Genuine Students* JCWI 22 November 2011), about

450 colleges had their status revoked during the previous year, affecting about 11,000 students. Where a sponsor's licence is withdrawn, no new leave will be granted for a CAS issued by that institution and entry clearance will be cancelled if the student has not yet travelled.

There is also power to curtail leave of those already present under para 323A of the rules. The leave of any student already present and who 'was involved in the reasons why the Tier 4 sponsor's licence was withdrawn' will be cancelled immediately. *NA and Others (Cambridge College of Learning) Pakistan* [2009] UKAIT 00031 found that the burden of proof in these circumstances is on the government on the balance of probabilities but 'critical' or 'anxious' scrutiny would be appropriate. Where such complicity is not established, students who have more than six months leave remaining will be given 60 calendar days (which runs from the date of curtailment) to find a new sponsor, which may be difficult in the middle of the academic year. If less than six months' leave remains, leave will not be curtailed (Tier 4 Guidance p. 62). The 60 days operates only to curtail the migrant's existing leave where this exceeds six months and does not create a new period of leave (*Patel (Tier 4 – no '60 day extension') India* [2011] UKUT 00187 (IAC)). Applicants who have applied in-country to a college whose licence is revoked after their prior leave expires but before the new decision are not entitled under the policy to the 60-day period (*Patel; SSHD v MM and SA* [2010] UKUT 481 (IAC); *JA (revocation of registration – Secretary of State's policy) India* [2011] UKUT 52 (IAC)). However the common law duty of fairness requires that such students, if they are not party to the reasons for revocation, be notified and allowed an equivalent period of time to find a new course (*Thakur (PBS decision – common law fairness) Bangladesh* [2011] UKUT 00151; *Patel (revocation of sponsor licence – fairness) India* UKUT 00211 (IAC)). As the Home Affairs Committee acknowledged in its July 2009 report, many students attending bogus institutions are not aware of the true position before entering the UK and will have invested thousands of pounds in a UK education. Having genuinely hoped to acquire a qualification, they are also victims of the fraud and usually lose the fees they have paid while the consequences for them may be very serious, particularly if they cannot find or afford to switch to another course.

A new application is required if an applicant wants to change sponsor (see para 323A of the rules). This represents a new form of control and s 50 Border, Citizenship and Immigration Act 2009 added a new sub-paragraph to s 3 Immigration Act 1971, permitting restrictions to be placed on studies. The rules now also require a new sponsor to confirm that the course of study for which the CAS has been assigned represents academic progress from previous study on a student visa (para 120B Appendix A) although a transfer is permitted. The Select Committee on Home Affairs (2011) recommended provision for students wishing to study for a second masters' degree.

10.7.3 General students

There are two categories of applicant under Tier 4; general students who are over 16 entering for studies in further or higher education and child students who must be between 4 and 18. There is thus some overlap between the two categories. General students who are under 18 must have their parents' support and consent for the arrangements.

The rules for leave as a Tier 4 (General Students) are found from para 245ZT onwards. All new entrants need entry clearance. Applicants need 30 points for attributes under Appendix A and 10 points for maintenance under Appendix C. The 30 points for attributes are awarded for the CAS, provided a number of other conditions are met. The CAS must contain the information required by the Sponsor Guidance and be issued by an approved sponsor no more than six months before the application, which itself must be made no more than three months before the course begins. The sponsor must not have withdrawn the CAS and must still hold its licence. The applicant must produce all the original documents cited in the CAS as evidence of the applicant's suitability for the course unless the applicant is sponsored by a Highly Trusted Sponsor or is a national of one of the countries listed in Appendix H, in which case documents need be produced only if requested. Since April 2011, applicants must demonstrate competence in English to at least B2 CEFR for degree level courses or B1 CEFR for courses below degree level. This may be demonstrated in a number of ways, and may be tested as part of the application process.

The course applied for must meet minimum academic criteria. The minimum academic level is NFQ level 3 (below degree level) or its Scottish equivalent. Since April 2010, CAS below degree level for these may only be issued by Highly Trusted Sponsors. English language courses, other than pre-sessional courses or where the student has government sponsorship, must now be at level B2 CEFR or above. B2 is equivalent to a high A level grade so that only non-EEA nationals who already have a good knowledge of English may now enter to study English on a student visa although short courses at the lower level may be undertaken as a student visitor for up to 11 months (see chapter 11). Entry for recognized foundation programmes for doctors and dentists, pre-sessional courses at the same institution as the main course and short-term study abroad programmes from an overseas institution are also permitted. Applicants may not spend more than three years after the age of 18 on sub-degree level courses. Where courses involve self-contained stages which may, incrementally, result in a higher award, it should not be assumed that a student is only applying for the first stage and an overall view should be taken (*R (on the application of Jawadwala) v SSHD* [2009] EWHC 802 (Admin)).

Courses must be full-time. A course at degree level or higher has no minimum requirement for contact hours. Other courses must involve a minimum of 15 hours per week organized daytime study and, except in the case of a pre-sessional course, lead to a qualification below bachelor degree level. The Sponsor Guidance defines daytime study as being between 08.00 and 18.00 Monday–Friday. There are restrictions on the time that may be spent on work placements and only Highly Trusted Sponsors may provide these on courses below degree level. Applicants for postgraduate qualifications in the scientific, medical, and engineering disciplines listed in Appendix 6 of the rules must also obtain an Academic Technology Approval Scheme (ATAS) Clearance Certificate. This is designed to ensure that applicants are not associated with programmes contributing to the proliferation of weapons of mass destruction.

To show adequate maintenance under Appendix C, the applicant must have the requisite level of funds available. The documents proving this must either be provided with the application or, if the applicant is sponsored by a Highly Trusted Sponsor or is a national of a country in Appendix H, they must be confirmed by the applicant and produced if required. Funds may be held in parents' bank accounts provided evidence of the parents' consent is also provided. After *Pankina,* the meaning of 'available' is determined according to the immigration rules and most restrictions in the guidance no longer apply. Thus funds held by the applicant's husband may be available to the applicant irrespective of the guidance (*FA and AA (PBS: effect of Pankina) Nigeria* [2010] UKUT 00304 (IAC)). Funds held in an overseas account are also available even if they cannot easily be accessed (*HM and others (PBS – legitimate expectation – paragraph 245ZX(1)) Malawi* [2010] 446 UKUT (IAC)) as are funds in the form of a credit card limit (*Ejifugha (Tier 4 – funds- credit) Nigeria* [2011] UKUT 00244 (IAC).

The amount needed varies according to the place of study, the length of the course, whether the applicant is already in the UK, and the applicant's personal circumstances. For instance, someone entering for a degree course in London who has a partner and a child would have to show possession of the first year's course fees and £7,200 for him- or herself. The partner and child would each need £4,797 so a total of £16,794 plus the first year's fees would have to be available. Following allegations that some financial institutions made insufficient efforts to prevent fraud, the rules were amended so that funds must be held by an institution with which UKBA can make satisfactory verification checks. Students may also be sponsored by the UK or their own government, the British Council, or other independent organizations.

Leave is granted for the length of the course plus a short additional period at either end. If further leave is needed, a new application must be made and the same points earned as on entry (although the maintenance requirements are less rigorous). Students may not apply in-country for a course that commences more than one month after their leave expires (para 245ZX(l) HC395). Leave includes leave granted under s 3C Immigration Act 1971 pending a decision on an application made before but decided after leave expires on the original visa (*QI (Pakistan) v SSHD* [2011] EWCA Civ 614.

As leave is granted for the whole course, most students should not need further leave for the same course and immigration officers no longer engage with questions of progression within courses as they did under the old rules. However, a student may sometimes fail to complete their studies within the time permitted in the visa so that further leave is needed. This requires a new application and a new CAS. Appendix A provides that, if the applicant is re-sitting examinations or repeating a module, this must only be their second attempt unless the sponsor is a Highly Trusted Sponsor. The student must also be engaged in study or revision classes; in other cases, they are expected to leave the UK and return as a student visitor for the resit examinations (*RS (Pakistan) v SSHD* [2011] EWCA Civ 434).

Switching into student status is permitted only from student or work related categories. This replicates a problem that existed under the previous rules in which those who enter in another capacity such as the family member of a worker and begin their studies cannot, if that leave expires, switch to student status but must instead leave the country and apply for entry clearance. A letter of 14 December 2000 from the Home Office to an International Student Adviser at Sheffield University stated that this was not a suitable case for a concession. In this instance, the student, who was writing up her PhD, would need to leave the country to obtain entry clearance to return and complete it, as her husband's student leave would expire before she had finished.

Students on degree level courses may work on placements that form up to half of their course (unless more is required by UK law) or for up to 20 hours per week during term-time and for an unlimited period during vacations. Students studying below degree level may work for 10 hours per week and full-time during vacations. The limitation on hours worked applies even if a student is writing up his thesis and has no scheduled classes (*OG (Student-thesis-term time employment)* [2008] UKAIT 00057). Self-employment is not permitted and the student must not fill a permanent full-time vacancy, work as a doctor in training except on a recognized Foundation programme or provide services as a professional sportsperson or entertainer. In *Strasburger v SSHD* [1978] Imm AR 165 the appellant was an art student who wanted to stay in the UK as a self-employed artist. She needed to show that she could maintain herself as an artist and relied on sales of her work while a student as evidence of that capacity. The Tribunal held that this did not represent a breach of the condition against self-employment.

The partners and children of students admitted for more than 12 months onto degree level courses may also work. Leave as a student is not a route to settlement.

10.7.4 Child students

Special rules apply to children between 4 and 18 coming to be educated in the UK. They need 30 points for attributes under Appendix A. This requires the applicant to have a CAS supplied by an independent, fee-paying school (unless the child is 16 or over) that holds a sponsor's licence. The student must be pursuing a course that is taught in accordance with the national curriculum or the National Qualification Framework or is subject to OFSTED or equivalent or the independent school inspection regime. They also need 10 points for maintenance. The precise amounts required depend upon whether the child is to attend a boarding school, is to stay with relatives or foster carers, or is 16 or 17 and living independently. This money may, unsurprisingly, be held by the parents rather than the child.

The child's parents or guardians must support the application and consent to the child's entry. If the child is to stay with relatives or in a foster care arrangement, there must be satisfactory evidence of the arrangements. Child students may not be accompanied by a partner or by their own child. Indeed, an applicant who has a child living with them or for whom they are financially responsible may not enter as a child student. A parent may accompany a child student under 12 under special rules for visitors (see chapter 11). A child student may not work under the age of 16. After that age, 10 hours weekly work in term-time and unlimited hours during the holidays are permitted. Switching is only permitted from other student categories.

10.8 Tier 5 (Temporary Workers)

This tier came into effect in November 2008, replacing a long list of entry routes including some very popular schemes such as the Working Holiday Maker. There was also a long list of smaller schemes that have now either disappeared or been subsumed into Tier 5 (for a full list, see the UKBA's Statement of Intent for Tier 5).

There are two sub-categories within Tier 5: Temporary Workers and Youth Mobility. These types of scheme, which aim to establish cultural, sporting, and other links, do not sit easily within a points-based system that is predicated on short-term economic benefit. Schemes such as the Working Holiday Maker had long-term and often intangible benefits in terms of establishing connections and relationships with individuals and countries but the arrangements for Tier 5, particularly Youth Mobility, seem to be over-concerned with control. It is arguable that this type of migration has been the least well-served by the introduction of the PBS and there have been several reports of dissatisfaction.

10.8.1 Temporary workers

The rules for temporary workers are found in paras 245ZM onwards, which, as always, have to be read in conjunction with the Appendices. The route is 'for certain types of temporary worker whose entry helps to satisfy cultural, charitable, religious or international objectives' (para 245ZM). Entry clearance is always required with an exception for non-visa nationals entering for up to three months for creative or sporting engagements, although these will still need a Certificate of Sponsorship. This is critical. In one well-reported incident, the Canadian singer, Allison Crowe, was detained and then removed from Gatwick after she arrived without a Certificate of Sponsorship. The

Manifesto Club has published numerous case studies of artists who have fallen foul of the Tier 5 (and other immigration) requirements (*Deported: Artists and Academics Barred from the UK*).

Thirty points are needed under paras 105–112 of Appendix A and 10 points for maintenance under Appendix C. Appendix A awards 30 points for possession of a Tier 5 (Temporary Worker) Certificate of Sponsorship issued, in most cases, no more than three months before the application. Much of the detail about the Tier 5 (Temporary Worker) route is found in the Sponsor Guidance. Even a small organization or charity who wishes to bring in an artist or volunteer for a short period must now go through the application process and fulfil the duties of sponsorship. The guidance for Tiers 2 and 5 is contained in one 103-page document and such organizations, even non-profit-making ones, are subject to the same requirements and obligations as large employers even if there will often not be an employment relationship between the sponsor and the migrant. In fact, according to the Sponsor Guidance, '[w]here a migrant is not your direct employee, we will look especially closely at your arrangements, and monitor you to ensure that you are fulfilling all of your sponsor duties. We will take action against you as set out in this guidance if we find that you are not fulfilling all of your sponsorship duties.' These duties include record-keeping and reporting obligations and a duty of cooperation. Sponsors are required to guarantee aspects of applicants' compliance although it is impossible to see how a sponsor can know for sure whether an applicant intends to comply. There have been reports that small sponsors are reluctant or ineligible to engage in the bureaucracy and cost of the sponsorship process, leading to a loss of small-scale and experimental work (Manifesto Club *UK Arts and Culture: Cancelled, by Order of the Home Office*).

The maintenance requirements require £800 of personal savings or a maintenance guarantee by an A-rated sponsor. Sponsors must advise migrants that they are ineligible for and must not claim state benefits and a benefits claim made with the sponsor's knowledge may result in suspension or removal of the licence. Switching is possible but only within the sub-category in which they entered and for the maximum time permitted. The only exception is for international footballers who can switch to Tier 2, subject to meeting Tier 2 requirements, including the English language requirement. The Select Committee (2009) regarded this as a case 'where money has spoken louder than merit' and urged removal of the exemption.

There are five sub-categories within the Temporary Worker scheme.

10.8.1.1 *Creative and sporting*

According to the guidance, this sub-category is for applicants entering for short-term contracts or engagements in this sector. Creative sponsors must operate or intend to operate in the creative sector, for example, as a national body, event organizer, producer, venue, agent or similar. Sponsors operating in dance, theatre, film, and television must follow a code of practice in recruitment and, in other fields, must take steps to ensure a resident worker is not available for the post. Group certificates may be issued to an entourage provided each member has proven technical or other specialist skills. Multiple engagements may be covered by the same sponsor or by multiple sponsors, in each case, on condition that no more than 14 days elapses between engagements. Otherwise, the applicant is expected to leave the UK and reapply for entry clearance.

Sponsors in the sporting sector must be a sporting body, sports club, events organizer, or other organizer operating or intending to operate in the sporting sector. The sponsor must gain an endorsement from the governing body of the sport confirming that the applicant is established at the highest level and/or that their employment will make a significant contribution to the sport in the UK and the post could not be filled by a suitable settled worker. In issuing the Certificate of Sponsorship, sponsors guarantee that the applicant is seeking entry to the UK to work or perform in the relevant sector, is not intending to base themselves in business, poses no threat to the resident labour force, and will comply with their visa.

Leave is for up to 24 months for sports people and 12 months for creative artists with the option to extend to 24 months upon issue of a new Certificate of Sponsorship. Family members may also enter and may work. Those who have leave for six months or more may leave and re-enter the UK during the currency of their leave. There have been numerous reports of artists experiencing difficulties under this route, although it is not always clear whether this is due to the rules themselves, the obligation to provide biometric data or the attitudes of entry clearance staff, who are now solely responsible for decision-making. Creative visas are often needed at short notice and this conflicts with the need for biometric data to be acquired and processed. If, for example, an international opera singer falls ill, a replacement of similar stature, who knows the work and is available must be found at very short notice, perhaps less than 24 hours, but the visa will usually take much longer to process if biometric data is needed. Delays can be particularly problematic for large groups whose members must apply individually and in person and problems are exacerbated where, as in many parts of Africa, biometric collection points are sparse. This may require the entire group to relocate for the duration of the process. One report to the Home Affairs Select Committee in 2009 involved Malian musicians who had to travel for three days to their nearest visa application centre in Dakar and then wait for up to ten days while their applications were sent to Banjul in the Gambia for processing, all the time being separated from their passports and relevant documentation. For artists from poor countries or engaged in worldwide travel, such expense and delay may make the visit untenable.

Other artists have complained about bureaucratic and obstructive attitudes experienced during entry clearance process. The Iranian film director, Abbas Kiarostami, cancelled plans to direct a London-based opera due to the difficulties of obtaining a visa. The Home Affairs Committee recommended that more biometric collection points be established, that visa issue times be reduced, and that a streamlined procedure be introduced for emergency applications (see also Manifesto Club *Deported: Artists and Academics Barred from the UK*).

10.8.1.2 *Charity workers*

Migrants coming as charity workers should only be undertaking voluntary activity and not paid employment. The migrant should intend to carry out fieldwork directly related to the purpose of the sponsoring organization' (Sponsor Guidance p. 66). In issuing the Certificate of Sponsorship, the sponsor guarantees that the applicant intends only to do this, will receive only reasonable expenses, will not take up a permanent position and will comply with their visa. Charity workers may enter for up to 12 months and their family members may also enter and work.

10.8.1.3 *Religious workers*

This is for those coming temporarily to do preaching, pastoral or non-pastoral work, to work in the same capacity as they already worked overseas or as a member of a religious order. The sponsor must be a charitable body and here 'the structure for a faith-based community', which is defined at some length and complexity in the Sponsor Guidance. The religion must not 'exclude from its community on the basis of gender, nationality or ethnicity' and must not 'operate against the public interest, or in a way that has a detrimental effect on personal or family life as these are commonly understood in the UK'.

In issuing the Certificate of Sponsorship, the sponsor guarantees that the applicant is qualified to do the job in question and will work only at the specified location. The sponsor also undertakes to accept the responsibilities of sponsorship, that it will support the applicant through sufficient funds and/or accommodation, that the applicant will not be displacing a suitably qualified resident worker, and will comply with the conditions of the visa. Leave is for up to 24 months, supplementary working is permitted, and family members may also enter and work.

10.8.1.4 *Government authorized exchange*

This category is for applicants coming 'through approved schemes that aim to share knowledge, experience and best practice' (Sponsor Guidance p. 68). Entry is for up to 24 months and family members may enter and work. This scheme cannot be used to fill job vacancies or to bring unskilled labour to the United Kingdom and the government will only approve schemes for skilled work (usually at NVQ level 3 or above) that do not damage the resident labour market.

With the exception of sponsored researchers and government departments, there are no individual sponsors. Instead, sponsorship functions are undertaken by an overarching body supported by a government department (or executive agency), which is expected to contribute to the cost of enforcement if there is significant non-compliance. As at December 2011, there were around 70 approved schemes, involving organizations such as the Law Society, the British Council, and various educational institutions. In issuing the Certificate of Sponsorship, the overarching body guarantees that the applicant is seeking entry to work or train temporarily here through an approved exchange scheme, does not intend to establish a business and meets the requirements of the individual exchange scheme.

10.8.1.5 *International agreement*

This category is available for migrants coming to provide a service covered by international law, including those coming under the General Agreement on Trade in Services (GATS) and similar agreements, employees of overseas governments and bodies, and private servants in diplomatic households. The sponsor of government employees and private servants will be the diplomatic mission or international organization or body in question not the individual employer. The sponsor must give various undertakings according to the type of agreement that is relied upon. For example, the sponsors of domestic servants in diplomatic households must confirm that the employee is over 18, will be employed full-time on domestic tasks in the diplomatic household, will take no other work, and will leave the UK at the end of their visa. Sponsors of migrants under GATS or other international agreements confirm that the migrant works for an employer or organization of a country that is a member of the World Trade Organization or has a bilateral agreement with the UK or EU or an EU member, will be engaged in work that accords with the international agreement and will work or provide services for the employer or client.

Migrants entering under GATS and related agreements obtain leave for up to 24 months. Employees of overseas governments, international organizations and diplomatic households may have an initial leave of up to 24 months with the ability to extend in-country for up to 72 months. At the end of that period, only private servants in diplomatic households may apply for indefinite leave to remain although the government has proposed capping their leave at 12 months and removing that right (Home

Office/UK Border Agency (2011) *Employment-Related Settlement, Tier 5 and Migrant Domestic Workers: A Consultation*).

10.8.2 Youth Mobility Scheme

The immigration rules say that the Youth Mobility Scheme (YMS) 'is for sponsored young people from participating countries who wish to live and work temporarily in the UK' (para 245ZI). It replaced the Working Holidaymaker scheme, which was both popular and controversial. Evaluating the YMS requires an understanding of the issues that were associated with its predecessor.

10.8.2.1 *Working Holidaymakers*

The Working Holidaymakers scheme was seen as one way of maintaining Commonwealth links. Applicants had to be a national of one of around 50 Commonwealth countries listed in the immigration rules or a British Overseas Citizen, a British Overseas Territories Citizen, or a British National (Overseas), and aged between 17 and 30. They could take only employment incidental to a holiday (para 95; now deleted). The scheme was, for many years, dominated by old Commonwealth countries. In 2000, 96 per cent of applicants were from New Zealand, Australia, Canada, and South Africa. In 2002, the Home Office consulted on reform of the scheme. Respondents noted its discriminatory effects while the Home Office suggested that there was abuse by people working full-time during their stay. The result was rule changes including more freedom to work.

After these changes, some posts experienced significant increases in applications, including over 1,000 per cent in South Asia. Refusal rates fell but were still high in some regions (62.6 per cent in South Asia, for instance, compared to between 0.2 and 0.3 per cent for Australia and the South Pacific). In February 2005, the rules changed again to limit work to one year of the applicant's two-year stay, a change that would particularly affect applicants from poorer countries less able to fund a prolonged holiday. The changes also partially restored other restrictions on working during and after the working holiday (for more details, see earlier editions of this book), reflecting government fears that the scheme was used for economic migration rather than cultural exchange. In April 2005, the government suspended applications from a number of developing countries, although an attempt to prove race discrimination failed in *SK India* [2006] UKAIT 00067.

Near the end of the period discussed here, there were moves towards making the scheme subject to bilateral agreements. This prefigured the Youth Mobility Scheme, which reflects the government's concern both to prioritize control and to avoid debate about culturally laden questions such as the meaning of 'holiday'. Unfortunately, the result is a scheme so restrictive that nationals of developing countries are likely to be indefinitely excluded from it.

10.8.2.2 *Requirements of the Youth Mobility Scheme*

The rules governing the scheme are found in paras 245ZI onwards but, as always, these are relatively uninformative and the Appendices and other documentation need to be consulted for a proper understanding.

Paragraph 245ZI says that: '[t]his route is for sponsored young people from participating countries who wish to live and work temporarily in the UK'. Entry clearance is compulsory. The applicant must be a national of a country listed in Appendix G of the rules or a British Overseas Citizen, British Overseas Territories Citizen, or British National (Overseas). As at December 2011, only Australia, Canada, Japan, New Zealand,

and Monaco were listed in Appendix G. Taiwan was added in January 2012. All other nationalities are ineligible.

The applicant must have 40 points under Appendix A for attributes and 10 points for maintenance under Appendix C, no children under 18, and not have previously spent time in the UK under this scheme or as a working holidaymaker. A partner may accompany the applicant only if they qualify under the scheme in their own right. Entry is for two years with no recourse to public funds and most types of work may be undertaken. There is no restriction on the proportion of time that may be spent working.

Under Appendix A, 30 points are awarded for having the necessary nationality and 10 points are awarded for being between 18 and 30. There is a quota for each country which must not be exceeded at the time the application is granted. These vary from between 1,000 places for Japan and Monaco to 32,500 places for Australia. It is not clear how applicants can know if the quota has been reached before they submit their application and pay the fee. The maintenance requirement is met by having £1,800 available.

The scheme is thus quite straightforward but the critical issue is why so few countries currently participate. The Sponsor Guidance does not explain how a country may become a sponsor. More information was contained in the Statement of Intent for Tier 5, written when the scheme was in the process of being established, but there is no longer a live link available on the UKBA website.

The Statement of Intent established that countries are eligible for inclusion only where they meet criteria as to immigration risk, returns and reciprocity. A country must not be subject to a mandatory UK visa regime (thereby excluding most developing countries) and have an acceptable risk value according to undisclosed formulae. It must have effective return arrangements and cooperate in that process. By the date it joins the scheme, the country must provide reciprocal youth mobility arrangements for UK nationals (either aged between 18 and 30 and/or who are undergraduates or graduates) that allow a minimum stay of 12 months, a minimum period of 12 months' work (with some minor restrictions permitted), and an annual minimum quota of 1,000 UK nationals. Where, for reasons of public policy, the UK government does not wish to admit a country to the YMS, that country will be deemed to be ineligible.

Given the restrictiveness of these criteria, it is perhaps surprising that any countries have qualified. Even qualifying countries may be removed from the list if their risk increases or they do not comply in other ways. The government may also temporarily suspend issuing entry clearances under the Scheme at specific entry clearance posts for operational reasons. The outcome is that individuals who are entirely honest and who otherwise meet the criteria for entry are disbarred under the scheme only because of their nationality. As the discrimination is contained in the immigration rules, it is lawful under the Equality Act 2010 (see chapter 8). This restrictiveness and lack of transparency suggests that the YMS is seen primarily as a tool of international relations rather than as providing an opportunity to travel. It also reinforces the point that, despite increases in transparency in some areas, immigration remains an area in which the executive may retain almost unlimited power.

Participating countries sponsor their own nationals and governments are licensed by UK Borders Agency. British Overseas Citizens, British Overseas Territories Citizens, and British Nationals (Overseas) do not need sponsorship. Low risk countries may be deemed sponsors and possession of a passport will be sufficient. Otherwise, governments must issue certificates of sponsorship to each applicant. The narrowness of the YMS was criticized by the Home Affairs Committee after representations from the National Farmers' Union that the Working Holidaymaker Scheme had been a source of semi-skilled agricultural labour and that the maintenance threshold of £1,600 was a deterrent. The Committee recommended that the YMS be made more user-friendly, although specific recommendations were confined to reducing the maintenance requirement and the narrowness of the scheme was not addressed.

10.9 Working outside the points-based system

There are still a few schemes that continue to operate outside the PBS and which permit entry for work or study.

10.9.1 A8/A2 nationals

Until May 2011, and as discussed in chapter 5, nationals of the A8 countries that acceded to the EU in 2004 had restricted access to the labour market. They did not need permission to work but they had to register with the Workers' Registration Scheme for the first year of employment. Workers and employers found registration onerous and did not always comply but this could have serious consequences. In *Zalewska v Department of Social Development* [2008] UKHL 67, the House of Lords found that the requirement to reregister if employment changed during the first year was proportionate and the appellant was therefore lawfully refused welfare benefits. As well as the possible refusal of benefits, non-registered workers were also liable to general exploitation by employers operating outside the system. As transitional measures could not be applied for more than seven years, the scheme was abolished on 30 April 2011.

A2 nationals (from Bulgaria and Romania) will not have the same rights as other EEA nationals to work in the UK until the end of 2013, although they may exercise other free movement rights such as self-employment or study. Their position is determined by the Accession (Immigration and Worker Authorisation) Regulations 2006/3317 as amended. A2 nationals who have already worked for 12 months, who have entered in another capacity that gives permission to work or who can establish that they are highly skilled according to the criteria for the Highly Skilled Migrant Programme (still applicable because of standstill requirements) do not need permission to work. A2 nationals with certain qualifications granted by UK higher education institutions are also exempt. Otherwise, they must have permission which may take two forms.

10.9.1.1 *Work authorization*

This takes the form of an Accession Worker Card. This will be issued only when the applicant has a letter of approval which will be issued only in respect of the categories of work set out in Schedule 1. This lists the work opportunities available to migrants at the time of accession, including work permit employment and the sectors based scheme. The criteria for issue of work permits (which used to apply to all non-EEA nationals) are discussed in more detail in earlier editions of this book.

10.9.1.2 *Seasonal Agricultural Workers Scheme (SAWS)*

This scheme was retained outside the PBS for A2 nationals. Migration for seasonal agricultural work is an old practice in the UK and, in 1990, was formalized through SAWS. It is a short-term programme with maximum six months' leave and no option to bring dependants or to settle.

The government's proposals to phase out temporary schemes for entry for work under the PBS were opposed by the agricultural sector. Rogaly (2006) describes how pressure from supermarkets to deliver standardized, high-quality goods to tight timescales resulted in a preference for migrant workers, perceived as more reliable, faster, and willing to work long hours. Rogaly also notes in this context their increased vulnerability to exploitation.

Since January 2008, the SAWS scheme has been restricted to Bulgarian and Romanian workers although that is not apparent on the face of the rules. The quota for 2010 and 2011 is 21,250. After representations from the sector about the continuing need for a circular migration system, the Home Affairs Select Committee (2009) recommended the replacement of SAWS if it is to be abolished.

10.9.2 Representative of an overseas business

Revised immigration rules (paras 144–151), which took effect in October 2009, created a new category, 'representative of an overseas business'. They replace the previous categories of sole representatives of a business and overseas media representative. The principal difference is that applicants must now demonstrate some English language competence.

The category is aimed at long-term entrants who do not qualify as business visitors (discussed in chapter 11). Entry clearance is mandatory, leave is for three years initially with extensions, dependants can accompany the main migrant, and settlement is possible after five years. The overseas business must have its headquarters and principal place of business outside the UK and no existing branch, subsidiary or other representative in the UK.

10.9.3 Domestic workers

The rules under discussion here do not permit UK residents to recruit domestic staff from abroad but apply to workers accompanying their employer from abroad. About 17,000 enter each year under this route. In 1980, the Department of Employment stopped issuing work permits for unskilled workers. From then until 1998, domestic workers were permitted entry as a visitor under a concession, although they were, in reality, entering for paid domestic work. In consequence, the employee could not change employer as their entry clearance formally prohibited paid work.

Such resident domestic workers were vulnerable to abuse and exploitation. Their feudal situation was changed in 1998 when the concession was altered to permit employees suffering abuse or exploitation to change employer. From September 2002, this was incorporated into the rules and the prohibition on changing employer and the limitation of entry to those undertaking skilled work were removed altogether. According to the current IDI, overseas domestic workers may include cleaners, chauffeurs, gardeners, cooks, those carrying out personal care, and nannies.

Under the current rules, found in paras 159A–159H, applicants must be between 18 and 65, have worked in the sponsor's household under the same roof or in a household that the sponsor uses for himself on a regular basis for one year prior to the application, and there must be a connection between the employee and the sponsor. The employee must travel with the sponsor or their family and intend to work full-time only as a member of the sponsor's household. There must be adequate maintenance and accommodation, which is assured through an undertaking from the sponsor who must also provide a signed statement of the main terms and conditions. The employee will be interviewed separately and given a leaflet explaining their rights under UK law. The employer will also be asked to undertake to pay the minimum wage but refusal is not grounds for refusing a visa.

Use by the sponsor of the household on a regular basis means that it must be 'habitually or customarily used' (*NG Bulgaria* [2006] UKAIT 00020), although a temporary hiatus for good reason is acceptable (*BO (Nigeria)* [2007] UKAIT 00053). Use by other relatives is not use by the sponsor 'for himself' and the 'connection' between the employer and the worker must amount to more than a contract of employment. The requirement to travel with the sponsor is intended to ensure that the employee migrates as part of the sponsor's household (*JF (Domestic Servant) Philippines* [2008] UKAIT 00085; *Wusa (para 159A (ii) "Connection") Nigeria* [2011] UKUT 00483 (IAC)).

Leave is for 12 months (unless the employer is entering as a visitor) and dependants may also enter. It may be extended if the applicant is still working as a domestic worker, their services are still required and the applicant still meets the requirements of entry, although it is not necessary for the employer to be the same. Where the applicant changes employer, they should notify the immigration authorities but failure to do so is not grounds for refusal of further leave although the applicant must explain the reasons for the change. Settlement is possible after five years provided the same conditions are met, including that he or she is still required by their employer although, once indefinite leave is granted, the applicant may work freely.

Domestic workers in private households were initially not included in the plans for the PBS but the government later proposed that they should be permitted entry for six months only on amended business visitor visas, as 'domestic assistants', rather than as 'domestic workers'. They would thus have lost all their hard-won protection. While this was consistent with the government's plans to prevent the long-term entry of unskilled workers, the consequences would have been catastrophic for this group. Migrant domestic workers often have close caring relationships with their employee's family, particularly children, and many of them cannot easily return to their country of origin. The likely consequence would have been underground working and increased exploitation. From the employer's perspective, the inability to retain long established domestic staff might influence them against choosing the UK as a destination. Following extensive campaigning, the government was persuaded to retain the current rules for a period of two years, pending research into possible new arrangements. The Home Affairs Committee in its report, *The Trade in Human Beings: Human Trafficking in the UK* (Sixth Report of Session 2008–9 HC 23–I), believed that the current arrangements would need to be retained for much longer than two years. However, in the Settlement Consultation (Home Office/UK Border Agency (2011) *Employment-Related Settlement, Tier 5 and Migrant Domestic Workers: A Consultation*), the government proposed capping leave at six or 12 months and removing the right to change employers. This was justified by the recent establishment of the National Referral Mechanism for trafficking. However, critics have argued that this is inadequate protection and the proposal would leave such workers highly vulnerable (see, for example, the response of Kalayaan to the consultation dated 5 August 2011).

10.9.4 Commonwealth citizens with UK ancestry

This is a special category in the immigration rules, HC 395 paras 186–193, which provide that a Commonwealth citizen aged 17 or over, one of whose grandparents was born in the UK may enter for five years if they intend to seek work in the UK and can maintain and accommodate themselves and any dependants without recourse to public funds.

Settlement is possible after five years, even if employment has not been continuous. The Home Office suspended applications from Zimbabweans in 2004, having decided that they were abusing the scheme, although they were resumed in November 2005. The rule appears to have survived implementation of the points-based system and the government announced its plans to retain it in the 2011 settlement consultation, noting both that 96 per cent of applicants come from Australia, New Zealand, Canada, and South Africa and that numbers entering and settling appear to be declining due to changed emigration patterns in the UK.

10.10 Illegal working

In the immigration context, 'illegal working' means working by those subject to immigration control who do not have leave to work or who work in ways not permitted by their leave. Illegal employment is often associated with other unlawful practices such as low pay, breach of health and safety regulations, failure to pay income tax and national insurance contributions, and so on.

Sanctions against employers for employing those not entitled to work are an aspect of the extension of immigration control, which has been intensified by the PBS. It is an offence under s 21 Immigration, Asylum and Nationality Act 2006 knowingly to employ a person who does not have permission to work. Section 15 of the Act also created a system of civil penalties for employing someone without permission to work, regardless of knowledge, although there is a statutory defence if the employer complied with a list of prescribed actions. There is a risk of race discrimination if employers become reluctant to hire those who, in their view, may be subject to immigration control and there is a code of practice for employers issued under s 23 of the 2006 Act. Nonetheless, employers may be torn between their duties to their employees and their fear of sanctions under immigration laws, particularly given the complexity of the latter. It is perhaps not surprising that the Migrants' Rights Network (2008) found that the regime adversely affected a much wider group than those who do not have permission to work. For example, in *Okuoimose v City Facilities Management (UK) Ltd* UKEAT/0192/11/DA, an employee of Nigerian nationality was suspended because the endorsement on her passport permitting her to work as an EEA national family member had expired. UKBA had failed to decide her application to renew the endorsement and advised the employer that they were liable to civil penalties if they continued to employ her. They later confirmed that the employee should be treated as able to work until her application was determined and she was reinstated. The Employment Appeal Tribunal found that her suspension had been unlawful as she had always been entitled to work and she was awarded compensation.

Under s 134 Nationality, Immigration and Asylum Act 2002, the Secretary of State may require an employer to supply information about an employee whom the Secretary of State reasonably suspects of having committed particular offences under the Immigration Act 1971. Reporting obligations are now, as discussed earlier, even more extensive under the PBS. These sanctions and obligations may have an effect on well-established employers but it is more difficult to assess the effect on less well-regulated sectors. Many migrants work through operators who supply them for short-term work in particular sectors. Following the death of 24 Chinese cockle-pickers in Morecambe Bay in 2004, the Gangmasters Licensing Authority was established to protect workers from exploitation in agriculture, horticulture, shellfish-gathering, and food processing and packaging. It is an offence to operate as a gangmaster without a licence or to use an unlicensed gangmaster. Licensed gangmasters are under a number of obligations which aim to prevent exploitation and dangerous working. However, those working unlawfully will not receive the protection of licensed gangmasters.

While estimating the number of irregular migrants is difficult for self-evident reasons, there are possibly more than 700,000 in the UK, many of whom will be working unlawfully and often in conditions of exploitation, leading to calls for a regularization programme (Migrants' Rights Network 2009). There is a connection between unlawful working and trafficking which is discussed in chapter 14, in the context of criminalizing activities connected with immigration.

10.11 Conclusion

The more positive, if highly instrumental, attitude towards migration which appeared to be heralded by the 2002 White Paper has vanished in the face of recession and public disquiet. Meanwhile, the system of entry for work and study has undergone its greatest change since its inception. While the concept of a points-based system has virtues, the system that has been implemented demonstrates few of them, lacking as it does, flexibility, transparency, and accountability. It suggests that the current priority is to establish a complex instrument of control. This has been exacerbated by the Coalition government's drive to curtail migration which has caused the end of the few remaining elements of flexibility.

There is a contradiction between the avowed intention to 'make migration work' for Britain, and the submission of applications to enter for work, study, or cultural exchange to an unresponsive and rigid decision-making process. It suggests a narrow vision of policy that is tied to short-term political calculations, a preoccupation with control, and administrative convenience. This is arguably inappropriate as regards economic migration but is surely even more so when applied to students, travellers, artists, academics, and sportspeople who wish to spend time in the UK, exchanging ideas and developing ties whose benefits may be intangible but are vital and long term.

QUESTIONS

1 Does the points-based system 'work for Britain'?
2 How accountable is government for the operation of the points-based system?
3 What is the justification for special categories of non-PBS employment?
4 Has the government satisfactorily addressed the problem of illegal working?

For guidance on answering questions, visit www.oxfordtextbooks.co.uk/orc/clayton5e/.

FURTHER READING

Beynon, Rhian (2007) 'Highly Skilled, No Longer Wanted' *Catalyst*, 22 January.

Bhabha, J. et al (eds) (1985), *Worlds Apart: Women under Immigration and Nationality Law* (Women, Immigration and Nationality Group (WING)).

Castles, Stephen (2000) *Ethnicity and Globalisation: From Migrant Worker to Transnational Citizen* (London: Sage).

Cohen, Steve (2000) 'Never Mind the Racism... Feel the Quality' *Immigration and Nationality Law and Practice* vol. 14, no. 4, pp. 223–226.

Devine, Laura (2007) 'Is the New Highly Skilled Migrant Programme "Fit for Purpose"? If Not, the Government's Proposed Points Based Immigration System is Fundamentally Flawed' *Journal of Immigration, Asylum and Nationality Law* vol. 21, no. 2, pp. 90–108.

Devine, Laura and Barrett-Brown, Sophie (2001) 'The Work Permit Scheme – An Analysis of its Origin and Scope' *Journal of Immigration, Asylum and Nationality Law* vol. 15, no. 2, pp. 92–101.

Dobson, Janet et al (2001) *International Migration and the United Kingdom: Recent Patterns and Trends*, Research, Development and Statistics Occasional Paper no. 75.

Dummett, Ann and Nicol Andrew (1990) *Subjects, Citizens, Aliens and Others* (London: Weidenfeld and Nicholson).

Geis, W. et al (2011) 'Why Go to France or Germany, if you Could as Well Go to the UK or the US? Selective features of immigration to the EU "big three" and the United States' *Journal of Common Market Studies* vol. 49, no. 4, pp. 767–796.

Gillespie, Jim (2000) 'Review of Work Permits' *Journal of Immigration, Asylum and Nationality Law* vol. 14, no. 2, pp. 75–76.

Harvey, Alison (2011) 'The Cap on Immigration' *Journal of Immigration, Asylum and Nationality Law* vol. 25, no. 1, pp. 7–9.

Holmes, Colin (1988) *John Bull's Island: Immigration and British Society 1871–1971* (Basingstoke: Macmillan).

Home Office (2006) *A Points-Based System: Making Migration Work for Britain* (London: Home Office).

Joint Committee on Human Rights, *Highly Skilled Migrants: Changes to the Immigration Rules* Session 2006–07 Twentieth Report HL Paper 173, HC 993.

Joint Council for the Welfare of Immigrants (2003) *The Politics of Managed Migration* JCWI Bulletin. Autumn Issue.

Joshi, Shirley (2002) 'Immigration Controls and Class' in S. Cohen et al (eds) *From Immigration Controls to Welfare Controls* (London: Routledge), pp. 47–58.

Kalayaan/Oxfam (2008) *The New Bonded Labour: The Impact of Proposed Changes to the UK Immigration System on Migrant Domestic Workers* (London: Kalayaan/Oxfam).

Kofman, Eleonore et al (2009) *The Equality Implications of Being a Migrant in Britain* (London: Equality and Human Rights Commission).

McLaughlan, Gail and Salt, John (2002) *Migration Policies: Towards Highly Skilled Foreign Workers* (London: Migration Research Unit, University College London).

Migrants' Rights Network (2008) *Papers Please: The Impact of the Civil Penalty Regime on the Employment Rights of Migrants in the UK* (MRN Migration Perspectives Paper).

—— (2009) *Irregular Migrants: The Urgent Need for a New Approach* (London: MRN Migration Perspectives Paper).

Momsen, Janet Henshall (ed.) (1999) *Gender, Migration and Domestic Service* (London: Routledge).

Paul, Kathleen (1997) *Whitewashing Britain: Race and Citizenship in the Postwar Era* (New York: Cornell), chapters 3, 4, and 5.

Portes, Jonathan and French, Simon (2005) *The Impact of Free Movement of Workers from Central and Eastern Europe on the UK Labour Market: Early Evidence* DWP Working Paper no. 18.

Puttick, Keith (2006) 'Welcoming the New Arrivals? Reception, Integration and Employment of A8, Bulgarian and Romanian Migrants' *Journal of Immigration, Asylum and Nationality Law* vol. 20, no. 4, pp. 238–254.

Rogaly, Ben (2006) *Intensification of Work-Place Regimes in British Agriculture: The Role of Migrant Workers* Sussex Migration Working Paper no. 36 (Sussex Centre for Migration Research).

Stalker, Peter (2000) *Workers Without Frontiers: The Impact of Globalization on International Migration* (Geneva: Lynne Reiner/ILO).

Stephenson, K. and Wilkins, C. (2011) 'The 2011/2012 Immigration Overhaul and the Impact on the Education Sector' *Education Law Journal* vol. 12, no. 3, pp. 197–207.

Wray, Helena (2009) 'The Points Based System: A Blunt Instrument' *Journal of Immigration, Asylum and Nationality Law* vol. 23, no. 3, pp. 231–251.

11

Visitors: entry for temporary purposes

SUMMARY

This chapter deals with those coming to the UK as visitors for short-term or finite purposes such as tourism, business visits, sporting and entertainment engagements, or for private medical treatment. An important issue, covered here, is the right of appeal against refusal of entry clearance to visit family members.

11.1 Introduction

The majority of passengers arriving in the UK do so not for settlement but for temporary purposes, and the most common reason for temporary entry is as a visitor.

Of around 12.3 million non-EEA nationals admitted to the UK in 2009, around 56 per cent were visitors, i.e., they came for a brief period for reasons such as business, tourism, or visiting family. The largest group (43 per cent of the total number of visitors) was from the Americas. The next largest group came from Asia (excluding South Asia) and the Middle East (nearly 21 per cent), followed by Oceania (11 per cent) the Indian sub-continent (10 per cent), and Africa (9 per cent). It follows that many visitors will be from non-visa countries such as US, Australia, Japan, Argentina, and Brazil. These visitors may obtain leave to enter at the border and do not need to obtain a visa prior to entry although they may still choose to do so.

The law relating to visitors is not much concerned with these individuals. While non-visa nationals must meet the requirements of the immigration rules, it is rare that the entry of, for example, American or Japanese tourists raises any issues when they request leave to enter. The immigration statistics for 2009, for example, show that 8,445 individuals from the Americas were refused entry at the port and subsequently removed. It is probable that not all were non-visa visitors but, even if they were, they still represent only a tiny fraction (less than 0.3 per cent) of all visitors from the region. This can be compared with refusal rates for visa applications at posts such as Abuja in Nigeria where, according to the Chief Inspector's report of July 2009, there was a refusal rate of 43 per cent for applications with limited rights of appeal (around 75 per cent of which were visitor applications). Certainly, acceptance and refusal rates seem to be connected to larger global issues. Following the terrorist attacks in New York in 2001, the overall refusal rate for family visitor applications increased considerably with particularly large rises in regions such as the Middle East and South Asia (Dunstan 2004).

The law relating to visitors is therefore principally concerned with the same issues as much of the rest of immigration law, and which are associated with particular regions and countries: deterring illegal and unwanted entrants, overstaying, and asylum claims.

It operates on the basis of discretionary judgements challengeable by limited appeal rights. It affects not only those who want to spend time in the UK as a tourist or on business but also the family lives of UK residents of migrant origin seeking to maintain relationships with relatives abroad. While not overtly expressed as a requirement of the rules, the credibility of the applicant is a major factor in determining the outcome of the application and lack of credibility is frequently the underlying reason for refusal. Of course, there are more matters involved in visitor applications than these but these familiar themes are clearly present.

The visa regime itself, as we have already seen (chapter 7), is designed to prevent illegal entry and deter asylum claims. No more will be said about this here. The right of appeal against refusal of entry clearance for visitors was removed by the Asylum and Immigration Appeals Act 1993. From then, the only possibility of challenging refusal of entry clearance was by judicial review. As we have already noted, judicial review is concerned not with the merits of the decision but with the decision-making process. Usually, in the case of refusal of a visa, this is the question of whether the entry clearance officer's decision was unreasonable, and it is rarely possible to show that this was the case (see, for instance, *R v SSHD ex p Kurumoorthy* [1998] Imm AR 401 or *R v ECO Accra ex p Aidoo* [1999] Imm AR 221). One effect of a lack of appeal right is that decision-making receives little scrutiny. There are few recent Tribunal cases, and given the limitations of judicial review, there is a relatively small body of case law on the application of the rules.

The Immigration and Asylum Act 1999 ss 59 and 60 reinstated a right of appeal for family visitors. This is of particular importance to families of migrant origin who want relatives to come for holidays and for family events such as weddings and funerals. In these latter instances, not only the right but the timeliness of the appeal is critical. In practice, an appeal may not be decided until after the family event in question has taken place but it may still be brought to avoid the adverse consequences of a refusal on future applications. Human rights issues may also arise in relation to visitor applications that affect family life while policies on refusal may raise race discrimination questions which, until implementation of the Equality Act 2010, could form the subject of an appeal although this was relatively rare. In its family migration consultation (Home Office/UK Border Agency (2011) *Family Migration: A Consultation*), the government proposed removing the enhanced appeal rights of family visitors, a proposal discussed further at 11.5.

The relationship between border control and visitor visas is highlighted by the inclusion of plans for reform of the visitor visa rules in the previous government's strategy document, *Securing the UK Border: Our Vision and Strategy for the Future,* published in March 2007, which set out the government's plans for expanding the border. It made a number of proposals to codify and regulate visitor status more tightly, some of which have been implemented. The government also announced an intention to create, to use its own consumerist terminology, 'a new family of visa products' for short term-visits and a new category of 'Business Visitors'. A category of 'Student Visitor' had already been established. In 2008, criteria for 'Business Visitor', 'Sports Visitor', and 'Entertainer Visitor' were introduced, the latter two regularizing previous concessions. These categories, together with the pre-existing categories of 'Child Visitor' and 'Marriage Visitor' and categories for those seeking medical treatment or visiting children at school suggest that the government wants to exert tighter control over each group of people permitted to enter. Yet it is impossible in practice to envisage all the possible circumstances in which a person might legitimately wish to make a short visit to the UK. The retention thus far of the 'General Visitor' category, said in para 40 HC 395, to include a tourist, as against the introduction of a specific 'Tourist Visa', as suggested in the Consultation, may be a recognition that attempts to define all types of possible visit are doomed to fail.

11.2 Requirements of the rules: General Visitors

The rules for General Visitors are found in paras 41–46. They are relevant not only to those coming as 'General Visitors' but also to other types of visitors who have to meet most of the criteria of a General Visitor as well as the specific requirements of their category. The actual requirements for a General Visitor are set out in para 41 and include the following.

11.2.1 Is genuinely seeking entry as a General Visitor

As the 'General Visitor' category is a generic one, the visitor is not required to spend their time in a particular way but certain activities are prohibited. Paragraph 41 requires that the visit must not be for the purpose of taking employment in the UK, producing goods or providing services in the UK, including selling goods or services direct to members of the public, or undertaking a course of study. Nor must the applicant intend to carry out activities provided for in the other visitor categories. Thus, provided the individual is not excluded for a general reason under para 320 (see chapter 7), a visit may be for any purpose which does not contravene these requirements. In *Gusakov* (11672), the applicant intended to stay with a family to improve her English and help look after their children. The ECO refused the application on the basis that, in substance, she was coming as an au pair but, as a Russian citizen, fell outside the au pair scheme. The IAT held that, as a matter of law, there are few restrictions on what a visitor can do. The authorities could not prevent her spending her time as a visitor in looking after children or improving her English although, of course, she could not be paid to do this. More recently, the Upper Tribunal came to a similar conclusion in relation to a family carer *Oppong (visitor – length of stay)* Ghana [2011] UKUT 00431 (IAC).

11.2.2 Duration of visit

The visit must be 'for a limited period as stated by him, not exceeding 6 months' (para 41(i), with an exception for some visitors accompanying Academic Visitors who may receive up to 12 months). There is no automatic entitlement to six months' leave, but it is usually given (Entry Clearance Guidance VAT 1.3). A visitor who has been given less than six months and continues to satisfy the requirements of para 41 may apply before the expiry of their leave for a further period up to the maximum, although the modernized guidance to immigration officials published on the UKBA website says that enquiries must be made to find out why a shorter period was given in the first place. Extension beyond the maximum period is possible under the rules for Medical Visitors (no limit) and, by concession, to 11 months for Student Visitors and to 12 months for those volunteering on archeological digs.

Paragraph 44(iii) requires that, in an application for leave to extend stay as a visitor, the previous leave must also have been as a visitor. This means that a period as a visitor cannot be tacked onto the end of another stay. In *YT (HC 395 paragraph 44 – extension of stay) Belarus* [2009] UKAIT 00003, the applicant asked to stay on after working under the sectors-based scheme, so that he could have 'the opportunity to travel in the United Kingdom'. The Tribunal found that this was permitted under the rules as they then stood. However, after that application had been made, para 44 was amended so that an individual in these circumstances would have to leave the UK and reapply for entry as a visitor.

The modernized guidance advises that there is no restriction on the number of visits a person may make to the UK and there is no requirement that a specified time must elapse between each visit so that brief intervals between visits should not, on their own, constitute grounds for refusal, although the guidance tells officials to consider the stated purpose of the visit against the length of time that has elapsed since previous visits in order to satisfy themselves that a person is genuinely seeking entry as a visitor. For example, a visitor should not normally spend more than six out of any 12 months in the UK unless there is a good reason, such as receiving private medical treatment. Nonetheless, the sole fact that someone wishes to spend more time in the UK, while inviting rigorous scrutiny to ensure compliance with the rules, is not, in itself, a reason for refusal (*Oppong (visitor – length of stay) Ghana* [2011] UKUT 00431 (IAC)). Applicants who can show a need for repeated visits and whose circumstances and travel history are considered appropriate may be given multi-entry visas for up to 10 years, permitting any number of entries within the currency of the visa (see Entry Clearance Guidance VAT 1.4). In other cases, a new application for leave will be needed for each visit.

11.2.3 Maintenance and accommodation

Paragraph 41(vi) requires that the visitor can maintain and accommodate himself and any dependants adequately out of resources available to him without recourse to public funds or taking employment. In the alternative, the visitor and any dependants may be maintained and accommodated adequately by relatives and friends. Under para 41(vii), they must also be able to meet the cost of the return journey. The modernized guidance says that a sponsor's undertaking may be taken into account and that it may be requested under para 35 of the rules, while refusing to give one is grounds for refusal of the application under para 320(14). However, the current definition of 'sponsor' in para 6 of the rules is confined to those involved in certain family applications and does not include visitors.

While some assurance about the applicant's financial circumstances is necessary, the purpose is only to show that the applicant has the capacity to maintain themselves and return and their finances do not need to be a model of clarity (*Osibamowo* (12116)). The assessment of this requirement involves an examination not only of the means of the visitor but also, where applicable, of those who will support them.

The proportionality of the cost to the applicant's means is regarded as relevant to questions of credibility. The paragraph in the guidance on credibility says that officials must consider whether the proposed purpose of a visit to the UK is reasonable, taking into account the applicant's financial means and their family, social, and economic background. This is a contentious area as it means that those from modest backgrounds may be treated more sceptically. The problem is illustrated by the case of *Hussain* (10037), in which the ECO refused entry clearance on the basis that the cost of the trip was out of all proportion to the applicant's income. The IAT found that the satisfaction of seeing family was quite sufficient reason for the trip and the expenditure involved. The visit did not need to be a demonstrably wise financial move. However, the appellant still lost in this case because he could not show that he could afford the airfare home. There was a similar approach in *Kaur v ECO New Delhi* [2002] UKIAT 05692, in which the Tribunal said that the emotional value of the trip might well mean that the visitor would pay more than strict economics might dictate. However, in *Iskola* (11334) it was held to be relevant that the price of the air tickets was equivalent to one year's income from the applicant's business, and refusal of entry clearance was justified. The difficulty here is that the difference in the standard of living between the applicant's home country and the UK may make it very difficult for the applicant to show that the trip is financially viable. This is not really because of this part of the rule taken alone, but because of the way it interacts with the requirement to show intention to leave. If an individual has allocated a substantial proportion of their resources to the trip, it may be suspected that it is because they hope to remain long-term.

11.2.4 Intention to leave

Under para 41(ii), an applicant must intend to leave the UK at the end of the period of the visit. As with all the immigration rules, the burden of proof is on the applicant to a civil standard of proof. Given that a person's intentions are, of necessity, difficult to prove, the applicant will have to adduce circumstantial evidence from which the immigration officer will make a judgement. Decision-makers will consider matters such as what incentive the applicant has to return, e.g., whether they have family and work commitments in their home country. In *Aye* (10100), the Tribunal said that an apparent lack of incentive to return should not of itself be treated as a reason to refuse but could be taken into account as part of all the circumstances used to decide the applicant's intentions. Evidence from the sponsor may also help to build a picture of the applicant's intention (*DM* [2005] UKIAT 130). Entry clearance officers often expect a prospective tourist to have some idea of what they will see and reject an applicant whose plans are seen as excessively vague or inaccurate. However, it is not necessary to have a detailed itinerary for a family visit. In fact, the Tribunal has commented that too much concern with sightseeing might suggest that a family visit is not really intended (*W (Ghana)* [2004] UKIAT 00005).

In considering incentive to return, the economic circumstances in the applicant's home country by comparison with those in the UK may be taken into account. There are many cases in which this reasoning is demonstrated; see *Ashfaq Ahmad v ECO Islamabad* [2002] UKIAT 03891 at 11.2.5 in the context of intention not to work). Such considerations are fraught with the potential for stereotyping and discrimination. In *R v ECO ex p Abu-Gidary* CO 965 1999, the argument was advanced for the applicant that the ECO's reasoning in this respect, if taken too far, could result in no young single women from developing or poor countries being able to obtain entry clearance as visitors. The applicant for entry clearance had made numerous previous unsuccessful applications. She was now a graduate who had a job to return to. Given local conditions, this was a considerable achievement but the ECO did not regard it as sufficient incentive to return, describing her income as 'modest'. The view of the High Court was more sympathetic. That sympathetic approach is also found in Tribunal decisions such as *Ogunkola v ECO Lagos* [2002] UKIAT 02238, in which the Tribunal endorsed the view that:

> if lack of economic incentive to return to the country of origin were sufficient to found a refusal of a visit application, then no person living overseas whose standard of living was lower than that prevailing in the UK could ever come on holiday here, or visit relatives settled here. That is not the law. (para 7)

In reality however, for those whose home lives are neither settled nor prosperous, there may be little concrete that can be put forward besides statements of good faith whose value depends on the subjective concept of credibility. The guidance paragraph on credibility illustrates the difficulty of proving intention for these individuals: 'Having a return ticket and other supporting evidence does not guarantee that a visitor intends to comply with their conditions of stay or that they intend to leave at the end of their visit.' As the Tribunal said, in a decision on intention to return in the sectors-based scheme, it is wrong to assume that 'anyone who has the opportunity to commit an offence will do so' (*AA and others (Sectors Based Work: General Principles) Bangladesh* [2006] UKAIT 00026 para 32). Yet, decisions can easily end up being made on such a basis and, where general appeal rights do not exist as in non-family visitor applications, they are difficult to challenge even where other evidence exists. In the past, the Independent Monitor for Entry Clearance has been deeply critical of the way such decisions have been made in poor countries (F. Lindsley *Report by the Independent Monitor* November 2005 pp. 33–45).

11.2.5 **Intention not to work**

Paragraph 41(iii) requires proof of a negative, that the visitor does not intend to take employment in the UK. This is not necessarily proved by evidence that they can be maintained and accommodated. In *Ashfaq Ahmad v ECO Islamabad*, the Tribunal found that, while the sponsor could maintain and accommodate the visitor, he could not control the actions of the visitor. Whatever the sponsor's own intentions, the visitor, as a free adult, may make other choices, such as working during their stay. The sponsor could not prevent this and the application for entry clearance could be refused because of the incentive to work, given the applicant's financial circumstances.

The Tribunal in *Mistry v ECO Bombay* [2002] UKIAT 07500 put the matter rather starkly as follows: 'It comes down to the question of whether someone making a modest living in India must inevitably be regarded as too much prey to the temptations of doing much better here, at least in cash terms, to be regarded as a genuine short-term visitor' (para 7). The implied answer here was 'no', but the possibility of making such a blanket, and potentially discriminatory, judgement is clear and invokes the earlier point made about the difficulty of proving an intention in the absence of compelling evidence, which will not often be available, particularly for young, relatively poor, first-time travellers.

11.2.6 **Credibility**

The immigration rules do not contain a heading of 'Credibility' but, as already indicated, this issue lies behind the requirements we have discussed earlier. The modernized guidance does contain a brief section on credibility, some of which has already been discussed. It goes on to say that, under the heading 'Grounds for doubting credibility and intentions' these may be doubted where the applicant or sponsor have clearly attempted to deceive the immigration authorities or there are clear discrepancies between statements made by the visitor and the sponsor particularly on points where the sponsor could reasonably be expected to know the facts.

Even where discrepancies do not go to the question in issue, they may be seen as relevant to credibility. However, they may also easily arise for legitimate reasons. In *Singh* (10139), the applicant was a 40-year-old married man in India who had applied to visit his brother in the UK. There was a discrepancy between him and his brother as to the ages of the brother's children and whether the brother paid maintenance to his former wife. The Tribunal held that a negative assessment of his credibility based on such discrepancies was unreasonable, given that he might well be unaware of them.

There were other more relevant factors supporting his credibility, for instance that he had visited before and had left before his allotted time, and these should have been given more weight.

Previous guidance included reference to the '[p]revious immigration history and evidence of a pattern of family migration, both here and abroad'. The practice of taking family migration history into account has been the subject of challenge particularly in family visit cases where, by definition, there will be a history of migration. It was approved in two judicial review cases, *Aidoo* and *Kurumoorthy* cited previously, which both held that these were relevant to credibility. In *Aidoo*, the sponsor and applicant's half-brother had overstayed and there was suspicion that the applicant might do the same. In *Kurumoorthy*, the ECO thought that the applicants, who were a couple, might consider following the wife's sister's example. She, however, had not acted unlawfully, having come on a visit to her children and applied, while in the UK, for indefinite leave to remain, which was granted. In *Gurgur v ECO Istanbul* [2002] UKIAT 024626, the Tribunal found that a history of lawful migration in a family should not be used to prevent the appellant from visiting her children and grandchildren in the UK: 'if a pattern of legal migration by members of a family excluded per se other family members from visiting them, it is difficult to see why the visitor visa system was put in place at all'. In this case, the applicant's own declared intention was to return. Of course, if she herself had shown any intention to remain that would have been grounds for refusal, irrespective of credibility issues.

Credibility is clearly relevant to subjective questions such as intention. However, it is easily elevated out of its rightful place and treated as the overriding factor. At worst, poor findings as to credibility may mean that the rest of an applicant's evidence is disregarded even where this is of good quality. Time and time again, the Tribunal has stated that the issue of credibility should not be so used. Yet, as with intention to return or not to work, poor decision-making on this question cannot easily be challenged in the absence of a general right of appeal.

The Chief Inspector of the UK Border Agency, in recent reports (for example, Chief Inspector (2010) *An Inspection of Entry Clearance in Abu Dhabi and Islamabad*, Chief Inspector (2011) *An Inspection of the UK Border Agency visa section in Amman, Jordan*, and Chief Inspector (2011) *A Short-Notice Inspection of Decision Making Quality in the Istanbul Visa Section*), has been particularly critical of how evidential issues are determined, suggesting that decision-making is sometimes over-influenced by a generalized risk profile so that decision-makers rely too heavily on applicants' personal characteristics (including, in the case of Pakistan, nationality) rather than on the contents of their application. Certain applicants are also subject to more onerous evidentiary demands. In such situations, applicants are effectively treated as having low credibility from the outset.

11.3 Other visitors

As already indicated, there is a range of special visitor categories, which are now briefly considered in turn.

11.3.1 Child Visitor

Rules for Child Visitors were first introduced into the rules in 2006 by HC 819 and amended under HC 120 from the beginning of 2010 to provide for educational exchange visits as well as to meet the UK Border Agency's obligations under s 55 of the Borders, Citizenship and Immigration Act 2009. This requires the UK Border Agency to take into account the need to safeguard and promote the welfare of children in the UK when carrying out its functions.

The Child Visitor rules apply to all visitors under 18, as that is the minimum age to qualify as a General Visitor. In addition to most of the usual requirements that a General Visitor must meet, there are other criteria: suitable arrangements must have been made for the child's travel to and reception and care in the UK (which arrangements, if not provided by the child's own parents, must comply with the UK Border Agency's guidance); the child has a parent or guardian in the country of origin who is responsible for their care and consents to the arrangements; if a visa national, the child has been given entry clearance as an accompanied Child Visitor and is travelling with the adult identified on the entry clearance, or has been given entry clearance as an unaccompanied Child Visitor. These provisions aim to protect children who might enter the UK under private fostering arrangements, such as those used in the case of Victoria Climbié, who was ill-treated and killed by her carers, or for trafficking.

The modernized guidance says that, unless there are grounds for concern, arrangements for the travel, reception, and care of a child will be regarded as satisfactory where they are accompanied by parents, relative, or friend, where they have a letter from a relative or friend inviting them to visit, or where suitable arrangements for private foster care exist. More investigation is likely if a child is accompanied by someone other than a parent, guardian, or close relative or is unaccompanied. A child on an accompanied child visa must travel with the adult named on the visa.

11.3.2 Business Visitor

Until November 2008, those wishing to conduct business in the UK entered as an ordinary visitor and the range of permissible activities was not defined. New rules were then inserted under HC 1113, creating separate General and Business Visitor categories. To qualify as a Business Visitor, the applicant must, in addition to meeting most of the requirements of a General Visitor, be intending to carry out one or more of a range of activities. These are listed in the rule itself and include taking part in a location shoot as a member of a film crew, undertaking media assignments, acting as an academic visitor or visiting professor, secondment to a UK company, undertaking preaching or pastoral work or consultancy or training for a UK branch of an overseas business, or a one-off training assignment. In all cases, the visitor must not take employment or be paid by a UK source.

In addition, a Business Visitor may undertake a 'Permissible Activity' which is defined in para 6 of the rules as being those listed in separate UKBA guidance. The modernized guidance states these to include attending pre-arranged business meetings, conferences, interviews, or trade fairs; signing agreements and contracts; carrying out fact-finding missions or site visits; working as a tour group courier; representing a computer software company or foreign manufacturer; or providing interpretation and translation facilities for colleagues who are Business Visitors.

The rationale for the creation of a separate category of Business Visitor was to 'make it clear what business visitors can do when they visit the UK and what they cannot' (Government Response to the Consultation on Visitors, p. 10). However, even if an activity is not within the list of permissible activities, the *Pankina* principle, discussed in chapters 1 and 10, means that an application might still succeed provided none of the requirements of the immigration rules is breached.

In practice, the critical requirements for a Business Visitor are those in the General Visitor rules that they do not undertake paid work, produce goods, or provide services or sell to the public. Ignorance of this can have serious consequences. It was reported that an American artist who arrived at Heathrow for a free five-day festival was detained, refused, and removed because she was carrying two small paintings which she had hopes of exhibiting or selling. In other cases, immigration officials have appeared to adopt an excessively sceptical attitude. Chinese artist Huang Xu was refused a Business Visitor visa to attend his own exhibition because it was suspected that he would sell his work, even though the exhibition was organized by the gallery who would, as is commonplace in the art world, act as vendor (Manifesto Club (2010) *Deported: Artists and Academics Barred from the UK*).

11.3.3 Sports and Entertainer Visitors

These two categories, which were inserted into the rules with effect from November 2008, permit applicants to enter the UK to take part in sporting or entertainment events and reflect previous concessions. As with Business Visitors, there is a list of activities in the rules and reference to a list in the guidance.

Under para 46M, a Sports Visitor may take part in a one-off charity sporting event, join an amateur team, or serve as support staff for a visiting sportsperson. In addition, a Sports Visitor may participate in a particular sporting event as defined in guidance. The guidance says these are specific events or tournaments such as Wimbledon, personal appearances or promotions, 'trials', or training. Sports Visitors are bound by paras 41(iii) and (iv) of the General Visitor rules and may not take employment or provide or sell services. The guidance says that those coming for exhibition matches and charity events may not receive a fee or sponsorship but may receive cash prizes, board, lodging, and living expenses.

Under para 46S, an Entertainer Visitor must intend to take part as a professional entertainer in one or more music competitions, fulfil engagements as an amateur, take part in a cultural event listed in guidance, or provide support functions to another Entertainer Visitor. The guidance lists well-established cultural events and festivals (such as the Edinburgh, Glyndebourne, and Glastonbury Festivals) where artists are allowed to enter as a visitor and are not required to apply under Tier 5.

Like Sports Visitors, Entertainer Visitors are bound by paras 41(iii) and (iv) of the General Visitors rules that prohibit employment and provision or selling of services. The guidance says that both amateur and professional performers may enter as Entertainer Visitors provided they do not receive payment by way of fees or sponsorship (except presumably those attending permit-free festivals) although they may receive cash prizes, board, lodging, and living expenses.

11.3.4 Visitors seeking private medical treatment

It is not permissible to come to the UK in order to receive National Health Service treatment and a person present as a visitor may not take advantage of the National Health Service unless they belong to one of a limited list of countries with which there are reciprocal arrangements, although treatment in emergencies and for certain infectious diseases is always free. However, visitors may come for the purpose of receiving private medical care. An applicant does not need to show that their visit is for a fixed period of less than six months, provided it will be of finite duration and they will leave at the end of that period. Instead, the duration of the visit is linked to the duration of proposed treatment and, exceptionally for visitors, extensions beyond six months are available provided the requirements are still met.

A Medical Visitor must meet most of the requirements for a General Visitor and show that there are sufficient funds to pay for treatment. They must also show that they intend to leave the UK at the end of their treatment, and, if they have a communicable disease, they must satisfy the medical inspector that their entry is not a danger to public health. The immigration service may require evidence of the nature of the illness and treatment, of the arrangements for treatment including frequency, duration, and cost, and availability of funds to meet those costs (para 51). The treatment must be shown to be finite, but the decision-maker should take a reasonable view of this and a precise time-scale is not needed provided there are sufficient funds and the patient needs to be in the UK for the treatment. The Tribunal in *LB (medical treatment of finite duration)* [2005] UKAIT 00175 held that treatment may last for years in a suitable case. The limit is the duration of the treatment, and, although this must be finite, it need not be short.

11.3.5 Visitors entering for marriage or civil partnership

Government scepticism about the intention of visitors to return home is illustrated by the ban implemented in 2003 to prevent switching from visitor to spouse status. The preceding *White Paper, Secure Borders, Safe Haven* (Cm 5387) said:

> In 1999, 76 per cent of those granted leave to remain on the basis of marriage had been admitted to the UK for another purpose and 50 per cent of those who switched into the marriage category did so within six months of entry. As it seems unlikely that such a large percentage of this number would develop permanent relationships within such a short period of time, the indication is that many of these persons had intended to marry all along but had not obtained leave to enter on this basis and had therefore lied about their intentions to the entry clearance officer. Alternatively, they may have entered a bogus marriage to obtain leave to remain after arrival. (para 7.11)

The failure to announce an intention to marry prior to entry may be explicable in many different ways and does not, in itself, indicate dishonesty or a bogus marriage. The applicant may, for example, wish to spend more time with their partner before deciding to marry. A person who has entered as a bona fide visitor and formed a relationship in that time has to choose between marrying or leaving the UK with the attendant expense and delay before returning. While some bogus marriages do take place, as the House of Lords found in *Baiai*, discussed in chapter 9, it is wrong to assume that these can be detected purely on the basis of immigration status.

The ban on switching was followed by the controversial Certificates of Approval scheme, also discussed in chapter 9, which aimed to prevent those with short-term or no leave from marrying within the UK. The purpose of both that scheme and the ban on switching was to force aspiring spouses to leave the UK and make an entry clearance application from abroad. Consistent with this policy, the Marriage Visitor rules provide for a visa that permits entrants to enter for marriage if they do not intend to remain in the UK after marriage. As well as demonstrating plans to marry or form a civil partnership in the UK, the applicant must also intend to leave the UK after the ceremony. If the intention is to live in the UK after the ceremony, the more demanding fiancé(e) visa is needed. As discussed in chapter 9, the Certificates of Approval scheme has now been scrapped. Those entering marriages outside the Church of England and who are subject to immigration control still have to meet additional notification requirements under ss 19–24 Asylum and Immigration (Treatment of Claimants, etc) Act 2004 although permission to marry may no longer be refused on the basis of immigration status.

Moreover, after *Chikwamba* (also discussed in chapter 9), spouses without the proper leave may no longer be routinely required to leave the UK and reapply for entry. The continuing function of the Marriage Visitor rules in these circumstances is limited although they may assist in identifying marriages that have already received some official scrutiny and are therefore considered less likely to require investigation as bogus.

11.3.6 Carers

There is no provision in the rules for those who want to care for a sick friend or relative in the UK. The Tribunal has found that, provided the applicant meets the requirements of the General Visitor rules, the fact that she intends to spend her time in the UK caring for a relative is not a reason for refusal (*Oppong (visitor – length of stay) Ghana* [2011] UKUT 00431 (IAC)). Article 8 ECHR may apply to such applications. In *R (on the application of Fawad and Zia Ahmadi) v SSHD* [2005] EWCA Civ 1721, the Court of Appeal held that an Article 8 claim of a brother to remain to look after his younger brother was not bound to fail and thus should be considered.

Family members who intend to care for children may be refused on the basis that they are working as a child minder. According to the Tribunal in *Jumawan* (9385), if the intention is to take over domestic responsibilities to enable another family member to work, then refusal may be justified as this is a task which may be undertaken by a third party employed for that purpose. However, merely because a person intends to occupy some or all of their visit in the care of their grandchildren, which could be done by an employee, it does not follow that domestic employment is the applicant's object. Leave to enter as a visitor may still be granted if other conditions are met.

The modernized guidance says that applicants may enter as visitors and care for children where they are close relatives, neither parent is able to supervise daytime care of the child, and neither parent has an immigration status leading to settlement. This is therefore of relevance only to the relatives of temporary migrants.

11.3.7 Student Visitor

This category has become more important now that Tier 4 visas are no longer available for students wishing to take lower level English courses. Paragraph 56K provides that, as well as meeting the usual requirements of the visitor rules as to maintenance, limitations on activity, and intention to leave the UK, the applicant must have been accepted on a course of study provided by a Tier 4 sponsor or an institution accredited or inspected by UKBA-approved bodies or by an overseas higher education institution offering part of a degree level programme in the UK. Entry under the rules is for a maximum of six months but a concession in the guidance permits entry for up to 11 months for those coming to do an English language course.

11.3.8 Other categories

There are some other categories that are mentioned here for the sake of completeness. Under paras 47–50, transit visas are available to those who are entering the UK en route to another destination outside the common travel area and have the means to continue their journey, are assured of acceptance at their destination, and intend and are able to leave the UK within 48 hours. Under paras 56A–C, parents may enter to visit a child under 12 who is attending an independent day school in the UK, provided the parents can afford to maintain a second home in the UK and do not intend to make the UK their main home. Unlike most other visitors, the maximum leave is 12 months but employment is prohibited. Paragraph 56G provides that, under the Approved Destination Status agreement with China, short-term visas of up to 30 days may be issued to members of a tour group. Paragraphs 56N–Q, implemented in April 2011, introduced a new visitor category of Prospective Entrepreneur, from which it is possible (exceptionally under the Visitor rules) to switch into Tier 1 (Entrepreneur).

11.4 Entry clearance

The requirements set out in para 41 apply to all visitors. Where they are met the applicant may be granted leave to enter at the port. Where entry clearance has been obtained beforehand, this will also function as leave to enter (Immigration (Leave to Enter and Remain) Order 2000, SI 2000/1161; see chapter 7). A visa national must obtain entry clearance for any purpose, including a visit. Visa national countries include a number of Commonwealth countries, so the belief which is sometimes held, that Commonwealth citizens may visit their UK relatives without prior entry clearance, is a false one. It depends on the Commonwealth country from which they come. For instance, Australian nationals have no such restriction; Indian nationals do.

The rate of refusal of leave to enter at the port to visitors from some non-visa national countries (notably in the Caribbean) is higher than for visitors from other countries. It can therefore be advisable for nationals of those countries to obtain entry clearance even though it is not obligatory, as it will ease the traveller's passage through immigration control and help to avoid wasted airfares and the distress of refusal at the port. There is a further advantage in applying for entry clearance where the visit is to a close family member, which is that refusal will attract a right of appeal. There is no appeal against refusal of leave to enter without entry clearance (Nationality, Immigration and Asylum Act 2002 s 89(2)).

11.5 Family visit appeals

As mentioned previously, the Immigration and Asylum Act 1999 reinstated a right of appeal against refusal of entry clearance for visits to family members. The right is now contained in Nationality, Immigration and Asylum Act 2002 s 88A, and provides a right of appeal when the application is 'for the purpose' of visiting a qualifying family member. These are defined in Immigration Appeals (Family Visitor) Regulations 2003, SI 2003/518, reg 2(2) as the applicant's:

(a) son, daughter, grandparent, grandchild, uncle, aunt, nephew, niece or first cousin;

(b) own or their spouse's parent, brother or sister;

(c) own or their son or daughter's spouse;

(d) step-parent, step-child or step-brother or sister; and

(e) any person with whom they have lived as a member of an unmarried couple for at least two of the three years before the application for entry clearance was made.

In *GB (family visitor – half-brother included)* [2007] UKAIT 00063, the appellant was denied an appeal against refusal of a visa to visit her half-brother on the basis that this was not a family visit. The Tribunal noted the inclusion in the regulations of step-siblings, where there is no blood tie, and the anomaly of excluding half-siblings who are related by blood. Half-siblings are therefore included in the references to 'brothers' or 'sisters' in the regulations. However, while the regulations permit an appeal against refusal to visit the applicant's spouse's brother or sister, the right does not extend to a sponsor who is the spouse of the applicant's own brother or sister (*SB (family visit appeal: brother-in-law?) Pakistan* [2008] UKAIT 00053), although, in both cases, the term brother or sister-in-law is appropriate.

A further question is which facts should be considered in deciding whether a visit is 'for the purpose of' visiting qualifying relatives, particularly if these are not specifically stated in the application. In *RK (purpose of family visit)* [2006] UKAIT 00045, the appellant (A) and her husband (B) planned to visit the UK, primarily because B's great-nephew had been very ill. On reconsideration, B's appeal was allowed. Although he had said in interview that his purpose was to visit his great-nephew, a non-qualifying relative, he would stay with the boy's mother, his niece, who was. However, the Home Office maintained its challenge to A's appeal right as a spouse's niece is not a qualifying relative. However, it became clear that A would also be seeing her sister-in-law, the niece's mother and a qualifying relative. Indeed, it was improbable that the couple would go to the UK and not see the sick child's grandmother who lived nearby and was herself elderly and unwell. The Tribunal held that the purpose of a family visit must be to visit the designated relative and incidental visits to other qualifying relatives did not make the visit a family visit.

This was an unfortunate decision in that it took a narrow and technical view of family relationships. A and B were childless and very close to the niece and her family. In fact, the great-nephew had been described at interview as a grandson. The decision certainly did not reflect the overall view of family life taken in the later Article 8 decisions of *Beoku-Betts* and *ZB*, discussed in chapters 4 and 9. This was a visit whose purpose was to offer support and practical help to the family as a whole. When applying for a visit visa, the importance of designating a financially sound sponsor and satisfactory accommodation means that the focus of the application is on the practical arrangements for the trip rather than on identifying the purpose of the visit and applicants may not be aware that they need to explain its purpose in such specific terms if they are to preserve their right of appeal. Fortunately, a more recent Upper Tribunal case has adopted a more sympathetic view.

Key Case

***Ajakaiye (visitor appeals – right of appeal)* Nigeria [2011] UKUT 00375 (IAC).**

The Upper Tribunal held that the starting point for deciding whether there is a right of appeal is the application form itself. However, the Tribunal was critical of the form's design which does not specifically elicit the necessary information. In the absence of sufficient information on the form, recourse may be had to extraneous sources. Here, the applicant stated on the form that she was visiting her brother-in-law (her sister's husband), who was not a qualifying relative, presumably because he was paying for her accommodation and food during the visit. However, she mentioned elsewhere that she was going to see the 'kids', i.e., her nephews and nieces, who were qualifying relatives, and further enquiry would rapidly have elicited that she was intending also to visit her sister who lived at the same address as the brother-in-law and the children. She was therefore entitled to an appeal.

When appeal rights were reintroduced, a fee was charged to appellants. Although it was refunded if the appellant won their case, it was seen as a disincentive to use the system and discriminatory given the profile of those likely to use appeal rights. The fee was reduced, and finally abolished, with effect from 15 May 2002 (SI 2002/1147). However, fees for first tier immigration appeals were re-introduced in December 2011 (First-tier Tribunal (Immigration and Asylum Chamber) Fees Order 2011, SI 2011/2841). The fee is higher if there is a hearing than if it is decided on papers. Gelsthorpe et al (2004) have shown that oral appeals are far more successful than those decided on papers only, having a success rate of 73 per cent compared with 38 per cent but appellants were often unaware of the implications of choosing a paper or an oral appeal.

The issue of family visit appeals is a controversial one because of the controversy surrounding the variable refusal rates and claims of inconsistent decision-making between posts. In December 2009, it was reported that the highest rate of refusal of family visits was in Pakistan (41 per cent), followed by Bangladesh (31 per cent). The refusal rate in Pakistan has been stated to be as high as 90 per cent (Notes of Entry Clearance User Panel 22 July 2010 in ILPA members mailing August 2010). There are well-established communities from both these countries in the UK, and the inability to invite family members to important events such as weddings and funerals or merely to provide a holiday is a major cause of resentment and creates a perception of discrimination (see 'Visa rules "blocked our reunion"' at: http://news.bbc.co.uk/1/hi/uk/8409117.stm and 'Pakistanis are most likely to be turned down for UK visas' at: http://news.bbc.co.uk/1/hi/uk/8407298.stm).

Nonetheless, successive governments have been uneasy about the continuation of Family Visitor appeals. In the five-year strategy published in February 2005, there was a proposal to end oral appeals, and a consultation paper in December 2007 asked if the appeal right should be 'revisited'. The current government has recently again proposed removing the general right of appeal for family members so that, in line with other visitors, appeals might be brought only on human rights grounds (Home Office/UK Border Agency (2011) *Family Migration: A Consultation*). It argued that most successful appeals are based on new evidence that should have been presented with the original application, that appeals represent a considerable public expense, and that some successful family visit appeals result in asylum applications.

These arguments fail to take account of the findings of the Chief Inspector of UKBA that applicants are not given clear guidance about the evidence required when an application is made and that visa officers fail to take proper account of the evidence that is submitted (see, for example, the reports on Abu Dhabi and Islamabad, Amman and Istanbul cited earlier). As already discussed, the refusal rate in some countries, notably Pakistan, is very high and the visa service there has been particularly criticized by the Chief Inspector for its discriminatory decision-making (see the report on Abu Dhabi and Islamabad cited earlier). These criticisms may be contrasted with the more favourable findings at, for example, the New York Post (Chief Inspector (2011) *An Inspection of the UK Border Agency Visa Section in New York*).

In these circumstances, independent appeals represent a necessary quality control mechanism and a way to maintain public confidence. As already noted, a fee is now payable for a first instance appeal and the 480 asylum claims that were made in 2010 after a successful family visit appeal are a tiny fraction of the 350,300 family visit visas issued in that year.

11.6 Family visits and Article 8

It may be recalled from chapter 4 that what respect for family life requires, or what constitutes an interference with family life, depends to some extent on the nature of the relationship. In a sense, the very specification of family members in regulations gives rise to questions under Article 8. As the cases previously discussed show, the list may be criticized as being insufficiently comprehensive, as concepts and experiences of the family differ widely (see *Review of Family Visitor Appeals*, June 2003).

As we have seen, Article 8 cannot be used to *establish* family life if it does not already exist. We noted this in the case of *ECO Lagos v Imoh* [2002] UKIAT 01967, in which an Article 8 application for a girl to join her aunt failed because there was no family life in this case but rather an attempt to create one. It said: 'Article 8 requires that there is as a matter of fact family life in existence and the mere payment of money for the care of a child and one visit to see that child, is not capable of creating a family life' (para 5 of the judgment).

One might ask, though, whether Winsome Imoh would have been refused entry clearance just to visit her aunt rather than to join her as a dependant, and if so, whether she could have challenged this successfully using Article 8. The case of *Praengsamrit v ECO Bangkok* [2002] UKIAT 02791 may be considered by way of comparison. In this case, an aunt applied to visit her niece, and was turned down on the basis that there had been insufficient contact between the two of them. Article 8 was not argued, but the Vice President of the Tribunal held that:

> There is no need to prove contact as an expression of devotion which one might expect between husband and wife. They are relations whose family life goes back over the period of the niece's life. That sort of relationship does not to my mind require to be demonstrated by evidence of frequent contact. It is of the essence of family life that the bond is there to be renewed as and when the occasion arises when members of a family are separated by considerable distances as in this case.

This must be a familiar idea to anyone with relatives who live at a distance from them. It suggests that the better way for the courts to approach Article 8 cases is not to consider whether family life exists, but rather what respect for family life requires in the particular instance. As discussed in chapter 4, this will vary from one situation to another. It may not require a government to respect the choice of residence of a married couple who could live elsewhere, but it is difficult to see how it would not require at least the possibility of contact between family members. In *Ramsew v ECO Georgetown* 01/TH/2505, the Tribunal confirmed that family visit cases do normally engage family life. On the other hand, in *Hussain and Noor v ECO Islamabad* (01/TH/2746), the Tribunal held that family life was not interfered with by refusing a visit. It could be carried on by other means, for instance letters and phone calls. The approach in *Ramsew* is implicitly endorsed in *Ashrif v ECO Islamabad* 01/TH/3465, in which the Tribunal held that there did not have to be a particular reason for the visit at a particular time. 'The whole point of family visits is that the existence of the family ties of themselves will normally furnish the reason for the visit' (para 14).

11.7 Change of circumstances

As we have seen in chapter 7, where there is a change in circumstances after the grant of entry clearance this may justify cancellation of leave to enter under HC 395 para 321A(1). The modernized guidance says that the paragraph applies when the change of circumstances means 'that they can no longer get leave to enter in the category for which they were granted entry clearance'. The example given is the withdrawal of a job offer. However, in the context of visit visas, circumstances might change (for example, a family wedding might be cancelled) and the applicant would still qualify as a visitor. In that case, para 321A(1) should not apply. Nonetheless, refusals where the applicant still qualifies as a visitor have sometimes been upheld by the Tribunal. *Dapaah* (11823) upheld the principle established in *Eusebio* (4739) that the question of the effect of a change of circumstances is a question of fact and degree, particularly when the applicant is seeking entry under the same rule as the one under which they obtained entry clearance. In a visitor case, a change of sponsor does not warrant cancellation of leave to enter. However, leave to enter may be refused or cancelled, even when the change of circumstances does not take the journey outside the visitor rules. In *Hiemo v Immigration Officer Heathrow* (10892), the appellant's original application had been to visit his sister. On arrival at Heathrow, he sought instead 20 days to attend a training course at the Church of Scientology in East Grinstead. His sister had gone to Germany. The Tribunal held that the change of circumstances was fundamental and the refusal was justified.

The grounds for cancelling leave to enter under para 321A are narrower than the grounds for refusing leave to enter under para 320. As most visitors now receive leave to enter at the same time as their visa, they cannot be refused leave to enter at the port but can only have their leave cancelled. This limits the options available to an immigration officer who discovers that a visitor with leave to enter may not comply with the terms of his visa after entry. If deception was used at the time of the application, leave may be cancelled under para 321A(2) (submission of false representations or false documents or non-disclosure of a material fact). However, where the application was made in good faith but the visitor has made new, non-compliant plans since it was granted, the immigration officer's powers under para 321A are confined to showing a change of circumstances under para 321A(1). The meaning of 'change of circumstances' is therefore critical and was considered by the Court of Appeal in *SSHD v Boahen*.

Key Case

***SSHD v Boahen* [2010] EWCA Civ 585**

Mr Boahen had a multiple entry visitor's visa. There is no suggestion in the court report that he had been dishonest at the time the original application was made although, after the visa was granted, he overstayed by about nine weeks. On the next occasion that he attempted entry, he was refused after admitting plans to undertake paid work for his uncle. The legal problem at the heart of the case was that, as he already possessed leave to enter, he could be refused entry only after such leave had been cancelled. It therefore had to be determined if the power to cancel leave under para 321A(1) applied and there had been a change of circumstances such as to justify cancellation of leave to enter. The Court pointed out that a change of purpose is not a change of circumstances. Paragraph 2A(2A) of Schedule 2 of Immigration Act 1971 permits cancellation of a visa for change of purpose but, for some reason, this had not been reproduced in the immigration rules. As the immigration officer had not purported to exercise his power under para 2A(2A) but under the immigration rules, only facts amounting to a change of circumstances could be taken into account. The Court found however that the circumstances had changed sufficiently to justify cancellation under para 321A(1), as the relationship between Mr Boahen and his uncle had apparently become that of employee and employer.

11.8 Switching immigration categories

For a visitor, opportunities to enter as a visitor and obtain further leave under a different immigration rule have almost vanished. The only exceptions within the rules now are Prospective Entrepreneurs who can switch to Tier 1 (Entrepreneur), family cases involving a child or dependent relative who fulfils the requirements of Part 8 of the rules, as discussed in chapter 9, or where an Article 8 claim succeeds. In the Family Migration Consultation, discussed earlier in this chapter in relation to family visit appeals, the government proposed removing the right of visitors to switch into the dependent relative category.

There is no provision in the rules for spouses to switch from a visit visa but appropriate Article 8 claims stand a greater chance of success following *Chikwamba* (see chapters 4 and 9). Applications outside the rules are possible in other suitable cases.

11.9 Conclusion

Non-EEA visitors are an important category of migrant numerically and in terms of their contribution to tourism and to enabling British residents to maintain family links with those living abroad. Yet, for a government preoccupied with preventing illegal working and overstaying, controlling access via the visitor visa route is critical and recent changes seek to define as tightly as possible the possible circumstances of entry. Proposals to remove rights of appeal for family visitors fail to acknowledge the importance of oversight, particularly given well-documented instances of poor quality decision-making at some entry clearance posts, including those that receive substantial numbers of family visit applications.

QUESTIONS

1 What is the purpose of creating different categories of visitor? Will the recently created categories fulfil these purposes?

2 What is the issue to be decided in Article 8 appeal in a visitor's application? Does this differ from Article 8 appeals in other contexts?

3 Should family visitor appeals be removed? Should appeal rights for all visitors be reinstated?

online resource centre

For guidance on answering questions, visit www.oxfordtextbooks.co.uk/orc/clayton5e/.

FURTHER READING

Duheric, D. (2009) 'Immigration – Business, Sport and Entertainer Visitors' *Employment Law Bulletin* vol. 89, February, pp. 5–7.

Dunstan, Richard (2003) 'Family Visitor Visa Applications: An Analysis of Entry Clearance Officer Decision-making in 2002' *Journal of Immigration and Nationality Law and Practice* vol. 17, no. 3, pp. 170–178.

—— (2004) 'Family Visitor Visas: ECO Decision-making 2000–2003' *Journal of Immigration, Asylum and Nationality Law* vol. 18, no. 2, pp. 100–105.

Gelsthorpe, Verity, Thomas, Robert, Howard, Daniel, and Crawley, Heaven (2004) 'Family Visitor Appeals: An Examination of the Decision to Appeal and Differential Success Rates by Appeal Type' *Journal of Immigration, Asylum and Nationality Law* vol. 18, no. 3, pp. 167–185.

Gillespie, Jim (1994) 'The New Immigration Rules: Visitors and Students' *Immigration and Nationality Law and Practice* vol. 8, no. 4, pp. 126–128.

McKee, Richard (2007) 'Tightening up? "Managed Migration" May Manage to Make Migration more Messy' *Immigration Law Digest* vol. 13, no. 2 Summer 2007, pp. 7–9.

Thomas, R. (2004) 'Immigration Appeals for Family Visitors Refused Entry Clearance' *Public Law* Autumn, pp. 612–642.

SECTION 5

The asylum claim

12

The asylum process and appeals

SUMMARY

This chapter describes the asylum process from application through to cessation of refugee status, including the use of fast-track systems of decision-making and the New Asylum Model. It discusses the problems of fairness and evidence that have arisen in the asylum process, including the concept of credibility, and the safe third country and country of origin provisions which may prevent a claim or appeal from being heard at all.

12.1 The nature of an asylum claim

Millions of people face persecution worldwide. This is often on account of their political or religious beliefs, their race or nationality, or another fundamental quality such as their gender or sexuality. The purpose of refugee law is to protect people in this position. In the UK, whilst someone is applying for this protection, they are called an 'asylum seeker', although the term 'refugee' is also still correct, as refugee status is declaratory, and a refugee is someone who is forced to leave their home. It is a descriptive term. The asylum process and appeals system are the stages that an asylum seeker goes through in order to establish their claim to refugee status. Asylum or refugee status is unique in the legal and political order, and we begin this chapter with examining some of its particular characteristics.

12.1.1 Asylum and migration

The distinction between seeking asylum and other reasons for migration is a modern one. It is a distinction which is imposed in present-day law, politics and administration. In the experience of migrants, however, the distinction is not necessarily clear cut, and in earlier times, no such distinction was made even in law. Stevens (in Nicholson and Twomey 1998) says:

> There is evidence to suggest that England was acting as a country of refuge from as early as the 13th century. Until the late 18th century, however, the word 'refugee' had not become a generic term; rather, individuals fleeing from persecution or oppression were viewed, alongside other foreigners, as 'aliens' with nothing to distinguish the normal migrant from those with cause to escape their countries of origin.

In Shah's discussion of the consequences of the Africanization polices pursued by Kenya, Tanzania, and Uganda in the 1960s he makes the point that those Asian citizens of the UK and Colonies who were forced to leave East Africa were in a practical sense refugees (2000:77). The focus at the time was on Britain's obligations to its nationals, but the phenomenon of flight from serious discrimination is in reality a search for asylum. As we have seen in chapters 1 and 3, the situation was dealt with by way of immigration restrictions. However, the Africanization policies which forced them out may be compared with the Serbianization policies which forced those of Albanian descent to leave Kosovo in search of asylum in the 1990s and who were treated as asylum seekers in the UK. The policies were characterized by favouring Africans (or Serbs) over Asians (or Albanians) in matters such as employment, business, and public office.

The House of Commons Home Affairs Committee noted:

> The difficulty of distinguishing between economic and non-economic causes of migration is compounded by the fact that the two categories may frequently overlap. Some refugees are undoubtedly motivated solely by the impossibility of continuing to live without persecution in their own countries. Some may be fleeing persecution in their homeland and be seeking a better job and income than is available there. Some may be primarily seeking to improve their economic position which is limited by the political or economic instability in their country of origin. Yet others will have identified the asylum system as a means of gaining access to the economic prosperity and welfare systems of Western Europe. (Session 2003–04 Second Report, Asylum Applications, HC 218 para 42)

Whether a person gets refugee status is as much a matter of whether they fit the legal definition as it is to do with the personal circumstances which led to their claim for asylum. It may be, for instance, that someone has been severely tortured in detention but, if that is not on account of one of the reasons provided for in the definition of a refugee, they will not be granted refugee status. In the UK legal system, asylum claims are dealt with in the same government department as border control (the UKBA). However, unlike for instance applications to visit a relative or study in the UK, it is very rare for someone to be able to enter the UK with the intention of claiming asylum without breaking immigration law in at least some respect. Asylum seekers fit into the immigration legal structure mainly as people who are subject to enforcement, and so the integration of asylum and immigration law facilitates the detention and removal of asylum seekers rather than protecting them.

This emphasis is shared in the EU:

> We are concerned that EU Member States and institutions are placing far greater emphasis on practical cooperation in border control than on refugee protection. Recent events in those EU states bordering the Mediterranean highlight the need to address the pressures faced by their asylum services and reception capacities. (Joint Refugee Council, Scottish Refugee Council and Welsh Refugee Council submission: House of Commons Home Affairs Committee inquiry on EU issues, September 2006)

12.1.2 A right to asylum?

The legal concept of asylum is nowhere near as old as the practice of seeking it. Dummett and Nicol (1990:143) say that 'the granting of asylum to refugees is as old as the concept of sovereign states'. The legal idea was originally conceived as a matter between states, not, as we tend to see it now, as a matter of an individual's claim for protection from a particular country. This original idea still has importance in the development of asylum law.

A national has the right to expect protection from their government. One way of looking at refugee status is that it steps in when that relationship has broken down to the extent that the state is not giving protection. Traditionally, the right involved in asylum is said to be the right of the state to grant asylum, not the right of the asylum seeker to receive it (see, for instance, Grahl-Madsen, *The Status of Refugees in International*

Law (1972)). The state owes its nationals a duty of protection, and nationals owe a duty of allegiance, but the state cannot insist on its nationals being returned to its territory (except in legally controlled extradition proceedings); another state can assert the right to give them asylum. The Universal Declaration of Human Rights 1948 Article 14 recognizes the right to 'seek and enjoy' asylum, but this is not a right to be granted asylum. Indeed, Shah (2000:61) recounts how at the stage of negotiating the terms of the Declaration a British amendment removed the words 'to be granted', substituting 'enjoy'. This means to be able to benefit from the status once it is granted, but not to be granted it. Member States of the European Union are now bound by the Refugee Qualification Directive Article 13, which says that Member States 'shall grant' asylum to those who qualify for it. Also, in the EU, Article 18 of the Charter of Fundamental Rights, which now has 'the same legal value' as the main Treaties, says that the right to asylum 'shall be guaranteed with due respect for the rules of the Refugee Convention'.

12.1.3 Refugee Convention

The 1951 Refugee Convention sets out the internationally agreed definition of who is a refugee and standards for treatment of refugees. The Convention was originally drafted to deal with the displacement of people as a result of the Second World War. It restricted the definition of refugees to those whose fear of persecution arose from events occurring in Europe before 1 January 1951. The Protocol of 1967 removed the time restriction and promoted a gradual removal of the geographical restriction but the refugee definition was not changed. The Convention was also drafted in the light of growing tension between East and West Europe, and was an instrument by which Western governments could prevent Communist ones from compelling the return of political dissidents.

The main present-day causes of refugee movements are armed conflict, large-scale human rights abuses, and environmental degradation. This last is an increasing cause through the escalating and mutually reinforcing phenomena of conflict and climate change. Thus, refugee recognition through the 1951 Convention is only a small part of the international phenomenon of people seeking refuge. Flight from war and drought were not in the mind of the drafters of the Refugee Convention. Its terms do not lend themselves easily to these situations, and the vast majority of uprooted people in the world do not apply for legal status through the Refugee Convention.

The UNHCR is the body given the task, worldwide, of protecting refugees and addressing the issues which give rise to refugee movements. People who have fled intolerable conditions but not used the Convention are referred to as de facto refugees, a much larger group than Convention, called de jure, refugees. By the end of 2010, the total population of concern to UNHCR, including internally displaced people, was just under 34 million. It is difficult to tell what proportion of displaced people eventually receive refugee status, partly because governments do not keep full statistics on outcomes. Some are granted protection under other international instruments, and some are granted refugee status on a group basis. Many are internally displaced (i.e., within their home country) and may return home soon, or after many years, or never. In Europe, the majority of grants of status are on the basis of an individual determination process, and it is this process and the law governing it that we are studying. According to UNHCR figures, in 44 industrialized countries, there were 370,358 such applications made in 2010.

Inevitably as the case law of the Refugee Convention is developed in signatory states rather than an international court, there have been some differences in interpretation between states. Consistency, however, is considered desirable. As the House of Lords in *Adan v SSHD* [2001] 1 All ER 593 affirmed, the meaning of the Convention is an autonomous meaning, in accordance with its purposes to provide an effective system of refugee protection, and should not differ between states. In the European Union, it is intended that there will be consistency of meaning to give effect to the Common European Asylum System (CEAS). The relationship between the Refugee Convention, EU, and domestic law is considered at 12.1.5.2. Case law of other jurisdictions, particularly New Zealand and Australia, is referred to in UK courts and tribunals as an aid to developing the law on new or contested points.

There are calls from a number of quarters for the Convention to be amended, but these come from opposing viewpoints. Some would like to see the Convention widened to include more contemporary forms of refugee movement, and situations that are at present difficult to bring within the Convention, such as the oppression of women and the abuse of children. Others would prefer to narrow the definition and so reduce the numbers of refugees that states can be obliged to take. Just as the Convention definition is a product of its time, a redraft would be the product of the present time.

The *UNHCR Handbook on Procedures and Criteria for Determining Refugee Status* is a recognized aid to interpretation of the Refugee Convention, as endorsed by the House of Lords in *T v SSHD* [1996] 2 All ER 865.

12.1.3.1 *Non*-refoulement: *Refugee Convention, Article 33*

The obligation which is central to the whole scheme of refugee protection is that of non-*refoulement*, imported into the Qualification Directive by Article 21. Article 33 says:

> No Contracting State shall expel or return (*refouler*) a refugee in any manner whatsoever to the frontiers of territories where his life or freedom would be threatened on account of his race, religion, nationality, membership of a particular social group or political opinion.

This means that, whether or not a state has an obligation to grant refugee status, it does have an obligation not to return someone on its soil to persecution. *Refoulement* can happen directly, by putting someone on a plane to their home country, or more controversially it is said that it may be done indirectly, by making their life so miserable and impossible that the better choice is to return and risk persecution. In this latter respect, some of the UK's legal provisions denying welfare support to asylum seekers have attracted adverse comment (see, for instance, Harvey in Twomey and Nicolson 1998). The obligation of non-*refoulement* applies to people seeking refugee status as well as those who are granted it, as the status is declaratory, in other words, to be granted refugee status means to have it recognized that one is a refugee, rather than to be made a refugee (Goodwin-Gill 1996:141).

One of the most difficult issues in present refugee law is the question of whether Article 33 is limited to those who have arrived in the territory of the contracting state. It is clear that the Refugee Convention does not apply to people who are still in their country of origin (*R v Immigration Officer at Prague Airport ex p European Roma Rights Centre* [2004] UKHL 55) and does apply once the asylum seeker reaches the territory of a destination state. However, the question of responsibility when asylum seekers are in transit is less clear. The US Supreme Court in *Sale, Acting Commissioner, INS v Haitian Centers Council* 113 S Ct 2549 (1993) ruled that the Convention did not apply outside the US territorial waters, and so the US did not act unlawfully in intercepting refugees on board ships from Haiti and returning them to Haiti. This decision has been criticized but no binding alternative authority has been established, although an Advisory Opinion requested from UNHCR cogently argues that the prohibition of *refoulement* applies 'wherever a State exercises jurisdiction, including at the frontier, on the high seas or on the territory of another State' (UNHCR 2007:12).

Den Heijer argues that the US Supreme Court placed too much importance on minority comments in the drafting history of the Convention, that it mistook the meaning of the word *refoulement,* and that the decision conflicts with the generally accepted notion that that obligations in human rights treaties not usually restricted to the territory of contracting states.

This view is not supported by an important decision by the ECtHR in which that court held that it was a breach of the Protocol 4 prohibition against the collective expulsion of aliens when Italy intercepted refugees at sea and took them to Libya (*Hirsi Jamaa v Italy* Application no. 27765/09). We have seen in chapter 7 how visa rules, airline liaison schemes, juxtaposed controls, and carrier sanctions can also prevent asylum seekers from ever reaching their territory in the first place (see Blake in Twomey and Nicholson 1998). Australia has openly adopted policies of offshore processing (the 'Pacific solution'), beginning with its notorious refusal to land the Norwegian ship the Tampa, which had rescued hundreds of asylum seekers from drowning. Despite international criticism and partially successful constitutional challenges in the Australian courts, the Refugee Convention did not avail the travellers.

12.1.4 Political nature of asylum

The grant of asylum implies criticism of the state of origin, as recognized by the Court of Appeal in *Krotov v SSHD* [2004] EWCA Civ 69: 'it is in the very nature of adjudication upon asylum issues that the tribunals or courts concerned with them are, for the purposes of surrogate protection underlying the 1951 Convention, obliged to examine and adjudicate upon events internal to another state' (para 42). Accepting that someone has a well-founded fear of being persecuted in their country of origin is an acknowledgement that the host state is offering protection where the country of origin has failed to do so. This is a humanitarian act, and thus should not be construed as a hostile action. As Dummett and Nicol say, quoting Lauterpacht: 'An enemy of his government is not an enemy of mankind' (1990:144). Unfortunately, sometimes an asylum claim which fails is treated as a hostile act committed by the asylum seeker themselves. In such a case there is a risk that someone whose asylum claim has failed may face persecution on returning to their country of origin for having made a claim. The question then is whether the failed asylum claim itself can give rise to a claim for asylum (see, e.g., *BK (DRC) v SSHD* [2008] EWCA Civ 1322, discussed in the next chapter).

It follows from Lauterpacht's principle that, not only must a home state allow an asylum claim to be made without taking revenge, but also that governments should not band together against the asylum seeker. Lauterpacht also says that the international community is not one of mutual insurance for the maintenance of established governments and that treason is not an international crime. However, in today's political climate, countries increasingly work together in the interests of national security and the fight against terrorism. For instance, the definition of 'national security' used in the House of Lords judgment in *Rehman v SSHD* [2001] 3 WLR 877 asserts that a threat to the security of one nation is a threat to all. This theme is explored more in chapter 14 in the context of exclusion from asylum and membership of organizations proscribed as terrorist.

Despite the humanitarian principles, there is no doubt that the grant of asylum is intimately connected with politics at all levels. Macdonald makes no bones about this:

The recognition rate for refugees has less to do with merits than with politics. Thus between 1989 and 1998 Canada granted refugee status to over 80% of applicants from Sri Lanka, France to 74%, and the UK to 1%: Refugee Council response to the Home Secretary's Lisbon Proposals, January 2001. (2001:468 n 2)

More recently, the European Court of Human Rights observed that '[a]n asylum system with a rate of recognition not exceeding 1 percent is suspect *per se* in terms of the fairness of the procedure', contrasting Greece's 1 per cent recognition rate with that of 60 per cent in Malta (*MSS v Belgium and Greece* [2011] ECHR 108). This example illustrates that the politics of recognition may be international in terms of the relationship between the host state and state of origin, but also regional.

As another example, at the outbreak of war with Iraq in March 2003, the hearing of Iraqi asylum appeals was suspended by the Immigration Appellate Authority, initially for six weeks. At a legal level, it is possible to see reasons for this as it could be difficult to assess the risk of persecution to an individual when the country to which they would be returned is in chaos. At a political level, to grant asylum to those individuals at that stage could be seen to undermine confidence in the outcome of the war.

12.1.5 Legal nature of the refugee claim in the UK

The system for claiming asylum has become integrated into the legal systems of signatory states and has become a branch of law in its own right. In the UK the choice was made at an early stage to give this responsibility to the Home Office, the same government department that deals with immigration, rather than an independent body. This is by contrast with countries such as Canada and New Zealand, where, although the same government department is often involved in immigration and asylum, there is a separate status determination and appeal process. As the Joint Refugee Councils' submission to the Home Affairs Committee said, 'the immigration controls introduced by the UK and other EU states are a blunt instrument that do not distinguish between those fleeing persecution and irregular migrants seeking to enter a country for other purposes'. Once this merging has taken place, it appears less controversial to make extensive use of detention and other draconian control measures, such as the removal of welfare support, because dealing with asylum claims is seen as part of managing migration and policing a frontier (see, for instance, Kostakopoulou and Thomas 2004 and Cornelisse 2004).

12.1.5.1 *Jurisdiction and appeal rights*

The Aliens Act 1905 gave the courts jurisdiction over the question of whether a person's circumstances would exempt them from deportation where political asylum could be claimed. However, when the 1905 Act was repealed and replaced by the Aliens Restriction Act 1914 and 1919, the exemption for refugees disappeared. Refugee status was a matter for the Secretary of State (*Bugdaycay* [1987] AC 514), not an independent body and not the appeals authority.

Immigration statutes continued to omit any provision for refugees until the Asylum and Immigration Appeals Act 1993 defined a claim for asylum as a claim that it would be contrary to the UK's obligations under the Refugee Convention for the claimant to be removed from the UK. This refers to the non-*refoulement* obligation under Article 33, and gave a statutory meaning to an asylum claim. When an application for asylum is refused, the appeal is not against refusal of asylum as such, but rather against the associated immigration decision. So for instance, a person may appeal against refusal of leave to enter the UK or a decision that they are to be removed from the UK (Nationality,

Immigration and Asylum Act 2002 s 82) *on the ground that* 'the removal of the appellant in consequence of the immigration decision would breach the UK's obligations under the Refugee Convention' (2002 Act s 84).

This means that the Tribunal hearing an appeal can only say that leave to enter should be granted, or that the appellant *should not* be removed. They cannot grant refugee status (*SSHD v R (on the application of Bakhtear Rashid)* [2005] EWCA Civ 744 para 37). In a successful case, it is the Home Office that sends the letter out granting asylum after the Tribunal office has sent its decision and reasons for allowing the appeal. In practice, if the Secretary of State does not go on to appeal to a higher court, the grant of asylum will follow the determination and reasons as a matter of course. There is no escaping that 'in asylum cases the appellate structure…is to be regarded as an extension of the decision-making process' (*Ravichandran v SSHD* [1996] Imm AR 97 at p.112). The procedures and principles by which asylum claims are decided are set out in the immigration rules paras 327–352 and in the Asylum Policy Instructions (APIs) and Asylum Process Guidance (APGs), disclosed on the Home Office website. The procedure should be in conformity with the Procedures Directive, which takes precedence over any inconsistent domestic provision.

12.1.5.2 *Directly effective EU law*

In the European Union, the Refugee Qualification Directive 2004/83 governs the interpretation of the Convention in Member States and has been implemented in the UK by the Refugee or Person in Need of International Protection (Qualification) Regulations 2006, SI 2006/2525 and changes to the immigration rules. The effect is that asylum law, which until 2006 was based solely on the Refugee Convention, general immigration rules and case law, has been placed on a legislative footing and the Home Office and courts must follow the regulations which implement the Directive. Additionally, with the Lisbon Treaty, the Court of Justice of the EU acquired jurisdiction in immigration and asylum matters. Accordingly, judgments of the CJEU are binding. There have been so far very few such judgments as the jurisdiction is new, but their impact is considerable. See *NS* at 12.11.3 and *Elgafaji* at 12.10.

After a major overhaul, the immigration rules now set out in unprecedented detail the criteria for granting asylum or humanitarian protection in the UK. They state that asylum claims will be decided in accordance with the Refugee Convention (para 328) and that asylum will be granted if the claimant is found to be a refugee in accordance with the regulations (para 334).

Where there are gaps in the rules or regulations, the Directive is directly effective and can be drawn upon (e.g., in *AD* [2007] UKAIT 00065 the Directive's definition of 'family member' was relied upon as there was not one in the immigration rules).

The Qualification Directive gives an EU-wide interpretation of all aspects of the definition of a refugee. We will discuss elements of the Directive when examining the refugee definition in the next chapter. It became binding on states on 10 October 2006 and applies to all asylum claims in a Member State after that date. If it appears in a particular case that the Refugee Convention and its case law are more generous than the Qualification Directive, it may be that the Convention will still be regarded as the authority. Symes suggests this is the case on the basis of Preamble 3 to the Directive: 'The Refugee Convention provides the cornerstone of refugee protection.' Lambert suggests the same on the basis of the EC treaty which provides for the primacy of treaty agreements entered into before conflicting European ones where these agreements are between Member States and third countries (Article 307 EC). This would apply to the Refugee Convention. An issue of this kind could now be referred to the CJEU.

Where the Directive is more favourable to refugees than the Refugee Convention and its case law, because it represents an agreed minimum standard, then it is binding (*SS (Libya) v SSHD* [2011] EWCA Civ 1547 para 25). The rights for refugees once status is awarded are, in the Qualification Directive Article 20, made explicitly subject to any greater rights granted by the Convention. This includes, in Article 21, the right to non-*refoulement*.

The new CJEU jurisdiction over immigration and asylum matters offers the first binding supranational source of refugee law. The Court's judgment in *NS* shows the potential of the Court to establish Europe-wide norms which integrate human rights protection into immigration and asylum law. The implication of *R (on the application of Pepushi) v Crown Prosecution Service* [2004] EWHC 798 (Admin), (see re Article 31 in chapter 14) was that Parliament could legislate its way out of international obligations which were not covered by the Qualification Directive. However, the CJEU held that a domestic statute governing asylum which allowed for violations of Article 3 ECHR was not compatible with EU law (see C–411/10 *NS v SSHD* at 12.11.3).

Challenges to secondary legislation need not go as far as the EU. The Court of Appeal in *EN (Serbia) v SSHD* [2009] EWCA Civ 630 endorsed the conclusion of the Parliamentary Joint Committee on Human Rights that delegated legislation which conflicted with the Refugee Convention and was made under a statutory power that purported to give effect to the Convention was ultra vires (see chapter 14 re Specification of Particularly Serious Crimes Order 2004, SI 2004/1910).

12.1.6 **Asylum and human rights claims**

Arguments under the European Convention on Human Rights, as enacted in the Human Rights Act, run alongside an asylum appeal and must be put forward at the same time as the grounds of appeal against a refusal of asylum by completing a form called a 'one stop notice'. This one-stop appeals system means that asylum seekers have one hearing at which their asylum and human rights claims are heard.

The Qualification Directive deals with some of the human rights protected under the ECHR as well as the Refugee Convention. Arguments that an asylum seeker will face treatment contrary to Article 3 ECHR, or Article 2 the right to life, are submissions that they merit 'subsidiary protection' under the Directive. The conditions for subsidiary protection appear in Article 15 of the Directive, and are that the individual is at risk of a violation of Article 3 ECHR, namely torture or inhuman or degrading treatment or punishment, or the death penalty or execution, or a 'serious and individual' threat to their life as a result of 'indiscriminate violence in international or internal armed conflict' in their home country (see discussion of C–465/07 *Elgafaji* in 12.10). The protection given is more limited than that to a refugee, but it is the first time that this kind of human rights protection has been collectively recognized by European states. Subsidiary protection does not cover other human rights claims such as a breach of Article 8 through separation from one's family by a threatened removal. These rights will still be governed by the safety net of the Human Rights Act.

Following the Qualification Directive, asylum and human rights cases involve consideration of at least three broad grounds (Symes 2006):

- First, that the Appellant deserves refugee status under the Directive.
- Second, that they merit subsidiary protection.
- Third, other human rights issues which could prevent their removal from the UK albeit not falling with the Directive's confines (e.g., Article 8).

Detailed provisions on granting humanitarian protection are found in the immigration rules (rules 339C–H).

12.2 Process of making an asylum application

The outline of the process of making an asylum application will be described in this section in order to give the context for the legal issues. Even before deterrent provisions were as fully developed as they are now, Schiemann J in *Yassine v SSHD* [1990] Imm AR 354 at 359 said that there were 'substantial obstacles in the path of refugees wishing to come to this country'. This was because:

1. Visa nationals require a passport before coming here;
2. You [sic] cannot get a visa on the basis of being a refugee in a country where you are being persecuted because at that stage you [sic] are usually not outside the country of nationality and thus do not fall within the definition of refugee and there is no provision for such situation in the immigration rules;
3. By reason of the 1987 Act carriers are disinclined to carry those without visas.

The Asylum and Immigration (Treatment of Claimants, etc.) Act 2004 has introduced further obstacles which will be discussed later in this chapter and in chapter 14.

Asylum applications may be made at the port of entry or at a later stage after legal or illegal entry. The latter are known as 'in-country' applications. Since March 2007, all new asylum claims must be made in person and are considered under the 'New Asylum Model' (NAM). In this model, the first interview is a screening interview which does not deal with the substance of the claim, but determines which route the claim is to follow. The NAM involves five routes, or 'segments', which determine: the speed at which the claim is processed; how the asylum seeker can obtain legal advice; the type of accommodation where they are required to live; how and where they are to remain in contact with the UKBA; and whether they are subject to electronic monitoring. At the screening interview the applicant is required to produce their identity documents, particularly their passport, which will be retained for the duration of the claim. As discussed in chapter 14, coming to the interview without a passport may be an offence. They will have fingerprints and photographs taken and be given an application registration card (ARC) which holds biometric details. A decision is taken on whether to detain the applicant or admit them on temporary admission (see chapter 15). Applicants from countries deemed safe or whose claims can be decided quickly may be detained immediately in Harmondsworth Removal Centre or Oakington Reception Centre and subjected to the 'fast-track' procedure (see 12.4).

The five segments of the NAM are shown in Table 12.1.

A key objective of the NAM was speed, and each segment was allocated a tight timetable with the aim of processing the majority of claims within two months, and all within six months. Although new claims are now decided more quickly, this objective has not been met.

In the NAM, each asylum claim is allocated to a 'case owner', who in theory, though not always in practice, sees the claimant through from arrival to refugee status or removal. The substance of the asylum claim is explained by the claimant at interview. Where, as in the majority of cases, the application is refused, the applicant receives what is known as a 'reasons for refusal' letter. These are discussed later in relation to the quality of decision-making.

Table 12.1 New Asylum Model (NAM)

Segment	Definition
1. Third country	People who the Home Office believes have, or could have, applied for asylum in a third country and are thus deemed ineligible for asylum in the UK. Some of these people are detained whilst others are not.
2. Minors	Unaccompanied minors and children in families who apply in their own right. Separated children may require a social services assessment to confirm their age and if they are accepted as a minor they are accommodated by social services. Until a social services age assessment determines that an age disputed young person should be dealt with as an adult their case will be processed through this segment, although they may be provided with support as an adult during this time. Case Owners dealing with cases in this segment have been specially trained to deal with children.
3. Potential non-suspensive appeal (NSA)	Nationals from one of the countries designated as generally 'safe'. Cases are considered on their merits but may be certified as clearly unfounded in which case the right of appeal has to be exercised from outside the UK. Individual asylum claims may also be certified clearly unfounded and attract only the NSA right. Some people in this segment are detained whilst others are not.
4. Detained fast-track	Any asylum claim, whatever the nationality or country of origin of the claimant, may be fast-tracked where it appears, after screening to be one that may be decided quickly.
5. General casework	Cases that do not come into any of the other categories. Some may be detained.

Reproduced with permission from the Refugee Council, *New Asylum Model* August 2007, showing the NAM as at that date (minor amendments made).

Minors are dealt with through a different process, as in the table. The conduct of children's asylum claims is now subject to the duty in s 55 Borders Immigration and Citizenship Act 2009 to have regard to the need to safeguard and promote the welfare of children. *ZH (Tanzania) v SSHD* [2011] UKSC 4 makes it clear children's welfare must be a primary consideration. This supplements one of the innovations brought by the Qualification Directive, which makes the best interests of a child a primary consideration in implementing social rights for refugees (Article 20.5), and recital 12 says that the best interests of the child should be a primary consideration in implementing the whole Directive. A lesser obligation has been transposed into UK law. Paragraph 350 of the immigration rules says that 'particular priority and care' is to be given to the handling of claims of unaccompanied minors.

12.2.1 Asylum interviews

The asylum interview is the time when the refugee gives their story, and the body of information upon which the claim will be decided. The quality of interpretation, the fairness of the interview, the skill and understanding of the interviewer, the resources given to the interview process, are all vital to the proper determination of the claim. The interview is a critical step in exercising the international obligation to determine an asylum claim and protect refugees, and if used properly, is not a judicial or adversarial function.

The *UNHCR Handbook* says,

> While the burden of proof in principle rests on the applicant, the duty to ascertain and evaluate all the relevant facts is shared between the applicant and the examiner. (para 196)

The Qualification Directive echoes the UNHCR's approach:

> Member States may consider it the duty of the applicant to submit as soon as possible all elements needed to substantiate the application for international protection. In cooperation with the applicant it is the duty of the Member State to assess the relevant elements of the application. (Article 4)

The API on interviewing says that:

> The purpose of the asylum interview is to establish the facts of an asylum claim. Whilst an asylum claimant might have submitted information to the Home Office previously, the asylum interview will be the principal opportunity for a claimant to set out their claim and for the caseworker to examine any details they consider necessary. (para 2.2)

Numerous inquiries into the asylum process have nevertheless commented on the poor and combative quality of asylum interviewing. For instance, Amnesty International recorded a perception by Home Office caseworkers of the interview as an opportunity to obtain material to attack the applicant's credibility by noting inconsistencies between the interview and the SEF and storing them up for a later refusal letter rather than putting the inconsistency to the applicant then and there (2004:20). The current APIs are a model of good practice in this respect, advising that any such discrepancies 'are thoroughly probed at interview', but it is clear from repeated studies of decision-making that the high standard of the APIs is not entirely maintained in practice. Interviewers have also been criticized for chaotic questioning, not dealing with the relevant issues, appearing adversarial and intimidating, and not dealing sympathetically or appropriately with those who have suffered trauma such as rape or torture (e.g., Asylum Aid 1999; Amnesty International 2004; and the Independent Asylum Commission 2008).

Since 1 April 2004, it has not been possible in most cases for an applicant to have public funding for a representative to be present at their asylum interview. The Court of Appeal in *R (on the application of Dirshe) v SSHD* [2005] EWCA Civ 421 held that where the applicant had no public funding either for a representative or for their own interpreter, the overall fairness of the process required that the applicant be able to tape record the asylum interview, so that there is some record of it independently of that kept by the Home Office. *Dirshe* has been interpreted as an obligation to record the interview 'on request by the claimant', and the Asylum Process Guidance (APG) says that where no advance request has been made, every effort should be made to arrange recording to enable the interview to go ahead. However, if the interview is not recorded, admission of the interview record is not automatically unfair (*MB (admissible evidence; interview record) Iran* [2012] UKUT 00019 (IAC)). Applicants may also request an interpreter or interviewer of their gender, and such requests should be acted upon.

From November 2010 UKBA is testing a new initiative, the Early Legal Advice Project, in which a lawyer is publicly funded to advise the asylum seeker before the initial interview, and to work with the refugee and UKBA to identify agreed and disputed issues at an early stage. The objective of the ELAP process is to 'get more cases right first time, identify those who are in need of protection earlier, manage public funds effectively, and increase confidence in the asylum system' (Early Legal Advice Project Guidance 2010). Paragraph 333C of the immigration rules, in force from 7 April 2008, provides that where an asylum seeker does not attend for interview, their claim may be treated as abandoned unless they show within a reasonable time that non-attendance was for reasons beyond their control.

12.2.2 Quality of initial decision-making

The immigration rules, para 339J, set out in general terms the matters which the Secretary of State must take into account in determining an asylum claim. A good quality initial decision is crucial. It is difficult for the applicant to obtain legal representation to appeal a wrong decision, and once poorly founded decisions go unchallenged, it becomes more difficult later on to address the contested issues.

The actual quality of asylum decision-making has by no means matched its importance as an implementation of an international protection treaty. Criticism of the process has been sustained from a variety of sources. Since 1995, numerous major reports from governmental and non-governmental organizations have been published which are critical in varying degrees of the asylum decision-making process. Some are listed in the reading at the end of this chapter. The reports on quality focused broadly on three areas: the interview, the reasons for refusal letter, and information about asylum seekers' country of origin. This last subject is treated separately at 12.7.4. Across all the reports, concerns are found in common, including:

- medical evidence corroborating horrific abuse was dismissed or misunderstood;
- proof was required to an excessively high standard (see chapter 13 for the asylum standard of proof);
- minor ambiguities or discrepancies were used to discredit the applicants, even when these had no bearing on the basis of the asylum claim;
- insensitivity in interviewing about serious trauma, particularly torture and rape;
- ignoring evidence relating to an individual;
- but also turning down claims on the basis that country-wide human rights reports documented abuses did not refer to the applicant personally;
- unreasonable assertions about individual credibility;
- inappropriate use of standard paragraphs in reasons for refusal letters;
- making findings at odds with the evidence.

The following example is extreme, and was recorded some years ago, but it makes the point. An asylum seeker had over a hundred burn marks on his back, and bruises where he had been held down. The reasons for refusal letter opined: 'Taking into account your appalling lack of credibility the Secretary of State considers that in fact these wounds were inflicted at your request in an attempt to strengthen your claim' (Asylum Aid 1999:19).

Since the first highly critical report by Asylum Aid in 1995, the quality of decision-making has improved. Despite the evidence of bodies including Asylum Aid, Freedom from Torture (formerly the Medical Foundation), the Constitutional Affairs Committee, the Home Affairs Select Committee, the House of Commons Public Accounts Committee, and the Independent Asylum Commission, there has been reluctance by governments to invest in the initial decision-making process. The Early Legal Advice Project (see 12.2.1) is the first exception. For instance, the Home Affairs Select Committee noted a 'steep rise in initial-level appeals', accompanied by a significant rise in the proportion of appeals which were successful (Second Report 2003–04 HC 218 para 122). The Committee took this as an indication of 'grounds for concern about the poor quality of much initial decision-making by immigration officers and caseworkers' (para 143). The government took the view that the way to deal with an increase in the number of appeals was to cut down the right of appeal. Thus, in the Asylum and Immigration

(Treatment of Claimants, etc.) Bill which became the 2004 Act they proposed reducing the appeals system to one tier. The Home Affairs Select Committee said in their comments on this proposal that '[t]he real flaws in the system appear to be at the stage of initial decision-making, not that of appeal' (First Report 2003–04 HC 109, para 43), and repeated this view in its report on asylum applications (HC 218 para 143). The Constitutional Affairs Committee ((HC 211 recommendation 5) also concluded that the problem did not lie in the arena of appeals but in the quality of initial decisions. The Home Affairs Committee recommended that there should be 'greater "front-loading" of the applications system, that is, putting greater resources into achieving fair and sustainable decisions at an early stage' (HC 218 para 144). It recommended more good-quality legal advice and interpretation at an early stage, recruitment of more caseworkers with specialist knowledge of asylum seekers' countries of origin and review of the 'overall calibre and training' of those who take initial decisions (para 144).

In 2005, the report of the Independent Race Monitor said:

> I reviewed samples of initial decisions and concluded that there was evidence of inappropriate decision-making. In some instances, caseworkers disbelieved claimants who told 'similar stories' about events, assuming they must have learned the details from others. Several refusal decisions were based on caseworkers' assumptions about what should have occurred, or on small discrepancies and inconsistencies in accounts of events, giving the impression that there was a tendency to disbelieve, and whatever the applicant's experience, some grounds for refusal would be found. (para 18)

The Independent Asylum Commission in 2008 found that 'the style and content' of substantive interviews often fell short, citing matters including inappropriate use of leading questions and failure to implement guidelines when interviewing traumatized women. The House of Commons Public Accounts Committee report on the Management of Asylum Applications (28 Report of Session 2008–09 HC 325) disclosed an improvement in decision-making, but that still in 136 of 580 refusal letters sampled the decision was rated as 'not fully effective' or 'poor'.

The UNHCR's Quality Initiative worked with UKBA from 2004 to 2009 to improve the quality of initial decision-making. They noted improvements made and the need for more. At the end of the programme, UNHCR remained involved to try to integrate good practices. After a pilot scheme in Solihull, the ELAP, mentioned earlier, is the first extensive attempt to devote resources to the initial decision-making process. The Solihull pilot had indicated the potential benefit, and it may be that ELAP heralds real change.

Numbers of appeals have dropped again, but the successful percentage at Tribunal stage has continued to slightly increase, reaching 27 per cent in the last quarter of 2010.

Where decision-makers lack the training or information to make a lawful decision, the consequences can be dire. See for example *R (on the application of Bakhtear Rashid) v SSHD* [2005] EWCA Civ 744, discussed in chapter 8, in which the claimant had been refused asylum in contravention of a Home Office policy apparently unknown to any caseworker or lawyer for the Home Office at each of the six decision-making points in his claim and appeal. The Court of Appeal held that this was unfairness amounting to an abuse of power.

12.2.3 Non-compliance refusals

Paragraph 339M of the immigration rules allows the Secretary of State to refuse an asylum or human rights claim where there is 'failure, without reasonable explanation, to make a prompt and full disclosure of material facts, either orally or in writing, or otherwise to assist the Secretary of State in establishing the facts of the case'. This includes failure to report for fingerprinting, or to comply with a request to attend an interview or report to an Immigration Officer for examination.

In *Haddad* (00HX00926), the Tribunal held that refusal must not be for non-compliance alone. The rules require, as we have seen, that applications must be determined in accordance with the Refugee Convention. Therefore even in a case of non-compliance, whatever evidence is available about the claim, even if it is in the form of brief notes taken by the immigration officer on arrival, must be considered (API on non-compliance). See Macdonald (2009: 279–280) for further discussion of the law surrounding these refusals. However, this must now be read in conjunction with para 333C referred to earlier, which allows the Secretary of State to treat the claim as abandoned if the applicant does not attend the interview.

12.3 'Clearly unfounded' – non-suspensive appeal

Under Nationality, Immigration and Asylum Act 2002 s 94(2), the Secretary of State has the power to certify that an asylum claim is 'clearly unfounded'. The result is that there will be no appeal in the UK. These are known as 'non-suspensive appeals' (NSAs), i.e., the appeal does not suspend the removal. As the claim will be refused (because the Secretary of State is saying it has no merit) the asylum seeker faces removal. An appeal from abroad, especially in a country where the person fears persecution, is worthless.

The decision to certify cannot itself be appealed, but only challenged by judicial review. In view of the serious consequences, the courts have maintained a demanding standard for the Secretary of State to show that the claim is unfounded. Case law has established that 'clearly unfounded' means 'bound to fail' (*R v SSHD ex p Thangasara and Yogathas* [2002] UKHL 36, concerning an earlier similar provision) or that the case is 'unarguable' (*R (on the application of Razgar) v Secretary of State for the Home Department* [2003] EWCA Civ 840, not overturned by the House of Lords). 'If the…claim cannot on any legitimate view succeed, then the claim is clearly unfounded, if not, not' (*ZL and VL v SSHD* [2003] 1 All ER 1062). The Court of Appeal put it in *NA (Iran) v SSHD* [2011] EWCA Civ 1172 that the claim is 'incapable of succeeding before an independent judicial tribunal' (para 40). In *ZT (Kosovo) v SSHD* [2009] UKHL 6, Lord Phillips said that the question of whether the claim was clearly unfounded could only have 'one rational answer. If any reasonable doubt exists as to whether the claim may succeed then it is clearly not unfounded.' Evidently, where evidence is still awaited, the claim cannot be certified. Home Office Statistics suggest that about 9 per cent of asylum claims are certified (Asylum data tables Immigration Statistics April–June 2011 Volume 1).

12.3.1 'Safe' countries of origin

Some countries are treated as 'safe', so that if an applicant is from one of these countries the Secretary of State must certify their claim unless satisfied that it is not clearly unfounded (s 94(3)).

The basis upon which a country or part of a country is designated as 'safe' is that the Secretary of State is satisfied that there is 'in general' in that state or that part of the state 'no serious risk of persecution' (s 94(5)). Blanket statements of safety sit rather uneasily with the requirement to investigate whether the particular applicant is at risk. Returning someone before their appeal is heard to a country where they fear persecution risks a breach of the principle of non-*refoulement*, and so the standard for designating a country as safe must be a rigorous one.

In making the decision to designate, the Secretary of State:

(a) shall have regard to all the circumstances of the State or part (including its laws and how they are applied), and

(b) shall have regard to information from any appropriate source (including other member States and international organisations). (s 94(5C))

This requirement was inserted by the Asylum (Procedures) Regulations 2007, SI 2007/3187, implementing Council Directive 2005/85/EC of 1 December 2005 on minimum standards on procedures in Member States for granting and withdrawing refugee status (the Procedures Directive). The Directive permits certification only where 'it can be shown that there is generally and consistently no persecution...no torture or inhuman or degrading treatment or punishment and no threat by reason of indiscriminate violence in situations of...armed conflict'. There is opposition within the EU to the concept of safe countries of origin and accelerated or suspensive procedures (see ECRE March 2005 and Statewatch 2004). The new subsection requires the Secretary of State to consider a broad base of evidence, whereas the section as originally enacted made no specifications as to how the Secretary of State should reach this view. Still there seems to be a gap between what the Directive requires and the amended UK statute. This may give scope for challenge in an individual case where it can be shown that the standard of the Directive is not met. There is an obligation in s 94A to make a 'European Common List of Safe Countries of Origin', if the Secretary of State thinks it necessary for the purpose of complying with the UK's obligations under Community law. However, the designation of countries as 'safe' is not agreed within the EU, and has been shelved for the time being.

Under the 2002 Act the Secretary of State is obliged to certify the claim unless satisfied that there are reasons to the contrary.

Section 94(3) says:

If the Secretary of State is satisfied that an asylum claimant or human rights claimant is entitled to reside in a State listed in subsection (4) he shall certify the claim...unless satisfied that it is not clearly unfounded.

The burden of proof is therefore on the claimant to show that the claim is not clearly unfounded. Proposals for revising the Procedures Directive emphasize the importance of an individual having an opportunity to demonstrate that their country of origin is not safe for them (COM(2011) 319 final). The UK is not opting into this revised Directive. In *ZL and VL v SSHD* and Lord Chancellor's Department [2003] 1 All ER 1062, the Court of Appeal set out the decision-maker's process of reasoning to certify a claim clearly unfounded:

(i) consider the factual substance and detail of the claim
(ii) consider how it stands with the known background data
(iii) consider whether in the round it is capable of belief
(iv) if not, consider whether some part of it is capable of belief
(v) consider whether, if eventually believed in whole or in part, it is capable of coming within the Convention. (para 57)

They concluded that there was 'no intelligible way' of certifying a claim from a listed country except by this same process (para 58). The burden of proof on the claimant and the practice of fast-tracking 'NSA' claims, discussed at 12.4, illustrate that in practice it is difficult to compel this individual consideration. However, see the case of *MD (Gambia)* at 12.3.2.

There is a power in s 94 to add to or remove from the list by Order made by the Secretary of State. The grounds for addition are that the Secretary of State is satisfied that:

(a) there is in general in that State or part no serious risk of persecution of persons entitled to reside in that State or part, and

(b) removal to that State or part of persons entitled to reside there will not in general contravene UK's obligations under the Human Rights Convention (s 94(5)).

States designated under Orders now in force are:

- Albania, Jamaica, Macedonia, Moldova, Bolivia, Brazil, Ecuador, South Africa, Ukraine (Asylum (Designated States) (No. 2) Order 2003, SI 2003/1919),
- India (Asylum (Designated States) Order 2005, SI 2005/330),
- Mongolia (SI 2005/3306),
- Bosnia-Herzegovina, Mauritius, Montenegro, Peru, Serbia (SI 2007/2221)
- Kosovo and South Korea (SI 2010/561).

The 2004 Act contains a further power for the Secretary of State to certify a state or part of a state safe in relation to a group of people (s 27(5), inserting s 94(5A) in the 2002 Act). The power was used for the first time in December 2005 to designate Ghana and Nigeria safe for men, and in 2007 also in respect of men: Gambia, Kenya, Liberia, Malawi, Mali, and Sierra Leone.

Criticisms could be and have been made of the inclusion of a number of these countries. For instance, it is difficult to reconcile the inclusion of Albania with the UK government's commitment to improve its policy and practice in relation to the protection of women trafficked for sex, Albania being one of the major centres of organized crime of this kind. The speed with which a claim may be refused and the person returned without an appeal hearing may give rise to real risks in individual serious cases such as that of A. In *Atkinson v SSHD* [2004] EWCA Civ 846 (see chapter 13) the Court of Appeal held that there was at least an arguable case that the criminal justice system offered insufficient protection for the applicant in Jamaica. The claim should not have been certified.

12.3.2 Challenging designation

There are two levels of decision which may be challenged. One is the specific decision to certify the particular claim, as in Atkinson's case, as clearly unfounded. The more fundamental challenge is to the designation of a country within s 94. The designation of Bangladesh was successfully challenged in *R (on the application of Zakir Husan) v SSHD* [2005] EWHC 189 (Admin). Wilson J held the inclusion of Bangladesh to be irrational and therefore unlawful in the light of a volume of evidence about widespread human rights violations in the country. The picture painted by official reports at the time was that violence in politics was pervasive, the use of torture was widespread, abuse of children and violence against women and religious minorities was common and widespread and corruption endemic (*Husan* para 55). Bangladesh was removed from the list of safe countries (Asylum (Designated States) (Amendment) Order 2005, SI 2005/1016).

The arguments in *Husan* raised questions about the basis for designating a country as 'in general' one in which there is no serious risk of persecution. The Secretary of

State relies in part on the low number of successful asylum claims from a country in determining whether it can be designated. Wilson J exposed the fallacy in this reasoning. He pointed out that poor economic conditions might well drive some people to make asylum claims which would be refused, but that this did not indicate a low risk of persecution in the country. It was disclosed that in Parliament a minister had replied that concerns about human rights in Bangladesh did not mean that 'the vast majority' of Bangladeshi nationals were at risk of having their human rights abused, apparently confusing the question of whether there was in general a serious risk of persecution with a risk of general serious persecution. The Minister advanced the reason for designation that 'it gives people the message that it is not worth coming unless they believe that they have a genuine claim' (para 21). The certification process does not, of course, test the genuineness of the applicants' beliefs.

In the case of Sri Lanka, the government removed the designation following many challenges to the certification of individual Sri Lankan claimants. The designation of Sri Lanka followed a peace accord in that country, but conflict broke out again very shortly after the order was made. In 2004, the UN Human Rights Committee called on the Sri Lankan government to cease using confessions extracted by torture (Advocacy.net news bulletin no. 23, 2 November 2004). Human rights groups continued to press that Sri Lanka was not a safe country. In December 2006, the government repealed the designation of Sri Lanka on account of the deteriorating situation there.

In *ZL and VL v SSHD and Lord Chancellor's Department* [2003] 1 All ER 1062, the Master of the Rolls held that the inclusion of a country in the so-called White List did not mean that there was no risk of any breach of Convention rights. It seems to be easier to identify what inclusion in the List does not mean rather than what it does mean. Persecution is only in the most extreme cases a phenomenon encountered 'in general' in a country. This is inherent in the concept of discrimination. In *Husan*, the evidence was that Bangladesh ranked worst in the world on a Corruption Perceptions index (UK Foreign and Commonwealth Office 2004) and was either second or fourth worst in the world for violence against women (Immigration and Refugee Board of Canada). The widespread nature of torture and police brutality and corruption meant that any individual could be at risk. So, whatever a country is in which there is 'in general' no serious risk of persecution, it is not this, following *Husan*.

An earlier challenge to the inclusion of India failed (*R (on the application of Balwinder Singh) v SSHD and Special Adjudicator* [2001] EWHC Admin 925) on the basis that, although Sikhs (in that case) may be persecuted, they were too small a percentage of the population to mean there was a risk of persecution 'in general'. 'In general' did not mean 'recurring', 'ongoing', or 'predictable'. It referred to the spread of persecution over the population. Burton J also found that there was nothing illegal in the Secretary of State having a policy of this kind, and that this did not interfere with each case being decided on its merits.

The first challenge to designation was in *R v SSHD ex p Javed and Ali* [2001] Imm AR 529, in which the designation of Pakistan under an earlier statute was found to be unlawful. The claimants relied in particular on the House of Lords' judgment concerning women in that country in *Shah and Islam* (see chapter 13) and the recorded position of Ahmadis there. These were evidence of persecution of women and religious minorities. The challenge raised a constitutional question. The Secretary of State argued that the designation could not be challenged as it had been made by affirmative resolution in Parliament, which was argued to be a proceeding in Parliament. To interfere with it would therefore be a breach of Article 9 of the Bill of Rights 1689 which prohibits proceedings in Parliament from being questioned in the courts. The Court of Appeal did not accept that argument. By approving the Order, Parliament had not debated its justification in detail or examined the evidence for it. Even though the Order was made by affirmative resolution it was still delegated legislation and as such open to judicial review in the usual way. Having disposed of the constitutional point the Court of Appeal found that, on the evidence concerning women and Ahmadis, the Secretary of State's decision to include Pakistan in the White List was irrational.

The most recent challenge to designation was that of Gambia, in *R on the application of MD (Gambia) v SSHD* [2011] EWCA Civ 121. The challenge to the designation of Gambia failed. Although there was accepted evidence of human rights abuses, the Court of Appeal held that they were not such as to enable them to regard the Secretary of State's designation of Gambia as irrational. However, the Court held that this evidence was relevant in the individual case, and the certificate relating to MD was quashed. It could not be said that his case was bound to fail.

12.4 Fast-track procedures

In parallel with the non-suspensive appeal, from 2000 onwards there has been a policy of detaining people whose claims appear to be ones that can be decided quickly. The Joint Committee on Human Rights, in its Report on Treatment of Asylum Seekers, explained that:

> the Home Office Five Year Strategy sets out plans to process up to 30% of new cases using detained fast track. IND states that the process is geared to claimants being detained pending a quick decision on their asylum claims, and that the average timescale from making a claim to removal is one month, including any appeal.

Certain detention centres, renamed 'removal centres', were designated to detain people on a 'fast track'. Initially, this was a system run only at Oakington Reception Centre, where the asylum decision could be made quickly. The claimant might then be released. The legal foundation for the Oakington system is discussed in chapter 15. In 2003, a new fast-track system was set up which included the initial decision and appeal process, all to be completed within less than two weeks. The system was first implemented for men at Harmondsworth, then extended to women at Yarl's Wood. Now it operates at a number of centres.

Until early 2008, selection of claims to pass through the fast track was based on a departmental list of countries of origin, compiled under the authority of a ministerial authorization to discriminate on the basis of nationality (Race Relations Act 1976 s 19D, see chapter 8). The list included some countries from which claims could be certified as NSA, but also some that could not. The list has since been abolished, and replaced with a policy that

> any asylum claim, whatever the nationality or country of origin of the claimant, may be considered suitable for DFT/DNSA processes where it appears, after screening (and absent of suitability exclusion factors), to be one where a *quick decision* may be made. This assessment must be made on a case by case basis. (DFT & DNSA – Intake Selection (AIU Instruction) para 2.2)

The guidance goes on to give a list of situations in which detaining in the fast track would be inappropriate, for instance, people who are seriously mentally ill, women in the late stages of pregnancy, and families including children. Claims are decided in three days. Appeals are heard on the premises. Two days are allowed to give notice of appeal, two days for a respondent's notice, and the hearing must be fixed within two days after that (Immigration and Asylum Appeal (Fast Track Procedure) Rules 2005, SI 2005/560). Legal representation is not automatically available.

Concerns about the fairness of this system have been expressed by UNHCR, BID, the Independent Asylum Commission, the Joint Committee on Human Rights and Detention Action. They argue that the two-day time limit for appealing is too short, and runs the risk of returning someone to persecution, thus contravening the Refugee Convention (*Asylum and Immigration Tribunal – Fast Track Procedure Rules, Response to Consultation* CP(R) 05/05 Department for Constitutional Affairs). Some key findings of the BID research were:

- 77 per cent of detainees did not have publicly funded representation at their appeal hearing
- There was inadequate time to prepare the case
- Claims of torture were made but not investigated
- Detainees did not know why they were in the fast track or what it entailed
- 60 days after the appeal hearing, one third of the detainees were still detained. (2006:8).

The Joint Committee on Human Rights concluded:

> 226. We are concerned that the decision to detain an asylum seeker at the beginning of the process simply in order to consider his or her application may be arbitrary because it is based on assumptions about the safety or otherwise of the country from which the asylum seeker has come. It is self-evident that some asylum seekers – most obviously torture victims and those who have been sexually abused – are unlikely to reveal the full extent of experiences to the authorities in such a short-time period, and that this problem will be exacerbated where they are not able to access legal advice and representation, and the support of organisations able to help them come to terms with their experiences.
>
> 227. We are also concerned that although fast track detention for anything more than a short, tightly controlled period of time is unlawful, some asylum seekers find themselves detained at the beginning of the asylum process for periods in excess of this. The act of claiming asylum is not a criminal offence and should not be treated as such. If asylum seekers are detained at the beginning of the asylum process, then the period of detention should be limited to a maximum of seven days.
>
> 228. We recommend that asylum seekers who are detained as part of the fast track and super fast track processes should be provided with free, on-site legal advice – for example, on the model previously provided by the Refugee Legal Centre and the Immigration Advisory Service at Oakington – to ensure that victims of torture and other forms of abuse are identified and taken out of the process; and that claims for asylum are properly considered. (Tenth Report 2006–07: Treatment of Asylum Seekers)

The lawfulness of the fast track was challenged by the Refugee Legal Centre, but the Court of Appeal held that, although the system was not operating with sufficient flexibility and improvements should be made, it was not inherently unfair and therefore could not be said to be unlawful (*R (on the application of the Refugee Legal Centre) v SSHD* [2004] EWCA Civ 1481 at para 25). Operational instructions were revised to respond to the Court of Appeal's comments, to make provision for such contingencies as, for example, the illness of the applicant, non-attendance or lateness of representative, and the need for more evidence to be gathered.

Although the legal process is fast, once the claim has been denied and the appeal lost, the claimant may then face a considerable period in detention before being removed.

BID found that two months' detention following failure of the claim was common, and reported an instance of 10 months of such detention (BID to Des Browne, Minister for Citizenship and Immigration 15 March 2005). Detention Action's findings in 2010–11 were similar, including an average wait of 58 days spent after the process was over, awaiting removal.

Harmondsworth, the main site of fast-track detention, is only for single men, interpreted by the Minister for Citizenship and Immigration as 'men who have no dependants on their claim' (HC Debs 16 September 2004 col 158WS). The claimant argued in *Kpandang v SSHD* [2004] EWHC 2130 Admin that his detention in Harmondsworth was unlawful because he had a partner and child. McCombe J was persuaded that 'single' meant that the detention facilities were for men on their own, not that they were unmarried. He also held that short detention in reasonable circumstances was not a breach of Article 8, given other justifications for detaining the claimant (and see *R v SSHD ex p saadi* [2002] UKHL 41, discussed in chapter 15).

Harmondsworth has had a very troubled history. The Chief Inspector of Prisons has found the centre 'unsafe' (2003), and there have been a number of hunger strikes and suicides. In 2006, there was a major disturbance and the centre was closed for several months. The 2008 and 2010 reports suggested that after partial re-opening problems were being addressed, with detainees feeling more respected, though there was still some way to go. After an extension, Harmondsworth is now the biggest immigration detention centre in Europe, with 615 beds.

Yarl's Wood is for women and families. Research into the experiences of women there suggests that there are serious problems with the fairness of the system, for instance:

> Applications to be taken out of the Detained Fast Track were rejected in the following cases: a complex case involving torture, suicidal tendencies, sexuality, and a lack of medical evidence; sexual violence; exceptional circumstances based on sexual assault; pregnancy (the appellant was 26 weeks pregnant). (Cutler 2007)

By way of example, one woman's claim based on forced marriage, rape, and threat of female genital mutilation (FGM) was adjourned for one hour to be examined by the detention centre doctor. She was refused the same day at the hearing where the medical evidence was not considered (2007:11). Legal representation is available at public expense to all women for their initial asylum claim, using a rota system maintained by the Legal Services Commission (LSC). Representatives without a fast-track contract cannot undertake fast-track work using legal aid, although privately charging lawyers can and do. The data gathered by BID suggests that the quality of legal representation on the rota is varied. Allocation to a lawyer is administered by the Home Office. Should women be unhappy with the quality of work or a decision not to represent them at their appeal, the timetable continues, leaving detainees without representation and vulnerable to refusal and removal.

Applications to take cases out of the fast track do not always succeed, even when the detainee is a torture survivor (see, e.g., *R (on the application of MT) v SSHD, GSL UK Ltd, Nestor Health Care Services plc* [2008] EWHC 1788 (Admin) and *R (on the application of Ngirincuti) v SSHD* [2008] EWHC 1952 (Admin)). In *R (on application of Sidibe)* [2007] EWCA Civ 191 the applicant's solicitors had applied on at least three occasions within a few days to have the case taken out of the fast track. An expert confirmed that there were complex issues that needed more evidence, but the Secretary of State still refused to take the case out of the fast track on the basis that the right of appeal (within the fast track) would be enough to deal with issues. Moses J held that this was not so. Following evidence given in the *Refugee Legal Centre* case, the claim should have been taken out of the fast track as soon as it was apparent that more evidence was needed (*Re Sidibe*, see also chapter 17).

In *R (on the application of Suckrajh) v AIT and SSHD* [2011] EWCA Civ 938 the Court of Appeal held that the DFT could be used to carry out examination of someone who was at liberty in the UK, where new evidence suggested his asylum claim could be decided quickly. Mr Suckrajh's claim was under consideration, and he had been at liberty for nearly a year when he was detained under the fast track. Protection of the public and risk of absconding were clearly also reasons that he was detained. The Court of Appeal held that these were legitimate reasons, and as the new evidence indicated the case could be decided quickly, it was not unlawful to use the fast track.

This is a new departure, as the detained fast track had previously been regarded as limited to detention on arrival.

12.5 Credibility

Credibility is the term used to refer to whether or not the decision-maker believes the applicant is telling the truth about their claim. An assessment of an applicant's credibility is made by the Home Office, and then upheld or overturned by the immigration judge at the appeal. Arguably, the subject of credibility could fill a chapter on its own, or be dealt with in the next chapter, or chapter 14, or this one, or not at all. In determining refugee claims the question of credibility is both everything and nothing. It is not an aspect of the refugee definition to be satisfied, like the matters covered in the next chapter, and yet the majority of asylum claims which are lost are lost precisely because of adverse findings on credibility – in other words the decision-maker does not believe the applicant's story.

Credibility can be considered alongside 'well-founded fear' as discussed in chapter 13. A fear will only be well founded if it is genuine. As the main source of evidence is usually the asylum seeker themselves, the assessment of whether that person is to be believed is crucial. If the decision-maker does not believe the asylum seeker's account, they are found not to be credible and their claim will fail. Difficulties arise where decision-makers disbelieve asylum seekers too readily and make negative credibility findings very early on in the process without assessing all the evidence.

What must be credible is the main part of the asylum seeker's story. Unfortunately, the issue of credibility has become entangled with the question of assessing whether they are afraid. This issue is discussed further in the next chapter, where it is contended that decision-makers should not be looking to establish that the refugee has a subjective state of trepidation about what they might face if returned to their home country. This is not what proves they are at risk. It is not appropriate to require the decision-maker to assess the inner state of a person whose culture and circumstances may be very far from their own. Hathaway and Hicks (2005, see further reading for chapter 13) describe how this impossible quest leads decision-makers to attempt to 'objectify' the asylum seeker's state of mind with questions such as 'did you claim asylum at the first opportunity?' The implication is that, if not, the asylum seeker was not genuinely afraid. This kind of subjective objectivity has found its way into the immigration rules (see 12.5.2) and presents a major difficulty in asylum claims. A very important principle in asylum law is that, although the asylum seeker has to prove their case, there is no requirement for their evidence to be corroborated from another source, as there would be in a civil case (*SSHD v Karakas* [1998] EWCA Civ 961). The standard of proof is a reasonable degree of likelihood or a 'real risk' (see Sivakumaran and Karanakaran, chapter 13). This is particularly important given that an asylum seeker may well have quickly fled their country in fear of persecution and not have been in a position to collect relevant documentation before their departure. Furthermore, when travelling clandestinely in order to avoid the authorities, it would not be desirable to be holding information on their person, such as an arrest warrant, which would identify them as wanted by the authorities if they were stopped en route. It is often the case, therefore, that the asylum seeker's evidence consists of their written statement and objective country information but little else. To penalize them for this is to undermine asylum. In *TK (Burundi) v SSHD* [2009] EWCA Civ 40, the Court of Appeal held that, where corroboration was easily available, it should have been produced. The context was that the appellant's asylum had failed on an earlier occasion because he had not been believed; in the current appeal, he had failed to produce corroboration of his family life claim in the UK. Whether this simple principle can be extended to evidence of the asylum claim itself is debatable. A judgement about what is easily available could risk entering the same territory as judgements of what is 'inherently' probable, a practice which will shortly be shown to be problematic.

The case of *Chiver (10758)* is an authority on the proper approach to credibility. The adjudicator in that case pointed to the discrepancies in the respondent's story in order to, in the words of the Tribunal:

> list the matters which were adverse to the respondent's case and to reflect his belief that they did not affect the kernel of his story. He adopted the approach which is urged upon adjudicators i.e. to weigh up the evidence and to indicate that which is believed and that which is not.

From this it may be gleaned that some inconsistencies are not fatal to the claim. The question is whether the immigration judge believes the core of what is claimed, or, in the oft quoted words in *Chiver*, whether 'the centerpiece of the story stands'. In the same case the Tribunal pointed out that there may be perfectly valid and understandable reasons for exaggeration or not telling the truth, which do not mean the asylum claim is not valid. For instance, a claimant may embroider their story if they fear it is not strong enough or change facts which they fear will be thought implausible. Gorlick (2002) quotes Hathaway as making the same point, that dishonesty, though not to be encouraged, is explicable for instance 'when bad advice is received from traffickers or others viewed by an asylum seeker as an expert'.

Immigration judges are warned about judging facts to be implausible. Hathaway (1991:81) points out that it is not in the nature of repressive societies to behave reasonably. Decision-makers should not place weight on their own subjective and culturally bound views about a claimant's demeanour or way of giving a statement or evidence.

This was evident in *HK v SSHD* [2006] EWCA Civ 1037, where the Court characterized the facts as 'unusual and remarkable'. Nevertheless, the evidence was consistent and there was no contradictory evidence. The Court gave important guidance:

> Inherent probability, which may be helpful in many domestic cases, can be a dangerous, even a wholly inappropriate, factor to rely on in some asylum cases. Much of the evidence will be referable to societies with customs and circumstances which are very different from those of which the members of the fact-finding tribunal have any (even second-hand) experience. Indeed, it is likely that the country which an asylum-seeker has left will be suffering from the sort of problems and dislocations with which the overwhelming majority of residents of this country will be wholly unfamiliar. (para 29)

The mere concept of inherent improbability is inappropriate where one has no real grasp of what would be inherent in a situation. The Court of Appeal in *Gheisari v SSHD*

[2004] EWCA Civ 1854 took a slightly different but related tack, saying that just because something is inherently improbable does not mean it is not true.

It is still legally permissible to find the claimant's account inherently implausible, even though such a conclusion should be reached with extreme care. In *MM (DRC – Plausibility) Democratic Republic of Congo* [2005] UKIAT 00019, the appellant claimed to have escaped leaving his clothes in the hands of a soldier who was restraining him, and then have vaulted a six-foot wall while six other soldiers were outside the house in which he and his family had been seized. His advocate at the Tribunal advanced possible explanations, but the Tribunal held that, where there were possible explanations, these should be advanced by the claimant, not speculated upon by his representative. In the absence of such alternative explanations, the adjudicator had not been wrong to find this account inherently implausible, and to do so it did not need to be outside the realm of human experience, thus declining to follow an Australian decision, *W148/00 A v Ministry for Immigration and Multicultural Affairs* [2002] FCA 679.

In *MM*, the Tribunal gave further guidance on the treatment of the claimant's evidence. A decision-maker should be wary of relying on the demeanour of a witness. Conclusions drawn from this are too likely to be subjective and rely on interpretation of behaviour. It is the content of evidence rather than the way it is given that should inform credibility.

It is difficult to overturn credibility findings on appeal, because appeals are restricted to points of law, and it is difficult to establish that an immigration judge's decision on credibility amounts to an error of law. However, in *NM (Afghanistan) v SSHD* [2007] EWHC 214 (Admin), the Court held that the immigration judge's finding on credibility was not soundly reasoned because he had made an error in interpreting the legal relevance of the claimant's passport application, and it could not be ruled out that his understanding of these events had affected his view of the claimant's credibility. This is not to say that reasons must always be given for all aspects of a credibility finding. As the Court of Appeal said in *B v SSHD* [2006] EWCA Civ 922, 'inadequate reasons may be a guide but they are only a guide to the ultimate question which... is whether or not the decision is one which the Tribunal was entitled to reach on the evidence which was before it' (para 18).

In *Koca v SSHD* [2005] CSIH 41, the Court held that the Adjudicator should have put to the appellant the discrepancies upon which she based her adverse credibility findings. Remarks of the Court of Appeal in *HH (Somalia) v SSHD* [2010] EWCA Civ 426 offer an important corrective to placing too much reliance on credibility. The Tribunal suggested that the finding that the appellant had lied and disabled them from reaching a conclusion on the Article 3 risk. The Court said this was mistaken:

> They first have to ask whether there is other evidence, independently of his unreliable testimony, casting light on the appellant's particular situation. If so, they must have regard to that evidence. (para 118)
>
> Even a mendacious appellant is entitled to protection from *refoulement* if objective evidence shows a real risk that return will place his life and limb in jeopardy. (para125)

12.5.1 Credibility and expert evidence

In *Slimani* 01/TH/00092, in a starred determination, the Tribunal restated the principle that decision-makers should give reasons for finding evidence, in this case expert evidence, to be implausible. The issue of credibility is bound up with the conduct of hearings and the whole question of fairness in the decision-making process. Expert evidence should be assessed on its merits.

The Amnesty International report on initial decision-making noted a practice of forming a negative view of the claimant's credibility based on a subjective response to the claimant, then discounting other evidence in the light of that view. This practice appeared in the decision of an adjudicator in *Mibanga v SSHD* [2005] EWCA Civ 367. The Court of Appeal found that the adjudicator should have looked at all the evidence, including that from the Medical Foundation and a professor with extensive knowledge of the Democratic Republic of Congo, before forming a view of the claimant's credibility. It was not appropriate to treat the claimant as not credible and then discount other evidence on the basis of that. This continues to be the proper approach (see, e.g., *KM (Somalia) v SSHD* [2009] EWCA Civ 466). *Mibanga* was distinguished in *SA (Somalia) v SSHD* [2006] EWCA Civ 1302, where the medical report did no more than repeat the claimant's explanation for the scars. The immigration judge formed a negative view of the claimant's credibility and the medical report did not provide independent evidence of that.

AJ Cameroon [2005] UKIAT 00060 warned against immigration judges making their own assessment of scars. In the rare case where an immigration judge 'has specific skills, qualifications, knowledge and experience, then he or she should disclose them to the parties and make clear what use, if any, it is intended to put them to in the course of the hearing and determination process' (para 34). An immigration judge should not conduct physical examinations in the hearing. Conversely, a medical expert should not draw conclusions on credibility (*HH (Ethiopia) v SSHD* [2007] EWCA Civ 306). This conclusion is less obvious than that in *AJ Cameroon*. The Medical Foundation and other organizations which support torture victims say that insufficient attention is given to the effects of trauma on memory when assessing inconsistencies. The UN Committee Against Torture also advise that these effects should be taken into account. Jane Herlihy and Stuart Turner draw attention to 'a great deal of empirical literature concerning the tendency for repeated interviews to introduce inconsistency, particularly in the more vulnerable applicant' (2009:187). They cite, for instance, Juliet Cohen (2001), an experienced medical examiner at the Medical Foundation, who describes processes by which new memories of actual but forgotten events and innocently constructed memories of things that never happened can be introduced by repeatedly interviewing a claimant.

The evidence of psychologists and psychiatrists has an important role to play in explicating for decision-makers the psychological effects of trauma, with potential effects on the assessment of credibility. One difficulty that the legal system has had with evidence of psychological symptoms is that, to a greater extent than physical, they are self-reported. However, psychiatric reports should not be dismissed on this account (*XS (Serbia and Montenegro)* [2005] UKIAT 00093). The weight to be given to psychiatric evidence must depend upon the authority of the witness and their independence.

Expert evidence about conditions in a country may be very significant to the claim. The Tribunal in *LP (Sri Lanka CG)* [2007] UKAIT 00076 held that significant weight should be given to evidence from the British High Commission as it was 'compiled by professional diplomats who are skilled and trained in the observation and acquisition of knowledge in the countries in which they are based' (para 205).

12.5.2 Section 8 AITOC and the immigration rules

The immigration rules in HC 395 para 339L, implementing Article 4 of the Qualification Directive, provide a demanding standard for credibility. Where aspects of the person's statements are not supported by documentary or other evidence, those aspects will not need confirmation when all of the following conditions are met:

(i) the person has made a genuine effort to substantiate his asylum claim...;

(ii) all material factors at the person's disposal have been submitted, and a satisfactory explanation regarding any lack of other relevant material has been given;

(iii) the person's statements are found to be coherent and plausible and do not run counter to available specific and general information relevant to the person's case;

(iv) the person has made an asylum claim...at the earliest possible time, unless the person can demonstrate good reason for not having done so; and

(v) the general credibility of the person has been established.

How this rule operates depends very much upon where the emphasis is placed. According to *UNHCR Handbook* para 196, the applicant should be given the benefit of the doubt in establishing their claim where supporting evidence is not available.

Asylum and Immigration (Treatment of Claimants etc) Act 2004 s 8 creates a new obligation for a 'deciding authority' to take into account as damaging the claimant's credibility factors which that authority 'thinks' are deliberately misleading. It further sets out a list of behaviours which *shall* be treated as designed to conceal information or mislead. These include failure to produce a passport, destruction of documents and failure to answer a question, in each case without reasonable explanation. Other matters are listed without provision for a reasonable explanation: production of a document which is not a valid passport as if it were and failure to claim in a safe third country or make a claim before an immigration decision or arrest under an immigration provision.

This extraordinarily draconian provision (so says Macdonald 2008:948) contradicts the core principle that an evaluation of all the facts is necessary, and deception about one matter does not necessarily mean that the claim itself is false. In *SM Iran* [2005] UKAIT 00116, an early case on the use of s 8, the Tribunal made it clear that it was not going to be overly bound by this parliamentary attempt at inroads into the decision-making process, saying that there was:

> no warrant at all for the claim...that the matters identified by section 8 should be treated as the starting point of a decision on credibility. The matters mentioned in s 8 may or may not be part of any particular claim; and their importance will vary with the nature of the claim that is being made, and the other evidence that supports or undermines it. (paras 7 and 9)

The Court of Appeal in *JT (Cameroon) v SSHD* [2008] EWCA Civ 878 is the present authority, endorsing that approach.

Key Case

***JT (Cameroon) v SSHD* [2008] EWCA Civ 878**

The appellant was a citizen of Cameroon who arrived in the UK using false papers. He used two identities while in the UK. He claimed asylum following his arrest for offences connected with the use of false documents. His claim was refused. On appeal, the Tribunal did not accept that the appellant had escaped from detention in the way he had described, nor that he had any political profile in Cameroon or faced serious harm on return. The Tribunal said that very serious damage had been done to the appellant's credibility by the operation of section 8.

The Court agreed that the statute required that the matters listed in section 8 must be taken into account when assessing credibility, and were capable of damaging it, but the section did not dictate that damage to credibility inevitably resulted. The section could be read as if it said 'potentially damaging the claimant's credibility'. Section 8 was no more than a reminder to fact-finding tribunals that conduct coming within the categories stated should be taken into account in assessing credibility. The weight to be given to it was entirely a matter for the fact-finder. The case was remitted to a different tribunal.

12.6 Asylum appeals

As explained at the beginning of this chapter, an appeal against the refusal of an asylum claim is made by appealing the underlying immigration decision on asylum grounds.

There are differences between appeals on asylum grounds and other appeals. The Tribunal also carries the obligation of non-*refoulement*, and there is some obligation in the direction of a more inquisitorial process, rather than being simply an arbiter between two arguments. This should not be taken to the point of excessive intervention in cross-examination, taking hostile points against the appellant which the Home Office had not thought fit to raise (*XS Serbia and Montenegro* [2005] UKIAT 00093). In *AM (Pakistan) v SSHD* [2011] EWCA Civ the Court of Appeal did not accept an argument that the immigration judge had been in error for failing to view a video which was central to the appellant's claim. Neither the appellant's representative nor the Home Office had asked for it to be viewed. When it finally was viewed by the Upper Tribunal it became clear that it would have made a substantial difference to the case. The Court of Appeal declined to place any responsibility on the Tribunal for the examination of evidence. The procedure of asylum appeal hearings is governed by the Asylum and Immigration Tribunal (Procedure) Rules 2005, SI 2005/230 as amended.

As the House of Lords said in the case of *Bugdaycay v SSHD* [1987] AC 514, an asylum claim involves matters of such great importance that judicial bodies should subject each case to 'the most anxious scrutiny'. Evidence should be admitted of 'any matter which the Tribunal thinks relevant to the substance of the decision, including evidence which relates to a matter after the date of the decision' (2002 Act s 85(4)). This is particularly important and relevant in asylum claims where the question to be determined is what may happen to the asylum seeker in the future.

Asylum appeals have the particular characteristic that the determination of claims is not an establishment of facts but an assessment of risk and 'there is a two way obligation of fairness' (Thomas 2005). The claimant alone possesses all the relevant knowledge about their asylum claim, but the state is better placed to investigate conditions in the country of origin.

Particular to asylum appeals is the case management review hearing, at which the appellant and Home Office must give details of witnesses they intend to call, interpreters, the timescale for evidence to be ready, and any other necessary steps to ensure that all will be ready for the hearing date.

12.7 Evidence

We have already considered the question of credibility, which depends on the assessment of evidence. This section will consider the admission of late evidence and the evaluation of evidence about the claimant's country of origin.

12.7.1 Late evidence

Although matters up to the date of the hearing may in theory be relevant in an asylum claim, as in other litigation the parties are still required to comply with procedure rules and serve evidence on the other side within a specified time before the hearing. This time is set by the Tribunal giving directions at the case management review hearing. Tribunal cases are now listed and heard quite quickly, which can put considerable pressure on lawyers and experts.

The procedure rules say that the Tribunal 'must not consider any written evidence which is not filed or served in accordance with those directions unless satisfied that there are good reasons to do so' (r 51(4)). The 'anxious scrutiny' which should be applied to asylum appeals is relevant in determining whether such good reasons exist. So said the Tribunal in *MD Pakistan* [2004] UKIAT 00197, in which the appellant was present and ready and willing to give oral evidence. Although his statement had been filed late, there was no prejudice to the Home Office in admitting the statement. In *SA Sri Lanka* [2005] UKIAT 00028 the Tribunal held again that the anxious scrutiny required in an asylum claim meant that the adjudicator should have admitted a medical report which had a bearing on the appellant's credibility. The Home Office had not sent a representative to the hearing but the Tribunal held that by this omission they had deprived themselves of the opportunity to comment on it, and the appellant should not be penalized on that account.

12.7.2 Fresh evidence

The earlier points raise the question of finality in legal proceedings. When does the asylum claim cease? If it is focused on future risk, and there is a substantial change in the asylum seeker's country of origin the day after she has lost her appeal in the Tribunal, what then? What if new evidence comes to light before she is removed which substantiates the risk she feared? Although the Tribunal is concerned with the risk to the appellant of persecution on return, the state of affairs which is under consideration is that at the date of the hearing. If this were not so, the matter could go on being re-opened indefinitely. However, the decision must be made on the best evidence as to the facts, and new facts may come to light.

The first appeal to an immigration judge from the decision of the Home Office is a hearing of all the issues. Any further appeal must be on a point of law, not a question of fact. This may make it difficult to argue that any challenge can be made solely on the basis of new evidence, as evidence usually contributes to a finding of fact rather than law. However, as discussed in chapter 8 in relation to *E and R v SSHD* [2004] EWCA Civ 49, a mistake as to fact may, in the circumstances stipulated, amount to an error of law and thus be appealable, particularly in asylum cases.

In civil litigation generally, evidence can be admitted on the principles derived from the case of *Ladd v Marshall* [1954] 1 WLR 1489. These are: that the fresh evidence could not have been obtained with reasonable diligence for use at the trial (here, the Tribunal hearing); if given, it would probably have an important influence on the result; it is apparently credible thought not necessarily incontrovertible (*E and R* para 23). These principles may be departed from in asylum cases in exceptional circumstances when the interests of justice so require (*E and R* para 91).

12.7.3 Fresh claim

If new evidence comes to light *after* an appeal has been lost, a fresh claim for asylum may be made. This will only be considered when new submissions are significantly different from the material which has been previously been considered, as prescribed in para 353 of the immigration rules:

The submissions will only be significantly different if the content

1. Has not already been considered;
2. Taken together with the previously considered material creates a realistic prospect of success, notwithstanding its rejection.

Given the length of time spent in the UK by many asylum seekers whose claim has failed, and the developments that can happen in that time, the opportunity to make a fresh claim is important. As there is no right of appeal against a decision not to recognize representations as constituting a fresh claim, the only avenue to challenge refusal is judicial review. Such challenges constitute a significant percentage of the work of the High Court. As discussed in chapter 8, this is the one group of immigration and asylum judicial reviews which is transferred to the new Upper Tribunal (s 53 BCI Act 2009).

R (on the application of MN)(Tanzania)) v SSHD [2011] EWCA Civ 193 confirmed that the proper approach for the courts when considering a challenge a refusal to treat representations as a fresh claim is the usual judicial review standard (the *Wednesbury* standard) applied with 'anxious scrutiny'. This means in this context that the Court must ask itself whether the Secretary of State was entitled, on the evidence, to reach the conclusion that there was no realistic prospect of an immigration judge, applying the rule of anxious scrutiny, thinking that the appellant would be exposed to a real risk of persecution on return. The House of Lords in *ZT* (Kosovo) held that the Secretary of State should have applied para 353 to further submissions made in a case where the earlier claim had been certified as clearly unfounded. The difference in practice between certifying a claim certified as clearly unfounded and using para 353 is that the former attracts an out of country right of appeal, whereas a refusal to treat further submissions as a fresh claim attracts no right of appeal. The majority thought that there was a difference between the question of whether there was no realistic prospect of success (para 353), and whether a claim was clearly unfounded (s 94). The Court of Appeal in *MN (Tanzania)* endorsed that difference.

In *ZA (Nigeria) v SSHD* [2010] EWCA Civ 926 the Court of Appeal held that the refusal to treat further submissions as a fresh claim did not amount to an immigration decision attracting a right of appeal. Furthermore, the Court held that the existence of the power to certify clearly unfounded claims (s 94 of the 2002 Act) did not deprive para 353 of meaning, because s 94 referred to claims which had been decided on their merits, whereas para 353 gave a power not to consider submissions to be a claim at all. This decision followed on the Supreme Court judgment in *BA (Nigeria) and PE (Cameroon) v SSHD* [2009] UKSC 7 that where there had been an appealable decision (here, a refusal to revoke a deportation order) the Secretary of State could not deny the appellants a right of appeal by treating the appellants' representations as further submissions not amounting to a fresh claim.

A fresh claim may be on the basis of a breach of human rights as well as an asylum claim. For a full account of the law relating to evidence in asylum appeals and the challenging and technical, but important, issues concerning fresh claims, reference should be made to a practitioner work such as Macdonald.

12.7.4 Country of origin information

The availability, reliability, relevance, and scope of information about an asylum seeker's country of origin are enormously important in asylum decisions and appeals (see

Tsangarides). The claim is that the asylum seeker fears persecution in their country of origin. To succeed, they must be able to show, as required by the Refugee Convention, that their fear is well-founded. To substantiate or refute this there must be evidence of relevant state practices, and this may be gleaned from governmental reports and non-governmental organizations, particularly those that monitor human rights.

12.7.4.1 *Country reports*

Common sources relied on are the Home Office's own country reports and human rights reports from the US Department of State, Amnesty International, Human Rights Watch and other international organizations. It is rare for such a report to mention the asylum seeker personally, although this may happen, and there may be references to others with whom she is associated. However, reports deal with a wide range of issues, including the use of torture and detention, the accountability of officials for wrongdoing, freedom of the press, and notable events such as demonstrations, uprisings, severe repression of dissent, and so on. It is rare that an asylum seeker will have resources to compile substantial country information on their own behalf, and although independent experts may be instructed, the asylum seeker will often be reliant on information produced by organizations who do not have them or their case in mind.

The Home Office has its own Country of Origin Information Service which produces reports about countries of origin of asylum seekers. In view of the revival of the practice of listing safe countries of origin, the 2002 Act provided for an Advisory Panel on Country Information which reviewed the reports produced by the Home Office and offers advice and constructive criticism. The work of the panel has been subsumed within a new body, the Independent Advisory Group on Country Information (IAGCI), which is part of the Office of the Chief Inspector of UKBA.

> The IAGCI reviews the efficiency, effectiveness and consistency of approach of COI material collated by the COIS and assesses the sources, methods of research and quality control used by the Agency to help ensure that these support the production of COI material which is as accurate, balanced, impartial and up-to-date as possible. (Chief Inspector July 2011 para 4.9)

Reports by the Immigration Advisory Service had been highly critical of Home Office COI reports, citing inaccuracies, misquoting and omission of relevant information, reliance on secondary sources, and a tendency to use Home Office opinion in the reports, which purport to be factual. For a robust approach by the ECtHR to assessment of background material, see *Said v Netherlands* Application no. 2345/02. The work of ACPI and then IAGCI has brought about an improvement in the quality of country information, but the Chief Inspector's report on the use that is made of it by UKBA indicates that to a significant extent this is selective and uncoordinated (Chief Inspector July 2011).

12.7.4.2 *Country guidance cases*

As may be imagined, not infrequently the same background issues fall to be proved in different cases. Laws LJ in the Court of Appeal in *S v SSHD* [2002] EWCA Civ 539 noted the waste of judicial and other resources in hearing evidence about similar factual issues repeatedly, and the need for consistency in decision-making, which is also an aspect of justice. As a remedy for this situation, Laws LJ proposed the unusual idea of a factual precedent, which might, in asylum cases, he thought, be 'benign and practical' (para 28). From this judgment was born the practice of declaring 'country guidance' cases, which are binding as to a factual situation.

As Laws LJ pointed out in *S*, the notion of a precedent which is binding as to fact is 'foreign to the common law' (para 26). For this reason alone, the proposition should be treated with caution that findings of fact made in one case should be binding in another. However, one can readily see that asylum cases present the law with a new phenomenon. *S* laid down a number of provisos, which should be strictly applied if factual precedents were to be allowed as a possibility:

- In making a decision which is intended to give guidelines on conditions in a country, the Tribunal must apply the duty to give reasons 'with particular rigour'.
- Such a decision must be 'effectively comprehensive. It should address all the issues capable of having a real as opposed to a fanciful bearing on the result, and explain what it makes of the substantial evidence going to each such issue.'
- The facts of an individual case must still be examined.
- Country guidance cases may provide a backdrop against which that individual examination takes place, recognizing that 'the impact of the political reality may vary as between one claimant and another'.

The practice of promulgating and following country guidance cases (designated CG in the case name) grew quickly after *S*. The Immigration Advisory Service carried out research and consultation on the use and nature of country guidance cases. Their work revealed concerns including the following:

- Country guidance cases may be out of date for the case in hand, or worse, based on obsolete material.
- Factual findings specific to a particular claimant may be elevated into country guidance.
- Country guidance decisions may not be referenced properly, so that a future claimant is unable to distinguish their case from the CG because they cannot identify the evidence.
- '[T]he judiciary operate under severe time constraints and a reference to a country guidance case is sometimes used as an alternative to giving reasons rather than an aid to decision-making' (p. 20).
- Some country guidance cases have been designated where the dismissal of the claim was based on a *lack* of evidence.
- Even in a CG case, evidence was sometimes used and dismissed selectively without objective reasons being given, particularly by preference being given to government reports over other sources. (IAS 2005)

The IAS challenged the concept of country guidance cases as importing an artificial degree of certainty 'on an uncertain and often rapidly changing country situation'. Thomas criticizes the CG system as 'naïve' – different conclusions may be drawn from similar facts (2005:476).

Despite these doubts, the Tribunal has embraced the notion of country guidance cases. There are now hundreds in relation to particular issues such as 'risk on return – Ivory Coast', 'Trafficked women – China', 'Undocumented Kurds – Syria' which are listed on the Tribunal's website. The relevant practice direction goes much further than *S* in relation to their weight as precedents. It says that the most recent CG case 'shall be treated as an authoritative finding on the country guidance issue identified in the determination... so far as that appeal:

(a) relates to the country guidance issue in question; and

(b) depends upon the same or similar evidence' (2010, para 12.2).

Even more unequivocally: 'any failure to follow a clear, apparently applicable country guidance case or to show why it does not apply to the case in question is likely to be regarded as grounds for review or appeal on a point of law' (para 18.4 endorsed in *R & others v SSHD* [2005] EWCA Civ 982). The exception is when there is other, inconsistent authority that is binding on the Tribunal.

Country guidance cases were described by the Court of Appeal in *HM (Iraq) v SSHD* [2011] EWCA Civ 1536 as having 'a status and significance comparable to that which declarations can have in public law cases' (para 39). The Court quashed the Tribunal's country guidance in the unique situation that representation had been withdrawn for all the appellants in the proposed country guidance case just before the Tribunal hearing. The case concerned the critical and controversial issue of the safety of return to Iraq, relying on Article 15(c) of the Qualification Directive, and it was essential to have proper argument, not only on the law 'but also the drawing of relevant materials to the attention of the tribunal and the making of submissions as to the effect of those materials, so that the determination is based on as full and informed an analysis as possible' (para 39).

The effect of a country guidance case is to establish the factual position until it is proved to have changed. This means that the Tribunal must consider new evidence and make a new decision. In the case of Zimbabwe, the Home Office declared itself not bound by country guidance case *RN (Returnees) Zimbabwe CG* [2008] UKAIT 00083, on the basis of its view that violence in that country had reduced, although this issue had not at that point been tested in the Tribunal. The Home Office announced that it would not follow *RN* on the basis that it anticipated that the forthcoming decision in the case of *EM* would change *RN*. Accordingly, it declared that *RN* need not be rigorously followed. This announcement highlighted the tensions inherent in having a system of factual precedents. In *PO (Nigeria) v SSHD* [2011] EWCA Civ 132 the Court of Appeal criticized the Tribunal's assessment of evidence and quashed two aspects of the guidance. In other cases too there are indications that the courts as well as the Home Office are feeling the disadvantages as well as the advantages of being bound to a factual precedent in a fast-changing situation (see, e.g., *HH Somalia* [2010] EWCA Civ 426).

12.8 Refugee status

In the cases where refugee status is granted (around 10 per cent of initial decisions and 22 per cent of appealed cases), the Refugee Convention and now the Qualification Directive set out the legal consequences of recognition. Refugees have a right to the issue of a travel document, an important right bearing in mind that they may well not have a passport of their country of origin or be able to travel using it. They are entitled to social rights on favourable terms and the intention of the Convention is that they should be integrated into the host society. The rights listed in the Convention include civil and political rights and fundamental freedoms such as that of religion and religious education (Article 4). The Directive concentrates on social and economic rights: employment, education, accommodation, health care, and social welfare. Denial of fundamental rights would be unconstitutional in the EU, but social and economic rights have very limited protection. Some social rights in the Directive are granted on the same terms as to nationals – e.g., education for children. Some are on the same terms as other third country nationals – e.g., accommodation. For a really comprehensive account of Convention provisions, see Hathaway 2005.

In *ST (Eritrea) v SSHD* [2012] UKSC 12 the Court of Appeal held that the appellant, who had been granted refugee status in relation to her country of nationality, Eritrea, could nevertheless be removed to her country of former residence, Ethiopia, where it was found that she was not at risk. The grant of asylum does not result in a right of residence even in the country which granted it, if the refugee can be safe elsewhere.

12.9 Cessation

The Refugee Convention Article 1C makes provision for refugee status to end in certain circumstances. Most refer to the voluntary actions of the refugee. The exception is Article 1C(5), that 'because the circumstances in connection with which he has been recognized as a refugee have ceased to exist' he can no longer 'refuse to avail himself of the protection of the country of his nationality' or, if stateless, his former residence. The host state bears the burden of proving this, and refugees should not be subject to continual examination of their status as this undermines the very security the Convention aims to give (see the *UNHCR Handbook* para 135). These conditions are reproduced in the Qualification Directive, and in the immigration rules implementing it. The rules include that there has been a 'significant and non-temporary change' in the conditions in the refugee's country of origin. The Directive and rules omit one provision of the Convention, which is that there are 'compelling reasons arising from previous persecution' for not returning to the country of origin. This means that the Directive and rules do not give the refugee the opportunity to argue against losing their refugee status because of the severity of their previous experience. However, in the first case exercising its new jurisdiction in refugee law, the CJEU has set a high standard for domestic authorities who wish to assert that refugee status has ceased:

Key Case

(C–175/08) *Aydin Salahadin Abdulla*

The appellants in the main proceedings had been granted refugee status in Germany, as people subject to persecution from the former regime in Iraq. When the regime changed, their refugee status was revoked. The German courts referred the interpretation of the cessation clause to the CJEU, which ruled that:

- refugee status ceases to exist when, having regard to a change of circumstances of a significant and non-temporary nature in the home state, the circumstances which justified the person's fear of persecution no longer exist and that person has no other reason to fear being persecuted within the meaning of Article 2(c) of Directive 2004/83;
- for the purposes of assessing a change of circumstances, the competent authorities of the Member State must verify, having regard to the refugee's individual situation, that the actors of protection have taken reasonable steps to prevent the persecution, that they operate an effective legal system for the detection, prosecution and punishment of acts constituting persecution, and that the national concerned will have access to such protection if he ceases to have refugee status.

UK practice used to be to grant indefinite leave to remain to those granted refugee status. On 30 August 2005, UK policy changed to giving five years' leave instead. At the end of that period the need for protection may be reviewed. In practice, since the first such periods of leave came up for review in August 2010, the claim for asylum has not been re-opened, and the usual practice has been to grant indefinite leave to remain. As in other areas, the main use of the five-year review is to give the opportunity to exclude those with serious criminal records. The Qualification Directive provides that only a three-year residence permit need be given to refugees and their families (Article 24).

In *ZN (Afghanistan) v ECO (Karachi)* [2010] UKSC 21 the Supreme Court ruled, on interpreting the immigration rules, that a refugee who had obtained British citizenship did not need to fulfil the more onerous requirements for maintenance and accommodation in order for their family members to join them in the UK. They were still a person who had been granted refugee status, and as such should benefit from the more favourable rules applying to refugees. The government responded to this by changing the immigration rules, so as to reverse the effect of *ZN (Afghanistan) v SSHD*. The rules now say that refugee status automatically ceases upon acquisition of British citizenship (para 339BA), and that the more favourable family reunion rules only apply to those with current refugee status.

12.10 Subsidiary protection

Many signatory states to the Refugee Convention make provision for a safety net status where a person is held not to qualify for asylum, but there are compelling reasons why they should not be returned to their home state. The Refugee Qualification Directive 2004/83 provides for 'subsidiary protection' (Article 18) where there are 'substantial grounds' for believing that the person concerned, if returned to their country of origin, would face a real risk of serious harm (Article 2(e)). Serious harm is defined as:

(a) death penalty or execution;
(b) torture or inhuman or degrading treatment or punishment;
(c) serious and individual threat to a civilian's life or person by reason of indiscriminate violence in situations of international or internal armed conflict.

One of the first decisions in the ECJ on the interpretation of the Qualification Directive concerned this Article.

Key Case

***Elgafaji* C–465/07**

Mr and Mrs Elgafaji were nationals of Iraq. Mr Elgafaji, who was a Shiite Muslim, had worked for a British firm providing security for personnel transport between the airport and the 'Green Zone' in Baghdad. Mr Elgafaji's uncle, employed by the same firm, had been killed by militia, his death certificate stating that his death followed a terrorist act. A short time later, a letter threatening 'death to collaborators' was fixed to the door of the residence which Mr Elgafaji shared with his wife, a Sunni Muslim.

Mr and Mrs Elgafaji applied for temporary residence permits in the Netherlands but were refused. They challenged the refusal, arguing that Article 15(c) did not require the high degree of individualization of the threat required by Article 15(b). The Raad van State referred the question to the ECJ for a preliminary ruling.

The ECJ found that:

- the existence of a serious and individual threat to the life or person of an applicant for subsidiary protection did not require proof that the applicant was specifically targeted because of factors particular to them;
- the existence of such a threat could exceptionally be established where the degree of indiscriminate violence characterizing the armed conflict reached such a high level that there were substantial grounds for believing that a civilian would, solely on account of their presence, face a real risk of being subject to that threat.

This judgment was applied in the UK in *QD and AH (Iraq) v SSHD, UNHCR intervening* [2009] EWCA Civ 620. QD was a former Ba'ath Party member, and feared reprisals. AH's claim concerned the level of violence in his locality. The Court of Appeal held that the Directive must be given an autonomous meaning. Protection under Article 15(c), which was additional to that given by the Refugee Convention or ECHR, was derived not from international humanitarian law (as the Tribunal had found in an earlier case) but from the practice of states. The Court accepted UNHCR's submission that, for the purposes of Article 15(c), there was no requirement that the armed conflict itself must be exceptional. What was required was an intensity of indiscriminate violence great enough to meet the test spelt out by the ECJ. It followed that 'civilian' meant, not simply someone not in uniform – which might include terrorists – but only genuine non-combatants. Article 15(c) could be invoked whether the source of the violence was a single entity or two or more warring factions.

In October 2009, the Tribunal reversed its previous country guidance and determined that there was no longer in Afghanistan such a high level of indiscriminate violence that a civilian would, solely by being present there, face a risk which entitled them to protection under Article 15(c).

Subsidiary protection is called humanitarian protection in the UK, and is incorporated in the immigration rules at paras 339C–N. The Directive requires that a year is the minimum leave given as humanitarian protection. In the immigration rules, five years is the norm, as for asylum. The rights that go with humanitarian protection are less than for refugee status in the Directive. In the immigration rules, both are unrestricted in employment and have a right to a travel document.

Principles of internal flight and sufficiency of protection (see next chapter) are applied in considering whether to grant humanitarian protection. Exclusions also apply, but are more severely drawn than for refugee status (see chapter 14). Persons excluded from humanitarian protection may be considered for a six-month period of discretionary leave.

It is still possible on human rights or other grounds for the Secretary of State to grant leave outside the rules. Where this is because of family ties or private life in the UK, the leave granted will be discretionary leave, the conditions for which are set out in policy and guidance. Discretionary leave may also be given where return would generate medical or severe humanitarian risks which would breach Article 3 and in very limited circumstances where other human rights violations are feared on return. The initial grant of discretionary leave is normally three years but may be less. It does not lead to settlement until six years have elapsed. In *R (on the application of Shahid) v SSHD* QBD Admin 13 October 2004, Gibbs J held that it was reasonable to grant three years' discretionary leave, and if there was no significant change in circumstances, the claimant could eventually expect to obtain indefinite leave to remain. Not immediately granting indefinite leave did not interfere with his Article 8 right beyond the allowable interference under Article 8.2. The Supreme Court has referred to the CJEU the question of whether the EU legal principle of equivalence requires a minor refused asylum/humanitarian protection but granted discretionary leave to be afforded a right of appeal not only against the asylum refusal, but also against the subsidiary protection decision (*FA (Iraq) v SSHD* [2011] UKSC 22).

The previous API provided that discretionary leave will not be granted 'on the basis that, for the time being, practical obstacles prevent a person from leaving the UK or being removed, for example, an absence of route or travel document'. See the discussion of the case of *Khadir* in chapter 15 for the significance of this. Discretionary leave does not give a right to be joined by family members.

12.11 Safe third country

Finally, we consider the application and development of safe third country provisions. The basic contention is that the claimant may be safely sent somewhere other than their country of origin or where they fear persecution. At the initial screening interview, questions are asked to determine whether an asylum seeker has travelled through another country which could have heard their claim. If it is decided that this is so, a safe third country decision is made, and the Home Office arranges for the asylum seeker to be returned to that country. Any further consideration of their claim in the UK is halted (although, if facts which would found a safe third country decision only come to light at a later stage, this cannot stop an appeal that is already in process: *AM (Somalia) v SSHD* [2009] EWCA Civ 114).

The notion of 'burden-sharing', now a key element in the development of policy in Europe, has always been a function of international refugee law. Indeed, one of the preambles to the Refugee Convention is to this effect:

> the grant of asylum may place unduly heavy burdens on certain countries, and that a satisfactory solution of a problem of which the United Nations has recognized the international scope and nature cannot therefore be achieved without international co-operation.

The use of safe third country provisions is widespread. For instance, Canada implemented a safe third country agreement with the USA, thereby closing its land border to most asylum claims and effecting a significant reduction in asylum claims overall. The Canadian Council for Refugees refers to this as 'the government's unstated purpose' (2005:26). The third country means one that is neither the refugee's home state nor the country where they have sought asylum, and the designation 'safe' means that it will not be a breach of Refugee Convention Article 33, the obligation of non-*refoulement*, to send them there.

12.11.1 Development of safe third country provisions

Prior to any statutory provisions, the decision to remove an asylum claimant was a matter of administrative discretion, subject only to the obligation of non-*refoulement* under Refugee Convention Article 33. The case of *Musisi v SSHD* [1987] AC 514 established that the doctrine of non-*refoulement* applies to indirect as well as direct return. In that case the appellant sought asylum from Uganda, but had travelled to the UK from Kenya and applied to enter as a visitor. The immigration service proposed to remove him to Kenya, but there was evidence that Kenya would not accept him and would send him back to Uganda where he feared persecution. The House of Lords found that, although the decision was within the discretion of the Secretary of State, he had failed to consider the question adequately, having not addressed the question of danger.

Protection against indirect *refoulement* as laid down in Musisi found its way into the immigration rules as an obligation to return the asylum seeker to a country through which they had travelled, if it was safe to do so. This set the basic principles of safe third country decisions, which still underlie the provisions that are in place today:

- the applicant has not travelled directly from the country of persecution;
- there is another country to which they could be sent as they could have made their asylum claim there; and
- this would be considered safe in the sense that the life or freedom of the asylum applicant would not be threatened (within the meaning of Article 33 of the Convention) and its government would not send the applicant elsewhere in a manner contrary to the principles of the Convention and Protocol.

Making such a decision required a lot of fact-finding on the part of the Secretary of State. Information was needed about the third country, not only about its systems of refugee protection, but also about the asylum claimant's travel route and their experiences. The Secretary of State had a discretion under this rule but one which it is difficult to exercise properly.

The Secretary of State was under no obligation to consult the authorities of the third country before returning an applicant to them, and they were under no obligation to deal with the claim. So for some years there was a phenomenon known as 'refugees in orbit' whereby asylum claimants were shunted from one unwilling country to the next and back again. Both Tuitt (1996:119) and Macdonald (2001:547) suggested that this in itself might constitute inhuman or degrading treatment contrary to Article 3 ECHR.

The Asylum and Immigration Appeals Act 1993 was the first statutory provision allowing the Secretary of State to certify removals to a safe third. Following many legal challenges to these certificates, the 1993 Act was succeeded by the Asylum and Immigration Act 1996, in which s 2 provided that if the Secretary of State certified that the safe third country conditions were met the claimant could be removed to European or designated countries *before* any appeal took place.

Challenges to safe third country certificates by judicial review became a forum for examining the compatibility of refugee law in European Member States. To put a stop to such challenges, the Immigration and Asylum Act 1999 s 11 introduced a deeming provision which entailed that Member States of the European Union were *'to be regarded as'* places in which the safe third country provisions were met. This in turn was replaced by the current provision.

12.11.2 Current legislation on safe third countries

Asylum and Immigration (Treatment of Claimants, etc.) Act 2004 Sch 3 repeals previous safe third country provisions. It establishes three kinds of lists of safe third countries. The only one which is active is the first list, which consists of 28 other countries of the European Economic Area, i.e., all except Liechtenstein. Where a claimant has travelled through a country which might be regarded as safe (e.g., Canada or Switzerland (API Dec 2008)) but which is not in the EEA list, claims may be certified on a case-by-case basis under Part 5 of Sch 3.

The 28 EEA countries are deemed to be safe places to return an asylum claimant whom the Secretary of State certifies is not a national of that country. They are deemed to be safe in three respects:

- the applicant will not face persecution contrary to the Refugee Convention in that country
- that country will not send the applicant to another country where there is a risk of such persecution
- that country will not send the applicant to another country if the removal would give rise to a risk of human rights violations.

The Secretary of State is also obliged to certify that a human rights appeal concerning the immediate consequences of removal to that country would be unfounded, unless s/he is satisfied that it would not be. This refers to any other human rights implications of removal aside from the possibility of onward removal from the destination state, for instance a claim that family or private life in the UK will be infringed by the removal (Article 8), or that the applicant faces a risk of degrading treatment in the receiving state (Article 3). The effect has been that anyone who may be returned to a European country was returned without an appeal unless the Secretary of State was persuaded that there would arguably be a breach of human rights by the UK in doing so. The only judicial forum in which this may be argued is judicial review.

The Parliamentary Joint Committee on Human Rights doubted the compatibility of these provisions with the UK's obligations under the Human Rights Act and ECHR in 'precluding any individual consideration of the facts of a particular claimant's case and conclusively ousting the jurisdiction of the courts to hear a claim that removal to a third country on the First List would breach the claimant's rights because of the risk of onward removal' (Session 2003–04 Thirteenth Report HL 102, HC 640). The Committee's critique has in effect been endorsed by the European Court of Human Rights, and by the Court of Justice of the EU, in considering the impact of the Dublin Regulation.

12.11.3 The Dublin Regulation

Safe third country provisions are a key element in the Common European Asylum System. The European Union attempts to prevent 'refugees in orbit' by ensuring that at least one Member State accepts an application for asylum, thus also stopping asylum seekers moving around the European Union in search of the country which seems to them to offer the best prospects and precluding multiple claims by one person in different Member States. The first mechanism adopted across the Union to do this was the Dublin Convention (OJ C 254 19.8.1997), which came into force in 1997. The Dublin Convention had no direct effect in the UK as it was a Treaty entered into under the Third Pillar of the European Union (*R v SSHD ex p Behluli* [1998] Imm AR 407), although it was given effect in individual cases.

Council Regulation (EC) No 343/2003 OJ 2003 L 50/1 replaced the Dublin Convention and is directly effective and directly applicable in national law without implementing measures (TFEU Article 249). The Regulation, known as 'Dublin II', or the Dublin Regulation, came into effect on 1 September 2003. Its purpose, like that of the Convention, is to establish the criteria and mechanisms for determining the Member State responsible for examining an asylum application lodged in one of the Member States. The criteria stipulate that a state takes responsibility for an asylum claim where a claimant has a family member who is a recognized refugee or an asylum seeker legally resident in that Member State, providing the persons concerned agree (Articles 7 and 8). Unaccompanied minors should be dealt with in the country where they make their application (Article 6). Also, a Member State which issues a residence permit or visa will be responsible normally for a claim from the holder of that permit or visa (Article 9). Where there is evidence of illegal entry into a Member State, the state so entered remains responsible for processing the asylum claim for 12 months. After that, or in the event of there being no evidence of illegal entry, the Member State in which the asylum seeker was living for the last five months is responsible (Article 10). Except where these and other provisions apply, the claim should be processed in the first Member State at which the asylum seeker lodges an application (Article 13).

In *R (on the application of Mosari) v SSHD* [2005] EWHC 1343, Lightman J held that where the claimant had entered Hungary as a minor with his adult cousin, and made an asylum application there, Hungary remained the country which had responsibility under Dublin II to determine which state should hear the asylum claim. The fact that the claimant was now living with his uncle in the UK did not mean that the UK had to take responsibility under Article 6. His entry to the EU and first claim was made in Hungary, and family life here would not displace that unless to proceed with the return to Hungary was disproportionate. Lightman J held that it was not. The High Court in *T, MA and A v SSHD* [2010] EWHC 3572 (Admin) held that Dublin transfers applied to minors in the same way as adults. Article 6, the Court thought, confirming *Mosari,* did not mean that the minor could choose in which country they made their application, but referred to the first state of entry.

Article 15 provides that '[a]ny member state... may bring together family members, as well as other dependent relatives, on humanitarian grounds based in particular on family or cultural considerations'. This appears to be a route for an asylum seeker to argue for family unity, not necessarily in the country which would otherwise be responsible for deciding their claim. However, in *R (on the application of G) v SSHD* [2005] EWCA Civ 546, the Court of Appeal held that Article 15 did not create a right for asylum seekers, but was only intended 'to regulate the relationship between two or more member states' (para 25). Similarly, in relation to procedural provisions such as time limits for action, in *Omar v SSHD* [2005] EWCA Civ 285 the Court held that these did not have direct effect as there were no clear words to create the rights which would then flow for the asylum seeker. Mr Omar could not insist that the UK take responsibility for his claim when there was a delay in transferring responsibility back to Italy. The High Court in *R (on the application of YZ, MT and YM v SSHD* [2011] EWHC 205 (Admin) held that this absence of individual rights for the asylum seeker in the Dublin Regulation applied also to challenging fingerprint matches in EURODAC, the fingerprint database which provides the regular source of evidence that an asylum seeker entered the EU elsewhere. The Court rejected the argument that the match was a precedent fact, i.e., a challengeable factual basis for the operation of the Dublin Regulation.

Mota v SSHD [2006] EWCA Civ 1380 illustrates the working of Eurodac. The appellant arrived in the UK in 2005 and claimed asylum. A fingerprint match revealed that she had claimed asylum in the Netherlands in 2003. She claimed that in the intervening period she had been back in Sierra Leone, but suffered atrocities which made her flee and renew her claim for asylum. The Dublin Regulation provides that, if the claimant had left the EU for more than three months, then the responsibility for the claim lapsed. The two governments did not accept that she had left the EU. This meant that her claim would still be the responsibility of the Netherlands. The Court held that this finding was not irrational and she could be returned to the Netherlands.

Once the third country has accepted responsibility, the question of whether the claimant has in fact left the EU for three months has been held in High Court decisions to be no longer the business of the state which issued the third country certificate. The repercussions of this have been that the UK was not obliged to pass on to France the asylum seeker's claim that she had returned to China (*R (on the application of Yong Qing Chen)* [2008] EWHC 437 (Admin)), and the rationality of the Secretary of State's belief that the claimant had not been back to Sri Lanka was no longer a challengeable issue in the UK Court (*R (on the application of Santhirakumar) v SSHD* [2009] EWHC 2819 (Admin)).

Both the Dublin Regulation and the UK's statutory list of safe EEA third countries have been thrown into question by the European Court of Human Rights' judgment in *MSS v Belgium and Greece* [2011] ECHR 108.

Key Case

Application no. 30696/09, *MSS v Belgium and Greece*

MSS was an interpreter who had fled Afghanistan after, as he claimed, an attempt on his life by the Taliban. His first entry to Europe was through Greece, where he was fingerprinted but did not claim asylum. He made his asylum claim in Belgium where his fingerprints, registered on Eurodac, showed that he had passed through Greece. Pursuant to the Dublin Regulation, an order was made that he be returned to Greece. MSS lodged unsuccessful challenges with the Belgian Aliens Appeals Board. In parallel, he applied to the ECtHR to have his transfer suspended. The Court refused to make a provisional measures order (Rule 39), but informally required the Greek government to honour its obligations under the ECHR and comply with EU legislation on asylum.

MSS was removed to Greece. He was detained on arrival in a small space with 20 other detainees, had access to the toilets only at the discretion of the guards, was not allowed into the open air, was given very little to eat, and made to sleep on a dirty mattress or the bare floor. When he was released he was required to report to the Attica police station to declare his home address so that he could be informed of the progress of his asylum application. Being homeless, and believing that an address was a condition of proceeding with his claim, MSS did not report to the police station. There were other deficiencies in the procedure applied to him. For much of his time in Greece the applicant had no means of subsistence, and slept in a park.

MSS complained to the ECtHR about his treatment by both Greece and Belgium. Against Greece he alleged breaches of Article 3 ECHR by reason of his conditions of detention, his conditions of living, and a breach of Article 13 ECHR because of the deficiencies in the asylum procedure and the risk of his expulsion to Afghanistan without any serious examination of the merits of his asylum application or access to an effective remedy. His complaint against Belgium was that Belgium had breached Articles 3 and 13 by sending him to Greece and exposing him to these risks. The Court found in his favour and held that both Greece and Belgium were in violation of their obligations under Articles 3 and 13 ECHR.

This decision by the ECtHR cast doubt on the continuing operation of the Dublin Regulation as Belgium was ruled to have breached Article 3 by sending MSS to Greece, and not enquiring, given the level of evidence about conditions in Greece, whether MSS would be at risk of *refoulement* or of breaches of Article 3 in Greece itself. While *MSS* is an important judgment, there is a binding impact on the Dublin system in the subsequent judgment of the CJEU in *NS v SSHD* C–411/10 (see also chapter 4).

In C–411/10 *NS v SSHD* the CJEU found that there is an obligation on Member States to operate the Dublin Regulation in a manner consistent with fundamental rights. It follows that Member States may not operate a conclusive presumption, such that in the UK's Asylum and Immigration (Treatment of Claimants, etc) Act 2004 Sch 3, that a transfer to another Member State will not entail a breach of fundamental rights. In order to ensure that rights are effective, there must be a meaningful channel through which an asylum seeker can adduce evidence that there is a serious risk to them in the destination state. Member States may not transfer an asylum seeker to the 'Member State responsible' within the meaning of the Dublin Regulation 'where they cannot be unaware that systemic deficiencies in the asylum procedure and in the reception conditions of asylum seekers in that Member State amount to substantial grounds for believing that the asylum seeker would face a real risk of being subjected to inhuman or degrading treatment' (*NS* para 94).

12.12 Conclusion

This chapter may illustrate that the procedural hurdles to be overcome are just as much of a challenge to establishing a refugee claim as satisfying the legal definition.

QUESTIONS

1 What would be your priorities for change in the asylum system?
2 Judith Farbey says, 'there is no difference between asylum claimants in Harmondsworth and elsewhere, save that the Home Office has decided that Harmondsworth cases can be speedily processed' (2004:199). Consider the justification for the difference in treatment of an asylum claimant in the DFT and one who is not detained on arrival.

For guidance on answering questions, visit www.oxfordtextbooks.co.uk/orc/clayton5e/.

FURTHER READING

Amnesty International (2004) *Get it Right: How Home Office Decision-making Fails Refugees*, Amnesty International UK.

Asylum Aid (1995) 'No Reason at all'.

—— (1999) 'Still no Reason at all'.

Bail for Immigration Detainees (2006) 'Working against the Clock: Inadequacy and Injustice in the Fast Track System'.

Barnes, John (2004) 'Expert Evidence: The Judicial Perception in Asylum and Human Rights Appeals' *International Journal of Refugee Law* vol. 16, no. 3, pp. 349–357.

Briddick, Catherine (2010) 'Trafficking and the National Referral Mechanism' *Women's Asylum News* (London: Asylum Aid), pp. 1–4.

Cohen, Juliet (2001) 'Questions of Credibility: Omissions, Discrepancies and Errors of Recall in the Testimony of Asylum Seekers' *International Journal of Refugee Law* vol. 13, no. 3, pp. 293–309.

Constitutional Affairs Committee Second Report 2003–04, Asylum and Immigration Appeals HC 211.

Costello, Cathryn (2005) 'The Asylum Procedures Directive and the Proliferation of Safe Country Practices: Deterrence, Deflection and the Dismantling of International Protection?' *European Journal of Migration and Law* vol. 7, no. 1, March 2005, pp. 35–70 (36).

Den Heijer, Maarten (2010) 'Europe Beyond its Borders: Refugee and Human Rights Protection in Extraterritorial Immigration Control' *Extraterritorial Immigration Control: Legal Challenges* Ryan, Bernard and Shah, Prakash (eds) (Leiden: Martinus Nijhoff).

Detention Action (2011) *Fast Track to Despair; The unnecessary detention of asylum seekers* (London: Detention Action).

European Council on Refugees and Exiles (ECRE) (March 2005) Comments on Amended Proposal for a Council Directive on Minimum Standards on Procedures in Member States for Granting and withdrawing Refugee Status, as Agreed by the Council on 19 November 2004 (Brussels: ECRE).

Ensor, Jonathan, Shah, Amanda and Grillo, Mirella (2006) 'Simple Myths and Complex Realities – Seeking Truth in the Face of Section 8' *Journal of Immigration, Asylum and Nationality Law* vol. 20, no. 2, pp. 95–111.

Errera, Roger (2011) 'The CJEU and subsidiary protection: reflections on *Elgafaji* and after' *International Journal of Refugee Law* vol. 23, no. 1, pp. 93–112.

Good, Anthony (2004) 'Expert Evidence in Asylum and Human Rights Appeals: An Expert's View' *International Journal of Refugee Law* vol. 16, no. 3, pp. 358–380.

Hathaway, James C. (2005) *The Right of Refugees under International Law* (Cambridge: Cambridge University Press).

Herlihy, Jane and Turner, Stuart W. (2009) 'The Psychology of Seeking Protection' *International Journal of Refugee Law* vol. 21, no. 2, pp. 171–192.

Home Affairs Committee Report on Asylum Applications Asylum Applications, Second Report of 2003–04, HC 218, 26 January 2004.

Independent Asylum Commission (2008) *Fit for Purpose Yet?*

—— (2008) *Saving Sanctuary*.

Lambert, Helene (2006) 'The EU Asylum Qualification Directive, its Impact on the Jurisprudence of the United Kingdom and International Law' *International and Comparative Law Quarterly* vol. 55, no. 1, pp. 161–192.

Millbank, Jenni (2009) '"The Ring of Truth": A Case Study of Credibility Assessment in Particular Social Group Refugee Determinations' *International Journal of Refugee Law* vol. 21, no. 1, March, pp. 1–33.

National Audit Office (2004) *Improving the Speed and Quality of Asylum Decisions*, report by the Comptroller and Auditor General HC 535 Session 2003–04 23 June 2004.

Norman, Steve (2007), 'Assessing the Credibility of Refugee Applicants: A Judicial Perspective' *International Journal of Refugee Law* vol. 19, no. 2, pp. 273–292.

Refugee Council (2007) *New Asylum Model* (London: Refugee Council).

Rhys-Jones, David, and Verity-Smith, Sally (2004) 'Medical Evidence in Asylum and Human Rights Appeals' *International Journal of Refugee Law* vol. 16, no. 3, pp. 381–410.

Ryan, Bernard and Mitsilegas, Valsamis (2010) *Extraterritorial Immigration Control: Legal Challenges* (Leiden: Martinus Nijhoff).

Smith, Ellie (2004) *Right First Time* (London: Medical Foundation).

Statewatch (2004) EU Divided over List of 'Safe Countries of Origin' – Statewatch Calls for the List to be Scrapped, accessed at: www.statewatch.org/news/2004/sep/safe-countries.pdf.

Sweeney, James (2009) 'Credibility, Proof and Refugee Law' *International Journal of Refugee Law* vol. 21, no. 4, pp. 700–726.

Symes, Mark (2006) 'The Refugee Qualification Directive' Electronic Immigration Network.

Thomas, Robert (2005) 'Asylum Appeals: The Challenge of Asylum to the British Legal System' in P. Shah (ed.) *The Challenge of Asylum to Legal Systems* (London: Cavendish), pp. 205–226.

Tsangarides, Natasha (2009) 'The Politics of Knowledge: An Examination of the Use of Country Information in the Asylum Determination Process' (2009) *Journal of Immigration, Asylum and Nationality Law* vol. 23, no. 3, pp. 252–263.

—— (2010) *The Refugee Roulette: The Role of Country Information in Refugee Status Determination* (London: Immigration Advisory Service).

Trueman, Trevor (2009), 'Reasons for Refusal: An Audit of 200 Refusals of Ethiopian Asylum Seekers in England' *Journal of Immigration, Asylum and Nationality Law* vol. 23, no. 3, pp. 281–308.

UNHCR (2007) Advisory Opinion on the Extraterritorial Application of *Non-Refoulement* Obligations under the 1951 Convention relating to the Status of Refugees and its 1967 Protocol 26 January 2007.

—— (2011) Statistical Online Population Database, United Nations High Commissioner for Refugees (UNHCR), Data extracted; 12/10/2011.

Woodhouse, Sarah (2004) *The Annual Report of the Certification Monitor* (London: UKBA).

Yeo, Colin (ed.) (2005) *Country Guideline Cases: Benign and Practical?* (London: IAS).

13

The refugee definition

SUMMARY

This chapter examines the definition of a 'refugee' found in Article 1A of the UN Convention Relating to the Status of Refugees 1951 and the Refugee Qualification Directive EC 2004/83. Although at the time of drafting the Convention this paragraph may not have been the main preoccupation of contracting states, every phrase of it has now been extensively examined in courts and tribunals worldwide.

13.1 Definition of 'refugee'

Refugee status is determined by applying the definition found in Article 1A(2) of the Refugee Convention, which says that a 'refugee' is a person who:

> Owing to a well-founded fear of being persecuted for reasons of race, religion, nationality, membership of a particular social group, or political opinion, is outside his country of nationality and is unable or, owing to such fear, is unwilling to avail himself of the protection of that country; or who, not having a nationality and being outside the country of his former habitual residence... is unable or, owing to such fear, is unwilling to return to it.

As explained in chapter 12, this definition is now applied in the EU as interpreted by European Directive 2004/83, referred to here as the Qualification Directive. The Directive is implemented in the UK by the Refugee or Person in Need of International Protection (Qualification) Regulations 2006, SI 2006/2525. Case law on Article 1A which predates the Directive is still applicable and remains a key source of refugee law.

The Qualification Directive provides for refugee claims only from third country (i.e., non-EEA) nationals and those who are stateless. The UK's implementing regulations apply to anyone who is not a British Citizen, although a claim from an EEA national would be likely to be certified as clearly unfounded. The rest of this chapter consists of an exploration of the refugee definition as it has been interpreted by courts and tribunals.

13.2 The fear

The centrality of the requirement of fear places a greater emphasis on the experience and circumstances of the individual than the refugee protection measures which preceded the 1951 Convention. Arguably, the fear has both a subjective and objective aspect. The *UNHCR Handbook* paras 37–50 suggests that both are necessary.

13.2.1 Subjective fear

The subjective aspect is the refugee's own experience of fear. Paragraphs 40 and 41 of the *UNHCR Handbook* discuss the way in which the subjective element may be evaluated, and suggest that the requirement of subjective fear gives scope for taking account of the effect of circumstances on an individual. For instance, 'one person may have strong political or religious convictions, the disregard of which would make his life intolerable; another may have no such strong convictions' (para 40). Similar circumstances may bear differently on different people. The assessment of the subjective state of fear, according to para 40, involves engaging in 'an assessment of the personality of the applicant... since the psychological reactions of different individuals may not be the same in identical conditions'. However, tribunals tend to steer away from too intense a psychological scrutiny of the subjective fear. The proper and usual approach was expressed as follows by the Tribunal in *Asuming v SSHD (11530)*:

> we understand 'fear' in an asylum claim to be nothing more nor less than a belief in that which the appellant states is likely to happen if he returns to his country of origin... one should not approach the issue on the basis of a need to assess whether a person is 'afraid' in the sense of being fearful rather than courageous.

In law and practice, subjective fear is secondary to objective fear. The objective aspect of the fear is the question of whether or not it is well-founded, i.e., whether or not the events that the claimant fears are indeed likely to come about.

Hathaway says that 'the use of the term "fear" was intended to emphasize the forward-looking nature of the refugee claim, not to ground refugee status in an assessment of the claimant's state of mind' (1991:75). This approach supports the purpose of the Convention which is to protect people from actual persecution and was approved in the leading Tribunal case of *Gashi and Nikshiqi* [1997] INLR 96. The same standard of proof applies to the subjective and objective aspects of fear (*Asuming*). The third colloquium on challenges in international refugee law produced the Michigan Guidelines on Well-Founded Fear (adopted 28 March 2004). These took a further step in this same direction by suggesting that the different psychological effects of the same circumstances should be considered not in relation to establishing the 'fear' but only in relation to persecution. The Guidelines in effect develop *Gashi and Nikshiqi* and Hathaway's earlier work by saying, not only that there is no need to look for a state of trepidation, but that doing so is harmful, discriminatory, and wrong (see Hathaway and Hicks 2005). For a contrary view, see Tuitt (1996:96–97) who argues that the central importance accorded to the test of objectively well-founded fear may be seen as part of a legal trend which enables the state to make generalized statements about safety to defeat an asylum claim.

We can summarize by saying that the subjective aspect of the fear is an anticipation that persecution would result if the asylum seeker returned to their home country. In general it will not come into question where there is evidence that the fear is well founded.

13.2.2 Objective fear

The applicant has the burden of proving that their fear is well founded, i.e., that there are objective grounds for believing that the fear will materialize. In proving that they face a risk of persecution in their country of origin, the refugee faces substantial difficulties. Not only are they outside their country of origin, in an unfamiliar environment, without access to common reference points, witnesses, or documents, but also, communication with their country of origin may be difficult or impossible. The very nature of their claim means that governmental sources in their own country will not be willing to provide supporting evidence. The refugee is not likely to have substantial documentary evidence proving their claim; they may not even have documents proving their identity. On the other hand, the consequences of refusing a valid claim could be extremely serious. As the Tribunal said in *Asuming*, 'Asylum cases differ from most other cases in the seriousness of the consequences of an erroneous decision, in the focus of the decision on the future, and the inherent difficulties of obtaining objective evidence.' In such a situation, the question of what standard of proof must be reached by the asylum claimant is all-important. Are they required to prove beyond reasonable doubt that they will be persecuted on return (the criminal standard) or on balance of probabilities (the civil standard) or on the lower standard that there is a risk of persecution or a reasonable likelihood (the standard formerly used in the 1993 Act in relation to whether torture may have occurred)?

13.2.2.1 *Standard of proof*

The House of Lords' judgment in *R v SSHD ex p Sivakumaran* [1988] AC 958 established that the asylum seeker should be required to establish a reasonable degree of likelihood that their fear will materialize, i.e., that persecution will take place. The standard of proof to be applied was variously described in that case as 'a reasonable chance', 'substantial grounds for thinking', 'a serious possibility', and 'a one in ten chance'. The standard has remained the same since that time, but is now usually more simply expressed as a 'real risk' (see *PS (Sri Lanka) v SSHD* [2008] EWCA Civ 1213).

What has happened in the past is an important indicator of what may happen in the future. The Qualification Directive says:

> The fact that an applicant has already been subject to persecution or serious harm or to direct threats of such persecution or such harm, is a serious indication of the applicant's well-founded fear of persecution or real risk of suffering serious harm, unless there are good reasons to consider that such persecution or serious harm will not be repeated. (Article 4.4)

It must still be determined what *has* happened in the past, and in the case of *Kaja (11038)*, an experienced Tribunal convened for the purpose of resolving the question held that the *Sivakumaran* standard of proof should be applied to the question of whether past events had taken place as well as to whether persecution would take place in the future. So, if the applicant claimed that they had been beaten in custody and that this would recur, both matters need to be proved to be a reasonable likelihood. In fact, the Tribunal said, past events and future risks were all part of the same question. To divide past events from assessment of future risks is artificial as assessment of future risk will depend to a great extent on an evaluation of what has happened in the past. *Kaja* has been relied upon since as authority for the proposition simply as stated earlier, that the lower standard of proof should be applied to past events as well as the chance of future occurrences. Brooke LJ in *Karanakaran* [2000] Imm AR 271 suggested that this is an oversimplification of the Tribunal's judgment which amounts to mis-stating it, and that the decision should be applied using its full reasoning. This was that a decision-maker in an asylum claim will be faced with four kinds of evidence:

1. evidence whose validity they are certain about;
2. evidence they think is probably true;
3. evidence to which they are willing to attach some credence, but would not go so far as to say that it is probably true; and
4. evidence to which they are not willing to attach any credence at all.

The contentious area is the third category of evidence, as this falls below the standard of proof which would warrant reliance upon it in a civil claim. The Tribunal's view in *Kaja* was that the asylum decision-maker should not exclude such evidence from their mind.

Karanakaran steers decision-makers away from a mechanistic approach to the standard of proof. It is not that the asylum seeker must prove the matters alleged to the standard of reasonable likelihood. In itself, this can become a rather meaningless word game, as though the phrase had the precision of a percentage and as though events and risks could be proved to a quantifiable degree. A refugee claim is not like a civil claim in which there are two competing sets of evidence, one of which the judge must prefer. A refugee claim is not an adversarial process at all. Rather, although *Sivakumaran* and *Kaja* represent appropriate standards if standards are required, the inherent uncertainty of future possibilities and of the evaluation of evidence must be understood. Assessing an asylum claim is not a matter simply of fact-finding but, crucially, of evaluation. It must be approached as a whole, as a public law enquiry into the need for protection rather than as an exercise in proving facts to a standard. The risks of over-applying a formulation were identified by Sedley LJ in *Batayav v SSHD* [2003] EWCA Civ 1489: 'Great care needs to be taken with such epithets. They are intended to elucidate the jurisprudential concept of real risk, not to replace it' (para 38). He used the example of a faulty type of car, quoted in chapter 4 (the real risk standard applies also to Article 3 claims). Even if only one car in ten actually crashes, most people would think there was a real risk of travelling in such a car. There do not have to be frequent or routine failures for this to be the case. In *PS (Sri Lanka)* the Court of Appeal said:

> The single test of whether a fear of persecution or ill-treatment is well-founded is whether on the evidence there is a real risk of its occurrence or recurrence. This straightforward formula now replaces the sometimes confusing variants which have been used over the years.

The application of this approach is a question of assessing the evidence in every case. Evidence of likelihood or of risk involves evidence of context and surrounding factors which may suggest for instance trends of behaviour by police or security forces. Asylum cases therefore rely not only on evidence concerning the particular applicant, but also on evidence of what has happened to people who are in a comparable situation in the country concerned. As discussed in the previous chapter, these kinds of evidence are procured by using expert evidence and regularly produced reports on the overall situation in particular countries by organizations such as Human Rights Watch, Amnesty International, the US State Department, and the Home Office's Country of Origin Information Service.

In *Hariri v SSHD* [2003] EWCA Civ 807, the Court of Appeal said that the appellant's case depended entirely on whether he would suffer ill-treatment as a member of a class, either of draft evaders or of those who had left Syria without authority. Therefore, the question of whether there was generally a pattern of ill-treatment of such people was crucial to establishing whether there was a real risk to the appellant.

13.2.3 Timing of fear

The well-founded fear must, at the time of the claim, be an operative cause of the asylum seeker's being away from their country of origin. In the case of *Adan* [1998] Imm AR 338, the House of Lords considered whether historic fear, i.e., fear in the past, would be sufficient to found refugee status, and concluded that it would not. Article 1(A)(2) says that it is 'owing to a well-founded fear' that the refugee 'is' outside their country of nationality. In Mr Adan's case, he could not, at the time of his claim, avail himself of the protection of his country (Somalia) as there was no effective government to offer that protection. However, the initial fear which had caused him to flee had subsided as President Barré had fallen and the risk to him of persecution was accordingly lessened. The House of Lords said that there were two parts to a refugee claim, the 'fear test' and the 'protection test', and held that Mr Adan could not obtain refugee status because the fear did not still exist, even though no governmental protection was available and there were risks to him consequent on the continuing civil war.

In *In re B; R v Special Adjudicator ex p Hoxha (UNHCR intervening)* [2005] UKHL 19, the House of Lords considered an argument centred on the cessation clause in Article 1C of the Refugee Convention. As discussed in the last chapter, this clause provides for the ending of refugee status when there has been such a radical change in the circumstances in the refugee's country of origin that they can no longer fail to avail themselves of their country's protection. There is an exception in Article 1C where a refugee is able to 'invoke compelling reasons arising out of past persecution'. The appellants in *Hoxha* had not obtained refugee status because of the changed circumstances in Kosovo. They argued that the persecution they had suffered in the past was nevertheless so severe that they should not be obliged to return. The House of Lords rejected this argument. An exception to the cessation clause could not be used to achieve refugee status for someone who had not achieved it on their asylum application. Their fear was not current, as was required in order to obtain protection.

13.2.4 Refugee *sur place*

The opposite situation also arises, where a refugee has left their country of origin without fear for some other purpose, e.g., a holiday or study, but during their absence an event such as a change of government takes place which causes them to fear persecution should they return. In this case the fear is the operative cause of their remaining outside their country of nationality, even though it was not the cause of their leaving it. They are thus entitled to claim refugee status and are referred to, following the French, as a refugee '*sur place*'.

It follows that if events since the applicant's arrival in the UK may give rise to a well-founded fear, these events may take place not only in the applicant's home country but equally in the UK, in fact they may be the actions of the applicant themselves. This was established by the Court of Appeal in *Danian* [2000] Imm AR 96, in which it was confirmed that refugee status could be granted after the applicant was at risk of persecution in his country of nationality because of his activities in the UK.

This decision does not necessarily mean that a person may create their own refugee status cynically by undertaking political activities in the UK when they have no genuine political motive. This question has been considered in a number of cases since *Danian*. The Court of Appeal in *Iftikhar Ahmed v SSHD* [2000] INLR 1 explained that *Danian* simply brings the decision back to the essential question, 'is there a serious risk that on return the applicant would be persecuted for a Convention reason?' In *Danian* itself, the Court endorsed the view of the UNHCR:

> it should be borne in mind that opportunistic post-flight activities will not necessarily create a real risk of persecution in the claimant's home country either because they will not come to the attention of the authorities of that country or because the opportunistic nature of such activities will be apparent to all including to those authorities.

Cases may turn on evidence of monitoring by the home country's government of nationals abroad. See for instance the cases on appeal in *TM (Zimbabwe), KM (Zimbabwe) and LZ (Zimbabwe) v SSHD* [2010] EWCA Civ 916 discussed at 13.6.5. It follows that it is a mistake to dismiss the claim without considering the effect of activities in the UK on the applicant's prospects on return (*R v IAT ex p Mafuta* [2001] EWCA Civ 745).

Mr Danian himself ultimately lost his appeal when the case came back to the Tribunal, after the Court of Appeal decision. The Tribunal considered that lack of good faith undermined the credibility of a well-founded fear of persecution. It took the view that if Mr Danian's motives were cynical, then he did not have a fear, and on the facts of his political involvement in the UK, the Nigerian authorities would not impute to him a political opinion. The *sur place* option is left open by the Qualification Directive, which says that a fear of being persecuted may be based on events which have taken place since the applicant left the country of origin and on activities undertaken since then by the applicant, in particular where these 'constitute the expression and continuation of convictions or orientations held in the country of origin' (Article 5.2). This leaves all aspects of Danian intact. In *YB (Eritrea)* [2008] EWCA Civ 360 Sedley LJ applied the Qualification Directive, observing that even if the sole or main purpose of *sur place* activities was to create the conditions for international protection, the claim should succeed unless the authorities in the home state were likely to treat the activities as insincere and opportunistic.

Where a first claim for asylum has failed and the applicant submits a further application, the Directive permits Member States to introduce a presumption against the grant of refugee status on such a basis (Article 5.3). The UK government made it known that it would not instate such a presumption, and there is none in the implementing rules or regulations.

13.2.4.1 *Rejected asylum claims*

A related issue is the effect of the asylum claim itself on what treatment the individual might face on return. The Home Office occasionally accepts as a matter of policy that returning people to particular countries may not be possible because the fact of having made an asylum claim may bring reprisals from their home government. In the case of Libya, the Home Office previously adopted a policy of this kind in 2001 (see *Hassan* [2002] UKIAT 00062). More recently, the only country to which, as a matter of acknowledged public policy, removals did not take place for some years has been Zimbabwe (letter Des Browne to Keith Best IAS published 12 July 2004). Amid protest, in November 2004 the Home Office lifted this moratorium. In Zimbabwe, some politicians welcomed the move, but Information Minister, Jonathan Moyo, considered that returnees should be treated with suspicion as they could be 'trained and bribed malcontents', sent to disrupt the election (newsvote.bbc.co.uk 17 December 2004). The resumption of returns caused not only a political and legal storm, but also scores of asylum seekers to go on hunger strike in detention. Eventually, the Home Secretary was forced to concede that removals to Zimbabwe could not continue at least until the hearing of a test case. Interestingly, on the same day, the European Parliament issued a far-reaching resolution on Zimbabwe, calling for the strengthening of sanctions and condemning the regime but making no reference to the return of failed asylum seekers (7 July 2005). After five Tribunal determinations and four Court of Appeal judgments, the legal situation at the time of writing is that failed asylum seekers per se are not held to be at risk on return to Zimbabwe, but some of those whose claim has failed may be at such risk. These are mentioned in the context of political opinion at 13.6.5.

Comparable arguments were made in the case of failed asylum seekers returning to the Democratic Republic of Congo, and the High Court asked the Home Office to suspend removals to DRC while this matter was under consideration. The Court of Appeal eventually endorsed the Tribunal's decision that there was insufficient evidence that people returning were at risk simply by virtue of being failed asylum seekers (*BK (DRC)* [2008] EWCA Civ 1322). As signatories to the Refugee Convention and with intelligence personnel active in the UK, the DRC government could be taken to know that asylum procedures were conducted in private and did not involve public denunciation of the state of origin. The accounts of failed asylum seekers would by definition have been disbelieved and so would not have brought discredit on the DRC government. While it is clear that there is no rule in law or policy that people from a particular country whose asylum claims have failed are thereby at risk, concerns over the same countries continue. A Report by Justice First found evidence of ill-treatment on return to DRC (*Unsafe Return* 2011). Flights returning refused asylum seekers to Iraq were stopped in June 2011 after evidence given in the High Court of ill-treatment of returnees at Baghdad airport. NGOs lobby for monitoring of what happens to refused asylum seekers who are returned, but the government accepts no formal responsibility for monitoring, having not opted into the Returns Directive 2008/115/EC (*House of Commons* 2011 *Hansard Written Answers for 21 June 2011* Col. 208W Damien Green MP).

In addition to general country policies, it may be necessary to argue that the return of a particular failed asylum seeker is not safe. In *Degirmenci v SSHD* [2004] EWCA Civ 1553, the Court of Appeal held that there needed to be a full assessment of the evidence relating to the treatment on return to Turkey of a Kurdish failed asylum seeker such as the appellant. Where, for instance, as in *Yapici* (see 13.3.2.1) the appellant had left the country in breach of reporting conditions, this would increase the risk of their coming to the notice of the authorities. Risk may also be established where the asylum seeker left their country illegally (e.g., *MO (illegal exit – risk on return) Eritrea* CG [2011] UKUT 00190 (IAC)).

13.3 Persecution

The concept of persecution is central to the recognition of refugee status. It is not conclusively defined, and in fact the *UNHCR Handbook* expressly avoids attempting to lay down any such definition, saying that whether threats or actions will amount to persecution 'will depend on the circumstances of each case' (para 52) and 'it is not possible to lay down a general rule as to what cumulative reasons can give rise to a valid claim to refugee status' (para 53).

The Qualification Directive Article 9 says that to amount to persecution acts must be 'sufficiently serious by their nature or repetition' to constitute 'a severe violation of basic human rights' particularly those which are non-derogable under the ECHR (see chapter 4), or must be an accumulation of measures, including violations of human rights, which is severe enough to affect an individual similarly to a severe violation of non-derogable rights. The second paragraph of the Article is an important development in refugee law in Europe:

2. Acts of persecution as qualified in paragraph 1, can, inter alia, take the form of:
   (a) acts of physical or mental violence, including acts of sexual violence;
   (b) legal, administrative, police, and/or judicial measures which are in themselves discriminatory or which are implemented in a discriminatory manner;
   (c) prosecution or punishment, which is disproportionate or discriminatory;
   (d) denial of judicial redress resulting in a disproportionate or discriminatory punishment;

(e) prosecution or punishment for refusal to perform military service in a conflict, where performing military service would include crimes or acts falling under the exclusion clauses as set out in Article 12(2);

(f) acts of a gender-specific or child-specific nature.

We shall return to this list as the matters arise.

One approach to identifying persecution, in a line of cases of which *Jonah* [1985] Imm AR 7 is the oft-quoted authority, has been reliance on the dictionary definition: 'to pursue with malignancy or injurious action'. However, this requires a focus on the motive and actions of the persecutor. It might be said that a person tortured once in a police station and then released has not been 'pursued' and that a person who would be prosecuted for any expression of their sexuality is not the target of malignancy but of government policy. Whereas the dictionary definition would work for some cases, it does not for others. This approach has been falling into disuse in favour of an emphasis on the acts or their effects rather than the motive. The Qualification Directive does not attempt to define persecution as such, but only acts of persecution, as described previously.

The Tribunal in *Gashi* adopted the submission of the UNHCR that: 'for the Convention to be a living instrument of protection, the term "persecution" must be interpreted in a manner that best achieves its humanitarian object and purpose'. The Tribunal went on to say that 'it would be a mistake to attempt a definition of persecution which could in any way restrict its power to meet the changing circumstances in which the Convention has to operate'. A simple formulation is that persecution = serious harm + failure of state protection (set out in this way by the Refugee Women's Legal Group (*Women as Asylum Seekers* 1997:9)). This is a workable formulation which underscores the crucial aspect of state responsibility and has been used by the courts, for instance by Lord Hoffmann in *R v IAT & SSHD ex p Shah and Islam v IAT* [1999] 2 AC 629.

There must be an analysis of whether what is feared in a particular case is persecution. However, the decision-maker does not so much *define* persecution as *identify* it. The difference is that a definition is an attempt to provide in the abstract a statement that will apply in a wide range (preferably all) circumstances, whereas identification starts with a set of circumstances and asks whether these amount to persecution. The Qualification Directive approach to acts of persecution is consistent with the commonly used starting point proffered by Hathaway:

> The sustained or systemic violation of basic human rights demonstrative of a failure of state protection in relation to one of the core entitlements which has been recognized by the international community. The types of harm to be protected against include the breach of any rights within the first category, a discriminatory or non-emergency abnegation of a right within the second category or the failure to implement a right in the third category which is either discriminatory or not grounded in the absolute lack of resources. (1991:112)

The three categories to which he refers he sets out in the following way:

> *Category one*:
> Freedom from arbitrary deprivation of life, from torture, cruel, inhuman or, degrading treatment or punishment, from slavery, imprisonment for breach of a contractual obligation, retroactive criminal prosecution, freedom of thought, conscience and religion, and the right to be recognized as a person in law.
>
> *Category two*:
> Freedom from arbitrary arrest and detention, right to a fair trial, equal treatment including in access to public employment, freedom of expression, assembly and association, of movement

inside a country, to leave and return to one's country of origin, to form and join trade unions, to take part in public affairs and vote, and protection for privacy and the family.

Category three:
The right to work, including just and favourable conditions of employment, to an adequate standard of living including food, clothing and housing, to the highest attainable standard of health, to education, and to engage in cultural, scientific, literary, and artistic expression.

This human rights approach to persecution was broadly adopted by the UNHCR and from them by the Tribunal in *Gashi and Nikshiqi*. It has been used and endorsed by the higher courts for instance the House of Lords in *Horvath v SSHD* [2000] 3 All ER 577 and *Sepet and Bulbul v SSHD* [2003] UKHL 15. It is an extremely useful framework though not final or definitive, and it has some limitations (see for instance Wilsher 2003). Goodwin-Gill proposes a formulation of 'reasons, interests and measures': the reasons for persecution would be race, religion and so on; the interests affected would be fundamental ones such as life and liberty; and the measures are the infliction of harm, arbitrary arrest and so on (2007:132). This formulation steers away from focusing on persecution as a special kind of activity, but rather emphasizes the actual consequences and the denial of rights.

Whatever approach is taken to identifying persecution, it requires both 'serious harm' and a failure of state protection.

In the leading case of *Horvath*, Lord Hope said: 'The general purpose of the Convention is to enable the person who no longer has the benefit of state protection against persecution for a Convention reason in his own country to turn for protection to the international community'. This is known as the principle of surrogacy. The underlying idea is the breakdown in the relationship between citizen and state, so that the citizen can no longer rely on the state for the protection which is their due, and must look instead to the international community. This may entail that the state is actively the persecutor, as when the police torture people in their custody. Alternatively, it may entail that others perpetrate the serious harm, as when skinheads attack Roma people, but the state fails to protect them. When persecution is carried out in this way by non-state actors, further legal problems arise, and these are discussed at 13.3.4.

Professor Hathaway's reference to the 'systemic violation' of rights suggests that the violation is part of the functioning of the state system, the state endorses the violations, implicitly by not providing redress or explicitly by for instance oppressive legislation, or covertly, by promoting brutal interrogation by security services.

This may be distinguished from, although it is connected to, the question of whether ill-treatment must be *systematic* to amount to persecution. This is sometimes used in the same way as 'systemic', but may also be used to mean 'repeated' or 'persistent', which will often be appropriate but not always. Where the violation feared is sufficiently serious, e.g., killing or torture, there is no necessity for repetition in order for this to be persecution.

The Qualification Directive follows the earlier EU Joint Position of 4 March 1996, in saying that acts feared will be persecution if sufficiently serious by reason of 'their nature or their repetition'. Either severity or repetition is required, but not both.

The authorities on a single instance of ill-treatment as persecution were comprehensively reviewed in the case of *Doymus* 00/TH/01748, expanding upon the Court of Appeal judgment in *Demirkaya* [1999] Imm AR 498, where Stuart-Smith LJ said:

At one end of the scale there may be arbitrary deprivation of life, torture and cruel, inhuman and degrading treatment or punishment. In such a case the conduct may be so extreme that one instance is sufficient, but less serious conduct may not amount to persecution unless it is persistent. (para 15)

That a single violation of a first category right would constitute persecution is so, not only in common sense (a single threat to life is enough) but also by reference to the human rights instruments from which these standards are derived. For instance 'no one shall be subjected to torture or to cruel, inhuman or degrading treatment or punishment' (Article 9 ICCPR as well as Article 3 ECHR). This does not allow an exception if the torture happens only once, and case law under these Articles treats single acts of torture or cruel, inhuman or degrading treatment, or punishment as violations. The Tribunal in *Doymus* cited other academic writers, the UNHCR, and case law of other jurisdictions also as authorities that, while persistency is a usual characteristic of persecution, it is not an inevitable one.

There is no requirement to be 'singled out' for persecution (*R v SSHD ex p Jeyakumaran* [1994] Imm AR 45). If the persecutory treatment is for a reason included in the Convention (see 13.6), the fact that others who share the same characteristic are treated similarly may be evidence that supports the asylum claim but it does not detract from it. As Lord Lloyd said in *Adan* at 348: 'It is not necessary for a claimant to show that he is more at risk than anyone else in his group, if the group as a whole is subject to oppression.' Conversely, there is no need for all those sharing the characteristic to be persecuted (*Shah and Islam*). However, in situations of civil war, there will not be a refugee claim where *all* sections of society are similarly in fear (*SSHD v Adan* [1999] 1 AC 293). Where the refugee's country of origin has been in a state of armed conflict for many years, there are particular difficulties in assessing an asylum claim. The House of Lords in *Adan* required, for a successful claim, that where society had broken down into continual conflict 'the individual or group has to show a well-founded fear of persecution over and above the risk to life and liberty inherent in civil war' (para 349). However, as discussed in chapter 12, Article 15c of the Qualification Directive contains a provision which has created a new possibility of protection in limited instances as a result of war.

13.3.1 Severe ill-treatment

As discussed in *Doymus* and *Demirkaya*, a single instance of sufficiently severe ill-treatment may amount to persecution. Loss of life and torture admit of no justification or derogation. This was made very clear by the House of Lords in *R v SSHD ex p Sivakumar* [2003] 1 WLR 840 where even the applicant's suspected involvement in terrorism could not justify the appalling torture he had experienced. The recent attempts by governments to justify torture have already been discussed in chapter 4.

The UN Convention against Torture and Other Cruel Inhuman or Degrading Treatment Article 1(1) defines torture as:

> An act by which pain or suffering, whether physical or mental, is intentionally inflicted on a person for such purposes as obtaining from him or a third person a confession, punishing him for an act which he or a third party has committed or is suspected of having committed, or intimidating him or a third person, or for any reason based on discrimination of any kind, when such pain or suffering is inflicted by or at the instigation of or with the consent of public officials or other person acting in an official capacity.

This Article has not been widely referred to in refugee cases, though it was used as guidance by the High Court in *R v SSHD ex p Javed and Ali* [2000] EWHC (Admin) 7.

It suggests that not only the conduct but also who carried it out and the reason are significant in determining whether it amounts to torture. However, Goodwin-Gill and McAdam (2007:96) point out that there is no need for an asylum claimant to prove any particular intention on the part of their persecutor, nor that any particular person carries it out. Indeed, as *Sivakumar* makes plain, intention may be irrelevant, and the discussion which follows will show that who carries it out is less important than whether the state can provide protection.

In *Doymus*, the Tribunal recognized that it was not just the level of ill-treatment that was relevant but also the psychological effects. The applicant had described being stripped naked, sprayed with cold water from a hose, and beaten with a stick while his hands were tied behind his back. The Tribunal held that this was likely to 'give rise to feelings of fear, anguish, and inferiority capable of humiliating and debasing him and possibly breaking his physical and moral resistance'. This would be a breach of Article 3 ECHR or Article 9 ICCPR, it was degrading treatment, and it was unnecessary to determine whether it amounted to torture. The judgment in *Doymus* thus links an act of persecution explicitly to human rights norms. In *Demirkaya* the Court of Appeal expressly disapproved trying to categorize behaviour such that a particular level of ill-treatment would amount to persecution. The question should be looked at in the round. 'Is this person at risk of persecution for a Convention reason?' The Court said that this was a question of fact.

In a case such as *Doymus*, there is no examination of the motives of the police. It was an essential and undisputed element of Mr Doymus' claim that he was at risk because of his political affiliations, and the precise anticipated motives of the police on any particular occasion do not require inquiry. This is all the more so the case as torture cannot be justified and so even if their motive was to preserve law and order this would not prevent the feared action being persecution. If motive is unimportant, rape and other serious sexual assault receive anomalous treatment in refugee law.

13.3.1.1 *Rape and other sexual violence*

The Qualification Directive and UK implementing regulations include, in their list of acts of persecution, 'acts of physical or mental violence, including acts of sexual violence'. Although this is not new in law, in practice there has been a persistent failure at all stages of asylum decision-making to recognize rape and other sexual violence as forms of persecution (see Ceneda and Palmer 2006, Asylum Aid 2011). Various organizations have produced guidelines on gender issues in asylum claims, including sexual violence, e.g., the Refugee Women's Legal Group in 1998, the Immigration Appellate Authority in 2000, and UNHCR in 2002. UKBA developed their own guidance to decision-makers (API Gender issues in the asylum claim, revised 2010).

The guidelines produced by a small group of immigration judges for the Immigration Appellate Authority in 2000 addressed directly and with authority the use of sexual violence as a form of torture or cruel inhuman or degrading treatment or punishment, refuting 'the myth that rape is sexually motivated – it is usually intended to inflict violence and humiliation' (Assistant Commissioner Wyn Jones of the Metropolitan Police).

They cited the Statutes of the International Tribunals for Former Yugoslavia and Rwanda, which list rape as a crime against humanity, and the Article 3 ECHR case of *Aydin v Turkey* (1997) 25 EHRR 251 para 83 in which the Court said:

Rape of a detainee by an official of the State must be considered to be an especially grave and abhorrent form of ill-treatment given the ease with which the offender can exploit the vulnerability and weakened resistance of his victim.

The IAA gender guidelines however were quietly dropped. A Parliamentary Question on 7 February 2007 (HL 1596) elicited the response that the gender guidelines were out of date, replaced by case law, and non-binding in any event. There is now a Joint Presidential Guidance note (no. 2 of 2010) on the conduct of hearings involving child, vulnerable, or sensitive witnesses. This gives some guidance on the assessment of evidence from people who have been traumatized. The Home Office guidance, represented by the API also deals with sensitivity to trauma, in the context of the asylum interview. However, neither the guidelines for tribunals nor for Home Office caseworkers cover the same ground as the IAA guidelines in that they do not explain the political uses of sexual violence (Ceneda and Palmer 2006 and see Women's Asylum News no. 96).

In the absence of this understanding, the research shows that the harm to the asylum seeker is often minimized. Also, there is much confused thinking about the motivation of the persecutor. This may be illustrated by the case of *R v Special Adjudicator ex p Okonkwo* [1998] Imm AR 502, where Collins J supported the distinction made by the adjudicator between rape committed 'merely to seek sexual gratification' and rape committed for some other motive. If it was 'merely to seek sexual gratification', then it was a common crime on a par with assault, and would not amount to torture unless repeated. It was argued for the applicant that rape constituted torture in part because the psychological effects can be similar to those referred to in *Doymus*, namely of fear, anguish, humiliation, and inferiority, and also because of the severity of the physical ill-treatment. Of course, the necessary element of state involvement must exist, as a crime which is investigated and punished is not persecution. In *Okonkwo*, the assailant was an army officer who had previously threatened the applicant. She had suffered violence before from the authorities. She was not in detention at the time of the rape, but was attacked by the roadside and left there. The location and the lack of formal relationship between the assailant and applicant influenced Collins J in his agreement with the adjudicator. However, this leaves out of account the exercise of power by a member of the military forces and the lack of redress.

The reasoning in *Okonkwo* has been followed in later cases, for instance in *Farhat Saeed Chaudhary* 00/TH/00304, in which the adjudicator found and the Tribunal accepted that rape by police could have been for sexual gratification and was therefore not persecution. Again, in *R v IAT ex p Arafa Shaban* [2000] Imm AR 408, the motive of the rapist who was a member of the ruling political party, the applicant being associated with the opposition, was regarded as relevant. In *Bajraktari* [2001] EWHC Admin 1192, Harrison J found that rape did not constitute torture because it was not used to extract information.

The case law in this area in the UK has been slow to recognize the political nature of much sexual violence. Even systematic rape by armed forces has not necessarily been recognized as persecution, as in *R (N) v SSHD* [2002] EWCA Civ 1082, where the claimant had suffered double rape by armed forces who took away her son (and had probably killed him). The adjudicator had found that the rape was for sexual gratification, and this argument prevailed before the Court of Appeal, who saw the situation as one of uncontrolled lawlessness by soldiers and did not construe this in the light of discrimination. *PS (Sri Lanka) v SSHD* [2008] EWCA Civ 1213 departed from this trend.

Key Case

***PS (Sri Lanka) v SSHD* [2008] EWCA Civ 1213**

The appellant was a Tamil living in the Jaffna Peninsula, where the insurgent LTTE was active. In 2006, she was raped in her home, which was also her father's grocery shop, by two Sri Lankan soldiers who used to make purchases there. Five days later, one of them returned with another soldier, and both of them raped her. A week or so later, the same two returned and again raped her, holding her father at gunpoint so that he would witness it. The appellant tried to kill herself. She failed, and her father took her to the home of her uncle with a view to her fleeing the country. Before she was able to do so, she found herself pregnant and then miscarried or aborted. In the interim, the soldiers had returned to her home, looking for her. In the UK, she was refused asylum and humanitarian protection.

The Tribunal on reconsideration upheld the Home Office's refusal, saying that the fact that she had been raped three times had no bearing on whether it would happen again; the rapes were the actions of rogue officers not sanctioned by the authorities, and if they did come back she could seek the protection of the authorities.

The Court of Appeal overturned that decision. Sedley LJ said that with perpetrators in the uniform of the state, there was no sensible possibility of state protection. The characterization of the soldiers' conduct as no different from that of civilian rapists was unsustainable. The whole point was that, unlike ordinary criminals, the soldiers were in a position to repeat their crime with no apparent prospect of detection or punishment.

This case is important in considering the issue of state protection, discussed at 13.3.4, and also demonstrates the issue under discussion. The UNHCR Global Consultations Summary Conclusions on gender-related persecution say that one of the main problems facing women asylum seekers is 'failure to recognize the political nature of seemingly private acts of harm to women' (para 4).

As appears from this, the recognition of sexual violence as persecution is bound up with the recognition of gender-based persecution, which is discussed further in relation to the Convention reason for persecution at 13.6. A fundamental issue is that much violence perpetrated on the basis of gender is socially sanctioned either by law or by practice, whether or not it is violence committed by a sexual act. Recognition of an asylum claim on such a basis therefore involves a political judgment which may go against the tide of public thinking either in the country of origin or the host country or both. An example of increasing importance is the practice known variously as female genital cutting or mutilation, or female circumcision (FGM). Case law concerning this practice went in all directions until the Court of Appeal in *P and M v SSHD* [2004] EWCA Civ 1640 accepted that forcible subjection to female genital mutilation was severe ill-treatment which, combined with the absence of state intervention to prevent or punish it, amounted to persecution. This has now been put beyond doubt in the House of Lords' judgment in *SSHD v Fornah* [2006] UKHL 46, in which Lord Bingham described FGM as 'an extreme and very cruel expression of male dominance'. This case is discussed further at 13.6.4.1.

The use and effects of sexual violence as a weapon of war are simply and eloquently described in an obiter passage of the judgment of Baroness Hale in *In re B & R v Special Adjudicator ex p Hoxha* [2005] UKHL 19. She explains that the effect may be compounded by a society which:

adds to the earlier suffering she has endured the pain, hardship and indignity of rejection and ostracism from her own people. There are many cultures in which a woman suffers almost as much from the attitudes of those around her to the degradation she has suffered as she did from the original assault. (para 32)

13.3.2 Second category rights

In relation to violations of rights in Hathaway's second category, for instance detention, ill-treatment in detention short of torture, or denial of a fair trial, international human rights' instruments give states some limited power to derogate or to justify infringements. For example, detention may be justified for one of a number of listed reasons in Article 5 ECHR. This is reflected in refugee law. The leading case which demonstrates this is *Sandralingham and Ravichandran* [1996] Imm AR 97, CA.

Key Case

Sandralingham and Ravichandran **[1996] Imm AR 97, CA**

This case arose from periodic round-ups by the Sri Lankan police of young Tamil men and their detention for questioning, sometimes for periods of days. The appellants had been so detained, and had also been ill-treated in custody. They alleged that ill-treatment in custody and arbitrary arrest and detentions each separately constituted persecution. It was accepted that the situation had improved since the time when they were detained. There was therefore no reasonable likelihood of repetition of ill-treatment in detention and so this part of the claim fell out of the picture.

In considering detention as possible persecution, the Court of Appeal held following factors were relevant:

(i) the frequency of round-ups and the length of the detentions resulting;
(ii) the situation prevailing in Colombo at the material time and the Sri Lankan government's undoubted need to combat Tamil terrorism;
(iii) the true purpose of the round-ups and the efforts made to arrest and detain only those realistically suspected of involvement in the disturbances.

The Court of Appeal endorsed the respondent's argument that:

young male Tamils are not arrested and detained because they are Tamils but rather because they may have been involved in some outrage. The round-ups are not arbitrary. The very fact that the particular sub-groups identified by the Amnesty Report are especially vulnerable to arrest shows that the true objective of the round-ups is to combat terrorism rather than discriminate against Tamils as such. (at 108)

It accepted that the authorities' attempts to control disorder had affected Tamils the most because more of the disorder had occurred in areas where Tamils lived. Detention of excessive length could amount to persecution, repeated detention of the same person could amount to persecution if it was not justified by an appropriate level of suspicion of that individual's having committed a criminal offence, and ill-treatment in detention would normally amount to persecution. However, if innocent people were accidentally caught up in a legitimate policing exercise, this was not persecution even if they were likely to be of a particular minority. This last point shows that it is difficult to consider persecution separately from the reason for the persecution. The reason for persecution is discussed later under the heading of 'Convention reason'.

In *Ravichandran*, Staughton LJ said that '[p]ersecution must at least be persistent and serious ill-treatment without just cause'. It is apparent how this arises from the facts of *Ravichandran* in which a single instance of detention was not held to be persecution, but the statement should not be taken out of context to require that persecution must *always* be persistent. The Qualification Directive list of acts of persecution includes 'legal, administrative, police, and/or judicial measures which are in themselves discriminatory or which are implemented in a discriminatory manner'.

13.3.2.1 *Prosecution or persecution?*

Continuing the consideration of second category rights, it is undeniable that the state has a right to prosecute its citizens, even a duty to do so in order to maintain law and order for the benefit of others. The *UNHCR Handbook* puts it in this way:

> Persecution must be distinguished from punishment for a common law offence. Persons fleeing from prosecution or punishment for such an offence are not normally refugees. It should be recalled that a refugee is a victim – or potential victim – of injustice, not a fugitive from justice. (para 56)

However, prosecution may amount to persecution in certain circumstances. If a punishment is excessive, this may turn prosecution into persecution. For instance, it may be within lawful bounds of state action for there to be some penalty for adultery, but stoning to death goes beyond that (*Shah and Islam*).

The discriminatory application of the law may also turn prosecution into persecution, as suggested in the quotation from *Ravichandran*. If people had been detained because they were Tamils, then this could have amounted to persecution. The *Handbook* gives the example of prosecution for an offence of public order for the distribution of pamphlets, which could be 'a vehicle for the persecution of the individual on the grounds of the political content of the publication' (para 59). In *Sivakumar* in the Court of Appeal [2002] INLR 310, Dyson LJ used the following words which were quoted with approval by the House of Lords:

> Where a person to whom a political opinion is imputed or who is a member of a race or social group is the subject of sanctions that do not apply generally in the state, then it is more likely than not that the application of the sanctions is discriminatory and persecutory for a Convention reason. (para 30)

The House of Lords added the caveat that this should not be used to suggest a rebuttable inference in the legal sense. There are many examples of cases in which the reason for prosecution is the political opinion imputed to the applicant, and this renders the prosecution persecutory for Convention purposes (e.g., *Asante* [1991] Imm AR 78).

The issue is less clear when an individual is not targeted for enforcement for a discriminatory reason, but enforcement of the law has a discriminatory impact. On the face of it, the claims of Turkish Kurds for refugee status on account of conscription into the military raise this issue as a significant proportion of the work of the military may be engaged in action against the minority to which they belong. However, these claims have on the whole not been successful. This is dealt with further at 13.6.5.1 in relation to the Convention reason for persecution and the implications of objection to military service.

Prosecution may also amount to persecution where there is a lack of due process or fairness in the criminal process. Hathaway says that where 'the decision to prosecute, the process under which the charge is heard, or the nature of the sentence imposed is politically manipulated' (1991:172) then the prosecution may found a refugee claim. The allegations were of this kind in *Khan v SSHD* [2003] EWCA Civ 530 where the appellant fled Bangladesh after a violent demonstration, as a result of which he had been charged and a warrant issued for his arrest. He believed that he would not be granted bail, would be detained in inhuman and degrading conditions for a long period of time, and would not receive a fair trial. The adjudicator had held that what he feared was prosecution rather than persecution, but the Court of Appeal agreed that the case must be reconsidered by the IAT when Mr Khan was able to prove that he had been sentenced to ten years' imprisonment in his absence. Where an individual is prosecuted for exercising fundamental human rights, then the prosecution may well be persecutory, but this will depend additionally on whether, in the circumstances, some curtailment of freedom is justified in the public interest, and if so, whether the curtailment imposed by the criminal law has exceeded what is justified. In Mr Khan's case, there may have been grounds for charging a public order offence, but this could not justify an unfair trial. The Qualification Directive recognizes this form of persecution by listing 'prosecution or punishment which is disproportionate or discriminatory' including if through 'lack of judicial redress'.

A conviction in their absence will not always prevent an asylum seeker from being removed from the UK or create a new ground of asylum where a previous one has failed. In *QJ (Algeria) v SSHD* [2010] EWCA Civ 1478 the issue before the Court was the appellant's deportation following offences relating to terrorism in the UK. He had also been convicted in his absence in Algeria. There was no evidence that a second trial in Algeria would not comply with the standards required by Article 6 ECHR, and the Court held that double jeopardy, while normally prohibited in UK law, was not prohibited as such by Article 6.

As mentioned earlier in relation to failed asylum seekers, many cases have concerned the question of whether dissidents will attract the attention of the authorities on return and so be at risk. In *Yapici v SSHD* [2005] EWCA Civ 826, the Court of Appeal held that a proper decision must have regard to the effect of the appellant's leaving the country in breach of reporting conditions. Although the appellant was in breach of an administrative requirement, his reason for being in breach and the fact that it could bring him to the notice of the authorities were relevant to whether he would be at risk on return. As mentioned earlier, a fear of prosecution that may amount to persecution on return is punishment faced by a refused asylum seeker who left their country illegally, as for instance in *MO (illegal exit – risk on return) Eritrea CG* [2011] UKUT 00190 (IAC).

13.3.3 Discrimination as persecution

The violation and threatened violation of rights in Hathaway's third category gives rise to difficult questions in refugee claims. The Refugee Convention protects against persecution, but not against discrimination in delivery of social rights. In an age of bitter inter-ethnic wars and discrimination against minorities so fundamental that in some cases they have been obliterated from social and political life, when does one become the other? This is one of the challenges to the international framework of human rights and refugee protection which was probably not contemplated in this form when the Convention was first drafted.

A formative case on this issue is *Gashi and Nikshiqi* [1997] INLR 96.

Key Case

***Gashi and Nikshiqi* [1997] INLR 96**

The appellants were ethnic Albanians from Kosovo. They had evaded military service, and their claim was based in part on the consequences for them of this evasion if they were to return and in part on the level of discrimination they would face as ethnic Albanians in Kosovo. There was an abundance of evidence before the Tribunal about the situation of ethnic Albanians in land, such as Kosovo, under Serb control. The government policy was referred to as 'Serbianization', implemented by, for instance (quoting from the Tribunal's summary of evidence):

> the removal of senior Albanians in the courts and public sector generally and restrictions in even the most menial of employment, e.g. street vendors. 80% of Albanians lost their posts... There is no control or evidence of any intended control by the central authority of the police in Kosovo and the police are all Serbians. There is a systematic state policy which, it is said, permits this police misbehaviour. In day to day life Albanians are harassed, subjected to house searches, beating, torture at police stations, constant checks carried out at random without any recourse to courts with an effective system to provide adequate remedies and protection to ethnic Albanians.

As a consequence, the Tribunal found that Mr Gashi and Mr Nikshiqi, in addition to prosecution for draft evasion, faced physical abuse, inability to obtain employment, and constant and persistent harassment by police uncontrolled by government.

In considering whether this would amount to persecution, the Tribunal drew on the internationally accepted view of the Convention as a living instrument. It said, 'it would be a mistake to attempt a definition of "persecution" which could in any way restrict its growth to meet the changing circumstances in which the Convention has to operate'. The prospects faced by Mr Gashi and Mr Nikshiqi amounted to persecution. The Tribunal's decision adopts the reasoning of the UNHCR on the question of discrimination without alteration. *Gashi and Nikshiqi* was by no means the first case to recognize denial of third category rights as a basis for refugee status, but the extensive judgment made it an authoritative and important turning point.

Where discrimination in social rights is feared, the assessment of whether this amounts to persecution and whether the individual will be protected necessarily involves questions that are concerned with the normal functioning of a society. In the case of, for instance, torture, any nation would say that this was an out of the ordinary occurrence. In the case of, for instance, exclusion from mainstream schooling, an assessment of social policies and practices enters the frame. These are highly political decisions as they are potentially more intrusive on the values and government of the country of origin than cases based on non-derogable rights. For instance, a number of Roma people from Eastern European countries made asylum claims in the UK based on severe life-long discrimination. The British Home Office Minister, Mike O'Brien, appeared on television to say that the majority of these claims would not be entertained as it was the job of the asylum seekers' own governments to resolve issues of discrimination, and they would not interfere in the internal matters of another state.

Applications from European Roma continued to be turned down, though it was questioned by academic commentators (see, for instance, O'Nions 1999) whether claims were genuinely considered on an individual basis. Evidence of severe discrimination against Roma continues to appear in cases in the ECtHR. For instance, in *DH v Czech Republic* (Application no. 57325/00) Judgment 15 November 2007, the ECtHR found by 13 votes to 4 that there had been discrimination against Roma children in the provision of education by placing the majority of them in special schools for children with learning disabilities or particularly low intelligence. In *Kalanyos v Romania* (Application no. 57884/00) Judgment 26 July 2007, the houses of Roma people had been burned down after threats to do so and the prosecution of the attackers was closed down partly on the basis that the Roma had brought it on themselves. The families affected lived in stables without heat or water as no alternative housing was provided. The case was settled because the Romanian government accepted that there had been violations of Articles 3, 6, 8, 13, and 14 of the ECHR. The emphasis in the Qualification Directive is on non-derogable rights, but there is scope for persecution to arise from 'an accumulation of various measures, including violation of human rights, which is sufficiently severe as to affect an individual in a similar manner to' severe violation of basic human rights. The Directive allows for claims based on discrimination, but only with reference to 'legal, administrative, police or judicial measures'. This seems to indicate a retreat at European level from countenancing claims with an economic basis. The *UNHCR Handbook* suggests that discrimination may amount to persecution where:

> measures of discrimination lead to consequences of a substantially prejudicial nature for the person concerned, e.g. serious restrictions on his right to earn a livelihood, his right to practise his religion, or his access to normally available educational facilities. (para 54)

The question, according to the Tribunal in *Gujda (18231)*, was whether the denial of social rights, education, housing, and so forth, is such that it interferes 'with a basic human right to live a decent life'. It must also be grounded in discrimination, not an absolute lack of resources in the state; citizens of countries where the majority live in extreme poverty cannot claim asylum on this basis. In *Harakal (also known as Harakel) v SSHD* [2001] EWCA Civ 884, the Court of Appeal found that a lifetime of serious discrimination should be taken into account in allowing the asylum claim of a Roma from the Czech Republic. The Court of Appeal described it as 'significant discrimination in all facets of his life throughout his life'. In *Chiver* (10758), the asylum application succeeded before the adjudicator where the claimant was a miner from Romania who had refused to take government orders to take part in breaking up anti-government demonstrations. He was dismissed from his job as a result, and refused a work card. Without this he was unable to obtain a job or any state benefits. He went on hunger strike, and was arrested and beaten by a policeman. His claim was based substantially on the denial of the right to a livelihood, and succeeded on this. It is noteworthy that although discrimination amounting to persecution is on the whole a more recent use of the Refugee Convention, a claim like this is a classic political refugee claim such as might have been envisaged by the drafters of the Convention.

Finally, as findings of discrimination require significant evidence of the law and practice in the refugee's country of origin, questions of discrimination are quite often dealt with by way of country guidance cases. For instance, in *SA (Divorced woman – illegitimate child) Bangladesh CG* [2011] UKUT 00254(IAC) the Tribunal was concerned with the question of what level of discrimination an unmarried mother might face in Bangladesh.

13.3.4 Effective state protection

So far we have been considering the serious harm aspect of persecution. This is closely bound up with the second aspect, that of lack of state protection. Assessing state protection requires consideration of three questions:

- Who will perpetrate the feared harm?
- What kind of protection is available against that?
- What kind of body is capable of delivering effective protection?

13.3.4.1 *Perpetrators – agents of the state*

This is the most obvious situation, where the feared persecution will be carried out by those who are part of the state machinery. Examples are the police, the military, security services, or perhaps a combination of branches of government, such as when the judiciary implement discriminatory laws passed by the legislature. An agent of the state may remain an agent of the state for Convention purposes, even though their actions do not necessarily reflect official government policy. For instance, the Turkish police who tortured Mr Doymus were not implementing a policy which the Turkish government would acknowledge; in fact, rather the reverse, as Turkey is anxious to improve its human rights record. However, if such actions are not controlled and prevented, then they amount to persecution by the state. Where there is proper redress for such incidents then there would be no fear of repetition and thus no real risk of persecution in the future. The crucial question is whether the individual can obtain protection.

Key Case

***Svazas v SSHD* [2002] 1 WLR 1891**

Both appellants were Lithuanian communists who had been repeatedly detained. Ms B had been raped in custody by the police. Mr Svazas had been beaten and kicked. The evidence before the Tribunal 'depicted a police force which systematically or endemically abuses its power despite the law and the will of the government to stop it'.

Sedley LJ said:

> Whether singling out Communist prisoners for assault…is systemic or endemic or sporadic, it necessarily represents an initial failure of protection on the part of the state. If so, the critical question…will be whether what the state does to stop it happening reaches a practical standard appropriate to the duty it owes all of its citizens…[this] does not require a guarantee against police misconduct, but it does…call for timely and effective rectification of the situation which is allowing the misconduct to happen.

Simon Brown LJ said:

> The ultimate question in all cases is whether or not the asylum seeker can establish the need for surrogate protection by the international community for want of sufficient protection in his home state…[T]he more senior the officers of state concerned, and the more closely involved they are in the refugee's ill-treatment, the more necessary it will be to demonstrate clearly the home state's political will to stamp it out and the adequacy of their systems for doing so and for punishing those responsible, and the easier it will be for the asylum seeker to cast doubt upon their readiness, or at least their ability, to do so.

The legal questions have been more complex where those from whom the refugee fears persecution are not agents of the state.

13.3.4.2 *Perpetrators – non-state actors*

Goodwin-Gill and McAdam point out that 'neither the 1951 Convention nor the travaux préparatoires say much about the source of the persecution feared by the refugee, and no necessary linkage between persecution and government authority is formally required' (2007:98). The *UNHCR Handbook* at para 65 says: 'where serious discriminatory or other offensive acts are committed by the local populace, they can be considered as persecution if they are knowingly tolerated by the authorities, or the authorities refuse, or prove unable, to offer effective protection'. Thus, in *R v SSHD ex p Jeyakumaran*, Tamils resident in Colombo were the victims of reprisals by local Sinhalese (majority ethnic) residents, and were not protected by the state. Although the victims were not 'singled out' for persecution by the government, the High Court held that they were nevertheless persecuted, as the state failed to protect them.

13.3.4.3 *What protection is available*

The leading case on the question of persecution by non-state actors is the House of Lords case of *Horvath v SSHD* [2000] 3 All ER 577.

Key Case

***Horvath v SSHD* [2000] 3 All ER 577**

The appellant was a Roma from the Slovak Republic who based his asylum claim on fear of violence by skinheads and on discrimination in employment, the right to marry, and education. The Tribunal concluded that any failure of these social rights in his case did not amount to persecution. The Court of Appeal agreed, and the appeal went to the House of Lords only on the question of the failure of state protection against the skinhead violence.

Three questions were considered by the House of Lords.

First: does the concept of 'persecution' refer simply to serious harm, or does it necessarily incorporate a failure of state protection?

Second: the refugee definition requires that a person is 'unwilling' to avail himself of state protection. Does this mean that they fear being persecuted precisely because they have gone to the police?

Third: if persecution implies a lack of state protection, what is the test for determining whether there is sufficient protection against a person's persecution in the country of origin? Is it sufficient that there is in that country a system of criminal law which makes violent attacks by the persecutors punishable and a reasonable willingness to enforce that law on the part of the law enforcement agencies? Or must the protection be such that it cannot be said that the applicant has a well-founded fear? The first alternative focuses on whether the state is doing its best, the second on whether risk is actually minimized or eliminated for the applicant.

Lord Hope said that the proper approach to this task was not 'to construe its language with the same precision as one would if it had been an Act of Parliament' but rather to give the words 'a broad meaning in the light of the purposes which the Convention was designed to serve'. He identified the key relevant Convention purpose as:

to be found in the principle of surrogacy. The general purpose of the Convention is to enable the person who no longer has the benefit of protection against persecution for a Convention reason in his own country to turn for protection to the international community. (at 383)

This approach is known as the protection theory. It is to be contrasted with the attribution theory previously followed in, for instance, France and Germany, according to which persecution is not recognized as such unless it can be attributed to the state. This way of setting out the issue by Lord Hope seems to be a classic endorsement of the protection theory. However, there is a curious contradiction. The House of Lords found, in relation to the three questions, that:

1. persecution included by definition a failure of state protection,
2. the applicant needed to be unable or unwilling to avail themselves of the protection of the state because they feared persecution for doing so, and
3. a system with a reasonable willingness to enforce it was sufficient for protection.

The net result of this is much closer than Lord Hope's statement suggests to the attribution theory. The effect is not to focus on the failure of state protection for the asylum seeker, but rather on whether the state should be regarded as culpable, which, judging by the preamble to the Convention, is not its purpose. As Lord Hope stated in the beginning, the purpose is to protect where state protection has failed. The focus in Horvath has turned from the refugee to the state.

The effects of *Horvath* have been mitigated and refined in later decisions. Schiemann LJ in *Noune v SSHD* [2000] EWCA Civ 306 made these points in relation to Horvath:

As a study of the many judgments and speeches in that case shows, the law in relation to persecution by non-state actors was unsettled and difficult to understand... [if it was interpreted to mean]...that where the law enforcement agencies are doing their best and are not being either generally inefficient and incompetent (as that word is generally understood implying a lack of skill rather than a lack of effectiveness) this was enough to disqualify a potential victim from being a refugee [this would be] an error of law. (para 28)

Schiemann LJ goes on to say that the crucial question is whether there was a reasonable likelihood of the appellant being persecuted for a Convention reason. This case, too, concerned the sufficiency of state protection, but the Court of Appeal, while bound by *Horvath*, came back to that central question of the risk to the appellant. *Horvath* has been more explicitly followed in other cases, for instance *Banomova v SSHD* [2001] EWCA Civ 807 CA in which on comparable facts the Court of Appeal held that the police were willing to protect the appellant who had withdrawn her complaint after death threats and so, following *Horvath*, there was sufficient protection.

On the other hand, in the case of *R (Bodzek) v Special Adjudicator* [2002] EWHC 1525 Admin, an adjudicator's decision that there was no evidence that the Polish state was unwilling to protect a Jewish family who had been the target of anti-Semitic attacks was held to be *Wednesbury* unreasonable. They had suffered from acts of personal violence, vandalism, and graffiti of their property for ten years, and had been forced to move house. They complained that the police response was inadequate as no attempt was made to identify the perpetrators. The adjudicator had accepted that the state was not unwilling as it was difficult to pursue a prosecution when the identity of the assailants was not known. The applicants' case was that it was a policing job to investigate and identify the assailants, and they had given what information they could. Horvath was followed by the Administrative Court, which on the evidence of years of police inaction, held it could not be rational to say that the state was not unwilling to act.

The Court of Appeal in *Bagdanavicius v SSHD* [2003] EWCA Civ 1605 emphasized that punishment after the event was not sufficient protection. The Court also incorporated the principle from the ECtHR case of *Osman v UK* (1998) 29 EHRR 245 that where the authorities were or should have been aware of the applicant's particular protection needs but failed to do anything about it, then there was a failure of state protection. These points bring the questions back in the direction of the situation of the particular applicant, though without changing the main findings in Horvath. Furthermore, the House of Lords in *Bagdanavicius* gave an unqualified endorsement of the application of the *Horvath* approach to an Article 3 case ([2005] UKHL 38).

A number of cases before and after *Horvath* elaborate the requirement for both willingness and effectiveness. The Federal Court of Canada in *Annan v Canada (Minister for Citizenship and Immigration)* IMM 215–95 said that 'pious statements of intent' about outlawing genital mutilation had not resulted in any action to do so and so not in protection for the asylum claimant. The Court of Appeal in *R (on the application of Atkinson) v SSHD* [2004] EWCA Civ 849 held that a lack of effectiveness would entail a systematic failure applying to individuals in the same group as the applicant, here, people who were or were seen to be informers for the People's National Party. It was not just a failure in relation to some individuals.

In *P and M v SSHD*, the IAT held that evidence that the police prosecuted due to public pressure after a woman had been killed by her husband and another had been seriously burned with acid suggested there was state protection against domestic violence. The Court of Appeal said this was to 'miss the point'. Where the police had to be compelled by such extreme circumstances to act (para 26), this did not amount to protection.

The requirement for an effective legal system has been taken as a starting point by some decision-makers: if there is an effective system, then this applicant would not be at risk. The Court of Appeal in *Mishto v SSHD* [2003] EWCA Civ 1978 advised against taking this approach. In this case, the adjudicator had considered the protection system for women in Albania and concluded it was sufficiently effective, therefore whatever the strength or weakness of the appellant's case, there was no real risk to her so he did not need to investigate the facts in order to find against her. The Court of Appeal held that in this particular case, there was no injustice done to the applicant, but as a rule this approach would be unwise. General conditions in a country must be evaluated in the light of the circumstances of the particular applicant. The Court of Session's decision in *Hussein v SSHD* [2005 CSIH 45] illustrated how the general meshes with the particular and cannot be considered aside from it. The appellant stated that he had not proceeded with a complaint to the police about shooting at his house because a bribe had been required. The Tribunal found that Pakistan had a sufficiently protective legal system, but made no findings on whether the bribe had been requested by a single corrupt officer or whether the appellant could not expect protection without a bribe because of the system. In the latter case, there would be no effective protection. The Court on appeal held that it was essential to go back and investigate this question. In *DK v SSHD* [2006] EWCA Civ 682, the Court of Appeal held that evidence about the capacity of the KDP police to protect DK from being killed in a blood feud had not been properly considered. The question was not whether they had provided a sufficiency of protection within their capacity but whether the KDP police were actually capable of providing DK with adequate protection. DK is another case which shifts the focus from the state's performance to the individual's protection. Following *Noune*, it was not necessary to show that the state machinery had collapsed before being able to claim refugee status (para 27). See also *PS (Sri Lanka)* discussed at 13.3.1.1. Finally, in *SM (Afghanistan)* [2011] EWCA Civ 573 the Court of Appeal accepted that the authorities could not offer protection 'to the *Horvath* standard'.

The question of non-state actors was a question which divided European countries in the course of the negotiations over the Qualification Directive. France and Germany did not recognize persecution by non-state actors, which was one of the reasons for challenges to France and Germany as safe third countries (see chapter 12). The Qualification Directive 2004/83 recognizes persecution by non-state actors where the state is unable or unwilling to protect (Article 6), though differences may remain over the meaning of this. Article 7 states that there will be protection when reasonable steps are taken to prevent the suffering or persecution by, inter alia, the operation of an effective legal system, in effect following Horvath and leaving open the questions considered previously.

13.3.4.4 *Sources of protection*

The final question here is whether protection must be offered by the state itself, or whether it may be offered by an entity which is capable of providing protection. *R (on the application of Vallaj) v Special Adjudicator and Canaj v Secretary of State for the Home Department* [2001] INLR 342 CA concerned the proposed return of the appellants, who were Kosovar Albanians, to Kosovo. The Court held that UNMIK (the United Nations Interim Administration Mission in Kosovo) supported by KFOR (the internal security force in Kosovo) had an international law obligation to protect Kosovans, which it was in fact discharging with the host country's consent, and this was enough to satisfy the Convention requirement for protection.

The Qualification Directive, followed by the UK's implementing regulations, goes further than *Vallaj and Canaj*. The Directive allows that protection may be provided by 'parties or organisations, including international organisations, controlling the State or a substantial part of the territory of the State' (Article 7.1b). The European Council on Refugees and Exiles (ECRE) is disturbed by this inclusion on the grounds that such authorities 'are not and cannot be parties to international human rights instruments and therefore cannot be held accountable for non-compliance with international refugee and human rights obligations' (ECRE information note October 2004). This argument was considered by the Tribunal in *DM (Majority Clan Entities can Protect) Somalia* [2005] UKAIT 00150, which concluded that all that was essential was effective protection. It could, in that case, be provided by a majority clan which had a militia. Somalia was a state in international law, and even if the function of government was fragmented, if a majority clan militia could provide protection, issues about the effectiveness of government would not need to be decided. Although drug barons or armed militia might be less effective than an army and police subject to law, this went to the question of effectiveness, and did not demand protection by the state. This conclusion is implicitly endorsed in later cases concerning Somalia, for instance *HH, AM, J and MA (Somalia) v SSHD* [2010] EWCA Civ 426, in which the Court of Appeal accepted that unless an individual was 'fortunate enough to be able to obtain protection by virtue of having close connections with powerful people in Mogadishu, he or she will face a real risk of persecution sufficient to engage article 3' (para 95).

13.4 Internal relocation

The concept of internal flight or internal relocation completes the consideration of persecution and state protection. Simply put, the internal flight or relocation doctrine, also called the internal protection alternative, is an assertion that, although they risk persecution in their home area, the asylum seeker could find safety somewhere else in their own country. If established, then the asylum claim will be lost as there is no well-founded fear of persecution. The Michigan Guidelines on the Internal Protection Alternative (the product of an international consultation and colloquium in 1999) say that internal protection analysis must be 'directed to the identification of a present possibility of meaningful protection within the boundaries of the home state' (para 8).

The foundational case in relation to internal relocation is that of *Robinson* [1997] 3 WLR 1162.

Key Case

***Robinson* [1997] 3 WLR 1162**

The appellant was a Tamil from northern Sri Lanka and had connections with the LTTE (Tamil Tigers). He claimed asylum in the UK following the assassination of the President of Sri Lanka by Tamil militants in May 1993, but his claim was refused. The Special Adjudicator held that, while he might risk persecution in an area controlled by the Tamil Tigers as he might be recruited against his will to support them, he could safely return to Colombo as it was controlled by the Sri Lankan authorities. He was in Colombo at the time of the President's assassination and had been briefly detained there. The Special Adjudicator did not expressly consider whether it was *reasonable* to expect the appellant to relocate in Colombo on the basis that this was an unreviewable matter of the Secretary of State's discretion.

The Court of Appeal decided that appellate authorities do have jurisdiction to consider the reasonableness of the internal flight alternative. As for the question of what is reasonable, that must be decided by looking at all the circumstances.

The Court of Appeal took guidance from the Australian case of *Randhawa* 124 ALR 265, suggesting that factors to be taken into account in determining whether it was reasonable to expect the appellant to relocate would include, for instance, the accessibility of the 'safe' part of the country, any danger or hardship of travelling there, the quality of internal protection in the country, i.e., does it meet 'basic norms of civil, political and socio-economic human rights'? To this one might add that safety of re-entering the country at all is relevant for internal flight as for any return (*Degirmenci v SSHD* [2004] EWCA Civ 1553).

The question to be answered was, it suggested, that posed in the Canadian case, *Thirunavukkarasu* (1993) 109 DLR (4th) 682, namely: 'would it be unduly harsh to expect this person, who is being persecuted in one part of his country, to move to another less hostile part of the country before seeking refugee status abroad?' The Canadian court had given the following examples:

> While claimants should not be expected to cross battle lines or hide out in an isolated region of their country, like a cave in the mountains, a desert or a jungle, it will not be enough for them to say that they do not like the weather in a safe area, or that they have no friends or relatives there, or that they may not be able to find suitable work there.

These are extremes to illustrate the principle, which has been expanded upon in English case law. Nolan J in *R v IAT ex p Jonah* [1985] Imm AR 7 considered that it was unreasonable to expect a senior Ghanaian trade union official to go back to what was in effect a hideaway, a very remote village accessible only by a 15-mile walk through the jungle. On the other hand, in both *R v SSHD ex p Yurekli* [1991] Imm AR 153 (CA) and *R v SSHD ex p Gunes* [1991] Imm AR 278, the courts held that it was not unreasonable to expect

Turkish Kurds to relocate in a part of Turkey away from the villages where they faced persecution. In *El-Tanoukhi v SSHD* [1993] Imm AR 71, the Court of Appeal held that it was not unreasonable to expect a claimant who lived in a part of Lebanon under Israeli control to relocate in a different part of Lebanon. On the other hand, in *MM (Lebanon) v SSHD* [2009] EWCA Civ 382, the Court held that it was unrealistic to talk of the appellant being safe in an area of Lebanon not controlled by Hezbollah. It was a small country without restrictions on freedom of movement, every part of which was within 30 minutes' drive of a Hezbollah stronghold.

Since Robinson, case law has not changed the basic question of whether it would be unduly harsh to expect the claimant to relocate, but the quality of life and of protection that the claimant should be expected to accept in the area of relocation has been hotly contested.

13.4.1 Replicating persecution in 'safe haven'

The internal protection alternative must not be used so as to require the refugee to live in a way that replicates the persecution they flee if they live normally, exercising basic human rights. The case of *Iftikhar Ahmed* is discussed at 13.6.2 in the context of religious persecution. It was held on the facts that Mr Ahmed would continue to proclaim his Ahmadi faith wherever he went. There would therefore be a reasonable likelihood of persecution in any part of Pakistan. The Court of Appeal held that no internal protection alternative was viable. The Court held in *Hysi v SSHD* [2005] EWCA Civ 711 that the Tribunal had given insufficient consideration as to whether it would be unduly harsh to expect a young man to return to Kosovo and hide his mixed ethnicity. The Court thought that the Australian case of *Appellant S 395 v Minister for Immigration and Multicultural Affairs* [2004] INLR 233 cited the correct principle:

> It would undermine the object of the Convention if a signatory country required [refugees] to modify their beliefs or opinions or to hide their race, nationality or membership of particular social groups before those countries would give them protection.

In a similar vein, the Tribunal in *SA (political activist – internal relocation) Pakistan* [2011] UKUT 30 (IAC) held that:

> [r]equiring a political activist to live away from his home area in order to avoid persecution at the hands of his political opponents has never been considered a proper application of the internal relocation principle: see e.g. Nolan J in *R v Immigration Appeal Tribunal, ex p. Jonah* [1985] Imm AR 7. And (since October 2006) such a requirement cannot be considered to be consistent with para 339O of the Immigration Rules (Article 8 of the Qualification Directive). Indeed, the pitfalls of requiring a person to act contrary to his normal behaviour in order to avoid persecution have been further emphasised by the Supreme Court in *HJ (Iran)* [2010] UKSC 31.

In *HC v SSHD* [2005] EWCA Civ 893, the Court of Appeal held that the adjudicator, in considering that the appellant could return to a different part of Lebanon, had failed to take sufficient account of the cumulative effect of being homosexual and a Palestinian refugee. She had also not taken into account significant evidence of conditions in that country for homosexuals when holding that he would be safe in a place other than the refugee camp where he grew up.

In a similar vein, UNHCR Guidelines on Internal Protection 23 July 2003 say:

> Where internal displacement is a result of 'ethnic cleansing' policies, denying refugee status on the basis of the internal flight or relocation concept could be interpreted as condoning the resulting situation on the ground, and therefore raises additional concerns.

This guideline was not followed in the case of *AE Sudan* [2005] UKAIT 00101. The appellant was internally displaced because of the activities of government backed militias, who were carrying out so-called ethnic cleansing, i.e., killing, raping, and destroying the homes of whole populations of a particular ethnicity. The Tribunal held that even though to live in a part of the country where he would not be persecuted by the militia was doing what the militia wanted, as he could be safe there he would not be able to claim refugee status outside Sudan. This was so even though he could not be said to be obtaining the protection of his government, as the government allowed the militia action and it was not through their protection that he could live elsewhere, but simply because the militia did not operate there.

13.4.2 Past persecution by the state

Is internal protection automatically debarred when past persecution was by the state? The Michigan Guidelines on the Internal Protection Alternative (para 16) say that there should be 'a strong presumption against finding an "internal protection alternative" where the agent or author of the original risk of persecution is, or is sponsored by, the national government'. UNHCR Guidelines 2003 take a similar position.

The authority now is *Januzi, Hamid, Gaafar and Mohammed v SSHD* [2006] UKHL 5, in which Lord Bingham said 'there is no absolute rule' or presumption (para 21). He referred to the spectrum of state responsibility we noted earlier in the case of *Svazas*, and said that the relationship between the state and the act(s) of persecution must be assessed: 'The more closely the persecution in question is linked to the state, and the greater the control of the state over those acting or purporting to act on its behalf, the more likely (other things being equal) that a victim of persecution in one place will be similarly vulnerable in another place within the state' (para 21). Lord Hope said that 'where the state is in full control of events and its agents of persecution are active everywhere' internal relocation is obviously not an option (para 48).

The severity of past persecution has repeatedly been argued to have a bearing on internal relocation. Amnesty International evidence to the New Zealand Refugee Status Appeals Authority suggested it should (see Symes and Jorro p. 219). The reasons for this are indicated by Elias J, in *R v IAT ex p Sellasamy* CO/3238/99:

> the fact that on his return he is protected by a state which has, albeit through a different agency and in a different area, inflicted great pain and humiliation on him, is potentially highly material to the question of whether it would be unduly harsh to expect him to return. (para 33)

Such a person might have developed a 'distrust of the country itself and a disinclination to be associated with it as its national' (Grahl-Madsen, quoted in *In re B & R v Special Adjudicator ex parte Hoxha* [2005] UKHL 19). In *FK (Kenya) v SSHD* [2008] EWCA Civ 119, Sedley LJ remarked, obiter, that there might be cases where, objectively, the appellant could be safe, but was so traumatized by past events that she remained in genuine terror of being returned there. This could be relevant to whether relocation was unduly harsh.

Where the persecution is feared from non-state actors, a careful evaluation of the evidence of their reach and influence is needed. In *PO (Nigeria)* [2011] EWCA Civ 132 the Court of Appeal considered that the Tribunal's failure to evaluate the evidence correctly infected their view that internal relocation was reasonable. The evidence included for instance that the man who arranged the appellant's trafficking was a 'professional violent criminal with a power base in Nigeria and probably in the UK'.

13.4.3 Risks in site of internal protection and basis of comparison

A case can be made that the Refugee Convention sets the standard of protection that is appropriate for a refugee. This standard should therefore be available in the site of alternative protection. The Michigan Guidelines and a number of New Zealand authorities support this view (see Symes and Jorro p. 218). However, in *E v SSHD* [2003] EWCA Civ 1032, the Court of Appeal held that what is required in the site of relocation is protection from persecution, not delivery of other human rights. The House of Lords in *Januzi, Hamid, Gaafar and Mohammed* agreed. It endorsed the UNHCR Guidelines in saying that relocation:

> requires, from a practical perspective, an assessment of whether the rights that will not be respected or protected are fundamental to the individual, such that the deprivation of those rights would be sufficiently harmful to render the area an unreasonable alternative. (para 28, in [2006] UKHL 5 para 20)

The Refugee Convention requires delivery of political and socio-economic rights, and integration into the host state. However, in internal relocation, the question would be whether what is lacking is the 'the real possibility to survive economically'. The Refugee Convention was not intended to define rights in the claimant's home country.

In reaching its conclusion, the Court was supported by the Qualification Directive which, it said, imposed a 'standard significantly lower' than the Michigan Guidelines and New Zealand cases would require (para 17). The Qualification Directive permits internal relocation 'if in a part of the country of origin there is no well-founded fear of being persecuted...and the applicant can reasonably be expected to stay in that part of the country'. In order to determine this, the Member State must 'have regard to the general circumstances prevailing in that part of the country and to the personal circumstances of the applicant' (Article 8).

Januzi disposed of a further question which had hovered over internal protection cases: the basis of comparison in assessing internal protection is between the proposed location and the refugee's home area, not with the country of asylum. The appeal of Mr Januzi was dismissed, but the appeals of Messrs Hamid, Gaafar, and Mohammed were sent back from the House of Lords to the Tribunal for decision. In the space of 18 months, the cases went back up the appeal chain and were heard again in the House of Lords. The cases are politically sensitive ones as they concern the situation of people from Darfur. While, on the one hand, the situation in Darfur has caused alarm worldwide and has been characterized as one of the greatest human rights disasters of the present age, on the other hand the question of whether such a situation can or should be contained within Africa, what kind of material standards a rural Sudanese person can expect, and whether refugee camps are tolerable places, all raise issues that go to the heart of global inequities.

Key Case

***AH (Sudan), IG (Sudan), NM (Sudan) v SSHD* [2007] UKHL 49**

All three appellants were black Africans formerly living in Darfur in western Sudan. They had been victims of serious persecution by Arab bands known as the Janjaweed, persecution which the government of Sudan had connived in or at the very least not restrained. It was accepted that by reason of the well-known facts about the desperate situation of black Africans in Darfur, all of the appellants were *prima facie* entitled to international protection.

The Secretary of State's case was that they could safely return to Sudan, provided that they return not to Darfur but to Khartoum. The appellants' case was that they would still be in danger of persecution in any part of Sudan; alternatively, even if they were not in danger of persecution if returned to Khartoum, it would be unduly harsh to require them to return there. They were village people and subsistence farmers. If they returned to Khartoum they would be in a camp outside the city in conditions of urban or sub-urban poverty. In the judgment, one expert is quoted as follows:

> In the Al-Fatah camp where the victims of forced relocation were living at the time of my visit, I was struck with their most desperate situation and appalling conditions of extreme poverty. They had scarcely been able to erect makeshift huts from plastic sheets and cardboard as they had been left without any building material. While there was a water bladder no food or other life-sustaining goods had been provided...The camp is situated some 50km outside of Khartoum in the desert, where without water agricultural activities are impossible. (para 43)

The Tribunal held that they would not be at risk of persecution anywhere in Sudan, and conditions in Khartoum would not be unduly harsh because they were no different from the conditions of rural poverty elsewhere in squatter camps and slums. The appeal continued to the Court of Appeal and House of Lords on the question of whether return to Khartoum was unduly harsh.

The Court of Appeal held it would be unduly harsh to expect them to relocate to Khartoum, including a principle that '[t]raumatic changes of life-style, for instance from a city to a desert, or into slum conditions, should not be forced on the asylum-seeker' (para 33).

The House of Lords allowed the Secretary of State's appeal. Their only criticism of the Tribunal's decision was that it came close to equating the standard of what was unduly harsh with a breach of Article 3. It did not actually do so, but this would have been an error. The Court of Appeal had introduced questions that were not necessary into the consideration of internal flight. The proper approach remained that in *Januzi*:

> The decision-maker, taking account of all relevant circumstances pertaining to the claimant and his country of origin, must decide whether it is reasonable to expect the claimant to relocate or whether it would be unduly harsh to expect him to do so. (para 21)

Lord Bingham agreed that 'enquiry must be directed to the situation of the particular applicant, whose age, gender, experience, health, skills and family ties may all be very relevant'. However, this did not mean that certain considerations should be mandated, prohibited or prioritized:

> There is no warrant for excluding, or giving priority to, consideration of the applicant's way of life in the place of persecution. There is no warrant for excluding, or giving priority to, consideration of conditions generally prevailing in the home country. (AH para 5)

Internal relocation in Sudan continues to be contentious. In *KH, QA, BK, AA and KA (Sudan) v SSHD* [2008] EWCA Civ 887, the Court of Appeal held that *AH (Sudan)* [2007] UKHL 49 had not undermined the country guidance given by the Tribunal in *HGMO (Relocation to Khartoum) Sudan CG* [2006] UKAIT 00062. It was still the case that asylum claims submitted by non-Arab Darfuris faced with return to Khartoum should be considered on their individual merits. Reasonable internal relocation could be to any place which offered sufficient safety from persecution and was not unduly harsh for the individual concerned.

An example of a holistic assessment in a very different context may be seen in the case of *AB (Jamaica) v SSHD* [2008] EWCA Civ 784, where it was not considered unduly harsh for the appellant to return to Jamaica in a different area from her violent former partner and his associates. The Tribunal had considered her circumstances, including her psychological state, the absence of social welfare support, stigma attaching to the claimant, and her concerns for her daughter's safety. The Court of Appeal upheld their decision.

13.4.4 Safety of home area

Finally, if persecution has ceased in the home area, refugee status is not available, even if conditions remain risky elsewhere in the country (*Canaj and Vallaj v SSHD and Special Adjudicator* [2001] INLR 342). However, risks elsewhere in the country may make the home area inaccessible and thus invoke the doctrine of non-*refoulement*. Formerly, this issue arose in numerous cases of planned return to the Kurdish Autonomous Area of Iraq (KAA) as there were no direct flights to the KAA and an asylum seeker would need to travel through Baghdad which was regarded as unsafe. The question of safe routes of return is often critical and is considered in more detail in chapter 17. In addition, asylum seekers may be refused documents by their country of origin to enable them to return. This was held by the Court of Appeal in *MA (Ethiopia) v SSHD* [2009] EWCA Civ 289 not necessarily to amount to persecution. That problem is also discussed in chapter 17.

13.4.5 Internal relocation and human rights claims

As mentioned in chapter 12, a claim for protection on the basis of a feared breach of human rights may be made together with an asylum claim. The Qualification Directive applies the internal relocation doctrine to such claims where 'there is no real risk of suffering serious harm' (Article 8). The doctrine is applied in exactly the same terms, whether the failed claim is for asylum or humanitarian protection. The question is whether return would be unreasonable.

13.4.6 Summary and burden of proof in relation to internal flight

As the internal flight alternative is raised by the Secretary of State, it could seem appropriate that the Secretary of State would have the burden of proving that it would not be unduly harsh to return the claimant. This is strongly suggested by the Michigan Guidelines (para 14). Alternatively, if the Secretary of State raises the point, does the burden then shift to the claimant to show that it would be unduly harsh, and if so, to what standard of proof? The Court of Appeal in *Karanakaran v SSHD* [2003] 3 All ER 449 held that there was no standard of proof in the civil sense, as discussed earlier in relation to establishing a well-founded fear of persecution. The claimant did not have to prove to a certain standard that particular events were likely to occur, but the decision-maker should take into account all the evidence and decide whether it was unduly harsh for the claimant to return to a different area. This point was refined by Sedley LJ in *Salam Jasim v SSHD* [2006] EWCA Civ 342, where he said that:

> Once the judge of fact is satisfied that the applicant has a justified fear of persecution or harm if returned to his home area, the claim will ordinarily be made out unless the judge is satisfied that he can nevertheless be safely returned to another part of his country of origin. Provided the second issue has been flagged up, there may be no formal burden of proof on the Home Secretary (see *GH*

[2004] UKIAT 00248); but this does not mean that the judge of fact can reject an otherwise well-founded claim unless the evidence satisfies him that internal relocation is a safe and reasonable option. (para 16)

The risks of persecution in the claimant's home area must be considered first, because it is against these that the proposed location must provide protection. Symes and Jorro (p. 221) point out that this means a claim should not be certified as unfounded (see chapter 12) on the basis of internal protection.

Reading case law on internal flight can be confusing. Who is arguing what? It may be seen like this:

Step 1: Asylum claim is assessed and risk is found of persecution in home area.

Step 2: Secretary of State asserts that the claimant would not face persecution or a real risk of serious harm in another area of their home country.

Step 3: Secretary of State, looking at all relevant factors, determines that it would not be unduly harsh for the claimant to return to a different area.

Step 4: In reply the claimant *may* argue that there is a risk of persecution or serious harm elsewhere.

Step 5: Whether or not there is a risk of persecution or serious harm elsewhere, the claimant may additionally argue that it would be unduly harsh to return them to that area.

Step 6: Undue harshness is assessed, bearing in mind whether the risks in the alternative site would amount to indirect *refoulement*, and the effect on the individual, as set out in *AH, IG and NM (Sudan)*.

Step 7: The refugee claim may succeed if the claimant would face persecution in their home area *and* it would be unduly harsh to force them to return elsewhere.

Step 8: A claim for humanitarian protection may succeed, even if the refugee claim has failed, if the claimant would face a real risk of serious harm in their home area *and* it would be unreasonable to return them elsewhere.

13.5 Causal link

Returning to the Article 1A definition, we see that a refugee is one who is 'outside his country of nationality, and owing to a well-founded fear of being persecuted for reasons of...', and then the list of Convention reasons appears. This apparently simple connecting phrase has significance in the case law of the Convention and in the determination of who is a refugee. The Qualification Directive requires only a 'connection' between the Convention reason and the persecution. The UK's implementing regulations require that the act of persecution is committed 'for' Convention reasons. The Tribunal in *SB (Moldova CG)* [2008] UKAIT 00002 reviewed these formulations and that of Baroness Hale in *ex p Hoxha*, who said persecution must be 'for reasons which are related to one of the Convention grounds', and accepted that in that case it was sufficient that the persecution was related to the Convention reason.

As the *UNHCR Handbook* points out, 'Often the applicant himself may not be aware of the reasons for the persecution feared. It is not, however, his duty to analyze his case to such an extent as to identify the reasons in detail' (para 66). The reasons in detail in fact may not all be important as there is no requirement that the persecution is carried out solely for Convention reasons (see *SB (Moldova CG)* [2008] UKAIT 00002). Reasons may in reality be very mixed and the personal motivation of the persecutor is not the key (see Goodwin-Gill and McAdam 2007:101). For instance, in the case of *Sivakumar* referred to earlier, the House of Lords were aware that the persecutors might have the suppression of terrorism among their motives for torturing the appellant. However, the reason that he was tortured was a mixture of his ethnicity and supposed political stance. The personal motivations of the persecutor are an aspect of individual criminality but are not connected with the failure of the state to protect. The relevant reason for the persecution is the structural reason in that society, not the personal reason of the persecutor. Again, we can see that the case of sexual attacks is treated quite differently as in *Okonkwo* and other cases discussed earlier, the supposed personal motive of the persecutor was regarded as overriding. Musalo (2003) proposes that some of this inconsistency in relation to gender-based claims would be resolved by a more widespread adoption of what she calls a 'bifurcated approach' to causation – namely, that there will be persecution for a Convention reason if either the ill-treatment or the failure of protection is for a Convention reason.

The question of the causal link, or nexus, was considered at length by the House of Lords in *Shah and Islam*. It considered the Canadian approach which is to use the 'but for' test, as in UK discrimination law. This is by asking the question: 'but for their gender, would these people be persecuted?' It is tempting to say that this is sufficient, and that in *Shah and Islam* (see 13.6.4) the two women would not have been persecuted but for their gender. However, this approach is not favoured as, following its use in tort law, it brings with it the question of how much of the cause the Convention reason needs to be, i.e., 60 per cent, 40 per cent, etc. (see discussion in Hathaway and Foster 2003). This is a fruitless path which, it is generally accepted, is better not to tread.

Lord Hoffmann suggested that drawbacks in the 'but for' test were revealed by the example of women raped in a situation of general lawlessness. The women would not be raped but for their gender but the reason for this treatment would also be the breakdown in law and order, and not their gender. This analysis is open to question in that men are subject to rape, but the power imbalance between men and women suggests that women are more likely to be raped, therefore one might argue that women would not be raped but for this imbalance which is left uncontrolled by the breakdown of law and order. They would not be raped but for their gender not because they are women but because they are women in a society where lawlessness exposes them to the underlying power imbalance. Nevertheless, one can disagree with the example and still see the point Lord Hoffmann is making, which is that causation should be sought at the structural level, in the lack of protection. He demonstrates this with the example of a Jew in Germany punished for failing to obey the racial laws, who is thereby persecuted for their race. The reason for this is that there is no state protection against such punishment and the state's lack of protection is also grounded in race. Whether the individual who initiates the prosecution hates Jews or not is irrelevant. Whether there are additional reasons, such as conducting a census, for identifying Jews is irrelevant. The reason in that society in which that person is suffering that treatment is that they are a Jew.

The effects of taking a subjective approach to causation are illustrated in the case of *Omoruyi v SSHD* [2001] Imm AR 175, in which the appellant sought asylum following death threats from the Ogboni cult as he refused to comply with their demands in relation to his father's burial. The Court of Appeal found against the appellant on the grounds that the Ogboni were not motivated by the appellant's religion (Christianity) to persecute him but by his non-compliance with their requirements. Anyone else who had similarly failed to comply would be treated in the same way. Simon Brown LJ said: 'The Nigerian State Authorities in the present case were not unable or unwilling to protect the appellant because of his being a Christian but rather because he was at risk for having crossed this particular cult.' Simon Brown LJ thus looked for motivation, first in the non-state persecutors, and, second, in the state, and finding none, concluded that there was no causal link to the appellant's religion. Hathaway and Foster (2003) provide a different analysis of this decision. The question, they suggest, should be 'why is the applicant in the predicament he is in?' rather than 'why does the persecutor wish to harm the applicant or the state refrain from protecting him?' The answer then would be 'because he was a Christian'. Hathaway and Foster contrast *Omoruyi* with the similar Australian case of *Okere v MIMA* 157 ALR 678 (Aust Fed C Sept 21 1998). In this case, the Court held that the causal nexus was satisfied. It noted that religious persecution often takes indirect forms, and if this form of causation were not accepted:

> Persons who have a well-founded fear of persecution for reasons of their refusal to work on the Sabbath could be found not to have a well-founded fear of persecution for reasons of their religion; the persecution feared by them would be related to their refusal to work and not to their religion.

Lord Hoffmann in *Shah and Islam* also identified a fallacy in the judgment of the Court of Appeal, namely the idea that all members of a group have to be persecuted in order for the reason for persecution to be membership of that group. The reason these two women were persecuted was because they were women in a society which discriminates against women. Not all women in the society need to be discriminated against for this to be the case.

The question of causal nexus was briefly considered by the House of Lords in *Sepet and Bulbul*. The result is not entirely clear. Lord Bingham reiterated the generally accepted view that the motive of the perpetrator is not the reason. The question is, 'what is the real reason?' It is not clear how the real reason is ascertained, though the question may be approached consistently with *Okere*. In *Gaoua v SSHD* [2004] EWCA Civ 1528, the Court of Appeal held that the question of what was the real reason for the risk of detention and persecution upon return could be answered in the following way. If it was because he was perceived to hold radical opinions, this would found an asylum claim. If it was 'just' to obtain information about Algerian terrorists in the UK, then 'arguably' it would not. This case should be compared with *Sivakumar*.

Reference was made earlier to the particular difficulties of proving a refugee claim in the context of a war, and this was evident, for reasons related to causation, in *XZ (Russia) v SSHD* [2008] EWCA Civ 180. A Chechen mother and son were subjected to horrific atrocities, but the Tribunal did not consider it proved that they had been targeted because of their husband and father's political activities in the Chechen Parliament. The atrocities were carried out during the Chechen War. The perpetrators were believed to be Russian security forces. The Court of Appeal accepted there had been no error of law. If Hathaway and Foster's question had been asked – 'why are the appellants in the position they are in?' – it is at least possible that the outcome might have been different.

The question of causal nexus may be simplified under the Qualification Directive, but will still overlap with a key question in refugee law, identification of the Convention reason for the persecution.

13.6 Convention reason

Persecution only gives rise to refugee status if it is 'for reasons of race, religion, nationality, particular social group or political opinion'. The first three reasons can be briefly dealt with, the other two require closer examination.

13.6.1 Race

Convention law does not require a technical definition of race. The *Handbook* says that race 'is to be understood in its widest sense to include all kinds of ethnic groups that are referred to as "races" in common usage' (para 68). It is not impossible for there to be persecution of members of the same race for reasons of race. The Federal Court of Australia in the case of *Perampalam v Minister for Immigration and Multicultural Affairs* (1999) 55 ALD 431 notes that the LTTE (Tamil Tigers) would approach Tamils for financial support. The implication is that pressure could be brought to bear.

The *Handbook* also emphasizes the seriousness of racial discrimination, and that where such discrimination interferes with the exercise of fundamental rights, or has serious consequences, this is likely to amount to persecution. Goodwin-Gill comments that 'Persecution on account of race is all too frequently the background to refugee movements in all parts of the world' (2007:70). For instance, Buxton LJ identified the persecution in Darfur which has given rise to many asylum claims as 'one of the most serious and extensive examples of racial persecution to have occurred in recent years' in *AH (Sudan), IG (Sudan), NM (Sudan) v SSHD* [2007] EWCA Civ 297.

It may be recalled that the European Commission on Human Rights found the state's action in passing racially discriminatory legislation capable in itself of amounting to a violation of Article 3 ECHR (*East African Asians v UK* (1973) 3 EHRR 76). Claims of persecution of Roma have been accepted as being for reasons of race (e.g., *Horvath*, *Harakal*), although also commonly Roma cases have failed, and in the case reports the emphasis is rather on questioning or establishing the seriousness of the violations of other human rights (to physical security, housing, etc.). The racial dimension, rather than being seen as an aggravating factor, seems invisible.

Claims by Palestinians have also not succeeded on this basis. In *MM and FH (Stateless Palestinians – KK, IH, HE CG reaffirmed) Lebanon* [2008] UKAIT 00014, the Tribunal held that differential treatment of Palestinians in refugee camps in Lebanon did not arise from their race, but from their statelessness. It could be justified under international conventions and human rights norms.

A recurring issue faced by Palestinian refugees is the difficulty of actually obtaining re-entry to their homeland. In *MA (Palestinian Territories) v SSHD* [2008] EWCA Civ 304, the Court of Appeal held that it was not persecutory to turn a stateless person away at the borders of his country of former habitual residence. MA had lived all his life in the Palestinian Territories. According to the law of Israel, he had no nationality, and could not compel any state to grant him entry after the failure of his asylum claim. This in itself, the Court held, was not persecutory. The appellants in *MT (Palestinian Territories) v SSHD* [2008] EWCA Civ 1149 and *SH (Palestinian Territories) v SSHD* [2008] EWCA Civ 1150 argued that the Court in *MA* had not considered the refusal of entry in the light of its being for reasons of race (being a Palestinian Arab). The Court disagreed. They held that this must have been in the contemplation of the Court in *MA*.

13.6.2 Religion

Religion is widely defined in the Qualification Directive, to include atheistic beliefs and both participation in and abstention from worship. The definition of religion has not been a major issue in asylum case law. More common issues have been what degree of self-restraint might be expected of the asylum seeker, what level of constraint is acceptable by a government, and therefore what kinds of religious activities should be absolutely free from state interference.

Although Hathaway places freedom of religion in his first category of rights, both the International Covenant on Civil and Political Rights (Art 18) and the ECHR (Art 9) allow some limitations by the state on that freedom where these are prescribed by law and 'necessary to protect public safety, order, health, or morals or the fundamental rights and freedoms of others' (ICCPR Article 18(3).

The ICCPR Article 18 also provides: 'No one shall be subject to coercion which would impair his freedom to have or to adopt a religion or belief of his choice.' The freedom therefore includes the freedom to change faith, or to hold a different faith from the official state religion, and this has arisen in numerous cases, for instance *Beshara* (19443) concerned a Christian under pressure to convert to Islam. Mr Beshara lost his claim because the Tribunal were satisfied that the Egyptian government took steps to protect its citizens from undue pressure by religious groups.

A number of the key issues have been addressed in claims brought by those of the Ahmadi faith, regarded variously as a sect of Islam or as a separate faith. In *Ahmad v SSHD* [1991] Imm AR 61, the Court of Appeal had held that the state of the law was not in itself persecution. Proclaiming the Ahmadi faith was illegal under the terms of a Presidential Ordinance no XX of 1984, however, Slade LJ accepted the Secretary of State's evidence that 'most Ahmadis live ordinary lives, untroubled by government, despite the existence of the Ordinance'. Mr Ahmad failed in his claim. This had been based partly on the assertion that if he did proselytize he would be subject to persecution. However, the Court of Appeal held that there was insufficient evidence to show that he would do in future what he had not done before.

The case of *Ahmed (Iftikhar) v Secretary of State for the Home Department* [2000] INLR 1, was somewhat different in that Mr Ahmed had suffered intense harassment personally before leaving Pakistan and regarded proselytizing as an essential element of his religion. The Court of Appeal accepted that he would not be likely to desist. It referred to *Ahmad* and to *Mendis* but distinguished this case because Mr Ahmed had already demonstrated what he would do and it was not a question of speculation, nor of the state of the law in itself being regarded as persecution. He did not fear prosecution under the Ordinance, but rather a continuation of the harassment he had already experienced. If the state intervened at all, it would be to prosecute him rather than protect him. The case of *Danian* should be used to decide that even if Mr Ahmed's behaviour was thought unreasonable, the real question was whether he was likely to face persecution on return. It is, of course, highly relevant that in the behaviour which some may think unreasonable he was exercising a fundamental right. This approach has in effect been confirmed by *HJ (Iran) and HT (Cameroon* [2010] UKSC 31 (see 13.6.4.3), applied in *R (on the application of Yameen)* [2011] EWHC 2250 (Admin) in which the Court agreed that the key question was the actual behaviour of the claimant, as an Ahmadi who had taken a leading role in his community and was dedicated to spreading his faith.

13.6.3 Nationality

This Convention reason is given a loose interpretation, not restricted to citizenship, as in the Qualification Directive Article 10(1)(c) which includes 'cultural, linguistic or ethnic identity, common geographical or political origins or its relationship with the population of another State'. The *UNHCR Handbook* notes that in conflict within a state where there are 'two or more national (ethnic, linguistic) groups... It may not always be easy to distinguish between persecution for reasons of nationality and persecution for reasons of political opinion.'

Persecution on grounds of nationality can in theory include where citizenship is denied to a minority. Though Czech and Slovak Roma have been in this position (see O'Nions 1999), once again there was little evidence of this being used to their advantage in asylum claims. As was clear at 13.6.1, Palestinians denied any nationality have also not been able to obtain protection through the Refugee Convention.

13.6.4 Particular social group

This Convention reason has given rise to more litigation than any other and it is more open to interpretation than the preceding ones. It has the capacity to some extent to enable the Convention to meet needs not originally envisaged, but is not a cure-all or catch-all category. As the Tribunal said in Montoya [2002] INLR 399 para 24:

> The convention is not intended to protect all suffering individuals, only those who can show that the risk of persecution in their case is for an enumerated Convention ground. If ignoring this principle the PSG grounds were read too widely, the enumeration of grounds would be superfluous; the definition of 'refugee' could have been limited to individuals who have a well-founded fear of persecution without more.

As a starting point for determining whether a claimant comes within a social group which could be protected by the Convention, it is useful though not essential to consider the principle of *ejusdem generis*. In other words, to construe 'particular social group' as being of the same kind as the other Convention reasons. This does not mean that social group repeats the other reasons, but that by having regard to the defining characteristics of the other reasons it may be possible to identify a social group for Convention purposes.

The key characteristics of the other Convention reasons were identified by the US Board of Immigration Appeals in the case of *Acosta* (1985) 19 I and N 211 as follows:

> Each...describes persecution aimed at an immutable characteristic: a characteristic that either is beyond the power of the individual to change or is so fundamental to individual identity or conscience that it ought not to be required to be changed...The shared characteristic might be an innate one such as sex, colour, or kinship ties, or in some circumstances it might be a shared experience such as former military leadership or land ownership.

Very similar qualities were identified in *Attorney General for Canada v Ward* (1993) 2 SCR 689, an application by a member of the Irish National Liberation Army for asylum in Canada. The Supreme Court suggested the following 'working rules' for identifying a particular social group:

1. groups defined by an innate or unchangeable characteristic;
2. groups whose members voluntarily associate for reasons so fundamental to their human dignity that they should not be forced to forsake the association;
3. groups associated by a former voluntary status, unalterable due to historical permanence.

None of this should be regarded as cast in stone. However, what we shall refer to as the *Ward* criteria have been extensively relied on by the courts.

The leading case in the UK on identifying particular social group is *Shah and Islam v SSHD* [1999] 2 AC 629, to which reference has already been made in the context of causal nexus. The case resolved a number of disputed points.

Key Case

***Shah and Islam v SSHD* [1999] 2 AC 629**

Mrs Shah's husband was violent and turned her out of their home in Pakistan. She arrived in the UK and gave birth to a child shortly afterwards. She was afraid that her husband might accuse her of adultery and denounce her under Sharia law for the offence of sexual immorality. The Court accepted evidence from an Amnesty International report on the position of women in Pakistan that the legal system discriminated against women in particular in its rules of evidence, and for the most severe charges of sexual immorality the evidence of women would not be heard. Arrests on such a charge could be made without preliminary investigation and could result in prolonged detention. For those convicted 'there is the spectre of 100 lashes or stoning to death in public' (549e).

Mrs Islam also had a violent marriage, but she had remained in it for 20 years. She was a schoolteacher. One day, a fight broke out at the school between two young supporters of rival political factions. She intervened and one faction became hostile and accused her of infidelity. These accusations were repeated to her husband, who was a member of the same political faction. Mrs Islam's husband assaulted her and she was admitted to hospital twice. She left her husband and stayed briefly with her brother, but unknown men then threatened him and she could not stay.

The Court of Appeal held that they were not members of a particular social group. One reason for this was a doctrine propounded that the members of the group must associate with each other, there must be some cohesiveness, interdependence, or cooperation, this was what made them a social group. None of the possible ways of defining a group of which Mrs Shah and Mrs Islam were members produced groups with this characteristic. The House of Lords dealt with this unambiguously. Contact among group members was not required. The examples given in *Ward* of characteristics which might form a social group (e.g., language, sexuality) do not suggest such contact. The groups are social groups in the sense of being recognizable in the context of the society in which they arise (per Lords Hoffmann, Hope, and Millett at 571a and 569e).

The second reason that the Court of Appeal held that the women were not part of a social group was the difficulty of defining the group without reference to the persecution. It is settled law, e.g., in *Savchenkov* [1996] Imm AR 28, that the group must exist independently of the persecution, and groups such as 'women subject to death by stoning for adultery' or 'women subject to domestic violence without redress' incorporate the persecution into the definition.

The problem was resolved by asking what the reason was for the persecution. It was because they were women, but not only this. They were women in a society which discriminates against women. This was not to use the persecution as a way of defining the group, but to use discrimination, and to acknowledge that women may be perceived as a group in a society which discriminates against them. Their Lordships explained by taking the example of left-handed people in a society which discriminates seriously against left-handedness. It may readily be seen that, in such a society, left-handed people would be regarded as a group in a way that they are not in a society which does not so discriminate.

To summarize, the group is a social group in the sense of being a group in the context of a society. The group may (but need not) be identified by discrimination against them in relation to a characteristic identified in the *Ward* criteria. There is no need for social cohesiveness in the group. The upshot in *Shah and Islam* was that the social group was found to be 'women in Pakistan', or 'women in a society that discriminates against women'.

13.6.4.1 *Gender-based persecution*

In the absence of gender as a listed reason in the Convention itself, case law has developed ways of including gender-specific persecution, and Shah and Islam was a significant step in this process. Women have faced enormous difficulty in establishing asylum claims. As discussed earlier, decision-makers at all levels have been very slow to recognize the political uses of rape and its place in the persecution of women. The nature of much gender-based persecution of women has not been recognized and neither have the forms of political activity in which women frequently engage. The Home Office's Guidance on Gender Issues in the Asylum Claim sets out some of the issues.

A woman may experience:

i) gender-specific persecution for reasons unrelated to gender (e.g. raped because of her activity in a political party)
ii) non-gender-specific persecution for reasons relating to her gender (e.g. flogged for refusing to wear a veil)
iii) gender-specific persecution because of her gender (e.g. female genital mutilation).

In connection with political opinion the API identifies that:

gender roles in many countries mean that women will more often be involved in low level political activities, for instance hiding people, passing messages or providing community services, food, clothing or medical care. Decision-makers should beware of equating so-called 'low-level' activity with low risk.

As discussed earlier in relation to sexual violence, although the guidance is limited, research also reveals a widespread failure to follow the guidance. Decisions still fail to recognize the political activities of women as political, or the possibility of applying *Shah and Islam* to identify a particular social group of women, persecuted for reasons connected to their gender (Ceneda and Palmer 2006).

While *Shah and Islam* broke new ground, especially for women's asylum claims, to succeed in a refugee claim, a woman must still show that she is a member of a particular social group which can be defined without reference to the feared persecution. This requires evidence of the situation of women in a comparable situation to herself in the society she is in. Where extensive evidence is given of social conditions, cases concerning the risks facing women may become country guidance cases, for instance in 2010 a new country guidance case on women in Pakistan found that

[t]he Protection of Women (Criminal Laws Amendment) Act 2006...has had a significant effect on the operation of the Pakistan criminal law as it affects women accused of adultery...Most sexual offences now have to be dealt with under the Pakistan Penal Code rather than under the more punitive Offence of Zina (Enforcement of Hudood) Ordinance 1979. Husbands no longer have power to register a First Information Report with the police alleging adultery; since 1 December 2006 any such complaint must be presented to a court which will require sufficient grounds to be shown for any charges to proceed. A senior police officer has to conduct the investigation... However, Pakistan remains a heavily patriarchal society and levels of domestic violence continue to be high.

The tribunal then considered and made findings about the protection available to women who suffered domestic violence (*KA and others (domestic violence – risk on return) Pakistan* [2010] UKUT 00216 (IAC)).

In Bangladesh, the Tribunal in 2011 found:

> There is a high level of domestic violence in Bangladesh. Despite the efforts of the government to improve the situation, due to the disinclination of the police to act upon complaints, women subjected to domestic violence may not be able to obtain an effective measure of state protection by reason of the fact that they are women and may be able to show a risk of serious harm for a Refugee Convention reason. Each case, however, must be determined on its own facts. (*SA (Divorced woman – illegitimate child) Bangladesh* CG [2011] UKUT 00254 (IAC)

Prior to the country guidance system, in *Kaur* [2002] UKIAT 03387, the Tribunal considered the case of a woman from rural India who had had an adulterous relationship in the UK which resulted in the birth of a child, and noted evidence that honour killings were still common in rural India; it concluded, 'looking at the Appellant's background in rural India in the light of the social, cultural and religious mores, women in the Appellant's circumstances are identifiable as a particular social group'.

In *P and M v SSHD*, P had been subject to serious violence by her husband including death threats and received no state protection. Her husband was a police officer who had friendships with high-ranking police officers. The evidence was that violence against women was taken as normal in Kenya, and that death or life-threatening injuries would have to occur before police would take action. The particular social group was 'women, who are disadvantaged in Kenya because of their position in society' (para 21, quoting the adjudicator).

R (on the application of N) v SSHD [2002] EWCA Civ 1082 was mentioned earlier in the context of rape. The Court of Appeal saw no merit in the argument that women in that locality where rape was common and uncontrolled were a social group. They saw the situation as one of general lawlessness by soldiers and did not construe this in the light of discrimination.

Claims based on FGM may succeed where societal discrimination and lack of protection is proved. In *P and M*, the Court defined the particular social group of which M was a part as women in Kenya, particularly Kikuyu women under 65 years of age. They had immutable characteristics of age and sex which existed independently of persecution and could be identified by reference to their being compelled to undergo FGM (para 41). The appellant's father had joined the Mungiki sect which enforces FGM. He and about 20 other members of the sect had performed a forced FGM on the appellant's mother, who died as a result. He then married another member of the sect who insisted that the appellant and her sister should be circumcised. Both refused. Five members of the sect were involved in raping M and violently assaulting her. Her sister was forcibly circumcised and M was told she would be next.

In the light of *P and M*, it was surprising that another FGM case went as far as the House of Lords (*Fornah v SSHD* [2006] UKHL 46).

Key Case

***Fornah v SSHD* [2006] UKHL 46**

In 1998, the Appellant and her mother were living in her father's family village to escape the civil war, and she overheard discussions of her undergoing FGM as part of her initiation into womanhood. In order to avoid this she ran away, but she was captured by rebels and repeatedly raped by a rebel leader, by whom she became pregnant. An uncle arranged her departure from Sierra Leone to the UK. She feared that if she was returned she would have nowhere to live except her father's village, where she feared she would be subjected to FGM. It was common ground that FGM constitutes persecution if the appellant was found to be a member of a particular social group. The Secretary of State argued that women in Sierra Leone could not be a social group because the cutting only happened once, and once it was done such women could no longer be in fear of persecution. But to hold that uninitiated women were the social group would be to define the group by the (fear of) persecution, therefore they could not be a social group for Convention purposes.

Baroness Hale pointed out the fallacy: 'It is the persecution, not the fear, which has to be "by reason of" membership of the group... [and]... It is well settled that not all members of the group need be at risk' (para 113). She defined the group as 'Sierra Leonean women belonging to those ethnic groups where FGM is practised' (para 114) although she added that 'it matters not whether the group is stated more widely, as all Sierra Leonean women, or more narrowly, as intact Sierra Leonean women from those ethnic groups. For all of them, the group has existence independent of the persecution' (para 114).

The House of Lords found that Ms Fornah was a member of a particular social group, though they defined it in a variety of ways. Lord Bingham's approach was interesting:

> women in Sierra Leone are a group of persons sharing a common characteristic which, without a fundamental change in social mores is unchangeable, namely a position of social inferiority as compared with men. (para 31)

This is an interesting integration of the *Ward* criteria. Lord Bingham found the social group, on the basis of this reasoning, to be women in Sierra Leone. Most of their Lordships added some further qualifying characteristic such as not having undergone FGM (being 'intact' or 'uninitiated').

The discrimination in *Shah and Islam* was in part because of the law itself, which was discriminatory. In many cases, however, the question is not the law but the practice. In *P and M*, P could not obtain protection because of social attitudes and the power and practice of the police, not because violence was formally legal. In *RG (Ethiopia) v SSHD* [2006] EWCA Civ 339 the societal discrimination against women was combined with the non-enforcement of the law, and with a particular law which provided immunity from prosecution for rapists if their victims could be persuaded to marry them. The Court followed *P and M* in saying that societal discrimination and lack of police protection were crucial, and found that young women in Ethiopia were a particular social group.

The Court of Appeal in *Liu v SSHD* [2005] EWCA Civ 249 said that 'the need to establish a particular social group should not become an obstacle course in which the postulated group undergoes constant redefinition' (para 12). The Court remitted the case to the Tribunal with guidance as to the treatment of Chinese women giving birth or becoming pregnant in breach of China's one-child policy. Relying on cases in Canada and Australia, the Court was of the view that the direction of development was in favour of finding a particular social group in such cases. They also said that persecution may form part of the means of identifying the group, though not the sole means.

In *NS (Afghanistan CG)* [2004] UKIAT 00328, the Tribunal found that lone women in Afghanistan were at risk of abuse, without adequate judicial redress and protection, and that the appellant could establish a fear of persecution as a member of the particular social group of women in Afghanistan (see Women's Asylum News issue no. 49 February 2005). In *HM (Somalia)* [2005] UKIAT 00040 the Tribunal held that '[w]omen in Somalia form a PSG not just because they are women, but because they are extensively discriminated against'. In *NM and Others (Lone women – Ashraf) Somalia* CG [2005] UKIAT 00076 the Tribunal found that a woman on her own and of a minority tribe would be at risk in Somalia. However, in *AI (Nigeria) v SSHD* [2007] EWCA Civ 707, the Court of Appeal rejected an argument on behalf of a young single woman with a child. She might well face discrimination, but this did not amount to persecution. The generally stated evidence of Amnesty International that violence against women was widespread did not, the Court thought, give sufficient evidence that the appellant was at risk from 'harmful practices'.

13.6.4.2 *Social perception*

The UNHCR Guidelines identify two approaches to the recognition of a particular social group. One is the 'protected characteristics' approach, which we have used and referred to as the application of the *Ward* criteria. The other is based on social perception. They recommend the adoption of a single standard that incorporates both approaches (2002 para 10). Goodwin-Gill and McAdam suggest that there is a value in recognizing 'groups in society, in the ordinary everyday sense'. By way of example, they refer to 'the landlord class, the working class, the ruling class' (2007: 85). Even without the connection to fundamental characteristics required by the *Ward* criteria, the identity of the group might be well-known and acknowledged in society.

A requirement for recognition *by* the society in which the persecution arises would present serious pitfalls. For instance, it is unthinkable that Pakistani society, whether government or otherwise, should be required to identify women in that country as discriminated against and thus a social group. Opinion on the matter would obviously be divided. The particular social group is a legal construct in the hands of the decision-maker in the refugee claim, not a naturally arising phenomenon. Its identification is a matter for those decision-makers *in the context* of the society in which it is said to arise. In non-state actor cases, it cannot be acceptable to identify a social group simply on the attribution of some members of society. *Shah and Islam* suggests that the group should be identifiable *within* that society, and of course that will often mean that members of that society would be able to identify the group. However, to say that they must be identified *by* that society is open to the (perhaps mis-)interpretation that if the society is unaware of what it is doing to a group of people then they cannot be a social group. It introduces an unnecessary element of subjectivity and risks replicating the very discrimination from which the asylum claimant seeks redress. The Australian case of *S v MIMA* [2004] HCA 25 sets out the difference between recognizing a group in the context of that society (here, young, able-bodied men in Afghanistan, who might as a consequence be subject to forcible recruitment by the Taleban), and their recognition as a group *by* that society. The latter was an unnecessary requirement, they thought, for a refugee claim.

The Qualification Directive seems to require the group to be recognized using both approaches. It says that a group shall be considered to form a particular social group where in particular the *Ward* criteria are met, *and* 'that group has a distinct identity in the relevant country, because it is perceived as being different by the surrounding society'. The UK implementing regulations repeat the two approaches, though say that groups will be recognized 'for example' where these are met, instead of 'in particular', which softens the requirement to apply both approaches. Lord Bingham in *Fornah* regarded an interpretation of the Directive which would require both the *Ward* criteria *and* the social perception approach as wrong, although these remarks were obiter (as the Tribunal noted in *SB (Moldova CG)* [2008] UKAIT 00002). In the House of Lords' judgment, the group is recognized in the context of the society, but the group that would be recognized by the society is uninitiated women, who were regarded as particularly inferior.

The Tribunal in *AZ (Trafficked women) Thailand* CG [2010] UKUT 118 (IAC) noted that the Qualification Directive permits Member States to apply standards more favourable to the applicant than the minimum laid down'. Also, they noted that UNHCR advised that 'to avoid any protection gaps, member states should reconcile the two approaches to permit alternative rather than cumulative application of the two concepts'. The Tribunal declined to accept that they should do this; nevertheless, in reliance on the 'broad humanitarian purpose' of the Refugee Convention, as described by Sedley LJ in *Shah and Islam* and Lord Hope in *Hoxha,* they found that the appellant was a member of a particular social group of 'young women who have been victims of trafficking for sexual exploitation' ((*AZ* para 140).

Having considered some of the follow-on from Shah and Islam and the construction of social group, we shall now consider some other particular social groups, and issues in defining social groups which arise in these contexts.

13.6.4.3 *Sexuality*

Shah and Islam expressly laid the foundation for resolving some of the inconsistencies that had bedevilled claims of asylum based on sexuality. Claims from homosexuals had been denied and granted on the basis of particular social group, but there had been no authoritative judgment on the matter. Although the comments of their Lordships in *Shah and Islam* must be regarded as obiter, it is the inescapable conclusion of their reasoning in the case, that homosexuals may constitute a social group if, as a group defined by their sexuality, they suffer discrimination. Sexuality is clearly within the *Ward* criteria, either as an innate or unchangeable characteristic or else as something fundamental to human dignity which a person should not be required to forsake (see, e.g., New Zealand Refugee Status Appeals Authority *Re GJ* [1998] (1995) INLR 387, 420).

This is confirmed by the Qualification Directive, which says 'depending on the circumstances in the country of origin, a particular social group might include a group based on a common characteristic of sexual orientation' (Article 10(1)(d)). This does not include acts considered criminal in the national law of Member States. So, for instance, a common sexual orientation as a paedophile would not constitute a particular social group.

In *SSHD v Z, A v SSHD, M v SSHD* [2002] Imm AR 560, Schiemann LJ emphasized that such cases are very 'fact sensitive' and that general pronouncements about particular countries should be avoided. However, the advance of country guidance cases has made inroads upon this view. Indeed, social attitudes and governmental or legal penalties relating to sexuality are an obvious field for general evidence, with the risk to the individual being case-specific. For instance, in *SW (lesbians – HJ and HT applied) Jamaica CG* [2011] UKUT 00251(IAC) the Tribunal held that:

> Jamaica is a deeply homophobic society. There is a high level of violence, and where a real risk of persecution or serious harm is established, the Jamaican state offers lesbians no sufficiency of protection. Lesbianism (actual or perceived) brings a risk of violence, up to and including 'corrective' rape and murder.

The Tribunal went on to examine and describe factors which might reduce, mitigate, or enhance the risk to any particular woman.

A recurring issue in claims based on sexuality has been the question of whether the claimant may be required to 'exercise discretion', i.e., conceal their sexuality, on their return. The Court of Appeal in *Z v SSHD* [2004] EWCA Civ 1578 accepted that the implication of *Danian v SSHD* [1999] INLR 533 and *Ahmed v SSHD* [2000] INLR 1 was that an asylum claim could be established where to live in their own country a person would be required to modify their behaviour to a level that constituted persecution, but the case law suggests that where lesser adaptation is anticipated, the claim would fail.

The law on this point has now been settled by *HJ (Iran) and HT (Cameroon)* [2010] UKSC 31.

Key Case

***HJ (Iran) and HT (Cameroon)* [2010] UKSC 31**

The Court unanimously overturned the Court of Appeal's judgment, and set out the proper approach to an application for asylum on the ground of a well-founded fear of persecution for being gay:

- Is the decision maker satisfied on the evidence that the applicant is gay, or would be treated as gay by potential persecutors in his country of nationality?
- If so, is the decision maker satisfied on the evidence that gay people who live openly are liable to persecution in the applicant's country of nationality?
- If so, the decision maker must consider what the applicant would do if he were returned to that country.
- If the applicant would in fact live openly and thereby be exposed to a real risk of persecution, then he has a well-founded fear of persecution – even if he could avoid the risk by living 'discreetly'.
- If, on the other hand, the applicant would in fact live discreetly and so avoid persecution, the decision maker must ask *why* he would do so. If the applicant would choose to live discreetly simply because that was how he himself would wish to live, or because of social pressures, then his application should be rejected. If a material reason for the applicant living discreetly would be a fear of persecution which would follow if he were to live openly as a gay man, then such a person has a well-founded fear of persecution. To reject his application on the ground that he could avoid the persecution by living discreetly would be to defeat the very right which the Convention exists to protect – to live freely and openly as a gay man without fear of persecution (para 82).

The Supreme Court judgment represents a new era in treatment of refugee claims on the grounds of sexuality. Other important statements in the judgment include:

- The use of the word 'discretion' is a euphemism and the more accurate description of what is being discussed is 'concealment' (para 22).
- A straight person is not required to conceal their sexual identity – neither should a gay one be required to do so (para 76).
- In any event, a decision maker in the English legal system cannot lay down such a 'requirement'. There can be no such requirement; all that there is is a prediction of how the applicant will in fact behave, and what will be the consequences of that.

Their Lordships remarked that the Court of Appeal judgment would return Anne Frank to the attic, on the basis she could stay there and avoid persecution. This made the point clear that she was not afraid of being in an attic, but of persecution by the Nazis as a Jew. So with a gay man required to conceal his identity for fear of persecution.

Finally, although the judgment is phrased strongly in terms of men and their relationships, there is no apparent reason not to apply the judgment equally to women.

13.6.4.4 *Families*

The identification of a family as a particular social group has slowly been established in the courts. Clearly, the first element in the *Ward* criteria is satisfied. There is an innate characteristic which is the blood tie, or there is a characteristic so fundamental that the person should not be required to change it in marriage or a comparable relationship. Lord Bingham in *K v SSHD* [2006] UKHL 46 (heard and decided with *Fornah*) said, 'the family is the quintessential social group' (para 3). The family has civil status in that its ties are recognized and even created by law. Article 23 International Covenant on Civil and Political Rights says: 'The family is the natural and fundamental group unit of society and is entitled to protection by society and the State.' However, prior to *K*, cases on family as a social group have often failed.

One reason, now disposed of in the UK by *K*, was the argument that if Y is persecuted for being a family member of X, X must have been targeted for a Convention reason in order for Y to claim the family relationship as a Convention reason (*Quijano v SSHD* [1997] Imm AR 227, in which the first person in the family was targeted because he had refused to cooperate with a drugs cartel, which was not a Convention reason). The House of Lords in *K* preferred the earlier case of *R v IAT ex p De Melo* [1997] Imm AR 43, in which Laws J found two sisters to be members of a particular social group as the family members of a Brazilian farmer who had refused to grow drugs. K feared persecution because her husband had been detained and ill-treated, and after his detention the Revolutionary Guard had visited their home and raped her. She and her family were royalists associated with the late Shah of Iran. The adjudicator had not found evidence that the husband's persecution was for a Convention reason. The House of Lords held that this was an unnecessary requirement. Likewise, it was unnecessary that all members of the family should be at risk for the same Convention reason or that all members of the family should be at risk at all. The reason in K's case was that she was a family member of her husband. Lord Rodgers of Earlsferry said:

> Even if Mr K was detained for completely valid reasons, singling out the members of his family for mistreatment simply because they are members of the family of a detainee would amount to persecution for the purposes of the Convention. (para 63)

It may be that K will have an impact on the blood feud cases, of which many have failed. For instance, in *Hurtado* [2002] UKIAT 03158, there were 92 members of each family who had been killed in a feud that had gone on since 1983, for obscure reasons, possibly connected with an argument over a bunch of bananas. The Tribunal commented: 'The Hurtado family were simply an ordinary family which had got involved in a feud.' Then, less surprisingly: 'It would be artificial to regard it as a particular social group.' Often, a 'straightforward blood feud' has been said not to be based on a particular social group. This means where no other Convention reason can be identified behind the feud, and may well be different after *K*. It is still the case that this Convention reason is not always clearly identified. For instance, in *MQ (Afghanistan) v SSHD* [2009] EWCA Civ 61, the appellant appeared to be targeted because he was the son of a former Mujahideen commander who had been executed, but this potential Convention reason is not discussed in the case.

It is certainly a mistake to require that all members of the family be at risk in order to qualify as a particular social group. This was already the case following *Shah and Islam*, and *K* reinforces the point.

13.6.4.5 *Other status*

There is a wealth of case law relating to a wide range of possible social groups. Here, we seek to give an understanding of some further categories which demonstrate general principles.

The quotation given earlier from *Acosta* is a principle that those people protected from persecution are those who cannot, if they remain in their homeland, make a choice which would prevent the treatment they fear. This was addressed directly in *Ouanes v SSHD* [1998] Imm AR 76, a Court of Appeal case concerning an Algerian midwife who, as she was required to do, gave contraceptive advice as part of her practice. As a result, she received threats from religious fundamentalist groups opposed to this advice. The question was whether her employment was something so fundamental to her conscience that she should not be required to change it. The leading judgment was given by Pill LJ who said at 82:

> A common employment does not ordinarily have that impact upon individual identities or conscience necessary to constitute employees a particular social group within the meaning of the Convention. I accept the possibility that fellow employees may constitute a particular social group if, by reason by the nature of their employment or the addition of other links to those of employment, the above principle applies. Employment as a member of a religious order could be an example.

Examples of others who have applied on the basis of particular social group are a Colombian landowner (Montoya), a wealthy educated Sierra Leonean mine owner (*Diallo* 00/TH/01231), a rich Lithuanian entrepreneur (*R v Special Adjudicator ex p Roznys* [2000] Imm AR 57). The words of Burton J in the last-named case probably sum up the courts' and tribunals' approach: 'I do not consider that it is arguable that possession of money puts you into a particular social group, namely a particular social group with money as opposed to those who do not have money.' Montoya 'seeks to clarify post-Shah and Islam criteria for establishing whether there exists a particular social group'. In that case, the adjudicator had accepted the existence of a particular social group of private landowners, but the Tribunal accepted the Secretary of State's view that Mr Montoya was targeted because he had money, and this, as expressed by Burton J, is not a social group.

The third limb of the *Ward* criteria, in the words of the Qualification Directive, sharing 'a common background that cannot be changed', opened the way to an important identification of a particular social group in the case of *SB (Moldova CG)* [2008] UKAIT 00002. The claimant was held to be a member of the particular social group of 'former victims of trafficking for sexual exploitation' in Moldova. She had given evidence against her trafficker in his prosecution in the UK. After his prison sentence he was now free, and she feared reprisals from his network if she were to return to Moldova. The Tribunal confirmed that discrimination did not need to be an identifying characteristic of the group, providing it was formed according to the *Ward* criteria (here, common history) and (following the Qualification Directive) the group was recognizable in that society. This decision paved the way for other decisions concerning former victims of trafficking, with groups defined on the basis of evidence concerning their treatment in the particular society (as in *AZ (Trafficked women) Thailand*, see 13.6.4.2).

13.6.5 **Political opinion**

A political dissident was a typical figure of a refugee who was the focus of the Refugee Convention when it was first drafted and political dissent continues to play a significant part in establishing refugee claims. Political opinion as a Convention reason however goes much wider than this.

Political expression is valued as an essential requirement of democracy as without debate and freedom of political speech, democracy cannot thrive. In the case law of the ECHR, political speech is protected more fully than other forms of expression as the Court allows a narrower margin of appreciation to states which seek to restrict it (see, e.g., *Lingens v Austria* (1986) 8 EHRR 407). In refugee claims, the question arises as to whether an opinion is political. Sometimes, this is obvious, such as support for a political party. Sometimes, it is less obvious, for instance a woman in Iran who refused to conform to a strict dress code and wore make-up was regarded by the Tribunal in *Fathi and Ahmady (14264)* as expressing a political opinion. Guidance was given in the Tribunal case of *Gomez* 00/TH/02257 on the characteristics of a political opinion: 'To qualify as political the opinion in question must relate to the major power transactions taking place in that particular society.' This makes it clear that not only party politics is intended, so, for instance, attending an anti-globalization protest would be an expression of political opinion.

A political opinion may be expressed or it may be imputed by the persecutor. Hence, it is not the holding of the opinion which is important, but how the claimant is perceived by the persecutor. This is not to reverse all that was said earlier about the motivation of the persecutor. A detailed enquiry into their motives is not required. What is required is to ascertain what the reason is for the persecution.

A number of relevant principles are cited in the case of *Noune v SSHD* [2000] All ER (D) 2163.

Key Case

Noune v SSHD **[2000] All ER (D) 2163 CA**

The appellant was an Algerian worker with a responsible position in the national Post Office. She was approached on numerous occasions by masked men asking her to send messages to Japan and the Soviet Union, offering her 'protection' in return. She was threatened with violence or other serious consequences if she did not comply and the suggestion made to her was that it was her duty to help. Those who approached her wore religious dress, whereas her appearance and demeanour were of a Westernized woman. There was plentiful evidence of killings by religious extremists in Algeria, and there was evidence of 'Westernized' women being targeted, but no evidence that she had been threatened for this reason, rather for her non-cooperation.

The Court of Appeal held inter alia that:

(i) The motives of the persecutor may be mixed, and they can include non-Convention reasons: it is not necessary to show that they are purely political.

(ii) Political opinion may be express or imputed.

(iii) It follows that in order to show persecution on account of political opinion it is not necessary to show political action or activity by the victim: in some circumstances mere inactivity and unwillingness to co-operate can be taken as an expression of political opinion. (*UNHCR Handbook* para 80)

(iv) If it is shown that there is a reasonable likelihood that the persecutor will attribute a political opinion to the victim and persecute him because of it, the fact, if it be a fact, that the persecutor would be in error in making that attribution does not disqualify the victim from refugee status. (para 8)

The Court of Appeal held that the facts were capable of giving rise to a claim on the basis of political opinion and remitted the case to a tribunal for decision.

As referred to previously, cases concerning witnesses of crimes and people refusing to cooperate with criminal activity have been argued under both social group and political opinion. For such claims to be seen as relating to the 'major power transactions in a society', the criminal activity in question must have a relationship to those power transactions. Like social group, political opinion must be construed in the context of the society in which it arises. In the UK, for example, it would not constitute political opinion to refuse the request of a common criminal to kill for him. However, to refuse to do the same at the request of say, Special Branch, could be a political action and might suggest a political opinion. Goodwin-Gill suggested a wider definition of political opinion as one 'on any matter in which the machinery of the state, government and policy may be engaged' (Goodwin-Gill and McAdam 2007:87). This definition has been approved by the courts. The Qualification Directive definition is wider, as it includes holding an opinion, thought or belief on a matter related to the potential actors of persecution, which includes non-state actors (Article 10(1)(e)).

In *Acero-Garces (21514)*, the appellant had witnessed the murder of a policeman and since then had been subject to serious threats and harassment. This had to be seen against the background in Colombia of the drugs cartels, in the words of the Tribunal 'a power unto themselves. The links between the narcotic industry, crime and the government is very thoroughly documented.' The Tribunal found that she risked persecution for reasons of political opinion, 'that the appellant is seen to be on the side of law, order and justice and against disorder, chaos and injustice; and it is these dark forces that control government'.

There was a different result in *Storozhenko v SSHD* [2002] Imm AR 329, CA. Here, the appellant had witnessed drunken police officers driving a speeding car which knocked down and injured a young girl. When he remonstrated with them, one of them hit him in the face with a baton, breaking his jaw. He made a formal complaint at the police station but there was no action taken, and after this he began to receive serious threats and was attacked. The Court of Appeal accepted that he was being persecuted for attempting to bring a police officer to justice, but said it was 'manifestly artificial to talk in terms of imputed political opinion' (para 44).

The case of *Gomez v SSHD* is a starred appeal which sets out a number of points intended to clarify issues in cases where some attitude may be imputed to the victim by a non-state perpetrator but it is arguable as to whether this is a political opinion. *Gomez* was heard before *Storozhenko* but would support the conclusion in that case.

The Tribunal confirmed established case law that the fundamental rights of the victim must be protected. So a person should not be in fear because they have exercised the rights to freedom of thought, conscience, opinion, expression, association, and assembly. To qualify as political an opinion must relate to the major power transactions taking place in that particular society. Where a non-state actor is not itself a political entity the Tribunal thought it would be difficult to regard an opinion imputed by them as political, but this is superseded by the Qualification Directive. Where social group has been used in these kinds of situations it has tended not to be a successful argument, as, for instance, in *Savchenkov* [1996] Imm AR 28 CA, the appellant argued unsuccessfully that he was a member of the group of individuals whom 'the mafia seeks to recruit and who refuse'.

As mentioned earlier, political opinions may be imputed to asylum seekers by their country of origin because they have made a failed asylum claim elsewhere. The risks of returning to Zimbabwe have been challenged on this basis. The latest country guidance says:

> the evidence does not show that...the return of a failed asylum seeker from the United Kingdom, having no significant MDC profile, would result in that person facing a real risk of having to demonstrate loyalty to the ZANU-PF. The position is, however, likely to be otherwise in the case of a person without ZANU-PF connections, returning from the United Kingdom after a significant absence to a rural area of Zimbabwe, other than Matabeleland North or Matabeleland South. (*EM and Others (Returnees) Zimbabwe CG* [2011] UKUT 98 (IAC))

In the case of Zimbabwe, that requirement to demonstrate loyalty gave rise to a question as to whether the Supreme Court's decision in *HJ (Iran)* would apply to political opinion too. Will a returned asylum seeker from the UK lie about their political affiliation on return to Zimbabwe and should they be expected to?

In *TM (Zimbabwe) v SSHD* [2010] EWCA Civ 916, the Court's provisional view (the point was not fully considered) was that as the appellants had been found not to have strong political views, any dissembling on their part to protect themselves on arrival in Zimbabwe did not violate the core of their right to freedom of political opinion, and was not analogous with *HJ*.

The Court of Appeal in *RT (Zimbabwe) and others* [2010] EWCA Civ 1285 held that the distinction was immaterial between having to lie on isolated occasions 'about political opinions which one does not have', and long-term concealment of an immutable characteristic. The question was the reason for the feared ill-treatment:

> If the reason is political opinion, or imputed political opinion, that is enough to bring it within the Convention. In this case, we are concerned with the 'imputed' political opinions of those concerned, not their actual opinions (see para 4 above). Accordingly, the degree of their political commitment in fact, and whether political activity is of central or marginal importance to their lives, are beside the point. The 'core' of the protected right is the right not to be persecuted for holding political views which they do not have. There is nothing 'marginal' about the risk of being stopped by militia and persecuted because of that. If they are forced to lie about their absence of political beliefs, solely in order to avoid persecution, that seems to us to be covered by the *HJ (Iran)* principle, and does not defeat their claims to asylum. (para 36)

13.6.5.1 *Conscientious objection*

Conscientious objection as a form of political opinion has generated a volume of case law from which certain principles may be distilled. Guidance is found in paras 167–174 of the *UNHCR Handbook*, though in places this is tentative.

Conscription and conscientious objection

There is a tension between the right of the state to demand military service from its citizens, and the right of the individual not to be forced to do something which goes against their conscience. All states have the right to demand military service from their nationals; some have a system of compulsory military service for all, some employ conscription only in times of war. In each case, it is usually a criminal offence either to refuse to join up or to desert the armed forces. An exemption from prosecution and an alternative to military service is given in an increasing number of countries to those who can establish a genuine conscientious objection to military action. In *Bayatyan v Armenia* [2011] ECHR 1095 the ECtHR noted that only two members of the Council of Europe did not have provisions for conscientious objection.

Prosecution for avoidance of normal military service for reasons other than conscience is not regarded as persecution unless the punishment is disproportionate or is inflicted or impacts in a discriminatory way. For instance, some countries, including the USA, still maintain the possibility of the death penalty for refusal to serve. In some countries, avoiding military service for whatever motive is seen as political dissent which warrants severe punishment. Country guidance cases on Eritrea hold that people who will be perceived as draft evaders are at risk on return to Eritrea, and that 'the issue of military service has become politicised and actual or perceived evasion of military service is regarded by the Eritrean authorities as an expression of political opinion' (*IN (Draft evaders – evidence of risk) Eritrea CG* [2005] UKIAT 00106).

Key Case

***Sepet and Bulbul* [2003] UKHL 15**

The two appellants were Turkish Kurds who objected to military service for the Turkish government. They did so because they opposed the Turkish government's policy towards the Kurds, and feared that they might be sent to a Kurdish area and required to commit atrocities against their own people. Turkey provided no alternative to military service. Draft evaders were liable to a prison sentence of between six months and three years, which was not thought disproportionate.

Their claim was framed as conscientious objection, but it was clear that they did not have a conscientious objection to military service as such, but only in the present circumstances. Nevertheless, their objection was evidently a political opinion and could not unreasonably be regarded as a reason of conscience. The Convention reason was therefore established, but the question was whether imprisonment because of this political opinion could amount to persecution, when imprisonment for refusal not based on such an opinion would not.

Their Lordships considered the submission for the appellants that there was a recognized human right of conscientious objection, for instance implied in the Universal Declaration of Human Rights Article 18. If there was such a right, then it could be argued that a discriminatory denial of the right could amount to persecution. They concluded that the weight of the evidence was that to date there is no such human right although there were developments in that direction.

The House of Lords made the distinction between 'absolute' and 'partial' conscientious objectors. Absolute objectors would object to all military action for reasons of conscience. This would include people who were pacifists without a religious belief, and people whose pacifism arose from a belief system which normally entailed it, such as Quakers or Buddhists. There was authority to suggest that in the case of absolute objectors at least that prosecution could amount to persecution (*Zaitz v SSHD* [2000] INLR 346). In the light of their finding that there was no human right of conscientious objection their Lordships considered that punishment for refusal of military service would not amount to persecution per se, reversing *Zaitz* to the extent that that case could be regarded as deciding otherwise.

Partial objection referred to people such as the appellants in these cases whose objection was a political one based on the practices and policy of the Turkish military, not on military action as such. In this case, the greater includes the less, because if there is no right of conscientious objection then even less will punishment of 'partial objectors' amount to persecution.

As the appellants Sepet and Bulbul were partial objectors, the case must be taken to decide that partial objection per se will not found a claim to refugee status. Comments that absolute objection does not give rise to a refugee claim must be regarded as obiter and would now be subject to review in the light of the ECtHR's Grand Chamber judgment in *Bayatyan v Armenia*.

Key Case

***Bayatyan v Armenia* [2011] ECHR 1095**

The applicant was a Jehovah's witness who objected to engaging in military action on the basis of his religious faith. He avoided conscription by leaving home, and was convicted for draft evasion. The Court held that 'opposition to military service, where it is motivated by a serious and insurmountable conflict between the obligation to serve in the army and a person's conscience or his deeply and genuinely held religious or other beliefs, constitutes a conviction or belief of sufficient cogency, seriousness, cohesion and importance to attract the guarantees of Article 9'.

The Court found that Article 9 had been violated.

In effect, in this judgment, the ECtHR, in harmony with the EU Charter of Fundamental Rights and Freedoms and the interpretation given by the UN Human Rights Commission to the ICCPR, found a human right to conscientious objection.

Action in breach of international norms

Refusal to undertake military action which is against international law can found refugee status. Lord Bingham in *Sepet and Bulbul* states established law in this way:

> There is compelling support for the view that refugee status should be accorded to one who has refused to undertake compulsory military service on the grounds that such service would or might require him to commit atrocities or gross human rights abuses or participate in a conflict condemned by the international community, or where refusal to serve would earn grossly excessive or disproportionate punishment. (para 8)

This is partly endorsed in the Qualification Directive, where the acts listed as persecution include prosecution or punishment for refusing to perform military service which would entail committing war crimes, crimes against peace, crimes against humanity or against the purposes and principles of the UN or serious non-political crimes. In such cases the political opinion of the refuser would readily be imputed if not expressed. Earlier drafts of the Directive allowed for broader grounds of conscience to found a refugee claim, but these were lost in the negotiation process. The cases of *Radivojevic and Lazarevic* [1997] 2 All ER 723 concerned objection to military service in the former Yugoslavia in an action that was internationally condemned. However, it was held in the Court of Appeal (and this point was not pursued to the House of Lords) that even in such a conflict, the individuals themselves must object to the condemned action on principle, not just be 'opportunistic draft evaders' in order to obtain asylum.

Paragraph 171 of the *UNHCR Handbook* suggests that where military action has drawn the condemnation of the international community, punishment for refusal may amount to persecution. In *Krotov v SSHD* [2004] EWCA Civ 69, the Court of Appeal considered a Russian soldier's refusal to participate in the Chechen War. The Secretary of State argued that the British asylum decision-making and appeal process could not be drawn into the kind of international judgments that would be required in order to grant refugee status on this basis. The Court of Appeal disagreed. They held that there were plenty of norms of international law to which reference could be made, and refugee status could be founded on objection to military service where that service would involve participation in acts which were contrary to basic rules of conduct as defined by international law. It was not necessary to wait for formal condemnation of the conflict by the international community. The claim could succeed if combatants could be punished for refusing to act in breach of basic rules of human conduct or if the genuine fear of such punishment was a reason for refusing to serve.

This was applied in *BE (Iran) v SSHD* [2008] EWCA Civ 540, where an Iranian soldier repeatedly refused orders to plant landmines in a populated area, despite three months' imprisonment, demotion, and death threats. There was no state of war or insurgency in Iranian Kurdistan at that time. The appellant did not want to cause civilian deaths. He deserted and fled to the UK.

His asylum claim reached the Court of Appeal, where he argued that the irreducible minimum of civilized conduct should not be lower in peace than in war, and his refusal to go below that minimum made him a refugee.

The Court said that the seeding of terrain with anti-personnel explosive devices was one of the most vicious tactics in modern warfare and also in state security. Sedley LJ reviewed research on the effect of landmines, and drew the conclusion that anyone who, and any state which, sowed unmarked anti-personnel mines in terrain from which civilians were not excluded was responsible for the deaths and injuries that would result.

The Home Secretary had defended the case mainly on the basis that there was no breach of 'hard law'. The Court held, however, that international agreements showed that by 1999, the almost universal condemnation of anti-personnel mines had placed their use in the category of gross atrocities or gross abuse of the human right to life and bodily integrity. In *Sepet and Bulbul*, Lord Bingham said:

> There is compelling support for the view that refugee status should be accorded to one who has refused to undertake compulsory military service on the grounds that such service would or might require him to commit atrocities or gross human rights abuses, or participate in a conflict condemned by the international community, or where refusal to serve would earn grossly excessive or disproportionate punishment. (para 58)

This was BE's case, and he was entitled to asylum.

The case of *Aydogdu* [2002] UKIAT 06709 also succeeded because the appellant left Turkey at a time when the military action he would have been called upon to undertake would have been condemned by the international community. This was in 1997–98 when, in the Tribunal's words, 'The policy of the Turkish army, albeit against a determined and vicious enemy, did result in international condemnation as it involved a programme of compulsory village clearances and the large-scale displacement of the Kurdish civilian population' (para 18).

A number of American conscientious objectors to the war in Iraq sought refugee status in Canada but have been refused. Other soldiers who objected to the war but did not flee have been sentenced in the US to imprisonment or hard labour (Amnesty International press release 13 May 2005).

A soldier cannot claim refugee status on account of risks from terrorists (*Fadli v SSHD* [2001] Imm AR 392). Being a soldier entails taking the risk of losing one's life in the service of one's country, and this is no different if the enemy is an internal one (here, the GIA, a fundamentalist group in Algeria). However, conditions of military service may be such as to amount to persecution if they are inhuman (*Foughali* 00/TH/01513 and now see *ZQ (serving soldier) Iraq CG* [2009] UKAIT 00048).

13.7 Conclusion

This chapter has given an introduction to refugee law in the UK, but no more. This field is now so vast, that a glance at some key issues and an examination of some of the key cases is all that is really possible in a small part of a larger book. The next chapter examines some of the legal restrictions upon refugee claims.

QUESTIONS

1 What are the benefits and the problems of operating with an international definition of who is a refugee?

2 Should gender be a Convention reason?

3 Is discrimination in relation to social rights a suitable basis for an asylum claim?

For guidance on answering questions, visit www.oxfordtextbooks.co.uk/orc/clayton5e/.

FURTHER READING

Ceneda, Sophia (2006) 'The Role of Gender Guidelines in the Determination of Asylum Claims' *Immigration Law Digest* vol. 12, no. 2, pp. 23–25.

Ceneda, Sophia and Palmer, Clare (2006) 'Lip Service or Implementation? The Home Office Gender Guidance and Women's Asylum Claims in the UK', *Refugee Women's Resource Project* (London: Asylum Aid).

Chaudhry, Mehvish (2007) 'Particular Social Group Post *Fornah*', *Journal of Immigration, Asylum and Nationality Law* vol. 21, no. 2, pp. 137–146.

Crawley, Heaven (2001) *Refugees and Gender* (Bristol: Jordan & Sons).

Cutler, Sarah (2010) *Women's Asylum News* Issue 91 'Rape and Sexual Violence: the experiences of refugee women in the UK' (London: Asylum Aid) pp. 1–5

Gil-Bazo, Maria-Teresa (2006) 'Refugee Status, Subsidiary Protection and the Right to be Granted Asylum under EC Law', Refugee Studies Centre, University of Oxford).

Goodwin-Gill, Guy and McAdam, Jane (2007) *The Refugee in International Law*, 3rd edn (Oxford: Clarendon Press).

Hathaway, James (2002) 'The Causal Nexus in International Refugee Law' *Michigan Journal of International Law* Winter, vol. 23, pp. 207–221.

—— (2003) 'The Causal Connection (Nexus) to a Convention Ground' *International Journal of Refugee Law* vol. 15, no. 3, pp. 461–476.

Hathaway, James and Hicks, William S. (2005) 'Is there a Subjective Element in the Refugee Convention's Requirement of 'Well-founded Fear?' *Michigan Journal of International Law* Winter, vol. 26, pp. 505–525.

Kelly, Brendan, 'What is a 'Particular Social Group'? A Review of the Development of the Refugee Convention in England' *Journal of Immigration, Asylum and Nationality Law* vol. 24, no. 1, pp. 11–25.

Krivenko, E. (2010) 'Muslim Women's Claims to Refugee Status within the Context of Child Custody upon Divorce under Islamic Law' *International Journal of Refugee Law* vol. 22, no.1, pp. 48–71.

Lambert, Helene (2001) 'The Conceptualisation of "Persecution" by the House of Lords: *Horvath v SSHD' International Journal of Refugee Law* vol. 13, no. 1/2, pp. 16–31.

Muggeridge, Helen and Maman, Chen (2011) *Unsustainable* (London: Asylum Aid).

Musalo, Karen (2003) 'Revisiting Social Group and Nexus in Gender Asylum Claims: A Unifying Rationale for Evolving Jurisprudence' *DePaul Law Review* vol. 52, Spring, pp. 777–808.

—— (2004) 'Claims for Protection Based on Religion or Belief' *International Journal of Refugee Law* vol. 16, no. 2, pp. 165–226.

O'Nions, Helen (1999) 'Bona fide or Bogus? Roma Asylum Seekers from the Czech Republic' *Web Journal of Current Legal Issues* 3.

Pearce, Hannah (2002) 'An Examination of the International Understanding of Political Rape and the Significance of Labelling it Torture' *International Journal of Refugee Law* vol. 14, no. 4, pp. 534–560.

Schnöring, Katharina (2001) 'Deserters in the Federal Republic of Yugoslavia' *International Journal of Refugee Law* vol. 13, pp. 153–173.

Shah, Prakash (2000) *Refugees, Race and the Legal Concept of Asylum in Britain* (London: Cavendish).

Stevens, Dallal (2004) *UK Asylum Law and Policy* (London: Sweet & Maxwell), chapters 1 and 2.

Storey, Hugo (2008) 'EU Refugee Qualification Directive: A Brave New World?' *International Journal of Refugee Law* vol. 20, no. 1, pp. 1–49.

Symes, Mark and Jorro, Peter (2010) *Asylum Law and Practice*, 2nd edn (London: Lexis Nexis Butterworths).

UNHCR *Handbook on Procedures and Criteria for Determining Refugee Status* (UNHCR; re-edited, Geneva: UNHCR, 1992).

—— (2002) 'UNHCR Guidelines on International Protection', 7 May 2002, Membership of Particular Social Group and Gender-related Persecution (UNHCR), accessed at: www.unhcr.org/3d58ddef4.html.

—— (2003) 'Guidelines on Internal Protection' (UNHCR), accessed at: www.unhcr.org/3f28d5cd4.html.

—— (2011) *Safe at Last? Law and Practice in Selected EU Member States with Respect to Asylum Seekers Fleeing Indiscriminate Violence* (Brussels: UNHCR).

Wilsher, Dan (2003) 'Non-State Actors and the Definition of a Refugee in the UK: Protection, Accountability or Culpability?' *International Journal of Refugee Law* vol. 15, no. 1, pp. 68–112.

Yeo, Colin (2002) 'Agents of the State: When is an Official of the State an Agent of the State?' *International Journal of Refugee Law* vol. 14, no. 4, pp. 509–533.

—— (2006) 'Qualification Directive: A new Era?' *Immigration Law Digest* vol. 12 no. 3, pp. 26–27.

14

Criminalization and excluding an asylum claim

SUMMARY

This chapter is concerned with the process of increasing criminalization of migration and of making an asylum claim, and with the provisions whereby an individual can be excluded from refugee status because of their conduct. It shows how powers of wide application are developed on the basis of policies of deterring asylum claimants and combating terrorism.

14.1 Immigration and criminal law

Immigration offences are not covered in detail in this book on the basis that they are part of criminal law. However, the creation and prosecution of such offences has an impact on migrants and an interrelation with immigration law. There are three principal kinds of interrelation: immigration enforcement (i.e., removal) may be used for an immigration infringement instead of criminal sanctions; a person subject to immigration control who commits a criminal offence, whether related to immigration or not, may be deported and so be subject to immigration sanction as well as a criminal penalty; immigration and asylum-seeking may themselves be highly restricted and in effect criminalized by the multiplication of sanctions in the name of policy objectives such as deterring asylum claims or illegal working. In this chapter, we will first of all briefly consider the interrelation of immigration and criminal enforcement, then focus on the impact of criminal provisions which are related to asylum deterrence. Deportation is discussed in chapter 16.

Immigration-related offences range from the purely regulatory, such as doing paid work in excess of permitted hours as a student, through to severe crimes of abuse such as human trafficking. In that immigration-related offences are often breaches of immigration control (though not necessarily so in the case of human trafficking), it is unsurprising that many are contained in immigration statutes rather than in criminal justice statutes. Where this means that the state's response, as it were, leapfrogs the criminal law and engages immigration enforcement, the immediate consequences are very different. For instance, a person prosecuted and convicted for working for a different employer from that authorized in their leave to enter or remain in the UK (an offence under s 24(1)(b) Immigration Act 1971) would receive a maximum criminal sentence of a fine and six months' imprisonment. This after standard remission would drop to three months and any time on remand would also be deducted. They would then be released, albeit with a criminal conviction. If immigration enforcement is applied, they may be removed from the UK, perhaps without an in-country appeal, and may be detained pending removal. That detention is for whatever period is reasonable to effect the removal, and they may then be debarred from re-entry to the UK for up to ten years (see chapters 7 and 17).

In accordance with the priority given to enforcement in immigration policy, the Immigration and Asylum Act 1999 gave enhanced powers to immigration officers very similar to those possessed by the police in the investigation of crime and the apprehension of suspects. These enhanced powers apply, both to dealing with people suspected of immigration offences (Immigration Act 1971 Part III), and to carrying out immigration functions under Sch 2. Powers of entry, search of people and premises, seizure of documents, and fingerprinting apply in relation to investigation of immigration status and to investigation of criminal offences. Section 145 provides that in exercising any power to

(a) arrest, question, search or take fingerprints from a person,
(b) enter and search premises, or
(c) seize property found on such person or premises,

an immigration officer must have regard to specified codes of practice. These are the Codes of Practice issued in relation to the Police and Criminal Evidence Act 1984, as modified and specified by the Immigration (PACE Codes of Practice) Direction 2000 and the Immigration (PACE Codes of Practice No. 2 and Amendment) Directions 2000. PACE Codes of Practice are revised from time to time, the most recent revision being from 1 January 2009 by the PACE Codes of Practice Order 2008, SI 2008/3503.

Immigration-related offences are numerous and far-reaching. In addition to those which may be committed by the person subject to immigration control, there are many offences which may be committed by others who give them shelter, advice, employment, or arrange false documents or illegal entry. Offences which may be committed by employers and advisers are dealt with in chapters 8 and 10. This chapter focuses on offences which are connected in some way with the government's policy to reduce the number of asylum claims in the UK.

14.2 Criminalizing seeking asylum

There is a right in international and EU law to seek asylum (UDHR 1948 Article 14, and EU Charter Article 18) but, as we have seen, it is difficult to exercise within the law. In *R v Naillie* [1993] AC 674 HL, the House of Lords held that arriving in the UK and requesting asylum without attempting to deceive did not make the defendants illegal entrants. However, in *R v SSHD ex p saadi* [2002] UKHL 42, the House of Lords held that detention of asylum claimants was lawful 'to prevent unauthorized entry' (HRA Art 5(1)(f)). It did not go so far as to say that unlawfulness was contemplated. Indeed there was clear evidence that it was not. As Collins J said at first instance, the claimants were doing all they could to enter lawfully, but were detained pending determination of their claim (see chapter 15). Adding *Saadi* to *Naillie*, it seems that entry to seek asylum is not illegal but is also not authorized. Despite this, the interlocking effects of criminal and immigration provisions make it almost impossible to enter the UK and seek asylum without some breach of the law.

Schiemann J in 1989 described the difficulties faced by asylum claimants in the face of visa regimes, carrier sanctions and now we would add border control measures such as the placement of airline liaison officers and juxtaposed controls and prosecution for not producing a passport. As a consequence, he said, an asylum seeker has the option of:

1. lying to the UK authorities in his country in order to obtain a tourist visa or some other sort of visa;
2. obtaining a credible forgery of a visa;
3. obtaining an airline ticket to a third country with a stopover in the UK. (*Yassine v SSHD* [1990] Imm AR 354 at 359)

We might add a fourth option: clandestine entry.

These sanctions combine with judicial acceptance that asylum seekers may be treated in a punitive manner even without any wrongdoing (*Saadi*) to create a murky zone between legality and illegality within which an international law right exists, but can hardly be exercised without risk of penalty. Equally troubling, the boundary between asylum seeker and criminal is blurred in the minds of officials who deal with them and of the public.

As Schiemann J commented, asylum seekers may be forced to resort to the use of false documents. The use of deception to seek or obtain leave to enter or remain in the UK is an offence contrary to Immigration Act 1971 s 24A (as inserted and amended by the 1996 and 1999 Acts), carrying a maximum penalty of two years in prison. The use of false or altered documents is an offence contrary to s 26(1)(d), and people in this position have also often been charged with the offence of using a false instrument contrary to s 3 of the Forgery and Counterfeiting Act 1981 or possessing one contrary to s 5. In *R v Kolawole* [2004] EWCA Crim 3047, the Court gave guidance that, because of increased public concern on these matters, the appropriate sentence for having a false passport with intent to use it, 'even on a guilty plea by a person of good character, should usually be within the range of 12 to 18 months' imprisonment'. The maximum sentence is two years, and ten years for an offence under s 3.

In 2006, the government introduced biometric identity documents for foreign nationals in conjunction with proposals for identity cards for nationals also. The proposals for national identity cards have been dropped, and the provisions of the Identity Cards Act 2006 concerned with offences have been re-enacted. Section 4 of the Identity Documents Act 2010 creates an offence of having in one's possession an identity document that is false which the holder knows or believes to be false, or that was improperly obtained (i.e., by the use of false information: s 9(3)) and which the holder knows or believes to have been improperly obtained, or that relates to someone else. This offence also requires the *mens rea* of intention to use the document to establish personal information about the holder or purported holder, including name, address, nationality, and immigration status. There is a further offence in s 6 of simply possessing such a false document without reasonable excuse. The s 4 offence carries a maximum sentence of ten years' imprisonment; the s 6 offence carries a maximum sentence of two years. An identity document is defined in s 7 to include a passport, a driving licence, and an immigration document of any kind.

In *Attorney Generals' Reference nos. 1 and 6 of 2008* [2008] EWCA Crim 677, the Court of Appeal considered two unconnected cases in which the Attorney-General argued that the sentences passed by the Crown Court judges had been too lenient. The trial judges had declined to follow *Kolawole*. Mr Laby had been found to be in possession of three forged passports with intention to pass them on to those who would use them, and the judge held that he should impose a lighter sentence because the sooner Mr Laby was deported back to DRC the better. The Court of Appeal held that the prospect of deportation was irrelevant. It would be insufficient deterrent to others if Mr Laby were to serve a short sentence and then return to his country of origin.

The other defendant, Mr Dziruni, had come from Zimbabwe and claimed asylum in the UK, promptly, and with full disclosure. His immediate family already had refugee status in the UK. His claim and appeals failed. He made a fresh claim, and did not realize that he would have been entitled to support while waiting for a decision. He eventually bought a false passport to enable him to work. The Court suspended his six months' prison sentence and also ordered voluntary work. The Court of Appeal considered that this was appropriate. Mr Dziruni had not been evading immigration control by his use of a false document and had pleaded guilty. They said:

> he was not someone hiding or trying to avoid removal...His status may appear clear enough in law but in practice it was, to put it neutrally, confused...what is clear is that the authorities in this country were not prepared to, and did not intend to do anything to procure his removal because of the situation in his home country.

The Court of Appeal held that the Crown Court judge's sentence was appropriately merciful. The judge had described him as a 'decent person' who was caught in an impossible limbo. The distinction between using false documents to avoid immigration control and using them for other purposes has been maintained in later cases, though the Court of Appeal in *R v Ovieriakhi* [2009] EWCA Crim 452 confirmed the validity of guidance in *Kolowole*.

The Refugee Convention itself recognizes what drives asylum seekers to use unlawful means, and limits the use of penalties as discussed in 14.3. First, we review the penalties for assisting entry, and another statutory penalty imposed on asylum seekers after entry by the Asylum and Immigration (Treatment of Claimants, etc.) Act 2004.

14.2.1 Those who assist or arrange entry

Section 25 Immigration Act 1971 was originally titled 'Assisting illegal entry and harbouring'. It consisted then of knowingly being concerned in 'making or carrying out arrangements for securing or facilitating the entry into the United Kingdom of anyone whom he knows or has reasonable cause for believing to be an illegal entrant' and of harbouring such a person. The maximum sentence increased from 7 to 10 years in 2000 (1999 Act s 29) and to 14 years in 2003 (2002 Act s 143). These sentences, and the powers in ss 25C and D to seize vehicles owned by a person convicted, are aimed at those who profit from arranging illegal entry, and show the prominent place that this offence plays in the government's campaign to prevent people smuggling and organized deception. By its nature, this offence may be committed abroad. Section 25(5) therefore provides for British nationals to be liable for the offence whether committed inside or outside the UK.

The Nationality, Immigration and Asylum Act 2002 greatly extended this offence and split it into three parts. The offence in s 25 now is to do an act 'which facilitates the commission of a breach of immigration law by an individual who is not a citizen of the European Union'. The definition of immigration law is wide, covering any provision which controls entitlement to enter or be in a Member State. A British citizen in Albania organizing a marriage of convenience in Italy could be charged under this section. The new offence in s 25B is assisting entry in breach of deportation or exclusion orders by European citizens. This complements the new s 25 and is more restricted, reinforcing the more limited controls that exist in relation to EEA nationals.

Section 25A has the extraordinary heading of 'helping asylum seeker to enter UK'. Amended by the UK Borders Act 2007, the offence is 'knowingly and for gain' to facilitate the arrival or entry of someone the defendant knows or has reasonable cause to believe is an asylum seeker. There is a defence for someone acting on behalf of an organization which aims to help asylum seekers and does not charge for its services, but none for an individual. For instance, a married couple who facilitated the entry of the man's brother and his friend were each sentenced to two years' imprisonment for that offence. The fact that the two entrants claimed asylum the day after their entry was irrelevant (*R v Javaherifard and Miller* [2005] EWCA Crim 3231). This means that, in terms of criminal liability, the good faith of the asylum claim, its merits, and the defendants' beliefs in relation to those matters are not relevant, except as mitigation of sentence.

Controlling those who profit from arranging illegal entry is a matter of some priority in the emerging immigration law of the EU (see generally chapter 6). Relevant European provisions here are Directive 2002/90 (Defining the Facilitation of Unauthorised Entry, Transit and Residence) and Framework Decision 2002/946 (on strengthening the penal framework for unauthorized entry etc), and the UK has opted in, but the offences under the expanded s 25 go beyond what is required by European measures. Notably, the s 25A offence of 'helping an asylum seeker to enter the UK' does not entail that the entry be illegal, simply that the entrant is an asylum seeker, whereas the Directive and Framework Decision require criminal sanctions for the facilitation of entry or transit 'in breach of the laws of the state concerned', not penalties on the travel arrangements of asylum seekers *per se*. Directive 2002/90 Article 1.2 allows any Member State not to apply sanctions where the 'aim of the behaviour is to provide humanitarian assistance to the person concerned'. The British defence is limited to organizations which do not charge for their services.

14.2.2 Asylum and Immigration (Treatment of Claimants, etc.) Act 2004 s 2

A practice which has troubled the Home Office has been that of asylum seekers who destroy their documents while on their journey to the UK. This may be on the advice of agents who have organized their travel. The act of destroying a document does not of course give any indication in an individual case of why a person concealed their identity or their means of travel, as the case might be. The desire to start a new life anonymously, or conceal a deception, or fear of persecution are clearly all possible motives.

In order to prevent this practice, the Asylum and Immigration (Treatment of Claimants, etc.) Act 2004 introduced a new offence of attending an asylum interview without a passport or similar document (s 2), unless it is produced within a three-day grace period after the interview (s 2(3)(b)). Statutory defences include:

- To produce a false immigration document and to prove that this was used for all purposes in connection with the journey to the UK.
- To prove that he travelled to the UK without, at any stage since he set out on the journey, having possession of an immigration document.
- Reasonable excuse, which does not include destruction of the document unless that was for a reasonable cause or beyond the claimant's control.
- Reasonable cause in this context does not include delaying an asylum decision, increasing one's chances of success, or complying with the instructions of a facilitator (smuggler) unless it would be unreasonable to expect noncompliance in the circumstances (s 2(7)(b)(iii)).

It is hard to imagine when it would be more reasonable to rely on a speculation about the needs of a system the asylum seeker has not yet personally encountered than on the advice of the person who has got them this far. The instructions to immigration officers implementing the section suggest that it would be unreasonable to expect noncompliance with advice where the asylum seeker has been threatened or intimidated so that this amounted to force.

In *R v Bei Bei Wang* [2005] EWCA Crim 293, the appellant had travelled for six months through several countries with an agent who had retained her passport at all points except for the moment of going through passport control. The Court of Appeal commented that her situation was not very different from that of someone who had not had possession of a travel document at all, or someone who travelled on forged documents. In the latter case, there would be a defence under the 2004 Act, and s 31 of the 1999 Act would provide a defence to a different criminal charge in the event of a successful asylum claim (see 14.3). In view also of the fact that Ms Wang was only 18 years old, a lighter sentence was appropriate.

The sentence was also reduced in *Lu Zhu Ai* [2005] EWCA Crim 936, in which the Court reiterated the very specific purpose of this offence, the distinction between s 2 and offences of fraud, etc., and, as in *Bei Bei Wang*, the significant deterrent element in the sentencing. The Court also noted that it was difficult in these cases to take full account of individual circumstances. The components of the alleged offence could be considered, i.e., the journey and to what extent the defendant had control of their travel document, but the merits of their asylum claim could not be considered at all by the criminal court. The case of *Thet v DPP* [2006] EWHC 2701 (Admin) began to set the limits of prosecutions under s 2.

***Thet v DPP* [2006] EWHC 2701 (Admin)**

The defendant had entered the country on a false passport which, after passing through immigration control, he immediately handed back to the person who facilitated his entry, as instructed. As a former political prisoner, he had been unable to obtain a genuine passport in Burma. The Lord Chief Justice held that Mr Thet could rely on the defence in s 2(4)(c) – that he had a reasonable excuse for not being able to produce a document at interview of the kind referred to in s 2(1), namely one which is 'in force' and 'satisfactorily establishes his identity and nationality'. The Court held that the passport referred to in s 2 is a valid passport, not a false one.

The prosecutor wanted to rely on statements in Parliament under the rule in *Pepper v Hart* [1993] AC 593 to show that there was a parliamentary intention to prosecute people who disposed of false documents en route. The Lord Chief Justice held that the section was 'ill-drafted but not ambiguous' and so there was no *prima facie* case for using *Pepper v Hart*. If there had been, it would have been at least arguable that, where a criminal statute was ambiguous, the defendant should have the benefit of the ambiguity.

Similar facts in *R v Mohammed and R v Osman* [2007] EWCA Crim 2332 gave rise to a finding that, where the defence in s 2(4)(e) was relied on, which is that the person never had an immigration document, a defendant cannot argue that they were never in possession of an immigration document throughout the journey because the only one they had was false. This would give a defence to a possessor of a false passport who destroyed it before arrival where a possessor of a genuine passport would have no such defence, an unlikely proper effect of the statute, the Court thought. The convictions were overturned because the jury had not been properly directed on whether the defendants' reasons for giving their passports back to the agents were reasonable ones (the same defence as *Thet*), but this was too late to be of benefit to the appellants, who had already served prison sentences. Indeed, Mr Osman had been served with a deportation order, and it was only by intervention of the Criminal Cases Review Commission that his conviction had come before the Court.

Despite the speculation in *Mohammed and Osman*, in *R v Hudarey* [2008] EWCA Crim 1761, the Court of Appeal held that the appellant's guilty plea should never have been accepted, because it was clear that he had a defence under s 2(4)(c). He had not been able to obtain a genuine passport, but had, on the instructions of his agent, torn up the false one on which he travelled and flushed it down the toilet during the flight. He had a reasonable excuse for not being in possession of a genuine passport. These various outcomes can appear confusing, and, indeed, in *Thet*, Lord Phillips described the section as 'ill-drafted' and 'difficult'. It helps to be aware that the defences are alternatives, not cumulative. Therefore, for instance, failure to retain a false passport, though depriving the applicant of the defence in paragraph (d), does not deprive them of the opportunity of arguing that they had a reasonable excuse, perhaps because of their politics as in both *Thet* and *Hudarey*, for not being in possession of a *genuine* passport.

Destruction of a passport makes it more difficult to return a person to their country of origin against their will. The s 2 offence is based on the proposition that it is not legitimate to obstruct one's return without reference to whether this is based on fear of return rather than a cynical desire to obstruct the legal system. No *mens rea* is required. The defendant is in an invidious position. If they have destroyed their passport in an attempt to ensure their own safety this fear is very relevant to the success of their asylum claim, but admitting its destruction will make them guilty of an offence and liable to imprisonment.

As Macdonald points out (2005:975), where the facts are in dispute, in the light of tightening controls by carriers, the Court may disbelieve a passenger's assertion that they never had a travel document. Section 2 may force a person fleeing persecution to prove a negative in the criminal courts. It does not target a person who attempts to remain hidden, but rather one who makes an application for international protection. The underlying mischief is the destruction of travel documents but there is no requirement on the prosecution to prove this as the actus reus is simply presentation at interview without the document. The burden of proof is on the defendant to show they never had one.

The Parliamentary Joint Committee on Human Rights considered whether this reverse burden meets the requirements of Article 6(2) ECHR. They did not reach a concluded view on that matter, but accepted that in principle it could be justifiable to place the burden on the defendant of showing an excuse for the destruction of a passport. This was with the caveat that immigrants should have access to information on the effect of destroying travel documents (para 23). The Committee also voiced their concern (Session 2003–04 Fifth Report HL paper 35 HC 304, para 10) that like the offences of forgery and falsification of documents, s 2 might be wrongly used, thus penalizing even more asylum seekers and breaching Article 31 (see 14.3).The defence of never having had a travel document was introduced to go some way towards alleviating the Committee's concerns. Nevertheless, many of the people who have been convicted under s 2 were in comparable positions to Mr Thet. His solicitor commented:

> this Act... had an effect of criminalising genuine asylum seekers who often can only leave their own country using a false passport for which they have had to pay an agent. Due to the power the agent has over them, they usually have to return the passport to the agent or destroy the passport on arrival in the United Kingdom. (Refugee Council briefing, October 2006)

The press reported 230 asylum seekers arrested and 134 convicted in the first six months of s 2 being in force ('Asylum seekers jailed for having no passports' *The Guardian* 18 March 2005).

14.3 The defences under Article 31 and section 31

Article 31 of the Refugee Convention says that refugees coming directly from the country of persecution should not be punished on account of their illegal entry or presence, provided they present themselves without delay and show good cause for this. In the case of *R v Uxbridge Magistrates Court ex p Adimi, R v Crown Prosecution Service ex p Sorani, R v SSHD ex p Kaziu* [2000] 3 WLR 434, three people who travelled on false documents were prosecuted. The purpose of Article 31 was to provide immunity for genuine refugees whose quest for asylum reasonably involved a breach of the law. The Court recognized that this could be a matter of necessity, and therefore the Secretary of State rather than the Crown Prosecution Service should decide when asylum seekers should be prosecuted for travelling on false documents. It was a matter relating to conduct of immigration and asylum, not to the need to punish criminal activity generally. They could use Article 31 to stay the criminal proceedings.

This meant that where there were grounds to believe that Article 31 would apply, a prosecution should not be brought. A joint Memorandum of Good Practice on this subject, giving guidance for liaison between the police, the Home Office, CPS, and the Law Society, was never published (Macdonald 2009:368). UKBA's Asylum Policy Instructions incorporate some of that guidance.

Following the judgment in *Adimi*, a statutory defence to forgery, deception, and falsification of documents was enacted in Immigration and Asylum Act 1999 s 31. It provides that there is a defence for a refugee charged with an offence to which the section applies if he or she

(a) came to the UK directly from a country where their life or freedom was threatened;
(b) reported to the authorities in the United Kingdom without delay;
(c) showed good cause for their illegal entry or presence; and
(d) made a claim for asylum as soon as reasonably practicable after arrival.

Section 31 is more restricted than Article 31 and the *Adimi* judgment. For instance, the defence is available only to someone whose refugee claim succeeds, whereas *Adimi* applied Article 31 to asylum seekers. This has the effect that there is no defence for someone whose claim is made on what they themselves consider to be proper grounds, but who does not succeed in law. This elides the genuine but unsuccessful claimant with the dishonest one, and confuses deception in the means of obtaining entry with deception as to the substance of the claim. The Court of Appeal in *R v Kishientine* [2004] EWCA Crim 3352 made it clear that the criminal court could have no part in assessing the merits of the asylum claim so as to deal with any of these objections. The API on Article 31 and s 31 say that 'it would normally be appropriate' for a decision on whether to prosecute to be deferred until the asylum decision and any appeals are concluded (API Oct 2006, rebranded January 2009, para 7).

Article 31 refers to people 'coming directly' from the country of persecution, but the Court in *Adimi* did not take this too literally. They held that there could be some element of choice by refugees as to their destination, and a short-term stopover on the journey could not be used to say that the refugee had not come to the UK directly. The Divisional Court in *R (on the application of Badur) v Birmingham Crown Court and Solihull Magistrates' Court* [2006] EWHC 539 (Admin) held that Article 31 would have permitted other considerations, for instance that the appellant was a minor at the relevant time, which might have had a bearing on whether he could have claimed asylum in a safe country. Section 31 does not allow for these factors. It limits the defence to situations where the defendant can show that in any third country at which they have stopped on the way to the UK they could not reasonably have expected to obtain refugee protection.

Section 31 as interpreted by the API takes a more restrictive approach than *Adimi* to the question of whether someone has presented themselves as soon as possible. UNHCR says that 'delay caused by an asylum seeker's wish to approach a lawyer or a voluntary organization first to seek advice is not unreasonable and should not preclude the protection of s 31'. They were concerned that account be taken of proper reasons for delay, such as the effects of trauma, language differences, lack of information, previous experiences which have resulted in a suspicion of authority, and a feeling of insecurity. UNHCR issued detailed advice on the API, but this has not been implemented, and the Home Office relies on the primacy of s 31 as statute over and above the provisions of the Refugee Convention. In *R (on the application of Pepushi) v Crown Prosecution Service* [2004] EWHC 798 (Admin), the Court held that there is no scope to claim the protection of Article 31 Refugee Convention, even though the protection offered by Immigration and Asylum Act 1999 s 31 is explicitly narrower. Mr Pepushi had stopped in France and Italy long enough to claim asylum. Section 31 gave no scope to extend the defence. The Court had an obligation to read the words of the statute which was intended to give effect to the Convention compatibly with the Convention; where this was not possible, parliamentary sovereignty entailed that the statute prevailed. Unlike the Human Rights Act, there is no domestic provision for a declaration of incompatibility, but the new jurisdiction of the CJEU in asylum matters opens up the possibility of a reference to that Court on the compatibility of s 31 with EU law. The Refugee Qualification Directive does not contain its own version of Article 31, but says that where refugee status is refused, revoked, or terminated, the rights set out in Article 31 apply (Article 14.6).

A strict interpretation of s 31 had a different result in *Badur*, where the Court held that the defence could only apply to offences to which it explicitly refers. Therefore it could not apply to the offence of seeking to obtain entry by deception as set out in an earlier form in Immigration Act 1971 s 24(1)(a)(aa). Mr Badur should have been charged under s 24A(1)(a), but as he was not, he should have had the benefit of Article 31.

The defence in s 31 was extended to cover the offences under first the Identity Cards Act 2006 and then the Identity Documents Act 2010 (see 14.2). Despite *Badur*, the Home Office have interpreted *Pepushi* to mean that Article 31 has no further application in any situation, with the result that a person may be prosecuted for an offence not mentioned in s 31, though based on the same facts as one for which the person would have a defence. The House of Lords addressed this practice in the case of *R v Asfaw* [2008] UKHL 31.

Key Case

***R v Asfaw* [2008] UKHL 31**

The appellant was an Ethiopian national who had very good grounds for an asylum claim. She left Ethiopia to claim asylum in the US, travelling via the UK. On arrival at Heathrow Airport, she passed through immigration control on her own passport, but was then provided with a false passport by her agent, which she presented at the check-in desk for a flight to Washington. The official on the desk informed the police. She was arrested and charged with using a false instrument with intent contrary to s 3 of the Forgery and Counterfeiting Act 1981 and attempting to obtain services by deception, namely a Virgin Atlantic flight. She pleaded not guilty to the first count, relying on the defence in s 31 Immigration and Asylum Act 1999 and was acquitted. She was convicted on the second count which was not an offence listed in s 31.

In the House of Lords, the Secretary of State raised a new argument, that s 31 and Article 31 did not apply to offences committed in the course of leaving a country rather than entering it.

The House of Lords by a 3:2 majority held that Article 31, and accordingly s 31, which sought to implement it, covered the situation where the refugee was leaving the UK as a transit passenger if she was still in flight. This was so, even if there was no danger to the refugee in the transit country. The drafters of the Refugee Convention had not contemplated air travel nor the implications of briefly entering a country to change planes as part of flight from persecution. Their Lordships also held that, although the CPS was not wrong to bring a charge not covered by the s 31 defence, once it was clear that s 31 applied, it was an abuse of process to continue with a prosecution on a charge not covered by it.

The House of Lords judgment in *Asfaw* contains an extended examination of the history and purpose of Article 31. It also refers to how carrier sanctions were influential in the case, the rigorous checks by Virgin Atlantic being motivated by their vulnerability to penalties if they carried a passenger using false documents. The judgment is important for its further definition of the extent of Article and s 31, and because of the House of Lords' grounding of that decision firmly in the humanitarian purpose of the Refugee Convention.

These principles, though argued, did not avail the appellants in *Sternaj v DPP and CPS* [2011] EWHC 1094 (Admin). Their convictions for offences under ss 25 and 25A were upheld for facilitating the illegal entry into the UK of the second appellant's two-year-old son. The Divisional Court held that the s 31 and Article 31 defences did not apply to offences under these sections, and it was not an abuse of process to prosecute. The Court observed in concluding that if the child had presented his own false passport, he would have had a defence, and in such a case it might be questioned whether a prosecution was in the public interest. But this was not such a case.

In *R v Kamalanathan* [2010] EWCA Crim 1335 the Court of Appeal held that a month's stay in the UK meant that the appellant was not still in flight, and not therefore in a situation like that of Ms Asfaw. The API, though rebranded in January 2009, have not (at October 2011) been updated to take *Asfaw* into account.

The Joint Parliamentary Committee on Human Rights noted that 'a significant number of people have been wrongfully imprisoned' for offences to which s 31 should have provided a defence. Estimated figures ranged between 1,000 and 5,000 (Session 2003–04 Fifth Report HL paper 35 HC 304, para 10). People who were wrongly convicted and imprisoned have received average compensation of £40,000, but few claims have been made (Macdonald 2008:1,133). Cases in the Court of Appeal have revealed that solicitors and barristers have failed to advise individuals that the s 31 defence was available to them. Where the defence was clearly available and would have been likely to have been upheld, convictions have been quashed (see *R v M, MV, M and N* [2010] EWCA Crim 2400 and *R v Jerdi* [2011] EWCA Crim 365).

14.4 Trafficking

Like Article 31 and s 31, immigration provisions related to trafficking are concerned with protection. Trafficking is defined in the United Nations 2000 Protocol to Prevent, Suppress and Punish Trafficking in Persons, especially Women and Children (the Palermo Protocol) Article 3 as:

> the recruitment, transportation, transfer, harbouring or receipt of persons, by means of the threat or use of force or other forms of coercion, of abduction, of fraud, of deception, of the abuse of power or of a position of vulnerability or of the giving or receiving of payments or benefits to achieve the consent of a person having control over another person, for the purpose of exploitation. Exploitation shall include, at a minimum, the exploitation of the prostitution of others or other forms of sexual exploitation, forced labour or services, slavery or practices similar to slavery, servitude or the removal of organs.

It is important to distinguish between people smuggling and human trafficking. The Joint Parliamentary Committee on Human Rights (twenty-sixth report 2005–06) identifies some differences, which can be elaborated as shown in Table 14.1.

People smuggling is treated as a criminal matter with a significant migration dimension. Trafficking entails human rights violations over and above the migration and criminal issues involved. Increasing international concern and domestic pressure has brought about an increase in criminal penalties, but a slower development of human rights protection. The deaths of 23 Chinese cockle-pickers who drowned in Morecambe Bay in February 2004 focused public attention on labour exploitation by traffickers and gangmasters. The Asylum and Immigration (Treatment of Claimants etc) Act 2004 introduced a new offence of trafficking for exploitation. Exploitation includes slavery

Table 14.1 Smuggling and trafficking

Smuggling	Trafficking
The smuggled person in broad terms consents or agrees to what is done by the smuggler. They may have no control over specifics such as route or documentation, but they want to make the journey. Any deception is practised on third parties, such as an immigration officer	Trafficking is carried out by coercion or deception of the trafficked person
Relationship with smuggler ends when smuggled person reaches their destination	Trafficking entails subsequent exploitation of trafficked person
Smuggling entails movement across international borders	Trafficking can take place within and across national frontiers
Entry is illegal. If legal entry were possible, the smuggler would not be required	Trafficking may entail legal or illegal entry

and forced labour, using threats or deception or someone's youth or vulnerability to force them to provide benefits or services, and encouraging the sale of human organs (s 4). The UK Borders Act 2007 amended this offence and the offence in the Sexual Offences Act 2003 of trafficking for prostitution so that acts abroad were included. Legislation was also introduced in the form of the Gangmasters (Licensing) Act 2004 to regulate the activities of those who employ casual migrant workers in agricultural work and the shellfish industry. After extensive discussion and lobbying, the UK opted into EU Directive 2011/36 on preventing and combating trafficking in human beings and protecting its victims, which requires the Member States to have criminal penalties for trafficking offences and powers to refrain from prosecuting victims of trafficking for offences committed 'as a direct consequence' of coercive acts of traffickers.

Similar provisions are contained in the Council of Europe's Convention against Human Trafficking, which was ratified by the UK in December 2008, and took effect in the UK on 1 April 2009. In *LM, MB, DG, Talbot and Tijani v R* [2010] EWCA Crim 2327 the Court of Appeal held that the defence should have been available to women forced into prostitution who then controlled others. The case reveals how details of the women's own experience of being trafficked only emerged slowly through the legal process, and demonstrates the need for caution in prosecuting women where there is a suspicion that they themselves may have been trafficked.

While criminal penalties are part of the picture, there is also a vital need to protect the victim. The Convention requires automatic reflection periods, i.e., a period during which immigration enforcement will be held in abeyance while the victim considers their situation, and residence permits for trafficking victims. The UK has implemented this by means of asylum process guidance issued to decision-makers. Once a decision has been made that there are reasonable grounds to think that someone is a victim of trafficking, they are to be given 45 days' temporary admission. They will be maintained on asylum support. At the end of that period, a decision must be made on whether to grant further leave. This can be refugee status or humanitarian protection or discretionary leave if the usual grounds are made out. The only special provision in relation to trafficking at this stage is that, regardless of other grounds, if the person decides that they will assist the police with their enquiries about the trafficker(s), and they do not wish to return home, 12 months' discretionary leave is to be granted.

Remedies for victims of trafficking not only relate to immigration status. Damages have been awarded in civil actions for false representations, false imprisonment, battery, assault, and harassment (*AT, NT, ML and AK v Dulghieru* [2009] EWHC 225 (QB)). The claimants' mental health was still suffering some years after these events, and for this they were awarded damages for pain, suffering, and loss of amenity: £125,000, £117,000, £82,000, and £97,000 to the claimants, respectively. The judge awarded further sums for injury to feelings, humiliation, loss of pride and dignity, and feelings of anger or resentment: £35,000 each to AT and ML and £30,000 each to NT and AK by way of aggravated damages.

As mentioned previously, an international protective status such as humanitarian protection or asylum is also possible. The ECtHR in *Siliadin v France* [2005] ECHR 545 held that Article 4 entailed a positive obligation to penalize slavery and forced labour. In that case, a domestic worker had been held in conditions akin to slavery. The proposed withdrawal of the immigration rules concerning domestic workers (commented upon in chapter 10) has provoked concern about an upsurge of abusive practices in the UK, including from the Joint Parliamentary Committee on Human Rights in their report on human trafficking. Humanitarian protection on the basis of a feared breach of Article 4 is warranted where there is a real risk of being re-trafficked if the person is returned to their country of origin.

The protective obligation has been reinforced by a historic case in the ECtHR, the first on cross-border human trafficking in Europe.

Key Case

***Rantsev v Cyprus and Russia* Application 25965/04, [2010] ECHR 22**

The applicant was the father of a young Russian woman who had obtained an artiste's visa to work in Cyprus. After a short while, she announced to her flatmates that she was leaving her employment in a cabaret. Her employer found her and took her to the police, asking for her to be deported. They checked their list of those who were wanted, declared that her status was not illegal, but held her in detention until her employer came to collect her. He took her to his colleague's apartment. Just over an hour later, she was found dead on the pavement, having fallen from the balcony of the apartment.

The ECtHR found Cyprus to have violated Article 4. They accepted that trafficking was prohibited under Article 4. They noted that the police had failed to investigate whether she might have been trafficked, for instance by enquiring about her reasons for wanting to leave her employment. They had also failed to release her, even though they had concluded that they had no outstanding matter to pursue with her and therefore had no authority to detain her. They had, instead, insisted on delivering her back into the hands of the person who might have trafficked her.

The Court's judgment in *Rantsev* contains a careful consideration of the facts, and identifies a number of ways in which the authorities failed in their protective duties under Article 4. It is potentially groundbreaking in establishing a strong human rights standard as a benchmark for states' protection duties.

The High Court held in *OOO and others v The Commissioner of Police for the Metropolis* [2011] EWHC 1246 (QB) that *Rantsev* defined the duty of investigation for UK police to 'carry out an effective investigation of an allegation of a breach of Article 4 once a credible account of an alleged infringement had been brought to its attention. The trigger for the duty would not depend upon an actual complaint from a victim or near relative of a victim. The investigation, once triggered, would have to be undertaken promptly' (para 154).

Following its ratification of the Trafficking Convention the UK instituted a National Referral Mechanism to identify and protect victims of trafficking. Where there is no cross-border element, the competent authority in the UK is the UK Human Trafficking Centre. Where there is a cross-border element, the competent authority is based in UKBA. For a critique of the process, see Briddick (2010).

In the UK, *SB (Moldova CG)* [2008] UKAIT 00002 was a significant decision in that the appellant was held to qualify for refugee protection because of the risks of reprisals she faced as a formerly trafficked person who had given evidence against her trafficker. She was held to be a member of a particular social group of formerly trafficked women in Moldova, and this reasoning has been followed in the case of Thailand and Albania. Country guidance cases in relation to each determined that women who had formerly been trafficked were capable of constituting a particular social group but whether they would face persecution for that reason depended on many other factors in their social situation (*AM and BM (Trafficked women) Albania* CG [2010] UKUT 80 (IAC) and *AZ (Trafficked women) Thailand CG* [2010] UKUT 118 (IAC)).

Although the law has developed since ratification of the Council of Europe Treaty, practical difficulties remain in attaining protection for victims of trafficking. The Joint Committee on Human Rights reported that 'evidence provided to us suggests that people who have been trafficked into the UK may not be asked appropriate questions by officials, and as a result will fail to be identified as victims' (para 145). Through mistrust of officials, not understanding what is happening to them, fear of reprisals or of being returned to their home state, victims may also be unwilling to talk about being trafficked. The JCHR report cites instances of trauma to victims in giving evidence when their privacy was not respected. The Committee emphasizes the role to be played by support workers. In *IO (Congo) v SSHD* [2006] EWCA Civ 796, social workers asserted that the appellant had probably been trafficked. All the circumstantial evidence pointed to this. The appellant herself denied it. The Court of Appeal held that there was 'real risk' that she had been trafficked, but that in order to treat this as established for the purposes of assessing her asylum claim it would have to be proved on balance of probabilities as it was against her own assertions. Lawyers may not be aware of the protections available, as appeared in the prosecutions of LM, MB, and DG where the prosecutors had not been aware of the defence.

When the domestic system does not protect the victim, the ECtHR may step in, as it did in *LR v UK* Application no. 49113/09, in which the ECtHR granted a Rule 39 order to LR, preventing her expulsion to Albania, where she was at risk of harm from her own family and from those who had trafficked her. LR had cooperated with the police but through no fault of hers, this did not lead to a conviction, leaving her vulnerable to retaliation from her traffickers. After the Rule 39 order, the applicant was granted refugee status.

14.5 Exclusion, expulsion, and anti-terrorism

This chapter now moves away from criminal and enforcement issues to exclusion from refugee status. The Refugee Convention provides both for the exclusion of individuals from initially obtaining refugee status (Art 1F), and the expulsion of recognized refugees and asylum seekers from the host state as a result of their actions there (Articles 32 and 33(2)). These provisions are also in the Qualification Directive Articles 12, 14, and 21.

These powers have been used increasingly often in the context of the escalation in international action and domestic legislation against terrorism. The interpretation and application of these powers has also been more tightly controlled by governments: in the UK by the Anti-Terrorism, Crime and Security Act 2001, the Nationality Immigration and Asylum Act 2002, and the Immigration Asylum and Nationality Act 2006. These statutes link with the Terrorism Acts of 2000 and 2006, to which reference must also sometimes be made in order to interpret and apply Article 1F.

Exclusion from refugee protection is not only a question of refugee law. As advised by the Lisbon Expert Roundtable, held as part of the 2001 UNHCR Global Consultations on International Protection, 'there is a need, in the interpretation and application of Art 1F, to draw on "developments in other areas of international law since 1951, in particular international criminal law and extradition law as well as international human rights law and international humanitarian law" ' (para 34). The provisions for expelling recognized refugees are considered later in this chapter. We begin with the examination of Article 1F Refugee Convention (Article 12 of the Qualification Directive). Article 1F makes exclusion from refugee status mandatory for a person with respect to whom there are serious reasons for considering that he has committed:

(a) A crime against peace, a war crime, or crime against humanity as defined in international instruments.

(b) A serious non-political crime outside country of refuge prior to admission to that country as a refugee.

(c) Acts contrary to purpose and principles of UN.

Some general principles have evolved in the application of Article 1F.

14.5.1 Restrictive interpretation

The *UNHCR Handbook* says that the Article should be construed restrictively because it deprives a person of protection who would otherwise qualify for refugee status (para 180). This principle has in practice been applied by the Courts, though without referring to it as such, in the sense that the Court has required a rigorous application of the provisions of the Article. This is apparent in the cases discussed in this chapter. The theoretical notion of a restrictive construction has not remained intact. The Tribunal in *Gurung (Exclusion – Risk – Maoist) Nepal* [2002] UKIAT 04870 suggested that 'the greater the scale of the violation of the human rights of others by those who perpetrate acts or crimes proscribed by Art 1F, the less rationale there is for a restrictive approach', although it also reiterated that exclusion clauses should be applied restrictively (para 151). More radically, the Immigration Asylum and Nationality Act 2006 requires an interpretation of Article 1F(c) which is wide rather than restrictive. The Court in turn has read down that requirement. These points will be visited again later.

14.5.2 Inclusion before exclusion

Another established principle was that inclusion should be considered before exclusion. In other words, the question of eligibility for refugee status should be considered before the question of whether the person should be excluded from it. The Lisbon Expert Roundtable conclusions give a number of reasons for this:

- Exclusion before inclusion risks criminalizing refugees.
- Exclusion is exceptional and it is not appropriate to consider an exception first.
- If a person does not qualify for refugee status, it is not then necessary to address the question of exclusion, thereby avoiding having to deal with complex issues.
- Inclusion first enables consideration to be given to protection obligations to family members.
- Inclusion before exclusion allows proper distinctions to be drawn between prosecution and persecution.
- Textually, the 1951 Convention would appear to provide more clearly for inclusion before exclusion.
- Interviews which look at the whole refugee definition allow for information to be collected more broadly and accurately.

However, in the UK, the Immigration, Nationality and Asylum Act 2006 s 55 enables the Secretary of State to certify that an asylum claim is excluded under Article 1F or 33(2), which prevents the claim for inclusion in the Convention from being heard at all. The statute makes no concession to the principle of 'inclusion before exclusion' as once the Secretary of State has certified, the Tribunal must begin by considering the statements in the Secretary of State's certificate. If the Tribunal agrees with those statements, it must dismiss the claim for asylum (s 33 of the 2001 Act, replaced by s 55 of the 2006 Act). However, as Cases C–57/09 and C–101/09 *Bundesrepublik Deutschland v D and B* and *BA (Afghanistan) v SSHD* [2010] EWCA Civ 1085 make clear, the Tribunal may then go on to consider an Article 3 claim (see 14.5.6).

14.5.3 Standard of proof

The standard of proof of allegations which would lead to exclusion is a matter of importance, even more so following the statutory provisions just discussed. The Article says that a person will be excluded if 'there are serious reasons for considering' that they have committed one of the acts discussed. The Lisbon Expert Roundtable says this should be interpreted as a minimum to mean 'clear evidence sufficient to indict'. The UNHCR in its statement for the CJEU references C–57/09 and C–101/09 suggests that the standard of proof is a high one:

> Although the application of the exclusion clauses does not require a determination of guilt in the criminal justice sense, and therefore the standard of proof required would be less than 'proof of guilt beyond reasonable doubt', it must be sufficiently high to ensure that refugees are not erroneously excluded.

In *Al-Sirri v SSHD* [2009] EWCA Civ 222 Sedley LJ rejected the appellant's argument that the standard of proof should be the criminal standard. He said that Article 1F set a standard above mere suspicion; beyond this, it was a mistake to paraphrase the straightforward language of the Convention: it should be treated as meaning what it said (para 33). This approach was endorsed by the UK Supreme Court in *JS Sri Lanka* [2010] UKSC 15 and the New Zealand Supreme Court in *Tamil X* [2010] NZSC 107, the burden lying upon the Secretary of State.

14.5.4 Proportionality

The question of whether proportionality has a role to play in exclusion decisions is partly settled in UK law by s 34 of the Anti-terrorism, Crime and Security Act 2001 (ATCSA). This section says that Article 1F 'shall not be taken to require consideration of events or fear by virtue of which Article 1A would or might apply to a person if Article 1F did not apply'. In other words, the asylum seeker cannot argue that they should not be excluded from refugee status because of the severity of the persecution they would face.

UNHCR, in Cases C–57/09 and C–101/09 *Bundesrepublik Deutschland v D and B*, argued that the degree and likelihood of persecution feared should be measured against the seriousness of the acts committed. They say that this balance is derived from 'the nature and rationale of the exclusion clauses and the overriding humanitarian object and purpose of the 1951 Convention'. However, the CJEU did not accept this view, and held that the question of exclusion was separate from the question of whether the person would be returned to their country of origin.

In the UK, if the Secretary of State certifies that exclusion is warranted, following ss 55 of the 2006 Act, the refugee claim may not be heard. A balance cannot be struck if the feared persecution has not been fully considered.

The Tribunal in *Gurung* suggested that it was the duty of immigration judges to raise Article 1F even where the parties had not, if its application to the facts of the case was 'obvious' (para 47). This approach was followed by the Court of Appeal in *A (Iraq) v SSHD* [2005] EWCA Civ 1438, in which the appellant's asylum claim had been based on fear of reprisals because he had personally tortured many people under Saddam Hussain's regime in Iraq. The Court held that it was obvious that he was liable to be excluded under Article 1F and the adjudicator should have raised it.

We will consider each of the Article 1F grounds in turn.

14.5.5 **Article 1F(a): Crime against peace, war crime, crime against humanity**

As Article 1F(a) suggests, the definition of these crimes is to be found in international instruments. The main contemporary source is the statutes of international tribunals. These incorporate key provisions of the UN Convention on the Protection and Punishment of Genocide (1948) and the four 1949 Geneva Conventions for the Protection of Victims of War. The Rome Statute of the International Criminal Court 1998 (ICC) contains extensive definitions of crimes against humanity and war crimes. The Statute of the International Criminal Tribunal for the former Yugoslavia (ICTY), (1993 but amended numerous times) has generated significant case law and is also an important source.

The statutes create jurisdiction to try the crimes of genocide, crimes against humanity, war crimes, and crimes of aggression. The Rome Statute's definition of war crimes includes, for instance, intentional attacks on undefended civilians, humanitarian bodies and buildings dedicated to religion, education, art or science, and killing prisoners of war. The ICTY established that war crimes may be committed during a civil war (see *Dusko Tadic* case no IT 94 I T). The ICC Article 7 enumerates crimes against humanity, including murder, extermination, enslavement, deportation, imprisonment, torture, rape, enforced disappearance of persons, the crime of apartheid, persecutions on political, racial, and religious grounds; and other inhumane acts committed knowingly against any civilian population.

Article 6 of the Charter of the International Military Tribunal includes in the definition of a crime against peace 'planning, preparation, initiating or waging a war of aggression, or a war in violation of international treaties, agreements or assurances'. In *JS Sri Lanka* (see 14.5.5.1), JS' claim was excluded by the Home Office under Article 1F(a) on the grounds that he had been complicit in war crimes and crimes against humanity. The Court of Appeal held that there could not be such exclusion without evidence of actual war crimes or crimes against humanity having been committed. In order to establish this, reference should be made to the ICC statute, and the crimes alleged should be identified. This is now the accepted approach, entailing findings in lower courts and tribunals about atrocities in other countries. Although these findings carry no legal weight outside the particular case, they demonstrate in a striking way the international context in which asylum law operates. For instance, in *AA (Art 1F(a) – complicity – Arts 7 and 25 ICC Statute) Iran* [2011] UKUT 00339 (IAC) the Upper Tribunal found that the First Tier Tribunal did not err in law in holding that the Bassij, whom they defined as a 'volunteer paramilitary force', committed crimes against humanity falling within Article 7 of the ICC Statute (para 51). In *B v Refugee Appeals Board & another* [2011] IEHC 198 the Irish High Court had no doubt that the Taliban committed crimes against humanity.

14.5.5.1 *Complicity*

Case law so far in the UK has turned to a great extent on the question of complicity. The most structured approach to Article 1F(a) has been in *JS (Sri Lanka) v SSHD* [2010] UKSC 15, which is also the authority on complicity.

Key Case

***JS (Sri Lanka) v SSHD* [2010] UKSC 15**

The appellant had served as second-in-command of the LTTE Intelligence Division's combat unit. The main issue was what degree of responsibility JS could be said to have for any international crimes that had been committed or planned by the LTTE. There was no evidence that he had committed such crimes himself, so any responsibility had to turn on the question of his complicity in the acts of others. The Court held that this must be determined by reference to the detailed provisions on liability in the Rome Statute. These dealt with the whole range of involvement in a criminal act, for instance, acting as a principal or co-principal, soliciting or procuring the crime, engaging in a joint criminal enterprise (Article 25). All the authorities were agreed that mere membership of an organization some part or members of which had committed crimes against humanity did not make a person liable for those crimes. This was the case in refugee law as well as criminal law. Article 1F required 'serious reasons for considering' that the person had committed such a crime. The Court of Appeal concluded:

> The fact that he was a bodyguard of the head of the intelligence wing... shows that he was trusted to perform that role, but not that he made a significant contribution to the commission of international crimes or that he acted as that person's bodyguard with the intention of furthering the perpetration of international crimes.... there was no evidence of international crimes committed by the men under his command for which he might incur liability under article 28. His own engagement in non-criminal military activity was not of itself a reason for suspecting him of being guilty of international crimes.

The Supreme Court rejected the Secretary of State's appeal, but held that the Court of Appeal's approach to complicity was too restricted. Lord Brown said:

> I would hold an accused disqualified under Article 1F if there are serious reasons for considering him voluntarily to have contributed in a significant way to the organization's ability to pursue its purpose of committing war crimes, aware that his assistance will in fact further that purpose. (para 38)

In *MH (Syria) and DS (Afghanistan) v SSHD* [2009] EWCA Civ 226, the Secretary of State had held that DS was excluded from refugee status under Article 1F(a) on the basis of atrocities committed by the KhAD, the Afghani intelligence service. It was found on the basis of the evidence that the torture and brutality of the KhAD was directed towards insurgents, not towards civilians. Accordingly, the Court of Appeal found that these acts did not constitute crimes against humanity according to the international statutes. DS' refugee claim could not be excluded on this basis. By contrast, in *BA (Afghanistan)* the appellant did not dispute that the KhAD had been responsible for crimes against humanity, namely, the extraction of intelligence information from the civilian population by torture. Refusing permission to appeal, Pitchford LJ held that the appellant, given his high rank and long service, must have been complicit in the common design to extract information by torture. Similarly, in *AA (Art 1F(a) – complicity – Arts 7 and 25 ICC Statute) Iran,* the Upper Tribunal held that even though the appellant had not himself tortured or abused civilians, as a long-serving local commander of the Bassij, on his own evidence he had handed individuals over knowing that they would be seriously ill-treated and 'closed his eyes' to abuses by others. Applying the test laid down in *JS Sri Lanka,* the appellant's own subjective religious motivation could not save him from a finding of complicity. He had 'contributed in a significant way to the organisation's ability to pursue its purpose of committing war crimes, aware that his assistance will in fact further that purpose' (*JS (Sri Lanka)* para 38).

In *Attorney General (Minister of Immigration) v Tamil X* [2010] NZSC 107 the New Zealand Supreme Court held that the respondent could not be regarded as complicit in crimes against humanity for having worked on board a ship which was transporting arms for the LTTE. Although acts committed by the LTTE in the past could be identified as crimes against humanity, it could not be shown that Tamil X's conduct had contributed to these acts, bearing in mind that the LTTE was engaged in armed struggle, and that his knowledge of the ship's cargo was not established prior to the last voyage.

The CJEU in *Bundesrepublik Deutschland v D and B* took a similar view to that in *JS* and *Tamil X*:

> Any authority which finds... that the person concerned has – like D – occupied a prominent position within an organisation which uses terrorist methods is entitled to presume that that person has individual responsibility for acts committed by that organisation during the relevant period, but it nevertheless remains necessary to examine all the relevant circumstances before... excluding that person from refugee status... the finding... is conditional on an assessment on a case-by-case basis of the specific facts. (paras 98 and 99)

14.5.5.2 *Can a private individual commit such a crime?*

Usually, crimes against humanity are committed by governments or by individuals in their capacity as members of military or paramilitary organizations. However, in rare circumstances private individuals may also commit such a crime. Linden JA in *Sivakumar v Canada (MEI)* [1994] 1 FC 433 refers to the Flick Trial, US Military Tribunal at Nuremberg, Law Reports of Trials of War Criminals, vol. IX, p. 1 when several industrialists were convicted of crimes against humanity for using slave labour in their factories. An individual will only be responsible however if they engaged in a positive act with a conscious intention (UNHCR Guidelines para 39).

14.5.6 **Article 1F(b): Serious non-political crimes**

A serious non-political crime may be so either because it never had any political connection or motivation, or because the consequences of it are so severe that it can no longer be treated as political.

Key Case

T v SSHD **[1996] 2 All ER 865**

T was a member of an organization in Algeria that intended to secure power, was prepared to use violence to achieve its ends, and had been declared illegal in 1992. The special adjudicator found that the appellant was involved in and had had prior knowledge of a bomb attack on the airport in Algiers in which ten civilians had been killed, although there was a dispute about the level of intended damage and of the appellant's knowledge of that. He had also been engaged in planning a raid on an army barracks to seize arms in which one person had died. The House of Lords endorsed the *UNHCR Handbook* paras 151–161 which suggests that a 'serious' crime in this context 'must be a capital crime or a very serious punishable act' (para 155). The common law character of the crime must be weighed against its political nature. The killing of ten civilians was too great a crime to warrant being called 'political'. Lord Lloyd suggested that for a crime to be political it must be committed for a political purpose, 'that is to say, with the object of overthrowing or subverting or changing the government of a state or inducing it to change its policy'. Second, there must be:

> sufficiently close and direct link between the crime and the alleged political purpose. In determining whether such a link exists, the court will bear in mind the means used to achieve the political end, and will have particular regard to whether the crime was aimed at a military or governmental target, on the one hand, or a civilian target on the other, and in either event whether it was likely to involve the indiscriminate killing or injuring of members of the public. (at 787)

T had not planted the bomb or carried out the raid, but he had planned the raid and was a political organizer for the group which planted the bomb. He had sufficient knowledge of the plan to exclude him from refugee status, even if it did not extend to details.

The Qualification Directive says that 'particularly cruel actions, even if committed with an allegedly political objective, may be classified as serious non-political crimes'.

The approach of the Tribunal to implementing these principles has not always been consistent. In *Hane* [2002] UKIAT 03945, the appellant was a Maoist Party member in Nepal who had been involved in an armed raid on a police station in which two policemen were injured. There was a high level of violence between Maoists and state authorities. For a period of time reported by Amnesty International, the official figures were 548 Maoists, 3 soldiers, and 1 policeman killed. The appellant was excluded from refugee protection by Article 1F, as the criminal nature of his act outweighed the political context in which it was committed. By comparison, in *Gnanasegaran* [2002] UKIAT 00583, the appellant was an active member of the LTTE (Tamil Tigers) in Sri Lanka. He and two other members were wanted for the murder of one or two policemen. The Tribunal concluded, following *T*, that this was a political crime. It concluded:

> Disturbing though we find it in the circumstances of this case that 'the perpetrator of a repellent crime should insist on the hospitality and protection of any nation whose borders he can manage to penetrate' (from the judgment of Lord Mustill in *T*...) we consider that this appeal must be allowed.

The comparison of *Hane* and *Gnanasegaran* illustrates the old adage that 'one person's terrorist is another's freedom fighter'. This is now a key issue in the application and interpretation of Article 1F. The UK government, in common with other governments, since September 2001 in particular, has attempted to exclude from refugee status people who for a range of reasons might be given the label 'terrorist'.

Key Case

Joined Cases C–57/09 and C–101/09, *Bundesrepublik Deutschland v D and B*

B had been a sympathizer of Dev Sol (now DHKP/C) when a schoolboy and had supported armed guerrilla warfare in the mountains. After being arrested he had been subjected to serious physical abuse and had been forced to give a statement under torture and sentenced to life imprisonment. In 2001, while he was in custody, B confessed to killing a fellow prisoner suspected of being an informant. D had been a guerrilla fighter for the PKK and one of its senior officials. Because of political differences with its leadership, D had left the PKK in May 2000 and since then had been under threat. He had been granted asylum in Germany, but after a change in the law this was revoked.

The German court sought a preliminary ruling which the CJEU answered as follows:

- the fact that a person has been a member of an organisation which, because of its involvement in terrorist acts, is on the [proscribed] list...and that that person has actively supported the armed struggle waged by that organisation does not automatically constitute a serious reason for considering that that person has committed 'a serious non-political crime' or 'acts contrary to the purposes and principles of the United Nations';
- the finding...that there are serious reasons for considering that a person has...been guilty of such acts is conditional on an assessment on a case-by-case basis of the specific facts, with a view to determining whether the acts committed by the organisation concerned meet the conditions laid down in those provisions and whether individual responsibility for carrying out those acts can be attributed to the person concerned, regard being had to the standard of proof required under Article 12(2) of the Directive.

The New Zealand Supreme Court in *Attorney General (Minister of Immigration) v Tamil X* [2010] NZSC 107 revived the recognition of serious *political* crimes. Tamil X had been recruited to work on board a ship, the *Yahata*. He claimed to be unaware that in addition to its legitimate commercial activities the ship transported arms for the LTTE. He was aware of this on what became its last voyage. When challenged by the Indian navy there was an exchange of fire, and those on board, including Tamil X, scuttled the ship. The Court held that this was a serious crime, involving risk to the life of the Indian navy, but its purpose was clearly political. It did not consist of indiscriminate violence to civilians such as in the case of *T*, and Tamil X should not be excluded from refugee status.

Paragraph (b), unlike the other two paragraphs, only applies to acts that were committed before entry to the country of refuge. This in part explains the recent increased resort to para (c) (discussed at 14.5.8).

The Qualification Directive makes a significant extension to Article 1F(b):

> He or she has committed a serious non-political crime outside the country of refuge prior to his or her admission as a refugee; which means the time of issuing a residence permit based on the granting of refugee status...(Qualification Directive) Article 12.2(b)

This seems to mean that a crime committed while waiting for refugee status to be granted may give rise to liability for exclusion under Article 1F(b), presumably still providing it was committed outside the country of refuge.

14.5.6.1 *Complicity*

The question of complicity in the context of para (b) is not necessarily settled by reference to the international statutes as discussed earlier, as the matter under consideration is generally not covered by the international statutes. It is still a question of how implicated the claimant is in the wrongful acts. In the case of *T*, although the appellant had not planted the bomb or carried out the raid, he had taken part in the planning and preparation of the latter and as a political organizer had at minimum an incriminating level of knowledge of the former. The degree of complicity which will result in exclusion is related to the nature and seriousness of the offence. Knowledge in advance that a demonstration may well erupt into stone-throwing and damage to property is a very different matter from knowledge in advance that a bomb will be planted in a densely populated area. In *Gurung*, the main evidence against the appellant was his membership of a Maoist organization which used violent means. The Tribunal in *Gurung* posed the question: 'is mere membership at the time of the commission of acts or crimes proscribed by Article 1F enough to entitle an adjudicator to conclude that an appellant is excluded...?' (para 103). The CJEU's judgment in *D and B* now answers that question, but makes it clear that membership of certain organizations is an important factor. What then becomes critical is how such an organization is identified.

14.5.7 Membership of proscribed organizations

The list that was relevant in the judgment in *D and B* was an EU list, forming the Annex to Common Position 2001/931/CFSP on the application of specific measures to combat terrorism. The UK uses a national list of organizations which are proscribed. The UK's list is made under the Terrorism Act 2000. The grounds for proscription are that the organization is concerned in terrorism (s 3) and this is defined as committing, participating in, promoting or encouraging, or otherwise engaging in terrorism. The Terrorism Act 2006 added that an organization promotes or encourages terrorism if it glorifies it. This means to praise or celebrate it in such a way as to give people to understand that such conduct should be emulated (see chapters 2 and 16). At the date of writing, 60 organisations are proscribed. These include Al-Qa'ida, the LTTE, the PKK, and ETA.

The Secretary of State has publicized the following as the criteria for proscription:

1. the nature and scale of the organization's activities;
2. the specific threat that it poses to the UK;
3. the specific threat that it poses to British nationals overseas;
4. the extent of the organization's presence in the UK; and
5. the need to support international partners in the fight against terrorism.

By Terrorism Act 2000 ss 11, 12, and 13 it is an offence to belong to a proscribed organization or to profess to do so, to invite support for a proscribed organization which is not restricted to money or other property, to arrange or support or address a meeting in order to support a proscribed organization, or to wear an item of clothing or display an article suggesting support for a proscribed organization.

There is a defence under Terrorism Act 2000 s 11(2) that the organization was not proscribed when the person charged became a member and that the person has not taken part in the activities of the organization since it was proscribed. However, such defences can only be raised in the course of prosecution of an individual, and challenging proscription of an organization is a more difficult process. David Anderson QC, Independent Reviewer of Terrorism Legislation found that proscription was 'at best a blunt instrument', and that the expense and complexity of applications made it unduly difficult to challenge a designation which was politically advantageous to government but damaging for the organization.

The use of the word 'terrorist' as a description of an organization begs the questions that must be answered. In *MH (Syria)*, the Court of Appeal approved the idea of the Tribunal in *Gurung* that an organization could be placed in a continuum from violence to working for democratic change in order to determine whether it should be described as 'terrorist'. The Court of Appeal in *JS (Sri Lanka)* did not regard that as helpful because, firstly, the Tribunal had 'rolled up a number of factors which might cause somebody wedded to the ideals of western liberal democracy to take a more or less hostile view of the organisation and to use an assessment of where the organisation stood in relation to those values in deciding whether its armed acts were "proportionate"'. This provided a subjective and unsatisfactory basis for determining whether as a matter of law an individual was guilty of an international crime. Secondly, some of the factors identified were not relevant to the question of guilt of an international crime, for example, whether the organization's long-term aims embraced a democratic mode of government. Thirdly, the continuum approach took the decision-maker's eye off the critical questions of whether the evidence provided serious reasons for considering the applicant to have committed the actus reus of an international crime with the requisite mens rea (Toulson LJ paras 112–114). The Supreme Court has now expressly disapproved the continuum approach.

In general it is not so easy to identify 'an extremist terrorist group'. There is an all too obvious danger that a national list will include groups for political reasons. Without scope to recognize that 'one man's terrorist is another man's freedom fighter', the Refugee Convention would be undermined, as persecution for reasons of political opinion is an archetypal qualification for refugee status. It is easy to recognize the events of 11 September 2001 as an atrocity, but it is not easy to derive a generalizable principle from this.

The judgment of the CJEU in *D and B* makes it clear that membership of an organization deemed 'terrorist' is not enough in itself to warrant exclusion from refugee status. The application of this judgment is complicated by rules permitting closed evidence where national security is in issue. In *SS (Libya) v SSHD* [2011] EWCA Civ 1547, SS was excluded from refugee status. The only open allegation against him was that he was a member of the Libyan Islamic Fighting Group (LIFG). He denied this, but the remaining evidence was closed and so he did not have access to it (see chapter 8). As mentioned, the LTTE and PKK are included in the UK's list, but the Supreme Court in *JS (Sri Lanka)* said that the LTTE was neither 'predominantly terrorist in character' nor an 'extremist terrorist group' (para 27). A number of Turkish claims are brought by members of the PKK or, indeed, other proscribed groups. B himself was a PKK member and guerilla fighter, initially awarded refugee status in Germany. In the UK membership of the proscribed organization is a crime, but this in itself cannot be regarded as grounds for exclusion under Article 1F(b) as the crime is clearly political, and goes nowhere near the level of seriousness described by Lord Mustill in *T*.

14.5.8 Article 1F(c): Acts contrary to purpose and principles of UN

The purpose of this paragraph was summarized in the Canadian case of *Pushpanathan* [1998] 1 SCR by Bastarache J: 'The rationale is that those who are responsible for the persecution which creates refugees should not enjoy the benefits of a Convention designed to protect refugees' (para 63). UNHCR and others suggest that the drafters of the Convention had in mind 'those operating on a state level and perpetrating crimes of national or international significance' (Pretzell et al 2002:149 and UNHCR Guidelines 2003). Recently the Court of Appeal voiced sympathy with this view (Pill LJ in *DD (Afghanistan)*). However, Pushpanathan countenanced an important extension:

The category of persons covered by Art 1F(c) was not, however, restricted to persons in positions of power. Although it may be more difficult for a non-state actor to perpetrate human rights violations on a scale amounting to persecution without the State thereby implicitly adopting those acts, the possibility should not be excluded.

In just a few years, Article 1F(c) has become the exclusion clause most often used, and the Court of Appeal has confirmed that an individual who is not a state actor is capable of being guilty of acts contrary to the purpose and principles of the UN so as to come within Article 1F(c) (*Al-Sirri v SSHD* [2009] EWCA Civ 222).

Another contested limitation on paragraph (c) was to actions committed before arrival in the country of refuge. If its purpose was as stated earlier, this limitation would be too obvious to need stating, and the reason for limiting paragraph (b) to acts before arrival would be that serious non-political crimes could be committed after entry, but the remedy for that would lie in Article 33.2 which permits *refoulement* in such a situation. However, case law has established that no such limitation exists, and paragraph (c) is now used to deny or revoke refugee status where refugees are suspected of international terrorist activity in the country of refuge.

These developments began with *Singh and Singh v SSHD* (SIAC 31 July 2000), where the Special Immigration Appeals Commission held that Sikh activists who were supporting armed struggle in India from the UK could be excluded from refugee status under Article 1F(c). They had conspired to commit acts of violence in India and had been involved in transporting explosives. The fact that these actions were in pursuance of a fight for self-determination did not provide a defence against exclusion (though see the doubts now expressed by Pill LJ in *DD (Afghanistan)*). They could not have been excluded under Article 1F(b) because these acts were committed after arrival in the country of refuge. The SIAC found that as there was no express limitation of Article 1F(c) to individuals carrying governmental authority, none should be implied. The crucial finding was that the UN unequivocally condemns terrorism. The actions of Singh and Singh could be brought within the definition of terrorism in the UK (Terrorism Act 2000 s 1). Therefore terrorist acts such as these were contrary to the purpose and principles of the UN.

Singh was followed in the Immigration and Asylum Tribunal in *KK (Article 1F(c)), Turkey* [2004] UKIAT 00101. The claimant had been active in Kurdish politics while living in Turkey, had been arrested, detained, and interrogated on seven occasions, and had fled after being implicated in a serious bombing incident. He had been active in the PKK (Kurdistan Workers Party) and Dev Sol, which became DHKP-C. Both are proscribed organizations in the UK. The Secretary of State accepted that he had a well-founded fear of persecution in Turkey because of his political opinions. Before his asylum claim was determined, KK was found guilty of arson and conspiracy to commit arson in relation to attacks in London on a Turkish travel agent and Turkish bank. No-one was injured in the attacks.

The Secretary of State sought to exclude him from refugee status under Article 1F(c). UNHCR argued that the crimes referred to in this paragraph were those with an international or global dimension, capable of affecting relations between states. The use should be exceptional and usually confined to those in positions of power or influence. The Tribunal held that the act was political, as it was continuing the fight against the

Turkish government in which the claimant had been involved in Turkey. However, in the country of refuge no distinction should be drawn between common crime and political crime. The Tribunal concluded:

> there are some acts which, despite being political or politically-inspired, do not depend for their criminality on the individual matrix of power within a particular state. These acts, in our view, are those which are intended to be covered by Article 1F(c). That subparagraph does not apply to every crime, nor to every political crime. It applies to acts which are the subject of intense disapproval by the governing body of the entire international community. (para 85)

The act that KK had committed came within the UK's controversial and wide definition of terrorism under Terrorism Act 2000 s 1. The UN condemned terrorism and so his action brought him within Article 1F(c).

KK was followed in *AA (Palestine)* [2005] UKIAT 00104, in which the appellant had been arrested while on a suicide-bombing mission. The Tribunal held that para (c) contains no requirement that the crime in question be non-political in order to attract exclusion, therefore if an act is accepted to come within this paragraph there does not need to be any enquiry into whether the common law criminal element outweighs any political motivation. Ironically, this now seems to result in a lesser crime giving rise to exclusion under Article 1F(c) than under 1F(b), even though the apparent intention is the other way round. The matter is put beyond doubt by Immigration, Asylum and Nationality Act 2006 s 54:

> In the construction and application of Article 1F(c) of the Refugee Convention the reference to acts contrary to the purposes and principles of the United Nations shall be taken as including, in particular –
>
> (a) acts of committing, preparing or instigating terrorism (whether or not the acts amount to an actual or inchoate offence), and
>
> (b) acts of encouraging or inducing others to commit, prepare or instigate terrorism (whether or not the acts amount to an actual or inchoate offence).

In *MT (Algeria), RB (Algeria) & U (Algeria) v SSHD* [2007] EWCA Civ 808, it was argued for the appellants that acts in the country of refuge could not exclude a person from refugee status under Article 1F(c), but the Court of Appeal disagreed (these issues did not form part of the appeal to the House of Lords). In *Abu Qatada v SSHD* [2007] UKSIAC 15/2005 the SIAC simply said that 'the acts which the SSHD relied on showed that the Appellant had been guilty of acts contrary to the purposes and principles of the UN' (para 104). These deportation cases were based on national security assessments by the Secretary of State. By their very nature, such assessments do not necessarily require past actions to be proved against the appellant (see chapters 8 and 16). This was treated as sufficient also to discharge the burden of proof for Article 1F, that there were 'serious reasons for believing' that acts contrary to the purpose and principles of the UN had been committed. This case law is consistent with the view of Sedley LJ in *Al-Sirri* that an individual may be excluded from refugee status on a lower standard of proof than would be required in a criminal trial to convict them of the same matters. At the same time, the Court of Appeal in *Al-Sirri* held that s 54 of the 2006 Act must be read down so as to comply with Article 12 of the Qualification Directive which defines acts contrary to the purpose and principles of the UN by reference to the UN Charter. The scope of such acts was more restricted than in s 1 Terrorism Act 2000 which was imported by s 54. The Court confirmed that, nevertheless, there was no doubt that acts of terrorism as internationally defined were included.

The question following s 54 and Al-Sirri is what acts will constitute such acts of terrorism? In *MH (Syria)*, MH joined the PKK at the age of 13 because of the constant harassment her Kurdish family suffered from the Syrian authorities. She was elected to carry a banner and to march in front of the crowd. Her other actions for the PKK were to resolve disputes within a refugee camp and carry out nursing duties there. She volunteered to be armed, and from then on carried a gun, though apparently had not used it. Her asylum claim in the UK was turned down on the basis of Article 1F (c).

The Court of Appeal said that the case 'fell well short of engaging Article 1F(c)'. The only basis on which it could be argued to do so was simple membership of the PKK, as the appellant had committed no act herself which could be construed as falling within the exclusion. The nature of the PKK was not such that mere membership would implicate a person in acts contrary to the purpose and principles of the UN.

In *SSHD v DD (Afghanistan)* [2010] EWCA Civ 1407 the Court of Appeal confirmed that 'participation in military actions against the government was not terrorism' (para 54). This had been doubted by SIAC in *SS* but the Court of Appeal may have stemmed the tide that was turning towards the erosion of even the concept of 'freedom fighter' by asserting 'it is difficult to hold that every act of violence in a civil war, the aim of which will usually be to overthrow a legitimate government, is an act of terrorism within the 2000 Act' (para 55). As they said, 'terrorism is indiscriminate'.

DD was nevertheless excluded from refugee status under Article 1F(c), because in Jamait-e-Islami, the Taliban, and Hizb-e-Islami he had fought also against the ISAF, the International Special Assistance Force. This force, said the Court of Appeal, was present in Afghanistan pursuant to the mandate of the UN, 'to assist in maintaining security and to protect and support the UN's work in Afghanistan so that its personnel engaged in reconstruction and humanitarian efforts can operate in a secure environment' (para 64). Direct military action against forces carrying out that mandate was contrary to the purposes and principles of the UN.

14.5.9 **Article 33(2)**

One argument against Article 1F applying to acts in the country of refuge is that, if it does, it duplicates Article 33(2), which certainly fills that role. Article 33(2) of the Refugee Convention provides an exception to the non-*refoulement* obligation. This is where there are 'reasonable grounds' for regarding the refugee as 'a danger to the security of the country in which he is' or in relation to a person 'who, having been convicted by a final judgment of a particularly serious crime constitutes a danger to that country'. The CJEU in *D and B* made the distinction plain between Article 1F and Article 33.2 by holding that exclusion from refugee status pursuant to Article 12(2)(b) or (c) of Directive 2004/83 (equivalent to Article 1F(b) and (c) of the Refugee Convention) was 'not conditional on the person concerned representing a present danger to the host Member State'.

Until 2003, this paragraph was not often used. It can be applied in case of serious common crime as well as threats to national security. For example, it was applied to the appellant in *A v SSHD* CA 16/2/2004, who had been convicted in the UK of a serious sexual assault on his daughter, and of the rape of a woman.

The emphasis is on danger to the country, i.e., conviction of a particularly serious crime should not of itself warrant exclusion if the person would not constitute a danger to the country. Goodwin-Gill says:

> an exception to non-*refoulement* ought necessarily to involve an assessment of all the circumstances, the nature of the offence, the background to its commission, the behaviour of the individual, and the actual terms of any sentence imposed. (2007:240)

The Qualification Directive Article 14 permits Member States to 'revoke, end or refuse to renew' refugee status on terms similar to Article 33.2, and Article 21 provides additionally for *refoulement* in the same circumstances as Article 33.2. The effect of Article 33.2 is to allow *refoulement,* rather than, as with Article 1F, exclusion from refugee status; because of the absolute nature of Article 3 ECHR, the distinction is rather theoretical. The presumption of Article 33 is that the offender is a person whose life or liberty is in danger if they are returned to their home state. If the risk of this is accepted at the time of a decision under Article 33.2, Article 3 will prevent their actual return. Of course, the need for protection from danger to the individual on return cannot be a licence for them to inflict serious harm on the host state. The creation of a 'special immigration status' by the 2008 Act, discussed at 15.5.10, is part of the UK's response to this tension.

14.5.9.1 *UK legislation related to Article 33.2*

UK statute contradicts the principles of proportionality and individual assessment. First, as mentioned earlier, ATCSA s 34 entails that this question of proportionality need not be taken into account in *refoulement* under Article 33(2). Section 34 is generally worded, and despite its inclusion in a statute rushed through Parliament as an emergency response to terrorism, it is not restricted to terrorist cases.

Second, Nationality, Immigration and Asylum Act 2002 s 72(2) resiles from the obligation to make the necessary judgement under Article 33(2) as to danger to the community. It says:

> A person shall be *presumed* to have been convicted by a final judgment of a particularly serious crime and to constitute a danger to the community of the United Kingdom if he is –
>
> (a) convicted in the United Kingdom of an offence, and
>
> (b) sentenced to a period of imprisonment of at least two years. (emphasis added)

By s 72(11) this does not include a suspended sentence but does include a hospital order. The offence of belonging to a proscribed organization under Terrorism Act 2000 s 11 carries a maximum sentence of 10 years. This risks making membership of the LTTE, PKK, and so on grounds for *refoulement* without the commission of any serious non-political crime. What saves it from this is that the presumption in s 72(2) is rebuttable (*IH (s 72 'Particularly Serious Crime') Eritrea* [2009] UKAIT 00012 confirmed in *EN (Serbia) v SSHD* [2009] EWCA Civ 630). However, s 72(8) provides that the gravity of the fear or threat of persecution, as in s 34 ATCSA, is not to be taken into account in considering whether the presumption is rebutted.

In *AQ (Somalia)* [2011] EWCA Civ 695 the Court of Appeal held that the presumption in s 72 applies whether or not the Secretary of State issues a certificate. However, in order to apply and test the presumption, the issue must be raised one way or another before the Court or Tribunal. It was held to be an abuse of power to issue a s 72 certificate *after* judicial proceedings were concluded. (*TB v SSHD* [2008] EWCA Civ 977). Where for instance the danger of reoffending is low, the presumption can be rebutted (*Mugwagwa (s.72 – applying statutory presumptions) Zimbabwe* [2011] UKUT 00338 (IAC)).

The Nationality, Immigration and Asylum Act 2002 (Specification of Particularly Serious Crimes) Order 2004, SI 2004/1910 was made under the power in s 72(4) to specify further crimes, having the same effect as a conviction under s 72(2). The order specified 183 offences, including not only rape, murder, and stockpiling biological weapons, but also theft, entering a building as a trespasser intending to steal, and aggravated taking of a vehicle. Section 72 is stated to be 'for the purpose and construction of article 33.2 of the Refugee Convention'. The Parliamentary Joint Committee on

Human Rights advised the government that the Order was incompatible with Article 33(2) of the Refugee Convention 'because it includes within its scope a number of offences which do not amount to "particularly serious crimes" within the meaning of Article 33(2)' (Joint Committee on Human Rights Session 2003–04 Twenty-second Report). As the Human Rights Committee pointed out, legislation which is designed to give effect to international obligations must be interpreted compatibly with those obligations. If the order is incompatible with the Convention, then it follows that it is ultra vires the 2002 Act. This has been held to be so in *EN (Serbia) v SSHD* [2009] EWCA Civ 630.

Key Case

EN (Serbia) v SSHD **[2009] EWCA Civ 630**

EN was a national of Serbia who claimed asylum in the UK. After appeals, he was granted indefinite leave to remain. In 2002 and 2005, he was convicted of minor offences and in 2006 of burglary and possessing an offensive weapon. The longest of his prison sentences was 12 months. The Secretary of State decided to deport him. After he had given notice of appeal, the Secretary of State notified EN that it had been decided to issue a notice under s 72 of the 2002 Act against him and that he was not entitled to humanitarian protection.

The Court of Appeal confirmed that Article 33(2) imposed two requirements: conviction by a final judgment of a particularly serious crime *and* constituting a danger to the community. Both of these must be present in order for the person to be subject to *refoulement*. The Court held that a rebuttable presumption could in principle be compatible with Article 33.2. More importantly, a rebuttable presumption was compatible with Article 14 of the Directive. The Court said that the 2004 Order specified not only offences that could sensibly be regarded as particularly serious crimes, but also many that could not. Even on the basis that the presumption was rebuttable, the 2004 Order was objectionable. The power conferred by s 72(4)(a) was impliedly qualified by its context and purpose. The Order was ultra vires.

The Joint Committee on Human Rights had expressed doubts about the compatibility of s 72 itself with the Refugee Convention (their report predated the Qualification Directive) on the grounds that a presumption undermined the case by case basis of refugee determination, reversed the burden of proof as stated in Article 33.2, and precluded the application of a proper proportionality test to each case (paras 32–36). Goodwin-Gill and McAdam consider the section incompatible for these reasons (2007:183). The provisions also drew strong criticism from the UNHCR (see press release 7 November 2004). The Court of Appeal, however, as the case summary shows, did not go as far as saying that the presumption contained in the section conflicted with the Directive. They accepted the earlier decision of the Tribunal in *IH (s 72 'Particularly Serious Crime') Eritrea* [2009] UKAIT 00012, that the presumption in s 72 should be read as rebuttable, and this was enough to make it compatible with the Directive and the Convention.

In fact, the Qualification Directive Article 14.4(a) seems to provide a looser possibility for the revocation, ending or refusal to renew refugee status in that it provides for this where 'there are reasonable grounds for regarding him or her as a danger to the security of the Member State'. The UK's immigration rules para 334(iii) reflect Article 14.4(a).

14.5.10 Immigration status after s 72 and the Criminal Justice and Immigration Act 2008

Given the ineradicable obligation not to return a person to their own country to face treatment contrary to Article 3 ECHR (see in particular chapter 4), what is the practical impact of exclusion from refugee status or a decision under s 72, applying the exception to *refoulement*?

The immigration rules, in accordance with the Qualification Directive, provide that exclusion and Article 33.2 apply to humanitarian protection just as to refugee status. Humanitarian protection is the status which may be granted to a person whose return would breach Article 3, and, as mentioned in chapter 12, a person excluded from humanitarian protection by Article 1F may be granted a shorter period of discretionary leave. This is renewable, but short term and insecure, and may cause additional chaos and instability in the person's life if reviews and renewals do not take place.

A more draconian option is now available, since ss 130 to 137 of the Criminal Justice and Immigration Act 2008 created a new status of being a 'designated person'. Such a person has no leave to remain in the UK and is not on temporary admission (see chapter 15). They may be subject to conditions as to residence and work, reporting conditions, and electronic monitoring. They are not entitled to mainstream welfare benefits, but may be supported by way of vouchers. This 'special immigration status' (which is the heading to this Part of the 2008 Act) may only be imposed on someone who falls within the exclusion criteria of Article 1F of the Refugee Convention, or has been convicted of a crime to which s 72 of the 2002 Act applies. Falling within one of these groups makes the person a 'foreign criminal' according to the terminology of s 131. The other condition for designation is that the person is liable to deportation but cannot be removed from the UK because to do so would breach their human rights under the ECHR. These provisions are not yet in force.

14.5.11 Article 32

This Article, in contrast to Article 1F and 33(2), gives a refugee protection against expulsion and in that respect complements Article 33(1), but its terms are surprisingly weak. It applies to recognized refugees, lawfully present, and says that they shall not be expelled save on grounds of national security or public order. Proper legal process for appeal must be allowed. In effect, this makes a refugee in the UK liable to deportation like any other foreign national, but with a higher threshold to be reached by the state to justify expulsion. Also, this is not a *refoulement* provision. The state must allow the refugee a reasonable period within which to seek admission to another country.

In *SSHD v ST (Eritrea)* [2012] UKSC 12 the Supreme Court held that a refugee was not entitled to the protection of Article 32 unless she had been granted 'lawful presence' in the state in question, in other words, leave to enter and remain. ST was an Eritrean national who had lived most of her life in Ethiopia. She was granted refugee status on the grounds of fear of persecution in Eritrea, but the Supreme Court agreed that she could still be removed to Ethiopia. The destination country must however be safe for the refugee, and a place from which they will not be refouled to the country from which they have been granted asylum *(RR (refugee – safe third country) Syria* [2010] UKUT 422 (IAC).

14.6 Conclusion

The trend is towards a less secure status for refugees and a greater willingness to exclude by reason of the threat posed by individuals. The linkage made between asylum and terrorism has been demonstrated in this chapter to be not only a matter of politics but also a matter of law.

QUESTIONS

1 Why does the Refugee Convention exclude from protection those who have committed a serious non-political crime? Is there still a justification for limiting this exclusion to non-political crimes? What would be the effect of excluding people from protection for any serious crime?

2 How does the Qualification Directive's extension of Article 1F(b) to the time waiting for a claim to be processed implement the policy behind Article 1F? Or is it addressed to a different consideration?

3 Why might an asylum seeker travel on a false document?

online resource centre

For guidance on answering questions, visit www.oxfordtextbooks.co.uk/orc/clayton5e/.

FURTHER READING

Anderson, David (2011) *Report on the Operation in 2010 of the Terrorism Act 2000 and of Part 1 of the Terrorism Act 2006*, July 2011,

Bowring, Bill and Korff, Douwe (2004) 'Terrorist Designation with Regard to European and International Law: The Case of the PMOI', Paper for International Conference of Jurists, 10 November 2004.

Briddick, Catherine (2010) 'Trafficking and the National Referral Mechanism' *Women's Asylum News* (London: Asylum Aid), pp. 1–4.

Bruin, René and Wouters, Kees (2003) 'Terrorism and the Non-derogability of Non-*refoulement' International Journal of Refugee Law* vol. 15, no. 1, pp. 30–67.

Dungel, Joakim, (2009) 'Defining Victims of Crimes against Humanity: Martic´ and the International Criminal Court' *Leiden Journal of International Law* vol. 22, pp. 727–752.

Finch, Nadine (2002) 'Refugee or Terrorist?' *Journal of Immigration, Asylum and Nationality Law* vol. 16, no. 3, pp. 144–147.

Gilbert, Geoff, (2003) 'Protection after September 11th' *International Journal of Refugee Law* vol. 15, no. 1, pp. 1–4.

Saul, Ben (2004) 'Exclusion of Suspected Terrorists from Asylum: Trends in International and European Refugee Law' Institute for International Integration Studies, Discussion Paper, no. 26, July 2004.

Symonds, Steve, (2008) 'The Special Immigration Status' *Journal of Immigration Asylum and Nationality Law* vol. 22, no. 4, pp. 333–349.

UNHCR (2002) *Addressing Security Concerns without Undermining Refugee Protection* (UNHCR) accessed at: www.unhcr.org/refworld/docid/3c0b880e0.html.

—— (2003) 'Guidelines on International Protection: Application of Exclusion Clauses: Article 1F of the Convention Relating to the Status of Refugees' (UNHCR), accessed at: www.unhcr.org/3f7d48514.html.

Walker, Clive (2007) 'The Treatment of Foreign Terror Suspects' *Modern Law Review* vol. 70, no. 3, pp. 427–457.

SECTION 6

Enforcement

15

Detention

SUMMARY

The deprivation of liberty is one of the most serious infringements of fundamental human rights. In immigration law, individuals may lose their liberty through the exercise of a statutory discretion by the Home Office or immigration officers, and so guidelines and safeguards for the exercise of this discretion are crucial. The statutory powers and executive guidelines are examined here, together with the human rights and common law rules which apply. Legal provisions are set in the context of empirical research into detention decisions. The use of detention is seen as an increasingly frequent phenomenon in the asylum process, and the key role of temporary admission is examined. The former use of indefinite detention for foreign terrorist suspects is discussed at the end of the chapter.

15.1 Introduction

'In English law every imprisonment is prima facie unlawful, and...it is for a person directing imprisonment to justify his act.' These well-known words of Lord Atkin in the wartime internment case of *Liversidge v Anderson* [1942] AC 206 at 245 are still a proper statement of legal principle. Detention is not lawful unless authorized by law. This is the reverse of the usual rule in English law, whereby anything is lawful providing it is not specifically prohibited. Detention, however, interferes with one of the most basic human rights, that of physical liberty, and the advent of the Human Rights Act 1998 strengthens the common law by providing in Article 5 a statutory right which may only be infringed in prescribed circumstances. The deprivation of physical liberty is regarded as the most serious punishment available in the criminal justice system in the UK. Nevertheless, in the immigration and asylum system, detention may be imposed upon people who are not charged with any crime nor even suspected of committing one.

In this chapter, we shall consider, first, human rights law having a bearing on immigration detention; second, who is detained in the UK presently under immigration powers; and third, the parameters of the domestic law power to detain.

15.2 Human rights standards

International human rights instruments show unanimity on the issue of detention. United Nations Declaration of Human Rights Article 9: 'No-one shall be subjected to arbitrary arrest, detention and exile'; International Covenant on Civil and Political

Rights Article 9(1): 'Everyone has the right to liberty and security of person. No one shall be subjected to arbitrary arrest or detention'; European Convention on Human Rights Article 5: 'Everyone has the right to liberty and security of person. No one shall be deprived of his liberty save in the following cases and in accordance with a procedure prescribed by law...'

All these three international human rights documents prohibit detention which is arbitrary. The United Nations Human Rights Commission's Working Group on Arbitrary Detention said that detention is arbitrary when:

- there is no legal basis for the detention.
- detention is imposed as a state response to the exercise of a fundamental right.
- the total or partial non-observance of the norms of a fair trial is of such gravity as to make the resulting detention arbitrary.

The UNHRC Working Group visits countries to investigate their detention practice. They visited the UK in 1998 to examine the situation of migrants and asylum seekers in detention, and identified a number of concerns relating to:

- reasons for detention,
- duration of detention,
- availability of independent review of detention,
- and limited consideration of other options before resorting to detention.

In terms of the qualities of arbitrariness identified by the UNHCR Working Group, these concerns in the UK mainly relate to the first criterion – the legal basis for detention. These concerns have persisted in critique of the UK's detention practices.

The Human Rights Act principles, contained in Article 5 ECHR, are concerned with similar issues:

- Detention must be for a reason specified in Article 5, and no other.
- Detention must only imposed through a procedure prescribed by law.
- That law should protect the individual from arbitrariness, both in content and process.
- The detained person has a right to reasons for their detention.
- They must be able to challenge their detention.

15.2.1 Article 5 ECHR

Article 5 ECHR begins with a presumption of liberty: 'Everyone has the right to liberty and security of person'. The principles upon which this liberty may be curtailed, as contained in Article 5, begin with the following:

- Article 5.1 'No-one shall be deprived of his liberty save in the following cases...

In other words, detention must be for a reason specified in Article 5, and no other. Unlike the qualified rights in the Convention which may be interfered with in the interests of broad public policy objectives, the right to liberty may be interfered with for specified purposes only. Two of these relate to immigration: 'to prevent unauthorized entry' into the country, and 'detention of a person against whom action is being taken with a view to deportation or extradition' (Article 5(1)(f)). The meaning of 'to prevent unauthorized entry' was considered for the first time by the ECtHR in the Grand Chamber in the case of *Saadi v UK* [2008] ECHR 79.

Key Case

***Saadi v UK* [2008] ECHR 79**

The appellants were Iraqi Kurds who claimed asylum on arrival. They were detained for seven days in Oakington Reception Centre. This was a new procedure initiated in the UK, whereby people whose claims were thought to be capable of being decided quickly were detained to enable that decision to be made. They challenged their detention on the basis that it was not 'to prevent unauthorized entry'. The ECtHR found, with the Court of Appeal and House of Lords, that until a state has 'authorized' entry to the country, any entry is 'unauthorized'. So, detention of a person in order to enable that authorization to take place can be to 'prevent his effecting an unauthorized entry'.

The Court rejected the argument which had been accepted in the English High Court, that, having presented themselves to the immigration authorities, stated their need to claim asylum, and complied with requirements, the claimants were in fact doing everything they could to make an *authorized* entry. As the House of Lords had also held, the entry was unauthorized until it was authorized. In the case of 'detention of a person against whom action is being taken with a view to deportation or extradition', the ECtHR in *Chahal* had decided that there was 'no requirement that the detention be reasonably considered necessary, for example to prevent the person concerned from committing an offence or fleeing' in order for it to be permitted by Article 5. In *Saadi*, the Court noted that, to avoid arbitrariness, detention for some other reasons permitted under Article 5.1 – to secure compliance with a court order, of a minor for supervisory reasons, and those which concerned public health and safety – required an assessment of whether detention was necessary to achieve the stated aim. They held that this did not apply to detention for immigration reasons, and held that the first limb of Article 5.1(f) should be interpreted in the same way as the second, so that detention was not required to be necessary in order to be lawful. The second part concerned control of the residence of aliens, and the first part concerned their entry. The state had the right to control both equally, so it would be 'artificial' to impose a different standard on entry from that on deportation.

The Court held by 11 votes to 6 that there had been no violation of Article 5.1. Helen O'Nions comments that 'the interpretation of the majority... appears to be at odds with the international legal provisions and also with regional statements from the Council of Europe and the European Union'.

15.2.1.1 *Arbitrariness*

- Article 5(1) says that detention must be '...in accordance with a procedure prescribed by law...'.

This means that the detention is in accordance with substantive and procedural rules of national law (*Conka v Belgium* (2002) 34 EHRR 54), and that the quality of that law is compatible with the rule of law (*Amuur v France* (1996) 22 EHRR 533 para 50). It requires that the legal provision in question be accessible and precise (see chapter 4).

These requirements are integral, *in the case of Article 5, to the principle that detention should not be arbitrary. This principle goes wider than* the requirement for the detention to be prescribed by law, and is fundamental to the protection given by Article 5. The ECtHR has said that detention 'should be in keeping with the purpose of Article 5, namely to protect the individual from arbitrariness' *(Chahal v UK, Amuur v France, Conka v Belgium). The case law of the ECHR on the question of arbitrariness shares some of the principles identified by that of the UN Working Group on Arbitrary* Detention: procedural fairness, limits on the duration of detention, the legitimacy of reasons for detention, and the availability of review. The Court in *Saadi* drew together authorities on the concept, saying that *detention would be arbitrary where, 'despite complying with the letter of national law, there has been an element of bad faith or deception on the part of the authorities' and where the detention did not genuinely conform with the purpose permitted by the relevant sub-paragraph of Article 5(1). There must be some relationship between the ground of permitted deprivation of liberty relied on and the place and conditions of detention.*

In *Conka v Belgium* the Court found a breach of Article 5.1 in that the reasons given for detention were misleading. Notices were sent to about 70 asylum seekers, requiring them to attend police stations to enable the files concerning their asylum applications to be completed. At the police station they were served with an order to leave Belgium, a decision for their removal to their country of origin, and notice of their detention for that purpose. They were detained and removed.

The ECtHR found that the wording of the notice which brought them to the police station was a deliberate ploy by the authorities to mislead the applicants in order to ensure the compliance of the largest possible number. The Court said that the action of the police in misleading asylum seekers about the purpose for which they were requested to attend the police station and thereby detaining them by deception could be found to contravene the principle against arbitrariness.

The mass nature of the deception practised by the police in this case attracted particular criticism by the Court. In addition to Article 5.1, the Court by a narrow majority found a violation of Protocol 4 Article 4, which prohibits collective expulsion of aliens.

These requirements for fairness and transparency have resonances in the UK's domestic case law, as appears later in this chapter.

15.2.1.2 *Limit on duration of detention*

In *Chahal*, the European Court of Human Rights held that where a person was detained with a view to deportation, the principle of lawfulness required that the deportation proceedings should be 'prosecuted with due diligence' (para 113). If they were not, the detention would cease to be lawful. Mr Chahal had been in detention for four years by the time of his application to the ECtHR. Two further years were spent waiting for his case to reach the Court, bringing his total detention to six years, though the Court could only consider the legality of the first four. The domestic proceedings were complex, involving deportation proceedings, two refusals of asylum, two applications for judicial review, the second of which was also refused on appeal by the Court of Appeal, and then refusals of leave to appeal to the House of Lords by both its Judicial Committee and the Court of Appeal. The ECtHR commented that the case involved 'considerations of an extremely serious and weighty nature'. It went on to say, 'It is neither in the interests of the individual applicant nor in the general public interest in the administration of justice that such decisions be taken hastily' (para 117). While a lack of due diligence could give rise to a breach of Article 5.1(f) as a violation of the principle of lawfulness, the Court here held that there had not been undue delay on the part of the government.

In *Amuur v France*, four asylum seekers were detained at an airport in the international zone. Their conditions were fairly comfortable, and they were free physically to board another flight out of France, although their safety in the event of this could not be assured. The government argued that this did not amount to detention. The Court said that such conditions were a restriction on liberty. This might be necessary to prevent unauthorized entry, but should not be unduly prolonged. In this case, they were restricted for 20 days. This length of time turned a restriction into a deprivation of liberty, which is detention.

Much of the case law in the UK on detention now concerns challenges to the length of time the person has been detained, and we revisit this subject later in the chapter.

15.2.1.3 *Quality of legal reasons*

Article 5.2 requires that everyone 'should be informed promptly' in a language that they understand, of the reasons for their detention. In *Saadi*, the ECtHR unanimously found a breach of Article 5.2 as a delay of 76 hours in giving reasons was held not to be prompt. The quality of legal reasons for detention also has a bearing on whether detention is arbitrary.

In *Dougoz v Greece* (2002) 34 EHRR 61, the ECtHR considered the quality of the domestic law which authorized Mr Dougoz's detention, in the light of the Court's principles on arbitrariness and the rule of law. Mr Dougoz had been released from detention after a criminal sentence on the explicit view of the indictments chamber that he was not a danger, would be unlikely to commit further offences, and need not be detained. This being the case, his detention was not actually authorized by domestic law, and so would have fallen at the first hurdle. However, there was a purported authorization in domestic law, in that the Deputy Public Prosecutor offered the opinion that an executive rule, which enabled detention of those who were subject to expulsion by administrative order, could be applied by analogy. The ECtHR did not consider that the opinion of a senior public prosecutor 'constituted a "law" of sufficient "quality" within the meaning of the Court's case law' (para 57). This case has parallels in the UK, as we shall see in the discussion of detention after a prison sentence.

The quality of legal reasons may initially be accepted, but may become unlawful if the reasons cease to apply. In the case of *Chahal*, the alleged threat to national security posed by Mr Chahal was accepted by the Court to be a sufficient reason, but to avoid arbitrariness there needed to be a check on the continuing application of this reason. This check was provided by the former advisory panel (see chapter 8).

15.2.1.4 *Review of detention*

The availability of review is a separate heading of challenge under the ECHR, as Article 5.4 provides:

> Everyone who is deprived of his liberty by arrest or detention shall be entitled to take proceedings by which the lawfulness of his detention shall be decided speedily by a court and his release ordered if the detention is not lawful.

In the case of *Chahal v UK*, the former advisory panel procedure (see chapter 8) was held to be a sufficient guarantee against arbitrary reasons, in that the panel could review the grounds for detention and check that it was still warranted in the interests of national security. There was therefore no breach of Article 5.1. However, it did not satisfy the requirements of Article 5.4 as the panel did not have the qualities of a 'court'. It lacked the normal qualities of judicial procedure, the right to representation, to notice of the case against the appellant, and so on. Even allowing for the need of the state for secrecy in national security matters, some fairer procedure could be devised. This decision led to the demise of the advisory panel and the creation of the Special Immigration Appeals Commission.

15.2.2 Detention of asylum seekers

Additional humanitarian considerations may apply in the case of asylum seekers, who may have been tortured or come from a war zone or have otherwise already suffered in detention. Additional human rights considerations also apply. Article 14 of the Universal Declaration of Human Rights provides that the 'right to seek and enjoy asylum' is a basic human right. Clearly, a person should not be detained for seeking asylum (see the UNHRC's criteria of arbitrariness, earlier). In the absence of lawful routes to enter and claim asylum, it is sometimes difficult in practice to see the difference between being detained as an illegal entrant and being detained as an asylum seeker, despite *Naillie* (see chapter 14). As UNHCR acknowledges, asylum seekers 'may not be in a position to comply with the legal formalities for entry' and may be 'forced to arrive at, or enter, a territory illegally' (*Guidelines on applicable Criteria and Standards Relating to the Detention of Asylum Seekers* (February 1999)). Detention of asylum seekers as illegal entrants, though widely accepted in Europe, looks like a prima facie breach of Article 31 of the Refugee Convention (see chapter 14). Article 31(2) permits 'necessary' restrictions on refugees' freedom of movement but only until their status is 'regularised'. Hathaway (2005:4.2.4) suggests that this means that the asylum seeker has satisfied formalities needed for status verification, for instance, ascertaining their identity and whether they present a security risk. After that, an asylum seeker may not be detained except on the same grounds as are applied to aliens generally (Article 26 of the Refugee Convention). This seems consistent with the UNHCR Guidelines. Although in the UK the same legal regime applies to all immigration detainees, and in this sense refugees are not treated less favourably, in practice the lack of practical recognition that making an asylum claim is a lawful act makes it difficult to compare the detention of refugees with that of other foreign nationals.

The UNHCR Guidelines say that, in exceptional circumstances, asylum seekers may be detained, subject to strict compliance with principles of non-discrimination and against arbitrariness. The fifteenth meeting of the Standing Committee in June 1999 suggested that exceptional reasons, which should be 'clearly prescribed in national law', would be:

(a) to verify identity;

(b) to determine the elements on which the claim for refugee status or asylum is based, but not 'for the entire status determination procedure, or for an unlimited period of time';

(c) in cases where asylum-seekers, acting in bad faith, have destroyed their travel and/or identity documents or have used fraudulent documents intentionally to mislead the authorities of the State in which they have claimed asylum;

(d) to protect national security and public safety.

Unaccompanied minors and pregnant and nursing mothers should not be detained, and alternatives to detention should be actively sought in the case of unaccompanied elderly people, those who have suffered torture or trauma, or who have a mental or physical disability. People in these groups should only be detained after medical advice that detention would not adversely affect their health or well-being.

The Guidelines advise that asylum seekers should not be detained in prisons, and that where this is unavoidable they should not be detained with those who are detained for criminal justice reasons, i.e., convicted or remand prisoners. Basic hygiene, medical, exercise, and legal facilities should be provided. There should be segregation of women and men and the opportunity for religious activity and contact with friends and relatives. While the Guidelines do not have any binding effect, Simon Brown LJ, in *R v Uxbridge Magistrates' Court ex p Adimi, R v Crown Prosecution Service ex p Sorani, R v SSHD ex p Kaziu* [2000] 3 WLR 434 at 444, said that they should be given 'considerable weight'.

UNHCR's submissions to the ECtHR in *Saadi v UK* argued that to assimilate the position of asylum seekers to ordinary immigrants and reject the application of a necessity test 'permitted States to detain asylum seekers on grounds of expediency in wide circumstances that were incompatible with general principles of international refugee and human rights law'. Article 12 of the ICCPR suggested that asylum seekers who were making a claim and complying with what was required of them were lawfully within the territory. This was also the effect of the EC Procedures Directive 2005/85/EC Article 7 and the House of Lords case of *Szoma v Secretary of State for the Department of Work and Pensions* [2005] UKHL 64. International law required that the detention of asylum seekers be necessary in order to be lawful. The Court's decision makes no distinction between asylum seekers and others, which was one of the points upon which the dissenting judges departed from the majority.

The reality is rather different. The Independent Asylum Commission criticized excessive use of detention as part of the asylum process (*Deserving Dignity* 2008). The impact of detention, with its lack of a fixed endpoint, yet the fear of removal, can be very severe for asylum seekers. In 1989, Kurdish refugees went on hunger strike in protest at their mass detention on arrival. One detainee, who was released and subsequently detained again after refusal of his asylum claim, was suffering from a profound depression at the prospect of return to Turkey and set fire to himself with fatal consequences (see Shah 2000:167). Between 1989 and 2007, there were ten suicides of asylum seekers in detention (www.ncadc.org.uk 6 December 2007), and three in quick succession in 2011 showed that the impact of detention on asylum seekers remains very severe. This figure in itself is the tip of an iceberg of self-harm. For instance NCADC ascertained there were 56 incidents requiring medical attention in the third quarter of 2009 (www.ncadc.org.uk/resources), and 444 individuals were recorded as being at risk during that quarter. Sometimes, deaths have sparked large-scale protests in removal centres. There have been other protests, too, about conditions in immigration detention, such as lack of legal advice and medical care, for instance the hunger strike in Yarls Wood in 2010. These have occasionally persuaded the Home Office to some temporary change of policy, but the trend continues to be one of increasing use of detention. The number of detention places available has increased to around 3,000 in 2011, and a second centre built near Gatwick, was to 'send a very clear message' to new arrivals (Immigration Minister 24 July 2007). There was fierce opposition in Parliament to this clear message when Nationality, Immigration and Asylum Act 2002 s 66 renamed detention centres as 'removal centres', but it was too late. It was revealed in the House of Lords that road and building signs had already been changed before the clause had even been debated in Parliament.

15.3 Who is detained in the UK?

While the majority of the policy described earlier focuses on the detention of asylum seekers, this is a more recent use of detention. In the first decade after the Immigration Act 1971 came into force, the power to detain, granted by that Act, was used mainly as a way of enforcing a refusal of leave to enter. For instance, a visitor or student who had been refused at the port might be detained overnight (see, for example, Weber and Gelsthorp 2000). Lengthy detention beyond this was rare.

From the mid-1980s, the number of asylum applications began to rise, and the Home Office was not able to process asylum applications quickly enough to prevent a backlog arising. A survey by the Joint Council for the Welfare of Immigrants revealed an increasing resort to detention as a matter of course to manage asylum applications (Ashford 1993). From a few hours to resolve some outstanding point, or to effect removal, immigration detention quite commonly extended to weeks or months. From the early 2000s until 2008, Home Office figures showed that although asylum seekers numbered less than a quarter of the people removed from the UK each year, they constituted nearly three-quarters of the people in immigration detention. Home Office figures for 2010 show that there were almost 26,000 instances of immigration detention (some people are detained more than once), with asylum detainees constituting half. Asylum detainees are those who have sought asylum at some stage.

Other immigration detainees include those who have served a criminal sentence and are to be deported, and people arrested for removal after overstaying their leave or perhaps working in breach of a condition.

Most of the eleven immigration removal centres are for men only. Three include facilities for women and children, and a twelfth 'family-friendly' centre is discussed at 15.8. The Home Office published a research paper in 2005 which examined in detail a sample of 'the illegally resident population in detention'. Three-quarters of those interviewed had worked illegally in the UK. Around half were in detention as a result of a raid on their workplace, for most it was their first immigration detention and they were previously not in contact with the Home Office (Home Office online report 20/05). The researchers attempted to distinguish between those illegally resident and asylum seekers whose claim had failed, but this distinction was difficult to make.

Other information about who is detained using immigration powers emerges from the case law discussed in this chapter.

15.4 Statutory basis of powers to detain

The power to detain for immigration purposes is found in Immigration Act 1971 Schs 2 and 3 and in Nationality, Immigration and Asylum Act 2002 s 62. No distinction is made in the statutes between asylum seekers and others. Powers to detain are possessed both by immigration officers and by officials in the Home Office, though as a matter of policy, the immigration officer's power to detain is normally exercised by a Chief

Immigration Officer. In broad terms, we can think of there being two stages at which detention may occur:

- before a decision is made to grant leave to enter; and
- in order to remove someone.

In terms of the legality of detention under domestic law, there are three main questions to consider:

- Does the power to detain exist in this situation? In other words, is the decision made 'pending examination' (before a decision to give leave is made), or pending removal or a decision to remove or deportation?
- Are there sufficient reasons to exercise the power?
- How long has this person been detained already?

Immigration officers have powers to detain which follow from their border control functions. They may detain pending examination, pending a decision whether to remove, and pending removal (Sch 2 of the 1971 Act). The original division of powers in the 1971 Act (see chapter 7) which made the Secretary of State responsible for 'in-country' decisions and immigration officers responsible for decisions on entry has, as we have seen, been largely eroded, and the Secretary of State now has similar powers (s 62(1) and (2)). The consequences for asylum seekers are shown in Table 15.1. These powers have been augmented in the UK Borders Act 2007 by a power for a designated immigration officer to detain someone for three hours at a port if they think that person may be arrestable under criminal law powers of arrest. This may have nothing to do with any immigration matter.

Until the 2002 Act, the Secretary of State only had power to detain pending deportation (Sch 3 to the 1971 Act) and this power remains.

Table 15.1 Circumstances in which an asylum seeker may be detained

AN ASYLUM SEEKER MAY BE DETAINED
1. ON ARRIVAL
(A) if claims asylum: Pending decision whether to grant leave to enter If either • Claim can be decided quickly, or • To verify identity, risk of absconding, etc.
(B) if does not claim asylum but enters clandestinely or on false docs: Pending a decision whether to remove
2. ON A LATER CLAIM As for 1A
3. ON REFUSAL OF CLAIM Pending a decision to remove
4. ON LOSING APPEAL Pending a decision to remove
5. ON DECISION TO REMOVE Pending removal
6. ON SETTING REMOVAL DIRECTIONS Pending removal

15.4.1 Detention on arrival – pending examination

This power to detain 'pending examination and pending a decision to give or refuse leave to enter' (1971 Act Sch 2 para 16.1) may be exercised by immigration officers or the Secretary of State whenever the decision or examination takes place. In other words, a person may be detained on arrival, perhaps as a clandestine entrant at a port, but they may also be detained at any stage before leave to enter is given (see Table 15.2). An asylum seeker may wait many months or even years for a decision on their application for leave to enter. The power to detain continues throughout this time. Although it is a discretion which must be exercised in accordance with proper criteria, the statutory power to detain persists. They may be required to report regularly to a police station or immigration reporting centre in the meantime, and for many asylum seekers the day of reporting is an anxious time, as it presents an opportunity for them to be detained.

The power to detain pending examination is mitigated by the Human Rights Act, even aside from the question of criteria for its exercise. The relevant specified reason for detention in Article 5 is 'to prevent his effecting an unauthorized entry', which, as we have seen, was widely construed by the ECtHR in *Saadi v UK*. In effect, the only constraint upheld by the Court upon the power to detain new arrivals in order to process an application was that implied by the principle against arbitrariness.

In the UK, the *Saadi* case was an unsuccessful challenge to a significant plank of government policy, the precursor of the present fast track. The new regime at the Oakington Reception Centre was for newly arriving asylum seekers in the UK who did not come within the existing criteria for detention because there was no risk attached to their being at liberty. The regime at Oakington was described in the Home Office Operational Enforcement Manual as 'relaxed'. It was a kind of 'soft' detention. However, residence there was compulsory (by an amendment to Immigration Act 1971 Sch 2 para 21), and there could be no doubt that in terms of Article 5, it amounted to a deprivation of liberty. The new Oakington criterion, as announced in Parliament, was that 'it appears that their application can be decided quickly' (HC written answers 16 March 2000 col 263). It was apparent from guidance issued on applications at Oakington that the expectation of dealing with a claim quickly arose chiefly from judging it ill-founded.

The detention was lawful in domestic law under Immigration Act 1971 Sch 2 para 16(1) 'pending examination'. Collins J in the High Court found it unlawful under Article 5, but the Court of Appeal and House of Lords disagreed (*R v SSHD ex p Saadi, Maged, Osman and Mohammed* [2002] 1 WLR 3131, HL).

Table 15.2 Powers to detain on arrival

Person arriving	May be detained in these circumstances
Entry clearance holder	Only if leave is cancelled or suspended and reasons exist*
Non-visa national visitor, requiring leave on entry	If further investigations needed in order to decide whether to grant leave to enter, and if reasons exist*
Claims asylum on entry	In order to decide whether to grant leave to enter and either claim can be decided quickly or reasons exist*
Clandestine entrant	Pending decision whether to remove, and reasons exist*
Arriving on false documents	Will depend on application made and nature of documents. May transfer into criminal remand if prosecution brought

* 'Reasons exist' refers to an assessed risk of absconding, the need to verify identity, etc.

The House of Lords resorted to the principle of sovereignty, which statute and human rights law are to a degree designed to mitigate, and quoted Oppenheim's International Law:

> The reception of aliens is a matter of discretion, and every state is by reason of its territorial supremacy competent to exclude aliens from the whole, or any part, of its territory. (para 31)

On this basis, the House of Lords reasoned similarly to the later decision of the ECtHR that: every entry is unauthorized until it is authorized. The entry of the appellants was therefore, quite simply, unauthorized because it had not been authorized. The House of Lords was influenced in its decision by considerations of proportionality. Lord Slynn, giving the only reasoned judgment, said that the methods of selection of Oakington cases ('are they suitable for speedy decision?'), the objective of speedy decision-making, and 'the way in which people are held for a short period... and in reasonable conditions' were not arbitrary or disproportionate and therefore did not fall outside the Article 5 requirements of lawfulness (para 45). He accepted the 'need for highly structured and tightly managed arrangements' in the interests of speed (para 46). The ECtHR took a similar view. The UNHCR Guidelines specifically exclude administrative convenience from being a legitimate basis for a detention decision, but the 'proportionality' of this detention for administrative convenience persuaded both the House of Lords and the ECtHR that it was lawful. It seems that somewhere between seven days at Oakington and 20 days in an airport, there is a boundary of what is lawful (*Conka v Belgium*).

Oakington closed in November 2010. However it established that the government was entitled to have a fast track policy, and was the forerunner of the fast-track procedures, discussed in chapter 12. In the fast-track system, unlike Oakington, detention is maintained throughout the decision-making process.

15.5 Detention pending removal or deportation

In the 1971 Act, as originally enacted, the power to detain pending removal was a power to detain someone 'in respect of whom directions may be given' (Sch 2 para 16(2)). In other words, someone who had already been deemed subject to removal, and before the Immigration and Asylum Act 1999 this meant someone upon whom notice had been served that they were deemed an illegal entrant. The 1999 Act, as well as widening the grounds for removal (see chapter 17), also amended para 16(2) to permit detention where there were 'reasonable grounds to suspect' that a person might be subject to removal. This means that, even where the removal decision has not been taken, for instance because the claim is not decided, or it is not clear to which country the claimant may be removed, they may still be detained. The discretion must still be exercised in accordance with the criteria discussed in 15.7.

One of the most pressing questions concerning the jurisdiction to detain pending removal is whether detention is lawful when there are obstacles in the way of removal. 1971 Act Sch 2 para 16 permits detention when there are reasonable grounds for suspecting that a person may be removed. However, what if the person may be removable at some point, but at present is not?

It is a breach of the Refugee Convention (Article 33) to remove an asylum seeker from the UK until their claim has been determined. This is confirmed in Nationality, Immigration and Asylum Act 2002 s 77, which prevents removal while an asylum claim is pending. As we have seen in chapter 12, an exception is made when an asylum seeker can be returned to a third country which is deemed safe. Where an asylum seeker is detained before their claim is finally determined, it could be argued that, as the removal cannot be implemented, detention on this basis is unlawful. However, the 2002 Act makes it clear that it is only the removal itself which cannot happen while the claim is pending. Removal directions can be issued, and other preparatory steps taken (s 77). This means that, despite UNHCR guidance to the contrary, a person may be detained for the entire duration of determination of the asylum claim, as is the case in the fast track, providing the common law and policy constraints are not breached, and providing either determination of the claim or removal is, in fact, pending.

In a Privy Council case, *Tan Te Lam and others v Superintendent of Tai A Chau Detention Centre and others* [1996] 4 All ER 256, the applicants were among those who fled from Vietnam to Hong Kong in the late 1970s, the 1980s, and early 1990s. They were of Chinese ethnic origin, and under the agreed repatriation arrangements it was the policy of the Vietnam government not to accept repatriation of non-Vietnam nationals. Therefore, although they were detained pending removal under the Immigration Ordinance of Hong Kong, as non-Vietnamese nationals they would not be removable. The Privy Council said there was no jurisdiction to detain 'pending removal' people whom there was no power to remove.

In *R (on the application of Sino) v SSHD* [2011] EWHC 2249 (Admin) the Algerian claimant served a criminal sentence and then was detained under immigration powers in 2006. He had been in immigration detention for 4 years and 11 months by the time his case came before the High Court. His detention was found to be unlawful from the beginning by John Howell QC as there were applications by UKBA for travel documents dating back to 2003 which had never been responded to by the Algerian authorities. When he was first detained there was no realistic prospect of deportation being achieved. Therefore the statutory purpose was not being served even at the very beginning of his long immigration detention.

Now, where an automatic deportation order has been made under s 32(5) UK Borders Act there is a duty to detain pending removal unless the Secretary of State thinks it is inappropriate (s 36(2)).

The majority of challenges to detention in the UK are to the length of detention pending removal. The UK is one of the few Western democracies which do not place a statutory limit on the length of time that at least certain categories of people may be detained for immigration reasons. Case law on the length of detention is discussed in 15.9.

15.6 Detention after a criminal sentence has been served

Continued detention after a criminal sentence has been served is authorized either when the criminal court which passed the sentence of imprisonment itself recommended deportation (Immigration Act 1971 Sch 3 para 2.1), or when the Secretary of State has made and served a decision to deport, which might or might not follow a recommendation of the Court (para 2.2). And now there is a more far-reaching power to detain 'while the Secretary of State considers' whether the automatic deportation provisions apply (s 36 UK Borders Act 2007). The effect of para 2.1 and s 36 is that a person may remain in detention at the end of their criminal sentence, but before the Secretary of State has decided whether to deport them. Such a person is in a kind of limbo between criminal and immigration powers. In *R (on the application of Sedrati,*

Buitrago-Lopez and Anaghatu) v SSHD [2001] EWHC Admin 418, Moses J granted a declaration to confirm an agreement reached between the parties that Sch 3 para 2 did not create a presumption in favour of detention upon completion of a sentence of imprisonment. The Supreme Court in *Lumba and Mighty* held that the correct interpretation of *Sedrati* was that it confirmed the statutory discretion to detain.

The effect of *Sedrati* is that the Secretary of State must actively decide in each case whether the prospective deportee should be detained, as demonstrated in *R (on the application of Vovk and Datta) v SSHD* [2006] EWHC 3386 (Admin). Mr Vovk was sentenced to 28 days in prison for using a false identity to gain employment. After his release date, he was detained for a further six weeks before being given notice of deportation which authorized his detention for that purpose. Mr Datta received an eight-month prison sentence for using a false passport. He was detained past his release date and later served with a notice authorizing his detention pending deportation. The High Court held that, until the decision had been made and notified to the two claimants, their detention was unlawful.

In *Vovk and Datta*, the Secretary of State argued that the claimants knew they were recommended for deportation, so it must have been obvious to them why they were not released (cf. *Dougoz*). There was jurisdiction, or power, to detain. However, the Secretary of State had acted unlawfully in his exercise of that power by not taking a decision and informing Vovk and Datta of it, and had breached Article 5 by not operating the presumption of liberty.

In s 36 of the UK Borders Act, the Secretary of State acquired the power that he seemed to aspire to in *Vovk and Datta*. Additionally, s 34 provides that a deportation order is made 'at a time chosen by the Secretary of State'. The JCHR pointed out the scope that this gives for detention in breach of Article 5. There is no requirement for the decision to be made even within a reasonable period, let alone a specified one. The first reported challenge to detention under that power was in *R (on the application of Hussein) v SSHD* [2009] EWHC 2492. The judge in the Administrative Court held that such detention did not breach Article 5. It was still detention with a view to deportation, even though the decision to deport had not yet been taken. The 2007 Act power is without regard to whether the criminal court has recommended deportation. It applies to anyone who has served a term of imprisonment (s 36(1)).

Before the 2007 Act was passed, as mentioned in chapter 2, a large number of foreign national prisoners were detained, under a blanket policy which was a response to press agitation. The Supreme Court held that this was unlawful.

Key Case

***Mighty & Lumba v SSHD* [2011] UKSC 12**

Mr Mighty was at liberty when he was served with a decision to deport him and then detained. Mr Lumba was serving a custodial sentence when the Secretary of State gave him notice that he was to be deported. The day before he was due to be released at the end of his criminal sentence he was detained under Sch 3 of the Immigration Act, pending deportation. In response to press criticism, the Home Office had in practice begun routinely detaining foreign national prisoners after the end of their sentence:

> Between April 2006 and 9 September 2008 the Secretary of State's published policy on detention of FNPs under her immigration powers was that there was a 'presumption' in favour of release ... In fact, during this period the Secretary of State applied a

> quite different unpublished policy which was described as a 'near blanket ban' by the Secretary of State... to the Prime Minister. (para 5)

This was not disclosed as a policy until September 2008.

On the evidence of internal Home Office correspondence the Supreme Court endorsed the conclusion of the Court of Appeal that this was a blanket policy admitting of almost no exceptions. This was in conflict with the basic rule of public law prohibiting rigid policies. The policy was also unlawful because it was secret, and in conflict with the published one. This breached the requirements of the rule of law for transparency.

Mr Lumba and Mr Mighty also challenged the policy on the basis that it entailed a presumption in favour of detention, contrary to common law principles and para 2 of Sch 3 to the 1971 Act as interpreted in *Sedrati*. The Supreme Court held that a policy could entail that it was normal practice to detain, provided that each detention was justified with reasons that related closely to the statutory purpose of effecting deportation. The concept of a presumption was not applicable, as a presumption applies to a burden of proof in judicial proceedings, not an administrative decision.

Although the policy was unlawful, the minority in the Supreme Court held that the detentions were not unlawful because there was a statutory power to detain, and if it had been correctly exercised then, 'detention of the appellants would have been inevitable in the light of the risk of absconding and re-offending that they both posed' (para 60). The majority in the Supreme Court held that the detention was nevertheless unlawful. The tort of false imprisonment required only that there was a detention without lawful authority. As with any trespass, no damage need to be shown for the tort to be committed. The fact that they would have been detained if the discretion had been exercised lawfully led the majority to conclude that they should only receive nominal damages, though a minority thought that a small award between £500 and £1,000 would have been appropriate.

In *R (on application of Hindawi & Headley) v SSHD* [2006] UKHL 54, the House of Lords, overturning the Court of Appeal, unanimously found that the right of prisoners who were subject to a deportation order to have their case referred to the Parole Board came within the ambit of Article 5. Denying referral to the Parole Board on grounds of their nationality (as prisoners subject to deportation, which British national prisoners were not) was discrimination contrary to Article 14. It was objectively unjustifiable, as individual decisions about prisoner release were for the body experienced in this task, and were not (interestingly) 'political' decisions to be made by a government minister.

15.7 Exercise of the discretion

The BID Submission to the UN Working Group on Arbitrary Detention argued for statutory criteria for detention. These would be subject to parliamentary debate and thus democratic control and would be more readily enforceable. However, the position remains that where the statutory power to detain exists, it is still a discretion, and the criteria for its exercise are contained mainly in policy and operational guidance. Additionally, the Detention Centre Rules govern a number of matters in the conduct of detention. The House of Lords' judgment in *Saadi* accepted that: 'the Home Office is entitled to adopt a policy in relation to procedures to be followed, a policy which may be changed from time to time as long as it does not conflict with relevant principles of law' ([2002] UKHL 41 para 11). Their Lordships did not elaborate on what these relevant principles are, but the principle against arbitrariness is undoubtedly one, and for the elaboration of this, reference should be made back to the human rights standards set out in 15.2. Helen O'Nions argues that 'what is required is not simply an assessment of legality but . . . should be defined as a broader test of substantive arbitrariness to include decisions which are unreasonable, unjust, delayed and unpredictable'.

As the government is entitled to adopt a policy to deal with asylum claims, the existence of a criterion referring solely to asylum seekers is not unlawful. The application of a more punitive criterion to asylum seekers is of much more doubtful legality (see Article 31 Refugee Convention and Hathaway's view, earlier) but the House of Lords' and ECtHR judgments in *Saadi* do not regard the Oakington criteria as punitive. Wilsher's conclusion is that the Refugee Convention has failed to protect refugees from arbitrary detention (2012:138).

Guidance to immigration officers on detention decisions may be found in UKBA's Enforcement Instructions and Guidance, chapter 55. Officers are advised:

> In order to be lawful, immigration detention must be for one of the statutory purposes for which the power is given and must accord with the limitations implied by domestic and ECHR case law.

The heart of the instructions is a list of factors to take into account in making a detention decision (55.3.1). Much depends on the immigration officer's perception of the width of their discretion. Weber and Gelsthorpe found that 38 per cent of officers thought they did not have a wide discretion, whereas 28 per cent thought that they did. As the researchers comment, within an organization decision-making rapidly becomes routinized so that decision-makers easily lose sight of the amount of discretion they actually (or theoretically) hold. Local practices develop, and this may account in part for the very different detention figures between different ports of entry. For instance, 32 per cent of all arrivals were detained overnight at Manchester's Terminal 2 as compared with 1.5 per cent at London Heathrow's Terminal 1 (Weber and Gelsthorpe 2000). This disparity was noted by Macdonald as grounds for concern about the arbitrariness of the UK's detention practice (2001:790).

The policy and guidance found in the Enforcement Instructions do not represent the total policy in relation to detention. Where statements and usual practices are communicated to practitioners they are entitled to rely upon these (*Nadarajah & Amirthanathan v SSHD* [2003] EWCA Civ 1768).

15.7.1 Disclosure of guidance

The disclosure of guidance upon which a detention decision is based is required by the principle that a constraint on liberty must be prescribed by law according to Article 5 ECHR (see *Nadarajah and Amirthanathan* in which the operation of unpublished policy rendered the detentions in breach of Article 5). Following *Lumba and Mighty,* detention pursuant to an undisclosed policy which is inconsistent with a published policy is unlawful in domestic law too, because it contravenes basic principles of public law.

15.7.2 Content of guidance

The three main approved policy reasons for detention, as set out in the 1998 White Paper, *Fairer, Faster and Firmer – A Modern Approach to Immigration and Asylum* (Cm 4018), together with the reason that the application may be decided quickly using the fast-track procedures, are still incorporated in current guidance as the policy foundation for detention decisions (EIG 55.1.1). These crystallize out as six approved reasons (EIG 55.6.3):

(a) The person is likely to abscond if given temporary admission or release
(b) There is currently insufficient reliable information to decide on whether to grant temporary admission or release
(c) Removal from the United Kingdom is imminent
(d) The person needs to be detained whilst alternative arrangements are made for their care
(e) Release is not considered conducive to the public good
(f) The application may be decided quickly using the fast track procedures.

In order to be lawful, detention must not only be based on one of the statutory powers and accord with the limitations set by human rights law, but must also be for one of these reasons. The decision to detain must also be taken in accordance with the principles which are set out in EIG 55.3:

1. There is a presumption in favour of temporary admission or temporary release.
2. There must be strong grounds for believing that a person will not comply with conditions of temporary admission or temporary release for detention to be justified.
3. All reasonable alternatives to detention must be considered before detention is authorised.
4. Each case must be considered on its individual merits, including consideration of the duty to have regard to the need to safeguard and promote the welfare of any children involved.

These principles give priority to the presumption of liberty. Particular factors which must be taken into account are also set out as follows:

- What is the likelihood of the person being removed and, if so, after what timescale?
- Is there any evidence of previous absconding from detention?
- Is there any evidence of previous failure to comply with conditions of temporary admission or bail?
- Has the subject taken part in a 'determined attempt' to breach the immigration laws (examples given here include attempted or actual clandestine entry)?
- Is there a history of complying with requirements of immigration control (e.g. by applying for a visa, further leave etc)?
- What are the person's ties with the UK? Are there close relatives (including dependants) here? Does anyone rely on the person for support? Does the person have a settled address or employment?
- What are the individual's expectations about the outcome of the case? Are there factors such as an outstanding appeal, an application for judicial review or representations which afford incentives to keep in touch?
- Is there a risk of offending or harm to the public (this requires consideration of the likelihood of harm **and** the seriousness of the harm if the person does offend)?

Ultimately, these enquiries must, if the person is to be detained, crystallize into one or more of the six listed reasons for detention which are ticked on a standard form (EIG 55.6.3). These reasons, and 14 listed factors which are used to determine whether the reason exists, were referred to in *Amirthanathan and Nadarajah* as 'an important part of the published policy' (para 55).

The policy also lists those who are unsuitable for immigration detention:

- the elderly, particularly where supervision is required;
- pregnant women, unless there is the clear prospect of early removal and medical advice suggests that there is no question of the baby arriving before this;
- people with serious disabilities;
- people with serious medical conditions or mentally ill;
- unaccompanied children and young people under 18;
- persons identified by the Competent Authorities as victims of trafficking;
- where there is independent evidence that they have been tortured.

Those with a violent or serious criminal background are among the very few immigration detainees who may or should be held in prison. Others include 'where there is specific (verified) information that a person is a member of a terrorist group or has been engaged in terrorist activities' (EIG 55.10.1). The fact that these listed factors and reasons exist does not mean that the detention decision can be reduced to a box-ticking exercise. The principles stated earlier are the basis of lawfulness, and without adherence to these principles oppressive practice may occur.

15.7.3 Challenging non-compliance with guidance

Although guidance does not have statutory force, failure to have regard to established guidelines gives grounds for challenge in administrative law (*R v SSHD ex p Khan* [1985] 1 All ER 40, and see chapter 8). Non-compliance with the detention criteria has been held to be a reason to grant a declaration that continued refusal of bail was unlawful.

Misuse of the power to detain was amply demonstrated in *Karas and Miladinovic v SSHD* [2006] EWHC 747 (Admin).

Key Case

***Karas and Miladinovic v SSHD* [2006] EWHC 747 (Admin)**

Mr Karas had lost his asylum claim, but made a request to have a fresh claim considered in 2001. Time passed. He married Ms Miladinovic. His solicitors wrote making representations about his family life and asking for her to be added to his asylum claim. There was no response. He continued to report weekly to the Croydon immigration office as he was required to do. Ms Miladinovic became pregnant. On 10 October 2004, he reported as usual. Unbeknown to him or them, on that day removal directions had been faxed to Heathrow for a flight at 7.40 a.m. on 12 October. At 8.30 p.m. on 11 October, the couple were detained by immigration officers at their home and told that they were to be removed the next morning. It turned out that Mr Karas' claim had been refused by fax sent to his solicitor shortly before the close of business on 11 October, four hours before the couple were detained.

Munby J. held that 'detention in the circumstances of this case was...oppressive, unreasonable and unnecessary' (para 65). It was done as it was in order to prevent the claimants from obtaining legal advice or being able to apply to a judge (para 81). The guiding principles of policy require detention to be used as a last resort. This detention was used in the opposite way – as a pre-emptive strike.

This case gives a flavour of what is meant by arbitrariness. There was no guiding rationale for the detention apart from to catch the claimants unawares and get them on the plane. It also gives an insight into practices which often do not reach the law reports. Munby J endorses the words of Collins J in a 'strikingly similar' case, *R (on the application of Collaku) v Secretary of State for the Home Department* [2005] EWHC 2855 (Admin):

> The Home Office practice involving delay in deciding a claim but then of arresting and serving the refusal at one and the same time with a view to removal within a day or two, often at weekends and frequently early in the morning, is one that is to be deplored. This court has deplored it on many occasions. It leads to unnecessary applications to the duty judge. It has the effect of preventing those who are to be removed from seeking proper legal advice to which they may be entitled and, even if the Home Office takes the view that there is no conceivable merit to be both found in any possible challenge, this is not the way to go about it. A reasonable time must be provided to enable representations to be made, if any are to be made, certainly to enable advice to be sought if the person to be removed wishes to obtain it. Quite apart from anything else, the approach to the duty judge will almost inevitably result in an order preventing the removal until the matter can be sorted out, either the following day or the next working day, when an application can be put before the Administrative Court. The result is that the flight ticket has to be given up – it is often more than one ticket because frequently an official will accompany the person to be removed – so public money is inevitably wasted. (para 14)

People who have been tortured are clearly among those who should not be detained. The issues are generally not whether that is a correct principle, but rather whether there is evidence which can be gathered within the time specified and what standard of proof is in practice employed. The current EIG says that where there is 'independent evidence' that a person has been tortured, they are 'normally considered suitable for detention in only very exceptional circumstances, whether in dedicated Immigration detention accommodation or elsewhere'. What was meant in this situation by independent evidence of torture was considered in *R (on the application of D and K) v SSHD* [2006] EWHC 980 (Admin).

Key Case

***R (on the application of D and K) v SSHD* [2006] EWHC 980 (Admin)**

D and K both sought asylum on arrival in the UK and were detained in Oakington. The Detention Centre Rules contained two provisions for medical examination on arrival. First, all detainees should be medically screened including an assessment for risks of self-harm within two hours of their arrival. Second, all detainees must have a physical and mental examination by a medical practitioner within 24 hours of arrival (rule 34). The Secretary of State initially argued that this did not constitute independent evidence of torture, but Davis J held that the emphasis placed upon the need for medical examination must mean that it was an essential part of the assessment as to whether a person was suitable to remain in fast-track detention. In that case, it must be capable of constituting independent evidence of torture.

This is an important outcome for detainees, who are not in a position to substantiate their claim of having been tortured in any other way at such an early stage after arrival, and it underscores the importance of the provision of medical services in detention centres. Despite this the Court of Appeal held in the same case that fast-track detention was not unlawful (*HK Turkey v SSHD* [2007] EWCA Civ 1357).

In 2000, the evidence of Amnesty International and the Medical Foundation was that those who have suffered torture were still being detained (Dell and Salinsky 2000), and it appears that up to the present this is still the case. In *R (on the application of RT) v SSHD* [2011] EWHC 1792 (Admin) the Court held that there was a breach of rule 34 where the claimant had said that she had been tortured, but had not been offered a medical examination. Scars she bore were later found to be consistent with the torture she described. Kenneth Parker J held that her detention was unlawful following *Lumba and Mighty* and *Kambadzi* as the breach of the rules in not examining her meant that the authority to detain her was assumed improperly. As a victim of torture she should not have been detained.

The claimant in *R (on the application of MT) v SSHD, GSL UK Ltd, Nestor Health Care Services plc* [2008] EWHC 1788 (Admin) was a national of the Democratic Republic of Congo (DRC). She arrived in the UK on 16 November 2005 and claimed asylum. Her asylum claim was based in part on rape and ill-treatment that she had suffered in detention shortly before her arrival in the UK. At the asylum-screening interview, she was not asked about this and did not disclose it. She was detained from the day after her arrival until 23 November under the fast-track procedure. Just under ten months later, she was given refugee status.

The judge in the Administrative Court held that a public authority had a duty to inform itself of all matters relevant to an exercise of discretion, but the extent to which it should make proactive inquiries depended on the context. Neither the statute authorizing detention nor policy required inquiries to be made on arrival as to whether the claimant had been tortured. Policy was rather that inquiries should not be made of a new arrival. Procedural fairness also did not require the Secretary of State to inquire about torture as an allegation of torture would not necessarily prevent someone from being detained in the fast track (as in *D and K*).

There is also evidence that other groups who should very rarely be detained, according to the instructions, are detained in circumstances which are not justified as being exceptional. These detainees include pregnant women and the mentally ill. For instance in *R (on the application of T) v SSHD* [2010] EWHC 668 (Admin) the claimant had made a number of suicide attempts, his criminal offences were not at the more serious end of the scale, and there were no exceptional circumstances justifying his detention. (See, for the effect of such detention on mothers and babies, 'A Crying Shame: Pregnant Asylum-seekers and their Babies in Detention' (2002) and, for the impact on mental health, 'A Second Exile: The Mental Health Implications of Detention of Asylum Seekers in the United Kingdom' (1996) and 'Fit to be Detained? Challenging the Detention of Asylum Seekers and Migrants with Health Needs' (2005).)

Challenges to detention on the basis, for instance, that the person has been tortured or is pregnant are made on the basis that this person should not be detained at all. If someone is not given a medical examination promptly, or their detention is not reviewed when it should be according to the Detention Centre Rules, clearly it is possible that they will be detained or continue to be detained when they would otherwise have been released. Thus, a breach of Detention Centre Rules may affect the fact of detention as well as its conditions. However, in *MT v SSHD, GSL UK Ltd, Nestor Health Care Services plc*, although the Court held that Nestor Health Care Services breached the rules in not giving the claimant a medical examination within 24 hours of arrival; the judge said that this breach did not cause the claimant's continuing detention because the outcome of the examination was speculative and would not necessarily have resulted in her release. The breach of rules thus did not make the continued detention unlawful. By way of contrast, the Administrative Court in *R (on the application of Beecroft) v SSHD* [2008] EWHC 364 (Admin), held that failure to examine the claimant medically on her arrival in detention was a breach of rules 34 and 35 of the Detention Centre Rules which rendered her detention unlawful according to Article 5 ECHR.

Key Case

***R (on the application of Beecroft) v SSHD* [2008] EWHC 364 (Admin)**

The claimant had been transferred to Yarl's Wood Immigration Removal Centre a week after her arrival in the UK. There, she was asked questions as part of a medical questionnaire, though not medically examined. She was recorded as having stated that she had been tortured. Two days later, she was interviewed at length, and stated that she had recently been tortured by gendarmes in Cameroon, and described the treatment to which she had been subjected. The following day, a nurse recorded on the claimant's medical records: 'Victim of torture form signed. Advise will book for a doctor tomorrow as she has not been seen since arriving.'

Two days later, her asylum claim was refused. The decision did not mention any consideration of medical records or of referring her to the Medical Foundation. The Court held that failure to refer her to the Medical Foundation was a breach of the Secretary of State's declared policy.

Despite this, the Court held that the breaches of policy did not invalidate the asylum decision.

That a breach of the Detention Centre Rules which goes to the basis of the detention renders the detention unlawful is now established in *Kambadzi v SSHD* [2011] UKSC 23.

Key Case

***Kambadzi v SSHD* [2011] UKSC 23.**

The claimant's detention had not been reviewed at the intervals required by the Detention Centre Rules. By the date of the High Court hearing, the claimant's detention should have been subject to 22 monthly reviews but in fact had had only ten. Of these, four were not carried out by an officer of the right level of seniority, and two were vitiated by errors of fact. The Supreme Court held that the reviews required by the policy were the authority on which the continued legality of the detention rested. Policy could be departed from if good reason were shown, but there was no such reason in this case. Following *Lumba,* there was a public law duty to give effect to the policy on reviews, and when this duty was breached, the detention became unlawful. Unless the authority to detain was renewed, the detention became unlawful. The Court accepted that if the reviews had been properly conducted, continued detention would have been warranted. Thus, Mr Kambadzi was not entitled to significant damages.

15.8 Detention of families

Prior to 2001, established policy in relation to the detention of families was that it should generally be avoided, and should, if at all, take place 'only to be as close as possible to removal so as to ensure that it lasted no longer than a few days' (Cm 4018 para 12.5). In October 2001, the Home Office announced an increase of family detention provision, and the detention criteria for families were brought more closely into line with the criteria for detention of people without children, although the Home Office also stressed that this would only be where it was considered necessary, particularly in view of the possible breach of Article 8 (see Cole 2003).

The reason for the policy change was obscure, except that the Home Office said that: 'families can be detained on the same footing as all other persons liable to detention' (earlier EIG 55.9.4). Family detention places in 2005 reached 456.

In December 2003, the government began to publish statistics on children in detention in the quarterly figures. The figures showed that at any one time there were scores of children in detention, and in 2009 over 1,000 children were detained. Inevitably, figures only show those children who are detained with their families, as those whose age was disputed would be shown as adults. Although the policy was that children should only be detained as a last resort, in a study done by BID and the Children's Society, 61 per cent of families were eventually released, their detention having served no purpose (Campbell et al 2011). Families were detained when there was little risk of their absconding. Families cited reasons to maintain contact with the Home Office: their children's welfare, access to health care, the need to avoid destitution, the desire to preserve their dignity, and pursuit of legal status. Often their removal was not imminent, and there were barriers to their removal – as with adults in fact. There was a significant adverse impact on the health of children, and the practice of detaining families was heavily criticized. The practice has begun to result in large compensation payments. In January 2010, the Home Office paid £100,000 in damages to a family that had been unlawfully detained for 42 days ('Family Wins £100,000 for Detention Ordeal' *The Guardian* 30 January 2010), and in January 2012 the Ay family settled out of court for a possibly higher figure.

The detention of children is now subject to the government's duty under s 55 Borders Citizenship and Immigration Act 2009, to make arrangements to ensure that in making any immigration decision affecting them the best interests of the child are taken into account. Guidance on implementing this section repeats that families must be encouraged to leave voluntarily and detention should be used only 'as a last resort and for the shortest possible time' ('Every Child Matters: Change for Children' November 2009).

The detention of children is clearly an interference with private and/or family life. In *R (on the application of Konan) v SSHD* [2004] EWHC 22 Admin, the six-month detention of a mother and her two-year-old daughter was unlawful. The detention was in breach of policy and of common law rules as the removal could not be effected because judicial review of it was pending. Detention was also a prima facie breach of Article 8. The Court held that if and to the extent that proportionality applied, the Secretary of State's policy should be taken as representing his view of what is proportionate.

In *S, C and D (by their litigation friend S) v SSHD* [2007] EWHC 1654 (Admin), baby D, who had his first birthday during his four-month detention, developed rickets and anaemia as a consequence of denial of medical and nutritional care during that time. The damage to his health was held to be a breach of his right to respect for private life, namely his physical integrity.

In *Mayeka and Mitunga v Belgium* (2008) 46 EHRR 23, the ECtHR found violations of Articles 3, 5.1, 5.4, and 8 in the detention of a five-year-old girl in adult detention facilities without the company of any adult known to her. Travelling with a relative she was due to join her mother who had been granted asylum in Canada. During the child's two months of detention, a legal tangle surrounding the child in Belgium even entailed her being deported, unaccompanied, back to the Democratic Republic of Congo before she was finally able to join her mother. The violations were of the mother's Articles 3 and

8 rights as well as the child's, since not knowing what was happening to her child and being unable to influence the course of events from Canada, despite daily telephone calls, was acutely distressing.

In May 2010, the new Coalition government announced that the detention of children for immigration purposes would be ended. However, detention of children did in practice continue. In December 2010 the government made a further announcement that child detention would end by May 2011. Arguably, the case of *Suppiah v SSHD* [2011] EWHC 2 (Admin) brought the matter to a head. The two families were detained as is often the case by immigration officers arriving unexpectedly at their home in the early hours of the morning. The families, including a two-year-old, were searched. The children quickly became sick in detention. They were detained on 10 February 2010 for removal on 13 February. The removals were cancelled, but the families were not released until 22 February. There was an enormous volume of evidence before the Court that 'detention is inherently and seriously harmful to the health and development of children' (para 106). The Court's judgment refers to the reports of the Children's Commissioner and the Chief Inspector of Prisons, both highly critical of the practice of detaining children, and to the report of the House of Commons Home Affairs Select Committee, which recommended a significant reduction in child detention. The Court quoted this passage from the HASC:

> We do not understand why, if detention is the final step in the asylum process, and there is no evidence of families systematically 'disappearing or absconding', families are detained pending judicial reviews and other legal appeals. The detention of children for indeterminate periods of time (possibly for 6–8 weeks), pending legal appeals must be avoided.

The criticisms and recommendations of the Chief Inspector of UKBA were also quoted in full.

The judge concluded that the families were detained initially for the purpose of removal, but he was not satisfied that they had been given any meaningful option of voluntary return, or that there was any significant risk of their absconding. UKBA had failed to have regard to their duty under s 55 of the Borders Citizenship and Immigration Act 2009, and this made the detention of the families unlawful.

The body of evidence and the unequivocal findings of the Court attracted press attention when the judgment was given in January 2011. Some commentators considered that this case was significant in actually bringing about a practical change of policy in relation to detention of children. In August 2011 the institution of a new process was completed with the opening of The Cedars, a 'last resort' detention facility for families.

The new process entails the following stages:

- **assisted return** including family conferences to discuss welfare and medical concerns and the availability of tailored assisted voluntary return packages to help families resettle;
- **required returns** for families who fail to take up assistance packages, allowing them to remain in the community, but giving two weeks' notice to board their flight, allowing self check-in without enforcement action; and
- **ensured return**, as a last resort.

There is an independent family returns panel to advise UKBA to ensure the welfare of the child is taken into account. Options include a limited notice removal, open accommodation, and the last resort 'family friendly, pre-departure accommodation'. The Cedars, the pre-departure accommodation for ensured returns, opened in West Sussex in August 2011. Its security is run by G4S, and there is a high perimeter fence, and 24-hour guards, escorting detainees to and from visitors' lounge. The Cedars is locked and detainees are searched on arrival. At the same time, The Cedars has play areas for small children, a library for different age groups, access to gardens, and a pets' corner and basketball court with equipment for ball games.

Numbers of children in detention have dropped since May 2010, but children are still detained. In the third quarter of 2011, 30 children have been detained, most in either The Cedars or Tinsley House.

The new policy on detention of children purports to respect the UNHCR Guidelines and the UN Working Group on Arbitrary Detention, which both state that children should not be detained.

The UN Convention on the Rights of the Child Article 22 says:

> States Parties shall take appropriate measures to ensure that a child who is seeking refugee status or who is considered a refugee in accordance with applicable international or domestic law procedures shall, whether unaccompanied or accompanied by his or her parents or by any other person, receive appropriate protection and humanitarian assistance in the enjoyment of applicable rights set forth in the present Convention and in other international human rights or humanitarian instrument to which the said States are Parties.

The UK has lifted its reservation to the Convention in relation to immigration and asylum matters, in tandem with introducing the duty under s 55 of the Borders Citizenship and Immigration Act 2009 to make arrangements to ensure that the best interests of the child are taken into account.

15.8.1 Age disputes and unaccompanied children

According to policy, an unaccompanied person under 18 is not generally detained or subject to fast-track procedures. If their asylum claim is refused, they may only be removed from the UK if adequate care and reception arrangements are in place in their country of return. Their support arrangements in the UK are different. The care of a person under 18 is the responsibility of a local authority under the Children Act 1989. Therefore, procedures for resolving whether someone is over 18 are crucial.

However, age assessment must be conducted with care, as this process itself can compound the suffering of a traumatized young person (*R (on the application of T) v London Borough of Enfield* [2004] EWHC 2297 (Admin)). It should be borne in mind that the fact of dispute does not necessarily reflect on the asylum seeker's good faith, as the measuring, recording, and concept of age may be treated differently in their country of origin from the UK. It is the UK's measure which is determinative.

Home Office guidance on the measurement of age and conduct of age disputes may be summarized as:

- A claimant *must* be treated as an adult only if their physical appearance or demeanour *very strongly* suggests that they are significantly older than 18.
- In all other cases an applicant who claims to be under 18 should be given the benefit of the doubt until an age assessment has been carried out.
- At this point the guidance applies on fulfilling the duty in s 55 Borders Citizenship and Immigration Act 2009 to ensure that arrangements are made to safeguard and promote the welfare of the child.
- 'Merton compliant' Social Services age assessments should be regarded as authoritative.

- Evidence submitted by the applicant *must* be considered and due weight given to it.
- Unaccompanied minors must only be detained in very exceptional circumstances and then only overnight, with appropriate care, whilst alternative arrangements for their care and safety are made (EIG 55.9.3.1 and APG on Assessing Age).

'Merton compliant' local authority age assessment is that which follows the judgment in *R (on the application of B) v Merton LBC* [2003] 4 All ER 280, namely:

- A local authority must make its own decision and not simply adopt the stance of the Home Office.
- There must be adequate information to make this assessment.
- This will include asking the child about their education, family, activities, and history.
- The assessment cannot normally be made on the basis of physical appearance alone except in an 'obvious' case.

In *A v London Borough of Croydon and SSHD, WK v SSHD and Kent County Council* [2009] EWHC 939 (Admin), Collins J held that the report of the consultant paediatrician was relevant and should be taken into account in the age assessment. However, neither UKBA nor the local authority was bound by it. Age assessment was a holistic and inexact process. He considered that paediatricians had no greater skill in arriving at a reliable conclusion than other experienced professionals.

In *R (on the application of A) v London Borough of Croydon* and *R (on the application of M) v London Borough of Lambeth* [2009] UKSC 8, the Supreme Court held that the question of whether a person was a child was a question of fact to be decided, in case of dispute, by the Court on the balance of probabilities. It was not an exercise of judgement of the kind which could be challenged only for irrationality. The limits of this decision were tested in *R (on the application of PM) v SSHD* [2010] EWHC 2056 (Admin). In this case a dental assessment had estimated PM's age as 19. By the time of his asylum Tribunal hearing this had not led to a reassessment of his age by the local authority, who had initially concluded that he was a minor. The tribunal judge made a decision on PM's age in the course of his judgment on PM's credibility, and decided that PM was over 18 and had lied about his age for the purposes of getting leave to remain in the UK. The local authority, in the light of the Supreme Court case, thought that the judge's assessment of age was binding upon them. PM challenged this by judicial review. The Court held that the Tribunal did not have jurisdiction to decide PM's age outside the context of a finding for the purposes of the asylum claim. The local authority for its purposes was still required to form its own judgement. The cases of *A and M* had been about the Court's jurisdiction on appeal to decide a matter in dispute, and did not mean that judges had jurisdiction to determine age 'against all the world'. UKBA in its guidance 'Assessing Age' says that where a tribunal judge finds that an appellant is a child, the Agency will generally regard itself as bound by this.

15.9 Length of detention

As mentioned at the start of this chapter, one of the chief concerns about immigration detention in the UK, voiced by many including the UN Working Group on Arbitrary Detention, is that there is no fixed statutory limit on the length of time a person can be detained. In July 1997, a research report considering treatment of asylum seekers in 12 countries found that 'the UK detains more people, for longer periods, with less judicial supervision than any other country we considered'. The Independent Chief Inspector of UKBA in a report of a thematic inspection of how UKBA manages foreign national prisoners found that the average length of detention had increased from 143 days in February 2010 to 190 days in January 2011. Twenty-seven per cent of foreign national prisoners who were detained after their custodial sentence had been detained for longer than 12 months.

In earlier case law challenging the length of detention, it was considered that lengthy detention could undermine the jurisdiction to detain, so that if obstacles to removal persisted, the power to detain a person expired, and they must be released. However, in *R v SSHD ex p Khadir (Appellant)* [2005] UKHL 39, Lord Brown of Eaton-under-Heywood, giving the only reasoned judgment, found that the '*Hardial Singh* line of cases', which revolved around the length of detention, referred to the exercise of the power to detain and not to its existence. In other words, length of detention affects the exercise of the discretion to detain, which becomes unreasonable if it goes on too long. It does not affect the power to detain: '"pending" in paragraph 16 means no more than "until"' (para 32). The significance of this distinction will become apparent shortly.

It is still the case that, if the purpose for which detention is authorized ceases to apply, then the detention is no longer authorized. For instance in *R v Special Adjudicator and SSHD ex p B* [1998] INLR 315, the Secretary of State was initially in doubt as to the applicant's true identity, and this was one of the reasons for detention. However, after the applicant had provided convincing proof of this, his detention became unlawful.

There is an implied limitation of a reasonable time to achieve the purpose sought by the detention, as was held in *R v Governor of Durham Prison ex p Hardial Singh* [1983] Imm AR 198. This case remains the authority on this point, though Lord Dyson's judgment in *Lumba and Mighty* clarified a number of issues about how it is applied. In *Hardial Singh*, Woolf J said, 'if there is a situation where it is apparent to the Secretary of State that he is not going to be able to operate the machinery provided in the Act for removing persons who are intended to be deported within a reasonable period, it seems to me that it would be wrong for the Secretary of State to exercise his power of detention' (at 200). Woolf J directed the applicant's release, finding that 'the Home Office have not taken the action they should have taken and nor have they taken that action sufficiently promptly' (at 202). Mr Singh had been in detention for five months and had attempted to take his own life. The Court similarly intervened in the case of *Wafsi Suleman Mahmod* [1995] Imm AR 311, in which Laws J held that ten months was too long to try to persuade Germany to take back a man granted asylum in Germany who had been convicted of a criminal offence whilst on a visit to the UK. The Home Office activity during the ten months was described as 'nothing but fruitless negotiations'.

In *Tan Te Lam*, in which the applicants had been in detention for 44 months, Lord Browne-Wilkinson summarized the law as follows:

> First, the power can only be exercised during the period necessary, in all the circumstances of the particular case, to effect removal. Secondly, if it becomes clear that removal is not going to be possible within a reasonable time, further detention is not authorised. Thirdly, the person seeking to exercise the power of detention must take all reasonable steps within his power to ensure the removal within a reasonable time.

The House of Lords regarded *Tan Te Lam* as an exception in which length of detention *did* remove the jurisdiction to detain, 'because there was simply no possibility of the Vietnamese government accepting the applicants' repatriation' (para 33).

The Court of Appeal applied these principles in *R (on the application of I) v SSHD* [2002] EWCA Civ 888, and added that the length of time a person has already been in detention was relevant to whether detention should be continued, taking into account whether there was a reasonable prospect that deportation would be achieved within a reasonable period. Like the applicants in *Sedrati*, *Buitrago-Lopez*, and *Anaghatu*, Mr I was detained under 1971 Act Sch 3 para 2 after the end of his criminal sentence and pending deportation. However, in his case, removal was not practically possible as there were no flights from the UK to his home country of Afghanistan. The Home Office was engaged in activity which might still have resulted in his removal in that they were engaged in negotiations with countries neighbouring Afghanistan for the return of Afghani asylum seekers whose claims had failed. The *Hardial Singh* point, the second in Lord Browne-Wilkinson's formulation in *Tan Te Lam*, was the crucial one for Simon Brown LJ in the Court of Appeal. He held that the Home Office's 'hope' that negotiations with neighbouring countries would bear fruit was not sufficient, given the time that Mr I had already spent in detention. By the time the case came before the Court of Appeal, he had been in administrative detention (i.e., after the end of his criminal sentence) for 16 months. Dyson LJ thought that the time already spent in detention was enough to justify release.

Appellant A v SSHD [2007] EWCA Civ 804 followed *Khadir* in the formulation that there must be 'some prospect' of A being removed within a reasonable period in order for the power to detain to exist. The level at which this prospect may be doubted was set extremely high. After two years of lawful detention, A was detained for a further 19 months during which he could not be removed because no airlines were willing to take enforced removals to Somalia, and he was not willing to go. The parties were agreed that this degree of practical obstruction and length of time did not affect the existence of the power to detain but only its exercise. There was still 'some prospect' of A being removed. Appellant A was distinguished from *I* in that the danger to the public posed by A was greater than that posed by I, and this was a factor which weighed in the exercise of discretion to continue to detain him.

In *Lumba and Mighty* Lord Dyson dealt with two further issues that commonly arise in cases based on *Hardial Singh*: detention during appeals pursued by the detainee, and the detainee's lack of cooperation. *R (on the application of Rostami) v SSHD* [2009] EWHC 2094 (QB) was a remarkable example of the latter. The claimant was detained in October 2006. He said that his father had been killed as a member of the Kurdish Democratic Party and his mother and sisters ill-treated by government agents. He had been unsuccessful in his asylum claims and had made suicide attempts in detention and refused to cooperate with steps to obtain travel documents to enable his return to Iran. He was convicted under s 35 of the Asylum and Immigration (Treatment of Claimants, etc.) Act 2004 (see chapter 12) of failing to cooperate with redocumenting procedures to effect his return. He was given a conditional discharge for 12 months.

He maintained his refusal to cooperate with redocumentation, and remained in detention, with no clarity as to whether he was on criminal remand or detained pending removal. He pleaded guilty to a further s 35 charge and breach of the conditional discharge, and received a prison sentence of four months. He refused again and was prosecuted again. He pleaded not guilty, and was sentenced to eight months in prison and recommended for deportation. Finally, in August 2009, the Administrative Court held that his detention had become unlawful. The Secretary of State had been unable to show that there was a reasonable prospect of removing Mr Rostami. He might abscond, but he was no danger to the public. His only breach of the law was his failure to cooperate with arrangements for his return to Iran.

Lord Dyson in *Lumba and Mighty* held that there was no exclusionary rule which prevented time spent in detention pending appeals from counting as part of the whole time spent in detention when this was considered for *Hardial Singh* purposes. The detainee's lack of cooperation was also just one relevant factor to take into account in deciding whether detention had gone on too long. It would be of limited weight and not conclusive, and would not be relevant if it was not in fact the reason for the extended detention.

Commonly, there are more complex obstacles to achieving deportation, including the lack of a safe route of return or the non-cooperation of home state embassies. Detention Action (then the London Detainee Support Group) carried out research on long-term detention and found that people who were in immigration detention for more than a year were unlikely to be removed. Of those surveyed, 44 per cent were from countries which had well-documented barriers to removal. They quote a possibly extreme but not unique example found by HM Inspectorate of Prisons:

> An Algerian man who had been held for over three years, had been refused travel documents by the Algerian Embassy three times, even though his UKBA caseworker accepted that he had been complying. Although not disclosed to the detainee, his file noted that there had been a number of cases where removal had not been possible due to the 'intransigence' of the Algerian embassy. (LDSG 2010)

The use of assurances to enable a removal which would otherwise breach Article 3 was discussed in chapter 4. Another aspect of the use of assurances is the length of time that a person may spend in detention while they are negotiated. Reading the judgment in *Youssef v Home Office* gives a rare insight into such negotiations. The claimant was a leading member of Egyptian Islamic Jihad, which mounted high profile terrorist attacks. He claimed asylum and was excluded under Article 1F, but faced likely torture on return, in breach of Article 3. For comment on the political process see, e.g., *The Guardian* 16 November 2004.

The Secretary of State sought to show that there was a realistic prospect of obtaining such assurances, so as to justify Mr Youssef's continuing detention until 9 July 1999, when negotiations were accepted to have failed and Mr Youssef was released. Detention remained lawful while it was reasonable for the UK to be negotiating with the Egyptian government, but ceased to be so, following *Hardial Singh*, when there was no realistic prospect of his being removed.

In order for detention to be lawful pending removal, the proposed removal must not only be foreseeably feasible at some point, but also lawful. In *R (on the application of K v SSHD)* [2008] EWHC 1321 (Admin), the Court held that the detention of the claimant was unlawful as it was said to be for the purpose of removing him to Irbil. His asylum claim had been turned down on the basis of a possible internal relocation (see chapter 13). It had been accepted that he was at risk in Irbil, so detention for the purpose of removing him there was unlawful.

Detention can become arbitrary if it continues 'beyond the period for which the State can provide justification'. So said the UN Human Rights Committee in finding Australia to be in breach of Article 9.1 of the International Covenant on Civil and Political Rights (*A v Australia* (1997) 4 BHRC 210). The UK has not accepted the right of individual petition for breaches.

15.10 Alternative to detention – temporary admission

The practical meaning and importance of cases like *Khadir* cannot be understood without appreciating the important part played in present-day immigration control by the status of temporary admission.

Wherever there is a power to detain there is also power to grant temporary admission (Immigration Act 1971 Sch 2 para 21 and Nationality, Immigration and Asylum Act 2002 s 62(3)). People are temporarily admitted when their applications for entry or asylum claims have not been determined. Once a claim is determined and refused, the person who was seeking asylum may remain on temporary admission. They were initially liable to detention pending examination. They are now liable to detention pending either a decision to remove or removal. The vast majority of asylum seekers are at liberty in the UK on temporary admission.

Temporary admission is granted for a fixed period which is normally renewed. The person admitted must report back to the Home Office or immigration service at the expiry of the period. Many people on temporary admission are required to report regularly, often monthly, to the Home Office. At this point there is a risk of detention, and there is no right of appeal against a refusal to extend temporary admission, because in itself it is not a status awarded, it is more like being on licence while being theoretically subject to a prison sentence.

Temporary admission may be subject to residence or employment restrictions and requirements to report to the police or an immigration officer (1971 Act Sch 2 para 21(2)). Residence restrictions may include the requirement to reside in accommodation provided under Immigration and Asylum Act 1999 s 4 or Nationality, Immigration and Asylum Act 2002 s 26. A prohibition on employment is routinely imposed. The restrictions may be varied, and the power to detain continues throughout the period of temporary admission. If a person is re-detained, although a breach of conditions is not specifically required by the schedule, the lack of such reasons would give rise to a finding of arbitrariness (see Macdonald 2001:780), unless, as is common, it is to carry out removal.

Temporary admission is a curious kind of limbo status, and this is where its importance lies. The person on temporary admission has no right to appeal against their limbo status, and only very minimal welfare rights. These are largely dependent on the stage of their asylum claim, and a person whose claim has failed may be without welfare support of any kind. Some rights to health and social assistance depend upon the claimant being 'lawfully present', and the government has maintained that people on temporary admission are not 'lawfully present' for these purposes. For a time, there was a legal fiction that people temporarily admitted are not present at all, let alone lawfully. This was scotched in *Szoma v Secretary of State for the Department of Work and Pensions* [2005] UKHL 64, in which their Lordships held that the appellant was lawfully present. The Court of Appeal in *MS (Ivory Coast)* [2007] EWCA Civ 133 gave a useful account of the difference between having discretionary leave and being temporarily admitted, showing the importance of the differences and the disadvantages of temporary admission.

The extended use of temporary admission creates a group of people without rights. Many people are in an uncertain situation; typically, their asylum claim has failed, but for practical reasons they cannot be returned to their country of origin. Prior to 2002, many people in this position would have been granted exceptional leave to remain (ELR). This status could, after some years, allow reunion with family members, and eventually indefinite leave to remain. It allowed the person to work and claim benefits. Although by nature temporary and insecure, it could be extended and could eventually bring security. This is the background to the case of *Khadir.*

Key Case

Khadir v SSHD **[2005] UKHL 39**

Mr Khadir's asylum application had been refused but he could not be returned to the Kurdish Autonomous Area of Iraq as there were no direct flights, and any travel via Baghdad would not be safe. The British government had been in negotiation with Turkey over the return of Iraqi Kurds, but they were not enthusiastic to permit travel of Kurdish people through their territory, and discussions had stalled. Usual practice at that time would have been to grant exceptional leave to remain, on the basis that return was not safe or possible. The Home Office's initial refusal to do so was quashed in the High Court. Mr Khadir was not in reality subject to removal and therefore it was not lawful to detain him. If there was no basis for detention, there was no basis for temporary admission. His status should change to ELR. This decision was overturned in the House of Lords.

When the High Court decision was given, the government was in the process of drafting the 2002 Bill and took the opportunity of inserting s 67(2) and (3). Section 67(2) provides that a reference to a person who is liable to detention shall be taken to include a person if the only reason why they cannot be removed is because of a 'legal impediment' concerning the UK's obligations under an international agreement, or practical difficulties in arranging the removal. This means that a person in Mr Khadir's situation may continue to be treated as liable to detention. In other words, they may remain on temporary admission despite the fact they cannot at present be removed. The subsection removed the obligation to grant ELR (now discretionary leave). Section 67(3) gave s 67(2) retrospective effect. The House of Lords held that the subsections were not even necessary. A person who could not for practical or legal reasons be removed was still liable to be removed and thus the power to detain existed.

The result dovetails with the Asylum Policy Instructions (see chapter 12): 'Discretionary leave is not to be granted on the basis that, for the time being, practical obstacles prevent a person from leaving the UK or being removed.'

Lord Brown raised a question, 'how the fact that someone has been temporarily admitted rather than detained can be said to lengthen the period properly to be regarded as "pending...his removal"' (para 31). Ironically, this is one effect of this judgment, as it is possible for people to be maintained for even longer periods in the limbo state of temporary admission, yet without the Home Office being required to concede that removal is unrealistic, and grant a more beneficial status. The periods spent on temporary admission can be far longer than any reasonable (and thus lawful) length of actual detention. On release from such excessive detention, however, removal would still be possible in law, and this appears to be Lord Brown's point. Length of time was not intended to displace the removal. Compatibility with Article 5 was not considered by the Court, as physical liberty was not in issue.

The importance of *Khadir* may now be appreciated. If their Lordships had accepted that length of detention affected the jurisdiction to detain, that would mean that temporary admission also could expire simply through length of time. There would come a point when a challenge in judicial review would accept that the jurisdiction to keep someone on temporary admission had expired because it had gone on too long. If length of time only affects the discretion to detain, as the House of Lords found, then there is always jurisdiction to detain while ever there is 'some prospect' of effecting a removal. Thus, temporary admission, which subsists along with the jurisdiction to detain, may continue even while it would be a wrong use of discretion to actually detain the person.

As we have seen, in the context of European law the ECJ was not prepared to regard someone on temporary admission as not having entered (C–357/98 *R v SSHD ex p Yiadom* [2003] ECR I–9265). She had been present in the UK for months and this was regarded as unreal. We have also seen that time spent on temporary admission may count towards a period of residence for obtaining British nationality (see chapter 3).

15.11 Judicial supervision

The availability of judicial safeguards is central to the lawfulness of detention, and the major criticism by the UN Working Party and others is that although these exist in the UK, none is automatic.

15.11.1 Judicial review

As there is no statutory appeal against the decision to detain (it is not listed in s 82 Nationality Immigration and Asylum Act 2002), challenges to the length and the legality of detention are made by judicial review. Although judicial review is not an appeal on the merits, in the case of challenges to detention a more liberal approach to the Court's jurisdiction is applied. 'Where the liberty of the subject is concerned the court ought to be the primary decision-maker as to the reasonableness of the executive's actions, unless there are compelling reasons to the contrary...' (*Youssef* [2004] EWHC 1884 QB). *Youssef* was a High Court case, and an action for false imprisonment, but its reasoning was adopted and approved by the Court of Appeal in *R (A (Somalia)) v SSHD* [2007] EWCA Civ 804, which is treated as 'binding authority that the court must assume the role of primary decision maker when considering the lawfulness of detention' (*Anam v SSHD* [2010] EWCA Civ 1140).

15.11.2 Right to reasons for detention

Notice of reasons for detention may help the detainee to challenge the decision. The Human Rights Act gives a right in primary legislation to reasons for detention in Article 5.2: a detained person 'shall be informed promptly, in a language which he understands, of the reasons for his arrest'. There is an obligation in secondary legislation to give reasons on initial detention, and monthly thereafter (Detention Centre Rules 2001, SI 2001/238 r 9). As mentioned previously, the UNHCR Guidelines on Applicable Criteria and Standards relating to the Detention of Asylum Seekers carries similar advice. The Home Office produces a checklist of reasons – those detailed in the EIG (see 15.7.2). This is given by immigration officers to detainees, with boxes ticked to show which standard reasons for detention apply in their case.

These standard forms were first introduced during the period of the Cambridge research project referred to earlier, and were discussed with immigration officers during the research. They represented an attempt to ensure that only sanctioned reasons were actually used. Failure to use appropriate reasons may invalidate the detention if it can be shown that there were in fact no sustainable reasons for it. For instance, in *C, S and D*, standard reasons that they were likely to abscond was ticked, but this was contrary to all the available evidence.

15.11.3 Bail

A crucial safeguard for anyone in detention is the possibility of applying for bail. A bail application may, but need not, address the question of jurisdiction to detain. In a bail application, the argument is principally that the discretion to detain should not continue to be exercised in the particular case; the applicant should therefore be released.

Immigration and asylum detainees have a right to apply for bail, but unlike the position in criminal cases there is no automatic bail hearing (Immigration Act 1971 Sch 2 paras 22 and 29 and Immigration and Asylum Act 1999 s 54). The exception is that those detained pending examination under 16(1) do not have a right to apply for bail until they have been in the UK for seven days (para 22 (1B)). The Immigration and Asylum Act 1999 contained a scheme for a system of automatic bail hearings, but this was never implemented and was repealed by s 68(6) of the 2002 Act. There is no statutory presumption of a right to bail. The previous Chief Adjudicator's Guidance notes confirmed that there was a common law presumption. In the Bail Guidance for Immigration Judges released by the Tribunal in July 2011 the common law right appears as the first point in the introduction, as a right enjoyed by all. However in the specific guidance this does not translate into a presumption in favour of liberty when making individual decisions. The guidance says:

> By contrast with criminal proceedings, there is no statutory presumption in favour of release in immigration detention cases. Nevertheless, bail should not be refused unless there is good reason to do so, and it is for the respondent to show what those reasons are... The immigration authorities have a policy stating that there is a presumption in favour of release... although not binding on an Immigration Judge a UKBA policy in favour of release would be a persuasive reason to grant bail.

The guidance characterizes a bail decision as a 'risk assessment'. The underpinning is the statutory power to detain, and whether it should continue to be exercised, not the liberty of the individual and whether this should continue to be restricted.

15.11.3.1 *Power to grant bail*

An immigration officer of ordinary rank does not have power to grant bail. Under paras 22, 29, and 34 bail may be granted by a chief immigration officer or an immigration judge. However, the Nationality, Immigration and Asylum Act 2002 s 68 takes away the power of the chief immigration officer to grant bail to anyone who has been detained for more than eight days, and gives it to the Secretary of State. Immigration judges retain the power to grant bail, however, there are difficulties in obtaining legal aid to be represented before them. The report of the Chief Inspector of UKBA noted that between February 2010 and January 2011 UKBA released 109 foreign prisoners from detention, compared with 1,102 released by the Tribunal (2011:24).

15.11.3.2 *Conditions for the grant of bail*

Bail may be granted on condition that the person bailed reports at a specified time and place, usually a police station or the immigration officer. Bail will be made subject to recognizances. These are pledges of money which will be forfeited if the person does not report to bail. Further recognizances may be taken from people who are willing to stand as surety for a fixed sum proportionate to their means. The guidelines for immigration judges make it clear that sureties are not essential, and should not be routinely required. Immigration judges are reminded that 'people recently arrived in the country may have nobody to whom they could expect to stand surety for them'. The guidelines advise that

> the purpose of requiring a surety is to increase confidence that the applicant will comply with all the conditions of bail. 'If there are no reasonable grounds for concluding that the applicant will abscond, a surety may well be unnecessary.' Research on the conduct of bail hearings together with the guidance notes for immigration judges make it clear that sureties can be excluded from the hearings, although some sureties are required to go to considerable lengths, even being asked to produce the deeds to their house.

Conditions may be fixed such as that the bailee resides in a certain place, and other conditions may be imposed, but only if they are strictly necessary. The Secretary of State may pay for travelling expenses incurred in meeting reporting restrictions or bail conditions (2002 Act s 69). Under s 4 of the Immigration and Asylum Act 1999 the Secretary of State also has power to provide accommodation to a refused asylum seeker who has no address to enable them to get bail.

15.11.4 Habeas corpus

The lawfulness of detention may be challenged by the prerogative writ of habeas corpus. This is an ancient remedy which has been regarded as constitutionally important as it is a means whereby a court can inquire into the reasons for any detention and order immediate release. The basis of the jurisdiction is 'a detention or imprisonment which is incapable of legal justification' (*Halsbury's Laws* vol. 1(1), para 208). Although a foreign national has as much right as a subject to apply for habeas corpus (see *Khawaja v SSHD* [1984] AC 74 at 111: 'He who is subject to English law is entitled to its protection'), it is of little use in challenging immigration detention. The reason for this is there is nearly always a jurisdiction to detain, i.e., the basic statutory precondition is in existence. The question is usually how that jurisdiction has been exercised. This is a matter for judicial review, not habeas corpus. The amendment brought in by Immigration and Asylum Act 1999 s 140(1), permitting detention where there is a reasonable suspicion that directions for removal may be given means that it is even more unlikely that jurisdiction can be questioned.

Where there is a question of the jurisdiction to detain, this can be argued in both judicial review and habeas corpus proceedings and where appropriate both sets of proceedings can be pursued simultaneously. The relationship between the two was considered by the Court of Appeal in *R v SSHD ex p Sheikh* [2001] Imm AR 219, who pointed out that habeas corpus proceedings may be brought at any time that an applicant is detained, and are not subject to the strict time limits applicable in judicial review. Furthermore, habeas corpus is a writ of right, whereas permission must be sought for judicial review. Where the challenge is really to the underlying immigration decision, e.g., the refusal of leave to enter, then judicial review is the appropriate procedure, not habeas corpus (*R v SSHD ex p Muboyayi* [1991] 4 All ER 72). Finally, Macdonald's view on the 1999 Act amendment was that 'this change sounds the death-knell for habeas corpus in removal cases, save where there is no reasonable suspicion (i.e. *mala fides* is alleged) or where detention is excessively lengthy (the *Hardial Singh* situation)' (2001:762). This latter point would now be displaced by *Khadir* in relation to immigration detention, but not where individuals are moved across borders against their will, as may be recalled from chapter 4: *Rahmatullah v Secretary of State for the Foreign and Commonwealth Affairs and the Ministry of Defence* [2011] EWCA Civ 1540.

15.11.5 False imprisonment and breach of statutory duty

At the time of *Youssef v Home Office* [2004] EWHC 1884 QB, an action in tort for immigration detention was relatively unusual. However, this is now an established cause of action, the basis for which was established more fully in *Lumba and Mighty* and *Kambadzi* (see 15.6 and 15.7). In these cases the Supreme Court accepted that errors of public law invalidated the detention such that it became unlawful. Without statutory authority, the tort of false imprisonment was committed. Following these two cases, where an error in the decision to detain or the procedure governing the detention is such as to remove the statutory basis of the detention, there may be remedies not only in public law but also in tort. In tort actions, damages can be claimed on a broader basis (although the claimants in the Supreme Court cases did not succeed in that respect) and there is greater scope for disclosure of evidence and cross-examination.

In *ID and others v Home Office, BID & ILPA intervening* [2005] EWCA Civ 38, the Court of Appeal reinstated particulars of claim which had been struck out in the lower court, allowing the appellants to proceed with an application for false imprisonment. A family on arrival in the UK had been detained in Oakington for a week. Following *Saadi*, they could not succeed in any action challenging that detention. Their asylum claim was then refused, and they were moved to Yarl's Wood detention centre. A major fire there started the night that they arrived. They lost their possessions, and were lucky to escape with their lives as they had been locked in and the guards forgot to let them out. In a state of shock, they were then transferred to Harmondsworth. The Court of Appeal held that their action in tort concerning the latter two periods of detention should be heard by the courts. The Home Office had argued that immigration officers were immune from suit in making decisions pursuant to statute. The Court of Appeal (Brooke LJ giving the only reasoned judgment) considered the limited immunities from suit still available in the case of decisions to detain, and concluded that there was no such immunity for immigration officers.

The Home Office relied also on an argument that 'the power of a state to control immigration... extends beyond the simple control of entry to encompass the treatment of aliens and the control of their activities while they are present or resident in the State' (para 71). This amounted to an attempt to argue that foreign nationals are not subject to the same law as nationals and do not have full redress in the courts. This argument was dealt with in *Khawaja* [1984] AC 74 and so the Court of Appeal held in *ID*. The Court also rejected an argument that the claim was an abuse of process: 'there is nothing in the slightest bit peculiar about an individual bringing a private law claim for damages against an executive official who has abused his private rights' (para 57).

15.12 Detention centres as public authorities

The management and running of detention centres, and of transport and escort services to effect removals, are contracted out to private bodies. An important question in terms of redress is whether these contractors act as public authorities for the purposes of the Human Rights Act 1998. In *R (on the application of D and K) v SSHD* [2006] EWHC

(Admin) 980, GSL UK (formerly Group 4 Total Security), the contractors running Oakington, accepted that they were bound by the Detention Centre Rules and were a functional public authority for the purposes of the Human Rights Act (see chapter 4). GSL contracted out the provision of medical services at Oakington to a company called Forensic Medical Services Ltd, a subsidiary of another company called PCFM. There was a failure to provide medical services according to the standard in the Detention Centre Rules, but this failure had been known to all parties for a long time. GSL said they were not funded to provide it. However, theirs was the obligation to ensure compliance with the contract, and so declarations were made against GSL and the Home Office, though not against PCFM.

Bacon (2005) examines the growth in involvement of private prison companies in running immigration detention centres. At that time, seven of the ten removal centres were run by private companies, but only 10 per cent of prisons. She cites the attractiveness of immigration detention to such enterprises, it being less regulated than prisons in the criminal justice system, and thus offering more opportunities for increasing the profit margin. No doubt the financial attractiveness of immigration detention is one reason why government policy to build more has been able to prosper.

On the other hand, there have also been some serious disturbances at detention centres, and in such a case, unsurprisingly, neither private contractors nor the government are eager to shoulder all responsibility for the cost of damage, for the causes of the problems or for human rights violations that may have occurred during disturbances. In February 2002, a riot occurred at Yarl's Wood Immigration Detention Centre. Group 4 and their insurers claimed to recover the cost of the damage from the Bedfordshire Police Authority under the provisions of the Riot (Damages) Act 1886. The claim had been quantified at some £32 million. The Police Authority resisted this on the basis that the Group 4 companies acted as public authorities in running the centre, and so were debarred from claiming against the police under the Act. As a preliminary issue, the Court of Appeal in *Yarl's Wood Immigration Limited; GSL UK Limited; Creechurch Dedicated Limited v Bedfordshire Police Authority* [2009] EWCA Civ 1110 held that such a claim was in principle allowable. If it were found that Group 4 were to any extent responsible for the riot or the damage, the Act itself made provision for exclusion or reduction of the police's liability.

Following disturbances at Harmondsworth Detention Centre, complaints were made by some uninvolved detainees, that they were:

> kept in confinement while water from the sprinkler system entered their cells, then ordered out into the exercise yard in the cold while many of them were still wet, then readmitted and locked into cells. There AM and others were affected by smoke from a fire started by other inmates in an adjacent room; others were soaked by the sprinklers; there was reduced ventilation and, for many, a complete absence of toilet facilities. Some inmates spent well over 12 hours in these conditions without food or water. Two of the claimants, HM and LM, were assaulted by detention officers or rapid response personnel. The dispersal of detainees which followed was in many cases carried out callously; some were transported long distances without their belongings. (*R (on the application of AM and others v SSHD and Kalyx, BID intervening)* [2009] EWCA Civ 219 para 7)

The three judges of the Court of Appeal each took different views of the responsibility of the Secretary of State and Kalyx Ltd, which managed the centre. Their majority conclusion was to make a declaration that the Secretary of State ought to have conducted an independent investigation when he was alerted to the possibility that the appellants may have been the subject of infringements of their Article 3 rights. The investigation that had been ordered was not independent and did not have a remit to investigate the impact on uninvolved detainees.

15.13 Indefinite detention in the 'War on Terror'

In a sense, the detention without trial of foreign nationals that took place from 2001 to 2005 does not belong in a textbook on immigration and asylum law. It has a place in this chapter because immigration powers were used to justify it. When that foundation in immigration law was held by the House of Lords to be a misuse the provisions were declared unlawful. Nevertheless, these provisions in the Anti-terrorism, Crime and Security Act 2001 (ATCSA) were not an aberration. They were only the most extreme end of a number of measures we have noted already, the designated status in the Criminal Justice and Immigration Act, and UK Borders Act provisions for detention pending automatic deportation. All these lead towards a limbo without rights for foreign nationals whom the government wishes to deport but currently may not.

The Anti-terrorism, Crime and Security Act 2001 was the UK Parliament's legislative response to the attack on the World Trade Centre on 11 September of that year. The government claimed that intelligence information suggested that there were people operating within the UK who had international terrorist connections, but against whom there was insufficient evidence to bring a prosecution. Against British nationals operating in such a way there would be no sanction. Foreign nationals could be deported on the grounds that their deportation was conducive to the public good (see *Rehman v SSHD* [2001] 3 WLR 877) but not if they faced torture or inhuman or degrading treatment or punishment contrary to Article 3 EHCR (*Chahal v UK*) in the destination country. ATCSA s 23 gave a power to detain a foreign national who could not be deported if the Secretary of State reasonably believed their presence in the UK to be a risk to national security and reasonably suspected that person of international terrorist activities or connections.

The provision clearly had the potential to breach Article 5.1 as detention was not pending deportation or extradition or a criminal trial. Accordingly, the UK government derogated from Article 5 to the extent that it would be breached by this Act (Human Rights Act 1998 (Designated Derogation) Order 2001). This meant that Article 5 was suspended to the extent that it conflicted with 2001 Act provisions, both for the purposes of action in Strasbourg (Article 15 ECHR) and under the Human Rights Act (HRA s 1(2)). The validity of the derogation was challenged by the first twelve people to be detained under s 23. The challenge initially came before the Special Immigration Appeals Commission (SIAC) who granted a declaration under Human Rights Act 1998 s 4 that the detention power was incompatible with Article 14 ECHR.

The Court of Appeal overturned SIAC's declaration (*A, X, Y and others v SSHD* [2002] EWCA Civ 1502). Its approach follows in the footsteps of the House of Lords in the national security case of *Rehman*, considering that in measures concerning 'a public emergency threatening the life of the nation' it was appropriate to accord deference to the Home Secretary who is in a special position to be able to assess the evidence and take the decision. It was therefore prepared to accept the Home Secretary's assertion that only the detention of non-nationals was necessary.

The UK's continued detention of eleven men under these powers attracted criticism from the committee of Privy Counsellors (the Newton Committee) convened to review the legislation, the Parliamentary Joint Committee on Human Rights (in its Fifth, Sixth, and Eighth Reports of 2003–04), the UN Human Rights Committee, the European Commissioner on Human Rights (Opinion 1/2002, August 2002), and many NGOs and other commentators.

The House of Lords overturned the Court of Appeal's decision in a momentous judgment (*A v SSHD* [2004] UKHL 56). The nine judges who sat in the Lords reiterated the fundamental constitutional importance of the right to liberty, and that the law applies equally to all.

They noted that SIAC had found as fact that 'there are many British nationals already identified – mostly in detention abroad – who fall within the definition of suspected international terrorists, and...there are others at liberty in the UK who could similarly be defined' (para 32). Also, 'allowing a suspected international terrorist to leave our shores and depart to another country, perhaps a country as close as France, there to pursue his criminal designs, is hard to reconcile with a belief in his capacity to inflict serious injury to the people and interests of this country' (para 33). The lack of rational connection to the aim to be achieved made the measures both disproportionate and discriminatory.

The derogation was not, they thought, limited to what was strictly required by the exigencies of the situation. Lord Bingham of Cornhill referred to the very strict bail conditions upon which one detainee had been released. These were less draconian than detention, but presumably considered sufficient. As the derogation was discriminatory and so in breach of Article 14, it was also in breach of Article 26 ICCPR and thus not consistent with the UK's other international obligations, as required by Article 15.

Lord Hoffmann alone found that there was no threat to the life of the nation warranting derogation under Article 15. The life of the nation should not be equated with individual human lives, but rather with the values and practices that constitute the collective life. He said, most memorably: 'The real threat to the life of the nation, in the sense of a people living in accordance with its traditional laws and political values, comes not from terrorism but from laws such as these' (paras 96 and 97).

The majority found that s 23 was disproportionate and thus in breach of Article 15, and discriminatory and thus in breach of Article 14. They issued a quashing order in relation to the derogation order and a declaration of incompatibility in relation to s 23. Only Lord Walker of Gestingthorpe dissented.

This conclusion was endorsed by the ECtHR in *A v UK* (2009) 49 EHRR 29, who additionally found the provisions unlawful under Article 5.1 in relation to 9 of the 11 applicants. The Court said that: 'one of the principal assumptions underlying the derogation notice, the 2001 Act and the decision to detain the applicants was that they could not be removed or deported "for the time being"'. Action 'with a view to deportation', as permitted by Article 5.1(f) could not therefore provide a reason for their detention (but see the contrary view of Finnis).

The Prevention of Terrorism Act 2005 was the government's response to the House of Lords' judgment, and this enabled the detainees' bail conditions to be swiftly transposed into control orders under that Act. A special provision exempted them from judicial oversight (PTA 2005 s 3(1)(c)).

A number of control orders have now been challenged in the House of Lords and the most draconian were found to be in breach of Article 5. These entailed confinement alone to a one-bedroomed flat in an unknown area for 18 hours a day, limited telephone, and no internet access, no visitors who had not been vetted by the Home Office, a limited radius of travel, a prohibition on attending any gatherings of people except once a week in an approved mosque, wearing an electronic tag at all times, and reporting to a monitoring centre on leaving and returning to the flat. The majority of the House of Lords thought that this amounted to a deprivation of liberty rather than merely a restriction on liberty. Baroness Hale said that the whole condition of someone's life had to be taken into account, and life under these control orders was similar to being in an open prison, but without association with other prisoners. None of the permitted reasons in Article 5.1 existed, so the control order breached the right (*SSHD v JJ* [2007] UKHL 45). In other cases of lesser restriction, no breach of Article 5 was found (*SSHD v MB and AK* [2007] UKHL 46). It may be doubted whether such a draconian system would have come into being without the more severe detention regime first being imposed on foreign nationals.

This section would not be complete without a reference to *R (on the application of Abbassi) v Secretary of State for Foreign and Commonwealth Affairs* [2003] UKHRR 76, a challenge to the Foreign Secretary's exercise of prerogative in interceding for the British prisoners held in the American military base in Guantanamo Bay, Cuba. In essence, the case concerns the impotence of the British government to intervene in the affairs of another nation and of the citizen to challenge that. However, it proceeded on the accepted basis that the detainees had access to no legal review of their detention, that detention was indefinite and that they had no access to legal advice or representation. Within the confines of the legal principles available to it, the Court of Appeal could only reiterate the primacy of liberty, and that every detention is a prima facie breach of law (para 60). They were powerless to intervene as the matter was political, not legal. As discussed in chapter 2, the impasse resulted in a break with constitutional convention when Lord Steyn spoke in a non-judicial setting to criticize the detentions (*The Independent* 26 November 2003). See also *R (on application of Al-Rawi) v FCO and SSHD* [2006] EWHC 972 (Admin), discussed in chapter 3.

15.14 Conclusion

We end this chapter as we began, *Liversidge v Anderson* dealing with wartime internment, and *A v SSHD* dealing with internment in a different kind of public emergency. In *Liversidge v Anderson*, although the House of Lords found for the executive, the case is remembered more for Lord Atkin's dissent than it is for its ratio. As *A v SSHD* takes its place in legal history, so far it is the majority judgment which has left a stronger print. The 8:1 decision that the detentions were unlawful has given the case a claim to be 'one of the most constitutionally significant ever decided by the House of Lords' (MLR Belmarsh special issue p. 654). Lord Bingham's leading judgment carefully marshalls international law to reach the majority conclusion, and this is important, not only for the outcome, but also because it shows that the UK is subject to international restraints upon government. The judgment of the ECtHR in *A v UK* upheld the right to liberty for the same appellants in one of the most politically charged of cases. They did so partly on the basis that lesser constraints could and should have been considered. However, the contrary effect is achieved by the ECtHR decision in *Saadi v UK*. Here, international law restraint is more or less abandoned, and remarkably, lesser constraints than loss of liberty were not considered. The Court's failure to distinguish between asylum seekers and other entrants can be seen as negating the lawful status of seeking asylum. Ironically, it also means that the same principles are in human rights law applicable to other lawful applicants at ports of entry, such as visitors without entry clearance.

In the UK, *Khadir* entrenches the capacity of the government to maintain a limbo status for asylum seekers. This chapter has shown that although prima facie unlawful, detention is on the increase, and even statutorily enshrined human rights can be defeated by a judicial assertion of the state's power to control foreign nationals. The administrative power to detain pending determination of a claim has grown far beyond its original use for visitors overnight, and become the foundation for a whole new system of detention. The Supreme Court's judgments in *Mighty and Lumba* and in *Kambadzi* place a legal stop on the expansion of executive freedom, but the absence of any real sanction may limit the effect on detention practice.

QUESTIONS

1 Do the judgments in the case of *Saadi* recognize the right in Article 14 UDHR to claim asylum?

2 Is it appropriate that the decision to detain should be a discretionary one without statutory criteria to guide its exercise?

3 Should asylum seekers have automatic bail hearings as criminal suspects do?

For guidance on answering questions, visit www.oxfordtextbooks.co.uk/orc/clayton5e/.

FURTHER READING

Amnesty International (1996) *Cell Culture: The Detention and Imprisonment of Asylum Seekers in the United Kingdom* (London: Amnesty International).

Bacon, Christine (2005) 'The Evolution of Immigration Detention in the UK: The Involvement of Private Prison Companies,' Refugee Studies Centre, Working Paper no. 27.

Bail for Immigration Detainees (BID) (2002) *Immigration Detention in the United Kingdom, Submission to the United Nations Working Group on Arbitrary Detention* (London: BID).

—— (2005) *Fit to be Detained? Challenging the detention of asylum seekers and migrants with health needs* (London: BID).

Bail for Immigration Detainees (BID) and the Children's Society (2009) *An Evaluative Report on the Millbank Alternative to Detention Pilot* (London: Children's Society and BID), accessed at: www.childrenssociety.org.uk/resources/documents/media/17148_full.pdf.

Black, Richard, Collyer, Michael, Skeldon, Ronald, and Waddington, Clare (2005) *A Survey of the Illegally Resident Population in Detention in the UK*, Home Office Research Paper 20/05.

Cole, Emily (2003) 'The Detention of Asylum-seeking Families in the UK' *Journal of Immigration, Asylum and Nationality Law*, vol. 17, no. 2, pp. 96–113.

Cornelisse, Galina (2004) 'Human Rights for Immigration Detainees in Strasbourg: Limited Sovereignty or Limited Discourse?' *European Journal of Migration and Law* vol. 6, no. 2, pp. 93–110.

Dell, Susi, and Salinsky, Mary (2001) 'Protection not Prison: Torture Survivors Detained in the UK' Medical Foundation for the Care of Victims of Torture, September 2001.

Finnis, John (2007) 'Nationality, Alienage and Constitutional Principle' *Law Quarterly Review* vol. 123, July, pp. 417–445.

Independent Asylum Commission (2008) *Deserving Dignity* (London).

Independent Chief Inspector of UKBA (2011) *Thematic Inspection Report of How the Agency Manages Foreign National Prisoners February to May 2011* (London: Independent Chief Inspector of UKBA).

Johnston, Connor (2009) 'Indefinite Immigration Detention: Can it be Justified?' *Journal of Immigration and Nationality Asylum Law* vol. 23, no. 4, pp. 351–364.

London Detainee Support Group (2009) *Detained Lives* (London).

McLeish, Jenny, Culter, Sarah, and Stancer, Cathy (2002) *A Crying Shame: Pregnant Asylum Seekers and their Babies in Detention* (London: Maternity Alliance, Bail for Immigration Detainees, London Detainee Support Group).

Modern Law Review (2005) 68(4) Cases Section: Special Issue on Belmarsh.

O'Nions, Helen (2008) 'No Right to Liberty: the Detention of Asylum Seekers for Administrative Convenience' *European Journal of Migration and Law* vol. 10, no. 2, pp.149–185.

Poole, Tom (2005) 'Harnessing the Power of the Past? Lord Hoffmann and the Belmarsh Detainees Case' *Journal of Law and Society* vol. 32, no. 4, pp. 534–561.

Pourgourides, Christina K., Sashidharan, Sashi P., and Bracken, Pat J. (1996) *A Second Exile: The Mental Health Implications of Detention of Asylum Seekers in the United Kingdom* (Birmingham: Northern Birmingham Mental Health Trust).

Sawyer, Caroline (2007) 'Elephants in the Room, or: A Can of Worms: Szoma v DWP' *Journal of Social Security Law* vol. 86, pp. 86–104.

Sawyer, Caroline, and Turpin, Philip (2005) 'Neither Here Nor There: Temporary Admission to the UK' *International Journal of Refugee Law* vol. 17, no. 4, December, pp. 688–728.

Shah, Prakash (2002) *Refugees, Race and the Concept of Asylum* (London: Cavendish), chapter 8.

UNHCR (1999) *Revised Guidelines on Applicable Criteria and Standards Relating to the Detention of Asylum Seekers* (Geneva: UNHCR).

Weber, Leane and Gelsthorpe, Loraine (2000) *Deciding to Detain: How Decisions to Detain Asylum Seekers are Made at Ports of Entry* (Cambridge: Cambridge Institute of Criminology).

Wilsher, Daniel (2012) *Immigration Detention: Law, History, Politics* (Cambridge: Cambridge University Press).

16

Deportation

SUMMARY

This chapter gives a brief history of the power of deportation, then discusses in some detail the application of the ground that the deportation is conducive to the public good. There is discussion of so-called automatic deportation and of national security cases.

16.1 Introduction

Deportation has a long history. The word conjures up images of forced removals, divided families, and poor conditions on board crowded ships. Deportations had become uncommon, but underwent a revival as the government introduced a policy in 2006 to increase deportations after media revelations that not all those were considered for deportation who might be (see chapter 2). Still the usual legal power used to remove someone from the UK is not deportation but administrative removal, which is dealt with in the next chapter. Deportation has traditionally offered more rights to the person removed than does the process of removal, though these have gradually been eroded almost to vanishing point.

Although the effects of deportation and removal have become more similar, it is still important to understand them as distinct legal processes. Deportation may only take place where the grounds for it are either proved or deemed proved by statute. Removal by contrast, despite its devastating effect, is in essence an enforcement process. The 'grounds' for it are regulatory and are concerned with immigration control. Deportation is based on the personal conduct of the person concerned, even though in national security cases wrongdoing need not be proved (see 16.7.3). A person with any kind of immigration leave, including indefinite, may be deported. Although this means that a person subject to immigration control is subject to a sanction following a criminal offence which does not apply to a British citizen, the ECtHR does not treat this as an unlawful double jeopardy because expulsion is regarded not as a punishment but as an administrative sanction (*Maaouia v France*). This approach has been confirmed in the UK courts. In *AT (Pakistan) v SSHD* [2010] EWCA Civ 567 the Court of Appeal rejected an argument that deportation was a punishment. It was 'preventative rather than punitive' (para 25). Extradition sometimes interacts with asylum claims but is a means of enforcing non-immigration criminal processes, and will not be considered in this book. Voluntary departure is considered later in this chapter.

16.2 What is deportation?

Deportation is an enforced departure from the UK, pursuant to an order which also prevents the deportee from returning to the UK unless and until the order is revoked. This continuing effect used to be a distinguishing characteristic of deportation, but changes to the immigration rules in 2008 amount to the imposition of a re-entry ban also after removal (see chapter 7). Paragraph 362 of the immigration rules sets out the effects of a deportation order:

(i) it requires the person who is the subject of the order to leave the UK
(ii) it authorizes that person's detention until they leave the UK (subject to a common law restraint on the length of detention, as discussed in the previous chapter)
(iii) it prohibits that person's re-entry for as long as the order is in force
(iv) it invalidates any leave to enter or remain given to the person before the order was made or while it was in force.

The first formal step in the deportation process is the notice of decision to deport, which gives the reasons for the decision, the country to which it is proposed to deport the person, and notice of appeal rights. Appeal is against the notice of decision to deport. Once the deportation order is signed, it takes effect and there is no further appeal, though it may be possible to appeal a refusal to revoke the order (Nationality, Immigration and Asylum Act 2002 s 82(2)(k)).

Entry while the deportation order is still in force makes that person an illegal entrant (Immigration Act 1971 s 33A).

16.3 History and development of the power to deport

As we have seen, in early times those regarded as enemies, such as Jews by Edward I or Irish by Elizabeth I, were expelled by royal decree. Deportation as a regulated process carried out by government officials was only instituted by the Aliens Act 1905. Under the statute, deportation could only take place after conviction of an imprisonable offence, or if a magistrates' court certified that the person had been sentenced elsewhere for an extradition offence, or had:

> [b]een found in receipt of any such parochial relief as disqualifies a person for the parliamentary franchise, or found wandering without ostensible means of subsistence, or been living in insanitary conditions due to overcrowding.

Criminality, poverty, and the spread of disease have often been mixed in with immigration policy, as discussed in chapter 1. The operation of appeal boards was suspended in 1914, and although for a short time there was a review panel, its decisions were unpopular with the Home Office and it was abolished again. Effectively, from 1914 to 1969, people who were to be deported had no access to appeal or independent review.

We have seen that the Commonwealth Immigrants Act 1962 marked an historic shift in the relationship between the UK and its Commonwealth citizens. Not only did it provide the first powers to refuse them entry and impose conditions, it also provided the first powers to deport Commonwealth citizens, though originally only for criminal offences on the recommendation of a criminal court (s 6). The 1962 Act s 7 provided protection against deportation for anyone who could prove they had been ordinarily resident in the UK for five years prior to conviction. This exemption was preserved by the Immigration Act 1971 for existing residents, but otherwise abolished. The importance of long-term residence has remained a live issue in Europe, both in debates in the Council of Europe (see chapter 18) and in increased protection for long-term residents in EU law (see chapter 5). Such protection has diminished in the UK. Long residence rules (discussed in chapter 7) may give settled status but give no protection against deportation.

The Immigration Appeals Act 1969 gave power to the Secretary of State to deport Commonwealth citizens who were in breach of their conditions of admission (s 16), again with an exemption for those who had been ordinarily resident for five years. This was a significant step as it developed deportation as a means of enforcing immigration rules, not only a means of excluding people who were considered socially undesirable. The Immigration Act 1971 made the position of aliens and Commonwealth citizens broadly the same, in that deportation became possible for both groups for breach of condition or overstaying, when conducive to the public good and after recommendation by a criminal court (s 3). From that time onwards, apart from the exemptions, the distinction between Commonwealth citizens and aliens for deportation purposes has vanished. The main distinction now is between EU nationals and others.

The Immigration Act 1988 s 5 restricted the grounds for appeal against deportation so that people who had been in the UK less than seven years who were being deported for breach of condition or overstaying could not argue their case on the merits of whether they personally should be deported, but only on whether there was power in law to deport them. The Asylum and Immigration Act 1996 added a further ground for deportation – obtaining leave to remain by deception. Despite the widened grounds and the restricted appeal rights, a person who was to be deported still had a right to appeal from inside the UK which the person to be removed did not. The Immigration and Asylum Act 1999 translated most of the grounds for deportation into grounds for removal, thereby substantially eradicating the distinction between deportation and removal. The same Act introduced the human rights appeal against removal and deportation.

In summary, until the implementation of the 1999 Act, the scope of the power to deport increased, while the rights of people who were to be deported decreased. In the Nationality, Immigration and Asylum Act 2002 a new right of appeal was introduced against a decision to deport following the recommendation of a criminal court (s 82(2)(j)). Interestingly, the Bill which preceded the 1999 Act had included this right of appeal, but it was removed by a late amendment sponsored by the government in the House of Lords.

Deportation powers were publicly linked to the national security agenda, though not for the first time, in 2005 in the Prime Minister's statement following the bombings in London that year. He proclaimed a 'list of unacceptable behaviours' and an intention to make these grounds for deportation and speed up the deportation process. The list includes writing, producing, publishing or distributing material; public speaking including preaching; running a website; using a position of responsibility to express views which 'foment terrorism, justify or glorify terrorism, foster hatred which may lead to intra-community violence in the UK or other serious criminal activity, or seek to provoke others to serious criminal acts'. This list is not exhaustive. It became a policy which could inform a decision to deport. In May 2006, the press disclosed that, over a seven-year period, 1,000 foreign national prisoners had been released without being considered for deportation (see chapter 2 for discussion of the incident). This turned out to be due to failures of management, organization, and communication within what was then the Immigration and Nationality Directorate. It was not that it would necessarily have been appropriate to deport these prisoners, but rather that whether they should be deported had not been considered. Over 100 were the subject of a court recommendation. As a response, the government announced that there would be automatic deportation of serious offenders, a proposal which was supported by the House of Commons Home Affairs Committee (Fifth Report 2005–06).

The immediate result was a rule change in July 2006, HC 1337, abolishing consideration of the merits of the case in favour of a presumption that a deportation which the Secretary of State considered to be conducive to the public good would be in the public interest. Most recently, UK Borders Act 2007 ss 32–39 created a statutory obligation to make a deportation order in many criminal cases, and deemed these to be conducive to the public good, as explained more fully in 16.7.2.

16.4 Rationale for deportation

The power to deport is most commonly used in relation to people who have been convicted of a criminal offence. The traditional and liberal view is that its use is not intended to be a further punishment for the criminal offence, but should only be considered when the person's continued presence in the country impinges on the life of the public in a way that is contrary to the public interest (Immigration Act 1971 s 3(5)(a) and *R v Nazari* [1980] 3 All ER 880). Every society contains a certain level of criminal activity and so crime in itself does not warrant deportation. The Court of Appeal in *Raghbir Singh* [1996] Imm AR 507 said that the Secretary of State should consider 'whether it is bad for the country for him to remain'. The rule change in 2006 and provision for automatic deportation in the UK Borders Act 2007 demonstrated that present executive policy tends more towards the view which in an extreme form would say that any non-British person who commits a criminal act should be removed. This view is an example of a policy which tends to creating categories of 'belongers' and 'non-belongers'. It is not really a penal policy as such, in that it regards criminality as secondary to nationality. It has echoes of the ATCSA experiment discussed in the last chapter, treating criminal matters as immigration matters wherever possible. Regarded as a penal policy, it could be summarized as 'out of sight, out of mind', rather like transportation of British subjects who had committed criminal offences to North America or Australia in the eighteenth century.

At the other end of the spectrum of opinion, it would be said that removing the criminal from society does not address the causes of crime and the wrongdoing of a non-citizen is no greater than the wrongdoing of a citizen. The possession of citizenship (and so exemption from deportation) is an irrelevant technicality given that one may apply for naturalization and so become a citizen after five years' residence in the UK, or on the other hand have lived here all one's life and still not have citizenship. Furthermore, nationality is now more easily removed (see chapter 3). The discrimination which results from the deportation of the non-citizen, combined with the harm to family and social networks, is a greater fracturing of the social fabric than the continued presence of someone who has committed a criminal offence. Punishment as meted out by the Court is already intended to deter others and prevent reoffending and if it fails to do so that is a matter for criminal policy, not immigration control.

Since deportation which interferes with Article 8 rights must be necessary in a democratic society, these underlying concepts of society and criminality inevitably affect decision-making.

16.5 Exercise of the power to deport

Section 5(1) Immigration Act 1971 expresses the power to make a deportation order as a power of the Secretary of State. However, in accordance with the Carltona principle (*Carltona Ltd v Commissioner of Works* [1943] 2 All ER 560 CA), properly authorized officials may carry out the function of the Secretary of State and in doing so their actions count as the actions of the Secretary of State. In the context of deportation, the Carltona principle authorizes deportation action to be taken by officials of the Home Office. In 1988, the Secretary of State authorized certain nominated immigration officers of the rank of inspector also to make deportation decisions. This delegation was challenged in the case of *Oladehinde and Alexander v Secretary of State for the Home Department* [1991] 1 AC 254, but the House of Lords upheld the delegation. The Court's concern about procedures being properly applied was met by the practice of making written records of the decision-making process, ensuring that immigration officers who had been involved in the investigation process were not involved in the deportation decision, and referring to the Home Office any proposed deportation where the person had compassionate circumstances or had been in the UK for a long time.

The Immigration Directorate Instructions (IDI 13.1.6 December 2007) say that deportation orders will usually be signed by the 'Chief Executive or Deputy Chief Executive', presumably of UKBA, and that 'certain' cases may be signed by the Home Secretary. Usual practice has been for the Home Secretary to sign deportation orders which are made on what we may loosely call national security grounds. These grounds are discussed in 16.7.3, and may only be challenged through the restricted appeal procedure before the Special Immigration Appeals Commission, discussed in chapter 8.

16.6 Who may be deported?

Section 3(5) Immigration Act 1971 says that 'a person who is not a British citizen' may be deported. Here, the term 'British citizen' has the meaning given to it by s 2 Immigration Act, as substituted by British Nationality Act 1981 s 39. It therefore includes, not only those who have British citizenship, but also Commonwealth citizens who retained right of abode when the British Nationality Act 1981 came into force, as discussed in chapter 3, namely those who married a British man before 1 January 1983, or who had a UK-born parent. However, s 2A Immigration Act 1971, inserted by the Immigration Asylum and Nationality Act 2006, now provides for this right of abode to be removed from Commonwealth citizens if the Secretary of State thinks that their removal or exclusion from the UK would be conducive to the public good – the same grounds as deportation.

There are other exemptions. By Immigration Act 1971 s 7, Commonwealth and Irish citizens are exempt if they were ordinarily resident in the UK on 1 January 1973 (the date that the 1971 Act came into force) and have been ordinarily resident for five years before the decision to deport was taken (s 7(1)(b) and (c)) (*Lawrence Kane v SSHD* [2000] Imm AR 250). Unusually in counting periods of residence, according to Immigration Act s 7(2), remaining 'in breach of immigration laws' counts towards this five-year period. Case law has established that this only applies to people who overstay their period of leave, and not to those who entered illegally in the first place. Time spent in prison however does not count (*Lawrence Kane*). Section 8(3) provides an exemption from deportation for diplomats and their families.

There used to be an exemption for Commonwealth wives of Commonwealth men settled in the UK before 1973, but this was abolished by s 1 Immigration Act 1988. The abolition of this security for Commonwealth women was in breach of a guarantee which had been given by s 1(5) of the Immigration Act 1971, that Commonwealth citizens would be no less free to come and go after the 1971 Act than they were before. The 1988 Act repealed that section and caused a furore by removing the rights of Commonwealth citizens. However, without constitutional protection, given the UK's doctrine of the legislative supremacy of Parliament, such promises cannot be relied upon. Even the Human Rights Act does not give a constitutional guarantee of the right to family life of Commonwealth citizens living in the UK (see generally chapter 9).

As discussed more fully in chapter 5, EEA nationals are only liable to be deported on the limited grounds allowed by Directive 2004/ 38. Developments in both EU and domestic law leave little room for doubt that EEA nationals have greater protection. Deportation of EEA nationals is an exception to the underlying right of freedom of movement and as such should be interpreted restrictively (Case 41/74 *Van Duyn v Home Office* [1974] ECR 1337). No such right can be claimed by non-EEA nationals. Leave to remain in the UK carries no protective power in itself comparable with European freedom of movement. Protection for an established life in the UK may only be argued through Article 8 ECHR. However, in *Omojudi v UK* [2009] ECHR 1942 the Court attached 'considerable weight to the fact that the Secretary of State for the Home Department, who was fully aware of his offending history, granted the applicant Indefinite Leave to Remain in the United Kingdom' (para 42).

16.7 Deportation 'conducive to the public good'

Since overstaying and breach of condition became grounds for removal instead of deportation, the remaining principal ground for deportation is that the Secretary of State deems the deportation to be conducive to the public good (s 3(5)(a)). In case law and literature prior to the 1999 Act, deportations under what is now s 3(5)(a) are referred to as 's 3(5)(b)' deportations.

It has been noted in the introduction to this chapter that deportation conducive to the public good has a long history. A controversial view is that of Finnis, who regards it as 'a constitutional principle that foreigners may be expelled for misconduct of sufficient weight' (2007:418). Whether or not that is the case, the power to deport on s 3(5)(a) grounds is a broad one, not confined to any one interpretation of the meaning of the public good. In *Raghbir Singh*, it was said that the ground 'covers a whole range of circumstances limited only by conventional public law and Wednesbury rules and the doctrine in *Padfield v Minister of Agriculture*', i.e., normal administrative law limitations of reasonableness and impartiality. As described earlier, the decision can now be based on the Secretary of State's judgement that someone has engaged in the 'unacceptable behaviours' which might foster terrorism. In practice, the commission of criminal offences is the most common basis.

Case law on the question of whether deportation is conducive to the public good has included evaluation of matters such as the seriousness of the offence, the likelihood of reoffending, and any deterrent effect on others. The evaluation of these factors entered a new era with the case of *N (Kenya) v SSHD* [2004] EWCA Civ 1094, which, although only a majority decision, has since been treated as a leading authority.

N (Kenya) required that weight be given to the Secretary of State's policy on the deportation of serious criminals. As the one holding government responsibility for deportation policy, the Secretary of State could be assumed to have developed a policy which took proper account of the deterrent effect of deportation, and its function as an expression of public revulsion at the crime(s) in question. There is a tension in evaluating the public good argument in deportation appeals between the impact of the actual individual's continued presence in the UK, most often considered to be demonstrated by their likelihood of reoffending, and the wider social impact of the deportation. This latter factor is evaluated, not only by the deterrent effect on other would-be offenders (which is inherently difficult to prove), but also, and particularly since *N (Kenya)*, by considering the deportation as a signal of society's revulsion at the crime(s). The ECtHR stresses taking all the circumstances into account, and would only weigh as one factor the use of deportation as a signal of revulsion at the crime. See *AA v UK* [2011] ECHR 1345:

> where, as in the present case, the interference with the applicant's rights under Article 8 pursues the legitimate aim of 'prevention of disorder or crime', the above criteria ultimately are designed to help evaluate the extent to which the applicant can be expected to cause disorder or to engage in criminal activities. (para 58)

Deterrence of others and the signal to society have little to do with the individual deportee, except to the extent that their crime may be described as belonging to a category. It is in relation to categories (e.g., 'violent crime') that the Secretary of State develops policy. In the case of deportees with families, the public interest in maintaining family unity and avoiding the social cost of severed families is rarely weighed on this side of the balance. Disruption of the family is mainly considered as it impacts on the Article 8 rights of the individual family in question (see chapter 18).

In *N (Kenya)* itself, the adjudicator had given decisive weight to the low risk of reoffending. The Tribunal on reconsideration had held that this was the wrong approach, and that more weight should have been given to the Secretary of State's policy of deporting those who committed very serious offences (as N had). The majority of the Court of Appeal agreed with the Tribunal. The application of this principle may be seen in the following cases. They illustrate that giving proper weight to the Secretary of State's policy is not at all the same thing as saying that all those who commit a serious crime should be deported.

In *AS (Pakistan) v SSHD* [2008] EWCA Civ 1118, the appellant, who had leave to remain as the husband of a British national, failed to stop his car at a pelican crossing on the Victoria Embankment during the early hours of the morning and ran down a young woman who was crossing on her bicycle. She was very seriously injured and died shortly after. The appellant was convicted of causing death by dangerous driving and sentenced to three years' imprisonment. He was a model prisoner and full of remorse for his actions. The Secretary of State decided to deport him. The Court of Appeal held that in the case of a serious offender, the public interest in favour of deportation lay principally in the protection of the public by the prevention of further offending in the UK and in deterrence of others who might be tempted to commit similar offences. In this case, there was little risk of reoffending and deterrence was less relevant as the offence was not deliberate. See *RG (Automatic deport section 33(2)(a) exception) Nepal* [2010] UKT 273 (IAC) (at 16.7.2) for how this approach has been applied under the 2007 Act.

In the opposite direction, though on very different facts, the Court of Appeal in *OH (Serbia) v SSHD* [2008] EWCA Civ 694 held that the risk of reoffending was only one aspect of the public interest. Other matters included deterrence, and as an independent factor, the view of the Secretary of State of the public interest. Where the Tribunal had not given due weight to this, their decision was not lawful. The appellant was a 19-year-old Kosovan refugee who had been severely traumatized by the violence he had seen in Kosovo. He had seen one of his brothers blinded in one eye by picking up a hand grenade, and Serbian troops shoot his grandfather in the head and killed him. He suffered flashbacks which brought back vivid scenes of these events. In the UK, he and a friend were accosted by two other youths and his friend was subjected to a brutal attack. When the assailants ran away, the appellant followed and, armed with a razor knife which he had in his possession, he slashed the neck of one, narrowly missing the jugular vein. The evidence was that this response was induced by the effect of trauma. The Court of Appeal held that the low risk of reoffending should not outweigh what they considered to be a deterrent effect, nor the policy of the Secretary of State that those who committed serious offences should be deported. In *AL (Jamaica) v SSHD* [2008] EWCA Civ 482, which on its facts is a more typical case than either of these cases, the Court of Appeal held, as in *OH (Serbia)*, that the immigration judge should not only consider their own assessment, but must also take into account as an independent element the Secretary of State's assessment of the public interest, and give appropriate weight to that. In this case, the appellant had been sentenced to a total of seven years in prison for drugs offences. He had a wife and child in the UK, but the Court of Appeal held that the Secretary of State's policy of deporting people who committed such offences must be given independent weight, and the deportation should stand. In *DS (India) v SSHD* [2009] EWCA Civ 544, the case of a reformed gambler was very finely balanced. The Court of Appeal upheld the Tribunal's decision that, even if he did not reoffend, the public interest extended to deterring serious crime generally, and to upholding public abhorrence of offences of dishonesty, and in particular the armed robbery he had committed to finance his gambling.

While the Secretary of State's policy is treated as important, in *SSHD v Omar* [2009] EWCA Civ 383, the Court of Appeal held that the Secretary of State's own actions also indicated the weight that the Court should give to it. She had delayed nine months in filing the notice of her appeal for which permission had been given. This delay did not indicate, in the view of the Court, that the Secretary of State was serious in her assertion that the public good necessitated removing Mr Omar from the UK.

The assessment that deportation is conducive to the public good may be based on reasons other than criminal offences. Deception of the Home Office resulting in a grant of leave (*Kesse* [2001] EWCA Civ 177) and abuse of the institution of marriage (*ex p Cheema* [1982] Imm AR 12) are reasons that have been used in the past. These kinds of deception would now bring liability for removal either for obtaining entry by deception or obtaining leave to remain by deception (see chapter 17).

16.7.1 July 2006 rule change

Deportation decisions may be divided into three eras or groups:

- Those which preceded the rule change in July 2006.
- Those made under UK Borders Act 2007 ss 32–39.
- Those made after July 2006 which do not come within the UK Borders Act.

Of the deportation decisions discussed in the last section, all except that in *DS (India)* were taken before July 2006, and thus were governed by what we may call the 'old' rules. Paragraph 364 of these rules required that the public interest in deportation be balanced against a list of factors relating to the proposed deportee. The weighting given by the Court of Appeal in *N (Kenya)* to the Secretary of State's policy prefigured the rule change in 2006, which abolished that list. The substance of the 2006 version of para 364 is as follows:

- where a person is liable to deportation
- the presumption is that the public interest requires it
- SSHD will consider all relevant factors in each case BUT
- only in exceptional cases will public interest in deportation be outweighed
- EXCEPT where deportation is contrary to Human Rights or Refugee Convention.

EO (Deportation appeals: scope and process) Turkey [2007] UKAIT 00062 was the first authority on interpretation of these rules. The Tribunal held that the first point, 'where a person is liable to deportation', entails a decision that the deportation is conducive to the public good, as a person is not liable to deportation until that decision has been made. Therefore, the presumption that deportation is in the public interest replaces the previous mandatory weighting of personal factors, but only comes into play once it has been determined that the deportation is conducive to the public good or the Court had recommended it and it has been decided that neither the Human Rights nor the Refugee Conventions would be breached. In *SSHD v HK (Turkey)* [2010] EWCA Civ 583, HK, a young man of previously good character, who had lived in the UK since the age of 6, had found the victim of a murder, dying in the street. Shortly afterwards, while paying his respects at that spot, he had got drawn into an impromptu revenge attack on someone said to be the killer. The Secretary of State argued that 'by considering the circumstances surrounding the committal of the offence the Tribunal was impermissibly trespassing on the nature and seriousness of the offence which was a matter for the Secretary of State'. But the Court of Appeal held that 'circumstances surrounding its committal were relevant in deciding whether it would be disproportionate to remove him' (para 29).

16.7.2 UK Borders Act 2007 ss 32–39

Section 32 provides that, where a person is sentenced to a period of imprisonment of at least 12 months, or is sentenced to a period of imprisonment of any length but has committed an offence specified under Nationality, Immigration and Asylum Act 2002 s 72(4) (none have been specified), their deportation is automatically deemed to be conducive to the public good and the Secretary of State is obliged to make a deportation order (s 32(5)). The main exceptions are where deportation would breach a person's ECHR rights or their rights under European Community law or breach the Refugee Convention, or the person was a minor at the date of conviction. The exceptions do not mean that no deportation order will be made (s 33), but rather that there is no duty to make the deportation order, and that there is a right of appeal on the grounds of the exceptions. There is no right of appeal against an 'automatic' deportation outside the exceptions, though the decision that s 32(5) applies is itself appealable (2002 Act s 82 (3A)). In the case of a minor there is also no presumption that the deportation is for the public good. It is strange that the presumption that deportation is conducive to the public good stands in the case of a proposed deportee protected by Community law, as in such a case Community law will prevail (see chapter 5). A further exception was introduced by s 146 of the Criminal Justice and Immigration Act 2008 for victims of trafficking.

Section 59(4) allows for the automatic deportation provisions to apply to people who were convicted before the UK Borders Act received Royal Assent (30 October 2007), if they were still in custody when these provisions came into force. Sections 32 to 39 came into force on 1 August 2008 as regards those sentenced to 12 months' imprisonment (UK Borders Act 2007 (Commencement No. 3 and Transitional Provisions) Order 2008, SI 2008/1818). In *R Hussein v SSHD* [2009] EWHC 2492, the claimant was convicted after the passing of the Act but before the commencement of ss 32 to 39. The Court held that to miss out people convicted between Royal Assent and commencement would be irrational, and that he was subject to automatic deportation. This was confirmed by the Court of Appeal in *AT (Pakistan) v SSHD* [2010] EWCA Civ 567, which also held that this retrospective application of automatic deportation was not a breach of Article 7 ECHR, which prohibits retrospective penalties, because deportation is not a criminal penalty.

In automatic deportations, the sentence of the Court has become a decisive factor, even though the sentence may well not have been passed with this consequence in mind, and, indeed, the Court should not take into account factors that are for the *Secretary of State (DA (Colombia) v SSHD* [2009] EWCA Civ 682). Paragraph 364 of the immigration rules, even in its new form, does not apply where the deportation is automatic (para 364A).

Automatic deportation goes in exactly the opposite direction to the development of EC law, in which, as we have seen in chapter 5, deportation must be based on the personal conduct of the individual and the risk they present to society, and is a last resort for very serious reasons, in fact intended to be rare where the individual has lived in the host country for more than five years.

In cases outside the UK Borders Act, the Secretary of State still has discretion to decide whether deportation is 'conducive to the public good'. These include minors, where the proposed deportee has not received a prison sentence of the kind covered by the section, or in cases not based on criminal convictions. In these cases, the reasoning applied is the old case law represented by the cases discussed previously applying *N (Kenya)*. Where deportation decisions are taken after 20 July 2006, the new form of the rules applies, including the presumption that a deportation which is conducive to the public good is in the public interest (amended para 364).

The critical factor in many deportation decisions remains whether they are arguably in breach of Article 8 (see chapter 18). In such cases, the matter will be decided principally according to that Article, the public interest in deportation being weighed as part of the justification under Article 8.2 for the deportation. This is so whether the decision is taken before or after July 2006, and before or after 1 August 2008. In *RG (Automatic deport Section 33(2)(a) exception) Nepal* [2010] UKUT 273 (IAC), RG, a 20-year-old man of previously good character, and son of a Ghurka who had retired to the UK, became involved with other young men in an incident in which a very drunk young man was thrown into the River Thames, where he drowned. He was sentenced to three years' imprisonment for manslaughter and violent disorder. The Tribunal found that he had a family and private life which required respect and which would be interfered with by deportation. They pointed out that neither the trial judge nor the Secretary of State had decided that deportation was the appropriate course. It had been deemed by statute. They said:

> There is a danger in equating the kind of seriousness of offence needed to justify deportation irrespective of any likelihood of re-offending and the criteria for automatic deportation subject to human rights claims under the Borders Act. Where automatic deportation arises in a case where there is a family and private life to which respect is owed, the task of the Immigration Judge is to carefully assess the factors that are identified in the case of *Maslov v Austria*. (para 39)

Additionally:

> The regime of automatic deportation where it has impact upon the family or private life of those lawfully resident here and deserves respect requires a very careful consideration of the seriousness of the offence and the extent to which the deportation can be said to enhance public protection on the one hand and the impact upon private and family life on the other. (para 43)

Although s 33 disapplies the duty to make a deportation order where the exceptions apply, in case of the exception for human rights, the deportation is still deemed to be conducive to the public good (s 33(7)). The Court of Appeal in *RU (Bangladesh) v SSHD* [2011] EWCA Civ 651 held that despite this, both the SSHD and any reviewing tribunal must take into account the public interest factors specified in *OH Serbia* when considering the proportionality of deportation. The Court must take into account that Parliament has deemed the deportation to be conducive to the public good, and in the light of this, determine the proportionality of the interference with Article 8 rights.

Perhaps surprisingly, the Court has still not considered directly whether, in an Article 8 case, these provisions of the UK Borders Act affect the weight to be given to the public interest, though referring to this question (see *RU Bangladesh* and in *AP (Trinidad and Tobago) v SSHD* [2011] EWCA Civ 551).

16.7.3 **Political reasons**

Interestingly, the deeming sections in the UK Borders Act do not necessarily apply to deportations under s 3(5)(a) where the ground of the decision is that deportation is conducive to the public good as being in the interests of national security or of the relations between the UK and any other country (Nationality, Immigration and Asylum Act 2002 s 97(2)). The reason for this is that proposed deportees do not necessarily have criminal convictions; the decision is based on the Secretary of State's assessment of the risk that the person poses to national security. Before the 2002 Act the national security ground also included 'other reasons of a political nature'. Unlike other deportations under s 3(5)(a), national security appeals do not go through the ordinary appeal process, but only to the Special Immigration Appeal Commission (SIAC). The Secretary of State also has power to take proceedings out of the ordinary appeal process and transfer them to SIAC if he or she certifies that the decision was made wholly or partly in reliance on information which ought not to be disclosed for reasons of public interest or national security or relations with other states (s 97(3)).

As in other areas of law, where national security is in issue, the balance between the state and the individual shifts further towards the state, involving curtailment of the rights of the individual.

16.7.3.1 *Basis of political deportation*

Although so-called 'political' or 'national security' deportations are treated differently from others, the formal grounds for such a deportation are still that the deportation is conducive to the public good. National security and international relations may overlap. The Secretary of State is not obliged to settle the allegations in such a way that they fit into one or another category (*SSHD v Rehman* [2001] 3 WLR 877. The decision to deport may be described for instance as being 'in the interests of national security, namely the likelihood of your involvement in terrorist activity'. The specificity of allegations depends upon the view that the Secretary of State takes of any risks of disclosing sources. See discussion of evidence in the next section and chapter 8.

Before the changes following on the case of *Chahal v UK* (1997) 23 EHRR 413 (see chapter 8), there was no right of appeal at all to a judicial body against a political or national security deportation. As described in chapter 8, the Special Immigration Appeals Commission (SIAC) resulted from this case, and the first case in the SIAC holds an important place in the development of the law on national security deportations.

16.7.3.2 *Rehman's case – standard of proof and evidence in national security cases*

Key Case

***SSHD v Rehman* [2001] 3 WLR 877**

Mr Rehman was a Muslim minister of religion who had limited leave to remain under the immigration rules in that capacity. He was married and had two children born in the UK. He was refused indefinite leave to remain on the grounds that the Secretary of State was satisfied that Mr Rehman was involved with a terrorist organization, and that in the light of that association his continued presence in the country represented a danger to national security.

The Secretary of State added that his deportation from the UK would be conducive to the public good in the interests of national security because of his association with Islamic terrorist groups. The organization was named, though the Secretary of State's view was formed on the basis of information received from confidential sources.

The SIAC found that the evidence did not establish the acts alleged, namely that Mr Rehman had recruited British Muslims to undergo militant training, or engaged in fundraising for Lashkar Tayyaba (LT), or knowingly sponsored individuals for militant training camps. It was accepted that he had provided sponsorship, information, and advice to people going to Pakistan for training. Such training he had regarded as purely religious and developmental. It had not been proved that he was aware of any militant content in such training.

In addition to the question of the jurisdiction of the Commission, two questions of law were appealed to the Court of Appeal and House of Lords. The first was the standard of proof to be applied. The SIAC took the view that these were serious allegations which had important repercussions for the individual involved and which impugned his good character. For these reasons, a standard of proof such as that laid down in *Khawaja* [1984] AC 74 should be applied, that is, a high civil standard of proof. Using this standard, they found that the matters alleged against Mr Rehman were not proved. The Court of Appeal and House of Lords approved the standard as applied to the appellant's actual involvement in alleged terrorist activities, but found that the question of danger to national security required an all-round assessment of the situation, not just a finding of, as it were, guilt or innocence in relation to past events. The Court of Appeal said: 'it is necessary not only to look at the individual allegations and ask whether they have been proved. It is also necessary to examine the case as a whole against an individual and then ask whether on a global approach that individual is a danger to national security' ([2000] 3 All ER 778 at 791). The House of Lords approved this view and said that the Secretary of State was 'entitled to have regard to precautionary and preventative principles rather than to wait until directly harmful activities have taken place' (para 22). In fact, the idea of a standard of proof was, said Lords Steyn and Hoffmann, not really appropriate to a case where the central question was not, as in a civil or criminal trial, whether something had happened in the past, but rather whether something was likely to happen in the future. It was an evaluation of risk. The effect of this is that the Secretary of State is entitled to make a decision that an individual who cannot be proved to have taken part in any unlawful activities should be deported because there is, in the words of Lord Slynn, a 'real possibility' that their presence may in the future constitute a danger.

The second issue in the appeals was the question of the definition of national security. First, there was the question of whether the SIAC had jurisdiction to engage in the question of defining national security. The House of Lords held that this could be within the jurisdiction of a judicial body; it was a question of construction and therefore a question of law. The area of contention between the parties was whether activities in the UK which furthered the cause of an organization abroad which could use violence which was not directed at the UK, could be said to endanger the security of the UK. SIAC accepted the appellant's argument that for an activity to endanger the national security of the UK there must be some direct link between the activity and a danger to the UK. The House of Lords and Court of Appeal rejected this view. They adopted the approach of Auld LJ in *Raghbir Singh* [1996] Imm AR 507, who said at 511, 'all sorts of consequences may flow from the existence of terrorist conspiracies or organizations here, whether or not their outcome is intended to occur abroad. Who knows what equally violent response here this sort of conduct may provoke?' and of Lord Mustill in the asylum case of *T* [1996] Imm AR 443, that 'terror as a means of gaining what might loosely be described as political ends poses a danger not only to individual states but also to the community of nations'. Lord Slynn said:

> It seems to me that, in contemporary world conditions, action against a foreign state may be capable indirectly of affecting the security of the United Kingdom. The means open to terrorists both in attacking another state and attacking international or global activity by the community of nationals, whatever the objectives of the terrorist, may well be capable of reflecting on the safety and well-being of the United Kingdom or its citizens...To require the matters in question to be capable of resulting 'directly' in a threat to national security limits too tightly the discretion of the executive in deciding how the interests of the state...need to be protected.

This approach is an international one, in which the fight against terrorism is seen as something in which nations have a common interest. National security is bound up with international security, and in the context of terrorism this enables the Secretary of State to justify a decision on national security by reference to damage to relations between countries.

The House of Lords made a distinction between deciding what national security is, which the courts could decide, and what is *in the interests of national security*, which they regarded as a matter for the Secretary of State to decide. In the words of Lord Hoffmann: 'the question of whether something is "in the interests" of national security is not a question of law. It is a matter of judgment and policy' (para 50). Such judgements should be made by someone who was democratically accountable, not by the courts.

The deference shown to the Secretary of State's view on what is in the interests of national security, combined with the abandonment of a standard of proof, to an extent undermines the jurisdiction of the SIAC. They can, indeed, review all questions of law, fact, and exercise of discretion, but issues of what is in the interests of national security are to be regarded as an exercise of discretion concerning risk, not one of establishing facts, and this is a discretion which the Secretary of State is best placed to exercise.

Macdonald commented on this case at the Court of Appeal stage: 'Not since the majority decision Liversidge and Anderson has the executive been given such deference; one can hear the Secretary of State saying "I can make national security mean anything I want it to mean"' (2001:724).

Macdonald was commenting in May 2001, and his comparison with *Liversidge and Anderson* [1942] AC 206 was prophetic. That decision is often explained on the basis that it was taken during wartime, when the government needs to be given more scope to act as it sees fit, even in breach of people's ordinary civil liberties. The response of the UK and US to the attack on the World Trade Center, on 11 September 2001, was to legislate in a way that is reminiscent of wartime, in the extent of inroads made into civil liberties.

This approach to the standard of proof and assessment of national security risk is similar to that used in refugee claims to assess future risk should the asylum seeker return to their country of origin, and the authority on that point, *Karanakaran*, is used also in national security appeals. For instance, in *Y v SSHD* [2006] UKSIAC 36/2004, SIAC held that the proceedings were not civil proceedings, requiring acts to be proved on a balance of probabilities. 'They are public law proceedings the focus of which is risk, that is an evaluation of what harm may happen in the future' (para 128). This draws directly on *Karanakaran*. Y was arrested on suspicion of being concerned in the instigation, preparation, or commission of acts of terrorism. He was tried as a defendant in the 'ricin' or 'poisons plot' trial but acquitted on all charges. Like other potential deportees on national security grounds, he did not hear all the evidence against him, as some was considered in 'closed' sessions of the SIAC. He was shown to be linked to militant organizations in Algeria, indeed facts related to this had formed the basis of his asylum claim which had succeeded on appeal some years earlier. Y could be shown to have connections and associations with people who were found culpable. For instance, he ran the bookshop at the mosque associated with extremist activity, and appeared to have photocopied the poison recipes. As the SIAC said, in isolation, each matter might be explicable as 'innocent'. Crucially, they decided that treating the matters as separate was not the right approach. They should be regarded cumulatively, and in that way they built a picture of someone the Secretary of State could legitimately regard as a risk. This approach was confirmed in *ZZ*, quoting from *Rehman*:

> the whole concept of a standard of proof is not particularly helpful in a case such as the present . . . the question . . . is not whether a given event happened but the extent of future risk. This depends upon an evaluation of the evidence of the appellant's conduct against a broad range of facts with which they may interact. The question of whether the risk to national security is sufficient to justify the appellant's deportation cannot be answered by taking each allegation seriatim and deciding whether it has been established to some standard of proof. It is a question of evaluation and judgment, in which it is necessary to take into account not only the degree of probability of prejudice to national security but also the importance of the security interest at stake and the serious consequences of deportation for the deportee. (para 56)

The deportation of Abu Qatada was held lawful on grounds of national security by the SIAC and upheld along with others by the House of Lords (*RB (Algeria), U and OO (Jordan) v SSHD* [2009] UKHL 10). The questions of law in these appeals did not turn on the question of whether the deportation was conducive to the public good, but on the nature of SIAC proceedings and admissible evidence, which is discussed in chapter 8, and on the government's reliance on assurances of fair treatment in the country to which they were to be deported, which is discussed in chapter 4. The Court of Appeal in *W (Algeria)* held that despite this, the approach of their Lordships to the evidence required before SIAC could be applied when the evidence required to justify a deportation on the grounds of national security was directly in issue (para 56).

Procedural rules are restrictive in national security cases. In some proceedings concerning national security, for instance those relating to control orders, case law has established a right to disclosure of an 'irreducible minimum' of evidence (see chapter 8). The UK courts have held that this does not apply where deportation or exclusion are challenged, because Article 6 ECHR does not apply (see *Maaouia*, chapter 4), and civil rights in the ECHR sense are not at stake (*W and others (Algeria v SSHD* [2010] EWCA Civ

898 and *IR (Sri Lanka)*). The appellants in *W (Algeria)* argued that the common law principles of a fair trial required the SIAC rules to be read down so as to enable disclosure of the gist of the case against them. The Court of Appeal held that they were not empowered to read down SIAC's explicit rules where the enabling statute clearly contemplated that priority could be given to the need to protect national security. Parliament had approved the rules by affirmative resolution (para 51). The only procedural right for the deportee or excluded person is to 'independent scrutiny of the claim' (*IR (Sri Lanka) and others* v *SSHD* [2011] EWCA Civ 704 (para 19)).

In *ZZ v SSHD* [2011] EWCA Civ 440 the Court of Appeal has made a reference to the CJEU asking whether the same standard applies to EU citizens, in the light of the principle of effective judicial protection in Article 30(2) Citizens Directive (Case C–300/11).

The Immigration, Asylum and Nationality Act 2006 includes a provision that deportation orders may be made on the grounds of threat to national security while an appeal is pending or may be brought, in contrast with other deportations in which no order may be made until the appeal process is exhausted (s 7, excluding application of s 79 of the 2002 Act).

16.7.4 Family members

Apart from deportations conducive to the public good, the only other people who may be deported since the implementation of the 1999 Act are family members of people who are deported under s 3(5)(a). Note that these deportations now take place under s 3(5)(b) of the 1971 Act, whereas in case law prior to October 2000 they will be referred to as s 3(5)(c). 'Family members' are defined by the 1971 Act s 5(4), as amended by the 1996 Act, as the husband or wife and children of the person to be deported. 'Children' include adopted children. When parents are unmarried, children are regarded as children of only their mother. Although the entry of second or further wives is not permitted under the immigration rules, in the context of deportation polygamy is recognized, as 'wife' includes each of two or more wives.

Paragraphs 365–368 of the immigration rules give guidance on the deportation of family members, including civil partners, though these are not mentioned in the Act. According to these paragraphs, the Secretary of State will not normally decide to deport the partner of a deportee where they have qualified for settlement in their own right or have been living apart from the deportee. If a child is living apart from the deportee either with their other parent or because they have established themselves on an independent basis, the Secretary of State will not normally decide to deport the child. This is also the case where the child married before the deportation 'came into prospect'. There are additional factors to be taken into account in the deportation of family members, and these are set out in para 367 as follows:

(i) the ability of the spouse or civil partner to maintain himself and any children in the United Kingdom, or to be maintained by relatives or friends without charge to public funds, not merely for a short period but for the foreseeable future; and

(ii) in the case of a child of school age, the effect of removal on his education; and

(iii) the practicality of any plans for a child's care and maintenance in this country if one or both of his parents were deported; and

(iv) any representations made on behalf of the spouse or child.

In *Njuguna v SSHD* [2001] EWCA Civ 688, the Court of Appeal held that these questions were irrelevant in relation to a five-year-old child. He was not, in any event, going to be able to make a life independently of his mother in the UK. If she were deported, he would be too, and issuing a notice and order in relation to him was simply taking the legal power which inevitably followed from his mother's deportation. Following *Beoku-Betts* and s 55 Borders Citizenship and Immigration Act 2009, these factors concerning the welfare of family members should have already been taken into account finalizing the deportation, and considering an Article 8 defence to it. Paragraph 367 provides a further safety net. *Njuguna* suggests that this does not avail very young children, but may need to be revisited in the light of *ZH (Tanzania)* (see chapter 9).

According to s 5(3) of the 1971 Act, a deportation order may not be made against family members if more than eight weeks have elapsed since the principal deportee left the country. Again, this in practical terms only applies where the family member has a viable life in the UK aside from their deported relative.

16.7.5 Criminal court's recommendation

Section 3(6) of the 1971 Act gives the power to the Secretary of State to deport following the recommendation of a criminal court. The power to make such a recommendation is a sentencing power which may be exercised by the courts in relation to a non-British citizen over the age of 17 who has been convicted of an offence which is punishable with imprisonment. Appeals against the recommendation itself are appeals against sentence and are made through the criminal appeals process.

The decision whether to follow the recommendation is a separate step, and this is the responsibility of the Secretary of State. The recommendation of the sentencing judge does not bind the Secretary of State. Case law held that he or she has a different constitutional role in the decision-making process and is better placed to take a wider policy-based view of whether deportation is the right course (*R v SSHD ex p Dinc* [1999] Imm AR 380 CA).

16.7.5.1 *Criminal courts and deportation*

The general powers of the criminal courts include sentencing for immigration offences. On the other hand, people who are liable to deportation for an offence which has nothing to do with immigration may not have a flawless immigration history. There is plenty of scope for confusion here. Macdonald used some choice words to describe an aspect of the problem:

> Matters have not been assisted by the tendency of the courts to describe any non-citizen guilty of an offence under the Immigration Act as an 'illegal immigrant'. The phrase is meaningless and has pejorative connotations of status that may be misleading. A student who fails to get the Department of Employment's permission before getting a summer job, a husband who forgets to apply in time for permission to remain with a wife, an alien who fails to inform the police of a change of address, are doubtless all guilty of offences which may be described as regulatory, but it would be as inappropriate to describe them as 'illegal immigrants' as it would be to describe the company which fails to make expeditious VAT returns as an illegal business. (1995:489)

Deportation as a sentence for an immigration offence is not appropriate unless it would be warranted in accordance with the proper criteria for deportation.

16.7.5.2 *Guidelines*

Guidelines for the criminal courts in exercising their power to recommend deportation were set out initially in *R v Caird* (1970) 54 Cr App Rep 499, CA and developed in *R v Nazari* [1980] 3 All ER 880. These, of course, now apply only in cases where the sentence is of less than 12 months' imprisonment, and yet the Court considers that deportation may be appropriate. The Court of Appeal in *R v Kluxen* [2010] Crim CA 1081 noted that such cases will be rare. The Court held that the threshold for a recommendation of deportation in *Nazari* is a high one, corresponding to the test in the leading EU case of *Bouchereau* (see chapter 5).

The first guideline from *Nazari* is that criminal courts are concerned with the potential detriment to the UK of the person remaining in the country. This has been regarded as nothing to do with their immigration status as the detriment is through criminal activity. However, in *R v Benabbas* [2005] EWCA Crim 2113, the Court of Appeal held that where deportation was for using a forged passport, immigration status is 'not entirely irrelevant: it is part of the defendant's personal conduct...a matter of public interest' (para 40) and 'detriment is intimately bound up with the protection of public order afforded by confidence in a system of passports' (para 41). The risk of reoffending is a key matter to be assessed, and the Court will also have regard to the nature of the offence and the defendant's past record.

Second, the Court in *Nazari* thought that they should not be concerned with the political situation or regime or any political threat in the defendant's home country. The Home Office rather than the criminal court was the place to assess such matters.

The Court in *Kluxen* then sets out the matters that a court recommending deportation should not take into account. These are:

i) The rights of the offender under the ECHR. As explained by Stanley Burnton J. in *R. v. Carmona* [2006] 2 Cr. App. R. (S.) 662: the Secretary of State and, in the event of an appeal, the Asylum and Immigration Tribunal, are able and better placed than a sentencing court to consider the offender's Convention rights.
ii) The effect that a recommendation for deportation might have on innocent persons not before the Court, such as members of the family of the offender concerned (*Carmona* overturned *Nazari* in this regard).
iii) The political situation in the country to which the offender may be deported (following both *Nazari* and *Carmona*).

The Court in *Kluxen* rejected the view that a criminal court, if considering a deportation order against an EU national, should take into account the period of the offender's residence in the UK, and other personal circumstances listed in Article 28 of the Citizens Directive. Taking a similar approach to the Court in *Carmona,* the Court held that these were matters to be considered when a deportation order was made, not when the Court made a recommendation for deportation. The same consideration applied to factors under the 2006 EEA Regulations. In any event, it was highly unlikely that the Court would be considering such a recommendation, as the Secretary of State's policy was that no citizen of the European Economic Area would be removed unless the prison sentence imposed was two years or more (para 30).

16.8 Revocation

A deportation order does not expire after a period of time. It runs until it is revoked, unless the person who is the subject of the order becomes a British citizen (1971 Act s 5(2)). However, it may be revoked on application in accordance with paras 390–392 of the immigration rules. The factors which will be taken into account are:

(i) the grounds on which the order was made;
(ii) any representations made in support of revocation;
(iii) the interests of the community, including the maintenance of effective immigration control; and
(iv) the interests of the applicant, including any compassionate circumstances.

In the case of deportation based on criminal convictions, para 391 provides for a normal minimum period of time that should elapse after making the deportation order before revocation is considered. This was three years until 2008, when rules were introduced to impose a re-entry ban for those removed or refused entry on grounds such as illegal entry or deception (see chapter 7). The normal minimum period for a deportation order was raised so that it equalled the longest period of exclusion. The new normal minimum is ten years in the case of offences which are capable of being spent under the Rehabilitation of Offenders Act 1974. In the case of offences which cannot be spent under that Act, deportation is indefinite, unless human rights or the Refugee Convention require otherwise.

The rule goes on to say 'in other cases' revocation will not normally be authorized, unless there is a change of circumstances or fresh information which might materially alter the situation. The passage of time in itself may amount to a change of circumstance. 'Other cases' are those not based on criminal convictions. Clearly, there is some discretion in criminal cases, too, as the ten-year and indefinite provisions are the norm, not the rule, and even without such provision in the immigration rules, public law principles would require it (e.g., *British Oxygen v Minister of Technology* [1971] AC 610). The IDI says that in 'exceptional' cases not covered by the Human Rights or Refugee Conventions, these same factors may be considered (IDI 13.5). Even before the 2008 rule change, the Home Office's internal guidance on deportation suggested that ten years should elapse before revoking deportation orders against people convicted of serious offences. These were defined as offences of violence, persistent, or large-scale burglary or theft, blackmail, forgery, drug offences, and public order offences including riot and affray. However, some of these offences could easily attract a sentence of more than 30 months' imprisonment – the maximum which permits the conviction to be spent – and now place the individual at risk of indefinite deportation. The period of exclusion was said by the Court in *AS (Pakistan) v SSHD* [2008] EWCA Civ 1118 to be relevant to the exercise of the discretion to deport.

Under s 82 of the 2002 Act, there is a right of appeal against the refusal to revoke a deportation order, but under s 92 this right may only be exercised from outside the country unless it is based on asylum or human rights grounds that have not been certified as clearly unfounded (*BA Nigeria v SSHD* [2009] UKSC 7). According to para 391 of the rules, time is counted before which an application can be made to revoke from the date of making the order. The IDI says, however, 'in cases where a person considerably delayed the enforcement of a deportation order through non-compliance, consideration should be given as to whether a lengthier exclusion period should apply'. This is a risk of attempting to stay longer, although occasionally successful public campaigns are mounted to avoid deportation even at this late stage (see, for instance, 'Resistance from Below' in *No-one is Illegal* (Cohen 2003)). An application to revoke a deportation order can be made on the basis of the impact that separation has had on family left in the UK (e.g., see *Lee v SSHD* [2011] EWCA Civ 348).

Revocation of a deportation order does not entitle the successful applicant to enter the UK. It only means that an application may be made for leave to enter under the immigration rules and this will be considered on its merits.

16.9 Voluntary departures

Once a person is aware that they may be subject to deportation, if there are no strong grounds to challenge the deportation they may wish to leave the country as quickly as possible to avoid a deportation order being made. If they leave before the order is made, even without contact with the Home Office, any deportation order made after that date will be invalid (IDI 13.1.2.2).

If the person leaves after the deportation order was made, they are still regarded as deported, even if they were not aware of it, and the order will have the same validity as if the Home Office had enforced it. Alternatively, a person may sign a formal disclaimer of appeal rights and agree to leave, which gives rise to the possibility of the immigration service paying for their passage (Immigration Act 1971 s 5(6)). This is known as 'supervised departure' (IDI 13.5.10.2).

The International Organisation for Migration operates voluntary return programmes for 'irregular migrants' as well as people whose asylum claims have failed. These are now conspicuously advertised by the Home Office in the case of failed asylum claims, but have no application in the case of deportation.

Voluntary departures still have an impact on re-entry. Those who have overstayed, breached a condition, used deception, or been an illegal entrant, but leave voluntarily at their own expense are refused entry under para 320(7B) for 12 months after return. Those who leave voluntarily at the expense of the Secretary of State are to be refused entry for five years.

16.10 Conclusion

The greatly increased use of deportation in recent years reflects a government policy of something approaching zero tolerance towards foreign nationals who commit criminal offences. The interaction of the automatic deportation regime with criminal sanctions for use of false documents and working without permission generates a further route to removing those whose asylum claims have failed, and who may resort to illegal working when they have no other means of support.

QUESTIONS

1 The European Court of Human Rights in the case of *Maaouia v France* said that deportation is not a criminal penalty imposed upon a foreign national. It is not a punishment for a crime for which they have already served a prison sentence, but is an administrative matter. Consider the arguments for and against that view.

2 Is it justifiable to treat European nationals more favourably in the context of deportation?

For guidance on answering questions, visit www.oxfordtextbooks.co.uk/orc/clayton5e/.

FURTHER READING

Bevan, Vaughan (1986) *The Development of British Immigration Law* (London: Croom Helm), pp. 305–309.

Clery, Elizabeth, Daniel, Nicholas, and Tah, Carolyne (2005) *The Voluntary Assisted Return and Reintegration 2003: An Evaluation, Home Office* (London: Research, Development and Statistics).

Cohen, Steve (2003) 'Resistance from Below', in S. Cohen (ed.) *No-one is Illegal* (Stoke-on-Trent: Trentham Books).

Farbey, Judith (2007) 'Foreign National Prisoners: Current Law and Practice' *Journal of Immigration, Asylum and Nationality Law* vol. 21, no. 1 pp. 6–13.

Shah, Ramnik (2007) 'The FNP Saga' *Journal of Immigration, Asylum and Nationality Law* vol. 21, no. 1, pp. 27–31.

17

Removal

SUMMARY

This chapter describes the development of the grounds in law for exercising the power to remove a person from the UK and the obstacles to removal both practical and legal.

17.1 Introduction

The power of removal is the clearest possible demonstration of the Crown's power to control the movement of foreign nationals, though this does not mean that it is an untrammelled power. It is exercised within a statutory framework, principally that of the Immigration Act 1971, amended and supplemented by the Asylum and Immigration Act 1996, the Immigration and Asylum Act 1999, the Nationality, Immigration and Asylum Act 2002, the Asylum and Immigration (Treatment of Claimants etc) Act 2004, and the Immigration Asylum and Nationality Act 2006. The power is tempered by human rights and asylum considerations; nevertheless, in 2010, 60,244 people were removed from the UK.

Directions for removal may be given without, necessarily, any kind of judicial process. A person may be put onto an aeroplane or a ship and taken to another country without any opportunity to challenge this course of action. Because of the abrupt and potentially speedy nature of this process, and its lack of judicial oversight, it can be described as 'summary removal'. It is difficult to imagine a more dramatic exercise of power by the executive over the individual, but its power may be mitigated by a right of appeal. Where there is an existing entry clearance and when human rights or asylum claims are made, there may be an in-country right of appeal , but not if the claim is certified as clearly unfounded by the Secretary of State (Nationality, Immigration and Asylum Act 2002 Parts 4 and 5). There are other limited appeal rights, but these may only be exercised after removal. As a consequence, resort has often been made to judicial review to suspend the implementation of removal.

17.1.1 Terminology

There is scope for a great deal of confusion in the use of the term 'removal' and associated phrases. One use of the term 'administrative removal' is to refer to removal on the grounds which used to be grounds for deportation, discussed at 17.2.3. This distinguishes it from removal of illegal entrants and those refused entry. Another use of the term 'administrative removal' is to refer to all removals, using 'administrative' to distinguish it from deportation. Finally, all enforced departures including deportation end in removal, as this term is used to describe the actual embarkation on transport which takes the person away, and all such departures are preceded by removal directions. These are served on the captain of a ship or aircraft or on a train operator, and on the person themselves, telling them when and where to report in order for their removal to take place. The term 'removal' is used in this chapter to refer to all removals as distinct from deportations. The term 'administrative removal' is not used.

17.1.2 Growth of the power to remove

The power of removal has existed in its present form since 1 January 1973, when the Immigration Act 1971 came into force. The Act made Commonwealth citizens and aliens subject to the same legal regime, and this included the power to remove anyone who had entered in breach of immigration laws (Sch 2 and s 33). *Azam v SSHD* [1974] AC 18 confirmed that this statutory power applied even to Commonwealth citizens who had entered before the Act came into effect, and who would have been immune from removal or deportation under the previous law.

The power to remove was implemented straight away. Evans charts the growth in its use from 80 people in the first year of operation to a peak of 910 in 1980, dropping again to 640 in 1981. The starting figure of 80 was, he points out, a significant increase on the steady annual figure of around 60 people removed each year from 1968 to 1972. As we shall see, the increased number of removals reflected expansion of the law governing removal at that time. After the 1971 Act extended power to Commonwealth citizens, the courts took hold of the concept of 'illegal entrant' and extended it in a way not foreseen by Parliament. In 1983, the House of Lords put the brake on this expansion. However, as described in chapter 16, with the 1999 Act many of those previously subject to deportation became subject to removal.

The number of people removed as illegal entrants doubled from 1987 to 1988, and the UK Immigration Advisory Service suggested that this increase was part of an attempt to curtail asylum appeals (Dummett and Nicol 1990:255). The number of removals combined with voluntary departures after enforcement proceedings reached a peak in 2008 at 67,980 (Control of Immigration Statistics 2008 Home Office August 2009). The Home Office explains that the drop since that peak:

> can be mostly accounted for by the significantly lower number of non-asylum cases refused entry at port and subsequently removed (from 29,162 during 2009 to 18,276 during 2010) and has also been affected by decreasing numbers of asylum cases (Immigration Statistics published August 2011).

Although the majority of people removed have never sought asylum, the desire to process asylum claims quickly and to remove unsuccessful applicants are significant policy drivers behind the law and practice on removal. It was considered in the Home Affairs Select Committee Report on Asylum Removals that the integrity of the asylum process relies on the capacity to effect the removal of those whose claim has failed (e.g., para 8). The Committee's report also describes the practical and legal complexities of effecting removals, and in 2010 only 10,394 of the 60,244 people removed had sought asylum at some stage (Immigration Statistics August 2011). See also the discussion in chapter 2.

Although governments repeatedly promise to increase the number of refused asylum seekers removed each year, there continue to be important questions about whether removals to certain countries are safe and feasible. See 17.8 on Viability of Return. The manner in which removals are carried out is also an issue of public concern.

17.2 Grounds for removal

There are two sets of powers of removal. Immigration Act 1971 Sch 2 gives power to immigration officers to remove people who have been refused leave to enter (para 8) and illegal entrants (para 9). Immigration and Asylum Act 1999 s 10 gives power to remove people who have overstayed the limit of their leave, or have breached conditions of leave or obtained leave to remain by deception. It also gives power to remove the families of such people.

We shall consider each of these grounds in turn.

17.2.1 Illegal entrants

It is extraordinary that such a draconian power as that of forcible removal is almost incidental in statute, and the many legislative changes since 1971 have not changed this. The definition of an illegal entrant is found in s 33, the definition section of the 1971 Act, and the power to remove an illegal entrant is in Sch 2. A power which forms a major plank of immigration control would be more appropriately located in the body of the statute. However, the power to remove was envisaged as an administrative matter, an action which could be taken speedily by immigration officers without judicial involvement.

An 'illegal entrant' is defined in s 33(1) of the 1971 Act, as amended by the Asylum and Immigration Act 1996, as a person:

(i) unlawfully entering or seeking to enter in breach of a deportation order or of the immigration laws; or

(ii) entering or seeking to enter by means which include deception by another person,

and includes a person who has entered by these means.

A person may be termed an 'illegal entrant' without actually entering, as s 33 covers those who 'seek to enter' as well as those who actually do. A person may be apprehended, say, at a port, and may be subject to removal as an illegal entrant if they were seeking to enter in breach of immigration laws but had not yet done so. A clandestine entrant may come within this category. The only kind of entry to the UK that is lawful without prior entry clearance is as a visitor. Any other application without documentation may be rejected at the port. If the immigration officer is not satisfied that the person is a genuine visitor there is no appeal against refusal of entry. If the passenger does not leave voluntarily, then removal will be arranged. The only appeal against this is on asylum or human rights grounds (2002 Act s 84). However, passengers are not routinely informed of this right. The Border Force Operational Manual puts it this way:

> Refusal in such cases should be notified on form IS82A, which does not advise the passenger of their limited appeal rights. However, any passenger who makes an unsuccessful residual claim must be refused again via service of the correct IS82AR series refusal form, which now notifies them of their appeal rights (in accordance with para 5(7) of the Regulations).

The meaning of this is that the passenger must raise the human rights, asylum, or discrimination grounds themselves.

Second, a person may be deemed an illegal entrant if they do actually enter illegally. We shall consider shortly what this means. Third, an illegal entrant is a person 'who has so entered'. The effect of this is that there is no cut-off date for designation as an illegal entrant. Under the Commonwealth Immigrants Act 1962, a person who remained undetected for 24 hours could not be removed; the 1968 Act extended this to 28 days but there are no such periods of grace in present law. Now, a person may live for years in insecurity, not knowing whether they will be subject to enforcement action. While a long residence in this country may affect whether enforcement action is taken or is successful (see chapter 7), the possibility of that action remains until their status is regularized. There are a number of ways in which a person may be considered to enter illegally.

17.2.1.1 *Entering without leave*

'Entering in breach of the immigration laws' was initially interpreted as meaning simply 'entering without leave'. The immigration laws were primarily concerned with the regulation of entry, so someone who entered in breach of those laws entered without having gone through that regulatory process. Specifically, 1971 Act s 3(1)(a) states:

> Except as otherwise provided by or under this Act, where a person is not a British Citizen (a) he shall not enter the UK unless given leave to do so in accordance with this Act.

Entry without leave by someone who needs leave is therefore a breach of immigration laws in that it is a breach of s 3 of the 1971 Act. Entry without leave does not require any particular state of mind or of knowledge in order to result in a person being an illegal entrant (*R v Governor of Ashford Remand Centre ex p Bouzagou* [1983] Imm AR 69). The breach of immigration laws does not need to be deliberate or even known to a person in order for them to have entered without leave and thus be deemed an illegal entrant.

This kind of illegal entry includes clandestine entrants who arrive in the back of lorries or land by night in a small boat on a secluded beach. It also includes people who mistakenly enter without leave, even if the mistake is that of the immigration officer. This surprising conclusion was reached in the case of *Rehal v Secretary of State for the Home Department* [1989] Imm AR 576 CA. Mr Rehal was a British overseas citizen. The immigration officer, glancing at his British passport, thought he was a British citizen and waved him through. Without a stamp in his passport, Mr Rehal had no leave to enter. The immigration officer's invitation for him to pass through was not a grant of leave but a (barely considered) decision that he did not need leave.

The same result comes about when the mistake, though still not the fault of the passport holder, is in the passport rather than the action of the immigration officer. This was apparent in the case of *Mokuolo and Ogunbiyi v SSHD* [1989] Imm AR 51 CA, in which the passports of two Nigerian sisters mistakenly stated that they were British citizens. Accordingly, they were not granted leave to enter on the assumption that they did not need it. Although, like Mr Rehal, they were not guilty of any deception or wrongdoing, they, like him, were found to be illegal entrants.

The Court of Appeal's decision in *Rehal* turned on the meaning they gave to 1971 Act Sch 2 para 6, the obligation to make a decision within 24 hours, failing which the entrant has six months' deemed leave. It applies where a person 'is to be given' limited leave. The Court of Appeal interpreted this to mean where the immigration officer intends to make a decision on the question of leave. This means that if the immigration officer has not thought about it because, for instance, as in Mr Rehal's case, they did not realize it was necessary to do so, the deemed leave provision does not apply, so the person is considered an illegal entrant. Macdonald puts forward an alternative and surely preferable interpretation that the words 'is to be given' refer to someone who needs leave, i.e., does not have right of abode (1995:70). This objective interpretation would bring within para 6 those who are deemed illegal entrants through the immigration officer's mistake. The UKBA's Enforcement Instructions and Guidance 2.3 says that the unwitting nature of any such illegal entry is a 'mitigating factor'. If a person enters using a British passport, the immigration officer has the burden of proving any suspicion that the person is not British.

Leave to enter is normally endorsed on a passport and will now usually have been granted by entry clearance in advance (Leave to Enter and Remain Order 2000, SI 2000/1161, see chapter 7). Therefore, the question of proof that it exists is reasonably straightforward except that leave to enter need not always be given in writing and need not be given to the traveller personally. It may be granted by fax or email or, for a visitor, even by telephone (2000 Order Article 8), and in the case of a group travelling together it might, for instance, be endorsed on a passenger list rather than a document produced by an individual (Article 9). In these cases, the burden of proof is on the person claiming that they have leave to enter to prove that is the case (Article 11). This reverses the burden of proof at precisely the point at which the entrant is most vulnerable, though it is unlikely that an oral grant of leave will often be given.

Section 11(5) of the 1971 Act provides that an air or sea crew member who seeks to remain beyond the time allowed (s 8(1)) will be treated as seeking to enter the UK. If they do so in breach of immigration laws they will be regarded as an illegal entrant.

17.2.1.2 *Entry in breach of a deportation order*

The s 33 definition of an illegal entrant includes someone who enters in breach of a deportation order. This means that any person who is the subject of a deportation order is subject to removal as an illegal entrant if they enter the UK while the deportation order is still in force against them. The order is in force unless it has been revoked. A deportation order completely prohibits re-entry, whether or not the person would normally require leave to enter, e.g., if they were an EEA national they would otherwise be able to enter without leave, but as a deportee they are an illegal entrant if they do so (*Shingara v SSHD* [1999] Imm AR 257 CA).

If the person who is the subject of the deportation order had leave when the deportation order was made the leave, whether limited or indefinite, is invalidated by the deportation order. Any leave granted during the currency of the deportation order, whether to enter or remain, is also invalidated (1971 Act s 5). The result of this is that if someone enters while a deportation order is in force against them, they enter without leave. This is the case whether they enter clandestinely or whether, by mistake or deception, they manage to obtain an apparent leave, as any such leave will have no effect.

It might therefore be objected that these words are redundant in the definition of an illegal entrant. A person subject to a deportation order is without leave anyway. This argument was advanced for the appellants in *Khawaja v SSHD* [1984] AC 74 (see next section) as evidence that 'in breach of the immigration laws' should be given a narrow interpretation, i.e., restricted only to those who entered without leave. If it was open to a wider interpretation, there would be no need to specify 'in breach of a deportation order', as that would be included. However, the House of Lords rejected that argument, opening the way to a wider interpretation of who is an illegal entrant.

17.2.1.3 *Entry by deception*

As indicated earlier, the possibility of becoming an illegal entrant by deception was not in the contemplation of Parliament at the time of the passing of the Immigration Act 1971. Illegal entrants were those entering in breach of a deportation order or without leave (see, for instance, discussion in Grant and Martin, *Immigration Law and Practice* (1982) and Evans, *Immigration Law* (1983)). The courts, however, began to interpret 'in breach of the immigration laws' as including people who had passed through immigration control and had obtained leave to enter, but had done so by deception. In a series of cases, leave obtained by deception contrary to s 26(1)(c) was treated as invalid. Section 26(1)(c) sets out a criminal offence, committed where a person:

> Makes or causes to be made... a return, statement or representation which he knows to be false or does not believe to be true.

The courts created a relationship between the definition of an illegal entrant and the criminal provisions of the Immigration Act. They decided that leave obtained in this way was obtained 'in breach of the immigration laws' and therefore not leave which would entitle a person to enter.

This judicial invention was ratified by the House of Lords in July 1980 in *Zamir* [1980] 2 All ER 768. Their Lordships held that leave granted through the use of deception was not leave granted in accordance with the Immigration Act and could rightly found a removal as an illegal entrant. Disturbingly, they considered that the duty of a potential immigrant was a 'duty of candour', analogous to the duty of utmost good faith imposed upon parties in the law of contract. This meant that the applicant must disclose all potentially relevant information, and was under a duty to volunteer information, not just to answer questions. This put the applicant in the position of being responsible for deciding what was relevant, and risking being removed as an illegal entrant if they made a wrong judgement on that matter.

This decision 'provoked widespread academic criticism and a storm of protest from the ethnic communities and bodies concerned with improving race relations' (Evans 1983:314). It was reversed in important respects by the House of Lords in *Khawaja* [1984] AC 74, which held that there was no duty of utmost good faith. There must be actual or attempted deception before illegal entry could be established, not just a failure to interpret correctly the requirements of the immigration rules. This judgment put beyond doubt that entry obtained by deception could give rise to removal as an illegal entrant, but tempered the more extreme aspects of the *Zamir* judgment. The House of Lords found that the burden of proof that the person was an illegal entrant was upon the Secretary of State, and the standard was the civil standard, but this should be interpreted as being at the high end of the balance of probabilities, bearing in mind the serious consequences for the individual and the quasi-criminal nature of the allegations. Importantly, the House of Lords in *Khawaja* reversed the 'hands-off' approach which had characterized earlier judicial decisions concerning illegal entrants. The courts had tended not to investigate the facts, and in judicial review held that such investigation was outside the Court's scope of enquiry as the jurisdiction is one of review of the decision-making process, not an appeal on the merits. The House of Lords in *Khawaja* held that the fact that someone was an illegal entrant was a matter which determined whether or not there was jurisdiction to act. Such 'jurisdictional facts' did, they said, come within the scope of the Court's inquiry. The Court would therefore examine for itself the evidence as to whether the person was an illegal entrant.

Following *Khawaja*, the inclusion of a person who gained entry by deception in the definition of illegal entrant was here to stay. Obtaining entry by deception became explicitly part of the statutory definition with the Asylum and Immigration Act 1996. The offence was created of using deception to obtain or seek to obtain leave to enter or remain in the UK (amending Immigration Act 1971 s 24, renumbered again by Immigration and Asylum Act 1999 so the offence is now found in 1971 Act s 24A). An offence under that section, like an offence under s 26(1)(c) is 'in breach of immigration laws' and so makes the perpetrator an illegal entrant as found in *Khawaja*.

However, this left open a number of issues surrounding deception. These included the effect of deception by a third party, the use of false documents, the relationship between any deception and the leave granted, and what conduct may give rise to a finding of deception, in the absence of a duty of utmost good faith.

Third-party deception and use of false documents

The Asylum and Immigration Act 1996 resolved the question of the effect of deception by third parties by adding to the definition of illegal entrant in s 33(1) para (b): 'entering or seeking to enter by means which include deception by another person'. This addition to s 33(1) puts beyond doubt that deception by a third party will make the entry illegal and means that earlier case law on this point no longer has any effect. Deception by a third party includes for instance preparing a false passport or a false offer of housing or employment.

The use of invalid documents is also covered by the statutory provisions introduced by the 1996 Act. If the entrant produces a false document knowing it to be false, this is deception contrary to s 24A(1). If they are not aware of its falsity but this is the result of the deliberate act of a third party, the deception is covered by s 33(1).

Relationship between deception and leave granted

The effect of the deception is a matter of some importance. At one extreme, some acts of deception might be about a quite peripheral fact, which had very little bearing on the decision to grant entry. It would be inappropriate then to regard entry as illegal. At the other extreme, misrepresentation about a central fact such as whether the sponsor and applicant did in fact intend to marry would render the entry illegal. The question to be addressed is whether, to make an entry illegal, the deception has to be the effective cause of leave being granted, or just a factor which contributed to the decision.

The question of the effect of the deception was addressed in *Khawaja*, in which the Court held that the deception should be the effective means of obtaining leave in order for the entry to be regarded as illegal. It relied on the earlier case of *R v SSHD ex p Jayakody* [1982] 1 All ER 461, in which the Court of Appeal had held that in order to render the entry illegal the fraud should be the decisive factor in the application. In other words, if there had been no deception then the application would probably have been refused. In *Bugdaycay v SSHD* [1987] 1 AC 514, the House of Lords said that the question was, if the true facts were known, whether the decision-maker would have been 'bound to refuse' the application. However, in *Bugdaycay*, the House of Lords also held that an applicant could not legitimize their entry by arguing that if they had put forward the true facts leave would still have been granted. In that case a person who applied as a visitor had not disclosed that he intended to apply for asylum. If he had applied for asylum he would not have been able to be removed. However, the House of Lords held that his argument could only be seen in the light of the application which he did in fact make, and that was deceptive, and so he was treated as an illegal entrant. An approach more consistent with *Bugdaycay* is the one that has been followed since then as the courts have tended to treat deception as creating illegal entry if it is material rather than decisive. For instance, in *Durojaiye v Secretary of State for the Home Department* [1991]

Imm AR 307, the Court of Appeal considered that giving false answers to questions about a student's attendance at college was 'material in the sense that it was likely to influence their decision'. This is not the same as saying that they were a matter without which a different decision would necessarily have been made.

Since 1996, the statutory formulation goes some way to resolving the question. At the time of *Khawaja*, a person was an illegal entrant by deception if they made representations which they knew to be false (1971 Act s 26(1)(c)). The causal relationship with the leave then granted was matter for the courts to consider. Since the 1996 Act, however, ss 24A and 33(1) both refer to entry obtained or sought 'by means which include' deception. It does not mean that, apart from the deception, the decision-maker would have been 'bound to refuse'. On the other hand 'by means' implies that the deception is operative. The net result is that, in order for the deception to give rise to a finding of illegal entry, it must have played a part in the decision to grant entry, but need not necessarily have been the only factor. Macdonald considers that the current statutory formulation of 'by means which include' is a decisive shift in the direction of materiality and away from the *Jayakody* test (2001:749).

Conduct – deception by silence

If the applicant says nothing about a relevant matter, it may be because they are deliberately concealing it or it may be because they are not aware that it is relevant and have not been asked about it. In the latter case, there is no deception. Which of these is the case is a matter of inference for the Tribunal from available evidence. To establish illegal entry from a failure to mention something, it needs to be established how much the applicant should have been expected to say. As there is not a duty of candour, what can the applicant be expected to know is relevant?

In *Cendiz Doldur v SSHD* [1998] Imm AR 352, the Court of Appeal held there was no duty on the applicant to disclose his marriage on arrival when he was not asked about it or about any change of circumstances. He was still dependent, in fact, on his father and could not be expected to know that this did not mean that he was still dependent in law after he had married. In *R v Secretary of State for the Home Department ex p Kuteesa* [1997] Imm AR 194, the applicant obtained leave to enter for two years as a student, subject to the condition that he was not to take employment. He decided not to enrol on the course for which he had been given leave, but enrolled on a later course and worked in the meantime. Shortly before he was due to start the new course his father died, and he went home to Uganda for the funeral. On his re-entry to the UK, he produced his passport and a letter from the college saying:

> This student is going home as a result of a bereavement in the family and will be returning to college to continue his studies. I confirm that [there is] a place reserved for him.

The High Court held that by his silent presentation of his passport he had made a representation that he had previously fulfilled his conditions of entry. As this was false, contrary to s 26(1)(c), he was an illegal entrant. He argued that if he had revealed the true facts, he would still have been granted leave to enter as to refuse would have been unreasonable. However, Harrison J disagreed. He found that the immigration officer would have refused leave to enter if he had known the full history. This was at least in part because the applicant had had leave to enter as a student on a previous occasion and had worked in breach of conditions. This argument illustrates how engagement with the question outlawed by *Bugdaycay* (whether leave would have been granted had the true facts been known) merges into the question of materiality (what was relevant) and, in this case, what would have been a proper exercise of discretion.

Unlike Mr Doldur, Mr Kuteesa had done something (presented his passport) which was a positive action and could thus amount to a representation. However, the case turned more on what the entrant in each case could be expected to have known was relevant. This kind of reasoning survives the amendments made by the 1996 Act as the question of whether there has been deception must involve the question of the entrant's state of mind. In *Durojaiye*, the passport holder obtained leave to remain, then left the country and returned again. The Court of Appeal held that the presentation of the passport on re-entry amounted to deception as the passport holder was aware that the leave stamped in it had been obtained falsely.

Standard of proof

The burden of proof that a person is an illegal entrant is on the Home Office. The standard of proof, first laid down in *Khawaja*, has been developed but not substantially altered by subsequent cases. It was said to be the civil standard, i.e., on the balance of probabilities, but at the higher end of that scale in view of the gravity of the matters in question. If the person is found to be an illegal entrant they are liable to detention and removal from the country; as liberty is at stake the burden of proof should be strictly applied.

However, an inference against the applicant may be drawn from the evidence if it meets the standard. For instance, in *Kesse* TH/00419, the appellant had obtained entry on the basis of marriage to a person who was subsequently found to have never been married. The Tribunal upheld the finding of deception, using the standard of proof laid down in *Khawaja*, which they described as being 'a high degree of probability'.

R (on the Application of Ullah) v SSHD [2003] EWCA Civ 1366 provided a more recent example of the application of this standard of proof. The case had proceeded without the benefit of a witness statement from the person who would have been the appellant's first wife had that marriage been valid. The Court of Appeal held that the Secretary of State could in theory proceed without such a statement, but in this case there was insufficient evidence to meet the high standard of proof that the appellant must have known of the invalidity of his marriage.

Reference may be made to chapter 7 on immigration breaches as a reason for refusal of entry, and the standard of proof that representations were false. The majority of recent case law concerning obtaining entry by what might broadly be called deception is brought and decided under provisions relating to false representations as a ground for refusal or cancellation of leave, or in the context of prosecution for documents offences. The law relating to illegal entrants is now relatively settled.

17.2.2 Refused leave to enter

As we have seen, a significant number of people are removed after being refused leave to enter. The Immigration Act 1971 Sch 2 para 8(1) says that where a person arriving in the United Kingdom is refused leave to enter, then they may be removed on the direction of an immigration officer. This rather stark provision, read in isolation, gives an impression that anyone refused leave could just be returned forthwith to the country from which they came. The UK Immigration Statistics show that 12,628 people were removed in this fashion from UK ports in 2010. This does not include those removed from juxtaposed controls.

In addition to those removed from the port, some people refused leave to enter have a right of appeal which they may exercise in the UK. The Nationality, Immigration and Asylum Act 2002 s 92 as amended by s 28 2004 Act gives a right of appeal in the UK to a person who holds an entry clearance, unless their leave is cancelled by an immigration officer on the grounds that the purpose for which they now seek leave is different from that for which they hold it. It also gives a right of appeal in the UK against refusal of leave to enter to an EEA national or their family member who claims that the refusal would breach their rights of entry or residence under European Community law and to someone who has made a human rights or asylum claim while in the UK. Section 78 provides that people who by s 92 have a right of appeal exercisable in the UK may not be removed while their appeal is pending. There is a further caveat to this, however, which is that s 94 gives power to the Secretary of State to certify asylum and human rights claims as 'clearly unfounded' in which case the appellant will lose their right of appeal in the UK, and be removable. Certificates of this kind will be issued automatically in the case of listed states of origin (see chapter 12). The 2002 Act therefore creates a kind of 'to and fro' motion, as in the following example:

> X applies for leave to enter as visitor – refused – no right of appeal (s 89) – X is removable.
> X claims removal breaches Refugee Convention – appeal s 92(4) – X is not removable (s 78).
> Secretary of State is satisfied that X is entitled to live in Mongolia, certifies claim clearly unfounded s 94 – X is removable.

An asylum seeker who may be returned to a safe third country may be removed without their asylum claim being considered (see chapter 12). If an asylum seeker is wrongly removed pending appeal, the Court may be prepared to grant an injunction to compel the Secretary of State to return the claimant to the UK so that his rights could be preserved pending the outcome of his appeal (e.g., *R (on the application of T) v SSHD* [2004] EWHC 869 (Admin)).

Removal under Immigration Act 1971 Sch 2 para 8 is therefore not necessarily permitted straight away, and the bare provisions of the statute give little indication of the very different circumstances in which they might apply. A swift removal might take place, for instance, in the case of a non-visa national applying unsuccessfully to enter as a visitor, and who has no asylum or human rights claim. On the other hand, there may be a lengthy process, perhaps an asylum claim with an unsuccessful appeal, and a person who is given temporary admission while their application is being processed and who has been in the UK for months or years without leave ever having been granted, is still subject to removal at the end of that process. In this case, the directions for removal would be made by the Secretary of State under Sch 2 para 10, as the Secretary of State has responsibility in any case where more than two months have passed since the refusal of leave (paras 8 and 10). Under the 1999 Act, removal directions could not be given (Sch 4 para 10) while an appeal was pending. However, the 2002 Act now permits removal directions to be given even while they cannot be carried out (s 78), and s 47 of the 2006 Act permits removal directions to be issued even while an appeal is still pending (see 17.2.3.2).

17.2.3 Removal for overstaying, deception, and breach of conditions

The courts had expanded the definition of 'illegal entrants', but from 1 January 1973 until 2 October 2000, those subject to removal were restricted to illegal entrants and people refused entry at the port. On 2 October 2000, Immigration and Asylum Act 1999 s 10 came into effect, and changed a number of grounds for deportation under Immigration Act 1971 s 3(5) into grounds for removal.

In the 1971 Act as originally passed, breach of condition and overstaying were grounds for deportation. Deportation carried a full right of appeal while summary removal attracted a right of appeal only from out of the UK, i.e., after the event. There was a rationale for that distinction as the original target of the removal provisions was those who were refused entry at the port and people who had arrived clandestinely but were apprehended soon after arrival. People who had overstayed or breached their condition have had some period of residence, and some connection with the UK, perhaps brief, but perhaps of many years. It would therefore be legitimate to treat them differently. However, in practice this rationale broke down because the courts developed the category of illegal entrant to include a person who had entered using deception. This could include a person whose original leave had been gained years earlier. This put a person deemed an illegal entrant and an overstayer in a much more similar position.

Parliament's response to this was to level down the rights of overstayers to those of illegal entrants. First, as discussed in chapter 16, by the Immigration Act 1988 s 5, then the Immigration and Asylum Act 1999. Section 10 made those who had overstayed, breached condition, or obtained leave by deception subject to removal and not deportation.

17.2.3.1 *Obtaining leave to remain by deception*

This was introduced into 1971 Act s 3 as a new ground of deportation by the 1996 Act but was changed into a ground for removal along with overstaying and breach of condition by 1999 Act s 10.

It refers to situations where, for instance, a person obtains indefinite leave to remain by misrepresenting that their marriage is still subsisting whereas in fact it has broken down, as for instance in *R v SSHD ex p Chaumun* CO/3143/95 (unreported). The 2002 Act s 74 has tightened this provision further by substituting a new s 10(1)(b): 'he uses deception in seeking (whether successfully or not) leave to remain'. It is difficult to see what is achieved by this attempt to cast the net even wider, as a person who did not succeed in obtaining leave to remain would presumably be without leave and so removable on another ground, probably overstaying. The words 'uses deception in seeking' seem to be intended to catch *any* level of deception, no matter how material it might or might not be to the application, though it is arguable that on principle, it should be treated as analogous to the illegal entry provisions, given that the consequences are similar.

It does not cover third-party deception; the words 'he uses' refer only to the applicant, so a person who was not aware for instance of the falsity of some evidence could not be removed under this provision. This may have been implicit in the withdrawal of the removal decisions which took place in the cases of *Anwar and Adjo v SSHD* [2010] EWCA Civ 1275. The ratio of the decision concerns the availability of in-country appeals, but the case was brought as a challenge to removal decisions. The Secretary of State had served removal decisions on Mr Anwar and another student, each of whom had entered lawfully as a student, but changed the college at which they were studying because the service offered by the college was substandard. Later on, the colleges the two students had left were removed from the register of training and education providers because they were found to be issuing bogus qualifications and providing no real training. The two students were then issued by the Secretary of State with decisions that they had obtained leave to remain by deception, and with decisions that they should be removed. The day before the hearing of the cases in the Court of Appeal the Secretary of State withdrew the immigration decisions, which Sedley LJ referred to as 'arbitrary and unjust'.

17.2.3.2 *Overstaying and breach of condition*

As mentioned earlier, these two grounds, applicable only to limited leave, were formerly grounds for deportation and are now, under Immigration and Asylum Act 1999 s 10 grounds for removal.

Staying beyond the time allowed by a grant of limited leave is a factual matter. There may be issues of proof, for instance of the duration of the leave, but there is little scope for legal interpretation. The only issue of interpreting the statute is a matter of making sense of what would otherwise be nonsense, making use of the golden rule of interpretation. The statute says 'having only a limited leave to enter or remain, he...remains beyond the time limited by the leave' (1999 Act s 10). This must mean 'having had', otherwise the leave has not yet expired and no overstaying has taken place (Macdonald 2001:756). When a person applies for a variation of their leave, the Immigration Act 1971 s 3C (as substituted by the 2002 Act s 118) continues the original leave until the end of the period set for appealing against a decision on the variation application. If an appeal is made, the same section continues the leave while the appeal is pending. It is only once these time limits are exhausted and the applicant has been unsuccessful that they may be treated as an overstayer. However, from 1 April 2008, s 47 of the Immigration Asylum and Nationality Act 2006 allows a decision to remove to be made during this period of extended leave, even though it cannot be enforced until the appeal is withdrawn or lost. This amendment, in accordance with the policy of both the 2002 and the 2006 Act, aims to speed up immigration processes. The removal decision is appealable. It seems to be made on a precautionary or pre-emptive basis in that the grounds for removal may not exist before the extended leave expires. The extended leave remains current after the service of the removal decision, although a removal decision under s 10 of the 1999 Act curtails any existing leave.

Section 10 of the 1999 Act extends removal to the breach of conditions imposed under 1971 Act s 3(1)(c). The conditions which may be imposed are: restricting employment or occupation, requiring the subject to maintain and accommodate himself and any dependants without recourse to public funds, registration with the police, reporting to an immigration officer or the Secretary of State, and a condition about residence. The UKBA's Enforcement Instructions and Guidance 50.6 say that a breach of conditions relating to work must be of sufficient gravity to warrant removal. Where private or family life would be interfered with by a removal, then the removal would in any event have to be proportionate under Article 8, and a trivial breach of any kind should not attract the sanction of removal.

In *SSHD v R (on the application of Lim)* [2007] EWCA Civ 773, Sedley LJ described as a 'colossal overreaction' an arrest and decision to remove Mr Lim who was found working for the employer for whom he had permission to work, but present in a different restaurant in the same city. He said he had gone there to collect food for the Lucky Star, his specified work place, but was disbelieved. Mr Lim would have had an out-of-country right of appeal, but attempted unsuccessfully a challenge by judicial review proceedings to protect himself and his wife from having to leave the country (see chapter 8). The Court of Appeal pointed out that a modest change to his work permit was the most that was needed.

The case of *Sabir* [1993] Imm AR 477 held that past breaches of condition could give rise to liability for deportation, but the policy is not to rely on old breaches that have in effect been cancelled out by a fresh grant of leave, and the Enforcement Instructions and Guidance 50.6 require evidence of a breach within the last six months to justify enforcement.

Family members of the person removed may also be removed, providing notice of this is given to them no more than eight weeks after the departure of their relative. Immigration and Asylum Act 1999 s 10 makes this provision in relation to s 10 removals. This was extended to illegal entrants by the Nationality, Immigration and Asylum Act 2002 s 73, inserting a new para 10A into 1971 Act Sch 2.

A peculiar feature of UK law is that children of a person to be removed or deported from the UK may be British. This may occur when the partner of the person to be expelled is British, or when one or both parents have indefinite leave to remain at the time of the child's birth (see chapter 3). This situation was addressed by the Supreme Court in *ZH (Tanzania) v SSHD* [2011] UKSC 4. The case is discussed more fully in chapter 9. The particular point of importance for this chapter is the potential that the case has to make inroads into the practice of removing British children. ZH's children, aged 12 and 9, were born in the UK and had lived all their lives here. The Supreme Court held that their British nationality was 'of particular importance' in determining what were their best interests. The Court said that the intrinsic importance of citizenship should not be played down:

> As citizens these children have rights which they will not be able to exercise if they move to another country. They will lose the advantages of growing up and being educated in their own country, their own culture and their own language. They will have lost all this when they come back as adults. (para 32)

Since *ZH (Tanzania)*, where British children are included in a removal decision, their British nationality is a factor of particular importance in determining whether the removal should go ahead.

17.3 Effect of decision to remove

If a person is actually removed, this has an effect on future applications for entry to the UK. Mandatory grounds for refusal of entry clearance and leave to enter, discussed in chapter 7, include that the person has previously been removed for overstaying, breach of condition, obtaining or seeking to leave to remain by deception or being an illegal entrant. This remains a mandatory ground for refusal for ten years from the actual removal (para 320 (7B)). The introduction of this re-entry ban in April 2008 eliminated one of the distinctions between deportation and removal. There remains an important distinction that mandatory refusal of entry after removal does not apply where the new application is to join family in the UK (para 320 (7C)), whereas an application for re-entry after deportation is not subject to that exception.

Section 48 of the Immigration Asylum and Nationality Act 2006 inserts a provision into s 10 of the 1999 Act, that a decision to remove made under s 10 invalidates any leave that had been granted. Obviously, this must mean extant leave. The effect seems to be that if a person, following receipt of the decision to remove them for breach of conditions, continues to work within what would have been their lawful limits, they are working illegally since they have no leave. Also, entitlement to any benefits stops on service of the decision. In this way, the 2006 Act radically increased the impact of a decision to remove, as a person can rapidly be in a position where they have no means of support. This enacts the government's policy of being 'tougher' on infringements of immigration law. If the person does not have the resources to travel, but leaves at government expense, they will be subject to the maximum ten-year period of restriction on re-entry (HC 395 para 320 (7B)).

The Tribunal in *CD (s. 10 curtailment: right of appeal) India* [2008] UKAIT 00055 held that where a student's leave had been in effect curtailed by service of a removal decision, he was entitled to an in-country right of appeal. It had been found in his favour by the first immigration judge that he had not used deception in his application.

The college for which he had leave had been unsatisfactory and he had moved. In these circumstances, he should not be denied an in-country right of appeal simply because the Secretary of State chose, as her enforcement method, to serve notice of removal. Conversely, in *R (on the application of Mirza and others) v SSHD* [2011] EWCA Civ 159 the Court of Appeal held that where workers had been refused variations of their leave to remain, they were entitled to have removal decisions so that they could argue why they should be permitted to stay for reasons other than the applications which had been refused. Without refusal decisions they would have no such right of appeal (confirmed in *Sapkota,* see chapter 8).

Similarly, once notice is given to a person that they are deemed to be an illegal entrant, any leave that they have no longer has effect, if it was obtained by deception.

Where a person does not disclose that they have already committed serious breaches of leave, and applies for further leave to remain, this may constitute obtaining or seeking to obtain leave to remain by deception and give liability for removal under s 10.

17.4 EEA nationals and removal

As EEA nationals may enter as of right on production of a passport or identity documents in order to exercise Treaty rights, it is rare that an EEA national may be deemed an illegal entrant. In C–215/03 *Oulane,* the ECJ held on a reference for a preliminary ruling that detention of a European national with a view to deportation was an unjustified restriction on free movement where his offence was principally lack of documentary proof of his status. So, while an EEA national may be deported on public policy grounds, removal is only likely to occur if the EEA national enters in breach of an exclusion or deportation order (*Shingara v SSHD* [1999] Imm AR 257 CA).

The Immigration (European Economic Area) Regulations 2006, SI 2006/1003 regs 19(3) and 24(2) provide that an EEA national or their family member who does not have or ceases to have a right to reside may be removed as if they fell within s 10 of the 1999 Act. This regulation may well be challenged as it appears to exceed sanctions that are permitted by the Citizens Directive 2004/38. Its application to a homeless Czech national was successfully challenged by the AIRE Centre in the First Tier Tribunal. The Tribunal found that the appellant was a jobseeker and had been self-employed selling the Big Issue. The Tribunal said that:

> such expulsions appear to be disproportionate in general because the only legitimate aim they might pursue, as a matter of EU law, would be to protect the social assistance system and this individual had never received social assistance. (AIRE Centre press release 30 July 2011)

17.5 Challenging a removal decision – immigration rules and policies

There are no immigration rules relating to the removal of illegal entrants or to port removals, but only to decisions to remove under s 10 Immigration and Asylum Act 1999 and s 47 Immigration and Asylum Act 2006. In these cases, the person to be removed could have spent some considerable time, maybe years, in the UK, and have established ties. Although this may equally be the case for illegal entrants, they have not received leave to enter, which makes it more controversial for the immigration rules to cater explicitly for their continued presence, though the Human Rights Act does not make these distinctions. Where in a standard form a Home Office employee had erroneously failed to delete s 10 from the heading, this did not make the removal of an illegal entrant subject to s 10 and thus the immigration rules (*MA (Illegal entrant – not para 395C) Bangladesh* [2009] UKAIT 00039).

Until 12 February 2012 the rules required the decision-maker to take into account all relevant factors in the case of proposed removal for overstaying, breach of condition, obtaining leave to remain by deception, and families of those people. These included age; length of residence in the UK; strength of connections with the UK: for instance, family ties, and business or employment interests; personal history, including character, conduct, and employment record; domestic circumstances (HC 395 para 395C). In *CM Jamaica* [2005] UKIAT 00103 and *CW Jamaica* [2005] UKIAT 00110, the Tribunal held that these factors were wider than those normally considered under Article 8, in particular by including the strength of ties with the UK, domestic, and compassionate circumstances. From 13 February 2012, para 395 is deleted from the rules. There is no new rule setting out factors to be taken into account in removal decisions. The explanatory statement to HC 1733 says that this is to enable refusal of an application for leave to remain and a removal decision to be made together (as *Mirza* and *Sapkota* required). Where a removal decision is contemplated after a fresh human rights or asylum claim has been made, a new rule says that, in place of the para 395C factors, account will be taken of the person's history of compliance with conditions, their 'character, conduct and associations, including any criminal record', and the length of time spent in the UK for reasons beyond their control after their asylum or human rights claim has been submitted or refused (para 353B).

Other immigration rules which may be relevant in any case of removal are those based on long residence, discussed in chapter 7. These apply whether or not a person has a family in the UK and so add a significant protection outside the Human Rights Act in limited circumstances. An important caveat is that if a removal decision has been issued, time has stopped running for the purposes of calculating the period of residence.

The decision to remove or deport a person is a discretionary one. An individual may have stayed beyond their leave or entered in breach of immigration laws, but this does not oblige an immigration officer to order their removal. Government pronouncements announcing targets for removal are open to the charge that they have lost sight of the principle that each case is decided on its particular merits. Where policies exist, discretion must be exercised in accordance with them and not arbitrarily (*Abdi v SSHD* [1996] Imm AR 148 CA).

UKBA's Enforcement Instructions and Guidance, available on the Home Office website, gives guidance on the conduct of deportations and removals, and contains relevant policy. Its 60 chapters include one called 'Extenuating Circumstances' (chapter 53) which now collects in one place at least reference to most of the policies which might protect a person from removal or deportation. Publication of a policy gives rise to a legitimate expectation that it will be applied fairly and rationally in the applicant's case (*Khan v IAT* [1984] Imm AR 68 CA). Where policies have not been published, they should still be fairly and rationally applied (*R v SSHD ex p Amankwah* [1994] Imm AR 240 and *Rashid v SSHD*). In *Baig v SSHD* [2005] EWCA Civ 1246, the Court of Appeal held that they did not just need to consider whether the Secretary of State had taken the policy into account, but the Court itself could apply the policy on appeal. This was held not to be the case in *AG (Kosovo) v SSHD* [2007] UKAIT 0082, but the Court of Appeal in *AB (Jamaica)* [2007] EWCA Civ 1302, while referring to both these cases, held it could apply the policy to a fairly clear-cut case. See chapter 8 for further discussion of challenges for failure to apply policy, and Glossop 2007. See chapter 15 for challenges based on procedure such as the policy to give 72 hours' notice of removal.

17.6 Removal directions

At some point, either at the same time as or, more usually, after the decision to remove or the deportation order, the person who is to be removed receives a copy of removal directions. These are instructions by an immigration officer or the Secretary of State to the captain of a ship or aircraft to remove the person in question to a country or territory:

(i) of which s/he is a national or citizen;

(ii) in which s/he has obtained a passport or identity document;

(iii) in which s/he embarked for the UK; or

(iv) to which there is reason to believe s/he will be admitted (Immigration Act 1971 Sch 2 para 8).

Removal directions have no duration or continuing legal effect beyond the moment when they are put into practice. They are enforceable in the very real sense that a person may be arrested and detained in order to give them effect. In law, they are themselves a form of enforcement (see, for instance, Burnton J in *SSHD v Kariharan* [2001] EWHC Admin 1004 likening them to a bailiff's warrant).

Removal directions could be appealed under 1971 Act s 16 and 1999 Act s 66, but only on the grounds that there was no power in law to issue them on the grounds stated, and only from outside the UK unless there was an asylum claim. These limitations on appeals against actual physical removal were particularly problematic where a lengthy claim, perhaps for asylum, ended unsuccessfully. If it had taken years to process, the asylum seeker could hardly be expected to refrain from making relationships in that time, but their asylum claim would have considered only the risk in their country of origin, and not any developing private and family life reasons for remaining in the UK. There would then be no forum for arguing these points, as the appeal against removal directions could only deal with the jurisdictional matter, and there would rarely be any dispute that the person was in fact an illegal entrant or perhaps an overstayer. An answer seemed to be provided by Immigration and Asylum Act 1999 s 65, which gave a right of appeal on human rights grounds against 'any decision under the Immigration Acts relating to that person's entitlement to enter or remain' in the UK. If the issue of removal directions was such a decision, then there could be a human rights appeal against it.

The Court of Appeal in *Kariharan v SSHD* [2002] EWCA Civ 1102 held that it was appropriate to interpret broadly a provision which related to human rights, so as to allow the possibility of a human rights appeal. It found that removal directions were discretionary and, as such, were capable of being determinative of entitlement to enter or remain. It did not consider that the comparison with a bailiff's warrant was apt because of this continuing discretion. The Court decided that the right to an appeal on human rights grounds applied to directions for removal. The Nationality, Immigration and Asylum Act 2002 s 82 reversed *Kariharan* by specifying 'immigration decisions' against which appeals can be made. Section 82(2)(g) and (h) permits an appeal against a 'decision that a person is to be removed by way of directions'. This means that all that is appealable is the immigration decision that the person is to be removed, not the removal directions.

As the 2002 Act does not include removal directions in its list of appealable decisions, there is no right of appeal against a destination named in them or on the grounds that the directions are invalid. Directions must specify a country to which the person can be returned, and must specify the time and date of removal (1971 Act Sch 2 para 8) and if these are wrong or non-existent, the only remedy is judicial review.

Key Case

***MS (Palestinian Territories) v SSHD* [2010] UKSC 25**

The appellant argued that the decision to remove him was not in accordance with the law because it said that he was to be removed by way of directions to the Palestinian Territories. There was evidence that he would not be admitted there. The Supreme Court confirmed that the destination must be stated in the removal decision, as required by reg 5(1)(b)(i) of the Immigration (Notices) Regulations 2003, because it was by reference to that destination that the asylum and human rights appeal against removal were judged. However, the destination was not part of the removal decision so as to make the removal decision appealable on grounds that the destination did not conform with Schedule 2 para 8 – i.e., was not one to which the appellant could be removed. A destination proposed at the date of the removal decision might not be the actual destination to which the Secretary of State finally intended to remove the person. That decision had to be dealt with at the time of its making, if necessary by judicial review.

By way of example, in *MA (Statelessness; removal; KF applied) stateless* [2005] UKAIT 00161, the appellant's asylum claim failed. Saudi Arabia was his country of habitual residence. His father was Somali, his mother Yemeni; the appellant was stateless. The decision being challenged was to remove him to Yemen. The Tribunal held, following *KF*, that the destination was relevant to whether the removal would breach the appellant's human rights as any risks in Yemen would need to be assessed. However, if they were satisfied that there were no such risks, they had to assume that Yemen was a country 'to which there was reason to believe the appellant would be admitted'. Travel documents would have to be arranged, and there would have to be negotiations with the Yemeni Embassy. If all this proved non-viable, then he would not be removed as Yemen could not be compelled to accept him, but the Tribunal could not deal with the practicalities.

Where the appellant is in detention, the consequences of the proposed destination not being one to which they can, in fact, be removed, may be detention protracted beyond all reason. For instance in *R (on the application of Raki) v SSHD and FCO* [2011] EWHC 2421 (Admin) the claimant, who said that he was Palestinian, had been in detention four years and seven months, pending deportation to Morocco – a destination to which he could not, in practice, be removed.

17.7 Human rights appeals

The argument that removal will breach Convention rights is now the most important basis of challenge. There is, as we have seen, no right to reside in the country of one's choice. Removal *per se* does not therefore infringe a protected right. The Convention rights most likely to be engaged by the threat of removal are Articles 3 and 8.

The operation of these articles is fully discussed in chapters 4 and 18, to which reference should be made.

17.8 Viability of return

Many of the more recent issues concerning removal have concerned the viability of return. As a thematic briefing for the Independent Asylum Commission relates, there may be practical and institutional barriers to removal. These include:

- lack of travel documents and identification
- lack of institutional coordination
- lack of an international airport, safe route or carrier (ICAR 2007).

Not all of these issues come before the courts or tribunals or can be considered within a legal forum when they do (see *MA (statelessness; removal; KF applied) stateless* at 17.6), but they are at least as important as legal issues in explaining why, although someone may be an illegal entrant or their asylum claim may have failed, they cannot necessarily be removed from the UK. The gap between the numbers of people who have no right in law to remain and the numbers removed is not just due to government inefficiency or non-compliance by those to be removed.

The Court of Appeal has considered the question of whether risks entailed in the actual route of return should form part of the human rights or asylum decision.

Key Case

***HH, AM, J and MA (Somalia) v SSHD* [2010] EWCA Civ 426**

The appellants challenged their removal to Somalia on various grounds, including that for some of the appellants there was no safe route of return. The Court of Appeal accepted their argument that 'in any case in which it can be shown either directly or by implication what route and method of return is envisaged, the AIT is required by law to consider and determine any challenge to the safety of that route or method' (para 58). This 'must be considered as part of the decision on entitlement' to international protection (para 81). 'Postponement of such consideration until the Secretary of State is in a position to set safe removal directions would effectively be to postpone the decision until . . . cessation' (para 81). This, the Court held (obiter), was consistent with the Qualification Directive and the Procedures Directive. Only technical matters such as documentation and availability of flights could be deferred until the moment of issuing removal directions (para 84).

The only point of return to Somalia from the UK was Mogadishu. Accordingly in order for someone to be safe on return it would need to be shown either that they were returning to Mogadishu itself, and would be safe there, or that they would have safe travel from Mogadishu to their home area. An Amnesty International report had described the road from Mogadishu to AM's home of Jowhar as 'one of the most dangerous', controlled by terrorist groups and freelance militias. This and other evidence must be considered by the Tribunal in determining whether he should be awarded a protective status.

The Court of Appeal said that its judgment in *HH and others* was consistent with that in *GH v SSHD* [2005] EWCA Civ 1182. Here, the Court held that, where removal directions are given as part of, or incidental to, an appealable decision, or where the Secretary of State adopts a routine procedure for removal or return so that the method or route is implicit in the decision to remove, the directions may also be considered as part of the appeal, though normal practice is to give the removal directions well after any appealable decision. *GH* concerned an Iraqi Kurd who, it was decided, could live safely in the area of northern Iraq from which he came, but who argued that he would face risks when travelling within Iraq from the point of arrival to his home area. As no removal directions had been set, the Court held that this question was 'academic'.

Note that in cases of internal relocation, discussed in the context of asylum claims in chapter 13, risks in travelling to the new safe area may be taken into account to determine that the proposed relocation is 'unduly harsh'. In cases such as *GH*, we are considering a different situation, where the appellant is held *not* to be at risk in their home area. In this case, risks on travelling there will only engage the UK's legal system of protection if they amount to a risk of violation of Article 3 (e.g., torture on return at the airport) or if, once removal directions have been set, they are so unreasonable as to be challengeable by judicial review.

In *AK v SSHD* [2006] EWCA Civ 1117, in a similar vein the Court held that as there were no proven obstacles to the appellant's re-entering the Palestinian Territories via Jordan, even though he might encounter some difficulty, this was not a matter the Court could engage with. Inconvenience is not an objection to removal, unless it amounts to treatment in breach of Article 3. The Supreme Court in *MS (Palestinian Territories)* held that nothing in its judgment affected *HH (Somalia)*, AK or *GH (Iraq)*.

A further practical difficulty in the way of removal may be obstacles to obtaining travel documents. Asylum and Immigration (Treatment of Claimants, etc.) Act 2004 s 35 makes it a criminal offence for an asylum seeker to fail to comply, without reasonable excuse, with obtaining a travel document. Guidance to immigration officers suggests that reasonable excuse would be something like a need for emergency medical care or transport problems which prevented a person from getting to an interview. This does not include the claimant's fear of contact with authorities in their home country (*R v Tabnak* [2007] EWCA Crim 380). It must be something which made the asylum seeker unable to comply, not unwilling. The Court of Appeal in *Tabnak* pointed out that the criminal court was not able to assess risks in the country of return, which would have already been assessed by the immigration authorities. There is a caveat to this, which is that if the asylum seeker's claim has not been finally determined, they should not be exposed to questioning by the authorities of their home state. This practice has been challenged in particular in relation to the questioning of Sudanese asylum seekers by embassy officials (see *Waging Peace* 2007).

Obstacles to obtaining travel documents to effect a removal may result in extended detention while the authorities attempt to resolve the problems. An atypical example was discussed in chapter 15 in the case of *Rostami*, where the claimant refused to cooperate with attempts to remove him because of his genuine fear of severe ill-treatment if he were returned to Iran. He was detained from October 2006 to August 2009, incurring three s 35 convictions during that time. He was finally released because the Court held that there was no reasonable prospect of removing him. Neither his refusal to go nor the requirements of the Iranian government as to documentation were likely to change.

Obstacles may equally come about because of the requirements of the proposed receiving state, which neither the individual nor UKBA can fulfil, or repeated delays and other obstructions raised by the authorities of the receiving state. When these factors are combined with the reluctance of the individual to go, it may be impossible to achieve a removal. Sedley LJ summarized the difficulties: 'Obstacles to return are commonly an amalgam of fact, governmental practice and policy, international law and local law, often in a form which is impossible to disentangle' (*R (MS, AR and FW v SSHD* [2009] EWCA Civ 1310 at 26). As we have seen in chapter 15, people may remain in detention for very extended periods because of these difficulties.

The other difficulty referred to by ICAR, and discussed by Phuong (see chapter 2) is that the airlines may be unwilling to take enforced removals. This was so in *Appellant A v SSHD* [2007] EWCA Civ 804, in which after two years of lawful detention, A was detained for a further 19 months during which he could not be removed because no airlines were willing to take enforced removals to Somalia, and he was not willing to go.

With the consent of the receiving government, alternative documentation can be used to effect a return. There are provisions for EU travel documents to be issued, or letters under the Chicago Convention, and UKBA publishes details of the documentation requirements of receiving governments from time to time.

It is obvious that steps to obtain a travel document from the appellant's embassy should not be taken before an appeal has been concluded because of risk to the appellant. In *R (on the application of Sidibe) v SSHD* [2007] EWCA Civ 191, Home Office officials had taken the claimant to the Guinean Embassy to arrange travel documents, despite the fact that there were serious allegations of the risk he faced as a member of the military, an expert's report was pending on the risk to him, and his appeal had not yet been heard. Moses J made it clear that this was highly irregular and that it would be necessary to discover:

> why it happened because if there was no good reason for it to be done that raises doubts as to the bona fides of those responsible for this applicant in the circumstances of his particular case, and may indeed add force to the contention that he was deliberately exposed to a risk by those responsible for his detention. (para 4)

The case law on practical obstacles to return is the tip of an iceberg. Under the water are many other factors which do not readily enter the court room. In addition to all the human reasons that an asylum seeker whose claim has failed may have for not wanting to return to their home country, are the interests of the country of return. It is easy to lose sight when studying the UK's system that the return of an asylum seeker is an international action. The country of return may have social, economic, or political reasons for not wanting to accept the returnee. As the ICAR report says, 'in times of conflict they may be reluctant to re-admit supporters of resistance groups' or they may fear that returnees will not be absorbed economically, or may compromise fragile security situations.

The other major issue which follows is the status of an asylum seeker once the legal process has ended unsuccessfully, where the UK is unwilling to give any leave to remain, but return cannot be achieved. Issues about lack of status and resulting destitution underlie some of the cases dealing with the feasibility of return. In *HH (Somalia)* the Court of Appeal referred to an important implication of its judgment. If the safety of the route of return is considered by the Tribunal, if a real risk is found of treatment that would violate human rights, this has the potential to change a refusal of asylum or humanitarian protection to a decision in the claimant's favour. This means that, although the individual may still be refused asylum, if there is currently no safe route of return the individual may be entitled to asylum support instead of being left entirely destitute. It also opens the possibility of some form of leave to remain, even if temporary.

Reference should also be made to discussion of temporary admission in chapter 15.

17.9 Carrying out removals

Practical and political aspects of this subject have already been discussed in chapter 2. Standard policy is to give 72 hours' notice of removal, including two working days, one of which must be the day preceding removal. This policy has been subject to various change and exceptions, including, in 2010, for shorter notice where there is a medically documented risk of self-harm, a risk of an unaccompanied child absconding, a risk of harm to others, in the interests of maintaining order and discipline in a removal centre, and where the person to be removed consents or removal is within seven days of refusal of entry at a port (Enforcement Instructions and Guidance, chapter 60).

Key Case

***R (on the application of Medical Justice) v SSHD* [2010] EWHC 1925 (Admin)**

Medical Justice challenged the 2010 exceptions to the policy of 72 hours' notice of removal. Silber J in the High Court upheld the challenge on the grounds that the policy failed to ensure the constitutional right of access to the courts. Given all the practical difficulties faced by someone detained without notice, the shortage of immigration and asylum lawyers, the constraints of the legal aid system, and the absence of evidence that the policy had ensured access to justice, he held that it did not do so and must be quashed. He did not accept the claimant's argument that the policy was irrational but did accept that the exceptions for people who were a suicide risk and for young people were unlawful for the additional reason that they had not been assessed as required for their discriminatory impact under the Disability Discrimination Act and Race Relations Act.

After some representatives achieved suspension of their client's removal by giving notice within the 72 hours of their intention to seek judicial review but then taking no further steps in the proceedings, the Home Office amended its policy so that removal would only be suspended if grounds were lodged in full (Policy notice, 2 March 2007). The other side of the coin is that even an injunction has on occasion not stopped a person being removed (see Thomas 2008).

For concerns about excessive force used in removals, see chapter 2.

17.10 Conclusion

Removal is a major plank of government immigration policy. There are 'targets' for removals, questions by Opposition MPs about number of removals, and promises to do more. The law on removal is a battleground. It is often tortuous and technical and its implementation may cause enormous human distress. Nevertheless, it has become a key measure of whether the government is able to maintain a firm immigration policy. There is no lack of legal powers to remove, and no increase in the law can answer questions such as 'Why are people willing to undergo significant hardship in the UK in order to avoid removal?' and 'Why is it that such a small percentage of people with irregular immigration status are in fact removed?'

QUESTIONS

1 Was it appropriate for the courts to develop the definition of 'illegal entrant' to include someone who entered by deception? What would have been the alternative?

2 Should removal directions be appealable? If so, on what grounds?

3 Should the power to remove the spouse of a British citizen be abolished?

For guidance on answering questions, visit www.oxfordtextbooks.co.uk/orc/clayton5e/.

FURTHER READING

Evans, John M. (1983) *Immigration Law*, 2nd edn (London: Sweet & Maxwell), chapter 6.

Granville-Chapman, Charlotte, Smith, Ellie, and Moloney, Neil (2005) *Harm on Removal: Excessive Force against Failed Asylum Seekers* (London: Medical Foundation).

Thomas, Robert (2008) 'Judicial Review Challenges to Removal Decisions' *Immigration Law Digest* vol. 14, no. 1, Spring, pp. 2–6.

Waging Peace (2007) *'I felt like I had been brought into a lion's den.' How Darfuri asylum seekers are being illegally interviewed by Sudanese Embassy officials at Home Office facilities* (London: Waging Peace).

18

Expulsions and Article 8

SUMMARY

The tension between the individual's right to respect for the private and family life and the right of the state to expel them for a range of reasons is one of the critical tensions governed by immigration law. In this final chapter, we apply the principles of ECHR Article 8, already set out in chapter 4, to deportation and removal decisions, and examine some of the principles that have developed in this area of human rights law specifically.

18.1 Introduction

People in a wide range of situations may be faced with a decision to expel them from the UK. They include people whose asylum claims have failed; people in relation to whom a deportation order has been made; people who have never had a legal status in the UK having entered illegally and perhaps worked illegally; people who have been working or studying legitimately and have overstayed; and people whose leave to remain has been revoked or cancelled. The only legal status they have in common is that they cannot, at the time of the decision to deport or remove, be British citizens. They may have been British previously, but then deprived of their nationality as described in chapter 3.

In theory, as we have seen in chapter 4, an expulsion can be opposed on the grounds that it will breach any Convention right (*Ullah and Do*; *ER Lebanon*). In practice, the vast majority of human rights challenges to expulsion are made under Article 3 or Article 8. Also in practice, Article 3 claims tend to be made after or in conjunction with an asylum claim or by someone facing deportation on national security grounds. These situations and uses of Article 3 have been considered in chapters 4, 8, and 16. Here, we focus on Article 8.

In chapter 4, we considered the basic elements of Article 8: identifying family or private life; identifying an interference; what is in accordance with the law; what is a legitimate aim; necessity in a democratic society and the concept of proportionality. We discussed some general principles in the structure of Article 8 including extraterritorial application and the question of the threshold. In chapter 8, we discussed the decision in *Huang* that a human rights claim does not have to be exceptional to make interfering with the right disproportionate, that the question of proportionality is a matter for the decision-maker at all levels, that the notion of deference has no place in an Article 8 appeal, and that the immigration rules do not embody human rights considerations. Here, we focus on the arguments that are used when applying Article 8 in cases of expulsion.

18.2 Proportionality – an evaluation of all the circumstances

While the courts have developed certain principles in addressing Article 8 claims, the hallmark of the application of proportionality in the ECtHR is the very detailed discussion of the facts, and the weighing of the elements of the applicant's life against the specific interest of the state advanced to support the expulsion. The Court does not rely on any presumption, and in each case a balance is struck to determine whether the harm done to the applicant is proportionate to the public interest served by the expulsion. There is an echo of that approach in the House of Lords in *Huang*, where the House said:

> We think, with respect, there has been a tendency, both in the arguments addressed to the courts and in the judgments of the courts, to complicate and mystify what is not, in principle, a hard task to define, however difficult the task is, in practice, to perform. (para 14)

A similar message came from their Lordships in *EB (Kosovo)*:

> there is in general no alternative to making a careful and informed evaluation of the facts of the particular case. The search for a hard-edged or bright-line rule to be applied to the generality of cases is incompatible with the difficult evaluative exercise which article 8 requires. (Lord Bingham para 12)

The remainder of this chapter should be read with these points in mind. These principles are superior to any categorization of common arguments in Article 8 cases, and should generally be treated as overriding. This also applies to distinctions made between cases on the facts. Although the question of proportionality is a fact-intensive inquiry, it is also an evaluative exercise. Therefore, to distinguish one case from another simply on the basis that a particular fact is different is also, while relevant, not an adequate performance of the 'difficult task' (e.g., in *JO (Uganda) and JT (Ivory Coast) v SSHD* [2010] EWCA Civ 10 para 52).

18.3 Settled people

There is a substantial body of case law in the ECtHR applying the principle of proportionality to the expulsion of individuals from a country where they are settled. As the House of Lords said in *Huang*, the Strasbourg cases 'are of value in showing where, in many different factual situations, the Strasbourg Court, as the ultimate guardian of rights, has drawn the line' (para 18).

The most extreme case is that of someone who has lived lawfully in that country for all or most of their life, and has been found guilty of criminal offences. People in this position are sometimes referred to as 'integrated aliens', or 'quasi-nationals'. In some cases, the fact that they are not a national of their country of residence may be because of that country's restrictive nationality law, or of decisions made by their parents. They may have longer residence in and greater ties with that country than some of its nationals do.

The ECtHR has considered this issue on many occasions, and the Grand Chamber laid down relevant principles in *Üner v The Netherlands* [2006] ECHR 873. The Court referred to Recommendation 1504 (2001), in which the Parliamentary Assembly of the Council of Europe recommended that the Committee of Ministers invited Member

States, inter alia, to guarantee that long-term migrants who were born or raised in the host country could not be expelled under any circumstances. A number of contracting states have enacted legislation or adopted policy or rules to that effect, but the UK has not, and has in fact moved in the opposite direction by introducing the power to revoke indefinite leave to remain (s 76 2002 Act), by weakening the presumption of a grant of indefinite leave after long residence (see chapter 7), and by introducing broader powers to deprive a person of their British citizenship (see chapter 3). The Court in *Üner* held that an absolute right not to be expelled could not be derived from Article 8 because it allows for exceptions to be made to the right (para 55). The Court considered that, even if a non-national held a very strong residence status and had attained a high degree of integration, his or her position could not be equated with that of a national when it came to the power to expel aliens (para 56).

However, the Court in *Üner* continued that its case law 'amply demonstrates' that expulsion could violate Article 8, and the Court would 'have regard to the special situation of aliens who have spent most, if not all, their childhood in the host country, were brought up there and received their education there' (para 58). As noted in chapter 4, the Court held that 'the totality of social ties between settled migrants and the community in which they are living constitute part of the concept of "private life" within the meaning of Article 8'. Thus, any long residence gives some protection against expulsion under Article 8, even if the person does not have family in their country of residence, though whether it will outweigh the reasons for expulsion is a matter which must be considered in the light of all the circumstances. The ECtHR in *Maslov* emphasized the importance of age and of youth spent in the host country:

For a settled migrant who has lawfully spent all or the major part of his or her childhood and youth in the host country, very serious reasons are required to justify expulsion; and this is all the more so where the person concerned committed the relevant offences as a juvenile (para 75).

Maslov was applied in the UK in *MJ (Angola) v SSHD* [2010] EWCA Civ 557 in which the Court held that:

> the fact that (i) the appellant had lived in the UK since he was 12 years of age, (ii) most of his offending had been committed when he was under the age of 21 and (iii) he had no links with Angola meant that very serious reasons were required to justify the decision to deport him. (para 42)

In *SSHD v HK (Turkey)* [2010] EWCA Civ 583 Sedley LJ said 'The number of years a potential deportee has been here is always likely to be relevant; but what is likely to be more relevant is the age at which those years began to run. Fifteen years spent here as an adult are not the same as fifteen years spent here as a child' (para 35).

18.4 Criminal offences

ECtHR cases commonly concern the expulsion of people because of criminal offences they have committed. In UK law, such expulsions are likely to be deportations (see chapter 16). In *Boultif* v *Switzerland* [2001] ECHR 497, the ECtHR gave guidance on factors to be considered when such an expulsion interferes with family life. These were:

- the nature and seriousness of the offence committed by the applicant;
- the length of the applicant's stay in the country from which he or she is to be expelled;

- the time elapsed since the offence was committed and the applicant's conduct during that period;
- the nationalities of the various persons concerned;
- the applicant's family situation, such as the length of the marriage, and other factors expressing the effectiveness of a couple's family life;
- whether the spouse knew about the offence at the time when he or she entered into a family relationship;
- whether there are children of the marriage, and if so, their age; and
- the seriousness of the difficulties which the spouse is likely to encounter in the country to which the applicant is to be expelled.

Üner v The Netherlands [2006] ECHR 873 added two more considerations:

- the best interests and well-being of the children, in particular the seriousness of the difficulties which any children of the applicant are likely to encounter in the country to which the applicant is to be expelled; and
- the solidity of social, cultural, and family ties with the host country and with the country of destination.

Before *Boultif* and *Üner*, in *Beldjoudi v France* (1992) 14 EHRR 801, a life of crime was held not sufficient to outweigh the fact that the applicant had spent almost all his life in France, and had a French wife with whom his marriage would probably be destroyed if he were deported. On the other hand, in *Boughanemi v France*, the retention of links with Tunisia meant that the deportation was proportionate, though in other respects the facts were quite similar. In *Bouchelkia v France* (1998) 25 EHRR 686, the applicant had lived in France since the age of two, and was living with his family of origin, but the ECtHR held that his deportation following conviction for rape was proportionate. In *Nasri v France* (1996) 21 EHRR 458, the applicant had been involved in a gang rape, and some petty offences. He was deaf and mute, and the ECtHR held that to deport him would interfere with his right to respect for family and private life under Article 8(1). The approach of ECtHR judges ranges between a search for principles respecting the lives of integrated aliens, to that exemplified in the minority judgment of Judge Pettiti in *Beldjoudi* that only Article 3 was capable of interfering with the state's right to deport an alien.

Rogers (2003) identifies *Boultif* as promoting a trend towards a more realistic assessment of the difficulties facing family members required to relocate and the actual harm which would be inflicted by continuing residence. She says: 'The judgement is significant for its recognition that in cases where there are real barriers such as lack of ties for some of the family members or language difficulties, the Court is likely to conclude that the family cannot be expected to follow the deportee' (p. 62). The development towards assessment of the actual harm risked by allowing the non-national to remain is confirmed in *Maslov v Austria*, where the Grand Chamber said that the criteria in *Boultif* and *Üner* were 'designed to help evaluate the extent to which the applicant can be expected to cause disorder or to engage in criminal activities' (para 70).

In the case of *Kaya v Germany* [2007] ECHR 538, the applicant's cruelty to his partner and another woman and his attempt to shift responsibility to a co-defendant suggested to the Court that, even though all his offending happened in a short period of time, it was not 'mere juvenile delinquency' and he was not taking responsibility for his actions. Although he was born and brought up in Germany, his removal to Turkey was not a violation of his right to respect for private life. By contrast, Mr Maslov's offences, though they were many, were committed within a short period of time and were typical of juvenile delinquency and to deport him was a breach of Article 8 (*Maslov v Austria* [2007] ECHR 224). Both *Kaya* and *Maslov* concerned second-generation immigrants, in relation to whom one can say that, but for the particular provisions of nationality law into which they were born, they would be nationals of their home state, and so not deportable.

There are numerous recent cases from the UK. By way of example, in *Grant v UK* [2009] ECHR 26, the applicant had come to the UK at the age of 14. He had four British children ranging in age from 12 to 25. He had last lived in Jamaica 34 years ago. Nevertheless, the Court took account of the 'sheer number' of offences and the time span during which they occurred. With the exception of 1991 to 1995, there was no prolonged period during which the applicant was out of prison and did not reoffend. There was no evidence that he had addressed the underlying problem of drug addiction, and deportation was proportionate. By comparison, in *Omojudi v UK* [2009] ECHR 1942, the claimant had committed a sexual assault which was also a breach of trust. However the short sentence revealed that it was not at the most serious end of the scale. The applicant and his wife had lived in the UK for 23 years, and had three children and a grandchild, who all lived with them. Mr Omojudi was deported, but the ECtHR held that deportation was disproportionate to the legitimate aim pursued.

The Court in *Üner* takes into account the effect of the deportation on the applicant themselves, given what they will face in their destination and their stage of life. In *Jakupovic v Austria* [2004] 38 EHRR 27, which concerned the proposed expulsion of a teenager with a fairly minor criminal record to Bosnia, the Court said, 'very weighty reasons have to be put forward to justify the expulsion of a young person (16 years old), alone, to a country which has recently experienced a period of armed conflict with all its adverse effects on living conditions and with no evidence of close relatives living there' (para 29). In *Grant v UK*, the Court took into account that deportation was not permanent. In a maximum of ten years, the applicant would be able to return. However, note that since the 2008 rule changes in the UK, only Article 8 could compel a return for someone with Mr Grant's record (see chapter 16).

18.4.1 UK Borders Act 'automatic' deportations

Where a deportation is rendered 'automatic' by the operation of s 32 of the UK Borders Act, the Court of Appeal in *RU (Bangladesh) v SSHD* [2011] EWCA Civ 651 confirmed that the judicial body on an appeal under Article 8 must go straight to the question of the infringement of Article 8 rights. The deportation has already been deemed to be conducive to the public good, and that question cannot be re-opened. Nevertheless, the Court held that the public interest as summarized by the Court in *OH (Serbia)* must be considered by the Court as the assessment of proportionality requires balancing those elements of the public interest against the appellant's right to respect for their family life (para 36). See chapter 16.

18.5 Can the family reasonably be expected to live abroad?

One possible result of removal is that the family is split; another is that the other family members leave with the person to be removed. In the UK, the question of whether this should be expected was for some years approached in a way that required the family to show 'insurmountable obstacles' to living abroad, rather than just whether it was reasonable, though the Court of Appeal in *Husna Begum v ECO Dhaka* [2001] INLR 115 had warned against this approach, derived from a misreading of *R (on the application of Mahmood) v SSHD* [2001] 1 WLR 840. As identified by the Tribunal in *VW and MO (Article 8 – insurmountable obstacles) Uganda* [2008] UKAIT 00021, ECtHR cases use a range of terms when considering the family's prospects of life elsewhere:

- 'whether there are insurmountable obstacles in the way of the family living in the country of origin of one or more of them' (e.g., *Da Silva and Hoogkamer*; *Headley v UK* Application no. 39642/03 1 March 2005; *Konstatinov*);
- 'whether the applicant's family could reasonably be expected to follow the applicant to...'(e.g., *Keles*; *Üner*); and
- 'the seriousness of the difficulties which the spouse is likely to encounter in the country to which the applicant is to be expelled'. (e.g., *Boultif*; *Üner*; *Keles*).

These terms are not used in the ECtHR as a 'test', but are context-specific. The proper approach now is referred to in *Huang* as the question of whether 'the life of the family cannot reasonably be expected to be enjoyed elsewhere' (para 20, and see chapter 9). This was repeated by the House of Lords in *EB (Kosovo)* who asked whether the individual could 'reasonably be expected to follow the removed spouse to the country of removal'. All the factors related to the possibility of family life elsewhere should be taken into account. These include, for instance, whether the spouse who is settled in the UK can speak the language of the other country or has any connections there; the impact on the couple's employment opportunities; their family ties in the UK; health needs; children's education; and so on.

The Court of Appeal has affirmed that, following *EB (Kosovo)*, assessing the proportionality of an interference with the right to respect for family life requires a judgement of what could reasonably be expected in the light of all the material facts, including whether a settled spouse could reasonably be expected to relocate abroad (see *VW (Uganda) and AB (Somalia) v SSHD* [2009] EWCA Civ 5, *TF (Angola) v SSHD* [2009] EWCA Civ 905 and *YD (Togo) v SSHD* [2010] EWCA Civ 214). The Court of Appeal in *SS (India) v SSHD* [2010] EWCA Civ 388 held that:

> the tribunal has to consider and assess as a whole how serious the difficulties would be if the family were to follow the deportee. As Richards LJ pointed out at paragraph 26 of *JO (Uganda)*, the precise wording used by a tribunal when making its decision is less important than whether it is clear that the matter has been examined as a whole and that no limiting test (such as 'insurmountable problem') has been applied. (para 52)

Many Article 8 cases opposing removal are of former asylum seekers whose claim has failed. The surrounding facts and context of that claim, even though they have not, for whatever reason, resulted in a grant of refugee status, may still be relevant in the question of proportionality, as seen in *Jakupovic* (see 18.4). In *AG (Eritrea)*, the fact that the appellant was recovering well from trauma played a part in establishing his private life and was considered as part of the proportionality question. In *MT (Zimbabwe) v SSHD* [2007] EWCA Civ 455, the Court accepted that 'because of shared experiences in Zimbabwe and the recovery from those experiences by mutual life together continuing in the UK, Ms T was more than normally emotionally dependent on Mr G and his family' (para 26).

Boultif gives the nationality of family members as a relevant factor. If a spouse is British, the Court in *AB (Jamaica)* [2007] EWCA Civ 1302 said that it was necessary to give:

> detailed and anxious consideration to the situation of a British citizen who has lived here all his life before it is held reasonable and proportionate to expect him to emigrate to a foreign country in order to keep his marriage intact. (para 20)

The position of British children has been changed by the case of *ZH (Tanzania) v SSHD* [2011] UKSC 4 (see chapters 4, 9 and 17). The rights of a child to preserve their national identity, with all that goes with this (see chapter 9), now weigh in the balance in considering an objection to removal under Article 8.

ZH (Tanzania) makes a significant addition to the protection which Article 8 gives to the residence of children. The Supreme Court drew on the ECtHR case of *Rodrigues da Silva, Hoogkamer v Netherland* (2007) 44 EHRR 34 in which the Court held that a mother who had had 'a cavalier attitude to the Dutch immigration rules' should nevertheless not be removed from the Netherlands. She and her daughter Rachael's father had separated, and the Dutch courts found that it was in Rachael's best interests to remain with her father and his family in the Netherlands even if this meant that she would have to be separated from her mother. In practice, her care was shared between her mother and paternal grandparents. The ECtHR concluded:

> In view of the far reaching consequences which an expulsion would have on the responsibilities which the first applicant has as a mother, as well as on her family life with her young daughter, and taking into account that it is clearly in Rachael's best interests for the first applicant to stay in the Netherlands, the Court considers that in the particular circumstances of the case the economic well-being of the country does not outweigh the applicants' rights under article 8, despite the fact that the first applicant was residing illegally in the Netherlands at the time of Rachael's birth. (para 44)

As discussed in chapter 9, the Supreme Court concluded that treating the best interests of a child as a primary consideration was required by s.55 BCIA 2009 and entailed asking whether it was reasonable to expect the child to live in another country:

> Relevant to this will be the level of the child's integration in this country and the length of absence from the other country; where and with whom the child is to live and the arrangements for looking after the child in the other country; and the strength of the child's relationships with parents or other family members which will be severed if the child has to move away. (para 29)

18.6 Alternative application for entry clearance

In cases where removal is founded not on criminality but on irregular immigration status, the government has often required the claimant to regularize their situation by leaving and applying for entry clearance (see discussion in chapter 9). If this option was available, then, the argument went, it was not disproportionate to remove that person if they chose not to avail themselves of it. However, such a return could in itself jeopardize the right that the individual was seeking to protect. If, for instance, the person would lose the job which supported the family (as in *Mahmood*), then their opportunity of living together might be destroyed. Also, the application to remain in the UK might be based on needs which made such a return impossible. For instance, in *Mukarkar v SSHD* [2006] EWCA Civ 1045, the appellant, who was a frail elderly man, would be unable to travel alone to make an entry clearance application, and no-one could reasonably be expected to go with him; these obstacles were held to be relevant to the question of proportionality.

In *A v SSHD* [2006] EWCA Civ 1144 [2007] Imm AR1, the Court of Appeal held that difficulties or dangers of travel to make an entry clearance application fell to be considered in relation to proportionality. The Home Affairs Committee report on immigration control recommended:

In view of the serious difficulties caused to some applicants by the requirement to return home to apply for permission as a spouse, we recommend that where the Foreign Office advises against all travel to a particular country, applications for leave as a spouse or unmarried partner from nationals of that country who are already living in the UK should be decided in the UK with an interview. (Session 2005–06 Fifth Report para 300)

The House of Lords judgment in *Chikwamba v SSHD* [2008] UKHL 40 established a new approach to these questions.

Key Case

***Chikwamba v SSHD* [2008] UKHL 40**

Ms Chikwamba's asylum claim had failed but removals to Zimbabwe had been suspended and she was not returned. She married a Zimbabwean refugee and had a child. Once removals were reinstated, the Secretary of State sought her removal, arguing that she could apply for entry clearance from Zimbabwe. The House of Lords upheld an appeal against that decision.

Lord Scott said:

> It is, or ought to be, accepted that the appellant's husband cannot be expected to return to Zimbabwe, that the appellant cannot be expected to leave her child behind if she is returned to Zimbabwe and that if the appellant were to be returned to Zimbabwe she would have every prospect of succeeding in an application made there for permission to re-enter and remain in this country with her husband. So what on earth is the point of sending her back? Why cannot her application simply be made here? The only answer given on behalf of the Secretary of State is that government policy requires that she return and make her application from Zimbabwe. This is elevating policy to dogma. Kafka would have enjoyed it. (paras 3 and 6)

Baroness Hale said: 'it must be disproportionate to expect a four year old girl, who was born and has lived here all her life, either to be separated from her mother for some months or to travel with her mother to endure the "harsh and unpalatable" conditions in Zimbabwe simply in order to enforce the entry clearance procedures'. (para 8).

The House held that it could be proportionate to dismiss an Article 8 appeal against removal on the basis that the appellant should return to their country of origin to seek entry clearance, but 'only comparatively rarely, certainly in family cases involving children' (Lord Brown).

Showing how this concept may be used, the House of Lords in *Chikwamba* accepted that there was in fact an insuperable obstacle to the appellant's husband returning to Zimbabwe as he had been granted refugee status, but such an obstacle was not required for removal to be disproportionate.

The implications and application of *Chikwamba* have been fully considered in chapter 9, to which reference should be made.

18.7 Other public interest

In terms of the general approach to proportionality, there is no hard distinction to be made between cases based on criminal behaviour and others, but some of the relevant factors of course are different, and the legitimate aim is likely to be different.

As discussed in chapter 4, in order for proportionality to be assessed, it is essential that the purpose of the removal is properly identified within a legitimate aim in Article 8.2. In *Abdulaziz*, the ECtHR accepted that the immigration policy which restricted entry of spouses was for the 'economic well-being of the country'. It is rarely possible to show that the removal of a person who is making an economic contribution fulfils this aim, particularly where removal would result in the loss of the only income and therefore leave a family reliant on state support. The underlying justification is that the maintenance of the immigration policy in question is for the economic well-being of the country. Therefore, it is not that the individual must be removed for the public good, but that they must be treated as one of a group in relation to whom there is a policy that serves that aim. This has repercussions for the question of proportionality if the harm to the individual is to be weighed against the need for the policy, but not a specific ill that would result from their remaining (see discussion in *ZH (Tanzania)* and 4.8.4.2).

Removals that do not follow upon a deportation order are, in essence, regulatory in the sense that they are conducted in order to enforce immigration control. In *Shevanova v Latvia*, the applicant had committed various immigration offences, such as having a false stamp placed in an invalid passport, failing to apply for regularization of her position in Latvia, and concealing her Russian citizenship. She had lived in Latvia for around 30 years. The ECtHR held that her offences were not criminal but regulatory, and making a deportation order against her was disproportionate even though it was not enforced. They held that the legitimate aim was the prevention of public disorder, as enforcing immigration control was for this purpose.

Chikwamba relativizes the actual importance of immigration control when balanced with severe disruption to a family life. This is not to say that the maintenance of immigration control is given no weight, but it is weighed against the interference in question. For instance, in *Nnyanzi v UK* [2008] ECHR 286, the Article 8 claim was rejected on the basis that, even if the applicant's ten years of residence in the UK and the connections developed in that time did amount to private life, the operation of immigration control justified refusing her leave to remain in the UK. Her human rights and asylum claims had failed and she had no other basis to remain. By contrast, see the Court's conclusion in *Rodrigues da Silva, Hoogkamer v Netherlands* (2007) 44 EHRR 729, quoted at 18.5.

The Court of Appeal stated the importance of correct identification of the legitimate aim (*JO (Uganda)* and *JT (Ivory Coast) v SSHD*):

> The difference in aim is potentially important because the factors in favour of expulsion are in my view capable of carrying greater weight in a deportation case than in a case of ordinary removal. The maintenance of effective immigration control is an important matter, but the protection of society against serious crime is even more important and can properly be given correspondingly greater weight in the balancing exercise. (para 29)

The Court of Appeal in *UE (Nigeria) v SSHD* [2010] EWCA Civ 975 held that the contribution of an individual to the life of the community could be taken into account in weighing the public interest in their removal. The basis for so doing was not completely agreed by the Court. Sir David Keene said:

I would expect it to make a difference to the outcome of immigration cases only in a relatively few instances where the positive contribution to this country is very significant. (para 36)

18.8 Delay as a factor in proportionality

In the case of people who have remained in the UK without leave, whether as asylum seekers waiting for their claims to be determined, or as people who have overstayed or not had any leave, delay in dealing with their case or in attempting to remove them (and recall the difficulties of this, discussed in chapter 17) can have very significant effects on their lives. *Shala v SSHD* [2003] EWCA Civ 233 established that delay can be a relevant factor in the question of proportionality. Not only the effect of delay is relevant but also whether the appellant or the Home Office is responsible for it. In *Shala*, delay by the Home Office meant that the application was not dealt with under an earlier policy that ethnic Albanians from Kosovo would generally be granted asylum. The individual's conduct in avoiding enforcement is also relevant. The Court of Appeal in *R (on the application of Ekinci) v SSHD* [2003] EWCA Civ 765 held that the claimant's poor immigration history should be taken into account in balancing an interference with private life against the public interest.

The trend since *Shala* has been to distinguish it as turning on its own facts, and binding guidance has now been given in *EB (Kosovo) v SSHD* [2008] UKHL 41. The House of Lords said that delay might be relevant in three ways:

- First, the applicant might develop closer personal and social ties and establish deeper roots in the community
- Second, the tentativeness with which a relationship may start, if both partners are aware that one has an insecure immigration status, will naturally fade with the passage of time
- Third, it may reduce the weight otherwise to be accorded to the requirements of firm and fair immigration control if the delay is shown to be the result of a dysfunctional system. (Lord Brown disagreed with the third point.)

The second point is addressed to the practice, following the case of *Mahmood*, of treating the fact that a relationship had been entered into with knowledge that one party had an insecure immigration status as weighing against the right to respect for family or private life.

A number of asylum claimants have attempted to rely on the third point, as delays in dealing with their applications often persist for years. However, it has not often been proved that delay was the result of a dysfunctional system. In *WB (Pakistan) v SSHD* [2009] EWCA Civ 215, there was a nine-year delay before deciding the appellant's asylum claim, which then failed. The Court of Appeal held that the guidance in *EB (Kosovo)* on delay could make a difference to the outcome of the Article 8 claim, and that the case should return to the Tribunal for rehearing on that point.

In *Mert v SSHD* [2005] EWCA Civ 832, the deportation order had been made six years earlier, but not carried out. The Secretary of State argued that if the deportation order was once appropriate it could not become inappropriate through passage of time. The Court of Appeal held that the adjudicator had carried out a proper proportionality exercise. He had taken account of the importance of the Secretary of State's policy of deterrence, but held that 14 years' residence, children born in the UK, a strong family life, and six years since the deportation order was made, meant that to carry out a deportation would be disproportionate.

Delay as an element in a public law challenge aside from Article 8 is discussed in chapter 8.

18.9 Conclusion

In this critical area of immigration law, a gulf has widened between the liberal and humane judgments of the House of Lords in *Huang, Chikwamba, Beoku-Betts, EB (Kosovo)*, and *JH (Tanzania)* and the restrictive policy which has produced the automatic deportation provisions of the UK Borders Act. The latter does not cancel out the former as human rights appeals are specifically preserved, and as shown in this chapter, a new area of debate has opened up about the effect of human rights when Parliament has deemed the basic requirement for deportation to be met. It remains to be seen whether the judiciary will be influenced by the climate of policy, or will continue to develop the direction that they have established.

QUESTIONS

1 Should the Secretary of State or the individual carry the burden of proof on the question of whether removal is proportionate to a legitimate aim?

2 Should the Council of Europe's proposal to protect long-term residents be adopted in the UK?

For guidance on answering questions, visit www.oxfordtextbooks.co.uk/orc/clayton5e/.

FURTHER READING

Berry, Elspeth, (2009) 'The Deportation of "Virtual National Offenders: The Impact of the ECHR and EU Law' *Journal of Immigration Asylum and Nationality Law* vol. 23, no. 1, pp. 11–23.

Dembour, Marie-Benedicte (2003) 'Human Rights Law and National Sovereignty in Collusion: The Plight of Quasi-nationals at Strasbourg' *Netherlands Quarterly of Human Rights* vol. 21, pp. 63–98.

Fasti, Maurice (2002) 'The Restrictive Approach Taken by the European Court of Human Rights: Deportation of Long-term Immigrants and the Right to Family Life, Part 1: Integrated Aliens and Family Rights: Involution versus Evolution' *Journal of Immigration Asylum and Nationality Law* vol. 16, no. 3, pp. 166–175; Part 2: 'Consensus Enquiry and Security of Residence of Long-term Immigrants in Europe' vol. 16, no. 4, pp. 224–236.

McKee, Richard (2008) 'Definite Article: Application of Article 8 in Removal Cases' *Immigration Law Digest* vol. 14, no. 1, Spring 2008, pp. 14–16.

Rogers, Nicola (2003) 'Immigration and the European Convention on Human Rights: Are New Principles Emerging?' *European Human Rights Law Review* vol. 1, pp. 53–64.

Steinorth, Charlotte (2008) '*Üner v The Netherlands*: Expulsion of Long-term Immigrants and the Right to Respect for Private and Family Life' *Human Rights Law Review* January, vol. 8, no. 1, pp. 185–196.

INDEX